The Book of
NEW ZEALAND WOMEN
Ko Kui Ma Te Kaupapa

Rita Angus, Self Portrait, 1929. *Rita Angus Loan Collection, National Art Gallery,
Reproduced with the permission of the artist's estate.*

The Book of
NEW ZEALAND WOMEN

Ko Kui Ma Te Kaupapa

Edited by
Charlotte Macdonald,
Merimeri Penfold and
Bridget Williams

First published in 1991 by Bridget Williams Books Limited,
P.O. Box 9839, Wellington, New Zealand
Reprinted 1992

ISBN 0 908912 04 8

Grants to assist with research and writing were provided by: ANZ Bank, Claude
McCarthy Trust, the Balivean Trust, the Manawatu Branch of the New Zealand
Federation of University Women, 1990 Project, the Victoria University Research
Committee. The Historical Branch of the Department of Internal Affairs assisted with
publication.

Cover design by Mission Hall Design Group
Typeset by Typocrafters Ltd, Auckland
Printed by South Wind Production Singapore Pte Limited

CONTENTS

Wetekia Elkington. *Tyree Collection, Nelson Provincial Museum*

INTRODUCTION

E rere e taku poi
Haria nga wairua e
Ki nga maunga
Ki nga tai
Ki nga iwi e tau!
Tau, tau, tau atu e!

———————

My poi in flight
Bear aloft the spirits of old
Beyond the mountains
Across the seas
There to land! to rest! to bide!
There the people!

The Book of New Zealand Women/Ko Kui Ma Te Kaupapa grew out of a desire to put together an alternative history – the history of women in Aotearoa/New Zealand.

Over the past fifteen years or so, women have begun to make an appearance in New Zealand history. Once relegated to an occasional reference (winning the vote in 1893, or entering the workforce during wartime), they now emerge as a part of the national history. As mothers, hotelkeepers, lobbyists and correspondents, their story is beginning to be told. Throughout the country people are finding out more about the women in their families, in their communities, or in organisations such as unions and voluntary societies. This book brings together some of that research by telling the life stories of over three hundred women.

It stretches back in time to the twelfth century, to a woman living at Palliser Bay on the southern shore of Te Ika a Maui (the North Island). She belonged to one of the first small communities known to have settled on the coast of Aotearoa. At the other end of the time scale, the book features women who belong to our own time, including several who lived into the 1980s, such as Helen Paske and Elizabeth Sewell. As an historical work, it does not include those who are still living.

We chose to tell the story of women in New Zealand through a series of biographical portraits for several reasons. First, research in women's history here, as elsewhere, has focused on recovering the lives of individual women. Second, although much research has been undertaken in the last decade, there are still considerable gaps which would make it difficult to construct a comprehensive narrative account. Finally, this seemed to us the best way of conveying a great deal of particular inform-ation while also providing a base from which generalisations could be drawn. Identi-fying general patterns in women's lives through examining individual biographies is a practice that underlies the current women's movement; it allows for the study of the complex interplay between the elements in women's lives, where the common distinction between 'life' and 'work' rarely fits.

The book brings together well-known historical figures and those who have never been known beyond their immediate circles. Alongside Rita Angus and Lady Pomare are Bessie Turnbull and Maggie Fraser. We did not set out to compile a collection of New Zealand's 'famous women', nor did we want to concentrate solely on those who had worked to advance 'the women's cause', although these women are certainly to be found within these pages. Our purpose was to present in as broad a sweep as possible the range of activities in which women have been engaged, and to illustrate the variety of courses that women's lives have taken.

Nowhere is this variety more evident than in the lives of Maori women. Under Merimeri Penfold's direction, the project has had a commitment to writing and researching the life stories of Maori women. Where possible, family members have written about their own people. These range from Hineamaru, a leader of Ngati Hine from the Bay of Islands in the late sixteenth century, to Maro Hoterene, a community leader from the far north, and the psychiatrist Dr Rina Moore, whose story is told by her daughter.

The stories of Maori women are an essential part of the book. The histories of these women need to be recorded if the true national character of New Zealand is to be portrayed. We acknowledge the contribution of those who believed in the import- ance of the stories of their kahui wahine (women kin). Traditionally these stories were transmitted orally through the various forms of waiata and story telling. Today our history is accessible through the written word.

Researchers Tui MacDonald and Raina Meha worked from documentary evidence to write biographies of women such as Rangi Topeora of Ngati Toa (one of the few women to sign the Treaty of Waitangi), the endurance swimmer Katerina Nehua, or politician Iriaka Ratana. Writers such as Judith Binney and Sandra Coney have also drawn on their research for biographies of Maori women – such as the three prophets from the Hokianga, and the YWCA leader Mary Geddes.

Some women's lives are recorded from the perspective of those who knew them. Cushla Parekowhai interviewed the descendants or friends of some leading Maori women of the past, and with them created life stories that link directly to the women themselves. Dovey Taiaroa speaks about composer Dovey Katene, Emily Schuster about Guide Rangi (Rangitiaria Dennan), Danny and Josie Tumahai about Tumanako Te Puna Reweti (Aunty Hope), the Auckland community worker and activist who died in 1980.

Entries on those few women whose lives have been studied in detail have been kept short. It is surprising how few these are. More numerous are those who, like Freda Du Faur, are associated with particular achievements but whose lives remain relatively obscure. More common still are women such as tennis champion Kate Nunneley or heroine Huria Matenga who enjoyed a considerable contemporary repu- tation but who have largely disappeared from historical memory. Some are known well within their own spheres – Nurse Cameron in the Women's Health League or town planner Nancy Northcroft – but remain virtually unknown beyond these circles. Others have been retrieved from the shadow of their more famous men: Bella King, Elizabeth Hocken and Maud Pember Reeves are three women whose lives are fascinating in themselves.

There are several women in the book whose lives have left no mark in the his- torical record. Yet their stories reveal much about the everyday texture of women's lives – in a country district in the 1930s (Mrs Walker of Cronadun), as a mother in the Hawke's Bay around the same time (Fanny Scott), or as a settler on the north Otago coast in the 1840s (Maria Kennard). Each has a chronicler. For Mrs Walker and Fanny Scott the portrait is based on the author's personal knowledge of her subject. Maria Kennard's life has been constructed from a few documentary sources and the evidence presented by a unique set of historical buildings preserved on the coast at Matanaka.

Sometimes the story is a partial one, as in the case of Meri Mangakahia. We know little of her beyond the fact that in 1893 she appeared as a petitioner before the Pare-mata Maori (Kotahitanga Parliament). We have included such women because the episode and the person are of considerable interest. Although we have been unable to discover more about her, we hope someone else will be prompted to carry on the research.

Space in any one book is limited. Many more names were considered than we could possibly include here. Emily Seideberg is not here, nor Learmonth Dalrymple. Readers will have their own ideas of who should or could have been included. That is good. We hope there will be other books of New Zealand women. This is a begin-ning on which we hope others will build.

Charlotte Macdonald
Merimeri Penfold
Bridget Williams

Farm buildings at Matanaka where Maria Kennard lived in the 1840s. *New Zealand Historic Places Trust*

SOURCES

The history of women, like other forms of history, is created rather than discovered. There is no one way to find out how women lived, or what they did, a hundred or five hundred years ago; there is no one place where information is gathered. Our task was to uncover sources, and then to interpret them.

The sources used in this book range from the conventional kinds found in archives and libraries (the minute books of organisations, political records, personal diaries, newspapers) to family testimony, both Maori and Pakeha, and other forms of oral tradition.

All sources reflect the pattern of the society that has generated them. Before women had the right to vote or the right to sit in parliament, for example, there were no women's words to be found in records of parliamentary debates; before women worked as journalists or editors, they had little control over what was included in the daily newspapers. When few women were employed in policy-making positions in government departments or large private organisations, they left little mark in the public records of these institutions. But these are not the only sources from which history can be written.

Women have, for a long time, been ready correspondents. Private letters exchanged between friends and family constitute an important source of historical evidence. For many Pakeha women in the nineteenth century correspondence was the means through which relationships with friends and family on the other side of the world were sustained. These letters were commonly full, expressive and detailed in their description. The letters written by Mary Hobhouse, Jane Maria Atkinson and Sarah Selwyn have given us rich insights into the world in which they lived.

Women have also been prolific writers of diaries and journals, and keepers of sketchbooks. They have often been responsible for compiling and transmitting family history. Some of this material has found its way into places such as the Alexander Turnbull Library in Wellington or the Hocken Library in Dunedin. Much also remains in family hands. In writing for this book, many contributors have drawn on papers held privately either by their own family, or by the subject's family – perhaps sometimes only a letter or two, sometimes a diary or collection of clippings. Even apparently slight documents can assist a researcher in establishing a history for women different from that left by the public record. The book has benefited greatly from access contributors were given to family papers.

In the record that remains, however, there is much unevenness. The range of sources left by men is much wider, drawing as it does on the history of public events and political record; these sources also tend to be better preserved. Even women who were prominent in the public domain, who wrote pamphlets and columns which were published in widely circulated periodicals, and who were well known by contemporaries can still be difficult to research. Kate Sheppard is a case in point. She left few personal papers. Although we know a great deal about her work for women's suffrage and for the feminist National Council of Women, we know little of her personal life. Our view of her remains a rather distant one.

Similarly, even in establishing such fundamental items of information as names of parents, difficulties are commonly encountered. Where possible we have included names of both parents; where only the father's name appears this is because we have been unable to locate the name of the mother. It is not a reflection of who was judged to be the significant parent.

The relative disadvantage women suffer in the documentary record does make the task of writing women's history more difficult. Researchers need to be more imaginative and infinitely more persistent. But the absence of sources does not preclude the writing of women's history. Many women in this book left no sources of their own and are beyond the reach of the recollection of those who knew them. Yet from the medical records we know something of Annemarie Anon; from archaeology, Little Papanui woman; from police records Opium Mag (Margaret Williams); from oral tradition Hine Poupou. Family sources have given us the letters of domestic servant Maggie Fraser; the Sweating Commission of 1889 the lives of two working girls at the end of last century. From such sources we can begin to piece together the history of women beyond the confines of conventional sources.

We have listed sources as fully as possible at the end of each essay for several purposes: to acknowledge direct quotations featured in the essay, to provide evidence for the portrait drawn, and to offer a guide to sources for subsequent researchers. In this last sense we hope that *The Book of New Zealand Women/Ko Kui Ma Te Kaupapa* will serve as the basis for the next stage in the development of women's history in this country. Much has been done in the last ten to fifteen years; there is much yet to do.

EDITORIAL NOTES

Information was checked thoroughly both by contributors and researchers; it has not been possible, however, to verify all facts absolutely. References to the Registrar of Births, Deaths and Marriages were omitted for reasons of space, but most essays drew on this source.

Maori words and phrases have been translated in the text on occasions when comprehension would have been difficult for most New Zealanders. Macrons have not been used, because of the difficulty of establishing consistent use throughout a range of texts.

Names used are those by which the women were most commonly known. The full names, and those of both parents, are also included wherever possible.

Quotations are sourced by paragraph at the end of the essay. A short title is given on the first reference, with the author's name only for following references. Full details of the document quoted are usually given in the *Unpublished Sources* and *Published Sources* following. On rare occasions when the document is used only for the quotation, full details are given in the quotation reference. Where two quotations from the same sources and same page appear in one paragraph, one reference only is given.

Sources list key items used for the essay, both published and unpublished (in archives and private collections). These are intended as useful guidelines to sources specific to the subject, not as comprehensive bibliographies.

The index identifies categories and topics as well as names. Cross-referencing through the index is a useful means of finding connections between women. All the names by which a woman has been known are given in the index; Maori women are indexed under both first and last names.

ABBREVIATIONS

The following abbreviations are used:

AIM   Auckland Institute and Museum
APL   Auckland Public Library
ATL   Alexander Turnbull Library
Hocken Hocken Library
NCW   National Council of Women
NZJH   *New Zealand Journal of History*
YWCA   Young Women's Christian Association
WCTU   Women's Christian Temperance Union
WEA   Workers' Education Association

In references to theses, universities are referred to by a short title, i.e. Auckland, Canterbury, Massey, Otago, Victoria, Waikato.

ILLUSTRATION SOURCES

We are grateful to all individuals who have provided illustrations, and to the following institutions and publications for permission to reproduce from their collections. All sources are credited in the captions.

Alexander Turnbull Library; Auckland City Art Gallery; Auckland Institute and Museum; Auckland Public Library; The Bath-house, Rotorua's Art and History Museum; Buddle Findlay; Canterbury Museum; *Dominion/Dominion Sunday Times*; Dorothy Neal White Collection, National Library; *Evening Post*; Hocken Library; *Te Kura*; Maori Arts and Crafts Institute; Metropolitan Opera Archives; National Art Gallery; National Dance Archive; National Museum/Te Whare Taonga o Aotearoa; Nelson Provincial Museum; NZ Drama School; NZ Film Archive; NZ Film Commission; NZ Forestry Institute; *NZ Herald*; *NZ Listener*; *NZ Woman's Weekly*; News Media; Otago Early Settlers' Museum; Our Lady of Compassion Archives; Palmerston North Public Library; *The Press*; Replay Radio, Radio New Zealand; Southland Museum and Art Gallery; Taranaki Museum; Waimate Museum; Wellington Public Library; Women's Health League; Young Women's Christian Association.

We have made every attempt to provide accurate information about illustrations used, and would be very glad to hear about any further information or omissions.

ACKNOWLEDGEMENTS

The Book of New Zealand Women/Ko Kui Ma Te Kaupapa was from the beginning a large project – one that touched many people during its life. The editors owe them much. By way of thanks we say simply: this book would not exist without you.

First, we would like to thank our sponsors. The initial grants from the ANZ Bank and the Claude McCarthy Trust made the project possible.

Other grants enabled us to continue: from the Balivean Trust, the J. V. Ilott Charitable Trust, the Manawatu Branch of the New Zealand Federation of University Women 1990 Project, the Victoria University Research Committee. The Historical Branch, Department of Internal Affairs, assisted with publication. The Stout Research Centre, Victoria University, provided a home for the project.

The advice and support of the advisory committee was crucial at the beginning of the project, in 1989. They were: Margaret Wilson (convenor), Miriama Evans, Penny Fenwick, Beryl Hughes, Dorothy Page, Margaret Tennant, Mary Ronnie, Anne Salmond, Pat Sargison.

Contributors in all parts of the country, who researched and wrote the essays, gave generously of their time, knowledge, and skills.

In Wellington a group of researchers formed a unit working primarily with Charlotte Macdonald: Bronwyn Labrum, Tui MacDonald, Raina Meha and Cushla Parekowhai.

Checking, proofing, and computer work was done by: Jen Barrett, Ilse Jacoby, Kate Kennedy, Pauline Russell, Alison Southby, June Starke, and Brenda Watson.

Alison Carew and Anna Rogers edited and proofed the book under difficult conditions, and the staff at Allen & Unwin, and then at Bridget Williams Books, provided invaluable assistance.

The index was done by Pat Sargison. Illustrations were provided by contributors, and by researchers; a central group of images was researched by Mary Louise Ormsby. Brett Robertson of the Photographic Section, Victoria University, reproduced many photographs. The book was designed by Lisa Noble of Mission Hall Design Group, and pasted up by Richard King of Edsetera Book Production.

There were many whose advice we sought, and it was given generously. There were others who listened, talked, cooked and provided other forms of support while we worked on the book. We would like to mention especially – Craig Cherrie, Vicky Duncan, Eve Macdonald, Jim Traue, Robin and Mary Williams, and librarians in all parts of the country but particularly those at the Alexander Turnbull Library in Wellington.

We would like to thank all those who have made this book possible.

Charlotte Macdonald
Merimeri Penfold
Bridget Williams

'The three graces': from left, Caroline Abraham, Mary Ann Martin and Sarah Selwyn, c.1865. *Alexander Turnbull Library*

CAROLINE ABRAHAM

1809–1877

Caroline Harriet Palmer was gently and piously reared within the High Church Anglicanism of a section of the English upper middle class. On the death of her father, Caroline with her mother and sisters left their home, 'Wanlip', in Leicestershire for Farnborough Hill in Hampshire. Here their near neighbours were the Abrahams of Frimley whose son, Charles, Caroline eventually married. Her cousin, Sarah Richardson, was to marry George Augustus Selwyn. This propinquity brought Caroline into the Etonian circle of friends of which Selwyn, the 'Royal George', was leader.

After the departure of Selwyn's party for New Zealand in December 1841, Caroline became bored. 'I cannot be content merely to glide down the stream of life', she wrote to Selwyn, offering herself as a companion to Sarah. Selwyn's off-hand reply was discomfiting, and so too was the apparent failure of her friendship with Charles Abraham to blossom into anything further. She thought of becoming an Anglican nun.

However, in 1850, Caroline was both married to Charles and off to New Zealand, where Abraham was to become Selwyn's right-hand man at St John's College, Auckland, and Caroline was to find work and friendship within the college community. She became a close friend of both Sarah Selwyn and Mary Martin; they were known as 'the three graces'.

Ill health punctuated by miscarriages kept Caroline largely confined to her couch during her first two years at Auckland. Later, when her physical health returned, she taught at the college and became involved in its mundane domesticity. She always tried to find satisfaction in the 'simple and all-sufficient employment of daily duties' – 'divine drudgery', Mary Martin called it. But from time to time 'deep gashes of memory' caused her to yearn for the quiet beauty of the English countryside and for the orderly services of an English cathedral. She saw colonial society as a 'caricature' of English society, 'quite respectable but snobbish'. Like many women of her social class she turned to water-colour painting as a pastime, and when her husband was absent on pastoral journeys, she noted, 'writing beguiles away the evening hours even more than reading'. Caroline continued to admire Selwyn but wished, as did many others, that he would limit his sphere to Auckland and the Maori mission, and thus avoid the '*rush* and scramble for time' caused by his forays to Melanesia.

In 1857, when Caroline was nearly forty-eight, her only child, Charles Thomas, was born. (Melanesian students at St John's were the first to say that he should have been named Isaac.) The following year her husband, at Lambeth, was consecrated Bishop of Wellington, and was enthroned at St Paul's, Wellington, in April 1859. Caroline, always intense and inclined to self-deprecation, worried over her role as a bishop's wife and, as a mother for the first time when some of her contemporaries were grandmothers, worried even more about her ability to be both Charlie's 'playfellow' and guide.

But when she turned her mind to public affairs, her opinions were pertinent and significant. She wrote of the 'folly' and 'injustice' of the part purchase and attempted survey of land at Waitara (Taranaki) which Wiremu Kingi Te Rangi-take had long maintained belonged to the whole of Te Ati Awa. She was highly critical of the 'short-sightedness of the grasping and covetous settlers', and indig-nant with the British government for entrusting the colony with its burgeoning land problems 'to a man [Thomas Gore Browne] whose governing powers had only been exercised on the rock of St Helena'. With prescience she wrote of the Taranaki war which followed the attempted Waitara survey:

What one chiefly mourns is the thought of our doing wrong to this people [Maori], and then supporting it by force and so beginning what may be a long chain of wrong and misery to both races; like all evil the beginning seems small.

One of Caroline's letters on Maori-settler confrontation, along with others from Mary Martin and Sarah Selwyn, was published in England in *Extracts of Letters from New Zealand on the War Question* (1861). Further comments on the war were contained in letters she wrote to English friends. It was in her letters that Caroline was outspoken; in Wellington society she and her husband were 'tongue tied for we can never speak on the subject'.

Caroline and her son left Wellington for England and Eton in April 1867. The break with New Zealand was made permanent in 1870 when Charles Abraham resigned the see of Wellington to become Selwyn's coadjutor at Lichfield.

Her last years of fragile health were spent in the cathedral close. This quiet sanctuary offered no protection against onslaughts made by Darwinism and 'Higher Criticism' (of the Bible), and Caroline's faith was tested. 'The line between the things of faith and the things of reason may be a fine one,' she wrote in one of her last letters, 'but I believe there is such a line and I had rather wish enlarging it on the side of faith.'   *Frances Porter*

Quotations

para.2 S. Marriott to Charles Abraham (son), 5 March 1898, Caroline Abraham Papers

para.4 C. Abraham to Mrs Marriott, 4 July 1851, Caroline Abraham Papers; M. Martin to E. Coleridge, 21 May 1852, Letters from Bishop Selwyn and Others, vol.4, p.699; C. Abraham to Mrs Marriott, 4 July 1851, 25 Feb. 1862, 4 April 1862; C. Abraham to E. Coleridge, 16 March 1855, Letters from Bishop Selwyn and Others, vol.5, p.787

para.6 C. Abraham, 24 April 1860, *Extracts of Letters from New Zealand on the War Question*; C. Abraham to S. Marriott, 1 Dec. 1860, Caroline Abraham Papers; C. Abraham, 24 April 1860, *Extracts of Letters*

para.7 C. Abraham to S. Marriott, 19 Aug. [1876], Caroline Abraham Papers

para.9 C. Abraham to S. Marriott 19 Aug. [1876], Caroline Abraham Papers

Unpublished Sources

Caroline Abraham, MS Papers 2395, ATL

Letters from Bishop Selwyn and Others, 1842–1867, qMS, ATL

Published Sources

Browne-Wilkinson, Virginia. *The Far Off and the Near*, Florence, 1983

Drummond, Alison (ed.) *The Auckland Journals of Vicesimus Lush 1850–1863*, Christchurch, 1971

Extracts of Letters from New Zealand on the War Question (printed for private circulation), London, 1861

Morrell, W. P. *The Anglican Church in New Zealand*, Dunedin, 1973

Tucker, H. W. *Memoirs of the Life and Episcopate of George Augustus Selwyn*, London, 1879

KUE-SUM AH-CHAN

1884–1967

Only the closest family members would know Yip Kue-sum by her own name. To most people, New Zealanders or Chinese, she was Mrs Joe Ah-Chan, wife of the 'Grape Man' and mistress of the Goldleaf Vineyard at Totara, near Thames. New Zealand's viticultural industry had long been a virtual monopoly of the Yugoslavs. In 1925, the Ah-Chans were the first Chinese grape-growers and winemakers breaking into the industry. Kue-sum came to New Zealand in 1920 to join her husband, who had been in the country for some time. Chan Hock Joe, better known as Joe Ah-Chan, started off in New Zealand as a fruit-and-vegetable hawker, selling from door to door in Wellington. Having accumulated some capital, he moved to Matamata and started a general store. Then he decided to send for his wife, whom he had left behind in his home village of Ha Kei in Tsengshing [Zengcheng], a county famous for its fruit, especially lychees.

Yip Kue-sum, Mrs Joe Ah-Chan, picture on her entry permit, 1920. *Family Collection*

Theirs had been a traditional arranged marriage, but the couple were very close. They had no children yet, and this made Kue-sum's life back home all the more unpalatable. At that time, the greatest hurdles for Chinese immigrants were a poll-tax of £100 and a literacy test of up to one hundred English words, picked at the pleasure of the customs officer (Immigration Restriction Act 1908). Most Chinese women were illiterate even in Chinese at that time, and the prospect of being tested face to face by some foreign man must have been hugely daunting. Kue-sum persevered, and went to a special private tutor in the village to study English. She brought all her textbooks and exercises with her to New Zealand, and referred to them frequently, keeping them all her life. She managed to pass the test and entered the country in 1920.

Her knowledge of English served her well when she had to run the general store in Matamata. Her first two children, George and Daisy, were born within twelve months of each other after she arrived. Her second daughter Anne was born in 1924. Kue-sum's life was busy and isolated, for there were only around 200 Chinese women in the country at that time.

After a couple of years, the family moved to Thames, where they set up a fruit shop and produce garden. In 1924 Joe Ah-Chan decided to lease land for a vineyard. The venture was possible only with the total support of his wife. Initially growing outdoor grapes for the table, he started winemaking in 1929 and was reputed to be the first Chinese winemaker in the Southern Hemisphere. Then the Depression set in, and since their land was only leased, the rent continued to rise. Fortunately for the Ah-Chans, a neighbouring landowner, who saw how hard they had struggled and how close they were to success, advanced low-interest loans and sold them a three-acre block next to their leased land. In 1935 a second Goldleaf Vineyard was established. As mistress of Goldleaf, Kue-sum oversaw all the cultivation, cutting and pruning, harvesting, and packing of the grapes, and sent them off by rail to Wellington. Her husband took charge of sales, and had his own grape shop in Cuba Street, Wellington. When the grapes were not in season, he ran a greengrocery store.

The grape season is early March to late May. In a few busy weeks Kue-sum had to see that the grapes were harvested and despatched to arrive at the Wellington shop before the holidays. Without refrigeration, transportation required meticulous planning and organisation on top of a lot of hard work. Kue-sum, the children, and half-a-dozen casual workers would work from dawn till dusk, picking the grapes and putting them in big boxes. Kue-sum also cooked three proper meals a day for the family and workers. Then after dinner the family worked on, wrapping and packing the highly perishable fruit. Bunches of grapes were trimmed and individually wrapped in tissue, then put into compartmentalised cardboard boxes before being carted away to the train. It meant working till after midnight most of the time.

When Joe Ah-Chan was away, often for months at a time, security was a problem. Burglars would cut open the wire-netting to strip the vines of such large quantities of grapes that the theft was obviously carried out on order. When the Alsatian watchdog barked, Kue-sum would unhesitatingly go to investigate. With only a broom as a weapon, she was totally fearless, telling her children that right would always triumph over might.

During the Depression, many impoverished people came by and asked to be employed for a few shillings a day. Although times were hard for all, Kue-sum would try to give work to the most needy. As a result, the Ah-Chans were popular among both Europeans and Maori, and did not suffer the bad racist abuse which was a common experience for many Chinese in the cities.

The Second World War and the arrival of the American soldiers in the South Pacific proved a blessing to the winemaking industry. Imports were restricted, and there was a demand for New Zealand wine. Joe Ah-Chan used to go round the countryside taking samples of his wines. Hotels often ordered in bulk from the Goldleaf Vineyard, and business flourished for the Ah-Chans.

Kue-sum was naturally generous and hospitable to the several Chinese bachelor gardeners scattered around Thames. These men congregated at the

Goldleaf partly because they had no family, and partly because they were eager to listen to the news which Joe Ah-Chan could tell them. Joe was well educated in Chinese by the standard of his time. His daughters recalled:

Father was always reading all these classical books at night. He also loved newspapers, we don't know where he got them from. Some were local Chinese papers from Wellington, but some were from China.

The men would be specially eager for the news of China after 1937, when Japan invaded China.

Joe Ah-Chan was intensely patriotic: 'Chiang Kai-shek and Soong Mei-ling were his idols! They could do no wrong.' Besides making large donations to the Chinese war effort, he overruled Kue-sum's objections and put most of their savings into war-bonds, believing that these could be cashed as money when they eventually retired in China. The children remembered their parents praying every morning, burning joss-sticks for peace to come to China soon. China was the motherland, with a way of life they had cherished and never forgotten.

When the war ended, many Chinese families came to New Zealand as refugees. Joe Ah-Chan, however, clung to his faith in the motherland, and bought a property in Canton in preparation for his family's return. He also offered his vineyard for sale. Business had been going well since the last years of the war and several astute buyers made offers. Joe Ah-Chan however sold to a distant clansman from the same village at the modest price of £6,000 because he preferred to 'help a kinsman'. In good faith he accepted a token down payment and gave up possession of the property. By then it was 1950, and the Communists had already taken over China, making it hazardous for the Ah-Chans to go back.

Kue-sum always had reservations about selling up the vineyard which they had worked on for twenty-five years. When Joe Ah-Chan moved to Auckland with their youngest daughter Anne, she chose not to move out of their property until payment was made in full. She stayed on alone, on the vineyard which was already stripped of all fruit, in the house without furniture, passing away the time by polishing pots and pans. Eventually the full sum was paid; only then did she leave the vineyard and move to the city, sixty miles away.

The Ah-Chans made their urban home in Blockhouse Bay. They bought a couple of glasshouses for tomatoes to keep them busy. Now they had more time to enjoy themselves, listening to their favourite Cantonese opera records on the old gramophone. Joe used to sing along while Kue-sum simply listened. It had been their one entertainment in the vineyard days. Then Joe suffered a stroke and died in 1959. Kue-sum stayed on in the family home, kept it immaculate, busied herself with the vegetable plots and the tomato glasshouses. The highlight of her week was Sunday dinner, when her children came with their families. Knowing there was little hope of any return to China, she bought a grave site adjacent to her husband's in the Waikumete Cemetery. She died in 1967, aged eighty-three, a brave and resourceful woman who spent most of her life making a place for herself and her family in a foreign land.   *Manying Ip*

Unpublished Source
Interviews with Daisy and Anne Ah-Chan, Kue-sum's daughters.

Published Sources
Ah-Chan, Anne. *Thames Grapes and Those Who Grow Them*, Thames, 1948
Ah-Chan, Anne. 'No Other Ways About It', *Leisure Magazine*, Oct. 1959, Penang, Malaya

MARY ALCORN   *1866–1928*

MARGARET ALCORN   *1868–1967*

The *Evening Post* on 5 May 1906 recorded the establishment of the 'Wellington branch of Liberty's London' by Mary and Margaret Alcorn in the new Kennedy Building on Lambton Quay.

The two sisters were born in Hokitika, the eldest of the nine children of Samuel, a draper, and Jane Alcorn (born Andrews), who were both from Ireland. In 1874 the family moved to Wellington, where Samuel bought property on Lambton Quay and set up a thriving draper shop opposite, and in opposition to, Kirkcaldie & Stains. The family lived above the shop, so the sisters had early experience of the daily running of a successful business.

Mary and Margaret had a governess, and then attended private schools. Their parents were well educated, cultured and prosperous, and their daughters would never have been expected to earn their own living had it not been for a disastrous fire in 1877 which destroyed Samuel's shop and killed a younger daughter, Winifred. Samuel never recovered, either financially or emotionally, from this double tragedy.

In the years of relative poverty which followed, the family moved to Ashburton where the sisters attended the local school. Later, Margaret became a dressmaker and Mary, it is believed, worked as a shop assistant.

In 1895, some of the family moved back to Wellington where Margaret attended night classes in art offered by the Wellington Technical School, renamed College in 1904. In 1903, she won a coveted prize in the 'national' art competition run from South Kensington, London, for a design worked on material. The accreditation of the local technical school to South Kensington had been of particular significance for women such as Margaret with limited financial means, who thus gained access to prestige training in a variety of marketable skills.

The two sisters never married, and both were determined not only to support themselves, but to have the security of their own business. The Liberty shop they opened in 1906 was not in fact a branch of Liberty's London, as the *Evening Post* reported; the two sisters owned the shop, and imported goods directly from Liberty's London. Some of the capital for the new business, which later became a limited liability company, was borrowed on their father's life insurance.

Mary, a hardworking and resourceful businesswoman, managed the shop. To get to work each day from their home in Oriental Bay she rode a bicycle – an unusual sight in those days. Margaret worked as a dressmaker at the shop while also continuing her art classes, becoming a proficient water-colourist.

ORIENTAL SILKS woven exclusively for LIBERTY & CO. Ltd.

"Liberty" Silks.

Hand-Block-Printed, in Varied Designs and colourings.
Dyed and Printed in England.   Woven in India.

THE PRINTED "LIBERTY" SILKS are woven in India, and imported in what is technically termed the "grey" state.

IN THE GREY STATE the Silks are Dyed (in England) and Printed by a special Hand-process, in which the latest Chemical and Scientific Knowledge is utilized to ensure the Stability of the Colouring Pigments applied.

THE CHARACTERISTIC AND BEAUTIFUL DESIGNS are the result of careful study and selection extending over a long series of years.

CONTEMPORARY DECORATIVE ARTISTS of acknowledged repute have been employed in the production of many of the Designs.

AMONG THE DESIGNS may be found reproductions of Ancient Indian, Persian, and other Classic Oriental Originals.   34 inches wide.

Price **28/6** per Piece of about 7 Yards.

Half-pieces cut without extra charge.

PATTERNS POST FREE.

A page from a Liberty's *Silks* catalogue, c.1895, a few years before the Alcorn sisters opened their shop in Wellington. *Lyndell Shannon*

The initial association with Liberty's London was probably suggested by Arthur Dewhurst Riley, formerly the founder and principal of the Wellington Technical College, whose importing business was also in the new Kennedy Building. Riley would have supported the Alcorn shop as a practical application of his philosophy that art and industry must interact.

The shop specialised in 'art furniture and furnishings'. Liberty's London then was selling mainly Art Nouveau designs and, in line with the Arts and Crafts Movement, trying to recapture the spirit and excellence of the handcrafted product in a machine age. An advertisement for Liberty's Wellington which ran along the bottom of successive pages of the 1911 annual exhibition catalogue for the local art society (the 'Academy') cites the extensive range of goods and services offered:

. . . Cretonnes, Linen, Silks, Etc . . . Art Pottery . . . Model Blouses . . . Designs and Estimates for Furniture . . . LIBERTY'S Silks are printed at their own works at Merton Abbey . . . Pewter and Silverware is specially designed and made at their Birmingham Works by Liberty Cymric . . . LIBERTY Carpets . . . LIBERTY'S Dress Muslins and Linens for the Summer Season . . .

Mary Alcorn extended the shop's business in 1913 with a trip overseas to visit

Liberty's London and to make other contacts. In 1921 or 1922, the shop moved further along Lambton Quay to the larger premises then occupied by Thomas Pringle's 'novelties and fancy goods' shop, and absorbed his embroidery business. The sisters were both skilled embroiderers, and are also known to have acted as interior decorators.

The sisters' talents and resultant success arose from a rare combination of taste and business acumen. They were both keenly interested in art, music, and the theatre, and were renowned for their generosity and hospitality, not only towards family and friends, but also strangers in need. Margaret, for example, was later to take in refugees from the Napier earthquake for months after the disaster.

After Mary died in 1928, Margaret managed the shop from her sewing-machine by the windows overlooking Lambton Quay, returning to Oriental Bay by tram each day for lunch, keeping her hat on to save time. In 1928 she opened another shop in the new Burlington Arcade at Cuba and Dixon Streets. Both outlets, being suppliers of luxury goods, were hard hit by the Depression and were forced into liquidation. Although legally Margaret Alcorn was under no personal obligation to clear the debts incurred by the business, she took in boarders until the debts were paid.

Margaret had earlier added the position of Arthur Riley's company secretary to her responsibilities, and she continued her involvement with his business, serving as a director until she was in her nineties. She died at her home in Oriental Bay in 1967, a few months before her hundredth birthday.

Ann Calhoun

Sources
Information came from interviews with Winifred Low, Pat Alcorn, and Armer Alcorn, niece and nephews of Mary and Margaret, and from family records in their possession.

FRANCES ALDA

1879–1952

In Victorian and Edwardian times the operatic stage provided one of the few avenues by which a gifted woman could reach the highest ranks of the musical profession. But although many aspired, few colonial-born singers achieved international status in this field. Lack of language skills, and of the cultural background their European contemporaries took for granted, handicapped their talents. The tyranny of distance meant they faced a highly competitive environment without family support. The first New Zealander to surmount these obstacles and carve out an international operatic career for herself was Christchurch-born Frances Alda.

Titian-haired, tempestuous and undeniably beautiful, she attracted critical acclaim from the moment of her European debut, as Manon in Massenet's opera of the same name, at the Paris Opéra-Comique on 14 April 1904. After three successful seasons as a leading soprano with the Brussels opera house, la Monnaie, she was invited to sing at London's Covent Garden, and at the Parma Verdi Fes-

Frances Alda in one of her sixty-three appearances at the Met as Mimi in *La Bohème*.
Metropolitan Opera Archives

tival, where she came to the attention of the management of Europe's greatest opera house – La Scala, Milan. Alda made her house début there in 1908, in the title role of Charpentier's *Louise*. She then sang Margherita to Chaliapin's Mefistofele in Boito's opera of the same name. It was a far cry from her first professional engagement as an eighteen-year-old supporting artist in a Sydney variety show. Strength of character, allied to talent and ambition, had enabled her to make the difficult transition from colonial novice to international opera star in less than a decade.

Alda was not her real name. It was a stage name bestowed upon her by the redoubtable Matilde Marchesi, with whom she studied singing for several months prior to her Parisian début. She had been born plain Fanny Jane Davis on 31 May 1879. Later, she amended her first names to the more elegant 'Frances Jeanne'. She also altered her date of birth, presumably in a bid to make herself appear more youthfully promising to operatic managers on her arrival in Europe. Entries in current dictionaries of music preserve this fiction, giving her birth date as 1883.

Alda's operatic aspirations were nurtured by family example. Her maternal grandparents, Fanny and Martin Simonsen, were notable operatic pioneers in Australasia. Both her parents were musical but while her father, David Davis, was content to be a talented amateur, her mother, Leonora, wanted to follow a professional singing career. She could not settle to life as the wife of a Christchurch businessman. The couple divorced some fifteen months after Alda's birth. Thereafter, the child travelled with her mother on operatic tours of New Zealand, Australia and America.

After her mother's untimely death in 1884, young Fanny found a stable home with her Simonsen grandparents in Melbourne. There she grew up surrounded by professional music-making. Her aunt, Frances Saville, had become an operatic star in Europe and, in her letters home, painted a glamorous picture of life as a successful prima donna. When Alda began singing professionally at the age of eighteen, she rose quickly from bit parts to leading roles in Gilbert and Sullivan productions. Her own ambitious nature made it inevitable she should want to emulate her aunt's success. Family connections ensured her acceptance as a Marchesi pupil, and so set her on the road that led to La Scala, and an international career.

It was at La Scala, in 1908, that Alda met two of the most important men in her life. The great conductor, Arturo Toscanini, became a lifelong friend. The general manager, Giulio Gatti-Casazza, became her husband on 3 April 1910. By then all three were employees of New York's Metropolitan Opera Company. Alda made her Met début as Gilda in Verdi's *Rigoletto* on 7 December 1908. Despite initial hostility from critics averse to Gatti's appointment as general manager, Alda quickly established herself as a leading prima donna in the world's most star-studded and wealthy opera company. She created the leading soprano parts in three contemporary American operas, but her reputation was based on established roles such as Desdemona in Verdi's *Otello*, Manon in Puccini's *Manon Lescaut*, Marguerite in Gounod's *Faust*, Nanetta in Verdi's *Falstaff* and, above all, Mimi in Puccini's ever-popular *La Bohème*. This she sang sixty-three times at the Met alone, partnering all the leading tenors of the day, from Caruso to Gigli.

Outside the opera house, Alda toured regularly as a recitalist and was an early participant in radio broadcasts. The brightness and warmth of her voice and her sure sense of style and line are preserved on over 130 gramophone recordings, made for the Victor Company between 1909 and 1928. These range from ballads and art-songs to operatic excerpts. After her retirement from the Met in 1929, she had her own radio programme and also taught singing. She was concerned about the position of women in the musical profession and was on the advisory committee of America's Musical Union of Women Artists.

Her marriage to Gatti she acknowledged as a mistake which had hindered her acceptance as an artist in her own right. The couple divorced in 1928 but remained on good terms. In 1941 Alda married a New York advertising executive, Ray Vir Den. An enthusiastic traveller, she died while on holiday in Venice on 18 September 1952.

Although she left New Zealand as a child and returned only once – for a recital tour in 1927 – Alda's allegiance was whole-hearted. She always described herself as a New Zealander and indignantly discounted Australian attempts to claim her. She wrote warmly of New Zealand in her entertaining autobiography, *Men, Women and Tenors*, published in 1937. Her most tangible tributes to this country are the gramophone recordings of Princess Te Rangi Pai's 'Maori

Slumber Song (Hine e Hine)' and Alfred Hill's 'Waiata Maori' which she made on 28 March 1928.

Colourful, temperamental and every inch the prima donna, Frances Alda made friends and enemies in equal proportion. She loved singing, prized professionalism in all things, and took pride in her own achievements. She was undoubtedly one of New Zealand's most successful international musicians.

Adrienne Simpson

Unpublished Sources
Clippings file on Alda, Music Department, New York Public Library
Metropolitan Opera Archives, New York
Robinson-Locke Theatrical Scrapbooks, Billy Rose Theatre Collection, New York Public Library
Small amounts of archival material on Frances Alda are also found in the archives of Théâtre de la Monnaie, Teatr Wielki, Covent Garden and La Scala. Simonsen family material is in La Trobe Library, Melbourne.

Published Sources
Alda, Frances. *Men, Women and Tenors*, Boston, 1937
Favia-Artsay, Aida. 'Frances Alda', *The Record Collector*, vol.6 no.10, Oct. 1951, pp.221–33
Simpson, Adrienne. '"This Country May Well be Proud of Her": Frances Alda's 1927 Tour of New Zealand', *Music in New Zealand*, vol.6, Spring 1989, pp.36–41, 61
Simpson, Adrienne. '"New Zealand's Most Famous Daughter", a Profile of Frances Alda (1879–1952)', *Women's Studies Journal*, vol.5 no.1, Sept. 1989, pp.61–73
Simpson, Adrienne. 'Frances Alda' in Adrienne Simpson (ed.), *Opera in New Zealand: Aspects of History and Performance*, Wellington, 1990, pp.91–104

HELEN ALLAN

1915–1972

The middle child of nine, Helen Edith Allan, daughter of Alexander and Edith Miller, grew up on an orchard in East Taieri. Doing well was highly regarded, and Helen developed early the desire to achieve academically and on the sportsfield.

As fast bowler in the New Zealand women's cricket team, 'this veritable demon at the bowling crease' was publicly applauded by the English captain during the women's test match of 1935.

A knee injury finished her sporting career, and her marriage in 1939 to Eric Allan, a fellow student at Otago University where Helen was one of the first women to study geology, prevented the completion of her degree.

Their marriage was a union of opposites: he was quiet and pragmatic; she the romantic idealist, intuitive and impetuous. Helen saw her husband as the anchor she needed, but was often frustrated by the very qualities that had first attracted her.

From 1948 they lived in Hamilton where Eric pioneered atomic absorption spectroscopy at Ruakura Animal Research Station. Knowing that his highly specialised work would keep them there, Helen felt trapped, and chafed at the restrictions of small town living.

Her answer was to look outwards, to forge her own identity while fulfilling the needs of her growing family. She chose friends who had come from Europe, cycled to night classes in Maori and Italian, and tried to complete her degree by correspondence. Family commitments made this impossible.

Once the youngest child was at school she taught geography and French, and eventually completed her BA at Waikato and Auckland universities. Teaching became an enthusiasm and was very fulfilling. She was head of the French department at Sacred Heart College when she died.

A large happy family was her goal as much as intellectual achievement, and family always came first. Here, too, she was determined to succeed whatever the cost. Ignoring medical warnings that more than three children could kill her, she had five, spaced judiciously. She did more than most: made clothes by hand when money didn't stretch to a sewing machine, filled the cupboards with jams, preserves and baking, took the children mountain climbing and fossil hunting, played Chopin as they fell asleep. But the price was high. Early photographs show her desperately tired and rashes, a sure sign of stress, periodically appeared on her arms.

A compassionate and loving woman, who could laugh with the exuberance of a child, her weaknesses were her virtues, carried to an extreme. Her intense love and pride in her children could also cause rejection if they failed to meet her high standards. In her later years her sensitivity to the suffering of animals and people became a burden which blighted her life.

Although she was often frustrated by her husband's introspection, their love sustained and nourished them both. The morning after his burial, having attended to all practicalities, she died in her sleep. *Rosemary Allan-Coleman*

Quotation
para.2 *Otago Daily Times*, 1935 (undated clipping in author's possession)

Sources
Material for this essay on Helen Allan came from the memories of her five children. The author is her eldest daughter.

RITA ANGUS

1908-1970

I like to paint the seasons, and devote time to the observation of skies, country, sea and peoples. In portraiture, I note the special personality of the sitter . . .

Aims: To show to the present a peaceful way, and through devotion to visual art to sow some seeds for possible maturity in later generations . . .

As a woman painter, I work to represent love of humanity, and faith in mankind in a world, which is to me, richly variable and infinitely beautiful . . . My paintings express a desire to unite with a great many individual artists everywhere . . . so as to create a living freedom from the afflicting theme of death.

Rita Angus was an innovative painter whose work has had a strong influence on New Zealand art. Born in Hawke's Bay, she was the eldest daughter of Ethel (born Crabtree) and William Angus, a building contractor. Her early interest in art was encouraged and in the 1920s she studied art at Palmerston North Girls' High. In 1927 she enrolled in a Diploma in Fine Arts course at Canterbury College School of Art. Influences at that time included local artists such as Archibald Nicoll, as well as European artists, especially Vermeer and Cézanne, whose work sharpened her interest in geometric composition and form. European art infiltrated Christchurch in the 1920s and 1930s not just through reproductions but also the experiences of artists returned from Europe. Angus was aware of modernism as well as traditional art.

Angus exhibited with the Canterbury Society of Arts for the first time in 1930. That year she married artist Alfred Cook, and gave up the diploma course. She spent six weeks attending life classes at the Elam School of Art in Auckland and then she and Cook both taught art in Napier, returning to Christchurch in 1931. Angus exhibited there regularly and also with the Auckland and Dunedin Societies of Arts and the New Zealand Academy of Fine Arts.

When Angus and Cook separated, in 1934, she began supporting herself through irregular sales of her work and jobs such as newspaper illustrating and part-time teaching. She was hard up financially, but her life was enriched by friendship with such artists as Olivia Spencer Bower, Leo Bensemann, and Louise Henderson. Three exhibitions in Christchurch in the 1930s particularly influenced her: the Empire Art Loan Collection of British Art and exhibitions of Japanese and Chinese art.

In 1939 Angus joined the Peace Pledge Union, a clear statement of her pacifist beliefs. The inclusion in the 1940 National Centennial Exhibition of *Cass* (1936) and *Self Portrait* (1936) signalled critical recognition, but the war years were difficult. Angus lived in various places, taking jobs such as picking tobacco and apples in Nelson. On a meagre income and often in poor health, she continued painting, doing a number of impressive portraits of friends, including Betty Curnow, Douglas Lilburn, Christine Cole Catley, and Theo Schoon. She began exhibiting with The Group in Christchurch in 1932, and continued until 1969. The group was formed by a number of Christchurch artists in 1927 for the purpose of exhibiting independently of the Canterbury Society of Arts; its early members included Evelyn Page (Polson), R. N. Field and Edith Collier.

Under the strain of poverty, anxiety, and living alone as a divorced woman, Angus's health deteriorated and in 1948 she produced only one painting. The following year she was committed to a psychiatric hospital where she stayed until Easter 1950. She emerged from this more withdrawn and introspective, but started exhibiting again that year. From then on she lived mostly in the North Island, though in the early 1950s she travelled frequently, In 1953 she went on a painting trip to Central Otago, a present from Douglas Lilburn, which resulted in her well-known *Central Otago* (1954–69). She settled in Wellington in 1955, buying the Thorndon cottage where she lived until her death.

It was not until 1957 that Angus had her first one-person exhibition. At the Centre Gallery, Wellington, it showed forty-three works. The following year a New Zealand Art Societies' Fellowship took her to London, where she attended life classes at the Chelsea School of Art and was a member of the Institute of Contemporary Arts. She also visited Scotland and Europe, studying both contemporary and traditional European art. She was greatly interested in Byzantine and Renaissance painting, noting the clarity and harmony of Piero della Francesca and the colour of Fra Angelico.

Back in New Zealand in 1959, Angus painted a mural for the Napier Girls' High School. In spite of increasing illness, she painted and exhibited, mainly in Christchurch and at the Centre Gallery in Wellington and the Auckland City Art Gallery.

Angus received little critical attention until 1960 when art critic Peter Tomory placed her with Tosswill Woollaston as a pioneer of modern New Zealand art in the 1930s and 1940s. Public acknowledgement came in 1965 when she was included in the first significant overseas exhibition of New Zealand art, 'Contemporary Painting in New Zealand', at the Commonwealth Institute in London. In 1969 she completed three paintings for an exhibition of New Zealand artists at the Smithsonian Institution, Washington. She painted until a few months before her death in January 1970.

Angus, living alone and childless, spent much of her life in ill health and poverty. She followed the same difficult path that Frances Hodgkins had chosen and described: 'Art absorbs your whole life and being. Few women can do it successfully. It requires enormous vitality.' Angus, like Hodgkins, did do it successfully. The Rita Angus Loan Collection at the National Art Gallery, the largest collection of her work, lists 620 works and sketch-books, a solid testimony to her ability, determination, discipline, and achievement. She painted landscapes, still lifes, portraits, and a remarkable series of fifty-five self-portraits: self as artist, nude, ideal, icon, woman, and, throughout, self in pursuit of spiritual and visual truth.   *Jane Clendon*

Quotations
para.1 R. Angus, *Year Book of the Arts in New Zealand*, no.3, 1947, pp.67–9
para.9 Quoted in E. H. McCormick, 'Frances Hodgkins: A Pictorial Biography', *Ascent*, Dec. 1969, p.8–28

Unpublished Sources
R. Brownson. 'Rita Angus', MA thesis, Auckland, 1977
Rita Angus MS Papers 1399, ATL

Published Sources
Eastmond, Elizabeth, and Penfold, Merimeri. *Women and the Arts in New Zealand*, Auckland, 1986
Friedlander, M. and Barr, J. and M. *Contemporary New Zealand Painters*, Vol.1, Martinborough, 1980
Paul, Janet. 'Biographical Essay', *Rita Angus*, Wellington, 1983 (National Art Gallery exhibition catalogue). The author acknowledges her debt to Janet Paul's work on Rita Angus.

ANNEMARIE ANON

c.1890

Annemarie's story offers us a brief glimpse of the shadowy side of some women's lives late last century. We know about her because she ended up under the care of Frederic Truby King in the Seacliff Asylum. Thanks to his meticulous note taking, and his interception of her mail, we can learn a little of the life of a disturbed young woman who was subjected to the most invasive of medical procedures, 'complete unsexing'.

Before entering first Ashburn Hall and then the Seacliff Asylum, Annemarie lived all her life in Invercargill. She was born around 1869 into a reasonably prosperous family and was regarded as a lively and clever girl. She was described as sympathetic to her schoolfellows, so much so that she was awarded, among other prizes, that for the most popular girl.

On Boxing Day in 1886, when Annemarie was aged seventeen, she went on a picnic and then to a ball in Invercargill. Around midnight she apparently began raving about love and religion and had to be brought home. Her mother reported that these events happened at her menstrual period. Cold baths followed by friction were tried in order to calm Annemarie from her bouts of singing, praying, laughing and crying. After a few months she 'lapsed into profound melancholy' and was eventually sent to Ashburn Hall, a private asylum in Dunedin.

The Ashburn Hall regime seemed to suit Annemarie, and after seven months she returned home reasonably well. But after eight months at home she 'became dull again' and was returned to Ashburn Hall where she remained for a further fourteen months. She was described as well for long periods but odd in that she liked to be solitary, she preferred to eat in private, and she bolted her food.

Annemarie's family consulted their local doctor about her condition; he suggested that some improvement might follow if she were completely unsexed by the removal of her ovaries and clitoris. It had been noted that Annemarie was given to masturbation and the doctor commented that the operation could only do good since 'there could never be any normal outlet for sexuality nor abandonment of the abnormal one'.

On 4 July 1890 Annemarie was committed to Seacliff where her preference

Seacliff Asylum, Otago, at the time Annemarie Anon was a patient, 1890. *Hocken Library*

for solitude and her habits of masturbation were observed. The latter was believed to be the root of her problem. Her father gave his assent to an unsexing operation and on 20 July, Dr Ferdinand Batchelor, one of Dunedin's leading medical luminaries, assisted by three other doctors including Truby King, removed Annemarie's fallopian tubes, ovaries and clitoris. Annemarie was anaesthetised with ether and the operation was carried out in the cottage by the Seacliff railway station. Truby King recorded that there appeared 'to be nothing abnormal in the state of the sexual organs'.

Nearly a month after the operation Annemarie exhibited no mental change. She had to be prevented from getting out of bed and removing her dressings, so her nightdress was sewn up between her thighs. By September Truby King noted that Annemarie no longer had any indecent sexual habits 'excepting an occasional tendency to expose herself' and by late November she was recorded as behaving 'quite sensibly'.

Annemarie's letters to her sister and father speak of her longing to go home. She said she was 'quite better now' and would be 'perfectly well' when she returned home. She was discharged in December having 'lost the downcast shamefaced look which she had when she came to the Asylum'. Her doctor in Invercargill reported on Annemarie's good health, her delight in being home, and expressed his thanks to Truby King for effecting her recovery.

The experiment upon Annemarie, which was regarded as a success, was related to Truby King and Batchelor's medical colleagues at an Otago meeting and recorded in the medical press. It is not clear whether it was repeated on other women who were judged to be suffering from 'masturbational mania'. And we can only speculate how Annemarie, 'unsexed' and denied the right to reproduce, fared for the rest of her life.   *Barbara Brookes*

Unpublished Sources

Seacliff Asylum, Casebook, No.2345–2441, Case No.2367, Seacliff Asylum Archives, Hocken. All quotations are from this source.

Published Sources

Batchelor, F. C. 'A Year's Work in Abdominal Surgery', *NZ Medical Journal*, vol.5, Oct. 1891, p.316
'Report of the Otago Branch'. *NZ Medical Journal*, vol.4, July 1891, p.300

MINA ARNDT

1885–1926

Hermina (Mina) Arndt sought to establish herself as a professional artist in New Zealand during the First World War. Forced to return to New Zealand by the war in Europe just as her career was gaining momentum in Europe, she found her painting derided here for its 'unrelieved dirtiness of colour'. When she died in 1926, at the age of only forty-one, her skills as a print-maker were being discovered by the local art fraternity. A retrospective exhibition at the Suter Gallery in Nelson, which established her innovatory place in New Zealand's art history, did not occur until 1960 and then was initiated by her children (her stepdaughter May and son John Manoy).

Mina was born on her father's estate, 'Thurlby Domain', near the Shotover River. Her father, Charles Henry Arndt, who was a merchant and a farmer, died before she was two. Her mother, Marie (born Beaver), moved herself and her four children (Edith, Jennie, Henry, and Mina) to Dunedin to live with her sister Laura Newman. Dunedin in the 1890s was a lively, cosmopolitan city; amongst women artists working there were Isabel and Frances Hodgkins, Grace Joel, the Wimperis sisters, and Mabel Hill, all offering exciting role models for an artistically gifted girl growing up at the time.

Mina's drawing talent must have been clear at an early age, for she is remembered as always having a pencil in her hand. In her teens she executed 'a most delightful pencil sketch of her sister Jennie'. There is in this early portrait, in pencil and charcoal, a certainty in the execution that is apparent again and again in the heads Mina drew and painted, giving them a strength that is quite out of the ordinary. The portrait suggests that Mina had already had drawing lessons. The family believe Mina attended Otago Girls' High School, where Fanny Wimperis was art mistress.

Marie Arndt seems to have encouraged her daughters' talents, and was probably aware that the family might need to use them to earn a living. Edith was to exhibit with the Otago Art Society and later with the New Zealand Academy of Fine Arts in Wellington. Jennie's abilities in dramatic recitation ensured her success during her subsequent brief stay overseas. To further Mina's training the family came to Wellington where new provisions for free places gave her access to Wellington Technical College in 1905 and 1906.

Mina took a prize for modelling 'from the antique' in clay or wax in the annual student competitions run by the New Zealand Academy of Fine Arts. (In this and other aspects, Mina's life parallels that of her fellow student, the sculptor Margaret Butler.) Between 1905 and 1907, as a student competitor and as a regular exhibitor, Mina exhibited *repoussé* (beaten) metal work, models, and a cabinet with modelled panels (as well as drawings of heads in charcoal and pastels). These applied arts were deemed suitable for 'ladies' – and most of the students in these classes at the Wellington Technical College were women. Mina developed during this time a variety of manual skills, as well as her impressive ability to present three-dimensional form in a range of fine art media.

In late 1906 or early 1907 an inheritance from a friend allowed Marie Arndt to take her daughters to London, where Mina attended the London School of Art. During the winter of 1907–8, Mina was in Newlyn in Cornwall at the School of Painting run by Elizabeth and Stanhope Forbes, at which several New Zealand artists had already studied. The ideas promoted by the artists' colony there, such as their choice of subjects from everyday life, accorded closely with ideas then current in artistic circles in New Zealand.

Stanhope Forbes encouraged Mina to submit work for the 1913 Paris Salon and Royal Academy exhibitions. The *Head of a Woman* is probably one of two heads in charcoal submitted to the Royal Academy and illustrates the artist's ability both to delineate and model her figures. The Paris Salons of 1912–14 and 1926 included Mina's work.

Mina's potential as an etcher was discovered during her first few years overseas. The German etcher Hermann Struck, on a visit to England, was 'so

Mina Arndt, 'Maori women washing',
charcoal, c.1918. *National Art Gallery*

impressed that he did something he had never done before or did afterwards. He
offered to teach her his art in Germany.' Mina's tuition with Struck in Berlin may
have started as early as 1907, and at various times between 1910 and 1914 she
returned to Berlin, where she also had the good fortune to be a pupil of the proto-
Expressionist painter Lovis Corinth. The powerful Expressionist brush-stroke
would have appealed to Mina's strong linear sense, well illustrated by *The Red
Hat* (in the National Art Gallery collection).

Mina became a prohibited alien in Germany with the outbreak of war. She
returned home and held an exhibition of work completed overseas (as Frances
Hodgkins and Dorothy Kate Richmond had done jointly in 1904). The Academy,
once so encouraging, now 'skyed' her paintings (that is, hung them above the
normal sight-line). Mina's dark palette did not accord with the parochial tastes
of the Academy selectors and the safe impressionistic colouring being used by
local artists at the time.

In 1917 she married Lionel (Leo) Manoy, whose first wife May had been
Laura Newman's daughter and Mina's cousin. A studio in the house in Motueka
was prepared for Mina and she had help in the house. Her husband's support
allowed her to continue working as an artist. Mina took up the 'peasant' theme
she had become familiar with in Newlyn and Germany, choosing Maori from
Motueka as her subjects.

She bore a son, John, in 1920 and made loving records of family life. Her
earlier passion for pastels was renewed. When prints again became popular in
New Zealand in the 1920s, her work as a print-maker was appreciated. A *New
Zealand Times* article on 1 December 1921 named Mina as one of six artists
'seriously setting forth individual expressions of national characteristics in our
scenery and life'. Subsequently she opened her own art school and became a vice-
president of the National Art Association of New Zealand. She continued her

contacts with the international art community and received a medal at the British Empire Exhibition at Wembley in 1924.

She died suddenly of nephritis, on 22 December 1926.   *Ann Calhoun*

Quotations
para.1 *Otago Daily Times*, 23 Nov. 1915
paras.3 and 8 Interview with May Manoy

Unpublished Source
Copies of taped conversations with May Manoy, the artist's stepdaughter, on 12 and 19 May 1988, are with the National Oral History Archives, ATL, and the archives of the National Art Gallery, Wellington.

Published Sources
Brown, Gordon. *New Zealand Painting 1900–1920: Traditions and Departures*, Wellington, 1972
Kirker, Anne. *New Zealand Women Artists*, Auckland, 1986

RITA ARNOLD

1900–1966

'I do it all by kindness', was the reply Rita Arnold gave when asked how she handled so easily the huge bulls she paraded in the Nelson Agricultural and Pastoral Show ring. For over twenty years, from 1932 to 1954, seeing shorthorn dairy stud owner Rita Arnold handle her animals was a highlight of the annual show at Richmond. Favourite among bovine personalities she exhibited was the huge bull, Greystone Gunner.

At the show you notice it takes two men to get an Ayrshire bull into the ring.
Another two men will bring in a Jersey. Then along comes a powerful
Shorthorn bull with only Miss Arnold in attendance

reported the *Weekly News* on 17 May 1961. Rita used to explain: 'It's just kindness really. Animals appreciate good treatment, I've never had any trouble.' Rita's kindness included a warm winter cover for every animal, and not letting her animals travel outside Nelson to be exhibited.

Rita was born in 1900 at 'Wilford Grove', Waimea West, about twenty-three kilometres from Nelson. The land her Irish grandfather, James Arnold, took up in the 1840s lies between the Wai-iti River and low foothills, and was then in dense native bush, some of which still remains to shelter stock. Rita's grandmother, born Hannah Wratt, named 'Wilford Grove' after a 'lovers' lane' in her native Nottingham.

Of James and Hannah's nine sons and one daughter, the seventh son Joseph took over the farm. Joseph married Clara Adeline Rutherford (a cousin of Ernest Rutherford); their three daughters were Eleanor (Nellie), Laura (called Lorna), and Rita. None of the three married. Their generation of New Zealand women knew that the loss of thousands of men in the First World War meant many of them could not marry.

But it was not just because she was single and without a brother that Rita entered a career unusual for a woman of her time. Her grandfather, James, who loved beautiful horses, passed on to her an affinity with animals which found a natural outlet in her work on the farm. She was also a superb horsewoman.

There had always been shorthorns on the farm, but in 1932 the pedigree stud was founded, with Joseph there to give encouragement, but with Rita as manager and official owner. Two fine in-calf heifers, Bon Accord Nancy Lee and Babmington Darcy, were bought from the Waikato to improve the gene pool, and they and their progeny helped Wilford Grove Stud win many trophies and establish shorthorn milk-fat records.

Her sisters were nearly seventy when Rita died at Nelson, aged sixty-five, on 12 January 1966. Nellie died the following year but, helped by stockmen, Lorna continued Rita's work for six years.

When Rita died she was the New Zealand Milking Shorthorn Association's only woman honorary life member.   *Elsie Curnow*

Quotations
para.1 *Weekly News*, 17 May 1961; *NZ Free Lance*, 19 Dec. 1945

Unpublished Sources
Information was provided by family members; the author is a cousin of Rita Arnold.

Published Sources
Nelson Evening Mail, 1932–66

SYLVIA ASHTON-WARNER*

1908–1984

To admirers Sylvia Ashton-Warner was a saint and a martyr; to critics she was a fraud and a poseur.

In 1958 her first novel, *Spinster*, became an international best-seller. She was ranked as one of the great educational innovators of the twentieth century following the publication of her third book, *Teacher*, in 1963. But the praise and admiration were by no means universal. Her emotive, introspective writing style, her unorthodox teaching methods, her flamboyant personality, and her non-traditional life-style polarised her audience.

Sylvia Constance Ashton Warner, the seventh child of a family of ten, was born at Stratford in Taranaki on 17 December 1908. Her crippled father, an impoverished English nobleman, was a dreamer and story-teller. Her proud, short-tempered, indomitable mother supported the family by teaching at sole-charge rural schools.

The Warners lived in social isolation. Without material goods or physical space at home and without friends outside, Sylvia turned to her siblings, to her imagination, and to the world of nature for entertainment.

She first encountered mainstream New Zealand in 1922 when she attended high school: one term at Wellington Girls' College, two terms at Masterton District High School, and three years at Wairarapa High School. She did not fit in easily and felt herself ostracised.

*She used the name Ashton-Warner, rather than Warner, once she began to publish.

In 1926 she became a pupil-teacher in Wellington, protesting then, and for the rest of her life, that she hated teaching and never wanted to be a teacher. She dreamt of fame and glamour overseas as an artist or concert pianist, and presented herself to the world as a flamboyant and temperamental actress.

Behind the actress was a child. Sylvia always insisted that she was, at heart, a five-year-old child, and often behaved like one: imaginative, petulant, spontaneous, selfish, creative, and insecure. Her preferred work – story-telling, art, music and drama – was the preferred work of all children.

She attended Auckland Teachers' Training College in 1928 where she met, and later married, fellow student Keith Henderson. After the birth of the last of their three children the Hendersons taught together in Maori schools: Horoera (two years), Pipiriki (four years), Waiomatatini (five years), and Fernhill (five years).

Following a nervous breakdown at Horoera, Sylvia became intensely aware

Eleanor David as Sylvia Ashton Warner with husband Keith (Tom Wilkinson) and child in Michael Firth's film *Sylvia. Bruce Jarvis, New Zealand Film Commission*

of her need for creative self-expression. For the rest of their married life Keith took primary responsibility for the childcare and housework, while Sylvia dedicated herself to developing her talents for writing and art in a series of studios she called 'Selah', and to practising the piano for hours at home.

As her own creativity bloomed, she began to recognise in Maori children the same powerful drives, both positive and negative, which motivated the artist/child in herself. Then at Fernhill her creative energy fused with her rapport with children – and the Key Vocabulary was born. The essence of the Key Vocabulary is that for every child there are certain powerful words related to his or her life and feelings; words that excite and words that terrify. Sylvia found that children who had struggled for months over 'See Spot run' in the Department of Education's *Janet and John* readers took one look at gutsy, down-to-earth words like 'drunk' and 'kiss' – and suddenly they could read. The fact that the Key Vocabulary made the teaching of reading easy, effective, and fun was almost incidental to Sylvia; its importance to her lay in the way those words captioned and defused the violent images of the undermind and nurtured each child's creativity.

The Key Vocabulary had far-reaching implications, but the uncontrollable forces in Sylvia's own undermind prevented her from developing it to its full potential. For most of her adult life she used alcohol, and an array of prescription and over-the-counter drugs, to ease her inner torment. At Fernhill her addiction surged out of control, and in 1955 she resigned from teaching. In 1957 the Hendersons moved to Bethlehem, near Tauranga, where the most productive writing years of Sylvia's life began.

The underlying theme of all her writing, and indeed of her life, was the search for unconditional love and admiration, coupled with a conviction that every loving relationship would end in betrayal. She often fell passionately in love with both men and women, but with the notable exceptions of her husband Keith and Joy Alley (the public health nurse at Pipiriki) her love affairs existed only in her imagination and in the pages of her books.

Sylvia also sought unconditional love and admiration from her mother country and its Department of Education, and bitterly accused both of rejecting her when her expectations were not met.

Her life was shattered in 1969 by the death of her husband; within weeks she left New Zealand vowing never to return. Her travels took her to Mauritius, Israel, England – and back to New Zealand.

In 1970 she left again to spend a troubled year at the newly established Aspen Community School in Colorado. At the end of 1971, she found the recognition she had always longed for when she was appointed Professor of Education at Simon Fraser University in Vancouver. Her teaching formula ('Release the native imagery of our child and use it for working material') and her creative formula ('"Touch the true voice of feeling and it will create its own style and vocabulary": its own power and pace') inspired scores of student teachers, but Sylvia did not find contentment.

Homesickness compounded by heavy drinking drove her back to New Zealand in 1973. She spent her last years living in semi-seclusion in Tauranga and died at home on 28 April 1984.

Her published work includes five novels (*Spinster*, 1958; *Incense to Idols*, 1960; *Bell Call*, 1965; *Greenstone*, 1966; *Three*, 1970), two books on teaching (*Teacher*, 1963; *Spearpoint*, 1971), two works of autobiography (*Myself*, 1966; *I Passed This Way*, 1970), one book of children's songs and stories (*O Children Of The World*, 1974) and a collection of short stories (*Stories of the River*, 1985).

Lynley Hood

Quotations
para.15 S. Ashton-Warner, *I Passed This Way*, p.450

Unpublished Sources
Sylvia Ashton-Warner archives, Mugar Memorial Library, Boston University

Published Sources
Ashton-Warner, Sylvia. *I Passed This Way*, New York, 1979
Ashton-Warner, Sylvia. *Teacher*, London, 1963
Hood, Lynley. *Sylvia! The Biography of Sylvia Ashton-Warner*, Auckland, 1988

ATA-HOE*

c. 1790–1810

A princess of New Zealand, one of the Daughters of Tippahee [Te Pahi], has arrived within these few days in Calcutta, accompanied by her husband, an Englishman of the name Bruce.

The year was 1809 and this was the opening sentence of an article published in the *Calcutta Monthly Journal*, when George Bruce and his young wife, Ata-hoe, arrived in Bengal.

The little we know of Ata-hoe's short life begins about three years before this chronicled arrival in Calcutta. In 1806, when Ata-hoe was about fourteen years old, her father, the northern Maori chief, Te Pahi, had made the return voyage from Sydney to New Zealand in the *Lady Nelson*. During the crossing, Te Pahi became ill and was cared for by a crew member called George Bruce, a former convict who had been transported for life at the age of ten for petty theft. Bruce left the ship with Te Pahi at the Bay of Islands. Over the next two years, by his own account, he was tattooed, became a high-ranking warrior in Te Pahi's tribe, mediated between European traders and Maori, and was given Ata-hoe as a wife. She became known as Mary Bruce.

In 1807 the *General Wellesley* left Sydney for Penang, calling at New Zealand for spars. Her master, Captain Dalrymple, obtained Bruce's assistance to load a cargo of spars. He then asked Bruce to board the vessel and accompany him to North Cape, in a quest for gold dust. Bruce embarked with Ata-hoe, on condition that the captain return them to the Bay of Islands. Dalrymple did not find gold and, unwilling to wait for favourable winds so that he could land Bruce and Ata-hoe, he became impatient and sailed instead for India, via Malacca on the west coast of the Malaysian peninsula, where they arrived in December 1808.

The name Ata-hoe appears variously in the sources as Aetockoe, Etoki, and Atahoe. Ata-hoe ('row carefully') is preferred as the most likely form.

At Malacca, Bruce went ashore to complain to the governor about Dalrymple's actions. While he was away, the captain raised the anchor and sailed to Penang with Ata-hoe still on board. Three or four weeks later the governor at Malacca received news that the ship had arrived at Penang. He gave Bruce permission to make the passage there on a gunboat.

On arrival at Penang, Bruce found that his wife had in the meantime been bartered to a Captain Ross. The governor of Penang intervened, Ata-hoe was returned to Bruce, and they went to Malacca to await a ship bound for New South Wales. No ships came and it was decided that they should go instead via England aboard a homeward-bound East Indiaman. After various vicissitudes they were taken by the *Sir Edward Pellew* back to Penang, and then on to Calcutta where Bruce and his wife, the affectionate companion of his distress, as the *Calcutta Monthly Journal* claims, were received hospitably.

After a brief stay there, they returned to Sydney via Tasmania on board the *Union*. A few days out of Bengal their daughter was born. In February 1810, barely a month after their arrival, Ata-hoe died of dysentery without ever returning to her native land or seeing her people again. Her daughter was left in the care of the Female Orphan School in Sydney. Bruce returned to England and, before his death in 1819 at the age of forty, dictated the story of his life to a fellow pensioner at the Greenwich hospital.

The broad outline of events in Bruce's memoir is probably correct, but a rather different interpretation is suggested by Governor Macquarie of New South Wales, in an official despatch of 12 May 1814:

George Bruce . . . deserted from the Government vessel Lady Nelson *at New Zealand, where he remained, and afterwards married the daughter of the chief Tippahee . . . he went to Bengal . . . and practised gross impostures on that Government, representing himself as a prince of New Zealand, and a man of great consequence there, by which means he obtained considerable sums of money from the Bengal Government, and a passage back to this colony . . . it is not true that George Bruce . . . possesses any interest or authority in New Zealand, where he is, on the contrary, much despised and disliked, on account of his ill usage and neglect of his wife [who] . . . was most shamefully and cruelly neglected in her last illness.*

The convict and the governor speak, but of Ata-hoe's view there is no record. Tossed hither and thither in a foreign world, she must have suffered considerably. She remains, in these accounts, a shadowy, and haunting presence.

Carol Legge

Quotations
para.1 *Calcutta Monthly Journal*, 10 May 1809, in 'Extract from *The Calcutta Monthly Journal*'
para.6 Governor Macquarie to the Under-Secretary of State, 12 May 1814, in R. McNab (ed), *Historical Records of New Zealand*, vol.1, Wellington, 1908, p.322

Unpublished Sources
Edward Robarts, 'Narrative of a voyage to the South Seas, 1797–1824', Micro MS 757, ATL
George Bruce, 'The Life of a Greenwich Pensioner by Himself', Micro MS 533, ATL
J. S. C. Dumont D'Urville, '*Les Zélandais Histoire Australienne*', in Isabel Ollivier, 'Research Notes on French Explorers in New Zealand', Micro MS 779, ATL

Published Sources
Australian Dictionary of Biography, 1788–1859, vol.1, Melbourne, 1966 (George Bruce)
Calcutta Monthly Journal. Extract from *The Calcutta Monthly Journal*, January–May 1809 pp.558–62,
    TL 3/1, 17 May 1969, ATL
Dumont D'Urville, J. S. C. *Voyage Pittoresque Autour du Monde*, Paris, 1839
Lee, Jack, *'I have named it the Bay of Islands . . .'*, Auckland, 1981

JANE MARIA ATKINSON

1824–1914

If Maria Richmond had remained in England she would, on the whole, have enjoyed life because it was in her nature to do so. She would, quite likely, have become a governess, more instructive and more adventurous than most, and would have married, perhaps not 'suitably', for she was impulsive and romantic as well as sensible. All her life she would have been irked by the restraints and artifice imposed on women by the conventions of polite society. There may have been, too, a persistent if faint niggle that she was 'doing nothing useful'. 'Really,' her mother once expostulated, 'Maria is too vigorous for civilized life, she has not half enough to employ her energies in an old country.'

To Maria, New Zealand was both discovery and recognition. She wrote shortly after arriving at New Plymouth in 1853, 'I may have failed to express the intensity of satisfaction I feel in this new home . . . I can say most emphatically that I am disappointed in no single particular.' And when she was employed as the general factotum of 'the mob' (her name for the kin group of Richmonds, Atkinsons, and others who were to settle in the back bush of New Plymouth), this discovery of a homeland led to a recognition of her own natural resources:

I am afraid I have the soul of a maid of all work, and whether I shall ever be anything better seems doubtful. Lely [her mother] seems rather disgusted seeing me scrub about and look dirty as I do when at dirty work, but I consider myself a much more respectable character than when I was a fine lady, did nothing for anybody but made a great many people do things for me. The worst part of my life is that it makes me feel fearfully conceited; I am so proud at finding how easy it is to be independent . . . I am much more in my element here than I ever was before.

It was her brothers' well-being and prospects – bleak in England – that drew the family to New Zealand. Her father, Christopher Richmond, a barrister of Lincoln's Inn, had died at forty-seven, leaving his widow Maria (or Lely, as she was known within her family) with a modest competence and four young children: William (ten), James (nine), Maria (seven), and Henry (two). It was an unenviable position for Lely but, possessing considerable intellectual and spiritual stamina, she set about managing her income to ensure that her sons were educated for the professions and that her daughter was at least well read. What her brothers read, from a wide range of contemporary political and economic writing, Maria read too, and added novels, although for the prolific but jejune work of some of the minor women novelists of the age she had nothing but contempt. Of one of them she wrote, 'I should say . . . she had fed on sponge cake and walked on lawns at least half her life (I mean mental sponge cake and moral lawns) . . . There was such a want of health and vigour in her book.' The Richmonds were Unitarians, members of a religious body which demanded that truth and morality be searched for in every human situation, and which bolstered a radical independence in its followers. This belief gave Maria a mental toughness and resilience which were to serve her well in New Zealand.

Maria's aunt, Helen Hursthouse, had been a reluctant emigrant in 1842. Her husband, John, had set his mind on 'emancipation' in New Zealand, and she and her young family had no choice but to go along with his plans. For Helen, life in Taranaki was domestic slavery set in near poverty in a frightening and alien land. Two of Maria's brothers, James and Henry, followed the Hursthouses to Taranaki in 1850, primarily to reconnoitre for the others. In 1853, Maria's elder brother, William, a struggling London lawyer, married Emily Atkinson of Frindsbury in Kent. Two of Emily's brothers, Harry and Arthur, were also determined to emigrate, and at the end of that year Maria and her mother, with William and Emily, Harry, Arthur, two Richmond cousins, and some other Atkinson friends, set out in the *Sir Edward Paget* to join their kin folk at New Plymouth.

On the voyage Maria and Arthur Atkinson fell in love. The phrase is apt, for the intimacy was outside the bounds of conventional propriety: Arthur was a 'lad of nineteen', Maria was twenty-eight. She wrote to her confidante, Margaret Taylor, that she contemplated 'marrying her grandson' if he did not see the 'error of his ways in preferring old age to youth hereafter'. The unofficial engagement prospered and they were married at New Plymouth at the end of 1854. The age difference was a key factor in their relationship, at least for the first part of their years together. Arthur had a precocious intellect, untrained and therefore unchannelled by any formal education. Maria, although she made no secret of her wish for him to become, eventually, a lawyer, allowed him freedom to explore various avenues and pursuits. Such understanding might have been beyond the capacity of a younger wife.

By 1858 the mob had made clearings and built houses on land along the Carrington Road, outside New Plymouth. The community at Hurworth (as they called it) was a busy one: cricket and horse riding, classes in German, and Maori, madrigal singing and debating, interspersed with forays into local politics, competed with farming, mail-carrying, and cheese-making. Maria and Arthur whiled away the winter months by producing a periodical in the pastoral mode.

The mob was willingly and ardently caught up in the events which led to the Taranaki wars of the 1860s. Maria was among the most vociferous as she berated her unfortunate brother, William (adviser on Maori affairs within the Stafford ministry), over the government's tardy, even pusillanimous attitude (or so it seemed to her) about buying land from Maori of any rank who seemed willing to sell. In her opinion, and that of the majority of Taranaki settlers, the 'right' to private property – the very bulwark of 'civilised' society – was endangered by increasing Maori intransigence. Maria's letters at this time show the expectations of an early and convincing British victory and, when that did not occur, the frustrations and finally the weariness of the long-drawn-out conflict in which all but one of the Hurworth houses were virtually destroyed.

After a sojourn in Auckland where Arthur was employed in the Native Office, he and Maria returned to New Plymouth in 1862. Maria spent the second part of the Taranaki war at 'Beach Cottage' (originally built for Emily and William Richmond), where her only son and third daughter were born. Disease (the result of overcrowding within the township) and the hazards of childbirth (which were accepted as normal) cut a swathe through the women and children, and Maria nursed and cared for many of the mob's young. It was the healthy situation of 'Beach Cottage', she declared, which kept her own immediate family from debilitating illness and death.

While Arthur was variously employed as a farmer, Bushranger (with the Volunteers), editor, journalist, and member of parliament, or chose to seclude himself in his study with Greek and Latin authors, Polynesian philology, spiders, and insects, Maria spent her time 'baby tending' and 'surrounded by little ones'. She was warmly affectionate and, when Arthur was out with the Bushrangers or away in Auckland or Wellington, found her charges an 'antidote to morbidity'. But the company of young children could scarcely provide the intellectual stimulus and companionship she needed. In America at this time Elizabeth Cady Stanton was speaking out against the 'bondage' which tied women to their roles of wife, mother, nurse, and household drudge. Maria would have regarded this view as neither tactful nor common sense. However, if one looks at this period of her life when she described herself as 'tied by the leg', and contrasts Arthur's freedom and opportunities with her lack of them, then the distance between the ardent pioneer feminist and Maria's own experience seems to narrow.

Arthur finally determined to become a lawyer and 'apprenticed' himself as judge's associate to his brother-in-law, C. W. Richmond. The family shifted to Nelson in February 1868 and, after Arthur had entered into a legal partnership with C. Y. Fell, moved to 'Fairfield' in Nelson. Enlarged and refurbished (and today still standing), this became Maria's final home.

Maria had no wish to leave New Zealand permanently; 'young folks and sunshine' were not to be exchanged for the gloom of the crowded 'old country'. But one essential was lacking in the colony – 'higher education for our girls'. To compensate for this lack, Maria spent the years from 1877 to 1881 in England and Europe with various groups of the mob's children. She renewed her friendship, hitherto sustained by letters, with English Unitarian friends and relatives, in particular with Margaret Taylor, who lived in a castle in Germany. Margaret, acting as a friend and counsellor to the older girls, immersed and nurtured them in European culture at Dresden. 'Whatever influence I might have in the world I should wish to use in the cause of education', Maria once wrote. She wanted her girls 'to have a boy's education because it is a better education than what is called a girl's'. She continued:

My experience in the Colony shows me that the most solidly educated women are the most useful in every department of life, and that so called 'feminine refinement' is fatal to female usefulness.

Jane Maria Atkinson was determined to defy old age as long as possible, believing that 'torpor not sin was *the* crime against the soul'. *Jinny Atkinson*

Maria saw education as making women 'fitter for their own special work', and maintained that their true workplace was within the family structure. She did recognise that drastic change was needed to the status of women: 'The ordinary life of women is either constant drudgery or complete frivolity out here.' When Margaret Taylor imagined that 'liberty would lead our sex into all sorts of wild vagaries' Maria replied, 'I have more confidence in *us.*' Politics, whether New Zealand or European, intrigued her; democracy she was not so sure about, and her comments on the political representatives of 'the masses' are pungent and pertinent.

In Nelson Maria busied herself with the welfare of Nelson College for Girls, of which she had been an early and keen advocate, the Temperance Movement, and its close associate, women's suffrage. She was determined to defy old age 'in spirit' for as long as possible, believing that 'torpor not sin was *the* crime against the soul'. She was in no way dismayed by the turmoil following Darwin's theory of evolution and the 'Higher Criticism' of the Bible, which together shook the authoritarian stance of the Church, nor by the agitation for women's 'rights'. However, she had little sympathy with the American women's movement: 'Our worthy brethren and sisters there have a knack of dressing up the most important truths so nauseously that they turn the strongest stomachs.' 'I rejoice in living in such exciting times,' she wrote, 'when all science and philosophy seem to be bent on searching to the root of things.'

Maria died at 'Fairfield' at the age of ninety, outliving Arthur by thirteen years. Rheumatism had increasingly laid hold of the outward woman, and it is evident from the handwriting of her last extant letters that it was finally crippling her fingers. Vigorous, always in an 'energetic scramble' with body and with spirit, having also a well-informed incisive mind, Maria, through her letters, travels well, and with good humour, confidence, and faith (she would insist on a measure of scepticism) looks forward. *Frances Porter*

Quotations
para.1 Maria (Lely) Richmond to M. Taylor, 6 Aug. 1851, Acc 77–253, vol.2, p.94, ATL
para.2 J. M. Richmond, 24 Sept. 1853, vol.13, ATL
para.3 J. M. Richmond to M. Taylor, Jan. 1850, vol.38, p.119, ATL
para.5 J. M. Richmond to M. Taylor, 27 May 1853, Discards, ATL
para.11 J. M. Atkinson to M. Taylor, 23 March [1870], Addl. 1870/2, ATL
para.12 J. M. Atkinson to M. Taylor, 23 March [1870], Addl. 1870/2, ATL
para.13 J. M. Atkinson to M. Taylor, 20 Jan. 1864, vol.38, p.537, ATL; J. M. Atkinson to M. Taylor,
    23 March [1870], Addl. 1870/2, ATL

Unpublished Sources
Ann Paterson private collection
Arthur Richmond Atkinson MS papers 204, ATL
Hursthouse family letters 1788–1854, MS 042, Taranaki Museum (microfilm at ATL, Micro MS 449)
Jinny Atkinson private collection
Richmond-Atkinson family papers (45 volumes plus the 'additional' and 'discards' letters), Acc 77–253,
    ATL
Richmond family papers, Acc 77–173, Acc 84–56, Acc 85–50, ATL

Published Sources
Porter, Frances. *Born to New Zealand: A Biography of Jane Maria Atkinson*, Wellington, 1989
Scholefield, Guy (ed.). *The Richmond-Atkinson Papers* (2 vols), Wellington, 1960

MOTHER MARY JOSEPH AUBERT

1835 – 1926

Marie Henriette Suzanne Aubert, the disfigured daughter of a wealthy Lyonnais family; Sister Joseph, the embattled French nun, defying episcopal displeasure to continue teaching Maori girls in Auckland; 'Meri', lay sister, missionary, teacher, and nurse to the Maori of the Hawke's Bay and Wanganui areas; the Very Reverend Mother Mary Joseph Aubert, founder of the New Zealand Sisters of Compassion, a national figure revered by Protestant and Catholic alike for her work among the urban poor and destitute.

These were just four personae of New Zealand's most famous female religious figure. Aubert's long and varied life gave more opportunity than most for fact and fiction to become intertwined, and for stories attesting to her saintliness to proliferate, but the reality of her remarkable career needs no embellishment.

In 1860, Aubert travelled from France to Auckland with Bishop Jean Baptiste Pompallier. She and three other French women formed the Congregation of the Holy Family, and undertook the education of Maori children. The venture was very much under Pompallier's personal protection, and the vicissitudes surrounding his departure in 1868 caused it to fall apart. Aubert was ordered by the new bishop, Dr Croke, to abandon her school, to desist from wearing religious habit, and to return to France.

Aubert defied the bishop on this last count, and it was as a lay sister that she commenced the second stage of her work. In 1871 she responded to a request from the Marist father Euloge Reignier to join his missionary work at Meanee in Hawke's Bay. There she developed an interest in Maori herbal remedies (which would later lead to their commercial production under her name), and in 1879 she published a Maori language prayer book and catechism. Despite the physical hardships, Aubert was later to describe her years in Hawke's Bay as the happiest in her life.

Aubert's persistent representations were largely responsible for the revival of the Marist mission to the Maori elsewhere in the Wellington diocese, and in 1883 she was sent to reinforce one such endeavour at Hiruharama (Jerusalem) on the Wanganui River. Conditions in that isolated community were harsh, but it became apparent that there was a place in New Zealand for a new religious order, one specifically adapted to pioneering conditions in the colony. Aubert gathered around her a group of young women postulants, most of Irish extraction, and in 1892 Archbishop Redwood sanctioned the formation of the diocesan congregation named 'The Daughters of Our Lady of Compassion'. Aubert was first superior of this, New Zealand's indigenous Catholic order of nuns.

Before the 1890s Aubert's activities were centred mainly on the Maori population. In 1891 her work developed in another direction, with the admission to Jerusalem of Pakeha children, many of them illegitimate or abandoned. Aubert came under fire then and in later years for insisting that the identity of her small charges be kept secret. She was accused of denying children knowledge of their parentage, and allowing young women to escape the consequences of vice. Aubert's defenders argued that by taking in such babies she reduced the likelihood of infanticide and gave single mothers a new start in life. However, a spate of deaths in the mission during 1898 did little for Aubert's cause and may have convinced her of the difficulty of managing such an establishment at isolated Jerusalem, far from medical facilities and cut off from public awareness.

Besides these considerations, Aubert had long been urged by Wellington Catholics to undertake nursing and social work in the capital. In January 1899 she and three of her sisters left for Wellington to begin a new era of social work among the urban poor. From district nursing among the sick poor, the sisters moved into the institutional care of the old, the ill and disabled, of sick children, and of 'foundlings'. St Joseph's Home for Incurables was opened in 1900, the Home of Compassion at Island Bay in 1908, and an Auckland home for 'foundlings', St Vincent's, in 1910 (closed by episcopal decree in 1916).

However, Aubert's work was never narrowly institutional: a soup kitchen functioned in Wellington's Buckle Street, and a day nursery was established in 1902 in recognition of the needs of poor working women. Throughout, Aubert was distinguished by the breadth and variety of her social outreach, by the fact that her efforts were extended to some of the least attractive, least prepossessing and, some thought, least 'deserving' members of New Zealand society. She also refused to restrict her work to Catholics, earning the displeasure of potential benefactors and of members of the Catholic hierarchy.

The fact that some of Aubert's greatest conflicts were with members of her own church shows something of the difficulties faced by church women at that time. In Australia and New Zealand at the turn of the century there was a marked expansion of religious sisterhoods, Catholic and Protestant, combining practical social work with the salvation of souls. In such communities women were able to seize responsibility, to achieve results, and to act in ways that would not have been open to them as individuals. Yet Aubert's experience shows the constraints that could be placed on women's initiatives by unsympathetic male hierarchies within the churches. It took an individual of Aubert's unsurpassed determination, confidence and uncompromising nature to prevail against such forces. In 1913, at the age of seventy-eight, she travelled to Rome to gain papal recognition of her congregation. The appropriate Decree of Praise was obtained in 1917, freeing Aubert from the jurisdiction of local bishops.

Mother Mary Aubert in later life.
Our Lady of Compassion Archives

Aubert retained a close interest in her sisters' activities in Wellington and Jerusalem and, although less personally active, remained very much their spiritual mother. In 1926 this 'little old nun', tiny and bespectacled, died. Her funeral, attended by politicians and church leaders of many denominations, was said to be the largest ever given a woman in New Zealand.

Margaret Tennant

Unpublished Sources
Daughters of Our Lady of Compassion, Archives, Home of Compassion, Wellington
Paul Bergin, 'Hoani Papita to Paora: the Marist Missions of Hiruharama and Otaki 1883–1914', MA thesis, Auckland, 1986
Margaret Tennant, 'Women and Welfare; the response of three New Zealand women to social problems of the period 1890–1910', BA Hons research essay, Massey, 1974

Published Sources
Evening Post, 2 Oct. 1926 (obituary)
Harper, Barbara. *Unto These Least: The Story of Mother Aubert and her Great Work*, Wellington, 1962

Manawatu Daily Times, 4 Oct. 1926 (obituary)
Rafter, Pat. *Never Let Go! The Remarkable Story of Mother Aubert*, Wellington, 1972
Simmons, E. R. *In Cruce Salus: a History of the Diocese of Auckland 1848-1980*, Auckland, 1982

ANNIE AVES

? - 1938

Isabel Annie Aves achieved notoriety by being brought to trial four times for murder. Despite the best efforts of the Crown prosecution, Mrs Aves was never convicted because the all-male juries consistently failed to agree on a verdict.

Mrs Aves lived in a typical suburban house in Fitzroy Avenue, Hastings. She was well known to women in the town and the surrounding area of Hawke's Bay as an abortionist – a speciality that made her much in demand in the Depression years. In one eighteen-month period when she dealt with 183 persons, Annie Aves earned £2,232/10/-. We do not know how she learned her trade, or whether she was motivated by greed or humanity, but we do know that she provided a service that many women wanted.

Unlike other abortionists who preferred to operate before the third month of pregnancy, Mrs Aves did not hesitate to perform later abortions. She mostly used the sea-tangle tent which, when inserted into the neck of the uterus, absorbed moisture and so caused dilation and eventually miscarriage or premature labour.

When the police raided the Fitzroy Street premises in June 1936, they found twenty-two separate collections of foetal remains buried in the garden. A number of women were willing to admit they had consulted Mrs Aves about having an abortion, how much they had paid her, and that she had induced miscarriage. There was no evidence in the house, however, of sea-tangle tents to prove that it was Mrs Aves who had been responsible for the abortions. Another difficulty was that the women who gave evidence against Mrs Aves were accomplices to the crime, and juries were reluctant to convict abortionists while the women who used their services went scot-free.

Mrs Aves was defended by Mr C. G. Barker, a well-known Napier barrister and a former member of the House of Representatives for Hawke's Bay. Her inconclusive trials were followed avidly by the press, and few doubted that, when no verdict could be reached and she was released, Mrs Aves would return to her former trade.

On her release Mrs Aves moved to Westshore, Napier. It was there, in September 1938, that she was visited by a young woman who preferred an abortion to a hastily arranged marriage. Mrs Aves took the young woman in on a Thursday, performed the abortion, and she returned home on Saturday. By Sunday the young woman was very ill. Her boyfriend, who had delivered her to Mrs Aves, insisted that she see a doctor and she was admitted to Waipukurau Hospital. The young man was led to believe that his girlfriend, whom he had wished to marry, was about to die. Collecting a gun, he retraced his steps, knocked on Mrs Aves's door and, when she answered, shot her. Annie Aves died the next day. The young woman survived and gave evidence at her boyfriend's trial, which resulted in a verdict of manslaughter and an eight-year sentence.

Barbara Brookes

Published Sources
Evening Star, 17 Feb. 1937, p.8
Lynch, P. P. *No Remedy for Death: The Memoirs of a Pathologist*, Victoria, 1970, pp.91-8

AMELIA BAGLEY

1871–1956

District nursing in New Zealand owes much to Amelia Bagley, whose warm and energetic presence was felt throughout the country during her long working life. Born in 1871 to Amelia (born Prictor) and Benjamin Bagley, a Dunedin chemist, she trained at Dunedin Hospital during the years 1892–5. The next seven years she spent as a ward sister at Auckland Hospital. State registration for nurses was introduced in New Zealand in 1902 and her name was entered on the register in March of that year. Her leadership qualities were soon recognised and in her early thirties she became matron of Masterton Hospital from 1903 to 1905.

Amelia Bagley's lifelong interest in midwifery began when she was among the first intake of trainee midwives at the new St Helen's Hospital in Wellington. In December 1905, soon after the register of midwives opened, she obtained her midwifery registration.

After two years of private nursing she was appointed Assistant Inspector of Private Hospitals and Midwives, and travelled New Zealand to inspect and supervise the many small maternity hospitals in both urban and rural areas (often in private homes). In an effort to improve the standards of midwifery, she was particularly concerned to advise midwives who were registered by the Midwives Registration Act (1904) but who had not had the benefit of formal training.

By mid-1911, however, she was concentrating on establishing in remote rural areas nursing stations at which nurses could be based to work with the Maori people. She personally set up bases at Te Karaka and Te Araroa on the East Coast, living and working in these (and other) places, often with horses as the only means of transport, until after the appointed nurse had arrived and had been introduced to the local people.

Amelia Bagley continued and developed this work when appointed as superintendent nurse of the Native Health Nurses in 1912. To be nearer the centre of her work in the upper part of the North Island she was based in Auckland at the District Health Office. She travelled extensively, establishing new nursing bases, and supporting nurses already working in isolated communities.

When outbreaks of typhoid fever and smallpox occurred in the north during 1913, she was despatched to provide immediate help and assisted in setting up camp hospitals in several communities. During the height of the smallpox epidemic she was reported to have 'almost lived in the saddle' for two months as she rode from one settlement to another, providing nursing care and advice, supervising quarantine, and other activities.

Amelia Bagley's district nurses provided primary health care and advice to people in remote areas and were forerunners to public health nurses such as Miss E. Norton, pictured here at Porirua Pa. *National Publicity Studios, Alexander Turnbull Library*

During the First World War Amelia Bagley was granted leave for active service abroad. She served first as matron of the hospital ship *Maheno* on its third commission in 1917, and later as matron of the *Marama*. On her return to the Department of Health in mid-1918, she continued to develop and supervise the rural nursing service in the northern and eastern parts of the North Island until her retirement in 1931.

Throughout much of her professional life and well into her retirement, she was active in the New Zealand Trained Nurses' Association. She represented the Auckland area on the Central Council in the 1920s and 1930s, and held office in the Auckland branch of the association; in 1930, she convened the newly formed Public Health Nursing Section. She wrote for *Kai Tiaki* (which later became the *New Zealand Nursing Journal*) on her experiences in district nursing work, and other topics such as 'Nursing Precautions in Typhoid' and the 'Economic Position of Nurses'. For a short period in 1915 while the editor of the journal, Hester Maclean, was on active service, Amelia Bagley was a member of the editorial committee.

During the early years of her retirement she also maintained an active interest in the New Zealand Returned Army Sisters Association. The last years of her life were shared with her sister Mary, also a nurse. Amelia died at their home in Turama Road, Royal Oak, Auckland, on 30 January 1956 at the age of eighty-five. Her obituary records a warm and generous personality which won her the love and admiration of those who worked with her.

Amelia Bagley's pioneering work in rural district nursing laid the foundations for our present public health nursing service, which continues to serve many of the communities in which she first established a nursing base.

Marie Burgess

Unpublished Sources
Register of Nurses, Nursing Council of NZ, Wellington

Published Sources
Gibson Smith, Margaret. *NZ Nursing Journal (Kai Tiaki) Index, volumes 1-62, 1908-1969*, Wellington, 1980
NZ Nursing Journal (Kai Tiaki), vols.1-49, 1908-1956

WILHELMINA SHERRIFF BAIN

1845 -1944

Wilhelmina Sherriff Bain was president of the committee which called the inaugural convention of the National Council of Women (NCW) in Christchurch in 1896.

She was about thirteen years old when her parents, John and Elizabeth Middlemiss Bain, came to Southland from Scotland with their seven children in 1858. They had sufficient means to buy a country estate and to build an impressive house in Invercargill. As a young woman she was engaged to be married, but her fiancé, John Clark, died and she remained single until she was sixty-nine.

Locally known as 'Minnie' Bain, she taught in Southland schools from 1880 to 1894. She complained to the education board that, being a woman, she received little more than half the salary of the male second assistant, and that she was teaching eighty-nine pupils in standard three, leaving insufficient time for study to improve her qualifications. However, she was a very well-informed member of the NCW, arguing for protective laws for workers, women on juries, prison reform, and proper financial provision for the dependants of propertied men.

Her absorbing passion was peace. She delivered the papers on 'Peace and Arbitration' to successive NCW conventions. In 1897 there were only three dissentients from her resolution declaring war to be 'a savage, costly and futile method of settling disputes, hostile to that realisation of brotherhood which is essential to the progress of humanity'.

Unhappily, when the Dunedin convention met in 1900, New Zealand was involved in the Boer War. Kate Sheppard, presiding, was anxious not to split the council and a compromise resolution was passed, regretting but not opposing the war. But Wilhelmina's prepared paper had been read, and cries of outrage in Dunedin followed her declaration that she was 'neither pro-British nor pro-Boer, but pro-humanity'. Undaunted, she wrote to the *Otago Daily Times*:

I confess that I am imbued with a sense of the sacredness of human life as compared with property, however enormous and however vested . . . beautiful as is the sense of patriotism, the solidarity of mankind is a still greater ideal. There is no opposition between the two conceptions; one is simply included in the other.

After leaving Southland, Wilhelmina taught at different places including Queen Victoria School for Maori girls in Auckland, and also travelled. That she

35

was an accomplished speaker is indicated in her pamphlet *Human Betterment*, printed in Gisborne in 1901, an address 'delivered . . . in various parts of the colony'. In that year she was chosen to represent the NCW on the standing committee on peace and arbitration of the International Council of Women. In 1904 she attended the International Congress of Women in Berlin, and she told the Thirteenth Universal Peace and Arbitration Congress in Boston that 'the love of peace for its own sake is becoming more and more freely expressed among us'.

When the Defence Acts of 1909 and 1911 introduced compulsory military training, Wilhelmina was keen to be part of the widespread 'anti-militarist' action; but she was now in Riverton caring for an invalid sister. With the help of friends she initiated a Women's Peace Society in Invercargill, and the Aparima Peace Society with a membership of twelve; and issued her own leaflet, *Compulsory Militarism*, reprinted from the *Southland Times*. Her verse collection *Riverton Sands & Other Verses* (undated) reflects her horror and grief when war broke out (evidently the Balkans War):

> *Armies and navies on land, on the sea,*
> *and in the air*
> *Fearing - boasting - evoking enmity,*
> *Everywhere:*
> *Cabinet ruptures, and men marched away,*
> *Knowing not why;*
> *Drilled to mutilate, to torture, to slay,*
> *And doomed to die.*
> *'Lo! The Glad Morn!'*

Her writing at this time showed her love of wild places, and she urged 'Speed the day when Aparima Estuary and Aparima Bush shall become sanctuaries for all unoffending life!'

In 1914 she married a widowed farmer of Fortrose, Robert Archibald Elliot. As the war proceeded, she apparently accepted its realities. Her song for the Fortrose Red Cross extolled the heroism of Gallipoli, but there was no anti-German sentiment. The war was a universal tragedy, a 'wilderness of woe'.

After her husband's death in 1920, Wilhelmina returned to Auckland and also travelled again. In England she published *Service, a New Zealand Story* (1924), a short fiction work, and her collected poems, *From Zealandia* (1925). Her verses reveal the breadth of her interests and human sympathies. She continued to believe in universal brotherhood as the alternative to war, and maintained her links with fellow-thinkers including the Revd J. H. G. Chapple and Ada Wells.

She died in Auckland on 26 January 1944, in her hundredth year.

Elsie Locke

Quotations
para.4 *Lyttelton TImes*, 2 April 1897, p.21
para.5 Quoted in B. Holt, *Women in Council*, pp.36–7
para.6 *Official Report of the Thirteenth Universal Peace Congress*, Boston, 1904, pp.127–8 (in Women's Archives, AIM)
para.8 'Riverton', undated article from *Otago Witness* in author's possession

para.9 W. S. Bain, *From Zealandia*, London, 1925, p.95

Unpublished Sources

Information about the Bain and Elliot families came from the Wallace Early Settlers Association, Riverton.

Bona Pankhurst, letter to the author, 9. Dec. 1977

C. R. N. Mackie Papers, corres. files 29, 208, Canterbury Museum

K. W. Sheppard Papers, Canterbury Museum

Megan Hutching, 'Turn Back this Tide of Barbarism': New Zealand Women who were Opposed to War, 1869–1919', MA thesis, Auckland, 1990

Teacher register, Southland Education Board

Published Sources

Auckland Star, 27 Jan. 1944 (obituary)

Bain, W. S. 'Compulsory Militarism', *Southland Times*, 22 Aug. 1911

Hall-Jones, F. G. *Invercargill Pioneers*, Invercargill, 1946

Havelaar, M. G. *A Short History of the Christchurch Branch of the National Council of Women of New Zealand from 1896–1950*, Christchurch, 1950

Holt, Betty. *Women in Council: A History of the National Council of Women of New Zealand*, Wellington, 1980

Lyttelton Times, 14–19 April 1896 (reports on NCW Convention); 3 April 1897; 20 May 1901

Mataura Ensign, 7 June 1892

Otago Daily Times, 27 Jan. 1944 (obituary)

The White Ribbon, vol.10 no.115, Dec. 1904

NOELINE BAKER

1878–1958

Isabel Noeline Baker was a Christmas child, born in Christchurch on 25 December 1878 to John Holland Baker, a surveyor, and his wife Isabel (who was a second cousin of the biographer Lytton Strachey). In 1891 the family moved to Wellington, where John Baker became Commissioner of Crown Lands for the Land District of Wellington and a year later became Assistant Surveyor-General in the Department of Lands and Survey.

When Noeline was eighteen, the family set off for foreign parts – Australia, India, Burma, Hong Kong, China, North America, and England. In 1899 Noeline enrolled at the Slade School of Fine Art, University College, London. By 1907, however, art was forsaken for women's suffrage.

In 1905, the Bakers moved to Guildford, where in 1910 Noeline was a founder member of the Guildford branch of the National Union of Women's Suffrage Societies (NUWSS). As honorary secretary she organised demonstrations, obtained signatures for petitions, spoke at meetings, convened a Sweated Industries Exhibition in 1911 and conducted fund-raising events, including a great sale of plants which came from famous gardens of Surrey. In the wider sphere she was a member of the London Society for Women's Suffrage (LSWS) and, from 1914, on its executive committee. Again, her organisational skills brought 'comfort and assistance'.

At the outbreak of the First World War in 1914, Noeline took charge of a register of voluntary workers at the London office of the LSWS, but her important contribution to the war effort was in Surrey. Women workers were required for farms to overcome the critical shortage of labour. As the honorary secretary of the Surrey Committee for Women and Farm Labour, Noeline organised training and found work on farms for women. In 1917, as the food crisis deepened, the British Board of Agriculture founded the Women's Land Army. Noeline was appointed the organising secretary for the county of Surrey. In 1920 she received the MBE for her work.

When the war was over, she had more time for gardening, painting, and travel. But her political activity continued. She presented a scheme for post-war agricultural reconstruction to the labour sub-committee of the War Agriculture Committee. In 1920 she became a member of the executive committee of the National Association of Landswomen, formed after the Women's Land Army disbanded, and later assisted in the amalgamation of the National Association of Landswomen and the National Federation of Women's Institutes. She was an active member of the League of Nations Union. When her mother died in 1920, Noeline cared for John Baker at Guildford until his death in 1930.

In 1931 Noeline returned to New Zealand and made her base on Stewart Island (which she had visited in 1921 while on holiday with her father). During her stay she edited her father's diaries for the book *A Surveyor in New Zealand 1857–1896*. She returned to England the following year, but she must have missed the beauty and tranquillity of that remote place, because by 1934 she had decided to lease her Guildford home and was having a house built on Stewart Island. When she moved into her new home in 1935, a Maori friend named the property 'Moturau Moana', meaning 'islands of bush above the sea'.

Stewart Island's botany fascinated Noeline. The island has an unusual number of endemic species, and many of its vegetation patterns remain unchanged. Already she was familiar with garden design through her acquaintance with Gertrude Jekyll, the English garden designer. At 'Moturau Moana', however, Noeline wanted to create something different. She aimed to grow everything indigenous to the island, as listed by the botanist Leonard Cockayne in 1909. Over a fifteen-year period, many people collected plants for her and a unique botanical garden was established. In the process Noeline became an expert on New Zealand plants. She was invited to attend the Dominion Bush Preservation and Amenity Conference in 1937, and in 1949 was awarded the Loder Cup in recognition of her dedicated conservation work on Stewart Island.

When the Second World War began, Noeline was visiting England. The British Ministry of Agriculture and Fisheries invited her to return to her old job with the Women's Land Army. She found, however, that the work-load was now too great. While in England she was greatly influenced by the writings of Sir Norman Angell. He believed people had to think carefully about the kind of peace they wanted if a lasting world peace was to be achieved.

On her return to New Zealand Noeline promoted study groups for the Post-War Reconstruction Society. A Wellington group was formed in 1941 and another in Christchurch during 1943. Noeline also became the honorary secretary of the Women's Active Service Club, Christchurch, in 1942.

At a special ceremony on Stewart Island in 1948 Noeline Baker handed over 'Moturau Moana' and nearby Baker Park to the New Zealand government, to be used for the encouragement of learning and as a centre for botanical study and research. She had a cottage built for herself nearby. In 1952 she purchased a house in Nelson where she began to spend the winters,

Noeline Baker died at Stewart Island on 25 August 1958. The house at 'Moturau Moana' was destroyed by fire in 1967, but the botanical garden, now in the care of the Department of Conservation, remains as a living memorial to a remarkable woman.   *Leah Taylor*

Unpublished Sources
John Holland Baker, diaries, 9 June 1875 to 17 March 1897, ATL
Letters to the author from: University College, London 8 Feb. 1989; Col. the Lord Freyberg, 14 May 1989; S. Natusch, 27 Sept. 1987; L. Kennedy, 12 Sept. 1989; Hugh Wilson, 22 May 1989
J. H. Baker, newspaper clippings, ATL (this includes material on N. Baker)
Noeline Baker, papers connected with NUWSS activities, Women's Land Army, and Post-War Reconstruction Society, Hocken

Published Sources
Baker, N. (ed.) *A Surveyor in New Zealand 1857–1896: The Recollections of John Holland Baker*, Auckland, 1932
Dempsey, G. *The Little World of Stewart Island*, Wellington, 1974
Dominion, 1 July 1941
Evening Star, Dunedin, 26 Aug. 1958 (obituary)
Natusch, S. *Moturau Moana*, Christchurch, 1956
NZ Woman's Weekly, 7 Jan. 1943
Otago Daily Times, 9 Dec. 1948
Phillips, G. A. R. *The History of the Loder Cup: A Review of the First 25 Years*, Wellington, 1960
The Press, Christchurch, 8 April 1943
Southland Times, 29 June 1940; 3 June 1967

JANE BANNERMAN

1835–1923

Of all the 247 passengers the *Philip Laing* brought up the Otago harbour on a sunny day in April 1848, none can have been more excited than thirteen-year-old Jane Burns. Independent of temperament, yet secure in her close family, she revelled whole-heartedly in the great adventure of founding a new colony. Her reminiscences offer us a unique insight, from the fresh perspective of a young teenager, into what migration meant for our first settlers.

For Jane's family it was the culmination of six years of effort and difficulty which had begun when her father, the Revd Thomas Burns, broke with the Church of Scotland to help found a more austere Free Church. His family at once left the elegant manse where Jane and her older sister Clemie had spent an idyllic childhood. While Thomas Burns gave himself over to promoting his vision of a model settlement — Scottish and Free Church — in distant New Zealand, the family moved from one cramped and dingy house to another, pressed for money and dogged by ill health.

Then came the burden of packing and the misery of parting. 'Let no one think,' wrote Jane, 'it was a light or easy matter to get ready to emigrate . . . it was a heavy undertaking . . . ' When at last the family boarded ship, it was in relentless rain and amidst a confusion of weeping women and homesick children crowding the deck.

Jane's account skims lightly over the voyage itself. She found it tedious ('I sewed all the time and read instructive books') but was pleased that the health of her mother and little sisters benefited from the sea air.

The first night the family spent on shore in New Zealand was unforgettable: the weather was bitter, the house unfinished, and the blankets missing, so Jane and Clemie, dressed in outdoor clothes, huddled under a piece of carpet to keep off the snow.

For the next eight years Jane's life centred on home ('as sweet and lovely a home as heart could desire') and family. Clemie sailed away with her new husband, the captain of the *Philip Laing*, leaving Jane her mother's mainstay in caring for her two, later three, younger sisters. 'In my own way,' she said, 'I cast in my lot with our new land.'

In May 1856 Jane married the Revd William Bannerman, one of two new ministers sent from Scotland to help her father in his fast-growing charge, and set off with him to begin a thirty-year-long shared ministry. William Bannerman's parish covered most of South Otago and Southland, but its heart was at Puerua, near Balclutha. Here volunteers from the congregation built a 'little church in the bush' and later a manse. Jane delighted in the unspoiled beauty of the place, the 'unbroken wilderness all around and fern ten feet high on the slope to the river'. Through the open door of the church on Sundays bird-song mingled with the songs of praise.

It was also lonely. William Bannerman walked extraordinary distances over his sprawling parish (3,600 miles in the first year) and was often held up by snow or swollen rivers, forced to sleep in the open in remote areas. Jane was left alone with her children – there were to be four girls and two boys – for up to a month at a time. When her husband was away, she would herself conduct divine service for family and any guests. Gradually, closer settlement led to the subdivision of the huge parish and the Bannermans' pastoral work became confined to the Puerua district. William's retirement in 1884 marked the end of this phase of their lives.

The couple returned to Dunedin and, while William took a leading part in church administration and mission work, Jane threw herself into a multitude of church-related activities: sewing circles, mothers' prayer and study meetings, YMCA, Sailors' Rest. To all of these she brought the energy and charm that had made her so admired and loved in every community she had lived in. Above all, with persistence and passion and in countless laborious ways, she raised money for the church's New Hebrides mission. A visit to the mission with her husband in 1889 touched her pioneering spirit deeply and she wrote of it as a high point of her life.

Jane continued her work for missions after William's death in 1902. She became the first president of the Presbyterian Women's Missionary Union and, in spite of increasing deafness, remained its international secretary for the rest of her life.

Jane Bannerman died in 1923, surrounded by children and grandchildren, in a Dunedin that bore scant resemblance to the little settlement she had come

Jane Bannerman in later life, and a page from her sketchbook, probably made while on holiday. *Dix Family Collection*

to three-quarters of a century before. A plaque in her honour sits alongside that to her husband in First Church, a tribute to a shared vocation.

Dorothy Page

Quotations
para.3 J. Bannerman, 'Reminiscences of her Life to 1855', p.35
para.4 J. Bannerman, 'Reminiscences', p.41
para.6 J. Bannerman, 'Reminiscences', pp.45, 44
para.7 J. Bannerman, *Jubilee Memorial*, p.8; J. Bannerman ('Nissi'), 'Looking Back', ch.5

Unpublished Sources
J. Bannerman, Diary and letters, 1889, of the New Hebrides trip, held by the Dix family, Waitepeka
J. Bannerman, 'More Reminiscences. The Life and Work of Rev William Bannerman', Typescript, held by the Dix family
J. Bannerman, 'Reminiscences of her Life to 1855', Typescript, M. I. 536/B, Hocken
J.(?) Bannerman, Short sermons and commentaries, held by the Dix family

Published Sources
Bannerman, J. 'Looking Back', *Clutha Leader*, 31 Aug. 1900 (under the pseudonym 'Nissi')
Bannerman, J. *Jubilee Memorial of the South Clutha Parish, comprising Puerua, Port Molyneux and Romahapa Part I, 1854–84* (held at Knox College)
Harvest Field, 17 Dec. 1923 (obituary)

ETHEL TE TUMANAKO BARCLAY

1885–1968

Ethel Harriet Te Tumanako Barclay was the product of a mixed marriage. She was the eldest child of Ngaone Pomare ('aboriginal native woman') and David Francis Glenville Barclay ('Gentleman'), as they are described on the marriage certificate from the registry office at Tauranga.

Such marriages were not common in the latter half of the nineteenth century. David Barclay's father was Captain William Malo de Rune Barclay, youngest son of a Scottish baronet. He served in the British army in Burma, and came 'out to the colonies' in 1881 to settle in Te Puke along with his family of six sons and three daughters.

Ngaone was the daughter of Ngarongo Pomare and Te Aongahoro Te Papa of Ngaiterangi and Ngati Ranginui. The relationship between Ngaone and David was a matter of great concern to both families, especially after the birth of the children – Ethel (Te Tumanako), Frances (Hauauru), and Glenville (Punga). By the time Ngaone and David married, Captain Barclay had transferred the rest of his family to Wellington and another settler witnessed the marriage with Ngaone's father.

David and Ngaone also moved to Wellington, where David's knowledge of the Maori language brought him employment as an interpreter to parliament. Ethel grew up as the indulged only daughter with four brothers. Ngaone died when Ethel was only twenty.

Just over a year later she was married, to Frederick William Moore, a post office worker, who had little knowledge of Maori culture and traditions. Ethel had no mother to advise her, and it was generally considered that she had done

Ethel Te Tumanako Barclay with her father David Barclay and three brothers, from left, David, Francis, and Glenville. *Rae Julian*

well for herself. These were the times of assimilation policies, so marrying a Pakeha was a way of bettering herself. One assumes that the kaumatua from Ngaone's marae, Hairini (in Tauranga), were not consulted.

By 1912 Frederick and Ethel had four children, all girls, born over a period of five years. Ethel had little time to remember her heritage and any 'Maori ways', such as going barefoot, were discouraged by Frederick. He was a kindly man, but he believed that all Maori should aspire to be like Pakeha in order to prosper in New Zealand.

But by 1912 Ethel could no longer cope with the pressures of a Pakeha life-style. She ran away. Some accounts say she abandoned her children, although she did try to come back. Frederick's pride, however, was such that he could not accept her back as his wife or as the mother of his children – and she got little sympathy in other quarters.

Frederick and Ethel were divorced in 1915, and little is known of her life for some years. She married Aubrey Beauclerc-Martin in 1915 and had a fifth child who was raised by another family. Later she married Albert Knap, a bushman from the country near Rotorua. They had four children, three of whom survived her. She also linked up again with some of her Maori family, especially with the Ngati Whakaue people at Waiteti marae, near Ngongotaha.

During the Second World War, Ethel came into prominence in Rotorua. She joined the St John's Ambulance Transport Unit and started driving an ambulance. She had been driving since the age of eleven and is reported to be one of the earliest women in New Zealand to hold a driver's licence.

A grandchild recalls Ethel's story of driving across the Mamaku Ranges in the fog, navigating with her head out the window. In another incident Ethel was summoned to a house where the baby was having convulsions. Her daughter recalls:

the only hot water available was in an oval cauldron on the stove with corn beef cooking. So she threw out the meat, poured some cold water into the cauldron and put the baby into that. Later she took the mother and baby to the doctor.

She was on call twenty-four hours a day, running the ambulance for 600–700 miles a week, with never an accident. For this she was paid only expenses, and eventually she was provided with a free 'home' – a couple of linked army huts in the Rotorua Transit Camp.

A transit camp was usually a short-term place for people waiting for a state house. Ethel stayed there for seven years, during which time Albert died. She went on driving the ambulance, covering much of the Bay of Plenty region, between Hamilton, Tauranga, Taupo, and Rotorua. No job was too difficult, from pulling people from boiling mud-pools, to transporting dead bodies, often without an assistant in the ambulance. In her own words:

I've helped people to live and when they have been going to die, I've held them so that they can get their breath and helped them to die peacefully. That's all I've ever thought about it.

When Ethel finally retired in 1955, at the age of seventy, her reward was a proper home at last – a state house. However, she was not yet ready for a quiet life, and took a job as night supervisor at Gardenholm, a rest-home for elderly men. Her home was also a refuge for those in need of a sympathetic ear or some ready money, and of course for the family, especially her many mokopuna. Three of her daughters from her first marriage had met up with her again when they were grown women. Their children, however, called her 'aunt', in order not to upset her ex-husband by letting him know inadvertently that they were meeting their grandmother.

Ethel died in 1968, mourned by her extensive family and by the grateful people of Rotorua – not the wealthy from the lakeside and the elegant suburbs, but the down-and-outers, the sick and the needy – to whom she had been a ministering helper for so long. *Rae Julian*

Quotations
para.11 'One Woman's Work: Record of Mrs Knap with Rotorua Ambulance', *Rotorua Post* (undated clipping, at time of Ethel's retirement in 1955), in author's possession

Unpublished Sources
Information was provided by family members, especially Rona Bradley, Maureen Meyer, and Jill Harvey. The author is a granddaughter of Ethel Te Tumanako Barclay.

MARY BARKAS

1889-1961

On 29 April 1961 the *Hauraki Plains Gazette* announced the death of Dr Mary Barkas, who for the past thirty years had lived in retirement at Tapu, on the Thames coast, prior to which she had been superintendent of the Lawn Hospital in Lincoln (England). The obituary is short and tells us little about Mary Barkas, how she came to enter the medical profession during the early years of this century, or why she retired at the relatively early age of forty-three. Fortunately Mary's letters to her father, now held at the Alexander Turnbull Library, tell us more.

Mary Rushton Barkas was the only child of Fred Barkas and Amy Barkas (born Parker), both the children of middle-class English families with academic and medical connections. Amy and Fred met and married in Christchurch in 1887, where Fred had taught at Lincoln College and then from 1883 worked for the New Zealand Loan and Mercantile Company. Amy had travelled extensively and worked as a governess and music teacher. She was thirty-eight when she married, and a strong character with ideas on the place of women in society, particularly colonial society, which were far from conventional for Christchurch in the 1890s.

Not surprisingly, given her family background, Mary's tastes from an early age were of a scholarly nature. In 1904 Amy took Mary to Europe to learn French and German and to visit the great cultural centres of the world. During the trip Mary maintained a rigid self-imposed study timetable concentrating on chemistry, botany, and mathematics. Invitations to participate in lighter social activities were turned down if they threatened to interfere. Mary was fourteen years old and determined that in adulthood she would be capable of working to earn her own living. Her heart was already set on becoming a doctor.

In 1905, at the age of sixteen, Mary was dux at Christchurch Girls' High School, gaining the fifth-highest marks in the Junior Scholarship Examination. She went on to study at Victoria University College and was awarded a BSc in 1908 and an MSc with second-class honours in chemistry in 1910. Amy now decided that she had finally had all she could take of colonial life and returned to England. Mary chose to remain in New Zealand with her father and turned down a Government Research Scholarship on Taranaki petroleum to keep house for him.

A career and independence were not, however, forgotten, and in 1913 Mary left her father to study domestic science at King's College in London. Domestic science had recently become accepted as a university discipline in New Zealand, and included medical studies. Shortly after the outbreak of the First World War, Mary enrolled at the Royal College of Surgeons in London, and 1918 she qualified MRCS (Member of the Royal College of Surgeons), LRCP (Licentiate of the Royal College of Physicians).

Mary worked briefly at Bethlem, a private psychiatric hospital which she left in August 1919 in order to study psychological medicine at the University of London. That year she gained the Certificate in Psychological Medicine of the

Medico-Psychological Association and passed the examination for the Bachelor of Medicine degree of the University of London.

Finding another job at this stage proved extremely difficult. The war years had been a time of opportunity for women, but by 1919 thousands of medical people were being demobilised and returned soldiers had preference. Mary spent some months out of work before taking a temporary position as house physician at the National Hospital for the Paralysed and Epileptic in London. In March 1921 Mary again found herself unemployed. Another temporary position followed, at Hellesdon Hospital, a public psychiatric hospital in Norwich.

At the end of 1921 Mary travelled to Europe to continue her studies in psychoanalysis. After spending two months in Germany gathering material for her Doctor of Medicine thesis, she moved to Vienna where she began studying under Dr Rank, one of Freud's pupils. She returned to England in mid-1922, and after six months of yet more temporary employment she secured an appointment on probation for one year as assistant physician at Maudsley Hospital, a large psychiatric hospital run by the London County Council. The appointment was extended but Mary found the work routine, with no opportunity for research or further promotion. It was at this point that Mary became aware that in most hospitals women were not allowed to advance beyond junior positions. When she was eventually 'promoted' to second in charge at the Maudsley, it was on condition that she would accept the new position on a temporary basis. The London County Council made it clear to her that a woman in such a senior position would block the way for men wishing to move up and therefore could not be appointed permanently.

Mary held the position for one year, and then early in 1928 accepted a post as superintendent of a small private asylum, the Lawn Hospital in Lincoln, in the north of England. Mary's colleagues in London were astounded that she should bury her talent in such a small and isolated institution. However, Mary hoped that at the Lawn Hospital she would have the opportunity for research and to test her theories.

The reality was to prove quite different. The Lawn Hospital had been badly managed in the past and Mary's time was taken up with getting it onto a sounder financial basis. Initially she was successful. The number of patients was increased and debts were cleared. However, the hospital was poorly equipped and the financial situation was such that she was not able to raise standards to a level where she could make real improvements or compete with even the most backward of public institutions.

The effects of the Depression compounded the problem. By March 1931 the Lawn was again running at a loss, and Mary predicted bankruptcy by the end of the year. The suicide of a patient in August shattered Mary's already battered confidence. She wanted nothing more than to get away from the hospital and even from psychoanalysis itself, but at the same time could not bring herself to abandon the hospital when it was in such a precarious state.

The situation dragged on until September 1932 when Mary's father died. Having returned to New Zealand to wind up his estate, Mary decided to stay. Her resignation was sent from this country. Although Mary registered as a medical practitioner soon after her arrival in New Zealand, she does not appear to

have practised and the remaining years of her life were spent in retirement at
Tapu.   *Kay Sanderson*

Unpublished Source
Barkas Collection, MS Papers 9401, ATL

LADY BARKER

1831–1911

Images of fire and a burning landscape come readily to mind when conjuring up
a vision of Lady Barker, born Mary Anne Stewart in Jamaica in 1831, daughter
of W. G. Stewart, the resident Island Secretary.

Her achievements were many and exceptional, the most notable being the
book *Station Life in New Zealand*, which detailed life on a Canterbury sheep station of the 1860s in a most exact and illuminating way. There she writes vividly
of burning tussock – a common practice amongst early settlers in their efforts to
force pasture growth and run as many sheep as they could: 'It is a very exciting
amusement, I assure you, and the effect is beautiful, especially as it grows dusk
and the fires are racing up the hills all round us.' Her passion for such wanton
destructiveness is one which modern environmentalists can hardly applaud, but
it suggests the adventurer in her.

The high country tussock that Lady Barker loved; Manuka Point Station below the
Arrowsmith Range. *John Pascoe Collection, Alexander Turnbull Library*

Barker achieved her title through marriage to a decorated military captain when she was twenty-one. She joined her husband in India where he served in the Indian mutiny,. and on his death went to England to live with her parents. Left with two young sons and very little money, she thus turned to writing. In 1865, she met a young farmer-cum-poet called Frederick Napier Broome, eleven years her junior. The son of a Shropshire vicar, he had been despatched to New Zealand as a cadet farmer, and was on a brief return visit to England. Barker does not appear in photographs as a conventional beauty, her hair parted with severity in the centre of her head and pulled tightly back from a face notable for its heavy eyebrows and a somewhat enigmatic expression. But the attraction between the couple was instant and passionate, and soon afterwards they married.

The pair travelled to New Zealand leaving her two children behind in her family's care. It appears that she did not live constantly with them again. Interestingly, she persuaded Broome to accept her decision to continue calling herself Lady Barker. This may well have been on the pretext of her literary career, but it does not altogether explain why she would later become Lady Broome when Frederick received a title in 1884.

They lived in Christchurch while the purchase of a sheep station was negotiated. The station was Steventon, a run of 9,700 acres, situated on the south bank of the Selwyn River. Broome and a partner, H. P. Hill, bought the property from a Mr E. C. Knight who was a nephew of Jane Austen – Steventon had been named after the rectory in Hampshire where Austen was born. The Broomes called their new house 'Broomielaw'.

The introduction to New Zealand was harsh; a son born shortly afterwards died on the station when two months old, leaving Frederick in a frenzy of grief. Barker might well have succumbed to despair but instead decided to tackle life with extraordinary gusto and a good deal of ingenuity. The New Zealand sojourn lasted for only three years but it provided the material for four of her subsequent books: *Station Life in New Zealand* (1870); *A Christmas Cake in Four Quarters* (1872); *Station Amusements in New Zealand* (1873), and *Colonial Memories* (1904). All of her books were published in England, and the only one to sell in any great quantities in New Zealand was *Station Life in New Zealand* which went through a number of Whitcombe & Tombs editions.

Station Life in New Zealand was written as a series of letters to a sister in England. The author is very much the central character in her tales and the reader cannot help but admire her role. She displays fortitude in the face of loneliness, floods, and snowstorms. The couple took camping holidays with groups of young bachelor men, for whom Barker was highly inventive in devising witty diversions and activities, although she comments in one instance, 'what babies men are'!

The book made a substantial contribution to the records of language, botany, and ornithology. Her observations, which history confirms as being exceptionally accurate, are evidence of a true writer.

In the ten years following Barker's departure from New Zealand she bore two more children, wrote eight books (in all she wrote twenty-two), and was appointed Lady Superintendent of the newly opened School of Cookery in

London. Frederick pursued journalism for a time, and was then offered administrative posts which took the pair to Natal, Mauritius, and then, in 1883, to Western Australia where Frederick was governor of the colony. He was not always popular and it fell to his wife to smooth over some of his displays of irascible temper. The last appointment was in Trinidad, where he died in 1896. In a letter she wrote, ' . . . we have been such friends and companions as well as lovers all our lives', an enlightened view, then, of relationships between the sexes.

She died at Eaton Terrace, London, in 1911.   *Fiona Kidman*

Quotations
para.2 Lady Barker, *Station Life*, p.195
para.9 Lady Broome, *Remembered with Affection*, p.22

Published Sources
Acland, L. G. D. *Early Canterbury Runs*, Auckland, 1930
Barker, Lady. *Station Life in New Zealand* (with a new introduction by Fiona Kidman), London, 1984
Broome, Lady. *Remembered with Affection: A New Edition of Lady Broome's Letters to Guy* (with an introduction by Alexandra Hasluck), Melbourne, 1963

CONSTANCE BARNICOAT

1872-1922

Journalist, mountaineer, and traveller, Constance Alice Barnicoat was the seventh (and last) child of John Wallis Barnicoat and his wife Rebecca (born Hodgson). An early Nelson settler, her father took his civic duties seriously and was a Member of the Legislative Council. Constance was tutored at home in Latin, French, and German and became familiar with British magazines and journals, which her father would read aloud. She had a vigorous outdoor life on her parents' farm, becoming a skilful rider.

At fifteen she attended the newly opened Nelson College for Girls, and in 1890 went to Canterbury University College. After graduating with a BA, she spent nearly three years in the Wellington office of the Crown solicitor, Francis Dillon Bell, work which gave her a wide knowledge of New Zealand law and politics. She also prepared herself for journalism by learning shorthand and typing, which together with a knowledge of modern languages she saw as essential for women to obtain real success in business.

In 1897 she left for London, where she continued her study of shorthand, French, and German. She was later to gain a reading knowledge of Spanish and Italian. These skills, as well as her writing ability, earned her the appointment in 1898 as secretary and then editorial assistant to W. T. Stead, editor of the *Review of Reviews*. For the *Review* she attended (with Stead) the Hague Peace Conference in 1898, and read and reviewed new books in the major European languages. She also contributed articles and reviews to other weekly and daily newspapers, including the *Daily Express*, *The Times*, and *The Press* (Christchurch), and leading monthly magazines such as the *Empire Review*, the *Ladies' Realm*, and *Pearson's Magazine*.

Always adventurous, Constance had cycled since her student days in Christchurch, where she was a member of the Pioneer Club. In London she cycled to Fleet Street from her rooms in Battersea. Mountaineering she did not discover until the first of her two voyages back to New Zealand, in 1902 when her mother died. During her nine-month stay, in April 1903 she and another woman took part in one of the earliest crossings of the Copland Pass, near Mt Cook. As with many of her experiences she described this in an article, entitled 'Where No Woman Ever Went Before'.

It was after this visit that she instituted the Barnicoat Essay Prize for the boys' and girls' colleges in Nelson, to encourage the study of contemporary world history. She felt that 'one of the chief drawbacks of a colonial upbringing is that it often tends to a lack of interest in the outside world'. Her frank views about aspects of New Zealand life earned the comment that she was a 'competent journalist and rather terrible'.

In 1905 she began her European climbing in the French Alps, starting with a peak previously unclimbed by a woman. Over the next few summers she climbed regularly, her greatest achievement being a winter ascent in 1911 of the Great Schreckhorn ('peak of terror') in Switzerland. She loved a challenge and had strong views on mountaineering for women:

I am prepared for contradiction, and even abuse from feminists, when I state that the number of women who have climbed throughout a long series of years, long enough for them to acquire any real skill or knowledge of mountains and glaciers, always has been and still is exceedingly small . . . but given a good guide and a sufficiently strong, healthy woman, who should be thin, muscular and in good training even before starting on her holiday, I think nothing so invigorating, refreshing and fortifying as mountaineering, nothing so helpful in building one up to face another hard year's work in dismal London.

Through a mutual interest in mountaineering and journalism she met Julian Grande in 1910; the next year they married and Constance left the *Review of Reviews*. Constance had already travelled widely; now they set off together to Europe, Egypt, and Palestine, sending back despatches to the papers they represented, which included the *Observer*, the *Daily Telegraph*, and the *New York Times*. In 1913, with war looming, they chose to live in Switzerland to be 'at the centre of things'. In addition to their regular journalism, they worked for the International Peace Bureau in Berne, collecting information, translating, and editing the English edition of the monthly newsletter.

Once war started, Constance, fervently patriotic, maintained a constant vigilance on German newspapers; she and Julian wrote articles for the British, American, and New Zealand press exposing and criticising German war ideology and propaganda, and criticising also British pacifists and anti-conscriptionists. They joined the propaganda war themselves, publishing a monthly review which they translated into three languages, and numerous pamphlets and books which they distributed widely to counter German propaganda. Throughout this time she continued to write 'illuminative' articles for the Christchurch *Press*.

An imperialist from her student days, Constance wrote frequently about the

British Empire and its dominions. To her, true imperialism did not mean domination by Britain, but the mutual knowledge and friendship of the independent member countries of the Empire. She approved of the League of Nations, but felt that the British Empire was more important and had more substance.

In 1915 the long hours she put into her work began to take their toll on her health. After the war the Grandes moved to Geneva to follow the development of the League of Nations, but Constance soon became too ill to attend the League's assemblies and report on them. She longed to visit New Zealand, with its wilderness and open spaces, but died, after an operation, on 16 September 1922. Mt Barnicoat in Westland is named in her honour.   *Janet McCallum*

Quotations
para.5 J. Grande, *Constance Grande*, p.126; *NZ Free Lance*, 16 May 1908
para.6 J. Grande, pp.98–9
para.7 J. Grande. p.173
para.8 J. Grande, p.22

Unpublished Source
Information was provided by J. J. G. Barnicoat.

Published Sources
Barnicoat, C. 'Where No Woman Ever Went Before', *World Wide Magazine*, March 1904
Grande, Julian. *Constance Grande*, London, 1925.
NZ Free Lance: 15 Feb. 1900, 29 Nov. 1902, 27 Dec. 1902, 9 Jan. 1904, 2 Feb. 1905, 16 Feb. 1905, 23 Dec. 1905, 16 May 1908, 13 Sept. 1910
The Press, 20 Sept. 1922 (obituary)
Scholefield, G. H. *A Dictionary of New Zealand Biography*, Wellington, 1940, p.41

HANNAH WARD BARRON

1831–1898

Hannah Ward Barron was like many women in nineteenth-century New Zealand who found themselves responsible for supporting their families. Usually untrained for any occupation, they often fell back upon the domestic skills they had acquired and ran hotels, boarding-houses or shops. Hannah began with a small store and used her commercial talents to such effect that she eventually owned the best hotel in Bluff, then an important port. She had not planned to become a businesswoman; her life was shaped by a combination of emergencies and seized opportunities.

Hannah Dorney was born in 1831 in Cork, where she married William Thomas Ward when she was nineteen. Two children, William and Mina, were born before the young Wards emigrated to Melbourne in pursuit of the opportunities offered by the gold-rushes of the 1850s. In Melbourne, fortune eluded William, and Hannah bore seven more sons. All except one of these children died in infancy from diseases rampant in the overcrowded rooming-houses of South Melbourne. Gradually Hannah seems to have assumed the chief responsibility for keeping her family. She opened a store and later managed hotels, while William declined in status from accountant to bookkeeper to no stated occupation. He died, after a fall from a horse, in 1860.

The Bluff, where Hannah Ward Barron set up her empire of hotels, shops, and boarding-houses. *Southland Museum and Art Gallery Collection*

At the end of 1862, Hannah remarried but her second marriage, to John Barron, a butcher, was so ephemeral it left little trace on her life beyond a wariness in money matters and a watchfulness lest Barron reappear. She came to Bluff with her three surviving Ward children in 1863 and set up a store near the small gold-field at Greenhills.

The store was replaced by a boarding-house on the Bluff waterfront. That prospered sufficiently for Hannah to buy the freehold in 1870 and then to contemplate the bold move of borrowing money to build the Club Hotel directly opposite the end of Bluff's main wharf. Bluff was at that time New Zealand's link with Melbourne and served the rapidly developing agricultural hinterland of Southland. By the time Hannah's younger son, Joseph, was twenty-one, Hannah was able to lend him £800 to set himself up as a stock and station agent. The J. G. Ward Farmers' Association set up warehouses near the port and expanded throughout the district. Ward was mayor of Bluff at the age of twenty-five. Hannah meanwhile was collecting commercial property along and near the waterfront. By 1880 she was in her own right one of the town's leading citizens.

Business did not occupy all Hannah's attention. She was a devout Catholic, and a loyal supporter of her church's charitable and educational activities. She was a loving grandmother and an intelligent and supportive mother. When Joseph Ward became Colonial Treasurer in the Ballance and then the Seddon governments, Hannah helped his wife Theresa with their children and wrote short shrewd letters of encouragement to her beloved Joseph.

When Hannah died in 1898 the obituary notices included all the usual praise of her piety, charity, and maternal virtues. They passed over her strength of character, resilience, and a commercial shrewdness which was shown even in the probate records. She died in her daughter's house in Bluff, possessed of no personal property except an invalid chair. Everything else was invested in town property, bringing in income.

Judith Bassett

Unpublished Sources
Family papers in possession of the Ward family

Published Source
Bassett, M. E. R. 'In Search of Sir Joseph Ward', *NZJH*, vol.21 no.1, April 1987, pp.112–24

LESLEY BARTLETT

1913 – 1976

Like many women of her generation, Lesley Elizabeth Bartlett lived quietly, but her impact was strongly felt in her own circle.

Lesley Maddox was born on 19 March 1913 at St Clair, Dunedin. Her mother Dorothy (born Gurr), who had lived her early life in India, was a well-educated and cultured woman. Her father was a builder who, for health reasons, moved to Richmond, Nelson, in 1915. There he took a job as a sales representative for agricultural machinery and also bred pedigree jersey cows on his thirteen acres.

Lesley was the youngest of three daughters, all of whom had a great interest in books, music, drama, and art. She was educated at Richmond School and Nelson College for Girls, where she won a special prize for excellence in home crafts. Of slight build and vital personality, Lesley as a girl had the same understated elegance that was to be her hallmark later in life.

For most school-leavers in 1930 there was no regular work, so Lesley took whatever was available. She picked raspberries, picked and graded apples, and did market garden work, as well as helping in the home and on the farm. She also did a stint at one of the local psychiatric hospitals, which she found so harrowing that she stayed only five days.

At twenty-three years of age she married Leo Bartlett, eighteen years her senior, who farmed at Appleby. There were three children of this marriage, and after the birth of the third her health, never robust, deteriorated. The farm of eighteen acres provided a frugal living, which left its stamp in a somewhat austere and simple way of life. This was reinforced when Leo retired from active farming in 1955.

Books and records, however, continued to be central to Lesley's life, feeding her lively imagination and enriching her vocabulary. Her love of books, and an awareness of their importance to rural women, made her a driving force in persuading the county to upgrade the Appleby library. When a new library was built in about 1965, she became the (unpaid) librarian.

She was, at different times, secretary of the Richmond Women's Institute;

during the war a member of a patriotic group, with which she studied first aid, passing her St John's certificate; and a member of the Women's Division of Federated Farmers. These activities were combined with work on the farm and a concern for her children's education. She was for many years an active member of St Alban's Anglican congregation at Appleby, her quiet Christian convictions underpinning her daily living. A conscientious person, her high standards veered towards perfectionism, which was reflected in her home and beautiful garden.

Lesley was a woman of liberal views and a defender of women's rights, long before they became a rallying point. She was also well versed in politics, both national and international. A sensitive person herself, she was compassionate towards suffering in others, and felt strongly about all forms of deprivation, whether material, social or emotional. She was a long-serving member of the Richmond Labour Party, and its secretary for several years. Her signature appended to letters or minutes guaranteed their accuracy.

Essentially a private person, Lesley took her most public stance over the demolition of the Nelson Railway. In August 1955 the government threatened to close the railway, and the women of the Nelson area organised a protest under the leadership of Ruth Page, a former schoolteacher from Golden Bay. Lesley and Sonja Davies were both members of a core group of nine who staged a sit-in at Kiwi, the last station on the line some sixty-four kilometres from Nelson, where the demolition was due to begin. Most of the group were older women; one brought her knitting; they offered the demolition workers and government officials cups of tea. On 30 September they were arrested, and eventually fined £10 each for being on railway property without a ticket. The line was closed, for

Lesley Bartlett (seated front centre) protesting against the closure of the Nelson railway, 1955. Sonja Davies is seated at the right. *J. T. O'Connor*

good. But this early protest by women made its mark on the Nelson community, and provided models for later generations.

Lesley continued to care for her ageing parents, as she continued to work for her beliefs. But she was never strong. A broken ankle, a cancer operation, and the additional support her husband required when he broke his hip combined to undermine her stamina. She died somewhat suddenly on 12 June 1976, predeceasing her elderly husband by several years. She remarked to a neighbour in her last few months that 'death will come as a friend'.   *J. T. O'Connor*

Unpublished Sources
Information has been provided by Lesley Bartlett's daughter and sister, as well as friends. The author
    was a neighbour for twenty-six years.

Published Sources
Davies, Sonja. *Bread and Roses*, Auckland, 1984, pp.98–107
Nelson Evening Mail, Sept.–Oct. 1955

DAISY BASHAM

1879–1963

From a childhood in Victorian London to a long career as a much-loved radio personality in New Zealand – that was the life of Maud Ruby Taylor. She was born on 30 August 1879 and christened Maud Ruby to please her father, who was soon to die. However, she was always known as Daisy, and by her death on 14 July 1963 as 'Aunt Daisy'.

Her mother, Eliza Taylor, was a lively and attractive widow in an age of good conversation, theatre, music, pantomime, and art. The British Navy was supreme, and pageantry and pomp engendered patriotic fervour in most British hearts. Daisy, her two sisters and brother absorbed it all. Weekdays Daisy spent at the Academy for Young Ladies; Sundays saw the whole family at church – Church of England, of course.

Eliza Taylor was persuaded by friends to emigrate to New Zealand, where her son Albert had already settled. On 31 August 1891 the SS *Rimutaka* berthed at Wellington, and Eliza with her three daughters disembarked in their new country. Daisy was just twelve.

The family settled in New Plymouth, where Daisy attended New Plymouth Central School and New Plymouth High School, and in due course qualified as a schoolteacher. She joined the choir of St Mary's church, and took singing lessons. She was an extrovert who entered into everything with verve and enthusiasm, but often worried that she might not have done her best. She continually strove for excellence, and expected it of everyone else.

In New Plymouth there was plenty of scope for her talents – singing, reciting at concerts, acting in plays, debating in the Mutual Improvement Society, and living the 'gay nineties' life of a colonial town.

In 1904 Daisy Taylor married Englishman Frederick Basham, then assistant engineer with the New Plymouth Borough Council. Later he was engineer to the Hawera and Eltham Borough Councils and the Patangata and Hauraki Plains

County Councils. There were three children, Frederick, Geoffrey, and Barbara.

Daisy kept on with her singing engagements, and was renowned for her contralto role in Handel's *Messiah*. She was only 4′11½″ tall – 'the same height as Queen Victoria,' she always avowed – so audiences were surprised by her strong deep contralto voice when she began to sing 'He was despised'.

In the early 1920s, while on a singing engagement in Wellington, she was invited to take part in a broadcasting experiment and sang 'Il Baccio' into a horn, somewhat reminiscent of the HMV dog. Towards the end of that decade she was living on the Hauraki Plains, her children were growing up and the eldest two had left home; with her husband's full support she was writing and broadcasting programmes for 1YA Auckland on the lives of composers, illustrated with songs and duets. When 'Cinderella' (Ruby Palmer) of the children's session went on holiday, Mrs Basham was invited to take over and she became 'Aunt Daisy'. This was followed by an eighteen-month engagement at 2YA Wellington, where she continued as a popular 'aunt' for the children's programmes, as well as arranging classical programmes.

When the Depression deepened, Daisy was one of the staff dispensed with. Her engineer husband was also made redundant, and they both moved to Auckland in 1932. There Daisy joined Colin Scrimgeour ('Uncle Scrim'), Tom Garland ('Uncle Tom'), and the others at 1ZR, the privately owned station on which Scrim, in 1931, had inaugurated the radio church known as 'The Friendly Road'. In 1933, the Friendly Road and Aunt Daisy transferred to 1ZB (which Scrim had bought in a run-down state from the La Gloria Gramophone Company and had upgraded, and which the government subsequently bought). Being an early riser, Daisy put the station on the air each day with her cheery 'Good morning, everybody', which became her well-known and often parodied greeting.

Politics loomed large during the Depression, and Colin Scrimgeour became embroiled; Daisy kept aloof. She was even asked by both political parties to stand for parliament, and wisely declined both.

As a result of the Broadcasting Act of 1936, 1ZB became the first station of the new state-owned National Commercial Broadcasting Service. The ban on naming brands on radio was lifted. Now Daisy was able to talk about her favourite products. Her sales talk was irresistible, and a word from 'Aunt Daisy' on radio would clear a grocer's shelf in a couple of hours.

In 1937 Aunt Daisy moved to Wellington, the head office of the new nationwide commercial network. All New Zealand now heard her daily programme.

Her daily routine was to wake about 4.30 am and have a cup of tea and thin brown bread and butter, in bed. In the quiet before dawn she would read one of the quarterly books of the Bible Reading Fellowship; by the 6 am news she was bathed and dressed, and cooking her breakfast egg. The taxi came about 7.30 am and by 8 am she was in the studio, with the curtains drawn so she was not disturbed by onlookers. She would check all the details – the recipes, advertisements, hints, listeners' letters and stories; then at 8.50 am a last-minute look at the weather. As a committed optimist she always saw a patch of blue sky, even on the worst days. Then came the chimes to establish the radio link, the 'Daisy Bell' song, and the stirring 'Good morning, everybody'.

The style was set. She had no script; she just talked for half an hour, non-stop. She was once counted at 120 words a minute – yet each word was clear, thanks to her early singing and acting training. She skilfully wove advertisements in with recipes and hints, adding a serious verse or thought, and comments on the dean's Sunday sermon, a play or film, concert or other event. Her listeners trusted her, and were strengthened by her integrity and Christian principles. They knew she would not advertise any product she did not approve of.

Later, in her office on Lambton Quay, she sorted out the material for the next day's programme, discussed products with advertisers, and dealt with the mail, phone calls, and visitors. Then home to prepare dinner and early to bed, ready for the next day which was for her always full of excitement and challenge.

War followed the Depression. The government recognised Daisy's propaganda value, and sent her to navy, army, and air force stations to report on how the women of the forces lived. She helped with campaigns such as the apple pie competition to sell surplus produce. Her personal war effort culminated in a semi-official visit to the United States to foster friendship between the two countries.

During these years she had been writing a recipe and hint page for the *Auckland Weekly News*, then the *Radio Record* (which became the *Listener*). She published at least twelve recipe and hint books, and each year a selection of the 'scrap-book' pieces which she used at the beginning of each session.

Daisy was awarded the MBE in 1956, an honour for one who loved New Zealand and wouldn't live anywhere else. She always claimed, however, to be a Londoner at heart. The honour was also tinged with sorrow that her husband could not share her joy, for he had died in 1950.

One listener, who was born during the war, summed up Daisy's magic like this:

Aunt Daisy used to make Marmite sound like caviare, and I still use it. Isn't it amazing what an impact she had? There isn't a star in the world who could leave such a mark on the everyday culture of a whole nation. Marmite may seem trivial, but somehow it seems to me to stand for more than that . . . a set of values and attitudes that somehow relate back to her presence on the air waves for all those years, for all those isolated housewives and mothers especially in rural areas. And so for their children.

Barbara Basham

Quotations
para.19 Private letter to the author

Unpublished Source
The author, Daisy Basham's daughter, relied substantially on her own knowledge, checked against *The Aunt Daisy Story*. Peter Downes also supplied information.

Published Sources
Basham, M. R. *Aunt Daisy and Uncle Sam: Aunt Daisy's Wartime Journey to the United States*, Christchurch, 1945
Downes, P. and Harcourt, P. *Voices in the Air: Radio Broadcasting in New Zealand: A Documentary*, Wellington, 1976
Fry, A. S. *The Aunt Daisy Story*, Wellington, 1957
Gordon, J. N. *All the World's a Stage*, Wellington, 1981
Holcroft, M. H. *Reluctant Editor: The 'Listener' Years, 1949–67*, Wellington, 1969

JEAN BATTEN

1909-1982

Jean Gardner Batten was a pioneer aviator who established four world records in the mid-1930s – and became a legend in her lifetime. She was the first woman to make the return flight from England to Australia and to cross the South Atlantic Ocean and the Tasman Sea.

The daughter of Ellen (born Blackmore) and Fred Batten, she was born on 15 September 1909 in Rotorua, where her father was a dentist. At the age of four she moved with her parents and two older brothers to Auckland, where she was educated at Melmerly College, Parnell, and Cleveland House College, Remuera. Described as a small and dainty girl, she shared her parents' musical ability, and played piano at a ballet school, where she also became an instructor.

In 1930 she went to London with her mother to take her final Royal College of Music exams, with the stated intention of becoming a pianist. However, the flying bug had bitten her. Two years earlier nineteen-year-old Jean had been excited by the flight of Bert Hinkler from England to Australia; not long after she had her own first flight while on holiday in Australia. She was taken up from an aerodrome near Sydney by Charles Kingsford-Smith in the *Southern Cross*. Once in London, she decided to start training at the Stag Lane Aerodrome, headquarters of the London Aeroplane Club, and sold her piano to finance lessons. Her father and other relatives refused to give her any financial or other support in her new venture: her mother, with whom she had a 'strange and exclusive relationship', was her only ally.

Flying was not easy at first. Jean had a lot of trouble with her landings, crashing into fences and gates. However, she obtained the British Air Ministry's 'A' licence for private pilots – a first for New Zealand women. At the beginning of 1931 she returned to New Zealand, and flew at Mangere Aerodrome, gaining her 'A' licence endorsement, which enabled her to carry non-commercial passengers. On returning to England in July 1931, with her mother's support and the financial help of Fred Truman, her close friend and a Royal Air Force pilot, she secured a 'B' licence, allowing her to carry commercial passengers. She now had the qualifications and skills that would help her to obtain sponsorship – and, more important, to fulfil her dream of a solo flight from England to New Zealand.

In 1933, with the help of another pilot, Victor Dorée, she bought a second-hand De Havilland Gipsy Moth, and had it fitted for long-distance flying. In April she attempted her first solo flight to Australia, but the old plane, which had already flown about 100,000 miles, got into trouble over India. Jean was forced to land several times because of sandstorms, and crashed on the outskirts of Karachi, following engine failure. A year later, on her second attempt, she ran out of petrol near Rome, and crashed. On 8 May 1934 she set off again and landed successfully in Darwin, in just under fifteen days, beating Amy Johnson's record by four and a half days.

She brought the Gipsy Moth back to New Zealand by ship, and toured the country – where she was fêted, and given a grant of £500 by the government.

Jean Batten. *New Zealand Free Lance Collection, Alexander Turnbull Library*

She went on to break more records. Taking the plane by ship to Australia, she flew back to England, this time in seventeen days, sixteen hours and fifteen minutes, becoming the first woman to fly from England to Australia and back. In November 1935, with a new craft, a silver Percival Gull monoplane, she crossed the South Atlantic Ocean from Africa to Brazil, braving constant storms and a failed compass, in a record time of thirteen and a quarter hours. That flight was part of another record journey between England and South America. Jean landed in Buenos Aires, having flown the fastest time for any aeroplane, covering the 5,000 miles in sixty-one and a quarter hours. Along the way she made an unconventional landing: a petrol leak forced her down on a beach fifty miles from Rio. To get away from the rising tide, she tried to taxi onto the high grass, but the plane tipped, damaging the propeller. She eventually found the house of a fisherman, and was rescued by Brazilian Army planes.

In 1936 Jean created the world record which was to give her an enduring place in the record books. She left England on 5 October in the Percival Gull on a solo flight to New Zealand – her flight to New Plymouth took a record ten days, twenty-three hours and forty-five minutes. The last leg, across a stormy Tasman Sea with a threatening petrol leak, broke the Tasman crossing record by two hours. Yet she didn't land at New Plymouth, but went on to reach Mangere by late afternoon, making her total time eleven days and forty-five minutes. The crowd that greeted this glamorous, white-helmeted twenty-seven-year-old had earlier caused one of Auckland's biggest traffic jams.

Often cramped and uncomfortable during her flights, Jean was either very cold or extremely hot. She related one story:

. . . the heat was so intense that the crepe rubber on my soles started to melt and the rubber around my goggles softened, forcing me to remove them, which made my eyes and face burn. After a few hours of intermittently holding the control column and the map with my left hand and working hard with the petrol pump with my right, I began to think I should melt completely.

Nautical tables were not available at the time, so she had to compile a reference book before each flight containing everything from times of sunrise and sunset to the value of the currency at each stop.

Jean carried minimal personal luggage: her white flying suit ready to wear on arrival, one frock, changes of underwear, soap, and a toothbrush. During the flights she lived on milk and meat tablets and barley sugars, and had a tiny fluid intake. Yet she stepped out of her plane immaculate, discreetly dabbed with cologne and lipstick.

Honours and awards were heaped upon Jean. She received the CBE from the New Zealand government in 1936, was made a Chevalier of the Legion of Honour and an officer of the Order of the Southern Cross of Brazil, and was given the freedom of the City of London. Aviation societies and aero clubs around the world gave her trophies and medals, which are now held in the Museum of Transport and Technology in Auckland. One of the few women to have public monuments in her honour, she has a street and a building in downtown Auckland named after her. In 1990 a full-length ballet about her life was performed.

On the lecture circuit in New Zealand after her 1936 flight, she made it clear that love of adventure was not the motivation for her extraordinary feats. She foresaw modern commercial air travel and wanted to show that long-distance flying had arrived. 'That is how record-breaking is complementary to aviation. The records of one decade are the service times of the next.'

In October 1937 she flew from Sydney to Croyden in five days, eighteen hours and fifteen minutes, becoming the first person to hold both England-Australia out and back solo records simultaneously. She began to lecture in England and Europe, and published two books, *Solo Flight* (1934) and *My Life* (1938). She gave up flying during the war, having failed the eye test for the Air Transport Auxiliary of the RAF, and did not fly again. Instead, she drove ambulances in France for the Anglo-French Ambulance Corps, and then worked in a munitions factory in Dorset.

After the war she lived quietly with her mother in Jamaica, Spain, and Tenerife in the Canary Islands. Successful lecturing tours and careful investment allowed her at this time to live comfortably. Always careful of her appearance and figure she swam daily, enjoying a small bottle of champagne afterwards.

Her mother died in 1966, and Jean increasingly withdrew from society. She was last seen in London in late 1982. Since she was regarded by now as a recluse, her disappearance was at first linked to her stated desire to 'go to ground for a while'. Although the facts were not discovered until 1987, she had died five years earlier on 22 November 1982, from an untreated dog bite. She had been found fully dressed on the bed of her Majorca apartment. Her body was taken to an unmarked pauper's grave; her death was registered under her middle name, Gardner, thus prolonging the mystery of her disappearance.

Jean Batten was a complex person. Elegant and beautiful, strong and intelligent, the focus of warmth and admiration the world over, she was also self-contained, ruthless, and single-minded, using people to achieve her own ends. She died alone with one last ambition unfulfilled: to fly on board the first Concorde flight to New Zealand.   *Bronwyn Labrum*

Quotations
para.3 *Evening Post*, 19 Feb. 1990
para.8 *NZ Herald*, 15 Oct. 1966
para.11 *NZ Herald*, 15 Oct. 1966
para.14 *NZ Woman's Weekly*, 26 Oct. 1987, p.15

Published Sources
Dannevirke Evening News, 3 Sept. 1986
Evening Post, 19 Feb. 1990
Grayland, E. *More Famous New Zealanders*, Christchurch, 1972, pp.80, 90
Lainé, Shirley. *Silver Wings: New Zealand Women Aviators*, Wellington, 1989, pp.45–52
Mackersey, Ian. *Jean Batten: Garbo of the Skies*, Wellington, 1990
NZ Herald, 15 Oct. 1966
NZ Listener, 9–15 April 1990, pp.112–3
NZ Woman's Weekly, 26 Oct. 1987, pp.14–5
Notable New Zealanders: the Pictorial Who's Who, Auckland, 1979, p.31
Wordsworth, Jane. *Leading Ladies*, Wellington, 1979, pp.80–3

BLANCHE BAUGHAN

1870–1958

Blanche Edith Baughan was born in 1870 in Putney, the daughter of a London stockbroker. By her own account, she graduated from London University in 1891 with a BA, majoring in Greek. She travelled widely, and came to New Zealand at the age of thirty for health reasons. 'I have never found any country with finer scenery, or a kindlier, more sensible and happier humanity than New Zealand', she wrote later. Apart from occasional trips to England, she was to remain here for the rest of her life, mainly on Banks Peninsula near Christchurch. A celebrated poet, she was one of the writers who began to establish an authentic New Zealand voice in the years preceding the First World War.

Blanche Baughan had already produced two books before she reached New Zealand: *Verses*, and *Reuben and Other Verses*. Like her English readers, at least one reviewer of *Shingle-short and Other Verses*, published in New Zealand in 1908, assumed the author was a man: 'Mr Baughan may not be considered to rank very high as a poet . . . Mr Baughan has a helpful message for those who are willing to listen.' In 1909 the poet's real identity brought out another critic: 'Miss Baughan claims Welsh descent, but there is in her verses no "imagination of the Celt" . . . Just a woman writing – a woman of poetical temperament, yet no poet – a woman talking, wondering, grieving, interpreting herself and others, mothering New Zealand.'

Blanche Edith Baughan. *J. Burns Collection, Alexander Turnbull Library*

Published in 1912, Baughan's *Brown Bread from a Colonial Oven* was a collection of prose sketches 'of colonial life'. She claimed later that by 1914 'my writing gift, gradually dwindling, had left me – as it proved for ever'. This was an exaggeration, for in 1923 she produced *Poems from the Port Hills, Christchurch*. She also wrote for periodicals in Britain and Australia as well as New Zealand, and continued to write her very successful travel guides. 'The Finest Walk in the World' (about the Milford Track) was first printed in the London *Spectator* in 1909. *Studies of New Zealand Scenery* collected together her travel booklets in 1916; her *Arthur's Pass and The Otira Gorge* had a print run of over 4,000 in 1925 (compared with 625 and 100 for *Shingle-short* and *Brown Bread* respectively). She was no armchair traveller, being one of the few early women mountaineers and a foundation member of Canterbury Women's Club in 1913.

Baughan had private means, giving her an independent position which, she believed, obliged her to care for the oppressed.

I regard social service as an art you know: my contribution to society is still to try and educe Beauty from Ashes. In religion, I am definitely a Mystic (nobody knows what that is(!)

This belief was perhaps associated with her longstanding interest in eastern religions, expressed in her last collection of verse. (She also corresponded from time to time with Hindu swamis in India and California.) Above all she was a humanitarian, concerned about civil liberties and dedicated to reforming the prison system. She had supported the suffrage movement in England, where she had also done welfare work in London's East End.

She had been a member of the Howard League for Penal Reform in London and established the first New Zealand branch in Christchurch in 1924. Her indignation was first aroused by the attitude of the authorities when she clothed, fed and sheltered two absconders from the Te Oranga Reformatory for Delinquent Women in 1917. Later she joined the staff of a women's reformatory for an inside view of the problems, and she encouraged understanding women to become prison visitors. She became known as 'the prisoners' friend' to the inmates of both women's and men's institutions.

In 1936 she wrote *People in Prison*, with F. A. de la Mare, under the pseudonym of 'TIS'. New Zealand's identity was obscured by calling it Dominia: 'a good place for the study of prisoners because she has, in proportion to population, an undue share of them. Moreover, she really believes in imprisonment.' Baughan was scathing about the inhumanity of the prison system and its total failure to reform its victims. One of her proposals, forward-looking for her time, was that the prisoners themselves should suggest reforms, and her book contains case histories and prisoners' comments. She was a strong advocate of employing psychologists (unheard of in New Zealand) and trained 'social servants' to establish not what the prisoner 'has *done* but what he *is*', and give appropriate treatment. It was a common claim by judges at the time that a prisoner was at war with society. Baughan wrote: 'Society is at war with this man.'

Margot Roth

Quotations
para. 1 'The Prisoner's Friend', p. 12

para.2 Undated clipping, *The Press*, Lawlor Collection, Hocken; A. G. Stephen, *The Press*, 13 March 1909

para.3 'The Prisoner's Friend', p.12

para.4 B. E. Baughan to J. C. Andersen, 6 March 1936, J. C. Andersen, MS Papers 148, folder 31, ATL

para.6 T.I.S., *People in Prison*, pp.170, 134

Unpublished Sources

Lawlor Collection, Hocken

Published Sources

Alcock, P. M. 'A True Colonial Voice: Blanche Edith Baughan', *Landfall*, vol.26, June 1972, pp.162–76

Bagnall, A. G. (ed.). *NZ National Bibliography*, vol.2, 1890–1960, A–H, pp.102–3

McLauchlan, Gordon (ed.) *Bateman New Zealand Encyclopaedia*, 2nd edn, Auckland, 1987, p.114

McLintock, A. H. (ed.) *An Encyclopedia of New Zealand*, vol.1, Wellington, 1966, pp.170–71

'The Prisoner's Friend' (unattributed), *NZ Listener*, 12 Sept. 1958

Regional Women's Decade Committee, *Canterbury Women Since 1893*, Christchurch, 1979, p.69

Summers, John. 'In Memoriam B. E. Baughan', *NZ Poetry Yearbook*, ed. Louis Johnson, vol.8, 1958–59, pp.91–2

'T.I.S.', *People in Prison*, Auckland, 1936

THE PADDOCK

Tomorrow? Same old sorrow!
Cook, clean – the same tame humdrum. . . I forgot –
Churning's thrown in – it's Friday. Every Friday . . .
Yes! Four whole years except that trip to Aunt's
I've churned! I've wash'd on every possible hour –
Ironed each Tuesday, Wednesday, clean'd the house –
Oh haven't I done enough? And, when it's done,
What does it all amount to? where's it gone?
That is the worst of all! If one had slaved
Straight on at anything else that monstrous time,
I guess there would be something at the end,
Done, and to show for it. But just look at me!
Four years . . . Say seven-and-forty solid months,
Over a thousand days . . . I've faithfully
Roasted and fried, made beds and bread-and-butter,
Scrubbed, rubb'd, and all the rest – with what result?
What's in the house this moment? Tumbled beds,
An empty larder and a foot-marked floor!
That's all. With all the doing, nothing's Done;
With all the endless making, nothing's Made;
There's nothing come of all the eternal drudge,
Except – the need to drudge all over again!
Oh, who'd be a housekeeper?

Shingle-short and Other Verses (1908)

MILLICENT BAXTER

1888–1984

Before I married I was often referred to as the daughter of Professor John Macmillan Brown, one of the founding professors of Canterbury University College, or the daughter of Helen Connon, the first woman graduate with honours in the British Empire. In more recent years I have found myself known as the mother of James K. Baxter.

I am myself, but I remain Mrs Archie Baxter. In this book I should like to show that it is possible to have an ideal marriage.

In her memoirs Millicent Baxter tells one of the most unlikely and most enduring love stories. But her life is also a tale of determination, independence, and self-reliance, overshadowed only in the public eye by her famous family.

Millicent Amiel Brown was the daughter of John Macmillan Brown and his wife Helen Connon. Her father had emigrated from Scotland to become one of the founding professors at Canterbury University College. He was an inspiring and formidable man: 'one of the intellectual dynamos and steam rollers of his time', wrote the poet Charles Brasch. Helen Connon was a brilliant student, who became principal of Christchurch Girls' High School. Millicent was born on 8 January 1888 – in time, she was to note later, to give her mother three weeks' respite before the summer term began. Her mother continued to work at the school, as the baby could be cared for by household or school staff.

Millicent and her sister Viola, nine years younger, grew up in 'Holmbank', the large family home in Fendalton with its five acres of gardens and orchards. Millicent had a governess and her mother also taught her for two hours a day. After her mother's death she had a tutor at home; her father also coached her, an experience she described as 'pure hell'.

From the beginning the family travelled extensively in New Zealand and abroad, 'educational touring' as it was then called. A lifelong passionate interest in botany, particularly in wild flowers, began when Millicent was a young child. Into her nineties she was still exploring remote parts of the South Island with groups interested in natural history.

When her much-loved mother died in 1903, a pall of grief descended on the family. Millicent's relationship with her father, never close, deteriorated, and became even worse when he, with unduly high expectations, coached her for university scholarship examinations. She was rescued by relatives in Sydney and was educated there at the Presbyterian Ladies' College and at Sydney University, graduating BA in 1908. After this distancing from her father, Millicent found she was better able to stand her own ground: 'I came to terms with him.'

He continued, however, in his attempts to control her life – preventing her, for example, from taking a teaching position at Wellington Girls' College in 1920. He insisted that she come with him instead to Dunedin, where he was to take up a temporary position as Professor of English at Otago University; he could not manage without her, he declared. 'I felt resentful about it, but I was accustomed to trying to do what my father wanted.' In 1909 father and daughter travelled to England and through Europe together, a life of academic receptions in pre-war London society.

Millicent then went up to Cambridge to Newnham College, a residential college for the higher education of women. Her name duly appeared in the Tripos list, but women there did not have degrees conferred on them until 1921. She then went to Germany to study the language and Old French. This double undertaking proved too much, and she abandoned plans for a PhD. But she continued, as in England, to travel and enjoy the artistic and intellectual life of Europe.

She had little wish to return to New Zealand but her father required her to come home, just as the First World War was breaking out. She did war work – rolling bandages and making up Red Cross parcels, 'the usual sorts of things that girls did then'. Atrocity stories about the Germans circulated everywhere. Millicent, with her very recent and happy experiences in Germany, found it hard to credit them.

Then came something which changed her life. She was shown a copy of a remarkable letter written to his parents by a New Zealand farmer, Archibald Baxter, a conscientious objector who was being tortured by the military at the front lines in France. This letter, she said more than seventy years later, 'altered my whole outlook on politics and on everything in life. I keep it in my handbag to this day.'

Eventually she sought out Archie and his family of five brothers and sisters on the family farm in Otago. To him she was little Miss Brown – she was slight, and only 5'1" tall – and to her he was Mr Baxter. 'He was everything I had hoped for.' To him, he later said, she was the woman he had dreamed of all his life and never found. Professor Macmillan Brown, soon to be chancellor of the University of New Zealand, was far from pleased: their backgrounds were so completely different that a marriage could not possibly succeed.

They married in 1921 when Millicent was thirty-three, and went to live in a primitive farm cottage at Kuri Bush with no electricity or other conveniences. She had never cooked more than scrambled eggs and shortbread, but she taught herself from European cookbooks, using New Zealand wine, learned to garden and to sew, and became a housewife. Terence was born in 1922 and Jim, the poet James K. Baxter, in 1926.

Government officials and some local people continued to harass Archie for his pacifism, but Millicent wrote:

Life was delightful. People have said that the change in my way of living must have been rather like the fairy tale of the princess and the peasant. What they didn't know was that Archie was the prince. What had been done to him in the war had only strengthened his nobility and his character.

Before Jim began primary school the family sold the farm, moved to Brighton, and Archie became a shearer. Whenever they could they explored the backblocks of the South Island, sleeping in tents.

Decades later, Millicent Baxter talked of the effects on children if their parents are intensely involved with each other: 'We loved our sons dearly but I sometimes wonder if I, for one, did not sometimes make them feel left out of our so very close relationship.'

They travelled to Europe as a family in 1937–8, on money left to them by Macmillan Brown who had died in 1935. In England they visited some of the camps where Archie had been imprisoned by the army for his pacifism, and there at her urging he dictated to her the classic story of his struggle against war, *We Will Not Cease*. It was published by Gollancz just as the Second World War broke out.

Millicent Baxter — 'I am myself'.
The Memoirs of Millicent Baxter

Archie and Millicent Baxter lived on in harmony, staunch workers for peace, and for organisations such as Amnesty International. James the poet became a Catholic in 1958. His parents followed him into the faith in 1965. Archie Baxter, who had never fully regained his health since his brutal treatment as an army prisoner, died in 1970. James died in 1972. Terence, living in Dunedin nearby, visited his mother regularly until her death in 1984.

On the last page of her memoirs, Millicent Baxter wrote:

Jim said once, 'I would like to change the emotional climate of this country, make it one per cent warmer before I die.' I think perhaps this is what we all must strive for, and first to have a change of heart in ourselves.

Christine Cole Catley

Quotations
para.1 M. Baxter, *Memoirs*, p.11
para.2 M. Baxter, p.30
para.5 M. Baxter, interview with the author
para.8 M. Baxter, p.49
para.9 M. Baxter. p.51
para.10 M. Baxter, p.58
para.12 M. Baxter, p.61
para.14 M. Baxter, interview with the author
para.17 M. Baxter, p.144

Unpublished Sources
The author is the publisher of Millicent Baxter's memoirs, and drew on interviews and personal
   information.
Published Sources
Baxter, Archibald. *We Will Not Cease*, London, 1939; reprinted Picton, 1980
Baxter, Millicent. *The Memoirs of Millicent Baxter*, Picton, 1981

EMMA BEAUFOY

1857–1931

Emma Langstaff was born in 1857 in the village of Langthorne, Yorkshire. She came alone to New Zealand in 1873 under an organised emigration scheme to a pre-arranged post as a housemaid in the Wairarapa. Two years later she was married at Greytown to Herbert Beaufoy. The newly married couple moved to Tolaga Bay where Herbert managed a farm and two children were born. A move to Te Arai Station proved very successful for Herbert, who found a comfortable niche in the station organisation. But after the births of a further five children, Emma found the life at Te Arai restricting and took steps to fulfil her ambition to become a farmer.

With an initial down payment of £80 which entitled her to three years' occupation rent-free, she took up a 1600-acre block on the route of the projected railway at what is now called Rakauroa, inland from Gisborne. Although he signed the deeds, Herbert remained in his employment at Te Arai.

Miles away from civilisation, and with access only by pack-track from Whakarau, Emma did much of the physical work herself to clear the homestead site. The 'homestead', which was a 12′ by 14′ slab hut with a clay floor, remained the family home for a long time and, although additions were made to accommodate the growing family, the clay floor was retained. Cooking was done in camp ovens and kerosene tins in a huge fireplace that was big enough to burn five-foot lengths of tawa. Wild pigeon and pork appeared regularly on the table, to the delight of her frequent visitors.

Emma was especially interested in dairying. Her prize-winning bull, Fisherman, and cow, Footstep, became the nucleus of a hill-country herd. The family established the first dairying plant in the region, starting with fourteen cows and expanding to sixty-five. Their butter, which Emma made herself from an old family recipe, was exported to England. Before Rakauroa had a rail connection with Gisborne, the butter had to be taken by pack-horse to Willow Crossing at Te Karaka, where it was transferred to the Cassidy Coach Service and taken to Gisborne for shipment.

More settlement was taking place in the area, and before the public school was established, the young Beaufoys were able to attend classes for three days a week at the home of the neighbouring Redpaths. Emma, believing some kind of musical instruction to be essential to her children's education, had her piano transported to Rakauroa from Te Arai, an undertaking that would have daunted a less determined person. Wrapped under two layers of mattresses, the piano was laid on a sledge and, with the aid of relays of draughthorses and many men, was delivered undamaged.

The homestead, which had been called 'Langthorne' after Emma's birth-place, was renamed Rakauroa when it was given the status of a post office. This resulted in numerous visits from neighbouring settlers and, as railway construction came closer, it became the centre of communications in the district. The family also provided a variety of services for later high-country settlers, including the supply and delivery of essentials such as fencing materials and grass seed.

The slab hut was something of a social centre too. Emma was famous for the kindly and generous hospitality offered to all comers, not only to local people, but also to bishops, ministers of the Crown, and all sorts of travellers.

At a time when women were expected to play a role secondary to their husbands, Emma Beaufoy displayed unusual enterprise and determination. Virtually a solo parent, she brought up her family of seven, established her farm, and provided essential services and a base for further community development, all in remote and very difficult country. When 'old Lady Beaufoy' died in 1931 she had become an almost legendary figure among pioneer bush settlers.

Avis Korver

Sources

Information provided by Ralph Beaufoy, Emma's son, for a pamphlet entitled 'A Bush Country Woman's Fight for a Footing', forms the basis of this essay. Another family member, Mrs Gates, also provided information (letter to the author, April 1990).

Conditions here at Matamau c. 1880 are similar to those encountered by Emma Beaufoy at Rakauroa, further north on the eastern side of the North Island. *E. R. Williams Collection, Alexander Turnbull Library*

JEAN BEGG

1887–1971

'Unstoppable' was an epithet frequently applied to New Zealand's most notable YWCA worker, Jean Begg. As director of British war services in the Middle East and North Africa, she earned a reputation as a woman of formidable determination. Even the fiercest general quailed at the mention of Jean Begg, for she tended to get her own way. But perhaps no tale better sums up Jean's character than an incident from closer to home – the Wairarapa in 1956.

Jean was aged nearly seventy at the time. Invited to speak to a Returned Services Association (RSA) women's group, she set out in her car. On the way, the car went over a bank, rolled several times, and landed at the front door of share-milker's cottage. The vehicle was a write-off, but Jean emerged from the wreck, hat still firmly in place, to ask the astonished share-milker's wife for a sticking-plaster to repair her broken glasses. She hitched a ride to the women's meeting and, apologising for her dishevelled state, mounted the stage to speak. Her address lasted an hour, during which time Jean's alarmed audience observed the relentless development of a large black eye and bruises all over her face, while one leg swelled visibly. The RSA women called a doctor. The *Dominion*, reporting this incident, noted that Jean was 'now back at home showing bruises from head to foot but serenely carrying on'.

Born in Dunedin on 7 October 1887, Jean was the daughter of Eliza and John Begg, a tanner and his wife who had emigrated from Scotland in 1879. She was the eighth of ten children and the birth was a difficult one, exhausting her mother. When a wet-nurse was sought, the only person available was a local prostitute. Her mother always maintained that Jean's sense of adventure and curiosity came not from her, but had been imbibed with her foster-mother's milk.

Jean attended Otago Girls' High School, then the University of Otago, but one year short of completing her arts degree she made a decision to become a missionary. After two years at the Presbyterian Missionary Training Institute in Dunedin, the twenty-three-year-old Jean sailed for the tiny island of Tutuila in Samoa.

This was being thrown in at the deep end. There was no electricity, supplies came twice yearly from Sydney,, and Jean was expected not only to teach school, but also to deliver the island's babies. Her first delivery, a difficult breech birth, was made with the aid of a home nursing manual open beside her.

In 1919, after nine years in Tutuila, Jean came to the conclusion that, although she loved them dearly, the Samoans did not need her. '[They] have everything they want and have every chance,' she said. 'I know that I can and will do better work amongst white women and girls'.

Jean had made contact with Jane Addams, the famed founder of Hull House, a model settlement in the slums of Chicago. Addams counselled Jean to train as a social worker in New York, and for the next two years Jean studied for a social work diploma, supporting herself by working in factories and restaurants before winning a scholarship. Jean's thesis for her course was an innovative scheme for the reorganisation of Inwood House, a New York reformatory for delinquent girls at which Jean had worked during her vacation. To her astonishment, she was offered a good salary by the board of the house to implement her plan. Jean firmly believed there was good in everybody and in the power of friendship, something she said she learned in Samoa. She had advanced ideas about social work, arguing that juvenile offenders needed to be integrated into the community. 'Teach girls to fight temptation where it lies,' she said, 'in the community – not behind closed walls and doors.' Her plan for Inwood House involved selling it and replacing it with a home for young single mothers with an attached creche, so that they could take up employment. By 1924 Jean had carried this out, but her health had suffered and she returned to New Zealand.

After undertaking a report on child welfare for the New Zealand government and organising the women's court at the 1925–6 New Zealand–South Seas Exhibition in Dunedin, Jean was recruited by the Auckland YWCA to assist its general secretary, Jean Stevenson. At the end of 1926, Jean Begg took over the secretaryship. In the YWCA, Jean had found her home. She was still 'on the King's Business', as she put it, but through the YWCA she could impact on a far wider community than was possible as a social worker. It was a time of accelerating change for women. In the wake of war, young women were taking on paid employment in increasing numbers. According to Jean:

The task of the YWCA is to wisely guide the new woman power that is gradually being released into the community . . . The church has been the haven of women, and is the inspiration of us all. But the voice of the church is usually the voice of men, and if we judge by their utterances, many of these men do not recognise that the situation has greatly changed for women . . . Our women are realising the release of their power, and are now confronted with the big task of preparing youth to take its place as well-balanced and perceptive leaders in the home, workroom or office.

Jean Stevenson had established a solid foundation for the association which Jean Begg built on and expanded. In the 1928 annual report, Jean Begg recorded that the Auckland YWCA had nearly 2,000 members, with 655 enrolments in the gym, while it had accommodated 964 local girls and 700 immigrants in the hostels. A further 652 girls had stayed at the Holiday House. There were nearly fifty clubs, a downtown businesswomen's lunch-room serving one hundred daily, and 64,000 meals had been served in the main building. Jean accomplished this with a staff of only thirteen, with an additional 150 volunteers organised through fourteen committees.

This demonstrated phenomenal organisational abilities, but the real explanation for Jean's success lay in her charismatic leadership. There was something larger than life about Jean. Tall, angular, and powerfully built, she had physical presence, but it was her personality that made the deepest impression. Her enormous vigour and zest for life inspired people to take on and carry through the tasks she set. A friend eloquently described Jean's persuasive powers as combining

a bracing, forthright charm, that no man or woman of any race could resist,

*with the cunning of a serpent. If she decided on a certain plan of action, how-
ever astonishing, it became possible, even easy to achieve . . .*

In her first two years in Auckland, Jean stayed at the YWCA's Holiday
House on the shores of the Manukau Harbour. One of her contemporaries
recalled that 'crowds came out to the Holiday House simply because she was
there'. Jean's story-telling ability is legendary and Holiday House residents and
visitors loved hearing tales of her adventures. But although Jean was often the
centre of attention, she also possessed the ability to focus on and support the
individual, whether it was a young woman who was 'down and out', as she put
it, or a member of her staff.

Audrey Owen, a junior member of Jean's staff, recalled her arrival at the
YWCA:

*. . . the building seemed huge, dark and empty, but there she was, waiting and
waiting to greet little me, with a wide smile of welcome. She could quite easily
have delegated this job to someone else, but she didn't. There was a personal
tour of the building and we ended up in the cafeteria, where Jean raided the
pantry and produced two red jellies, bidding me never to reveal what she had
done. Any nervousness I might have had was banished by being part of this
little conspiracy.*

Jean was deeply religious, but she combined her faith with a feminist and
egalitarian vision. On her arrival in Auckland, she quickly became a vice-
president of the National Council of Women (NCW) and was an active and outspoken member, attending national conferences. In the 1920s she became one of
the first women justices of the peace, an advance fought for for years by the
NCW. She was the leader of the New Zealand delegation to the 1930 Pan-Pacific
and South-East Asia Women's Association and, in the same year, with the onset
of the Depression, took up the issue of government neglect of unemployed
women through both the YWCA and NCW.

Pioneering Auckland sportswomen described Jean Begg as being a good
friend to women's sport. She made the YWCA building available for their
meetings, fought for a sportsground for Auckland women, headed the Auckland
Girls' Athletic Association, and with a handful of others was instrumental in
establishing cricket as a women's sport in the city.

Jean was an ardent champion of her sex. Answering criticism of the 'modern
girl' in the media, she said the young woman was merely trying to sort out her
life 'free of dogma':

*She is accused of a number of things – recklessness, love of excitement and a
disregard of authority. All the faults said to be peculiar to the modern girl have
really been characteristics of each new generation . . . If Joan of Arc had been
older and had more sense, she might not have led an army.*

She deplored distinctions of class or race. Arguing for the abolition of
private schools, she said that 'New Zealand is a democratic country and anything
that tends towards class distinction should be done away with'. Her years in
Samoa had made her alive to racial prejudice. She had formed enduring friend-

ships in Samoa, and at the end of her life always worshipped at a Samoan church. She maintained that:

The feelings of white superiority and the use of nicknames for native peoples must pass. The white races had to understand that their own ways were not necessarily the best and both races had much to learn from each other.

In 1931 Jean went to India to reorganise the Indian YWCA, which had lost its American funding. She was still there in 1940 when Lady Churchill invited her to take on a special assignment, the provision of recreational facilities for WAACs (Women's Army Auxiliary Corps), WAAFs (Women's Auxiliary Air Force), and nurses serving in the Middle East. This was the work for which she would become internationally renowned, for in time she developed a vast network of no fewer than sixty-five clubs, stretching from North Africa, Palestine, Iraq, and Italy to India, Burma, and Japan. Wherever the troops went, Jean Begg was very close behind.

From the very beginning of this task, Jean determined that women who were putting their lives on the line for their countries, often working under appalling conditions, should have nothing but the very best. The first club, at Tahag Camp in Egypt, had the only grass for miles around. There were tennis courts, trees, solid walls (rather than canvas), and a bird-bath made by Italian prisoners of war. The club was an instant success, something Jean put down to her policy of not excluding anyone because of their rank. The British nursing sisters, for instance, were forbidden to go out with any men but commissioned officers, but could meet friends of any rank at the YWCA clubs.

Leave houses were established in other places, often in the most luxurious buildings. Nurses on furlough from the war zones stayed in exotic palaces, where they had breakfast in bed served on fine china. When Jean arrived in Italy to establish more clubs, a witty British officer signalled army headquarters in Naples: 'Inform Miss Begg that Vatican not available.' In South Burma, Jean had the Royal Engineers shave the top off a mountain to create a building site for a leave house where nurses could rest away from the steamy jungle.

At the end of the war, Jean was put in charge of the repatriation of women war prisoners in Singapore, taking over the famed Raffles Hotel for her purposes. She wrote home at this time that:

owing to my age (58), I'm a bit deafer, blinder, stiff at the joints, wrinkled at the neck and my memory isn't all that it should be. I've been dog-tired many a time, but a few hours of natural sleep always sets me to rights again . . .

Tired or not, after Singapore Jean went on to Japan to assist women with reconstruction after the war. When she left in 1948, the Japanese women presented her with an album of photographs and the following testimonial:

She is at the back of us to support us so that we might not falter and turn back. She is by the side of us to show, guide and lend a leading hand. When she is in front she is paving the way with a hammer and paint brush in hand. She never ceases to help. She is very weary. One thing is accomplished, she looks forward to something new. She is ever so young.

Jean was now sixty-one, but she next took over the revitalisation of Helen Graham House, the main hostel of the British YWCA in London. On her return to New Zealand, she worked for Corso in Wellington, before returning to Dunedin to care for her now aged two older sisters.

Jean always made her friends for life. She was given a tumultuous welcome when she revisited Samoa late in her life, discovering at least fifty babies who had been named Jean! The Auckland YWCA called its first hostel for female university students after her, and, in 1970, 200 of her old colleagues from Auckland gathered for a grand reunion. When an appeal was made for Jean's airfare, so much was collected that Jean was able to visit her friends in Samoa again and travel to Norfolk Island to see one of her workmates from the 1920s. 'For once,' said Jean, 'I've seen everyone I wanted to see.'

Within three months, Jean was dead. Several days after an operation for kidney stones, she died suddenly of a blood clot. She was given a full military funeral and her ashes were buried in the soldiers' cemetery at Andersons Bay, Dunedin.

For her war services, Jean was given the status of colonel, and awarded the MBE, OBE, and CBE. *Sandra Coney*

Quotations

para.2 *Dominion*, 17 Aug. 1956
para.6 R. Begg, *Jean Begg*, p.45
para.7 R. Begg, p.62
para.8 R. Begg, p.46, S. Coney, *Every Girl*, p.121
para.10 R. Begg, p.98
para.11 R. Begg, p.222
para.12 R. Begg, p.71
para.15 S. Coney, p.113
para.16 S. Coney, p.223; S. Coney, p.223
para.20 R. Begg, p.127
para.21 R. Begg, p.141
para.23 S. Coney, p.227

Unpublished Sources

Auckland YWCA Archives, MS 1131, AIM
Minutes and Scrapbooks of the Auckland Branch of the NCW, AIM
NCW, Auckland Branch, 'History: 1918 to 1938', AIM
Women's Archives, NCW, AIM

Published Sources

Begg, Rewa. *Jean Begg CBE: Her Story*, Wellington, 1979
Coney, Sandra. *Every Girl: A Social History of Women and the YWCA in Auckland*, Auckland, 1986
History of the New Zealand Branch of the Pan-Pacific and South-East Asia Women's Association 1928–1978, Christchurch, 1978
Law, Ethel. *Down the Years*, Wellington, 1964

ETHEL BENJAMIN

1875-1943

In 1897 Ethel Benjamin became the first woman in New Zealand and the British Empire to qualify as a lawyer. A committed feminist and self-professed rebel, she became one of a handful of progressive women who managed to step outside the limited roles nineteenth-century society prescribed for them.

She was born in Dunedin in 1875, the eldest in a family of five girls and two boys. Her parents, Harry and Lizzie Benjamin (born Mark), had emigrated from England in the late 1860s. Harry became a prominent mercantile businessman and sharebroker.

Education was held in high regard by her Orthodox Jewish family and Ethel had an excellent scholastic record. She attended Otago Girls' High School from 1883, and during her time there she won Learmonth Dalrymple's 'Victoria' prize for order, diligence, and punctuality, and an Education Board Junior Scholarship. Her education prepared her well for her chosen career. Not only did Otago Girls' High School provide an unusually thorough education for girls in New Zealand at that time, it also focused specifically on exam preparation. In addition, students were taught the merits of a university education.

Ethel set her heart on being a lawyer from the beginning. 'Because in my own mind, I saw that any talent I had lay in that direction, and because, even as a child, I loved to study the law.' In 1892 she won a university scholarship and enrolled for a law degree at the University of Otago the following year. Since the first woman had been admitted to the university nearly twenty years earlier, all of the thirty women who had taken degrees had gained general qualifications which led to traditional fields of female employment, especially teaching.

Ethel's boldness is even more remarkable in that throughout her degree she did not know if she would be able to put her training into practice.

When I heard that being a woman, I could not be admitted to the practice of the law, I was very indignant, and I suppose, being a true daughter of Eve, the fruit, because forbidden, became all the more attractive and desirable, and I grew all the more determined to follow the legal profession.

In 1896, the last year of her degree, the Female Law Practitioners Act was finally passed, after several similar bills had been introduced unsuccessfully into parliament.

Compared with her contemporaries at the medical school, Ethel faced little discrimination from fellow students. Although she frequently gained the highest marks in her class, most of the men appeared to welcome her presence. It was the Otago Law Society which put most of the barriers in her way. Its members denied her access to the Supreme Court Library and only allowed her to read in the Judges' Chamber Room and borrow books with the consent of a member of the society's council.

At her graduation in 1897, Ethel replied on behalf of the graduates, the first time a current graduate and a woman had made such a speech. In an incisive

Ethel Benjamin at her graduation in 1897. *Hocken Library*

address, she argued that there must be a wide range of employment options open to women in order for them to have economic independence and become 'self-actualised, fully integrated beings'. Yet she also cautioned women against using a 'masculine' approach. In an attempt to head off a frequent criticism, she claimed that '[t]he heart must be developed as well as the brain. The ideal new woman will perfect herself, body, mind and soul.'

Once qualified, Ethel seems to have set up in practice on her own. Again she had no help from the profession. Established lawyers refused to help her and did not readily pass on briefs. The Law Society continued to make things difficult. They attempted to regulate her dress and refused to invite her to their annual dinner. At the opening of the new law courts in 1902, she almost did not have a partner for the formal procession through the streets, but was saved from humiliation at the last minute.

Despite the fact that she was supported by the Jewish community, and by a number of married women clients with financial interests, and had her premises in a good location in Princes Street, Ethel's practice grew only slowly.

She had to advertise for new clients, a method which drew strong objections from both the Otago and later the Wellington law societies.

Not surprisingly, Ethel did a lot of voluntary work on behalf of women. She was a founding member of the Dunedin Society for the Protection of Women and Children from 1899, and acted as its honorary solicitor. The objectives of the society were to initiate proceedings in cases of cruelty, seduction, outrage or excessive violence towards women or children; to give advice and aid to women who had been cruelly treated; to provide neglected children with homes; and to lobby for improvements in the law with respect to women and children. Thus much of Ethel's case work involved threatening legal action against abusive husbands and, if divorces were granted, ensuring ex-husbands paid maintenance. She also acted as an intermediary in adoption cases between birth mothers and prospective adoptive parents, and spent a lot of time on affiliation cases trying to obtain child maintenance from the fathers of illegitimate children.

Much of her other work was for the hotel industry. Ethel was one of the minority of prominent nineteenth-century feminists in New Zealand who did not advocate temperance. She managed the business affairs of several hotels and acted for several publicans' associations in the battle over prohibition.

By 1906 she was frustrated with law in Dunedin and took over a restaurant in Christchurch's International Exhibition. The following year she returned to Dunedin, conducted legal business, and prepared to move to London. But instead, she met and married Alfred de Costa, a Wellington sharebroker and real estate agent. Ethel set up a new practice in Wellington and moved into the field of property speculation.

In 1908 the de Costas went to live in England. Ethel's family had returned to England in the late 1890s, and she had always intended to join them there. The de Costas had no children, and enjoyed a comfortable middle-class life in London, travelling frequently to Europe in their holidays. Ethel joined a legal firm on her arrival, but could not fully practise law until the Sex Disqualification (Removal) Act was passed in 1919.

After Alfred's death just prior to the Second World War, Ethel continued to live and work as a lawyer in London. During the war, when bombing became severe, Ethel went to her sister's house in Middlesex, but was fatally injured one night during a black-out when a building she was in collapsed. She was admitted to hospital and died on 14 October 1943.

Ethel expected that other women would build quickly upon her success. However, it was not until 1911 that another woman completed a full law degree in New Zealand. Women did not begin seriously to enter the profession until after the Second World War. The problems she encountered remained serious obstacles.

Bronwyn Labrum

Quotations
para.4 C. Brown, 'Ethel Benjamin – New Zealand's First Woman Lawyer', p.5
para.5 C. Brown, p.13
para.7 C. Brown, p.20
Unpublished Source
Brown, Carol. 'Ethel Benjamin – New Zealand's First Woman Lawyer', BA Hons research essay, Otago, 1985

AGNES BENNETT

1872–1960

Agnes Bennett, one of the first women doctors in early twentieth-century New Zealand (and perhaps the most distinguished), was born on 24 June 1872 in Sydney. Her father, William Bennett, an able Irish engineer, was Commissioner of Roads and Bridges for New South Wales. Her mother Agnes (born Hays), born in London and brought up in New York, was a woman of strong character. Agnes spent a happy early childhood, enjoying the freedom of a spacious house and garden. She was a healthy active child whom her father considered the brightest of the children.

In 1878, her mother took Agnes, her two sisters, and four brothers to England to further their education. Agnes attended Cheltenham Ladies' College, where the headmistress was Dorothea Beale, a pioneer in girls' education, and then Dulwich Girls' High School in London. The children returned to Sydney in 1881, after their mother died of smallpox. Agnes attended Abbotsleigh School and later Sydney Girls' High School.

After gaining a state scholarship, she became a student at Sydney University, where in 1894 she became the first woman to gain a science degree with honours. She found that, while men with only a pass degree in science could find employment, she could not. She decided to make a fresh start by studying medicine at Edinburgh University, which attracted her by its Medical College for Women. She sailed for Scotland in 1895.

Although women were taught separately from men students and faced special difficulties, Agnes enjoyed her time at Edinburgh and graduated in 1899 with the degree of MB ChM. Rejected for a post in Edinburgh Infirmary because she was a woman, she became medical officer at a psychiatric hospital in Larbert, Stirlingshire; positions in psychiatric hospitals were unpopular but women doctors were glad to take them. After fifteen months she returned to Sydney, where she tried unsuccessfully to establish a medical practice and then fell back on another appointment in a psychiatric hospital.

Her prospects improved in 1905, when she bought the practice of Ella Watson, in Upper Willis Street, Wellington. The city was then relatively short of doctors, so women doctors did not meet the hostility from male doctors that they often encountered elsewhere. In 1908 she was appointed medical officer of St Helen's Hospital, Wellington, a position she held with great distinction until 1936. She worked hard to reduce the number of infant and maternal deaths, and collected material on breast-feeding which was the basis of her 1911 MD degree from Edinburgh. She became honorary physician to the children's ward in Wellington Hospital in 1910, the first woman doctor to be appointed to the hospital.

In her early years in Wellington, Agnes Bennett publicly defended the right of women to higher education. In 1909, she wrote an article in the *Dominion* attacking the speeches by Dr Frederic Truby King and the obstetrician Ferdinand Batchelor which claimed that higher education for girls was dangerous to their health and that of their future children. A few years later, she persuaded

Dr Agnes Bennett. *New Zealand Free Lance Collection, Alexander Turnbull Library*

a medical conference to set aside Truby King's motion attacking higher education for women.

By the beginning of the First World War, she had made many friends and was financially well established. She did not hesitate, however, to offer her services to the government. When these were refused, she sailed for Europe in 1915, intending to work for the Red Cross. She was offered work in Cairo and was attested for service in the New Zealand Medical Corps with the pay and status of captain, although she was not formally commissioned. She worked in hospitals in Cairo and then, from August 1916 to September 1917, was in charge of a medical unit of the Scottish Women's Hospitals in Serbia, which were financed by the National Union of Women's Suffrage Societies in Britain. She ran an extremely efficient and well-kept unit in difficult and dangerous conditions until illness forced her to resign. The Third Order of St Sava and the Royal Red Cross of Serbia were given to her for her work. After recovering from her illness, she worked for a time in hospitals in Britain.

On returning to Wellington in 1919, she resumed her general practice and her position at St Helen's. Always interested in social issues, she had time, now that her early struggles were over, to work for a number of causes. She helped to found a hostel (Victoria House) for women students and to establish the Wellington branch of the Federation of University Women. She was the first president of the branch and in 1936 was the New Zealand delegate at an international Federation conference in Poland.

In 1931, after a slight heart attack, Agnes Bennett decided to retire from general practice, but responded immediately to the news of the Hawke's Bay earthquake. Collecting equipment, she drove to the area and reported to the Red Cross in Wellington on what was needed. With the help of friends, she organised a retreat in Lowry Bay (Wellington) for expectant mothers from Hawke's Bay.

After retiring from her position at St Helen's in 1936, she worked for a year in the flying doctor service in Queensland.

Back in New Zealand, she helped to establish the Women's War Service Auxiliary on the outbreak of the Second World War, and then worked with the Women's Voluntary Service in London during the blitz. After serving as a medical officer in English hospitals she returned to New Zealand in 1942. She travelled around the country, lecturing on sex education to servicewomen. A sergeant-major declined to enter her birth date as 1872, since a recruit aged seventy-two might suggest a mistake in the records.

In 1947, Dr Bennett responded to an appeal for a temporary replacement for the resident doctor in the Chatham Islands. For five weeks she went on horseback through heavy mud and severe cold to visit patients. It was probably this work which led to the award of the OBE in the following year.

Dr Bennett lived from the early 1930s at Lowry Bay in a house called 'Honda' after her childhood home. She gave this house in 1947 to the Women's Division of Federated Farmers as a holiday centre. For herself she built a smaller house nearby.

Agnes Bennett died in 1960 after a life full of more activities than can be mentioned here. Her friends had included some of the most outstanding women in the country: Grace Neill, Mother Aubert, Dr Ada Paterson, Hester Maclean.

Throughout her career she had visited hospitals overseas to widen her knowledge. Although not an extreme feminist, she worked consistently to help women, by standing up for their right to educational opportunities, by trying to improve conditions of childbirth, and by helping many individual women in practical ways. Her independent and courageous life showed what women could do.

Beryl Hughes

Unpublished Source
Agnes Bennett Papers, MS Papers 1346, ATL

Published Source
Manson, Cecil and Celia. *Doctor Agnes Bennett*, London and Christchurch, 1960

FLORENCE BENNETT

1882–1962

Florence Catherine Wratt was born at Bulls in 1882, the eldest of ten children of John and Harriet Wratt, early settlers in the Manawatu district. Florence married John Bennett in 1903 and moved to his farm in the Te Arakura district, near Feilding, where she lived for the rest of her life, bringing up a family of nine children. In addition, the Bennetts were foster parents throughout their lives, incorporating additional children into farm and family life.

Many of their foster children came from the Child Welfare Division of the Education Department (established under the Child Welfare Act of 1925). In the 1920s the division encouraged fostering as an alternative to institutional care, and with the absence of support for single mothers, many children passed into foster care. It was not uncommon for large families to take in children, who would sometimes help on the farm if they were older. Foster parents were given approximately 15/- per week for each child; outfits were provided initially, but thereafter foster parents were expected to clothe the children.

Florence's care for these children was clearly well beyond the basic requirements of Child Welfare, and she was unusual in her willingness to take on very small children and babies. She also fostered on a more informal basis, taking in unwanted children from the local community. Two of the children were formally adopted by the Bennetts, and two others remained part of their extended family into adulthood.

Fostering was a family enterprise, with John Bennett nursing and singing children to sleep as well as providing his share of discipline. A bunk room out the back held four large bunks, two or three children to each. As well as caring for the children, Florence made both soap and bread, and the Bennetts grew all their own vegetables. Florence also knew a great deal about herbal cures, which she used effectively in looking after people in the district as well as her own family. She was also a midwife on call in the district, using her bike for transport. An educated woman, she did all the farm accounts and handled any major written transactions for the family: John Bennett could neither read nor write. But the work took its toll, and both John and Florence had breakdowns after their son Hersal died of tetanus at fifteen in 1920. After a year's rest Florence recovered, and the Bennetts renewed their work with children, continuing until the late 1950s.

Their daughter writes:

One of the first memories of my mother was her love and care of babies. She was a great follower of Sir Truby King's Plunket system. I remember at one stage we had seven dress baskets with babies in, on our dining-room table. Several were babies of parents who died tragically of the dreadful epidemic after the First World War. Also young girls, unwed mothers. Their parents had disowned them and the babies were put up for adoption. Then there were a few babies of war brides. They got homesick and went back to England. The Child Welfare Department brought them to my mother until the father decided what to do. They were sometimes adopted out but quite often the grandparents took them.

I remember one young soldier who brought home a music hall singer from London. She had a voice like an angel. But she had no idea at all about caring for a baby. When the baby cried, she cried. The father had worked for us when he was a boy, and he knew about my mother's caring for babies. I will never forget the sight of the baby. He was just like a wizened little old man. My mother had one look at him; he smelt, and it was hard to imagine a baby looking so dreadful and still being alive. My mother looked at the parents and said: 'I'll do my best. Now go home and I don't want to see you for three months.'

So off they went back to Dannevirke, where the young man worked on a farm. The first thing my mother did was to starve the baby for twenty-four hours, just boiled water to drink. Then gradually she started him on the Plunket humanised milk. Very weak at first, and gradually strengthened. When the three months were up and the parents came back, I have never seen such delighted parents: he was just a beautiful bonny baby. The parents came and stayed for a week so that my mother could give them practical lessons in childcare.

Another baby girl was brought to us by the Child Welfare people. They called her Ida. We didn't know where she came from but we were told that no baby in New Zealand had better breeding. She was the highest in the land. Her layette was just beautiful; we had never seen such clothing. We loved her, but eventually they found suitable parents, when she was nine months old. We didn't see them, or know who they were. That was the hardest thing about caring for babies – the parting when they were eventually adopted or found homes for.

Then there were the children of welfare homes who were sent to us for care and correction. We found that good food and discipline and given jobs to do, worked with most of them. Although there were a few real naughty boys who took longer than others to learn how to behave themselves, Mum and Dad didn't try to make little angels out of them, that was impossible. But just to know right from wrong and cut out swearing and having clean habits and just a little Christianity for good measure. No way were they preached religion every day; but that bad habits and naughtiness didn't pay. I think it was the family feeling and love and kindness that worked most. Some got work in the district when they were older, or they were moved on when the Welfare knew they could be trusted.

How many children were cared for: I think there must have been more than 200 altogether.

Elvera Carthew & Bridget Williams

Source

Information was provided by family members and Margaret Tennant. Elvera Carthew is Florence Bennett's daughter.

URSULA BETHELL

1874–1945

Mary Ursula Bethell, poet of the New Zealand landscape, was born in England, and divided the first fifty years of her life between the two countries. She then settled at 'Rise Cottage' on the Cashmere Hills, above Christchurch, with her close friend, Effie Henrietta Dorothea Pollen. Here she created a sheltered garden looking across the plains to the Southern Alps and wrote the poetry which secured her a place in New Zealand literature.

The first child of Isabel (born Lillie) and Richard Bethell, Ursula was born at Horsell, Surrey, on St Faith's Day, 6 October 1874. She lived in England, Tasmania, Nelson, and Christchurch before moving with her parents, brother Marmaduke, and sister Rhoda to Rangiora at the age of seven. Rangiora provided a childhood in the outdoors, and an appreciation of the Canterbury landscape which was later reflected in her poetry.

> *It was the river, the river. We played there,*
> *out, out of the house, out of the garden, out under the wide sky.*

'By The River Ashley'

Her parents remain shadowy figures in the background as she writes of the Rangiora Show, rides in their 'two-ponied cart', visits to the seaside, and 'the guardian Mt Grey' casting 'a spell of greatness'.

She wrote and illustrated stories for her brother and sister, and more formal compositions for their governess. When her father died in April 1885, the family returned to Christchurch, where Ursula attended Mrs Crosby's school in Park Terrace before enrolling at Christchurch Girls' High School. Two years later, in 1889, Ursula left her mother, brother, and sister to attend the Oxford High School for Girls in England. From Oxford, and then from Nyon in Switzerland, Ursula sent home letters full of detail about her life, combining humorous description with astute observations of human nature.

Wherever she went, she formed close friendships and made lasting impressions on all she met. Short-term acquaintances continued to write to her for many years. She took her correspondence, her friendships, and life seriously, and she wanted to play her part in helping people. When she returned to Christchurch in 1892 at the end of her formal education, she became involved in Sunday school work and in social work among working boys.

But cultured Europe beckoned, and Ursula returned to study painting and music for two years. Then in 1897 she joined the Women Workers for God (the 'Grey Ladies') in South London, an Anglican community, where she engaged in parish work, caring for the sick, visiting the needy, and teaching mothercraft, as well as running boys' and girls' clubs.

A life-threatening bout of pneumonia in December 1901 forced Ursula to withdraw from the Grey Ladies and she left England to spend several months convalescing in the Santa Cruz Mountains of California before returning to New Zealand, where she spent a year principally at 'Pahau Pastures', the family property near Culverden, farmed by her brother since 1900.

Mary Ursula Bethell, front left, with her sister and brother. *Mr and Mrs D. Bethell*

Back in England in 1904, Ursula returned to a mixture of social work and frequent visits to her many friends and relations in Scotland, France, Italy, and Switzerland, a pattern she had established while a Grey Lady. The brief possibility of marriage was dismissed and not regretted later in life, and she put her energies into establishing her home at 'The Wilderness', Hampstead, as a retreat for Christian workers. Effie Pollen, newly arrived from New Zealand, helped her run the house for three years.

Several months after Effie returned home to care for her father, Ursula also travelled to New Zealand, and in March 1910 purchased 47 Webb Street in St Albans, Christchurch. As a Grey Lady, Ursula had formed many friendships and had accomplished worthwhile work, but she had not tolerated well the muddle-headed ways of the community. Now, at 'Villa Jobiska', she could organise her social work and boys' club work in her own way.

Returning to England again in 1914, she spent several months visiting Java and India, and was in Switzerland when war broke out. In the ensuing five years in London, she was a Cub mistress, an observer in a Montessori school, a member of the School Care Committee, a night supply waitress at the New Zealand Soldiers' Club, and a helper at an Information Office for Soldiers, despite continuing concern for her health.

After the war Ursula returned to Christchurch. Five years later, in August 1924, she bought 10 Westenra Terrace which she named 'Rise Cottage', and which she shared with Effie for ten years, broken only by a visit to England in 1926 and hospitalisation in Sydney for an operation to her nose, eyes, and cheeks on the way home. At 'Rise Cottage' she created a garden (as she had also done at 'The Wilderness' and at 'Villa Jobiska') out of the steep, clay slope. She also began writing poetry in a manner hitherto unforeseen.

Her first collection, *From a Garden in the Antipodes* (1929), celebrates the garden, its inhabitants, and their activities:

> I said: I will go into the garden and consider roses;
> I will observe the deployment of their petals,
> And compare one variety with another.
> But I was made to sit and scrape potatoes.
>
> The morning's rosebuds passed by unattended,
> While I sat bound to monotonous kitchen industry.
> Howbeit the heart of my consort was exhilarated,
> And for virtuous renunciation I received praise.
>
> The taste of the potatoes was satisfactory
> With a sprig of fresh mint, dairy butter,
> and very young green peas.
>
> 'Discipline'

The young men who visited their home saw little of Effie, while Ursula gave them time, support, and encouragement in their creative endeavours and a vision of a wider cultural life than they had yet seen. Young women artists were also among their visitors, and the Church and the training of women for the ministry remained important to Ursula.

Ursula's poetry continued to develop, and her second and third collections, *Time and Place* (1936) and *Day and Night Poems, 1924–1934* (1939), comprise distillations of her experience, education, and faith, prompted by the Port Hills, the Canterbury Plains, the Southern Alps, and by picnics and outings with her beloved Effie, whose head was just visible above the driver's window of the big, black Essex.

For the first collection and for poems submitted to *The Press*, the *North Canterbury Gazette*, and *The Home* (an Australian journal), Ursula used the pseudonym 'Evelyn Hayes'. However, she later consented to a volume of her collected poems being published under her own name.

In 1934, Ursula and Effie celebrated Ursula's sixtieth birthday with a picnic and a meal together. Little more than a month later, on 8 November, Effie died suddenly of a brain tumour, leaving Ursula bereft and lonely. Many letters express her difficulty in accepting her loss and in retaining her faith. Subsequently, Ursula wrote very little poetry, apart from the six memorials to Effie, which movingly express her continued grief.

Ursula pressed forward with plans made while Effie was still alive, and gave 47 Webb Street, now named 'St Faith's', to the Church of England as a 'House of Sacred Learning' for deaconess training. It was to a small, two-roomed flat, where domestic chaos reigned, at St Faith's that she retired in 1935. She then devoted herself to helping her 'young friends' in their artistic ambitions, maintaining a lively correspondence with each one. She travelled more frequently – to Akaroa, Kaikoura, Mapua, Wellington, the glaciers, 'Pahau Pastures' – to escape the flat, dreary city she disliked so much. She also spent increasingly frequent periods in hospital as a cancer of the cheek-bone developed.

St Faith's failed and was closed down at the end of 1943, but Ursula continued to live there with her young friends, Kathleen and Merlin Davies. They gave her the support she needed as she prepared for her death, sorting through her papers and writing letters of farewell to her many friends.

Mary Ursula Bethell died on 15 January 1945, and is buried with her parents in the Rangiora Church of England cemetery, below 'the guardian Mt Grey'. 'Rise Cottage' still stands and is cared for, but her poetry is her lasting memorial – to her love for Effie, to her garden, to her faith in God, and to the grandeur of the Canterbury landscape which inspired it.

Alison Mary & Valerie Laura

Researched with the assistance of the Literature Committee of the Queen Elizabeth II Arts Council of New Zealand.

Unpublished Sources
Family papers, in the possession of the Bethell family, 'Pahau Pastures', Culverden
Ursula Mary Bethell, papers, MS 38A, Canterbury University Library

Published Sources
Bethell, Mary Ursula. *Collected Poems*, Auckland, 1985

JESSIE BICKNELL

1871-1956

Jessie Bicknell was described at her death as a dignified, reserved Victorian gentlewoman with a keen sense of right and wrong and a dry sense of humour. In a long and active career, she helped improve standards of maternity care and the education of nurses, and worked for a strong professional organisation for nurses.

She was born in Oamaru in 1871, the daughter of Frederick and Elizabeth Bicknell (born Armstrong). Educated in Oamaru and Melbourne, she trained at Nelson Hospital, coming first in the state examination for nurses in 1903. During the next three years she was employed as a sister at Wairau (Blenheim) and Waipukurau Hospitals. Training further at St Helen's Hospital in Dunedin, she registered as a midwife in 1906.

Two unidentified contemporaries of Jessie Bicknell, c. 1903. *Jones Collection, Nelson Provincial Museum*

After a short period of private nursing, she was appointed to the position of Assistant Inspector of Hospitals in May 1907, working with another assistant inspector, Hester Maclean. In those early years, she spent a lot of her time inspecting small private hospitals and supervising and advising midwives, particularly those who were registered by the Midwives Registration Act (1904), but trained only by experience. Travel to these remote areas was often difficult; road and rail services were poor, and she would frequently use coastal steamers instead. Improved standards in midwifery practice at this time owed much to the intrepid spirit and dedication of Jessie Bicknell and her colleague, Amelia Bagley.

Jessie Bicknell spent twenty-five years (from 1907) with the Department of Health, becoming deputy director of the Division of Nursing when the department was reorganised by a change in legislation in 1920. When she succeeded Hester Maclean as director in March 1923, she became the first New Zealand-trained nurse to hold the position.

Before the outbreak of the First World War, the New Zealand Army Nursing Service had been established. Jessie Bicknell became the deputy matron in chief of the service in 1915 and from 1922 was matron in chief. Released for active war service from January 1916 through to the following year, she served as matron on the hospital ship *Maheno*, and in 1917 received the award of Associate of the Royal Red Cross (ARRC).

Like Hester Maclean, Jessie Bicknell worked hard for the fledgling national organisation of nurses. When the New Zealand Trained Nurses' Association was formed in 1909 she became the first honorary secretary, a position she held until 1923. Throughout her professional life and well into retirement, she maintained an active interest in the organisation, serving on committees of the Wellington branch of the association and also as branch president. At meetings of the International Council of Nurses (ICN) in Copenhagen (1923) and Montreal (1929), she represented the national association. In 1923 she became a member of the ICN Education Committee. During her retirement she was elected Dominion President of the Registered Nurses' Association (as it was then called).

Jessie Bicknell was a strong advocate of higher education for nurses, proposing university preparation at a Registered Nurses' Association conference in 1923, and subsequently helping to establish the postgraduate course for nurses. She was also influential in furthering the scheme of superannuation for hospital nurses and in a major review of the legislation affecting nurses. With the passing of the Nurses and Midwives Act (1925), nurses gained greater control of the Nurses and Midwives Board. Jessie Bicknell was a member of the first board by virtue of her position as director of the Division of Nursing, and as such was the registrar of the board.

Jessie Bicknell retired from government service in March 1931 and in later years lived in Remuera in Auckland. She was eighty-five when she died on 13 October 1956 in Greenlane Hospital.   *Marie Burgess*

Unpublished Sources
Register of Nurses, Nursing Council of New Zealand, Wellington

Published Sources
Gibson Smith, Margaret, and Shadbolt, Yvonne T. (eds). *Objects and Outcomes: New Zealand Nurses'
     Association 1909–1983*, Wellington, 1984
NZ Nursing Journal (Kai Tiaki), vol.1–49, 1908–56

FAN BLANCH

1859–1939

The versatility and ingenuity of many New Zealand women affected only their immediate families and communities. Since their achievements were not public they were seldom recorded and, once their immediate families died, such women were forgotten. Frances Boniface Blanch contributed significantly to her family's survival and to the social fabric of the central district of Southland. Her story is evocative of the lives of hundreds of women in rural New Zealand at the turn of the century.

Fan Boniface was born in 1859 at Gummies Bush in Southland and in 1880 married John Blanch, a man much older than herself, at Riversdale. In 1887 the couple came to the new farming area around Drummond where John Blanch owned a five-acre township section. Fan reared ten of her twelve children (two died in infancy) in a cottage on this land, and later nursed her ailing husband, who died in 1909. Her first 'career' as a labourer's wife ended and a valiant battle for independence began. The many aspects of this part of Fan's life were later lovingly recorded by her youngest son Albert, then her five-year-old helper. The oldest Blanch boys were married or working on farms. Albert, the child of Fan's middle age, followed her about, helping where he could.

On her small patch of land Fan kept six cows. She milked by hand, feeding the skim milk to the pig and making butter from the cream. Bacon and hams were home-cured. Butter and eggs from the free-range hens went to the store to credit against purchases. 'No cash money was ever in her hands', wrote Albert in his memoirs. Fuel for the household consisted of sacks of cones from the pine plantations or dray-loads of roots laboriously ploughed up from the swampy fields. Sometimes Fan did a day's wash for better-off families in return for a sack of coal.

Cooking was done on an open fire and all her bread was produced from a camp oven. The weekly wash was an outdoor task, in a wood-fired copper under the trees, using an old tin bath for a tub. Another fire heated the heavy flat-irons. 'The work continued to late hours, as mother's day seemed to overflow', wrote Albert.

Vegetables, fruits, and berries were grown in the garden. Fan made wonderful jam, making the jam jars herself by beheading beer bottles using a hot iron ring and a bucket of cold water.

Experience gained from the births of her own children and from nursing her husband was put to use as Fan's services were called upon by her neighbours. As the district became more settled, a third career opened up. Fan became a maternity nurse in the district from Otautau to Riverton to Drummond. She delivered babies, helped the local doctors, and usually stayed for a week or a fortnight (fee £4 a week) as cook, housekeeper, and caregiver.

Two of her boys, Walter and William, were killed in France in 1916, but her descendants are still to be found in Southland. In old age Fan retired to Invercargill, where she died on 15 January 1939.   *Judith Bassett*

Unpublished Sources
Information was provided by Fan Blanch's grandson, J. J. Blanch, Invercargill.

Published Sources
Blanch, A. G. 'Frances Blanch, My Mother', in Drummond Historical Committee, *History of Drummond and Gladfield: One Hundred Years More or Less*, Drummond, 1978, pp.73–4. All quotations are from this source.

AMY BOCK

1859-1943

Doubt about Amy Maud Bock's 'real' identity sets in with her birth: the police records compiled for her spectacular trial for false pretences in Dunedin in 1909 cite her place of birth as Gippsland, Victoria, and the year variously as 1861 or 1864. In fact, she was born in Hobart on 18 May 1859, the daughter of Mary Ann (born Parkinson) and Alfred Bock, and baptised at Holy Trinity Church.

It is likely that the other stories about her childhood which were in popular circulation in 1909 are as fanciful: she may or may not have been the daughter of a photographer with a passion for amateur dramatics and a demented mother convinced that she was Lady Macbeth. She may or may not have been musical, a good horsewoman, well educated at a ladies' seminary in Melbourne, and a primary teacher who occasionally behaved erratically, forging cheques to buy goods which she promptly gave away, or ordering items such as a pile of coffins to be delivered to an astonished and healthy local family.

What is certain is that for twenty-five years, between 1884 (when she arrived in New Zealand) and 1909 (when she took centre stage in a scandalous trial), she was the country's most notorious confidence trickster. As Miss Lang, Mrs Merry, Miss Barrett, Miss Crisp, Miss Bruce, Miss Cameron, Miss Sherwin, Miss Shannon, Miss Chanel, Agnes Vallance, Charlotte Skevington, and as Percy Carol Redwood, son of a wealthy widow and nephew to an archbishop, she acted out a series of extraordinarily complicated scenarios, all, it seems, for the purpose of stealing trifling sums of money. She remains without peer as New Zealand's most unusual and energetic con-artist.

The source for much information about her is a pamphlet, *The Adventures of Amy Bock*, by R. W. Robson, published by the *Otago Daily Times* in 1909 to cash in on the interest aroused by the trial. Even the author admitted that his work could at best only be described as 'fairly reliable'; he was writing to a tight deadline and dependent on fallible witnesses. His style does nothing to increase confidence, blending straight reportage with amateur psychological analysis and some lip-smacking speculation. Robson is the source of the photographer father, the mad mother, and the coffins. His version of Bock's later progress is more reliable and can be confirmed by reference to court records and daily newspapers.

The first definite sighting is in the Auckland Magistrates' Court in late 1884, when Bock pleaded guilty to charges of theft from her employer in Otahuhu, dissolved in tears, mentioned her mother's sad kleptomaniac history, and was discharged by a sympathetic magistrate. The pattern was set: for the next twenty-five years she would find employment as a cook, housekeeper or companion, always giving complete satisfaction, delighting her employers with her diligence and charm. Within a few weeks, however, she would become restless. She would begin to fabricate a story, generally highly dramatic, involving a dying mother, sick brother, and desperate friends, and would then obtain money for their relief from some kindly soul, usually no more than a few pounds, whereupon she promptly disappeared. She made little attempt at concealment, and within a week or two would be caught and taken to court, where the pious regrets were repeated and she received her sentence.

Amy Bock spent almost half of her twenty-five-year career in prison for the following crimes:

April 1886, Christchurch. One month's hard labour after obtaining goods on false credit.

July 1887, Wellington. Six months' detention in Caversham Industrial School on fraud charges. (She so impressed the superintendent with her intelligence and 'lady like deportment' that he offered her employment as a teacher. This lasted till she was discovered attempting to engineer her escape by forging letters from an affectionate but, alas, fictitious aunt.)

April 1888, Dunedin. Two months' imprisonment for obtaining goods on false credit. (She had bought cosmetics at a pharmacy and charged them to the account of Mr Titchener, supervisor of the school.)

April 1890, Dunedin. Three years' imprisonment with hard labour for pawning her employers' furniture while they were off on holiday.

October 1892, Timaru. Six months' imprisonment for defrauding a local woman of £1. In November when she was discharged, Bock joined the Salvation Army and lived with various members in Timaru, but by Easter 1893 she was in trouble again for selling her landlady's watch (six months).

November 1894, Oamaru. Three months for attempting to defraud a furniture vendor.

August 1895, Dunedin. Three months for leaving a house owing a week's lodging.

March 1902, Waimate. Two years' imprisonment for fraud. In 1901 Bock had reappeared in Waimate as 'Miss Sherwin', run up a few debts, and departed for Sheffield, where as 'Miss Shannon' she borrowed substantial amounts of money to finance the 'purchase of a poultry farm'.

February 1905, Rakaia. Three years for 'altering a cheque'.

In June 1907 Bock was released and for a year lived quietly in Christchurch, but in May 1908 she returned to Dunedin (as 'Agnes Vallance') where she pawned her employer's furniture and went to ground, after delaying pursuit via a complex series of letters from Miss Vallance's concerned 'friend', 'Charlotte Skevington'. It was at this point that she found the perfect disguise, as 'Percy Carol Redwood', a wealthy young man who went on holiday to Port Molyneux and paid court to the landlady's daughter, Agnes Ottaway. They became engaged within a few weeks and were married at an elaborate ceremony attended by 200 guests including the local MP. Throughout the engagement, Bock managed to maintain the appearance of wealth by defrauding a woman in Dunedin and creating an elaborate fiction about a lost wallet which was not detected till the night after the wedding. The trial in 1909 made headlines

Con artist Amy Bock at her infamous peak in
1909 as Percy Carol Redwood, son of a
wealthy widow and nephew to an archbishop.
Otago Witness, 28 April 1909. *Hocken Library*

throughout the country, and this time Bock was declared an habitual criminal.

Robson's record ends here, but according to a 1949 *Taranaki Herald* article
Bock apparently moved north after serving her sentence, and worked as a housemaid at Mokau, where she 'organised many plays and entertainments and was
the life of the district'. She married Charles Christofferson on 16 November 1914,
but they parted within the year because of Amy's debts. Bock then moved to
Hamilton, where she made her final appearance in court on 28 October 1931 on
five charges of false pretences. She died at Bombay, 29 August 1943, and is
buried in the Pukekohe cemetery.

Bock could not be described as a successful con-artist. She never made much
money from her efforts and seems at the time to have been generally liked,
regarded as a nuisance, but tolerated as one of the Dominion's 'characters'.

She was lucky. In contemporary Europe, psychologists were diagnosing
similar women as victims of 'pseudologia phantastica' – describing them as typically highly intelligent, romantic, verbally fluent, and 'sexually confused' (that
is, too 'masculine' and behaving inappropriately). Reading the good doctors'

analyses and 'cures', one can only feel relief that Amy Bock was able to live out her fantasies, hard labour and all, in a less civilised environment.

Fiona Farrell Poole

Quotation
para.8 W. Christophel, 'Amy Maud Bock'

Published Sources
Christophel, W. 'Amy Maud Bock', *Taranaki Herald*, 29 May 1949
Healey, W. and Healey, M. T. *Pathological Lying, Accusation and Swindling*, Criminal Society Monograph No. 1 (Supplement to the *Journal of the American Institute of Crime, Law and Criminology*), London, 1915
Robson, R. W. *The Adventures of Amy Bock*, Dunedin, 1909

VIOLET BOYD | *1888–1985*

ANNE ABRAHAM | *1827–1927*

Violet Boyd lived in Kaikoura for almost a century. She had stored not only memories of her own early life, but also her grandmother's records of Kaikoura during the early 1860s, when there was no wharf, no coast road, and only three white women in the area.

Violet's grandparents, Anne and Luke Abraham, had jobs arranged on the Cheviot Hills sheep station, south of Kaikoura, as general hand and cook/housemaid. But soon after they arrived there in 1860 they moved on to the Kahutara run, nearer Kaikoura, so they set out again on horseback, along the beach and the rough tracks over the hills. Anne had never been on a horse before, but clung to a blanket strapped in front of the saddle. The men took the couple's two-year-old child and six-month-old baby in front of them. When they arrived at the station that night, Anne had to set to work and wash for the baby in the tub, they had so few clothes. All she had to cook on was a colonial oven: an oblong box about thirty inches long, ten inches high, and eighteen inches wide. A wood fire was kept burning on top of the oven, and when a good heap of red embers had built up they were shovelled underneath.

Eventually Anne and Luke got their own small piece of land at the foot of the mountains west of Kaikoura, put in a vegetable garden, and started work on their whare. This was slow work as all supplies had to be carried on horseback from the whaling base. Timber was scarce, so the whare was built 'Maori style', with split spars and poles, thatched roof and walls, mud lining, and a clay floor. They built two rooms but lived in only one, and stored food, tools, and farm equipment in the other.

All the cooking was done in a camp oven over an open fire in the living room. Beds were made of long manuka rails, with stripped bulrushes for mattresses; a slice chopped off a huge fallen totara tree was their table.

For three years Anne never went off that piece of land, and saw no one except the occasional man who called, perhaps once in six or twelve months. The only woman she ever saw was a Mrs Keene, who also came to the area in 1860 and made a habit of riding around and seeing all the isolated women.

Soon Anne had another baby, which was born on the mat by the bed. Her husband promptly fainted, and Anne recalled: 'I just had to lie there and wait until he came round, then he lifted us onto the bed.'

They were still so poor they could not afford a cow, but they were later given a goat, so at last the children had enough milk. Generally, however, food was plentiful, with their own vegetables, fruit, and chickens, and also wild pigs, trout, pukekos and wekas and their eggs, and gulls' eggs. All they had to buy was flour, tea, salt, and sugar, all ordered and transported from Wellington by boat. Kaikoura's first shop was not built until 1867.

As new settlers gradually came to the area, they began pit-sawing timber, and the couple made a decent home with two mud-lined rooms, a floor, and a shingle roof. They bought two iron bedsteads and feather mattresses, and installed a colonial oven and a 'fountain'. The latter was a six- or eight-gallon kettle with a tap instead of a spout, hanging on a chain from an iron bar up in the chimney. That was the hot water supply.

Luke got all these new gadgets up to the house on a sledge, which was real progress as before that everything had to be packed in on a horse. Anne then had a forty-gallon cask sledged in and cut in two for washing the clothes. Before that she had had only a small baby's bath and a bucket, with a kerosene tin for a copper. She was often short of soap too, so invented a substitute: she would line a large box with fern or hay, pile in dry wood ashes, and pour over a kettle of boiling water. The liquid that dripped out was quite good for washing but severe on the hands.

Anne was only five feet high, but an active, strong woman. She reared five children, drove the horse and buggy around the district when well into her eighties, and lived over one hundred years. She had come through the famine and the plague back in Tipperary, Ireland, and often stated: 'I had been brought up to expect hard times, so you must not imagine I thought I had any reason to complain.'

Violet, her granddaughter, was similar: in her later years a dignified old lady yet fiery, full of fun. She explained: 'It was in the breed. All four of my grandparents were Irish. Then I had an Irish husband to cap it all off.' They waited five years before they married, until Alexander had paid off his piece of land north of Kaikoura. Every morning he would milk sixteen cows by hand, take the milk to the factory on the horse and cart, drive back, and clean the cans. Then it would be inside to cook breakfast, wash the clothes, and do the housework.

This long engagement gave Violet time to gather her glory-box together, and eventually they married when she was twenty-nine, late in life for those days. 'I've been here ever since, on this block of land. I've had a lifetime of getting up early and milking cows.'

Violet was up before the sun every morning for twenty years, except once when she had mumps, and when her two babies were born. She would get out of bed at half-past four, have a cup of tea, change and feed the babies, and take them out to the shed. Once milking was finished she would come in and get breakfast, her husband would take the milk to the factory, and she would get on with the housework.

Violet's life appeared to be as rigorous as her grandmother's had been. She was married six years before she had a living baby. 'I had one stillborn, that was a shock, and several miscarriages. In the end I had two children living, and we adopted a first cousin. No, I wasn't lucky with my children.'

She lived through the Boer War, two world wars, and the Depression of the 1930s, which she recalled in detail. By that stage they had their farm freehold, were producing nearly all their own food, and her husband was working sixteen hours a day, but

still we weren't able to keep our heads above water. There was just no sale for stock. You'd send bullocks or steers to the market and all you'd get back would be the bill for the transport. During one year of that Depression our total income was two hundred pounds, and we had to pay all sorts out of that: keeping the farm going, tax, unemployment tax, food for the five of us.

When sugar was very scarce Violet decided to give up sugar in tea. 'I did that for three months, then I gave up tea! Just drank hot water after that.' She remembered many families worse off than they were, some unable to afford bread. One father would cut firewood and travel around in a horse and cart trying to sell it, while the mother walked four miles to the hospital to do a day's washing. She would get a decent meal there in the middle of the day, but their kids would run home a mile from school at lunch-time and all they would get was a plate of swedes or potatoes. They might have a few vegetables in the garden or even a cow or some hens, but the problem was feeding the hens, to make sure they laid well.

In the towns where they couldn't grow their food, the hunger was even worse. Violet recounted:

The government announced that anyone who had a shepherd's hut or shearers' cookshop was to let people use them in return for work of some kind, and the government would pay a nominal price towards their food. One farmer near here took on nine or ten men. He picked them up from the station in his wagon.

One chap fainted on the platform, through hunger. There were all sorts came – doctors, accountants, dentists – and the farmer said that for ten days they just couldn't get enough food. He got tired of rounding up sheep and killing them, so he went out the back and shot a huge wild steer. That lasted them a week.

Violet outlived her husband by twenty-four years. As an old woman in the 1980s she disapproved of much she saw around her: the violence, materialism, and pollution. She was 'modern' in many of her concerns:

It's about time there was a law passed about plastic bags. You don't know what to do with them. They don't decompose; you've got to bury them. Who wants to go out and have a funeral every day? We'll all be strangled in plastic bags before we're done. And look at the number of people making a fat million with those plastic bags. I detest them.

By the age of ninety-five she was blind and almost deaf, had little sense of taste or smell, yet was still very talkative, still cooking up her own orange and lemon peel on the wood stove and 'keeping a fruit cake on the go'.

Above all she had retained her sense of humour: 'As soon as my eyes are fixed I'll be jumping around like a lamb. Perhaps they made a mistake about my age!'

Christine Hunt Daniell

Sources
The author interviewed Violet Boyd before her death in 1985. Anne Abraham's diary is in private possession. All quotations are from these two sources.

MAGGIE BRIGGS

1892–1961

Equestrian star Margaret Jane ('Maggie') Briggs was born in Otahuhu on 17 April 1892 to Robert Ephraim Briggs and his wife Linda Elsie (born Stevens). On 29 November 1896, Briggs was drowned in a boating accident, leaving his 'wife and young child totally unprovided for'. In 1898, however, Maggie's mother married an Inaha farmer, John Robertson, and Maggie's childhood was spent 'near the top of Yorks Hill, from which you get one of the world's most magnificent views'.

Maggie was trained by Manaia horse-breeder Alex Mitchell; his 'clever little nag' Czarina was Maggie's mount at her début in Hawera in 1903. Already displaying 'the makings of a wonderful horsewoman', she won both pony leaping contests and took third place in the women's jumping event. The following week in New Plymouth, 'little Miss Maggie Briggs, wearing a divided skirt, had no difficulty in winning' again. To ride astride was just becoming usual for women and Maggie was in the forefront of those adopting this riding style.

Maggie continued to compete in both children's and women's events at shows around Taranaki, though she does not seem to have travelled outside the province. From the beginning she was never unplaced, holding her own with older, more experienced riders in hunting, leaping, wire jumping and dual jumping events, and bareback riding. The sums of money accumulated in prizes were considerable. She regularly won the accolade of 'Best lady rider', an event sometimes judged on the flat and sometimes over jumps. She was a particularly graceful rider and possessed an excellent seat. In 1906 she accomplished on that 'marvel of miniature horseflesh', Rawhiti, 'a probably unprecedented feat in winning the high jump competition without a saddle'.

In 1913 Maggie moved to Clevedon, where she apparently engaged in training racehorses, acquiring a New Zealand Trotting Association licence. She began competing at the Auckland Show in 1913, winning championship honours that year and again in 1917, 1919, 1920, and 1921. In 1922, however, she was unplaced. A remark from the judge led her to believe that officials now intended giving other riders a chance, so she decided to move to Australia.

Maggie made her first appearance at the Sydney Royal Easter Show in 1923. Australian show-jumping courses were generally easier than those in New Zealand and she swept the field, winning all six events for which she entered.

'She sat beautifully straight and has splendid "hands",' remarked the judge, 'presenting a striking contrast in style to the Australian riders.' Maggie won prizes again in 1924 and 1925, and gave a display of wire jumping in 1924. She then organised for the Sydney police a riding event for women trained 'the New Zealand way'.

Invited by American millionaire Guy Woodin, Maggie moved to Los Angeles in October 1925. Although riding Rudolf Valentino's Arabian stallion, Jadaan, made her 'one of the most envied women in Hollywood', she found America disappointing. Show-ring riding was almost unknown there and she suffered a hip injury which incapacitated her for years. In 1933 she was stricken with tuberculosis, followed by nervous shock and paralysis. Offered no hope of permanent recovery, she rehabilitated herself with the help of radio personality Bill Perry and his record session. No longer permitted to ride but still an exceptionally attractive woman, she modelled for the American Artists' Association and published poetry under the pseudonym 'Pakeha'.

Maggie returned to New Zealand in 1948 and settled in Otaki. Her interest in show-jumping never waned and she donated almost all of her trophies as prizes to encourage others. But she often felt herself to be alone and largely forgotten. In a poem given to Wally Ingram, she looked back wistfully over her life:

> *Now I have lost through Fate*
> *That friendship won through Fame . . .*
> *My honour and glory all forgot*
> *That early fame had bought . . .*
> *Now Fame's flame has ceased to burn*
> *Will you too from me turn?*

Horse riding, Wellington, 1977. Maggie Briggs donated almost all her trophies to such young riders. *Evening Post Collection, Alexander Turnbull Library*

She died on 5 November 1961, New Zealand's first international equestrian success story.   *Patricia Sargison*

Quotations
para.1 *Hawera Star*, 30 Nov. 1896; W. Ingram, 'Maggie Briggs', p.21–2
para.2 *Hawera Star*, 1 Dec. 1902; 25 Nov. 1904; *Taranaki Herald*, 11 Dec. 1903
para.3 *Hawera Star*, 23 Nov. 1906
para.5 *Sydney Morning Herald*, 29 March 1923; *Sunday Times*, quoted by W. Ingram, 'Maggie Briggs',
      p.23; W. Ingram, 'Maggie Briggs', p.24
para.6 W. Ingram, 'Maggie Briggs', p.24
para.7 W. Ingram, 'Maggie Briggs', pp.25–6

Published Sources
Dominion, 7 Nov. 1961 (obituary)
Dwyer, T. *Showjumping Down Under*, Adelaide, 1973
Evening Post, 6 Nov. 1961 (obituary)
Hawera Star, 30 Nov. 1896 and 2 Dec. 1896; reports on Egmont A & P Show, Nov./Dec. each year,
      1903–12; reports on Stratford A & P Show, 1911 and 1912
Ingram, W. 'Maggie Briggs', in *Legends in their Lifetime*, Wellington, 1968
Ingram, W. 'Greatest Horsewoman', *NZ Listener*, 3 May 1968
Levin Chronicle, 6 Nov. 1961 (obituary)
NZ Herald, reports on the Auckland Show each year, Nov./Dec. 1913–7, 1919–22
Stratford Evening Post, 28 Nov. 1911 and 30 Nov. 1911
Sydney Morning Herald, reports on Royal Easter Show, 29 March to 4 April 1923, 21–24 April 1924,
      and 9–15 April 1925
Taranaki Herald, reports on Taranaki A & P Show, Nov./Dec. 1903–8; report on Stratford Show, 29
      Nov. 1912

ERENA AHUAHU BROWN

1896–1975

Erena Ahuahu Brown was born Erena Hatea Maynard in Manutuke, Gisborne, in 1896. Her people were Ngati Maru, Ngaitawhiri, and Rongowhakaata. When Erena was born, her marriage had already been arranged. After long consultation and debate, her whanau had decided that should the expected child of Motoi Tapunga and Paku Brown be a boy, then Erena would be betrothed to him. Eru Brown was born six weeks later and both children grew up knowing that one day they were to marry.

Erena and Eru had fifteen children. Her eldest child was a girl who was left in the family home to be raised by Erena and Eru themselves. A number of Erena's subsequent children became tamariki whangai (foster children) and were cared for by other members of the extended family group. It was thought entirely proper that in order for Erena to have many, many children she should 'not be worried with bringing them up'.

After her marriage Erena lived near the sea at Muriwai. She was an accomplished weaver and kete maker who learned the craft from her kuia. Erena died in 1975, and is buried at Te Maheni, Manutuke.

Erena Brown tells her own story, in a recording made in 1974:
I was born in Manutuke, brought up in Manutuke. My mother died when I was

*young. I don't know what my mother's like. The people who brought me up is
a negro. This old lady – she was very dark with fuzzy hair. Don't know where
she came from . . . she must have come on the boats. Those days a lot of
Europeans came on the boats, all sorts come on the boats. She was a very tall
powerful woman. Very powerful.*

*We had our good times, when we were small. We all grew up together
with a big family. Like we all friends those times. We were all mixed up. We
stay in a pa those days. We didn't have a house like this.*

*We have a raupo place. One room house. One window, one door, that's
all, in my time when I was small. We had a big fire. The ashes outside, so I
bring the ashes inside and we made like a hole. But there was no floor those
days, just got a raupo on it. Oh, very nice, but different now. The inside of the
raupo. They use that for mattresses, you know, like kapok. Raupo is very good.
Every year you change, get a new lot. Comes out very nice, the raupo.*

*We used to go out swimming, fishing, get some cockles. We used to have a
kit to collect the pipis. We have different things for fishing – they make their
own those days. But I haven't got any. I used to have some, but oh, I throw it
away. We make a paua – remember the paua – they cut him up in nice squares
like that, and they make their own hook out of wire and tie him up. When you
fish, you throw the fishing line into the water, this paua, the colour go into the
water, it go like that. It flickers. They catch the crayfish too, but I don't, the
younger people are frightened to catch a crayfish.*

*Different, those days – it was nice. I enjoyed it when I was young, say
about thirteen to seventeen, eighteen. I went to stay with my grandmother. My
grandmother used to do weaving – all the old people do. We used to sit with
them and say, 'What do you do?', you know what kids are like. Well, they say,
'Oh go away, go away.' No. We go back in and learn what they're weaving.
The only thing I can't weave is a mat. But I can make a kit, all different kits.
Can't make whariki, not the mat. I can do in the middle, but the end with the
whariki is pretty hard.*

*The women do a lot of weeding and plant. They make their own hole for
the seed, put him in the ground, and wait till it comes up. But if they kei te
mate wahine,* they couldn't go to the kumaras. They were no good, eh? They
always say there's a tapu on the kumara place. Koina hoki te tapu ki a ratou
kare haere te mate wahine, things like that. You couldn't just plant any old
days. Different days no good and some days were all right. Plant east to west.
That's what the Maori plant, always towards the sun, but they don't bother this
time. But those days they were very particular to do it right. It comes all right,
very good.† The kumara pit in those days mostly they near the hillside. They
dug quite a big hole and then they make a ground and make a door to it and
pack all the kumaras in.*

*For Maori, women were unable to participate in some activities while they had their period.
†Planting was determined by the Maori calendar. Some days were seen as more propitious than others.
It was important to have the root of the kumara pointing east.

Quite a few women had mokos those days. But no moko now. They all gone. They would do it when the girls was about sixteen, I suppose. Sixteen upwards. How they used to do it, they got something pronged, got all sizes, a little one too. This prong it's got three little very sharp things, like a tooth. Old Maori made it I think but they put it in this black stuff and make it go black. Then hammer it on you, bang. They hammer, hammer, but the blood comes out when you're doing it. It's sore they say, that's what the old people say. It's very sore. They don't just hammer away with nothing. They say with words.‡

The Maori tattoo is all over the face. All over – the old people, gee, some of them got tattoo around the back. The moko won't fade. It last. Best thing. Oh, the moko got a story to it. All those things, curves over here and over here, down there, all different curves. They got a story. I saw the old people with the tattoo all over the face.

The Maoris have their own medicine. The Maori used herbs a lot. Those days there were no doctors. Nothing at all. The Maori had their own medicine for everything. Even headache, vomiting and diarrhoea, and all those things, if you got sores and when you get burnt they have something.

Those days we were starting to have European things. We have a bit of bread and things like that. Before that I don't think they had bread. They go into the bush and get different things to eat. But they had corn. They have put corn in the water to get rotten and dry them up. When it's dry just like a flour. One thing, you won't believe it, the Maori eat the rotten potato. It's quite good. Maori in times like now get the blight in the potatoes. Those days there was not blight. I suppose the Maori knew, oh well – January/February you put your potato into the pit. End of March you start taking them out of the pit, packing him away. Well, some of them go rotten in the pit. That's the one you use. Well, some of them very dry when they got rotten in the pit and when you cleaned outside of it you used the white part inside, just like flour. So the Maori would mix them all up and make bread, things like that. Quite nice, you know.

Those days I could hardly get butter. When you're going to school you just take fat from the pork. Those days we have pork, most meat we have, pork. But you melt the fat down and go get the honey, the wild honey, mix it up, that's your butter for you. Put on your bread, whatever. Sometimes we might have only one piece of bread, or sometimes nothing.

If you got nothing to go to school with, oh well, your grandmother, your mother will give you a maize. Cook the maize, give it for your lunch. That's your lunch for school those days. But still you were quite healthy. We did eat a lot of fruit and things like that. But not all the time. There would be different things too. The wild briar – we used to get the berries. They're very sweet. It goes a sort of orangey colour. That's when they were really ripe. You open it up, tip all the seeds, just eat the inside. No, we eat all those things those days. We get chewing gum out of puha.

‡*It was the custom to chant karakia while the moko was being done.*

Erena Brown. *Brown Family Collection*

When the puha grew very high, they start to flower. Those days we used to go and pinch all the top of it and you see the juice comes out very white like milk. And you pick every one of them. Roll it up. You have quite a big chewing gum. It's a bit bitter when you're chewing it, and you spit it out, the bad taste. After a while it's just like the chewing gum you buy from the shop. I've seen it in my own life. I did it myself. It is sour to kick off but after a while it's good as anything.

Now when these sweet things, cakes and all sorts came, well, you get rheumatics, you get cancer and everything. Maori didn't get cancer those days. Fish, potatoes, and fresh food are good. Old Maori ate anything – but healthy Maoris. I'm nearly eighty. I'm quite healthy yet.

Erena Brown & Cushla Parekowhai

Quotation
para.2 Judith Binney, *Nga Morehu: the Survivors,* Auckland, 1986, p.112

Unpublished Source
Erena Brown, Tape VI, Oral History Archive, Gisborne Museum. Erena Brown was interviewed by
    Gretchen Mettner in 1974. Permission for the interview to be reproduced was given by Erena
    Brown's daughter, Heni Sunderland, who was present at the interview.
Gretchen Mettner, 'Daily Activities in the Life of a Kuia', Te Hukatai, Maori Studies Library, Auck-
    land University

ELIZABETH BRYANT

1888–1972

Miss Bryant (for thus she was always addressed) was appointed as a temporary assistant in the lending section of the Dunedin Public Library on 3 June 1912 at the rate of £50 per year. She was the most junior of the six staff members employed at that time. Dunedin born, she had attended St Dominic's Priory

School, was a devoted but not bigoted Catholic and one of a close-knit family. Her appointment had been confirmed and her salary raised by £2 per year when she was transferred to the reference library as assistant in February 1913. Dunedin Public Library had been established a mere five years earlier, its Carnegie grant ensuring that it would be a 'free library'. Its energetic librarian had just achieved its four main functions: a reading-room with current periodicals and newspapers, the reference library, a children's reference and lending service, and finally an adult lending library.

The reference library was to be Miss Bryant's home territory and her command post from 1919. There she developed a standard of service and staff training which gained her a wide reputation, so much so that she was offered a position in the Municipal Library of Calle Corrientes in Buenos Aires in 1921. She refused this for personal reasons, doubtless much to do with her role as unmarried daughter caring for her mother.

While in charge of the reference library in Dunedin, and before the New Zealand Library Association had begun formal education for its certificate, Miss Bryant developed a course which served as the basis for in-service reference training for many years. Her attitude to the purposes of libraries is expressed in the course's introduction:

. . . the need for authoritative books for reference is continually felt, and it is the first duty of the assistant to be familiar with such books . . . bibliographical research is the keynote of all reference work, however humble the resources of

Lower Hutt Public Library, 1948. High standards of service in New Zealand's city libraries were set by such women as Elizabeth Bryant, deputy city librarian in Dunedin from 1941 to 1949. *Alexander Turnbull Library*

the library may be . . . a trivial answer is a breach of library etiquette. Equality of assistance is the key to good librarianship.

Certainly scholars visiting the library in later years spoke warmly of the encouragement Miss Bryant had given to their studies when they were at school or university in Dunedin. (The introduction shrewdly concludes, however: 'Not all library assistants are suited to reference work.')

Her reference library was not just a place for abstract scholarship. In a brisk article in *New Zealand Libraries* in 1942 she describes its role in the war effort. Books which ought to be in stock included *The Bren Gun Pocket Book*, *The Lewis Gun Pocket Book*, and *The Vickers Gun Simplified*, along with more defensive texts on *Elementary Drill for the Home Guard,* and the *New Zealand Emergency Standard Code for Air Raid Shelters*. Prices of these invaluable pamphlets ranged from 9d to 1/3d.

In 1941, when Miss Bryant moved from the now much changed reference service to become deputy city librarian, the newspaper of the day recorded her to be the only woman in New Zealand to occupy such a position in a city library (this was still the time of the four main centres). A year later she was appointed acting city librarian when the city librarian went off to organise libraries for the armed services. She held this position until his return in 1945, a period with its particular war-time problems. Despite these, Mr Dunningham was able to list special projects successfully concluded in his absence: revision of the card catalogue, the organisation of serials storage, and the staff training programme.

Miss Bryant was designated associate librarian and when she retired from this position in 1949, the *Otago Daily Times* rightly described her as 'one of the Dominion's library personalities'. But her major contribution was as a reference librarian rather than an administrator. The gift by Dr Robert McNab of his collection to the Dunedin City Council in 1913 created a new speciality within the library. It generated a very important interest in the collection of New Zealand materials, and Miss Bryant proved to be a splendid and persistent collector. She also set standards of library service to the public, whoever they were. In a small way her success was permanently recorded when three of Dunedin's botanists discovered new specimens in the Lawrence area and named them in honour of Miss Bryant and her assistant, *Veronica Bryantia* and *Veronica Elioti*.

After retirement Miss Bryant retained her connection with the library as secretary to the Dunedin Public Library Association (Friends) in one of its liveliest periods. Ill health forced her retirement from this position in 1965 and she died in 1972, aged eighty-six.   *Mary Ronnie*

Quotations
para.3 E. D. Bryant, Introduction to 'Course of Training'
para.6 *Otago Daily Times*, 4 Feb. 1949

Unpublished Source
Elizabeth Dunbar Bryant, 'Course of Training in Reference Work', Reference Department, Dunedin Public Library

Published Sources
Books in Dunedin, April 1949, p.11; June 1965, p.1
Bryant, E. D. 'The City Reference Library and the War Effort', *NZ Libraries*, vol.5 No.9, April 1942, pp.133–6
Otago Daily Times, 30 April 1921, 24 May 1941, 4 Feb. 1949

JESSIE BUCKLAND

1878-1938

Jessie Lillian Buckland was born at Waikouaiti in 1878, daughter of Caroline (born Fairburn) and John Channing Buckland, who came from a wealthy merchant family in Auckland. Jessie lived with her parents and siblings in or near Dunedin, until they moved to Central Otago in 1896, first to Taieri Lake sheep station, near Hyde, then to nearby Rock and Pillar. In March 1899 Jessie was appointed resident governess at Otago Girls' High School at a salary of £30 per annum. She left this position about the middle of 1902, when she apparently moved with the family to 'The Glen', near Akaroa.

Photography and painting seem to have been pursued by most of the women in the Buckland family. The Hocken Library holds a folio of water-colours painted by Jessie during the years 1903–14. A family album bears witness to prizes won from 1895 onwards for photography in New Zealand and Australia by Jessie, her sisters, and her aunt, Elizabeth Mary Buckland. Although it is difficult to be certain who took some of these photographs, family tradition has it that Jessie composed the shots. She arranged her siblings into humorous poses, frequently resorting to 'dressing up' and sometimes appearing herself in male attire. The album is a fine document of family life in New Zealand around the turn of the century.

At 'The Glen' Jessie had a studio ('Jay's room') where she kept her extensive collection of books on photography, and where she did most of her retouching (always done on the negative). By 1908, however, she had set up her own professional studio in Akaroa, travelling the two miles to the township by bicycle until 1923 when she acquired and learned to drive a Morris Cowley. She worked from this studio until 1935.

Her first professional camera was a half plate, and at Akaroa she also used a full plate camera, and a large camera that produced postcard-size prints. Postcard views were popular items in the family albums of the early twentieth century, and the Buckland series of views of Akaroa found their way into many New Zealand albums. As well as developing her own films, Jessie processed films as part of her business (her nephew remembers her delight with her first developing tank, imported especially from Kodak).

The success of her studio portrait work, the sale and processing of amateurs' films, and the very profitable postcard business enabled her to maintain the independence she valued so highly and to contribute a large measure of support to her mother and sister after the death of her father in 1904.

After 1935 she travelled overseas and during her return voyage home in 1938 she died of cancer. She was buried at sea. Her nephew thought she had planned it that way.

Annette Facer

Unpublished Sources
Album 121, Photograph Collection, Hocken (copied from album lent by Geoffrey Orbell)
J. L. Buckland, Folio of Sketches, 1903–1914, Pictures Collection, Hocken
Letter from Jessie Buckland's nephew Geoffrey Orbell, to William Main, 16 April 1980 (copy held in Photograph Collection, Hocken)

ROSINA BUCKMAN

1881-1948

'If you make any reputation at all in music, it will be in Grand Opera'.

These words, spoken by her singing tutor, George Breedon, in Birmingham in 1903, must have echoed in Rosina Buckman's mind as she stood beside Melba, acknowledging the appreciative audience at Covent Garden's opening night of *La Bohème* in April 1914.

Rosina was born in Blenheim in 1881, the daughter of John Buckman, a builder, and his wife Henrietta. The family left Blenheim in 1885, when Rosina was four years old. There were to be many more moves before they finally settled in the Manawatu in 1889, where Rosina went to school for the first time, and joined the Methodist church choir.

The choirmaster, James Grace, gave Rosina singing tuition. He was later to be the catalyst for her going to England in 1898 for professional training first with Dr Charles Swinnerton Heap, and later at the Birmingham and Midland Institute's School of Music. In Birmingham she sang in many concerts, both at the school and locally, winning excellent notices and predictions of a successful operatic career.

In 1903 Breedon offered her the role of Queen of the Night in Mozart's *The Magic Flute* but she turned it down, believing she had neither the talent nor the ambition for such a role. She continued accepting professional engagements, but subsequently became ill and returned home to her family in New Zealand.

On her return her father organised a tour of some North Island towns which, though moderately successful, did not lead to other needed engagements. Rosina taught singing as a source of income.

In September 1905, Alfred Hill offered her the lead in his romantic opera *A Moorish Maid*. This successful production was taken a year later, to Australia where Rosina was to stay for six years, singing with the J. C. Williamson Opera Company. In 1911 she made her début with the Melba Grand Opera Company, where her roles included Musetta in *La Bohème* and Suzuki in *Madame Butterfly*. From this point on she became a protégé of Melba.

The British tenor, John McCormack, a member of Melba's company, toured New Zealand in early 1912 with Rosina Buckman as guest artist. Both Melba and McCormack advised Rosina to return to England to take up an operatic career there. This advice she took, sailing from Auckland on 8 July 1912.

Singing engagements were slow in coming. It was after meeting Melba again at a concert in London in 1913 that an audition was secured at Covent Garden. This led to Rosina's first appearance on that famous stage in February 1914 as a Flower Maiden in Wagner's *Parsifal*; she returned in April as Musetta to Melba's Mimi in *La Bohème*. A few months later war broke out and the theatre was taken over for furniture storage. Five years were to pass before Rosina sang there again.

Her interpretation of Cio-Cio San in *Madame Butterfly* in 1915 with the Robert Courtneidge Company was praised by the critics. That same year saw the formation of the Beecham Opera Company. In 1915 Beecham invited her to

Rosina Buckman as Cio-Cio San in a 1916
production of *Madame Butterfly* with the
Beecham Opera Company. *Anne Morrison*

become principal soprano, a position she was to hold until the company disbanded in 1920.

In these years she sang in many famous and not-so-famous operas, including
the première of Dame Ethel Smythe's *The Boatswain's Mate*, in which she
created a brilliant Mrs Walters. Her success was due in part to Thomas Beecham,
who was a perfectionist and encouraged Rosina's own skills to a high degree. She
was often called on by him to perform tasks that she considered impossible – such
as learning Isolde in *Tristan and Isolde* in twenty-seven days, or Mimi for *La
Bohème* in Italian in four. During the war years she also gave free concerts for
servicemen.

Whilst on tour in May 1919 she was called back by Thomas Beecham, then
artistic director at Covent Garden, to take the lead in *La Bohème* as Melba was
unable to appear. This was her first appearance there as principal soprano;
before the end of the year she was to take the lead in two more operas including
de Lara's *Naïl*, in which she created the title role. She repeated her success during
1920 in *Madame Butterfly*..

Rosina gave a farewell concert at the Royal Albert Hall in 1922 to an
audience of 10,000, before embarking on a world tour with her husband, tenor
Maurice d'Oisly, whom she had married in December 1919. This included an
extensive tour of New Zealand, where she was enthusiastically received.

On her return to Britain in 1923 she continued to sing in opera, including
five performances of *The Boatswain's Mate*. After a serious illness in 1925, she
decided to concentrate on concerts and recitals. She felt that her breathing had
been affected, and she was becoming too stout for many operatic roles. During

the 1920s she also made a number of recordings which captured her 'clear generous voice' and enjoyed 'considerable popularity'.

After her election in 1937 as an honorary member of the Royal Academy of Music, an unusual honour for a woman, she became a professor of singing at the academy, remaining there until her death. She was an excellent teacher of interpretation, always willing to give of her time and talent to those intent on a musical career, as long as her pupils were willing to work hard.

She was one of the greatest Isoldes of her age, remarkable also as Aida and Butterfly, and a notable Mimi. Her voice had a rare intensity, and great emotional range and power. Rosina Buckman died on 30 December and is buried in Marylebone churchyard, beside her husband. *Anne Morrison*

Quotations
para.1 S. Grew, *Favourite Musical Performers*, p.98
para.13 *New Grove Dictionary*, vol.3, p.411

Unpublished Sources
Information used in this essay has been accumulated by the author in preparation for a biography of Rosina Buckman.
Newspaper clippings describing the career of the singer Rosina Buckman, 3 vols, ATL
Rosina Buckman, Acc 81–114, ATL
Scrapbook of cuttings in the possession of J. M. Thomson, Wellington

Published Sources
Downes, P. *Top of the Bill: Entertainers Through the Years*, Wellington, 1979, pp.40–8
Grew, Sydney. *Favourite Musical Performers*, Edinburgh, 1923, pp.95–100
Macgregor, M. *Petticoat Pioneers: North Island Women of the Colonial Era*, Book 1, Wellington, 1975, pp.14–20
The New Grove Dictionary of Music and Musicians, vol.3, London, 1980, p.411
Thomson, J. M. with Anne Morrison, 'Rosina Buckman' in Adrienne Simpson (ed.) *Opera in New Zealand: Aspects of History and Performance*, Wellington, 1990, pp.105–19

MARGARET BULLOCK

1845–1903

The nineteenth-century women's movement owed much to the diverse talents of Margaret Bullock, journalist, writer, painter, voluntary welfare worker, and campaigner for women's rights. Although little is known about her early life, records establish that she was born in Newton, Auckland around 1845, the only daughter of Scottish immigrants Mary (born Kennedy) and James Carson. On 10 February 1869 she married warehouseman George Bullock. They settled in North Auckland and had five sons.

In 1877, after George died, Margaret took her young boys to Wanganui, where her brother Gilbert Carson edited the *Wanganui Chronicle*. In order to support herself and her young family, she joined him as a partner in the newspaper, working as a reporter and assistant editor. She continued there for about ten years.

Margaret was also one of the pioneers of the ladies' press gallery at parliament and worked as a special parliamentary correspondent for several colonial newspapers. 'She was a very bright writer of sessional notes, observations and comments.' This experience 'only whetted her earnest desire to see legislation passed to enable woman to take her part in righting the many wrongs women then had to bear.' Indeed she was able to play a key role in facilitating the course of the Women's Franchise Bill in 1893, when its success hung in the balance, by warning Kate Sheppard of impending political action.

Margaret's other means of livelihood was writing. She contributed to both English and colonial magazines under the pseudonym of 'Madge'. In 1894 she published her first and only novel, *Utu: A Story of Love, Hate and Revenge.* Later she returned to writing tourist handbooks for the government, producing guides to Wanganui and Rotorua in 1897 and one for Taupo in 1899. She became well known throughout the colony as a 'clever descriptive writer'.

Her interest in things Maori is also revealed in her paintings. In 1885 she exhibited three works at the Auckland Society of Arts, including 'A Maori Hebe' and 'Kawana Tiwhitorangi, A Wanganui Chief'.

In June 1893, Margaret founded the Wanganui Women's Franchise League (known later as the Women's Political League), which spearheaded the campaign for the vote in Wanganui and enabled women to educate themselves about public life. She believed that women lacked men's knowledge of methods, public affairs, political questions, and the world's needs. Margaret was president of the league from 1893 until 1896, when ill health forced her to resign, and served as a committee member from 1898 to 1900. She was also prominent in the National Council of Women, and was elected vice-president in 1900.

As a feminist she believed passionately in the removal of 'women's disabilities', as the civic and political face of discrimination against women was then called. 'Subjugated by brutality, dominated by fear, or cajoled by specious words, and held fast by silken fetters, women for ages, had dumbly sighed for opportunities of self-development.' In 1895 Margaret and two other members of the Women's Political League formed a deputation to discuss with Premier Seddon the removal of barriers to women's employment in the civil service and to equal pay. She also advocated economic independence for women, a stance which was undoubtedly prompted by her own experience. However, she did not support prohibition and unlike most feminist contemporaries was wary of the Temperance Movement.

In common with other politically active women in this era, she was concerned about welfare. In 1896 Margaret became an official visitor to the female department of the Wanganui prison. She also worked for the elderly residents of Wanganui's Jubilee Home, soliciting donations of magazines and publicising the bad conditions in which they lived. These activities, along with her feminist lobbying, did not always endear her to the public.

Pain and suffering, constant companions since her arrival in Wanganui, continued to afflict her. In 1902 she underwent an operation which appeared to cure successfully an 'internal complaint'. However the illness recurred, and gradually incapacitated her. She died on 17 June 1903 at her residence in Sydney Place.   *Bronwyn Labrum*

Quotations
para.3 *NZ Free Lance*, 27 June 1903, p.3; *The White Ribbon*, July 1903, p.5
para.4 *Evening Post*, 17 June 1903, p.5

para.7 H. K. Lovell-Smith, MS Papers 1376, folder 3, NCW Conference, 1900 Session, p.38, ATL

Unpublished Sources

B. Labrum, '"For the Better Discharge of our Duties": The Women's Movement in Wanganui 1893 1903', BA Hons research essay, Massey, 1986

B. Labrum, '"For the Better Discharge of Our Duties": Women's Rights in Wanganui, 1893–1903', *Women's Studies Journal*, vol. 6 nos. 1 & 2, Nov. 1990, pp. 136–152

Published Source

Evening Post, 17 June 1903

LYDIA BURR

1838–1930

Lydia Harris Hoskins was born at Cheltenham, England, on 31 March 1838, the eldest daughter of John Hoskins, a cobbler, and his wife Lydia (born Harris), the daughter of a tailor. The family arrived at Nelson on the *Poictiers* on 11 July 1850, moving to Wellington in 1851 where John Hoskins established his cobbling business.

Lydia (Hoskins) Burr as a young woman. This portrait was probably taken before her 1855 marrige to Amos Burr. *Palmerston North Public Library*

When Lydia was seventeen, her father insisted she marry Amos Burr, a double amputee, fifteen years her senior, whom she barely knew. Even the day before the wedding she still swore she would never marry him. After the wedding on 29 October 1855, the couple travelled by bullock-wagon to Amos's one-hundred-acre farm at Whirokino, near Te Awahou (renamed Foxton in 1866).

Amos's accident had occurred on 22 January 1840 on the *Cuba*, during the salute to the arrival of the *Aurora* and the founding of the Wellington settlement.

The cannon misfired, finally going off as he withdrew the charge. The seventeen-year-old lost both arms, one above and one below the elbow, and wore hooks in their place thereafter. Despite the physical and visual disadvantages, he recuperated well and there was little he could not do. He established himself in the Manawatu where he was highly regarded by Maori and Pakeha alike. He often worked as an interpreter.

Lydia had to adjust to life with a disabled husband, and then motherhood, on the partially broken-in, swampy, and frequently flooded farm. She found it hard initially living amongst a large Maori population, which included Amos's blind tubercular son by his defacto wife, the daughter of Te Raotea from the Ngati Raukawa village of Te Papa Ngaio. After his mother's death around 1850, Amos's Maori son lived with her people. Lydia is understood to have taken an interest in him until his death a few years later.

The arrival of Amos's widowed mother, sister (Eliza-Ann Staff), and the latter's three children made Lydia's life a little easier. She soon learned to take advantage of domestic skills to supplement her growing family's income. She sewed for her Pakeha neighbours and also bartered her work with the local Maori women.

There were periods of tension between Maori and Pakeha, and sometimes, in Amos's absence, Lydia had to cope alone. Once, in the midst of jam-making, she defended their storehouse from a would-be raider by claiming to have encircled it with gunpowder. Another time she anxiously watched eight men drive off their milking cows, with one threatening to brain her if she didn't call off her little dog. The cows soon returned home to their bellowing calves. But such scares led to a brief adjournment to Wellington in 1864.

The Burrs' home had burned down in 1862; then in 1863 the farm was sold and Amos declared bankrupt. The couple by this time had four living children. Things improved in 1865: Amos was appointed overseer of Maori labourers in the Manawatu and then Lydia, a staunch Anglican, was appointed proprietress of the Adelaide Hotel at Te Awahou, to clean up its image. The job included managing the Foxton ferry. The family lived at the hotel for three years.

During this time Lydia and Lady Fox (wife of Sir William Fox, four times premier of New Zealand) rode inland with a survey party to the Papaioea Clearing, thus becoming the first European women to see what is now Palmerston North. Amos opened the Palmerston Hotel there in 1867, intending that Lydia would run it. But the small town of Foxton was growing, and she refused to uproot her children and start again. The Palmerston Inn soon closed for lack of custom.

As settlement spread through the Manawatu, jobs for an ageing, armless man became scarce and further afield. Frustration took its toll on Amos, and Lydia is known to have borne much of the brunt. The burden of supporting the family fell increasingly on Lydia in Foxton, although Amos (living and working mainly at Palmerston) sometimes had the older boys. Lydia took in boarders and juggled domestic responsibilities with sewing. When the marriage finally crumbled in the late 1870s, the family consisted of ten children, three others having died as babies. The children recalled their mother regularly sewing by lamplight until 2 am to make ends meet. In 1880 she was declared bankrupt.

Although her oldest daughter was now married, she still had five children under the age of thirteen, including the frail asthmatic Sidney and three-year-old Hester. She was fortunate to have her sister-in-law, Eliza-Ann Nye, still living nearby (Eliza-Ann had married George Nye, later mayor of Foxton), and family friends such as local ferryman Harry Hillary, whose kindness endeared him to the younger children thereafter.

Lydia worked as a dressmaker and milliner from her home in Main Street, Foxton, before moving to Palmerston North in 1896. There she became head of the dressmaking department for Leopold Simmons, a 'Draper, Dressmaker and General Outfitter' in the Square and then the largest shop of its type in the town. She designed, cut, and fitted clothes ranging from wedding outfits and ballgowns to overcoats, and was regarded as very good at her job. She always dressed well herself, as photographs confirm.

While Lydia's life improved after the separation, Amos's did not. But after the split their relationship had become fairly amicable, and she attended his small funeral gathering at Karori Cemetery in 1906. Following her retirement, Lydia intended to travel between the homes of her children, and she spent time in Christchurch and Auckland, and a year in Australia. After a severe stroke in 1910 she spent twenty years physically, but not mentally, disabled and confined to a wheelchair. She lived in Palmerston North with her daughter, Hester Rogers, and her family, almost never leaving the house, until her death on 23 August 1930. She is buried at Terrace End Cemetery, Palmerston North.

Valerie Burr & Vera Lydia McLennan-Boman

Unpublished Source
This article is based substantially on the work of Vera Lydia McLennan-Boman and was compiled by her niece Valerie A. Burr. It also includes research carried out by Valerie Burr after a 1990 family reunion.

Published Source
McLennan-Boman, V. L. *Glimpses into Early Manawatu: The Saga of Amos and Lydia Burr*, Waikanae, 1985

NELL BURTON

1892–1979

Helen Augusta (Nell) Tizard was active in youth work and, after her marriage to Ormond Burton, in Christian pacifism and pastoral caring.

Born at Waitara, Taranaki, on 11 July 1892, she later moved to Auckland. She attended the Auckland Technical College and was a Bible Class member at St Luke's Presbyterian Church in Remuera. Here, she used her talents as a pianist and singer and gained leadership experience. Being the eldest daughter among five children, with a mother in poor health, she was tied to family responsibilities till her late twenties when she began voluntary work for the YWCA, taking over the secretaryship in 1924.

Nell's engagement in 1926 followed the revival of an old friendship with Ormond Burton, and a long and testing courtship. Burton had been away at the war for four years and had come back to work out and strengthen his Christian beliefs. Nell came gradually to share his views. Straight after their marriage in January, 1927, they went to live at Whangarata near Tuakau where Nell led a busy life as the wife of a sole-charge teacher, entering into community activities as well as teaching and accompanying singing in the school.

Her husband not only put a great deal of energy into his work for the school but also wrote a thesis on 'creative history' and, in 1928, stood unsuccessfully as a Christian Socialist in the parliamentary elections. It was on election night that Nell gave birth to their son, Robert. In 1929, they moved to Paerata where Ormond taught at Wesley College. Here, in 1932, their daughter, Mary, was born. Meanwhile, Ormond was writing a great deal and strengthening his commitment to pacifism and Christian Socialism. He discussed his views in depth with Nell, and she became his strongest supporter. She encouraged him when he entered the Methodist ministry in 1935.

This meant a move to Wellington where they lived in the parsonage of the Methodist church in Webb Street, and together they exercised an innovative and caring ministry. The area was a poor one and the church run down, but down-and-outs soon came to know they could come to the Burtons for help. Nell kept a pile of clean blankets in their detached wash-house which became a night shelter for the homeless. The story that she kept a pair of trousers and lent them out to her husband on Sundays so that he would not give them away illustrates the nature of their work among the poor. At the same time, Nell built up the Sunday school, encouraged the use of song and drama in worship, and led the Webb Street choir which gave regular radio broadcasts.

During the Second World War, Nell stood firmly behind Ormond in his courageous stand for Christian pacifism. While he served four prison sentences, she carried on much of his work, speaking from a soap box in the Basin Reserve on Sunday afternoons, running his boys' club, preaching in the Webb Street church and attending meetings of the District Synod. At the same time, she accepted

Nell Burton addressing a Sunday afternoon open-air meeting at the Basin Reserve, Wellington, early in 1940. Such meetings were later disallowed. *Alexander Turnbull Library*

invitations to speak to church women's groups and others such as the Nurses' Christian Fellowship and the Lower Hutt Men's Fellowship. She cared for her two children and took in boarders to make ends meet.

Ormond Burton's controversial dismissal from the Methodist Conference in 1942 meant that Nell had to move her family to a house in Aro Street. She wrote to Ormond in prison telling him how she had planted a garden and laid down a concrete path. When Ormond was released in 1944, they carried on the Webb Street way of life, but worshipped at St Peter's Anglican Church. Ormond worked as a janitor, then teacher, then headmaster at Wellington Technical College.

In 1955, when Ormond was reinstated by the Methodist Church and appointed as minister to Otaki, Nell, though suffering from lumbago, picked up again the role of minister's wife, providing hospitality at the parsonage, addressing meetings and leading the women's organisations. Though at times impatient, even disgusted, with the church, Nell maintained an unwavering faith.

After her husband's death in 1974, Nell Burton went to live with her daughter in Wellington, where she died on 4 June 1979.

Ruth Fry

Unpublished Sources

Letters from Nell (Helen) to Ormond Burton, Ormond Burton Papers, MS Papers 438 (mostly folder 14), ATL

Methodist Archives, Christchurch

Published Sources

Coney, Sandra. *Every Girl: A Social History of Women and the YWCA in Auckland*, Auckland, 1986, pp.142–5

Crane, Ernest. *I Can Do No Other, A Biography of Ormond Burton*, Auckland, 1986

AGNES BUSBY

1800–1889

Visiting Agnes and James Busby at Waitangi in 1834, the traveller Edward Markham recorded his impression of life at the home of the British Resident:

Busby's dinner The same as any other in the Island. Pork and Potatoes, and we had Bread the first I had seen for five months, and a bottle of Port, A rare treat in these days . . . Mrs Busby is very pleasant, he is rather too formal, and Religious for me to be quite at my ease with, but was particularly kind and civil . . . NB Too many prayers at Why tanghie, but the Port was good, and the Reception good and a glimpse of Civilisation.

Agnes's struggle to achieve a standard of gentility befitting the British representative is a major theme of her husband's letters to his family in New South Wales. Under the primitive circumstances of life at the Bay of Islands, it was an uphill battle and a far cry from the life she had left behind. There is no hint, however, that Agnes ever regretted her decision to marry James and emigrate. Like many other early women settlers, she appears to have relished the challenge of her life, despite the hard work. She emerges as a self-reliant and emotionally robust woman, unfazed by the dramas which surrounded life at Waitangi. Few letters by Agnes survive; consequently her life is largely mediated to us through her husband, James, who conducted a voluminous correspondence.

Agnes was born in 1800 to Jessie (born Campbell) and John Dow, a well-connected Scottish couple who emigrated to the Hunter River district of New South Wales in 1830. The only description we have of Agnes is provided by her niece, who said she was 'a very handsome woman with a beautiful complexion, splendid hair, sweet manners and a great nobility'. Agnes met James Busby, then a prosperous and ambitious young civil servant with an interest in viticulture, at a tea-party at his family home at Potts Point, Sydney. In November 1832 they married. Busby had lobbied assiduously for the establishment of a British government presence in New Zealand, with his own career prospects in mind. In May 1833 he took up his post in New Zealand, and three months later Agnes joined him, arriving on HMS *Nereus*.

The famed Treaty House was the Busbys' first home but in 1834 it consisted of only four rooms (the present two front rooms, an entrance hall, and a back bedroom), shipped from Australia. Official support for Busby was consistently parsimonious, reflecting a lack of commitment to involvement in New Zealand. Most of James's letters home in the first ten years contain references to the 'ruinous state' of the house.

The Busbys had continual problems with servants and Agnes spent long periods without domestic help. James wrote to his brother:

You express the hope that the Black Cook continues with us . . . he has been gone these two months and we have had no other – Jane has been two nights in succession in the Bush . . . [she] was found early next morning trying to make her way through the long fern in the direction of Waimate . . .

James described Agnes's life as 'slavish'. 'I often think she is a little lonely here', he wrote to his brother, 'although she never complains.' In another letter he thanked God for 'providing me such a *help-meet* in my circumstances'. There was an endless round of cooking, cleaning, gardening, and sewing. Supplies were limited and months might elapse before basic goods such as clothes, teas, fish-hooks or mousetraps arrived from Sydney. Writing to her friend Charlotte Brown at the Tauranga Mission, Agnes commented that good health was 'such a blessing . . . in this country where our domestic comfort depends so much on our own exertion'.

Waitangi was isolated and in 1839 Agnes wrote that visits to Paihia were 'few and far between'. Her pregnancy had kept her at home through the winter and she said that, since the birth of the baby two months earlier, she had not been to church as 'neither the season nor the weather are suitable for boating with so young a charge'.

But Agnes spent time with the local Maori women, providing medical help and teaching sewing and cooking. Family tradition tells that the latest Busby baby might share its cradle with a Maori baby while its mother helped cook in the kitchen. Agnes had three young Maori girls who visited to learn knitting and

A miniature painted before Agnes Dow became Agnes Busby. *Alexander Turnbull Library*

sewing and these were her 'inseparable companions'. She was saddened to learn they were wagging school to do it.

Agnes also had a formal role, entertaining important visitors to the Bay of Islands, providing food for visiting Maori who came to the residency with grievances and disputes, and helping James write his despatches to the Colonial Office. When Tamati Waka Nene came to dinner to discuss lawlessness in the Hokianga area, Agnes served kumara and pork with mustard. A family story relates that, despite Agnes's warning, Nene took a lavish helping of mustard. Rendered speechless, with tears streaming from his eyes, he was led from the room by James. When he resumed his meal, he quizzed Agnes about each forkful before putting it in his mouth.

Agnes bore six children in nine years, although a son and a daughter died in childhood. She enjoyed motherhood, writing to Charlotte Brown that she was 'happy in the midst of my little flock'. The fourth baby was delivered by James, the doctor being slow in arriving. Agnes described this baby, George, as 'a fine healthy child and I think the stoutest infant I have had'. The first birth was attended by a visiting ship's surgeon and Marianne Williams, wife of the missionary Henry Williams and a trained maternity nurse. James wrote a detailed account of the birth to his brother, but Agnes tore it up and 'said you had no business to know anything more than that, "I am the happy father of a most lovely baby."'

Thirty-six hours after the birth there was a dramatic fracas at the residency when local Maori attempted to raid the store-room. James was shot at and a splinter of wood from the door lintel cut his face. According to James, Agnes's 'conduct was a mixture of courage, patience & resignation which you might imagine in an angel'. Marianne Williams, however, described arriving at the house and finding Agnes 'greatly agitated'.

After this disturbing incident, Busby attempted to employ a Maori guard but could not retain it. As Busby was unable to guarantee his wife's safety, she left for Australia, returning later in the year. This was not the only time Agnes retreated to Australia, nor the only drama she weathered. In 1836 fighting broke out between two parties of Maori who had gathered at the Busby residence to settle a land dispute. One group, who were unarmed, rushed into the residency for safety, ripping up bed clothes to staunch their wounds. Frantically trying to round up her children, Agnes discovered that the baby was missing from her cradle. To her immense relief, she spotted the baby's white robe protruding under the cloak of an old Maori chief who was crouched in the corner of the room. Fearing for the baby's safety, he had concealed her.

In 1839, James learned that the British government was to dispense with his services. In official circles he was generally regarded as ineffectual, but this may have had more to do with his lack of resources than with particular deficiencies in his abilities. Agnes wrote to Charlotte Brown of the British government's

inconsideration for Mr Busby who has given the best fifteen years of his life to their service. He is far however from blaming the secretary of state for his removal indeed he does not well see how he could do otherwise – after the character that has been given of him from one source and another.

James was deeply disappointed, but helped his replacement, Lieutenant-Governor Hobson, draw up the Treaty of Waitangi. The lawn of the residency was the setting for the historical signing. For the occasion Agnes had a new dress and a mob-cap, sent from Sydney.

A number of disastrous business ventures led to a severe decline in James Busby's financial fortunes. He was foreclosed by the bank, and his cattle, horses, and much of his furniture were sold at below their true value. Agnes was alone at the Waitangi house when agents for the bank arrived to remove his property; she was allowed to keep only her clothes and jewels and furniture not exceeding £50 in value. James spent the next twenty years fighting the invalidation by Hobson of massive land purchases he had made during his term as British Resident. He died after a cataract operation in London in 1871.

Agnes returned to Waitangi and lived at the residency with her son and his family. 'The longer I live', she wrote to her granddaughter in 1872, 'the more I miss him here at Waitangi where no one else can fill his place.' She died at Pakaraka in 1889, aged eighty-nine, and is buried in the churchyard at Paihia.

Sandra Coney

Quotations

para.1. E. Markham, *New Zealand*, p.64–5

para.3 Letter from Jessie Campbell Sempill, June 1897, quoted in letter, E. M. Wynne-Lewis to author, 1974

para.4 J. Busby to Alexander Busby, 26 Jan. 1838, AIM

para.5 J. Busby to Alexander Busby, 9 April 1839, AIM

para.6 J. Busby to Alexander Busby, 29 July 1839, AIM; J. Busby to Alexander Busby, 9 Aug. 1836, AIM; Busby Family History, AIM; A. Busby to C. Brown, 1 May 1838, A. N. Brown Papers, ATL

para.7 A. Busby to C. Brown, 23 Sept. 1839, A. N. Brown Papers, ATL

para.8 Busby Family History, AIM

para.10 A. Busby to C. Brown, 9 July 1840, A. N. Brown Papers, ATL; A. Busby to C. Brown, 23 Sept. 1839, A. N. Brown Papers, ATL; J. Busby to Alexander Busby, 17 May 1834, AIM

para.11 J. Busby to Alexander Busby, 17 May 1834, AIM; Mrs H. Williams, Journal, 30 April 1834, quoted in G. Ramsden, *Marsden and the Missions*, p.53

para.13 A. Busby to C. Brown, 23 Sept. 1839, A. N. Brown Papers, ATL
para.15 A. Busby to A. L. Williams, 1872, Agnes Lydia Williams Papers, ATL

Unpublished Sources
Agnes Lydia Williams, MS Papers 9579, ATL
Alfred Nesbitt Brown, Micro MS 756, ATL
Busby Family History, MS 1522, AIM
Busby Papers, MS 46, AIM
Correspondence by the author with descendants of Agnes Busby: E. M. Wynne-Lewis, Helen Busby,
    James Busby, 1974
Nora Bayly, 'James Busby: British Resident in New Zealand 1833–40', MA thesis, Auckland, 1949
Sandra Coney, 'The Trials and Tribulations of Mr James Busby', research essay, Auckland 1969

Published Sources
Lee, Jack. *'I have named it the Bay of Islands . . .'*, Auckland, 1983
Markham, Edward. *New Zealand or Recollections of It*, ed. E. H. McCormick, Wellington, 1963
Ramsden, George Eric. *Marsden and the Missions: Prelude to Waitangi*, Dunedin and Wellington, 1936
Ramsden, George Eric. *Busby of Waitangi*, Wellington and Dunedin, 1942

ALICE BUSH

1914–1974

Fired by a commitment to the society in which she lived, Dr Alice Bush was one of the few women to gain public and professional prominence in New Zealand in the mid-twentieth century.

Born in Auckland on 7 August 1914, Alice Mary Stanton was the second of the five children of Marjorie and Joseph (later Sir Joseph) Stanton, an Auckland lawyer who was to become a Supreme Court judge. She spent her early years in a close and supportive family, where humanitarianism was fostered along with perseverance and self-discipline. Educated at Hill Top School and Diocesan High School in Auckland, Alice completed an MB ChB at the Otago Medical School in 1937, one of four women in a graduating class of sixty-three. Although her academic record was excellent, it was only after intervention by Dr E. Gunson, a member of the hospital board, that she was appointed a resident medical officer at Auckland Hospital in 1938.

The beginning of the Second World War provided increased professional opportunities for women doctors. Early in 1940, after a second resident year at New Plymouth Hospital, Alice became the locum for Dr Edward Sayers, an Auckland physician, during his absence on overseas service. She took up not only his private practice, but also his appointment as a visiting physician to the Auckland Karitane Hospital, and his interest in the diagnosis and treatment of allergies and asthma. In June the same year she married a schoolteacher, Faulkner Bush, and before his departure for overseas service in 1943 she gave birth to a daughter, taking only a short maternity leave.

By 1944 Alice had gained a position as assistant visiting physician to the children's wards at Auckland Hospital. She was also taking an active role in local division meetings of the New Zealand branch of the British Medical Association (BMA), the Medical Women's Association (MWA), and educational seminars for postgraduates. As part of her formal 'war effort' she acted as medical officer for the Women's National Service Corps, and in 1944 published a booklet, *Personal Relationships*, based on her series of wartime sex education lectures at the YWCA. She had also become involved in a small study group of medical professionals. Dissatisfied with the opposition to change which they believed had blighted the medical lobby in its negotiations with the Labour government over the medical provisions of the 1938 Social Security Act, they published a suggested alternative in *A National Health Service* (1943).

Towards the end of 1944, Edward Sayers returned to Auckland. He now proposed a professional partnership. Alice's years in the practice had been stimulating and satisfying, if exhausting. After correspondence with her husband, she entered into a three-year agreement with Sayers and began to study for her first formal postgraduate qualification, membership of the Australasian College of Physicians. Despite the tragic death of her infant daughter three months before the examination, she became the first New Zealand woman member of the college in February 1946, shortly after her husband's return to New Zealand. The immediate post-war period brought some tension for the couple, as they acknowledged the growing demands of Alice's career as a permanent part of their relationship. By the end of 1947 it had been agreed that Alice would have her husband's continued support in obtaining further specialist qualifications, and they spent the next eighteen months in Britain where she gained membership of the Royal College of Physicians and a Diploma in Child Health from the Great Ormond Street Hospital.

By April 1950, when Alice commenced private practice in Auckland as a specialist in child health, the couple had two children. With family support and domestic help, she balanced the demands of her roles as wife, mother, and medical specialist. She was appointed a senior visiting children's physician at Auckland Hospital, where she served on various professional committees, taught sixth-year students, and with her fellow paediatricians began to work for improved child health services, with the ultimate aim of establishing a properly designed and serviced children's hospital. She once again attended BMA and MWA meetings, and fostered the newly emerging field of paediatrics through the Paediatric Society of New Zealand, of which she was a founding member and later an office-holder. In 1955 she became the first New Zealand woman to be elected a Fellow of the Australasian College of Physicians.

Aspects of medical practice, however, continued to frustrate her. She believed that the profession was failing the people by not being more receptive to new ideas. These attitudes led to her support for Parents' Centres and the Family Planning Association (FPA), lay organisations providing services such as preparation for childbirth and contraception, of which a significant proportion of the medical profession disapproved. Matters came to a head in the late 1950s when the two organisations applied for formal recognition from the BMA and Alice assumed national presidency of the FPA, as part of a campaign to counter professional disapproval of that body.

During the 1960s Alice continued to further the causes she believed in, readily taking on speaking engagements and expressing her opinions in the press. Her public profile rose accordingly. A growing concern with violence in the home reinforced her involvement with lay groups which provided counselling for parents and children. She was active in a number of women's organisations, including the National Council of Women and Zonta. Her work for Karitane and her interest in sex education continued, as did her concern for child health, where she supported moves towards the greater involvement of social workers, child psychologists, and play therapists in medical diagnosis and therapy.

Over the same period she became particularly concerned with the welfare of Maori and Pacific Island children. The answer, she felt, lay in family spacing. Working through the FPA, the Health Department, the Maori Women's Welfare League, and community groups in South Auckland, she supported efforts to provide Polynesian women with the same access to birth control techniques which Pakeha women enjoyed. She also prodded manufacturers and importers to provide the special food products which her allergic patients required; travelled overseas to medical conferences and regional meetings of the International Planned Parenthood Federation; and in 1968 spent three months studying advances in paediatrics in Canada and the United States. In 1970 she became the first New Zealand woman to be elected Fellow of the Royal College of Physicians.

Despite her undoubted achievements, many of her activities provoked criticism. Her theories on allergies, her outspokenness and reforming zeal, and her role in the FPA could antagonise as well as inspire. Although her views on contraception for the unmarried and abortion liberalised over the years, her commitment to the ideal of constraint in sexual activity outside marriage, and her unshaken belief in the value of family life, were considered old-fashioned by a generation shaped by the revolutionary sixties.

In mid-1973 Alice suffered a coronary and was warned to curtail her activities, but caution was not her creed. She embarked on a programme as demanding as before. On 11 February 1974 she completed her day's work before admitting to signs of another coronary. She died in hospital the following day. The considerable public response to her death underlined the contribution Alice Bush had made to society, as a woman and as a doctor.   *Fay Hercock*

Unpublished Sources
Alice and Faulkner Bush papers, in the possession of the author
Family Planning archives, NZ Family Planning Assn Library, Auckland
Health Department files, H1 13/20/30, National Archives, Wellington
Meikle Collection, in the possession of the author
National Council of Women records, at NCW headquarters, Wellington
NZ Medical Women's Association records, in the possession of Auckland branch, MWA
Paediatric Society of NZ papers, held by the Executive, Paediatric Society of NZ

Published Sources
Bush, A. *et al. A National Health Service*, Wellington, 1943
Bush, A. *Personal Relationships*, Auckland, 1944

MARGARET BUTLER

1883-1947

Margaret Butler's sculpture was shown and praised in Europe, but received little recognition in New Zealand. She is now principally known through the collection of bronzes and plaster casts bequeathed to the National Art Gallery.

She was born at Greymouth, of Irish descent. Her father was a civil engineer. Attending Wellington Technical College, Margaret was a successful student. Her modelling talent was evident first when she won a prize for a Study in Relief, a Human Head from Life or Antique in Plaster in 1910.

Modelling at this time was seen as a suitable accomplishment for 'ladies'. Not until after the Second World War was modelling distinguished from sculpture, and the latter described as a form of art rather than a craft. Modelling in wax or clay is, however, a preliminary step in the creation of bronze or plaster sculpture – and an excellent preparation for a developing sculptor like Margaret Butler.

There is no record of her in Wellington from 1910 to 1917, but between 1917 and 1923 Margaret Butler exhibited regularly with the New Zealand Academy of Fine Arts. Her *Grannie* and *Pioneer* heads of 1922, both of Grannie Bolton who arrived in New Zealand in 1868, suggest that she had a good modelling technique before she left in 1923 for further studies with Antoine Bourdelle in Paris. She was then forty.

Bourdelle had trained with the French sculptor Auguste Rodin. After working with Bourdelle, Margaret Butler had her sculpture accepted in a number of very competitive exhibitions – the Salon des Tuileries, Salon des Beaux-Arts, and the Paris Salon – between 1927 and 1930. It was warmly reviewed in Vienna, where she lived and worked in 1931:

Her work lives and glows; it is imbued in all her portraits with a fine and mysterious life of its own, which the French call 'interieur' and the Germans 'verinnerlicht'.

She exhibited also at the Royal Academy in London in 1935 (after her return to New Zealand), and again at the Salon des Tuileries in 1938. The sculptures exhibited in Paris included an Arab's head, an old *Bretonne*, an old sailor, a child's head, and romantic genre portraits (studies from life).

On her return to New Zealand in 1934 the Academy of Fine Arts permitted Margaret Butler to use its rooms for a private exhibition, but failed to recognise her ability. Her most important sculpture (1938) was a portrait of Mariama Heketa, titled *La Nouvelle Zélande*. The pride of the sitter is idealised to make a forceful visual statement – an 'expression of nationhood'.

Her work remained unrecognised in New Zealand, as traditional suspicion of women sculptors continued. The two local sculptors, Joseph Ellis and Nelson Isaac, did not endorse her work. And her age and health may have hindered her acceptance as a sculptor. The academy purchased one work in 1939, but cited casting problems as an excuse for their belated acknowledgement.

Margaret Butler, 'La Nouvelle Zélande',
1938. *National Art Gallery*

Public resistance, however, seemed to strengthen her resolve. Throughout her life she had the support of her sister, Mary, and she continued to work. On her death in 1947 she left a substantial number of sculptures, which form a record of her strength, determination, and talent.   *Ann Calhoun*

Quotations
para.5 A. Kirker, *New Zealand Women Artists*, p.162
para.6 A. Kirker, p.164

Unpublished Source
Margaret Butler scrapbook, MS 17, National Art Gallery Archives

Published Sources
Dunn, Michael. 'Aspects of New Zealand Sculpture', *Education*, vol.26 no.3–5, 1977
Kirker, Anne. *New Zealand Women Artists*, Auckland, 1986

NURSE CAMERON

1892–1971

I first met Nurse Cameron, founder of the Women's Health League, at a meeting of the league held in the Rukuwai Dining Room, Ohinemutu. My aunt had persuaded me to go, promising that if I joined this organisation (about which I knew nothing) I would learn to make kits. We met this small dynamic nurse, as Guide Rangi described her, and with the formation of the Rotorua branch of the league, there began an association that was an education and an enrichment for all who joined.

Robina Thomson Cameron was born in Edinburgh in 1892. She came to New Zealand in 1911, training as a nurse at the Cook Hospital, Gisborne. At the outbreak of the First World War she returned to England, where she worked in a war hospital. Later she was sent to Egypt, where for three years she nursed the sick and wounded as a member of the (English) Queen Alexandra Nursing Service. For her work there she was awarded the Royal Red Cross.

On her return to New Zealand in 1919, Nurse Cameron became a district nurse (now known as a public health nurse) and covered the East Coast as far as Cape Runaway. For Maori, she was a doctor, nurse, friend, and a link with the outside world. After eleven years she was transferred to Rotorua, where the health problems were even worse as there were more Maori settled there.

Nurse Cameron was appalled at the frightening decline in Maori health. Housing was crowded, unemployment high, and sanitation poor; the diet of the Maori people was changing and they were now exposed to diseases such as tuberculosis, measles, and other illnesses brought by the Pakeha. Infant mortality was high. Nurse Cameron spoke to the chiefs, and was able to set up health clinics on the marae. With the help of concerned Europeans, she gave lectures and presented films on health, and helped the Maori women to form health committees.

All this meant travelling around a district that stretched from Whakatane to Putaruru and across Rotorua and around the lakes, on roads that were sometimes nothing but dirt tracks. She was given a car, and became known as 'the little woman in the Model T Ford'. Where the car could not go, she went on foot or horseback, as she had back on the East Coast. Such was the enthusiasm of the women, that after much talk the Women's Health League was formed on 2 September 1937 in the same Rukuwai Dining Room where we were to meet twenty years later. It was the first Maori women's organisation.

Members of the Women's Health League founded by Nurse Cameron at the opening of the Janet Fraser Memorial Hostel, Rotorua, 1948. From left: Mrs Puhi Royal, Mrs Hina Kameta (behind), Mrs Wena Whata, Mrs Tawhito Whata, Mrs Makarena Curtis and others.
Women's Health League

The changes achieved were amazing. Proper water supplies were laid on in the pa, and sanitation was improved. The Maori Housing Act of 1935 had been passed but never implemented, so Nurse Cameron, with a housing committee of league members, harried the Arawa Trust Board and local members of parliament. The league's patron, Janet Fraser (wife of Prime Minister Peter Fraser), worked as their representative in Wellington. The Department of Native Affairs began to build houses in Whakarewarewa, Ohinemutu, and Koutu. After the years of hard work and dedication, there was a vast improvement in the health of the Maori people, especially the children and babies. For her services to the Maori people Nurse Cameron was awarded the MBE, and later the OBE.

In the early 1940s, Nurse Cameron asked the Health Department to provide milk for pupils of Native Schools. This scheme was so successful that the government extended it to include all state schools – half a pint for each pupil every day.

Concerned that Maori visiting Rotorua to see relatives in hospital were refused accommodation in hotels and boarding-houses, the league planned to build a guest-house. Nurse Cameron told members that they must raise money themselves before asking for help. After seven years of fund-raising, on 28 August 1948, Peter Fraser opened the Janet Fraser Memorial Guest-house. In 1970 the guest-house became a hostel for young apprentices, and today it offers accommodation for young men and women working and studying in the city.

After the Second World War, Rangi Royal, Controller of Maori Welfare, came to Rotorua to ask league members to join an organisation he was forming with government backing. Nurse Cameron, Guide Rangi, and Mrs Ruihi, representing the league, went to parliament to refuse. They preferred to remain an independent voluntary organisation with their own identity. In 1951 Rangi Royal formed the Maori Women's Welfare League.

In 1971 Nurse Cameron died, a rangatira with great mana. On 30 August 1986, the Tunohopu Health Centre was opened and dedicated to the memory of the league's founder and president for thirty-four years, Nurse Cameron. Another league project, this marae-based health centre is situated in Ohinemutu, and offers to the community the services of doctors and nurses as well as traditional Maori healers.

Naomi Brell

Source
This is a personal account by Mrs Naomi Brell a member of the league for many years.

BETTY CAMPBELL

1917–1989

Elisabeth Joyce Peill was born in Tientsin, China, to missionary parents Roy (who died when Betty was twelve) and Freda Peill. She was educated in China, England, and Switzerland; she then worked for the BBC in the early days of television, transferring to the Monitoring Service when the Second World War began. Later she served four years in the Women's Auxiliary Air Force. In 1943 she married Peter Coopman of the RAF, who died in an air crash three months after their wedding.

In 1947 Betty sailed to New Zealand as an assisted immigrant, bonded for two years' work in government departments. She met Duncan Campbell, a journalist covering the arrival of her ship, and they were married ten weeks later.

Betty joined the Plunket Society after the birth in 1949 of the first of her three children. As president of the Hataitai sub-branch, she drummed up a large attendance at the 1957 annual general meeting by playing a Grantly Dick Read record on natural childbirth. Her success was not appreciated by the hierarchy, however, and an unrepentant Betty, having previously failed to forge links between Plunket and the newly-formed Federation of New Zealand Parents' Centres, left to join the latter.

Parents' Centre, which began in New Zealand in 1952, emphasised parent education and especially antenatal education for mothers and fathers. The movement gave full rein to Betty's abilities, efficiency, and capacity for dedication. She held various positions at branch and federation level, and devised a postal course for expectant mothers unable to attend antenatal classes.

As Parents' Centre was making little headway in its push for hospital reforms, Betty decided to join the decision-makers. She was voted onto the Wellington Hospital Board in 1965. Her aim in joining the board was to see childbirth in hospitals humanised and to enable fathers to be present at their babies' births. This policy was adopted by the board in 1971. She also worked for: the appointment of a play-leader for pre-schoolers in the children's ward; the production of a leaflet, *Your Child in Hospital*; the liberalisation of visiting times, especially of and by children and their parents; and the approval of emergency beds for mothers to live-in with their children.

Betty worked ceaselessly for what she believed in. She rarely accepted the status quo, looking always for new concepts and approaches. This progressiveness earned her much ridicule from other hospital board members – she was once called a bull in a china shop – but won the admiration of those who appreciated her struggles.

In 1968 the Citizens' Association asked her to be a candidate for the Wellington City Council. Betty agreed reluctantly, and was voted into office. The highlight of her fifteen years as a councillor was the establishment of a community services section. There was considerable resistance to this from both councillors and council officers, but Betty's determination to speak her mind, and the fact that she had no party allegiance, helped her cause. She was in touch with the real needs of the community through her involvement in many voluntary organisations, and slogged to see them met.

On the council, Betty started and worked with the anti-litter committee; organised civic consciousness-raising bus tours; helped set up the Green Cottage for pensioners, the Johnsonville and Newtown community centres and citizens advice bureaux, and a shoppers' creche. She also chaired or participated in national and local seminars on the needs of the elderly and youth, and local body responsibilities in community development and social planning. Betty's ideas required the changing of values rather than the spending of money.

From 1983 to 1986 she served another term on the Wellington Hospital Board. By then, she was keen to have a permanent home set up for voluntary agencies, with affordable rent and shared facilities. Such a home was built by the Wellington City Council in 1988, with offices for forty-eight agencies. It was called the Betty Campbell Community Office Complex.

The naming of the complex came as a surprise to the self-effacing Betty, as did her MBE. Her guiding motto was if a thing was worth doing, it was worth doing badly. That is, if no one else was tackling a job that needed doing, she was willing to have a try herself. She had been raised with the ethic that duty must be done, duty before pleasure, and that was how she lived.

Betty Campbell, Wellington city councillor.
Dominion/Dominion Sunday Times

When she retired from public life in 1986, Betty began to relax. Duncan had died in January 1985 after a long illness and her children all had homes and off-spring of their own. In late 1987 she was diagnosed as having inoperable cancer – caused, she suspected, by all the battles she had fought. Undeterred, she flew again to see family and friends in the United Kingdom and visit Crete and Hungary with her sister.

Her activities became increasingly restricted in her last months, but she had always been committed to the Christian faith and now looked forward to discovering what lay ahead. *Fiona Campbell*

Sources
Information has been provided by Betty Campbell's colleagues and family; the author is her daughter.
   Diaries and other papers in the author's possession have also been used.

ELIZABETH CARADUS

?1830-1912

The 1880s saw the emergence of groups of women throughout New Zealand dedicated to improving the position of their sex. Against the codes of proper behaviour for women, they sat on numerous committees, took deputations, held public meetings, and stood in the streets collecting signatures for their petitions. They had certain characteristics in common, being primarily middle-class women, the wives of businessmen and ministers, and most had small families or were childless.

Elizabeth Caradus differed from many of her fellow suffragists. She was working class and always had been, and she bore fifteen children, although seven of them died in infancy. What Elizabeth had in common with her colleagues was her strong Christian faith, her abhorrence of alcohol, and her commitment to her sex. Like them, she was prodigiously energetic and hard-working.

Elizabeth was a young girl when she arrived in Auckland on the *Jane Gifford* in 1842 with her parents, David and Elizabeth Russell. Her father was a carpenter, and when she left school Elizabeth went to work for a cobbler in Queen Street. Her descendants tell of her walking all the way from Auckland to the Tamaki River delivering farmers' boots.

At the tender age of seventeen, Elizabeth married James Caradus who had arrived in Auckland with his family on the same day as the Russells in 1842, though on the *Duchess of Argyle*. James was a rope-maker, and like Elizabeth was a devoted Methodist and later an active campaigner for prohibition.

Prosperity eluded James. Although his dressed flax, shipped to England for the Crystal Palace Exhibition in 1851, was judged good enough to win a medal, the supply from the Maori was erratic and James was forced to look elsewhere for work. He walked to the gold-fields in Dunedin, he followed the gleam of gold to Ballarat and the Thames. Meanwhile, to keep body and soul together, Elizabeth ran a shop in Napier Street, Freemans Bay, and had a baby every year or two.

Eventually James took up carpentry, building a number of houses around Freemans Bay which were rented out, and the family had a more settled though modest existence. The Caradus children all went out to work, finding employment in printing, dressmaking, boat-building, and other industries.

Elizabeth's first involvement outside her home was with the church. The Methodist historian, William Morley, writes that James and Elizabeth Caradus spearheaded the Freemans Bay Mission 'for a generation'. It was an area where 'the residents were of the poorer class, the houses being small and the rents lower than elsewhere'. From 1860, the mission held cottage prayer meetings and out-door services. Elizabeth also worked for the Ladies' Christian Association, the forerunner of the Young Women's Christian Association (YWCA) in Auckland, holding mothers' meetings in Freemans Bay at which women sewed, talked, and prayed.

Eighteen-eighty-five was a signal year for women, for it marked the beginning of a movement away from purely philanthropic work. In Auckland the

YWCA was formed, initially providing a lunch-room and recreational facilities for working girls, but also concerning itself with accommodation for young women and the safety of female immigrants. A few months earlier, in February 1885, the Women's Christian Temperance Union (WCTU) had been established. It was predominantly Methodist women who formed the backbone of these organisations. Elizabeth Caradus was a founding committee member of the YWCA, a vice-president until 1900, and one of the first life members. She was also at the first meetings of the WCTU and quickly became a key member.

When the Auckland Women's Franchise League (WFL) was formed in 1892, for the purpose of drawing into the suffrage campaign women who would not work in an overtly Christian organisation, Elizabeth Caradus was involved and later became an office-holder in the organisation. Her descendants record that Elizabeth was part of a delegation to parliament, pressing for the franchise.

Amey Daldy tells us that Auckland women approached their first public meeting on the topic of female suffrage nervously. It was unusual for women to speak publicly and take the chair. The foundation meeting of the WFL, chaired by a local minister, had been something of a fiasco. Even the normally sympathetic *New Zealand Graphic* had described it as a 'hopeless muddle'. There was no agenda and the chairman had 'to ask the women present to address the chair rather than each other'.

The women learned from their mistakes and a large meeting later in 1892, chaired by Amey Daldy, was judged by the *Graphic* to have been a huge success:

. . . the ladies speeches were infinitely better than their best friends had hoped. Public speaking is an art only acquired after long practice . . . in point of logic and conciseness the ladies of Auckland would set an example to many members of the House.

At this meeting Elizabeth Caradus thanked the press for their support and expressed her opinion that the vote would enable women to stop men gambling.

By the time of their second public meeting, a year later, the suffrage campaign had intensified, and the women of the WFL did not get such a good reception. The meeting was a rowdy one with heckling and booing. When comparative order was restored, Elizabeth Caradus, apparently unfazed by the commotion, successfully put a resolution that 'those in whose hands the earliest and most important part of the training of our future legislators lies, are certainly entitled and fitted to exercise the franchise.'

It is difficult to make an assessment of Elizabeth Caradus's personality and politics from the surviving record. Although acknowledged as an important figure in the suffrage campaign and the later National Council of Women (NCW), she never held the highest offices. When she took on a position in the WFL it was as treasurer, a post involving hard work but not attracting the public profile and demands that came with being president, a position she turned down in the WCTU. Her financial position may have made her acceptance impossible, for the leaders of these organisations often funded their own travel and expenses.

The resolutions Elizabeth framed at meetings showed that she was strongly behind the moral reforms advocated by the women's organisations, and that she saw the vote as necessary to achieving them. It is hard to know what support she gave to broader feminist aims, although her involvement in the WFL and NCW imply a commitment to social progress for her sex.

Some comments in the minutes of the Auckland branch of the WCTU point to a certain grittiness and forcefulness in her character. Mrs Caradus, they record, 'with accustomed zeal earnestly pleaded that a protest be sent to the Licensing Committee against the extension of time to eleven o'clock'. On another occasion, Elizabeth led a WCTU deputation to the Auckland City Council protesting about the Contagious Diseases Act and 'it is reported that she spoke so forcible [*sic*] that one member of the Council acknowledged himself converted'. Such passion for the cause was needed in the suffrage campaign.

Elizabeth Caradus died on 5 November 1912, aged eighty-two years, and is buried in the Symonds Street cemetery. *Sandra Coney*

Quotations
para.7 W. Morley, *History of Methodism*, p.219
para.10 *NZ Graphic*, 11 June 1892
para.11 *NZ Graphic*, 9 July 1892
para.12 *Auckland Star*, 18 July 1893
para.15 Minutes of Auckland Branch of WCTU, 24 June 1896, and 25 May 1898, ATL
Unpublished Sources
Ailsa Caradus, 'Courage and Perseverance, the Russell-Caradus Story', Du 417.1, AIM
K. R. Dreaver, 'Women's Suffrage in Auckland 1885–1893', MA research essay, Auckland, 1985
Minutes of the Auckland Branch of the WCTU 1889–1898, Acc 79–57, ATL
Published Sources
Auckland Weekly News, 11 June 1892
Coney, Sandra. *Every Girl: A Social History of Women and the YWCA in Auckland*, Auckland, 1986
Grimshaw, Patricia. *Women's Suffrage in New Zealand*, Auckland, 1972
Morley, Revd William. *The History of Methodism in New Zealand*, Wellington, 1900

UNA CARTER

1890–1955?

Woman today is expected to be a veritable encyclopaedia of general knowledge. Often the housewife is hard put to it to find a recipe or hint just when it is wanted and this book has been compiled in a spirit of helpfulness to furnish recipes which apply to every section of domestic life.

The foreword to *Una Carter's Famous Cookbook* is a good summary of her work. Through her lectures, demonstrations, and books, she provided down-to-earth, practical advice for housewives.

Una Isabell Carter was born in 1890 in Tutaenui, north of Marton. She was one of four children of William and Selena Carter. On Una's birth certificate, William Carter listed his occupation as farmer.

Relatives do not recall Una undertaking any formal cooking training, but do remember that Selena Carter was an excellent cook who spent a great deal of time sharing her knowledge with her daughters.

In 1913 Una established her own cookery school in Wellington. Classes were held several times each week and were for varying levels of ability. In October

1913, a course of eight lessons was advertised for 11/-. Shortly after this, Una Carter was employed by the Wellington Gas Company to give weekly demonstrations in their showroom, with its model gas kitchen, to show the benefits of cooking with gas. It was one of several promotional techniques used by the company – an advertisement in the *Evening Post* in 1915 announced that on Friday evening the Wellington Gas Company Orchestra would 'render Musical Selections' in the 'Brilliantly Illuminated Showroom'.

Women who attended these demonstrations recall Una Carter's deftness and skill in the kitchen as well as her friendly and informative style. Newspaper descriptions stress the usefulness and practicality of the demonstrations.

Yesterday Miss Carter gave a very interesting and instructive lesson, and wisely made it in tune with the times, as it taught economy as well as good cooking and serving. The art of using scraps was cleverly demonstrated in several directions . . . There was a good attendance yesterday and after the lecture those present had an interesting time in the showrooms seeing the latest developments in the use of gas, notably the use of a 'press button' to light the gas without match or pilot.

The demonstrations covered a wide variety of foods and techniques, from baking to lunch and dinner dishes. The recipes were simple and did not require a great deal of equipment – some of those who attended Una Carter's demonstrations recall seeing her cut up small pieces of cardboard to use as spatulas.

Una demonstrated for the Wellington Gas Company at the annual Wellington Show and at the 1940 Centennial Exhibition, in Wellington. She also undertook several cooking tours of New Zealand and Australia.

Her first book, *The National Cookery Book* containing over 400 recipes, was published sometime before 1918. It was extremely successful, running to at least ten editions. In her preface, Una explained why she had written the book:

At the solicitation of the many pupils who have attended my School of Cookery and my Public Lectures and Demonstrations as well as to satisfy an ever increasing demand for a simple, economical, practical up-to-date cookery book, I have been induced to compile the following pages.

The book was later republished as *Una Carter's Famous Cookbook* and was expanded to over 800 recipes, household hints, and simple home-made remedies. Like Una's demonstrations, the recipes stressed practicality and thrift. 'Do not waste anything in the way of food. Food thrown away is money thrown away.'

Una Carter also produced a second book, entitled *Home Made Sweets*, which was published during the First World War. She hoped that readers would 'be surprised to find out how easily and cheaply really good and wholesome sweets may be made in the ordinary household kitchen.' This was especially important while the country was at war:

Now that New Zealand has so large a number of men away from home, what could be nicer than to send them a tin of home made sweets . . . if they are sent in small tins the men can carry them in their pockets and enjoy them when feeling tired and lonely.

Una Carter continued her demonstration work until at least 1940. Later she married Bert Stanley and went to live in Auckland. Upon his death she returned to Wellington, where she lived on the Terrace. She was a popular and hospitable member of her family, introducing nieces and nephews to sweet-making, and encouraging them to cook the catch after a day's fishing.

After a period of illness, Una Carter died while on holiday in England. Well-thumbed copies of *Una Carter's Famous Cookbook* are to be found today in New Zealand kitchens.

Jean-Marie O'Donnell

Quotations
para.1 U. Carter, Foreword to *Una Carter's Famous Cookbook* (9th edn)
para.5 *Evening Post*, 28 Sept. 1915
para.6 *Evening Post*, 28 Oct. 1915
para.9 U. Carter, Preface to *The National Cookery Book*
para.10 U. Carter, *Una Carter's Famous Cookbook*, p.228
para.11 U. Carter, preface to *Home Made Sweets*, pp.3, 4

Unpublished Sources
Information was provided by family and friends of Una Carter.

Published Sources
Carter, Una. *Una Carter's Famous Cookbook* (9th edn)
Carter, Una. *Home Made Sweets*

JANE HEAD CHERRINGTON

1908–1989

Seini (Jane) Cherrington combined many rare qualities. Hers was a tolerance and a generosity that pierced both racial and ideological prejudices.

Born on 4 September 1908 at Tuapa, Niue, to Francis (a trader) and Tolitagaloa ('Climber of the Rainbow') Head, Jane was the second of seven children. She came from a line of courageous women, and often retold the story of how her great-grandmother, Tanita, withstood custom. In Niue during times of war the crying of babies was thought to allow attackers to discover the people's whereabouts. When an attack was feared, a baby was put into a canoe and let drift out to sea in order to get rid of the potential noise-maker. Tanita averted this fate for her baby, Pelenise, by hiding with her in a cave until the danger was past.

Saved from the sea, Pelenise came to marry one delivered from the sea. An Englishman, Robert Henry Head, was shipwrecked on Niue in 1867 and stayed to work with the mission. An arranged marriage with Pelenise took place the same year. Early in the marriage Pelenise decided she didn't want to stay with her *papalagi* (European) husband but her father Apelamo chased her all the way back to her house with his *takalo* (spear stick). The couple had fifteen children, all taught by Robert Henry until they were old enough to be sent for further education in England, Australia or New Zealand.

Jane's early childhood was shaped in the household of her grandparents, Pelenise and Robert Henry (known affectionately as Misi Hale). Throughout the years Pelenise never got used to *papalagi* housekeeping. At first her unmarried

Jane Cherrington, aged twelve, when she left
Niue to live in New Zealand. *Dawn Kennedy*

daughters took turns to go back to Niue to housekeep. Eventually, Jane's parents
moved their family to the grandparents' house.

It was there that Jane formed her lifelong commitments to God and to
education. Robert Henry had served fifteen years in the Royal Navy in England
and he recreated its strict disciplines in his home. A ship's bell called his family
to daily prayers and to meals. Jane recalled that if the children could use cutlery
and behave properly, they could sit at the main table. It was an honour Jane
achieved twice.

One day when Jane was nine years old, she was watching her mother
making calico *fi hui* (pants) on a hand sewing-machine. Tolitagaloa asked her
if she wanted to go away to school. The love of learning that Jane was later to
implant in her own children was evident in her reply, 'I don't want to be a *goa
goa* [ignoramus] all my life.'

Before Jane left Niue for New Zealand her father, Francis, gave her two
responses to use in her new land. If anyone asked, 'What's your name?' she was
to reply, 'Jane Head'. If anyone asked, 'How are you?' she was to answer, 'Very
well thank you'. Towards the end of her life Jane still recalled how she would
get these answers muddled up. She soon learned that people smiled when she got
it wrong, so she didn't answer at all.

In 1917, at the age of nine, Jane left Niue on the schooner *Awanui*. She was
to return only once, for a visit in 1933. In New Zealand, she attended Manga-
papa School at Gisborne, where she stayed with her aunt and uncle, Frances and
Glen Barnes. While she was befriended at school by May Gough, some of the
other children called her names such as mangu mangu taipo ('black black devil')
because she was darker skinned and different. She also had to cope with the
major handicap of being unable to speak or understand English, and of being the

oldest and biggest child in her class. Although her aunt then sent her to another school, Jane was very homesick and for two years she cried every night and wished she could walk home to Niue.

In 1920 Francis came to visit and took Jane on the ship *Arahura* to Auckland where other family members had a house in Balmoral. After finding Jane a suitable new school, Francis left for Niue; his ship, the *Jubilee*, was lost without trace. Jane's last sight of her father was of him waving his white handkerchief in the distance. She was not quite twelve years old.

At Balmoral Jane boarded with her aunt and uncle, Bessie and Ernest Vaile, her sister Opa and cousin Faiola. She was in her teens when she finished at Maungawhau primary school; she went on to Brain's Commercial College and then began work as a shorthand typist in an Auckland solicitor's office.

But Jane's growing desire was to become a nurse. Her guardian family opposed her as they did not consider nursing a good profession. In tears Jane stated, 'I will go nursing when I turn twenty-one.' And so she did.

Jane began her general training at Auckland Hospital in 1929. She did her maternity training at Thames in 1933, and in 1934 at St Helen's Hospital in Wellington she completed her midwifery training with honours. She went on to nurse at St Helen's Hospital in Auckland.

During a function at Queen Victoria School, Jane met her future husband, Hoterene Te Rangaihi (Joe) Cherrington, son of Canon W. H. Keretene (Cherrington). She later nursed Joe in hospital. He had been training for the ministry but because of health problems was not ordained. Against advice from her mother-in-law that Joe was 'no good', the couple married on 28 April 1937 at Ngararatunua in Northland, where they began living in the family home.

After the birth of two sons, Peter and Lupo, the couple moved to Motatau Base Farm, near Kawakawa. There Jane learned to ride horses, the only form of transportation. Three more children followed – Paki, Dawn, and Vera – and the family were living again at Ngararatunua in a rented house. There were many difficulties because of Joe's continuing mental illness. However, Jane was both courageous and a hard worker. She raised the family virtually as a solo mother. She planted vegetables, chopped wood, and carried water.

Then tragedy struck. Northland in the late 1940s was hard hit by the polio epidemic that swept New Zealand. When Jane's eldest son, Peter, became ill she nursed him at home until she herself became sick. At the hospital Jane and Peter were both diagnosed as having poliomyelitis. Peter recovered but Jane's case was more serious. A night nurse asked her where she was affected. With her characteristic blend of courage and humour, Jane replied, 'Everywhere but my tongue'. Completely paralysed down one side, Jane was told she would never walk again. She rejected this pronouncement because she was determined to get her family back together again. After eleven months in hospital, she refused to leave in a wheelchair. She used crutches.

For the rest of her life, Jane remained paralysed down her right side. With the same determination that got her out of a wheelchair and walking, she relearned how to write, knit, crochet, bake, and garden; everything had to be done not only left-handed, but also one-handed. Her children had been cared for by whanau while she was in hospital; she collected them all and brought them home (refusing to budge from the car until the last one had been collected). Often in the early days she fell down in her house or in her vegetable garden. However, she refused to let her children help with her tasks. 'If you do it for me even once,' she told them, 'I'll never do it for myself.'

Jane's courage was only one aspect of her character. She loved reading and fostered a love of books and education in her children. Tragically, her eldest son, Peter, died while at Auckland University. Lupo became a qualified carpenter, while Paki, Dawn, and Vera all became certificated teachers and passed university papers. Paki graduated with a BA from Massey University in 1973. The tradition established by Pelenise and Robert Henry was continued in Jane's children and her mokopuna.

Throughout all the years Jane also stood by her husband, Joe, until his death in January 1984. She once described her marriage as a 'living hell', but she said she had made her vows before God and would never break them.

When Jane first began living at Ngararatunua, she was not totally accepted because she was an outsider and not afraid to speak her mind. As in her early school-days at Gisborne, she was dismissed by some people as that 'coconut'. Yet Jane persisted in her tolerance and aroha for others. She was a lone guide (a member of the Girl Guides by correspondence) before her polio and a member of the Matarau branch of the Women's Division of Federated Farmers for many years. People grew to love and respect Jane's honest responses, her laughter, her caring, and her rejection of either Pakeha or Maori 'humbug'. She was a true kuia.

Throughout the many tributes paid to her, Jane's personal humility and humour never changed. These qualities are reflected in a response she wrote to a poem in her praise by her son, Paki:

Dear Mr Man
Gosh! What kind of a pedestal have you placed poor old Seini of Niue on? A wonderful bit of writing, your poem . . . but it cannot be an ordinary biddy like Seini of Tuapa of Niue. This here fuakau [kuia] does not look too well on a pedestal, likely to topple off without any pushing – being such a wobbly person.

In April 1988, Jane left her home of fifty years in Ngararatunua to stay with her daughter Tagaloa Dawn Kennedy in Auckland. At this time, though her love and determination were as strong as ever and her mind clear and alert, her physical strength was waning. Seini of Tuapa of Niue died at Dawn's home in Auckland on 19 April 1989.

Haere atu e kui ki o tatou tupuna kua hinga atu i te po
Tatari mai koe mo matou nga morehu. *

Dawn Kennedy & Suzann Olsson

*Farewell kui, join our ancestors who have fallen to the night. And there wait for us who remain.
Sources
Dawn Kennedy is Jane Cherrington's daughter; Suzann Olsson is Jane's former daughter-in-law.
   Information was also provided by other family members.

GRETE CHRISTELLER

1895–1964

Grete Reiche was born into a solicitor's family in Berlin in 1895. Early in life she was attracted to a career in healing. She trained as a nurse, and as such served in the First World War. In 1918 she married Erwin Christeller, a doctor who soon became head of the Institute of Pathology at the Virchow Hospital in Berlin. His death ten years later left Grete a widow with two young children, Gert and Eva.

In order to be independent, and to support her family, Grete studied massage and, after the family's move to Switzerland, trained as a psychoanalyst with C. G. Jung. During the next two years, having by then acquired a good knowledge of Italian, she worked at Genoa and Rome, patients being referred to her by local medical practitioners.

By the mid-1930s Europe was becoming increasingly difficult for people with Jewish connections like the Christellers (although the whole family was in fact Protestant). Gert's schoolteacher, a New Zealander, encouraged them to emigrate, and in 1939 the family arrived in Auckland.

New Zealand in the 1940s and 1950s was not an easy place for a woman on her own to establish herself, especially during the years of war when Grete was a registered alien. Also her profession as a psychoanalyst was in those days surrounded by a great deal of ignorance. Yet she was anxious to fit in with her surroundings and formed strong friendships with the New Zealanders she worked with. She worked first in Auckland and then moved to Christchurch, where she had her own practice for many years. She was thus able to support her children and give them a good education, and lessons in art and music.

Grete Christeller in the garden of her
Christchurch home, c.1962. *Gert Christeller*

Grete Christeller died in 1964 – a woman who brought to New Zealand a rare gift for healing through her knowledge of the human psyche, her intuitive grasp of the problems of her patients and the sympathy she showed towards them. *Gert Christeller & Ngawi Thompson*

Source

Information was provided by friends and family members.

KEN CHUNYU

1926–1978

Ken Chunyu was one of the first New Zealand Chinese women to succeed academically and professionally in the mainstream society beyond her immediate family and community. In so doing, she had to overcome both subtle and overt discrimination.

Ken was the fifth child of the Tse family. She had three elder sisters, one elder brother, and three younger brothers. Their father, Tse Yue-Hoe, had come to New Zealand in 1908 as a market gardener. At the immigration office, his surname was taken to be 'Hoe'; such mix-ups seem to have been extremely common with Chinese immigrants of the time. Thereafter the Tse family became the Hoe family. Their mother came in 1920, having studied English so hard beforehand in order to pass the 'literacy test' that she absolutely refused to speak a word of English for years afterwards. Ken's full name was Ken-Ching Hoe; it was shortened to Ken to simplify things for the Europeans, who found Chinese names confusing. After she grew up, she often found it highly amusing when people asked to see 'Mr Ken Hoe' and it turned out to be a woman.

Ken was born in Te Kuiti. She started school in Wellington where the family had a fruit shop in Newtown. Like her siblings, Ken started helping in the family shop – tidying, arranging displays, and serving customers – from about seven or eight years of age. The children were also sent to the Chinese mission school in Frederick Street to learn some rudimentary Chinese reading and writing. At home they spoke the village dialect of Ha Leung [Xialiang], which was a small village in the Poonyue [Panyu] county.

The family then moved to Wanganui. Ken's father started the Nanking Fruit Mart in Victoria Avenue and business grew steadily. Ken's days were fully occupied with helping around the stop, looking after her younger brothers, and pursuing her studies at school. The shop was open from 6 am to 11 pm six days a week, and the children routinely worked before and after school. Family duties never seemed to interfere with the Hoe children's ability to excel academically, for they all did exceedingly well. Ken, for example, was dux of Queen's Park School in 1937 and then dux of Wanganui Girls' College in 1944. She also served as a school prefect and was in the top basketball team.

A great blow came to the family when their father died in 1942. It must have been the most heart-breaking decision for the mother to make, choosing which son or daughter should give up their studies in order to keep the family shop running. Mrs Hoe had always encouraged her children to study well, looking at academic success as the only avenue by which a Chinese could rise above 'traditionally Chinese' work in a fruit shop or market garden. Ken's eldest brother was top student at the medical school, so the family decided he should keep going. Of her three elder sisters, two were at university, and one finishing the seventh form. Cruel common sense dictated that the sister who had just started at university and the one who was finishing school should pull out and come home to keep the family business running. Ken and her younger brothers were allowed to continue with their studies.

Her consciousness of the great sacrifice her elder sisters had made for the family influenced Ken's choice of career. She excelled in languages and her favourite subjects were English, Latin, and French. Yet she decided to pursue a science degree at Victoria University College on the grounds that science was more 'useful' than the arts. Although science was not really what she wanted to do, she did well. While still a student she also worked part time in the Department of Scientific and Industrial Research (DSIR) central library from 1948 to 1953, where it became quite clear that library work was her vocation.

Meanwhile, her elder sisters got married and a younger brother took over the family fruit shop. But when her mother fell seriously ill, family loyalty compelled Ken to return to Wanganui, quitting her work as DSIR librarian and her last university subject before she could get her degree. On leaving her job, she was told that she would not get it back because she was Chinese! The early 1950s were years of Macarthyism, and the Chinese were once again regarded with distrust and suspicion. Ken returned to Wanganui and worked very hard for years keeping the family business afloat.

In the early 1960s, with the last of her children graduated and established, Ken's mother decided to fold up the business and retire. Ken's eldest brother had gone to Singapore after postgraduate studies in London and now he invited his mother to go over for a holiday. But disaster again struck. Mrs Hoe suffered a severe stroke while in Singapore and since she had not been formally naturalised as a New Zealand citizen, she was classified as a 'stateless person' by the Singapore authorities and her visitor's visa could not be extended. On the other hand, although she had been resident in New Zealand for over forty years, she was told that as a Chinese she needed to have a re-entry permit before she could be allowed back into this country. Lengthy wrangles with the New Zealand Department of Immigration made this an extremely stressful time for the family. As the legal negotiations went on, Mrs Hoe's condition worsened, and Ken, as the only unmarried daughter, eventually went to Singapore to keep her mother company. By the time Mrs Hoe got special dispensation to return she was too weak to make the final journey, and she died in Singapore in 1965.

Ken then went to Hong Kong, where she worked in the Technical Bureau of the School of Architecture at the university. In 1968 she gained the Joint Certificate in Librarianship of the Hong Kong University and Hong Kong Library Association. She then married Yin Hsu Chunyu, a northern Chinese and ex-Nationalist solider who already had a young son by a first marriage, and the couple returned to New Zealand.

Once back in the country, Ken completed her science degree and took her New Zealand Library School Diploma to supplement her British qualifications.

She worked in the Victoria University library for a while, and also enrolled in Chinese language courses for beginners. In 1972 she was appointed to the newly created position of head of the reference section at the University of Waikato library, a post she held until her sudden death in 1978.

On top of her demanding library job, Ken also ran a carnation nursery business with her husband. Her day started well before 5 am, when she had to cut and pack the carnations ready for delivery to the auctioneers and flower shops. She routinely did the delivery rounds with her husband before starting work at the university. At home, she had to do all the business correspondence, attend to the legal, financial, and purchasing details, and keep the accounts, all aspects that required a knowledge of English beyond her husband's grasp. She also helped with the physical labour of spraying, clipping, and bunching. Friends often remarked how tired she looked, and marvelled that she could hold down two full-time jobs so competently. The greatest blessing was that her relationship with her husband was extremely harmonious, although their backgrounds were vastly different. Their one hobby was preparing meals together, often entertaining friends who dropped in. Ken was always hospitable, and was especially kind to overseas students in their early settling-in days.

Early in February 1978, Waikato's chief librarian was shocked to find Ken Chunyu writhing in pain on the floor of her office. 'Just back pain!' she insisted, but the doctor was sent for. It was diagnosed as cancer of the ovaries which had spread to the lungs. Ken Chunyu died on 18 February, with fewer than ten days' sick-leave on her work record.

Her funeral service was held at the Waikato University Chapel, and the love and esteem which she commanded was amply demonstrated by the huge attendance. Colleagues and friends all remember Ken Chunyu as a warm, affable, and extremely helpful person whose unfailing modesty masked a sharp intelligence. At the time of her death, she was working on a bibliography of Chinese mathematics with her brother Jock. *Manying Ip*

Unpublished Sources
Curriculum vitae and work records of Ken Chunyu, Waikato University
Interviews with Jock Hoe, Ivy Whitmore, Jeanette King, Jenny Stubbs, and Yin Hsu Chunyu

Published Sources
King, Jeanette. 'Obituary – Ken Chunyu', *NZ Libraries*, no.1, 1978

KATE McCOSH CLARK

1847–1926

Kate Emma McCosh Clark is known as a writer, especially for children, but she was also an accomplished artist and took an active interest in several charitable institutions in Auckland.

She was born Kate Woolnough in 1847 in Ipswich, Suffolk, where her education included the study of art. In 1875 she married James McCosh Clark, and came with him to New Zealand the same year. Her husband was a wholesale merchant in Auckland, president of the Chamber of Commerce, and, from 1880 to 1883, Mayor of Auckland. The couple had five children.

As prominent citizens they lived in a house known as 'The Tower' in Remuera, and were well known for their hospitality. The Bishop of Auckland, the Rt Revd W. G. Cowie, and his wife were visitors in the mid-1880s:

It is always . . . a special pleasure to accept Mrs Clark's invitations . . . Having a large house and extensive grounds well laid out, situated in one of the most beautiful districts of Auckland, overlooking the sparkling waters of the Waitemata harbour and islands near and distant, [Mr Clark] was able during his long term of office to exercise most acceptable hospitality to the people of Auckland and many distinguished visitors. Mrs Clark is specially gifted as a hostess, being gracious to everybody, desirous of helping all who need her aid, and most interesting as an accomplished painter and a woman of rare good sense.

Kate took a particular interest in the St Mary's Home for Women. She served many years on the committees of the Home, the Blind Institute, the Girls' Friendly Society, and other institutions. She was also a skilled musician and a member of the Auckland Art Society, with which she regularly exhibited.

In 1889, the Clarks went to London for several years and there Kate had three books published. The first, completed before she left New Zealand, was *A Southern Cross Fairy Tale*, which she states was written for the 'generations of children . . . growing up under the Southern Cross . . . with English speech and English hearts, to whom the Yule log at Christmas is unmeaning and the snows unknown' as well as for those in the 'older land', on the other side of the world.

With a young Santa Claus (because he is in the new world), and goblin and fairy characters, the book presents a guide to the natural features and wildlife of New Zealand, from geysers and glaciers to the huia and the tuatara. The text is amplified with notes on geological wonders such as the Pink and White Terraces, by Professor A. P. W. Thomas, and on the birds, by Andreas Reischek. The illustrations of the birds are by Kate Clark herself, drawn from specimens lent to her by Reischek. The writing shows a lively sense of humour and includes poetry in the form of verses sung by the fairy characters. The book was published in London in 1891.

Her next work, published in 1894, was a collection of poetry, *Persephone and Other Poems*. Often using classical themes, she shows a feeling for natural beauty and the innocence of childhood, as well as a strong sense of nostalgia, not surprising in someone whose life alternated between New Zealand and England.

Her last book, *Maori Tales and Legends* (1896), made no attempt to dress up its material:

I have endeavoured to adhere to the true spirit of the tales themselves, and to give them the form, expression and speech characteristic of the country and clever native race.

Her social position allowed her access to sources such as Sir George Grey and King Tawhiao, 'whom I had several opportunities of meeting and from whom I heard much that was valuable regarding the Maoris'. Her aim was to *give pleasure . . . to the young people, and awaken and increase their interest in the beautiful islands of New Zealand and in the native race, who still, in spite of the presence of the white man, keep up their numbers and retain much of their powerful individuality.*

Kate McCosh Clark returned to New Zealand in 1900, two years after her husband had died in London. She spent the rest of her life in her adopted land. Through her writings she did much to educate young people about its people and environment, of which she had a deep appreciation.   *Janet McCallum*

An illustration from Kate McCosh Clark's *A Southern Cross Fairy Tale*, 1891. *Dorothy Neal White Collection, National Library*

Quotations
para.3 W. G. Cowie, *Our Last Year in New Zealand*, p.154
para.5 K. McC. Clark, preface to *A Southern Cross Fairy Tale*
para.8 K. McC. Clark, preface to *Maori Tales and Legends*
Published Sources
Clark, Kate McCosh. *A Southern Cross Fairy Tale*, illustrated by the author and Robert Atkinson, London, 1891
Clark, Kate McCosh. *Maori Tales and Legends*, London, 1891
Clark, Kate McCosh. *Persephone and Other Poems*, London, 1894
Cowie, W. G. *Our Last Year in New Zealand*, London, 1888
Gilderdale, Betty. *A Sea Change: 145 Years of New Zealand Junior Fiction*, Auckland, 1982
NZ Herald, 28 Jan. 1898 (husband's obituary); 1 Dec. 1926 (obituary)
Scholefield, G. H. (ed.) *A Dictionary of New Zealand Biography*, Wellington, 1940, pp.158-9

MATILDA CLIMO

1896-1988

Matilda Brunning was born in 1896, and lived most of her ninety-two years in the Puponga area, at the base of Farewell Spit in Golden Bay, Nelson. She was raised in Lower Moutere, then moved over the Takaka Hill as a young girl to work as a housekeeper.

In 1913 she married James Climo of Puponga. Her early married life was spent in the even more remote Kaihoka lakes area, accessible only by horse and cart over the mud-flats, then sledge through the bush. The family lived in a home-made slab cottage with three rooms: a kitchen with a bedroom on each of three sides. Cooking facilities were primitive: an open fire and a camp oven. Matilda produced all their food, including bread, in that camp oven. The nearest shop was at Collingwood, about twenty miles away, and 'we only really ever went out there when I wanted to have a baby . . . once a year!' They would often get locked in with floods and slips, and food could not be sent in, so for weeks on end they would live solely on eels out of the creek, and quail, kaka, and pigeons, which were not protected in those days. They also ate wild nikau – raw, boiled or made into pickles – and now and again would find a hive of bees in the bush and get honey. Eventually they became established with a vegetable garden, a cow, and some ducks, and even a copper boiler to replace washing the clothes in the creek.

Initially Matilda was satisfied with this existence.

We had plenty of everything really, except food now and then. We went in there in 1913 when we got married. Then I had a baby in 1914 and another in 1915. I'd have had two kids couldn't walk. So when I went out to Collingwood to have the second one I said, we're staying out. Matter of fact, then I had another baby in 1916, a miscarriage in 1917, another baby in 1918, another in 1919, and I went on like that till I had ten of them altogether. I remember they used to sleep four to a bed, top and tail . . . except one time when all the kids got whooping cough and I put them sideways in the beds, so when they started to cough I was able to handle them all together.

Women panning for gold in the Aorere River, c.1935. Matilda Climo's family were goldminers and farmers in this area for many years. *Nelson Provincial Museum*

Her only assistance at these births was from Granny Wigzel in Collingwood, who had had the basics of midwifery passed on to her from her mother: she would take women into her home and dose them up with castor oil.

Matilda's own mother had had twelve babies at home and completely on her own, except for one birth which Matilda remembered vividly:

One day when I was about twelve my Dad came to me and said, Mum wants you in the bedroom. So I went in and Mum was down on her knees. She said, when I tell you to, put your hands up between my legs, take hold of the baby and put her gently on my chest. Well I didn't know anything at all about babies. I didn't even know Mum was pregnant. I just collected the baby when it came out. That's the first I knew about where they came from. I didn't even know how they got there. Then Mum said, go out, I can manage now. So she cut the cord and all that herself.

Obedience was demanded, and given. No questions were asked, or explanations offered. 'No, I just went out. I didn't ask her about anything.' Similarly, Matilda's father expected to play no part in the drama:

No, my Dad didn't help, I don't think he ever did. Mum must have had trouble with this one or she'd have managed all of it herself, like the other eleven babies. But those days they didn't talk about things like births.

Eventually the stress told on Matilda's mother:

*Mind you, she died in the mental, my mother, when she was only forty-seven.
The doctor told me she'd had such a hard life, and with all that childbearing
she couldn't take any more.*

However, Matilda remained philosophical about life generally, and practical about her own existence. You just didn't stop having babies so there was no
time to get depressed, with big families to cater for and men coming home from
the bush or the mines.

*It's been a good free life. I wouldn't be here at this table talking about it if I'd
had to put up with the city life. We just kept ourselves amused here, didn't
think of going off into towns like Collingwood for entertainment. You just
headed for the bush.*

Matilda described her kids as woodhens, heading off in the morning and
sometimes staying away overnight. Other times they'd head down the coast and
spend several days fishing. They never took food with them, just ate what they
could catch or find, such as berries and nikaus. Sometimes they would take a
rope and bring back a goat or a kid, and they would be kept as pets. Other times
they would play hockey at home, with a manuka stick and an old condensed milk
tin.

Matilda remembered Puponga before the First World War as being a busy
place, with two hundred men working the coal-mine, seven streets, a school, a
hall, a post office, and a boarding-house. There were grocer's and butcher's
shops, a bakehouse, a sly grog corner and billiard-room, a racecourse, and two
football fields. Then the miners went on strike in 1918 and everything closed
down.

Now there is nothing at Puponga, just the scrub, the remains of a few huts,
and the cottage where Matilda lived with her elderly son. 'There's only us living
here now. There's nothing but us two and the gorse.'

Christine Hunt Daniell

Source
This essay is based on the author's interview with Matilda Climo.

MARY COLCLOUGH

1836–1885

Mary Ann Barnes, born in England in 1836, arrived in Auckland in the
mid-1850s. In 1861, she married Thomas Colclough, a 'gentleman settler' twice
her age, and six years later was left a widow with two young children. A highly
educated, well-paid teacher, she supported the family single-handed. She taught
in Auckland country schools and ran her own school for girls in Auckland township. In 1874, after seventeen years in the colony, she left for Melbourne.

To Auckland in the early 1870s she became a public figure – a social reformer, lecturing on the evils of drink, working for the rehabilitation of women ex-prisoners and prostitutes. Above all, it was her championing of women's rights that rocked Auckland and made her a household name. As 'Polly Plum' she carried on an exhaustive public correspondence in the local press, taking on all comers. She spoke on public platforms in Auckland township and environs, and as far afield as Ngaruawahia, Hamilton, and Thames, an unheard of activity for a woman at that time. One Auckland husband bemoaned the lamented hour when he took his wife to hear 'Polly Plum'. His domestic felicity was no more. Converted by the writings of John Stuart Mill, 'Polly' targeted the legal position of married women: no independent legal status, no control over their property, no guardianship of their children. It was 'iniquitous,' she argued, 'that in a Christian country, anyone, male or female, should have it in their power to wrong and oppress others, under the shelter of the law.' Men would not tolerate such a crippled, dependent position, but women were supposed to be used to it 'as eels are to skinning'.

She spoke from bitter personal experience. Her own husband had not been unkind or ever wilfully wronged her, but he was 'a thoroughly unbusinesslike, unenergetic man' who spent his wife's earnings 'in ruinous speculations'. Once,

---

FEMALE EDUCATION.

To the Editor of the HERALD.

SIR,—Will you allow me space for a few words relative to your article in Monday's issue, on Female Education ? You advocate many sensible views on the subject, but make the great mistake of urging that women shall be improved and raised without any corresponding rise being permitted in their legal position. The whole experience of society is opposed to such a view. Though female education is far from so good or so general as it ought to be, women, even with the limited knowledge they have acquired through the more general diffusion of learning, have become discontented with existing institutions, and there can be no doubt, the more they are educated, the more will be their objection to legal subjection. All Christian women who think in accordance with Scriptural doctrine, hold that the rational subordination of a wife is the right and orderly position for her to occupy, but in the present day hundreds and hundreds of women, many of them in our very midst, and in all respects worthy of trust and honor, hold the doctrine that legal subjection is a frightful wrong, that whilst it continues it forms the most effectual bar to progress ; for what is the use of knowing how to act rightly, and guide a family properly, when it may so happen that you may be joined to a man who may choose to nullify all you would gladly accomplish ?—and who, in the present state of society, *can* do so, simply because he wills it so, without being obliged to assign any reason for his acts.

The more women are educated the less willing they will be to submit to this state of things. As to men losing respect for them, directly power over them is taken out of their hands, I can hardly understand that. It seems hard to believe that men are so essentially mean and unchivalrous that unless they hold women almost entirely at their mercy, they cannot consent to be civil and respectful to them. It may be so ; I cannot tell. I am not a man, and can no more enter into their feelings than they into woman's, though they so frequently pretend to do so, then often try to terrify us with the threats that there is this ugly, ungenerous trait in their character. Still, I am fain to hope that they are unjust to themselves, and that an alteration in the law would in no way affect those whom love has joined together. Mutual self-sacrifice in such a case is the highest happiness of both, and no mere legal attractions can or will alter their feelings. Only the bound-down, the ill-matched, and the unjustly-treated will find the freedom of woman affect them in any way. Of this I feel sure.

POLLY PLUM.

Mary Colclough writing as 'Polly Plum' in the *New Zealand Herald*, 2 August 1871.
Alexander Turnbull Library

she and her two babies 'were left on the bare floor', all the household furniture which she had bought with her own earnings having been seized through her husband's mismanagement. 'I was breadwinner,' she said, 'whilst he had all the breadwinner's powers and privileges.'

What of education, careers, the vote? She did not question, at this time, the importance of women as wives and mothers, but it was absurd to educate girls purely for a domestic life. As single women, widows or wives of improvident husbands, many would have to support themselves. Self-reliance and self-help were the goals. There should be no legal barrier to women rising as high in the world as their talents would take them. Let them have fair field and no favour! Education was the answer. Finally, women should have the vote. It was a question of justice. They should not be subject to laws they had no part in making.

How did Aucklanders react to all this? Both men and women were outraged. Both men and women cheered and applauded. The *Herald* wrote of the 'absurd and demoralizing theories' of female lecturers. The mere mention of women's rights 'excites the risibility of one and all', one correspondent claimed. A political woman was 'a "female monstrosity"', argued another (a woman). Many tried to patronise her. Male opponents 'threw the Bible' at her – the supporters of slavery likewise used St Paul's epistles, 'Polly' retorted. Many charged her with impropriety of conduct. 'Polly' was 'totally destitute of those two female characteristics, docility and modesty,' one man put it. Many women agreed.

But many cheered. Encouraged by 'Polly's' example, women supporters were astonishingly outspoken in the press. 'Ah me!' wrote one. 'I wish I was nearing eighteen instead of eighty.' Large, enthusiastic audiences packed her lectures. One of her strongest supporters was a remarkable non-conformist minister, Revd Samuel Edger, father of Kate, the colony's first woman university graduate. The *Herald* was ambivalent, calling her 'a very talented lady' and warmly wishing her well after the public farewell concert on 'Polly's' departure for Tuakau, in 1872.

Last news of 'Polly' is in late 1874, from Melbourne. She had become an 'advanced thinker' on the subject of marriage, the *Herald* reported. She was lecturing in the city. She had roused a storm of controversy in the press. She attacked the marriage ceremony. She appeared to ignore the absolute necessity of the conjugal tie. Women should not be bound down all their lives by a set of doctrines they did not believe in. She challenged the Melbourne public: 'Let all my opponents muster strongly and dispute with me face to face when I lecture next week.'

'Polly' later returned to New Zealand. She died in Picton in 1885, at the age of forty-nine, after a severe accident.

Mary Colclough shook Auckland society for five years – then disappeared. She was a hundred years ahead of her time.   *Judy Malone*

Quotations
para.2 *NZ Herald*, 14 Aug. 1871
para.3 *NZ Herald*, 18 Aug. 1871; *NZ Herald*, 21 Aug. 1871
para.5 *NZ Herald*, 29 Feb. 1872; 24 June 1870; 2 Aug. 1871; 25 Aug. 1871
para.6 *NZ Herald*, 7 July 1873
para.7 *NZ Herald*, 21 Nov. 1874; 1 Dec. 1874

Unpublished Sources
J. Elphick (now Malone), 'Auckland 1870–74: A Social Portrait', MA thesis, Auckland, 1974, pp.140–55

Published Sources
Elphick (now Malone), J, 'What's wrong with Emma? The Feminist Debate in Colonial Auckland',
    NZJH, vol.9 no.2, Oct. 1975, pp.126–41
Letters by Mary Colclough and press reports about her are found in the following newspapers:
NZ Herald 24 June 1870, p.5; 27 Oct. 1870, p.3; 27 June 1871, p.2; 12 July 1871, p.3; 15 July 1871,
    p.3; 24 July 1871, p.2; 31 July 1871, p.3; 2 Aug. 1871, p.3; 5 Aug. 1871, p.3; 7 Aug. 1871, p.3;
    14 Aug. 1871, p.3; 18 Aug. 1871, p.3; 21 Aug. 1871, p.3; 25 Aug. 1871, p.3; 30 Aug. 1871, p.2;
    21 Oct. 1871, p.1, p.3; 10 Nov. 1871, p.3; 20 Dec. 1871, p.1; 6 Jan. 1872, p.1; 9 Jan. 1872, p.3;
    15 Jan. 1872, p.3; 29 Feb. 1872, p.2; 2 March 1872, p.3; 21 March 1872, p.2; 27 Sept. 1872, p.3;
    14 April 1873, p.2; 7 July 1873, p.2; 21 July 1873, p.4; 28 July 1873, p.2; 21 Nov. 1874, p.2; 1 Dec.
    1874, p.2; 10 Mar. 1885, p.5
Daily Southern Cross 8 Jan. 1871, p.3; 17 Jan. 1871, p.3; 23 Jan. 1871, p.3; 31 Jan. 1871, p.3; 6 Feb.
    1871, p.6; 4 April 1871, p.3; 8 April 1871, p.3; 13 May 1871, p.3; 8 June 1871, p.3; 4 Oct. 1871,
    p.5; 12 Oct. 1871, p.3; 1 Nov. 1871, p.6

ELIZABETH COLENSO

1821–1904

'This is the story of a woman, sincere, humble, unselfish and generous', wrote Elizabeth Colenso's granddaughter at the beginning of her biography of her grandmother. 'One who lived for others and never spared herself in any way.' It is a story of a woman's devotion to God and of her dedication to His cause.

Elizabeth Fairburn was born in Kerikeri on 21 August 1821, the daughter of William Thomas Fairburn and his first wife, Sarah (born Tuckwell). The Fairburns had come to New Zealand with the Church Missionary Society in 1817, serving at Paihia, Puriri, and Maraetai. Elizabeth was thus brought up to mission life from the beginning.

New Zealand in the 1820s was no place for the squeamish. Mrs Fairburn gave Sarah Mathew in 1840 'a dismal account of their terrors and suffering when they first settled among these savage tribes'. Maori frequently assaulted the mission stations and Elizabeth 'nearly fell a victim . . . when a wild posse rushed in over her'. She also apparently witnessed 'an act of cannibalism which filled her with terror'. Nevertheless, 'There was not much monotony in the life . . . The wit and sense of humour possessed by the Maoris kept up a happy genial spirit.' The children learned to speak Maori 'better than English', and inherited the strict evangelistic religion of their parents where one could 'never forget your duty to God'. Elizabeth attended Marianne Williams' school in Paihia, and from there returned to Maraetai to teach 'reading the scriptures . . . the catechism and hymns . . . and writing' in the Maori school. She had natural aptitude for teaching, and her intelligence and capacity made an excellent impression on the new bishop, George Selwyn. She also learned from her mother the use of homeopathic medicines, an invaluable skill in a land without doctors.

In 1842, Elizabeth and her father received letters from William Colenso, the mission's printer, proposing marriage. Colenso was about to begin training as a missionary and was seeking 'a suitable partner particularly in mission work . . .

this I plainly told Miss Fairburn in my first letter . . .'. Despite this cool approach and although she had seen him perhaps only twice in her life, Elizabeth accepted the offer. The serious, austere girl and her energetic, quick-tempered fiancé finally met in January 1843. Both seemed doubtful as to their suitability for each other and agreed to postpone the wedding till after William's ordination. But it was not to be. Selwyn, needing a teacher for his new girls' boarding-school at Waimate and a competent Maori scholar to assist in revising the New Testament, 'requested [Colenso] to get our affair concluded as soon as possible'. Thus, a reluctant Colenso set out for Otahuhu, while Elizabeth wrote nervously to Charlotte Brown: 'do you approve the step I am about to take? I am fully alive to the importance of it . . .' The couple were married on 27 April 1843 and left for the north immediately.

Despite the inauspicious start, Elizabeth was soon to write of her 'dear kind husband', trusting they would indeed 'esteem and love one another'; and within weeks she was pregnant. She found, however, that 'it would take all her ability to cope with the onerous duties entrusted to her [at Waimate] . . . she had to break in, to unaccustomed and often unsuitable rules . . . a large number of "half-wild things" . . . The work was incessant and unremitting.' She had almost no time alone with her husband, and found 'their unsettled state continually reminds us that here we have "no abiding city"'. William detested Waimate and they both longed to be 'somewhere amongst the natives'. But his ordination was constantly deferred, primarily, William believed, because Selwyn could find no replacement for Elizabeth. Bitterness created tension and increasing estrangement between the couple, which the birth of Fanny in February 1844, after a difficult confinement in William's absence, did little to improve.

A chance to bring about a happier state of affairs was offered by William's appointment as missionary at Ahuriri in September 1844. The Colensos arrived in Hawke's Bay in December, after a horrendous voyage to 'the most disagreeably situated mission station in all New Zealand'. In a land constantly under flood and eighty miles from the nearest white woman, Elizabeth began eight years of missionary endeavour. Her life was 'spent in the service of others', teaching, housekeeping, and nursing the sick, and 'never being able to depend on having a moment to herself'. Her only break from the station was in July 1845 when, seven months pregnant, she was 'obliged to clamber up and down very steep hills and precipices . . . more than doubly hazardous in the . . . wet winter season' on her way to Turanga for the birth of her son.

After this time, her relationship with William became, at her request, one of form only, with communication between the two largely confined to mission tasks. William undertook long journeys for over half of each year, while Elizabeth was left to 'that solitary responsibility which he maintained she always preferred'. Matters came to a head in 1851 when the Colensos' servant, Ripeka, gave birth to William's son, Wi. Elizabeth was shocked at this transgression of her husband's role as Ripeka's guardian and as God's representative, yet no immediate action seemed possible. To leave the station would be difficult and perhaps an unacceptable abrogation of the mission responsibilities which gave Elizabeth's life its meaning.

So, shored up by 'that imperious sense of duty which firmed the will and straightened the back' of so many missionary women, she found herself committed to silent acquiescence. She even 'brought [the baby] up, showing it great kindness', but the friction caused by Ripeka's determination to return to her own people with the child and William's refusal to allow them to go made life almost untenable. Recrimination, threats, attempts to kidnap the baby, and William's intransigence finally left Elizabeth 'too weak and ill in bed for discussion'. She intended to go with her children in 1852, when her brother took them to Auckland, but 'circumstances prevented me'. Not till William was suspended from the mission in 1853 was she able to leave, forced, through a fantastic compromise between her husband and Selwyn, to take Wi with her. Her only reference to the 'deep fountain of sorrow', 'the wounded, bruised and battered spirit' left by those bitter years, was recorded in her diary some twenty years later: 'the deep springs [of feeling] . . . were well nigh frozen by the unkindness and ingratitude of those . . . whose bounden duty it was to show every kindness and attention.' Neither Elizabeth nor Fanny ever saw William again, and in her scorn for her husband, she also prevented him from seeing either of his sons for many years.

In 1854, having placed her children in school in Auckland, Elizabeth rejoined the mission, at Taupiri in Waikato, teaching for seven years at Taupiri, where 'her influence with the native children was very great . . . She was sedulously at work, not only for the school but for the natives generally.' No doubt she needed occupation but financial reasons may also have played a part. 'I have not received a penny from [Mr Colenso] since I left, nor would I under any circumstances', she wrote to her agent, seeking rents from the land settled on her by her father at the time of her marriage, 'but I do feel anxious about the children's education.'

When the station was abandoned in 1861, Elizabeth decided to take her children to England. Here she spent the following five years, the highlight of which was undoubtedly her meeting with Queen Victoria at Windsor in December 1863 when she acted as interpreter for the parents of Albert Victor Pomare, the Queen's godson. A description of this event fills well over half her autobiography. She also spent much time in welfare work, made two visits to Europe, and, as 'an able and intelligent Maori scholar', was actively involved in the revision and printing of the Maori Bible. A book of her own, *Scriptural Stories*, was delivered to the printer in 1864.

In October 1866, Elizabeth and Fanny returned to Auckland, and in 1869 they settled at the old Mission House in Paihia where Elizabeth started a school at Te Ti marae. Fanny's marriage in 1870 left Elizabeth alone but, at the end of 1875, Bishop John Selwyn of the Melanesian Mission 'asked me to go to Norfolk Island . . . I gladly went, it being work which I liked'. Thus, at the age of fifty-four, Elizabeth learned a new language, Mota, at which she became extremely proficient, and 'settle[d] down with great content to spend the rest of [her] life helping the good work'.

Life at Norfolk followed 'the usual routine': teaching, sewing clothes for the pupils, nursing both Europeans and Melanesians, and writing innumerable letters of thanks to supporters of the mission. She found the place beautiful, 'the absence of the world and its wearisome conventionalities . . . a happy feature'. The people were congenial and, although at times she was lonely, 'weary of moving about', and longing for a 'settled home', she was able to see her family fairly frequently. In 1893, her eldest granddaughter came to care for her, as she suffered from rheumatism, asthma, and sciatica, but 'was still so useful as a teacher that the Mission did not want to lose her'. She was always tired in these last years, but continued to work 'conscientiously and unselfishly to the limit of her strength'. By 1898, she was confined to a bath chair, and finally decided she must retire, 'being afraid her failing health might make her a burden on the Mission staff'. She died at her daughter's home in Otaki on 2 September 1904, having continued with translation work to the end. Benjamin Ashwell had written: 'It was impossible for anyone to take a greater interest in missionary work'. She had indeed given to it her whole life.   *Patricia Sargison*

Quotations
para.1 F. Swabey, *Elizabeth Colenso*, title page
para.3 F. & S. Mathew, *The Founding of New Zealand*, p.139; E. Hickson, *Reminiscences*, p.2; F. Swabey, p.1; E. Hickson, p.21; F. Simcox, *One Hundred and Twenty Five Years in NZ*, p.19; F. Swabey, p.3; F. and S. Mathew, p.153
para.4 A. G. Bagnall and G. C. Petersen, *William Colenso*, p.150; F. Swabey, p.6; E. Colenso to C. Brown, 5 April 1843, Brown Papers, folder 74, No.10
para.5 E. Colenso to C. Brown, 30 Aug. 1843, Brown Papers, folder 74, No.14; F. Swabey, p.8; Letter, 30 Aug. 1843, Brown Papers
para.6 D. H. McIntosh, *William Colenso*, pp.34–5; F. Swabey, p.14; W. Colenso, *Journal*, pp.201–3
para.7 A. G. Bagnall and G. C. Petersen, p.226
para.8 F. Porter (ed.), *The Turanga Journals*, p.27; A. G. Bagnall and G. C. Petersen, p.334; F. Swabey, p.20; F. Simcox, p.15; F. Swabey, p.73
para.9 B. Y. Ashwell, *Recollections*, p.19; E. Colenso to J. Newman, 5 Jan. 1856, Newman-Buttle Papers, folder 6
para.10 H. Carleton, *Henry Williams*, appendix to vol.1, p.xii; F. Swabey, p.42
para.11 F. Simcox, pp.22–3; F. Swabey, p.50
para.12 F. Swabey, p.73; F. Simcox, p.47; F. Swabey, p.24; F. Swabey, p.24; B. Y. Ashwell, p.19

Unpublished Sources
A. N. Brown, Papers, folders 73 & 74: miscellaneous letters to Charlotte Brown, Micro MS 756, ATL
Doris H. McIntosh (Pow), 'William Colenso: The Man and his Work, 1811–1899', MA thesis, 1931, ATL
Elizabeth Colenso, Correspondence, 1836–1881, MS Papers 1070, ATL
Elizabeth Colenso, Diaries, letters and notebooks, 1862–1895, 21 vols, MS, ATL
Esther (Fairburn) Hickson, 'Memories of the War time in 1868' and 'Reminiscences of Old Days in Auckland', in private possession
Frances Simcox (compiler), *One Hundred and Twenty Five Years in New Zealand*, MS, ATL. Includes: 'Recollections of Mrs Elizabeth Colenso' and those of her daughter (F. Simcox) and granddaughter (F. Swabey).
Frances Edith (Simcox) Swabey, *Elizabeth Colenso*, MS, ATL
Newman-Buttle family papers, MS Papers 402, ATL
William Colenso, Journal, 1833–1852; Correspondence, 1833–1863, qMS, ATL

Published Sources
Ashwell, B. Y. *Recollections of a Waikato Missionary*, Auckland, 1878
Bagnall, A. G. and Petersen, C. G. *William Colenso, Printer, Missionary, Botanist, Explorer, Politician: His Life and Journeys*, Wellington, 1948
Carleton, H. *The Life of Henry Williams, Archdeacon of Waimate*, vol.1, Auckland, 1874
'Elizabeth Colenso on Norfolk Island', *Auckland-Waikato Historical Journal*, no.29, Sept. 1976, pp.9–12
Evening Post, 7 Sept. 1904 (obituary)
'The Fairburn-Colenso Story', *Auckland-Waikato Historical Journal*, no.27, Oct. 1975, pp.10–15 and no.28, April 1976, pp.31–3
Macgregor, Miriam. *Petticoat Pioneers: North Island Women of the Colonial Era*, Book One, Wellington, 1973

Mathew, Felton and Sarah. *The Founding of New Zealand: The Journals of Felton Mathew and his Wife, 1840-1847*, Dunedin, 1940

NZ Herstory 1984, Auckland, 1983

Porter, Frances (ed.). *The Turanga Journals: Letters and Journals of William and Jane Williams, 1840-1850*, Wellington, 1974

Wordsworth, Jane. *Women of the North*, Auckland, 1981, pp.39-44

CHARLOTTE COLLARD

1874-1944

> *The whole family belongs to the railways (at least that's how it seems);*
> *It dominates our waking hours, and then invades our dreams.*

These lines from the anonymous poem 'The Trials of a Locomotive Man's Wife' are an apt description of the world Charlotte Williams entered when she married William Collard, a young railwayman, in 1890. For the next forty years she and William and their family were to move regularly between railway construction sites all over the country.

Charlotte was one of eight children born to Henry Williams, a bullock driver, and his wife Jessie (born Bagley). She was only sixteen when she married William, leaving behind a childhood spent in farming communities in the Wairarapa. They were married in Wanganui where William was working at the time, but when their first child was born a year later they were living in Timaru.

Eight daughters of Charlotte and William Collard mourn the death of a younger sister, thirteen-month-old Jessie, at Stratford in 1907. Five of the Collards' twenty-one children died in infancy. *J. McAllister Collection, Alexander Turnbull Library*

The following year their second child was born in New Plymouth. They had twenty-one children in all, born in fourteen different locations. Often these were railway construction sites in remote areas, and William would have to take a jigger to fetch the midwife when Charlotte went into labour. On at least two occasions she had to deliver the baby herself when the midwife didn't arrive in time.

It was not an easy life. Five of their children died at an early age and another died in her teens. Sometimes the family was separated when William went ahead to a new work-site and the rest of the family had to wait until a railway house large enough to accommodate them became available.

Fortunately railway houses were usually surrounded by enough land for Charlotte to keep fowls, a pig, and sometimes a cow, enabling her to provide some of the food the family needed. She also had her own sewing-machine and made all their clothes.

Not only did she take care of her own family, but also found time to care for others, particularly the sick, sometimes nursing children in her own home. Her concern for others may have influenced her decision to join the Salvation Army in 1908. She was an active member of the church for many years. She also read the entire Bible during the latter half of her life, even though she had little schooling and had signed her marriage certificate with a cross.

Despite the hardships and frequent upheavals associated with railway life, Charlotte was able to bring up a large family successfully and be involved with activities outside the home. She worked hard all her life, even after suffering a stroke a few years before her death, at the age of seventy, in 1944.

Charlotte and William settled in Auckland in their later years but their association with railway construction work continued. All but one of their sons followed in William's footsteps; the family still belonged to the railways.

Rosanne Livingstone

Quotation
para.1 'The Trials of a Locomotive Man's Wife', in Rex Hancock, *My Forty Footplate Years*, Wellington, 1987

Unpublished Sources
Information came from interviews with three of Charlotte Collard's children: George Collard, Auckland; Evelyn Kerr, Manurewa; and Alice Aydon (now deceased).

Published Sources
Pierre, Bill. *North Island Main Trunk*, Wellington, 1981
Troup, Gordon (ed.). *Steel Roads of New Zealand*, Wellington, 1973

HELEN CONNON

1860–1903

Helen Connon was the first woman in the British Empire to graduate MA with honours. Later, her pioneering work as an early principal of Christchurch Girls' High School helped create a new model for education for girls in New Zealand.

She was born in Melbourne in 1860, the daughter of a builder, but when she was five her family emigrated to New Zealand. Even at this early age it was obvious that she had remarkable ability.

Helen had made so much impression on her teacher that he came down to the ship, when she was leaving Melbourne, to see her off, and said to her mother, 'Never grudge any trouble that is taken for that child's education; she will repay everything that is done for her.'

Her mother was to heed this advice, making many sacrifices in her commitment to her daughter's education.

The family went first to Dunedin, where Helen was taught by Robert Stout, who later became Chief Justice of New Zealand. After two years they moved to Hokitika, then a rough mining township, where the only girls' school was so elementary that Helen soon passed its limits and went for a while to a church school for boys.

When James Scott arrived from England to start a boys' high school, Mrs Connon tried to persuade him to teach her daughter, 'but the schoolmaster was not inclined to waste his energies on the inferior sex'. A meeting with Helen changed his mind: '. . . when I first saw her, she was a very beautiful child. Her usual expression was that of one who has something important to do and meant to do it.' She became his star pupil, surpassing her male class-mates, despite their six-month start, to win the top prize. It says a good deal about her character that, although she stayed several more years at the school, she refused to take any more prizes – that sort of rivalry did not interest her. Instead, she was put in charge of a class for girls which Scott decided to start at the school. Her success had convinced him that women were worth educating.

He was in the process of arranging for her to open a separate girls' school when the family moved to Christchurch. There, in 1875, the indefatigable Mrs Connon approached John Macmillan Brown, who had just taken up his post as Canterbury College's first professor of English and classics, and asked if he would accept Helen in his classes. He agreed, and Helen was enrolled as the college's first matriculated woman student.

Macmillan Brown claimed in his memoirs that his move had made Canterbury the world's first co-educational institution. It had, in fact, been preceded by several American universities, but it is almost certain that it was the first in the British Empire.

It was as well that no formal application was made by a woman to the Canterbury College Board of Governors, though the admission of women to Collegiate Union classes in 1872–74 was a strong precedent. There were some opinionated members of the board, and a well-publicised row could have brought to the surface unpleasant prejudices in Christchurch society. It was better that admission should be achieved quietly . . . through some side door.

Taking part in a college Dialectic Society debate on higher education for women, Helen was so upset to find her serious arguments met with juvenile male advice to stick to cooking and nursing that she never took part in the debates again. She herself was 'totally devoid of sex antagonism', Edith Grossmann recalls. 'She went calmly on her own way, apparently without effort, and without aggressiveness and by "a sweet attractive kind of grace" won over more to sympathise with her cause than she would have done by any arguments.' She took her BA in 1880 and an MA with first-class honours in Latin and English the following year.

Macmillan Brown found her the ideal scholar and, before long, his ideal woman. After she graduated, he asked her to marry him, but she set the offer aside. 'She wished to show independently what a young woman could do in life.' She was already involved in building up the new Christchurch Girls' High School, as well as educating her two younger sisters, who followed her to university.

The school had been founded in 1877, and, while she was still studying, Helen was employed as an assistant mistress, teaching English literature. Margaret Lorimer remembers her teaching style:

She was not a teacher in the modern sense. She seldom used the blackboard, or made any attempt at demonstrating. She merely talked quietly and interestingly, often assuming in us a knowledge which we did not possess, and thereby stimulating us to remedy any deficiencies.

Helen Connon became the school principal in 1882. Although she was only in her early twenties, she was already an able administrator with progressive ideas. At a time when colleges for young ladies were concerned largely with teaching accomplishments such as needlework, dancing, and music, she emphasised the importance of a good general knowledge of languages, literature, science, history, and mathematics. She once said she thought it most vulgar and foolish for girls to learn accomplishments when they had only a miserable stock of general knowledge; it was like putting jewellery over a ragged dress. Between 1879 and 1883, the school won more honours than any other in the country, girls' or boys'.

As well as training the most able girls for university, the school endeavoured to train them to be 'earnest, cultured and intelligent women, able to take an independent stand in life and at the same time to manage a household'. She started Saturday classes in practical cookery and dressmaking; she also abolished homework because, as she told a pupil, 'You are only preparing yourself now, what good can you do if you exhaust yourself before you begin your real work in life?' Her school was one of the first to adopt drill for girls, as well as swimming classes, gymnastics, and tennis. She herself was fond of physical exercise, especially walking, rowing on the Avon, and riding on the hills of Banks Peninsula.

Professor Macmillan Brown was sent to examine the school and noted the powerful influence she had over the girls.

. . . their attitude to her was little short of worship. She never needed to give commands; her look was enough to ensure perfect discipline . . . I had never seen anything in all my experience of teachers to compare with her serene power.

Pupils at Christchurch Girls' High School c.1900–08, soon after Helen Connon retired as principal in 1896. *Canterbury Museum*

Although she married him in 1886, she continued as principal, even after the birth of their first daughter, Millicent, in 1888. But by 1894, according to her biographer Edith Searle Grossmann, the strain of running a home and a school was getting too much and she retired. Since the household was well supplied with servants, it seems unlikely that the strain was physical. There may have been a psychological strain, since by combining marriage, motherhood, and a professional career she was at odds with the conventions of her time. Perhaps the ebullient and egotistical John Macmillan Brown was not the easiest husband for a woman in that situation. In 1898 a second daughter, Viola, was born.

Helen's life after retiring from teaching was marked by insomnia and frequent moves from one house to another, and between New Zealand and Europe. She was unwell for some time before her death in 1903, at the age of forty-three. The official cause of her death was diphtheria, but some of her family doubted that this was correct. Her husband erected a broken column over her grave. It was a recognition of the unfulfilled promise of her life, which had begun brilliantly and fruitfully, and then, after her retirement at the age of only thirty-four, contained much sadness.

Her name is perpetuated in Helen Connon Hall, a hall of residence for women students at Canterbury University, and in a memorial prize at Christchurch Girls' High School. In a school assembly sixty years after her death, Eileen Fairbairn, a teacher, summed up Helen Macmillan Brown's impact on women's education.

Her dignity, her calm, her very great beauty were answers to those who feared, and said, that educating girls was freeing them to ape men, making them hard and unfitted to be wives and mothers. By sheer personality, she achieved for women a

153

place in scholastic life, which was unique at that time in the world, and put all her energy into building up this school of ours into one where learning was held in respect.
Mavis Airey

Quotations
para.2 E. S. Grossmann, *Life of Helen Macmillan Brown*, pp.10–11
para.4 E. S. Grossmann, *Life*, p.12
para.6 W. J. Gardner, *Colonial Cap and Gown*, p.82
para.7 E. S. Grossmann, *Life*, p.24; E. S. Grossmann, 'In Memoriam', p.4
para.8 E. S. Grossmann, *Life*, p.30
para.9 B. Peddie, *Christchurch Girls' High School*, p.30
para.11 E. S. Grossmann, *Life*, pp.36, 37
para.12 *The Memoirs of John Macmillan Brown*, p.180
para.15 B. Peddie, *Christchurch Girls' High School*, p.48

Published Sources
Christchurch Girls' High School Magazine, no.121, 1963
Gardner, W. J., Beardsley, E. T., and Carter, T. E. *A History of the University of Canterbury, 1873–1973*, Christchurch, 1973
Gardner, W. J. *Colonial Cap and Gown*, Christchurch, 1979
Grossmann, Edith Searle, *Life of Helen Macmillan Brown*, Christchurch, 1905
Grossmann, Edith Searle. 'In Memoriam Helen Macmillan Brown', *Lyttelton Times*, 4 March 1903
McLintock, A. H. (ed.) *An Encyclopedia of New Zealand*, vol.1, Wellington, 1966
Macmillan Brown, J. *The Memoirs of John Macmillan Brown*, Christchurch, 1974
Peddie, Barbara. *Christchurch Girls' High School 1877–1977*, Christchurch, 1977
The Press, 8 May 1973 (interview with Millicent Baxter)
NZ Herstory 1978, Dunedin, 1977

FREDA COOK

1896–1990

If anybody was doing somebody an injustice she would be in there, saying something about it.

This was one friend's description of Freda Cook, a staunch and inveterate campaigner for civil rights and for a wide range of community, environmental, and peace issues.

Freda Pym was born in Alfordscott, Oxfordshire, in 1896. She was educated at Cheltenham Ladies' College, one of the first secondary schools for girls, whose principal was Miss Beale, a pioneer in higher education for girls. Freda won a scholarship to Oxford University and graduated with honours in English language and literature. 'There I did begin to understand a little about the socialist movement which appealed to me because of its apparent aim of justice for all . . .'

In 1924 she followed her brother out to New Zealand, where she worked first as the girls' work activity secretary for the YWCA in Auckland. There she became more aware of the problems of imperialism, through people who were involved with international issues such as India's struggle for independence and Japan's growing ambitions towards China. From Auckland she went to Christchurch, and then to New Plymouth, where in 1931 she met her future husband,

Englishman Eric Cook, a teacher and member of the Unemployed Workers' Movement (UWM). When they married she gave up her work for the YWCA and took a year off to decide what to do next.

In 1934 she joined the national UWM in Wellington and was particularly active in fighting for the rights of unemployed women. By the following year she was secretary of the Wellington women's branch of the NUWM. During one campaign, Freda was one of twelve women who created the first recorded 'disturbance' in the House of Representatives.

We shouted from the Gallery every time a member made some speech attacking the unemployed and the poor . . . I was the first to shout, as secretary, and the policeman who escorted me out was really shocked and told me that the lady sitting next to me was a Presbyterian minister's wife and that one ought to behave more decently in such company. But I knew she was the next one on the list to start shouting.

An early member of the New Zealand Communist Party, Freda became active in the Working Women's Movement and attended its first conference in October 1934. She helped organise the second national conference in 1936. At this time she also set up discussion groups involving different women's organisations – one of these being the Sex Hygiene and Birth Regulation Society, from which the Family Planning Association eventually emerged.

Soon after the first Labour government was sworn in, the Cooks returned to England, 'hoping to get some further education in communism and the way forward'. Freda became involved in 'play centres' (which, unlike New Zealand playcentres, were places where children could play after school) and the Workers' Educational Association (WEA). She sent back occasional articles on international issues to *Woman Today*, a feminist publication promoting economic, social and political rights for women. She also wrote for the *Workers' Weekly* (the Communist Party newspaper), *Working Woman* (a communist women's newspaper which preceded *Woman Today*), and for *Tomorrow* (an independent left-wing magazine). She continued her association with the Communist Party in England, while her husband became a member of the British Labour Party and involved himself in local body politics.

During the Second World War, she and her husband ran, from London, an alternative news service called Democratic and General News:

I did the foreign correspondence of the news agency and was able to go to many countries in Europe, such as Poland, Hungary and Czechoslovakia, directly after the war, to see how they were getting on.

During one year of the war Freda also drove trucks at different air-bases around England. She joined the China Campaign Committee, which supported the Chinese against the Japanese, and worked with Krishna Menon in the English headquarters of the India League.

Eric and Freda were living apart during the war, but still worked closely together. When he died in 1948, and the news service had to be wound up, Freda returned to New Zealand. She taught at Wellington College and did various other jobs in between. Freda also travelled extensively in the 1950s. She taught English in Italy and toured Czechoslovakia.

In 1960 Freda went to North Vietnam as the first full-time teacher of English at the University of Hanoi. Her time there was 'next in line to the UWM as the most absorbing, interesting and beautiful periods of my life'. For eight years she wrote articles for the *New Zealand Monthly Review* on the Vietnam war and the life of the Vietnamese people. She was vocal in her disapproval of the United States' intervention in Vietnam.

Freda Cook at an anti-Vietnam War demonstration, 1972. *Ans Westra*

In 1968 she returned to New Zealand to address the Peace, Power and Politics in Asia Conference. Unable to go back immediately to battle-ravaged Hanoi, she revisited it in 1974 and 1976. Meanwhile she retired from teaching, but continued working as an activist in the community. She lived in various communes in Wellington and worked for HART (Halt All Racist Tours), CARE (Citizens' Association for Racial Equality), and Corso, amongst other groups. A member of the Committee on Vietnam and the National Anti-Apartheid Committee, Freda joined the Maori land protests at Bastion Point in the late 1970s and marched in the anti-Springbok tour rallies in 1981.

A woman of prodigious energy and commitment, a 'battler, always in the front line', she was also witty and a good listener. 'Perhaps most important of all, her general concern for humanity is also reflected in her own personal relationships'. Finally, her age began to catch up with her. She lived in a rest home in Wellington from 1981 until her death in 1990.   *Bronwyn Labrum*

Quotations
para.1 *Evening Post*, 23 Jan. 1990
para.2 *Broadsheet*, no.24, Nov. 1974, p.24
para.4 NZ Biographies, p.189
para.6 *Broadsheet*, p.25

para.8 *Broadsheet*, p.26
para.10 *Evening Post*, 23 Jan. 1990; *City News*, 5 March 1975
Unpublished Sources
NZ Biographies, 1976, vol.2, p.89, ATL
Published Sources
Broadsheet, no.24, Nov. 1974 (interview with Freda Cook), pp.25–27
City News, 5 March 1975
Evening Post, 23 Jan. 1990 (obituary)
NZ Herstory 1984, Auckland, 1983
Otago Daily Times, 24 Jan. 1990 (obituary)
Watchdog, April 1990 (obituary)

HELEN CRABB

1891–1972

Adopting the anagram 'Barc' for most of her professional life as an artist and teacher, Helen Crabb energetically nurtured the nascent creative talents of many women and men in the Wellington region during the 1940s and 1950s. One of her students, Elva Bett, wrote an apt tribute upon her death: 'Her wise counselling, philosophy, superb draughtsmanship and above all her teaching were respected widely.'

One of a family of six children, Helen Crabb was raised at Waituna West, a rural settlement in the Manawatu, where her parents managed the general store and later took up farming. At first Helen was interested in both music and art, not unusual for young ladies being groomed for society in the Edwardian era. After secondary school in Wanganui, she opted for art and took drawing classes at the technical college in Palmerston North before travelling to Australia for further study. The Sydney Art School under Julian Ashton promoted drawing from the antique, and later the life model, as a sound basis for aspiring painters and sculptors. Barc trained there until 1916, afterwards spending nine months at the Royal College of Art, London. Her studies were interrupted by the First World War, when she took on volunteer work, but by 1919 she was back in Australia recommencing classes with Julian Ashton. It was there that she formed friendships with Dorrit Black, Grace Crowley, Adrian Feint, and Thea Proctor, active participants in Sydney's contemporary art movement.

Her apprenticeship over, Barc concentrated on what was to become her special forte: numerous studies from the figure in water-colour and rapidly executed pen and ink studies. At the same time she began her teaching career and for most of the 1920s and early 1930s she taught art at private colleges for girls in New South Wales. Clearly skilled in this respect, she was appointed to the staff of the Sydney Art School in 1937, serving there for two years.

Barc decided to return to New Zealand in July 1939 and chose central Wellington as her base. She became a distinctive sight in art circles with her tall commanding stature, long skirts, and swirling capes. Equally unconventional in her life-style, Barc cared little for domesticity and rarely had a fixed address until 1944 when she settled at 25 Hobson Street, Thorndon, her home for the next ten

Helen Crabb, 'Barc', 'Seated woman, reading', 1913, pencil drawing. *Alexander Turnbull Library*

years. In the large room she occupied upstairs, 'practice nights' and day classes were conducted for artists, including Patricia Fry who recalled:

From October 1947 I usually managed three times a week at Barc's and steadily drew the lay figure, chairs upside down, the cast of Venus often foreshortened, a large branch of a tree, Barc posing in different positions.

Many of her students were married women with children and, although choosing to remain single herself, she urged them to keep drawing: 'You need not hurry, but you must not stop.'

In 1949, the artist exhibited with the Group of Nine at Helen Hitching's gallery in Wellington. T. A. McCormick, Helen Stewart, Evelyn Page, and Stewart Maclennan were among this assembly of local painters. Barc's name also became regularly linked with the annual shows put on by the New Zealand Academy of Fine Arts. Her distinctive pen and wash studies of people relaxing or engaged in their daily routines were often published in the *Year Book of the Arts* with titles such as *Drowsy, Civvy Street, Instrumental Trio*, and *Travellers*. The June 1954 issue of *Landfall* featured four such works. Barc knew her subjects intimately, frequently staying with the families of friends and students who were duly recorded on paper.

In recognition of her significance as an artist and mentor, the National Art Gallery purchased a folio of her drawings from the solo exhibition she held in 1959 at Wellington's Architectural Centre. On the proceeds Barc travelled to

Australia, refreshing herself at life classes in Sydney before moving to Tasmania, where she settled for the next decade.

By 1960 the artist had decided to devote her energies almost solely to preparing a manuscript on art instruction. This evolved from lengthy letters she had already sent to her former students, and repeated her favourite maxims such as: 'A phrase I want you to understand is: *THE HABIT OF RESEARCH*. I give you the right ideas for a lifetime. Performance is your own affair but your grammar is *my* affair.' Before compiling her teaching code, Barc had been a contributor of articles and reviews to *Art in New Zealand*, signing them with her anagram, 'H.P.C.' or 'The cheil'.

At the end of the 1960s she returned to Wellington, continuing to work on her manuscript which is now held at the Alexander Turnbull Library. Barc held a final exhibition of her work with three others at the Bett Duncan Gallery in 1971.
Anne Kirker

Quotations
para.1 Elva Bett, *Evening Post*, 11 March 1972
para.4 Patricia Fry, manuscript in preparation on Helen Crabb, in private possession
para.7 Barc, 'Artists' Magic (Teaching Notes on Art)', MS Papers 1939, folder 5, ATL

Unpublished Sources
Helen Crabb, Papers 1952–1969, MS Papers 1838, ATL

MARGARET CRUICKSHANK *1873–1918*

CHRISTINA CRUICKSHANK *1873–1939*

When Dr Margaret Cruickshank died in the influenza epidemic of 1918, the people of Waimate grieved at the loss of a friend who had devoted her life to them. They raised a monument to her in Seddon Square, said to be the first erected to a woman in New Zealand.

Margaret and her twin sister, Christina, were born on New Year's Day in Palmerston (South). Their parents, Elizabeth (born Taggart) and George Cruickshank had emigrated from Scotland. Their father was a contractor, but their mother died her large family was still young. Because of their family responsibilities, the twins apparently took turns going to school, week and week about, the one who had been to school teaching the other. From Palmerston High School they went on to Otago Girls' High School, where they were joint duxes in 1891 and gained university scholarships.

Christina graduated from the University of Otago with an MA in 1896 and an MSc in 1906; she decided upon a teaching career. Margaret was at first undecided between teaching and medicine. It was only in the year before they left school that the first woman had been admitted to medical school – Emily Siedeberg, who had been a fellow pupil. After discussions with her, Margaret decided on medicine. She graduated as a physician and a surgeon in 1897. The first woman to go into general practice, she joined Dr H. C. Barclay in Waimate as his assistant, later his partner. She took her MD in 1903, and in 1913 did postgraduate studies in Edinburgh, travelling also in Europe and America. Apart from this trip, she was to spend the rest of her life in the little South Canterbury town.

Her personal qualities and professional skills were such as to 'remove the prejudice and want of confidence felt in female doctors in the days of her early professional career'. And a journalist from *The White Ribbon* wrote in 1900: 'There can be no doubt that the skill and kindliness of Dr Cruickshank have quite won the hearts of the people in her district.'

Dr Margaret Cruickshank of Waimate. *Waimate Museum*

The journalist had hoped for an interview with Dr Cruickshank, but had been refused. Margaret Cruickshank said that she hated publicity: 'I have quite enough in my daily life without seeking after the avoidable.' And she disliked the essentially egotistical character of an interview: 'Though I may have had a little measure of what the world calls success, I am on a very lowly rung of the ladder yet, and from such have a very circumscribed outlook so that I feel myself hardly fitted to speak very dogmatically about questions affecting women practitioners.' But she dwelt particularly on 'the absence of anything like hostility to women practitioners among the medical men of the colony'.

During the First World War, Dr Barclay went to work for the Red Cross overseas, and Margaret Cruickshank took on his workload as well as her own. She was also involved with Red Cross work. She did her rounds as far as possible by bicycle, the more distant ones by horse and gig.

When the influenza epidemic broke out, she worked night and day. M. J. Leonard, the son of her housekeeper, remembered: 'Where the mother was laid low, she fed the baby, prepared a meal, and in many cases where whole families were laid low she would milk the family cow to obtain milk for their sustenance.' Inevitably the workload placed considerable strain on her physique, and she herself fell victim to influenza and pneumonia. She died on 28 November 1918.

Christina, too, had a distinguished career. She was principal of Wanganui Girls' College from 1911 to 1932, and instituted many changes. In her first report to the board of governors, she referred to the ideal of education shifting more and more 'from that of the mere acquisition of knowledge, either as an end in itself or as a personal decoration to that of development through bringing to bear in a practical way what knowledge we have on the yet unknown'. In her time, all girls studied the core subjects of arithmetic, composition, history, geography, literature, physiology, and a foreign language, but were then able to choose from courses leading to university or a teacher's certificate, or improving their home skills with needlework and dressmaking, cookery and nursing classes, science, hygiene, drawing, elocution, and singing. She was, she said, 'feeling towards a course that will constitute at once a practical and liberal education for girls who are, sooner or later, to be in charge of homes of their own'.

Her time at the school spanned the upheavals of the First World War, the influenza epidemic, and the Napier earthquake, as well as financial stress and educational change. When she retired, the school magazine described the way in which she met difficulties with 'the courage and quiet dignity of a sensitive and deeply reserved nature. At other times difficulties have been dissolved by the quick wit and delightful humour of which we could never have enough.'

Christina Cruickshank kept an interest in the school for the rest of her life; her memorial there is a specially carved table, chair, and lectern in Southland beech. *Mavis Airey*

Quotations

para.4 *Timaru Herald*, 29 Nov. 1918 (obituary); *The White Ribbon*, April 1900, pp.1–2
para.5 *The White Ribbon*, April 1900, pp.1–2
para.7 M. J. Leonard, *Waimate Advertiser*, 27 Nov. 1981 (NZ Biographies, 1981, vol.6, pp.29–30, ATL)
para.8 C. Cruickshank, report to the Board of Governors, Wanganui Girls' High School, 5 Dec. 1911, in *The Adastrian*, 1911, p.65

para.8 *The Adastrian*, 1911, p.64
para.9 *The Adastrian*, 1931, p.93
Published Sources
The Adastrian (Wanganui Girls' College Magazine), 1911–31
The Cyclopedia of New Zealand, vol.3, Christchurch, 1903, p.1068
McLintock, A. H. (ed.) *An Encyclopedia of New Zealand*, vol.1, Wellington, 1966, p.422
Morrison, Elizabeth. *Dr Margaret Cruickshank*, Christchurch, 1923
NZ Herstory 1977, Dunedin, 1976
NZ Herstory 1978, Dunedin, 1977
Wanganui Chronicle, 18 Sept. 1947

EVELINE CUNNINGTON

1849–1916

Social worker, feminist, and Christian Socialist, Eveline Willett Cunnington worked, to the end of her life, for social change.

She was born on 23 April 1849 in Wales, the twelfth and youngest daughter of the wealthy, upper-middle-class Leach family of Devizes, Wiltshire. As a young girl, she 'climbed trees, collected butterflies, frogs and white mice', but as she got older, the isolation created by her family's insistence on its superiority and her father's injunction to 'stay at home and read and write and dress nicely', made her restless in her 'gilded cage'.

She went to school in France and travelled in Germany and Italy, continuing her education at Queen's College, London, for 'three wonderful years of rapid and rich intellectual growth'. In London she met James Hinton, a doctor, who was her introduction to the ideas that became basic to her Christian Socialism. He taught her to 'fling away . . . all affectations, pretences, shams, unrealities', and to recognise the 'oneness of Humanity and . . . that nothing must separate one from one's fellow creatures'.

In 1875, aged twenty-six, Eveline emigrated to New Zealand, where her cousin, Mr S. Sanders, was editor of the *Lyttelton Times*. 'From being a rich man's daughter [she] became the wife of a poor man', marrying Capel Baines in 1896. They went to South Australia to the gold-fields, but on her husband's sudden death eight years later, Eveline came back to Christchurch with their two children.

Within two years she married Herbert Cunnington, an electrical engineer. Her second marriage returned Eveline to some comfort and status. But with her knowledge of poverty and her developing Christian Socialism she was committed to working for the well-being of others. She visited the 'lunatic asylums' and the prisons, being appointed one of the two first women prison visitors in 1896. The *Lyttelton Times* described her work:

It is at the gaol gates that she has chiefly laboured . . . taking in hand the helpless women and girls who are constantly appearing in the Police Courts, cheering timid witnesses, protecting frightened children and finding homes for neglected girls.

As well as helping individuals, Eveline Cunnington campaigned publicly for structural change, writing letters and newspaper articles, addressing meetings, and petitioning influential figures in the community.

Her participation in the campaign against the 1869 Contagious Diseases Act was one aspect of her concern for the women and girls who came before the courts. (Ostensibly aimed at controlling venereal disease, the act permitted the forcible vaginal examination and imprisonment of any woman the police defined as a 'prostitute'.) Her campaign for women police to process female offenders was another. 'We must have women police, if possible women lawyers, women on the grand and petty juries, women detectives.'

She advocated a number of prison reforms, such as the training of prison officials, the separation of first-time prisoners from recidivists, and the provision of trade-training for inmates.

She also agitated for the raising of the age of consent for girls, for women's suffrage, and for the entry of women into parliament. Eveline was a member of the National Council of Women and a founding member of the Canterbury Women's Institute, set up in 1892 to promote women's emancipation in all spheres. Eveline was elected to the Christchurch Hospital and Charitable Aid Board in 1910, topping the poll. By now, however, this work was beginning to be a distraction from what she considered to be her 'soul's work' – teaching.

A severe illness during her long visit to England (1904–6), where one of her sons died, had diminished her ability 'to help on the world by service', but she could still 'help people to think'. Recognising 'a tremendous opportunity for work among . . . leisure class girls and through them to the men', she initiated courses of 'good hard study' on social questions, setting up the Girls Social Science Club in Christchurch in 1908. They met weekly for a lecture followed by discussion. She saw this as her 'last work on earth', but in 1910 she went to hear a socialist speaker and organiser from Australia and 'was appalled at the ignorance, the spite, the pettiness, the back number style of the lecture'.

Fearful of the consequences of such leadership, Eveline decided that 'an organised army of trained, educated lecturers' was needed. The Christchurch Fabian Society, founded in 1896, met regularly in her home at 38 Papanui Road and she encouraged its members to develop their educative and propagandist work. She herself lectured, wrote socialist articles for the *Maoriland Worker*, and contributed regular 'Fabian Notes' to the *Lyttelton Times*.

A devout and lifelong Anglican, she perceived her socialism to be an inevitable outcome of her Christian ideals and wanted clergymen to join with the Fabians in educating working people. At the inaugural meeting of the Church Socialist League in the Anglican Cathedral in 1913, she was the only woman present.

Eveline Cunnington was a very popular speaker, and her credibility with the trade unions and at the Socialist Hall enabled her to introduce speakers from church and university who might not have reached working-class audiences without her. By the First World War, an extensive programme of lecture/discussions and study courses had been established in Christchurch. The next step was the formation of a Workers Educational Association (WEA). Eveline's ill health and her husband's death restricted her direct contribution to the initial proposals, but she lived to see the WEA set up. She died at Sumner on 30 July 1916.

The public memory of Eveline Cunnington is now faint: she resisted public recognition herself, and the focus of her work was local rather than national. But she was regarded as a 'truly great woman' by those who worked with her. Her letters and lectures were published by her children after her death: some of her words survive.   *Claire-Louise McCurdy*

Quotations
para.2 E. Cunnington, *Lectures and Letters*, p.5; p.3
para.3 E. Cunnington, p.7
para.4 E. Cunnington, p.7
para.5 *Lyttelton Times*, 25 Feb. 1904
para.6 E. Cunnington, p.65
para.8 E. Cunnington, p.121
para.9 E. Cunnington, p.112; p.119; p.114; p.113; p.20
para.10 E. Cunnington, p.120
para.13 Jessie Mackay obituary in E. Cunnington, p.1

Unpublished Source
Plumridge, E. W. 'Labour in Christchurch: Community and Consciousness, 1914–1919', MA thesis, Canterbury, 1979

Published Sources
Cunnington, Eveline. *The Lectures and Letters of E. W. Cunnington*, edited by her children, W. G. Roberts, Freda Cunnington, & A. Baines, Christchurch, 1918
Holt, Betty. *Women in Council: A History of the National Council of Women in New Zealand*, Wellington, 1980
Macdonald, Charlotte. 'The Social Evil: Prostitution and the Passage of the Contagious Diseases Act (1869)', in Barbara Brookes, Charlotte Macdonald and Margaret Tennant (eds), *Women in History: Essays on European Women in New Zealand*, Wellington, 1986
Parsloe, N. A. *Eveline Willett Cunnington and the Origins of Canterbury W.E.A.*, Wellington, 1971
Regional Women's Decade Committee. *Canterbury Women Since 1893*, Christchurch, 1979
NZ Herstory 1984, Auckland, 1983

AMEY DALDY

1829–1920

From beneath her customary white bonnet, the strong handsome face of Amey Daldy gazes uncompromisingly from photographs of gatherings of nineteenth-century feminists. The character and opinions of the woman herself were every bit as strong as her appearance suggested. Minutes of National Council of Women (NCW) meetings regularly recorded her dissenting voice, while to men she threw down a challenge:

[A]t present we are only in the chrysalis state, hardly knowing our own capabilities, yet feeling we could accomplish something if only we were free, free as the other sex. And why should we not be? Who has given to man the prerogative to say what a woman shall do or what a woman shall not do? Let him produce his authority and we may consider it.

She was born Amey Hamerton in 1829 at Yarwell, England, the daughter of Charles Hamerton, a farmer. In 1860 she emigrated to New Zealand with her brother John, arriving at Auckland on the *Caduceus* in October. In 1865 she married William Henry Smith, but the marriage was short-lived, for by the following year Amey was listed as a school teacher and was living alone in a central Auckland boarding-house. She was clearly not wealthy, for the other occupants were a carpenter and a labourer.

By 1872 Amey was running a secondary school for girls in Karangahape Road, one of the earliest in Auckland. She also took a girls' bible class at the Beresford Street Congregational Church and it is here that she probably met widower William Crush Daldy, whom she married in 1880. Besides both being Congregationalists, they also shared an interest in philanthropy and social reform. William was always Amey's staunchest supporter.

At fifty, Amey was past childbearing age, but Captain Daldy had had four children. Soon after Amey and William's marriage, William's widowed son-in-law James Wrigley died, leaving eight orphans. The Daldys inherited the task of rearing the Wrigley children, then aged from three to nineteen years, and installed them in a house next door to their own in Hepburn Street, Ponsonby, with two housekeepers. All the children regarded Amey as their grandmother, and many years later May Wrigley recalled accompanying Amey in the buggy as she visited the businessmen of Auckland, lobbying for support for female suffrage. 'The businessmen seemed to enjoy her visits', she wrote, 'as she was never bitter and always ready with her answers to their arguments.'

The marriage was distinctly advantageous to Amey's feminist work, for William Crush Daldy was a powerful figure in the colonial business and political worlds. He had built up a substantial business as a gum and timber trader and shipper, and was on the boards of numerous companies. He was at various times a member of parliament, provincial secretary, Auckland city councillor, first captain of the Volunteer Fire Brigade, and first chairman of the Auckland Harbour Board. William could provide Amey with useful connections, and guarantee that when she went in to battle she would at least get a hearing.

When Mary Leavitt of the American Women's Christian Temperance Union visited New Zealand in 1885, Amey Daldy was one of the women inspired to form a branch in the city. Prohibition was clearly dear to Amey's heart, for at successive meetings of the Auckland Women's Christian Temperance Union (WCTU) she raised the issues of the use of alcohol at Auckland Hospital ('their drink bill for the year was higher than any other hospital in the colony'), the violation of the law prohibiting the sale of liquor in the King Country, and the sale of alcohol to 'natives in the Cook Islands', about which Amey was 'to write to the Queen for further information'. She was clearly unafraid of adopting unpopular stances, for she also wrote to the newspaper condemning the proposal to give alcohol to soldiers departing for the Boer War.

Although the primary goals of the WCTU were control of alcohol and the woman's vote, the union was also involved in charitable and social reform work. According to the temperance paper, *The Leader*, the WCTU was concerned about 'juvenile prostitution and Auckland hoodlums of both sexes', and the propensity of the police for arresting the girls, but 'allow[ing] the males to escape'. Its response was the establishment of 'Lad's Own' evening recreation classes in Newton for 'the children of neglectful and vicious parents', under the stewardship of Amey Daldy. Amey put out a request for puzzles, games, and illustrated magazines for the one hundred boys who attended, and reported that a gymnasium had been started. But it was uphill work, and there were pleas for helpers to keep it going.

Amey Daldy's background as a teacher made her aware of new ideas in education, including the pre-school field. In Auckland a kindergarten 'to rescue very young children of poor parents from the streets and prepare them for going to public schools' and a creche 'for infants of mothers who have to wholly or partially support their families' were established in association with the WCTU in 1887. By the year's end, seventy children were attending the kindergarten and three babies were in the creche.

But Amey Daldy's activities extended beyond social work. She took a leading role in the struggle for the suffrage at a national level, working closely with national WCTU president Annie Schnackenberg and the national franchise superintendent Kate Sheppard. In 1893 she resigned as Auckland franchise superintendent of the WCTU, as the previous year she had been elected founding president of the Auckland Women's Franchise League, the secular arm of the suffrage campaign. She led deputations, chaired large public meetings, and argued the suffrage case forcibly through the media.

Amey was noted as 'a very good speaker' and 'a strong and popular chairwoman', and on many occasions she needed to be. The presence at suffrage gatherings of 'high-spirited males . . . with a super abundance of cheap wit' was, said the *New Zealand Graphic*, 'as inevitable as the dog on the racecourse'. The *Auckland Star* reported one town hall meeting where a heckler was removed by the police, a suffragist attempted to pull an interjector off the stage by his coat-tails, and the meeting periodically broke into 'stamping, hissing and hooting'. Above the din, Amey Daldy said that 'she was not surprised they were refused the franchise if that was a specimen of the mankind of Auckland'.

The *New Zealand Graphic* had a policy of supporting the suffrage; other publications lampooned it mercilessly. Amey featured prominently in a series of unkind cartoons in the *New Zealand Observer*. Although she did not flinch from taking a public role, there were aspects of it which caused her pain. 'I still sometimes shrink from the odium of publicity and an unpopular movement,' she wrote to Kate Sheppard.

In September 1893 the suffrage campaign was rewarded with a victory. May Wrigley wrote that she would 'never forget the pleased look on [Amey Daldy's] face as she held the telegram in her hand from Mr Seddon saying "Parliament has granted the vote to women!"' Six days before women were to cast their first vote, Amey chaired a packed public meeting at which she uttered the memorable lines: 'Let not the babies, the wash-tub, or even dinners prevent the women going to the polls', adding practically that baby-sitters had been organised for mothers.

There was no rest for the suffrage feminists once the vote had been attained. They moved on to other items in the feminist agenda. The name of the Women's Franchise League was changed to the Women's Political League, with Amey

Daldy continuing as president. The establishment of the National Council of Women (NCW) in 1896 provided another forum for feminist concerns, and Amey Daldy attended the first meeting. She was elected vice-president in 1897 and held office until the NCW went into recess in 1905. In 1898, she was national president.

At NCW conferences Amey Daldy promoted the issues that were nearest to her heart. Although she had argued against including the right of women to stand for parliament in the suffrage agenda on tactical grounds, fearing that it would 'frighten the public', in the NCW it became one of her main platforms. Moving the motion for 'the removal of women's disabilities' in 1900, she said that

it had fallen to her lot to move the motion at every session, and she hoped she would not have to do so again . . . They must have equality all the way through.

It is difficult at this distance and with such scant surviving records to make an assessment of the political position of Amey Daldy, but essentially she held *laissez-faire* and conservative views, at the basis of which was individualism. She was not always in sympathy with the economic and social reforms of Seddon's Liberal government. One of her co-workers, Emily Gibson, described how she and a group of others broke with the Women's Political League:

Mrs Daldy's opinions were all right from a feminist point of view – she wanted absolute equality with men but she did not approve of the Government's policy on some points connected with Labour and the workers.

Mercutio, the *New Zealand Herald* columnist, noted that 'Mrs Daldy . . . usually complains of the State interfering . . . in the daily life of the people and becoming a second Providence to them . . .' Her voting position at meetings showed that she disapproved of excessive social welfare or curbs on the freedom of employers. But she believed passionately in equality of opportunity, and was one of a minority of NCW women to oppose the exclusion of Asian immigrants from New Zealand.

Just as modern feminism contains radical and conservative elements and contradictions, so too did nineteenth-century feminism. Although conservative on many issues, Amey actively supported the fledgling Tailoresses' Union.

Other apparent contradictions are explained by the social purity ethos which was the well-spring of nineteenth-century feminism. This held that feminine values, epitomised by the mother in the home, had the potential to cleanse society of degradation. The traditional gender-based division of labour in the home was never questioned. Amey Daldy went so far as to argue that no woman should have a legal right to marry unless she obtained from the state a certificate to say she had a thorough knowledge of domestic duties. Commenting on this, Mercutio wrote that:

this takes the sentiment out of the whole business, but Mrs Daldy says that sentiment does not wear well, and the outcome of untidy homes, with bad cooking thrown in, is the Divorce Court or purgatory.

But Amey Daldy also argued that 'old maidism' should be esteemed as highly as married life, and was adamant that women had a right and a duty to be out in the world, active in public life. 'No one who has read history can doubt woman's capacity for public duties,' she said, reminding her fellow workers of Boadicea, Ethelfleda, and other powerful women in the past.

How can [woman] thoroughly recover the position she once held? We unhesitatingly say, by her own effort. Though Acts of Parliament may give authority and encouragement, they cannot give to women fitness, ability, and willingness to suggest or to carry out measures for the improvement of the human race.

She was an ardent supporter of equal rights for both sexes to divorce, saying that marriage should not be regarded as 'an infinite contract which only eternity could cancel'. She also believed that wives had a right to an equal share of the household income. To critics of the latter proposal, Amey produced a series of counter-arguments which were typical of her blunt style and clear thinking. Some people claimed 'it is placing a wife on the level of a paid housekeeper,' she said. 'In that cause she would have fewer duties, more leisure and more pay.' She dismissed arguments that women could not manage money by referring to government finances, which '. . . are manipulated by men with the result that every country has a national debt'. For men to control the household purse amounted to tyranny, 'and how can a tyrant be a partner?' she asked. 'What would be said of a business firm if one partner absolutely refused to share in the profits?' In her presidential address of 1899, she said:

Future generations will be as shocked at the dependent condition of many present day wives as we are when we read the miserable conditions of serfs under the feudal system . . .

Amey Daldy's marriage provided her with a model of an equal partnership. William accompanied her to NCW conferences and spoke publicly in favour of suffrage. She never really recovered from his death in 1903. She wrote to Kate Sheppard:

I do sometimes think a few friends did realise his worth . . . he was so unlike the common men of humanity in not wishing to place his best commodities in the window . . . I was proud of him and am still, and but few, if any, of our women know how much they owe to his influence in keeping me up to my duty . . . What I can do without him I do not know.

The suffragists were growing old. Amey had been fifty-five when the suffrage campaign began; she was now in her seventies and could no longer face the long journey to the annual NCW conventions. The secretary, Christina Henderson, wrote: 'We shall miss you very much, no one fills just the place you do.'

Henderson was one of the few younger NCW members. To Amey's intense disappointment, there was no host of women poised to take over the reins. She wrote wistfully to Kate Sheppard:

I have heard nothing of our women's movement for so long a time that I am wondering if the past has been all a dream and nothing more . . . Why, oh why, do the women not rouse themselves from their love of ease and do something for the betterment of the race?

She had left the house in Hepburn Street because it was too full of old memories, sold her pony, and 'coiled down for the remaining months or years of this life'. But, despite the sad tone, she was planning to 'attend a few public meetings and encourage others by my presence', was writing to the local council about men spitting on the pavement, and had organised a public peace meeting.

In 1905 she turned down the presidency of the NCW and wrote to Wilhelmina Sherriff Bain that she felt she had 'aged recently'. Shortly after this she suffered a severe and disabling stroke and was confined to her bed under the care of a nurse, paralysed and unable to speak, until her death on 17 August 1920. Even in death, Amey remained committed to her sex. Under her will, considerable bequests were left to women's organisations such as the Auckland YWCA, the WCTU, the NCW, and two local homes for unmarried mothers.

Sandra Coney

Quotations
para.1 A. Daldy, 'The Disabilities of Women Civil and Political', *The White Ribbon*, vol.2 no.22, April 1897, p.9
para.4 May M. Wrigley, 'Memories of my Grandmother, Mrs Daldy', *Women's Viewpoint*, July 1960
para.6 Minutes of Auckland branch of WCTU, 14 July 1892, ATL; 11 Aug. 1897, ATL
para.7 *The Leader*, 6 Nov. 1886, p.7; p.8
para.8 *The Leader*, 9 April 1887, p.5
para.10 Unidentified, undated newspaper clipping, NCW scrapbooks, AIM; *NZ Graphic*, 9 July 1892, p.689; *Auckland Star*, 18 July 1893, p.2
para.11 A. Daldy to K. Sheppard, 4 Feb. 1904, Sheppard Collection, Canterbury Museum
para.12 M. Wrigley, 'Memories'; *NZ Herald*, 23 Nov. 1893, p.6
para.14 *Auckland Weekly News*, 11 June 1892; *NZ Herald*, 19 April 1899
para.15 C. Purdue, *Women in the Labour Cause*, p.9; Main Scrapbooks, AIM
para.17 Main Scrapbooks, AIM; A. Daldy, 'Marriage, Economic Independence of Women and Divorce', Annual Report of NCW, Third Session, 1898, p.22, in H. K. Lovell-Smith Papers, ATL; A. Daldy, 'The Disabilities of Women', p.8
para.18 B. Holt, *Women in Council*, p.25; A. Daldy, 'Marriage, Economic Independence', p.25; A. Daldy, The President's Address, Fourth Session of the NCW, 1899, p.9, in H. K. Lovell-Smith Papers, ATL
para.19 A. Daldy to K. Sheppard, 4 Feb. 1904, Sheppard Collection, Canterbury Museum
para.20 C. Henderson to A. Daldy, 14 April 1903, Daldy Papers, AIM
para.21 A. Daldy to K. Sheppard, 14 April 1905, Sheppard Collection, Canterbury Museum
para.22 W. S. Bain to A. Daldy, 14 April 1905, Daldy Papers, AIM

Unpublished Sources
Amey Daldy Papers, MS 94, AIM
H. K. Lovell-Smith Papers, MS Papers 1376, ATL
Lesley Dugdale, correspondence with the author
Main Scrapbooks, AIM
Margaret Tennant, 'Matrons with a Mission: Women's Organisations in New Zealand 1893–1915' MA thesis, Massey, 1976
Minutes of the Auckland Branch of the WCTU 1889–1898, Acc 79–57, ATL
K. W. Sheppard Papers, Canterbury Museum
Women's Archives, NCW, AIM

Published Sources
Auckland Star, 17 May 1892; 18 July 1893; 19 Aug. 1920 (obituary)

'Captain Daldy: Sailor, Trader, Timberman, Businessman, Pioneer of Local Governement', *Journal of the Auckland-Waikato Historical Societies*, no.26, April 1975, pp.1–6

Coney, Sandra. *Every Girl: A Social History of Women and the YWCA in Auckland*, Auckland, 1986

Grimshaw, Patricia. *Women's Suffrage in New Zealand*, Auckland, 1972

Holt, Betty. *Women in Council: A History of the National Council of Women of New Zealand 1896–1979*, Wellington, 1980

NZ Herald, 2 June 1892; 23 Nov. 1983; 13–24 April 1899

Purdue, Connie. *Women in the Labour Cause: The History of the Auckland Women's Branch of the New Zealand Labour Party 1925–1975*, Auckland, 1975

PEARL DAWSON

1887–1987

When Pearl Howard Dawson went into action, on the sports field or off it, people took notice. Tough and blunt, with an acerbic wit, she was just the kind of person women's sport needed in its formative years.

In 1887, the year Pearl was born in Auckland to Walter and Elizabeth Dawson, most sports were barred to women. Only golf and tennis were regularly contested and the players were hampered by voluminous skirts. Pearl's passion for sport was aroused as a little girl when she saw schoolgirls playing hockey in a field. 'I loved sport,' she said towards the end of her life. 'I would have sold to Satan for sport.' Her first hockey stick was such a prized possession she took it to bed with her. At Wellesley Street Primary School she wrestled, boxed, and played cricket with the boys. 'I learned my sport,' she said, 'playing with the boys.'

Pearl had ambitions to be a doctor when she left Auckland Grammar School, but her father would not hear of it. Instead, she apprenticed herself to an Auckland veterinary surgeon. Pearl said she really thought she liked animals better than humans. At the time of the Napier earthquake, she set off in a car packed with veterinary supplies to minister to the stricken city's animals. Undertaking part-time study, Pearl earned the diploma which enabled her to work as the first woman veterinarian in Auckland. She specialised in farm work, developing the strong arms and shoulders which made her such a formidable opponent on the hockey field.

Pearl was one of 'The Flying Five', the forward line of the Mt Eden club which won the Auckland senior championship with monotonous regularity. She captained the Auckland side but also moved into hockey administration, chairing the Auckland Ladies Hockey Association executive from 1921 to 1946. In the early years, hockey was under the thrall of the men, with the male-dominated Auckland Hockey Association extracting exorbitant fees from the women for the use of their roughest fields and severely restricting the hours women could play.

'The men always gave us the grounds out in the backblocks,' said Pearl. 'Number four was always given to the ladies. We got the dirty end of the stick all the time.' The women broke with the men's association and then set about finding a sports ground for themselves.

Raising money by penny trails and bring-and-buys, the women succeeded in outbidding the men for the lease of their Remuera hockey ground in 1928. The men were furious, but the women were unmoved and, adding salt to the wound, renamed the ground the 'Girls' Sports Ground'.

After the women failed to maintain the lease during the Depression, Pearl and two other sportswomen determined to solve the problem for good and all. A park was being developed by relief workers in Mt Eden, and the women successfully lobbied the council to make it a women's sports ground. In gratitude for the support given by councillor Ellen Melville, Pearl persuaded the council to name the ground after her. Melville Park opened in June 1939, a permanent home for Auckland's sportswomen.

Cricket was Pearl Dawson's second love, even though she said that 'you run the danger of wearing out the seat of your pants'. She was one of the women who founded the Auckland Girls' Cricket Association in 1928. She also captained the Auckland team but typically was not content just to play. In the formative years of the sport, she visited all the local schools recruiting players, she chaired the executive of the association from 1932 till 1944, and was association president several times.

'I would have sold to Satan for sport' — Pearl Dawson, wearing the New Zealand Women's Hockey Umpires' Association cap, c.1950s.
Dot Simons

At a national level, Pearl was president of the New Zealand Women's Hockey Association on two occasions and was the first New Zealander to be appointed vice-president of the International Federation of Hockey Associations. In 1969 she was awarded the British Empire Medal for her services to sport.

Melville Park was like a home to Pearl and over the years she became a familiar sight, with her short hair, tailored suit, and man's tie. Not a few players were a little in awe of Pearl because of her forthright views and habit of calling everyone by their surname. As she grew older, she became an honoured guest at Melville Park, often bowling the first ball at the beginning of the cricket season. Pearl died on 16 May 1987, two weeks after her one hundredth birthday.

Sandra Coney

Quotations
All quotations are from an interview with Pearl Dawson in 1986.

Unpublished Sources
Auckland YWCA archives, MS 1131, AIM
Dot Simons, interview with the author, 1986
Pearl Dawson, interview with the author, 1986
Women's Archives, NCW, AIM

Published Sources
Coney, Sandra. *Every Girl: A Social History of Women and the YWCA in Auckland*, Auckland, 1986
Dawson, Pearl. 'History of Women's Hockey in Auckland', *65th Jubilee of the Auckland Ladies Hockey Association*, Auckland, 1968
NZ Sportswoman, April 1949, May 1949, June 1949
Simons, Dot. 'Women Blazed the Trail', *NZ Sportsman*, June 1953
Women in Sport, July 1948

MINNIE DEAN

c. 1840–1895

On 12 August 1895 Minnie Dean became the only woman ever hanged for murder in New Zealand.

Little is known about her life prior to her 'baby farming', though she is believed to have been born in Edinburgh around 1840. Accompanied by two small daughters, she came to New Zealand from Tasmania in the late 1860s as Mrs McCulloch, the well-educated young widow of a physician. Initially she lived with her aunt in Invercargill and taught school.

In 1872 she married Charles Dean, an innkeeper at Etal Creek, near Otautau. He went bankrupt in the depression of the 1880s and the couple moved to Winton. They took possession of an abandoned two-storeyed house which burnt to the ground soon after they moved in. Charles Dean then built a two-roomed cottage with a lean-to, and began raising pigs. Minnie Dean began taking in unwanted babies in return for payment.

The practice of 'baby farming' was a necessary evil in colonial New Zealand; contraception was unavailable, abortion was dangerous, mothers of illegitimate children were ostracised, and no provision was made for the care of their offspring. Many desperate women replied to Minnie Dean's discreet newspaper advertisements:

RESPECTABLE Married Woman (comfortable home, country) Wants to adopt an INFANT – address, childless, Times office.

Minnie Dean kept up to eleven children at a time, ranging in age from a few weeks to eleven years, in her cottage. After the deaths of two children in 1891, the coroner advised her to reduce the numbers and improve the living conditions, but she continued as before. No more deaths were reported but rumours abounded of children mysteriously disappearing. The police were frustrated by inadequate child welfare laws: they had no right to enter or inspect the Dean property and Mrs Dean was not required to keep any records. But they watched her every move.

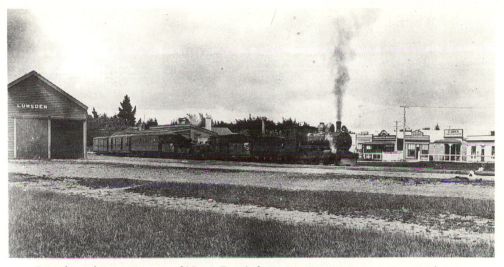

Lumsden railway station, one of Minnie Dean's destinations in suspicious train journeys that caused the police to lay charges for the murder of infants left in her care. *Godber Collection, Alexander Turnbull Library*

In May 1895 she was seen boarding a train carrying a one-year-old child and a large tin hat-box. At Lumsden she disembarked (and the next day re-embarked) carrying only the hat-box. Later in the journey she was handed a younger baby, but when she left the train at Winton she was carrying only the hat-box and a parcel.

A few days later the police unearthed the bodies of the two missing babies and the skeleton of a third in Minnie Dean's garden. At the inquest the older baby was found to have died from an overdose of laudanum (an opiate used to soothe fractious children), the other was found to have died of asphyxiation. Minnie Dean was publicly branded as a murderess by the coroner and community feeling against her ran high.

At the lower court hearing charges against Charles Dean were dismissed, but in the Invercargill High Court Minnie Dean was found guilty of murder and sentenced to death.

Major advances in New Zealand's child welfare legislation were enacted in response to the public concern aroused by the Dean case. *Lynley Hood*

Unpublished Sources
Certificate of Title (Transfer no.1265) Wairaki District, sect.4, Lands and Deeds Office, Invercargill
Justice Dept, J1 1895/917; 1895/643, National Archives, Wellington
Police Dept, P1 1895/845, National Archives, Wellington
Published Sources
Southland Times, May–Aug. 1895

JANE DEANS

1823-1911

Jane McIlraith was born into a farming family at Auchenflower, in Ayrshire, Scotland. The oldest child of Agnes (born Caldwell) and James McIlraith, she valued throughout her life the values of her Scottish upbringing. A profound faith in God, kindness and love were accompanied by a strict discipline and frugality. She was to write later that self-denial was one of the requirements for a contented colonial life.

John Deans entered the McIlraith household in 1839 as a 'gentleman boarder', to learn farming. During his two years with the family, affection grew between the two young people. John, a notary's son, wanted to farm, but prospects were bleak in Scotland. He emigrated to New Zealand, settling in Canterbury in 1843.

With his brother William, John sought permission to squat at Putaringamotu (now Riccarton) on the Canterbury Plains. They later leased the land, first from Ngai Tahu, and later from the Crown and the New Zealand Company. With the colonisation of the Christchurch area, the Deans brothers moved their farming operation up to the Morven Hills, retaining the homestead at Riccarton.

Some years later, John Deans asked Jane McIlraith to share his life in New Zealand, and returned to Scotland for the wedding. Jane arrived at Lyttelton in the *Minerva* on 2 February 1853. 'Besides wearing apparel and furniture, we had the old dog cart, threshing mill, the water-wheel belonging to it.' She was very weak from prolonged seasickness and expecting her first child; nevertheless, she set off up the Bridle Track on horseback, spending the first night at Heathcote Parsonage.

Jane was delighted with her new surroundings at Putaringamotu. 'My curiosity was excited to see how a joint could be roasted at an open fireplace. The fires were all on the hearths then; no manner of grates or stoves.' Her son John was born in August 1853.

Less than a year later her husband died, after a serious illness. At thirty-one Jane was left on her own, in charge of an extensive pastoral property in New Zealand. She had the choice of returning to family and friends in Scotland. She said:

He gave me my choice, so that he might alter his will accordingly. He was afraid I might regret having come here with him away from all my friends. That I never did . . .

Though lonely enough, I did not sit down and mope. I had a mission in life to carry out or see carried out – the wishes and intentions of your grandfather, both in respect of your father personally and also in respect of the property, left in charge of myself and co-trustees for your father's benefit when he came of age. With the property I had kind assistance from my co-trustees and managers, but no one interfered with your father, which was a great comfort to me. I had to set myself to work, and will now tell you how I got on. Not being

174

*well acquainted with business, I looked up and studied all the written
documents I could find, and well I did so, for the knowledge I thereby gained
was of much service to me afterwards.*

Jane had little knowledge of farming, but she was clearly a woman of great
purpose. She became a good judge of stock, especially horses and Shorthorn
cattle. To the end of her long life she took a keen interest in the stud stock at Riccarton. As her skill developed, the trustees were content to leave the administration of the property largely in her hands, with the help of her half brothers, Hugh
and George McIlraith.

Jane loved music, particularly Scottish songs: she played Scottish reels on the
piano all her life. She also loved trees, and planted many at Riccarton and at
Homebush. The drive plantation at Riccarton House was designed 'to be my
masterpiece in the art of planting and . . . my memorial as a Scotswoman'. She
wrote to her grandchildren: 'You will say: 'The vanity of our grandmother.'
Never mind . . . It cost me a great deal of thought . . . how to manage to bring
out the colouring of checks of tartan with trees to make them blend.'

She was a devout Presbyterian, and active in the church throughout her life.
Her faith in God helped her through the tragedy of the early death not only of
her husband, but also of her son, at the age of forty-nine in 1902.

Jane Deans died in 1911. The story of her life is told in *Letters to My Grandchildren* – the family who gave her so much joy.   *Mandy Natusch*

Unpublished Sources
'A Few Notes Relating to First Settlers on the Canterbury Plains and the Peninsula', Deans family papers
   in private possession

Published Sources
Deans, Jane. *Letters to My Grandchildren*, Christchurch, 1923. All quotations are from this source.
The Deans Family, 1840–1990: Sesquicentennial Commemorative Booklet, Christchurch, 1989
Harper, Barbara. *Petticoat Pioneers: South Island Women of the Colonial Era*, Book 3, Wellington,
   1980

JEAN DEVANNY

1894–1962

Jean Devanny's life embodied many of the contradictions of the period through
which she lived. She was widely perceived as a sexual liberationist, though she
was also a devoted mother. She was a crusading reformer and revolutionary, but
encountered harsh treatment at the hands of the bureaucracy of the Communist
Party of Australia (CPA). Though centrally a women's liberationist, she also
retained a strong class consciousness developed in her childhood and early adulthood, as the daughter and then the wife of men who were miners. She was a
writer of fiction which focused on the lives of working-class women and/or the
figure of the 'New Woman', and was later to write what she described as 'the
first really proletarian novel in Australia'.

Jane Crook was born in the small mining settlement of Ferntown, near
Collingwood, in Golden Bay. Her father, William, was a miner, but her mother,

Jane, was from the middle classes, being the daughter of a colonel who had fought in India and subsequently in the New Zealand wars. The family had ten children – and the only piano in the settlement.

Jane left school at thirteen to care for her mother, whose health was delicate. On the suggestion of her schoolteacher friend Rose, she changed her name to Jean. In 1911, aged seventeen, she met Hal Devanny at a miners' dance in Puponga, and they were married the same year. Hal Devanny was heavily involved in the politics of the Miners' Union, one of the most radical unions in New Zealand. In many mining towns there were small Marxist study groups, and the Devannys belonged to one in Puponga.

The Devannys' first child, Karl, was born in 1912, and two daughters, Patricia and Erin, followed in quick succession. Jean Devanny managed to combine caring for three small children with playing the piano and reading widely in left-wing and revolutionary literature. In the early 1920s the Devannys were living in Fairfield near Dunedin, and it was there that Erin died. Jean Devanny was grief-stricken and gave up playing the piano. The family moved to Wellington so that Hal could join Bob Semple's tunnelling party driving a tunnel through the Orongorongos. Because the job was well paid, the family was able to buy a boarding-house in Wellington; this experience provided the background to Devanny's second published novel, *Lenore Devine*.

Jean Devanny was writing fiction during the early 1920s, and in 1926 her first novel, *The Butcher Shop*, was published in London. The novel won instant fame, being banned in New Zealand, Australia, and several other places. It also sold 15,000 copies, an impressive total by any standards. It was banned in New Zealand because of 'its frank portrayal of farm conditions [which] was considered detrimental to the Dominion's immigration policy'. *The Butcher Shop* uses the format of the romantic novel to explore the economic and sexual subjugation of women in marriage. The solution to female oppression is seen to lie in socialism: in a socialist state, women and workers will be freed from slavery, and a 'race of emancipated women, free in body and mind, economically independent, choosing their own mates' will march onwards to a goal which cannot yet be visualised.

During these years, Devanny was courted by the Labour Party (whose opinion was that she could have become a prominent Labour politician). While she rejected reformist directions, she did not apparently join the organised Left until shortly after she and her family moved to Australia in August 1929. This was the period when the real impact of the Depression was being felt in Australia, as in New Zealand. Mass meetings in the streets and marches of the unemployed were the stuff of everyday life. After one march in 1930, Devanny was arrested and jailed for four days; she then decided to join the Communist Party.

She rapidly became one of the party's best-known public orators and remained so through the 1930s, making several speaking tours along the east coast of Australia. She was also involved in building up the organisation and solidarity of writers, and was instrumental in the setting up of various writers' and artists' groups in Sydney and Melbourne in the 1930s and 1940s.

When she arrived in Australia, Devanny had already achieved some reputation as a novelist. She had published four novels and a volume of stories before she left New Zealand; three more novels with New Zealand settings were published before work set in Australia began to appear. Her best-known novel in Australia is probably *Sugar Heaven*, published in 1936; this is a 'socialist realist' account of the 1935 cane-cutters' strike in North Queensland. *Sugar Heaven* is also notable for a focus on the lives and political activity of working-class women only rarely found in Australian and New Zealand fiction of this period. Devanny's earlier interest in the representation of non-British characters, including several Maori in her earlier novels, is developed in this novel in her depiction of an Italian activist, Tony, and in her creation of the Yugoslavian Toni Muranivich in the 1938 novel, *Paradise Flow*, which was also written as a play.

Devanny's stance on sexual liberation was always well ahead of her time. While still in New Zealand, she had written a large work on the theory and history of women's oppression, which remains unpublished. Some of the problems she encountered in the Communist Party derived from her birth control lectures in Broken Hill, and her refusal to conform to the public facade of a 'respectable' sexual morality required by many CPA leaders.

Devanny's expulsion from the CPA in the early 1940s is murky. Her own account can be found in her autobiography, *Point of Departure*. Despite her long record as a public party figure and organiser, and her longstanding relationship with J. B. Miles, the general secretary, she was expelled — primarily, she said, as a result of rumours about her sexual morality. She was subsequently re-admitted in 1944.

Partly as a result of continuing tensions with the party and partly because of ill health, Devanny devoted herself much more to writing than to organising during the 1940s. She published 'travel books' (primarily what we now call 'oral history') about Queensland, and began work on a planned trilogy set in the Queensland canefields. Only the first volume, *Cindie*, was published; the second volume, *You Can't Have Everything*, was never published, and the third never written. Devanny left the CPA in 1950 when the party leadership claimed that *Cindie* did not represent fully the semi-slavery of 'Kanaka' workers on the Queensland canefields. As a fervent opponent of racial oppression, she found this hard to accept.

In the early 1940s Devanny began to write her autobiography, analysing her experiences with a view to understanding her own formation and to producing changes in the party. She was plagued by doubts about publishing it, however, because of its potential to feed the anti-communist ideologies of the 1950s. Along with many of her other manuscripts, it remained unpublished when she died of leukaemia in Townsville in 1962.

Devanny has several roles in the history of women in New Zealand and Australia. Her work for the class struggle and also for women's liberation was considerable; she was one of a number of feminists working and writing in New Zealand in the 1920s who believed that the solution to female oppression would come about through socialism. Her contribution to New Zealand literature is beginning to be recognised with the republication of some of her fiction in New Zealand, as well as in Australia and Britain. She was also a pioneer in the use of oral history, both in her later novels and in her 'travel books', particularly in relation to Aboriginals, Melanesians and migrants.

Carole Ferrier & Heather Roberts

Quotations
para.5 M. B. Soljak, 'Outspoken New Zealand Novelist', *NZ Observer*, 16 Dec. 1935, p.9

Unpublished Sources
Jean Devanny papers (including many unpublished manuscripts), James Cook University Library, Townsville

Published Sources
Devanny, Jean. *Point of Departure*, Queensland, 1986
Ferrier, Carole, Introduction to *Cindie*, London, 1986
Ferrier, Carole. 'Jean Devanny's New Zealand Novels', *Hecate*, vol.6 no.1, 1980
Hecate, vol.13 no.1, 1987 (contains a complete bibliography of Devanny's work)
Roberts, Heather. Introduction to *The Butcher Shop*, Auckland, 1981

AIRINI TONORE
AIRINI DONNELLY

?1855-1909

Airini Donnelly, or Airini Tonore as she was known to her Ngati Kahungungu people of Hawke's Bay, was an articulate and resourceful woman who, during the latter part of the nineteenth century, became renowned for her efforts in the Native Land Court and for her grasp of Land Court procedures, land legislation, and whakapapa. 'Her keen and able defence of her people's rights in the Native Land Court was acknowledged to be a revelation of advocacy and understanding of the law.'

Born around the year 1855, she was one of five children of Haromi Te Ata and Karauria Pupu of Puketapu, near Napier. Airini's whakapapa links her closely to several of the noted chiefs of the Ahuriri area. Her father, Karauria, was one of the leaders of a force involved in pursuing Te Kooti in 1868, after his escape from the Chathams. During that campaign, Karauria was seriously wounded and died a few days later. From that time, Airini, then aged about thirteen, went to live with Renata Kawepo, principal chief of Omahu pa (near Hastings) and an uncle of her mother.

Another uncle was Tareha Te Moananui who, during the early 1860s, had built a school at Waiohiki, south of Napier, and employed a teacher. (This was some years before the Native Schools were established.) Airini was probably a pupil there at some stage of her childhood. She was known to have been a fluent speaker of English from an early age. She would have had contact with many Pakeha visitors as Renata Kawepo was well known for his generous hospitality.

One day in 1876 while she was out riding, Airini had a chance encounter with the man who was to become her husband. George Prior Donnelly was born in 1847 in County Tipperary, Ireland, and emigrated to New Zealand with some of his family during the 1860s. When he met up with Airini he was managing 'Gwavas', a large Hawke's Bay estate. An energetic and personable man,

Donnelly pursued Airini with determination. The following year the couple were married, and farmed at 'Crissoge', near Hastings. In 1878, Airini gave birth to a daughter, Maud Airini Tiakitai. A son, Henare Paraea, was born in 1883 but lived for only three months, dying just two weeks after Airini had buried her mother, Haromi.

Both Airini and George were hospitable people. As well as entertaining their friends, neighbours, and relations, they frequently hosted visiting politicians, officials, and dignitaries of the time. They kept a staff of servants, including a gardener and a chauffeur. Balls, dinners, and golfing parties were a regular and enjoyable part of Airini's life. During the Duke and Duchess of Cornwall's visit to New Zealand in 1901, George and Airini were prominent participants in the Rotorua welcome for the Royal couple. Seated beside them in the grandstand, Airini must have made a favourable impression. During a tour of Europe in 1904, she was presented at the Royal Court in London in a formal gown, a diamond tiara, and a head-dress of ostrich plumes.

Over the years, Airini succeeded to land in several different blocks. Together she and George successfully farmed thousands of acres in Hawke's Bay. But it was for her involvement in Native Land Court hearings that Airini became celebrated. While still a young woman, she gradually acquired a detailed working knowledge of Native Land Court procedures and of the relevant legislation. Over a period of some thirty years, Airini appeared many times on behalf of her people before the Land Courts, as well as other judicial bodies. The minute books of the Native Land Courts contain many references to the name of Airini Tonore.

The following story is often related in accounts of Airini's life:
A Native Land Court was sitting in Rangitikei district when word was received that the case was going against her people. The chief Renata, her grand-uncle was ill and could not attend. Suddenly Airini Tonore announced that she would go and represent her uncle and her people. At first her determination to go was opposed. She was quite a young girl at the time and unaccustomed to court procedure. She went, however. When she reached the court the case was practically over, and judgement was about to be delivered in favour of her opponents. She claimed to be heard. The Court demurred. Council objected. But she persisted and insisted on her right to speak for and represent herself and her absent people. Courage won the day and after eight or ten hours of argument and pleading, worthy of Portia, a judgement was recorded recognising substantially the claims of Renata, Airini and those associated with them.

From the 1880s on she was involved in protracted litigation concerning the tenure of the Waimarama Block. Airini, who was eventually to become the principal owner of the block, made every effort to restrict the expansion of European leasehold interests in order that more of the land could be taken up and farmed by other Maori owners. The case against the lease renewals was heard in the Native Land Court, the Native Appellate Court, the Supreme Court, and finally the Court of Appeal. Eventually Airini's interests did prevail, but only after some expensive litigation. Fortunately, the Donnellys had the resources to fund the lengthy legal proceedings.

Airini Tonore is remembered as a warm, charming, and attractive woman with a forceful and determined character, who enjoyed playing golf and attending race-meetings. Very aware of the responsibilities to her people which came with her birth, Airini accepted and continued the tradition of leadership which was her inheritance. She showed great foresight in the importance she placed on retaining tribal land and the control over its use. Airini could be either a strong ally or a very formidable adversary.

On 6 June 1909, Airini, in her mid-fifties, died of cervical cancer at 'Otatara', the family homestead at Taradale. Her tangi was held the following day at Omahu, attended by several thousand mourners. Airini Tonore was laid to rest beside her infant son Henare in the cemetery of St Johns, Omahu.

Tui MacDonald

Quotations
para.1 *M. MäcGregor, Petticoat Pioneers*, p.116
para.7 *Hastings Standard*, 7 June 1909 (obituary)

Unpublished Source
P. H. Garrett, 'Te Whakaruruhau o te iwi: Airini Tonore 1855–1909', research essay, Te Hukutai, Auckland University

Published Sources
Grant, Sydney. *Waimarama*, Palmerston North, 1977
MacGregor, Miriam. *Petticoat Pioneers: North Island Women of the Colonial Era*, Book 1, Wellington, 1973

ELIZABETH DONNELLY

c. 1842-1926

Elizabeth was born in Ireland to a farming couple, James and Mary McCluskey. When she was nineteen she married Felix Donnelly, some seven years older than herself. They moved from County Tyrone to England, and their first child, Mary, was born in Lancashire. They sailed for New Zealand, possibly via Australia, and arrived in 1863 or 1864. The first Otago rush was over, but there was still gold to reward the steady worker.

Thomas Christopher was born 25 December 1865, at the Devonshire diggings at the foot of the Dunstan Mountains in Central Otago. Tinkers, Sugar Pot, and Drybread diggings lay to the north. All four place names have disappeared but Tinkers remains as Matakanui, where the Donnelly family settled.

In the next fifteen years Elizabeth gave birth to ten more children – so few words for so much gestation, labour and plain hard work, or for so much joy. They were the young Elizabeth and the young Felix; Francis; Kate, who became a nun; Margaret, who remained single too, and lived to ninety-eight; three more boys, who did not marry; and two more girls, who did.

In the 1860s and 1870s, as the children were growing in number and size, Tinkers diggings had become a township. There were other families settled nearby, a school, more than one hotel, and a racetrack with an annual race meeting. In 1877 there were five events at the races on 2 January and six the next day. Drybread had a spring meeting as well as one at Christmas, and doubtless Ophir, Ida Valley, and St Bathans held theirs at intervals to suit the wider community.

In 1879 Felix was part-owner of a ground sluice mine known as the Mountain Race Claim. In later years his son Tom would manage the Undaunted Gold Mining and Water Race Company, whose founders had spent three laborious years building twenty miles of fitted stone water-race, and then another ten months sluicing before their first 'wash-up'.

Felix and his fellow-workers used two water jets against a twenty-five-foot face. By night, if not by day, each man working these was out of sight of the other. On the night of Friday 31 October 1879, Felix began his shift at ten o'clock and by half past eleven he was dead, suffocated under a fall of clay and earth. Elizabeth's latest pregnancy withstood this shock, and when the child was born the following March she named her Felicia.

Even with their own home, how would a widow and twelve children survive in the 1880s? Perhaps by a dairy cow, hens, and a vegetable garden, with cash for clothes and shoes coming from a dividend on her late husband's shares in the gold-mine.

Elizabeth did more than survive. By 1885 she owned 200 sheep at Ophir. Numbers and places varied, but for the next forty years she farmed sheep: two spells at Ophir, over ten years at Matakanui, and her last twenty years at Lauder, where she counted her biggest tally – 1,861 sheep – in 1909.

Before farming at Lauder she was also the owner-licensee at the Blacks Hotel at Ophir, where 'the travelling public were well catered for'. By the time the railway was put through she had prospered enough to build the Railway Hotel at Lauder. Her son Daniel was still there in 1916, but it was later sold.

Elizabeth was then living on the farm at Lauder with her single 'children' and small granddaughter, who was the youngest of the eight children of her daughter Elizabeth, who had died in 1907 when the child was only two months

St Bathan's, Central Otago, 1879, was similar to the gold town where Elizabeth Donnelly lived and raised her twelve children. *National Museum/Te Whare Taonga o Aotearoa*

old. At sixty-five Elizabeth Donnelly was fending still for her family, and shouldering the responsibility of a new generation.

Elizabeth died aged eighty-four, and was buried beside Felix at Omakau on the Wednesday before Easter, 1926. *Mavis Donnelly-Crequer*

Quotation
para.9 *NZ Tablet*, 12 May 1926 (obituary)

Unpublished Sources
Information came from family sources.
Inquest on death of Felix Donnelly, J 79/3869, National Archives, Wellington

Published Sources
AJHR, 1885–1928, Annual Sheep Returns
Dunstan Times, 5 April 1926 (obituary)
NZ Tablet, 12 May 1926 (obituary)
Wise's Directory, 1890–91, 1894–95, 1900, 1905, 1910, 1916

UNUI DOO

1873–1938

Unui Doo, matriarch of the Thomas Wong Doo clan, came to Auckland around 1915. One of the few Chinese women in the country, she worked in her husband's Chinese general store, located first in Wakefield Street, then Victoria Street, and finally in Hobson Street. The centre of her activities, in other words, was Auckland's old Chinatown.

She was born Chan Yau-nui, a humble name simply meaning 'daughter of the Chan family'. 'U Nui' (daughter) was the name she was called by her parents. Her home county was Sunwui [Xinhui], one of the four counties collectively known as Szeyap [Siyi] in the southern province of Kwangtung [Guangdong]. It was from this area that most of the Chinese in the United States, Canada, Australia, and New Zealand came. Like many who emigrated from Sunwui, Unui was from humble peasant stock. Her family must have been comparatively well-to-do, however, for she had the tiny and dainty bound feet which might entitle her to an upper-class marriage.

When Unui was nineteen by Chinese reckoning she married Thomas Wong Doo, a young man from the 'New Gold Mountain', as New Zealand was known. (The Chinese use the lunar calendar for counting their age. The baby's gestation period is also counted. So a baby born in the last month of the Chinese year will be three when the new year comes.) Her husband was from the same county, and had emigrated to New Zealand as a teenager. His family, the Wongs, had been extremely poor, and Thomas Wong Doo was on the verge of being sold by his parents when the harvests were especially bad one year. Fortunately, his two elder brothers had already started up as market gardeners and Chinese grocers in Auckland, and the eldest brother, Wong Ngong Gi, sent for the boy and brought him up. Wong Ngong Gi had come to New Zealand as a gold-miner in the late 1880s, and had saved up enough to start market gardening when the gold ran out.

By the time Thomas Wong Doo returned to China to find a wife, he was a hard-working market gardener still making his way in the world. The match-makers, however, viewed anyone from the 'Gold Mountains' as an eligible bach-elor. After their marriage, Unui and Thomas Wong Doo spent a year together in their home village, a well-earned holiday for the 'Gold Mountain Man'. Soon after the birth of their eldest son, he left again for New Zealand. Unui and the baby stayed behind in China, as was customary for the families of New Zealand Chinese men. Besides the New Zealand government's restrictive immigration laws (£100 poll-tax and an English test), the social climate in New Zealand was also intensely anti-Chinese.

Unui Doo looked after her in-laws, and reared the baby single-handed. She lived frugally on the remittances sent by her husband, consoling herself that if he worked hard enough he might be able to come home for a visit after another five or ten years. He did not let her down; he saved enough to buy a market garden in West Auckland, in an area known as 'Chinaman's Hill', then bought farms in Mangere and Pukekohe as well, leasing them out to fellow countrymen who had come as bachelor workers.

Around 1914, Unui received her husband's letter asking her to come to Auckland. His elder brothers were getting old and, like all Chinese men of the time, wanted to 'go back to the Tang Mountains' to spend their last years. Thomas Wong Doo saw his opportunity. He bought their grocery shop, the Wong Ngong Gi, and sent for his wife. Luckily for Unui Doo, her husband had the foresight to become a naturalised New Zealand citizen before the 1907 Nationality Act, which denied citizenship as well as permanent residency to all Chinese people.

When Unui Doo arrived in Auckland in 1915, she was in her early forties. She had two boys by then, Thomas and Norman. Photographs show her as a tall, strong woman, with a square face, broad forehead, bright eyes, and firm lips. She had tiny bound feet, which she unbound after coming to New Zealand. Since the insteps had been broken, they never grew back to normal size. But she moved quickly about on her foot stumps, carrying out her household chores and con-siderable social duties.

Unui Doo lived and worked in her husband's Chinese grocery shop in Wakefield Street. They imported Chinese foodstuffs, rice, soya sauce and other necessities, and served their countrymen well. The shop became a kind of com-munity centre, social club, pseudo-bank, and post office, as well as an immi-gration advice centre. The Chinese people from as far north as Whangarei and as far south as Ohakune congregated there for their provisions and to exchange news. In time, New Zealand immigration officials also turned to the Wong Doos for help in interpreting and in other dealings with the Chinese. Unui was always present in the shop, an indispensable figure in the Auckland Chinese community.

As mistress of the Wong Doo household, Unui looked after the family as well as tending the shop. Baby Willy, later to become the famous acupuncturist William Wong Doo, was born in 1916. The children were always immaculately dressed in Western-style clothing, all sewn by Unui. She herself preferred darker coloured clothes, either navy blue or brown, in simple Western style, often covered with an apron. Her hair was always drawn back tightly into a bun. She played gracious hostess to all visitors, Chinese and Westerners, who called in for

Unui Doo with her sons Thomas and Norman before leaving for New Zealand. *Family Collection*

various reasons. Her grandson Thomas recalled 'the extremely colourful days when all the market gardeners called in for their provisions, stayed for meals and drinks before going their separate ways' to various rural centres in the North Island. Unui had to be a great cook, for she was expected to turn out memorable meals for men who normally ate simply and had no time to cook. She was a mother figure to all those lonely single Chinese men, too. 'She was the community's cloth-mender and haberdasher. Anyone with a ripped coat turned to Grandma Doo.' She also cared for them when they were sick: 'It was not that she wanted to be a Florence Nightingale, but without their own women in New Zealand, where could the men turn to?' Like many of her contemporaries, Unui had considerable knowledge of herbal medicine. Her son Norman remembered how she would brew up bitter-tasting health drinks in a big copper and put it outside the shop for passers-by to drink for free during the 1918 influenza epidemic.

A few years after Unui's arrival, the Thomas Wong Doo shop moved to 109 Victoria Street. The importing business was going well, and the family decided to export to China dried fungus, which grew wild in New Zealand and was considered a great delicacy in China. Business boomed, and the shop attic became the temporary living quarters of Chinese men landing in Auckland or waiting for ships to take them back to China.

No, of course you don't charge people board and lodging, they might leave a red-packet of 'lucky money'. But you never charge them . . . Grandma was quite astute, looking back, I think her graciousness and warmth must have helped to promote good business connections for the family shop.

From such comments by her descendants one can glean what a hectic life Unui led. She started her day early, preparing cooked breakfasts for her family and house guests. Late into the night she would still be sewing and darning. Her chores were considerably lightened when she acquired her daughters-in-law. Unui was illiterate, and she disliked using outsiders for business correspondence. Nor was her son's Chinese good enough for business transactions with Chinese suppliers. So Unui decided that her daughters-in-law must be fluent in written and spoken Chinese. Like other young Chinese men in New Zealand, her eldest son Thomas Doo Junior returned to China to look for a bride in 1922. Unui and her husband both went too. Matchmakers would usually seek good-looking girls from reputable families, but the Wong Doos introduced a literacy and calligraphy test for the prospective brides as well. They chose Lily Lam, a Canadian Chinese girl who had returned to China for a proper education. Lily was only seventeen when she joined her mother-in-law's house. She remembers Unui as stern and demanding, but very fair and loving as well. All household duties were quickly taught to the young woman. Lily gave birth to all her babies at home, which was the upper storey of the shop. Unui would make sure that her daughter-in-law stayed in bed for a complete rest of two weeks, and prepared all the special ginger concoction and rice wine to restore her health.

In 1932, Unui acquired her second daughter-in-law. By then the family's business was booming. The three sons had recently started the British and Eastern Wholesalers, mainly importing and distributing Chinese curios, camphor chests, and tablecloths to all over New Zealand. Unui and her husband decided to stay in China in semi-retirement, leaving the business for their sons to run.

By 1936, however, the whole family had returned to Auckland. This time Unui brought back third son Willy and his new bride Helen, a graduate of Canton's famous True Light Girls' College. The Japanese had started their invasion of Manchuria in 1931, and by 1936 there were rumours of further Japanese encroachment into China.

Unui was active to her last days. She presided over three daughters-in-law and passed on to them the family rules of frugality and loyalty. She strictly observed ancestral worship, and paid homage to Lord Kwan, a god of righteousness and honesty in the popular Chinese pantheon. She had his image fitted in the kitchen and performed rites religiously. She believed that it was because her husband and sons had treated their friends with righteousness that the Doo family was especially blessed. Parties became ever bigger, 'often twenty to thirty guests, all the men eating in the front, and the womenfolk ate in the kitchen'. People stayed for chats and played mahjong with great merriment, but the Doo women never played.

Unui Doo died in 1938, the year after Japan invaded southern China. She was sixty-six by Chinese reckoning. Her funeral was said to be one of the most lavish and spectacular that Auckland had ever witnessed. 'The procession was three miles long.'   *Manying Ip*

Unpublished Sources
Interviews with Lily, Norman, Helen, Thomas, Dennis, and Winnie Doo; and with James Letcher, Auckland customs officer, 1927–33. All quotations are from these interviews.

Certificate of Registration (re-entry permits) of Chinese persons leaving Auckland, A/234, National Archives, Auckland

Published Sources

Ip, Manying. 'The Story of Lily Doo', *Home Away from Home*, Auckland, 1990, pp.50–65

FLORA DORLING

1875–1954

My mother Flora was the third of eight children of Samuel and Ngawini Yates. She and her brothers and sisters were all born at Paua on the shores of Parengarenga Harbour in the far north. Virtually all the land from Te Kao northwards was either owned or controlled by Samuel and Ngawini. Ngawini was of the Te Rarawa tribe from the southern end of the Aupouri Peninsula; her mother Kataraina is buried at Ahipara and her father John Murray and brother David (Reewi) are buried at Pukepoto, just a few miles away. Samuel Yates, an English Jew who had been educated to be a solicitor, came to the far north in 1863. He later met and married Ngawini and together they built up their large farming and kauri gum business.

Ngawini Yates, left, with her daughter Flora Dorling, c.1900. *Gwen Cameron*

At Paua there was a wharf, a general store, a butcher's shop, a gum-sorting shed, and a boarding-house – all part of the family 'empire'. When the gum trade was at its height, around 1890, there were 300 diggers bringing gum to be sorted, many of them Yugoslavs who were to become major settlers in the north. From Paua the gum was sent to Auckland for export.

Life for a young girl at Paua was carefree, among the bustle of the large happy family and thriving business interests. Flora spoke only Maori until, when she was seven, Miss Pringle came from England to be the children's governess. She taught them to speak and write English. Later the older girls were sent to board at Miss Laws' school in Portland Road, Auckland. Emily, two years older than Flora, was quick and clever; Flora was slower and dreamier.

Holidays at home were spent riding and rowing – it was nothing to ride all the way down Ninety Mile Beach and across to Mangonui to dance all night, then ride home the next day. Flora, a big girl, was a strong rower, but she hated to be in the sea – the 'tide' as she called it. There were frequent long visits from friends and family.

After leaving school, Flora returned to Paua to work in the general store as postmistress. It was there that she met her future husband, Captain Edward Dorling, a handsome young Englishman who worked for the Northern Steam Ship Company, trading goods and transporting gum for the Yates family. They were married on 30 May 1900 at the registry office in Auckland. In September of that year Flora's father, Samuel Yates, died.

In the early years of their marriage Ted and Flora were to shift house several times. Their first two daughters, Alma Esther Ngawini and Annette Rachel, were born in Ponsonby. From there they moved to Onehunga, handy for coastal shipping men, then to Mt Eden, where Flora ran a poultry farm. She travelled to Paua with the little girls for summer holidays. But in 1910 Ngawini, Flora's mother, died and the extensive family property up north was sold.

After a disastrous fire at the poultry farm, a new home was built in Epsom, from heart kauri Ted brought from the Hokianga. He established a large garden and there were just enough chooks to keep the family in eggs. John Hongi, their son, was born in 1912. He was to live only three weeks, and Flora grieved sorely for his death. The following summer Ted announced to Flora, Alma, and Annette that he had bought tickets for them all to go 'home' to England to spend some time with his family at Bacton, Suffolk. A voyage round the world in 1913 went via Sydney and Suez; Ted and Flora also spent some precious time on their own in Scandinavia.

A third daughter, Gwen Yates, was born in 1916. Flora found the new baby a handful, but was later to say she was 'one of the best things that had happened to her'. Nineteen-twenty saw the family move again to another heart-kauri house in Remuera. A second fire gutted the garage and the car, and the family moved for the final time to 116 Great South Road, Remuera. Flora was forty-nine and beginning again. But after only a few years they were devastated yet again by fire, while Ted was away at sea. When the house was rebuilt, Flora and Ted nurtured on flat land a large and beautiful garden. Visitors were always taken for a 'turn' around the garden and never left without a gift of flowers, fruit or vegetables. Always an early riser, Flora would gather flowers and maidenhair fern, walk into Newmarket to sell them to Sibun's the florist, and be home in time to prepare breakfast. Nieces en route from Wellington to the north would be met at Newmarket station by Aunty Flora, carrying a basketful of breakfast for them.

When Ted retired, there was more time to spend together, gardening, walking, motoring, drinking tea in the sun. Alma, with her husband and daughter, lived next door. Annette, recently widowed, returned to live with her parents. When Gwen's husband was away at war, she and her small daughters came to stay. Maori was spoken, especially with family and friends from 'up north' who came to stay. Flora used to teach her granddaughters Maori and remained a fluent Maori speaker all her life.

There were games of cards – patience, five hundred, and bridge. Flora was not above cheating at times, especially when a hand of patience was proving stubborn. She overbid recklessly to capture kitty at five hundred. Friday night was family night; dinner was served in the big dining-room and everybody helped, scrubbing down the kauri kitchen benches at the end. Sunday was church at St Mark's, always sitting on the same pew, walking there and back on a fine day.

Ted died in 1945 and there were nine years of widowhood ahead, although Flora's family were always close by. On Easter Sunday 1954, Flora died in the bed she had shared with her husband, her children, and her grandchildren. She is buried beside her son, her son-in-law, and her husband. A gracious, beloved, and loving lady: I am lucky she was my mother.   *Gwen Yates Cameron*

Unpublished Sources
Papers in possession of the Yates and Dorling families
Published Sources
The Cyclopedia of New Zealand, Wellington, 1894
Keene, F. *Under Northland Skies: Forty Women of Northland*, Whangarei, 1984

CATHERINE DOUGLAS

1874–1946

Catherine Douglas campaigned indefatigably for the rights of mothers and poor families, particularly during the Depression of the 1920s and 1930s.

Like many women of her time, she had a hard life. Born Catherine Gaffney in Shannon, Ireland, she was orphaned young, and raised and educated in Blackrock Convent, Dublin. She came to New Zealand in 1894 at the age of twenty on the SS *Gothic*. An uncle in New Zealand paid her passage and she worked in his hotels until 1903, when she married George Douglas, an Australian who worked on the railways and later as a parliamentary messenger. In 1908 the couple moved to Johnsonville, Wellington, where Catherine was to spend the rest of her life. Despite unemployment caused by the Depression and illness, the marriage was happy, and produced eight children. At times the family was forced to live off the produce of their two acres of land where they had a good vegetable garden, and kept hens and a goat for milk.

While being practical in her help for others less fortunate, Catherine also wrote letters to newspapers and a booklet entitled *The Chastener: A Book for Mothers*, which she entered into a competition for the prevention of crime in America in 1925.

Poverty was the source of many problems in Catherine's opinion, and she believed that mothers should receive a wage to enable them to feed and educate their children adequately.

Mothers work eighteen hours a day . . . foster mothers get paid . . . why the real mothers' worth is not recognised is a mystery. Some mothers were earning high salaries before marriage. When we get married, we give up all . . . every mother should have a small wage as she has to provide when her husband is ill or out of work.

Catherine believed that children were the country's greatest resource and potential, and that parents should have the money to care for them properly. (She admired the spirit of Michael Joseph Savage who voiced publicly her own beliefs.)

Her Irish farming background made her feel strongly about the usurpation of land, and she was critical of those in New Zealand who had 'grabbed [their land] for a few sticks of tobacco' and still wanted more. She believed that every family should have enough land to grow their own fruit and vegetables.

Appalled by the pain and futility of the First World War, Catherine wrote letters to the editor of the *Evening Post* denouncing war and promoting peace.

Men are drilled like dumb driven cattle . . .
All went to war with the firm belief that we would have better conditions to live under. The war has failed hopelessly, and workers are worse off now than before the war.

Catherine believed that if Christian principles were followed, the world's problems would be solved or at least eased. She was one of the pioneers of the Johnsonville parish of SS Peter and Paul, and 'in a quiet and unobtrusive manner . . . worked unceasingly for the establishment of the church, school and presbytery'. She imparted her strong Catholic faith to her eight children, three of whom entered religious orders. One son, Francis Vernon Douglas, became a Columban missionary in the Philippines. During the Japanese occupation of the Philippines, he was arrested and tortured for three days by the Japanese military police for information. Although devastated by the death of her son, Catherine was proud that he had withstood torture and died rather than betray those who had trusted him.

Catherine Douglas's life and writing exemplified her never-ending fight to make the world a better place for working-class families.   *Patricia Brooks*

Quotations
para.4 C. Douglas, *The Chastener*, p.9
para.6 C. Douglas, p.12
para.7 C. Douglas, pp.16,13
para.8 *Zealandia*, 5 Sept. 1946

Published Sources
Douglas, Catherine. *The Chastener: A Book for Mothers*, Wellington, 1925
Evening Post, 24 Feb. 1934; 11 March 1934; 28 Sept. 1934
Zealandia, 5 Sept. 1946 (obituary)

MARY DREAVER

1887–1961

Mary Manson Bain, the eldest of a family of thirteen children, was born in Dunedin on 31 March 1887. Her Irish mother, Hanna Josephine (born Kiely), is remembered as a pleasing singer. Her father, Alexander Manson Bain, had been involved in working-class politics in Scotland, and became well known in this field in New Zealand. Mary grew up in Dunedin where from the age of eighteen she competed with considerable success in oratory, elocution, and dramatic art competitions. Her early plans to become a Methodist missionary came to an end in 1911 with her marriage to Andrew James Dreaver, a grocer and former Otago-Southland featherweight boxing champion. They lived in Auckland where their six children were born between 1912 and 1925. During these years Mary studied at Seddon Memorial Technical College, took extension classes at Auckland University College, and gained a licentiate of the London College of Music for the pianoforte.

Mary was involved in numerous community activities and in local music circles. Her teaching of music, drama, public speaking and elocution was an important source of income for the family during the Depression. In radio, she earned a high profile hosting programmes directed at women from the late 1920s, as 'Maorilander' ten years later, and again as a director and welfare officer of 1ZB's Happiness Club in the late 1950s. Another interest was astrology; she hosted a radio slot on Radio 1ZM and wrote a column for the *New Zealand Woman's Weekly*. She also lectured for the Theosophist Society and in about 1938 became the first woman ordained as a pastor of the National Spiritualist Church of New Zealand. She served as president of the People's Health Society, and she was proud that she was able to swim and play hockey and billiards until late in life. In 1931 she was appointed a justice of the peace, having actively campaigned for women's right to serve. A keen painter, she exhibited her work and served as vice-president of the New Zealand Fellowship of Artists.

It was not until around 1918 that she became widely associated with industrial and political activities in Auckland. Strong, determined and energetic with a well-developed self-esteem, Mary aimed for political prominence as she actively promoted women's rights and articulated their needs. Health care and the plight of the unemployed were particular concerns. There were few women with a public profile at the time and she became a positive role model for other women.

In 1922 she joined the Women's International Political League (which in 1925 became the Auckland Women's Branch of the Labour Party). As the league's delegate to the National Council of Women, her agreement with the council's objectives for politically independent women became a source of conflict with the league; her advocacy of support for the election to parliament of women regardless of political persuasion led to her expulsion from the branch in September 1931. Nevertheless, she spent many years as an active member of the New Zealand Labour Party. She was a member of the Auckland Labour Party Executive for a number of years – a powerful party position.

In 1938 she was a successful Labour candidate on the Auckland City Council and held office until 1944 and again from 1953. During a period of over twenty years she served on an impressive range of boards, including the Auckland Hospital and Charitable Aid Board, Drainage Board, Power Board, and Harbour Board. In 1939 she became the first woman member of the Auckland Transport Board, serving for five years.

Mary stood (unsuccessfully) as the Labour candidate for the Remuera seat at the 1938 general election. The experience proved useful, however, when she was selected as Labour candidate for the Waitemata by-election in 1941. Mary Dreaver became the third woman member of parliament, joining her contemporary, Catherine Stewart. She was an active MP and made numerous speeches on a wide range of issues, being particularly associated with social security measures and the Women Jurors Bill. Unfortunately she remained there only two years before losing her seat by a narrow margin. She was appointed to the Legislative Council in 1946 and remained there until the Upper House was abolished. Her maiden speech identifies clearly her role as a Labour MP, working for women in parliament:

It has often been said that the making of laws is a job for men only and that women should keep to their homes. I know many men have had that thought in their minds for generations, applauding masculine politics when they were good and keeping discreet silence when they were bad . . . I feel that I have the goodwill of many women in New Zealand, as well as that of the people in my own electorate, and I venture to add that the economic experience of women in the home provides the best reason for their taking a parliamentary part in the shaping of what I would call 'domestic' legislation . . .

In October 1942 two women members of parliament – Mary Dreaver and Mary Grigg – donned uniform and travelled through the country promoting and recruiting for the Women's Land Service (Army). Recognition of her work culminated in the award of an MBE in 1946 for her contribution to the community. During the 1950s she maintained her public profile as an Auckland City Councillor, as director of the New Zealand Happiness Club, and as an active minister and president of the National Spiritualist Church. She died in July 1961 at the age of seventy-four, remembered as a very pleasant woman, a loyal supporter of the labour cause, and an activist on behalf of the under-privileged.

Liz Gordon

Quotation
para.7 *NZ Parliamentary Debates*, 7 Aug. 1941, vol.260, p.25

Unpublished Sources
H. M. Chandler, 'Mary Manson Dreaver – Political Woman', MA research essay, Auckland, 1984

Published Sources
NZ Herald, 20 July 1961; 10 Aug. 1973
NZ Listener, 22 Aug. 1941
Scholefield, G. H. (ed.) *Who's Who in New Zealand*, 5th edn, Wellington, 1951
Woman Today, 1 May 1938

HYPATIA DREWET

1886-1978

Hypatia (Patia) Morrell, named for Charles Kingsley's heroine, came with her parents and five older siblings to remote bush-clad Waimamaku, near the Hokianga, in 1888. Her father, James Morrell, one of the main instigators of a co-operative socialist community there, the Christchurch Village Settlement Association, set up to take advantage of the government's land settlement scheme and to put into practice ideals of co-operative living and working. Her mother, Susan Morrell, acted as the small community's midwife and nurse for many years. The last daughter, Marama, was born in 1889. James Morrell was killed in an accident in 1895.

Like many other country children at that time, Patia finished her schooling at Form Two. For the next few years she participated fully in community life, often helping the overburdened women of the area.

The family was passionately musical. All of them played at least one instrument and several of them performed in public. Patia played the piccolo and her first public performance was with her brother and sisters at a farewell dance in 1901 for her former schoolteacher, Mr Cahill. 'We played a waltz. Such a few boys to dance.'

All the Morrells kept daily diaries. Patia, always outgoing and gregarious, noted all the parties, dances, and concerts in the district, as well as the doings of her older sisters and of her beloved brother and music teacher, Lou.

In about 1906–7, she married Frank Drewet, a farmer who lived near the community. They had four daughters: Hilda, Mabel, Nell, and Sylvia (Tibby). In 1917, when Patia was thirty-one, Frank died of cancer. She applied for the job of postmistress at Waimamaku; a house was built for her opposite the post office.

For the next twenty-two years, she worked to bring up her daughters, as well as being a central figure in Waimamaku. Postmistresses were paid a very small wage but, with skilful management, the family system of trading garden and farm produce, and the support of her ever-strong mother nearby, Patia and her family coped well. Her daughter Tibby recalls: 'The only thing she ever bought on time payment was a piano.'

Some thought her bold when she cut her hair short for convenience, but no one ever questioned her integrity. Honest to the point of bluntness, she was also unfailingly generous and hospitable. Not one of her thousands of visitors ever left her house without a bite to eat.

In 1939, her daughters now all married, Patia retired from the post office. She refused to become a justice of the peace. The next few years she spent doing

Hypatia Morrell (later Drewet), right, c.1906. Riding on the jigger with her are her sister Rose, Frank Drewet and George White. Hypatia later married Frank; Rose married George. *Mason Family*

various jobs in Auckland, taking bus tours round the country, keeping up with her family, and of course playing music and writing her dairy.

Her last years were spent in Dargaville, involved in many community groups, including the Dargaville Orchestra. Elderly as she now was, she won a musical competition playing the tin whistle. Her granddaughter remembers her in her eighties hearing small children do their reading.

She died in Dargaville in 1978. Practical to the end, she donated her body to science.

Janine McVeagh

Unpublished Sources
Family members have supplied information for this essay.
Hypatia Drewet, Diaries, AIM (the quotation in para.3 is from this source)
Louis Morrell, Diaries, AIM

MARIA DRONKE

1904–1987

Actor, voice teacher, and producer, Maria Dronke was born in Berlin in 1904, the daughter of Dr S. Kronfeld, a barrister, and his wife, Laura Liebmann. Educated at the Dorotheen Lyceum where she became dux, she went on to study philosophy and modern literature at the University of Berlin. She was trained in voice by Professor Daniel at the Berlin Conservatory of Music, and later taught there.

In 1924 she gave her first public literary recital at the Meistersaal, Berlin. From this performance she was contracted to work in the theatre, taking the stage name Maria Korten. For seven years she played leading classical roles in major theatres: Ophelia, Portia, Titania, Gretchen as well as Helena in *Faust*, Minna in *Minna von Barnhelm*, Elisabeth in *Don Carlos*. For two years she was engaged in Vienna at the Burgtheater, and in Berlin was directed in the role of Juliet by Max Reinhardt.

In 1924 she also took religious instruction and was received into the Catholic Church.

On a holiday cruise Maria was seated at table with a young judge, John Dronke. She hoped he wouldn't interrupt her reading schedule. He decided she was Spanish and wondered why this young foreigner had launched herself into such esoteric and literary volumes in German. They were married in 1931: it was to be a successful and enduring love-match. Their two children were born in Germany, Peter Ernst Michael in 1934, and Maria Gabriele in 1935.

Maria Dronke, c.1944, 'volatile, brimful of temperament and never tepid'. *Photographed by Bristow Morley, Marei Bollinger*

With the rise of the Nazi Party, Maria and her children, with their Jewish blood, were no longer secure. With difficulty they escaped to England and waited to be assigned a new country.

Finally the stiff doors of immigration creaked open and New Zealand accepted the Dronke family. Maria, John, Peter, and Marei reached Wellington, the city that became their much-loved home, in August 1939. Frieda Burkhardt ('Lohlein'), the fifth member of their party, had been with Maria from the start. As governess, dresser in the theatre, nanny to the children, she now held the home together in all the ways the word 'housekeeper' implies. It was Lohlein who enabled Maria to earn the major part of the family income where her talents were so effective – voice training, and working with young actors.

By admitting these and other refugees, New Zealand allowed a different light to penetrate, an expansion to living that left the careful natives gasping, exhilarated. I was sixteen when I met Maria. I was supposed to be learning German, but this soon overflowed into literature, both English and German, and finally I became one of her acting students. I remember a woman of particular beauty, and a voice of extraordinary quality: trained, but blessed by nature. Maria had a sure, energetic intellect, with a vitality that left a sixteen-year-old in need of a good rest after some hours in her company. She was volatile, brimful of temperament, and never tepid.

Theatrical entrepreneur Dan O'Connor recognised Maria's value, and created many opportunities, touring her in *Cradle Song* and *Deirdre of the Sorrows*. Most important were her poetry recitals. On her poetry reading tours (managed by O'Connor) Maria discovered and revealed to New Zealanders their own poets: R. A. K. Mason, Ursula Bethell, A. R. D. Fairburn, Allen Curnow, Denis Glover, Louis Johnson, and the young James K. Baxter. Maria also acted in and produced many plays. Apart from Shakespeare, she was most interested in the plays and poetry of T. S. Eliot. She had the ability to elucidate and distil the essence of the drama for both players and audiences.

Maria's influence on young people was important to the development of professional theatre in New Zealand. It was for 'services to the performing arts' that she received an OBE in 1979, a deserved acknowledgement of the Dronkes' contribution to New Zealand. She returned to university (at Victoria) in her later years and took an MA with honours in English and German.

John meanwhile was employed in the Justice Department; he also played double bass in the National Orchestra. When he died in 1982, the honey was gone from Maria's life. She lived on for five years in a nursing home, confiding once to me that she liked to be alone in her room where memories flooded back and old poems revived themselves in her mind.

> *At night she filled*
> *The arid hospital room*
> *With dreams and memories*
> *Her beautiful aged face cradled*
> *In crossed regulation pillows.*
> *She laughed and confided with shadows*
> *Held out her hands to admirers*
> *And to the one deep and only love*
> *Who waited for her in the dark*
> *Only a few heart beats away.*

Maria died in 1987. She lives on in the hearts of the people she touched and influenced, and her remarkable voice will sound in their minds forever.

Edith Campion

Sources
Family and friends have provided information. The poem is by Edith Campion.

FREDA DU FAUR

1882-1935

Emmeline Freda Du Faur was not the first woman to climb New Zealand's mountains, and she has been followed by many outstanding female mountaineers since. But her exploits made immediate history, and she has captured the imaginations of New Zealanders through the decades. The first ascent of Mt Cook by a woman (and at that time the fastest ascent on record) and the first ever traverse of the three peaks of Mt Cook are credited to this diminutive, camera-shy woman.

Freda, the daughter of Blanche (born Woolley) and Frederick Du Faur, a wealthy Sydney engineer, lived in typical Edwardian comfort at her family home in suburban Turra Murra, near what is now the Kuringai Chase National Park. It was the rocks, gullies, and unexplored sandstone ridges criss-crossing the reserve that set free her adventurous, courageous spirit as she explored and scrambled with her little dog 'Possie'. The skill gained here was to reward her well on high icy ridges across the Tasman Sea.

Freda came to New Zealand in 1906 when she visited the Christchurch Exhibition. Here she saw a photograph of Aorangi (Mt Cook), 'The Cloud Piercer', which set her hopes on fire. She travelled to 'The Hermitage' at Mt Cook and lost her heart to the mountains:

From the moment my eyes rested on the snow-clad Alps I worshipped their beauty and was filled with a passionate longing to touch those shining snows, to climb to their height of silence and solitude, and to feel myself one with the mighty forces around me . . . The greatest peaks towering into the sky before me touched a chord that all the wonders of my own land had never set vibrating . . .

Freda had time only for a walk up on Sealy Ridge that year, before a cablegram called her away. Family matters occupied her in Sydney for the next year, along with her uncompleted nursing training. Her mother's sudden death in 1907 was a shock she shared with her father, but it also freed her from some family responsibilities. In 1908 she returned to the Southern Alps for a fortnight of low-level walks and climbs. Chief guide Peter Graham, who was to become her mentor and teacher, saw her ambition and ability, and did not hesitate to support her quest to become a mountaineer.

The 1909 season heralded Freda's real début in the Southern Alps. Preliminary fitness training on a traverse of Mts Kinsey and Wakefield led to ascents of Mt Sealy and the Nun's Veil, but not without being confronted with unwanted advice from the self-appointed moral doyennes of 'The Hermitage' resort who were steeped in the prudery of the day.

At the moment there was no one in the hotel who could or would climb Mount Sealy; there was not the ghost of a climber on the premises, only women who found a two-mile walk quite sufficient for their powers. This they could not deny, but they assured me in all seriousness that if I went out alone with a guide I would lose my reputation.

The fact that the guide in question was Peter Graham, whose reputation as a man was one at which the most rigid moralist could not cavil, made no difference.

Freda replied gently but firmly that: 'if my reputation were so fragile a thing that it would not bear such a test, then I would be very well rid of a useless article.'

She flouted convention and, with a little compromise, went on her way. To protect her guides and to prevent gossipers from getting too enthusiastic, she paid

Freda Du Faur on one of her numerous visits to the Southern Alps, 1906–13.
Guy Mannering Collection

197

extra for a second guide to act as 'chaperone'. This was an unwelcome drain on her limited capital, which seems to have originated from family sources.

Freda completed her season with climbs of loose-rocked Mt Malte Brun and the heavily crevassed Minarets, which gave her a first taste of 'real ice work'. She wrote, in her book *The Conquest of Mount Cook and Other Climbs*, of her feelings while navigating the glacial maze below the Minarets:

My mind was chaos, my nerves on edge, but fortunately neither of these are exposed to an unsympathetic world; and my face, thanks to the long training of two brothers who jeered at me for a girl baby if I dared funk anything, was no doubt smiling and bland . . .

She did not always find the going easy, but had a strength of will to match the rugged terrain.

As if geographical difficulties were not enough, there was a sartorial problem to solve. Freda's climbing outfit was a knee-length skirt, described by Peter Graham as 'a frill', over knickerbockers; if the skirt got in the way she would remove it and just climb in the trousers – a decadent act according to contemporary propriety. Sleeping in a separate tent to her guides was often cold, and these factors, plus the additional expenses of 'chaperones', made her almost wish to take the easiest solution – a husband.

The news that Freda was going to attempt Mt Cook generated disapproval and criticism. It was 'madness' and 'an unjustifiable' risk. The first attempt, in February 1910, was foiled by bad conditions on the mountain, so it was not until 3 December that year that she stood on the summit, 'feeling very little, very lonely, and much inclined to cry'. All her detractors were now silenced.

Freda went on over the next few seasons to climb Mts De La Beche, Silberhorn, Green, Walter, Chudleigh, Sebastopol, Tasman, Dampier, and Lendenfeld, and to make traverses of Mts Cook and Sefton. Her achievements are commemorated in three peaks in the area – Mt Du Faur, Mt Cadogan which she named after a great friend, Muriel Minnie Cadogan, and Mt Nazomi which she also named. The summer of 1913 was the last to see Freda Du Faur high among alpine peaks. She bid farewell to New Zealand, took her memories to Australia and soon after to England, where she lived until about 1930. Life was never the same again for Freda. Her courageous battle against social convention had taken its toll. The death in 1929 of Muriel, her long-standing friend and companion, was a great distress from which possibly she never recovered. Freda died, lonely and unhappy, at her home in Sydney in 1935. *Pip Lynch*

Quotations
para.3 F. Du Faur, *The Conquest of Mount Cook* (1915 edition), p.27
para.5 F. Du Faur, p.36
para.7 F. Du Faur, p.36
para.9 F. Du Faur, p.58

Published Sources
Du Faur, Freda. *The Conquest of Mount Cook and Other Climbs*, London, 1915; Christchurch, 1977
NZ Herald, 9 June 1984

EILEEN DUGGAN

1894-1072

Repudiating D'Arcy Cresswell's criticism of Eileen Duggan's poetry in 1931 Robin Hyde commented in the *New Zealand Observer*, 'Mr D'Arcy Cresswell isn't fit to tie up Miss Duggan's shoe laces.' The Irish critic and friend of W. B. Yeats, A. E. (G. W. Russell), said of her first volume, 'She has the entry to the lovely places of the spirit . . . If she keeps to her own place people will come to her in due course and she will get due recognition for what is in her.' Yet seventy years later, it seems Pat Lawlor was right when he commented regretfully after her death that Eileen Duggan 'could almost be listed . . . as New Zealand's forgotten poet.'

Born on 21 May 1894, Eileen May Duggan was the daughter of Irish immigrants John and Julia Duggan from County Kerry, who settled in Tua Marina near Blenheim. As a child, the fourth and youngest daughter, she grew up in her family's Catholic faith, and spent much of her time listening to the stories of the early settlers, to the folk tales and tragedies of Ireland and exploring the countryside around the Wairau. These early experiences were central to her poetry as one of her most successful lyrics illustrates:

> The tides run up the Wairau
> That fights against their flow.
> My heart and it together
> Are running salt and snow . . .

> 'The Tides Run Up the Wairau'

Winner of a Junior National Scholarship, she attended the Tua Marina school and Marlborough Girls' College before enrolling at Wellington teachers college. In 1918 she graduated from Victoria University College with an MA (first class honours) in history. The recipient of a Jacob Joseph Scholarship, she returned to Victoria as a junior lecturer after a short period of secondary teaching. Describing herself as 'the worst lecturer they had', she proved herself to be not only exceptionally intelligent but willing to express her views clearly and independently, even when they were not particularly popular in the history department.

In 1921 Evelyn, the sister to whom she was closest, died suddenly; two years later her parents had died within five months of each other. Troubled by ill health and this loss, wearied by the demands of teaching, Eileen Duggan decided to remain in Wellington but to retire and to write full time, in spite of financial difficulties.

In 1921 her first volume *Poems* was published, followed by *New Zealand Bird Songs* (1929), *Poems* (1937), *New Zealand Poems* (1940) and *More Poems* (1951). In September 1927 she began writing the women's page for the *New Zealand Tablet*. Despite some reservations, she continued her idiosyncratic 'Pippa's Page' – 'from a woman's point of view' – for over forty-five years while contributing to papers and magazines in Australia, America and New Zealand.

The last article by 'Pippa', 'Memories of Mother Aubert', appeared in the same issue as her obituary by Pat Lawlor.

Her poetry won Eileen Duggan international recognition; she was awarded an OBE in 1937 and a government annuity (on the recommendation of Peter Fraser) in 1942, yet she continued to avoid publicity. Part of her reserve and self-consciousness may have been due to physical frailty (which was wrongly presumed by some to be Parkinson's disease), and part of it to the fact that she spent much of her life in boarding-houses, reluctant to accept hospitality she could not return. Her letters, however, reveal a warm, caring and non-judgemental woman with a delightfully witty sense of humour and an unexpected worldliness. Particularly important to her were her friendships with Jessie Mackay (although she was unwilling to share the older poet's commitment to prohibition), and with the Australian writer Nettie Palmer, with whom she corresponded although they never met.

Eileen Duggan's rather dreamy, mild manner contrasted with her practical skills, revealed when she wrote *Pippa's Cookery Book* to assist the Missionary Sisters of the Society of Mary. Nor was it wise to underestimate her – Pat Lawlor recalled with amusement a PEN meeting where someone unwisely criticised the Irish and was quietly but firmly 'obliterated'. Although Eileen Duggan avoided large social gatherings, she was always supportive of friends, concerned for those in need and for the future of New Zealand and the modern world, recognising that 'The worst burn is to come . . ./ Peat burns underground' ('Post-War').

In her work there is no nostalgia for 'Home' on the other side of the world. Her early poems were often concerned with Ireland but it was New Zealand that mattered most:

> *For if I held the freehold of this land*
> *From Cape Reinga to Oreti Beach*
> *I could not feel that it was more my own.*
>> *'Invasion'*

Her concern was not for Empire but for an independent New Zealand, and she was anxious about the erratic development of its national consciousness:

I feel as if I want to stop every child in the street and say – 'This is your country – you can see it – touch it – love it. What do you know of Empire?' If I could myself see New Zealand as an entity I would love it better than Ireland. Five years ago it was a healthy rosy child peeping from behind mother's apron. Now it is a simpering debutante, paying calls and echoing mother's phrases.

Her passionate commitment to New Zealand, her concern for the disadvantaged and for the rigours of women's lives, and a genuine interest in the Maori people were common concerns in her poetry, while her religious faith underpinned her life and work.

Eileen Duggan believed, like Yeats, that poetry is the product of the heart not the head. Some derided her work as Georgian romanticism; Denis Glover mocked her for her 'solemn saints'; for A. R. D. Fairburn she was one of 'the Menstrual School of Poetry', although he had earlier admired her; the young

Allen Curnow considered that her early work, like Robin Hyde's, showed 'how talents above the commonplace could be drawn into the habit of sentimental posturing'. Further complications led to the omission of her work from the two anthologies he edited (*A Book of New Zealand Verse, 1923–45*, 1945, and *The Penguin Book of New Zealand Verse*, 1960). But for her '"Fame is dead men's bread." The real joy is in the craft.'

The first New Zealand poet with an international reputation, Eileen Duggan died in 1972. She had once warned an interviewer, 'About my work say whatever you like, good or bad, but about me nothing.' Robin Hyde dared to do both, describing her as: 'New Zealand's first poet – if not a great poet, a true poet . . . I think she could be fierce in her defences and protection of what needs help, her dislike of banality and exploitation.'   *Gill Boddy*

Quotations
para.1 Robin Hyde, 'A Poetaster on Poets', *NZ Observer*, 26 Feb. 1931; 'AE', quoted in F. M. McKay, *Eileen Duggan*, p.11; Pat Lawlor, *NZ Tablet*, 20 Dec. 1972, p.2
para.3 *NZ Woman's Weekly*, 11 Feb. 1937, p.1
para.7 P.Lawlor, p.2
para.8 E. Duggan to Nettie Palmer, n.d. 1924?, E. M. Duggan Papers
para.9 Denis Glover, *The Arraignment of Paris*, Christchurch, 1937, p.1; A. R. D. Fairburn to D. Glover, 8 June 1935, in Lauris Edmond (ed.), *The Letters of A. R. D. Fairburn*, Auckland, 1981, p.95; Allen Curnow, introduction to *A Book of New Zealand Verse 1923–1945*, Christchurch, 1945, p.24; E. Duggan to Nettie Palmer, n.d. 1938, E. M. Duggan Papers
para.10 Bernice May, *Australian Woman's Mirror*, 8 Jan. 1929; Robin Hyde, 'New Zealand Authoresses', *Mirror: New Zealand's National Home Journal*, vol.18 no.18, 8 Feb. 1938, p.20

Unpublished Sources
A. Mulgan Papers, MS Papers 224/19, ATL; Alan Mulgan, 'Eileen Duggan. A Critical Appraisal' (broadcast talk); J. Reid, talk; press cuttings file
E. M. Duggan Papers, 1924–1964, MS Papers 801/2, ATL
Robin Hyde's letters to Eileen Duggan, in the archives of the Archdiocese of Wellington

Published Sources
Burgess, Grace. *A Gentle Poet: A Portrait of Eileen Duggan, O.B.E*, Masterton, 1981
Lawlor, Pat. *Books and Bookmen, New Zealand and Overseas*, Wellington, 1954
McKay, F. M. *Eileen Duggan*, Wellington, 1977
O. M. A. 'Eileen Duggan poet', *Dominion*, 4 Feb. 1937
Palmer, Nettie. *The Bulletin*, 5 Dec. 1928

KATE EDGER

1857–1935

Kate Milligan Edger was born in England on 6 January 1857, the third daughter of the Revd Samuel Edger, a Baptist minister, and his wife, Louisa (born Harwood). She was to be the first woman graduate in New Zealand and an outstanding leader in women's organisations.

When she was five, the family emigrated to the Albertland settlement in Northland and then later moved to Auckland. An intelligent and industrious student, Kate was taught at home with her sisters. As she grew older, she was confronted with a lack of scholastic opportunities for women. Furthermore, it was not clear that women could be admitted to a university education in New Zealand, since the issue had not yet been raised specifically. Fortunately for her, her father, a graduate of the University of London, was knowledgeable and supportive. On his advice, she applied to the senate of the University of New Zealand for permission to sit for a university scholarship, giving her age and qualifications but not her sex. In her application she wrote:

I am a candidate for one of the mathematical scholarships of the University of New Zealand to be awarded at the examination in May. My age is within the specified limits and I have received instruction privately and also in Latin and Mathematics at the Auckland College Evening classes.

The senate accepted her application, which in effect allowed her to proceed towards a degree. In the words of the historian, W. J. Gardner, 'The whole episode was virtually a non-event.' J. C. Beaglehole, however, described the situation from a different perspective, saying that she 'walked into the open citadel and took possession of the heritage of her sex'. The senate apparently acted pragmatically, believing that to refuse the application might cause more trouble than to allow her to proceed. The only girl present, Kate worked in the highest class at Auckland College and Grammar School, which was affiliated to the University of New Zealand (Auckland University College was yet to be established).

Three years later, in 1877, she graduated with a Bachelor of Arts degree (specialising in mathematics and Latin) from the University of New Zealand, the first woman in the British Empire to earn a BA. (A Canadian woman had graduated with a Bachelor of Science degree two years earlier.) The *New Zealand Herald* commented when she graduated in the presence of nearly a thousand people, 'Let us hear no more of the intellectual inferiority of women.'

Her first teaching post, in 1877, was at Christchurch Girls' High School, where Helen Connon (later Helen Macmillan Brown) was soon to join the staff. The testimonial from the headmaster of Auckland Grammar School had praised Kate's power of winning the affection of the young and her indomitable perseverance. While teaching at the high school, she gained a Master of Arts degree at Canterbury College and was capped in 1882 with her sister Lilian.

In 1882, Kate Edger was appointed as headmistress of Nelson College for Girls, which opened the following February. She had to sustain the school through its teething troubles, cope with problems presented by badly designed buildings, establish her position in relation to her staff, and deal with the difficulties presented by the boarding establishment. In addition to her duties as headmistress, she taught English grammar, composition and literature, physical science, Latin, geography, and singing. She also prepared girls for university scholarships. Out of her annual salary of £350, she sometimes bought equipment for the school and on one occasion financed a scholarship to allow a senior girl to stay on at school.

The burden was heavy for a young woman who was only twenty-six years old when appointed. But Kate Edger's ability, quiet determination, and the experience she had gained as second mistress at Christchurch Girls' High School, itself a new institution, enabled her to establish Nelson College for Girls on a

Nelson College for Girls staff, 1888. Kate Edger is at the extreme right. *Hocken Library*

sound footing and to win the appreciation of the board of governors. The girls loved and admired her from the beginning.

Kate's sister Lilian had followed Kate into teaching, and taught with her at Christchurch Girls' High School and under her at Nelson College for Girls. From about 1887 to 1894, Lilian was headmistress of her own private school, Ponsonby College, in Auckland.

The arrival in Nelson in 1889 of the Revd W. A. Evans, a Welsh Congregationalist minister, changed the course of Kate Edger's life. She married him in the following year and soon afterwards resigned her position. She frequently preached in her husband's church, both in Nelson and later in Wellington.

The couple moved to Wellington in 1893, where they both became active in the Forward Movement, in which religion, philanthropy, and adult education were combined. Kate visited people in the slums and helped them in a practical and unobtrusive manner; with her husband and Sir Robert Stout and others she also lectured for the movement. As her husband was working full time for the movement, Kate seems to have become for some years the principal breadwinner. By this time she had three sons, and motherhood was not easily combined with teaching in the kind of schools where she had previously worked. So during the late 1890s and early 1900s, she ran her own private school in Mt Victoria and also did private coaching. During the First World War, she worked in the Department of Education and for thirty years she examined for University Entrance at intervals.

Kate Edger played an active part in the campaign for women's suffrage in New Zealand, chairing meetings and making speeches. She was Dominion recording secretary of the Women's Christian Temperance Union from 1916 to 1928 and edited its newspaper *The White Ribbon* for some time. She was also Dominion president of the League of Nations Union, foundation president and vice-president of the Society for the Protection of Women and Children and foundation member of the Prison Reform Association. The family moved to Newtown in 1904 after her husband had been appointed minister of the Congregational church there and Kate became a member of the Newtown school committee.

When Kate attended a social function with her sister at Auckland University College in 1917, an observer commented that with their dowdy holland clothes and their old-fashioned hats on top of their old-fashioned buns they 'typified the best of early Auckland – plain living had to accompany any effort at high thinking . . . in them in this old worn building there was the spirit of a true University.' In 1923, Kate Edger headed the women graduates in the procession to mark the golden jubilee of Canterbury University College. No one had a better right to that place.

Although Kate Edger was quiet and reserved, she was widely admired and loved. She showed determination, a high degree of physical stamina, and a zeal for education and the creation of a better life for all people. At a time when marriage and motherhood usually severely limited the lives of women, she continued to teach and to work actively for women's interests. She was not a feminist by the standards of the present day, as an article she wrote on the occasion of Canterbury College's golden jubilee shows:

Has the higher education of women justified itself? It is too soon yet for a complete answer to be given to this question, but thousands of university women are proving by their lives that it has not unfitted them for homemaking, the noblest sphere of women's work.

But she herself had combined marriage, motherhood, and career with an unusual degree of success.

Kate Edger spent the last few years of her life in the home of her second son. She died in 1935, twelve years after her husband.   *Beryl Hughes*

Quotation
para.2 J. C. Beaglehole, *The University of New Zealand*, p.75 n.73
para.3 W. J. Gardner, *Colonial Cap and Gown*, pp.80–1; J. C. Beaglehole, p.75
para.4 *NZ Herald*, 12 July 1877, cited in K. Sinclair, *A History of the University of Auckland*, p.14 n.4
para.12 K. Sinclair, pp.60–1
para.13 *Lyttelton Times*, 12 May 1923, cited by W. J. Gardner, p.110

Unpublished Sources
Letters from Miss Beryl Evans, Kate Edger's granddaughter, to the author, 1988–90

Published Sources
Beaglehole, J. C. *The University of New Zealand; An Historical Study*, Wellington, 1937
The Cyclopedia of New Zealand, Christchurch, 1897, vol.1, part 1, pp.406–7
Freedom, 20 March 1946
Gardner, W. J. *Colonial Cap and Gown*, Christchurch, 1979
Hight, James and Candy, Alice. *A Short History of the Canterbury College*, Christchurch, 1927
NZ Free Lance, 12 Jan. 1901
Scholefield, G. H. (ed.) *A Dictionary of New Zealand Biography*, Wellington, 1940 (under Kate Evans, W. J. Evans, and Samuel Edger)
Sinclair, Keith. *A History of the University of Auckland 1883–1983*, Auckland, 1983
Voller, Lois C. *Sentinel at the Gates*, Nelson, 1982

WETEKIA RURUKU ELKINGTON

1879–1957

Wetekia was born 19 June 1879 on Rangitoto (D'Urville Island). Her father, Roma Hoera (Ruruku), was a full-blooded Maori of Ngati Koata, who had travelled down from Kawhia with other members of his tribe, including his brother Matiu. These two eventually settled on D'Urville Island, marrying sisters from Te Ati Awa who owned land on the island. Wetekia's mother was Maria Tuo Hukaroa. From these marriages come the families who claim D'Urville Island as their home place.

Her mother died when Wetekia was very young, leaving her, the eldest, to look after her brothers, one a baby born not long before their mother died. They were then living at Ohanga, on D'Urville Island, and although other people living there had cows, they would not give her milk for her baby brother. She struggled to keep the baby alive even though she could not have been more than ten years old herself. She would put flour in the bottom of a camp oven and roast it. When it was roasted, she would put boiling water in, cook it up as a custard and then feed the baby. But the baby died despite her efforts. Even if they had had milk to give him, he would not have lived, as he had pneumonia. After that everything she learned, she learned from her father. For example, he taught her to wash blankets by putting them in the water, soaping them, then getting in and washing them with her feet. Life was rough, but her father was a man of great character.

Religion had a major influence in Wetekia's life and she was a visionary woman. Once she had a dream in which she was lying on her back looking up and she saw a bird flying across the sky. The wings of the bird turned into a book and she heard a voice saying in Maori:

O house of Israel how oft have I gathered you as a hen gathereth her chickens under her wings, and ye would not . . . I will gather you as a hen gathereth her chickens under her wings. if ye will repent and return unto me.

Not long after this there was a tangi at Ohanga. A family from the North Island came down and brought a book with them, *The Book of Mormon*. When Wetekia saw the book, she told her father that was the book in her dream. After the tangi her father travelled to Wellington and brought the missionaries back with him to Ohanga where the whole pa was baptised into the Church of Jesus Christ of Latter Day Saints (Mormons). Four generations of her family have now been brought up in the church.

Wetekia also dreamed of her future husband. In her dream she saw a fair man and a voice told her that this was the man she would marry. Around 1893-5 she married John Arthur Elkington. His father was an Englishman who had come out with the 91st Regiment of the British Army to fight in the New Zealand Wars and ended up marrying a Maori woman. John was born on 6 October 1866.

Wetekia and John had thirteen children. Their first baby was born in Matapihi, outside beside a river. He was ten days old when he died of whooping cough. The second baby, a girl, died when she was three years old. Eleven more children were born, of whom two more died.

Despite the hardships she endured, or perhaps because of them, Wetekia had a strong perception of where her family should go and what they should accomplish. My father was always impressed by the fact that she gave her children and grandchildren a vision of what can be achieved. For instance, education has always been important in our family and this comes from Wetekia. She taught herself to read and write in both Maori and English. In Nelson Provincial Museum there is a copy of a book written in Maori by Wetekia which traces her family's genealogies from the 'seven canoes'.

Wetekia was always very proud of who she was – Ngati Koata and Te Ati Awa, and her links to Tainui. Once when Te Puea needed a rest from Waikato, she came down to stay with her relations on D'Urville Island. They, being aware of how important she was, went to her at the end of two weeks and said, 'You've had a rest but you're needed back. We're telling you, you should be making your way back up to Waikato, to do what you have to do up there.' And of course she went, but in appreciation for the hospitality she had been given, the family received a mere, Pare Waikato. As you go on to Turangawaewae there are the two houses offering hospitality, Pare Waikato and Pare Hauraki. One of Wetekia's daughters was named Pare Hauraki and now they had the mere, named Pare Waikato.

Wetekia was an expert in the genealogy of Tainui, although in her book the descent finishes with King Rata, which means others of the Kingitanga movement are missing. The grandchildren used to sit around and listen while their grandparents told them stories of Tainui, Waikato, the Kingitanga, and the wars. These stories gave their grandchildren a base from which to feel proud, something which could not be taken away from them.

It has been asserted that Maori society is sexist, but Maori know that women are the font of life and consequently accord women their rightful place. Wetekia demonstrated this when she taught her children to whakapapa on the female side as well as the male. But then she always recognised her place, which most certainly was not as a subordinate.

Just before she got married, an uncle of John Arthur gave him the advice that 'you've got to let her know right from the start who's the boss'. So the first morning after they were married John Arthur kicked Wetekia out of bed and told her to go and get him his breakfast. Wetekia got up, put her clothes on, walked down to the beach, and swam home. John Arthur waited for her to come back: after two weeks he went down to see when she was coming home and her father told him, 'You can't treat her like that, she's ariki.' He learned he had to treat his wife with respect.

Wetekia was often heard to repeat the quotation:

> *Ana koe ka tuohu*
> *Tuohu ki te maunga teitei.*
>
> *If thou must bow*
> *Bow only to the highest mountain.*

This was used to raise the self-esteem of her people and her family.

For the last seventeen years of her life she was paralysed and bedridden, but this did not stop her from asserting herself. Another aunt remembers that when they were children and their grandmother wanted to punish them, because she was paralysed she would tell the kids to 'come here so I can hit you'. And they went. Such was the strength of her character there was no question that they would disobey her, even when she was confined to a wheelchair. She was a strong-minded, strong-willed woman. But she was also just a normal Maori grandmother. In Maori society grandmothers taught the children. My father remembers that once when he was a small child she asked him, 'Do you want to be fit? I can teach you.' He asked how, and her advice was to take a dip in the sea every morning. As my father says, if a person can take that, they must be fit. He also remarks that kohanga reo is only giving back to the grandmothers their traditional role as educators of the children.

Like the rest of Maori society Wetekia practised the concept of matua whangai (foster-parenting). People used to whangai children to give them a better chance in life. Once her cousin Tiro, knowing she was dying, brought her children to Wetekia and asked her if she would look after them because she did not know who else could. Wetekia, of course, said yes. With all her own children as well as her cousin's she had a large family to look after, so she had to devise some means for dealing with this myriad of kids. Her method was to pair them and then give them all jobs to do, working in rotation shifts. In the meantime she would be up felling timber or cooking for the men who were digging the roads of D'Urville Island on contract work.

Another time Wetekia went up to the Waikato and saw a sickly little boy who had been born to her niece. She told them she thought she had better take him back with her and feed him up with fish, and that she would be able to offer him more. Her niece agreed to let him go, so Wahanui Tupaea was brought back down to the South Island where he was brought up with other whangai. Later on when Wetekia was paralysed, Waha, who was still only a teenager, became her main nurse, caring for her, changing her, and cooking her meals.

The story goes that one time Wetekia was annoyed with Waha and said to him, 'If it wasn't for me you'd be dead,' and Waha replied, 'If it wasn't for me *you'd* be dead.' And she recognised this. She was so appreciative of the care that Waha took of her that she adopted him so that he could be counted as one of her children and take his share of her land.

Summing up Wetekia I would have to say that family, church, and Maoritanga were the most important things in her life. They were all inter-related. She got a lot of joy out of her religion and her Maoriness. This made her a traditional person but she was also a modern person, up with the latest – with kohanga reo, matua whangai. Only thirty years after she died they brought in all these 'new' things which she had lived and practised in association with other kuia.

Joy Hippolite

Sources

Information came from family members: Maria Tuo Poto Elkington Hippolite (daughter), John Te One Hippolite (grandson), Emily Hippolite (granddaughter), Puhanga Hemi Tupaea (granddaughter), Cissy Hemi Harvey (granddaughter), Wana Selwyn Tari (granddaughter). The author is the great-granddaughter of Wetekia Ruruku Elkington. Records in Nelson Provincial Museum were also consulted.

ELLEN ELLIS

1829–1895

Ellen Elizabeth Colebrook was the second of seventeen children of William Colebrook, tenant farmer of Great Tangley Manor, near Guildford, Surrey. The family were fervent 'chapel' (Methodist). Ellen was educated at a 'seminary for young ladies' run by Misses Priddie and Patterson in Guildford, and she herself later set up, with two sisters, a 'boarding school for young ladies' in Guildford, in which she was the sewing mistress.

In 1852 she married Oliver Sydney Ellis, a businessman, and had three sons: John William, Alec (who died within a few months), and Thomas. The family emigrated to New Zealand, arriving in Auckland in July 1859 on the *Whirlwind*, with Ellen's brother Tom and cousin John. Her husband was involved, not very successfully, in business and property speculation in Auckland. Ellen returned to England in January 1864 to put her sons in school. Thomas fell overboard on the voyage back, and was drowned. Leaving her remaining son William in England, Ellen returned to Auckland in February 1865.

In the 1870s, with the encouragement of the Revd Samuel Edger, she followed a programme of self-education, joined the Good Templars (a temperance group originating in the USA), and did welfare work with the wives and children of drunkards. She wrote:

Even before they had reached the point of admission to the asylum, the conditions of their lives would have been quite dreadful. Such women would be beaten repeatedly by their drunken husbands. Even if the unfortunate creatures had spirit enough to take the children & go, the law would allow them nothing. There came a moment when I knew I must do more than merely sympathise with them. I must actively fight to ensure that in future, women should never be brought to such shame and degradation through no fault of their own.

She decided to write a novel.

God had denied me a happy marriage, so that I should not become inturned on my own satisfactory life. He had taken Alec & Little Tom to Himself, to free me from the responsibility of looking after them. He intended me to drink to the dregs of sorrow's cup. He had given me my present freedom, so that I could devote my every effort toward lifting the heavy burden of my less fortunate sisters.

Her only novel, *Everything is Possible to Will*, was published in London in 1882. No reviews of the novel have been traced and her son William, upset at the supposed portrayal of his father as the alcoholic husband of the heroine, bought up and burnt as many copies as possible. (Ellis's husband died a year later, in 1883.)

The novel is directly autobiographical. The heroine is a spirited intelligent girl whose life is limited by the poor education offered to girls. She marries a businessman who turns out to be an alcoholic, and goes with him to New

Zealand. Ellen's biographer, Vera Colebrook, describes Oliver Ellis as a 'social drinker' and talks of Ellen as an 'implacable teetotaller', but the novel vividly depicts an alcoholic husband who is certainly far more than a social drinker, and whose alcoholism has disastrous effects on the marriage:

The Drunkard's wife and little ones are the slaves legally of the vilest slave
holder that ever owned human cattle, or disgraced his kind. They are his, body
and soul; there is no limit to his power, so long as he spares life.

The novel's primary concerns are exposing the evils of drunkenness in men, the need for the government to control the sale of alcohol, and the need for women to have a good education and legal freedom, so they can use their superior moral and emotional influence:

Denied a liberal education, the greatest of all wrongs, the majority of women
are incapable of putting their thoughts in such logical sequence as shall
command the public ear. Trained by repression however, woman is slowly
beginning to realise her power to manufacture public opinion by direct appeals
to her own sex, to whom facts are more potent than reasoning drawn out to
infinitude.

The novel argues, in what is for its time an outspoken way, for birth control through abstinence: 'Man must be taught that he can and must control his animal passions, and women must refuse to be sacrificed to his lust.' The heroine limits her family, refusing to follow the example of her mother who 'loved her husband . . . but . . . could never forgive him the suffering her seventeen children occasioned her'. Ellis's mother had indeed seventeen children. Ellis had three, presumably limiting her family size as the novel suggests. She argues that 'an amount of mock modesty highly reprehensible hangs about the population question' and attacks the medical profession for keeping women ignorant. The novel ends on an appeal:

Public opinion can, if it will, strike the chains of slavery from woman's intellect
and heart and make woman's emancipation the greatest trophy of Victoria's
reign.

Ellis had her sons taught Maori and believed the government had failed to realise the need to understand Maori culture. In a letter of 1860 she writes:

I still feel the great importance of 'tapu' is not sufficiently realised. In preaching
against it the missionaries in the past appear to have done much damage since
'tapu' is not only a matter of spiritual belief for the Maoris, it also acts to
protect the power & prestige of the heads of the tribes &, especially their
dignity: it also protects their communal fishing & hunting rights: their hygiene
and cooking arrangements.

In this as in other matters she was a woman truly ahead of her time. In 1860 she wrote an impassioned plea for peace, occasioned by the land wars:

O! When will men learn to dissolve their differences through discussion rather than destruction, through education rather than elimination! And when will women band together to insist that there shall be no more war.

When she died of bronchitis in 1895, the Auckland newspapers did not consider her worthy of an obituary; a hundred years later her words still ring true of many women. *Aorewa McLeod*

Quotations
para.3 V. Colebrook, *Ellen*, p.145
para.4 V. Colebrook, p.146
para.5 V. Colebrook, p.40; E. Ellis, *Everything is Possible to Will*, p.124
para.6 E. Ellis, p.70
para.7 E. Ellis, pp.73, 135, 223
para.8 V. Colebrook, p.106
para.9 V. Colebrook, p.101

Published Sources
Colebrook, Vera. *Ellen: A Biography*, London, 1980
Ellis, Ellen. *Everything is Possible to Will*, London, 1882

MARGARET ESCOTT

1908-1977

Margaret Escott, born in London, was the fifth and last child in her family. The parents and two of the children, including Margaret (then eighteen), emigrated to New Zealand in 1926. Margaret spent a year as a pupil-teacher at Seddon Technical College in Auckland and in 1928 returned to London for eight years. During that time she wrote three novels. Two – *Insolence of Office* (1934) and *Awake at Noon* (1935) – were published under the pseudonym of C. M. Allen, and were set in London. The third, *Show Down* (1936), was published under Escott's own name and was set in New Zealand.

Escott returned to New Zealand in 1936, and lived in Auckland until her death. She was heavily involved in amateur drama, teaching it at Epsom Girls' Grammar School and for the Department of Adult Education, and producing many plays for dramatic societies. For her, drama was 'a genuine way of learning, a kind of rehearsal for life'. Though she continued to write, nothing was published after *Show Down*. In an interview in 1970, she explained her reluctance to publish by saying: '[I] couldn't face reading what I'd written.'

Show Down is the love story of David Hawkes, a farmer near Hamilton, and Anna Trove, a rich Englishwoman who comes to New Zealand to hand over an inheritance to her wayward brother. For some time the things that David and Anna share outweigh the differences between them, differences of which both are aware:

we knew many things together . . . we took the best of our own separate worlds and gave them to each other – not consciously, but just inevitably, because we were so close to one another.

But in the end the relationship disintegrates; David rekindles an affair with a woman in the neighbourhood and Anna goes off with a rich English farmer living nearby.

It wasn't circumstances, it wasn't her money and her friends and her class that drove a wedge between us. It was ourselves – and me more than her because I was older and should've been wiser . . . I was an underling. I had those weaknesses that love was going to show up in such a blaze of light that the sight of them turns me sick for what I've held dark in my heart for so long.

At the beginning of their relationship Anna reads a line of Blake to David: 'Never seek to tell thy love . . .' This could be the novel's epigraph. At the heart of the book is Escott's conviction that language is inadequate to convey the important things. Although Escott realised the limitations, she used language in a way that is rare in New Zealand literature: a man's voice, introspective and analytical, examining his emotional life. Escott believed, and David Hawkes expresses this in the novel, that men are constrained in such examination and analysis only by the expectations of others.

Although there has been little dispute about the merit of Escott's one New Zealand novel, there has been difficulty in placing her book in any of the main streams of New Zealand fiction. A woman writer using the introspective technique and perspective usually associated with female writing, but doing so with a male voice, poses particular problems for those who look for consistent patterns. Apart from other strengths the novel has, *Show Down* demonstrates that there often are no patterns, and that the best writing may come from those who break the unwritten rules.

Heather Roberts

Quotations
para.2 S. Cornwell, 'Peg Escott', p.40
para.3 M. Escott, *Show Down* (1973 edition), pp.45–69
para.4 M. Escott, p.41

Published Sources
Cornwell, Sue. 'Peg Escott and her 30-year-old pal', *NZ Woman's Weekly*, 31 Aug. 1970, p.40
Escott, Margaret. *Show Down*, London, 1936; Auckland, 1973

ISABEL FIELD

1867–1950

By 1888 at the age of twenty-one, Isabel Jane Hodgkins had proved herself as an artist. A review of the annual Otago Art Society exhibition praised the composition and colouring of Isabel's *Flower Study* (daffodils and wallflowers), and talked of her 'considerable genius'.

Isabel's instruction came primarily from her father. William Mathew Hodgkins was a Dunedin solicitor and artist, and the centre of much artistic activity in the city. Hodgkins and his circle of artist friends were disciples of the English artist J. M. W. Turner and his atmospheric depiction of landscape. Isabel, with her deft touch, had the requisite 'aptitude for reproducing the transient effects of light amid foliage'.

In 1886 Isabel was the special guest of Katherine Holmes on a sketching trip to Lakes Manapouri and Te Anau. Katherine, also an artist, was in the Hodgkins' artistic circle and the first woman to be elected to the council of the Otago Art Society (1886). Her support for Isabel was always loyal but unassuming. An account of the trip, in a diary in Katherine's humorous and conversational writing style, coins the title 'The Bostress' for Katherine, and for Isabel, the youngest in the party, 'Baby' or 'Sissy'. Katherine on this and later occasions saw herself as *in loco parentis*, 'besides being deeply attached to the girl'.

Isabel had established herself sufficiently by 1888 to pay for, from the sale of her art, a trip to the 1888–9 Melbourne Centennial International Exhibition. Her work was also included in the 1889–90 New Zealand and South Seas Exhibition at Dunedin.

Katherine Holmes moved to Wellington in 1891. During a visit to Wellington, which included sketching excursions with Katherine, Isabel met her husband-to-be, solicitor and future parliamentarian William H. Field. Katherine in her diary displays constant concern for her protégé, and is ever mindful of the excitement of a young woman's courtship.

Isabel Hodgkins before her marriage to Will Field (on rug), with her sister Frances Hodgkins and her parents in the garden, Cranmore Lodge, Dunedin, 1892. *Alexander Turnbull Library*

Isabel married Will Field in 1893. After a few years she made an effort to resume her place in artistic circles. She was a member of the council of the New Zealand Academy of Fine Arts in Wellington in 1898, 1900, 1903, and 1904, and exhibited with the society during this period. After 1904, she exhibited with the Academy on only three further occasions.

A review of Isabel's art written after 1898 lowers her artistic efforts to a 'hobby', lacking 'the serious attention that art claims for its devotees'. No doubt Isabel put her five children and duties to her husband's position first. But she seems also to have wanted to continue painting. The pressures of her family duties must have conspired against this – and her style of art was no longer fashionable. Landscape had been her popular strength. Buyers now preferred genre portraits and figure studies from their women artists.

In 1927 Isabel chanced her arm and exhibited with the Academy for the last time. Frances Hodgkins, her younger sister and by now an *avant-garde* artist overseas, urged Isabel to 'take it up seriously Sis and "Come back" – It can be done – with your fine colour and sympathetic imagination you might be as strong as ever again.'

Isabel ceased painting almost entirely, and, despite the early talent she showed, her work is now largely forgotten. *Ann Calhoun*

Quotations
para.1 *Evening Press*, 19 Oct. 1888
para.2 *Evening Star*, 17 Nov. 1894, quoted in R. D. Collins, 'Otago Art Society Exhibition, 1894', p.19
para.3 K. Holmes diary, Folder 3/2, Field Family Papers
para.7 Unsourced clipping, W. H. Field Scrapbook, Art Collection, ATL, p.121
para.8 E. H. McCormick, *The Expatriate*, p.211

Unpublished Sources
Field Family Papers, MS Papers 113, ATL

Published Sources
Collins, R. D. 'Otago Art Society Exhibition, 1894', *Bulletin of New Zealand Art History*, vol.5, 1977
McCormick, E. H. *The Expatriate: A Study of Frances Hodgkins*, Auckland, 1954

MYRTLE FISHER

1878–1972

My Winter Garden (1923) was one of the first gardening books to be written by a New Zealand woman. Concealed behind the pseudonym 'Kowhai' was an experienced gardener, garden designer, teacher, and writer. Based on the idea that a garden in temperate New Zealand need not be bare for half the year like a Northern European garden, *My Winter Garden* contained advice on what to plant for winter flowers and foliage, and how to prepare during winter for spring and summer.

Myrtle Emily Fisher was born in Port Melbourne, Australia, in 1878, the daughter of Sarah and Frederick Platts. Her father was an Anglican clergyman who moved to New Zealand when his daughter was young to take charge of the Port Chalmers parish. Myrtle was educated at St Hilda's College in Dunedin, and then went on to teachers' training college. After teaching for a period, she met and married Horace Fisher, also a teacher, and they moved to Motueka. Their son Trevor Platts Fisher was born in 1908.

It was in Motueka that Myrtle Fisher began gardening, encouraged by a local mentor. She had further support when the family moved to Eastbourne and by the 1920s she was in a position to give advice to others. She wrote gardening notes for the *Dominion* newspaper, and edited a gardening magazine. She also organised the Gardening Centre, was an active member of the Pioneer Club, the first women's club to be established in Wellington, and gave lectures on gardening. In *My Winter Garden* she advertised her availability as a garden consultant.

From the mid-1920s to the mid-1930s she designed gardens in Wellington and wrote two more books. *Joan, Betty and the Seagull* (1931) was a children's story whose main adult character was a young woman who ran a fruit and poultry farm. The *Garden Book of the Wellington Free Kindergarten* (1933) was a compilation organised by the Wellington Horticultural Society and edited by Myrtle Fisher in order to raise funds for kindergartens which had just had their government subsidies cut.

In 1935 Myrtle Fisher moved to England in order to be closer to Trevor Fisher, who had been studying music in Vienna and later worked as a musician. She settled at Kew in London, both to be near the famous botanical gardens and to have room for another garden of her own. When the Second World War broke out, she was employed as a censor, and after the war she worked for the Ministry of Education in a clerical capacity. She maintained her interest in gardening and music, making frequent trips into London to attend concerts until the last months of her long life. She died in 1972, aged ninety-four.

Christine Dann

Unpublished Source
Information was provided by Myrtle Fisher's niece, Elizabeth Budden.
Published Source
My Winter Garden, Wellington, 1923

RUTH FRANCE

1913-1968

On her death, writer Ruth France was described by Monte Holcroft as one of 'the finest minds of her generation'.

She was born into a Catholic family at Leithfield, Canterbury, in 1913. Her mother, Helena Henderson (born Hayes), was a prolific writer of unpublished novels and plays, and had many essays, poems, and stories published in the local Christchurch newspaper. Ruth herself seems to have been, on the surface, a quiet, shy young woman. After leaving Christchurch Girls' High School, she worked as a librarian at the Canterbury Public Library until her marriage to boat-builder Arnold France (a non-Catholic). Her father, Francis Henderson, objected strongly to what he considered an unsuitable marriage, and faked a suicide attempt on the eve of her wedding. She later detailed this experience in one of her short stories, 'The Wedding'. Her father's narrow minded attitudes and violent actions were undoubtedly a factor in her rejection of Catholicism and subsequent life of spiritual uncertainty.

Ruth France was an intelligent, literate, and gentle woman, who seems to have led a life of apparent conflict and frustration. She wrote that she 'always had an adventurous spirit and an early dream was to be the first woman to reach the Antarctic'.

As a young married woman she lived for four years on a yacht anchored in Lyttelton Harbour, rowing ashore every day to take her husband to work, her son to kindergarten, and to do the shopping. When the family (which by now included two sons) built and moved into a house in Sumner, she spent the rest of her years leading what she herself called 'a rather retired life'. Her only close friend was writer and pacifist Elsie Locke, and her contact with other writers was spasmodic, as she felt alienated by the literary circle in Christchurch at the time. She thought that the members of this group treated women like chattels.

She was never happier than when writing – for her, a stimulating and necessary exercise of the mind, something she did 'because I can't help it'. But at the same time she was determined to be the 'good wife and mother' that the 1950s required women to be. Her chances to write were spasmodic, fitted in and around boat-building, house-building, family, and housework:

When I am writing, I am in better health and disposition than at other times and the world seems a nicer place to live in . . . the happiest times are those at the desk, preferably when one is alone in the house, but even when the family is banging in and out, and the Hit Parade is resonant on the radio.

Much of her poetry explored themes of life and death; of life as imprisonment; of impermanence; of lack of fulfilment. It was not all pessimistic, however. Many of her earlier poems, in particular, used her own garden and environment as a starting point for considering how the spark of life survives seasons and cycles. In both her poetry and her prose she was essentially a regional writer, believing firmly in the importance of landscape and a sense of place in people's lives and emotions. She also wrote some fine love poetry although, as in her novels, she stressed a sense of people's separateness from each other.

Ruth France published two volumes of poetry, *Unwilling Pilgrim* (1955) and *The Halting Place* (1961), under the pseudonym of Paul Henderson. Several of these poems have been anthologised both in New Zealand and overseas. It is not clear why she chose to use a male pseudonym for her poetry. She had previously written poetry under her own name. One of her poems (which had won her first prize in a national competition) had been criticised by letter-writers in the *Listener*. She always felt criticism very acutely, and perhaps felt the need for protective anonymity in her subsequent writing. Critics at the time also suggested that the masculine pseudonym contributed to her success and gave her poetry a freedom from 'poetess mannerisms'. Certainly her poetry seems to have been better accepted by many of the male literary establishment of the 1950s than were her novels (written under her own name).

Lyttelton boat harbour, c.1930s, the destination in Ruth France's novel *The Race*.
Canterbury Museum

Her two published novels both explored groups of people and the relationships between them, as they battled with themselves and the outside environment. *The Race* (1958) tells the story of a yacht race from Wellington to Lyttelton. A storm blows up during the race, wrecking some of the yachts while all the rest except *Shadow* seek shelter. The novel follows the struggles of the men on board and alternates this with an account of the anxiety and suspense of the women who are waiting for them. With its emphasis on people as members of a group, *The Race* was seen by some as breaking fresh ground in New Zealand fiction, especially in its departure from the tradition of writing about 'man alone'. Other critics, however, disparaged the 'tea and worry sessions' of the female characters.

Ice Cold River (1962) is about a family Christmas celebration on a Canterbury farm being shattered by a sudden flood which disrupts communications and maroons the family. France explores the relationships and tensions within the family, and contrasts this with the fury and destructiveness of the Waimakariri River. Once again, critics commented on the 'trivial round of domestic routine'. Ruth France was moved to ask: 'To receive any credit am I to write only of things which will interest men?'

Besides the novels and poetry, Ruth France wrote reviews for *Landfall* and the *Listener*; thoughtful articles for local papers; short stories for both an adult audience and for the *School Journal*; radio broadcasts about writing and books; and even advertising ditties for her husband's company, Arnold France Limited. A third novel, *The Tunnel*, was still unpublished at the time of her death from cancer in 1968.   *Sue Abel*

Quotations
para.1 *NZ Listener*, 27 Oct. 1968 (obituary)

para.3 R. France, in NZ Broadcasting Service 'Book Shop' programme, 8 Oct. 1958 (copy in R. France papers, Hocken)

para.5 R. France, in 'The Writer as a Person' radio talk series (copy in R. France papers, Hocken)

Unpublished Sources

Information was provided by family members; the author is married to Ruth France's son Paul.

Ruth France papers, MS 932, Hocken

P. A. French, 'Twelve Women Poets of New Zealand: Imperatives of Shape and Growth', MA thesis, Texas, 1967 (held on microfiche at University of Auckland)

Helena Henderson papers, Arch HEN, Canterbury Public Library

ROSE FRANK

1864–1954

Rose Frank collected history – about 200,000 pieces of it.

Born Rosaline Margaret Frank, the daughter of Christopher and Emma Frank of Nelson, she was educated by the Sisters of Our Lady of the Missions at St Mary's Convent.

As a senior pupil, Rose specialised in music and art. She was to remain a devout Catholic and worker for her church all her life. In 1886 at the age of twenty-one, when most young women were either marrying or staying at home 'to help mother', Rose started work as an assistant to William Tyree, the photographer, in his studio in Trafalgar Street, Nelson.

The Tyree Studio had been operating since about 1882, with the Tyree brothers, William and Fred, sharing the work. This was no small local venture. In 1895, the Tyree Studio was involved in tourist trade promotion with a series of views along the Newman's coach route from Blenheim through Nelson and on to Westport. These photographs were exhibited in principal hotels throughout New Zealand and distributed around the world by the Orion Steam Ship Company and the New Zealand Steam Ship Company.

Rose must have quickly become a competent photographer and business woman because in September of 1895 William Tyree gave Rose power of attorney, leaving her to manage the business while he went to Australia to pursue his career as an inventor.

William Tyree was a man of many talents. Not content with photography, he devoted many hours to his inventions – life-preservers which doubled as deck-chairs; a new, improved .egg tester; an apparatus for washing clothes; an improved mouse and rat trap; the Tyree Headline, an ingenious contraption for teaching writing; so the list goes on. One of his more successful inventions, 'The Improved Acetylene Gas Generator', was sold throughout New Zealand. William Tyree left Rose to manage both the photography studio and the generator business.

So here was Rose, aged thirty, running a photography studio, selling gas generators, and reporting to William in Sydney. He never returned. She managed the business for fourteen years and finally purchased it in 1914 for the sum of £750, keeping the name of Tyree.

By now the collection of negatives filling the strong-room was becoming

Rose Frank, studio setting, c.1910. *Tyree Collection, Nelson Provincial Museum*

history. Early days of European settlement; portraits of early European pioneers; scenes of Nelson in its infancy, including copies of earlier photographs not taken by the Tyree Studio. Over the years Rose added to the collection, although the photographic business showed a steady decline, very noticeable from the number of negatives taken each year after 1918.

In 1948 the Alexander Turnbull Library offered her £100 for the collection and selected over 1,100 negatives, including all Tyree's Wellington images.

Retiring in 1947 at the age of eighty-two, Rose Frank sold the Tyree Studio to Cecil Manson of London, but retained the massive collection of negatives. These she presented to the Nelson Historical Society in June 1954. Later the same year, this grand old lady of photography died and was buried in the Wakapuaka Cemetery, in Nelson, next to her sister.

The Tyree Studio collection numbers over 200,000 negatives. These are now in the care of Nelson Provincial Museum, along with the negatives of many other photographers.

To Rose Frank's devotion to photography, New Zealand history owes a considerable debt.

Carol Peters

Tyree shop, Trafalgar Street, Nelson, 1896. A plate from the studio where Rose Frank worked. *Tyree Collection, Nelson Provincial Museum*

Unpublished Source
Information was provided by Maurice Watson, photographer, Nelson Provincial Museum.
Published Source
Nelson Evening Mail, 18 Oct. 1954; 15 April 1947 (on Rose Frank's retirement)

MAGGIE FRASER

1866–1951

Maggie Fraser was born in December 1866 at Inveravon in Banffshire, Scotland. The sixth, and last, child in the family, she was named after her mother. Her parents were crofters living on a small piece of land running two cows, a few sheep, growing a little grain and a small orchard. Maggie's father, John Fraser, also worked as a tailor.

Soon after Maggie turned twenty-one, she and her brother left Inveravon and Scotland for good. They travelled by train to Plymouth, where they joined the *Ionic* to sail direct to New Zealand; they arrived in Dunedin in February 1888. Maggie's two eldest brothers, Alick (also known as Sandy) and Jim, had preceded them. Maggie and John disembarked and immediately went on by train to Christchurch, where Alick had bought a house (in Humbolt Street, Sydenham) and was working as a blacksmith. Maggie reported their arrival in a letter to her sister: 'When we arrived Sandy was at [the] station and his mate . . . was frying chopps and had the table laid out with gilt and white dishes.'

About a fortnight later Maggie went out to her first place as a domestic servant. For the next twelve years, with occasional breaks to keep house for her brothers, she was in service in houses in Canterbury and, at one time, in Wellington. Throughout these years she wrote regularly to members of her family back in Scotland, most often to her mother and her sister Chatty (Charlotte). A good number of those letters have survived. They provide a rarely obtained insight into the life of a young woman working in service in late nineteenth-century New Zealand. As a series they are believed to be unique. Maggie continued to write after she married in 1900 but only two letters from this period of her life survive.

Maggie's first job was a general servant (G.S.) to a Scots family named Carmichael who lived at Loburn in North Canterbury. She told Chatty how she got the job:

I answered an advertisment in the paper for a Scotch woman as G.S.; the lady wrote asking my references. I sent them and a note explaining that I had been a G.S. before . . . and I have a letter just now saying that they are quite satisfactory and that I will have £2.10s a month for three months and a rise then if both parties are pleased.

After six weeks with the Carmichaels she wrote again:

I am liking this place fine we have a little Scotland of our own up here they all speak braid Scotch at times of course with a good bit of the Dundee twang. Mrs

C. is better now, she is rather a jolly looking old wife with a good deal of pride. We have been very busy Autumn cleaning all last week and will be this one. I would like fine to stay here if they gave me my wages up to £40 or even £36 a year any how it is a good deal better than home as I have no more work here than I had at Kinermony and have more than double the pay – I have just got one months pay as yet. Did I tell you when I wrote last that we have only Prebesteryn service once a fortnight here in a small school at seven at night and there is generally half as many dogs as people attend, the C.'s belong to it.

She was with the Carmichaels for almost a year but left as she found it rather a lonely place. Also, Charlotte and Alick's wife Annie and their son were expected from Scotland to join them. Maggie's letters at this time are full of advice on what to bring and what to expect on the voyage. Both Maggie and Alick spent a lot of time preparing the house, curing hams, and making jam in readiness for the new arrivals whom they were still hoping would arrive early in 1890. But they were disappointed, as Charlotte and Annie decided not to come to New Zealand after all. From this time Alick's marriage ceased to exist in anything but law.

In the meantime Jim, one of the other brothers, married a New Zealander and it was Maggie who wrote to her mother with details:

I always thought that I told you Mrs J's age she was between six and seven over twenty when they were married so she is just the suit for Jim for age. I really could not in fairness say much about her otherwise, I saw so very little of her but I think they have gone to a very good place as they will of nessesity have to learn each others tastes. [They went to Pitt Island in the Chathams.] I think they will get on very well . . . I think Jim will be much better married but I am not so sure of his wife if she will be better or not.

Maggie spent most of 1889 keeping house for Alick, at one stage knitting him a pair of bicycle pants. At the beginning of August she went to a situation with a family at Ohoka, but she told her mother:

I can't say I like it much the family consist of Mr. & Mrs. White, two children, a governess, housemaid & myself, they are English & Mrs. W. is new to the colony . . . I don't think I will stay long the place is all right but Mrs. can never make up her mind what she is to have in time to have it done. Mr W. has what they call a station here – a large farm at home but all the farm bussiness is apart from us only I have the dairy (which is very little at present) to look after.

She stayed only a few weeks.

Early the following year she took up a situation in Riccarton which she held for over a year. Her feelings on leaving Alick's house were mixed:

I have been here between 2 and 3 months now and like the place fairly well but it is not a place one feels any wise settled or home like in. You might still address me to Humbolt St as I might be away from here before a letter came. Alic was out about a week ago he is getting tired of bachelouring again it must

221

be very uncomfortable just now and the house very cold and dark when he gets home from work. Sometimes I think it was very selfish of me to leave him but I wanted to be making my pile and it so difficult to know which way is best.

Details about wages and how she and her brothers were 'getting on' occur frequently in the letters. Maggie, and in the early years her brothers also, regularly remitted money back to their parents. This was usually a £5 money order sent once a year. In 1894, however, knowing her father's sight was deteriorating and her mother suffering badly from rheumatism in the winter, she sent £25 of her £50 savings so the croft at Inveravon could be re-roofed. The money was used to completely replace the old roof with new corrugated iron.

Maggie left her place at Riccarton when her mistress decided to return to England. Early in 1891 she moved to Wellington where she was servant to the Pearce family in Abel Smith Street. The Pearces were a young couple – only a few years older than Maggie herself; Arthur Pearce worked for Levin & Co. Maggie wrote:

they are very nice people but there is a good deal of work. There is only Mr. & Mrs. Pearce and one child, the nurse and myself in the family but they have had company staying with them ever since I came and then the moveing about makes a lot of bother. They have a house about twelve miles out of town [Lowry Bay] where they were when I came. It seems almost strange to be writeing home to me now I have felt so much alone lately.

At the time she was working at the Pearces' there was a private members' bill discussed in parliament which proposed that servants should work regular hours like shop and factory workers. Maggie comments on this while reporting that she is quite happy where she is:

I get along very comfortably here just now but we expect an addition to the family any day now so that will make a difference. They have one little girl now she is about two years old now and such a good little thing . . . one can't do much of an evening as they all have late dinner out here but I must say the people I am with are very good for waiting on themselves. After dinner at seven they don't often trouble us for anything. There was talk sometime ago of the slaveys having hours to work as other work-men I think the idea gave some of the ladies a scare.

In 1892 Maggie returned to Canterbury, spending some time with Jim and Grace on her way south. She kept house for them when their third child was born as she did two years later when the fourth arrived. In between she was in service in Hornby.

The letters become quite sparse in the late 1890s. In 1897 she went to Masterton to nurse Alick who had a bout of typhoid fever. She probably stayed there again a year or so later – keeping house for him and working in service.

It was while she was in Masterton that she met Bill (William Crawford) Johnston. He had been in New Zealand a couple of years longer than she had and had managed to save a good deal from working on farms in the Manawatu and

Wairarapa. In December 1899 Johnston was successful in a land ballot on the Te Matua block at Awahuri, between Palmerston North and Feilding. He built a simple four-roomed cottage and he and Maggie were married in April 1900. She was thirty-four, he was thirty-five. Alick gave his sister a horse and custom-built buggy as a wedding present.

The marriage had its trials. Bill Johnston was known for his fiery temper. Maggie considered leaving him at one point; she was away staying with friends in Christchurch when the second of her four children was born. The farm was undoubtedly a successful venture; they freeholded it in 1914, and retired to Rotorua in the mid-1920s. By this time Maggie was suffering from rheumatism, and the thermal springs at Rotorua gave her some relief. Bill had been stone-deaf since about 1914. He died in 1940. Maggie's daughter, by then married with five young children, was widowed the same year and went to live with her mother. From living for years in an extremely silent household, Maggie was plunged into the turbulence of a young family. She died in 1951 aged eighty-four.

Charlotte Macdonald

Quotations
para.2 M. Fraser to Chatty, 7 March 1888. The original spelling has been retained but occasional punc-
     tuation has been added to assist a modern reading.
para.4 M. Fraser to Chatty, 7 March 1888; M. Fraser to Chatty, 18 April 1888
para.6 M. Fraser to Mother, 11 Nov. 1888
para.7 M. Fraser to Mother, 18 Aug. 1889
para.8 M. Fraser to Mother, 10 May 1890
para.10 M. Fraser to Mother, 25 March 1891
para.11 M. Fraser to Mother, *c.* Aug. 1891

Unpublished Sources
Maggie Fraser's letters to her family, in the possession of D. T. Johnston (Maggie Fraser's son), Rotorua

Published Source
Carter, Ian. *Farmlife in Northeast Scotland*, Edinburgh, 1979

CAROLINE FREEMAN

?1856–1914

The ceremony, on 27 August 1885, at which Caroline Freeman became the 'first lady graduate' of the University of Otago, was a real celebration. As she accepted her diploma, and an essay prize won in a contest open to all New Zealand under-graduates, the audience clapped, sang, cheered, and threw bouquets onto the stage. They were celebrating not only one woman's achievement, but also the new opportunities higher education was opening to women in general. By this time there were eleven women at various stages of the Otago BA course, mostly matriculated students who had progressed smoothly from high school to univer-sity, supported by their families, sometimes holding scholarships. Caroline Freeman did not fit this model. She lacked the advantage of secondary educa-tion, and both her parents were dead. In our terms she was a mature student who had put herself through university.

Caroline Freeman, the University of Otago's
'first lady graduate', 1885. *Otago Early
Settlers' Museum*

Caroline was the daughter of William Freeman and his wife Lucy Jane. A small child when her family left Yorkshire in 1858 to settle in Otago, where her parents farmed at 'Abbotsroyd', Green Island, she had all her schooling at the one-teacher Green Island school. She was its dux in 1866 and returned to spend four years as pupil-teacher before moving, in a huge career leap, to a position as headmistress (as the infant mistress was called) at the large and growing Caversham school in Dunedin. She had thus attained, while still in her teens, the highest position open to a woman in the primary teaching service. While she was teaching at Caversham, Caroline studied for her matriculation exam; at the end of 1877 – the year the first woman received a degree in New Zealand – she left to enrol at the university.

It was not easy. At first she continued to live at Green Island, walking the eleven kilometres home each day after lectures. When her health suffered under this demanding regime, she took rooms in Dunedin, where she also conducted 'classes for ladies'. For almost two years she taught at Otago Girls' High School, part of the time as deputy principal. The goodwill apparent at her graduation was not evident in her student days; as a friend put it, she had to submit to 'many silent, if not openly expressed opinions' from staff and students. Caroline's degree was an achievement of will-power as well as scholarship. In 1885, however, she was well known and respected in educational circles and within a year of graduating was able to open her own girls' school in Dunedin, proudly named after the pioneering women's college at Cambridge, Girton College. From modest beginnings of four pupils in a disused hall, Girton flourished.

In 1897 Caroline accepted an invitation to open a Girton College in Christchurch. Both schools were up-market establishments, with a roll of about sixty each, enjoying a fine reputation for scholarship and accomplishments. Caroline, who was herself an outstanding teacher, especially of English literature, as well as a fluent public speaker, enjoyed the freedom the private school system gave her to train her own staff and put her own ideas into practice. As gleaned from her addresses at annual break-up ceremonies, these ideas encompassed the moral (to 'fit the girls for the battle of life') and the practical (to train teachers for the secondary schools).

In 1911 Caroline sold the Dunedin Girton to her co-principal, in order to settle in Christchurch. Her health collapsed soon after this and, in spite of a long recuperative sea voyage undertaken in 1912, she was not able to resume her responsibilities. She died of a heart attack in August 1914.

Caroline Freeman's schools were among the best private schools for girls during an exciting, expansionist period of girls' education in New Zealand. They show her a worthy 'first lady graduate' of Otago University.   *Dorothy Page*

Quotations
para.1 W. Brown, graduation address in *Otago Daily Times*, 28 Aug. 1855
para.3 Advertisement in *Otago Daily Times*, 3 April 1884 (also cited B. Harper, *Petticoat Pioneers*, p.67); H. Fodor, tribute to Caroline Freeman, photocopy given by family member
para.4 Address at Girton College break-up, *The Press*, 18 Dec. 1897

Published Sources
The Cyclopedia of New Zealand, vol.3, Canterbury, Christchurch, 1903, p.183
Gardner, W. J. *Colonial Cap and Gown*, Christchurch, 1979
Green Island School Souvenir Booklet, 73rd anniversary, 1853–1926, School Jubilee pamphlets, 206, Hocken
Harper, B. *Petticoat Pioneers: South Island Women of the Colonial Era*, Book Three, Wellington, 1980
Page, D. 'Otago University's First Woman Graduate', *Otago Daily Times*, 10 Aug. 1985

BRIAR GARDNER

1879–1968

Miss Gardner was a pioneer in her work . . . great credit was due to her, inasmuch as she carried the whole thing through from the designing to the finishing of the pot, work usually done by a series of experts. Great interest has been shown, and Miss Gardner deserves every encouragement.

Briar Gardner worked and exhibited as a potter some twenty-five years before the advent of the studio pottery movement in New Zealand.

Maria Louise Gardner, known as Briar, was the daughter of John and Louisa Gardner of Mataia Estate, Glorit (on the Kaipara Harbour). Her family had strong links with the pottery industry: her maternal grandfather, Rice Owen Clark, was the founder of the brick and pipe works in Hobsonville, an area renowned for its heavy clay soils. 'As a child Briar watched the pipes being extruded from the moulds and the flanges expertly turned. She could not resist dabbling in the lovely plastic stuff.'

Briar was educated at home, where she had a tutor; she also had lessons from her grandparents in Hobsonville, and access to their extensive library. Lessons included fine needlework, painting, and music.

In 1901, Briar moved to New Lynn to keep house for her three brothers, who were establishing their own brickworks. When her younger sisters took over her domestic duties in 1904, Briar was free to develop her interest in embroidery, tapestry, and painting. She spent some years in Australia studying these crafts, and in 1920 exhibited art needlework in Auckland.

Briar did not become a potter until she was in her mid-forties. After the First World War, one of her brothers introduced a pottery wheel to the brickworks, and brought William Speers, an expert thrower from the Royal Doulton factory in England, out to New Zealand to operate it. Briar watched him at work, and was inspired. She persuaded her brothers to let her use the wheel outside factory hours. In the cold early mornings at the deserted yard, Briar taught herself to throw her first pots, firing them in the corners of her brothers' kilns during brick firings. The results were coarse and often flawed, but she persevered, and hunted the libraries for information on ancient Greek and Roman pottery methods. Her brothers, though initially sceptical, were won over, and had a small coal-fired kiln built for her at the brickworks. There Briar experimented with firing and glazing, learning through trial and error. She had lessons in modelling clay from William Wright of the Elam School of Art, and learned about Maori design from Trevor Lloyds, a fellow member of the Auckland Society of Arts.

In December 1930, Briar held the first exhibition of Auckland pottery in the Auckland Society of Arts rooms, and during the 1930s exhibited her pottery regularly with the society.

Briar Gardner in front of her first pottery kiln, c.1927. *G. Louise Gardner*

One was struck by the soft harmonious colouring and lovely effects of flowing glazes. Her shapes were interesting and her colour good. Maori design used sparingly forms the basis for some of the most interesting pots, and New Zealand flora was seen effectively in quite a number.

Although she worked for years in almost total isolation, public interest in her pottery grew. Smith and Caughey provided a retail outlet for her pots, she gave lessons and radio talks, and demonstrated with her potter's wheel at winter shows. During the Second World War disabled ex-servicemen came to her studio for weekly occupational therapy.

Following the Second World War, the studio pottery movement began to flourish in Auckland. *A Potter's Book* by Bernard Leach had been published, disseminating knowledge of pottery-making. Formal instruction in pottery became established in New Zealand.

Arthritis in her hands forced Briar Gardner, now over seventy, to give up pottery. Turning instead to another love, speech and drama, she worked in film and radio, gained her LTCL at the age of seventy-three, and taught speech for several years. She died in New Lynn in 1968, aged ninety.   *Justine Olsen*

Quotations
para.1 *Art in NZ*, vol.4 no.15, March 1932, p.227
para.2 O. Jones, 'Early Potting in Auckland', p.19
para.6 *Art in NZ*, vol.9 no.2, Dec. 1936, p.109

Published Sources
Art in NZ, vol.4 no.15, March 1932; vol.9 no.2, Dec. 1936
Gardner, G. Louise. 'Briar Gardner, 1879–1968, Potter Extraordinary', *Auckland-Waikato Historical Journal*, no.44, April 1984
Jones, Olive. 'Early Potting in Auckland', *NZ Potter*, vol.3 no.1, Aug. 1960, pp. 19–23
Lambert, Gail. *Pottery in New Zealand*, Auckland, 1985.
Scott, D. *Fire on the Clay*, Auckland, 1979
Tizard, R. *The Auckland Society of Arts 1870–1970: A Centennial History*, Auckland, 1972

AILEEN GARMSON

1890s

A nurse and union organiser, Ida Aileen Marie Garmson came to Christchurch from New South Wales in the early 1890s. As with many nineteenth-century women, little is known of her private life; it is her public activity which has generated records and subsequent attention. Nor do we know what she did before coming to Christchurch and after she left. However, her time in Canterbury shows that Mrs Garmson, as she was always referred to, was principally interested in the plight of women workers and the unemployed, and was a leading union official at a time when even all-female unions had male leadership. She remains most famous for her efforts to stop New Zealand 'blacklegs' from breaking the shearers' strike in Australia in 1894.

Mrs Garmson's union activities began in Christchurch in July 1893 when she joined the local branch of the Amalgamated Shearers' and Labourers' Union

(ASLU), which in 1894 became the New Zealand Workers' Union (NZWU). She soon became a very active member, holding the offices of treasurer and then secretary until 1896, and attending the ASLU and NZWU national conferences as the Christchurch delegate from 1893 to 1895. However, at the 1896 conference she was criticised for failing to keep good, accurate minutes, and the *Otago Daily Times* reported that the executive strongly objected to her being appointed secretary again.

Mrs Garmson was also a Master Workman of the Christchurch Knights of Labour. She was constantly criticised in the newspapers both for her advocacy of unionism and for being a woman active in public life. For example, 'Cave' thought she did it all for self-glorification and to seek higher political office, and believed she controlled the Christchurch branch of the Workers' Union.

It goes without saying where a body of men like that cannot find one among them to take the office of secretary, but have to fall back on petticoats, the secretary will 'boss the show'.

She persuaded the union to endorse the organisation of women workers into trade unions, and to admit them into membership of the union at reduced rates. She also wanted to set up a Women Workers' Union branch of the New Zealand Workers' Union. At the same time, Marianne Tasker was organising women workers through the Wellington branch of the union.

As well as working within union structures, Mrs Garmson did a lot of work in the community. She addressed and chaired several local public meetings on labour matters and the advantages of unionism. Just after she joined the ASLU, when New Zealand and particularly Otago and Canterbury were experiencing a period of economic recession, she helped to organise a meeting of the unemployed in Christchurch's Cathedral Square. Forums were held regularly through the winter. The following year she was one of fifteen women who met with the mayor to support local endeavours to provide work for unemployed men in the city and suburbs, and formed a committee to canvass each district for subscriptions. She was also a committee member of the Canterbury Women's Institute and secretary of the Women's Section of the Canterbury Liberal Association.

Mrs Garmson's work on behalf of domestic servants and tailoresses earned her a lot of bad press, and it is in this connection that one sees evidence of her forceful personality and her unflagging championship of the cause. In March 1894 she chaired a meeting of domestic servants and women workers at the Temperance Hall. She reported that:

numbers of young girls were subjected to various impositions at the hands of some employers; some dressmakers . . . worked about ten hours a day and received nothing for twelve months, and at the end of that time they were only paid 2s 6d a week.

Mrs Garmson told her audience that a union provided a more effectual way for employees to bring their grievances before employers. Several months later she wrote:

Who can say that the lot of servants has fallen in pleasant places when they see

or know of a girl living from morn till night and late into the night for no other
purpose than work, work, work. No leisure for reading or recreation, and this is
what is styled a 'profession'. When the work of a house is done, what right has
an employer to control the actions of an employee? . . . Once more I ask the
domestic servants to stand up for themselves and let their voices be heard.

Her efforts to persuade them to unionise met with resistance from the workers themselves and from the public. Many servants did not think a union was necessary, because the continuing shortage of domestics made it easier for those who were badly treated to find another job. Long hours of work also made it almost impossible for meetings to be arranged, which did not assist unity. The first steps towards a union were taken in 1907 when an attempt was made to set standards. A circular was sent to employers demanding a maximum sixty-eight-hour week, with uniforms supplied and a well-ventilated bedroom. The Domestic Workers' Union was registered in 1908 with fifty-nine members, although numbers declined steadily until 1911 when no returns were sent and registration was cancelled.

Members of the public were virulent in their defence of existing practice, and Mrs Garmson was spirited in her replies in letters to the editor: 'No doubt our worthy friend believes in the dignity of leisure and makes others keep his pot boiling, for someone must work for he who does nothing.' She also came into conflict with other progressive women of the day, reminding us that women of the nineteenth century were no more unified in their political and social outlook than women today. In a series of letters to the editor of the *Lyttelton Times* during June and July of 1894, Jessie Mackay, a local poet and ardent feminist, challenged Garmson's efforts to unionise domestic workers. Although she thought relations between mistress and servant were not necessarily perfect, Mackay did not see how the aims and benefits of unionism could be applied to

such a necessarily varied and indefinite sphere as domestic employment . . .
Why then, when every atom of reformatory energy necessary is so urgently
required – why, in the name of common sense, does Mrs Garmson elect to
champion the one free and independent class in New Zealand?

Domestic service was the major source of employment for women in the nineteenth century, but an almost insatiable demand for servants exceeded the supply, especially when many women opted for factory work once the dressmaking and woollen industries were established in the 1880s. Thus, because of their strong bargaining position, servants here were often more independent and self-confident in spirit than their British counterparts – traits often referred to as 'servantgalism'. The well-to-do such as Jessie Mackay became concerned, as they had long found servants 'hard to find, cheeky when found and difficult to keep'. Mackay compared the servant favourably with the 'poor pupil teacher' or the put-upon 'shopgirl', and claimed that had Mrs Garmson, 'like many professional ladies, been obliged to relegate her maternal duties' to her servant 'we should certainly have heard nothing of fixed hours and formal rules'. In fact Mrs Garmson did have hired help, although she brought up her children herself.

Mrs Garmson achieved her greatest notoriety as a result of her involvement with the Australian shearers' strike. In 1894 Queensland shearers went on strike for better wages and conditions, and the Australian pastoralists advertised in the Christchurch papers offering free passages for those willing to go over and shear, and thus break the strike. Because of the high numbers of unemployed in New Zealand at the time, this was an attractive offer and 150 shearers were engaged to travel on the SS *Hauroto*. Mrs Garmson wrote to the *Lyttelton Times* urging New Zealand shearers not to 'cross the pond', but to stand firm 'each for all and all for each' with the strikers. The Christchurch NZWU appointed her its delegate to travel steerage with the men and talk them into changing their minds. She boarded the ship in August and by 'persuasion and sarcasm' managed to encourage many to return. Exact figures are disputed, with some sources arguing that Mrs Garmson overstated her success. Her exploits were recorded in a full page of ten cartoons in the *New Zealand Graphic* of 27 October 1894. The strike collapsed soon afterwards.

The last two glimpses we have of Aileen Garmson show her continued concern with labour and women's issues. In September 1896 she successfully gained a conviction against a local shopkeeper who was selling on the weekly half-holiday. Two years later, at a meeting in Auckland of the Women's Liberal League, she found herself at the centre of a controversy over whether the 'female franchise' was a failure and whether women's organisations were succeeding with their aims. The press, with characteristic venom, wrote that:

The principal offender, apparently, was our old friend . . . who was not ashamed to be described as 'molten lava' or as 'the terror of all the women of Christchurch'.

After this, no more is heard of this colourful and controversial woman.

Bronwyn Labrum

Quotations
para.3 *Lyttelton Times*, 3 July 1894
para.6 *Lyttelton Times*, 16 March 1894; 13 June 1894
para.8 *Lyttelton Times*, 13 June 1894; 18 June 1894
para.9 E. Olssen, 'Women, Work and Family', p.162; *Lyttelton Times*, 18 June 1894
para.10 *Canterbury Women*, p.54
para.11 *Lyttelton Times*, 21 Feb. 1898

Published Sources
Arnold, Rollo. 'Yeoman and Nomads', *NZJH*, vol.18 no.2, Oct. 1984
NZ Graphic, 27 Oct. 1894
Olssen, Erik, 'Women, Work and Family: 1880–1926', in P. Bunkle and B. Hughes (eds), *Women in New Zealand Society*, Auckland, 1980, p.162
Regional Women's Decade Committee. *Canterbury Women Since 1893*, Christchurch, 1979
Roth, Bert and Hammond, Jenny. *Toil and Trouble*, Auckland, 1981

ANNABELLA MARY GEDDES *1864–1955*

MARY A. GEDDES *1887–1968*

Annabella Mary Geddes was every inch the society matron. Elegantly groomed, stately and gracious, she hosted balls and tennis parties at 'Hazelbank', her Auckland mansion, travelled overseas to the watering places of Europe, and knew all the best people in town. But Mary was more than a fashionable woman. In the early years of the twentieth century, she was involved in virtually every philanthropic activity in the city, giving unstintingly of her wealth and her time.

Mary had not been born to status and riches, for her own beginnings were very much more humble. Her father, William Webster, was one of the earliest sawmillers in the Hokianga, an enterprise at which he did not prosper. His brother, visiting from Scotland, said that William was an 'easy going young man . . . and could not fight the battle of life'. Officers from a survey ship visiting the district were surprised to discover that William's major project was the construction of an organ, for which he was hand-cutting ivory for the keys.

In the early 1850s, Webster married Anabella Gillies, daughter of Maori and Pakeha parents, who had been working for Jane Hobbs at the Mangungu mission. Mary was born on 19 May 1864 and was educated at the mission school. She grew up speaking Maori and was perfectly bilingual all her life.

Sent to Auckland to finish her education, Mary met and married John McKail Geddes, a prosperous tea and coffee merchant. Seven children were born and the family lived in some style. When John died in 1910, Mary was left a

Annabella Mary Geddes, centre back, with her family. *Hanna photo/Alistair Geddes*

231

widow of considerable substance. She had already begun to involve herself in charitable work, was on the original Plunket committee of 1908, on the committee of the Society for the Protection of Women and Children, and from 1907 had formed recreational and training clubs for Maori girls coming to the city. Mary always maintained links with her Maori relatives from the Hokianga, entertaining them at her home. She trained their daughters in domestic work in her home before placing them with her friends, whom she cautioned that these were girls of status in their own culture and should be treated accordingly.

After her husband's death, Mary threw her energies into the Auckland YWCA, becoming its president in 1913 and holding the position for six years. It was Mary more than anyone else who fought for the fine new home the association built in Queen Street, campaigning at a time when war fever militated against such lavish expenditure on women.

Mary Geddes argued that girls deserved just as good as the boys, and her contacts with Auckland's businessmen meant she was highly successful when she went looking for sponsors. She supported the association in other ways: she lent her car, paid for the care of sick immigrant girls, purchased a hostel, and made her tennis court available.

Mary was not just motivated by philanthropy. She was forward-thinking in her views on women and was involved in the rekindling of feminism in Auckland at the end of the First World War. In 1917, she played a dominant role at a mass meeting of women called to discuss the perennial feminist issues: the age of consent, women's health patrols, and venereal disease. With the revival of the National Council of Women in Auckland, Mary sat on the executive and took a leading part in a deputation to parliament asking for legislation to allow women to stand for parliament.

Right through the period of Mary Geddes' greatest involvement with the Auckland YWCA, her daughter Mary A. Geddes also made her mark on the organisation.

Born on 24 February 1887, Mary Geddes was the oldest child in the family. An intelligent, able girl and a good sportswoman, she attended the Auckland Grammar School up the road from 'Hazelbank'. When Mary announced she wished to train as a doctor, a brave ambition at the time, her father, a man of strong views and overwhelming personality, deemed it a totally unsuitable pursuit for a girl.

Mary is described by those who remember her as a stern disciplinarian who didn't always manage to suppress her rage. She was quite different from her calm, sweet-natured mother, although both are described as strong willed. Denied her desire to be a doctor, Mary too began to work in the YWCA. In 1913, she went to the YWCA training school at Sydney, returning to Auckland to establish the Hearth Fire Movement, an early girls' movement which taught domestic skills and was based on an ideology of devotion to the home. In 1915, Mary took up the position of YWCA national girls' department secretary for Australasia, based in Sydney, a challenging role involving travel, public speaking, and leadership skills. Visiting Auckland, Mary told audiences that girls' work aimed at producing 'a competent worker and a useful citizen'. It was necessary, she said, to encourage in girls 'a belief in themselves, and co-operation in work and play, that brings out the best in both those who give and those who receive'.

Mary resigned her post in 1919, but maintained her interest in the YWCA by serving on the board and chairing the progressive girls' department. She was placed on the first New Zealand field committee (the forerunner of the YWCA of New Zealand), along with her mother, and represented the New Zealand YWCA overseas. Mary and her mother frequently travelled abroad, visiting the ski resorts of Europe. In her obituary Mary is credited with being the first woman to win the New Zealand women's skiing championship, in 1921.

The Depression struck the family firm a deathly blow from which it was not to recover. All the servants were laid off and Mary had not only to take over the care of her ageing mother, but also to set up cottage industries to try to pay the bills.

In 1939, 'Hazelbank' was sold to the university and a new home was established in Remuera. At the same time an exciting new career opened up for Mary. Dorothy Hawkins, head of the Women's Army Auxiliary Corps (WAAC) for the Northern Military District, enlisted her as commandant of WAACs at Papakura Military Camp. Mary trained at Trentham where she gained the rank of captain, then took over the Papakura 'Waacery' for the whole of the Second World War. She was never happier; she was just entering her fifties, and all her organisational and leadership qualities could be brought into play.

By the late 1940s Mary had returned to housekeeping and the care of her mother. Mrs Geddes died in December 1955, aged ninety-one. Her daughter died thirteen years later.   *Sandra Coney*

Quotations
para.2 J. Webster, *Reminisences*, p.240
para.10 *NZ Herald*, 30 April 1919, YWCA scrapbooks, AIM
Unpublished Sources
Auckland YWCA archives, AIM
Interview with Alastair Geddes, 1986
Minutes of the Auckland Branch of the National Council of Women, AIM
Published Sources
Auckland Star, 16 Nov. 1968 (obituary)
Coney, Sandra. *Every Girl: A Social History of Women and the YWCA in Auckland*, Auckland, 1986
Latham, Iris. *The WAAC Story*, Wellington, 1986
Lee, Jack. *Hokianga*, Auckland, 1987
NZ Herald, 7 Dec. 1955 (obituary); 18 Nov. 1968 (obituary)
Webster, John. *Reminiscences of an Old Settler*, Christchurch, 1908

HELEN GIBB

1839–1914

Cabbage Tree Flat Accommodation House, on the road between Amberley and Cheviot in Canterbury, was kept by a widow, Helen Gibb. Helen Lindsay was born in Forfarshire, Scotland, on 9 July 1839. From the age of nine she worked as a dairymaid. Later she became engaged to Stewart Gibb and had a son, James, in 1858. In 1860, Stewart Gibb sailed to Canterbury on the *Matoaka*.

Here he was employed as a shepherd on Teviotdale Station in North Canterbury. Helen did not leave Scotland until 1863, working right up to the day she left. With James, and Stewart's brother and his wife, she arrived in Lyttelton on the *Accrington* on 5 September 1863.

Stewart Gibb and Helen were married twelve days later at Cameron's Hotel in Kaiapoi on the way to Teviotdale. They were employed as a married couple on the station. Helen's second son, Stewart, was born in 1864. Already in labour, Helen set off on horseback with her husband to Amberley, but was obliged to stop; Stewart delivered the baby in a sod hut beside the road.

Helen was widowed while pregnant with her fourth child; Stewart Gibb drowned on 2 March 1867 while bathing in the Motunau River. He had purchased sixty acres at Cabbage Tree Flat near Motunau, and Helen decided to farm this land to support herself and her children. She had a sod cottage built, but later erected a four-roomed wooden house because the cottage was too damp and she suffered from rheumatism.

She wrote to Forfarshire for gorse seeds to plant as hedges. She planted an orchard and kept cows and sheep. Her sons helped her as they got older, but she remained always enterprising and independent. In the 1860s, seeing that discarded telegraph poles would provide much-needed firewood, she borrowed a horse, found out how to attach the chain to the poles, and with the assistance only of James, dragged them home.

In the early 1870s the main road to Cheviot was established – and it ran right past Helen Gibb's house. Previously she had supplied refreshments to travellers, but now she set up an accommodation house where travellers could stay overnight and stock could be confined in the paddocks close to the house. During the 1870s her house was virtually the only one on the Amberley-Cheviot

Helen Gibb, right, with her daughter Ella at the Accommodation House, Cabbage Tree Flat, Motunau, Canterbury, c.1888. *Canterbury Museum*

road and everybody stopped there. By 1882 she had purchased an adjoining seventy-five acres.

Helen, a Presbyterian, was a deeply religious person. Church services were held in her house until the Motunau school was built in 1893. She often prayed while she worked, and grace was said at breakfast and dinner, accompanied by Bible readings, no matter who was present.

She was a forthright woman who would speak her mind directly. When her neighbour, William Acton Adams, attempted to move the surveyed boundary line and build a fence, she confronted him with her Bible in her hand, and quoted scripture to him about boundaries, widows, and orphans. The boundary stayed in its original position.

Until 1902, when the railway reached Scargill, Motunau was the centre of the area, and Helen was the centre of life at Cabbage Tree Flat. She acted as postmistress from 1883 to 1899, and her house was the focus of much of the activity in the area. The coming of the railway changed all this as the centre then became Scargill. By this time Helen was sixty-three.

She never stopped working, and late in life would try to do all the things she had done previously. Her sons stayed in the same area, and grandchildren boarded with her while at school in Motunau. Her daughter Ella lived with her until she died on 28 July 1914, after eighteen months' illness.   *Jo-Anne Smith*

Unpublished Sources
Information was provided by Annie Denton, Helen Gibb's granddaughter.
G. R. Macdonald Biographies, Canterbury Museum
James B. Roberts, 'Reminiscences', MS typescript, Canterbury Museum
Published Sources
The Cyclopedia of New Zealand, vol.3, Canterbury, Christchurch, 1903, p.548–9
The Press, 7 March 1867
Roberts, T. E. L. *Motunau, or The Hills of Home*, Rangiora, 1946

EMILY GIBSON

1864–1947

Emily Patricia Ray was born in Dublin in 1864. From the age of fifteen she lived and worked in London until she embarked on the *Tongariro* with her widowed sister and two nieces, arriving in Wellington in 1891. A month later they moved to Auckland, her home until her death in 1947. As an experienced compositor and proof-reader, she found work with the *Auckland Star*, which had begun to employ women in 1875.

Emily and her sister, Clementine Kirkby, 'discovered that the movement of women's suffrage was in full swing, and we naturally joined up with the local Franchise League'. After the Electoral Act (1893) gave women the vote, Emily was in one of the first groups to walk between rows of jeering men to the polling-booth in Rutland Street. 'We were brave because we were together, but not one of us was not trembling and trying to hold back tears.'

At thirty-one she married William Edward Gibson, a bricklayer from

London who had spent some time in Australia before settling in New Zealand. The couple had two daughters and a son. Although Emily left her paid employment after the birth of her first child, her political interests and activities remained a lifelong commitment.

'The Woman's Place', a poem she wrote in 1907, made her own beliefs plain. She said of the woman at home:

> *Cosy and snug and warm*
> *. . . must all her life be centred*
> *Within that narrow space*
> *While sisters slave and sin for bread? . . .*
>
> *While Might is Right and Giant Greed*
> *Enslave the human race,*
> *In the vanguard by her brother –*
> *That is the woman's place.*

In 1897 she became a delegate to the newly formed National Council of Women (NCW), then a radical organisation. One of its campaigns was to put an end to the practice of many employers who refused to pay apprentices for their first twelve months' work.

We women were infuriated over this system and every woman's society from North to South showered appeals to the Government . . . until Mr Seddon was so pestered . . . that he passed an Act of Parliament . . . that every boy or girl employed in any industry in New Zealand must be paid a minimum wage of five shillings a week.

At the fourth annual convention of the NCW in 1899, Emily presented a paper advocating the formation of a union for domestic servants, a popular proposal which, however, never drew more than a token government response. The NCW was also critical of the failure of small businesses to observe the eight-hour day.

In 1912 Emily gave evidence before a Royal Commission on the Cost of Living. There were approximately 300 witnesses, only six of them women. She was described as 'a married woman engaged in home duties' and said she appeared as secretary of the Women's Political League (formerly the Franchise League). Her submission touched on the doubling of Auckland rents; the existence of coal and fish 'rings' that eliminated competition; the probable use of sweated labour among clothing workers; the expense of school books and uniforms; and scarce, therefore dear, butter.

Emily and some like-minded colleagues found the policies of the original Franchise League too conservative, and briefly formed a breakaway group, the Women's Political League, with policies based on socialist concepts of social justice, equality and world peace. In 1918 it amalgamated with the two-year-old New Zealand branch of the Women's International League for Peace and Freedom (WILPF) and in 1925 evolved into the Auckland Women's Branch of the New Zealand Labour Party (Emily had also been a foundation member of the Auckland West Branch). Then in 1930 WILPF (Emily was corresponding secretary) separated itself again from the Labour Party, and in the following year collected a remarkable (for the time) 44,000 signatures to a petition for disarmament.

Emily's writings reflected her wide interests. In addition to organisational letters and reports, she produced poetry, short stories, general articles, ran a children's page for the *Maoriland Worker*, edited the 'Women's Point of View' page in the *Auckland Labour News* and at one stage wrote a weekly column on music in the *Auckland Star* under the name of 'Orpheus'. (Her sister had been an opera singer in London and in her later years Emily used to sit at the piano every morning and play opera choruses very loudly.) Described as modest and unassuming, she was a small woman, only about five feet tall, who was never aggressive and never complained about her increasing deafness. Her passion for justice never faltered – in 1936 she was again advocating unions for domestic servants in an article in *The Working Woman* and condemning the idea of training institutions. 'The girls do not want to be trained, they want to be treated like human beings, not slaves.'

The next year, when she was seventy-three, she became a member of the advisory board of *Woman Today*, a new monthly magazine standing for 'Peace, Freedom and Progress', to which she also contributed. The most appropriate summing up of her beliefs is her own:

No one here is more enthusiastic about Socialism than I am – it embraces everything I have fought for and barracked for all my life – from Home Rule and Women's Suffrage to a municipal fish market.

Margot Roth

Quotations

para.2 E. Gibson, 'Then and Now', in *Woman Today*, Aug. 1939, p.12; *The Illustrated Encyclopaedia*, p.474

para.4 In C. Purdue (ed.), *Women in the Labour Cause*, p.2

para.5 E. Gibson, 'Then and Now', in *Woman Today*, Sept. 1939, p.14

para.6 *AJHR* 1912 II, H-18, pp.247–8

para.8 E. Gibson, 'The Position of the Domestic Worker'

para.9 E. Gibson, 'The Woman's Place', p.19

Published Sources

AJHR 1890, H-5, p.52; 1912 II, H-18 pp.247–8

Gibson, Emily. 'The Woman's Place' in Connie Purdue (ed.), *Women in the Labour Cause*, Auckland, 1975

Gibson, Emily. 'The Position of the Domestic Worker', *The Working Woman*, July 1936, pp.3–4

Gibson, Emily. 'Peace on Earth', *Woman Today*, April 1937, pp.6–7

Gibson, Emily. 'The Child Welfare Act', *Woman Today*, Aug. 1937, pp.29–31

Gibson, Emily. 'Then and Now', *Woman Today*, Aug. 1939, pp.12–13, Sept. 1939, pp.14–15

Holt, Betty. *Women for Peace and Freedom*, Auckland, 1985

McLauchlan, G. (ed.). *The Illustrated Encyclopaedia of New Zealand*, Auckland, 1989, p.474

NZ Rationalist, July 1947, p.15 (obituary)

ERENA RAUKURA GILLIES
TAUA FAN

1896–1989

> *He tohu aroha ki a koe te taonga o Ngai Tahupotiki.*
> *A sign of love for the treasure of Ngai Tahupotiki.*

The life of Erena Raukura Gillies of Ngai Tahupotiki spanned enormous social change in the story of her people. During her early infancy it was estimated that the average life span of Maori women was twenty-four years and that of Maori men twenty-seven years. The children born into Ngai Tahu between 1886 and 1896 stood a 58 per cent chance of not living until five years compared with the 90 per cent survival rate of their pakeha* counterparts. Raukura, born in 1896, survived.

In many respects she was a privileged child, particularly in the Ngai Tahu context. A member of a hapu which still had some reserve land, Raukura was able to grow up secure in the sense of her several papakainga and tura-ngawaewae. Because her family had a small land base on Banks Pensinsula secured to them after the infamous Crown negotiation of the 1848 Kemp purchase, she was insulated during her childhood from the hardest edges of colonial impact. Almost a hundred years later her mokopuna were to be deeply grateful for the solid strength and depth of Maoritanga in the life of their beloved Taua Fan ('I don't know how I got that name').

The political focus of her childhood was energetic and steady. Seriously depleted by the musket wars of the 1820s and the government land grabs from the 1840s onward, Raukura's family were constantly engaged in Maori nationalism. Her tipuna, Hoani Tikao, signed the Treaty of Waitangi under the name of John Love. He demanded a more realistic price (£5 million) for the transfer to the Crown of the ownership of the Canterbury Plains and, as surveyor and mathematician, he recalculated every boundary purchased by the government agent so that his descendants would not be deprived of any of their land.

Tikao's nephew Hoani Taare Tikao also devoted his life to the pursuit of justice for his disenfranchised people. In this work he was usually accompanied by his wife, Matahana Toko Solomon. Raukura was the youngest of their five girls and her life was to a large extent shaped by the political activities of her people.

Her mother's whakapapa placed Ruakura securely in the bosom of Ngai Tahu as a member of Ngai Tuahuriri and through her grandmother to the earlier tangata whenua peoples, notably the Waitaha of Murihiku. The whakapapa of he father took her through Tuhaitara and Marukore to Mataatua, Tuhoe, and to Ngati Awa and Te Ati Awa. Through her tipuna Tutekawa she went back to Ngai Tamanuhiri of Muriwai and through her tipuna Rakiaihikuroa she took descent from Ngati Kahungunu.

Her Ngati Kuri descent connected her back to Te Taitokerau, and through all her grandparents she belonged to the major hapu of Ngai Tahu, taking sub-

*The author uses 'pakeha' rather than 'Pakeha', as she regards the term as an adjective, not a proper noun.

238

stantial parts of her identity from Ngati Irakehu, Ngai Tutehuarewa, and Ngati Kahukura. She is buried with her family in the hapu of Ngati Wheke in the ancient pa at Te Rapaki o Te Rangiwhakaputa on the shores of Whakaraupo (Lyttelton Harbour).

Although the world around them was swirling with change, Raukura's family took strong measures to maintain their Maoritanga. 'My parents never spoke English in the house, I spoke Kai Tahu dialect right until I married and went north. My husband's folks used to tease me, I couldn't speak any other way.' Normal conditions of tapu prevailed. The cooking was always done in a kauta (outside cooking shelter), separate from the house. The same rules applied to sanitary arrangements. Raukura maintained both of these rules until late in her life when ill health forced her to bring stoves and lavatories under one roof.

Her father moved to Rapaki, closer to school facilities for his children. Raukura was eventually to make this her permanent home. Life was full; Raukura had the example of a strong mother and aunts, and knew clearly her own place in the community, as the youngest of the girls.

Her status prevented her from playing with all the other children and she was chaperoned by her Taua and provided with special companions in the same circumstances. Later she attended the taumau (betrothal) of her special friend Te Uira Te Heuheu to the son of King Mahuta of the Kingitanga at Waihi pa on Taupo Moana. 'Te Uira and I sat in the whare and tried to get a look at this man she was to marry.' They both watched as a huge display of bridal gifts were laid on the marae and listened to the whaikorero discussing the importance of this alliance. They embraced and whispered their farewells and Te Uira left to begin her new life. Raukura said, 'I said goodbye to my friend and went home to my people. Little did I know that soon the same thing was to happen to me.' Her family's part of that kopaki (presentation of gifts) was a number of gold sovereigns.

The Prince of Wales visited Rotorua in 1918. 'The government was giving fares to all the Maori to go to Rotorua.' Raukura had a wonderful wardrobe, and a chaperone. Her portmanteau was packed. Just before leaving, however, she was called to a gathering of her kaumatua which included the pakeha schoolmaster, who was the current Earl of Huntingdon. The great influenza epidemic had reached Rapaki, and someone was needed to turn the meeting-house into a hospital ward and supervise the nursing in the pa. Raukura was asked to stay home, and she did so. Over the time of the epidemic, every household in Te Wheke was checked. There were no deaths. And 'the Prince of Wales came to Christchurch and so I saw him there.'

Almost by chance, assisting at the birth of her niece led Raukura into the role of midwife to her whanau. In her later years, though, she was able to advise her descendants of the histories of their grandmothers and mothers. This special status as the gynaecological historian of her family was particularly valuable in a small, close community. There is a certain comfort, a sense of timelessness and continuity in being able to discuss your personal experience as a Maori woman with that midwife who shares the travail, joy and whakapapa with the women of one's whanau.

Raukura recalled a fishing camp almost eighty years ago, when she was delivering one of her nieces. 'There I was trying to get a light from a hurricane lamp and the baby was turned the wrong way.' But, she said, 'I never lost a baby.' Later, legislation giving pakeha doctors control over the childbirth process deprived her whanau of their midwife.

After the First World War, a tono (bid) was made for Raukura's marriage by the people of Ngati Kahungunu at Waimarama. Their son Robert Tukuewe Gillies had just returned from the war; he was to be married to Raukura. When questioned later about her response to this sudden question of her marriage she said, 'Hei whakamahanai nga toto.' The marriage was arranged between families to 'keep the blood warm' – to maintain longstanding political, land and family alliances. Raukura and Bob were married at Rapaki on 7 July 1920 and later moved to the North Island. The union lasted almost sixty years, terminated only by his death. True to the design of their old people, their children and grand-children move with great ease between Ngati Kahungunu and Ngai Tahupotiki to this day.

Erena Raukura Gillies.
Rosemary Fullerton-Smith-Haeata

As well as bringing up her four children, mokopuna and whangai, Taua Fan also gave home, shelter and love to whangai-pakeha. Her home was open and her love for people almost unconditional. Arthritis prevented much physical activity but with extraordinary patience she waited for her people to find their way to her. Occasionally there would be a reminder to tend to land matters, or support and encouragement for those caught in the turmoil of the pakeha legal or the complex and often painful educational system. As they came home to her, Taua Fan gave to her whanau, deepening and strengthening their own version of Maoriness, shaping with hers, providing a core. Many children over the years owe much of their identity to Taua Fan. Her great skill lay in being an arbiter without appearing to be so. Everyone looked to her for the leadership and knowledge she was able to give without controlling and disabling her people.

Having outlasted her contemporaries, and almost two generations of her people, Raukura was ready to die. Each death in the whanau was very painful to her and she felt she was being left past her useful time. In the way of her people she began to call to her old people and her siblings to take her. They came early in April 1989 and took a treasure of Ngati Irakehu back to themselves.

A lasting image of Erena Raukura Tikao is of a tiny white-haired woman, bent over the kitchen table with her mokopuna great-granddaughter, working on School Certificate Maori language.   *Irihapeti Ramsden*

Unpublished Sources
Information comes from family members and friends. The quotations are from these sources. The author is one of Erena Raukaura Gillies' mokopuna.
'A Brief Chronology of Health Among Maori and Pakeha', including a chronological survey of Maori and Pakeha health services in New Zealand, papers prepared by the Waitangi Consultancy Group, Wellington, 1989
'Reports of Dr Pomare, Health Officer to the Maoris, and of the Native Sanitary Inspectors, *AJHR*, H-31, vol.4, 1907, pp.52–9

Published Sources
Beattie, Herries. *Tikao Talks: ka taoka tapu o te ao kohatu: treasures from the ancient world of the Maori*, told by Teone Tikao to Herries Beattie, Auckland, 1990
Cowan, James. 'Tikao the Sailor', *Akaroa Mail*, 1 Jan. 1918
Poole, Ian. *Te Iwi Maori: A New Zealand Population, Past, Present and Projected*, Auckland, 1990

ELIZABETH GILMER

1880–1960

Elizabeth May Gilmer was born into public life, as the daughter of Louisa Jane Seddon (born Spotswood) and Richard John Seddon, Liberal politician and prime minister from 1893 to 1906.

She came from a family of strong personalities. Richard Seddon was a towering figure in New Zealand politics, but Elizabeth later spoke of her mother as the driving force in the family, 'The woman who was the power behind my father'. On women's issues Seddon was ambivalent. Opposed to the Women's Suffrage Bill of 1887, he spoke out against 'petticoat government', saying 'We shall have to look well to our laurels and assert our prerogative as the lords of creation before long.' Once the 1893 Electoral Bill granting women suffrage had been passed, however, he praised its results.

Elizabeth's early life was spent at Kumara, on the West Coast, where she attended the local school. In 1895 Louisa and the children moved to Wellington, to join Seddon. Elizabeth attended Girls' High School (later Wellington Girls' College). She took courses in typing and shorthand in 1902, with a view to entering the public service; then, with her sister Mary, acted as private secretary for her father, participating actively in public life.

In 1905 Elizabeth was engaged to Knox Gilmer, who was training to be a dentist. They married in 1907 after a year's mourning for her father's death in 1906. By this time her forthright manner was becoming well known: when the couple arrived in Sydney for their honeymoon, a newspaper commented:

Miss May Seddon, who is more like Maoriland's departed Dick as regards character, build and voice, than the whole of the remaining Seddons combined . . . is just as liable to board a car wearing a cotton blouse, a utilitarian skirt and her brother's cap, as she is to say exactly what she thinks of things in a voice remarkably reminiscent of the voice that died away for ever a little more than a year ago.

In the early 1930s Elizabeth began the public service for which she is remembered. Her two daughters, born in 1911 and 1914, were now old enough to take care of themselves, and Knox had died after a severe illness in 1921.

Her interest in conservation began in 1927 when she bought a log cabin at Te Marua, north of Wellington. The destruction of native bush there led her to work for conservation through groups such as the Forest and Bird Protection Society. Her interest was also practical: her own garden won the Bledisloe Cup twice for the best display of native flora, and she lobbied successfully for the reinstatement of tree planting on Arbor Day.

Local body politics was a natural field for her political and practical skills: she was a member of the Wellington Hospital Board from 1938 to 1953, and a city councillor from 1942 to 1953, both on the Citizens ticket. She worked to improve nurses' conditions, helped introduce 'meals on wheels', and argued for better library services in the city (particularly the free issue of books). She also served on school councils and boards in the region.

As a local politician, Elizabeth Gilmer was noted for her ability to cut through red tape and get things done. She was a formidable, and not always generous, opponent, who did not suffer fools gladly. In her personal capacity Elizabeth supported a number of community groups, particularly those concerned with women – the Unemployed Women's Association, the Home of Compassion, the City Mission Men's Shelter, and the YWCA all received her assistance.

On the outbreak of the Second World War she served on the central executive of the Women's War Services Auxiliary, established by Prime Minister Peter Fraser to co-ordinate the war effort. Fraser also appointed her to sit on the Loans and National Savings Committee. When, after the war, she was appointed to the Allocation Committee of Housing for the State Advances Corporation, she had established a reputation for political effectiveness rarely accorded women of that era.

In 1951 she became Dame Elizabeth Gilmer, in recognition of her achievements. She died in 1960, and was buried with her husband at Karori cemetery.

Bronwyn Labrum

Quotations
para.2 NZ Biographies, 1982, vol.2, p.118 (undated newspaper clipping), ATL; Patricia Grimshaw,
    Women's Suffrage in New Zealand, 2nd edn, Auckland, 1987, p.42, ATL
para.4 *The Bulletin*, 16 July 1907 (in 'Mother's Story')
Unpublished Sources
'Mother's Story as told by her daughter Jean, for her family', family publication in private possession

ESTHER GLEN

1881–1940

Alice Esther Glen, children's writer and journalist, had the gift of friendship that made her beloved of thousands through her work as 'Lady Gay' for the children's pages of Christchurch newspapers, and through the help she gave to many in the community.

Born in 1881 in Christchurch, she was the third of the twelve children of Robert Hogg Parker Glen, a merchant, and Alice Helen Glen (born White). Literary influence seems to have come from her mother's family. Esther produced a family journal and later she and her older sister Helen had short stories published. With the younger children and family friends, they organised all sorts of plays and entertainments. Another favourite family pastime was walking on the Port Hills.

It was this close and active family life which Esther used as the basis of her writing for children. She wrote the first truly New Zealand family story, *Six Little New Zealanders* (1917). Its sequel, *Uncles Three at Kamahi* (1926), and another story, *Robin of Maoriland* (1929), based more closely on her own family life in Gloucester Street, Christchurch, were published in England like the first. There was also a booklet of fairy stories, *Twinkles on the Mountain* (1919), and a story called 'Treasure of the Stars' which was serialised in the Christchurch *Press*.

A scene from Esther Glen's 1929 children's story *Robin of Maoriland*, which followed closely her own family life in Gloucester Street, Christchurch. The illustration, by Kathleen W. Coales, is captioned 'Maria hustled down the road, missing the cliffs more than once by nothing less than a sheer miracle'. *Dorothy Neal White Collection, National Library*

243

On first leaving school, she stayed home to help with the younger children for some years, then briefly ran a private kindergarten with her sister Helen. Then, until she became a full-time journalist, she worked as a typist and book-keeper for a legal firm in Christchurch, and also spent a short time in Australia. At the same time, she freelanced as a journalist and wrote poetry and her first two books.

From 1925, when she joined the staff of the *Sun* in Christchurch, her energies were mainly occupied with journalism and social service. The children's section of the *Sun*, started in 1922, was the first children's supplement in New Zealand, and under Esther as 'Lady Gay' it flourished. Not only did she encourage children to write and draw and share their hobbies, she also undertook to give them a grounding in civic affairs through the annual election of a child 'mayor', and to encourage them to become 'citizens of the world' through writing to pen-friends.

The idea of service to the community had been part of the children's page from the beginning. Esther carried on the 'Christmas mission' established by her predecessor, 'Sister Scatterjoy' (May C. Brown), when children would bake cakes and prepare presents for the children of poor families or for old people in need. She was capable of inspiring children to think of others and of 'investing the call for aid with the spirit and vitality of a challenge'.

While with the *Sun*, she also helped pioneer children's broadcasts, prepared classical stories for radio, and wrote radio plays. With her friend 'Breezy' (Georgina) Mackay, sister of Jessie Mackay, she wrote several children's panto-mimes which were produced in Christchurch. The actors were *Sun* children.

Her office, which she encouraged children to visit, was filled with their stamp collections, scrap-books, and pets, and she 'often incurred the wrath of the neat and orderly Lady Editor, with whom she shared an office, for the clutter of her belongings and for her habit of borrowing small items which she always forgot to return.'

In 1935, when the *Sun* folded, she moved to *The Press*, which added to its Thursday children's supplement the Saturday *Gay Gazette* under Lady Gay and her illustrator Joan Mayo, who had moved with her from the *Sun*.

But Esther was not interested only in children and old people; she would respond with her pen and her energy when a need arose. In 1929 she published a letter from a young woman who needed temporary work, and found there were many other girls and women with household services to offer. Through a public meeting, she brought them into contact with women who needed relief from home and children, and so the Christchurch Home Service Association began. Its purpose was: 'To promote a spirit of cooperation between employer and worker, and to raise the status of workers in the home.' By the time Esther Glen died, the organisation had hundreds of members, and its work was said to be 'a modest monument to her first quality – her constant interest in other people's problems and her anxiety to be of help in tackling them.'

During the Depression, she was also a member of the Women's Unemployment Committee, and it was at her prompting that the Christchurch City Council provided cottages not only for married pensioners, but also for 'spinsters'. As a single woman who lived alone for a time, she was well aware of their needs. Her own life, however, was rich in family and friends, who included writers such as Mona Tracy (who also had worked for *The Press*), Oliver Duff (editor of *The Press*), Edith Howes, H. C. D. Somerset, and Jessie Mackay.

Aside from her work for children, Esther Glen was considered one of the finest women journalists in the country. She was an expert on Canterbury history, especially that of Banks Peninsula, about which she wrote a good deal, and she was the only woman to receive an award in a New Zealand Journalists' Association competition in 1934. Generally, however, her journalism, like that of many other talented women at the time, was confined to the 'women's pages'.

Her special love always was children. As a radio tribute to her said:

. . . she possessed a remarkable gift for making a gay and festive occasion out of the most unpromising conditions . . . Her radiant personality was unique. She loved all children. Each individual child had an appeal for her. Her memory for children's names and faces was uncanny.

It was also said of her that 'children seemed to respond to her with warmth and devotion that few others could command'. True to her belief that colour and beauty are intended to cheer daily life, she would wear her prettiest frock to the many children's parties she attended. This spirit of fun and warmth was a feature of her books, her children's pages, and of her dealings with all who knew her.

When she died after a short illness in February 1940, children who had been contributors as 'sunbeams' or 'shipmates' flocked to her funeral with flowers.

The merit of her books for children was recognised by the Esther Glen Award for children's literature, set up in 1945 by the New Zealand Library Association. It continues to encourage the tradition she helped to establish of excellence in New Zealand children's literature. *Janet McCallum*

Quotations
para.6 M. B. Lovell-Smith, 'Esther Glen', p.2
para.8 C. M. Tremewan, 'Something for the Children', p.122
para.10 *The Press*, 10 Feb. 1940
para.13 M. B. Lovell-Smith, p.2; C. M. Tremewan, p.122

Unpublished Sources
Information was provided by Betty Gilderdale, Dorothy Bregmen, Robin du Fresne, John Sage, and Penny Tritt.
Lovell-Smith, Macie B. 'Esther Glen as a friend' (talk under the auspices of the National Council of Women), 3YA, Christchurch, 18 April 1940, transcript in possession of Penny Tritt

Published Sources
Ballantyne, Dorothy Neal. 'About Esther Glen', *New Zealand Book World*, no.3, Aug. 1973, p.34
Britten, Rosemary. 'When "The Press" Went "Gay" Once a Week', *The Press*, 9 July 1982
Dominion, 10 Feb. 1940 (obituary)
Gilderdale, Betty. *A Sea Change: 145 Years of New Zealand Junior Fiction*, Auckland, 1982
Gilderdale, Betty. 'Kotare Books: a new series of NZ Children's Classics', in *Children's Literature Association Year Book*, 1983
Hyde, Robin. 'Archives: The New Zealand Woman in Letters', *Women's Studies Journal*, vol.3 no.1, p.76
NZ Free Lance, 14 Feb. 1940 (obituary)
The Press, 10 Feb. 1940 (obituary)
Scholefield, G. H. (ed.). *A Dictionary of New Zealand Biography*, vol.2, Wellington, 1940
Tremewan, Christine M. 'Something for the Children', *Canterbury Women Since 1893*, Christchurch, 1979, pp.121–3

DORIS GORDON

1890-1956

Doris Clifton Gordon was born in Melbourne, Australia, in 1890, the daughter of Lucy Clifton Jolly (born Crouch) and Alfred Jolly, a bank manager. She moved to New Zealand with her family in 1894. Raised in Wellington and Tapanui, Otago, she graduated MB, ChB from the University of Otago in 1916, and later completed a Diploma in Public Health. At the age of twenty-six she married Dr William Gordon, with whom she entered a lifelong partnership in general practice.

Her first medical appointment was as a locum in the Ohakune and Raetihi district in 1918; she transferred to the Taranaki town of Stratford as locum to Dr Tom Paget in July of that year and in 1919, with her husband, bought Paget's Stratford practice and private hospital, 'Marire'(meaning 'peaceful'). There they continued to live and work for the rest of their lives; in 1942 a new 'Marire' was built to Doris's design, replacing the old hospital.

'Dr Doris', as she was known, was a dynamic force in New Zealand medicine and in the contemporary women's movement. Her mission was to raise the status of obstetrics and improve the quality of midwifery care by reforming the education of medical students, to work for the welfare of mothers and children, and to halt what she perceived to be a bureaucratic assault on private practice by public health officials.

Her interest in the care of women and children began early. In the male-dominated medical school, teaching about childbirth was poor, and Doris was critical also of the expectation that ministering to mothers and babies was women's work. Her belief in motherhood as women's destiny and her sense of service to humankind led her to dedicate herself to obstetrics. This was also a practical choice in the division of labour with her husband. 'I am not like a male doctor dependent on adequate pay for time given,' she wrote in 1937, 'hence I can do this work as a hobby, mission or research work, whatever you like to think it.'

Doris Gordon had four children, three sons and one daughter. She was active in the Plunket Society when her children were growing up and appreciated the advantages of having nurses to help from her own hospital. Her goal was to make women contented with their maternal lot, primarily by making them happy in pregnancy and by easing the pain of childbirth; by 1938 she advocated also domestic help and state housing.

In 1925 Doris Gordon was the first woman in Australia or New Zealand to be admitted a Fellow of the Royal College of Surgeons of Edinburgh. In 1954 she received 'the highest distinction', being elected Honorary Fellow of the Royal College of Obstetricians and Gynaecologists, 'the only woman to be so honoured, and . . . the only Honorary Fellow . . . in the Southern Hemisphere'.

As a doctor in country practice she was both a GP-surgeon and an obstetrician and, like other medical practitioners in isolated rural districts, she earned almost a cult following. In Taranaki she lived the mythology of the country GP, a mythology recorded in her two-volume autobiography, *Backblocks Baby-*

Dr Doris Gordon. *Alexander Turnbull Library*

Doctor (1955) and *Doctor Down Under* (1957). Mothers in Stratford might be recruited to bake a cake while at 'Marire', while those too distant for antenatal check-ups posted their urine samples to Dr Doris once a fortnight. During the war, with husbands away, mothers turned to her for advice.

From her provincial home, Doris Gordon led the New Zealand medical profession in the struggle with the Department of Health for the control of obstetrics in the 1920s and 1930s. Her ideal service was a full doctor service, that is, supervision by a medical practitioner of a mother in pregnancy, at the birth, and in the postnatal period. She believed that all births should take place in hospital.

Her powers as a lobbyist won public notice from 1927, when she galvanised her colleagues into founding the Obstetrical Society, of which she became honorary secretary. The society was formed in protest at state reforms in midwifery in the mid-1920s and represented the increasing ascendancy of doctors in obstetrics. As Doris Gordon explained, the society was 'first conceived as a banding together of doctors to refute allegations that obstetricians were a forcep-interfering pest-bearing coterie'. Under her leadership the society campaigned to stop midwifery from passing into state control.

While it was imperative to reform the training of medical students, Doris Gordon wanted the Obstetrical Society, not the Department of Health, to take the initiative in raising standards. She launched an Obstetrical Endowment Appeal to raise money for a professorship in obstetrics at the University of Otago in 1930. Aware that the Depression was about to cut public funds, she turned to the women of New Zealand to finance the obstetrical chair. She chose wealthy women throughout the country to lead the campaign ('eminently respectable ladies of the right tint of politics'), while she concentrated on 'big donations, addresses, and publicity'. The campaign raised £25,000. Her next target, a modern teaching hospital for the new professor, proved more difficult because it required capital expenditure by the government. Doris Gordon fought to keep this issue before politicians until the Queen Mary Hospital in Dunedin opened in 1938.

Dunedin, however, failed to provide enough mothers for the medical students. The pressing need for clinical teaching led Doris Gordon to lobby, from 1939, for a postgraduate obstetrical training school and modern women's hospital at Auckland. National Women's Hospital was opened on its present site in 1964, and the Postgraduate School of Obstetrics and Gynaecology set up in 1947.

It is perhaps ironic that, after opposing the Department of Health for twenty years, Doris Gordon joined its ranks as Director of Maternal and Infant Welfare from 1946 to 1948. But this was consistent with her philosophy that 'health can never be separated from happiness in the individual, and public health can never be dissociated from public welfare'.

On these grounds she campaigned against abortion in the 1930s. She gave evidence before the Committee of Inquiry into Abortion, established by the first Labour government in 1936, and (with Dr F. O. Bennett) wrote a book on the subject, *Gentlemen of the Jury* (1937). Here she revealed her strong pro-natalism and wish to 're-consecrate' motherhood. Doris Gordon was not alone in regarding the mother as the guardian of the race and the falling birth rate as a menace to the Empire and humanity. But her views on motherhood were influential because of her position within the Obstetrical Society and the esteem in which she was held by politicians, by the public, and by women's organisations.

At her hospital she administered the 'twilight sleep' drugs to her patients because she believed that painless childbirth was one way of persuading mothers to have more babies. She was an early practitioner of Caesarean section and quick to try the latest medical and surgical techniques. This enthusiasm helped to persuade women's groups and the Labour government in the 1930s of the advantages of childbirth in hospital with a doctor in attendance. By the time of the maternity services inquiry of 1937–8, for which she wrote the Obstetrical Society's submission, her goal was largely achieved.

Outspoken and pertinacious, Doris Gordon built her success as a fighter on what would now be called 'networking' with women activists, such as Janet Fraser, and her medical colleagues. She died at Stratford on 9 July 1956 – indefatigable to the end.

Philippa Mein Smith

Quotations
para.4 D. Gordon, Evidence to Committee of Inquiry into Maternity Services, National Archives
para.6 Sir Bernard Dawson, *Otago Daily Times*, July 1956 (quoted on dust-jacket of *Backblocks Baby-Doctor*
para.9 D. Gordon, *Backblocks Baby-Doctor*, p.207
para.10 D. Gordon, *Backblocks Baby-Doctor*, pp.181, 183
para.12 D. Gordon and F. Bennett, *Gentlemen of the Jury*, p.113

Unpublished Sources
Evidence of Doris Gordon, and NZ Obstetrical and Gynaecological Society, Report of Evidence Given Before the Committee of Inquiry into Maternity Services in New Zealand, 1937, H3, 3/7, National Archives
NZ Biographies, 1956, vol.2, p.31; 1957, vol.2, p.145–6; 1976, vol.3, p.130, ATL
NZ Obstetrical and Gynaecological Society, 'A Statement on the Dominion's needs for one well-equipped Hospital for Obstetrics and Gynaecology . . .', Women's Associations of NZ, Dec. 1940, NZ Women's Archives, AIM

Published Sources
Gordon, Doris. *Backblocks Baby-Doctor*, London & Wellington, 1955
Gordon, Doris. *Doctor Down Under*, London & Wellington, 1957
Gordon, Doris and Bennett, Francis. *Gentlemen of the Jury*, New Plymouth, 1937
Gordon, Doris. 'Comparative Obstetrics', *NZ Medical Journal*, vol.25 no.126, April 1926
Gordon, Doris. 'Further Problems of Obstetrics', *NZ Medical Journal*, vol.25 no.129, Oct. 1926
Gordon, Doris. 'Modern Problems of Maternal Welfare in N.Z.', *Kai Tiaki*, 18 Nov. 1936; 15 Jan. 1937
Gordon, Doris. 'Obstetrical Hospital: History of the Movement', *NZ Countrywoman*, vol.1 no.9, 20 Jan. 1934

ISABELLA GRAHAM

1837–1918

Isabella Kathleen Garland was born in Dublin on 31 July 1837, the only child of Dr and Mrs Garland. When she was only three years old, her parents died, and she went to live in London with an uncle (also a doctor) and aunt who adopted her. She had a happy girlhood n London, developing an interest in literature and the theatre. She was introduced to Dickens, who became one of her favourite authors. In 1851 she emigrated to Australia with her aunt, uncle, and governess, and settled in Victoria.

In 1859 she married a Mr Ford, who died a few months after the wedding. Shortly after that her aunt and uncle also died, leaving her 'stranded in a strange land without a relative of any kind to appeal to for comfort or help in her loneliness and distress'. However, she 'faced up to her difficulties, knowing that she had only herself to depend on for the future', and went to Melbourne where she trained as a nurse and midwife.

After several years of nursing in Melbourne she became ill, and was recommended to try the 'healthier' climate of New Zealand. She took ship to Hokitika, and for a while nursed privately in Ross. She then moved to Okarito (a town of four to five thousand people), where she continued nursing. In those days and in that context, nursing included housekeeping and cooking as well.

In South Westland she met David Millar Graham, a Scotsman who was gold-mining at Five Mile, south of Okarito. In 1869 they were married, and he worked as a baker and grocer in Okarito until he became ferryman at the Three Mile river crossing in 1879. Isabella continued nursing in between bearing and raising her own children – Margaret (1870), David (1872), John (1873), James (1875), Peter (1878), and Alexander, known as Alec (1881). Her children were later amused that she remembered their birthdays by recalling confinements she had attended before giving birth herself.

Isabella shared her love of literature with her children. Alec remembers that

times were hard when we were young, but we had a very happy family life, and we boys idolised our little mother. [Isabella was a tiny woman.] She was a great reader and could read aloud beautifully . . , We looked forward to our evenings with mother reading to us. We would do the washing up for her after our evening meal and would then make her cosy in an easy chair and bring the books she was reading . . .

Peter and Alec, the two youngest, benefited most from this informal education, as the older boys went away to work when they reached the age of thirteen or fourteen.

The death of their daughter Margaret in 1883 was a great blow to the Grahams; and in 1892 David Graham had a stroke which severely disabled him. Isabella cared for him, with help from family, until he died in 1900. She then moved to Waiho (now known as Franz Josef), where she lived in a curtained-off corner of a cottage with her unmarried sons. When her son Jack left South Westland, she moved into the cottage he had built earlier for his bride.

She continued to make herself indispensable, becoming the first postmistress at Franz Josef in 1907 – the post office was a room off the verandah of her cottage. Later it became a store as well, and in 1909 she began letting lodgings in her cottage. A woman in her seventies thus became a foremother of the tourist industry in South Westland, an industry her sons and daughters-in-law were to develop, eventually running a hotel as well as the post office and store, and offering a mountain guiding service.

A widely respected 'little mother' to three generations of Waiho relatives, friends, and neighbours, Isabella Graham remained active up until her death, at the age of eighty-one, in 1918. *Christine Dann*

Quotations
para.2 A. Graham and J. Wilson, *Uncle Alec*, p.15
para.5 A. Graham and J. Wilson, p.19

Published Sources
Graham, A. and Wilson, J. *Uncle Alec and the Grahams of Franz Josef*, Dunedin, 1983
Graham, P. *Mountain Guide: An Autobiography*, Wellington, 1965

PRUDENCE GREGORY

1925–1986

Mary Prudence Gregory was one of the key women broadcasters in the late 1950s and 1960s, and was responsible for introducing 'talk back' radio to New Zealand.

She was born in 1925 in Hamilton, the daughter of Cecily and Horace Gregory, and had one younger sister, Jocelyn. Both parents were very involved in local theatre, and their daughters were encouraged to perform and to write. Horace Gregory was a bank accountant, and later bank manager; the family moved several times, living mostly in small towns and rural areas.

Prudence spent the first years of her formal working life as a shorthand typist with the Lands and Deeds Office in Napier, and later with the Department of Maori Affairs in Gisborne. But she had from school days wanted to be a newspaper journalist. Undeterred by the view that newspaper reporting was no job for a woman, she started as 'lady editor' of the *Manawatu Evening Standard* in 1945. Her task was to compile a column called 'Women's World by Nanette'.

Dissatisfied by the limitations of her job, she wrote to the *Gisborne Herald* in search of a reporter's position, only to be told that they had to 'first settle all the soldiers who'd been on the staff'. A few months later, however, she was appointed general reporter on condition that she agreed to do the women's column as well. Court reporting, usually part of the general reporter's work, was not allowed: 'They thought I should be protected from the court,' she said later. She remained on the *Gisborne Herald* for several years until she left to travel to Australia.

On her return to Gisborne she approached the newly established local radio station, 2XG, and was hired, initially as an office assistant. A few months later the station advertised for a woman to prepare and present *Feminine Viewpoint*, a fifteen-minute daily programme for women listeners. Prudence was appointed.

The programme, like others of its kind on the commercial radio stations, consisted of interviews, fashion comments, book reviews, and other topics considered to be of particular interest to women. Most of the material was prepared by the local woman broadcaster but was sometimes supplemented by items prepared at the head office of the Broadcasting Service in Wellington. Prudence had no special training for the job, and found the first weeks in front of a microphone terrifying, an experience she later called 'mike fright'. However, with her journalistic experience and her initiative and drive, she developed the programme and began to enjoy the work.

In 1950 she moved to head office in Wellington to become assistant to the supervisor of women's programmes on the commercial programmes. The job included editing contributions from outside writers, as well as researching and preparing her own material for the women's programmes throughout the country.

During the 1950s, Prudence's broadcasting career continued to develop. She worked in a number of places, including Dunedin and later Invercargill, where she became one of four *Women's Hour* 'personalities' on national radio. The popular *Women's Hour* had developed in 1947 from an amalgamation of several smaller programmes which had presented household hints, shopping advice and advertising, 'home science', and interviews. The 'personality' prepared most of her own programme, and was expected to be 'both glamorous and motherly, well-fed but not over weight, tastefully dressed and intelligent'. Prudence also travelled overseas at this time, and observed the operation of public television networks.

The introduction of public television to New Zealand in June 1960 marked the beginning of a new era in communications. Prudence switched from radio to television, but after a year at the Wellington channel (WNTV1) she returned to radio work, which she preferred. By 1962 she had become the first supervisor of all the women's sessions – both commercial and non-commercial radio – numbering seventeen throughout the country.

The next four years were ones of innovation and change. She was instrumental in reshaping a ten-minute weekly programme, 'Background to the News' (broadcast as part of *Feminine Viewpoint* and a forerunner to the current affairs programmes of the late 1960s) to provide listeners with a more in-depth understanding of current affairs. Prudence regarded the women's programmes as 'windows on the world' for women at home, and aimed to produce programmes which were interesting and extending, rather than patronising. As part of her work, she travelled to radio stations throughout the country, training women broadcasters.

In 1965 she received an American State Department grant and toured the United States. There she observed talk back radio programmes, a concept she brought back to New Zealand. A talk back slot, 'Telephone Time', was introduced throughout New Zealand on the popular *Person to Person* programme, a two-hour afternoon session which had replaced *Women's Hour* in October 1965.

Listeners were invited at the start of each session to phone in with questions, advice, comments or ideas. It was enormously successful and Prudence later observed: '"talk back" took off from there and quite suddenly it seemed to be jumping out of the afternoon into other time slots all over the band.'

In spite of her professional successes, Prudence's personal life was difficult and conflicted. For most of her adult life she struggled with a depression that debilitated her emotionally and physically, partly through the prescribed drugs which became a regular part of her life and also through the guilt she experienced at not being able to meet the expectations of her family and of society. In one attempt to fit those expectations, she left broadcasting in 1953 to prepare for her marriage to Joe Cassins. She didn't go through with this, though, and he remained an ambivalent presence in her life until her death.

Prudence believed for some time that her depression was chemically based and kept hoping for a cure, even undergoing ECT (electroconvulsive therapy, or 'shock treatment'). Integral to this struggle was her realisation of her lesbianism. It was not until the early 1980s, late in her life, that she felt able to make contact with other lesbians. This contact was a source of great delight to her, and she enjoyed being able to share her many interests with other lesbians. However, she had a struggle with self-acceptance, with her Catholicism and her family being sources of deep conflict.

As a result of organisational changes within the new Broadcasting Corpora-tion, Prudence's position as head of women's programmes was disestablished. By 1000 she was working at a lower level as a senior public affairs officer, radio, editing the work of outside writers. In what seemed like another move sideways, she was then made responsible for the new two-year-long women's programme, *On Camera*, which was to begin on afternoon television in mid-1967. She became increasingly dissatisfied and the rest of her working life was spent in less public roles as a radio parliamentary reporter, promotions officer for television, and programme officer for radio. She retired on medical grounds in 1977. After 1983 she became involved in Wellington's Access Radio, a station set up by Radio New Zealand for use by community groups. She gave advice, criticism and encouragement to the feminist programme *Womanzone*, and to the Lesbian Community Radio programme.

By 1986 the years of psychiatric and medical treatment, along with the unresolved internal conflicts, had left a legacy she no longer wanted to carry, even though she was supported by many people, including women of the Well-ington lesbian community, during her last crises. She found the periodic lows of the depression cycle difficult and demoralising. She made several suicide attempts before finally succeeding with a drug overdose in Wellington on 18 February 1986.

Prudence was a woman of wide interests, especially in the theatre, films and music. She also loved outdoor activities, especially skiing and swimming. At a time when it was difficult for women to establish and maintain careers her sharp wit, drive and creativity enabled her to be a competent journalist and a broad-caster of some vision. Her later work was not accorded the same official recog-nition that she had won earlier in her career, but she was an innovator who was respected and admired by the thousands of women who were her audience.

Julie Glamuzina

Quotations
para.4 P. Gregory, interviews 1985, 1986
para.8 *NZ Listener*, 1 Oct. 1965
para.11 P. Downes and P. Harcourt, *Voices in the Air*, p.173

Unpublished Sources
A. Woods (de Lacey), interview with the author, 16 May 1990
A. J. Laurie, interview with the author, 15 May 1990
P. Gregory, taped interviews with Alison Laurie, Dec. 1985 and Dec. 1986, in private possession

Published Sources
Auckland Star, 23 Jan. 1967
Downes, Peter, and Harcourt, Peter. *Voices in the Air: Radio Broadcasting in New Zealand: A Documentary*, Wellington, 1976
Evening Post, 26 Jan. 1967
Gisborne Herald, 28 Jan. 1967
Lesbian Feminist Circle, Dec. 1985, Issue 44
NZ Listener, 18 Nov. 1949; 2 March 1951; 30 May 1952; 7 Aug. 1953; 24 April 1959; 15 Nov. 1963; 1 Oct. 1965; 15 July 1966; 27 Jan. 1967; 9 Feb. 1968
Southland News, 26 Jan. 1967

OENONE GREIG

1896–1987

Oenone – Noni or Nona to her family – was born in Wellington in 1896, the eldest of the three daughters of Euphemia and Charlton Morpeth. C. D. Morpeth was a successful accountant. He and Effie brought their daughters up to be 'ladies', not to work. But Nona had other ideas.

On completing her secondary schooling at Miss Baber's School, she asked to study at Victoria University College and, when her father refused, became a teacher at Wellesley Boys' School at Days Bay. She resigned to marry Esmond (Billy) Greig in February 1919.

During the war Nona had fallen in love with a cousin whom her parents would not permit her to marry. Billy may always have been a second-best choice. This was not helped when the young couple bought a back-country dairy farm in Taranaki and then were forced to walk off it by the 1921 depression.

Oenone Greig the 'new woman' emerges in 1935. Aged thirty-nine and with three teenage children, the eldest starting at university himself, she enrolled full-time at Victoria University College. She completed her BA in 1937, majoring in philosophy with a concentration in psychology. An MA with second-class honours came two years later.

Nona was one of the first women to begin undergraduate study at Victoria College as a 'mature student'. She was also unusual in that she was planning a professional career. By 1935 Nona had realised her marriage would not last, and she and Billy agreed she should train for a career before they parted. In contrast, the older married women who began to appear at Victoria College a few years later had usually been students before they married and were mainly seeking intellectual stimulation.

Nona recalled later the warm encouragement she received from 'Prof' Thomas Hunter. Under his tutelage she won a Jacob Joseph Scholarship and in 1940 became a demonstrator in psychology. While Nona's achievements became a college legend, she remained to her children a warm, caring mother.

Thus began a second working career which lasted forty-eight years. Since money was short (the Greigs were divorced in 1941) Nona took the first job offering, making scones in a tea-shop. Several years as a child welfare officer with the Department of Education followed.

During those years Nona gained administrative experience. She also worked on the Public Service Association's women's committee, the first of the groups of feminists whose campaigning led to the 1960 Government Service Equal Pay Act.

From 1946, Nona spent nine years in Greece on relief work, first for Corso and later for the World Health Organisation. She was fifty when she set off to see the world. During annual holidays she visited every country in Europe, a small carrying bag her only luggage.

On her return to Wellington two 'careers' still lay ahead. Nona joined the National Library Service, where her superiors regarded her so highly that she was quietly kept on some six years past the normal retiring age before the State Services Commission forcibly retired her.

In 1967–68 Nona moved to the law firm of Buddle Anderson Kent and Co. Telephone receptionist, then librarian, deeds custodian, and filing clerk, she became 'the vital point of reference for the whole office'. She moonlighted once a week at the Petone Library until she was seventy-nine.

Oenone Greig. *Buddle Findlay*

In her final years, work absorbed most of Nona's energy, but she retained her interest in people (especially her family), in books, and in the world around her. Her employer described her as 'the most knowledgeable woman that it has ever been my privilege to have met, and one of the wisest'.

'She was one of the oldest active employees in any office (legal or otherwise). She died as she would have wanted – sitting at the office computer seeking information. She was ninety-one.'   *Elizabeth Orr*

Quotations
All quotations are from the Buddle Findlay client letter, p.4.

Unpublished Sources
Buddle Findlay client letter, June 1988, in private possession
Correspondence from Kathleen Koten, Sept. 1989
Information from Mary Boyd, and from family members
Interview with Mrs Molly Parry, 7 April 1989
Oenone Greig's diaries, held privately

Published Sources
Ross, Kathleen. 'Who Are These Women?', *The Public Service Journal*, July 1945, pp.315–6

AIRINI GRENNELL

?1910-1988

Airini Nga Roimata Grennell was born in Wharekauri (Chatham Islands) in 1910. Her father was Harry Grennell and her mother was Mary Tikao. At an early age Airini and her family moved to Port Levy where she and her two sisters were sent to be educated at Sacred Heart College in Christchurch. While still at school, she showed remarkable musical promise and as a young woman began to earn recognition as a talented singer. She was also an outstanding sportswoman and represented Canterbury at both basketball and golf.

Airini Nga Roimata Grennell, painted by
Rudolph Gopas, early 1950s.

When Airini left school, she joined Seamer's Waiata Maori Choir which toured England and Australia in 1937. During this tour Airini and other choir members were presented to the recently crowned King George VI. There were three Tikao family members in the Seamer choir, including Airini's younger sister Linda Hinemoa. Other members included Inia Te Wiata.

Airini began her career in broadcasting in 1938 when she joined 4ZB Dunedin as a programme assistant. At that time she earned £175 a year with an additional allowance of £10 for her ability to perform as a piano accompanist. Airini once said of her early experiences on radio that:

Commercial stations were very new then, and everything you did was so much more exciting . . . we were rather a do-it-yourself station in those early days . . . often interviews were broadcast live . . . we worked much closer to the people in those days. We were young and the service was young.

From 4ZB Airini went to 1ZB Auckland. In the 1950s Airini returned to Te

Waipounamu (South Island) and worked for 3ZB and then 3YA in Christchurch. At 3YA, she became involved in organising a series of radio programmes for women. This initiative promoted by the National Stations Network recognised that in addition to being 'good cooks and housekeepers' the female target audience was also highly capable, 'intelligent and discerning'.

Airini was one of the women who pioneered the network of women's programmes on National Radio. These for the first time seriously attempted to provide a balance of entertainment and information on issues important to women.

Airini retired from broadcasting in 1966. She was married to the New Zealand painter Rudi Gopas and had one child. She died in 1988 and is buried at Port Levy.

Until her death Airini retained her sharpness of wit and clarity of thought. Her failing health forced her to relinquish golf but she maintained an interest in all sport to the end of her life. Her musical ability did not leave her and she continued to play the piano at whanau gatherings and was vigilant about her family's standards of speech, in both languages.

Airini Grennell was a woman before her time, born too early in many ways. She was an incisive, articulate, and brilliant Maori woman. As the revival began and our people became politically more active and outspoken, she moved with it. But even with her amazing talent, she remained curiously whakama (modest).

Irihapeti Ramsden & Cushla Parekowhai

Quotations
para.3 *The Press*, 29 April 1966
para.4 P. Downes and P. Harcourt, *Voices in the Air: Radio Broadcasting in New Zealand: A Documentary*, Wellington, 1976, p.158

Published Source
The Press, 20 Dec. 1988 (obituary)

ELIZA GREY

1822-1898

Eliza Lucy Grey spent only eight years in New Zealand, during the first governorship of her husband, George Grey. She did not enjoy her stay: she considered the climate unhealthy and the settlers ill-bred and materialistic. Her dissatisfaction with New Zealand was just one manifestation of a deeper unhappiness which was always to shadow her. Although she was privileged, she was also oppressed by convention, and when at length she defied it she found herself an outcast.

She was born on 17 December 1822 at Lyme Regis, Dorset, England, one of ten children of Ann Wardin Spencer (born Liddon) and her husband Richard Spencer, a former naval commander. In 1833 the family sailed for Western Australia, following Richard Spencer's appointment as government resident of Albany. In July 1839 he died suddenly, leaving his wife and children in reduced circumstances. The new government resident was twenty-seven-year-old

Captain George Grey, who had recently led several journeys of exploration in Western Australia. On 2 November 1839 George Grey married the sixteen-year-old Eliza Spencer.

In February 1840, George Grey was ordered to return to England. While the couple were there, George was offered and accepted the governorship of South Australia. On 16 February 1841, during the return voyage, Eliza gave birth to her only child, a boy, named George. The Greys arrived at Adelaide in May and shortly afterwards, on 25 July, their son died.

George believed that Eliza had neglected the child, thus causing his death. Discord between husband and wife was fuelled by a basic incompatibility. Curiously, they were similar in some respects: both were proud, sensitive, and prone to violent outbursts of temper. Yet these few shared characteristics probably brought them into conflict.

In 1845 George Grey was promoted to the governorship of New Zealand and in November he and Eliza arrived in Auckland, where they lived, with periods of residence at Wellington and New Plymouth. George made frequent visits to the Bay of Islands, leaving Eliza by herself. Her loneliness is evident in letters sent to her friend in Adelaide, Maggie Watts (later Bagot). In June 1846 she wrote: 'I really ought to be accustomed to live alone by this time. I am so constantly left now – & I am growing graver and gloomier than ever I fear.' A few poignant remarks in the letters reveal her lasting sadness over the loss of her son, and her childlessness. In February 1850 she told her friend, who by then was married with two children:

I am so glad you are using my cot, for 'twas useless to leave it idly to rot when it could be of use to your darling, & also bring me to your mind. If it ever please God that I should want it, I will write.

Eliza found solace in religion, and it seems that she taught in the St Paul's bible class in Auckland. She remained loyal to her increasingly aloof husband and acted as his filing clerk for correspondence. It may also have been tempting for her to seek refuge from her misery in the role of permanent invalid. While in New Zealand she suffered from a succession of rather vague illnesses which prevented her from taking much part in social life.

As the governor's wife, Eliza Grey (by 1848 Lady Grey) had a mixed reception. The two qualities consistently remarked upon were her beauty and her intelligence. On first meeting her, Sarah Selwyn wrote: 'Mrs Grey is a pretty person . . . I think she is clever too, with something in her.' However, the combination of attributes did not gain her automatic acceptance and indeed was sometimes regarded with suspicion. In a letter of 1850, Charlotte Godley found fault with Eliza's looks and her particular brand of shrewdness, and claimed that she had 'a very satirical expression, and way of talking about everybody, which is evidently the reason of her being so little liked'. Charlotte Godley was inclined to be harsh: she interpreted Eliza's affectionate interest in her young son, Arthur Godley, as an attempt to curry favour.

The Greys left New Zealand at the end of 1853 and, after a brief sojourn in England, embarked for the Cape Colony where George Grey was to be governor. In South Africa, relations between the couple deteriorated. George

Eliza Grey painted by William Gush in 1854, before her marriage to George Grey and the unhappy posting to New Zealand. *Alexander Turnbull Library*

went away on lengthy official journeys, on at least one occasion neglecting to correspond with Eliza. By this period, if not before, she had formed the impression that he was unfaithful to her.

She found diversion alternately in illness and in good works. Friendship provided some consolation. She was supported by Sophy Gray, wife of the Bishop of Cape Town, and became fond of Sophy's eighteen-year-old daughter Louisa. However, in June 1857 Louisa married and moved away. Soon afterwards George Grey's increased responsibilities led to domestic problems. Controlled in public, at home he allegedly gave vent to his emotions. Eliza Grey, who was herself in a fragile mental state, suffered a nervous breakdown. She went to England for a time to recuperate.

In late 1859 George Grey was recalled from South Africa, only to be reinstated. Returning with her husband to South Africa on the *Forte* in mid-1860, Eliza Grey confided her marital difficulties to the captain, Sir Henry Keppel. Notes between her and Keppel, discovered by George Grey, suggest that a romantic relationship developed, though it was probably unconsummated. George Grey immediately demanded that the ship return to Rio de Janeiro where he put Eliza ashore. He then proceeded to Cape Town and thereafter lobbied to have Keppel transferred from the Cape of Good Hope station, eventually succeeding after it was revealed that his wife and Keppel had remained in communication.

Though outwardly George Grey was motivated by 'honour', it seems possible that he used the situation to regain the governorship of New Zealand and, moreover, to rid himself of a wife who had become a liability. He had powerful support. When Eliza wrote to Samuel Wilberforce, Bishop of Oxford, for advice, stating in her defence that her husband had committed adultery, the bishop rejected her claims, replying bluntly: 'I do not admit for an instant that the *Sin* of infidelity in the wife is altered by the want of chastity in the husband.' He advised her to comply with George Grey's wishes for a permanent separation.

Eliza Grey spent the remainder of her life in England, supported by an allowance from George Grey. She had few friends and, after converting to Roman Catholicism, devoted herself to the Servite Order. In 1896 she returned to her husband who, failing in health, had retired to England. It seems she was motivated primarily by a sense of duty, but also by a need to secure her financial position. George Grey's health became worse and it emerged that his monetary affairs were in disorder. The couple were forced to live in cramped quarters at the Norfolk Hotel, London. Old animosities resurfaced and Eliza was advised to make extended visits to Bournemouth to relieve matters. As George had stopped her allowance, she was forced to live off her savings, a cause of further anxiety. The failure of the reconciliation confused and depressed her. It was at Bournemouth on 4 September 1898 that she died suddenly from the effects of a stroke. George Grey survived her by only two weeks. *Nancy Swarbrick*

Quotations

para.5 E. Grey to Maggie Watts, 21 June 1846, ATL; E. Grey to Maggie Bagot (Watts), 10 Feb. 1850, ATL

para.7 A. Drummond (ED.), *Married & Gone to New Zealand*, Hamilton, 1860, p.127; J. R. Godley (ed.), *Letters from Early New Zealand by Charlotte Godley, 1850–1853*, Christchurch, 1951, p.130

para.11 R. K. Pugh (ed.). *The Letter-books of Samuel Wilberforce, 1843–68*, vol.47, Oxford, 1970 pp.362–3

Unpublished Sources

Lady Eliza Lucy Grey, Letters 1845–1850, MS Papers 860, ATL

Aston papers, GL:AST, APL

Published Sources

Dalton, B. J. 'Sir George Grey and the Keppel Affair'. *Historical Studies*, vol.16 no.63, Oct. 1974, pp.192–215

Rutherford, J. *Sir George Grey KCB 1812–1898: A Study in Colonial Government*, London, 1961

ELSIE GRIFFIN

1884–1968

When the World's YWCA put out a call for university-educated Christian women to take up secretarial work in the YWCA, Elsie Griffin was one of a group of exceptional women who volunteered. Once trained in the association's methods, these skilled professional workers built the YWCA in Australia and New Zealand into a major women's organisation while they themselves became leaders of women in the community.

Elsie Griffin was born in 1884, the daughter of Mary (born Brown) and the Revd Cornelius Griffin, a minister of the Methodist Church. She was educated at Prince Albert College, a Methodist school in Auckland, and Auckland University College, where she gained a BA with first-class honours in botany, followed by an MA in botany in 1906.

For five years after graduating, Elsie was botany mistress at Auckland Girls' Grammar School, first in Symonds Street and then at the new school in Howe

Street. Elsie had the task of equipping the new botany laboratory, considered to be one of the most up-to-date in the country. Her progressive teaching methods did not involve studying European oaks from textbooks. Instead she took her girls to the kauri forest at Northcote and formed a field club whose members embarked on epic journeys into the Waitakere Ranges, tramping miles to collect botany specimens.

Elsie believed in the broadening influence of education. Throughout her life she was often a jump ahead of her colleagues in embracing new ideas. Some years later, on the National Council of Women (NCW), Elsie organised a study circle where the subjects were the economic position of married women, relations of the sexes, and labour and capital. In 1919, these were contentious subjects for an essentially conservative organisation, and attendance was so low the course was discontinued. Women had to 'wake up and think,' said Elsie:

There is an art in keeping alive. The majority of the people we meet walking the streets are dead, although they are not aware of the fact. They are in a groove. They have ceased to exist as a growing personality. They are dying from the inside onwards.

She cared little for convention herself. Tall and large, she dressed oddly, and was inclined to indulge in some boisterous good fun. This endeared her to her younger charges, who knew her as 'Griff', but was apt to raise eyebrows amongst her staider colleagues.

Elsie's first YWCA post was at Dunedin, following which she spent two years studying social work methods in America, particularly at the YWCA training school in New York. Her return to New Zealand to take up the post of general secretary at the Auckland YWCA occurred at a critical time, as the organisation was in the process of building splendid new premises in Queen Street. In the light of her knowledge of progressive methods of youth work, Elsie Griffin was able to suggest modifications to the building and establish a direction for the association which turned it into a Mecca for Auckland's girls. One member of the time wrote many years later that Elsie Griffin transformed the YWCA from 'a dull building where a few girls crept about and there were prayers and singing' into 'a busy swarm of girls going to classes of all sorts . . . .'.

Elsie's interest in young women was not simply philanthropic. Along with other feminists of the period, she saw women as the hope of the future and sought to inspire them to build a better world. The horrific years of the First World War had been the business of men; 'the reconstruction process,' said Elsie Griffin, 'was going to be far more in the hands of women'. In America she had seen the women's club system developing as a political force and she had visions that something similar could happen here. On arriving back in New Zealand, she had been shocked at the way women's long-standing campaign for women police was 'flouted with impunity'. This, she said, demonstrated the need for a strong movement of women. Such a call could not be ignored in America, for 'the clubs were co-ordinated and wield a powerful influence'.

The clubs formed at the YWCA never became a political force, although the training that the girls received enabled some at least to take on public roles in adult life. But beyond the YWCA, Elsie was involved in the establishment of a network of women's organisations, founded in the flush of confidence following the First World War. She was a charter and lifelong member of the Federation of University Women (FUW), the Pan-Pacific and South-East Asia Women's Association, the Lyceum Club, and one of a group of Auckland feminists (mostly single professional women including Ellen Melville, Dr Hilda Northcroft, Alice Basten, and Sarah Jackson) who were instrumental in reviving the lapsed National Council of Women. Elsie Griffin went to all the early national conferences of the NCW, was on the national executive, and her fellow NCW members remained her close friends for life. She was an active member of all the organisations she joined. Writing of her after her death, a FUW member said that:

her brilliant brain and ability for objective comment were fully appreciated by all the organisations with which she was connected. [As] she appeared didactic to untrained women who were unable to follow her reasoning, she consequently often encountered strong opposition, but always saw the other point of view and remained friendly and tolerant.

In 1925, Elsie accepted the position of national secretary for the YWCA of Australia, a position she held for ten years and in which she gained international recognition. She commented later: 'When you join the YWCA you inevitably become a globe trotter.'

At the height of her career, Elsie was called home to care for her ageing mother, a period described by her friends as 'exacting'. She spent her last thirty years in Auckland, faithfully attending meetings of the women's groups she had helped to found. She became a staunch member of the Food Value League, an organisation which distributed sensible advice on nutrition during rationing in the war years. A daughter of a league member remembers Elsie and her colleagues attending meetings at her family house:

Russian comfrey was talked of, for Vitamin C, and also the benefits of liver, for iron. It all sounded dreadful to the ears of a young child and I tried to close mine. Everyone wore hats and never used first names. The rules and conventions of those times offered much more protection than the superficial friendliness of today; those women were steadfast friends but never intruded on each other's privacy.

Members of women's groups of the post-war period remember Elsie as a distinctive figure:

She was a big person who moved like an elderly Queen Mary. She wore a big black hat, a big black scarf and a floppy coat. She created a vivid picture you would never forget. She was a strong person, kind to younger women, and was very respected.

She died in May 1968, leaving bequests to the YWCA and to Grafton Hall of Residence at the university.   *Sandra Coney*

Quotations
para.4 *Auckland Star*, 25 Aug. 1917, Auckland YWCA scrapbooks, AIM
para.5 Letter, Kathleen M. Luckens to *Women's Viewpoint*, Auckland YWCA scrapbooks

para.6 Unidentified newspaper cutting, 31 Aug. 1917, Auckland YWCA scrapbook; *Auckland Star*, 25 Aug. 1917

para.7 B. A. Jackson, 'Elsie M Griffin', 1969, in Women's Archives, AIM

para.8 *Auckland Star*, 9 March 1961, in Women's Archives, AIM

para.9 Christine Taylor, communication to the author, 1990

para.10 FUW member, communication to author, 1990

Unpublished Sources

Auckland YWCA Archives, MS 1131, AIM

Minutes and Scrapbooks of the Auckland Branch of the NCW, AIM

Women's Archives, NCW, AIM

Published Sources

Coney, Sandra. *Every Girl: A Social History of Women and the YWCA in Auckland*, Auckland, 1986

Holt, Betty. *Women in Council: A History of the National Council of Women of New Zealand 1896–1979*, Wellington, 1980

Law, Ethel. *Down the Years*, Wellington, 1964

Northey, Heather, *Auckland Girls' Grammar School 1888–1988*, Auckland, 1988

Price, Eric. *Pauline Tulloch Price: YWCA Secretary*, Adelaide, 1979

EDITH SEARLE GROSSMANN

1863–1931

Born at Beechworth, Victoria, Edith Howitt Searle came to New Zealand with her parents, Mary Anne and George Searle (a journalist) in 1878. She was educated at Invercargill Grammar School, Christchurch Girls' High (where she was head girl), and Canterbury College, graduating MA in 1885 with first-class honours in Latin and English, and honours in political science. Her mentor, who persuaded her to study for the Junior University Scholarship and to go on to university, was Helen Connon, then a teacher at Christchurch Girls' High.

After graduating, Edith became assistant mistress, then second assistant, at Wellington Girls' High until 1890, when she married Joseph Penfound Grossmann, formerly a fellow student at Canterbury College, now a master at Wellington Boys' High. In 1894 she had her only child, a son who was apparently mentally handicapped.

In 1892 Edith and her husband were among the founding members of the Canterbury Women's Institute, which was active in the struggle for women's suffrage. From 1896 to 1898, 'Joey' Grossmann was a lecturer in political economy at Canterbury College. In 1898 he was sentenced to two years' imprisonment for improper use of the money and shares of others. The marriage was reputedly unhappy. Joseph became a leader writer with the *Auckland Star* and a lecturer, later a professor, at Auckland University College. In 1932 he was dismissed by the university for financial dishonesty. He claimed that 'he had been struggling all his life to overcome the heavy expenses involved in the care of his mentally disturbed wife'. There is no evidence that his claim is other than self-justification.

Edith wrote articles for magazines in New Zealand and overseas – 'The Woman Movement in New Zealand' in the *Westminster Review* (1908), and 'Old Time Maoris – "Homes of the Silent Vanished Race" – Native Pas on Waiheke' in the *Auckland Star* (1919), among others. She also wrote four novels, the first of which (*Angela, a Messenger*) was published in 1890, and the last (*The Heart of the Bush*) in 1910. She travelled in Europe, and lived in London with her son, apart from her husband, for eleven years around 1906–17. Returning to New Zealand, she lived in separate houses from him in Auckland, dying there in 1931.

Edith Searle Grossmann.
Annals of New Zealand Literature

In her 1905 life of Helen Macmillan Brown (Heleṅ Connon), Edith Grossmann wrote:

She wished to prove that it was possible for a woman to have an independent career and yet to fulfill all the duties of wife, mother, and mistress . . . Her well-ordered household, where nothing seemed awry, her carefully tended children, her complete union with her husband, were all silent but unanswerable witnesses to the possibility of women managing a home and a profession at the same time.

But Grossmann ends by admitting that:

She held her position for eleven years; but the strain, though it never showed in her manner, must have been severe. Gradually the home duties demanded more and more of her time and strength. She began to be troubled with sleeplessness and in 1894 her husband persuaded her to resign. The rest of her life was devoted to him and her little girls. Perhaps the task she set herself was not to be accomplished under the circumstances of colonial life . . . But the full solution lies in the hands of the new generation.

This is not the usual obituary pamphlet. It is by a woman who is aware of issues we have not yet solved today – the conflicts presented by the prevailing ideology that a woman would make a full-time job as a homemaker, alongside demands for equality of opportunity in a country that was the first to give women the vote, and one of the first to admit them to university degrees. It is not a conservative voice.

Grossmann's 1893 novel *In Revolt* is the story of what can happen to a young girl who, refused a further education, marries at sixteen the man she loves, a wealthy squatter. The novel (set in Australia) is a convincing psychological portrayal of her gradual disillusionment and an overt attack on a society that condones a husband's complete power over his wife. Although the husband's brutality is associated with his heavy drinking, the primary focus is on male control over women and their bodies. The novel follows Hermione's despair and loss of faith. A friend says:

I was not to talk to her about Heaven or God. It was all lies men made up to keep children quiet and make women fools. She said, 'I found out long ago when I cried to God and no-one heard'.

It ends with her going into the wilderness ('crossing the Wallaroo ranges and the burning sands of the Cowla Euroka'), and the novel suggests that she dies there.

In Revolt came out in 1893, the year its author was thirty and New Zealand women got the vote. Fourteen years later, in 1907, Grossmann published the novel's successor – *Hermione: A Knight of the Holy Ghost*. This novel, written by someone who has lived through the women's movement, is much more self-conscious about its feminist message:

This novel is the life story of a woman who fought against subjection and against licentious and barbarous views of sex and love of life . . . We are today in the midst of a great struggle which aims at overthrowing the power of a small privileged class, and the power of one privileged class, and the power of one privileged sex, over a more dependent sex.

The story is set some thirty years earlier, before the late nineteenth-century divorce and property laws (such as the Australian 1884 Married Woman's Property Act, and the Victorian 1889 Divorce Act). But the purpose of the novel is to point out the impact of the women's movement over these years, and underline the fragility of any achievements:

The following narrative is based on a story from the past, before the Woman Movement had raised the condition of women; and it is produced now in view of a strong reactionary tendency towards re-subjection.

The impact of American feminism is apparent – Hermione travels to the States, where she studies feminists such as Elizabeth Blackwell, Susan B. Anthony, and Frances Power Cobbe. She becomes involved in the 'Woman Movement', and sets up a women's commune, which then moves back to Australia. Several chapters are devoted to commune members discussing their feminist principles, focusing on what Hermione calls 'free love' and the 'new morality'.

'Free love' is far removed from its later connotations. Hermione's aim is to

set women free from all but natural disabilities, and to do away with a

*dominion that was set up in a bygone savage age. And, most of all, I would
raise the idea of marriage, the union is marriage, and the union is the source of
the new race, the generation that shall surpass the one before it. The giving of
life should be consecrated. But now impurity goes almost free and unpunished
and when a man corrupts himself and some woman it is thought of as quite a
venial fault. Yet it is worse than murder. In the new age that I dream of, the
age that we are helping to build up, these infamies will be thought of as
horrible and impossible as the orgies of Fijian cannibals.*

'Free love' here is a demand for sexual purity and abstinence – perhaps more
in keeping with the Victorian moral code than a liberation from it. But the basis
of Hermione's argument is that sexuality is the instrument of man's dominion,
as 'power over' a woman's body. In this sense the demand for sexual purity can
be seen as a radical feminism. It is not unlike the second-wave feminists'
emphasis on rape, pornography, and incest. Sex, even with love, even in
marriage, is still seen as possession.

Hermione's arguments about equal education are a similar mixture of
radicalism and conservatism. Education should be

*not necessarily the same, but equally thorough. If a woman is to be trained for
the household and for management of a family, that wants as sound an
education as if it were for the state.*

Grossmann argues that motherhood is a profession (perhaps the most important
profession in the state), and that women are uniquely qualified for it.

In Grossmann's last novel, *The Heart of the Bush* (1910), the hero is a
rugged, uncultured, and handsome New Zealand farmer. The heroine is delicate, weak, and cultured. The passion between them is explicitly spelt out:

*He looked around on the river and the untrodden mountains, then took her
completely to himself – her heart beat in ecstasy – every nerve thrilled with self
consciousness. Her bridegroom was such a barbarian sometimes, and she felt as
if he were literally bearing her straight out of her civilized sphere to his
kingdom.*

The novel ends as a celebration of true love and heterosexual pair bonding.
It is an unexpected novel after the Hermione novels and their attitude to barbarous sexual passion. *The Heart of the Bush* seems to indicate a rejection of the
radical feminism of the earlier books, and of the women's movement and its
ideology of purity. Grossmann appears to be reclaiming passion and sexuality for
women, and accepting traditional sex-role stereotypes. Perhaps not surprisingly,
this is the novel most referred to in literary histories, and it is seen as transcending
the 'dogmatism' of her earlier fiction.

In her obituary, Alan Mulgan wrote:

*New Zealand is much indebted to Edith Searle Grossmann. She set examples of
an intellectual life lived long and consistently, and of service to shining ideals.
She enriched the small body of our creative literature . . . Generations of*

women graduates walk on the road that she and her contemporaries made.

Aorewa McLeod

Quotations
para.3 K. Sinclair, *History of the University of Auckland, 1883–1983*, Auckland, 1983, pp.146–50
para.5 E. S. Grossmann, *Life of Helen Macmillan Brown*, Christchurch, 1905, pp.52–3
para.7 E. S. Grossmann, *In Revolt*, London, 1893, pp.368, 425
para.8 E. S. Grossmann, preface to *Hermione: A Knight of the Holy Ghost*, 2nd edn, London, 1908, p.vii; E. S. Grossmann, preface to *A Knight of the Holy Ghost*, 1st edn, London, 1907
para.10 E. S. Grossmann, *Hermione*, p.181
para.12 E. S. Grossmann, *Hermione*, p.202
para.13 E. S. Grossmann, *The Heart of the Bush*, London, 1910, p.163
para.15 A. Mulgan, 'Edith Searle Grossmann Pioneer', p.279

Published Sources
Macmillan Brown, J. 'E. S. Grossmann: A Pioneer in Women's Education', *The Press*, 7 March 1931, p.13 (obituary)
Mulgan, Alan. 'Edith Searle Grossmann Pioneer', *Art in New Zealand*, vol.3 no.12, June 1931 (obituary)

ELIZABETH GUNN

1879–1963

The name of school doctor Elizabeth Gunn is engraved upon the minds of a generation of Wanganui and Manawatu children. Born in 1879, Elizabeth Catherine Gunn was the eldest daughter of William and Elizabeth Jane Gunn. She was educated at Otago and Timaru Girls' High Schools (staff even then noting her remarkably strong character) and in 1903 she completed her medical degree at Edinburgh University. Towards the end of that decade Gunn was one of at least five 'lady doctors' practising in Wellington. She does not appear to have engendered sisterly feelings in her medical peers, at least one of them complaining privately about Gunn's 'big talk' and exclaiming, 'Oh, she is a bounder!'

By 1911 Gunn was complaining about slackness of trade, and this may have influenced her decision to join the School Medical Service when it was established in 1912. Other women doctors, such as Eleanor Baker, were quite explicit about seeing the service as a means of assured income, even though this income was limited and the work was of low status, and frustratingly bound up with bureaucratic routine. With the exception of a period between 1916 and 1918, when she 'donned . . . uniform and went importantly off to war' (as Eleanor Baker put it), Gunn spent nearly three decades within the service, mostly based in the Wanganui district.

Visits by the school doctor were impressive occasions, and Elizabeth Gunn, with her autocratic manner, embodied all that was threatening about the School Medical Service to parents and to children. Mothers regarded the school doctors as potential critics of their maternal capacities; children feared the threat of tonsillectomy and removal to a health camp. One of Gunn's specialities was to knock out loose infant teeth with her spatula, a procedure which did not endear her either to children or to dental nurses. To the child's eye:

She was always dressed in a grey suit . . . with shirt, tie and a masculine style haircut. On her large bust she wore her war ribbons. Her voice was loud and she had penetrating eyes. She never talked softly . . .

Children to be examined would proceed to the Primer 1 classroom which was a hive of industry . . . We children were undressed to our 'bloomers' and the nurse in her flowing veil brought us forward to the doctor. Our chests were sounded, eyes and ears looked at also for skin lesions. Dr Gunn would depress our tongues and make cryptic remarks to the nurse. Everyone seemed in her opinion to have tonsils and adenoids in need of removal . . .

I was a skinny child and when Dr Gunn noticed a small bony prominence on my chest Mother explained I had fallen off her bed when small which had resulted in the lump. Poor Mother, Dr Gunn fixed her with her steely gaze and shouted 'Rickets, pure and simple'. However she gave my infant sister a gold star on her card for being a perfect baby. My mother had great respect for Dr Gunn's opinion and advice.

The fact that Gunn's name nearly rhymed with 'bum', and that she was at one stage accompanied by a 'Nurse Bullet', provided great potential for school-yard ditties, but friends had a more benign view of her. One remembers the doctor as 'Gunny', a tireless teller of stories and player of games, and an obituary notes how she helped during the Depression to outfit children with school uniforms.

But it is as a pioneer of the health camp movement that Elizabeth Gunn made her most notable contribution. She was convinced that if children could

Children gargling at the King George V Memorial Health Camp, Otaki, September 1948. This was one of a number of health camps set up by the formidable Dr Elizabeth Gunn of the School Medical Service. *National Publicity Studios, Alexander Turnbull Library*

only learn the simple rules of health and nutrition, and be provided with adequate rest and fresh air, many of their ailments would be cured. The first health camps were held at Turakina from 1919, with the aid of a local farmer, B. Lethbridge, teacher-volunteers, and camping equipment hired from the army. Gunn brought her full military experience to bear upon the camps, which resounded to bugle-call, included toothbrush drill, and involved a good deal of marching and flag-saluting. The majority of children were believed to leave the camps in much improved health (as evidenced by weight gain and sun-tan), and by the 1930s Gunn's initiative had been taken up by voluntary associations all over the country.

Gunn ended her official career as Director of the Health Department's School Hygiene Division. Described by a (male) contemporary as 'a rollicking sort of a woman', Gunn provided a contrast with her charming and conciliatory predecessor, Ada Paterson. Some of her more dogmatic public pronouncements involved her in controversy before her retirement in 1940.

Dr Gunn continued in private practice as a paediatrician, was awarded an MBE in 1951, and died in 1963. While her larger-than-life style may sometimes have worked to her disadvantage, she was at all times a battler for child health in New Zealand. It is an indication of her personality and forceful presence that there still resides in popular memory a host of 'Lizzie Gunn' stories.

Margaret Tennant

Quotations
para.1 Kate Hogg to Agnes Bennett, 18 May 1911, 27 July 1911, A. E. L. Bennett Papers
para.2 Eleanor Baker McLagan, *Stethoscope and Saddle Bags*, p.126
para.3 Letter to the author from Barbara Travers, 1 May 1989
para.6 Personal communication to the author

Unpublished Sources
A. E. L. Bennett Papers, MS 1346/201, ATL
Annual Report of the Department of Health, Division of School Hygiene, *AJHR*, H-31, 1920–40
Dental Nurses Oral History Archives, Transcripts of Interviews, ATL
Letter to the author from Dora Asher, 22 April 1989
NZ Biographies 1969, vol.3, p.34, ATL (*Christchurch Star*, 12 Aug. 1969)

Published Sources
Baker McLagan, Eleanor. *Stethoscope and Saddle Bags*, Auckland, 1965
McLintock. A. H. (ed.). *An Encyclopaedia of New Zealand*, vol.1, Wellington, 1966, pp.888–9
NZ Free Lance, 26 Feb. 1910
NZ Medical Journal, Feb. 1964, pp.108–10 (obituary)
'The Days Before Yesterday', *Onslow Historian*, vol.10 no.3, pp.6–8

KATE HADFIELD

1831–1902

Catherine (Kate) Williams, eighth child and third daughter of Archdeacon Henry Williams and his wife Marianne (born Coldham), was born at Paihia in the Bay of Islands on 24 February 1831. Her father had joined the Church Missionary Society after service in the Royal Navy. He arrived with his wife and three children in New Zealand in July of 1823, to serve as superintending missionary. Henry, an energetic, disciplined, and courageous man, won the respect and confidence of many Maori and acted as adviser and peacemaker on numerous occasions. He spearheaded the extension of Church Missionary Society activity throughout the North Island, and until 1840 exerted almost absolute control over the Church of England mission in New Zealand. Marianne supported her husband in full measure, reared their large family, and fostered missionary endeavour by training Maori women and girls in domestic arts.

Kate Williams helped her mother and later taught in the mission schools. A gay and practical young woman, she left Paihia in June 1850 for Otaki to assist her cousin Mary, wife of her brother the Revd Samuel Williams. Mary was recuperating from a severe illness; Kate taught in the mission school and cared for and trained in housewifery the Maori girls who lived in the Williams home. Her full and lively letters to her parents describe a busy life in the mission house, relieved by journeys to Wanganui, Wellington, and 'a very pleasant visit to Manawatu'.

The Otaki mission station had been established by Archdeacon Octavius Hadfield, who had joined the Church Missionary Society in October 1837 and in January 1839 became the first priest to be ordained in New Zealand. His aim of spreading the gospel began on the Kapiti coast in November of that year. From late in 1844 serious illness had confined him to the home of Henry St Hill, the magistrate in Wellington. He returned to Otaki in October 1849. Kate's marriage to the archdeacon was celebrated on 19 May 1852 at Rangiatea Church in Otaki by the Revd Richard Taylor of Wanganui, who recorded that 'there was a very large assemblage of Maoris in the noble church'.

The mission station at Otaki, sketched by Janetta Maria Cookson in 1853, a year after Kate married Octavius Hadfield at the Rangiatea Church. *Alexander Turnbull Library*

Kate was not to see her parents again until September 1853 when the Hadfields visited the Bay of Islands. They returned to Otaki overland from Auckland to Wanganui and Kate's journal records this December journey, the first undertaken by a European woman. With their infant son Henry Samuel, the family walked or travelled by horse, spring cart, litter, and canoe for almost three weeks. They went from one mission station to the next, with several nights spent in the cottages of lonely settlers or sleeping on fern beds in a tent at isolated kainga (villages), where the archdeacon invariably conducted a service and 'stayed talking with the Maoris a long time'. Kate describes the challenges and discomforts of the journey but adds that 'riding overland was nothing to the misery of seasickness'.

Hadfield spent a great deal of time away from the mission. Kate, as well as caring for her growing family, worked hard for the school. Girls lived in the Hadfields' small home and Kate taught at the school at times and nursed the children through more than one epidemic.

In 1858 the archdeacon declined the Bishopric of Wellington on the grounds of continued ill health which forced him to take a year's rest. On 28 April the Hadfields and their elder son Henry sailed for England on the *Southern Cross*. Kate records the birth of her daughter Anne on 7 June and the welcome rest and cossetting she received, and she regained her strength with the aid of 'Mrs Selwyn's concentrated beef tea' (presumably made from a recipe of Sarah Selwyn) and other delicacies provided by fellow passengers.

New Zealand born and bred, Kate felt some apprehension at meeting her husband's English family, but her fears were allayed by the welcome the Hadfields gave them on the Isle of Wight. A visit to the Church Missionary Society in Salisbury Square, London, drew her comment on a conversation with the secretary regarding 'the female part of the work':

I wished very much to have the opportunity of telling him it was impossible that I could do anything unless we had a better house, but perhaps it was better left unsaid.

Missionary wives were generally acquiescent of the conditions – frequently very difficult – in which they lived and worked.

The Hadfields returned to their home at Otaki in April 1859, after attending the consecration at Lambeth of Charles John Abraham as Bishop of Wellington. The golden days of the Otaki mission were waning, but the archdeacon was not yet ready to give up his work as a missionary. During the conflicts of the 1860s some missionaries withdrew from isolated stations, but Hadfield stayed at Otaki strengthened by the support of a wife born on a New Zealand mission station. She stood by him during the bitter days following Governor Gore Browne's enforcement (in response to settlers' pressure) of the purchase of land at Waitara despite tribal opposition. Hadfield always championed Maori rights, and knew himself to be the most unpopular man in New Zealand when he expressed deep anger at this denial of guarantees made under the Treaty of Waitangi and his conviction that war could have been avoided. His reaction included a direct and public appeal to the Duke of Newcastle, Secretary of State for the Colonies, with three pamphlets published in London in 1860 and 1861. In New Zealand he was summoned to the Bar of the House of Representatives on 11 August 1860 to justify his stand.

Early in the 1860s Kate and some of her Maori pupils made a large Union Jack painted on calico with washing blue and red raddle, and hoisted it on a ship's mast erected in front of Rangiatea Church in defiance of a Kingite flag flown nearby for a few days. In June 1865 when Hauhau supporters were in the district, Hadfield told Bishop Selwyn in a letter that Kate was 'not alarmed'.

After seventeen years of marriage and hard toil at Otaki, Kate and Octavius with their family (now numbering nine children) moved to Wellington, where the archdeacon took charge of the diocese while Bishop Abraham was in England. Hadfield was consecrated Bishop of Wellington on 9 October 1870 and elected Primate in 1890. The bishop's wife organised bazaars, entertained many visitors at Bishopscourt, including Maori friends from Otaki, and became known as 'a kind hostess'.

In 1893 Kate and Octavius retired to a rural home at Edale, Marton, where Kate died on 8 January 1902, and was buried in the churchyard at Tutu Totara. As her great-granddaughter records, Kate Hadfield's influence and personality extended to many places. An *In Memoriam* spoke of 'her quiet strength and force of character, her wise counsel, her helpful sympathy, and her faithful friendship'.

June Starke

Quotations
para.2 Kate Williams to her family, 2 Sept. 1851, O. Hadfield Papers
para.3 R. Taylor, Journal, 19 May 1852
para.4 C. Hadfield, Diary of a Journey from Auckland to Whanganui in 1853, O. Hadfield Papers 1833–1902
para.6 Kate Hadfield to her mother, 5 July 1858, O. Hadfield Papers 1833–1902, vol.5
para.7 Quoted by B. Macmorran in *Octavius Hadfield*, p.90
para.9 Hadfield to Selwyn, 8 June 1865, O. Hadfield Papers 1838–1952
para.11 B. Macmorran, *Octavius Hadfield*, p.139

Unpublished Sources
Catherine Hadfield, Early New Zealand, O. Hadfield, Papers 1838–1952, MS Papers 139, ATL
Catherine Hadfield, Diary of a Journey from Auckland to Whanganui in 1853, O. Hadfield Papers, qMS, ATL
O. Hadfield, Papers, 1833–1902, qMS, ATL
O. Hadfield, Papers, 1838–1952, MS Papers 139, ATL
R. Taylor, Journal 1833–73, qMS, ATL

Published Sources
Macmorran, B. *Octavius Hadfield*, Wellington
Ramsden, E. *Rangiatea*, Wellington, 1951

RUTH HALL

1898–1988

Ruth Hall spent most of her life on a farm in Dovedale, a valley not far from Nelson. Born in Nelson and educated at Nelson College for Girls, Ruth went teaching after leaving school and met her husband, Lance Hall, while on country service. When they married, in 1928, they moved to the farm at Dovedale and were among the first to become established as tobacco growers in the Nelson area. Ruth's life came to revolve around the seasonal work of cultivating and harvesting the tobacco leaf.

Her daughter-in-law writes:

When tobacco was first introduced into the Dove Valley the tobacco seedlings were grown commercially in a plant nursery, brought by the grower in boxes, 'pricked out' into tobacco beds covered with calico, and so the growing process would continue. As a grower's wife, my mother-in law would be expected to help with this work a well as provide morning and afternoon tea and a hot drink at lunch-time for all the workers.

Later, growers discovered they could sprout their own seed. Early in September the seed would be sown in small 'parcels' of old flannel. The hot water cupboard was an ideal spot to put the baby's bath with the seed on a bed of old material. Hot-water bottles would sometimes be filled to maintain an even temperature. This was another of Ruth's responsibilities. When the seed had sprouted sufficiently it would be sown in the tobacco beds and left to grow. If the strike was poor, seedlings would be bought from the commercial grower and 'pricked out'. Planting would commence in early November. Women would pull the mature plants from the beds and put them in boxes ready to plant out in the tobacco paddock. If the plants did not 'take' and died out in the paddock – and some always did – replanting would be necessary.

Harvesting would commence towards the end of January and could go on until late March, depending on the crop and the weather – tobacco is very susceptible to frost. Growers worked in gangs. One day of the week would be allocated to each of the five growers in a gang – too bad if it always rained on your allotted day! On each farm the wife would be responsible for providing a bucket of hot, soapy water, pot-mits, and towels for washing hands before morning and afternoon tea and lunch. Tobacco, when green, is very sticky with tobacco gum which needs to be peeled off the hands before washing with hot water. A bucket of tea, milk and sugar for a gang of about eighteen to twenty people would also be provided. Ruth always had at least one and sometimes two workers living in the house, so preparing meals for the extras was also part of her daily work.

Men did the picking of the leaf and the women worked at the tobacco kiln, tying the leaf onto sticks ready to be loaded into the kiln. The other four days of the week Ruth worked at the kilns of other growers in the gang.

From April to July the leaf was graded and tied in hanks, then loaded onto pallets to be taken to the buying sheds in Motueka. Help was needed at this time of year also so Ruth had extras in the house as well as her work in the shed from 8 am to 5 pm. In the winter a 'hot dog' stove heated the shed and boiled the billy for morning and afternoon teas as well as heating the occasional pot of soup.

Cooking, heating, lighting, and firing the kiln were all done without

*electricity until 1950 when power came to the valley. Like other women living
in the country at this time, Ruth did without many of the conveniences which
townspeople had. The telephone exchange operated from 7 am to 9 pm on
weekdays and 9 am to 10 am and 5 pm to 6 pm at weekends and public
holidays. A store cart from Wakefield, about eighteen miles away, called once a
week. After the war a shop opened in the area. The butcher called on a
Thursday and bread was delivered twice a week.*

*Ruth raised two children. She was also active in the community life of the
valley. Fifty years' service in the Women's Division of Federated Farmers
included a term as president of the local branch and secretary/treasurer on two
occasions. Ruth was also the Dovedale librarian for a number of years.*

*Travelling up or down the valley to meetings, or into Nelson for shopping,
meant a dusty journey by bus on a road which was unsealed until the 1960s.
The service ran three times a week (Mondays, Wednesdays, and Fridays).
Although the Halls owned a car, Ruth did not have a licence (only two women
in the valley did in the 1950s). Even getting to the road could be difficult. The
farmhouse was across the river, and to get out meant crossing a swing-bridge or
negotiating a ford.*

*Improvements came in the 1950s and 1960s. Working conditions on
tobacco farms changed markedly once mechanical pickers and tying machines
were introduced in 1958. But twenty years later tobacco growing was in
decline. The lower cost of imported leaf made New Zealand cultivation
uneconomic. The 1988–89 season, which followed Ruth's death in September
1988, was virtually the last in which tobacco was harvested commercially in
New Zealand.*   Robin Hall

Sources
Personal recollections of Robin Hall, Ruth Hall's daughter-in-law.

RHONA HASZARD

1901–1931

Rhona Haszard was barely thirty when she died, but she left behind a legacy of
paintings, drawings, and prints which are possibly the most interesting instances
of modernism achieved by a New Zealand artist. She was born at Thames, one
of five children whose father held a senior position with the Department of
Lands and Survey. She spent most of her youth in Hokitika and Invercargill.
When her mother died in 1918, the family moved to Christchurch and Rhona
enrolled at the Canterbury College School of Art under Archibald Nicoll.

In the 1920s opportunities were opening up for middle-class women. In
Christchurch the visual arts were burgeoning. The emphasis was on landscape
painting. Among Rhona's friends at the time were Evelyn Page, Rata Lovell-
Smith, and Olivia Spencer Bower, artists who would all achieve prominence in

later years. She herself was considered a brilliant student and by the early 1920s was exhibiting with the country's major art societies. In 1923 she married Ronald McKenzie, but the union was short-lived as two years later she met the Englishman Leslie Greener and was greatly attracted by his unconventional background and extroverted personality.

The couple weathered considerable family criticism, escaping to Europe soon after their marriage at Waihi in December 1925. Judging from correspondence between the two (covering the period 1925–30), the partnership seems to have been remarkably equitable for its time.

Leslie Greener was himself a painter but acknowledged that Rhona's artistic abilities far outstripped his own. There are many instances of praise and support in the letters he sent to her. During 1926 the two studied together at the Académie Julian in Paris, then cycled through France, stopping to paint in the Marne Valley. Although Rhona had begun to use thicker pigment and to flatten her forms before 1925, there is little comparison between the artist's more tentative New Zealand works and those she produced abroad. In Europe she developed a post-impressionist style where full brush-strokes were laid in a broken, divisionist manner which her commentators referred to as 'mosaic'. The colour

Rhona Haszard, 'Finistere, Spain', 1926. *National Art Gallery*

was high-keyed, with complementaries playing off against one another; in the interests of decorative unity, forms were distorted and simplified.

By the end of 1927, Rhona Haszard regularly attracted recognition. *Sardine Fleet, Brittany,* for example, was hung in the Paris Salon for 1927 before being sent out to New Zealand. Here it prompted the art critic for the *Otago Daily Times* to observe that 'one sees her experimenting in a direction which is peculiar to a foreign people'. She became associated with the Society of Women Artists in London, and was included in the comprehensive British Artists' Exhibition, shown at Manchester, Leeds, Bradford, and Glasgow.

When Leslie Greener was appointed art master and French instructor at Victoria College in Alexandria, Egypt, it gave Rhona the opportunity to produce a fresh series of paintings and water-colours. However, these tended to be less adventurous than her French paintings, and there were fewer of them. Several were included in the artist's survey exhibition at Claridge's Hotel, Alexandria in December 1928. Landscapes dominated the forty works on display, covering New Zealand, Brittany, Sark, the Marne Valley, and Egypt. There were also a number of still life studies and portraits.

In the summer of 1928 the artist had sustained a serious back injury while on a camping expedition to Cyprus and for several months the following year was compelled to seek treatment in London, choosing the unorthodox methods of Louis Doel. Although her spinal injury was cured, the period of considerable anxiety and loneliness in England left her drained both physically and emotionally. In an attempt to overcome the problem she became an avid champion of dietary reform, eating only vegetables and fruit.

Together with her husband she turned to print-making, producing a number of lively black and white linocuts based on earlier themes. These included *The Road to Little Sark,* the title of one of the artist's most accomplished canvases. They both exhibited their prints at the Galerie Paul in Cairo during March 1930. It was her oils, however, which earned Rhona most attention. In a show of contemporary British artists mounted at the Grafton Galleries, London in June 1930, she was regarded by P. G. Konody of the *Daily Mail* as a 'newcomer of considerable talent'. A further exhibition of her work took place in Cairo early in 1931, but before it was over the artist had met her untimely death, falling from the Victoria College Tower.

Appreciation of this artist is based chiefly on a survey of her work, selected by Leslie Greener, which circulated New Zealand in 1933.   *Anne Kirker*

Quotation
para.5 *Otago Daily Times*, 21 Nov. 1927

Unpublished Sources
Rhona Haszard File, Research Library, National Art Gallery
Rhona Haszard File, Research Library, Auckland City Art Gallery

Published Sources
Greener, L. 'Rhona Haszard'. *Art in New Zealand*, vol.5 no.17, Sept. 1932, pp.17–20
Kirker, A. 'Rhona Haszard: A Painter of the Twenties', *Art New Zealand*, no.34, Autumn 1985, pp.48–51

ANA HATO

1906-1953

When she died in December 1953, it was said of Ana Hato that she had the finest Maori voice of all time. She was born at Ngapuna, Rotorua, in 1906, the daughter of Riripati Eperima and Hato Ngamahirau. On her mother's side she was descended from the Tuhourangi people, and on her father's the Ngati-Whakaue, both sub-tribes of Te Arawa. She attended Whakarewarewa primary school, where Mrs Banks (the head teacher's wife) took singing classes, the only formal music tuition Ana would ever have. Although hers was a strong, clear, soprano voice, and she played the guitar, Ana did not read music nor did she write any of her own songs.

For most of her life Ana lived at the tourist resort of Whakarewarewa. She was one of the children who amused tourists by diving for pennies in the Puarenga Stream. She was a strong swimmer and hockey enthusiast, her voice joining the chorus on many a team excursion. Ana's parents were singers, well versed in traditional Maori music, and she grew up with a background of stage performance. By the time she was sixteen Ana had joined a Maori concert group. Her popularity as a talented young singer grew, and soon she was sought for public occasions where solo items were required.

Ana's fame was restricted to New Zealand until early in 1927, when the Duke and Duchess of York came to this country. Ana sang for them with her cousin Dean Waretini and her performance was greeted with much acclaim by both the royal visitors and the press. The Parlophone Company, which at that time took a particular interest in ethnic music in different countries, made the first recording of her songs in Rotorua. A recording arrangement was made and the two singers went to Australia. Soon their records were selling by the thousands – any New Zealand home that boasted a gramophone possessed a record of Ana and Dean singing such numbers as 'Pokare Kare', 'E Pari Ra', 'Hine e Hine', songs composed this century and set to popular tunes rather than traditional Maori waiata. Alfred Hill's 'Waiata Poi' was also a great favourite. In all they were to make fourteen recordings together.

Ana gave of her talent unselfishly. Many charitable organisations raised large sums at concerts at which she performed. A staunch Roman Catholic, she worked hard for the church, especially during the war years. Soon after the outbreak of the Second World War, her husband Pahou Raponi went overseas with the first Maori contingent. He died in a German prisoner-of-war camp.

Ana formed her own concert party, which performed throughout the country. She was usually asked to sing at special occasions such as the opening of the new 1ZB building in Auckland in 1941 and at the opening of Radio Station 1YZ at Rotorua in April 1949. Maori radio programmes were then in their infancy, but Ana took part in some of the early radio broadcasts featuring Maori music.

People who remember Ana Hato describe her as generous, fun-loving, and easy-going. They still marvel at the beauty of her singing voice. The songs she

Ana Hato. *The Bath-House, Rotorua's Art
and History Museum.*

sang were sweet, touching, with a melancholy plaintiveness sometimes evident
in Polynesian music.

During the last years of her life, Ana entered hospital periodically. Even
though her health was failing she continued to sing, sometimes entertaining her
fellow patients in Rotorua Hospital, where she eventually died at the age of
forty-seven.

Relatives regret that they no longer have any of Ana's recordings, but they
remember her voice. In December each year they place an 'In Memoriam' notice
for her in the Rotorua newspapers which says: 'The melody is ended but the
memory lingers on . . .'. *Alison Masters*

Published Sources
Dennan, Rangitiaria with Ross Annabell. *Guide Rangi of Rotorua*, Christchurch, 1968
Rotorua Post, 9 Dec. 1953
Shaw, Kate. *Just Ordinary People*, Rotorua, 1989
Waretini, Dean, and H. T. Mitchell. Notes on the record cover of the record *The Great Songs of Ana
Hato*, PMCM 6021

Unpublished Source
Williams, Ulrich. Tribute to Ana Hato, talk broadcast in the 1950s, Radio New Zealand (copy in private
possession)

SARAH HEAP

1871–1960

Sarah Heap, the pioneer of girls' physical education in New Zealand, was born
in 1871 in Ashton, Lancashire, where her father, Henry Miller, was a cheese
factory worker. Nothing more is known of her life before she arrived in New
Zealand in 1901 and married Harry Heap of Auckland.

Although the exact nature of the teaching qualifications she gained in England was never disclosed, Sarah Heap soon acquired a reputation as an expert drill mistress. In 1908 she was given charge of the physical training of girls at the Diocesan High School in Auckland, and by the time she was appointed as the visiting drill mistress at the Auckland Girls' Grammar School in 1909 she was also working part-time at the Mount Eden Collegiate School and the Technical College in Auckland. In 1910 she organised classes for girls of the Young Women's Christian Association and in 1911 began working as a part-time instructor in physical culture and swimming to women students at the Auckland Teachers' Training College. Through a special arrangement with the Auckland Grammar School Board, she was allowed to continue working at the training college after she was appointed to a full-time position at the grammar school in 1912.

At the grammar school, Sarah Heap established the most comprehensive system of physical training for secondary school girls in New Zealand. She gave lessons in drill, organised school games, conducted dancing classes and gave instruction in first aid and home nursing. Like her counterparts in English girls' schools, she monitored the health of her pupils through annual physical examinations and, whenever necessary, administered special courses of remedial exercises. During the First World War, she also organised and trained the grammar school branch of the Women's National Reserve.

Through her work in Auckland, Sarah Heap became recognised as the country's leading authority on the physical training of girls. In 1912 she was appointed to act on the Minister of Education's advisory committee on primary school physical education. As the only teacher on the committee, she played an important part in shaping the new system of physical instruction and medical inspection which was introduced to primary schools under the Education Acts of 1912 and 1914.

Girls' physical education became a central part of school routine under the impetus of teachers such as Sarah Heap. This class is at Port Chalmers District High School, 1900. *De Maus Collection, Hocken Library*

At the end of 1915, Sarah Heap resigned from her position at the training college to concentrate on her work at Auckland Girls' Grammar School where she had initiated a unique experiment in teacher training. After her first attempt to establish a physical training college for women had failed in 1907, she had managed to convince the Auckland Grammar School Board to allow a number of old girls to return to the school for training as assistants in physical culture and games. Although her instruction scheme never gained the official backing of the Department of Education, it remained the only form of training in physical education available to women in New Zealand for many years.

Sarah Heap, affectionately known to pupils and colleagues as 'Sally', retired from the grammar school in 1931. She enjoyed good health throughout most of her later life and retained a close attachment to the school where she had taught for twenty-three years. She died a childless widow at the age of eighty-nine on 14 July 1960.   *Margaret Hammer*

Unpublished Sources
Auckland Grammar School Board Records, NZ MS 824, APL
Education Department Files E 36/1/- and E 36/1A, National Archives, Wellington

Published Sources
Auckland Girls' Grammar School Magazine, 1909–1931, APL
Northey, H. with J. A. and M. Asher. *Auckland Girls' Grammar School – The First Hundred Years 1888-1988*, Auckland, 1988

PIRIHIRA RAUKURA WAIOEKA HEKETA

1884-1947

> *Ko Kahuranaki te maunga*
> *Ko Tukituki te awa*
> *Ko Ngati Kahungunu te iwi*
> *Ko Ngati Te Whatuiapiti te hapu*
> *Ko Keke Haunga te marae*
> *Ko Renata te tangata.*

Pirihira Raukura Waioeka Renata was born in 1884 at Patangata, daughter of Warena Te Whatuiapiti Renata and Ritihia. She spent most of her early life at Pukehou.

Very little is known about her early years except that her first marriage to Te Ua was arranged and they had three children, all daughters, and only one survived to sixteen or seventeen years of age and that was Winipere, who is buried on top of her father at Waipatu. It was not until after her marriage to Tuhi Te Okanga Keketa Te Awe and the birth of their daughter Miriama Warihia that they moved to Lower Hutt and then Wellington, where Nanny Pirihira died in September 1947.

Nanny Pirihira was a rangatira of Ngati Te Whatuiapiti and considered to be urukehu. She was a direct descendant of the marriage between Tohuangaterangi and Tapuhara and this line made her very proud of her close relation-

Pirihira Raukura Waioeka Heketa of Te
Whatuiapiti, Ngati Kahungunu, at the
opening of Tama Te Kapua, Ohinemutu.
Miriama R. Scott

ship to Pareihe, a paramount chief of Ngati Kahungunu, whose generous gifts
of land for church and educational purposes were often remembered. Nanny
Pirihira was steeped in tikanga Maori and it is said that she had 'mana to speak
on her marae' of Patangata and Keke Haunga.

Her depth of knowledge about tikanga Maori is reflected in her conversation
with John Lee Zimmerman, an American linguist who was an interpreter for the
Marine Corps and frequent visitor to 370 Tinakori Road, Wellington:

*In old days, Hone, when a girl learn about taniko and learn how to make mats,
she learn early in the morning, Hone, before the sun come up. Always one old
woman in the village, she know all that work and she tapu and the house tapu
. . .*

*When I was a young girl, Hone, I learn all these things. I know how to
make taniko and work flax, you see me make taniko, Hone, you see me fix flax
for piupiu. I know what tree make things yellow and where I get stuff to make
it black and red. We make oil for our hair in the old days, Hone, we take fat
from big bird and heat it many times and make it clear and nice. Then we take
little flowers off a low bush, I don't know what you call it in English and we
put them in the oil, we put lots of them in and we heat it again. Then we use it
on our hair and it smell nice . . .*

*So I like the old things, Hone, I learn the old things. I learn to make mats,
Hone, and the first mat I make, it's not so good, Hone, but I give it to the head
man anyway, to the chief, 'cause it's the first one I make.*

Nanny Pirihira had a very distinctive moko, which was used by Sister Mary
Lawrence in her painting of the Maori madonna. She recounted to Zimmerman
the tale of her moko:

My aunt, she had a fine one, and when I was young girl, I said to myself, I get

281

one, too. But the minister up there, he just hate it, Hone, and if any of the girls even talk about getting one, he give them the devil, Hone.

Well, Hone, one day I hear there's a good tohunga in the town, he know how to do the moko real fine, Hone, so all of a sudden I take the horse and the little buggy and I go in to the town and get the moko done. Then I go home, and it's all right. My aunt say it's a good one, Hone. Then somebody say I must go on an errand to the minister's house, Hone, and I'm scared, 'cause I know he going to be mad. So while I'm going over, I think hard, Hone, and when I get there, I wrap my scarf around my face and knock at the door.

He want to know what the trouble is, Hone, and I tell him I got a bad toothache, and I mumble when I talk, because my lip's all swelled up and sore, Hone, and anyway I can't talk plain like that. So I tell him I got a bad toothache, and everything all right.

Then I go away for a while and I don't see him for some time. Then I go to a hui, a big meeting, and my face all fine now, and the moko look good and I'm proud of it, Hone. Then all of a sudden I see him coming toward me and I think to myself oh-oh, here it come, here I get the devil for sure. And I can't run away because he already see me. So I just stand there.

But when he come up, he rub noses with me, the hongi, you know, Hone, and then he begin to call out the names of the dead like we always do when we meet old friends, and I know everything all right. But when he going away again he look hard at me and say, 'Toothache, eh? Huh.' So I think I don't fool him, e, Hone?

Aunty Aroha Johnson (Niania) recalls how in Nanny Pirihira's day, a women was not to have a liaison with a man unless she had a moko, to show her standing in the tribe.

One of our earliest recollections of Nanny Pirihira and Grandpa Oka is from our mother Miriama. She always told us of when Grandpa Oka was at Te Aute College, he used to watch Nanny Pirihira riding bareback on a horse across the hills at the back of the college. This admiration from a distance resulted in the marriage of our grandparents.

The most prominent memories of Nanny Pirihira are when she was in Lower Hutt and Wellington, in particular, her work in helping to form Ngati Poneke. Both she and Kingi Tahiwi strove very hard to ensure the club maintained its high standards of performance and tikanga Maori. This involvement earned her the revered title of 'Mama' and it is primarily for this work, especially during the years of the Second World War, that Nanny Pirihira was awarded the Order of the British Empire medal posthumously in 1947.

The commitment of Nanny Pirihira to tikanga Maori is reflected in the 'schooling' of the young people at Ngati Poneke, particularly the women. Aunty Aroha recounts how Nanny Pirihira would tell the young women not to sit in a meeting-house with their feet bare, that they must have something on their feet, even if it's a hanky and when asked 'why?' she would reply that by doing so they were insulting the men . . . 'they [the men] get funny ideas.'

Nanny Pirihira was also fiercely protective of the young women of Ngati

Poneke and Aunty Aroha recalls the stern reprimand that Nanny Pirihira delivered to Captain Kennie: 'you rude to my girls, you make my girls go funny.'
Apparently, the club went on board Captain Keenie's ship to give a concert and
drinks were served before the performance. Unfortunately one of the young
women was affected by the alcohol, which marred her performance slightly.

Aunty Aroha remembers how Nanny Pirihira had a good sense of humour,
even if a bit of a teaser and despite being a strong disciplinarian who stood no
nonsense.

But in Aunty Aroha's opinion, Nanny Pirihira loved her Maoritanga and
always in the back of her mind there was the need to satisfy her father and her
tribe. Perhaps the final words should be left to the then prime minister, Peter
Fraser, who recalled an association of many years with Nanny Pirihira, particularly during the war period, and he said in his tribute: 'Pirihira was not only
a Rangatira by brith, but she was a Rangatira in her way of life, and an inspiration to the younger generation.'

It is with deep gratitude that we thank our Aunty Aroha Johnson (Niania),
Uncle Jock McEwan and John Lee Zimmerman, who made our Nanny come
alive so that this account was possible. E nga matua keke, tena koutou. He mihi
aroha tenei ki a koutou mo a koutou pitopito korero mo to tatou kuia. No reira
noho ora mai.   *Miriama Ritihia Scott*

Quotations
para.3 Interview with Mrs Aroha Johnson (Niania), 24 Feb. 1990, Rotorua
paras.5ff J. Zimmerman, *Where the People Sing*, pp.181–83
paras.9ff J. Zimmerman, pp.172–73
para.14ff Interview with Mrs Aroha Johnson
para.21 *Evening Post*, 27 Sept. 1947

Unpublished Sources
Information was provided by Mrs Aroha Johnson, niece of Pirihira Heketa and one of the original
    members of Ngati Poneke, and Mr Jock McEwan, one of the original members of Ngati Poneke, and
    a colleague of Tuhi Te Okanga Heketa and Miriama Warihia Scott (Heketa) in the Department of
    Maori Affairs. The author is a mokopuna of Pirihira Heketa.

Published Sources
Evening Post, 25 and 27 Sept. 1947 (obituaries)
Laugesen, Carl. *Te Ahua: Maori Portraits*, Palmerston North, 1946
Zimmerman, John Lee. *Where the People Sing: Green Land of the Maoris*, New York, 1946

AMY HELLABY

1864–1955

Amy Maria Briscoe, born on 5 February 1864, was the only child of Elizabeth
and Walter Briscoe to survive diphtheria, which also left her motherless at the
age of two years. Her father remarried and they sailed to New Zealand on the
Great Britain in 1872, and thence to the Chatham Islands; fellow passengers on
the voyage were Mr and Mrs Anthony Trollope, and six-year-old Amy was much
impressed with the splendour of Mrs Trollope's evening attire.

She was entrusted to the nuns at Ponsonby Convent for necessary education, returning to the Chathams only for Christmas. She had no playmates there, and was thrown on her own resources, finding joy in beautiful sunrises and sunsets, and playing on the beach with shells. This self-reliance was to benefit her in later life.

In 1885 she married Richard Hellaby, the motivating force behind the retail butchery business of R. & W. Hellaby Ltd, which he had founded with his elder brother, William, in 1873. This veritable dynamo of a man, working twelve to fourteen hours per day, well liked and respected for his fair dealing and hard work, was aware that he had a cardiac condition, the legacy of a childhood illness. As his family grew and his business prospered, he made sure that his wife was familiar with the workings of the business. This proved essential, for he died suddenly, minutes after arriving home on 20 June 1902. Amy was thirty-seven, with six children, the youngest only three months old. It was then that her strong will and self-reliance came into their own. In addition to assuming control of the business and bringing up her own children, she supervised the care of five children of William and Rosina Hellaby, who had both died the previous year.

The business at the time of Richard's death was involved not only in retail butchery but also in tanning, canning, soap-making, ice-making, blood and bone manufacturing, and other allied activities; it was said to be 'the largest and most complete private business in the colony'.

Two trustees were appointed to manage the business; they reported to Amy who was in overall control of the financial affairs. To fulfil the wishes of Richard that his sons should carry on the business, she steadfastly refused many tempting offers to sell. Also in accordance with Richard's express wishes, she organised the building of a large house in Mountain Road, Epsom, in the style of an English manor house, naming it 'Bramcote' after their English home. It was here that she gave to her children the secure and happy family life that she had not experienced herself. She made numerous trips to Europe with each of her children as they came of age, in order that they knew and appreciated European culture.

The three sons were in England at the outbreak of war in 1914; all joined up immediately and were commissioned. Amy set up house in London, so that they had a home when on leave from France.

On their return from England in 1919, 'Bramcote' was sold and a smaller house built in Remuera Road. The family firm passed through many vicissitudes, but Amy fulfilled her pledge and saw two of her sons, John and Frederick, learn the business 'from the hoof'; the third son, Sydney, who was an artist, remained in France and England.

Amy was known for her charitable bequests, particularly to Kings College, Auckland. She was a healthy, active woman into extreme old age, and even though changing world conditions saw the decline of the business, she had steered it successfully; the name 'Hellaby' was known throughout the South Pacific. She died on 7 April 1955, at the age of ninety-one.

Freda Romer

Quotation
para.4 *The Cyclopedia of New Zealand*, p.389

Unpublished Sources
Information has been provided by family members; the late Freda Romer was the youngest daughter
  of Amy Hellaby.

Published Sources
Caughey, Angela. *An Auckland Network*, Auckland, 1988
The Cyclopedia of New Zealand, vol.2, Christchurch, 1902
Scott, Dick. *Stock in Trade*, Auckland, 1973

CHRISTINA HENDERSON | *1861–1953*

STELLA HENDERSON | *1871–1962*

ELIZABETH HENDERSON | *1873–1935*

The three Henderson sisters were remarkable women who throughout their lives worked for the rights of women.

Daughters of Daniel Henderson, a clerk from Wick, Caithness, Scotland, and Alice (born Connolly), from Adare, Ireland, they were born in Kaiapoi into a family of seven girls and two boys. Christina Kirk Henderson, the eldest of the three, whose life is least documented. was born in 1861. When she was 'barely in her teens', she began her career as an unpaid pupil-teacher. At that time there were not nearly enough teachers to cope with the steady influx of immigrants arriving in the colony, many of whom were uneducated. She then won a scholarship to Canterbury College and studied under Professor Macmillan Brown, graduating with a BA degree. Later she became first assistant at Christchurch Girls' High School, and founded the Canterbury Women Teachers' Association. Her tireless work for equal pay was prompted by the fact that, as a teacher, Christina earned half the amount men were paid for doing the same work with the same training. 'It is quite true', she wrote, 'that a woman manages to live on less than a man because her wants are fewer, but it is equally true, that her wants are fewer because her earnings are less.'

Christina also fought for women's suffrage, the right of women to become members of parliament, better legal protection for women and young people, and, most importantly, for temperance. These causes involved her in several key organisations. She was a founder member of the National Council of Women (NCW) in 1896, its president for seven years, and a chief instigator of its revival in 1916. At the 1900 NCW conference, she delivered a paper on 'The Ethics of Wage Earning' in which she wrote:

Sex does not disable woman being employed in the most arduous and dangerous occupations, but it does disable her from receiving what is regarded – if a man's wages are to be taken as a guide – as the efficient reward of those services.

Christina's commitment to temperance involved her in both the Christchurch Prohibition League and the Women's Christian Temperance Union (WCTU), where she was president of the local branch for twenty years. At a

Christina (left) and Stella Henderson (right) with another sister, Kathleen.
Canterbury Museum

national level, Christina was a Dominion officer of the WCTU, corresponding secretary, and legal and parliamentary adviser for over twenty years. Contemporaries greatly respected her opinions and noted her 'calm, clear and logical' speaking manner and the thoroughness of her knowledge.

She was also active in the Presbyterian Church, and held the offices of president and secretary of the Dominion Presbyterian Women's Mission Union, and the Christchurch Presbyterian Association. For thirty-five years she was assistant-editor and then editor of *Harvest Field*, the church's publication for women. Her long and varied public service was recognised when she was made one of the first women justices of the peace.

At an early age, Christina had developed strong socialist beliefs. She described the capitalist system as 'the most cruel, the most unjust . . . It demands . . . that there should always be an army of unemployed who may be used to restrain the demands of those who are in work'.

Although most accounts stress the prosaic side of Christina's character and her brilliant intellect, she had a warm and generous nature. She never married. On her death in 1953, *The White Ribbon* mourned the loss of her 'lively mind, pungent wit, her quiet courage and integrity . . . her real humanity and devotion, her earnestness yet gaiety of spirit.'

Stella May Henderson was born on 25 October 1871 and educated at Christchurch Girls' High School, where she was taught by Helen Connon. After a brilliant scholastic career that included winning a Junior Scholarship in 1888, completing a BA degree in 1892 and a MA degree with first-class honours in English and Latin in 1893, she decided to read law. With the help of William Izard and H. H. Loughnan, she began working for their law firm and attending law lectures at Canterbury College. Izard further assisted her by approaching the MP for Riccarton to ensure legislation would be passed to allow her to practise law. In 1898 she passed her final examination for her LLB degree.

Although she now had both a law degree and legal experience and all legal impediment to practise law had been removed by the Law Practitioners and New Zealand Law Society Acts of 1896, Stella chose not to practise law. She decided instead to accept an offer from the editor of the *Lyttelton Times*, S. Saunders, of a position as parliamentary correspondent and political leader-writer in Wellington. She therefore became one of the earliest New Zealand woman parliamentary reporters. But when she arrived at the press gallery in parliament she was rebuffed by the gallery members, who voted against her admittance. Undeterred, she bought a ticket to the ladies' gallery and proceeded to write notes with her notebook balanced on her knee. Eventually the editors of the newspaper protested that the journalists' vote had restricted their right to choose whom they employed for the press gallery. The matter was resolved by the decision of the Reporting and Debates Committee of the House to convert a portion of the ladies' gallery into a press gallery for her use. She continued in this position for nearly two years.

Like her elder sister, Stella was a convinced prohibitionist, fought for equal pay for equal work, and held socialist views. She was a member of the NCW and in 1898 presented a paper on local government to its annual conference. In it she demanded an extension of municipal powers and favoured nationalisation of the land, 'because it belongs to the people'.

In 1900 she married Edwin Frank Allan, senior leader-writer for the *Evening Post*. They moved to Australia when Edwin was invited to join the Melbourne *Argus*. Stella soon became involved in a number of organisations concerned with the health and welfare of women and children. She continued to write for newspapers, joined the Women Writers' Club, and became one of three women foundation members of the Australian Journalists' Association.

Stella became best known in Australia for her weekly 'Woman to Woman' column in the *Argus*. Writing under the pen-name of 'Vesta', she gave information and opinions on most issues relating to women, children's interests, and community welfare. 'Vesta' became a household authority.

As well as being a good writer, Stella was a 'witty, fluent speaker with a pleasant, well-modulated voice and direct manner'. In 1924 she was appointed a substitute delegate for Australia to the fifth assembly of the League of Nations, and was a delegate to the second Pan Pacific Women's Conference in Hawaii in 1930.

In 1939 she retired to England, where she continued to write for the *Argus* about the experience of women and children in wartime. She returned to Melbourne in 1947, and died there on 1 March 1962. She had four daughters.

The youngest of the three sisters, Elizabeth Reid Henderson, was born on 4 November 1873. She is best known as New Zealand's first woman member of parliament, being elected in August 1933 in a by-election following the death of her husband James McCombs, MP for Lyttelton.

Elizabeth's election to parliament came at the end of a life in public service.

Educated at Christchurch Girls' High, she became politically active soon after leaving school. She was secretary of the Canterbury Children's Aid Society and an executive member of the Canterbury Progressive Liberal Association. Throughout her life she was, like her sisters, an ardent prohibitionist and was president of the Canterbury Section of the Women's Christian Temperance Union, as well as Dominion treasurer.

She married James McCombs in 1903, and the couple had two children. Both Elizabeth and James were members of the Socialist Church, and helped to reform the Fabian Society in 1908. These were both moderate organisations, whose aims were educational rather than electoral. Elizabeth and James were members of the Social Democrat Party, before becoming foundation members of the Labour Party in 1916, with James being elected the new party's first president and Elizabeth a member of the national executive. James was the member of parliament for Lyttelton from 1913 to 1933, first as a Social Democrat and later representing Labour.

Elizabeth was heavily involved in local body politics. She was elected to the Christchurch City Council and the North Canterbury Hospital Board in 1921; in 1927 she became a member of the Tramways Board and Chairwoman of the Electricity Committee, which reduced the cost of electricity to consumers. The following year she unsuccessfully contested the Kaiapoi parliamentary seat for Labour, and in 1931 tried for the Christchurch North seat.

When James died in 1933, Elizabeth stood for the vacant Lyttelton seat as the Labour candidate and won by a large majority. She was nearly sixty when she took her place as the first woman member of parliament, just forty years after New Zealand women had won the vote. In the House as in all her public activities, she used her position to advance the status and welfare of women and children. She was uncompromising in her assertion of the contribution women could make to decision making. In her maiden speech, after thanking members for their kind reception, she stated that she hoped

. . . nothing will happen during my term of office that will disturb the harmony of the relations so created. I would like to warn honourable members, however, that women are never satisfied unless they have their own way. It happens in this case the women's way is the right way.

In that speech she argued passionately for the right of the unemployed to work, and in particular the right of the young unemployed. During her time in parliament, she also lobbied for reforms in the education and health systems, and strongly advocated the need for women to be appointed to the police force.

Unfortunately Elizabeth's parliamentary career was short-lived. Her health deteriorated and she died on 7 June 1935. Her son, Terence Henderson McCombs, succeeded her as member for Lyttelton and was minister of education from 1947 to 1949.

Although the first woman member of parliament, Elizabeth McCombs did not see herself as a token figure. Like her sisters she was a strong woman who advocated the rights of her sex. Yet Stella and Elizabeth, like other prominent inter-war feminists, argued from a position of 'domestic feminism', founded on a belief that 'women's major contribution to the world was as wives and mothers and that special training would improve their performance of that role'. As 'Vesta', for example, Stella stressed the need to train girls in the domestic arts. Similarly, Elizabeth was proud of being both 'a fully domesticated woman . . . splendid cook and dressmaker' and active in public life. After twenty years of political activism, she maintained that her constant mission had been 'to strengthen the institution of the home in our community'.

Contemporary views of Elizabeth give us some idea of the prejudice she and her sisters faced: for example, she was described as not being a feminist 'in the offensive sense'. Championing domestic feminism may therefore have been a tactic as well as a conviction. Nevertheless, the Henderson sisters helped to pave the way for future generations of women to enjoy greater equality and improved social conditions.   *Margaret Wilson & Bronwyn Labrum*

Quotations

para.2 *The White Ribbon*, Dec. 1953, p.4; quoted in *NZ Herstory 1984*, p.33
para.3 Quoted in *NZ Herstory 1984*, p.33
para.4 J. Cocker and J. Malton Murray, *Temperance and Prohibition*, p.184
para.6 Quoted in *NZ Herstory 1984*, p.33
para.7 *The White Ribbon*, Dec. 1953, p.4
para.10 Quoted in *NZ Herstory 1978*, p.67
para.13 B. Nairn and G. Searle (eds), *Australian Dictionary of Biography*, vol.7, p.39
para.19 *NZ Parliamentary Debates*, 236 (1933), p.156
para.21 K. Reiger, *The Disenchantment of the Home*, p.59; E. Plumridge, 'Labour in Christchurch', p.241; E. Plumridge, p.242
para.22 E. Plumridge, p.242

Unpublished Sources

E. W. Plumridge, 'Labour in Christchurch: Community and Consciousness, 1914–1919', MA thesis, Canterbury, 1979

Published Sources

Cocker, J. and Malton Murray, J. *Temperance and Prohibition in New Zealand*, Wellington, 1930
Gardner, W. J. *Colonial Cap and Gown*, Christchurch, 1979
Gustafson, B. *Labour's Path to Political Independence*, Auckland, 1980
McLintock, A. H. (ed.) *An Encyclopedia of New Zealand*, vol.2, Wellington, 1966
Nairn, Bede, and Searle, Geoffrey. (eds) *Australian Dictionary of Biography*, vol.7, Melbourne, 1979
NZ Herstory 1977, Dunedin, 1976
NZ Herstory 1978, Dunedin, 1977
NZ Herstory 1984, Auckland, 1983
Regional Women's Decade Committee, *Canterbury Women Since 1893*, Christchurch, 1979
Reiger, Kerreen M. *The Disenchantment of the Home*, Melbourne, 1985
The Press, 6 March 1962
The White Ribbon, Dec. 1953

JESSIE HETHERINGTON

1882–1971

Jessie Isabel Hetherington influenced the teaching of the humanities in New Zealand secondary schools in her day. Born at Thames in 1882, she was the daughter of Samuel and Rebecca Hetherington, both from Irish protestant families connected with the linen trade. Her father owned an importing business in

Thames, where the family were supporters of the Methodist Church and of the growing educational interests in the town. Jessie attended Mrs Hume's private school, and, at ten, went to Thames High School. She said of her childhood that school, church, and reading took up most of her time, and, though music-making was encouraged in the family, the pursuit of pleasure for its own sake was not. After her mother died in 1896, she was sent to Prince Albert College, a Methodist boarding-school in Auckland. She matriculated in 1897 and stayed on as a boarder for another two years while attending lectures at Auckland University College. She studied history, economics, Latin, and French and joined in the activities of the Korero Club where women could debate among themselves. After completing her BA degree, she studied law till 1903 when her father took his three daughters with him on one of his business trips to London.

Jessie was inspired to follow in the footsteps of other New Zealanders who had studied at Cambridge. In October 1904, with her father's blessing, she entered Girton College to read law. The only woman attending law lectures, she had to be chaperoned and was excluded from discussion tutorials. She gained a second-class pass in the Law Tripos and went on to read history.

For three years she taught at Blackburn Grammar School in Lancashire. At a vacation language course in Normandy in 1908, she was introduced to the use of phonetics in French teaching, a practice she was later to encourage in New Zealand schools.

Returning home, she was unable immediately to find work. Towards the end of 1908 she became headmistress at Burwood Ladies' College, a Methodist school in Sydney. The post was fraught with the kind of difficulties not uncommon in a girls' private school, and Jessie had a heavy teaching load, but she worked for three years at improving relationships amongst the staff and introducing new teaching methods.

With the aim of qualifying to train teachers, she went back to England to take a Diploma in Secondary Education at St Mary's College, Lancaster Gate. This was followed in 1913 by a one-year appointment as assistant lecturer at the Cambridge Secondary Training College for Women. She took a special interest in direct-method language teaching and observed with approval the introduction in some schools of the 'interest or play motive', though she warned against bad copies of the Play Way.

Jessie returned to New Zealand after the outbreak of war, sailing under black-out. She had wanted to stay in London but, she said, 'the plans and funds were my father's'. She was now thirty-two, and was welcomed by the principal of Wellington Training College, who said she had 'anticipated a felt need' in teacher education. She was appointed as tutor and librarian: the only other woman on the staff had been a part-time lecturer in infant method.

Always anxious to keep up to date, Jessie took a term's leave from training college to study in the United States, at Columbia University, and in New York. She observed developments in women's colleges, and was somewhat alarmed by 'the development of Free Discipline in full force' in several New York schools.

As the proportion of women students at the training college increased, Jessie advocated that there should be a senior woman's position on the staff. When the vice-principalship became vacant in 1923 she applied, but, learning that a decision had already been made on the basis of sex, she resigned in protest. The Federation of University Women and the Wellington Women Teachers Association came to her defence, and the matter was aired in the press, but the decision had been made. Jessie spent two and a half years 'in the wilderness'.

She spent this time in research for two volumes on *New Zealand's Political Connection with Great Britain*, which appeared in 1925 and 1926. They were not a success, but no doubt helped to secure her next appointment, in 1926, as the first woman inspector of secondary schools in New Zealand.

Her field work as an inspector involved yearly visits to all the girls' schools and half the mixed schools in the country, as well as to district high and independent schools. A marked difference in the tone of these inspections was observed now that a woman had joined the team of inspectors: from being brusque and authoritarian, they became more appreciative and co-operative. For some years, inspectors set and marked state examinations. For a month each year, Jessie would work at marking from 4 am to noon.

In 1937 Jessie took a year's leave to travel to Australia, India, and Europe, observing educational developments and, to her delight, attending the coronation of George VI. In her report to the Department of Education, she said that she saw examinations 'coming under suspicion and arrest'. She advocated smaller classes, more choice of subjects, a reduction in the number of inspectors, freedom for schools to develop their own curricula, and the establishment of a good departmental library and of permanent exhibitions of teaching materials in main centres.

Jessie Hetherington retired in 1941 and went to live in Auckland. Adult education became her main interest. She lectured for two years at the Adult Education Centre and represented the Auckland branch of the Federation of University Women on provincial and national adult education councils. She served on the Auckland Grammar Schools' board of governors, taking a special interest in Auckland Girls' Grammar School. She died in Auckland in 1971.

Jessie Hetherington had gained respect and authority in an area of educational administration where women had not previously taken part.

Ruth Fry

Quotations
para.6 J. Hetherington, 'Numbering my days', pp.59, 60
para.7 J. Hetherington, p.59
para.8 J. Hetherington, pp.63–4
para.11 Report to Director of Education, 4 Feb. 1938, MS Papers 644:5, p.32, ATL

Unpublished Sources
J. I. Hetherington. 'Numbering my days', typescript autobiography, MS Papers 644:2, ATL

Published Sources
AJHR, 1924, vol.3, E-2, Appendix D, p.iv
Dominion, 16 June 1923, p.6
Macaskill, P. (ed.) *Ako Pai*, Wellington, 1980

MABEL HILL

1872-1956

Mabel, the last of the seven children of Charles and Eliza Hill, was born soon after the family arrived in New Zealand in 1872. The Hills had been hatters in Bristol for generations. Charles Hill soon established a men's hatting business, first in Auckland, and later in Wellington.

Mabel shared the family's musical and acting talents. (One brother, Alfred Hill, was a composer, and another, Edwin, a tenor; Mabel herself performed with Rosina Buckman in *A Moorish Maid*, one of Alfred Hill's operas.) But she alone showed a propensity for painting and drawing. By eleven she had sailed through the elementary education provided by the Thorndon school, and she marked time for three years in standard seven until 1886 when she was old enough to study art at the Wellington School of Design (renamed the Technical College in 1891).

The Scottish painter James Nairn was appointed instructor at the college in 1891. He exercised great influence on Mabel as both a teacher and a colleague – for in the same year she herself became an assistant instructor. The Technical College was affiliated with the South Kensington Art Department in South London and, in 1894, she gained her South Kensington Diploma. During the 1890s she became a leading member of the Wellington Art Club, the anti-academic group devoted to exhibiting sketches as finished works of art. Their subjects were drawn mainly from rural landscapes around Wellington.

Nairn also encouraged her to go to Europe, to absorb modern art at first hand, and particularly the paintings of the Impressionists that had so influenced him. She began to save from her tiny salary, and from the sale of her paintings. By the mid-1890s she had nearly enough to take the plunge. On holiday in Dunedin, however, she met a good-looking Scotsman, and in 1898 Mabel Hill, artist, became Mrs John McIndoe, wife, and, in time, mother. The fine house her husband built for her included a studio, and she continued to paint, exhibited frequently at the New Zealand Academy of Fine Arts and the Otago Art Society as well as at major national exhibitions. She became, during this time, one of the foremost women painters in New Zealand.

These were happy years, but they lasted only until 1916 when John McIndoe died after a long illness. While war raged in Europe, she was left with little money, a failing printing business, and four children. Painting was put to one side as Mabel set about growing as much food as she could, cooking, cleaning, patching, darning, and attending to the education of her three sons and one daughter. (She continued to own the printing business until 1945, but took no part in its management. There were some years of business difficulties until her son John Leslie assumed management in 1924.)

As the boys left home, Mabel painted again, learned to etch, and exhibited regularly. In 1924 her still-life *Maori Curios* was shown in the New Zealand pavilion of the British Empire Exhibition at Wembley. It now hangs in the Dunedin Room of the Edinburgh City Chambers. To pay her daughter's school

Mabel Hill, self-portrait, 1896.
National Art Gallery

fees at Archerfield School, she became art mistress there. She also opened the Barn Studio with the artist A. H. O'Keeffe in Carroll Street where many young painters benefited from her gifts as a teacher. She was a passionate gardener as well, winning several awards for her small garden.

Meanwhile her sons had prospered. A visit in 1926 to Rochester, Minnesota, to her surgeon son, changed her life. She came home with new horizons, new feet, new teeth, cropped hair, short dresses, and minus a lot of weight. With her daughter (just out of school) she set off for a ten-month painting sojourn in Tahiti. Then, at last, came Europe, with painting in Brittany and on Capri, and visits to all the art galleries of London, Paris, Moscow, and Leningrad.

Some years before the Second World War she returned alone to Dunedin and continued painting and gardening. In 1945 she made her final trip to Britain, settling in Sussex near her beloved Archie (who had by now established his reputation as a plastic surgeon, through his work with pilots severely burned during the war). Painting almost to the end, in spite of advanced cataracts, Mabel McIndoe died at East Grinstead in 1956.   *Elizabeth Mason*

Sources
The author, who is Mabel Hill's daughter, drew on memories of her mother which have been published as: Mason, Elizabeth. 'Mabel Hill 1872–1956: A Memoir by Elizabeth Mason, annotated by Jane Vial', *Bulletin of NZ Art History*, vol.2, 1990

HINEAMARU

?1550–?1600

> *He Whakatauki: Ko Hineamaru te tupuna*
> *Ko Tokerau te maunga*
> *Ko Taumarere te awa*
> *Ko Ngati Hine te iwi*

Hineamaru te tupuna was a leader of great mana, who in her youth took part in a great journey from the Hokianga to the Bay of Islands. It was she who discovered the Waiomio Valley, which became the cradle of Ngati Hine.

Hineamaru was the first-born of Hauhaua and Torongare. Torongare was of Ngatikahu descent. He fell out of favour with his wife's people, Ngaitamatea, and was forced to leave their village at Waimamaku. So began a journey in search of land, which was to take many years.

With his wife and children and a group of faithful followers, Torongare departed from Hokianga. His party travelled slowly, spying out the land and testing it for fertility, but always moving on. There were other people on the land before them, so they were forced to continue their journey to avoid disputes. They were confronted by a mountain range to the east, which was named Whakatere (to set adrift or to float), after the 'drifting away' of Torongare and his family from Hokianga.

By the time the party had reached Papatahora, near the Motatau Ranges, Torongare was ailing, and unable to walk. There is no mention of Hauhaua ever reaching this final camp at Papatahora; it is thought that she may have succumbed to the rigours of the journey and perhaps died at Kaikou.

Hauhaua, daughter of Uenuku, had ensured that her children survived and reached the safe haven of Kaikou. The journey from Hokianga was not one of chance, for Hauhaua had set her heart on returning with her children to Taumarere, in the Bay of Islands, her place of birth and early childhood. Hineamaru was committed to carrying out her dying mother's intention.

On the death of her mother, the mana of leadership, power, and wisdom became Hineamaru's as of right, for she was the eldest child, and was great-granddaughter to Rahiri. From this time, the large tracts of land she would trek through to reach Taumarere would automatically become hers.

From their campsite at Papatahora, about fifteen miles south-west of Waiomio, Hineamaru led expeditions through the Waiomio Valley and along the south banks of the Taumarere River to the pipi banks and fishing grounds of the southern Bay of Islands.

At Paparata, Hineamaru set fire to some dead rata trees. She took some earth from the burnt-out site back to Papatahora to show her father. On her next visit to the coast, she brought some kumara seeds with her and planted a garden on the ground cleared earlier by the fire. On her autumn visit to the coast, she dug up the kumara and filled ten paaro (large food baskets) with a good variety of large, middle-sized and small kumara, and took them home to show her father. On seeing the quality and quantity of the kumara, Torongare declared, 'E ko! nana to taua whenua' (my daughter, behold our land). So they came to Waiomio, of the meandering, swirling waters, and settled in what was to become the land of the Ngati Hine tribe.

The lands in the southern Bay of Islands were occupied by Ngatitu, relatives of Hineamaru who were willing to share their lot with the newcomers. This happy relationship remains today, based on tolerance among equals, not domination by conquerors.

Torongare decided to settle in the valley next to Waiomio, which he named Mohinui after the large mohi (whitebait) which his children caught in the river. Hineamaru discovered an ana (cave) at Otarawa and made this her home. It became likened to a sacred chest or box, and was thus named Te Pouaka a Hineamaru.

Hineamaru married Koperu of Ngatitu, whom she met at his home in Te Wharau on the left shore of the Taumarere Inlet. A huge hangi was lit at Tapahina to cook seventy kits of pipi in her honour.

After her death, the cave became her urupa (burial place). Records handed down stated that 'I whakahokia atu ona koiwi ki te pouaka a Hineamaru' (the remains were returned to the cave of Hineamaru). Down the succeeding generations, the bodies of Ngati Hine leaders and warriors of great mana were returned to Otarawa, Te Pouaka a Hineamaru, to lie with their tupuna.

Ngati Hine's occupation of their land has never been seriously challenged during the 400 years since Hineamaru's time. Apart from the physical advantages of the terrain, there have been able warriors in every generation ready to defend it. These warrior leaders, commencing with Hingatuauru, great-grandson of Hineamaru, and ending with Kawiti, five generations after him, seemed to possess extraordinary qualities of leadership, daring, and wisdom. These, without a doubt, were inherited from Hineamaru, who, in displaying great endurance, determination, and foresight, discovered a fertile and permanent home on which to settle her ailing father, her homeless brothers and young sisters, and her many descendants.

Hineamaru occupies a place of honour, in the form of a carved pou (pillar), in many of the carved meeting-houses throughout the North today.

Kene Martin

Unpublished Source
Information came from family members.

Published Source
Kawiti, W. B. *Waiomio Limestone Caves*, Kaikohe, 1968

MARY HOBHOUSE

1819–1864

Mary Hobhouse was born on 31 March 1819, the second of the three daughters of General the Hon. John Brodrick, sixth son of Lord Midleton, an Irish peer, and his wife Anne (born Graham), of an aristocratic Scottish family. Mary did not come to New Zealand until she was almost forty and lived here for only a brief five years before her death in childbirth in 1864. However, her stature as a letter-writer and her position as wife of the first Bishop of Nelson give her a place in the history of this country.

Mary Brodrick, painted some years before her marriage to Edmund Hobhouse, first Bishop of Nelson. *J. Payne, Dorset*

Her early letters reveal glimpses of a remarkably well-educated woman, who had studied extensively in Europe, and travelled with an unusual degree of freedom, riding and climbing in the Pyrenees, visiting French friends and sketching. In a letter early in 1852 she sets out her ideas for opening a school for middle-class girls. 'I have always had the subject of education in one shape or other very much at heart, and had a great wish to put my hand to it.' Later she wrote:

Of course I shd. give the preference to clergymen's children or orphans. They would receive a thorough education as gentlewomen, and therefore if their circumstances required it, would be qualified for governesses. I should be thankful to do anything towards improving that unhappy race and raising the footing of even a few of them. I do not intend to aim at every acquirement and accomplishment under the sun, and would not promise to cultivate any talent in a girl in which she was positively wanting, but at any rate I would engage

296

that they should be taught nothing badly, and that, one knows from one's own experience, is an incalculable advantage. I shd. wish to make history a principal object – also language – not languages – I would give a much more thorough knowledge of English and English authors than is common (or than I possess myself), French of course must be taught, and I would substitute the tongue of Ancient Italy for that of modern Italy – considering it to be in every way a more profitable study. If a person has learnt one or two languages thoroughly they can easily teach themselves afterwards any others they may want.

By 1856 she was in charge of her own school at Oxford, where she presumably had the opportunity to carry out her educational principles. To set up such an establishment was no small undertaking, for any woman at that time. She sought sponsorship first from 'a clergyman on whom I could thoroughly depend to stand godfather to my project'. It seems that she eventually funded the school from modest fees and her own resources.

In the following year Edmund Hobhouse, the vicar of St Peter in the East (Oxford), was chosen as the first Bishop of Nelson in New Zealand. Edmund persuaded Mary to accompany him as his wife; she was to help him in the young colonial community, and to try 'to make a pattern Christian household, and in upholding in the Face of Society whatsoever things are pure, lovely etc.'. He told her she would 'have no unprofitable Function'. Her feelings are expressed to a friend:

I have promised to be his wife, and what is not quite so pleasant to think of, my dearest Maud, to go with him to N. Zealand. Well it can't be helped, and it's no good thinking of it or lamenting it.

They were married on New Year's Day 1858. Most of that year was spent planning and packing and travelling through the British Isles saying goodbye to friends and relatives. Just before they left, Mary's first pregnancy ended in a stillborn child and a severe illness. But she struggled to accompany her husband on the voyage and finally reached Nelson in March 1859.

From the beginning the bishop considered that hospitality was part of his vocation and there were often nine or ten assembled for meals in the house by the Maitai River, which she ruefully describes as 'this episcopal hotel and boarding house'. Guests included the bishop's resident chaplain, the Maori-speaking itinerant deacon, various young men who were recommended from friends in England as possible schoolmasters, and local settlers or their offspring who had failed to cope with the challenges of colonial life. In another letter Mary writes:

I must say when I sit down to pour out tea for them I feel very much as if I kept a school or an Inn . . . There is one consideration however that always stops my inclination to grumble at the destruction of all domestic privacy in this mode of life, and that is that it is broken up, not by people to whom one is obliged to be civil and who don't benefit much by the civility, but by those to whom a temporary home is a great comfort, or else by some unfortunate overworked woman to whom a few days' holiday is a treat, and if one has a house, which compared to the general run of houses here is luxurious, one is glad to extend its enjoyment to as many people as possible.

The bishop had plans for his wife to conduct a school for girls in their own house, and the letters frequently discuss the possibilities of a boarding-school for Maori children. However, by Easter 1860 Mary was pregnant again. Before the birth of her son in August 1860, Nelson was invaded by a large party of refugees from Taranaki. The outbreak of war in the North Island led the superintendent of Nelson to offer shelter and financial support to the women and children evacuated from New Plymouth. Like other Nelson households the bishop's home was stretched to its limits by the arrival of a family of four daughters and their governess, and two small boys and their nurse. To Mary's great joy her younger sister, Maria, arrived in time for her confinement. In the week before her baby's birth Mary was almost overwhelmed by 'Synodical hospitalities' forced upon her by the annual Diocesan Synod, and described herself as feeling 'very thronged' by feeding and entertaining so many synodsmen in a house which, though large by colonial standards, was cramped by hers.

There was always a domestic staff, consisting of an Irish cook who came out with the family, and two local girls, one of whom acted as butler.

The butler is a little damsel of fifteen or sixteen who is always good-humoured and generally (by dint of my lectures) tidy, so we are envied by our neighbours for so valuable an acquisition.

One of the most remarkable features of the Hobhouse regime was their determination not to compromise in any way the standards to which they had been accustomed, and which for them were a mark of 'civilisation'. Appalled by casual colonial ways, the bishop had written to his wife a few weeks after arrival that they would both need some time to get used to the change: 'and with Regard to some Things, e.g. Dirt and Untidiness, and *Unpunctuality*, you will feel it a Duty to keep up a perpetual Protest.'

Mary's happiest times were spent in the country, at Motueka and Spring Grove. She describes a gathering of neighbours to welcome her on a visit to Motueka:

the poor womenkind seldom leave their houses – but on this occasion there was a great gathering of people, who did not see each other once a year. They began arriving soon after 11 o'clock some on their feet, some on cart horses, some in carts drawn by oxen . . .

She describes the 'hospitable simplicity' which provided a table covered with roast fowls, 'for which the surrounding country had been scoured for the previous two days', and a following course of blancmange and jellies:

the production of which under present circumstances seemed fresh proof of the indomitable energy of the Saxon race of which one hears so much in new Countries. And all and everyone so thoroughly enjoyed their holiday and meeting their friends that a more triumphant success could not have been secured by the most splendid Dejeuner.

She was touched, too, to discover the warmth of colonial generosity.

No sooner was it known that we were bivouacing here, than kind and considerate people began pouring in supplies. One lady has bestowed on us a magnificent supply of home made bread and butter . . . Yesterday morning just as we were going to breakfast two children, a girl of eleven and a boy of nine arrived, having ferried themselves across the river in a ricketty canoe, to bring us a supply of all sorts of comestibles, including rashers of bacon, ready cut . . . – so that we are nearly as well off as the Officers before Sebastopol with their Fortnum and Mason supplies.

To a woman who had enjoyed climbing in the Pyrenees, the beauty of the mountains surrounding Nelson was a source of consolation, though she was disappointed that she was unable to climb them:

but almost all are covered with impenetrable forests . . . I wish I could send you a drawing of a grand panorama of the mountains behind Nelson with their snowy tops . . . and of the higher ranges that make the background of Motueka.

In 1862 her second son was born and for nearly a year there are glimpses of her delight in the development of her children and evidence of a very enlightened attitude to small children. In 1863 the episcopal headquarters was moved to the country parsonage at Spring Grove where, it was hoped, the tranquil atmosphere would help to restore the bishop's deteriorating health, which was frequently affected by overwork and migraine headaches. The final months of Mary's life were devoted to supporting and comforting her husband until her fourth pregnancy ended in another still birth on 10 October 1864 and her own death on 12 October. J. C. Richmond's editorial in the *Nelson Examiner* reflected the grief felt by the Nelson community, but perhaps this passage from an earlier letter best reveals the feelings of Mary Hobhouse herself, torn between two hemispheres:

I become daily more conscious that it is not the disagreeablenesses nor discomforts of colonial life that affect one, but the long long distance from all those one cares for, and this consciousness which of course never leaves one throws a shadow over everything. I am often aware whilst I am expressing my admiration of the beauties round one here and the charms of the climate, of something drawing at my heart and preventing my admiration from becoming delight. But I hope I shall never fall into the habit which I see many people have of decrying everything here, and denying the beauty of the mountains and the gloriousness of the skies, because they are not happy or comfortable here.

Shirley Tunnicliff

Quotations
para.2 Mary Brodrick to Revd W. Pennefather, 1 Jan. 1852; Mary Brodrick to Anne Pennefather [1852], both letters in family papers, Dorset
para.3 Mary Brodrick to Revd W. Pennefather, 1 Jan. 1852, family papers, Dorset
para.4 Edmund Hobhouse to Mary Brodrick, 6 April 1859, E. Hobhouse MS Papers 414, ATL; Mary Brodrick to Maude Williams, 14 Sept. 1857, family papers, Dorset

para.5 M. Hobhouse to F. Hobhouse, Nov. 1859, ATL

para.6 M. Hobhouse to Eliza Hobhouse, 4 Aug. 1860; M. Hobhouse to Eliza Hobhouse, 22 Aug. 1859, both letters ATL

para.7 M. Hobhouse to cousin Louisa, 21 May–2 June 1860; Edmund Hobhouse to M. Hobhouse, 31 March 1859, both letters ATL

para.8 M. Hobhouse to Eliza Hobhouse, 22 Sept. 1859, ATL

para.9 M. Hobhouse to Eliza Hobhouse, 23 Sept. 1859, ATL

para.10 M. Hobhouse to Eliza Hobhouse, 23 Sept. 1859, ATL

para.11 M. Hobhouse to cousin Louisa, 21 May–2 June 1860, ATL

Unpublished Sources

Edmund Hobhouse MS Papers 414, ATL

Family papers in the possession of Mrs Joan Payne, Dorset

Published Sources

Nelson Examiner, 13 Oct. 1864 (obituary by J. C. Richmond)

ELIZABETH HOCKEN

1848–1933

Elizabeth Mary Buckland (known as Bessie) was born in Auckland in 1848, the daughter of William Thorne Buckland and his wife Susan (born Channing). The Bucklands were a well-established Auckland merchant family, and Bessie was a wealthy woman in her own right, holding land in the Auckland area valued in 1882 at over £2,500.

In 1883 she married Thomas Morland Hocken, a general practitioner and coroner for the district of Dunedin. He had also a strong interest in the beginnings of the European settlement of New Zealand which led him to start collecting relevant documentary material. They settled in 'Atahapara', a house build by H. F. Hardy in Moray Place, Dunedin, and their only child, Gladys, was born in 1884.

Over the next thirty years Dr Hocken built up his collection of New Zealand and Pacific related manuscripts, monographs, photographs, maps, art works on paper, and artefacts, which he bequeathed to the public of New Zealand to be administered by the University of Otago. The collection, except for the artefacts which are held by the Otago Museum, forms the basis of the Hocken Library in Dunedin.

Bessie Hocken had many natural talents that were of great assistance in her husband's collecting, although he rarely acknowledged his debt. The original Hocken collection gives evidence that her expertise in oils, water-colour and photography enabled her to record material of interest to Dr Hocken, and to illustrate his historical work. She gained an award for flower painting at the New Zealand and South Seas Exhibition in Dunedin in 1889–90, and exhibited with the Otago Art Society from 1887 to 1914.

A well-travelled woman, she had some knowledge of languages and she assisted her husband in his foreign correspondence. Bessie Hocken's social skills, too, made her house a centre for the intellectual and social élite of Dunedin – and for travellers, for Dr Hocken's connections were international as well as local.

Although Bessie's contribution to his work received little acknowledgement, her husband regarded her business acumen highly enough to appoint her as one of the executors of his will. After his death in 1910, and Gladys's marriage a year later, Bessie moved first to England, and then to South Africa.

She continued a keen interest in the two collections, and made generous gifts to support them – despite the fact that she felt the bequest to her daughter was meagre in comparison to bequests made to the University of Otago, various churches, and the Dunedin Public Art Gallery. Dr Hocken, however, believed that 'about £1,000 a year [was] quite enough for a single woman . . . he was of the school of thought that women should not be burdened with too much money'.

Bessie died at Rondebosch, Capetown, on 19 April 1933.

Annette Facer

Elizabeth Mary (Bessie) Hocken. *Hocken Library*

Quotation
para.7 Elizabeth Mary Hocken to her legal advisers, Dunedin, 1922, Hocken
Unpublished Sources
E. M. Hocken, Sketchbook of Maori Material, Picture Collection, Hocken
Last Will and Testament of Thomas Morland Hocken, MS 648, Hocken
Published Sources
Hocken A. G. (no relation). *Dr T. M. Hocken 1836–1910, A Gentleman of his Time* (Hocken Lecture 1986), Dunedin, 1989
Otago Daily Times, 21 April 1933 (obituary)
Otago Witness, 28 July 1883
Platts, Una. *Nineteenth Century New Zealand Artists*, Christchurch, 1979

FRANCES HODGKINS

1869–1947

Expatriate painter Frances Hodgkins earned a significant reputation in France and more particularly in England during the early part of this century. Her courage and dedication have been an example to many aspiring artists.

Frances Hodgkins was born in Dunedin, one of six children whose father, William Mathew Hodgkins, was a leading light in art circles and highly regarded as a water-colourist in the English landscape tradition. Whereas his eldest daughter (Isabel Field) displayed a precocious artistic talent, Frances Hodgkins was slower to find her way. Encouraged by Girolamo Nerli, by whom she was first taught in 1893, she discovered her penchant lay in informal figure subjects such as that of the goose-girl, and portraiture. From 1895 she began to receive prizes from the Otago Art Society and the New Zealand Academy of Fine Arts, and increasingly committed herself to a career in painting and teaching. By the time Hodgkins left on her first trip to Europe in 1901 she had achieved considerable local success. Initially tentative and awkward, her water-colours became freer and more assured in their impressionistic treatment.

Europe brought fresh developments in her work, and she embarked on a life that would become increasingly peripatetic. Early on she attended Norman Garstin's sketching group in France and afterwards spent a profitable few months in Morocco. The Doré Gallery, London, featured her work in a solo exhibition, and in May 1903 she was hung 'on the line' at the Royal Academy. Back in New Zealand from late 1903 to 1906, the artist produced little work and faced the trauma of a broken engagement. Hodgkins' second sojourn abroad lasted nearly seven years, during which time she was based primarily in Paris. Her water-colours were accepted by the Paris Salon and the Société Internationale d'Aquarellistes. In January 1910 she became the Académie Colarossi's first woman instructor and the following year established her own classes. The Canadian artist, Emily Carr, and Australians Bessie Gibson and Vida Lahey were among the students who benefited from the summer excursions she took to Brittany and elsewhere during this period.

By 1912 Frances Hodgkins was stretching her colours to their full potential, laying them on in washes with big decisive sweeps. Her recent water-colours were triumphantly received when she took a number to Australia en route to New Zealand. A turning point had nevertheless been reached and Hodgkins decided, in spite of family allegiances, to pursue her career single-mindedly in the Northern Hemisphere. She left New Zealand permanently in October 1913.

Facing the repercussions of the First World War, the artist sought refuge in England, basing herself at St Ives until 1919. Although continuing to paint in water-colour, she began using oils during her enforced stay in Cornwall. Among the first of these larger works was *The Belgian Refugees* (c.1916), which heralded the years of courageous experimentation (especially between 1920 and 1927) when Hodgkins finally abandoned her former impressionistic style and searched instead for more innovative ways of organising her motifs. She most clearly referred to the example of Henri Matisse; his lyrical colour and calligraphic brushwork, for instance, are the hallmarks of her *Double Portrait* of 1922.

The period 1928 to 1939 firmly established the artist, now in her sixties, with a younger generation of progressive painters in England. She was elected a member of the Seven and Five Society in 1929, and was briefly associated with Paul Nash's group, Unit One. Although she was still to face economic hardship, her work began to sell through well known dealers in London: Lucy Wertheim, the St George's Gallery, Alex Reid, and Lefevre. Frances Hodgkins' name became linked with such painters and sculptors as Ben Nicolson, Barbara Hepworth, David Jones, Ivon Hitchens, John Piper, and Henry Moore. Her subjects, including *Two Plates* (1931) which combined landscape and still life, became a feature of the London art scene and later caused a critic for *The Times* to comment:

she borrowed, in fact, many tricks of modern painting, but what is extra-ordinary is that what had already become a formula with many other artists really served to free her sensibility, allowing her to become a subtle colourist and bringing out her genuine powers of imagination.

Always an artist to prize her independence, and one for whom travel was essential to her health and work, Hodgkins became more nomadic as the century progressed. She painted in France, the Balearic Islands, and Spain, but the English landscape often proved her most fruitful source of visual material, as for example in the Tate Gallery's version of *Wings over Water*, based on Cornwall. At the end of 1934 she set up her studio at Corfe Castle, a small village in Dorset, and began to work with gouache, a medium which merges the fluid qualities of water-colour with the density of oils. Forms were often left open in the land-scapes and unconventional still lifes she produced, allowing a rhythmic flow between objects and the spaces between them. *The Elevator* was one of the gou-aches shown at Lefevre's in April 1940, an exhibition which caused Eric Newton of the *Sunday Times* to acclaim her as 'A painter of genius'.

During her last years, Frances Hodgkins painted at Corfe, concentrating on gouaches with their distinctive calligraphic treatment of form. Her final oils, such as *Self Portrait: Still Life* (1941), were composed from personal possessions. Some measure of official recognition came at this point: in 1940 she was invited to represent Britain at the Venice Bienniale and shortly afterwards was awarded a Civil List pension. The peak of her career, however, was marked by the

Frances Hodgkins in England, 1920. *Alexander Turnbull Library*

Frances Hodgkins retrospective exhibition held at the Lefevre Galleries in November 1946, six months before her death. The London press then described her as one of the most remarkable woman painters of all time.   *Anne Kirker*

Unpublished Source
Frances Hodgkins, Correspondence 1875–1946, MS Papers 85, ATL

Published Sources
Evans, M. *Frances Hodgkins* (The Penguin Modern Painters), London, 1948
Frances Hodgkins commemorative issue of *Ascent*, 1969
Howell, A. R. *Frances Hodgkins: Four Vital Years*, London, 1951
Kirker, A. *New Zealand Women Artists*, Auckland, 1986
McCormick, E. H. *Portrait of Frances Hodgkins*, Auckland and Oxford, 1981
McCormick, E. H. *The Expatriate*, Wellington, 1954
McCormick, E. H. *Works of Frances Hodgkins in New Zealand*, Auckland, 1954

ALICE HOLFORD

1867–1966

As a young woman, Alice Hannah Holford had one ambition: to devote her life to nursing. In achieving this, she contributed in great measure to 'inventing the future', particularly in regard to the health of women and children, and the development of nursing as a profession.

Growing up in New Plymouth, she was one of six children of Port Taranaki's first harbour-master, Captain J. A. Holford and his wife. In 1886, at the age of nineteen, she applied to be a probation nurse at New Plymouth Hospital. She had to wait until 1897 before she was accepted, becoming the fourth nurse to be trained at the hospital.

Meantime, she nursed – looking after sick people in the community around her, while living at home. 'My aunt had thirteen children, and when any of them were sick she always said: "Send for Alice."' She went out too with the local doctors on their rounds, travelling over rough mud roads in horse-drawn buggies.

When she had completed her initial hospital training, she applied for registration under the Nurses' Registration Act of 1901 – the first nurse to do so. Then in 1902 she borrowed £200 in order to train as a midwife at Crown Street Women's Hospital in Sydney. On her return she faced severe censure from many of her nursing colleagues: the idea of an unmarried woman delivering babies was generally unacceptable at this time. Nor was midwifery itself held in high regard by the profession.

However, Grace Neill, who was responsible for the legislation concerning the training and registration of both nurses and midwives (1901 and 1904), was herself a midwife. She frequently consulted Alice Holford at this time, and they were both closely involved in establishing maternity hospitals called St Helen's. The first St Helen's hospital was opened in Wellington in 1905, and later in the same year Alice was appointed matron of the second St Helen's hospital in Dunedin. She remained in this position until her retirement in 1927 at the age

St Helen's Hospital staff, Auckland, c.1908. Alice Holford was closely associated with the establishment of St Helen's Hospitals. *Auckland Institute and Museum*

of sixty, and continued to reside in Dunedin, sharing her home with a much-loved niece, until 1956.

Her life is summed up in her own words: 'I have always been civic minded, but I wanted specially to help women and children.' But her work for people extended beyond nurses, and indeed beyond women. After the Second World War, when she was well over seventy, she answered an emergency call to take charge of Queen Mary Hospital at Hanmer Springs, which treated soldiers returning from the war.

Other activities included establishing the first Citizens' Day Nursery in Dunedin, and helping to fund a building 'where pregnant women or mothers with little ones could rest when in town and attend to their babies'. She understood the political process and used it with skill, both in relation to the nursing profession and in the wider community.

Alice Holford is perhaps most remembered, however, for her work for nurses. It was in 1907 that she convened the first meeting of the Trained Nurses' Club, which later became the Otago branch of the New Zealand Trained Nurses' Association. The national association was founded in 1908, and named subsequently the New Zealand Nurses' Association. Alice said over fifty years later: 'I little thought that it was going to grow into a national organisation.' She remained active in the association throughout her working life.

She was concerned from the beginning about training and education for nurses. She addressed this vigorously at the 1912 annual conference, arguing for a lower age of entry for nursing training, and more careful preparation at school level. In 1922, clearly exasperated by the lack of progress in nursing education, she delivered an address entitled 'Nursing as a Profession for University Women'. By mid-1923, nursing leaders were discussing with the University of Otago a

Diploma of Nursing to be associated with a proposed domestic science course. Alice Holford was an active protagonist – but it was to be nearly fifty years before her dream of university education for nurses was realised.

Many people continued to 'send for Alice', for both professional and personal reasons, for much of her forty odd years of 'retirement'. She died at the age of ninety-nine in 1966 at New Plymouth Hospital, where she had commenced her nursing training.   *Beatrice Salmon*

Quotations
para.3 *Weekly News* (Taranaki), 22 Nov. 1961
para.6 *Otago Daily Times*, 16 Nov. 1954
para.8 *Weekly News* (Taranaki), 22 Nov. 1961

Published Sources
Gibson Smith, Margaret. *NZ Nursing Journal (Kai Tiaki) Index, volumes 1–62, 1908–1969*, Wellington, 1980
Holford, A. 'The Development of the Nursing Profession' (includes text of her address, 'Nursing as a Profession for University Women'), *NZ Nursing Journal (Kai Tiaki)*, vol.15 no.5, Nov. 1922, p.210
Hughes, B. 'Nursing Education: The Collapse of the Diploma of Nursing at the University of Otago 1925–26', *NZJH*, vol.12 no.1 April 1978, pp.17–33
NZ Dept of Health. *Historical Development of Nursing in New Zealand, 1840–1946* (prepared by Mary Lambie), Wellington, 1951
NZ Nursing Journal (Kai Tiaki), vols.1–60, 1908–67
Otago Daily Times, 16 Nov. 1954; 12 Nov. 1957
Scanlan, A. B. *Hospital on the Hill: A Centennial History of the New Plymouth Hospital, 1867–1967*, New Plymouth, 1967
Weekly News (Taranaki), 22 Nov. 1971

MARO HOTERENE

1900–1937

Maro Motu was the eldest daughter of Mata and Motu of the Ngati Kuri tribe. Mamari is the canoe. She was born in Te Hapua, the most northerly village in the land, in the year 1900. She was one of a family of seventeen, nine of whom, five boys and four girls, survived to adulthood. Te Hapua, an isolated Maori community, had a population of approximately four hundred and had kauri gum digging as its main livelihood.

Maro attended the local primary school where she learnt English and how to read and write. At standard four level she left school. Like her peers she became adept at helping at home, setting yeast and baking bread, assisting in the care of her younger brothers and sisters, and doing the many chores on hand.

At the age of sixteen Maro became wife to Te Mutunga Hoterene, who had lost his wife and who was three times her age. Both her parents died during the 1918 influenza epidemic. Most of the members of her family were farmed out to relatives in the community and further abroad. Having married, Maro escaped this traumatic family upheaval.

The community would have considered Maro to have married well. She moved into a house of kauri with two bedrooms on either side of a corridor which went from the front door to the kitchen, the largest room in the house. Its length was the combined width of the corridor and the two bedrooms. The open fire-place, later replaced by a Shacklock stove, was set a few feet in from the back door and on the outside wall.

By the year 1920 Maro had had four children, two of whom died as young babies. Te Mutunga was a man of considerable means and therefore a good provider. The planting of his kumara and potato crops and his fishing and gathering of sea and other foods were for family and community consumption. He had annual musters of cattle he had out on 'the run' which he sold to visiting buyers. The kauri gum digging industry was at its height at this time. It paid good money. With occasional stints on road works, these activities were the sole source of income for the family of Maro and Te Mutunga. Maro was involved in all these activities except for mustering. She was indeed a breadwinner with Te Mutunga.

Kauri gum digging was an all-season occupation, slotted in between mustering, the planting and harvesting of crops, and fishing. Gum digging for Maro meant working areas of endless tracks of gum digging land. It was a life of hard slog. Often she stood knee-deep in water to retrieve chunks and pieces of gum in holes she had dug that were three to four feet in diameter and three to four feet deep. She would flush clean what she had collected, and carry it to a nearby clearing to dry over several days. Sieving and sorting into sacks followed in readiness for sale.

Kumara planting was as demanding of Maro. She assisted in setting beds of kumara tubers. She would also pick shoots when ready, create depressions at regular intervals along the tops of endless rows, and expertly place and heel a kumara shoot into each depression. Weeding and later harvesting followed. Kumara were dug manually, allowed to dry, and then sorted – seed tubers, bruised and cut ones for immediate consumption, good firm ones for storage, and the small tubers for the celebratory first kumara meal of the year.

Fishing with all its many and varied demands – boat rowing, netting, scaling, smoking, filleting and drying catches – were second nature to her.

Throughout the year Maro did much weaving, using flax, kiekie, kuta, hoihere, pingao, and toetoe. She wove fine mats of boiled flax and kiekie. How-ever, much of her weaving was with green flax. She provided many kits annually for harvesting kumara and potato crops and for the endless fishing expeditions that took place. Further, the floors of her home were well covered with mats she wove.

Despite her youth, Maro's involvement in the community manifested itself in the church, other functions at the community hall, and as midwife with other women. As an Awhina member (elder) of the Ratana Church, Maro led the hymns at the regular Sunday services and on other occasions. She attended Sunday afternoon sessions when new hymns were taught, thus adding to the church's choir's repertoire.

On occasions when issues of community concern arose – proposals of mar-riage, truancy, bad behaviour by the local youths, the invasion of Parengarenga Harbour by trawlers, land issues, and the banning (rahui) of resource areas – Maro and other women expressed their thinking freely.

She assisted in the delivery of many babies in the community. For her own confinements her husband was assisted by her midwife colleagues.

Maro died giving birth to her eighteenth child at the age of thirty-seven and was buried at Mailtu, the local wahi tapu or cemetery. Eight of her children, three boys and five girls, survived to reach adulthood.   *Te Kui*

Unpublished Source
Information came from members of Maro's community, and from the author's own memories of her
   mother, who died when Te Kui was seventeen.

MABEL HOWARD

1894–1972

Mabel was a woman of passion and strong political views. She cared most for women, the underprivileged, and for animals. She was a socialist and a feminist, yet she had little time for labels. People were her main concern.

Born in Adelaide in 1894, Mabel Bowden Howard came to New Zealand in 1903 with her widowed father and two sisters. In 1908, after leaving school, she attended Christchurch Technical College and took a commercial course. Her shorthand was to stand her in good stead in her parliamentary days. Several times she warned other members that she had a shorthand note of their remarks and they should watch what they said. She also joined the Christchurch Socialist

Mabel Howard outside her only ministerial home, Karori, 1960. As the first tenant, she had the house decorated very much to her own tastes — mostly yellow wallpaper and a guest room in black and mauve. *Evening Post*

Party, the forerunner of the Labour Party, in 1908 and thus began her lifelong involvement in politics.

Her father Ted Howard had been active in the trade union movement before he entered parliament as a Labour member. Mabel was devoted to her father and his work and principles. She joined him in the Canterbury General Labourers' Union office at the age of eighteen, and eventually held the position of assistant secretary and then secretary. She was appointed national secretary of the New Zealand Federated Labourers' Union in 1942 – the first woman to hold such a position in an all-male trade union organisation. At that time Mabel told the only other woman who worked with her at Trades Hall that she wanted to be treated like a male as she thought men had the best chances in life. Mabel's reputation for forthrightness and 'giving as good as she got' started there.

But she won these positions in her own right, not through following in her father's footsteps. She was passed over for his parliamentary seat when he died in 1939, but contested a by-election for the Christchurch East seat in 1943 and was elected as a Labour member. In 1946 she became the member for Sydenham, holding this seat until her retirement in 1969, during which time she became the first woman Cabinet minister in 1947, as minister of health and child welfare. When Labour returned to power in 1957, she was minister of social security and minister in charge of the welfare of women and children.

Throughout her life Mabel was what is called 'a character'. She is most famous for displaying outsize women's bloomers in parliament in 1944 to illustrate the poor quality of women's clothing and the fact that measurements should be given in inches so that people knew the real size. This 'outrageous' incident was typical of her colourful, down-to-earth personality. Before beginning an election campaign in 1961, Mabel said she intended to go round the country electioneering in a pair of slippers to show that it was impossible to get decent shoes. 'Those offered all have extremely pointed toes and stiletto heels, which ruined footpaths and carpets. It is time women woke up to this stupid fashion.' Earlier she had stated that 'I believe in the equality of the sexes. I truly believe that men are just as equal as women in the work they do. I believe that a man should have equal chances with a woman.'

She was very human, giving a lot of herself to people, but equally capable of being very difficult.

Her heart was of gold: but she could be vitriolic in speech, bitter in enmity, an unfair adversary in politics, ungrateful to friends. She was at times extremely generous, at others miserably stingy.

She knew what she believed in and was not afraid to advocate it. She once said, 'I went into the office and threw my weight about and it is not inconsiderable.' She believed in equal rights for women, particularly equal pay, and took up many issues, including social security, standardisation, the cost of living, and housing.

Her concern for animals motivated her successful fight to enact the first Prevention of Cruelty to Animals Bill in 1960. Mabel was famous for her cats. She never bought them but collected strays, having up to seven in her house at any one time. No expense was spared for the cats and she was loath to take holidays and trips away because she worried about their feeding. She was president of the Canterbury SPCA for nearly twenty years and visited strays in the local cattery.

In her last years Mabel caught pneumonia several times and, after retiring in 1969 from tiredness and ill health, ended up living alone with no interests, spurning friends. Mabel had always said that she wouldn't retire but would die in the harness. However, her memory faded and, after months of fighting with her family, they obtained a magistrate's order to commit her to Sunnyside. She died there in her sleep from hypostasis pneumonia.

Mabel Howard will be remembered as a woman who dared to be herself, who cared deeply for those with no political power or voice, and who had the courage to advocate their rights. From the risks and hardships of her life, many women in New Zealand have benefited. *Margaret Wilson*

Quotations
para.5 D. Gee, *Our Mabel*, pp.229–30
para.6 J. Wordsworth, *Leading Ladies*, p.5
para.7 D. Gee, p.276

Published Sources
Gee, David. *Our Mabel*, Wellington, 1977
NZ Herstory 1977, Dunedin, 1976
Regional Women's Decade Committee. *Canterbury Women Since 1893*, Christchurch, 1979
Wordsworth, Jane. *Leading Ladies*, Wellington, 1979

EDITH HOWES

1872–1954

Edith Annie Howes was a teacher and much-loved children's writer.

New Zealand landscapes and a 'didactic instinct' inspired her writing. 'Her book was in the running brook, her sermon in stones', wrote her friend Charles Allen. Hampered in the infant classroom by the lack of textbooks, and determined to interest children in the wonders and beauties of nature, Edith Howes explored sea and inland environments, indefatigably observing and recording the flora and insect life. After verifying her research, she wove it into simple but imaginative fairy stories, becoming known as 'New Zealand's fairy godmother'.

Her first book, *The Sun's Babies* (1910), was acclaimed by the Professor of Biology at the University of Otago, W. B. Benham, who testified to its scientific accuracy and charm. Its immediate success brought Howes life membership of the New Zealand Institute (now the Royal Society) in 1911; it also led to overseas editions and the motivation to produce *Fairy Rings* (1911), *Rainbow Children* (1912), *Maoriland Fairy Tales* (1913), *The Cradle Ship* (1916), *The Singing Fish* (1921), and *The Dream Girl's Garden* (1923), all published in London, New York, and Melbourne by Cassell or Ward Lock. *The Cradle Ship*, conveying the facts of life in a way considered a little excessive by some, was so well founded it was discussed at a medical conference in Paris and translated into several languages. *Silver Island* (1928, 1983), an Arthur Ransome type story set around Stewart Island, incorporated real-life adventures of the children of William

George Howes, Edith's favourite brother. An adaptation of this book and other titles were part of the *Whitcombe's Story Book* series. Also published by Whitcombe and Tombs in a series on New Zealand nature were *Stewart Island* (1913) and *Where Bell-Birds Chime* (1912).

The author's stories, Maori tales, and playlets for children appeared in *Red Funnel*, *New Zealand Artists' Annual*, *Art in New Zealand*, and the American *World Youth*. A series of 'Maoriland Fairy Tales' appearing in *The New Zealand School Journal* between 1907 and 1917 is thought to be Edith Howes' work. She also contributed to the *Otago Witness*, *Canterbury Times*, *Otago Daily Times*, and Dunedin *Evening Star*, the latter newspaper serialising weekly, from 14 August 1926, 'The Pebble Path', the haunting tale of a woman descendant of the Stuarts who is exiled on a sealers' island.

Edith Howes also wrote poetry, songs, and plays. *Rose Lane*, a three-act play about early Dunedin and the Central Otago gold-fields, won first place in the British Drama League's competition both in New Zealand and Britain. Active also in organisations such as the New Zealand League of Penwomen and the New Zealand Writers' and Artists' Society (of which she was a vice-president from 1932 to 1954), Edith Howes received the MBE in 1935 and the George VI Coronation Medal in 1937 for her literary work.

Born in Peckham, London, she was the third of eight children of Cecilia (born Brown) and William James Howes. Of her siblings, three died in infancy, leaving a sister and three brothers. Evening nature expeditions and a lifelong empathy with one brother, William George – a Fellow of the Entomological Society – were to be catalysts for Edith Howes' literary career.

She was educated at Kaiapoi and Christchurch schools, and became pupil-teacher at Kaiapoi Borough School from July 1888 to December 1892. After a year of teacher training in Christchurch in 1893, she gained her Normal School Training Certificate and between 1894 and November 1899 held teaching positions at Elgin School (Ashburton), Aratika School, and Makarewa School.

In December 1899 Howes began an important period of her life at Gore Public School. Here, she was infant mistress until 1912, managing classes of 220 children, assisted only by five or six young girls whom she had to train herself. After a year's leave of absence in 1913 (with a free government-granted railway pass to collect data for new books) she returned as headmistress until February 1917.

The writer's years in Gore were marked by a warmth and kindness that made her 'almost revered' by pupils, by her early use of Montessori teaching methods, and by the publication of books which were recognised internationally as textbooks and used widely in New Zealand and Australia. Former pupils remember her as small and pretty, a dainty well-dressed woman with a crown of red-gold hair, twinkling eyes, and a bright step. With her Peter Pan quality she appeared to some children 'no ordinary mortal . . . a kind of fairy herself'. Her warm infectious smile was especially attractive: 'life was good with Miss Howes' smile on us'. From her own perspective, life in Gore was

work and a little play, and more work; experimenting, weighing the right start for young lives, convinced that first necessities in education are health and a joyous outlook on knowledge and its acquirement; love for little children and their gentleness in return; flowers and gardens and walks and sunlight on the hills and the loveliness of snow . . .

Howes' love of the outdoors led her to found a Scout group for older girls. In uniforms of a dark-blue dress and khaki hat and scarf, they camped in Croydon Bush for instruction in the flora and in bushcraft.

From 1917 until 1919 Howes taught at Wellington Girls' College and in 1919 she published *Tales Out of School*, critical accounts of conditions in New Zealand schools. This was followed by a trip to South Australia. By 1921 she had settled in Dunedin, although she also spent a long period in Christchurch caring for her ageing mother. Gardening was a great love; so too were parties and dancing, play-readings, cooking, dressmaking, woodwork, and latterly bridge. A woman of enterprise, Edith Howes lived life to the full. She died in July 1954 in Dunedin.
Celia Dunlop

Quotations
para.2 C. R. Allen, unsourced newspaper clipping, Dorothy Thomson collection; P. Lawlor, *Confessions of a Journalist*, Auckland, 1935, p.211
para.9 Alex Dickie (former pupil) to Eileen Soper, 16 July 1983, Claire Schoon collection; M. B. Robertson, 'Edith Howes, M.B.E.', *Woman Today*, vol.2 no.1, 1938, p.304; Taped interview with C. Beardsley, Celia Dunlop collection; R. Fraser, *Gore Public School 50th Anniversary*, p.33

Unpublished Sources
Family records held by Dorothy Thomson, Waikanae
Letters/tape, and other research material, held by Celia Dunlop, Wellington
Records held by Claire Schoon, Dunedin (including those collected by Eileen Soper)

Published Sources
Bagnall, A. G. (ed.). *New Zealand National Bibliography to the year 1960*, vol.2, Wellington, 1969
Fraser, Robert N. J. (compiler). *Gore Public School 50th Anniversary 1878–1928, Commemorative Booklet*, Gore, 1929
Grinling, A. H. 'Edith Howes', *The Bookman*, Dec. 1914, pp.69–70
M.E.F. 'Miss Edith Howes', *The Lone Hand*, vol.1 no.3, 1914, p. 171
Otago Daily Times, 12 July 1954 (editorial)
Phillips, Enid B. V. 'New Zealand's Rich Store of Children's Books', *NZ Journal of Agriculture*, Dec. 1948, pp.629–633
Scholefield, G.H. (ed.). *Who's Who in New Zealand* (5th edn), Wellington, 1951, pp.115–16

FANNY HOWIE

1868–1916

Fanny Rose Howie, who used the stage name Te Rangi Pai, was a noted singer of opera and popular music in Britain from 1901 to 1905.

Fanny was born in Gisborne in 1868, the eldest daughter of Colonel Thomas Porter and Herewaka Te Rangi Paea. Her maternal grandfather was a high-ranking Ngati Porou chief, Tamati Tamaiwhakanehua, who signed the Treaty of Waitangi. From her mother, Fanny inherited the title Ariki Tapairu, and she added the title 'Princess' to her stage name overseas.

She was educated, along with her three sisters, at Mrs Shepherd's Ladies

College in Napier. Her father was mayor of Gisborne for four terms between 1878 and 1886, and her family often hosted touring entertainers such as the Pollard Opera Company. Introduced to fine singing at a young age, Fanny began in time to perform in public herself.

In 1891 she married a Scot, John Howie, and went to live in Nelson, where her singing continued and where she was soon at the forefront of amateur opera. In 1898, accompanied by her husband, she went to Australia with her sister Isabelle to study. The next year she toured there with the evangelists the Revds Charles Clarke and R. S. Smythe, before returning to New Zealand.

Early in 1901 she went to England with her husband, to study with (amongst others) the baritone Sir Charles Santley, who had toured New Zealand in the 1890s. Her first concert was at Liverpool, with Santley and Lady Halle. Her London debut was at the Queen's Hall, as part of the first concert given solely by New Zealand artists. She had a strong, warm personality, with a sense of humour and spirit, and 'her mana became something unusual'.

Fanny was to stay in England for nearly five years, appearing at all the major concert halls, with some of the leading singers of the day – such as Ada Crossley, Belle Cole, Watkin Mills, and Eva Foster. Fanny was basically a concert singer, whose repertoire included ballads, national and 'art' songs, with some excursions into comic opera and oratorio. She appeared too before royalty, and later described one of these occasions:

I think one of the most interesting episodes in my London experience was when I sang at an entertainment given by the Children's Protection League. I was on the committee of the League and was specially asked to sing for the tableau provided by Queen Alexandra and arranged by Lady Henry Somerset. I sang 'The Children of the City' and a number of children gathered from the East End slums formed the tableau. It was quite a special thing that I should be chosen for this, and of course, very gratifying. All the principal Court ladies arranged tableau [sic] from pictures by Royal Academy artists . . .

In 1903 she toured England, Ireland and Scotland with another Maori singer, Rangiuia, and the first New Zealand Representative Band. She later toured with a New Zealand concert party, and her version of 'Home Sweet Home' in Maori 'always captivated the English people'. She received excellent reviews, her voice being described as 'brilliant, warm, and colourful'.

John Howie had, meantime, returned home to his job in the Customs Department. Fanny, in spite of her success, sometimes earned little from her engagements, and from time to time went without food to provide necessary attire for her concerts.

At the end of 1904 her mother died, and a year later Fanny returned to New Zealand on what was intended to be a short trip. A return concert in the packed Wellington Town Hall in March 1906 was described as 'an unqualified success':

Her deep beautiful voice is so entirely musical and her refined, sympathetic treatment appeals at once to her audience . . . so few understand how to frame a programme that is acceptable to the majority of their audience.

Fanny Rose Howie, Princess Te Rangi Pai. *Tyree Collection, Nelson Provincial Museum*

However, she was overweight and suffering from diabetes, which prevented her from returning to England. Later in 1906 she undertook a tour of New Zealand with a concert party which included Maggie Papakura, May Moon, and accompanist Gertrude Hunt.

At this time she became interested in composing. On her last tour in 1907 she attracted crowded houses from Whangarei to Opotiki, and received tremendous applause for her lullaby 'Hine e Hine' (still known today from its use as the goodnight theme tune on television). Her interest in composing remained to the end of her life, and gives her an additional place in the history of New Zealand music. Compared with singers such as Rosina Buckman and Frances Alda, Fanny was a minor figure internationally, and her career was brief. At the age of thirty-nine, ill health caused her stage career to come to an end. By 1908 she had rejoined her husband in Gisborne, where she taught singing.

In 1910 her illness caused her to withdraw almost entirely from society, and she went to live near Te Kaha, in a house overlooking the sea which her husband and adopted son built for her. There she was visited in 1914 by Florence Harsant, who described her as a charming hostess and tremendous woman:

She was only just learning to housekeep and to speak Maori. Her father, Colonel Porter, had not allowed her to learn it when she was young . . . She had a glorious garden of roses and her great treasure, of course, was her grand piano. Here she had composed some exquisite little songs, which she would not publish, not being able to take out a copyright for she was not wealthy.

Fanny died in Opotiki on 20 May 1916. Her grave, near her house 'Kopua Koeae', is marked by an angel carved in Italian marble – fitting for a singer who had found her place on the international stage. *Janet McCallum*

Quotations
para.5 *NZ Free Lance*, 17 March 1906
para.6 *NZ Mail*, 14 March 1906
para.7 *NZ Mail*, 14 March 1906; *NZ Herald*, 31 Oct. 1970
para.9 *NZ Mail*, 21 March 1906
para.12 F. Harsant, *Historical Review*, Nov. 1982, p.112

Unpublished Sources
Information was provided by June Carson, Peter Downes, Dulcie Hunt, Jill Palmer (ATL), Adrienne Simpson, Annette Tootell, Maurice Watson (Nelson Provincial Museum).
Typescript on the death of Herewaka Porter, 1904, in private possession.

Published Sources
Bay of Plenty Times, 9 March 1981
Fuller, Joyce. 'Thoughts on Entertaining an Angel', *NZ Caravan and Camping*, July 1978
Harsant, Florence. *Historical Review*, Whakatane and District Historical Society, vol.30 no.2, Nov. 1982
Motueka-Golden Bay News, 14 Aug. 1985
NZ Free Lance, 1 Dec. 1900, 8 Dec. 1900, 11 Feb. 1905, 4 Nov. 1905, 17 March 1906, 26 May 1916
NZ Herald, 31 Oct. 1970
NZ Herstory 1982, Dunedin, 1981
NZ Mail, 6 April 1904, 14 March 1906, 21 March 1906

FLORENCE HUMPHRIES

1916–1981

When Florence (Flo) Humphries died, obituaries called her a 'battler', and battle she did, not only for herself but for everyone at the bottom of the social heap. The term 'organiser', however, better conveys her ability to unite people in a worthwhile cause. The trade union movement was central to her life and work, particularly as a means of encouraging solidarity among women. 'A true daughter of the working class', Flo herself said in an interview: 'The system that caused the heartaches and tragedy of the 1930s is still with us in the 1970s. I know because I was there.'

Flo Humphries, Auckland trade unionist.
New Zealand Herald

She was brought up on a farm in Taranaki, but her family was forced off the land during the Depression and went to Wellington. She began work at the age of thirteen, first in a milkbar, then in a shirt factory. She subsequently spent three years in hospital with rheumatic fever. Her first marriage ended in divorce – and in those days the stigma of divorce for women made jobs hard to find, especially for solo mothers like Flo, who had two daughters.

She worked as a housemaid, managed a Wellington private hotel, then a large Auckland tearoom. She remarried, was employed as a housemaid and then as a manager of an Auckland boarding-house. Her second husband was a waterside worker, locked out during the 1951 waterfront dispute. Flo was elected secretary of the Women's Combined Committee which set up sub-committees to help with feeding and clothing the watersiders' families. There was always food ready at her boarding-house for the hungry among them.

In 1954 Flo became secretary of the Auckland Drug and Chemical Workers' Union, a position she held for twenty-four years. She led campaigns for equal pay, maternity leave and the provision of child care, and was proud of being the first woman to represent the Federation of Labour at an overseas trade union seminar in 1971. She also continued with community work as a member of the Freemans Bay Residents' Welfare Association, and later, in Glen Innes, organised fund-raising for the Sunshine Free Kindergarten.

In 1966 she helped establish CARP (Campaign Against Rising Prices), a popular consumer movement. In less than four years, with Flo as first president, Auckland membership grew to almost 3,000.

Fragments of Flo's life and times have been permanently recorded in *Some of My Best Friends are Women*, a TV documentary commissioned by the government Committee on Women for 1975, International Women's Year.

Margot Roth

Quotation
para.1 *Tribune*, 26 March 1981; 13 March 1978
Published Sources
Auckland Star, 20 Oct. 1971; 22 Oct. 1971
CARP Newsletter (Auckland), no.1, Feb. 1971
NZ Herald, 11 April 1978
NZ Weekly News, 19 Oct. 1970, pp.3–4
Tribune, 13 March 1978; 26 March 1981 (obituary)

ROBIN HYDE

1906–1939

Iris Guiver Wilkinson, poet, novelist and journalist, was very much a New Zealand woman although she was born in a Dutch boarding-house in Capetown, and died thirty-three years later in a London flat. Neither parent was New Zealand-born. Adelaide Butler, an Australian nurse on her way 'Home', met and married in South Africa George Edward Wilkinson, an English colonial born in India. Iris, however, lived virtually all her brief, intense life in New Zealand. For her last thirteen years she wrote as Robin Hyde, a name she gave to, then borrowed back from, her first son, who died at birth in Sydney when she was twenty.

It is hard to extract the life from thousands of pages of autobiography, poetry, letters and novels, especially as she claimed to be a 'natural liar'. Some facts are sure. When Iris was a baby, the Wilkinsons came to Wellington, where they lived in rented houses in Newtown, Melrose and Berhampore. With her sisters Iris roamed the local hills and beaches and visited Newtown Zoo, where the lions gave 'their desolate yawning roar'. Her parents were poles apart, her mother admiring respectability, Lord Kitchener, bluebells, manners, and the British Empire; her father seeking controversy and the steamy companionship of mankind in Jack London and the workers. Iris brought home strange old men for tea. The attraction of dirty pinnies and life on the margins surfaced early.

The story of family struggles, the years at Berhampore school and Wellington Girls' College, the move to 92 Northland Road, her friendship with Gwen Hawthorn (later Mitcalfe) are told in her autobiographical novel *The Godwits Fly*. The landscape and people of her childhood are evoked again in *Houses by the Sea*.

At sixteen the 'schoolgirl poetess' of her school magazine became 'Aunt Mary' of the *Farmers' Advocate* children's page. Soon she graduated to the *Dominion*, 'razoring from foreign exchanges anything that might be considered a hot tip for women.' *The Godwits Fly* also offers a transparently fictionalised account of her early love affair with Harry Sweetman. They planned to go to Europe together but at eighteen she spent some months in hospital after a severe knee injury. She left hospital on crutches, lame for life, dependent on opiates for pain relief and knowing that Harry had gone without her.

Yet at nineteen, in the election year of 1925, she was in the Women's Press Gallery writing for the *Dominion* 'a column designed to show the more skittish side of the Houses of Parliament'. Although flippant (as her age, sex and the *Dominion* required), the column disclosed some of her concerns – for example, the brain drain and inadequate provisions for women's health. She met politicians like Downie Stewart, Harry Holland, Dan Sullivan, and John A. Lee, who became friends. Instructed to omit all mention of the Labour Party, she replied that one might as well ask for a snappy scenario about Adam and Eve without any reference to the Serpent. Once she leapt up from the press table to address an election meeting in the Wellington Town Hall and 'held two and a half thousand people spellbound with her Amazonian eloquence'.

At twenty her professional success was swiftly halted. A brief love affair left her pregnant. To conceal this she resigned and left for Australia. Six months of poverty in Sydney's Surrey Hills ended with the clandestine birth and death of her son Robin Hyde. She returned to find his father married. A physical and mental breakdown followed and in 1927 she spent five months in Hanmer Springs Hospital.

From there she began corresponding with J. H. E. Schroder, literary editor of the Christchurch *Sun*, who had published one of her poems. He became her literary adviser and friend. She returned to Wellington but as the 'boom' years of the twenties were descending into the 'bust' years of the thirties, work was hard to find. She wrote some descriptive travel articles, sub-titled silent films, had poems, reviews and stories published. But there was no steady work. Finally she was employed as secretary/contributor to *Truth*. There she wrote paragraphs for the women's page about socialites and suffragettes, brides and borstal matrons, alternately submitting to and subverting editorial expectations. After four months *Truth* sacked her without warning.

'I'll have to start again as barmaid, milkmaid or lady pickpocket', she wrote to Schroder, who helped her join Esther Glen on the women's page of the Christchurch *Sun*. There she inserted reports of Jean Devanny, Elizabeth McCombs and Jessie Mackay into the 'society' and shopping columns. She moved next to the Wanganui *Chronicle* where she produced a full page daily of political, film, drama and 'social' news, headed by an idiosyncratic 'Letter from Margot'. She hoped some day to 'get a backer to start a woman's sheet of my own'. She continued to write poetry. She was only twenty-three; neither the beauty of the river below her window nor the parties and seances she attended could console her for the losses she had experienced. *The Desolate Star* was published in 1929. Although it secured her reputation as a promising young poet, she was obliged to sell copies one by one to friends and colleagues. She became pregnant in a brief affair with a married journalist who offered to pay half the cost of an abortion. 'Well, I thought, you can't say we haven't got sex equality all right.'

Hyde refused the abortion and took six months' sick leave ('a dicky heart'). She went to the Marlborough Sounds, living under an assumed name. Her son Derek Challis was born in Picton in October 1930. She lost her job and returned penniless to Wellington, her son in a dress-basket, his existence still unknown to her family. She tried selling a new non-slip sanitary belt on commission, but was a dismal failure. Disappointing daughter, clandestine mother, sacked journalist, Hyde was 'saved' by a job offer as 'Lady Editor' of the *New Zealand Observer*, a popular Auckland weekly. The editor Gordon McLean covered sport and finance; Hyde was to write much of the rest – as book, film and drama critic, feature writer, fashion reporter, political commentator. In the deepening slump her articles on 'vagrant women' and soup kitchens contrasted with the 'society notes'. She called Mt Eden prison a grim anachronism – overcrowded, antiquated and fundamentally rotten; through the Prisoners' Aid Society she met Douglas Stark, protagonist of *Passport to Hell* and *Nor the Years Condemn*. She was present at the Queen Street riots in 1932. Shocked that unemployed women received no sustenance or relief work, although all working women were taxed, Hyde presented a petition on their behalf to the mayor of Auckland, calling for government action.

But the constraints were too much – deadlines for the social pages, Derek's needs, life in boarding-houses, the temptation of morphia. These drained her time and energy and even, she feared, her capacity for poetry. In mid-1933 she tried to drown herself. She was taken by the police to a cell for alcoholics in the basement of Auckland Hospital and later entered Avondale Hospital's Grey Lodge as a voluntary patient: 'perhaps I came to this asylum of yours . . . because I needed madness if I were to survive . . .' Janet Frame has written something frighteningly similar; both seem to be talking of economic as well as psychological survival. The Grey Lodge attic was a refuge for one 'frightened of the great steel winds pouring over the world, of being evicted, of having to pay one shilling in the pound unemployment tax, of being found out for having illegitimate babies . . .' After a year she could write poetry again, do research in the Auckland Public Library, visit family and friends in other cities yet return to the security of Grey Lodge.

Two pictures of this period emerge. One of retreat: 'I'm in the predicament of having no definite career merely a choice between two Alice-in-Wonderland rabbit-holes, the first being journalism and the second, months or even years of illness during which I've had time to write as I like.' The other picture from friends like Mary Dobbie is of a warm, generous, courageous woman able to 'mother' a younger journalist.

Between mid-1933 and early 1937, Hyde completed *Journalese* (1934), *Check to Your King* (1935), *Passport to Hell* (1936), *Wednesday's Children*, *The*

Conquerors, and *Persephone in Winter* (1937). She was already working on *The Godwits Fly* and *Nor the Years Condemn* (1938).

A marked change is visible in 1936–7. Hyde turned to New Zealand's history and stories, both Maori and Pakeha, for her poetry and journalism, and was more assertive about 'women's' issues. She now wrote for *Tomorrow* and *Woman Today*, a pioneer Marxist-feminist paper whose board she was on. She accused the *Herald* and *Dominion* of suppressing controversial articles. She saw the special vulnerability of the woman writer: 'Frank Sargeson would say 'starve' and be right: but women get no sustenance and do have babies.'

Her 1937 *Observer* articles and letters to Labour housing minister John A. Lee passionately advocated the cause of the Maori resisting eviction from their lands at Orakei's Bastion Point, wanted for a state housing development. In the *Observer* she wrote: 'In the interests of a garden suburb and a view the white residents of Orakei are perfectly willing to hunt the living natives from lands which have been their ancestral right and property for so many years.' She told Lee that 'dispossession would not be forgiven or forgotten'. Her words are quoted in the November 1987 Report of the Waitangi Tribunal on the Orakei land claim.

Hyde left the security of Grey Lodge in early 1937. In a year of 'penury and hard work', rarely earning more than a pound a week, she lived on 'bread and butter, tea and the tin opener' in various baches – in the Waitakeres, Whangaroa, and Milford. The drug experiences narrated in the 'A Night in Hell' fragment date from this time. But she also dined at the 'Golden Dragon' in Greys Avenue, and met friends – Rosalie and Gloria Rawlinson, Allan Irvine, Jane Mander, Frank Sargeson, Mary Smee (Dobbie).

In December 1937 she resolved to go to England via Hong Kong, Japan and the trans-Siberian railway. It was a journey to seek wider experience and recognition as a poet and novelist, to meet her publishers, to write about. But a brief stop-over in Hong Kong disclosed another world: China. Under Japanese bombs (during the Sino-Japanese War) she visited Shanghai and Canton, met Chinese generals and editors, Agnes Smedley, Edgar Snow and the New Zealanders Rewi Alley and James Bertram, obtained a pass for the front signed by Chiang Kai-Shek. Many articles, some of her finest poems and *Dragon Rampant* came from her extraordinary journey into the war zone. Petty obstacles still met her as a woman journalist – a party of pressmen rejected her as 'an encumbrance' on their visit to the front. In Hsuchowfu when it was bombed and captured, she limped fifty miles along the railway track towards Tsingtao, witnessing the agony, brutality and unexpected compassion of war. Assaulted by Japanese soldiers, she suffered a painful eye injury, which was treated by a Japanese doctor.

Hospitalised in Hong Kong, she was diagnosed as having the tropical disease sprue but still interviewed Soong Ching Ling (Mme Sun Yat Sen). She reached England by ship on the day of the Munich agreement between Hitler, Chamberlain, and Daladier. Ill and penniless, she immediately became involved in the China Campaign Committee, the Left Book Club and the Suffragette Fellowship. Renting a caravan in Kent, she wrote of China and 'the world we know, love and are probably about to destroy'. In letters she spoke of coming back to New Zealand to 'shove for a United Front as in China'.

Robin Hyde (Iris Wilkinson), 4 November 1936. *S. P. Andrew Collection, Alexander Turnbull Library*

Suffering from depression, dysentery and anaemia Hyde moved in and out of hospital, stayed with friends, kept on writing. Imminent war in Europe displaced public concern for China; there were no New Zealand reviews of *Persephone in Winter*, those of *Godwits* were 'spitballs', negotiations for dramatising *Wednesday's Children* dragged. In New Zealand John A. Lee arranged for government assistance to bring her home.

For England was in no way 'home' to her. 'Nothing of me belongs to this country . . . I feel if people die here they die stupidly.' She died on 23 August 1939, the day of the Nazi-Soviet pact. The verdict was suicide by benzedrine poisoning. Perhaps it was through stupid miscalculation; perhaps, after China, it was indifference to personal survival. Dr James Buchanan had once nicknamed her 'Mrs God' – 'on account of [her] desire to re-arrange the universe'. She expressed that desire in living and in her actions but above all in writing. Knowing 'the mesh and the naked flesh of words' Robin Hyde lived and died as a 'fighter with words'. *Jacqueline Matthews*

Quotations

para.2 R. Hyde, *A Home in This World*, Auckland, 1984, p.98; R. Hyde, *The Godwits Fly*, Auckland, 1970, p.14

para.3 R. Hyde, *The Godwits Fly*, p.139

para.4 R. Hyde to Eileen Duggan, 12 April 1935; Pat Lawlor, *Confessions of a Journalist*, Christchurch, 1935, p.213

para.7 R. Hyde, *A Home in This World*, p.36

para.9 R. Hyde, *A Home in This World*, pp.92, 94

para.10 R. Hyde to Eileen Duggan, 12 April 1935, Letters to Eileen Duggan

para.12 R. Hyde, undated letter, copy in author's possession

para.13 *Observer*, 8 July 1937; R. Hyde to John A. Lee, 18 Aug. 1937, Lee Papers

para.14 Gloria Rawlinson, introduction to Robin Hyde, *Houses by the Sea*, Christchurch, 1952

para.16 R. Hyde, *Dragon Rampant*, Auckland, 1984, p.12; R. Hyde to J. Schroder, 8 March 1939, J. H. Schroder Papers para.18 R. Hyde to J. Schroder, 25 March 1939, J. H. Schroder Papers; 'Words', *Selected Poems*, Auckland, 1984, p.55

Unpublished Sources

J. H. Schroder Papers, MS Papers 280, ATL

Lee Papers, NZ MS, APL

Robin Hyde, Autobiographical Fragment, NZ MS 412, APL

Robin Hyde, Journal 1935, NZ MS 837, APL

Robin Hyde, Letters to Eileen Duggan, Archives of the Archdiocese, Wellington

Sweetman Papers, MS Papers 2623, ATL

Published Sources

Boddy, Gill, and Matthews, Jacqueline. *Disputed Ground: The Journalism of Robin Hyde* (forthcoming)

FANNY IRVINE-SMITH

1878–1948

Fanny Irvine-Smith is remembered today for her book, *The Streets of My City*, and for her work as a training college lecturer. She was born in 1878 in Napier but lived for most of her life in Wellington. After attending Wellington Girls' College, she taught for a while in Miss Swainson's school in Thorndon and then became a student at Victoria University College, Wellington. She played an active part in student clubs and was a co-founder and co-editor of the student magazine, *The Spike*. Her degree of Bachelor of Arts was gained in 1908.

After graduating, Fanny Irvine-Smith taught in primary and secondary schools in Taranaki and Hawke's Bay for several years. Then she returned to Victoria University College to study for a Master of Arts degree in history which she gained in 1921. In 1928, she became a lecturer in history in Wellington Training College, where her personality, as well as her brilliant teaching, enthralled students. Tall and gaunt, she wore her skirts much longer than was customary then, apparently in an attempt to conceal her barely visible boots, which were another unusual feature. With an abundance of hair wound round her head and large, haunted eyes, she invited the creation of legends. One was that she was in mourning for her dead lover, the writer Robert Louis Stevenson. The two appear never to have met.

Her lectures at training college showed her to be well in advance of her contemporaries. She gave courses on Maoritanga at a time when this was hardly ever taught in Pakeha institutions, and presented the history of other peoples with a similar respect for social settings and everyday life. As women's warden, a post she held for five years, she enforced what she considered proper standards. Men students had to escort the women home after college dances, there was to be no *clutching*, and Kelburn residents were not to be disturbed by noise.

One of Fanny Irvine-Smith's interests was drama. She put her formidable energy and talents into the college dramatic society, for which she produced a number of plays. Her students in later life became the backbone of local repertory.

Local history was another of her passions and she aroused the interest of her

Courtenay Place, Wellington, c.1929, one of Fanny Irvine-Smith's streets. *Wellington Public Library*

students in early Wellington. After retiring from lecturing, she continued her research and then wrote *The Streets of My City*. In this book, she examined the names of Wellington streets and in doing so provided an historical commentary on the city, its character, customs, topography, and old identities. In order to find the information, she covered much of the city on foot and talked to many people, particularly those who could tell her stories about the early days.

Unfortunately, Fanny Irvine-Smith died shortly before the book was published in 1948. It was an immediate success, with the first edition selling out in two weeks. The royalties from the second impression went towards the purchase of books for the branch library in Khandallah, which the author's vigorous lobbying of Wellington City Council had helped to establish.

Fanny Irvine-Smith was an excellent lecturer who passed on her interest in Maori culture and society to her students, an enthusiast for drama at a time when few plays were produced in Wellington, and the author of a book which is still of value today.

Beryl Hughes

Published Sources

Bollinger, Alice, *et al*. 'History was written here: reminiscences about the historian', *The Onslow Historian*, vol.6 no.2, 1976 (Alice Bollinger was Fanny's half-sister)

Irvine-Smith, F. *The Streets of My City*, Wellington, 1948

Macaskill, Patrick (ed.). *Ako Pai*, Wellington, 1980 (See particularly the contributions of C. L. Bailey, D. G. Edwards, and Audrey Naumann)

LUCY JACOB

1896–1976

Lucy Atareti Winiata of Ngati Raukawa was born into a family of fourteen, eight boys and six girls. She was the thirteenth child of Ema Hapai Nicholson and Pataka Winiata. Her paternal grandmother was Erenora Taratoa.

A small child at the turn of the century, she saw the erection and completion of the first Ngatokowaru wharetupuna (meeting-house) as commissioned by her mother, her mother's sister and brothers, and three cousins. It was to have a lasting effect on her, instilling a lifetime's devotion to upholding the prestige and mana of her forebears.

In the same decade her parents built their large colonial-type homestead alongside the marae. Until then they had raised their family in a humble dwelling with earth floors covered by flax mats, and cooking facilities no more than open log fires.

From an early age Lucy accepted responsibility within the family. Her mother fostered many of her own grandchildren and Lucy assumed a motherly role in the care of many who were only a few years her junior. Her formal education was modest. Riding five miles on horseback, she attended the Levin primary school at a time when Maori language was discouraged.

Her brothers were able sportsmen and all played rugby for the Levin Wanderers Rugby Football Club. Their father was patron of the club, and because of their involvement the family homestead and marae was often the focal point for important rugby functions. Together with her sisters-in-law and other family members, Lucy was supportive of the menfolk. They were well known for their hospitality and catering for special occasions and hui at the marae.

In 1919 she married Harry Jacob, a returned serviceman of the Pioneer Maori Battalion and an outstanding sportsman, who was to become Horowhenua's first rugby player to gain selection in the New Zealand All Blacks. Together they farmed their property near Ngatokowaru. They lived with her parents, and cared for them in their twilight years.

In 1930 they moved to Otaki, where Harry was appointed caretaker for the Otaki Maori Racing Club. Still smarting from the effects of the Depression, they both worked tirelessly to upgrade the accommodation house and racing club facilities. As custodian, Lucy developed a high standard of accommodation for the racing fraternity. When race meetings occurred, as many as fifty-four people were accommodated, and there were three superb cooked meals each day.

All cooking was done on a coal range, and laundry was washed and boiled in a copper. She was never afraid of hard work, and understood many tasks beyond her calling. To supplement the necessities for a growing family of five children, she chose to do seasonal work in the nearby market gardens, and as each of the children became old enough to weed and harvest crops, they too worked there to help through the hard times. Especially during the Depression, Lucy was concerned for those less fortunate than herself and many times gave shelter and sustenance to the needy.

During the Second World War, she became involved with the Patriotic Society, devoting much of her time to knitting and baking for food parcels to send overseas to the local boys in the armed forces, sewing and recycling clothes for refugees, and organising fund-raising ventures for the war effort.

A devout Anglican, Lucy held strong in her faith. She was confirmed at Rangiatea Church at Otaki only by chance. When she was attending a confirmation service, some older members of the family decided on the spur of the moment to line her up with the other candidates. In contrast, when her own daughters were of a suitable age for confirmation, she made sure they received adequate preparation. Her daughters recall with fond amusement their surprise when they arrived at church for lessons after school to find their parents waiting for them. Their mother was equipped with wash basin, towel and soap, and hot water in a hot water bottle. When they were scrubbed up and their hair brushed, they were then free to enter the house of God.

Lucy upheld with humble dignity all aspects of Maoritanga. Well versed in Maori protocol and traditions, she was especially known for her performance of waiata and patere. In 1962 she made an archive recording of her grandmother's patere 'Poi atu taku poi' and other waiata. She became a familiar figure at hui throughout and beyond Ngati Raukawa. At her own marae, she not only set a high standard in food preparation and presentation but also took exceptional care that the lawns were kept tidy and toilets kept to the best possible standard of sanitation. She led by example, believing that it was even more important to have good management behind the scenes than it was to present a good image out front. Throughout her life she maintained her love for the marae she had helped to develop.

She was widowed in 1955 soon after she and Harry had moved back to Levin. By that time she had become involved in the formation of the Maori Women's Welfare League branches throughout Ngati Raukawa. She had represented the Okaroa District Council on the Dominion Council of the MWWL and became a driving force in fostering the aims of the organisation. In 1956 she received the MBE in recognition of her services to the Maori people and to the community. For the next twenty years she continued to work to create a better relationship between Maori and Pakeha.

While she cherished her Maori heritage, she also acknowledged and respected her English ancestry. She was effectively involved in her communities, serving on committees of the Red Cross, Country Women's Institute, the National Council of Women and the church vestry, to name just a few.

She realised full well that education of a higher level than her own would be the key for her children's future livelihood, and having reached their goals they showed little enthusiasm to become as well versed in Maori protocol as their mother. Her example perhaps was not in vain. Today many of her grandchildren and great grandchildren are bi-lingual and uphold with pride their family heritage.

With a vision of the twenty-first century, she saw the growing demands of an ever-increasing whanau, and in the early 1970s she helped initiate the rebuilding of a new Ngatokowaru meeting-house. She lived to see the old one demolished and the new one started.

Shortly before her death in 1976 she sat contentedly in a wheelchair watching the builders complete the exterior. As the last nail was hammered into the roof she smiled and said: 'Ka pai, kua pai, kua mau te koti o te tupuna' (Good, our ancestor's coat is fastened).

Her tangi was at Ngatokowaru marae. Because using an uncompleted meeting-house is not permitted by Maori lore, marquees had to be erected to accommodate the huge crowds who paid their respects. She was interred at 'Raumatangi', the family cemetery.

Hine Tamatea Morgan, Joanna Hoana Selby, Cynthia Tohe Bell &
Arohaana Sciascia

Sources
Lucy Jacob's daughters drew on their memories of their mother.

GRACE JOEL

1865–1924

Grace Jane Joel was born in Dunedin on 26 May 1865, the daughter of Catherine and Maurice Joel. Her family were Jewish merchants, her father being the proprietor of the Red Lion Brewery. He was also a cousin of Sir Julius Vogel, premier of New Zealand in the 1870s.

Grace was educated at Otago Girls' High School. In 1891 she went to Melbourne where she attended the National Gallery of Victoria School of Art, winning the Ramsay Prize for painting from the nude. Later, in Paris, she went to the Académie Julian, where she worked according to the precept that a finished drawing should be the result of many hours' study. However, when left to her own devices, she emulated the Impressionists in producing rapid oil sketches. It is probable that her knowledge of and early enthusiasm for Impressionism developed from her contact in Melbourne with the Heidelberg School, whose members introduced *plein air* Impressionism to Australia. In later years her work took on a Renaissance quality; in mother and child portraits she found a genre attuned to her interest in figure painting, which intensified during the years she spent in Europe.

Returning to Dunedin from Melbourne in 1895, she continued to paint, and exhibited with the Otago Art Society which she had joined as early as 1886. In addition she helped found the more bohemian Easel Club with Girolamo Pieri Nerli (who introduced the work of the *Macchiaioli* group of Italian artists into Australasia, and is remembered as the teacher of Frances Hodgkins), L. W. Wilson, Jane Wimperis, and A. H. O'Keeffe. Grace continued her contact with both groups until Nerli's marriage (to Marie Cecilia Josephine Barron) and departure from New Zealand. She too then sold up her paintings and left for Europe, where she is known to have lived in London and France.

It has been suggested that two of her works, titled *Under the Spell* and *The dead dead past is gone; the present . . . ,* mark the effect on her of Nerli's arrival in and departure from Dunedin. It has also been suggested that Nerli and she had an affair. Whether or not this is true, she continued to correspond with him in Europe.

Only once, in 1906, did she return to New Zealand. Her contact with fellow expatriates was also limited. Frances Hodgkins mentions seeing Grace Joel on two occasions. However, despite their closeness in age and interests, the two did not maintain an association. Joel's European connections seem to have been those of an independent-minded woman; she was acquainted with Sylvia Pankhurst, and through her the women's suffrage movement, and with Isadora Duncan.

Because she possessed independent means, and perhaps also because she disliked the public gaze, she did not attempt to live by selling her work. She exhibited at the Paris Salon, the Royal Academy, and the Royal Scottish Academy. But by the time of her death she still owned most of her work. She bequeathed paintings to those Australasian institutions which had tried to acquire her work. She died in London on 6 March 1924. *Rosemary Entwisle*

Published Sources
Dickinson, F. H. *Grace Joel. 1865-1924: paintings and drawings*, Dunedin, 1980
Entwisle, Peter, *Nerli, an exhibition of paintings and drawings*, Dunedin, 1988
Entwisle, Peter. *William Mathew Hodgkins and his Circle*, Dunedin, 1984
Kirker, Anne. *New Zealand Women Artists*, Auckland, 1986
McCulloch, Alan. *Encyclopedia of Australian Art*, Melbourne, 1984

EMELIA JOHNSTONE *1838-1911*

BERNICE JOHNSTONE *1871-1960*

Emelia Speedy was born at Kurnaul in India in December 1838. Her childhood was spent following her father's regiment around the Indian subcontinent. Seeking a healthier climate, the Speedy family emigrated to New Zealand in 1856 and settled at Mauku in South Auckland.

In January 1859 Emelia married Captain John Campbell Johnstone, a man much older than herself, and one of the earliest European settlers in the Raglan district. Her new home at Te Haroto was described by one visitor as primitive, and there were no servants. Adjusting to such conditions would have been difficult for Emelia, who had been brought up to be a 'gentlewoman'.

At Te Haroto she was isolated from her family and European society. It was probably in the first years of her marriage that Emelia learnt to speak Maori by mixing with people of the area.

During the Waikato war Emelia and her two children were evacuated to Auckland, but the family returned to Te Haroto in early 1865. The already marginal farm was further set back by being abandoned throughout the war. By the late 1860s the family was in severe financial difficulties, but could not afford to leave the land in which they had invested everything. During this time Emelia had further children. Ultimately she had eight, but a son died in infancy and a daughter aged eleven years.

Captain Johnstone's behaviour was becoming increasingly eccentric; this was attributed to sunstroke sustained in India, but it is likely that he had a drink problem. He frequently fell into conflict with his neighbours. Some evidence suggests that in the early 1880s Emelia may have left the family. She unsuccessfully applied for a teaching post, and gave an address near Whangarei. In 1882 Captain Johnstone moved out of the family home and was living nearby. In July 1882 he was depressed over the recent death of his daughter and, due to appear in court the next day on an assault charge, he committed suicide. Emelia was left with dependent children, and an almost unprofitable farm. The eldest boys were as yet unable to support the family.

At this point she disappears from historical view until 1886, when she was appointed the sole-charge teacher at the Waitetuna Maori School. She had no teacher training or experience other than teaching her own children, and her first inspector's report was a disaster. Amongst other things she was rebuked for speaking to pupils in Maori. Her teaching rapidly improved, and her relationship with the children was praised. On the closure of the school in 1888, the inspector recommended that she be given another position.

However, Emelia returned to her home at Te Haroto. After her house burnt down in 1891, she stayed with each of her adult children in turn. She remained active, and despite weighing some fifteen stone could ride the distance between Auckland and Raglan in two days. In the late 1890s she lived in Waiuku, where she kept house for a widowed son. She died in January 1911, aged seventy-two years.

Bernice Alexander was born in January 1871 at Howick. Her mother was Danish and her father English. When she was a year old the family moved to Mangapiko on the Waikato frontier. Bernice and her sister Nina were taught at home until Bernice was six, old enough to walk the four miles to and from Pirongia School. She enjoyed her education and was good at her lessons, especially singing.

When Bernice was sixteen or seventeen, her father decided she should leave school. She worked at home, then spent a few months as governess on an isolated Raglan farm. During this time she became engaged to Lindsay Johnstone, Emelia's third son and the brother of Nina's fiancé, Campbell (Cam).

Reluctant to marry so young, Bernice passed the probationer teacher examination, and spent the next two years as a pupil-teacher at Huntly and Ararimu. In 1890 her career was cut short when she was summoned home to keep her newly married sister company. Although bitterly disappointed, Bernice obeyed her parents.

Bernice and Lindsay were married in May 1893, and made a home near the site of Emelia's old house. Financially life was a constant struggle and the farm's debt flourished. The first of their eight children was born in 1896.

In 1901, in an attempt to clear the debts, Bernice and her husband sold up. Cam and Lindsay took a lease on a large tract of uncleared land in the ranges between Whatawhata and Raglan. The new house was perched on a mountain top ridge, on a road that was impassable to wheeled traffic for five months of the year.

The work of running a colonial farming household was unremitting, and Bernice set high standards for herself and her children. Her discipline was by today's standards extremely severe – perhaps an indication of the strain she was under.

In 1915 Cam and Lindsay decided to end their partnership, and a farm at Miranda was bought for Lindsay's family. Disaster struck shortly afterwards when Lindsay was drowned in the Waipa River. He died intestate, and Cam reneged on the unformalised division of the property. After a few years of increasing unhappiness, Bernice finally accepted Cam's proposal for division. According to her memoirs no one could be found to swear the division equal. Finally Cam's elder brother acted as witness, but stipulated extra concessions from Cam, which went unfulfilled.

Bernice retained her share of the leasehold and also bought some land at Whatawhata. She built a house on it and made a beautiful garden, transplanting trees from the threatened bush. She had a great love of native trees, and had no patience with people who asked her why she was planting kauri seeds when she was in her eighties.

On recovering from illness in her mid-seventies, Bernice became, in her own words, a 'difficult old lady'. She decided that an old hut on her mountain property would provide her with the sense of space she wanted, and a place where she could go and write her poetry and the story of her life without disturbance. She worked hard to make the hut comfortable, and called it 'Retrospect'. Desiring independence in her to-ings and fro-ings, Bernice took up riding again. However, she was very self-conscious about what she felt to be the lack of dignity

Bernice Johnstone and her three children making the first post-winter trip along the Old Mountain Road, c.1915. The youngest child, David, is retrieving the whip while his mother leans out holding onto his trousers. *Enid Lyons*

in a woman of her age riding astride. So she acquired an old side-saddle and had it restored.

In the late 1940s or early 1950s the hut was again used for its original purpose, to house farm workers. Bernice had not been consulted and, feeling her retreat to have been violated, she burnt it down.

Bernice died in her ninetieth year in a manner that matched the way she lived her life. She had a heart attack while chasing a nesting opossum down off her old buggy.   *Sally Maclean*

Unpublished Sources
Information for this essay has been given by family members.
Major James Speedy, Diary Extracts, 1863, Speedy Family Papers, MS Papers 2184, ATL
Manuscript by Bernice Johnstone of the story of her life, and notebook of advice/diary kept by John Campbell Johnstone, private collection
Sarah Speedy, Letters, Speedy Family Papers, MS Papers 2184, ATL
Return of Compensation Claims after Waikato war, Maori Affairs Series MA 61/3, National Archives, Wellington
Waitetuna Native School Buildings and Sites file 1883–1929, BAAA 1001/7216, National Archives, Auckland
Published Sources
AJHR, 1887–89, E-2 Native Schools reports
Franklin Times, April and May 1926 (the story of the Speedy family before they came to New Zealand by Emelia's mother, Sarah Speedy)
Johnstone-Smith, S. M. *Battles, Buggies and Babies*, Hamilton (privately published), 1975
Waikato Argus, 11 Jan. 1911, p.2 (Emelia Johnstone's obituary)
Waikato Times, 27 July 1882 (J. C. Johnstone's suicide); 27 July 1915 (Lindsay Johnstone's death); 14 March 1960 (Bernice Johnstone's obituary)

OLIVE JONES

1893–1982

Olive Jones and her sister Gwenda almost constituted a two-woman antipodean arts and crafts movement. Between them they painted, potted, wove, designed and made embroideries, stitched tapestry, bound books, made linocuts, and worked with copper and gemstones. Everything in the Jones household was made by hand, and Olive, one of the first studio potters in New Zealand, hand-crafted most of her tools.

The Jones homestead, where the sisters lived for most of their lives, was a rambling farmhouse in Onehunga, built by their father, a builder. High on a hill, it surveyed the wide grey waters of the Manukau. Behind the house, in what had been the stables, Olive built her pottery.

The daughter of Emily (born Rout) and Adam Jones, Olive was born on 20 June 1893 and, after attending Auckland Girls' Grammar School, studied with Gwenda at the Elam School of Art. But Olive needed to earn a living and in 1922 trained as a girls' work secretary at the Auckland YWCA. This was the Girl Citizen era of YWCA work, a mass youth movement which attracted thousands of girls and which taught good citizenship and promoted the comradeship of girls. Olive was part of the movement at its zenith, working first at Auckland and then, from 1924, at Palmerston North.

In 1930 Olive went to Adelaide for the YWCA, not realising that her life was about to change direction radically. In Australia, Olive saw her first studio pottery and decided this was the work she really wanted to do. Fortuitously, at the same time she learned that she and Gwenda had received legacies from a Rout aunt.

Olive enrolled at the London Central School of Arts, meeting up with Gwenda who had preceded her there. The school gave Olive a solid grounding in clays, kilns, firing, and moulds, but she decided she also needed some experience in production: 'We used to play around as one does in an art school, spending a whole day over one pot.' In the pottery town of Stoke-on-Trent, Olive found the experience she needed, taking lessons at Burslem School and also visiting commercial works such as Wedgwood.

When Olive returned to New Zealand in 1934, there was no such thing as a pottery supply shop and the only other Auckland studio potter was pioneering Briar Gardner. While still in England, Olive had purchased a wheel and muffle lining for a kiln, and ordered glazes and oxides from the Wengers catalogue, a publication which was virtually Olive's potting Bible: 'Their large catalogue chapter headings [were] almost as informative as a text book.'

Soon Olive's backyard studio had on oil-fired kiln, built with her father's help, and a double cone pottery wheel. Much experimenting was needed:

My ignorance was still colossal. I knew nothing of draughts – I just followed my plan and wasted much heat straight up the chimney, not to mention problems with opossums and starlings taking up residence in the new chimney.

Olive dug her own clay, scouting all over Auckland for suitable deposits and bringing it home by horse and buggy. Learning of a new building site, Olive would reconnoitre and was sometimes successful in persuading the foreman to send a truck-load of clay to her front gate. She would then move it to her studio by wheelbarrow and store it in drums. She was very orderly in her methods, recording her trials with glazes in a workbook. She methodically burned one wood at a time in the homestead fireplace, so that she had the right ash for her work.

Within a year of her return from England, Olive was able to earn a living with her craft, though a modest one. She lived frugally, grew everything, and always claimed she didn't earn enough to pay tax. She sold her pots through shops and from her studio, and also taught students. From 1962, Olive sold through the 12 Potters, a pottery co-operative started by a group of Auckland potters. Gwenda taught arts and crafts at Auckland schools, including at Auckland Girls' Grammar School for nearly twenty years. One of her personal projects was the design and embroidery of elaborate vestments and an altar cloth for the local church she attended.

Olive exhibited all her life; her first solo exhibition was with the Auckland Society of Arts in 1934. At the 1939 Centennial Exhibition she and Elizabeth Matheson, another early studio potter from Havelock North, drew fascinated crowds by demonstrating with the wheel.

Olive Jones began producing pots from her Onehunga kiln in 1934. *New Zealand Herald*

People were so intrigued to know how the clay came up when you squeezed it and you brought up your cone. They said was there something that came up out of the wheel inside there.

Olive's overseas apprenticeship meant she had learned her craft well. She was able to draw on that training all her life. In London, she had experimented with copper lustres and she continued with this, producing pots that were highly sought after. She also produced slipcast ware, having learned how to make moulds in London, often using Maori motifs. She didn't specialise in a particular style, but would experiment, perfect a technique, then move on to something new.

The last exhibition featuring Olive's work was held in 1979, when she was eighty-six. She died on 26 December 1982, having potted to the end of her days. Gwenda died five years later.   *Sandra Coney*

Quotations
para.5 *Kaleidoscope* interview sound tape
para.6 'Olive Jones Pioneer Potter', p.14
para.7 J. Parker, *Olive Jones*, p.3
para.10 *Kaleidoscope* interview sound tape

Unpublished Sources
Interview with Pauline and Murray Jones, 1989
Sound tape from *Kaleidoscope* interview with Olive Jones, in private possession

Published Sources
Jones, Olive. 'Early Potting in Auckland', *NZ Potter*, vol.3 no.1, Aug. 1960, pp.19–23
Macdonald, Iain. 'Pioneer in realm of craft pottery', *NZ Herald*, 31 Oct. 1979
'Olive Jones Pioneer Potter', *NZ Potter*, vol.20 no.2, 1978, p.14
Parker, John. *Olive Jones: A Profile*, Auckland, 1979

ANI KAARO, MARIA PANGARI, REMANA HANE

c.1880s

In the 1880s in Hokianga three Maori women prophets burst into public attention. Ani Kaaro was the daughter of Hohaia Patuone and his wife Harata. She was therefore the granddaughter of the senior Ngati Hao chief, Patuone, who had lived on the southern side of the Waihou River, and who had become well known to Pakeha. Her two rivals were the sisters Maria Pangari and Remana Hane. Maria and Remana were the daughters of Aporo ('Apostle') Pangari (Te Houhou). Their grandfather, Pangari, had also been a significant Ngati Hao chief at Orira on the northern side of the Waihou. The religious competition that developed between them probably had its roots in old rivalries among the Ngati Hao leaders, re-enacted by the women, although members of Ani's family would later become firm followers of Remana.

In 1885 Maria (who was also known as Maria Te Houhou and Mere Taipu) emerged as a prophetess predicting the end of the world on 28 March. She was then about twenty-four years old. Her followers (estimated variously at between 200 and 700) gathered at a camp on the Waioro Stream (about a mile north of the Kaikohe Maori settlement) to await the millennium. The camp was built in a square, and the inner area, enclosed by whare (homes), was considered a wahi tapu, a sacred place for the elect. Most of the people were kin to Patuone, and most, like Maria herself, were formerly Roman Catholic believers. Among them was her father, Aporo, and also Hohaia Patuone. Alcohol was banned for the people, many of whom had destroyed or sold their possessions in anticipation of the millennium. They waited until 31 March, and then quietly disbanded.

Two years later the same community of Ngati Hao again drew public attention. Maria had died at Patea, during a visit in May 1885 to Parihaka, the community of the prophet Te Whiti O Rongomai. Her place as prophetess in the north had been taken by her younger sister, Remana, who was married to Hipiriona Hi and was therefore also known as Remana Hi. Their father was still considered to be a leader in the movement, along with Hohaia Patuone. Another sister, Mata Kuku (Cook), and her son, Tame Kuku, were also involved, Tame being the priest for the movement. From the accounts of 1887 it appears that the followers of Maria and Remana (now estimated at between forty and fifty) had broken away from Ani.

Ani was generally considered the leader of Ngati Hao. In April 1885, immediately after the failure of Maria's apocalyptic prediction, she had persuaded Ngati Hao to enter into a compact with the Maori King, Tawhiao, when

Ani Kaaro, *New Zealand Graphic*, 6 July 1901.
Wellington Public Library

he visited Te Tii marae at Waitangi in an attempt to establish Maori unity. But Ngati Hao and Te Popoto were the only two Hokianga tribes prepared to enter such a union with the Kingitanga. It seems likely that Ani's rivals drew support from the more widespread suspicion of 'subordinating' the mana of the north to the Waikato leaders of the King movement.

Ani Kaaro was the wife of Ngakete, and had been considered a prophetess for some years. In 1887 she was seen as the founder of the religious movement at Waihou. She, too, had travelled with Maria to visit Te Whiti at Parihaka in 1885, and in 1886 her father and Aporo had 'declared themselves Te Whiti adherents'. But during Ani's subsequent absence at Napier, Remana seized the leadership and took Te Whiti's teachings as her own. She claimed to be spiritually married to him. Her followers wore only white clothing and white headbands, as statements of their peaceful intentions. At their camp near Okaihau they built a fenced enclosure, which they named Mount Zion (the place of deliverance). Inside the enclosure were the whare, and a tent for Remana, which stood apart. This enclosed area was considered to be a wahi tapu. There were also two flagpoles, bearing fluttering, small, white calico flags. The people had developed new rituals of worship: they did not observe any Sabbath, for all days were the Sabbath. They also apparently made burnt sacrificial offerings – sheep, dogs, and fowls, according to one account of Maria's earlier teachings, and a cat in an account of Remana's rituals. Remana's followers also cremated the body of a dead baby (cremation is antipathetical to traditional Maori attitudes) and asserted their belief that the body would rise from the ashes.

Conflict with the law occurred after the local Araturi storekeeper blundered into their tapu enclosure in a fog. Remana ordered him to be tied up and his boots and clothing burnt, because they were dark-coloured. His complaint to the police came hard on the heels of the extensive feuding with Ani Kaaro's followers. Remana's people had killed some cattle belonging to Ani's followers because the animals had wandered into their sacred enclosure. Complaints about the quarrels and confrontations, as well as hysterical rumours about Remana's revival of cannibalism, led to an armed police expedition being sent against her on 22 July 1887. She and her followers, including her father, her husband, her sister Mata, and Patu Hohaia, brother of Ani Kaaro, resisted their arrest because, they said, the dark uniforms and black horses of the police had violated their enclosure. They fought with axes and sticks, and the police retaliated with bullets. Five Maori and two constables were wounded; fourteen men and nine women were arrested.

Remana herself, described by the *New Zealand Herald* as 'a very intelligent woman', told the court that she had expected to be interviewed by the police on the previous day; the armed expedition at dawn had violated the community's tapu enclosure and had directly provoked their self-defence. The police inspector's account supports her evidence in this respect, but she was convicted and imprisoned for three months for resisting arrest and for assaulting the storekeeper. The separate community was broken up by the police raid, but the settlement began again at Orira, and was still gaining fresh adherents in 1889. In that year Remana and her followers waited for the Archangel Gabriel to bring them their deliverance. Ani Kaaro also maintained her monthly meetings, but from 1887 apparently disclaimed the role of prophetess and now observed the Sunday Sabbath. After 1890, when the resident magistrate commented that no new members had joined Remana's community, she vanishes from the written records of the Pakeha observers.

The three women inherited the cloak of leadership from the senior chiefs of the upper Hokianga region. They took on the role of matakite, or visionaries, in a time of considerable political activity in the Hokianga. This was a role a number of women assumed in the nineteenth century, particularly when the chiefs found their mana eroded by the Pakeha-created authority structures. The discontent in the Hokianga in the 1880s derived from the government's new land settlement and roading schemes. Ani Kaaro was seeking to establish a broad Maori unity in order to retain control over their destinies, while her rivals looked to a more immediate religious deliverance. The women all sought, in terms of the scriptural promises, the 'right paths' to ensure their survival. The social context which gave them a following was the extreme local poverty combined with extensive, recent land alienation in the Hokianga, the consequence of the government's policies to open up this region for European settlement. *Judith Binney*

Quotations
para.5 Letter, 21 July 1886, von Sturmer Letters, APL
para.7 *NZ Herald*, 26 July 1887

Unpublished Sources
Andrews, C. L. 'Aspects of Development: The Maori Situation 1870–1890', MA thesis, Auckland, 1968
Police 1/1889: 1545, National Archives, Wellington
Spencer von Sturmer, Letters to John Webster, NZ MSS 745, APL

Published Sources
AJHR, 1885, G-2; 1887, G-1; 1888, G-5; 1889, G-3; 1890, G-2
Auckland Weekly News, 28 March 1885, p.22
Elsmore, Bronwyn, *Mana from Heaven. A Century of Maori Prophets in New Zealand*, Tauranga, 1989
Gudgeon, W. E. 'Maori Religion', *Journal of the Polynesian Society*, vol.14 no.3, Sept. 1905
Lee, Jack. *Hokianga*, Auckland, 1987
NZ Graphic, 6 July 1901, p.23
NZ Herald, 23, 25, 26, 28, 30 March 1885; 4, 7, 8 April 1885; 11, 12 May 1885; 13 June 1887; 22, 23, 25, 26 July 1887; 15 Aug. 1887
Orange, Claudia. *The Treaty of Waitangi*, Wellington, 1987
Scott, Dick. *Ask That Mountain*, Auckland, 1975

KAHE TE RAU O TE RANGI

?1800–?1850

Kahe Te Rau O Te Rangi, also known as Te Rau O Te Rangi, is best remembered for her epic swim from Kapiti Island to the mainland.

Kahe was born probably in the early 1800s, either at Kaweka, in Taranaki, or at Kawhia Harbour. Her mother, Hautonga, was of the Ngati Mutunga tribe of Taranaki and her father, Te Matoha, was of the Ngati Toa and Te Atiawa tribes. During Te Rauparaha's great military migration in the early 1820s she marched from Kawhia Harbour through Taranaki down to the Wellington Province.

In the 1820s Kahe was living with some of her people at Waiorua, a large stockaded village at the north of Kapiti Island in a rocky bay facing the mainland. She was thought to be in her early twenties at the time. In about 1824 a great battle was fought at Waiorua, with tribes from both the north and south participating. The final outcome was to establish Ngati Toa firmly in the south of the North Island. Shortly after the battle, Kahe was warned by her slave that her father's pa near a stream south of Waiorua was to be attacked. The slave dreamed that an enemy tribe would succeed in killing her.

Kahe decided to raise help and save her first child. She would swim to the mainland and raise the alarm against the invaders.

I shall go to the mainland . . . but I shall not take a canoe, for it would be seen, even the smallest canoe. I shall swim the Strait – I shall take my little daughter with me; and I shall rouse the people to save Kapiti.

Her slave-woman, Rauhuihui, prepared her for the dangerous task. She anointed her from head to foot with oil and rubbed her body with kokowai or red ochre to protect her from the cold. A tohunga, Te Whataupoko, recited karakia to safeguard her trip. She swam at night when the mist blotted out the hills behind and the coast in front. With her baby daughter strapped to her back she braved the treacherous waters. She was supported by a raupo (bulrush) mat which was light and buoyant, so she was kept high and safe. She swam about seven miles and landed at Te Uruhi two miles south of Waikanae. She had safely crossed the channel to warn her people. In commemoration the channel is known as Rau O Te Rangi, but more correctly should be known as Otaheke.

It is said that Kahe's first husband was Tommy Westhorpe. She later married John Nicholl, a Scottish trader, on 10 November 1841. Her husband was also known as 'Scotch Jock', and she took the name of Betty Nicholl. According to some she had twenty or so children. One daughter, Heni, also known as Jane Brown, was born in 1835. Another daughter, Mere Hautonga or Mary Naera, was the mother of Sir Maui Pomare. Another daughter, born in the early 1840s, was looked after by Governor Grey and his wife and lived with them at Cape Town in South Africa, where she died sometime after December 1854.

Kahe has been described as a tall, strong woman. She did not mind cracking jokes and putting smart ones in their place. She was a 'beautifully proportioned woman of great muscular strength and endurance'. Kahe excelled in swimming and diving. No one in Kapiti was a more strenuous diver for shellfish, or could fill a basket more quickly or remain under water longer. In swimming races she outdistanced all her rivals, and in later years she defeated all Pakeha sailors who challenged her.

Kahe is also noted as one of the few women to have signed the Treaty of Waitangi, which reflects her position in the tribe. She signed on 29 April 1840 under the name Kahe, probably at Kapiti.

Kahe died in the mid-1800s at Paekakariki. She is said to be buried at Karewarewa, on the northern side of the Waikanae River.   *Raina Meha*

Quotations
para.5 J. Cowan, *Hero Stories of New Zealand*, p.11
para.7 G. Lindauer and J. Cowan, *Pictures of Old New Zealand*, p.206

Published Sources
Carkeek, W. *The Kapiti Coast*, Christchurch, 1978
Cowan, J. *Hero Stories of New Zealand*, Wellington, 1935
Grover, R. *Cork of War*, Dunedin, 1982
Lindauer, G. and Cowan, J. *Pictures of Old New Zealand*, Auckland, 1930

EMA UMURAU KARETAI

1865-1948

Born on 21 August 1865, Ema Umurau Karetai was the second daughter of Timoti Karetai and Hariata Rapatini, and granddaughter of Karetai (one of the signatories of the Treaty of Waitangi) and Te Koara. She attended school at Otakou on Otago Harbour, and was disappointed at not going on to secondary school because of family commitments.

At the age of sixteen Ema was selected by Sir William Larnach to teach his daughters the Maori language. Although none of them became proficient in the language, she stayed on at 'the Camp' (now known as 'the Castle') as companion to the youngest girl, Gladys.

As such, she travelled to Wellington with the family whenever parliament was in session, and had many stories to tell of life there. In summer, the family carriage would take Ema and Gladys on a picnic to one of the Wellington bays. Sometimes they went for walks or visits to Government House.

Ema married in the early 1890s, her husband being Frederick William Julius Waltsgott from Saxony, in South Germany. Married life began on a small dairy farm at Pipikaretu on the Otago Peninsula. During the early part of this century she acted as official interpreter at sittings of the Maori Land Court in the southern area of the country. She was also the unofficial midwife to the district for many years. These were the days before the advent of the motor-car, and the doctor was hours away, having to travel by ferry and horse-drawn vehicle. If he was sent for, the baby had usually arrived before the doctor did.

The Waltsgotts brought up a family of three daughters. One entered the teaching profession; the other two married and moved south to live, one at Bluff, the other at Stewart Island. So there was no one to carry on the farm. By this time, too, the pattern of farming was changing, cows being phased out in favour of sheep. So the parents leased the farm and went to live for a time at Stewart Island.

While there, Ema's husband died, and eventually she went to live with her teacher daughter, who had never married. Her last years were spent at Otakou, where she died in 1948, just one month before her eighty-second birthday. She now lies in the urupa (cemetery) there with her forebears.   *Magda Wallscott*

Source
The author is the teacher daughter of Ema Umurau Karetai. The name changed over time to the more easily pronounced Wallscott.

DOVEY KATENE

1912-1978

Hera (Dovey) Katene was born in Wellington in 1912. Her people were Ngati Toa, Ngati Tama, Te Atiawa, Te Rarawa, and Ngati Whatua. She was educated at Te Waipounamu Maori Girls' College in Christchurch.

Dovey Katene was the composer of many award-winning waiata. Her best known compositions include the songs 'I nga ra o mua' (The days gone by) and the lament 'Te ra pouri' (The day of grief), dedicated to the memory of Prime Minister Norman Kirk.

Throughout her lifetime, Dovey Katene worked hard to retain knowledge of tikanga Maori. These values she nurtured among all her people, but especially among the generations of Maori rangatahi (youth) that were to grow up in the city.

Dovey Katene was a driving force behind Ngati Poneke Maori Club in Wellington and founder of the Mawaihakona Maori Cultural Association. In 1978 she received a Queen's Service Medal for her contribution to the Maori community. Later in life she also received a moko.

Dovey Katene died in 1987 after a long illness and is buried at the Katene family cemetery, Pukerua Bay.

Her story is told by Dovey Taiaroa:
I was named Dovey because my mother, Teitei Winiata, and Aunty Dove were very, very good friends. Aunty Dove and my mother made a sort of pact that Aunty Dove would take my mother's second baby. But when I was born, Mum just couldn't give me up. I was the baby that my mother wanted all the time. My Mum said she'd do the next best thing and name me after Aunty Dovey.

Aunty Dove was quite old when she got the moko. She didn't have the black around the lips, she just had the outline because it was too painful. Unlike the other women that had their moko put on at the same time, Aunty Dove didn't have anybody to say karakia for her so she just had the chin tattoo. *

My first memory of Aunty Dovey was when I came down to Wellington and she was living in Johnsonville with a man called Whata Green. He was a champion axeman and they'd adopted the twins by then. The twins were Dorothy and Mary Enoka but we used to called them Maina and Taina. They were whangai, brought up by Aunty Dove from babies.

She talked really how a mother talks, or how an aunty talks, about growing up and how to look after yourself. She told us how we were to behave. She didn't make us feel bad about ourselves. She was like that. If we had our mate [period] at those times, we weren't to go in the water, at the beach. We were always taught not to go near the gardens then, not to do that kind of

**There was a ritual to having a chin tattoo, involving the support of elders, and chants.*

340

work, because that was the time we kept ourselves to ourselves.

Aunty Dove was an elder in the true sense of the word because she was ngawari [understanding] to all the young ones. She was one of the few that wasn't constantly growling and not telling us what she was growling at us for.

Dovey Katene in later life. *Stephen A'Court — Replay Radio*

One of my strongest memories of Aunty Dove was when we were waiting for the body of Bill Rourangi, one of the tutors of Ngati Poneke, to arrive. We were all there standing in line and at that time the old people were going to come up front. The next minute Aunty Dove came up beside me and took my hand. I looked at her. I sort of had an inkling of what she was going to ask me to do. She just said, 'You're going to do it for us.' I had to stand there all by myself and that was the first time I realised that I was to karanga.

But Aunty Dove was standing right behind me, encouraging me. It showed the rest of the people that I'd been given permission to do the karanga. I suppose I wouldn't otherwise be in the position that I am in now, of having confidence and knowing full well that I had got the support of my kuia. I think it's got to be that selection by elders. They've got to show the way.

Now, about her music. Aunty Dove had a passable voice. When she was writing songs, she didn't know music but she knew enough to know what kind of an air she wanted – what kind of rangi. But her club, Mawaihakona, had some singers with really good voices. They would pick up on what she wanted them to do. They made her songs, they really did.

You know most of Aunty Dovey's songs were original. They weren't songs which she composed lyrics for and then put them to Pakeha tunes. She tried as much as possible to have her own rangi. She composed these waiata-a-ringa

341

(action songs), which had a kind of Pacific Island beat. I love her songs that have that beat.

What stands out in my mind about Aunty Dovey was, I think, knowing that she was there. She was like a rock to me. She was somebody that I could go to. She was like another mother to me. She really was. I suppose it was because I had her name, that I felt that I could talk to her. So we'd have our talk and if Aunty Dove wanted me to keep anything just to myself she knew that would happen too.

When there was tragedy, Aunty Dove just got on with it. The last three times I went to see her, she couldn't come out in public, because everything was starting to play up. She had the cancer, but she still went on with her life and tried to make it full, she was that kind of person. So at the end there, I just didn't mind going to see her any time she wanted. I don't know what it was, but I felt that she was calling to me.

Even though she's gone, she's still a strength, because we know she's there. She's still there helping us and telling us to get on with it. She certainly was wahine toa.

She brought the past into the future. She joined them and it gave her the confidence that she had in her life and that she would wish for our young ones. She believed in things Maori. She proved that even though she wasn't fluent in Maori language, she certainly was wahine toa for wairua Maori, the quintessence of what we are.   Dovey Taiaroa & Cushla Parekowhai

Published Sources
Dominion, 29 Jan. 1987 (obituary)
Evening Post, 28 Jan. 1987 (obituary)
Ihimaera, Witi and Long, D. S. *Into the World of Light*, Auckland, 1982
Katene-Horvath, Dovey. *Nau mai ra e poi; songs by Dovey Katene-Horvath* (sound recording), Radio New Zealand, Wellington

ELIZA KAYE

1854–1923

Eliza Bannerman Maclaren was born in Lossiemouth, north Scotland. Her mother was Mary Maclaren (born Aitken), and her father was Peter Maclaren, a Presbyterian minister. She lived for a time in Port Adelaide, Australia, where her father had a parish. It was there that she met and married Albert Kaye in 1875 when she was twenty years old; he was a manager for a grain and shipping merchant company.

The young couple moved to Christchurch, New Zealand in November 1883, where Albert and his partner, a Mr Carter, established their own firm of Kaye and Carter, setting up premises in Cathedral Square. Eliza and her husband lived in a large home in Papanui Road.

Eliza served as president of the Christchurch Young Women's Christian

Association from 1901 to 1920; she probably became involved in the YWCA soon after her arrival, for the Christchurch association was founded in the same year.

Eliza Kaye was considered a woman of great vision, earnestness, and strong conviction. She gave the impetus for the separation of the YWCA of New Zealand from the YWCA of Australia (realised in 1926, after her death). A tireless worker, she was president of the New Zealand field committee of the YWCA from 1920 until her death in 1923. Now a widow in her late sixties, she left her long-established home in Christchurch to live in Wellington, travelling to as many local YWCAs as she could – Palmerston North, New Plymouth, Whangarei, and Gisborne.

Eliza was actively involved in her church, conducting a large bible class. She was also the editor of the Presbyterian Woman's Missionary Union paper, *Harvest Field*. But there is very little other information concerning the life of this dynamic woman.

Eliza Kaye died in Wellington on 4 October 1923, aged sixty-nine; she had no children. She bequeathed to the National YWCA her roll-top desk, her swivel chair (many times upholstered), and a carpet square.   *Clare Simpson*

Unpublished Sources
Canterbury Married Women Index, Canterbury Museum
G. R. Macdonald Biographies, Canterbury Museum

Published Source
Law, Ethel. *Down the Years: a record of the past for women of the present and future*, Wellington, 1961, p.17

LAVINIA KELSEY

1856–1948

Writing in 1914, Lavinia Kelsey said of the Dunedin Free Kindergarten Association that it 'was started for those children who needed an environment of joy and kindness'. Responding to the sight of unsupervised children playing in the area of Dunedin known as 'The Devil's Half-Acre', Lavinia Kelsey and Rachel Reynolds established New Zealand's first free kindergarten in the Mission Hall, Walker Street, Dunedin, in 1889.

Lavinia Jane Kelsey was born in London on 23 February 1856. Her mother died when she was three and her father remarried a year later. A broad education followed, the young Lavinia being tutored by such scholars as Henry Morley and Edward Aveling, later married to the daughter of Karl Marx. The other important influence in her early education was the Congregational Church, in which her father was a prominent minister.

In 1877 Lavinia and her two brothers, Thomas and Arnold, emigrated to Dunedin, where she set up a private school for girls. A move to Christchurch six years later was followed by a trip to England. Upon her return, she moved back to Dunedin and ran literature classes for women.

Lavinia's sister-in-law had been trained by the National Froebel Society in Great Britain. The influence of the ideas of Froebel, and her wish to guard the children of Dunedin from 'thriftlessness, disease, pauperism and crime', prompted Lavinia to ask the Revd Rutherford Waddell of St Andrew's Church in Walker Street to help her establish a free kindergarten. Responding to a donation from some of Dunedin's 'Little Folk' ('Dot's Little Folk' was a column in the *Otago Witness*), Lavinia wrote that:

Little children belonging to poor busy mothers will be made happy with work and play. They will be taught to be clean, and to love flowers and birds of sunshine.

The first directress of the Walker Street Kindergarten, Miss Wieneke, had been trained in the Froebel Method of early childhood education, which emphasised the powers of observation, association, and habit, and used systematic training to enhance the senses as well as the mental faculties of the child. The Walker Street Kindergarten teachers also instructed the children in domestic duties, using a doll to demonstrate to the girls the 'correct' way to keep house and care for a child.

Lavinia Kelsey. *Hocken Library*

Lavinia was a founding member of the Dunedin Free Kindergarten Association (1889). She was the honorary secretary of the association for some time, resigning only when she felt the work to be interfering with her teaching. She remained on the committee and was made the first life member of the executive. She was also a prime mover in the creation of the Free Kindergarten Union of New Zealand (1926).

A 'wander year' in Europe in 1905 resulted in a broadening of Lavinia's private classes in Dunedin. She took pupils in classics, literature, history, and French. One pupil remarked that 'but for Miss Kelsey Virginia Woolf would mean nothing to this community'. Her interest in the arts involved her in the Dunedin Public Art Gallery and the Free Library, particularly in the later years of her life.

During the First World War Lavinia established the Toy Makers' Society, a group of volunteer workers who visited wounded soldiers in Dunedin Hospital and involved them in rehabilitative activities. The programme was so successful that it spread to the consumptives' and children's wards, and continued until the influenza epidemic of 1918.

Lavinia Kelsey was a pioneer in the field of early childhood education in New Zealand. Although she began the Walker Street Kindergarten to help 'mothers [who] often find it very hard to give [their children] as much food as they need, or to clothe them warmly during the cold weather', Lavinia's career saw the spread of kindergarten education to the children of the middle class as well. However, her work did not significantly challenge contemporary trends in education. Indeed, the values instilled in the children who passed through the Walker Street Kindergarten reflected a growing concern for the moral tone of the nation, reinforced by the Temperance Movement and Charitable Aid authorities. Cleanliness, thrift, and hard work were emphasised.

One who 'sat under her in kindergarten' described Lavinia Kelsey as 'a bluestocking born to rule a salon'. She was influential in her tuition of large numbers of women in a variety of subjects, but these were, for the most part, within the realm of traditional 'female accomplishments'.

Lavinia Kelsey died on 16 June 1948, having continued her involvement in the kindergarten movement and the arts well into her ninetieth year. She was cremated, an appropriate ending as she had been a prime mover in the establishment of the local crematorium. *Karen Duder*

Quotations
para.4 L. J. Kelsey, 'Annual Report, 1889' in *Dunedin Free Kindergarten Association*, p.11; *Otago Witness*, 7 March 1895, p.45
para.7 *Evening Star*, 19 June 1948, p.9
para.9 *Otago Witness*, 19 Dec. 1895, p.14
para.11 *Evening Star*, 19 June 1948, p.9

Unpublished Source
D. Dempster, 'From Patronage to Parent Participation – the development of the Dunedin Free Kindergarten Association 1889–1939', DipEd thesis, Otago, 1986

Published Sources
Dunedin Free Kindergarten Association Semi-Jubilee 1889–1914, Dunedin, 1914
Evening Star, 26 Feb. 1944; 17 June 1948; 19 June 1948; 20 June 1959
Otago Daily Times, 17 June 1948, p.1; 10 July 1948 (obituary)
Otago Witness, 7 March 1895; 22 Aug. 1895; 5 Sept. 1895, p.47; 19 Dec. 1895, p.14

JANE KENDALL

1784–1866

Jane Quickfall was the daughter of Joseph and Jane Quickfall and was baptised in Brocklesby, Lincolnshire, on 21 March 1784. She married Thomas Kendall on 21 November 1803 in the nearby parish of Kirmington, where he was working as a tutor to a 'gentleman's' family. Jane and Thomas then returned to his home in North Thoresby, Lincolnshire, where he set up as a grocer and draper. However, Jane's life would be transformed when her husband was dramatically converted to Evangelicalism in 1805. He took her and their two small daughters, Susannah and Elizabeth, to London to live near the 'means of grace' which had opened to him through the passionate preaching of the Revd Basil Woodd of Bentinck Chapel, Marylebone. Under the sway of Woodd, Kendall applied to the Church Missionary Society to become a missionary settler in New Zealand.

Jane sailed for New South Wales with her husband and five children on 31 May 1813. Their sixth child, John, was born in the colony on 7 November 1813, but died shortly after birth. When Kendall went on an exploratory voyage to New Zealand in March 1814, Jane stayed behind. The first of the only two known letters she wrote arose out of this separation. It was probably written at her dictation; it seems she was illiterate, signing legal documents in 1840 with a cross. In the letter sent to her husband on 19 March 1814 she said:

My dearest love, I did not think I could bear your absence from me so long as we have lived ten years together so very happy God grant we may meet again and spend many more years together as happy. I do not care where I am if we are together, I cannot bear the thought of being parted.

Jane accompanied Kendall to found the first mission in New Zealand in November 1814. Their two elder daughters at first remained in New South Wales, but their three surviving sons, Thomas, Basil, and Joseph, went with them. The close communal living demanded of the missionary families and their convict-servants at Rangihoua created great stress. In about 1816 it was discovered by the missionaries that Jane was having an affair with Richard Stockwell, the convict who had been assigned as a helper to her family in New Zealand for three years, and who had also looked after them during Kendall's earlier absence. The discovery created a division between Jane and her husband which was never completely healed. The missionary William Hall accused her of bearing a child to Stockwell, and it is possible that Samuel, born to her on 5 June 1816, was Stockwell's child. Her next son, John, was born on 13 January 1818; he was followed by Lawrence, born on 31 August 1819. Both possessed a strong Kendall family resemblance as adults. Despite this evidence of a renewed relationship between Jane and her husband, it is clear that strains continued between them. They are revealed by Thomas's letter to her written on the voyage he made to England in 1820. He expressed the hope that the visit, by which he sought ordination, would also become the means of reconciliation between them – if she were willing.

Jane Kendall, aged seventy-three.
Judith Binney

Jane looked after her large family for sixteen months in New Zealand. She was later accused by the other missionaries of trading with muskets to buy pigs, which was contrary to the rules of the settlement. After Kendall's return in July 1821, harmony seemed to have been re-established between them. Her last child, Edward, was baptised on 30 May 1822. But before then, the scandal of Kendall's affair with their Maori servant girl, Tungaroa, had broken. Kendall's letters to Jane, written at this time, reveal both his love and the tension between them. On 24 May 1822, he wrote from Hokianga:

Sometimes I think to myself, that I am of all men the most unhappy, for when I am at home I am continually oppressed in my mind, and when I am so, I am led to seek for refuge in a distant place of abode; but when I am from you I am much worse. I dream of you almost every night, and am cast down, by the consideration of those many years of uninterrupted happiness that we have formerly enjoyed but which now are continually succeeded by years of sorrow and trouble.

In February 1823 the family moved to Matauwhi on the southern shores of the Bay of Islands in an attempt to start afresh, away from the mission. In September they prepared to leave New Zealand after Kendall was formally dismissed from the Church Missionary Society. However, they were shipwrecked in the bay itself and Kendall decided that Providence had determined that they should remain. They returned to Matauwhi. When the pre-eminent chief at the bay, Hongi Hika, tried in October to persuade Kendall to come to live at Kerikeri, near the second Anglican mission station but under his patronage, Jane refused to move. She told Hongi that her husband 'must not take the step', for it would reopen all the old conflicts derived from Kendall's intense involvement in the Maori world.

On 31 January 1825, the Kendall family left New Zealand suddenly. They went to Chile, but in 1827 returned to New South Wales. Shortly afterwards, Samuel died, on 21 November 1827. Kendall had purchased 500 acres at Kiama, New South Wales. He named it Retreat Farm, but subsequently he received a large government land grant at Narrawalla. Jane and Thomas lived there until his death in 1832, while their eldest son farmed at Kiama. It was at Kiama that Jane died on 22 April 1866.

Jane Kendall remains largely unknowable because she left only two letters, and her husband did not keep a journal after 1815. In New Zealand, the early missionary wives had to be strong of heart and mind to survive at all; Jane was certainly a survivor. If she violated the conventional sexual mores of her world, she also endured the opprobrium to which she was then exposed. She stood fast by her husband in his unending time of crucifixion by the missionary world, while also caring for nine children.   *Judith Binney*

Quotations
para.2 T. Kendall, Journal, Mitchell Library
para.4 T. Kendall to J. Kendall, 24 May 1822, Hocken

Unpublished Sources
Lincolnshire Parish Records, Lincolnshire County Council Archives Office, Lincoln
Thomas Kendall, Journal of proceedings, 7 March 1814 to 10 January 1815, MSS A1443, Mitchell
    Library
Thomas Kendall, Letters of Thomas Kendall, MS 71/28, Hocken

Published Sources
Australian and New Zealand Gazette, 17 July 1866, p.20
Binney, Judith. *The Legacy of Guilt: A Life of Thomas Kendall*, Auckland, 1968

MARIA KENNARD

1815–1903

Maria Kennard came to New Zealand in 1840, one of a small party of working-class immigrants selected by entrepreneur Johnny Jones in Sydney to found a farming settlement at Matanaka, Waikouaiti, on the Otago coast. Jones's attempt to establish a permanent community, comprised of families and based on agriculture, was a marked departure from the makeshift and generally rough groupings of sojourning traders and whalers then resident on the southern coasts, whose shore stays were frequently little more than occasions for unruly drunkenness. Jones's Matanaka farm predated by eight years the arrival of the main body of Scottish settlers at what was to become Dunedin.

When Maria Kennard boarded the *Magnet* to sail to New Zealand in February 1840, she was embarking on her second long sea voyage in as many years. Twenty-three-year-old Maria had set out from England in July 1838 with her husband William and two young children (Eliza aged four and William aged two), destined for Australia as assisted immigrants. Maria was born in Ewehurst, Sussex in 1815, the daughter of Mary (born Crouch) and labourer Thomas Baker. She worked as a farm and house servant before marrying William Kennard, an agricultural labourer from Kent, in the early 1830s.

Maria was seven months pregnant when the *Lady Nugent* set sail for New South Wales; she was dangerously ill for several days after her daughter Alice was born on board ship but, fortunately, recovered. Although William found work in Sydney the Australian climate proved trying. Maria and William were prepared to take a risk on the unknown prospect of Jones's Otago venture, with the promise of sixty acres at the end of two years' service. In the autumn of 1840 the *Magnet* landed Maria and her family, ten other families, a single man, twenty head of cattle, a large store of provisions, and a number of prefabricated buildings at the north end of Waikouaiti Bay. The buildings comprised a granary, schoolhouse, stable, privy, and farm shed, most of which are still standing.

Maria and her family were housed at first in temporary barracks at the foot of the hill known at the time as Matanaka-by-the-Beach. Conditions were fairly harsh – the barracks were damaged by fire and much of the settlers' initial efforts were directed toward building wattle and daub huts to live in. Their closest neighbours were the rough and predominantly male inhabitants of the whaling stations. The arrival of Methodist missionary James Watkin later in 1840 brought some moderating influence to the area. The Kennards were stalwart members of Otago's Methodist Church throughout their lives. A little over a year after first landing, in May 1841, Maria gave birth to her fourth child, Thomas.

The settlement was not an immediate success. Jones entrusted its management to his less able brother, under whose regime the first group of settler families dispersed, some even returning to Sydney. Maria and William spent some time a short distance away at Tumai, but were again at Matanaka in 1843 where their fifth child (Alfred) was born. They continued to live in the Waikouaiti area throughout the 1840s, much of that time working for Johnny Jones. Maria gave birth to another three children in these years: George in 1846, Samuel in 1848, and Robert in 1850. Soon after Robert's arrival William and Maria bought ninety acres at Goodwood, between Waikouaiti and Palmerston, naming it 'Brenzett' farm. Maria's ninth child, Sarah Ann, was born in 1852. The following year Maria and her family moved into the home which quickly became known as Kennards' Accommodation House. Here Maria offered hospitality to travellers and, from 1857 to 1862, ran a post office. The farm was known best for the bullocks which were bred from a prize shorthorn cow given to the Kennards by Jones in payment for their services. Bullock teams were the main mode of transporting people and goods across the hilly terrain.

At Goodwood Maria gave birth to the last three of her family of twelve: David (1854), Edwin (1856), and Aaron (1858). By this time her eldest children were married and starting families of their own. Like many women in the nineteenth century, Maria did not see all her children grow to adulthood. Tragedy struck in 1858 when two-year-old Edwin died from scalding. Eight years later her daughter Alice died in Australia when she was just twenty-seven years old. Alice's three surviving children returned to New Zealand without their father; one of these, Clara Morris, was taken in by her grandmother Maria.

Later in her life Maria moved into a small cottage while her youngest son Aaron took over the main homestead on the family farm. As one of Otago's earliest European residents, described as 'sturdy, hardy, strong-willed' and 'independent', Maria occupied place of honour in the Dunedin procession held to commemorate Queen Victoria's Diamond Jubilee. Maria died in 1903 at the age of eighty-eight, outliving her husband by nearly thirty years (William died in 1875). She is buried at Palmerston. *Charlotte Macdonald*

Quotations
para.7 O. M. Kennard, *With Those Who Came First*, p.5

Unpublished Source
Kennard family papers, Biographical/Genealogical Collection, Biog. Box 33, Otago Early Settlers Museum

Published Sources
'A Place You Can Visit: Matanaka Farm Buildings', *Historic Places in New Zealand*, no.4, March 1984, p.2

Kennard, O. M. *With Those Who Came First: A History of the Kennard Family in New Zealand from 1840 to 1967*, Invercargill, 1967

Knight, Hardwicke and Coutts, Peter. *Matanaka – Otago's First Farm*, Dunedin, 1975

Olssen, Erik. *A History of Otago*, Dunedin, 1984

THELMA KENT

1899–1946

In 1914 Thelma Kent was given her first camera. It was a gift which had a lasting effect on her private life and her career.

Thelma Rene Kent was born in Christchurch on 21 October 1899, the daughter of Catherine Maud Kent (born Hales) and John Robert Kent, a bootmaker. She was educated at Addington School and the Christchurch Technical School.

Using the box camera her uncle gave her, she won a newspaper photographic competition. With the prize she bought herself a newer camera. She began by taking photographs of her school friends, but as her interest in photography grew she concentrated more on pictorial work.

Although based in Christchurch, Thelma Kent spent several months of the year touring New Zealand in search of photographic subjects. With the 1/4 plate Zeiss Ikon camera she travelled by car (her Armstrong Siddley appears in several photographs), on horseback and on foot, to get her pictures.

As a 1939 article in the *Listener* noted,

Sooner or later you will see a car beside some lonely road, with a view nearby and a tent efficiently pitched, workmanlike gear around and, if you do not actually see her waving as you pass, you may guess that Thelma Kent and a friend are away out somewhere, looking for pictures, trying for this effect and that effect, worrying about depth of focus scales, trying to make up their minds whether the exposure should be shorter or the aperture closer. If she is satisfied with it – and she is hard to please – the result may get into print somewhere, and you will see just how well a sympathetic camera artist can interpret the New Zealand scene.

Thelma Kent, centre back, on a photography expedition with friends, c.1936. *Thelma Kent Collection, Alexander Turnbull Library*

She usually took a female companion with her on her trips to help with equipment and, quite frequently, to appear in her photographs – a lone figure set against the grandeur of the landscape. If she picked up hitchhikers, 'she would stand no funny business: male hitchhikers were to ride on the running board along with the gear'.

Not only were her pictures published, but Thelma Kent also wrote and illustrated her own articles for such publications as the *Auckland Weekly News* and the *New Zealand Railways Magazine*.

She had a particular love for the mountains of the South Island and made frequent tramps through the area. In an article published after a crossing of the Copeland Pass, she wrote:

Far away thoughts will visit a lover of the mountains, these thoughts gradually form themselves into a picture, then plans formulate and the picture eventually becomes a reality.

A trip to Cape Kidnappers produced a photograph of gannets which was published in the English annual *Photograms of the Year 1939* with the comment:

There is a wonderful rendering of the tones not only of the plumage of the birds, but also of the sea and sky. Nothing but photography could produce anything in the nature of an equivalent; and in a thing of this kind it stands supreme.

A French critic writing about another of her gannet studies remarked: 'in company with the elite of the whole world, Miss Kent fully justifies her reputation as an artist.'

Photographic work for the Cawthron Institute and the Canterbury Museum encouraged her interest in natural history and scientific work. Professor Robert Speight, curator at the Canterbury Museum, lent Thelma Kent a microscope, and after much experimentation in the laboratory at her home she became proficient at photomicrography, a method by which photographs are taken of minute objects with the aid of a microscope. Work for Christchurch Hospital and Canterbury University followed, including a photographic series showing the life cycle of the monarch butterfly photographed on colour slides as well as in black and white.

Thelma Kent was an enthusiastic member of the Christchurch Photographic Society. Her photographs were widely exhibited both in New Zealand and internationally. Many of her images won awards and in addition she was made an associate member of the Royal Photographic Society and, in July 1938, became a fellow of the Royal Society of Arts.

She encouraged interest in photography through articles and lectures and in 1938 and 1941 she gave a series of radio talks covering subjects as diverse as 'Hiking with a Camera' and 'Photographing the Unusual'.

Thelma Kent never married. She lived at home with her parents until her death from cancer on 23 June 1946. In 1948 her mother donated a collection of her negatives and prints to the Alexander Turnbull Library in Wellington.

Joan McCracken

Quotations

para.5 *NZ Listener*, 25 Aug. 1939, p.41; *NZ Herstory 1982*, Dunedin 1983, p.24

para.8 T. Kent, 'The Crossing of Copeland Pass and Graham's Saddle', pp.27–9; C. Symes, 'Photograms of the Year', 1939, p.14; 'A folio of best pictures', *The Monocle*, Dec. 1938, p.25

Published Sources

Anderson, A. R., and Casbolt, F. L. (eds). *Camera in New Zealand*, Wellington, 1967, pp.32–3

Blackley, Roger. *Two Centuries of New Zealand Landscape Art*, Auckland, 1990, p.80

Kent, Thelma. 'The Crossing of Copeland Pass and Graham's Saddle', *NZ Railways Magazine*, 1 Aug. 1935, pp.27–9

Kent, Thelma. 'Valleys in the Waybacks: the Region Beyond Lake Wakatipu', *NZ Railways Magazine*, 1 Dec. 1937, pp.38–9

McCracken, Joan, and Sullivan, John. 'Women Photographers in the Turnbull Library', *Turnbull Library Record*, May 1986, pp.52–60

NZ Listener, 30 May 1941, p.6; 25 Aug. 1939, p.41

ELSA KIDSON

1905–1979

Scientist Elsa Kidson achieved a considerable reputation within New Zealand and internationally for her work in the fields of soil chemistry and plant nutrition. She was responsible for establishing the importance of trace elements in soils and became a world leader in research on magnesium deficiency.

Born in 1905, Elsa Beatrice, along with her three brothers, was brought up by her mother, Kitty Kidson, and her grandfather, Charles Kidson, in Nelson. Her father died when she was three, and her mother worked as a schoolteacher to support the family. Elsa attended Nelson College for Girls, where she won a Junior National University Scholarship and starred on the tennis court. As a university student in Christchurch, Elsa lived with Christabel Robinson, a young teacher she had met in Nelson and a niece of the Henderson sisters, Stella, Christina, and Elizabeth – a family of remarkable women with tremendous intellect and drive. They presented Elsa with a strong and forceful model of what women could do and so reinforced her own confidence. For the rest of her life she admired achievers, especially women.

Scientist Elsa Kidson. *Family Collection*

After graduating in 1927, with an honours degree in chemistry, Elsa worked for two years as a demonstrator in chemistry at Canterbury College, and then in 1929 she joined the New Zealand Refrigerating Company at Islington, outside Christchurch. As a recent appointee she was one of the first to lose her job when the Depression hit. Elsa and her mother moved to Wellington where they lived with her eldest brother. In August 1931 Elsa joined the soil survey section of the Department of Scientific and Industrial Research, working at the Cawthron Institute in Nelson.

In 1930 the DSIR inaugurated a survey of the volcanic ash soils in the central North Island. Elsa, by now a skilled chemist, perfected highly sensitive methods for the determination of trace amounts of cobalt in soils and plants. This work, carried out in collaboration with Dr H. O. Askew and Dr J. K. Dixon, showed conclusively that cobalt deficiency in the soil was the cause of the wasting disease which occurred in sheep and cattle in parts of Nelson and Southland and also in some North Island volcanic areas.

In addition, Elsa carried out research on the defoliation of apple trees in the Moutere district and other problems of plant nutrition in crops in the Nelson area. From this work she developed an international reputation in the field of research on magnesium deficiency. The shortage of citrus fruits during the Second World War led to an investigation of the vitamin C content of apples,

353

tomatoes, and rosehips. Elsa tested many varieties of apples and tomatoes as well as rosehips from Central Otago briars. The outcome of this work was a study of apple juice concentrate and the fortification of jams with rosehip powder for use by the armed forces.

In 1952 she was awarded a Doctorate of Science from the University of New Zealand for her work between 1933 and 1950. She was the first woman fellow of the New Zealand Institute of Chemists, and was elected to the fellowship of the Royal Society of New Zealand. She was a member of the Nelson Photographic Society, the Nelson branch of the Federation of University Women, the Nelson Chamber Music Society, the Nelson Suter Art Society and the Nelson Fencing Club (she had been an expert fencer in her university days). She did not marry. After her retirement Elsa travelled to England where she studied sculpture at the Wimbledon School of Art. She showed special skill in sculpting life-size heads of children, many of which were exhibited. She was also an accomplished photographer whose interest lay in portraiture. She made a thirty-year photographic study of pianist Lili Kraus, who was a frequent visitor to Nelson. Her outlook and her nature inclined her towards the Quaker movement, whose meetings she attended in Nelson. She died in July 1979.

Margaret Campbell & Joyce Watson

Published Source
Campbell, Margaret and Watson, Joyce. 'Elsa Beatrice Kidson, DSc, FRIC, FNZIC', *Proceedings of the Royal Society of New Zealand*, vol.110, June 1982, pp.27–32

ISABELLA TRUBY KING

1860–1927

Isabella Cockburn Millar married Dr Frederic Truby King in 1887 at the age of twenty-six. She was his devoted wife for forty years. Her life is remarkable for her loyalty, for her dedication to her husband's cause, and for the ways in which her abilities in public relations and journalism greatly assisted the early work of the Plunket Society, which she helped to found in 1907.

Bella was the only daughter of Mr and Mrs Adam Millar of Edinburgh. Her father was a jeweller. Their middle-class home, well known in Edinburgh circles, was filled with books and learning. One of Bella's brothers became a writer to the Signet (a select body of solicitors who prepared Crown writs); as young adults, Bella and her four brothers invited their university friends home to discuss politics, literature, the sciences, and the arts. The night that Truby King entered the house, Bella was engaged to his friend, Dr Robert Smith; the next morning her fiancé was dead, a victim of typhoid. With time, and with Truby King's companionship, she overcame this tragedy. 'I think I fell in love with Fred's pale face and dark eyes', she wrote to a friend about the young New Zealander, three years her senior, who was a boarder for six years in her family home before she married him.

Bella was softly spoken but determined, just and sensible and everyone's friend. She is remembered as a 'little person' in height and weight. Rickets in childhood had left her physically deformed and unable to have children. Instead, the Truby Kings adopted a baby, Mary, in 1905. Throughout her life Bella was ill for months at a time with heart and rheumatic problems. Despite this, she nursed Truby King through his bouts of active tuberculosis and soothed him through periods of overwork and strain. It was as if her own battle against disease nerved her for the couple's crusade to improve the nation's health in body, spirit, and mind.

Bella King's partnership with Truby King was one of the intellect: she was extremely bright. She was dux of Edinburgh Ladies' College, and, because women were barred at that time from taking a degree, she attended lectures arranged by the Edinburgh Association for the University Education of Women, obtaining a First Class Honours Certificate in 1884. She was musical and good at languages. These linguistic and literary skills provided a fund of strength, professionally, for her husband. From her engagement in 1886 until 1923–24, when she was severely ill, Bella was Truby King's unpaid secretary. She was willing to accompany him anywhere, and against her mother's wishes emigrated to New Zealand in 1888, shortly after her marriage.

On all their travels she performed the role of tour manager; she knew that without her Truby King was soon hopelessly muddled. She travelled the length of the country with her husband on an official tour in 1912, answering innumerable letters and keeping him organised. She also wrote reports on his behalf, both on this tour and when at home. In 1913 she accompanied Truby King to England and helped him measure babies in London's slums in an effort to show that his feeding tables were better than those of an English rival, Dr Eric Pritchard, and that his schedules conformed to the laws of nature. In Europe, she acted as Truby King's interpreter and translated mothercraft pamphlets for him to read. As his personal secretary she spent much of her life answering his voluminous correspondence, writing individual replies to mothers and nurses who wrote from around the world; she would follow him around the house with a pencil, jotting down points that he dictated, gently bringing him back to the subject when he side-tracked himself.

One of Bella King's most important contributions in the public domain was as the author of newspaper articles on the feeding and care of babies and young children, which she wrote for many years under the pen-name of 'Hygeia'. By 1914 these articles, begun in the *Otago Witness*, were published in fifty newspapers. This baby column was of inestimable value in publicity terms to the Plunket Society. Such was its appeal that the idea soon caught on with infant welfare associations overseas.

As Truby King's wife, Bella was expected to support her husband's quests, but, as a tertiary-educated woman able to put people at their ease, she played a crucial management role in her own right, as a link and liaison between her husband and the Plunket Society headquarters in Dunedin and nurses and philanthropic women in local Plunket Society branches. It was Bella who wrote out lists of instructions for nurses. These, like her newspaper columns, were checked by Truby King. Matrons of mothercraft homes and Plunket and Karitane nurses in New Zealand and overseas wrote to Bella for advice because they knew that Truby King was often too busy; and Bella was their friend. Thus Matron McMillan in Sydney consulted Bella about arrangements for the first Baby Week in New South Wales in 1920, soon after the Truby Kings had returned from the doctor's first tour of Australia. The success of this trip, at the end of 1919, itself owed much to Mrs King's temperate influence on her husband, who without her was more wont to upset his hosts with his mood swings.

Truby King knew that his reputation as a public figure, as well as his private happiness, depended heavily on his wife's professional competence and devotion. Until she died, Truby King addressed his letters to 'my own little wifie', 'my dear wee wifie', and his manuals were dedicated to her. Still, he usually forgot to introduce her on formal occasions. In an incident recorded by Mary King, an official on a visit to Seacliff Mental Asylum remarked: 'Bright little thing, that', unaware that the 'little thing' was the medical superintendent's wife. Bella, selflessly adoring, was indispensable to him; she was his rock and she never complained when she was overlooked. She was convinced that her husband was always right.

She did not complain when Truby King forgot to come home for lunch or returned late for dinner, although his erratic hours made it difficult for her to retain servants. Truly, she was an 'ideal wife'. She accepted that her domestic world came second to her husband's work and mission. A keen botanist and gardener, she experimented on her own account with plants in the gardens at Seacliff and at 'Kingscliff', the Truby Kings' cottage at Karitane, on the coast north of Dunedin, where she had some success with hybridised daffodils.

Her health, always poor, deteriorated rapidly when she moved to Wellington with her husband and adopted daughter in 1921. In 1924 her health broke down completely. Bella King died on 15 January 1927 after a cerebral haemorrhage. Towards the end, in much pain, she watched from her new home atop the hill at Melrose, Wellington, the Karitane hospital being built further along the ridge. She did not live to see the hospital opened by the Duchess of York in March 1927. Her husband could not function well without her. From 1924 his professional powers began to disintegrate and with her death he was a broken man. 'Sir Truby King had always received the greatest assistance from his late wife in his well known work in connection with the health of women and children', understated the *New Zealand Times* on 17 January 1927. Bella King helped to make her husband famous; in this partnership the joint contribution exceeded the sum of their individual effort.   *Philippa Mein Smith*

Quotations
para.2 M. King, *Truby King*, p.48
para.8 M. King, p.95

Unpublished Sources
Letter to the author from Mary White (Mary King), Feb. 1990
Plunket Society Records, PS AG 38/9/1, Karitane, Dunedin, Newspaper Clipping Books, Sept. 1908–April 1911, April 1920–Sept. 1927, Hocken
Plunket Society Records, PS AD 7/128/931, Mary Truby King Files, Letters and Papers in Connection with the Establishment of Truby King Work in Australia, 1919–34, Hocken

Published Sources
King, Mary. *Truby King, the Man*, London, 1948
NZ Times, 17 Jan. 1927 (NZ Obituaries, vol.12, p.136, ATL)

MARTHA KING

1802/03 – 1897

Martha King, like so many of New Zealand's pioneer women, is now known chiefly through passing references in the letters of friends and acquaintances or occasional mention in newspapers of the day. But from these few comments a picture emerges of a warm and sociable woman, a capable teacher, a keen gardener, and a highly talented botanical artist. Martha King was, in fact, the first resident botanical artist in New Zealand, and the bare facts of her life here were pieced together only when the Alexander Turnbull Library acquired a collection of forty of her botanical water-colours in 1982. Until then her work was known only through five illustrations of New Zealand plants, ascribed to 'Miss King', in E. J. Wakefield's *Illustrations to Adventure in New Zealand* (1845). The originals for four of these lithographs were among the Turnbull collection.

We do not know the town where Martha King was born, or even the exact year of her birth. She is buried in Te Henui Cemetery and her death at the age of ninety-four is recorded on 31 May 1897. Presumably she must have been born in 1802 or 1803. She arrived in Wellington on board the *London* in December 1840 with her brother, Samuel Popham King (1793 or 1794–1869), and her sister, Maria (1796–1872). The family were Irish Socinians (a rationalist sect who denied the existence of the Trinity and the divinity of Christ) and their father had been a Protestant clergyman. In New Zealand Samuel married an Irishwoman, Mary Jane Quelivan (or Quenlivan) (1818–96). The two sisters never married and continued to live with their brother and his wife.

The Kings sailed on board the *Elizabeth* to Wanganui, arriving on 27 February 1841. Life was not easy for the foundation settlers. Mary Swainson, herself an artist and daughter of the naturalist and artist, William Swainson, records that the Kings' possessions were lost in the wreck of the *Jewess*, and they lived in tents until Samuel had built two whares. In one of these the sisters opened the first dame school in Wanganui. Present-day Maria Place, named for Maria King, marks the location of the school. Samuel King was Wanganui's second postmaster, a justice of the peace, and later, police magistrate.

In September 1842 Martha was commissioned by the Wellington Horticultural and Botanical Society to prepare two sets of drawings of New Zealand plants. The set drawn for the directors of the New Zealand Company is the one now in the Alexander Turnbull Library. Also in the library are sixteen pencil sketches of North Island landscapes dated between 1841 and 1859, and these are the only other surviving drawings known to be by Martha King. The botanical water-colours clearly demonstrate her artistic skill, depicting the flora of the new land with accuracy and a sure sense of composition. Their quality was appreciated by the directors of the New Zealand Company, as the *New Zealand Gazette and Wellington Spectator*, on 3 February 1844, records:

The thanks of the Court for the very elegant present of drawings of Native plants executed by Miss Martha King . . . The whole of these, forty-one in number . . . have excited universal admiration.

Martha King, 'The rata in flower',
lithograph, 1845.
Alexander Turnbull Library

Martha's artistic abilities are also referred to in the letters of fellow settlers
such as Jessie Campbell. The Wicksteeds had also been passengers on the *London*
and remained close friends. Emma Wicksteed, in a letter home, mentions that
she, Martha King, and George Duppa 'are to furnish sketches for Mr Wakefield's
journal'.

In 1847 the King family moved to New Plymouth, where the two sisters,
with their sister-in-law, again opened a school. They quickly became as popular
as they had been in Wanganui, including among their friends the Richmond and
Atkinson families. The school was the venue for dances and balls, and the hospitality of the Kings was described by many of their guests.

By mid-1860, it was apparent that the violence that had erupted between
Maori and Pakeha at Waitara would be widespread and prolonged. Already a
number of women and children had been sent for refuge to Nelson. Auckland
was another destination, and on 3 July, Maria and Martha departed for Auckland on board the *Airedale*. In her journal Jane Maria Atkinson recorded their
sorrow at leaving their garden, and added: 'it would please Miss Martha better
to be tomahawked in her own bed than sleep out of it.'

Martha King's love of nature was not expressed in her paintings alone. She
was a keen and capable gardener, and on her death left her garden to the New
Plymouth Recreation Grounds Board. In 1862 she gave up teaching to concen-
trate on her garden and on the fowls and animals that she also raised. Jane Maria
Atkinson was obviously impressed by her talents, for she wrote to Margaret
Taylor in 1855:

358

Miss King is a wonderful woman; besides doing all the cooking and household management and assisting in the school three days of the week she has found time to make a wilderness at the extremity of their garden blossom like the rose . . .

We do not know whether Martha King had received any formal training in art, but the botanical paintings are undoubtedly the work of an experienced artist and place her in the forefront of nineteenth-century botanical painters. Though no other botanical works are known to have survived, she presumably continued to paint in her retirement, because a report in the *New Zealand Mail* on 1 November 1879 refers to a botanical study exhibited by Miss Martha King at the International Exhibition, Sydney.   *Moira Long*

Quotations
para.5 T. M. Barrett, 'The Kings', p.6
para.7 Richmond-Atkinson family papers, vol.5, p.17
para.8 Richmond-Atkinson family papers, vol.3, p.63

Unpublished Sources
Richmond-Atkinson family papers, Acc 77–253, ATL

Published Sources
Barrett, T. M. 'The Kings', Whanganui Branch of the New Zealand Founders' Society Newsletter, no.27, 1964
Long, Moira. 'Martha King, Botanical Artist', *The Summer Book 2*, Wellington, 1983, pp.56–65
Sampson, F. Bruce. *Early New Zealand Botanical Art*, Wellington, 1985
Smart, M. T. 'The Early Private Dame Schools of Wanganui', *Historical Record*, vol.2 no.2, Nov. 1971, pp.21–6

MARY LAMBIE

1889–1971

'All of us to a very great extent are influenced by our home life and background', wrote Mary Lambie in introducing her memoirs, *My Story: Memoirs of a New Zealand Nurse* (1956). It was certainly true in her own life. Her grandfather and father had close links with the Presbyterian Church and her home life was that of a Scottish Presbyterian family. Mary was the eldest of five children. Her father was over fifty years of age when she was born, and her mother was frequently in poor health. Mary's secondary education was interrupted by her mother's illnesses; when her mother died in 1914 Mary, then aged twenty-four, left Christchurch Hospital where she had recently completed training as a nurse. She took full charge of a household which included an elderly invalid father, her younger sisters, and a family of six children her mother had taken into the Lambie household.

During the next four years Mary learned how to run a large household on limited finances. She quickly developed domestic and administrative skills, particularly during her next six years (1918–24) as a school nurse in a part of Christchurch which had widespread poverty. She had her first experience of assisting in a large-scale emergency in the 1918 influenza epidemic. During these years she was active in the Christchurch branch of the New Zealand Trained Nurses' Association and the National Council of Women. She also attended classes at the Christchurch Technical Institute and Canterbury University College.

By 1922 a five-year course for students of nursing at the University of Otago Home Science School, in association with selected hospitals, was under discussion. In 1924 Mary Lambie was one of two nurses selected to study abroad to enable them to teach in the new course. After completing her training as a Plunket nurse in Dunedin, she set forth from Auckland in January 1925 for the University of Toronto. Alas, she arrived at the wrong time of the academic year. The course in public health nursing in which she expected to enrol was almost completed. Communications between New Zealand and Canada were obviously not quite what they might have been in the mid-1920s. Special lectures and fieldwork in Ontario plus a summer course at Teachers College, Columbia University, New York, were arranged until she began the University of Toronto public health nursing course later in 1925.

In mid-1926 Mary Lambie returned to New Zealand after eighteen months of study and travel, only to find that the course at the University of Otago had not materialised and she was without a position. The disappointed traveller decided to undertake her midwifery training in Wellington, in spite of being very short of money and, by this time, thirty-seven years of age.

In April 1927 she was appointed as public health nurse in the Department of Health in Wellington. At the end of 1927 she was involved in discussions with Victoria University College concerning a course for registered nurses in collaboration with the Department of Health. Arrangements were finalised and in February 1928 twenty-eight students arrived at the New Zealand Post-graduate School for Nurses.

Mary Lambie taught at the school until she was sent to assist with the organisation of emergency services after the disastrous earthquake in Napier in February 1931. On her return to Wellington she was appointed director, Division of Nursing, Department of Health, a position she held with distinction until her retirement in 1950 at the age of sixty. In her capacity as both director, Division of Nursing, and registrar of the Nurses' and Midwives' Board, she undertook inspections of hospitals and schools of nursing, and laid the foundations of an efficient, generalised public health nursing service. She had a particular concern for the health of Maori people. She worked vigorously for improved conditions of work and remuneration for nurses and, where appropriate, enlisted the aid of the New Zealand Registered Nurses' Association. She was also influential in the training of other health workers, particularly occupational therapists, dietitians, and physiotherapists.

In 1938 Mary Lambie went to Samoa to reorganise the nursing service and to institute economies in the hospital, and the following year undertook similar responsibilities in Fiji. This marked the beginning of fifteen years' association with the health services of the South Pacific, including membership of the South Pacific Health Board from 1946 to 1949.

The election of the Labour government in 1935 and the passing of the Social Security Act in 1938 brought new responsibilities to Mary Lambie in a changing health service. The war years of 1939–45 presented added difficulties and scarcity of all resources. Post-war expansion was rapid and fraught with problems for the busy director: for example, acute shortage of hospital staff and coordination of public health nursing services.

Prior to the war, Mary Lambie was already well known in international nursing circles. But it was in the immediate post-war years that she made her major contribution. In 1946 she was elected president of the Florence Nightingale International Foundation, an influential organisation later associated with the International Council of Nurses (ICN). She was to guide the foundation through some very difficult years.

Probably the highlight of Mary Lambie's international activities was her participation in the International Council of Nurses' Congress in Atlantic City, New York in 1947, where she was elected first vice-president of the ICN. Various committees were set up to forge links with new post-war organisations, including the World Health Organisation (WHO). In 1949 Mary Lambie was invited to be a member of an Expert Nursing Advisory Committee of WHO to meet in Geneva in 1950. She was unanimously elected chairperson. The results of this committee's deliberations were published under the title *Expert Committee on Nursing Report of the First Session (1950)*. It was just thirty pages long but was to have a profound impact on organised nursing throughout the world.

Mary Lambie received the CBE on her retirement from the Department of Health. She continued to work on many projects in the community, was on a panel of WHO nurse advisers in the Western Pacific, and maintained her involvement with the New Zealand Registered Nurses' Association. She continued as first vice-president of the ICN until 1953 and played an important part in the organisation of a WHO International Nurses' Study Week in Wellington in 1952, the first to be held in the South Pacific area. She wrote of this occasion: 'I realised that truly a new era of international cooperation had begun in this part of the world.'

The personal qualities and leadership skills evident so early in Mary Lambie's youth remained throughout her life.

She had a magnetic personality and a genius for friendship. She was convincing because she was always well informed, and persuasive because she was never tentative in the expression of her convictions.

A severe illness in 1960 caused Mary Lambie to be an invalid during the last years of her life and she died at her home in Christchurch in 1971. A medical colleague once observed that Mary Lambie was 'not only a nurse. She was a national figure, a statesman of her time.'   *Beatrice Salmon*

Quotations
para.1 M. Lambie, *My Story*, p.1
para.11 M. Lambie, p.184
para.12 H. Campbell, *Mary Lambie*, p.92
para.13 Conversation with Dr John Jeffrey, 1972

Published Sources
Bridges, Daisy Caroline. *A History of the International Council of Nurses 1899–1964*, Toronto, 1964
Campbell, Helen. *Mary Lambie: A Biography*, Wellington, 1976
Gibson Smith, Margaret and Shadbolt, Yvonne T. (eds), *NZ Nursing Journal (Kai Tiaki) Index, volumes 1–62, 1908–1969*, Wellington, 1980 (see vols. 15–33, 1921–1960)

Lambie, Mary I. *My Story: Memoirs of a New Zealand Nurse*, Christchurch, 1956

Quinn, Dame Sheila. *ICN Past and Present*, London, 1989

Salmon, E. B. 'The International Idea' in *Objects and Outcomes: New Zealand Nurses' Association 1909–1983*, Wellington, 1984, pp.118–38

G. B. LANCASTER

1874–1945

In the issue for January 1901, the *New Zealand Illustrated Magazine* published the prize-winning story of the eighty-six entries in the New Zealand Literary and Historical Association's competition, the first of its kind, for 'original' stories about New Zealand life.

By a unanimous choice, the judges awarded the prize to a story by Keron Hale, 'His Work Before Him', a story praised for 'its excellence in the blending of these two elements – correct "local colour" and a strong appeal to human nature generally'. Its writer was, in fact, not Keron Hale of ambiguous gender, but Edith Lyttleton, a twenty-seven-year-old Canterbury woman, who had already published a number of stories and poems under her pseudonym, particularly in the *Bulletin* and *Lone Hand* in Australia, and the *Otago Daily Times* and the *New Zealand Illustrated Magazine* in New Zealand. When her pseudonym was discovered, Edith Lyttleton continued writing under the name G. B. Lancaster.

Edith Lyttleton was born near Epping, Tasmania, on 18 December 1874. Her maternal grandparents were described by an old family friend, F. de la Mare, as soldier settlers of the earliest Tasmanian days. This was the setting for Lancaster's best-known novel, *Pageant*, a world in which convicts provided the labour and the male settlers mounted guard as the ladies crossed the verandah for dinner:

a queer sour devil of a world, where the brutish eyes of beaten men came and went in the deep bush, watching, watching, and gentlemen and ladies, proud in silk and broadcloth, drove their four-in-hands, gave rollicking toasts, loved, bred up their children . . . and never forgot those watching eyes.

Lyttleton's father, Westcote McNab Lyttleton, took his family to New Zealand when she was a child, and they farmed at Rokeby, Canterbury, until 1908. During this time Lyttleton began writing stories and poems in large numbers, always published under a pseudonym. Apparently her family 'hated publicity in men and denied it to women'. From 1902, all Lyttleton's work was published under G. B. Lancaster. In her novel *Promenade* (1938), which is about the early settlement of New Zealand through the history of a family, there is a scene in which two children of the aristocratic Lovel family are found to have published a poem under their own names in a newspaper. On seeing it, their father

raged about the room like a judgement, shaking the paper. 'My daughter! The

*first time a female Lovel has ever been so abandoned as to get herself into print.
Even in death notices she should be merely "the wife of"'* . . .

All her novels and stories centre on class questions, and, from her earliest
publication, the existence of British class strata within colonial societies is clearly
affirmed. But her use of a pseudonym or unspecific gender also allowed her some
freedoms. G. B. Lancaster's early stories and novels deal with masculine activities and imply a male point of view. The stories she wrote for Australian and
New Zealand journals in the 1890s and 1900s are about male society, in which
male values and male activity are valorised. Anti-domestic, often anti-women as
in the prize-winning story 'His Work Before Him', they are demonstrably part
of the same cultural environment as Henry Lawson, Banjo Paterson or Rudyard
Kipling; stories of integrity and honour in new societies busy modifying the
hypocritical social systems of the old. *Sons o' Men* (London, 1904) was Lancaster's first collection. It is a series of connected stories about the men who work
an isolated South Island sheep station, and establishes a straightforward but
unconventional code of honour, represented by the plain-speaking, disreputable-
seeming man of integrity who dominates early Australian and New Zealand
writing.

In her later novels Lancaster deals with more complex multi-layered societies, but they consistently feature characters who display their unconvention-
ality and who do not fit comfortably within social categories. In that sense
Lancaster's work is always preoccupied with the colonial in writing; quite apart
from the settings of her novels, their narratives always present a conjunction of
colonial and Home which redefines the old in discovering the new.

In 1908 the Lyttletons left New Zealand for England and spent a number
of years travelling in Europe and the Americas. During this time Lancaster wrote
and published regularly, her novels describing a narrative journey through the
colonies of the British Empire. From 1905 to 1944 she published twelve novels,
and many magazines in England and America 'vied' to publish her stories. Her
novels are set variously in Tasmania, New Zealand, Canada, England, New
Caledonia, and South America; invariably they deal with some aspects of
colonial history.

As a prefatory note to her last novel, *Grand Parade*, published the year
before she died, Lancaster remarked:

*To try to put the beginnings of Canada between the covers of one book is like
trying to get an oak tree back into its acorn. I have done what I could for those
who do not know its history, and that history is as correct as diligent research
can make it.*

All Lancaster's work comes into the category of historical fiction. It is very much
the history of men that she wrote, and mostly from a male point of view, but
distinctively concerned with the effects and consequences of colonialism on
individuals, families, races, and nations.

Lancaster's best-known novel, *Pageant* (1933), was Book of the Month in the
United States and established her most successful narrative structure, the family
saga. When *Promenade* appeared in 1938, Lancaster was described as the

'Galsworthy of New Zealand', and the novel as 'New Zealand's *Gone With The Wind*'.

During the war Lancaster was occupied with war work and published only one more novel before her death in 1945.

In a number of ways, Lancaster perfectly illustrates the colonial woman writer. Her life is split between a number of countries and she wrote fiction that represented both her own itinerancy and the cultural stability of being an 'English gentlewoman'. All her work is built on ideas of class, race, and gender difference, but its other common feature is the insistence on the attainment of moral value in an individual's life. F. de la Mare wrote:

The standards she imposed upon her men and women she applied inexorably to herself. She had set herself a task, the task of painting in blood and bone the pioneers of the Empire's expansion and life.

Lancaster's work is about moral choice. There is perhaps no more subtle commentary on being a woman writing pseudonymously about colonial pioneering around the globe. *Lydia Wevers*

Quotations
para.2 'Some Remarks on the Recent Prize Story Competition', *NZ Illustrated Magazine*, Feb. 1901, pp.344–6
para.3 G. B. Lancaster, *Pageant*, London, 1933, pp.23–4
para.4 F. de la Mare, *A Tribute*, p.4; G. B. Lancaster, *Promenade*, London, 1938, p.163
para.7 F. de la Mare, p.7
para.8 G. B. Lancaster, *Grand Parade*, London, 1945, p.5
para.9 Reviews from the *Saturday Review of Literature* and the *New Yorker*, quoted in the order form for *Promenade*, issued by Thomas Avery & Sons Ltd, New Plymouth, 1938

Published Sources
de la Mare, F. A. *A Tribute*, Hamilton, 1945 (printed for private circulation)
NZ Illustrated Magazine, Jan., Feb. 1901

HORIANA TE KAURU LAUGHTON

1899–1986

Horiana Te Kauru Laughton was born in Nuhaka, near Wairoa, the fifth eldest child of Hohepa Te Kauru and Heni Te Kauru, on 19 November 1899. Eighteen children were born into the family. In some respects the family's life-style, in Horiana's early days, was a spartan one. The times were difficult for rural communities like Nuhaka. But the Te Kauru children grew up in a family in which education was highly valued, where religion was a celebrated feature of family life, and where discipline was firmly instilled. The resources of the land were nurtured and harvested. In conversation with her younger sister Messines, Horiana recalled the fruit trees and vegetables, so carefully tended, which provided the family's food.

The lessons she learned from her family provided Horiana with many useful life skills which she could call upon in her adult years. Later in life, for example, her gardens and home-grown produce would be a source of great pride to her and of enjoyment for the family. Visitors to the family home in Rotorua will remember how the garage was lined with shelves stocked full with preserved fruit and vegetables.

After an early education at Nuhaka Native Primary School, Horiana attended Turakina Maori Girls' College from 1915 to 1917. Her time at Turakina was significant for a number of reasons. First, it took her away from her whanau and hapu during a formative time in her life. The great distance from Nuhaka to Turakina meant that Horiana would not see her family for some years. Second, it educated her in the teachings of the Presbyterian Church, whereas her family had raised her in the Mormon faith. After her years at Turakina, Horiana lived her life strictly according to Presbyterian teachings. Third, Turakina provided Horiana with the education necessary to begin a career in teaching, and she was one of the few Maori women at this time to hold such a position. In 1917, she earned the coveted award of dux of Turakina Maori Girls' College.

Horiana continued a lifelong association with the school. In 1919 she returned as a teaching assistant; she served as a foundation member of the board of governors from its first meeting on 20 February 1957 until at least December 1970. She always encouraged young Maori women to attend Turakina, helped with fund-raising activities, and supervised the making of the tukutuku panels which decorated the new school chapel. A dormitory at Turakina is named the Laughton Dormitory after Horiana.

Horiana was also a pioneer educator in her own right. She experienced the challenge of being an early role model for other Maori women in education, and felt keenly the loneliness of being a highly educated Maori woman seeking to be accepted for her work amongst Maori people. When, many years later, one of her mokopuna was appointed to a university position, Horiana's counsel to the young woman was that Maori people, including her own relations, would be the most severe critics of her work and that she needed to be able to accept this if she was serious about an academic career.

After the completion of her studies at Turakina, Horiana became the first Maori woman to be appointed teaching assistant in the Presbyterian Mission Service. She took up her first position at Waihou in the Ureweras, when the school was opened there on 6 May 1918. In 1919 she returned to Turakina as a teaching assistant. On 3 October 1921, a new mission school was opened in the meeting-house at Matahi, also in the Ureweras, with Horiana as the teaching assistant.

In 1921 Horiana married the Very Revd John George Laughton (CMG), a Scotsman born in the Orkney Islands, who travelled to New Zealand as a young boy with his father. At the time of their marriage, he was serving as a Presbyterian missionary with the Tuhoe people, stationed at Maungapohatu. The Laughtons had five children: Mary (Evetts), John, Jean (Mundy), Kathleen (Cameron), and James. John Laughton became a famed Maori scholar and historian, known affectionately as 'the missionary on horseback' because of his work in the Urewera country amongst the Tuhoe. He became the moderator of the Presbyterian church, and a member of the Maori Bible Revision Committee and the Maori Purposes Fund Board.

John and Horiana shared a number of special projects – one was the creation of Te Maungarongo marae on its present site at Ohope; another was the trip to London when Horiana accompanied her husband to see the revised Maori Bible printed and helped with the meticulous job of proof-reading the script.

No account of Horiana's life would be complete without mentioning her passion for singing, for music, and for gardening. She was blessed with a strong beautiful soprano voice and a keen love of music. One of her dreams was to have devoted more of her life to her singing and music, although for many years she was able to enjoy working with church choirs. She was a great believer in the therapeutic value of music.

Gardening was also a pastime which brought her much joy. She revelled in attending to the needs of the trees, shrubs, and flower-beds of her gardens as well as to her vegetables, balancing creativity and beauty with survival skills learned early in her family life. She tended her own garden until the last few years of her life. A certain district health nurse once asked Horiana why she didn't come to some of the basket-weaving classes, designed as a kind of therapy for the older residents in the community: Horiana's reply left no doubt as to the importance of gardening as therapy!

Te Maungarongo marae is set in a beautiful location, giving the impression of a natural bush environment. In fact, the garden and layout of the complex were created by Horiana's vision; the bush was literally constructed tree by tree. Access to the marae is gained by walking up a slight incline, on a path through lovely bush, into a clearing in which the wharenui and wharekai are situated, again surrounded by native trees. The Laughton children, and some grandchildren, have told many stories about holidays given over to planting the multitude of trees necessary to create this haven of beauty.

Horiana Te Kauru Laughton photographed with her husband John in the grounds of Te Maungarongo, Ohope, 1954. *Kathie Irwin, Family Collection*

Horiana is remembered as a disciplined, hard-working, forthright woman with a keen intellect. Given what we now understand about life in the early part of this century and the combined impact of racism and sexism on Maori women, particularly those who are role models in their fields, we may well believe that she had to be strong and forthright to survive. She lived according to her chosen Presbyterian faith. This included a total abstinence from alcohol, smoking, and gambling, a discipline not always embraced with gusto by her children or mokopuna. She was also a vigorous exponent of the protestant work ethic.

Also, Horiana was married to a European minister in the early part of this century. We can never know how hard it was for her to satisfy her own high standards as well as the expectations of the communities they lived in. In a tribute at her funeral service, the Revd Jim Irwin said:

She once commented to my first wife that she [Alice] could get away with an untidy house sometimes but she [Horiana] never could because people would say 'what do you expect. He married a Maori' . . . Horiana was aware of the deeper subtler attitudes in later years that made life difficult and chafed a good deal.

Her sister Messines quotes Horiana as having said: 'Maori have to be as good as Pakeha, even better.'

One of her great-grandchildren has been named Horiana with her blessing to carry the name on in the whakapapa and as a gentle reminder of this wonderful woman, a pioneer educator in her own right, a woman of remarkable strength, courage, and dignity. Horiana Te Kauru Laughton lived the last period of her life in Rotorua, in the home that she and her beloved husband had retired to, a place in which she could cherish the memories of their life and work together. She died in Rotorua on 9 December 1986. *Kathie Irwin*

Quotation
para.13 Funeral tribute, copy in the author's possession
Unpublished Sources
Information was provided by family members: Mary Evetts (Horiana's eldest daughter); Messines Rogers (Horiana's younger sister); Tukiwaho Edwards (Horiana's youngest sister); Revd Jim Irwin. The author is a granddaughter of Horiana Laughton. Mary Evetts and Messines Rogers have given approval for this text to be published.
Turakina Maori Girls' School has assisted the author greatly in her research for this article, in particular with access to the school's records.

Published Sources
Binney, Judith, and Chaplin, Gillian. *Nga Morehu*, Auckland, 1986
Fry, Ruth. *It's Different for Daughters: A History of the Curriculum for Girls in New Zealand, 1900–1975*, Wellington, 1985
Laughton, Rev. J. G. *From Forest Trail to City Street: The Story of the Presbyterian Church among the Maori People*, Christchurch, 1960
Webster, Peter. *Rua and the Maori Millennium*, Wellington, 1979. John Laughton is named as one of Peter Webster's informants for this work; Horiana is described as 'an authority on the Tuhoe in her own right'.

MARY LEE

1871-1939

Mary Isabella Taylor was born in Airdrie, Scotland, on 18 June 1871, the eldest child of a 'fiery tempered' father and an alcoholic mother, Alexander and Alice Taylor. When she was six, in 1877, the family emigrated to New Zealand, arriving in Port Chalmers. Over the next ten years, they moved at least nineteen times between the cities and small towns of Otago and Southland, following jobs for Alexander Taylor, who was a baker. Mary's sister, Minnie, and two brothers, Benjamin and Alexander, were born in New Zealand. In part because of Alice Taylor's alcoholic bouts, during which she would use whatever money or household goods were at hand to buy liquor, they were never well off.

Her parents created a volatile and threatening domestic world which Mary did not escape until well into her adult life. Alice's drinking infuriated Alexander Taylor, who physically abused her and favoured Mary, arousing Alice's hostility to the child. When Mary was ten, her mother threw a tin mug at her, striking her on the head and wounding her far more than she had intended. In her autobiography, Mary wrote:

It was dined into me that if my Father found out how it had happened he would kill Mother . . . my Deafness Started from then & Before i was Eleven years. There were days when i could not See Either.

Mary became increasingly deaf and had periods of blindness and poor sight for the rest of her life. Her mother's violence, and the fear that her father would find out and in turn hurt her mother, remained a constant threat through her childhood. When still quite young, however, Mary seems to have exercised a steadying hand in the family, and to have taken over some aspects of her mother's role: certainly she was central to carrying out household work.

Sometimes the family stayed in one place for a year or more, and then Mary went to school, which she loved. Alice, however, wanted her to go out to work, and to work at home. At twelve, Mary went to work as a 'nurse girl', and was then apprenticed to a dressmaking firm in Invercargill, though the apprenticeship ended after three weeks when her mother realised that she would not earn for the first year. It was enough to equip her, however, for what became her main source of income.

At thirteen, Mary got her father a job with a former employer in Woodlands, returning the family to the relative tranquillity of the small Southland town, and herself to school, although she still had considerable household and childcare responsibilities. She would sit up with her mother after the youngest child was born and, unable to sleep because the light was on and she was liable to be called to help, 'took [her] Love for Reading', which she kept all her life.

The Taylors moved to Mataura when Mary was about fifteen, and she left school to work at the paper factory, but also went to picnics, dances, and the new Salvation Army meetings. Next came Dunedin, where Mary acquired a number of steady customers for her sewing, including Rachel Reynolds, a well-known

Dunedin benefactress, who 'till the Day of her Death in 1928 . . . was the Best friend of myself & Children'.

Her mother's physical violence had continued. When Mary was sixteen, Alice threw a kettle at her, scalding her. Mary left home, and one of her customers helped her to find a room in Royal Terrace in Dunedin – by far the most distinguished address she ever had. She lived there for a year, supporting herself by sewing, although some of her income still went to her parents. She was at this time very happy and records church picnics and 'teafights' which she greatly enjoyed. An attack of blindness at Easter 1888 hospitalised her for seven months, after which, still with limited sight, she went to her parents to convalesce. They had moved to Pukerau in Southland, but soon moved again to Waikaka, where Mary met Alfredo Lee and married him in September 1889. He was probably a Gipsy, though his family then lived in Napier. His usual employment was farm labouring, but he had recently travelled with his brother(s) doing tumbling and trapeze work.

Mary had two children by Alfredo: Alice in July 1890, and John in October 1891. She went to Dunedin for both confinements. On her return to Waikaka after Alice's birth she found that Alfredo had taken a lease on a surface coal-pit, and they lived after that on the land adjacent to it. The economic potential of the coal-pit, she soon found, was to be realised through her labour:

When a order came – if the day was fine i would have the Baby in a Old Box. If not i would fix the Rocking chair as a Bed – & put the Baby thier & Toby the Dog used to look after her & I would go over to the Coal with 2 Karosine Tins and fill them for the house & Then take the Pick & get as much coal ready in a heap – for when the men would come with the cart, if the men had to get the coal out themselves they did not pay so much.

She and the children did not always have enough to eat, relying mainly on eggs from the fowls they kept, and potatoes; she also made bread, and was sometimes given it; she tried to make sure, not always successfully, that there was milk for the children; and they ate the gooseberries which grew on the property when they were in season. When Mary was pregnant with John, she contracted typhoid fever because they had no clean water. The children, too, 'was Suffering from the effects of the Poor food & Bad Water'. Fortunately, Mrs Reynolds and Mary's mother sent clothes for the children.

Alfredo drank and gambled, to the detriment of the family income. The marriage collapsed one night when he returned from a labouring job. There was no food in the house, other than bread and dripping, and a bill at the grocer, but he departed for the hotel and spent most of his £25 cheque treating the customers. When he arrived home drunk, he aimed a blow at his vociferously protesting wife and hit his daughter by mistake, prompting Mary to attack him with a butcher's knife she used as a poker. He fled, returning next morning to make peace, but

somehow it Just came to me then that i could not Live there any Longer. I would get the Children & myself to Dunedin where i could get work to get food – he could come after me – or stay away I just felt I did not care.

It is not clear whether Alfredo did follow her and live with her for a short while in Dunedin, or whether the marriage ended finally at this point.

Mary sewed, once more, for many of the well-to-do families of Dunedin, including Dr and Mrs Hocken ('he was a funny little chap'), and Mrs Joachim and her sisters 'Miss Fanny & Miss Jane Wimpress' (i.e. Wimperis). John A. Lee records in his fictional account of this period, *Children of the Poor*, that although many of her customers were generous with left-overs and cast-off clothing, they were less so with payment for her work.

Mary had two further children: Fred in 1895, and Kathleen, who was born in September 1900 and died of bronchopneumonia at seven months. Mary set great store by the social form of marriage, and gives us few clues about the relationship(s) which produced these children. In her autobiography, she does not mention Kathleen at all. Childbirth made her very ill and restricted her earning capacity for a considerable period on both occasions.

Once she was settled in Dunedin, Mary tenaciously maintained her own household; to have and to keep a good house – she never owned one of her own – was of great importance to her. Her parents would often turn up and move in with her, however, and their tendency to 'rows' and the problems associated with Alice Taylor's drinking threatened some of Mary's tenancies. Her sister Minnie also lived with her at times, sometimes helping with the children and occasionally assisting financially. For periods between 1897 and 1901, rather against Mary's will, her parents took the three older children to live with them in Riversdale in Southland. Mary sent them food, clothing, and money.

From Alice's birth until at least 1911, Mary was often partly or wholly dependent on charitable aid. From May 1891 to December 1893 she received 7/6d a week in aid. In 1897, the Benevolent Society inspector reported that she earned between 3/- and 10/- per week by sewing. Her rent was 5/-, and she usually received 6/6d per week in charitable aid. During 1898–9, however, she was often 'not in good health', and sometimes unable to earn anything; at those times the Lees survived largely on aid, which was increased to 10/- in 1900. The birth of Kathleen put her relief under threat, the inspector noting that she

appears to be in need of relief – Although I am of opinion it is not right to give this woman Aid in its present form I am of opinion her 3 Children should be put in the School & let her do for herself.

The threat was not carried out but the next years were hard. They celebrated the New Year of 1902–3 on bread and treacle.

Mary continued to work at dressmaking until 1922. At times her poor sight prevented her from sewing, and she looked to other paid work, mainly washing or cleaning (she cleaned offices for one employer for nineteen years), or relied on charitable aid. Contributions from her father, who lived with her for most of the last ten years of his life, were very occasional. John and then Fred helped to collect wood and coal – by John's account he kept her well supplied with stolen coal for some years – and when they began to earn both contributed financially. John got a paper run with the *Star*, but began wagging school; later he was convicted of theft and 'was sent to Burnham [Industrial School]'. She saw him twice in the following fifteen years.

Mary Lee in later life. *Auckland Public Library*

Alice Lee, as her brother later recorded, 'never had a chance'. By the time she was fourteen, Mary found her difficult to control, and she had left school. The aid to the family was reduced from 10/6d to 7/6d between July 1904 and May 1905, concurrent with reports on Alice's behaviour: she was seen 'talking to about 1/2 doz youths' and

visiting & frequenting Chinamen's Houses & the neighbours have complained of Men being seen about her Mother's House 'till nearly 12 o'clock at night. She should be committed to some Home, if not recommend the relief be discontinued.

In 1906, when she was fifteen, she had a son, who was brought up by Mary after he was seven. Alice married Tom Rowe, who was probably the child's father, in 1910; their marriage was stormy ('But Oh they were always Rowing'). She became ill in April 1913, and this effectively ended the marriage. Alice returned to Mary's house and died of tuberculosis in December 1914.

Fred's career was never marked by the traumas which Mary and her older children experienced. He went to work at thirteen, spent a brief period in the army in 1918, and returned to buy a grocery business in Dunedin. Before Fred's marriage in 1922, Mary enjoyed the quieter life they led together (her mother having died in 1911, her father in 1919). She recalled that:

sometimes, at Tea Time, when we were By ourselves, he would get me talking about things i could Remember & we would Chat away telling each other Things – till it was so dark we could not see ourselves & he used to say for heavens Sake write these Things for me Mother so i will have a record of them.

When he married, 'It ment finish to me of home Life'.

In 1922, Mary's son John won the Auckland East seat for Labour. Having lost all trace of him, Mary found that 'he had been to the War & won his medals for Dash & Pluck: but a woman had got a hold of him'. Although Mary strongly disapproved of his politics, she went to live in Auckland with him and the 'woman', his wife Mollie Guy, for some of her last seventeen years; the rest she spent with Fred and his family. These were years of relative security and comfort. She is remembered as being very deaf, but able to lip-read well, and she had earned the deep devotion of both her sons. Days before her death in August 1939, John A. Lee wrote in his diary:

Mother ill, struggling to live, very weak. How like myself in face and tenacity! How she fought for her bairns in the years gone by! . . . I sat in her room last night watching her struggle for breath and wondering at the struggle made for us years ago, thought of her forty years of deafness.

Her pallbearers were members of the Labour Cabinet.   *Annabel Cooper*

Quotations
Except for the three noted below, all quotations are from Mary Lee's autobiography 'The Not So Poor'. Mary Lee's spelling and punctuation have been retained. Permission to quote from the autobiography has been given by Don Paton.
para.13 Otago Benevolent Society relief casebooks, p.4033
para.15 J. A. Lee, *The Children of the Poor*, p.90; Otago Benevolent Society relief casebooks, p.4584
para.17 J. A. Lee, *The John A. Lee Diaries 1936–1940*, p.170
Unpublished Sources
Interviews with Lyn Moses, October 1989; and with Doris Palmer, Don Paton, and Alice Hall, March 1990
Letter from D. Paton to author, 26 October 1989
Mary Isabella Lee. 'The Not So Poor' (an autobiography), APL (edition in preparation)
Otago Benevolent Society relief casebooks, vol.2, p.1028; vol.5, p.2400; vol.6, p.2936; vol.7, p.3516; vol.8, p.4033; vol.9, pp.4509, 4584, 4776, Otago Hospital Board archives, Hocken
Register of parish records, Lanarkshire
Published Sources
Lee, John A. *Children of the Poor*, London, 1934
Lee, John A. *The John A. Lee Diaries 1936–1940*, Christchurch, 1981
Olssen, Erik. *John A. Lee*, Dunedin, 1977.

LITTLE PAPANUI WOMAN

c. 1600

She was born in about the sixteenth or seventeenth century AD, locality unknown, tribal affiliation uncertain, died aged approximately thirty-five years, and was buried at the mouth of a small creek at the south end of Little Papanui Beach, Otago Peninsula. Her place of burial was within a small village or camp occupied periodically from about the twelfth or thirteenth century AD to possibly the eighteenth century. Because of the prevalence of artifacts in the various levels, this site was dug over extensively by curio collectors from the 1920s–50s. More organised excavations took place there from 1929–32 but the methods of the time did not do justice to the structural remains or stratigraphy. However, we know the details of her discovery by H. D. Skinner and Roger Duff on 6 September 1932; she was named Skeleton No.3. Many years later, H. D. Skinner (1960) and D. R. Simmons (1967) attempted to collate the surviving records from this site.

As an adult she had been 161 cm tall (about 5' 3½") and had given birth to only one child. Most prehistoric Maori women had three or four. Her spine shows surprisingly little degeneration for someone in their fourth decade, and this probably means that she did not have to work too hard.

Little Papanui was clearly a popular place to live because of its freshwater creek, coastal forest providing shelter and timber, and excellent food supplies. Yellow-eyed penguins and seagulls had rookeries at the northern end of the beach, and fur seals still haul out on the rocks at the foot of the high cliffs which protect the beach from southerly storms. Paua and mussels were available from intertidal rocks. The food refuse dumps within the site also contained many fish bones along with the broken bait hooks and lure points used to catch them. As well as the numerous seal bones, there were remains of birds (including albatross) and dogs. Because this woman lived too far south for tropical crops such as kumara to succeed, much of her energy needs would have been met by eating the oily flesh of marine creatures, supplemented with the beaten roots of the bracken fern and cooked cabbage tree roots. In summer her daily activities would have seen food preservation added to the tasks of collecting firewood, preparing food, weaving, and child-care.

The village in which she lived consisted of a tight cluster of small huts, each with a fireplace outlined by four stones. The floors of the huts and the ground between them served as workshops where red ochre was ground into powder and bones, ranging in size from whale to bird, were cut and fashioned into ear and neck pendants, tattooing chisels, hair combs, awls, needles, fish-hooks, and bird spears. Broken stone tools were discarded on the surface; the materials of which they were made provided evidence that this woman's group were able to obtain greenstone (for adzes and chisels) from as far away as the West Coast and obsidian (for flake tools) from the North Island.

Some of the ochre prepared at this village was used in their burial ceremonies. It was customary here to truss the bodies tightly and bury them in small graves with the head facing north. One of the eight people found here had been reburied with the skull painted red with ochre. This woman was buried without any apparent grave goods. *Helen Leach & Philip Houghton*

Published Sources

Simmons, D. R. 'Little Papanui and Otago Prehistory', *Records of the Otago Museum: Anthropology*, no.4, 1967

Skinner, H. D. 'Excavation at Little Papanui, Otago Peninsula', *Journal of the Polynesian Society*, vol.69 no.3, 1960, pp.187-98

JOHANNE LOHSE

1839-1910

Anyone can teach clever girls, but I like to help lame dogs over stiles, that is the real test of a teacher's power.

Johanne Lohse came to Canterbury in 1873 with the purpose of starting a school where she could carry out her advanced views on the education of girls.

Born on 12 May 1839 in Oldenburg, Germany, the eldest of sixteen children and for many years the only girl, Johanne had many household responsibilities from a young age. She was allowed to go to school, but was never a brilliant pupil, progressing by sheer hard work. Family demands meant her school work often suffered, and after leaving school in 1854 she spent the next four years at home. She eventually won her father's unwilling consent to train as a teacher, and went to Lausanne to study for her teacher's certificate. During these years she received no financial support from her family, and lived off her own savings.

Johanne went to England briefly as a governess, and in 1868 she returned to teach at a large girls' school, Culcheth New Hall of Bowden, Cheshire. She took this position on condition that she could live out of the house, have one day a week to herself, and take private pupils in her leisure time. Between 1869 and 1873, she worked from 6 am to midnight each day to gain enough money to start her own school. She wrote:

Show me a school which I can take over and in which I can work faithfully and honestly, without the constant dread that pupils may fail me, that I may get worsted by the keen, the unscrupulous competition. Show me a place where pupils will come to me without my having to beg for them; I will go to that place and establish a school of my own, even if it were at the uttermost ends of the earth.

Hearing that there was an opening for a superior private school in Christchurch, Johanne left for New Zealand in 1873. At the time she arrived, girls were taught either by governesses or at schools run by women, often without teaching qualifications, who took in a few pupils to support themselves. The other girls' school of standing in Christchurch at that time was run by Mrs Crosby, also from Germany.

With her savings of £1,000, Johanne bought land at Riccarton in Christchurch and built a house called 'Matlock Bank'. While the house was being built, she rented a farmhouse nearby and started her school in 1874 with five boarders and fourteen day pupils. Here she was free to teach girls as she wanted.

She advocated that every human being should have the right to an education suited to their capacities and condition in life and considered there were grave disproportions between the education of girls and boys. Girls were sent to school too late and taken away too early. She thought that girls should have a thorough knowledge of English language and literature, a good prose style, the art of reading, practical skill in arithmetic, insight into history, geography, and languages, including Latin, and have clear handwriting. They should also be taught drawing, music, and needlework. In addition to scholastic abilities she wrote:

My one object was to train good, faithful, conscientious workers to impart true knowledge and with it that love for all that is great and beautiful, which raises man [woman] above himself amidst the struggles and sorrows of life. This object was seldom understood. Too many parents wanted style, amusements, trivial accomplishments and what not.

It was important, she wrote, that teachers were qualified, but they should also have zeal, self-denial, conscientiousness, the power of imparting knowledge, good manners, refinement, and general culture.

These views were expressed in her book *Mistaken Views on the Education of Girls*, which was published in 1884, and reprinted the next year. Despite these beliefs about the importance and quality of girls' education, she also believed that women should not put intellectual development before the simple duties of life on which the happiness of every family depends.

When the school moved to 'Matlock Bank' the roll rapidly increased. Johanne had trouble getting trained teachers and also servants. She would rise early to do the housework before school began, teach all day, and stay up late to correct exercise books. She was also Examiner in Modern Languages for Canterbury University College, and gave advice and assistance to Christchurch Girls' High School, which opened in 1878.

She was an active, energetic woman who enjoyed the relative freedom from convention of colonial life. Miss Lohse on her chestnut mare was one of the familiar sights of the neighbourhood, and she was fond of telling how on one occasion she rode home carrying a broomstick. She was naturalised in 1875.

As a boarding establishment, 'Matlock Bank' was always vulnerable to the fluctuating price of wool: the first economy a father made when there was a downturn in the market was to take his daughters away from school. And it was also too far away from the centre of town for day-pupils. In 1880 Johanne purchased a house in Armagh Street near Cranmer Square and called it 'Oldenburg House'. The school moved into town, and the roll increased as well as the teaching staff. She had problems with her eyelids and, after an unsuccessful operation in Christchurch, went to Europe in 1882 for advice, returning the next year. Her health worsened, and increasingly the responsibility fell on her assistant, Miss Katherine Wilson. In 1890 she sold the school to Mrs Annette Bowen, and it later became the foundation of St Margaret's College.

Johanne Lohse. *Canterbury Museum*

She returned to Europe and travelled for two years before settling in Florence. She still kept in touch with her pupils from New Zealand. She had a great influence on the girls she taught and, although a strict disciplinarian, was loved by many. She died in Florence on 25 August 1910. In her will, she bequeathed the greater part of her estate for the foundation of scholarships (still in existence) to help the daughters of clergymen to continue their studies.

Jo-Anne Smith

Quotations
para.1 K. W., *Miss Lohse*, p.25
para.4 *ALB School Magazine*, 24 May 1902, p.5
para.7 *ALB School Magazine*, p.6

Unpublished Sources
G. R. MacDonald Biographies, Canterbury Museum
Jane Waymouth, 'A Study of Individualism: the Development of Private Educational Enterprise in Christchurch 1859–1948', MA thesis, Canterbury, 1948

Published Sources
ALB [Annette Laura Bowen] *School Magazine*, 24 May 1902 (Canterbury Museum)
Lohse, Johanne. *Mistaken Views on the Education of Girls*, 2nd edn, Christchurch, 1885
Lyttelton Times, 19 Oct. 1890
K. W. [Katherine Wilson]. *Miss Lohse: A Memoir by Her Friend*, London, 1911

IDA LOUGH

1903–1985

Weaver Ida Lough found her major vocation late in life. Born Ida Mary Withers, the daughter of Elizabeth (born Robins) and John Withers, a draughtsman, she grew up in Duvauchelle on Banks Peninsula and received her secondary education at Christchurch Girls' High School. She initially imagined she would have a career in literature, and wrote and published both children's books and poetry.

Her poem 'Questionings' appeared in the 1930 anthology of New Zealand verse, *Kowhai Gold*.

A lifelong admiration of things French took her to France in the early 1930s. She spent three years there working as a governess and acquiring proficiency in the language. It was while in Paris that she first saw and admired the *Mille Fleurs* tapestries in the Cluny Museum: 'Ignorant New Zealander that I was, I had no idea they were woven. I did know that they were the most beautiful things I had ever seen . . .' Many years later Ida Lough was to make an international reputation as a tapestry weaver.

Visiting Scandinavia in 1953, Ida Lough was impressed by the work of contemporary Swedish weavers. She returned to Christchurch determined to learn to weave, though at that time there were few classes, teachers, weaving yarns, and spinning-wheels in the city. Assisted by the occupational therapist at Burwood Hospital and several borrowed books, she eventually mastered the craft. Later, she learned to spin her own yarns and to experiment with dyes made from flowers, leaves, lichen, and fruit.

It was a time when there was a developing interest in crafts in New Zealand and gradually galleries such as New Vision in Auckland and shops such as Several Arts in Christchurch began to open. It was through these outlets, and Ballantynes, that Ida Lough first began to sell her table-mats, cushions, and rugs. Linen, cotton, silk, and wool were all used in her weaving, though she always said that her greatest love was wool from 'the rich fleeces from South Island hills'.

In the early 1960s, she helped establish a weaving room at the Canterbury Sheltered Workshop for the intellectually handicapped and taught there for nearly eleven years. She finally left to devote herself full time to tapestry weaving. From the 1960s her work was shown internationally through exhibitions of the New Zealand Craft Council and at the 1965 Commonwealth Festival in London. For over ten years she exhibited regularly with the Group (a distinguished association of Canterbury artists) in Christchurch and as a guest exhibitor at other New Zealand shows. Her weaving was bought by art galleries, museums, and private collectors both at home and abroad.

By the late 1960s she was producing outstanding work in series such as *Hagley Park*, *Water Grasses*, and *Princess Zalia of Khelima*. Several years later she received a major commission for a tapestry to hang above the altar in a small side chapel in the Cathedral of the Blessed Sacrament in Christchurch. This work (9' by 8') took a year to complete, and is entitled *Earth with Heaven United* (a quotation from the Mass). In 1976 Mrs R. Davis of the Metropolitan Museum of Modern Art in New York commissioned another in the *Water Grasses* series. Ida Lough felt that her life's experience went into what she made. When asked how long a work took, she would often reply: 'all my life'.

A founding member of the New Zealand chapter of the World Craft Council and early member of the Guild of Spinners and Weavers, Ida Lough was the patron of the Christchurch Guild until her death. She always felt a special affinity with other craftspeople and is remembered by many as an outstanding teacher and inspiration. She wrote in her poem 'The Weaver' (1982):

> *He who works with wood or stone, brush or clay or parchment skin,*
> *Gold or silver, jewel, jade – this my brother, sibling, kin.*

> For me the shuttle and the loom, heddle, hank and subtle dye.
> From Time's Beginning to the End, full sister to Arachne, I.

Ida Lough was married in 1947 to John Harold Welsh Lough, who died in Ballantyne's shop fire a few weeks later. *Coral Broadbent*

Quotations
para.2 *NZ Crafts*, Winter 1985
para.3 *The Press*, 21 July 1965
para.7 *The Press*, 14 July 1986

Unpublished Sources
Information was provided by J. Lough (stepson), Vivienne Mountford, and Rona Tovey (cousin), all of Christchurch

Published Sources
NZ Crafts (NZ Crafts Council Magazine), no.14, Winter 1985
The Press, 21 July 1965; 6 Dec. 1968; 14 Nov. 1969; 21 Jan. 1970; 16 Feb. 1976; 5 Dec. 1984; 21 Aug. 1985 (obituary); 14 July 1986

MOLLY MACALISTER

1920-1979

The sculptures of Molly Macalister can be seen in a number of public places in different parts of New Zealand. In these works she combined to an unusual degree sculptural excellence with general popularity. She was also able to endow smaller works with monumental presence and calm. Her sculptures are principally of human figures, heads, and animals, in attitudes of stillness and repose.

Molly Morell Macalister was born on 18 May 1920 at Invercargill. She studied with Francis Shurrock at the Canterbury College School of Art from 1938 to 1940, then became a land-girl on her uncle's Southland farm before going to work at the Otago Museum. There she made models of animals for agricultural displays, and researched, designed, and painted a diorama of the kakapo.

In 1943 she moved to Auckland where she met George Haydn, who had left Hungary in 1939. They were married in 1945; Molly's wedding present to her husband was a jarrah head of a Maori woman she had carved around 1941 – it is regarded as one of the strongest works in New Zealand sculpture of that time. Molly and her husband built a house in Takapuna and their son John was born in 1947. Molly exhibited work regularly in the Auckland Society of Arts' annual exhibitions from 1944 onwards.

In 1952 she entered an international competition for a sculpture of the *Unknown Political Prisoner*, organised by the Institute of Contemporary Arts in London. Her maquette was selected as the New Zealand entry and was exhibited at the Tate Gallery in 1953. It showed a standing figure with hands clasped above the head. Macalister continued to concentrate on the human figure as her subject, and exhibited seven works in the 1955 exhibition of contemporary New Zealand sculpture at the Auckland City Art Gallery.

Durable material for sculpture has always been a problem in New Zealand, where there is no marble suitable for carving and bronze is an expensive medium requiring the rare skills of a foundryman for casting. Most of Macalister's works in the 1955 exhibition were in wood or plaster, but she also showed a small bronze piece, *Birds*, and a kneeling figure of a man titled *Concrete figure for bronze*. Macalister had begun to experiment with concrete but still saw it as a second-best material.

New developments in her sculpture were precipitated by the arrival in New Zealand in 1957 of Ann Severs, an English sculptor who had worked in Italy with Marino Marini. The two women became friends and practised life drawing together. In July 1959 Macalister and Severs had a joint sculpture exhibition at the Auckland City Art Gallery with Alison Duff, who had returned to New Zealand from Australia. This exhibition marked the beginning of a new flowering of sculpture in Auckland.

Molly Macalister, sculptor, c.1947. *Auckland City Art Gallery*

The three women sculptors all began using concrete as a final material with intrinsic qualities and merits – no longer an interim stage on the way to possible bronze casting. Concrete had none of the preciousness or academic history of bronze – it was tough and modern. The concrete was both built up over steel armatures and cast from a plaster model. The women had to invent their own techniques and experimented with mixing and colouring the concrete. The resulting works were vigorously modelled and physically strong, and Macalister's figures became more compact and solidly grounded. Critical response was enthusiastic, and Macalister showed other concrete sculptures at successive contemporary exhibitions at the Auckland City Art Gallery in 1960 and 1962. One of these was *Bird Watcher*, a figure of a woman. Colin McCahon later wrote:

Molly gave us our Bird Watcher *who sits in the garden and watches birds on our grapefruit tree and a privet. She never looks down. She is a calm and detached figure who watches beyond the birds and the trees to something even more rewarding. It could be the sunset or rainbows lacing a passing storm or the world of clouds that hang heavily in the Auckland sky most times – a feeling of peace.*

Macalister first left New Zealand in 1962. She travelled with her husband to America, France, Germany, Hungary, and Italy, widening her experience of both current and historical sculptural practice. After her return to Auckland she began to receive commissions for public sculptures and these occupied much of her time over the next decade. She was also generous in her support of other artists, and a driving force behind organisations such as the New Zealand Society of Sculptors and Painters (established in 1961), and the 1971 International Sculpture Symposium in Auckland.

In February 1964 the Auckland City Council commissioned Molly Macalister to make a large sculpture of a Maori chief to stand at the bottom of Queen Street. She consulted with Ngati Whatua at Orakei and gained their support for the work. After a year of working on small models, Macalister began making the final plaster model which was built over reinforced steel in a plastic tent in her garden. The three-metre-high figure was then cast in bronze and was finally unveiled on 2 July 1967. *Maori Figure* is an imposing work, now a familiar and well-loved part of Queen Elizabeth Square.

In 1967 Macalister won a competition for a bronze sculpture to go in the Hamilton Gardens. In *Little Bull* she created a work that appeals to adults as sculpture and to children as something to play on. Other commissions included a head of John A. Lee for the Auckland Public Library; stone relief carvings representing the twelve tribes of Israel on the Ark in the new Auckland Synagogue; an untitled bronze for the State Insurance Company in Auckland; a work for the foyer of BP House in Wellington, and another for the crematorium in Schnapper Rock Road, Auckland. In these last two works she cast small shard-like fragments in bronze and assembled them on steel wires to form floating and shimmering arrangements of shapes in space. They marked an alteration in her work and were perhaps a response to changing ideas in contemporary sculpture. In her last works, however, Macalister returned to solid simplified forms made from the hard volcanic basalt of the Takapuna reef. They included a figure of the Buddha, a sheep, a bird, and a fish – small, self-contained and serene.

Molly Macalister died on 12 October 1979. Hamish Keith wrote: 'For twenty years Macalister has been a constant presence in New Zealand sculpture. She will be badly missed.'

Alexa M. Johnston

Quotations
para.7 C. McCahon, 'Molly Macalister: 1920–1979', p.26
para.11 H. Keith, 'Death of a Pioneer', p.25

Published Sources
Auckland City Art Gallery. *Molly Macalister: A Memorial Exhibition*, Auckland, 1982
Keith, Hamish. 'Death of a Pioneer', *NZ Listener*, 10 Nov. 1979, pp.24–5
McCahon, Colin. 'Molly Macalister: 1920–1979', *Art New Zealand* 14, pp.26–7
Tomory, Peter. 'New Zealand Sculpture', *Art and Australia*, Sept. 1965, pp.108–13

PHYLLIS McDONALD

1923–1984

When Phyllis McDonald was honoured with a fellowship of the New Zealand Library Association (NZLA) in 1981, the citation read:

For her contribution to the development of library services to children and teachers, for her participation in the N.Z.L.A. committees concerned with furthering school librarianship and for her leadership in promoting and extending National Library service to schools.

Phyllis Lockwood Jones was born in Gisborne in 1923. She qualified for her Teachers' Certificate in 1945, her Bachelor of Arts degree in 1946, and her Diploma of the New Zealand Library School in 1948. These two strands of expertise, in teaching and librarianship, were reflected throughout her working life.

She had two short spells in public libraries, at Auckland (before library school) and New Plymouth (from 1949 to 1954). In 1954 she married Walter McDonald and moved with her husband to Dunedin, where Phyllis worked for a year as head of children's services. She left the library to raise her two children, who were brought up with fond but not suffocating affection amidst some difficult times as Phyllis nursed her husband through his final illness.

She returned to the paid work force in 1963, joining the Dunedin office of the National Library's School Library Service. She transferred to the Wellington office in 1966, until Dunedin once more lured her back to be librarian of the teachers' college from 1969 to 1975. This variety of experience was to prove invaluable when she was appointed to be the head of the School Library Service in Wellington in 1975, a position she held until her retirement in 1983, first as an assistant-director and from 1979 as director.

This period of Phyllis McDonald's work was one of dual activity: the re-organisation of the service to cope with decreasing government funding and the staff reductions which resulted; and continued concern for the future of school libraries around the country, which included pressuring the government to employ trained teacher-librarians in state schools.

Phyllis was a skilled and innovative administrator, who regularly analysed methods, reviewed programmes, and reappraised goals and priorities. Never a respecter of 'sacred cows', she was adept at demolishing systems which had out-lived their relevance. Despite the fact that her staff was scattered from Auckland to Invercargill, she made every endeavour to canvass staff opinions widely and persuade the reluctant that change was beneficial.

She also ventured into new areas, such as support for children's services in public libraries; the establishment in 1979 of the Dorothy Neal White Collection of children's literature within the National Library; and the publication of the *School Library Bulletin* to review and advise on books and other materials for school libraries.

Outside the service too, Phyllis McDonald was an active campaigner for school libraries and for the education of teacher-librarians. In Dunedin and later in Wellington, she served on the local committee of the NZLA, and in 1975 on the association's national committee for the survey of library service to children and young people. In 1981 she was convenor of the School Library Action Group, set up to counter the government's failure to implement the recommend-ations of two major reports with which Phyllis had been involved: that of Sara Fenwick in 1975 for the NZLA, and the Foley Report, published in 1978 by the Department of Education's Working Party on School Libraries, of which Phyllis was a member.

Joint use school/community libraries also received her attention, although she was not hopeful of the co-operation such ventures would require. Writing in *New Zealand Libraries* in 1977, she expressed her hopes and misgivings:

For years the school has been isolated from its community . . . education cannot be regarded as 'schooling' but a function involving the total community . . . [But] New Zealand has special problems – lack of qualified staff working full time . . . different approaches by local authorities and central government to funding.

Such concerns were to feature in Phyllis's writing in *New Zealand Libraries*, and in her contribution to *Recent Advances in School Librarianship*, published in 1981.

Those who worked with Phyllis have warm personal memories of her: of staff parties in her home with her culinary skills in evidence; and of a placard-carrying Phyllis picketing in the rain the concrete-lined pit in Molesworth Street, Wellington, which one clever character had christened the Notional Library of New Zealand. The protest was directed at parliamentarians across the road, sug-gesting resumption of activity on the long-delayed National Library building.

These final energies were set against a very brave battle with cancer, from which she died in 1984.

Mary Ronnie

Quotations
para.1 Quoted in *School Library Review*, vol.3 no.4, 1983, p.2
para.9 P. McDonald, 'School/Community Libraries', *NZ Libraries*, vol.40 no.3, 1977, pp.51–5
Published Sources
Chandler, E. (ed.) *Recent Advances in Library and Information Services*, vol.1, New York, 1981, pp.187–94
NZ Libraries, vol.39 no.6, Dec. 1976, pp.206–10; vol.44 no.6, June 1984, p.114 (obituary)
Proceedings of the Library Assn. of Australia Conference, 1981, pp.381–9

MURIEL McINTOSH

1907–1989

Muriel McIntosh, artist, craftswoman and teacher, devoted a lifetime to the arts. The product of a New Zealand technical school education, she passed on her skills to generations of students.

Born in Wellington, Muriel Bernice Carter came from a family with craft skills. Her father, Herbert Carter, was established in trade as a book finisher and her great-grandfather, Edward Carter of Merton Abbey, Surrey, had been involved in the textile industry.

Muriel attended Wellington Technical School as a full-time art student from 1922 to 1926, studying under Linely Richardson, who was known to give his students sound academic training. Subjects taught included:

Drawing – Painting from the Living model – and the Antique, Poster Design, Book Illustration, Landscape, Painting and Still Life, Animal Drawing, Etching in Copper & Drawing for Lithography.

Nelson Isaac was head of the art school at the college and provided his students with firsthand knowledge of developments in the arts. He taught his students the principles of the arts and crafts movement, of which he was an exponent. Muriel's work was of such a high standard that it was included for exhibition at Wembley and Dunedin (probably the British Empire Exhibition in London in 1924, and the New Zealand and South Seas Exhibition of 1925–6). She exhibited metalwork in the New Zealand Academy of Fine Arts/First Arts and Crafts Exhibition in Wellington in 1934. She later assisted Frederick Coventry in the execution of four murals for the New Zealand Centennial Exhibition of 1939–40; these were considered to be the first large-scale murals undertaken in New Zealand.

After leaving Wellington Technical College, Muriel taught art and craft at schools in Hamilton and later at Samuel Marsden Collegiate School in Wellington, from 1942 to 1971. Her marriage to Graham McIntosh in 1932 caused her to be known by pupils as 'Mrs Mac'. She had two children, Ranald and Berenice.

Among the subjects Muriel taught were copperware, pottery, spinning, screen-printing, and embroidery. Her daughter, a pupil at Marsden, described Muriel's time there as being

a wonderful outlet for the seemingly endless energy, drive and ability to impart her skills to at least two generations of pupils. There was always a searching for new crafts, new ideas and constant updating. Each year brought exciting happenings to the Art Department.

Following her retirement from Samuel Marsden Collegiate School, Muriel continued with her craft work while remaining in touch with past school pupils and fellow staff members. She died in Auckland in 1989.   *Justine Olsen*

Quotations
para.3 L. Richardson's reference for Muriel Carter, 19 April 1926, McIntosh Papers

para.6 From reminiscences of Muriel McIntosh by her daughter, Berenice Veldhoen, McIntosh Papers

Unpublished Sources

McIntosh Papers, Index of NZ Craftspeople, Designers and Manufacturers, AIM

Published Sources

Brown, Gordon H. and Keith, Hamish. *An Introduction to New Zealand Art 1839–1967*, Auckland, 1969

Manawatu Art Gallery. *Harry Linely Richardson 1878–1947: painter, designer, illustrator and teacher*, Palmerston North, 1986

Murray, Tosti. *Marsden: The History of a New Zealand School for Girls*, Wellington, 1967

New Zealand Art: A Centennial Exhibition (catalogue), Wellington, 1940

Te Kura (Samuel Marsden Collegiate School magazine), Nov. 1972

JESSIE MACKAY

1864–1938

Jessie Mackay, the eldest surviving of the nine children of Elizabeth and Robert Mackay, was born at Rakaia Gorge, Canterbury, on 15 December 1864. Her Scottish parents had arrived in New Zealand the previous year. Robert Mackay, who managed successfully the Double Hill, Raincliff, and Opuha Gorge sheep runs, was a liberal with keenly humanitarian views and a fierce pride in his Scottish heritage; he had a strong influence on the character and ideas of his daughter. Jessie received her early education at home and was encouraged to read widely. Formal schooling began at the Normal School in Christchurch in 1879, followed by teacher training. She taught until 1898 when, after the death of her mother, the family home broke up and she went to Dunedin to become a professional journalist. In 1902 she was back in Christchurch teaching 'classes for ladies' at Inveresk School for two years. From 1911 she lived with her sister Georgina in a cottage at New Brighton until 1918 when they moved to a home on the Cashmere Hills.

Jessie Mackay was widely acclaimed in her lifetime as New Zealand's leading poet and was known outside this country. With William Pember Reeves she is recognised as producing 'the first clear signs of national self-awareness' in this country's literature. Her first volume of poetry, *The Spirit of the Rangatira and Other Ballads* (1889), was prefaced with the hope for 'the dawning of a national spirit' – that 'at least a few of the verses might have a flavour of the colonial soil from which they had sprung'. Six other volumes followed, the last, *Vigil and other Poems*, published in 1935. E. H. McCormick writes of Jessie Mackay as 'an inveterate romantic' whose 'allegiance was uneasily divided between the world of her parents and her immediate environment'. Her poems with a New Zealand setting, some of which are based on Maori legend, are interspersed with poems ranging through history and her own Scottish heritage. *Land of the Morning* (1909) contains some of her best work, including 'The Burial of Sir John McKenzie'. This lament for the champion of closer land settlement in New Zealand is inspired by the evictions of Scottish crofters.

While at school in Christchurch Jessie had attended bible classes held at Trinity Congregational Church led by Kate Sheppard, whom she greatly admired. She became an enthusiastic member of the Women's Christian Temperance Union, and in 1890 was actively involved in soliciting signatures for a petition on women's suffrage for presentation to parliament. Her second volume of verse, *The Sitter on the Rail* (1891), reflects the political situation in New Zealand and her activities in this field. In 1896 she was present at the inaugural meeting of the National Council of Women. At its 1905 conference she moved:

That all disabilities be removed which hinder women from sitting as members in either House of the Legislature, and from being elected or appointed to any public office or position in the Colony . . . and with regard to all positions, powers, duties and privileges of citizens to declare absolute equality as the law of the land for both men and women.

In 1900 she wrote for the *Otago Witness* the first of the fortnightly articles that were to continue over the next thirty years. From 1906 she was the editor of the ladies' page of the *Canterbury Times* as well as a regular contributor to the *Lyttelton Times* and the Christchurch *Press*. Her 'vigorous, trenchant articles' were written in support of prohibition, equal pay for women, women police, penal reform, a welfare state, internationalism, and vegetarianism, and against vivisection, bloodsports and an attempt to make domestic science a compulsory subject for girls for matriculation. She acted as New Zealand correspondent for *Votes for Women* and as assistant editor of *The White Ribbon*.

A defender of the rights of oppressed nations or minorities, Jessie argued for Irish and Scottish home rule. As early as the 1870s she had a youthful hero-worship of Charles Stewart Parnell, leader of the struggle for home rule in Ireland. In a series of articles published in the *Otago Witness* in 1903, she portrayed Ireland as 'The Woman of Nations', oppressed for centuries, as women had been. She saw the solution to international conflict in the play of a 'feminized intelligence', and declared in 1917 that: 'These events have kindled a flame of internationalism in women that will make wars for ever impossible – When the mother speaks in the councils of the nations these evil things will cease.' Sent as one of three New Zealand delegates to the Gael Race Conference in Paris in 1921, she met W. B. Yeats, Eamon de Valera, and (in England) Millicent Fawcett. Irish fanaticism affected her sympathy for the cause but she remained an ardent Scottish nationalist and a feminist: 'How willingly would I give up my little bit of fame if my causes might prosper.'

The first New Zealand woman poet to achieve fame at home and abroad, Jessie Mackay was a tall wraith-like woman with 'intense eyes, low toned speech and a slow smile'. She was an idealist and a romantic, a humanitarian with a deep sympathy for the oppressed. An illuminated letter in celebration of her birthday in 1934 voiced the gratitude of many New Zealand thinkers and reformers, who acknowledged their debt to 'the vision of the artist'. In 1936 she was awarded a civil list pension, and following her death in Christchurch on 23 August 1938, the New Zealand Centre of PEN established the Jessie Mackay Memorial Award for Verse as a tribute.   *Aorewa McLeod & June Starke*

Quotations
para.2 E. H. McCormick, *Letters and Art in New Zealand*, Wellington, 1940, pp.108–9
para.3 Quoted in N. F. H. McLeod, *A Voice on the Wind*, p.52

para.4 G. H. Scholefield (ed.) *A Dictionary of New Zealand Biography*, vol.2, Wellington, 1940, p.21

para.5 Quoted in N. F. H. McLeod, p.59

para.6 A. H. McLintock (ed.) *An Encyclopedia of New Zealand*, vol.2, Wellington, 1966, p.362

Published Sources

Lawlor, P. A. *Books and Bookmen*, Wellington, 1954

McLeod, N. F. H. *A Voice on the Wind: The Story of Jessie Mackay*, Wellington, 1955

Mulgan, A. 'Jessie Mackay, Poet and Crusader', *Evening Post*, 3 Sept. 1938 (obituary)

FLORA McKENZIE

1902–1982

Flora McKenzie was born in August 1902, the daughter of Sir Hugh McKenzie, long-time chairman of the Auckland Harbour Board. She grew up in prestigious circles, entertaining close friends of royalty and United States presidential figures. In 1927 Flora and her widowed father entertained the Duke and Duchess of York on Sir Hugh's launch on the Waitemata Harbour.

She qualified as a nurse, and was also a fine dressmaker, running a shop in Vulcan Lane which specialised in bridal gowns and, rumour has it, was patronised by an up-market clientele. Flora's notoriety, however, derived from her involvement in a business venture of a different nature.

For many years she ran an establishment in Ring Terrace, Ponsonby, which became the most famous brothel in Auckland. Her involvement in the prostitution industry seems to have begun more by accident than design – it is said that her father bought her a block of flats which she owned for six months before realising what they were used for. This was during the Second World War and

Flora McKenzie, well known in Auckland as the proprietor of an 'exclusive club' in Ring Terrace, Ponsonby. *News Media*

her female tenants were described as 'good time girls', in the business of entertaining American GIs.

Flora gradually drifted into the role of madam and developed a regular clientele. Her establishment has been described by one former member of the vice squad as being more like an exclusive club than a brothel, and Flora herself apparently never liked the word 'brothel' or 'prostitute'. 'Isn't every woman a prostitute?', she is quoted as saying. 'Married men pay their wives, don't they?' Instead, she preferred to describe her business as offering 'sex therapy'.

She ran the place in a very orderly manner, demanding good behaviour from both her 'girls' and the clients alike. While drinking was encouraged, narcotics were not, and Flora prided herself on running an establishment free from thefts and rip-offs. Her girls saw clients by appointment only, and all money was handed first to Flora who removed her commission before passing the rest on. The women she employed were characteristically sophisticated and well presented; they included teachers, nurses, and secretaries who worked there on a part-time basis. The clientele included leading figures from city and political life.

Between the years 1962 and 1976, Flora appeared in court six times on charges of keeping a brothel and was twice imprisoned for six months. She became a familiar face to Auckland's vice squad detectives, who reputedly held their Christmas parties on her premises. One of them, Alec Leyland, established a working relationship with Flora that lasted for nearly twenty-five years. It began in 1957 when Flora's neighbour, a woman justice of the peace, complained to the police that Flora had accused her of killing her Pekinese dog – Flora had turned up on the doorstep, whirled the dead animal's body around by the tail and, when the door opened, let it fly! Alec Leyland was sent to investigate and over subsequent years spent many hours drinking and swapping yarns with Flora in her antique-laden lounge.

He describes Flora as: 'a flamboyant, happy-go-lucky woman with an outrageous sense of humour who did not care a damn about what the so-called respectable people thought of her.' Their friendship survived the repeated raids on Flora's premises.

The magistrate who sentenced Flora on her last court appearance in 1976 accepted her lawyer's word that she could not be present because she had bronchopneumonia and a congestive heart condition. For that reason, said the magistrate, she was fined the maximum instead of receiving a prison term. When Flora died in 1982, the police were amongst the many who mourned her passing.

Jan Jordan

Quotations
para.4 *Sunday News*, 11 July 1982
para.7 A. Leyland in R. Myles, 'Flora McKenzie', p.13

Unpublished Sources
Interviews with ex-clients, working girls, and police officers

Published Sources
'Flora's Gone', *Sunday News*, 11 July 1982 (obituary)
Myles, Rex. 'Flora McKenzie: Part of Auckland Folklore', *Metro*, Dec. 1982, pp.13–14
'One of Ponsonby's Old Identities', *Auckland Star*, 9 July 1982 (obituary)

MONICA McKENZIE

1905-1988

Monica McKenzie was one of the pioneers of dietetics in New Zealand. She played a major role in the establishment of dietetic training, founded and was first president of the New Zealand Dietetic Association in 1943, and initiated legislation which made New Zealand one of the first countries to give state registration to dietitians. These were important milestones for the dietetic profession; for Monica McKenzie they were part of her campaign to improve the nutritional care of hospital patients.

Monica Beatrice McKenzie was born in Wellington in 1905, the daughter of Alexander and Ida Grace McKenzie (born Kenny), who were both schoolteachers. She was educated at Wellington Girls' College, and then went to the Home Science School, which had been established in 1911, at the University of Otago. She graduated in 1926 with a degree in home science and then taught for some years at Wanganui Girls' College. At the time there were few careers other than teaching open to home science graduates, although some trained as nurses and thus managed to get hospital positions as diet sisters. But there were promises of a new career. As early as 1921, concern about the standard of food service in hospitals had led to tentative plans for a dietitians' training course, but these plans came to nothing. Women who had set their hearts on a career in dietetics had to travel overseas, at their own expense, to get the requisite qualifications. Few of those who returned home found employment as dietitians.

Monica McKenzie changed all that. She had given up teaching to train as a dietitian at the Royal Northern Hospital in London, and in 1938 returned to a position as assistant dietitian, under the diet sister, at Wellington Hospital. The following year she was appointed senior dietitian and she soon built up a well-staffed diet department, the first in New Zealand to come under a dietitian's control. Her work at Wellington Hospital came to the attention of Mary Lambie, the Health Department's director of nursing, who wanted hospital patients to have the kind of nutritional care she had observed in modern hospitals overseas, especially in the United States. Together, Mary Lambie and Monica McKenzie negotiated with the Health Department and with hospital boards to establish four hospital training schools for dietitians, and worked with the Home Science School to develop the curriculum for the new courses.

The first trainees graduated in 1942, and within a few years all the larger hospitals had food service departments run by dietitians. When Monica McKenzie was appointed to the Health Department in 1947 to co-ordinate dietetic services throughout the country, she spent much of her time travelling to give guidance and support to these young dietitians.

Monica McKenzie was determined that dietitians should be given the same statutory recognition as other health professionals. She initiated legislation which resulted in the Dietitians' Act of 1951, giving state registration to dietitians and setting up national standards of training and practice.

By the time she retired in 1963, hospital food services had been revolutionised. The new well-equipped kitchens, which she had helped to plan, together with the many advances in food technology, provided both patients and staff with a much wider choice of food than had been possible in earlier days, when the menu was limited to what could be produced on the premises. Changing old ways had not always been easy, but Monica McKenzie, a quiet, patient, but determined woman, had a talent for getting even the most difficult people on her side and for inspiring confidence. She achieved what she set out to do, without fuss and without ruffling feathers.

Monica McKenzie was a very private person, whose life revolved around her work and her family. She is remembered as a 'gentlewoman' who was always delightful company, even in illness and old age. She died in 1988, at the age of eighty-three.

Flora Davidson

Unpublished Sources
Information was provided by Monica McKenzie's niece, Lesley Ferguson.
NZ Dietetic Association, 'Dietetics in New Zealand: A History', 1968 (cyclostyled)

Published Source
Journal of the NZ Dietetic Association, vol.43 no.1, April 1989 (obituary), pp.43–45

HESTER MACLEAN

1863 – 1932

Born in Sofala, New South Wales, in 1863, Hester Maclean was the daughter of Emily (born Strong) and Harold Maclean, the comptroller-general of prisons. Educated at private schools, she was inspired by the English nurse who cared for her father in his last illness to become a nurse herself. After training for three years at Prince Alfred Hospital in Sydney, she gained her certificate in 1893.

Over the next decade she was matron of a number of hospitals in New South Wales and Victoria, including a large private psychiatric hospital and the Royal Women's Hospital in Melbourne. She was also sister in charge of the District Nursing Associations in both Sydney and Melbourne, an experience she would find useful later in New Zealand.

Hester Maclean travelled to England and trained for her certificate in midwifery, which she obtained in 1905. Returning to district nursing in Sydney, she was soon encouraged by her friend Agnes Bennett in Wellington to apply for the position of assistant inspector of hospitals in Wellington – a position shortly to be vacated by Grace Neill.

Although Hester Maclean brought a wealth of nursing experience to her new position, she lacked Neill's broader social perspective. She was less involved with issues to do with women's welfare generally. 'My chief interest,' she wrote, 'was in the hospitals and especially the training schools for nurses.'

Between 1906 and her retirement in 1923 Maclean saw the foundations laid for the backblocks district nursing scheme, the appointment of native health nurses, the training of young Maori women as nurses to work among their own people, the development of the school nursing service, and the extension of

St Helen's hospitals for the training of midwives. For much of the time she was assisted only by two nursing colleagues, Jessie Bicknell (who was to succeed her) and Amelia Bagley. The Health Department was headed by Dr T. Valintine, with whom Hester Maclean enjoyed an excellent working relationship.

Maclean also held the post of deputy registrar of nurses and midwives, and for many years was the only nurse involved in this work. Registration for nurses was inaugurated in the Nurses Registration Act, 1901, and the Midwives Act, 1904; Hester Maclean was keen to extend registration for nurses, as a means by which their professional status was established and protected. She advocated the formation of a registration board on which nurses could be more adequately represented. Her work bore results; the Nurses and Midwives Registration Act, 1925, passed two years after Maclean's retirement, achieved this reform.

Hester Maclean's approach to nursing training was nevertheless conservative. She was cautious about university training, although she acknowledged the possible value of postgraduate courses for administrators and teachers. But she believed that for 'The nurse who means to devote her life to actual sick nursing the time needed to acquire a university degree would be better spent in gaining experience in the treatment of disease'. She argued vociferously against the introduction of an eight-hour day for nurses, and regarded a day off a week as a desirable but not essential condition of employment. Yet she believed wholeheartedly in the professional status of trained nurses and fought constantly for it.

'To create [the New Zealand Army Nursing Service] and see [it] suddenly develop into a large splendid service . . . was perhaps Miss Maclean's greatest achievement.' For her, it was 'the most interesting though strenuous period I have gone through'. In 1913 she became matron-in-chief of the service, a position she held until her retirement from the Department of Health. She led the first large contingent of nurses overseas in the First World War, aboard the transport ship *Rotorua* in April 1915. She returned six months later, after inspecting the hospitals in which the nurses were stationed, and winning for them the right to do actual nursing, rather than simply supervising male orderlies. 'The war years saw her at her best, her guiding hand at every turn, her forceful personality creating and developing new units and hospital staffs as needed . . .'

In 1907 she proposed the publication of a journal to enable nurses to exchange ideas and keep up to date with new trends both in New Zealand and overseas. 'Coming as I did from Australia, where two nursing papers were flourishing', she wrote, 'I quickly saw the need of some medium of communication in New Zealand.' The first issues of *Kai Tiaki, The Journal of the Nurses of New Zealand* (later the *New Zealand Nursing Journal*) appeared in January 1908, both funded and edited by Maclean. She continued to own and edit the quarterly journal until she retired in 1923, when it was sold to the Registered Nurses Association. 'Many evenings I spent . . . in writing addresses and wrapping journals for despatch', she wrote. She retained the editorship until her death. The journal still flourishes today.

At the time of Hester Maclean's arrival in New Zealand, associations of nurses were forming in the main centres, Wellington being the first. Through the journal and her travels nationwide, Hester Maclean was able to encourage the growing desire of nurses to form a national professional body. When the four

Hester Maclean led the first large contingent of New Zealand nurses to serve overseas. This group is at the Stationary Hospital, 1918. *Alexander Turnbull Library*

associations from Wellington, Auckland, Canterbury, and Dunedin came together to form the New Zealand Trained Nurses Association in 1909, Hester Maclean was elected the first national president, and she maintained an active interest in the association for the rest of her life.

She retired from the Department of Health in 1923. Her autobiography, *Nursing in New Zealand*, was written during her retirement; she continued also her interest in painting and gardening, and enjoyed the independence her own home gave her. Until the end she remained actively involved in the work for nurses and nursing to which she had dedicated her life. She is acknowledged within the nursing profession as one of its most influential and notable pioneers.

Marie Burgess

Quotations
para.4 M. Tennant, *Paupers and Providers*, p.51; H. Maclean, *Nursing in New Zealand* p.42
para.7 H. Maclean, p.106
para.8 *NZ Nursing Journal*, Sept. 1932, p. 197 (obituary); H. Maclean, p.125; *NZ Nursing Journal*, Sept. 1932, p.197
para.9 H. Maclean, p.73

Unpublished Sources
Register of Nurses, Nursing Council of New Zealand, Wellington

Published Sources
Gibson Smith, Margaret, and Shadbolt, Yvonne T. (eds). *Objects and Outcomes: New Zealand Nurses Association 1909–1983*, Wellington, 1984
McLintock, A. H. (ed.). *An Encyclopaedia of New Zealand*, Wellington, 1966, pp.371–2
NZ Nursing Journal (Kai Tiaki), vols.1–49, 1908–56
Tennant, Margaret. *Paupers and Providers: Charitable Aid in New Zealand*, Wellington, 1989

SARAH McMURRAY

1848–1943

Sarah Silcock was born in Nelson, where her father, Captain Simon Bonnet Silcock, had settled in 1842 after several voyages to New Zealand bringing immigrants under the Wakefield scheme. On one of these voyages he fell in love with Susannah, the fourteen-year-old daughter of William and Elizabeth Flower. On his next voyage he left the ship and married Susannah.

Sarah Ann, also known as Sallie, was the second of their fifteen children. In 1872, she, barely five foot tall, married six-foot Robert McMurray. They took up a small farm, 'Thorneycroft', in Nelson. Two years later Robert acquired a section in the Inangahua Valley, fourteen miles from Reefton on the West Coast. Leaving Sarah to manage 'Thorneycroft', he felled thick bush, pit-sawed the timber, and built 'Forest Home'. This took two years. Sarah, taking household goods, two pigs, six fowls, and six ducks, set out by sailing ship for Westport. They trekked for fifty miles up a narrow bush track following the turbulent Buller River, sometimes on horseback, sometimes on the punt carrying all their goods and stock.

At the farm Sarah saw no other woman for months. She wrote in early February 1875:

Dear Mother . . . We have such a nice place here, so quiet and comfortable . . . I have been here six months next Sunday and have only been away once . . . I began to think that you had all quite forgotten there were such people as us in the world.

As she wrote, her mother was ill and dying. On 15 February, Sarah's first child arrived two months prematurely. Alarmed, Robert galloped six miles to the nearest woman neighbour for help. She demurred, having no experience in such matters. He picked her up, put her on the horse, mounted, and they galloped, desperately anxious, back to 'Forest Home'. The baby survived. Three days later Sarah was up tending to her child and making dinner for her hard-working husband.

Three of their six children were born in their ten years' stay in the Inangahua Valley. Sarah made butter, cheese, camp-oven bread, candles, furniture, toys, hand-sewn clothes, even shoes. It rained nearly every day – drying the washing was an endless chore. Sarah made high clothes-horses which stood around the big open fireplace where logs burned continuously. She schooled the children and taught them music. In the 1880s the McMurrays moved to the North Island, first to a farm at Awahuri, near Feilding, and then to Wanganui. With her family growing up and no farmwork, Sarah found time on her hands. She enrolled at the technical school to develop her woodcarving skills. Beautifully carved mantelpieces and architraves began to adorn their Wanganui home. In 1914 Robert and Sarah retired to Palmerston North. In a shed in the garden she continued her woodcarving. Her output was prolific; working mainly in kauri, she carved wardrobe doors and panels, chairs, wash-basin stands, piano-stools, glory-boxes for her granddaughters, and large mirror and picture frames.

She created her own designs, meticulously charted on graph paper. They included grapes, trailing vine leaves, acorns and oak leaves, native raupo and flax, nasturtiums, daisies, and irises – all expressions of the wonder of life as she found it. For children she fashioned animals and toys – a kilted Scotsman who danced a highland fling was a favourite. She also excelled in needlework, making twenty-three large patchwork quilts, finely feather-stitched in varied materials and colours. These contrasted with the fine tapestries and pillow lace she also made. She won many prizes for her craftwork at agricultural shows over the years.

Sarah McMurray took up woodcarving when she 'retired' from raising six children and farming. *Phyllis Orwin*

In her later years, Sarah's daughter Minnie was her companion and helper. She died at ninety-five years of age.

Her life in early New Zealand was total dedication to family and to survival in the harsh conditions of the 'Coast'. She had great inner strength from her spiritual conviction to endure the challenges of everyday life. She was a great lady – so small – so serene. Sarah's motto was: 'A merry heart goeth all the day.'

P. M. Orwin

Quotations
para.3 S. McMurray, letter to her mother, Feb. 1875, in private possession
para.7 Valerie Ryan (Sarah McMurray's granddaughter), letter to author, 30 Jan. 1989, in private possession

Unpublished Sources
Information and written reports were provided by family members. The author is a granddaughter of
Sarah McMurray.

Published Sources
'Grand Old Lady of 95 Passes', *Manawatu Daily Times*, 23 Sept. 1943 (obituary)
'92 and Still Going Strong. A Pioneer with Many Accomplishments', *Manawatu Evening Standard*, 26
May 1940
The Summer Book 2: A New Zealand Miscellany, Wellington, 1983, p.108
'Talented Age! Lady Who Chisels her Home with Beauty', *Manawatu Daily Times*, 16 Sept. 1935

MARGARET MACPHERSON

1895–1974

Margaret Louisa Macpherson, pacifist, socialist, feminist, and writer, arrived in New Zealand at the beginning of the First World War. She was born in Leeds, and educated at a Quaker school and St Andrew's University in Scotland. Married to Alfred Sinclair Macpherson, she had six sons.

She was a socialist before she arrived, and already active in the suffrage movement in Britain. She described herself as 'a disciple of Marx, even though my friends do cruelly assert that they are never sure *which* Marx it is, Karl or Harpo'. She believed that women's emancipation could only come through socialism, but was sceptical about the Labour Party in its early years in New Zealand, believing that 'labour in power never brings in socialism'. However, after the experience of the first Labour government in the 1930s she revised her opinion, impressed by the achievements of the welfare state.

From 1916 to 1922 Margaret Macpherson compiled the women's column in the *Maoriland Worker* (the weekly paper of the Labour movement) under the pen-name of 'Wahine'. During the early years the column was primarily devoted to issues arising out of the war. Macpherson was strongly opposed to war, and published frequent articles on anti-militarism and pacifism. She also drew attention to the dramatically rising cost of living, and the effects of this upon women trying to manage their households on low wages. A large part of the column consisted of cheap recipes, such as 'Half Pay Pudding'. After the war, the column devoted more space to issues arising out of women's employment, such as equal pay for equal work and the difficulties faced by teachers and nurses. Organisations such as the Women's Christian Temperance Union (WCTU) and the Women's International League regularly published reports of meetings. However, the content of the column was challenged by Jean Devanny in 1919 and a spirited debate followed over the relevance to working-class women of WCTU reports. A later article on the issue of birth control also aroused controversy, following which many women wrote to 'Wahine' asking where they could obtain the books by Marie Stopes.

In the early 1920s, while living in Kaitaia, Margaret Macpherson edited *The Northlander* (a weekly newspaper of progressive leanings). She found attitudes towards women in the north very conservative.

Oh, how we shocked them, Colonel Bell and I, and our little party of progressives! When the infant town needed a sanitary system, they thought that the lady editor who could bring herself to mention so indelicate a subject was certainly no lady.

Robin Hyde described Margaret Macpherson at this time as the 'tam-o'-shanter lady', and recounted an occasion when an advertiser took umbrage at an editorial by Macpherson and withdrew his large advertisement:

Margaret made the space more prominent still. She left it 'blank as Death' save for a neat little caption explaining that Mr So-and-So's advertising had been withdrawn, and for what reason! Personally, I think the idea was funny, even if not profitable.

Margaret Macpherson evidently felt deprived of customary cultural pursuits in New Zealand. She told George Bernard Shaw, whom she interviewed when he visited New Zealand in 1934, that there was no art, drama, music or culture in New Zealand, although it was 'a dear country, fresh and wholesome and free'. Shaw, she recorded, rebuked her and told her to do a New Zealand journey and write about it. This she did, and her travels provided the material for much of her subsequent writing about the country. Her six published books tend to be idiosyncratic accounts of individuals she met and stories she heard along the way. With the exception of the account of her meeting with Te Puea, the books ultimately reveal little that was distinctive about New Zealand society.

Later, Margaret Macpherson left New Zealand and travelled widely overseas in her work as a journalist, living in the United States, Malta, and Britain at various times.

When Margaret Macpherson finally returned to New Zealand in the 1960s, after a long absence and in difficult financial circumstances, she 'was given a benefit in recognition of her services to this country in the form of the publicity which her best sellers gave the Pacific countries'.

She died in Kaitaia in September 1974.   *Anna Green*

Quotations
para.2 M. Macpherson, *Antipodean Journey*, pp.48, 133
para.4 M. Macpherson, *I Heard the Anzacs Singing*, p.336
para.5 R. Hyde, *Journalese*, pp.73–4
para.6 M. Macpherson, 'New Zealand Journey', *NZ Railways Magazine*, 1 May 1935, pp.32–3
para.8 *Northland Age*, 17 Sept. 1974 (obituary)

Published Sources
Hyde, Robin. *Journalese*, Auckland, 1934
Macpherson, Margaret. *A Symposium Against War*, Wellington, 1934
Macpherson, Margaret. *Antipodean Journey*, London, 1937
Macpherson, Margaret. *Australia Calling*, New York, 1951
Macpherson, Margaret. *I Heard the Anzacs Singing*, New York, 1942
Macpherson, Margaret. *New Zealand Beckons*, New York, 1952
Macpherson, Margaret. *The Love Horse*, New York, 1954

SUSIE MACTIER

1854-1936

Susie Mactier was one of a tiny handful of published women writers in colonial New Zealand. In the 1880s, she was well enough known to have earned the soubriquet 'The Takapuna Lake Poet', and she continued to write through marriage and motherhood, publishing three novels.

Her family was a prominent one on Auckland's North Shore. Thomas and Lydia Seaman arrived in Auckland on the *Andrew Jackson* in 1865 when Susie was eleven years old. Thomas took up farming at Takapuna and also ran two primary schools in the area. In 1876 Susie Seaman, who had been assisting him, took over as head teacher of the Lake School and, in 1879, when the school gained official status under the Education Act of 1877, she became the first headmistress of Takapuna primary school, a post she held until 1880.

Susie Mactier. *YWCA*

As census enumerator, first chairman of the Lake District Road Board, board clerk and rate collector, Thomas Seaman was busily involved in local affairs, as was Susie. With her sister, Annie, she ran a non-denominational Sunday school, and Susie and her father were part of a small group who promoted the cultural life of the district by founding the Takapuna public library in 1879.

Susie's interest in literature was not confined to reading other people's work. In 1884 she published a volume of poetry. Called *Thoughts by the Way*, the collection gives several clues to Susie's interests. Experiences as a teacher and religious sentiments influence the subject-matter of the more Victorian of the poems. But others are more revealing and original. The subject-matter and imagery in these are rooted in her own environment. They draw on the sights and sounds of the North Shore – the splash of a row-boat oar on the Piako and the silver sound of a tui calling his mate. There is also a romantic theme in the poems. Susie was a young woman and either passionate by nature, or highly imaginative!

Susie's real-life romance with Anthony Mactier led to their marriage in 1886. He was a doctor from Edinburgh who had taken up farming in the Awhitu district, south of the Manukau Harbour. The Mactiers lived first at Ponsonby, then settled in Hauraki Road, Takapuna.

Two daughters were born, Dora and Minnie, but over this period Susie also became closely involved with the Auckland YWCA, serving on the board from 1886 to 1912, with a term as president in 1910–11. With Annie Seaman, Susie organised the Flower Mission, which visited local work-rooms singing hymns and handing out religious tracts. The motivation for this exercise, said Susie, was 'a passionate desire to win girls for Christ'.

Although several prominent temperance feminists were involved with the YWCA through this period, Susie's efforts were more narrowly evangelistic. She appears never to have become actively involved in the Women's Christian Temperance Union, even though her writing at this time dwelled on the evils of alcohol.

Three novels appeared in the early years of the twentieth century: *The Far Countrie: A True Story of Domestic Life at Home and in the Bush* (1901), *The Hills of Hauraki, or The Unequal Yoke: A Story of New Zealand Life* (1908), and *Miranda Stanhope* (1911). Temperance is the major theme of Susie's writing, but Heather Roberts, writing of New Zealand's early women novelists, makes the point that, unlike feminist writers such as Edith Grossmann and Ellen Ellis, Susie did not embed her temperance theme in broader arguments about the powerlessness of women. Susie saw alcohol abuse as an affront to God and decent living, and accepted traditional gender relationships as a contract for life. In *The Hills of Hauraki*, Christina Beaminster is doomed from the moment she marries a man who 'was not a child of God'. The only escape for her is death. Miranda Stanhope, though a strong character, must continue to support her feckless drinking husband until released by his death in the Tarawera eruption.

Although Susie published no books after 1911 and at the same time gave up her YWCA work, she remained actively involved in her district, running a Sunday school from her home, and with her husband organising fund-raising for Dr Barnardo's. She also kept on writing, if for a more modest audience. The Mactiers' Christmas card always contained one of Susie's verses.

After her husband's death in 1925, Susie moved to Rotorua to live with Dora, a qualified nurse who was in charge of the Rotorua bathhouse. Even at the age of seventy-three, Susie's pen was not still. She wrote a long narrative poem about the Tarawera eruption, had it printed, and presented it to the Auckland Public Library. Susie died at Rotorua on 5 June 1936.   *Sandra Coney*

Quotations
para.6 S. Coney, *Every Girl*, p.23
para.8 S. Mactier, *The Hills of Hauraki*, p.142

Unpublished Sources
Auckland YWCA archives, AIM
Notes on the Seaman family, Takapuna Public Library
Obituary Scrapbook, 1936, AIM

Published Sources
Bartless, Jean. *Takapuna People and Places*, Auckland, 1989
Coney, Sandra. *Every Girl: A Social History of Women and the YWCA in Auckland*, Auckland, 1986

Mactier, Susie. *Thoughts by the Way*, Auckland, 1884

Mactier, Susie. *The Far Countrie: A True Story of Domestic Life at Home and in the Bush*, London, 1901

Mactier, Susie. *The Hills of Hauraki, or The Unequal Yoke; A Story of New Zealand Life*, London, 1908

Mactier, Susie. *Miranda Stanhope*, Auckland, 1911

Mactier, Susie. *An Idyll of Rotorua*, privately printed, 1927

Northcote Past Pupils. *Eightieth Anniversary Reunion Commemorative Booklet, 1877–1957*, Auckland, 1957

North Shore Times Advertiser, 4 Oct. 1961

NZ Herald, 7 May 1925 (obituary, Anthony Mactier)

Roberts, Heather. *Where Did She Come From? New Zealand Women Novelists 1862–1987*, Wellington, 1989

ELLEN MAHER

1849–1922

Ellen Maher was the middle child of an Irish family of the 1840s. Born in County Kilkenny she emigrated to Australia, where she spent a period in domestic service before coming to the West Coast of New Zealand. She was softly spoken, astute, and humorous.

At Hokitika in May 1872, she married Guiglio Piezzi, a Swiss-Italian baker. In 1873 a daughter, Helvetia, was born and in 1874 a son, Severino. Moving to nearby Goldsborough on the Waimea Creek east of Hokitika in 1875, the Piezzis opened the Helvetia Hotel. Not the standard grog shop this, but a two-storey inn of some distinction, incorporating bakery and store, ballroom, commercial and billiard rooms. Here R. J. Seddon gave his addresses; coach-horses were changed for the Christchurch–Hokitika run; brass and dance bands practised. The opening with its attendant ball was a great occasion for the young couple.

They were expecting a third child when Guiglio died from an untreated hernia. Flooded rivers had made access to a doctor impossible. Ellen Piezzi was only twenty-seven years old and pregnant. The child, born in December 1876, was a girl named Julia.

Indomitably, Ellen persevered with the hotel, her charm and common sense serving her well. But the task must have been daunting with trading hours from 6 am to 11 pm, young dependent children, and a clientele of rugged miners from all nations and stations. Goldsborough was then a town of about a dozen streets. Roads were rough, the climate and terrain harsh, and the supply port, Hokitika, twelve miles away.

Letters to her brother-in-law in California shed some light on the next years. She writes of family affairs, the headstone for Guiglio, the progress of the children. Troubled over rearing them in a public house, she decides to send Helvetia to St Mary's Convent in Wellington. Later letters depict the decline of the diggings and comment on the many people insolvent. (In 1879 R. J. Seddon filed for bankruptcy and Ellen was amongst his creditors.) By 1881 she writes of selling out.

Ellen viewed the hotel patrons as her guests and took pleasure in providing a good table. Herself a teetotaller, she assumed responsibility for her guests' sobriety – a quality not always valued in that environment – and would decline to serve those infringing her standards. A good billiard and card player, she would fill in as required. Later, her grown daughters would play the piano and sing for their visitors.

Though she was not disposed to self-pity, some lines in a letter written in 1881 denote her sense of exile: 'I got no one, neither of my own or Julius [Guiglio] near me but black strangers to talk to – God help me.' Her many friends among the Coasters belie this statement but her buoyant spirit seems for a time to have ebbed.

Fresh hope followed the finding of gold at Upper Woodstock (renamed Rimu), about six miles south of Hokitika on the Main South Road. Ellen went there to the new settlement, still under canvas, to take out a licence. In her absence the Helvetia Hotel was burnt down, a serious loss. In September 1882, she opened the Swiss Mountain Hotel at Rimu, while the Helvetia was rebuilt. The opening of a new hotel and the rebuilding of the old were considerable undertakings for a young widow.

A more radical change was in the offing. Probably at Rimu, Ellen met Dennis Maher, whom she married there in October 1883. A tall elegant Irishman, he had a great command of language which masked his lack of education, as he could barely read or write.

The first family was never happy with this alliance. There were three children of the second marriage: Veronica, John and Ellen. Uneasy years followed the return to Goldsborough. The strains of step-parenting may have been exacerbated by financial stresses in a township now holding little promise. So in 1895, while the Piezzis remained on the Coast, the Mahers moved to Wellington where Ellen had a brother and sister.

Ellen was now in her late forties and seems to have provided direction and business sense in the marriage. In Newtown the Mahers managed the Tramway Hotel and later the Panama in Taranaki Street. Ellen again established herself as a competent and responsible proprietress, making friends amongst customers, staff, and the business community.

In 1909 she retired and lived in Newtown where she kept a garden, a few hens, and a little dog. Children ranked high in her affections and, though constantly teasing them, she supplied them with sweets, materials for dolls' clothes, half-crowns, and on occasions sovereigns. Never wealthy, she was always open-handed and many spoke of Mrs Maher's assistance – a new suit for father, an operation for my sister, a start in business for my dad, tram fares for the needy or seedy, and a helping hand for any good cause.

From 1919 she endured a painful illness. Her bed was beside an upstairs window and the 'trammies' (tram drivers), who knew her from her business years, would clang the bell and wave to her in passing.

Arriving empty-handed in a harsh environment, Ellen Maher overcame adversities with resourcefulness, generosity, and humour, and earned the affection of many. She died in 1922 and is buried at Karori amongst her kin.

J. T. O'Connor

Unpublished Sources
Information was provided by family and friends. The author is Ellen Maher's granddaughter. The letters
   from Ellen Maher to her brother-in-law in California are in the author's possession.
Published Sources
Harper, Barbara, *Petticoat Pioneers: South Island Women of the Colonial Era*, Book 3, Wellington,
   1980
Seddon, T. E. Y. *The Seddons*, Auckland, 1968
West Coast Times, 16 Dec. 1875; 20 Sept. 1876 (obituary Guiglio Piezzi); 30 June 1882; 7 Sept. 1882

MAATA MAHUPUKU

1890-1952

Few New Zealand women have led more unusual lives than Maata Mahupuku.
She was born in Greytown in the Wairarapa on 10 April 1890, the only child of
Emily Mahupuku (born Sexton), aged nineteen, and Dick Mahupuku, aged
twenty-four, a Maori farmer of Longbush, near Gladstone. Dick was the son of
Wiremu (or Wi) Mahupuku, a wealthy sheep-farmer and chief, who was a
member of the Ngati Parera and Ngati Hikawera tribes which, in turn, were sub-
tribes of Ngati Kahungunu. He was to die in a farm accident in 1893. Just over
two years later, in February 1895, Maata's mother remarried, her second husband being Nathaniel Grace, a well-respected Gladstone farmer, aged fifty-five.

By the turn of the century, Maata had enrolled at Miss Swainson's School,
Fitzherbert Terrace, Wellington, where, at the age of ten or eleven, she became
friendly with Kathleen Beauchamp (who later assumed the name Katherine
Mansfield).

Within the next three or four years, Maata, now usually known as Martha
Grace, left for Paris in the company of a chaperone, a Miss Turton, to continue
her education. (The Beauchamp sisters in early 1903 had entered Queen's College, London.) Later in 1906 Maata and Kathleen met in London, a meeting
recalled by the writer in a journal entry of early February 1908: 'We were
floating down Regent Street in a hansom, on either side of us the blossoms of
golden light, and ahead a little half hoop of moon.' About the time of the London
encounter the two girls agreed to keep diaries. Maata later sent part of hers to
Kathleen, who wove it into a story called 'Summer Idylle, 1906', about Hinemoa
(probably Kathleen) and Marina (probably Maata) living by the sea. Hinemoa
loved to watch Marina's 'complete harmony'.

In November 1906 Maata, now aged sixteen, returned to New Zealand just
as details were published about the embezzlement of the large Mahupuku estate
which she had inherited following the death of her grandfather, Wi, and later
her great-uncle, Tamahau Mahupuku, in January 1904. (Eventually most of the
money was recovered.) Meanwhile, her stepfather, Nathaniel Grace, had also
died and her mother had married J. L. Laurenson, an accountant of Carterton.
Maata, probably unsettled, now spent a good deal of time visiting friends and
relatives.

For most of April 1907 she was in Wanganui, and a typed copy of a journal
she kept then has survived. Well-known Wanganui residents of the time are men-

tioned: Walter Empsom, then headmaster of Wanganui College, his wife, and his daughter, Judith, who was about Maata's age, and Dr Christie and his wife, obviously close friends. Maata falls in love in Wanganui but frequently suffers from 'the blues'.

From Kathleen in Wellington on her birthday on 10 April she received a letter and later a telegram. Maata wrote in her journal:

I am 17 today. It is extraordinary how young I am in years and how old in body – ugh! I am miserable and oh! so bored . . . I had a letter from K this morning . . . Dearest K writes 'ducky' letters. I like this bit. 'What did you mean by being so superlatively beautiful just as you went away? You witch; you are beauty incarnate.'

Maata continues: 'It's conceited of me to like it, but I do – I love admiration.'

Soon Maata was back in Wellington for the Beauchamps' house-warming party on 4 May at their new home in Fitzherbert Terrace. Edie Bendall, another friend of Kathleen, was also at the party, and, at least on the latter's part, this friendship was to become intense during the next few weeks. However, by the end of June Kathleen's thoughts had returned to Maata as a journal entry on 29 June revealed:

I want Maata – I want her as I have had her – terribly. This is unclean I know but true. What an extraordinary thing – I feel savagely crude – and almost powerfully enamoured of the child. I had thought that a thing of the past – Heigh Ho!!!!!!!!!!! My mind is like a Russian novel.

On 18 July Maata again visited and stayed with the Beauchamps for a dance given by Charlotte, Kathleen's older sister. However, a Wanganui romance now seemed to be the focus of her life and in November her engagement to George McGregor, a part-Maori farmer, descendant of well-known Wanganui residents, was announced. They were married in Greytown in January 1908 and, after a year or two in Wanganui, lived in a large brick house, today surrounded by a beautiful garden, in Kuratawhiti Street, Greytown. Until KM, the name by which she now wished to be known, left New Zealand finally in 1908, she and Maata still met from time to time in Wellington.

For at least eight years after her departure from New Zealand, Kathleen's stories revealed that thoughts of Maata still sometimes crossed her mind. In 1913 she began a story entitled 'Maata', although it was not in fact about Maata Mahupuku but about Kathleen herself. Three years later she wrote 'Kezia and Tui', clearly inspired by recollections of their friendship. In the same year (1916), after reading Dostoevsky's story of Nastasya, she noted that she was reminded of Maata – they both seemed to know 'how things are done in the world . . . With such women it seems to be a kind of instinct. (Maata was just the same. She simply knew these things from nowhere.)'

The McGregors were to have three children, and eventually many grand-children, but in October 1914 they were divorced. Within two weeks, Maata, then twenty-four years old, married Tom Asher, a widower of Maori, Dutch, and Jewish descent. They had two daughters, but ten years later this marriage also ended in divorce. Maata did not marry again.

Maata Mahupuku in Greytown, c.1920.
Chris Scanlon

On a visit to New Zealand in 1931 KM's first biographer, Ruth Elvish Mantz, met Maata, then forty-one. Mantz was impressed by her assured presence and warm personality, but thought she had lived mainly an unhappy life. Other glimpses of Maata in later life emerge in *The Mystery of Maata*, by Pat Lawlor (1946), and in a newspaper article by Eric Ramsden, a Pakeha journalist. She was, he thought, like 'an Italian marchesa, handsome, erect, dignified'.

Maata finally settled in Palmerston North, where she died of heart disease on 15 January 1952 aged sixty-two, leaving many descendants. She had lived through an eventful period in New Zealand race relations. In Eric Ramsden's opinion she was considered by the Maori people to be Pakeha in her outlook and ways. To the Pakeha, on the other hand, she seemed predominantly Maori. Her final resting place in the private burial ground of the Mahupuku family at Kehemane, near Martinborough, suggests that at the end of her life she had no doubts which heritage meant more to her. Her headstone is inscribed with her Maori name, Maata Mahupuku. *Barbara Angus*

Quotations

para.3 K. Mansfield, *Journal*, pp.35–6; M. Scott (ed.), 'The Unpublished Manuscripts of Katherine Mansfield. Part II', p.133

para.6 'New Zealand Journal by Maata', p.1

para.7 A. Alpers, *The Life of Katherine Mansfield*, p.401

para.9 K. Mansfield, *Journal*, p.110

para.11 E. Ramsden, *Evening Post*, 21 Jan. 1959

Unpublished Sources

'New Zealand Journal by Maata', typed copy in Mantz papers, Item 15, Harry Ransom Humanities Research Center, University of Texas

Published Sources

Alpers, Antony. *The Life of Katherine Mansfield*, New York, 1980

The Cyclopedia of New Zealand, vol.1 pt.2, Wellington, 1897, p.923

Evening Post, 30 Dec. 1946; 21 Jan. 1959 (articles by Eric Ramsden)

Fearon, Kevin J. *History of Gladstone and Surrounding Districts*, Carterton, 1976

Lawlor, P. A. *The Mystery of Maata*, Wellington, 1946

Middleton Murry, J. (ed.). *Journal of Katherine Mansfield 1904–1922*, 'Definitive Edition', Auckland and London, 1984

Middleton Murry, J. (ed.). *The Scrapbook of Katherine Mansfield*, London, 1939, p.41 ('Kezia and Tui')

O'Sullivan, Vincent. *Katherine Mansfield's New Zealand*, Auckland, 1988, pp.44–5

Scott, Margaret (ed.). 'The Unpublished Manuscripts of Katherine Mansfield. Part II', *Turnbull Library Record*, vol.9 no.3, Nov.1970, pp.128–36

Scott, Margaret (ed.). 'Katherine Mansfield The Unpublished Manuscripts: Part VII Maata', *Turnbull Library Record*, vol.12 no.1, May 1979, pp.11–28

TE WHIU MAITAI

1869–1960

Te Whiu Maitai was born in the Tolaga Bay area of the East Coast in 1869. Her people were Te Aitanga-a-Hauiti. She went to primary school for a short time but was withdrawn by her family after contracting pneumonia. Although she never learned to speak English, she was able to read it.

Te Whiu married a number of times. She had no children of her own but raised many whangai. She died in 1960 and is buried in Tolaga Bay.

Her story was told to John Walsh by one of her whangai, Kupere Sanders.
I don't know where she was born but I presume it must have been in Tolaga Bay. They used to live way out, probably Mangahei, somewhere around there. Her full name was Tau Tangiao Te Ao Marama, but most people just called her Emere or Piwi, whatever. Her mother I think was Atareta Paku and her father's name was Herini. She and Nanny Rangi were first cousins. Her and Aunty Rangi got on quite well. When I was a kid, they were really the old kuia of Tolaga Bay. Mum was very placid natured. Aunty Rangi was a fiery old devil when she got cracking and when they drank fire water together it made it worse still.

Aunty Rangi's father, I believe he was the one that wanted Mum to take up speaking on maraes and being the keeper of the whakapapas and things like that. But she didn't want that. She said that parties were more her line. I think that's what people remember about her most of all. Her mixing with them, and drinking with them. Even though she was quiet, she was a very commanding person. She had a great respect in the community and it's quite odd that she didn't take up the public life. She wasn't an assertive character. She loved people for what they were. Practically all Mum's life, people were more important to her than things. We always had somebody living in the house that didn't belong in the family. She collected them wherever they came from. She originally brought up five of us as whangais, but actually she collected people like nobody's business. Our house was always full of people. Europeans, Maoris, they were all there, and if she could have got Chinamen she'd have had those too but Chinamen are a bit thin on the ground in Tolaga.

Her legal husband was a Tautau. I think his name was Wiremu. They lived up at Ruatoria for a while. It was an arranged marriage. If the family say you've got to marry so-and-so, you have to. But Mum's never worked out so well. She had been married before and Tautau was a very jealous man. Mum was a very beautiful woman and when she was young and they all had their eyes on her, and of course, he used to beat her up a lot. So Mum would run away. He'd find her on the way between Ruatoria and Tolaga Bay and take her back, but finally she managed to escape. She came across country and once she got back into her own family she didn't go back.

When she got back to Tolaga, like every other young woman of that time, she found different men that she liked. One of them was a Pakeha, Eric Loisel. She lived with him for a long long while. He was a very wealthy man, a land-owner. He built her a little cottage just out of Tolaga and that was the place they used to meet. He'd come from the farm and they'd stay there together in this beautiful little place. Loisel wasn't married at that time and of course she couldn't get married because she was already married. So Mum and Eric just lived together. They were very happy. Then he went overseas, and I've still got a few of the love letters that he wrote. Mum could read English but she didn't speak it. It was while Loisel was over there that he met somebody else. He decided he was going to marry for convenience. I don't think he really was in love with the lady but I think he married her because he wanted children. He was a very rich man, he had a big farm, and he needed somebody to carry on. Mum couldn't have children, so she decided that perhaps somebody else will get him a baby. I think it was very traumatic for her.

She got her moko when she was about eighteen. It was done out at Kaiaua Bay. They've got a special place there where the old chief always used to do the mokos. They were isolated, and weren't allowed to have husbands there with them. They were absolutely isolated from everything. According to my Mum, the place where they lived while receiving the moko had a well. The old chief would go there to this well and bring the water out. She said most of the time she didn't feel it being done because he would recite some sort of prayer. It was as if you were being hypnotised by the sound of his voice. Her moko was done with the old tools. I don't know whether she was the last to be moko'd but she was the last of the moko'd ladies in that area, her and Ngaropi White. She was chosen to have the moko because of her nature. As I said, she was a placid-natured person and loved people. She had the potential that I guess those old people approved.

We used to have a dairy farm out at Mangahei. Most of us kids would go out and help to get the cows, and Mum was at home, doing all the cooking and so forth. During those times, all sorts of people would pass through our house. Mum was not only the cook, but she became the doctor too. It was miles to go to any doctor and Mum was a great herbalist. She took stuff out of the bush for all sorts of ailments. I remember one woman got her hair caught in the shearing machine. She had long hair, and the machine just ripped it out. Just peeled the scalp and left this horrible mess on the top of her head. I remember Mum just cut a great big hunk off the meat

Te Whiu Maitai. *Portrait by John Walsh*

*that had just been killed, and stuck it over that place that had been hurt and
held it there until the bleeding stopped. She treated that woman at home for
a week before they could get out to the doctor, but she was perfectly all
right by the time that Mum had finished with her. The scalp went back nice
but of course in some places she wouldn't have hair on. Her treatment was
all bush medicine. It was just one of the things that Mum did.*

*Mum used to love gardening. She lived in that garden practically. She
didn't like girls in her garden very much, because when girls menstruate and
they pass over the garden, it makes the food go funny. I guess Mum was one
of those old people who believed solely in the old ways of keeping gardens.
She had a great orchard. People for miles used to come and pick apples. Our
neighbours used to try and get the trees to grow like they say in the books
but their trees would shrivel up and die. Hers just seemed to go on and
on. She said it's because she uses all the rubbish lying around. She'd have a
lot of cow dung and so forth and she just put it all back into the ground
again. It was as simple as that.*

*She didn't have very much education. When she was little they used to
ferry the children over from the other side of the river, from Hauiti to the
school. Now it was a long way for her to come and she'd be sitting on a
bank waiting. Of course, when there was only a few of them waiting, the
ferryman wouldn't come over and pick them up until there was a lot of
children. This particular day she was there on her own and it was pouring
with rain, and she got pneumonia. Her father was so angry he wouldn't let*

her go back to school. I suppose he thought he was doing it to punish the education board or whatever, because of what happened to his child. But he also punished her in that she never learned about the European world. Although she hardly spoke English, she could make herself understood. There were some words that she wasn't quite sure of. Words like television and things that wouldn't have been part of her experience. Most times she spoke back to you in Maori. I don't know whether this was a good thing or a bad thing but whenever she went into a shop she couldn't help but teach that shopkeeper a little bit about Maori language.

She used to do the preservation of food. They didn't have any fridges and things in Mum's time, because we didn't have the power where we lived. I remember her and Dad going to the beach and getting pauas. We used to camp out for a couple of days or so, at the beach. Collect up all the seafood we needed because we lived inland in the country.

Mum was an excellent swimmer for somebody smallish. She swam right up until she was fairly old. We'd take her to the beach and she'd get in the water and show us where the crayfish holes and the paua places were. She'd walk out to where the blue waters were and that's a long walk for an old lady. She'd take her stick and point out where to get in the water. Once or twice she hopped in herself. Mum was great at catching octopus. You caught it by the stomach holding it from underneath and the legs just all folded up paralysed. After getting enough paua we'd go home. Mum would render pork fat down and she would cook all the pauas up and she'd fill those big earthenware jars with pork fat and pauas. Whenever you wanted paua, you just dug them out of the fat and recooked them. We fried them or whatever and they were perfect. She also dried parengo, the seaweed. She put it in a plastic bag and it would keep indefinitely in a dry place. The other thing was the drying of eels. They put a lot of salt on it because that keeps the flies away. Even during the war we were lucky on the farm, there was always something to eat. We had a hand separator and Mum used to make our butter at home. It was a wee bit salty but it was better than no butter.

The only thing I think Mum wished she could have made during the war was smoke. That was something that the older generation did was smoke. I don't think anybody ever found a substitute for smoke. Although there is this tree that has a very fine fabric just underneath the bark – it's very much like lace. It was the nearest thing they got to tobacco. Dad used to flay it. He hung it on the fence and flay the damn thing to get this very fine lacy material and he'd dry it. After it's been rolled up in the paper, you put a match to it. It didn't burn away but smouldered. Of course, it was a far cry from the real thing, but Mum she used to smoke something awful.

She also used to work – washing and housemaiding – in the hotel. Working in the pub where she met up with Eric Loisel and all that clan. She was a keen drinker. I remember finding her in that private bar sitting in a dark little corner, holding court down there. She drank a great deal, practically most of her life. As she got older, it was a way of meeting other people like herself. Most of the old people used to gather in one place. To be able to go and sit in a meeting-house and talk about old times only happened after certain functions. The only informal place they could meet was in the pub. I think they all went there for the company and of course some of them got hooked on the drug and really drank till it came out of their ears. Nevertheless I think Mum was a very religious person. A lot of the people from the apostolic churches used to come down on her and berate her about her drinking and so forth, telling her that she should be preparing a way for herself because she was getting old. All she'd say to them was that Christ was a happy man. He went to parties. He turned water into wine because they ran out of drink, so he must have been a gay blade like me, she says. When she drank, she always raised her glass and says, 'Here's to you, Jesus!' She never let booze get on top of her. The Christians used to tell her it was bad for her health to drink. She was dirtying the temple of God, they said. She says, 'Ah, no, it's the things that come from deep down inside that dirty the temple of God.'

To die at ninety-one is no mean feat. I guess she could have lived on a little longer but she was getting hoha. There was no one of her own age to talk to. They were all dead. She always used to say, 'I'm getting tired of talking to myself.'

John Walsh, Kupere Sanders & Cushla Parekowhai

MAKARIRI

c.1840

Some of the Pakeha who settled in nineteenth-century New Zealand formed relationships with local Maori women – relationships that presumably mixed in varying degrees convenience and affection. Some lasted a year or two, before the Pakeha moved on, to continue his trading, whaling, or seafaring elsewhere; some had a permanent basis. The women's view of these connections is rarely heard, but we have a glimpse of Makariri's life with George Willsher at Port Molyneux on the South Otago Coast.

Makariri was a young Maori woman living at Matau (at the mouth of the Clutha River), a daughter of the chief Tahu and his wife Toke. In the 1840s she shared a house with the squatter George Willsher, who arrived at Port Molyneux in 1840. He traded in cattle, and travelled to and fro between Otago and Sydney for the next few years. Makariri, it seems, took care not only of domestic matters, but of his land and animals.

In 1844, when the *Deborah*, a New Zealand Company vessel, called at Port Molyneux, seeking a place for the New Edinburgh Scottish settlement, a surveyor's assistant J. W. Barnicoat recorded in his journal a meeting with Willsher and Makariri:

In the evening we had the neighbouring Mouries around us, together with a native woman who lives with Mr Wiltshire. The latter displays the characteristic talkitiveness, liveliness and shrewdness of her sex and people. Overhearing her husband speak rather disparaging of the native women, she enforced the value of her own services in the following terms. 'By and by you go to Otago to Waihora – to Toutu. You stay three weeks – you stay five weeks – you stay two moons – you come back – you say Hullo where's the cow? Gone. Where the bull? Gone! Where the goatee? Gone! Where the chikeni? Gone. The blankety gone the stockeni gone all all gone. You get the Mourie woman, by and by you go to Otago. To Waikawa to Toutere – you stay three weeks – you stay five weeks – you stay two moons – you come back you say – Hullo where's the cow? Me say 'All right' You say Where the Bull? all right. You say where the goati – me say all right – You say where the chickini? Me say all right. The blankets all right the stockini all right – all all right – are very good the Mourie woman.'

In time George Willsher apparently tired of southern New Zealand, and of his Maori partner. He returned to Britain in 1859, with another local settler, A. O. Fuller. Makariri is said to have mourned his departure. The words that Barnicoat recorded are those of a woman of independence and spirit.

Sheila Natusch & Bridget Williams

'The Molyneux near Stirling', pencil and wash sketch by William Mathew Hodgkins. This was where Makariri lived with Willsher in the 1840s. *Alexander Turnbull Library*

Quotation
para.3 J. W. Barnicoat, Journal, 8 May 1844, p.56

Unpublished Sources
J. W. Barnicoat, Journal 1841–44, qMS, ATL

Published Sources
Marshall, Heather. *Balclutha to Molyneux Bay*, Dunedin, 1980
Natusch, Sheila. *On the Edge of the Bush: Women in Early Southland*, Invercargill, 1976, pp.35–6
Natusch, Sheila. *Southward Ho! The 'Deborah' in Quest of a New Edinburgh 1844*, Invercargill, 1985, pp.62–3
Otago Daily Times and Witness, Jubilee Issue, 1898
Waite, Fred. *Maoris and Settlers in Otago: A History of Port Molyneux and Its Surrounds*, Dunedin, 1980, p.52
Waite, Fred. *Pioneering in South Otago*, Christchurch, 1977, pp.32–3

JANE MANDER

1877–1949

Soon after Alice Roland arrives at her husband's remote sawmill up the Otamatea River, an arm of the Kaipara Harbour, she is visited by an English gentlewoman, Mrs Brayton, whose appearance reassures Alice that there is civilisation in the far north. Mrs Brayton is a reader. Before she leaves she recommends to Alice a 'wonderful new novel' – Olive Schreiner's *The Story of an African Farm*. Mander saw *The Story of a New Zealand River* as the New Zealand equivalent of Schreiner's novel. As a piece of regional documentation, *The Story of a New Zealand River* locates itself firmly in traditional colonial writing, recording a world of change for an English readership, with a remarkable landscape the subject of the novel.

Jane Mander spent her childhood moving around small rural settlements in the Kaipara district and on the outskirts of Auckland. Her father, Frank Mander, began his marriage to Janet Kerr with a hundred acres and a house he built himself, in which Mary Jane Mander was born on 9 April 1877. Mander estimated the family moved twenty-nine times while she was growing up, following Frank Mander's bush-felling and milling work. By the time she was fifteen and started as a probationary teacher at Port Albert, the Mander family had been associated with the logging of kauri forest all over the north. This activity and landscape were to provide the texture, incident, and literary environment for all Mander's New Zealand novels.

After ten years of teaching in Port Albert and various schools in Auckland, doing matriculation and teacher's exams at night-school, Mander went with her family to Whangarei where her father became the MP for Marsden in 1902. He also acquired the *Northern Advocate*, a paper he owned for four years. During this time Mander worked as a journalist.

At times I ran the department singlehanded from leader to proofs, and the proudest boast of my life is that I once brought out the paper four days running without a mistake and caught the four o'clock train.

Valerie Carr, Mander's heroine in *The Strange Attraction*, works on a paper in Dargaville and, like Mander throughout her life, is engaged with political issues.

25–26. Begin again. The new religion – socialism; the new god – humanity; the new Christ – the man, the carpenter; the new devils – poverty, capitalism; the new heaven and hell – the earth; the new Bible – Marx, Wells, The Fabian Society, the Economists.

When Frank Mander sold the paper and built a house in Whangarei in 1906, topped by a tower reached only by an outside ladder, Jane Mander retired into this to write a novel. She visited Sydney, and then spent some time editing Dargaville's *North Auckland Times*. While in Sydney friends suggested she go to the School of Journalism at Columbia University in New York; after persuading her parents, Mander left New Zealand in June 1912 and did not return for twenty years.

At the School of Journalism, one of the first professional schools to admit women, Mander found she was 'regarded as an "event of importance", the first New Zealander to enter there as a student . . . We were socialism without bloodshed: We were Utopia materialised!' Despite the 'pretty bad' grind of being a student, Mander revised the novel she began in New Zealand, took various paid employment, including prison research at Sing Sing, addressed street meetings, and wrote *The Story of a New Zealand River*, which was accepted in 1918 and published in 1920. It was followed by *The Passionate Puritan* (1921), *The Strange Attraction* (1923), *Allen Adair* (1925), *The Besieging City* (1926), and *Pins and Pinnacles* (1928). In 1923 Mander moved to London; her last two novels were set in New York and London respectively, her previous four in New Zealand. All were published in London.

Although the change in setting in her novels argues a shift of focus, Mander's fiction, including her rare stories (the first of which appeared in the *New Zealand Illustrated Magazine*, May 1902), is preoccupied with social politics. Mander's novels are romances. They are distinguished by their complicated treatment of the romance form, one designed to illustrate the constraints of conventional expectation and social habits upon women and to attack in general terms puritanism and materialism. Her novels progressively move away from marriage and children as the objective of a woman's life; a process begun in *The Story of a New Zealand River* when Asia Roland leaves the narrow limits of her mother's marriage and morality for an extramarital relationship with Allen Ross in Sydney. None of Mander's heroines end up in the inevitable association of wife and mother; all of them question the social and sexual roles of women and exhibit what in Asia is called 'mental restlessness'.

In New Zealand, reviews of Mander's novels were preoccupied with the questions they raised: the *Evening Post*'s London correspondent in 1923 regretted the 'combination of what one may call the "sex" novel and the New Zealand bush country as unnecessary and misleading'; the *Dominion* thought she was 'obsessed by sex problems'. Mander's fiction characteristically challenges narrow conceptions of morality, duty, and ambition. *Allen Adair*, the only novel to have a male subject, rejects conventional materialist Anglophile ambitions in favour of the freedoms and spiritual satisfactions of life on the gum-fields of the north; habitually Mander's novels feature a population of outsiders, those who have chosen to remove themselves from mainstream society. As Asia tells Ross, 'This is the land of the lost'. At the same time Mander's novels presuppose an English reader and a dominating cultural environment. Allen Adair is only one of four Oxford men on his gum-field, and it is the Oxford men who attract him; Mrs Brayton comforts Alice Roland by telling her she has both an Englishman and an English-woman to stand by her.

Jane Mander, 1937. *Alexander Turnbull Library*

But though the implied readership of Mander's novels is an English one, their location is firmly regional – North Auckland, the Kaipara Harbour in particular. Mander's four New Zealand novels all have definitively local settings – gum-fields, kauri dams, sawmills, the river systems and mangrove swamps of the northern harbours – and they abound, as Katherine Mansfield noted in her review of *The Story of a New Zealand River*, with 'magnificent scenery'. Although, as Mansfield said, she 'leans too hard on England', Mander's fiction is deeply engaged with a distinctive environment, which is differentiated from the world of 'Home' both physically and socially. The freedom experienced by Mander's characters in the small communities they inhabit is contrasted with the constraints of larger societies; Allen Adair's move up north illustrates the large-ness and generosity of his character, matched by the physical environment. In the 1880s and 1890s stories abound of Northlanders who drank themselves into oblivion; alcohol is an explicit social problem in Mander's fiction (as is sexually transmitted disease) but this does not detract from the value of the characters who are its victims. David Bruce, hero of *The Story of a New Zealand River* (in all other respects 'too good to be true'), wages successful battle against alcoholism and illustrates a preoccupation of Mander's novels, the moral distinctions that are most easily recognisable out in the bush.

When Mander's novels move to London and New York, they focus more acutely on the difficulties of combining career ambitions with marriage, and less on the association between physical and spiritual environments. When Mander returned to New Zealand in 1932, she was under contract to write both another novel and a book of reminiscences, but neither appeared. Back in Auckland Mander lived with and looked after her father alone after her mother's death, and was actively associated with a number of younger New Zealand writers – Frank Sargeson, Roderick Finlayson, D'Arcy Cresswell, and Robin Hyde among them.

Hyde in a letter to John A. Lee described Mander as 'almost the only literary female liked in Auckland for reasonable reasons. She is honest and tough as a nutcracker (outwardly)'; she talked about her 'holidaying in a tent, up north, trying to escape from the haunting thought of her father, who will play bridge with her'.

Jane Mander's importance as one of New Zealand's earliest novelists is matched by her willingness to question social conventions and affirm the value of free-thinking individuals open to change. Commentary frequently describes her as forthright, honest, unpretentious. Mander made no claims to great writing. In a letter to J. H. E. Schroder, she remarked of *The Story of a New Zealand River* that 'its crudities would hit me in the eye now', and it has often been noted that her imaginative writing failed to represent the intellectual conception of her work. But in her fiction as in her person Mander asserts the importance of truth-telling; her novels are a history, a record, and a re-enactment of 'that gum country of the north which is in my blood and bones'.

Lydia Wevers

Quotations

para.3 D. Turner, *Jane Mander*, p.22; J. Mander, 'A Diary of Evolution in a Small Country Town', *New Republic*, 25 March 1916

para.5 *The Press*, 15 Dec. 1934, quoted in D. Turner, p.26

para.6 J. Mander, *Story of a New Zealand River*, p.131

para.7 *Evening Post*, 1 Sept. 1923; *Dominion*, 6 Oct. 1923, both quoted in D. Turner, p.133; J. Mander, *Story*, p.271

para.8 K. Mansfield, *Novels and Novelists*, ed. J. M. Murry, London, 1930, p.219

para.10 Robin Hyde to John A. Lee, 8 May 1936, MS Papers 828, APL; R. Hyde to J. H. E. Schroder, 1937, MS Papers 280, ATL

para.11 J. Mander to J. H. E. Schroder, June 1938, quoted in D. Turner, p.38; J. Mander to Pat Lawlor, 1931, quoted in D. Turner, p.111

Published Sources

Mander, Jane. 'A Stray Woman', *NZ Illustrated Magazine*, May 1902

Mander, Jane. *The Story of a New Zealand River*, 1938

Turner, Dorothea. *Jane Mander*, New York, 1972

MERI MANGAKAHIA

c.1870–c.1920

Meri Mangakahia is remembered for the part she played in the Kotahitanga political movement towards the end of the nineteenth century.

In the early 1890s Kotahitanga expanded its tribal runanga to form an intertribal parliament, Paremata Maori, as an independent political institution. It was modelled closely on the existing parliament in Wellington. The first formal meeting was held at Waipatu marae, Heretaunga, in Hawke's Bay in June 1892. Over 1,000 people took part in the opening ceremony, including ninety-six representatives elected from eight districts. A prime minister, speaker, leader of the house, and ministers were subsequently elected.

In May 1893 Meri Mangakahia appeared before the assembled parliament to present a motion which would enable women to vote and stand as candidates for the parliament. These were her words:

I exult the honourable members of this gathering. Greetings. The reason I move this motion before the principal member and all honourable members so that a law may emerge from this parliament allowing women to vote and women to be accepted as members of the parliament.

Following are my reasons that present this motion so that women may receive the vote and that there be women members:

1. There are many women who have been widowed and own much land.

2. There are many women whose fathers have died and do not have brothers.

3. There are many women who are knowledgeable of the management of land where their husbands are not.

4. There are many women whose fathers are elderly, who are also knowledgeable of the management of land and own land.

5. There have been many male leaders who have petitioned the Queen concerning the many issues that affect us all, however, we have not yet been adequately compensated according to those petitions. Therefore I pray to this gathering that women members be appointed.

Perhaps by this course of action we may be satisfied concerning the many issues affecting us and our land. Perhaps the Queen may listen to the petitions if they are presented by her Maori sisters, since she is a woman as well.

Several members of the parliament spoke in support of Meri Mangakahia's motion. They acknowledged that women had an interest in land, that many women worked the land and, indeed, women who supported Kotahitanga were levied £1, the same as men. This entitled them to a vote. The only person to express some reservation was Akenehi (Agnes) Tomoana. She supported the motion but argued that priority should be given to gaining recognition for existing members.

Despite this support, and the speaker's expression of surprise that no women as yet had stood for election to the parliament, the subject was quickly put aside.

Reweti : Me unu tenei korero mo te 2 p.m.

Toroaiwhiti : E tautoko ana ahau.

Pika : Konga mea e pai ana me ki mai Ae. Paahitia ana.

Ka panuitia atu te motini a Meri Mangakahia, he tono kia whai mana nga wahine ki te pooti.

R. Aperahama : Me haere mai a Meri Mangakahia ki te whakamarama i tenei motini.

H. K. Taiaroa : E tautoko ana ahau i tenei motini, i te mea kanui nga wahine whiwhi whenua a ka mahi noa atu ko tatou ki te mahi ture atu mo o ratou whenua I oti hoki i tera tau kia kohi nga wahine i te £1 0s 0d, na reira me whai mana nga wahine ki te pooti.

Pika : Ka tonoa atu a Meri Mangakahia.

Mo te 2 p.m. ka noho te whare.

---

2 P.M.

Pika : Ko te kai motini i naianei.

Meri Mangakahia : E whakamoemiti atu ana ahau kinga honore mema e noho nei, kia ora koutou katoa, ko te take i motini atu ai ahan, ki te Tumuaki Honore, me nga mema honore, k a mahia he ture e tenei whare kia whakamana nga wahine ki te pooti mema mo ratou ki te Paremata Maori.

Ka whakamarama ahau i te take i tinotino ai ahau kia whakamana nga wahine maori ki te pooti, a kia tu hoki he mema wahine ki roto i te Paremata Maori.

1. He nui nga wahine o Nui Tireni kua mate a ratou taane, a he whenua karati, papatupu o ratou.

2. He nui nga wahine o Nui Tireni kua mate o ratou matua, kaore o ratou tungane, he karati, he papatupu o ratou.

3. He nui nga wahine mohio o Nui Tireni kei te moe tane, kaore nga tane e mohio ki te whakahaere i o raua whenua.

4. He nui nga wahine kua koroheketia o ratou matua, he wahine mohio, he karati, he papatupu o ratou.

5. He nui nga tane Rangatira o te motu nei kua inoi ki te kuini, mo nga mate e pa ara kia tatou, a kaore tonu tatou i pa ki te ora i runga i ta ratou inoitanga. Na reira ka inoi ahau ki tenei whare kia tu he mema wahine.

Ma tenei pea e tika ai, a tera ka tika ki te tuku inoi nga mema wahine ki te kuini, mo nga mate kua pa nei kia tatou me o tatou whenua, a tera pea e whakaae mai a te kuini ki te inoi a ona hoa Wahine Maori i te mea he wahine ano hoki a te kuini.

Akenehi Tomoana : Kia ora nga mema Honore e kimi nei i te ora mo tatou. E tu ake ana ahau ki te tautoko i tenei motini, engari e mea ake ana ahau kia riro rawa mai te Honore i nga tane katahi ano ka pai te korero i tenei motini.

Marara : Ko ahau tetahi e tautoko ana i tenei korero.

Paremata Maori O Nui Tireni, Proceedings of the Maori Parliament, May 1893, when Meri Mangakahia led a delegation of women seeking the right to vote and sit in the assembly. *Alexander Turnbull Library*

Debate turned to where the assembly should meet the following year. In the written records of Paremata Maori no further mention can be found of debate on the issue.

Meri Mangakahia was born Meri Te Tai in the Hokianga; she was of Te Rarawa, Taitokerau. She married Hamiora Mangakahia, who became one of the key figures in Kotahitanga. He was elected prime minister at the first meeting of Paremata Maori at Waipatu. They had four children: two sons, Mohi and Waipapa, and two daughters, Tangiora and Mabel Te Ao Whaitini. Hamiora Mangakahia continued to take a leading role in the Maori parliament until 1898, when he withdrew in protest at the direction of negotiations taking place with the government of the day.

Little else is known about Meri Mangakahia. Her elder daughter was married in 1914 and her name appears (as Meri Mangaraha) as a voter in the Western Maori electorate at the time of the 1919 election. She died sometime after this and is buried at Pangaru in the Hokianga.

Charlotte Macdonald, with translation by Charles Royal

Quotation
para.3 *Paremata Maori o Nui Tireni*, q499M, ATL

Unpublished Sources
Information was provided by Meri Mangakahia's granddaughter, Raukawa Lilian Adams, of Coromandel.

Published Sources
1919 Electoral Roll, Parliamentary Library
Huia Tangata Kotahi (newspaper), various dates, 1893
Paremata Maori o Nui Tireni, q499M, ATL
Walker, Ranginui. *Ka Whawhai Tonu Matou – Struggle Without End*, Auckland, 1990

KATHERINE MANSFIELD

1888–1923

In spite of her own belief that 'I shall not be "fashionable" long', Katherine Mansfield has gained an international reputation based on the publication of five volumes of short stories and editions of her letters and notebooks. The writer whose work has been translated into some twenty languages was born Kathleen Mansfield Beauchamp, the third daughter of Harold and Annie Beauchamp, on 14 October 1888 in Wellington. Her mother was beautiful, intelligent, and socially ambitious; her father, 'a self made man', gained success and prominence. Plump, inky-fingered, and moody as a child, Mansfield later described herself as 'the odd man out', but memories of her family, her childhood in Thorndon and Karori, and the sun, sea, and wind of Wellington remained a vital part of the pattern of her life, eventually acknowledged and recreated in her fiction.

Between 1903 and 1906 the three eldest Beauchamps attended Queen's College, London. During this stimulating period Mansfield decided to become a cellist, discovered the writing of Oscar Wilde and the Decadents, developed a relationship with Arnold Trowell, a young Wellington musician studying in Brussels, and began a lifetime friendship with a tall, awkward Rhodesian student, Ida Baker (L.M.).

In December 1906 Mansfield returned reluctantly to Wellington and a dual existence. She enjoyed the social life of the colonial capital: balls, tennis parties, five proposals, and playing the cello at various functions including the all-women's Red Cross dinner. Yet she also rejected these people who had not yet 'learned their alphabet', and the restricted, conventional life of her now socially prominent family. There were consolations: time spent with her younger sister Jeanne and brother Leslie, music, reading Marie Bashkirtseff and Elizabeth

Robins. Continuing an intense correspondence with Arnold Trowell, she was also involved in two passionate relationships, with Maata Mahupuku and Edie Bendall. She wanted only to return to London – 'it is Life' – and write. Publication of several pieces in Australia and New Zealand and the continued success of her cousin Elizabeth von Arnim, author of the best-selling *Elizabeth and her German Garden*, finally persuaded her father to allow her to leave. After an extraordinary camping trip to the Ureweras at the end of 1907 she eventually sailed for England in July 1908.

One of five letters written by Katherine Mansfield to Miss Putnam in 1908 announcing her intention to return to England. *Alexander Turnbull Library*

The next few years were an often chaotic search for experience. Little was published at first, and she fell passionately in love with Arnold Trowell's twin brother, Garnet, by whom she became pregnant. Yet she became engaged to George Bowden, a singing teacher, inexplicably marrying him in March 1909, dressed in black, with L.M. as the sole witness. She left Bowden immediately, later returning to him briefly and remaining his legal wife for nine years. Alarmed, Annie Beauchamp arrived in England. Separating her daughter from the ever-supportive L.M., she escorted her to Bad Wörishofen in Germany before returning to Wellington to arrange her eldest daughter Vera's fashionable wedding and delete Katherine from her will. The lonely six months in Germany and her miscarriage there were the basis for the stories which appeared in the *New Age* after her return to London and were collected in 1911 as *In a German Pension*. She had begun to build her literary reputation but was already dogged by illness; not only did she suffer from pleurisy but had already begun to experience the effects of a long-term infection, probably of gonococcal origin.

In December 1911 Mansfield met John Middleton Murry, the editor of the periodical *Rhythm*. At her instigation he became her lodger, then her lover. They loved each other deeply, admired each other intellectually, yet frequently failed to meet each other's needs. For the remainder of Mansfield's short life Murry and L.M. were both indispensable.

By 1914 *Rhythm* had failed, Murry had been declared bankrupt, and they had moved house constantly. They were by then close friends of Frieda and D. H. Lawrence, who were shocked by Mansfield's brief escapade in the war zone with the French writer, Murry's friend Francis Carco.

In October 1915, after spending much of the summer with his sister, Leslie Beauchamp was killed in Flanders. Mansfield fled to Bandol in the South of France where she was later rejoined by Murry. Determined to recreate that 'undiscovered country' she had known with Leslie, Mansfield began to rewrite *The Aloe*, which she had begun in Paris. Published later by Virginia and Leonard Woolf as *Prelude*, it established her reputation.

By 1917 Mansfield and Murry were frequently invited to Lady Ottoline Morrell's Garsington Manor. Fellow guests included T. S. Eliot, Aldous Huxley, Lytton Strachey, the 'Woolves', Bertrand Russell, and her close friends S. S. Koteliansky and Dorothy Brett. In 1918 she returned on medical advice to Bandol. There in February she had her first tubercular haemorrhage. Sensing immediately that 'perhaps it's going to gallop', she began a race against time – the search for health, for some kind of ideal happiness, and for the perfect short story. Haunted by the thought that she might die leaving '"scraps", "bits" . . . nothing real finished', she felt that even her marriage to Murry was a sad anticlimax.

The winters of 1919 and 1920 were spent in Italy and at Menton where, at the Villa Isola Bella, she wrote 'the only story that satisfies me to any extent', 'The Daughters of the Late Colonel'. By 1922 the stories written at the Chalet des Sapins in Montana-sur-Sierre, Switzerland, had won her the fame she dreamed of, but a series of painful X-ray treatments had failed. She now wished only to find the balance between the extremes that had plagued her life, to reject the many parts she had played: 'Risk! Risk anything! Care no more for the opinions of others·. . . . Act for yourself. Face the truth.'

Soon after her thirty-fourth birthday Mansfield entered Gurdjieff's Institute for the Harmonious Development of Man at Fontainebleau. Her last letters to her family, the bewildered L.M., and Murry show that she found something of the calm resolution she sought. Murry visited her on 9 January 1923: 'Katherine died suddenly on the evening I arrived . . . She had found happiness here – that is undoubted.'

Gill Boddy

Quotations

para.1 K. Mansfield to W. Gerhardi, Nov. 1921, *Letters*, vol.2, p.156; K. Mansfield, 'Juliet', Notebook 1, qMS 1242, ATL

para.3 K. Mansfield, *Collected Letters*, p.45; K. Mansfield, *Journal*, p.21

para.7 K. Mansfield, *Journal*, p.94

para.8 K. Mansfield, *Journal*, p.129; *Journal*, p.129

para.9 K. Mansfield, *Letters*, vol.II, p.185; K. Mansfield, *Journal*, p.333

para.10 J. M. Murry to S. Waterlow, 11 Jan. 1923, qMS 1157/4, ATL

Unpublished Sources

The Papers of Katherine Mansfield, 1901–1922, John Middleton Murry Collection, MS Group 38, ATL; and Sir Sydney Waterlow Collection, MS Papers 1157, ATL

Published Sources

Mansfield, K. *The Collected Letters of Katherine Mansfield*, 2 vols, ed. V. O'Sullivan and M. Scott, Oxford 1984, 1987

Mansfield, K. *The Letters of Katherine Mansfield*, ed. J. Middleton Murry, London, 1928

Mansfield, K. *Journal of Katherine Mansfield*, ed. J. Middleton Murry, London, 1954

ANNIE URUWHARANGI MARSH

1896–1982

For nearly fifty years Annie Uruwharangi Marsh longed to move the neglected meeting-house Hinerangi to her own land and have it restored.

Annie Uruwharangi, the daughter of Peina Tetohatoha and Taruke Merea Tetohatoha (born Nicholls), was born on 14 December 1896 at Tirohia, north of Te Aroha near Springdale.

As a young child she moved south to Okauia in the foothills of the Kaimai Range not far from Matamata. She attended Okauia primary school and spent the rest of her life in the district. In later years she recalled that, while the men were felling bush on contract, the women and children did the cooking and collected fungus which was dried, packed into bags, and sold to the Chinese for cooking.

In 1916, at the age of twenty, Annie Uruwharangi married Jack Hakunga Marsh, a farmer of Okauia. They spent the next twenty-seven years farming and raising a family of twelve children. After the death of her husband in 1943, Annie carried on with the milking and farm work with the help of her children. She was a strong woman and could carry a full can of cream on her shoulder.

She would put her son on the farm horse and walk behind guiding the scarifier, an agricultural machine used to earth up the potatoes. To feed her family she planted potatoes, kumara, and corn, and kept a few pigs as well. She was a firm disciplinarian and brought her children up with strong Christian principles.

Annie was an expert weaver. She not only taught members of her own family, but gave demonstrations to the local Maori Women's Welfare League on how to weave kono (food baskets) and headbands. Her beautiful kete (kits) are still treasured by the recipients.

A member of the Waharoa branch of the Maori Women's Welfare League, Annie attended conferences in Wellington and Invercargill. She became a respected elder and commanded much mana in the community. She was invited to perform the karanga to welcome visitors at a reception held by the Waharoa branch of the Maori Women's Welfare League when they were presented with a shield won at the Waikato Winter Show in 1971 for the best Maori court in the show.

The meeting-house Hinerangi Tawhaki had been built at Okauia by Tamatehura Rikihana for his family and officially opened in 1915. After his death, local elders wanted to move the meeting-house to their own land, but the money was needed to feed their families, and in the early 1930s the land was sold to a European owner. Annie feared that the meeting-house would never belong to her

Mrs Annie Uruwharangi Marsh, right, with Mrs Mary Douglass and Mr Walter Aoake in front of Hinerangi meeting-house in the Okauia district, c.1976. *Ruth Cummins*

people again. She would sit on a hill and weep for Hinerangi Tawhaki. She made approaches to several people but with no result. In 1976 a new owner, Russell Thomas, agreed that the Maori people could move the meeting-house, which had been used as a hay barn, back to their own land. It was Annie Marsh who instigated the move and within a week the money had been raised.

The meeting-house was moved a few kilometres down the road to Tawhaki Marae, opposite Annie's house. More money was raised and Hinerangi Tawhaki was restored and renovated.

Annie Uruwharangi Marsh's dream had come true not long before she died on 3 June 1982 at the age of eighty-five, the last of her generation of the Hinerangi Tawhaki sub-tribe. *Joan Stanley*

Published Source
'Elder Carried Much Mana', *NZ Herald*, 4 June 1982 (obituary)

Unpublished Sources
Information was supplied by: Ruth Cummins, George Harrison, Adam Marsh (son of Annie Marsh), and Finn Thompson (son-in-law), all of Matamata.
Collection of undated cuttings from the *Matamata County Mail*, *Matamata Chronicle*, and *NZ Herald* about Okauia and the Maori and Pakeha people who lived there, lent by Effie Douglas of Okauia.

NGAIO MARSH

1895–1982

Ngaio Marsh's life reflected her Renaissance spirit: she was an artist, journalist, actor, producer, novelist, traveller, and broadcaster. Although she is perhaps best known for her elegant, ingenious detective novels, her first love was always the theatre.

Edith Ngaio Marsh was born in Christchurch in 1895, the only child of Rose Elizabeth (born Seager) and Henry Edmund Marsh, a bank clerk. Her parents shared an active interest in the arts, especially in amateur theatricals; as a child Ngaio delighted in 'all the theatre talk' and in being taken to plays and concerts.

She grew up in an isolated house built by her father in the Cashmere Hills above Christchurch; at the age of twelve she described her childhood in her diary as 'the life of a girl who lives on the free hills goes without stockings in summer and runs about all day . . .'. Her early schooling, at a small select dame school, was made miserable by her natural shyness and her embarrassment about her height and her unusually deep voice. Although she learned to cope socially, and as an adult had a rare gift for friendship, she remained a very private person all her life.

Ngaio was then educated for a while at home, first by her mother and then by a governess; she also studied music, and was encouraged to paint, draw, and write stories. Although Ngaio's parents were not well-off, they made many sacrifices in order to give their daughter the best possible education. From 1910 to 1913 Ngaio attended St Margaret's College, a private High Anglican school for girls.

From 1914 to 1919, Ngaio studied at the Canterbury University College

School of Art. There her talents in oils and water-colour were encouraged by tutors Elizabeth and Richard Wallwork, who took her on painting trips to the West Coast and her beloved Southern Alps. Although engrossed in her art, she also earned money from writing articles, poems, and stories for the Christchurch *Sun*, and acted in a number of amateur theatrical productions, sometimes alongside her parents.

Her plans for a career as an artist were disrupted by the visit to Christchurch of the touring Allan Wilkie Shakespeare Company, which revived her love of the theatre and sparked a lifelong passion for Shakespeare. Impressed by a play which Ngaio had written and submitted to him, Wilkie invited her to join his company as an actress to gain practical theatre experience. Her New Zealand tour with Wilkie in 1919–20 and another with the Rosemary Rees Comedy Company the following year were to be Ngaio's theatrical apprenticeship, invaluable at a time when there was no drama school for young actors and producers to learn their craft.

I went on learning about the techniques of theatre . . . of the astonishing effects that may result from an infinitesimal change in timing, of how, in comedy, audiences are played like fish by the resourceful actor.

Returning to Christchurch, Ngaio continued to paint, sharing a studio in Cashel Street with some women friends from art school (which included Evelyn Polson, later Page, and Rhona Haszard) and exhibiting regularly. In 1927 'The Group' caused quite a sensation when it held its own exhibition in rebellion against the hanging strictures and Victorian atmosphere of the Canterbury Society of Arts. Ngaio became increasingly dissatisfied with her painting, however, and correspondingly more involved in the theatre.

During the 1920s she earned a modest living from selling her paintings, stories, and articles, coaching drama, and directing plays for amateur societies; this was at a time when financial independence was unusual for a woman without inherited wealth or a salaried position. But her yearning for 'home' and her European cultural roots was becoming too strong to resist; in 1928 she made the first of her many extended trips to England, supporting herself in London by writing a syndicated series of travel essays entitled 'A New Canterbury Pilgrim' for New Zealand newspapers.

Her urbane, aristocratic sleuth, Chief Detective-Inspector Roderick Alleyn, CID, made his debut in 1931 in *A Man Lay Dead*, the first of over thirty internationally acclaimed detective novels by Ngaio Marsh which were published in England and America and translated into many languages. The success of these beautifully crafted 'whodunnits' made Ngaio one of the few New Zealanders of her time earning a living from their writing.

Many of the novels were set in England (which in some respects was her literary home); a few had a New Zealand setting. The art and theatre worlds also featured as backdrops (in *Artists in Crime*, published in 1938, Alleyn falls in love with a painter, Agatha Troy, who closely resembles her creator). In 1977 she received (along with Daphne du Maurier and Dorothy B. Hughes) the highest accolade from the Mystery Writers of America – their Grand Master Award.

Her mother's final illness in 1932 brought Ngaio home to Christchurch, where she picked up the threads of her old life – painting with The Group, writing, and directing plays for the Canterbury Repertory Society and other amateur groups. She also cared for her widowed father, and developed an English country garden around their Cashmere home.

In 1941, Ngaio was invited to produce a play for the Canterbury University College Drama Society; this was the beginning of what was to be an exciting and successful partnership centred on the college's Little Theatre, and later referred to as a 'Golden Age' in New Zealand drama. Ngaio discovered the pleasures of working with young people:

. . . they started from zero and being extremely intelligent were soon passionately concerned with dramatic principles. Their gluttonous appetite for work and their responsiveness under a hard drive were a constant amazement and their loyalty . . . heartening above words. Their Little Theatre quivered with vitality.

It was at the Little Theatre that Ngaio was able to realise a long-cherished ambition – to produce Shakespeare. Her student production of *Hamlet* in 1943 was a legendary success, and was followed by *Othello*, *A Midsummer Night's Dream*, *Henry V*, and *Macbeth*. Her impact on her student cast and crew was profound:

She was creative and charismatic, and each production was a discovery and an adventure; she was an inspiration to young people discovering the theatre, and immense loyalty and affection developed . . .

Jack Henderson, one of the young actors who fell under her 'powerful Shakespearean spell', remembers her as

tall [5'10"], thin, mannish in appearance, flat-chested, rather gawky . . . dressed usually in beautifully cut slacks . . . large feet with shoes like canal boats, a deep voice – yet intensely feminine withal.

In 1945 and 1946, Ngaio Marsh and the Canterbury Student Players toured their productions of *Hamlet*, *Othello*, and *Macbeth*, sponsored by professional theatre manager Dan O'Connor. In 1949 he also backed their three-month tour of Australia, where they gave 140 performances and received ecstatic reviews; the Sydney *Sun* praised the players' 'inspiration and dramatic intensity, producing exhilaration and excitement – a rare phenomenon'. The tour marked Ngaio's transition from 'a small-town celebrity to an internationally known figure'.

Her flair with student actors did not however transfer readily to the professional stage. While in London again in 1950, Ngaio helped to put together a troupe of professional actors, the British Commonwealth Theatre Company, which toured Australia and New Zealand the following year under her direction. The tour was not a success, playing to poor houses and poor reviews, and leaving Ngaio exhausted and disillusioned. Two years later she faced another disaster when her beloved Little Theatre in Christchurch was destroyed by fire.

In the 1950s Ngaio's life settled into the pattern it was to follow for almost thirty years: nearly every year there was a new detective novel to write, another

Ngaio Marsh making up an actor in *Henry V*.
Hocken Library

Shakespearean play to produce, and every few years she indulged her passion for overseas travel, with London becoming her second home. She was much in demand both at home and abroad as a public speaker and broadcaster, and received many commissions for stories and articles. She also loved to entertain, and her home became a Mecca for her wide circle of friends of all ages.

The New Zealand literary establishment tended to be somewhat dismissive of Ngaio's detective novels, so on a visit to the United States in 1960 she was pleasantly surprised to find herself acclaimed by the *New York Times* as 'New Zealand's best-known literary figure', and fêted as a celebrity on the strength of '21 of the best whodunnits ever written'.

By this time the sales of her novels, plus serial and dramatisation rights, were providing a substantial income, although she complained that the taxman got more than his fair share. She was able to indulge her love of elegant clothes (she was a regular client of Hardy Amies in London) and of fast cars: she drove a powerful black Jaguar XK150, brought back from England in 1960, with great panache until she was nearly eighty.

In 1966 her autobiography, *Black Beech and Honeydew*, was published; it was a book that the reticent Ngaio found difficult to write. That same year she was made Dame Commander of the British Empire, an honour she jokingly referred to as 'me damery'.

For many years Ngaio had campaigned for a replacement for the Little Theatre, but it was not until 1967 that the Ngaio Marsh Theatre, named in her honour, was opened on the University of Canterbury's new campus at Ilam, with Ngaio herself directing *Twelfth Night* as its first production.

In 1972, at the age of seventy-seven, she directed *Henry V* for the opening of the James Hay Theatre, in Christchurch's new civic centre. It was to be her last Shakespearean production. Her health and her legendary energy (Bruce Mason had called her 'indestructible') had begun to fail; on her last trip to

England in 1974 she underwent major surgery for cancer, and her eyesight and hearing were fading. She commented: 'Old age has caught me completely by surprise'.

She maintained her close links with friends and activities in the theatre, however, and continued to write until a few weeks before her death. Her final novel, *Light Thickens*, set during a production of *Macbeth*, was published posthumously.

Ngaio Marsh died at her home on 18 February 1982 of a brain haemorrhage, and is buried at Mount Peel, in the foothills of the Southern Alps.

Annette Facer & Alison Carew

Quotations
para.2 N. Marsh, *Black Beech and Honeydew*, p.28
para.3 Quoted in M. Lewis, *Ngaio Marsh*, p.13
para.6 N. Marsh, p.138
para.12 quoted in M. Lewis, p.91; quoted in M. Lewis, p.92
para.13 quoted in M. Lewis, p.113
para.14 quoted in M. Lewis, p.113; quoted in M. Lewis; p.97
para.15 quoted in M. Lewis, p.120; M. Lewis, p.116
para.18 quoted in M. Lewis, p.168
para.22 quoted in M. Lewis, p.246

Unpublished Sources
Information came from conversations with and letters from Ngaio Marsh in the possession of Annette Facer, who was a friend of Ngaio Marsh.

Published Sources
Lewis, Margaret. *Ngaio Marsh: A Life*, Wellington, 1991
Marsh, Ngaio. *Black Beech and Honeydew*, Auckland, 1966

MARY ANN MARTIN

1817-1884

In the circle of friends of which George Augustus Selwyn was the acknowledged leader there were three remarkable women – Sarah Selwyn, Caroline Abraham, and Mary Martin. Henry Williams had little time for 'Selwyn's young men' who seemed to him no more than acolytes, but the women of Selwyn's company, although they admired and valued their bishop, were not so overawed by the 'Royal George'. Possibly their very willingness to accept the position of helpmeet enabled them (in their letters and journals) to stand back and evaluate. None of the three was physically strong, and Mary Martin was an invalid or semi-invalid all her life. But she even more than her two close friends – they were known as the 'three graces' – responded to New Zealand with a mental vigour and a resilience which took little account of physical frailty.

Mary Ann was born to Ann and William Parker on 5 July 1817. Her father was a vicar of the London parish of St Ethelburga, Bishopsgate, and a prebendary of St Paul's. Mary wrote later of her 'sickly childhood and youth' without giving any further detail about the nature of her disability. She would have had a good classical education, for in New Zealand she relished her access to Selwyn's library, enjoying in particular the writings of the early Christian theologian, Tertullian. On 3 April 1841 at her father's church she married William Martin, who also throughout his life struggled with indifferent health. William, ten years older than Mary, had been a contemporary of Selwyn at St John's College, Cambridge. He was called to the bar of Lincoln's Inn but, keen to escape both the drudgery of legal practice in England and the smoke and fog of London, he responded to Selwyn's suggestion and applied, successfully, for the position of Chief Justice of New Zealand. William Martin sailed for the colony in April 1841 and took up residence at Taurarua (Judge's Bay), Auckland.

Nine months later Mary Martin joined Selwyn's party on the *Tomatin*, bound for New Zealand. William Cotton, the Bishop's chaplain, wrote of her: 'she is a most charming person, very clever indeed and never says anything which is not worth hearing and has plenty to say.'

Later in New Zealand Caroline Abraham stated that her friend had a 'gift for skirmishing'. Both Caroline and Sarah Selwyn always wrote of her as cheerful – even 'bonny' – in spite of her life largely confined to a couch, wheelchair or litter.

When the *Tomatin* grounded in Sydney Harbour, Selwyn brought Mary on to New Zealand in the brig *Bristolian*. She rejoined her husband on 30 May 1842.

Before the Martins' arrival, Taurarua was a favourite camping place for Maori on their way to trade at Auckland. Using raupo huts and a blanket tent, Mary Martin organised a hospital below her house in 1842 which, for hospitality and care towards her Maori patients, outrivalled the government hospital established in 1847. She spoke Maori fluently having, like Selwyn, become proficient on the voyage out. According to Sarah Selwyn she soon gained a 'great name among Maori as a doctor'. She also 'trained' Maori women at her home and taught French and history to the daughters of settlers.

In September 1844 Mary and William visited Selwyn's headquarters at Waimate, in the Bay of Islands. Mary arrived from Kerikeri in an armchair slung on poles carried by Maori bearers. By litter or canoe she accompanied her husband on two further journeys – to Tauranga in 1846 and the Waikato in 1852. Although so much the invalid she wrote enthusiastically to her friend Edward Coleridge of the delight, 'not to be described, only felt, in being able to go out in the early morning and move about without pain or languor'. Proximity to St John's College, when the bishop moved his headquarters to Auckland, was another blessing, maintaining an 'agreeable excitement of comings and goings and messages and notes'.

William Martin was absent from home on circuit for six months of the year, and during this time Mary found the constant happy presence of Maori friends a welcome antidote to loneliness. One uses the words 'Maori friends' advisedly, for here Mary's attitude differed from that of many of the missionary wives. She did not condescend:

Have not Missions even suffered from a jargon of 'deluded heathens' – 'poor natives' – 'dark idolaters' and the like. Use these words long and the habit becomes formed of viewing them as a different species and we get the duty expressed by one of 'condescending to the natives', and with another, 'he is a nice man for a Native'!

She was aware too that, even if missionaries were 'dotted over the land like flax bushes', they would not be effective. 'They are still Pakehas. It must be by means of themselves that the Maoris will be raised.' But 'raised' the Maori had to be; Mary felt the moral imperative to colonialism as keenly as any missionary. At Taurarua 'good' wives were to be trained and suitably educated for their 'good' men. 'Continually', she wrote, 'a hopeful Maori is thrown back and damaged by his marriage with some idle dirty woman.'

Regarding the future of New Zealand, Mary Martin held two viewpoints simultaneously without apparently seeing any potential conflict. When travelling by canoe up the Waihou River and admiring the scenery, she thought 'some day, doubtless, stately mansions will be built there and the park-like ground stocked with deer'. In almost the next sentence she observed, when one of the paddlers mentioned that on that same land he had a crop of potatoes:

yet it is sometimes asserted that the greater part of the countryside is untilled and ownerless. As far as we could learn, every man had his share in the tribal property and knew as well as any old English squire what tracts belonged to him.

The Martins returned to England briefly in 1855, because of the deterioration in William's health; they were back in Auckland the following year. In 1857 William resigned as Chief Justice but, after another brief trip to England during which he was knighted, the couple lived on at Taurarua, maintaining their active interest in Maori welfare and the affairs of the Anglican Church.

The land wars of the 1860s gave an edge to Mary's 'gift for skirmishing', as she and her two friends Sarah Selwyn and Caroline Abraham took up their pens against the actions of their countrymen. 'A policy of intimidation', Mary wrote, 'will never prevail in this land among so brave a people as the New Zealanders', and later:

It is remarkable even now – while the Times *calls these people 'savages' and the* Guardian *dismisses them with a jaunty sentence to be exterminated like all 'savage races'! – that the New Zealanders shew such singular temper and forbearance . . . these men meet – speak – deliberate – send messages to the Governor, shew marvellous respect to law and order.*

The passion and the anger, however, were confined to her letters; in Auckland society, particularly at Government House, she felt 'obliged to turn my attention to the tea table and say that women did not meddle with politics'. Her caution probably resulted from Governor Gore Browne's censure, by imputation, of her husband for 'meddling' in politics. William Martin's pamphlet, *The Taranaki Question*, published towards the end of 1860, defended the stand taken by Wiremu Kingi Te Rangitake at Waitara. In reply the *Government Gazette* of 25 January 1861 stated:

The publication of opinions (especially when emanating from persons of high authority) impugning the justice and legality of the course pursued by Her Majesty's Government, has a most injurious effect on the minds of the native race.

At least the Martins' 'enthusiasm for the natives' was seen as a 'one-sided development of genuine philanthropy', and, unlike Octavius Hadfield, William Martin was not branded as a traitor. Nevertheless the news in July 1861 of Governor Gore Browne's recall, which Taranaki settlers received with gloom, was to Mary Martin a portent of deliverance. She wrote to Charles Abraham in England:

I must sit down at once . . . to tell you the wonderful news. We can't yet believe it, it is like a dream. Kawana, poor man, is recalled & Sir George Grey is coming & will be here in a month.

For Harriet Gore Browne she had more sympathy:

Poor woman she has played a desperate game to help him. Some day when she is calm she will think the last eighteen months over & wish she hadn't meddled so much.

But Governor Grey was no improvement; the war died down in one place only to spring up in another. No further Maori invalids were brought to be nursed at Taurarua hospital and it seemed to Mary that the 'pleasant intercourse . . . which for twenty-five years had made our lives so bright' was at an end.

Although the Martins lived mainly at Taurarua, Mary and William also worked for a time at the Melanesian Mission College of St Andrew's Kohimarama (Auckland) and at St Stephen's College (Auckland). On 14 April 1874 they finally left New Zealand to live quietly at Torquay, where Mary wrote her reminiscences of life in this country. She survived William by just over four years, dying at Torquay on 2 January 1884. For one so frail her life had been diverse, useful, and energetic.

Our Maoris, published in 1884, is an interesting and observant account of her time in New Zealand. The term 'Our' is not insensitively possessive; the affection was mutual. Mary wrote of those she knew personally, for whom she was 'our' mother. The warmth of this genuine relationship still shines through.

Frances Porter

Quotations
para.2 M. Martin to E. Coleridge, 2 Dec. 1846, Letters from Bishop Selwyn and Others, vol.4, p.688
para.3 W. Cotton to sisters, 30 Dec. 1841, Letters from Bishop Selwyn and Others, vol.3, p.634
para.4 C. Abraham to Sophia Marriott, 2 July 1863, Caroline Abraham Papers
para.6 S. Selwyn, Reminiscences, p.25
para.7 M. Martin to E. Coleridge, 1 Dec. 1846, Letters from Bishop Selwyn and Others, vol.4, p.688; 7 Dec. 1844, vol.4, p.674
para.8 M. Martin to E. Coleridge, 1 Dec. 1846, Letters from Bishop Selwyn and Others, vol.4, p.691
para.9 M. Martin to E. Coleridge, 7 Dec. 1844, Letters from Bishop Selwyn and Others, vol.4, p.674
para.10 Lady Martin, *Our Maoris*, pp.94, 95
para.12 M. Martin, *Extracts of Letters from New Zealand on the War Question*, pp.5, 35
para.13 Lady Martin, *Our Maoris*, p.165; *NZ Government Gazette*, 25 Jan. 1861; *Taranaki Herald*, 12 Jan. 1861; M. Martin to C. Abraham, 30 July 1861, Charles Abraham Papers, folder 2
para.14 Lady Martin, *Our Maoris*, p.163

Unpublished Sources
Caroline Abraham, MS Papers 2395, ATL
Charles J. Abraham, MS Papers 257, ATL
Letters from Bishop Selwyn and Others 1842–1867, qMS, ATL (vol.4 contains Mary Martin's letters to Edward Coleridge)
Sarah Selwyn, Reminiscences, 1809–1867, qMS, ATL

Published Sources

Extracts of Letters from New Zealand on the War Question (printed for private circulation), London, 1861

Martin, Lady. *Our Maoris*, London, 1884

NZ Government Gazette, 25 Jan. 1861

Ross, R. M. *Melanesians at Mission Bay*, Auckland, 1983

Taranaki Herald, Nov. 1860 to Jan. 1861

HURIA MATENGA

1841-1909

While still only a young woman, Huria Matenga of Whakapuaka, Nelson, became a national heroine after she played a leading part in rescuing the crew of a sinking cargo vessel during a violent storm.

It was 3 September 1863 and the *Delaware* was en route to Napier from Nelson. Caught in the storm, the vessel took shelter in Whakapuaka Bay off the Nelson coastline. Overnight the ship floundered during fierce gales and was driven on to the rocks. The *Delaware's* first mate Henry Squirrel attempted to swim with a line to shore, but was unsuccessful, so the crew of ten men remained with their stricken vessel as the storm continued to rage.

The residents of Whakapuaka had noticed the *Delaware's* plight and began making preparations for the rescue of the sailors. While some lit fires on the beach, and others prepared to receive the sailors, Huria, her husband, and Hohapata Kahupuku, took to the cold choppy waters of the bay and began swimming out to the site of shipwreck. The *Delaware* was a distance of some half a mile out from the shore. After a difficult swim, they were able to grasp the line thrown out by the crew.

These three were powerful swimmers, but the height of the waves meant their progress back to shore was slow. Eventually, cut and bruised by repeatedly being thrown against the rocky coastline, Huria and the two men swam ashore and secured the line to a large rock. One of the crew then attached a stronger rope to the line and one by one, the sailors left their sinking ship and began hauling themselves along the rope.

The rescue work was hampered by the continual rolling motion of the ship, caused by the strength of the waves, and progress along the rope was painstakingly slow. As the rope slackened or tautened with the movement of the vessel, the exhausted sailors would often fall off into the churning seas, or on to the many sharp rocks.

Huria, Hemi and Hohapata frequently re-entered the water, assisting the sailors along the rope until they reached shore. The last to make the journey was the *Delaware's* Captain Baldwin; he had no sooner been guided to safety, than the rope finally frayed and disappeared into the sea. The only casualty was the ship's mate. Badly injured, he had mistakenly been left for dead on board the *Delaware* and subsequently fell into the water, being swept away before any rescuer could reach him.

Hemi Matenga then set off on the lengthy ride into the Nelson township

Huria Matenga. *Tyree Collection, Nelson Provincial Museum*

with the news·of the incident. The settlers of Nelson acknowledged the courage of all the participants in the rescue. They raised a public subscription and Huria was presented with a specially inscribed gold watch, while Hemi and Hohapata received silver ones. Later, the Board of Inquiry which sat to investigate the episode praised Huria and all of the men for their selfless act of bravery and humanity.

Huria and Hemi Matenga and Hohapata received a reward of £50 each from the government and two others, Te Rei and Te Heirahi, the sum of £10 each. The rescue caused a sensation in the Nelson province, and gradually as the news spread around the country, Huria became celebrated as a national heroine. She was dubbed the 'Grace Darling of New Zealand', after the daughter of an English lighthouse keeper who had also saved several lives during a shipwreck.

Whakapuaka was where the chieftainess Ngarongoa Huria (Huria Matenga) was raised and spent most of her life. She was born there in 1841 and her tribal affiliations were Ngati Tama, Te Ati Awa, and Ngati Toa. Her father was Wiremu Katene Te Puoho, a chief who held lands in both Nelson and Taranaki and resisted the efforts of Chief Land Purchaser Donald McLean to buy them. Her mother was Wikitoria Te Amohau Te Keha, the daughter of the Chief Te Kaha. At the age of sixteen, Huria was married to Hemi Matenga, son of Metapere Waipunaahau (of Ngati Toa and Te Ati Awa) and George Stubbs, a whaler.

During the 1880s Huria succeeded to over 17,000 acres of her father's lands. She and Hemi farmed very successfully on a large scale. Several substantial blocks of land were leased long term to settler farmers. She remained a widely known and well-respected identity for the remainder of her lifetime. The portraits of Huria painted by Gottfried Lindauer show her to have been a strikingly beautiful woman. Amongst her own people, she was renowned for her leadership, strength, kindness and hospitality.

Over the years she made several trips to Taranaki, but she always returned to Whakapuaka. She died there on 24 April 1909, predeceasing Hemi by three years. Her tangi was attended by over 2,000 mourners, Maori and Pakeha, who came to pay their respects to a wahine toa of Whakatu.   *Tui MacDonald*

Unpublished Source
Information was provided by Janice Manson, a relative of Huria Matenga.

Published Sources
AJHR, 1936, G-6B
Ingram, C. W. N. *New Zealand Shipwrecks*, Wellington, 1974
NZ Herstory 1977, Dunedin, 1976

NURSE MAUDE

1862–1935

When Nurse Maude was crowned Queen of the Festival during Christchurch's fund-raising for Belgian refugees in 1915, she wore her coronation robes over her nurse's uniform, a 'nurse at the front and a queen at the back'. Her uniform was symbolic of 'her call for life', the 'trust remitted to her care for which she had to account'. She was never seen in any other garment; in July 1935, 'one of the best-known and best-loved women in the city', she was buried in it.

Emily Sybilla Maude was born on 11 August 1862, the eldest daughter of a well-known Christchurch settler Thomas William Maude and his wife Emily Catherine (born Brown). She wrote in 1908:

When I was a young girl, I used to be very fond of visiting among the poor and in the hospital, and I conceived the idea that by being trained as a nurse, I could best serve my fellow creatures.

Thus, in 1889, she became a paying 'lady probationer' at Middlesex Hospital, England.

Nurse Maude returned to Christchurch in 1893 to become matron of Christchurch Hospital. During her three years there, she achieved her major goals of professional nursing training programmes and a new nurses' home. But they were not happy years. Embroiled in the bitter debate between the new probationers and older, untrained nurses, and in constant friction with the board, her work was subjected to a commission of inquiry into the management of the hospital in 1895. Although exonerated of all charges, and her efficiency 'in the nursing business . . . unquestioned', the inquiry undoubtedly confirmed her dislike of her position. Blunt and uncompromising, unable to submit easily to authority and unwilling to delegate the nursing work to others, Nurse Maude was not suited to institutional management.

Nurse Maude began her district nursing work in November 1896, based at the Anglican Community of the Sacred Name and supported financially by Lady Heaton Rhodes and later by the St Michael's and Sydenham parishes. District nursing, 'services given to the sick poor in their own homes regardless of the religious denomination of the sufferers', was an English development and Nurse Maude 'worked it as nearly on English lines as I knew how'. By the end of that first year, she had made over 1,100 visits on foot to those unable to afford hospital or private nursing. Later transportation included a horse and buggy, bicycles and, after the First World War, a car, donated by local businessmen. From 1897, the service was based in an old shop in Durham Street. In March 1901, the Nurse Maude District Nursing Association was formed, with a committee of supporters organising financial backing. More nurses were employed as funds permitted. It was not until after the war that state assistance was received by the association, which depended entirely on subscriptions. However, Nurse Maude found she 'never appealed to the public without receiving a very generous response'. In 1918, a successful street appeal financed a new building in Madras Street.

From the first, Nurse Maude recognised the far-reaching nature of district nursing: 'sometimes to relieve, sometimes to heal, always to console'. Her social work services included the provision of clothing and food, and she never hesitated to interfere in her patients' lives or questioned the rightness of her decisions about them. Yet she had 'a definite policy that every family should maintain its independence . . . the most cruel thing a social worker could do,' she said, 'was to take away a family's self respect.' Thus clothing was always sold, for however little, and patients were invited to contribute to the association's funds if they

Nurse Maude's district nursing staff had to be 'the BEST nurses . . . thoroughly trained . . . women of tact, judgement and resource'. District Nursing Office Headquarters, South Durham Street, Christchurch, 1914. *Steffano Webb Collection, Alexander Turnbull Library*

were able. At a time when relief was often 'minimal, condemnatory and grudgingly given', Nurse Maude gave as one friend to another. 'I'd rather help ten men who abused my help, than refuse one who really needed it,' she said.

Nurse Maude believed that no nurse could be truly successful without developing her spiritual role, for the dying must be 'comforted and strengthened . . . with words of hope'. She was a firm believer in faith healing; all her visits began with prayers. Her service was, furthermore, 'not only to the living but to the dead', and from 1908 she accepted responsibility for preparing bodies at the public morgue for burial, 'with the same reverent attention being given to the known and the unknown'.

Nurse Maude regarded her role as a teacher as one of the 'fascinations' of district nursing. She believed that mothers in particular should learn the basic principles of cleanliness, ventilation, diet, home-nursing, and childcare, and in 1917 began a series of lectures on these subjects through the Mothers' Union.

The duties of a district nurse were thus manifold, and Nurse Maude's staff had to be 'the BEST nurses . . . thoroughly trained . . . women of tact, judgement and resource'. A foundation member of the Trained Nurses' Association, she worked hard all her life to gain recognition for professional nursing qualifications, although she regarded nursing as a 'vocation, not just a profession'.

Among the worst health problems of the early twentieth century was 'the great white plague of consumption'. Accepting 'the gospel of fresh air' as a possible cure for the disease, Nurse Maude, with the support of various working men's clubs, opened a camp at New Brighton in 1903 where working men in the early stages of tuberculosis could live in tents, getting plenty of rest and good food. A separate women's camp opened in 1905. Run on a shoe-string, facilities remained primitive. However the Canterbury district health officer regarded the camps as 'great sources of credit to those concerned', and it was claimed that the 'percentage of cures was as good as that at Cambridge' (that is, at the government sanitorium at Cambridge, Waikato). The enterprise ended in bitterness, with accusations of financial dishonesty and a public falling-out with the camps' honorary medical officer, but Nurse Maude was not held personally to blame and she received much praise for her efforts.

It was Nurse Maude's 'transparent simplicity of goodness' which enabled her to achieve so much. Despite her abrupt manner, her stern expression only occasionally lightened by 'the loveliest smile anyone could wish to see', she was 'someone of whose motives and purposes there could be no question whatever'. Even with doctors, always jealous of their prerogatives, there are almost no recorded clashes, no doubt at least partly because Nurse Maude saw the nurse's duty as obeying instructions without question. Upheld by a 'simple Christian faith', 'granite-like in its substance', and unhampered by any domestic ties, Nurse Maude pursued her goals with a single-minded and untiring devotion which could achieve miracles.

Nurse Maude was not by nature a good organiser, nor would she accept any interference in the running of her organisation. She did not believe in written records, committing all information about her patients to her phenomenal memory. 'Do you keep a list of your friends for fear of forgetting them?' she asked tartly. During the 1918 influenza epidemic, her inability to delegate finally caught up with her. Placed in charge of the central bureau sending out medical and nursing aid and deluged with requests for her personal help, she worked harder than anyone, doing everything herself. From that time on, her reserves of energy, once boundless, were never the same. A serious illness in 1925 forced her to give up direct nursing work, though she always remained closely involved in the service she had founded. She was awarded an OBE in 1934 and died on 12 July 1935. Her body lay in state at the cathedral before the funeral, which was attended not only by the notable but also by the thousands of people she had helped. The citizens of Christchurch stood in silent tribute as the funeral procession passed through the streets of the city to which Nurse Maude had devoted her life.   *Patricia Sargison*

Quotations

para.1 *Christchurch Star*, 20 April 1915; Sister Constance, NERF oral history project, *The Press*, 14 Dec. 1908; *The Press*, 13 July 1935

para.2 *Kai Tiaki*, vol.1 no.4, Oct. 1908, p.118

para.3 Report of the Commission of Inquiry into the Management of Christchurch Hospital, *AJHR*, 1895, H-18, p.13

para.4 *Kai Tiaki*, vol.4, Oct. 1908, p.118; *The Press*, 9 March 1901; *The Press*, 14 Dec. 1904

para.5 Motto of Nurse Maude District Nursing Association; M. Lambie, *My Story*, p.25; M. Tennant, *Paupers and Providers*, p.199; E. Somers-Cocks, *A Friend in Need*, p.153

para.6 *Kai Tiaki*, vol.1 no.4, Oct. 1908, p.119; *Kai Tiaki*, vol.5 no.2, April 1912, p.31

para.8 *Kai Tiaki*, vol.6 no.1, Jan. 1913, p.11; *The Press*, 10 Aug. 1905

para.9 *Kai Tiaki*, vol.27 no.2, May 1937, p.84; Annual Report of Department of Health, *AJHR*, 1905, H-31, p.41; *The Press*, 2 March 1905

para.10 *The Press*, 13 July 1935; Elsie Browne, NERF oral history project; *The Press*, 14 Dec. 1908, p.4d; Sister Constance, line 124; E. Somers-Cocks, p.156

Maude

para.11 E. Somers-Cocks, p.88

Unpublished Sources

Elsie E. Browne, 'Reminiscences about Nurse Maude', recorded by H. Campbell, NZ Nursing Education and Research Foundation (NERF) oral history project, tape 81, ATL

M. Tennant, 'Women and Welfare: The Response of Three New Zealand Women to Social Problems of the Period 1890–1910', BA Hons thesis, Massey, 1974

NZ Royal Commission on the Influenza Epidemic, 1919, Transcripts: Examination of Nurse Maude, p.982–8, National Archives, Wellington

Sister Constance, 'Reminiscences about Nurse Maude', recorded by J. Sutherland, NERF oral history project, tape 160, ATL

Published Sources

Lambie, Mary. *My Story: Memoirs of a New Zealand Nurse*, Christchurch, 1956

NZ Department of Health. *Annual Report: Report of Canterbury District Health Office*, AJHR, H-31, 1904, p.41; 1905, p.41; 1907, p.36

NZ Nursing Journal (Kai Tiaki), 1908–1935, especially articles by S. Maude: 'Hospital Etiquette', vol.1 no.2, April 1908, p.36; 'District Nursing', vol.1 no.4, Oct. 1908, pp.118–9; 'The Last Office for the Dead', vol.5 no.2, April 1912, p.31; on district nursing, vol.6 no.1, Jan. 1913, p.11. Also obituary, vol.28 no.4, Sept. 1935, pp.147–50

Somers-Cocks, E. *A Friend in Need: Nurse Maude: Her Life and Work*, Christchurch, 1950

Tennant, M. *Paupers and Providers: Charitable Aid in New Zealand*, Wellington, 1989

LUCY MEE

1857–1925

As New Zealand's Pakeha population grew in the later nineteenth century, and as the proportion of elderly people increased, there was an expansion in the number of local charitable institutions. Most of these were intended for the aged and infirm, but in the four main centres larger institutions catered for a range of 'social problems'. Nearly all the 'benevolent institutions' (the somewhat kindly name conferred on them, though 'workhouse' might have been as apt) were run by a married couple, the employment of one dependent upon the continued availability of the other. The husband's role was that of disciplinarian; the wife was both nurse and housekeeper. Mr and Mrs Mee, master and matron of the Otago Benevolent Institution at Caversham, were one such couple, but so essential was Lucy Mary Mee to the running of 'the Benny' (as it was popularly known) that she continued as matron for some years beyond her husband's retirement, only retiring herself after thirty-four years of service.

Mrs Mee had solid credentials for the position of matron of one of New Zealand's largest charitable institutions. As Lucy McDermott she was for some years charge laundress at the Dunedin Lunatic Asylum, and afterwards head nurse at Ashburn Hall Asylum (a progression not uncommon in nursing before the establishment of training courses and registration). In 1884 she married Edward John Mee, an Irishman who had been head warder at the Dunedin asylum. In 1886 the Mees were appointed to the Otago Benevolent Institution at a salary of £100 a year. At this time the institution contained an assortment of destitute children and adults, many of the latter unattached, alcoholic old men.

Since most of the cleaning and nursing in the institution was done by the inmates, old and young alike, Mrs Mee had to supervise their work and train the

434

children for domestic service outside the institution. In 1888 a lying-in ward for single and destitute women was opened and, at the same time as her own family was increasing in size, Mrs Mee added maternity nursing to her skills. She probably did the best she could, given the penny-pinching policies of the management committee and the obstreperousness of her elderly charges (some 300 by the 1900s), but there is no doubt that the institution was a bleak and uninviting place. In 1902 Grace Neill, the Assistant-Inspector of Charitable Institutions, compared it with an English poor-house of some forty years earlier, and denounced the 'pauper nursing' practised within. Recognising that an increasing number of inmates were chronically and terminally ill, and in need of advanced nursing skills, the management committee appointed a nurse to assist Mrs Mee in 1907.

For the first time, Mrs Mee had to share her domain with another female authority figure. After a prolonged dispute, the nurse's activities were restricted to the hospital wards, Mrs Mee retaining control of the rest of the institution. Further difficulties came in 1912, when the Mees' employment was terminated, apparently on account of Mr Mee's health (he was incapacitated for the next fourteen years, which meant that his wife had his needs to attend to, as well as those of the institution). Mrs Mee was reappointed in charge of the women's quarters and another master, a Mr Sinclair, appointed to take charge of the men. Again there was conflict, Mrs Mee apparently engineering Sinclair's dismissal in 1913. Some members of the management committee felt uneasy at Sinclair's treatment, but noted that Mrs Mee had been at the institution for a very long time, and that they appreciated her capabilities. Sinclair's replacement was appointed as Mrs Mee's subordinate, and all was well by 1916, when Mrs Mee was presented with a handbag in appreciation of her thirty years' service.

In 1920 Mrs Mee finally retired, then aged sixty-eight. Unlike the majority of her charges at the Benevolent Institution, she had family to care for her in her old age, and when she died in 1925 it was in a daughter's home. The bedridden Mr Mee died almost exactly one year later.   *Margaret Tennant*

Unpublished Sources
Cemetery Transcriptions, Dunedin Southern Cemetery, R. C. (Roman Catholic) Headstones
Otago Benevolent Institution, Relief Rough Minutes, 1886–1890 and 1893–1908, Hocken

Published Sources
The Cyclopedia of New Zealand, vol.4, Christchurch, 1905, p.150
Evening Star, 2 Dec. 1916; 19 July 1926
Otago Daily Times, 23 Jan. 1912; 20 April 1920

ELLEN MELVILLE

1882–1946

When Ellen Melville died on 27 July 1946, Auckland lost one of its most significant women. She was the longest serving councillor in the history of the Auckland City Council and one of the nation's leading feminists. Her contemporaries were in no doubt about her importance. The National Council of Women

(NCW) called a meeting of Auckland women to discuss some fitting memorial to Ellen. Speaking at the meeting, the mayor, John Allum, stated that 'her service will remain forever an example to all citizens and in particular to the younger women of our city and indeed of our dominion'. It was decided to commemorate Ellen's life and work by building a hall for women, an ambition achieved in 1962 after a marathon fund-raising. Ironically, few Auckland women passing the Pioneer Women's and Ellen Melville Hall today know anything about the woman who gave her name to it.

Born on 13 May 1882 at Tokatoka, Northern Wairoa, Eliza Ellen Melville was the third of the seven children of Alexander Melville and his wife Eliza (born Fogarty). Alexander Melville was a boat-builder and farmer. Eliza Colls and her sister Ellen had established a private school at Hokitika in the early 1870s, and Eliza had then been governess to the children of Judge Gillies in Auckland.

Ellen Melville's first schooling took place at home, and her mother's influence contributed to her lifelong belief in the value of education. She believed that 'knowledge meant power' and talked of the 'armour of education'. Although she never married or had children, she took a keen interest in the educational careers of her nieces and nephews.

At the age of seven Ellen began attending Tokatoka School, three miles' walk through mud and bush. In 1895 she sat her Junior District Scholarship and was placed second for New Zealand. This entitled her to three years' secondary schooling and the following year she began attending Auckland Grammar School, boarding with relatives in Auckland.

We do not know what fired Ellen's ambition to be a lawyer, although during her secondary school years, Ethel Benjamin, the first woman in the British Empire to become a lawyer, graduated from Otago University. In 1896 the Female Law Practitioners Act was passed in anticipation of Ethel Benjamin's graduation. She was admitted to the bar the following year. A year later Ellen Melville matriculated and passed the Solicitors General Knowledge Examination.

Ellen was under the requisite age to study law at the university, so she joined the firm of Devore and Martin as a clerk and received her early training there. Both partners in the law firm had progressive ideas about women and had a considerable impact on the young Ellen. Albert Devore had been a city councillor and mayor of the city. He encouraged Ellen to enter local body politics. Both partners later signed Ellen's application to the Supreme Court to become a solicitor.

In 1904 Ellen enrolled at Auckland University College for her professional examination. As her family could not support her financially, she attended night classes while working at Devore and Martin during the day. Ellen apparently approached her chosen course of study with some trepidation. She tried without success to persuade a friend to enrol with her and did not attend the first week of lectures. In the second week she was relieved to be met at the lecture room door by Geraldine Hemus, who had also enrolled. The two women attended all lectures together, studied together, and later were lifetime workers for the NCW.

In December 1906 Ellen Melville became the second woman in New Zealand to be admitted to the bar (Geraldine Hemus was admitted in the following year) and three years later she set herself up in sole practice, the first woman in New Zealand and probably the first in the British Empire to do so. Ellen's life is marked by such acts; although the anecdote about her nervousness in attending her first lectures shows that she was not immune to moments of hesitation, she consistently placed herself in positions where she was pioneering the way for her sex.

Her legal practice consisted primarily of conveyancing work. It provided her with a means of financial support, but John Allum was probably correct when he said she 'sacrificed her own personal professional interests for the general good of the community as a whole'.

Ellen Melville saw a wider role for herself than the advancement of her career. She believed that women had a duty to enter public life and to make progress for their sex. Her legal skills were put to work for the women's groups of Auckland. She had little time for frivolity and typically, despite being one of the founders of the Auckland Lyceum Club, declined to seek the office of president because she saw the aims of the club as too exclusively social.

In 1913 no women held public office in the major cities of New Zealand and the law prohibited women from standing for parliament. The NCW was in recess and it was a low point in feminist activity. When Ellen Melville acceded to a request from women in Auckland to stand for the Auckland City Council in that year, she had two aims. She believed that she could represent women's interests in the development of civic policy and she also hoped to inspire other women to exercise their political responsibilities.

To equip herself for public life, Ellen learnt skills which had hitherto been largely the preserve of men: the law, meeting procedures, and public speaking. She also actively encouraged other women to enter the public sphere. In 1913 she was involved in the setting up of the Civic League, a feminist group which provided a voice on local and national issues. In the 1930s she established a public speaking circle in the Lyceum Club to train women for public life; almost every member of it became active in community affairs. Later, in 1944, she co-founded the Women for Wellington movement to encourage women to stand for parliament. But her most outstanding tactic was to encourage women by doing it herself.

Ellen always publicly acknowledged the female constituency from which she had emerged and which supported her. In her first local body election, she stood with Dr Florence Keller (Hospital and Charitable Aid Board) on a Civic League ticket after being asked to do so by a public meeting of Auckland women. She saw herself as conduit by which Auckland women could lobby council; she introduced deputations of women's groups to council and took up their concerns. She fought discrimination during debates over issues such as the employment of women as tram conductors and the granting of taxi licences to women.

But she was careful never to allow herself to be marginalised. In accepting the support of women for the 1913 campaign, Ellen explained her philosophy that the 'best government' involved 'a partnership' drawing on the talents of both sexes and all classes. It was not possible, she argued, to leave women out of this partnership. 'Individual homes are conducted by men and women on a partnership basis . . . what is good for the home is good for the city full of homes.' Later, on the NCW, she talked of 'our mission of mothering the world', but despite putting forward arguments for women's participation based on their different perspective, she never argued that women should confine themselves to women's concerns. She took the opposite position. To the NCW in 1921 Ellen expounded her belief that 'women must act as Citizens rather than as members of one sex, and work not as women against men, but as men and women together'. Throughout her political life, she adeptly juggled her championing of women's issues with involvement in all aspects of civic work. On the council her membership of the key finance committee, her nearly thirty-year-long chairmanship of the library committee, and her parks work ensured that Councillor Melville was part of the mainstream of council business.

Her own personal qualities contributed to her political credibility. She understood meeting procedures, was a confident speaker and adept at handling even large public gatherings. Her obituary tells us that the 'contributions she made to debates were always models of their kind, brief, completely thought-out and containing original ideas of real value'. She got on well with men and her personal qualities obviated any tendency on their part to see women in public life as lightweight.

Her niece Beth Rushbrook remembers her manner as

matter-of-fact with a dry Scottish sense of humour. She talked to men very well. She was clever and didn't let men put it over her. If she thought something was nonsense, she could be very scathing, although never nasty. It was more a tone of voice. She was quite outspoken and very direct. Once she decided to do something, I couldn't imagine her being hesitant.

Ellen's personal style was a careful blend of sobriety and femininity. To *The Observer* she complained that she didn't see 'why apparently sensible men should be surprised to see her looking at the dress goods display in the shop windows merely because she is qualified in law'. She was well groomed and made her own dresses and hats, although in her public life she always wore subdued colours and tailored outfits. She used perfume, but not make-up. Writing about her for *The Observer* in 1931, Robin Hyde said she lacked 'any hint of frivolity and flapperdom which old gentlemen always seem to hope that women in office will represent'.

Hyde observed that Ellen and her male colleagues 'seem to mix quite well', but she also noted that in her first years of office Ellen was regarded by some as 'an improper joke. Several of them were pledged to be ponderously funny at her expense.' Ellen suffered blatant discrimination when she was passed over in 1938 and again in 1941 as deputy mayor, a position she should have won by virtue of her seniority in council and her ability. On the second occasion there was a storm of protest from women's groups who called it bluntly 'sex prejudice'.

Neither was Ellen entirely supported by her family. The Melvilles were a close family and for many years Ellen lived with her ageing parents and sister May in Mt Eden. Ellen tended a garden full of native plants, and at the family bach at Campbells Bay she planted more. She took care of the business side of family affairs, while May kept the household running smoothly. Beth Rushbrook says that generally the family regarded Ellen with great respect, but her parents

Ellen Melville, solicitor and Auckland city councillor. *Auckland Public Library*

had been unhappy about her decision to stand for council and, when she announced her intention to contest parliament, some family members tried to dissuade her. Her brother Randall, then parliamentary reporter for the *New Zealand Herald*, said he did not consider it a suitable place for women.

But her family's reluctance did not prevent Ellen from pursuing her political ambitions. Within days of the passing of the Women's Parliamentary Rights Act in 1919, she announced her intention to stand for parliament. She believed that

women would get nothing done for them in the legislation unless they had women in parliament. They knew what became of their conference resolutions which were forwarded to the Government, and went into the waste-paper basket. They would make no progress until they got women in the House.

Her first campaign was as Reform candidate in Grey Lynn. Despite the fact that this was traditionally a Labour seat, Ellen won 30.9 per cent of the vote to Labour's 36.5 per cent. This creditable performance added to her bitterness

439

when in the next election the Reform Party rejected her as a candidate in favour of a man, and a man who was a former Liberal to boot. 'The only conclusion to be taken,' she said, 'was that they did not want a woman in Parliament. They preferred a Liberal man to a Reform woman.' Later, in 1931, Ellen was caustic about the failure of the United-Reform Coalition to field any women candidates. 'The Ex-Kaiser's attitude to women was not much different to that of certain New Zealanders,' she said.

Her political career may have been checkered but it demonstrated enormous stamina. She stood a total of seven times, but was never ultimately successful. On two occasions she stood against her own Reform Party as an independent, in 1926 against the express wishes of Prime Minister Gordon Coates. On this occasion she split the vote in the Eden electorate, which allowed Labour to win. This damaged her reputation and finally put an end to her chances. She had put her feminism before party allegiance and for this she paid the price.

The issues promoted by Ellen during her electioneering campaigns were essentially those of the National Council of Women. Ellen had been a leading figure in the revival of the NCW, calling the inaugural meeting in Auckland in 1917 at the rooms of the Civic League, a feminist society formed by Ellen and other Auckland women active in political affairs. During the war Ellen was active on the Auckland Patriotic League. The war, she said, gave women

a stronger sense of the value of common effort, had drawn them more closely, the practical results to be derived from organisation having been seen and remarked. Their experience had removed their sense of inferiority to men.

She became the inaugural president of the Auckland NCW, was president nine times, and between 1919 and 1922 was Dominion president of the council.

Ellen's devotion to the NCW stemmed from her belief that women must band together to advance their cause. She had been instrumental in forming and nurturing many women's societies and clubs, commencing with her involvement in the Auckland YWCA's Women's Club for businesswomen, formed in 1911, of which she was secretary and later vice-president.

The 'club movement' had developed as a political force in America, and Ellen was always conscious of the place of New Zealand women in the world-wide feminist movement and the need to forge international links. In 1924 she and fellow NCW member Elsie Griffin travelled to Europe. In England Ellen helped Lady Astor, Britain's first woman member of the Commons, with her electioneering campaign. In Scotland she stayed with Lady Aberdeen, president of the International Council of Women. In 1934 she was a delegate to the Pan-Pacific and South East Asian Women's Association Conference in Honolulu.

Ellen urged the NCW to have 'a broader view' and to 'get in personal touch with the women's movement throughout the world'. It should 'avoid resolutions of a trivial character and see that matters we dealt with were of sufficient seriousness and weight. There is nothing women cannot do if they really combine'.

One of the most significant themes of Ellen's political career was her belief that there should be no favours for women because of their sex; she suspected such favours would confirm women in a subordinate position. Although she spoke of 'the dignity of the home' and the importance of women's role in it, she also argued that women had to earn their place in the world by competing equally with men and pulling their weight. During the Depression, she maintained that women should pay the same unemployment levy as men, because then the Unemployment Board would have to provide relief work for women and girls. She spoke against a NCW remit that domestic workers should not pay tax. In typically uncompromising style Ellen said that those proposing it had

allowed a lot of sloppy sentiment to influence them. The women who follow this employment are honoured and valued citizens who should be prepared to bear the burden of tax. If the National Council stands for the equality of women, it cannot endorse this pernicious exception.

'Sloppy sentiment' was something Ellen Melville could never have been accused of. Speaking at a meeting in 1919 soon after the revival of the NCW, Ellen chastised women for letting the NCW go into recess. This, she said, had resulted in New Zealand lagging behind the rest of the world in women's affairs.

Women were to blame for practically all the social disabilities under which they suffered in this country. If they would not work nor organise to remove them they simply had to suffer them . . . It was no use blaming men. It was women's own fault.

From men, Ellen demanded nothing more nor less than equality. But from women she expected more. She believed women owed a special obligation to their sex. During the Depression, she maintained that 'it was a woman's duty to help the women who were in difficult circumstances'. Ellen took this injunction personally. In the early years of the Depression she embarked on journeys in her Morris 8 car, taking with her a selection of New Zealand-made clothes, to promote local goods and keep the women who made them in jobs. 'The working woman has no one to champion her,' she said to the NCW.

She is an unknown quantity. No statistics, so far as I know, have been collected about her, and I think as a woman's organisation we should put forward some constructive proposals. We have only ourselves to blame that government and government departments take no interest in women.

In Ellen's view, it was up to women to prove and win their equality. She expected nothing to be handed to women on a plate. Her whole life was single-mindedly focused on this goal.

In 1946 Ellen learned she had stomach cancer. An operation was unsuccessful. It was typical of Ellen that she refused drug treatment for the pain, as she wished her mind to remain clear. Her secretary worked with her in hospital to wind up her affairs and leave her business in order. She died in an Auckland private hospital.

Her coffin was laid in state in the Auckland City Council chamber and a laurel wreath was placed on her desk. The flags on the Town Hall and all the city's libraries were flown at half-mast. Representatives of women's organisations and local bodies packed the church for her funeral service, at which the prime minister, Peter Fraser, gave an address, and a hundred people, unable to get inside, waited on the pavement outside. Three trucks were needed to take the wreaths to the graveside at Waikumete Cemetery.

Ellen Melville's life spans the interregnum between the campaigns of the suffragists and the so-called 'second wave' of feminism. She worked tirelessly to finish the work of the nineteenth-century feminists to remove women's political 'disabilities', campaigning actively to see women enter parliament, serve as jurors, and be appointed as justices of the peace. But she also represented the new breed of feminists: the predominantly single highly educated career women who sought reform by entering the mainstream of political and economic life. Even by modern definitions she was unquestionably a feminist. In some ways she was a conservative woman, standing for parliament on a conservative ticket and sometimes taking strong moral positions. But her belief that there should be no limits on women in public life or employment, her persistent efforts to organise women, and her absolute faith in her sex, all mark her as one of the most significant women of the twentieth century in the struggle for women's rights.

Sandra Coney

Quotations

para.1 J. Allum, speech notes, 9 Oct. 1946, Auckland City Council archives

para.3 F. J. Danaher, 'A Woman's Advocate – The Life History of Ellen Melville', typescript, APL

para.9 J. Allum, speech notes

para.14 Unidentified, undated newspaper clipping, Women's Archives, AIM; Report of Second NCW Conference, 1921, H. Lovell-Smith Papers, ATL

par.15 Obituary, unidentified newspaper clipping, 29 July 1946, NCW scrapbooks, AIM

para.16 Interview with B. Rushbrook; *Observer*, 26 April 1913, p.20; *Observer*, 10 Sept. 1931, p.15

para.17 *Observer*, 10 Sept. 1931, p.15; V. Kuitert, 'Ellen Melville', p.76

para.19 *Auckland Star*, 19 Sept. 1923, p.7

para.20 *NZ Herald*, 25 Nov. 1922, p.11; *Auckland Star*, 17 Nov. 1931, p.8

para.22 *NZ Herald*, 25 June 1919, p.8

para.25 Report of the Annual Conference of NCW, 1923, H. Lovell-Smith Papers, ATL

para.26 Unidentified newspaper clippings, 1 Oct. 1930, 31 March 1933, NCW scrapbooks, AIM

para.27 *Dominion*, 9 Sept. 1919, NCW scrapbooks, AIM

para.28 Unidentified newspaper clippings, 27 March 1931, 3 March 1931, NCW scrapbooks, AIM

Unpublished Sources

Auckland City Council Archives, held at Auckland City Council

H. K. Lovell-Smith Papers, MS Papers 1376, ATL

Interviews with Beth Rushbrook and Rod Melville, 1987

Melville family history and other documents held by Rod Melville and Beth Rushbrook

Minutes and scrapbooks of the Auckland Branch of the NCW, AIM

Veronica Kuitert. 'Ellen Melville 1882–1946', MA research essay, Auckland, 1986

Women's Archives, NCW, AIM

Published Sources

Bush, G. W. A. *Decently and In Order: The Centennial History of the Auckland City Council*, Auckland, 1971

Colgan, Wynne. *The Governor's Gift: The Auckland Public Library, 1880–1980*, Auckland, 1980

Coney, Sandra. *Every Girl: A Social History of Women and the YWCA in Auckland*, Auckland, 1986

Holt, Betty. *Women in Council: A History of the National Council of Women of New Zealand, 1896–1979*, Wellington, 1980

The Observer, 26 April 1913, p.20

Wilkinson, Iris (Robin Hyde). 'The City Council Through a Woman's Eyes', *Observer*, 10 Sept. 1931, p.15

NOLA MILLAR

1915-1974

I have held two of the most interesting reference librarian jobs in the country and I loved the work. My trouble was that I loved the theatre just as much.

In both fields Nola Leigh Millar broke new ground and made a lasting national contribution. She was a woman who 'touched and inspired everyone who [came] into contact with her'.

Nola was born in Wellington in 1915, into a family with strong theatrical influences on both sides. Her father, Frank W. Millar, was the secretary of the Public Service Association in the 1930s, and for many years produced the *New Zealand Theatre and Film Magazine*, a popular periodical. Her mother, who died when Nola was very young, was one of the nine gifted children of Richard Marshall, conductor of Wellington's Theatre Royal Orchestra, and later the theatre manager.

Nola gained her first practical experience of theatre with the Wellington East Old Girls' Dramatic Society, for which she acted; she later produced and even wrote plays for the society's entries in the festivals of amateur one-act plays organised by the New Zealand branch of the British Drama League.

Meanwhile, in 1934, she joined the Alexander Turnbull Library, rising from typist to reference librarian, and, on one occasion, acting librarian. By 1937, she had completed a BA degree at Victoria University College.

It was said of Nola that she cared less about audiences than about the intrinsic value of theatre for those participating, that she believed in its healing effects and ability to foster personal growth. She was involved with several theatre groups in Wellington in the 1940s, but it was through Unity Theatre that her beliefs found most expression. With Unity's policy of producing socially relevant plays and promoting New Zealand theatre, Nola was able to produce the works of dramatists such as Gorki, Gogol, Ibsen, and Brecht, which she continued once she had her own theatre group in the 1960s. For Unity she produced over twenty plays, including four by New Zealand playwrights.

From 1946, she began to be involved in drama administration: she became president of Unity Theatre, and secretary of the Wellington branch of the British Drama League. In the late 1940s, she received frequent requests to produce plays around the country, but was unable to accept because of her library job.

The challenge came when she was asked by Richard and Edith Campion to be manager of the New Zealand Players, a professional touring company which they set up in 1952.

I had to make a decision. I thoroughly enjoyed reference work, helping people who were doing research. But there was no real doubt in my mind what was the first thing I wanted – the theatre.

But, as she explained, what the company really needed was an accountant, and she was soon back in a library, this time at Victoria University College, where her research skills were again much in demand.

After three years, I decided I must try again to make a life in the theatre. Sink or swim, I would try my luck as a freelance theatrical producer and drama tutor. Since 1956, I've been swimming hard!

She lived on very little, supplementing her income with broadcasting and writing, for example as radio critic for the *Listener*. She was also an excellent public speaker.

Because of her belief in the value of performance for its own sake, she was also active in amateur drama circles: the British Drama League and the New Zealand Drama Council, which co-opted her onto its executive in 1959. She also edited its publication *New Zealand Theatre* from 1958 to 1967. She travelled to towns and cities from Whangarei to Alexandra, at the request of members of either organisation, to produce plays, but only those she thought worthwhile: 'It must be something I want to do and enjoy doing and I would not do a play that I did not care for.' She was the obvious person to preside over the amalgamation of the Drama League and the Drama Council to form the New Zealand Theatre Federation in 1969. This new body honoured her with life membership in 1971.

Nola felt strongly that the experience of theatre was important for young people. Remembering her pleasure as a child in seeing Shakespeare performed, she set up her own New Theatre Company in 1959 to put on Shakespearean productions for schools. There was an annual open-air event in the Wellington Botanic Gardens as well, and for three summers the company travelled as strolling players around motor camps, beaches, and theatres in the North Island. Nola also worked with Unity Theatre's under-twenty-fives group in the mid-1960s, and, in 1969, directed the first residential Youth Theatre School.

Nola Millar conducting a summer drama workshop in 1965. *Nola Millar Archive, New Zealand Drama School*

New Zealand training for actors was also a major commitment. She tutored at many workshops and schools of drama and after a successful summer school at Massey Agricultural College in 1964 she formed her 'most exciting and challenging' venture yet, the New Theatre School. It was to be the foundation of the first national drama school set up by the Queen Elizabeth II Arts Council in 1970.

In 1967 she took up an Arts Council travel grant, visiting theatre schools and attending performances in sixteen countries. Her experience of the tiny Traverse Theatre at the Edinburgh Festival inspired her to set up the New Theatre Club on her return. For a very low fee, members could attend six productions a year of new plays or rarely seen European theatre as well as New Zealand works. Professional actors and directors in Wellington were engaged, with New Theatre School drama students filling secondary roles.

It is a completely benevolent dictatorship. A one-woman show. This is one way amateur theatre can develop. The style of semi-professional theatre, with decisions made not by committees, but by one or two individuals.

Nola continued to run both the club and the school after being appointed the first director of the national drama school, a post she held until the month before she died, on 20 January 1974, at the age of fifty-nine. Fittingly, the library of what is now the New Zealand Drama School/Te Kura Toi Whakaari o Aotearoa is named after her.

Nola was unique in New Zealand theatre. Respected for her intelligence and perception, her warmth and dedication, she could draw the best out of people but came down hard on pretension. Her 'trademark' was the beret she frequently wore, and she had a passion for betting on horse races, for which she would travel miles on a Saturday. As she said of her decision to quit library work for an uncertain living in the theatre: 'But life is a gamble, anyway, and I believe that sometimes you must take a chance. I took the chance and I do not regret it.'

Janet McCallum

Quotations
para.1 D. Wiseman, 'A Beret is her Trademark', p.17
para.2 Quoted in P. Downes and P. Harcourt, *A Dramatic Appearance*, p.116
para.8 M. Firth, 'First Lady of the Theatre', p.27
para.9 M. Firth, p.27
para.10 M. Firth, p.27
para.13 Editorial, *Arts and Community*
para.15 D. Wiseman, p.17

Unpublished Sources
Nola Millar Papers, MS Papers 1563, ATL
The assistance of Ruth Graham, the Nola Millar Library, and Rona Bailey is gratefully acknowledged. The Nola Millar Library, New Zealand Drama School, provided much valuable material. In particular, the notes of John McCreary for his tribute to Nola Millar at her funeral service, and the typescript of the obituary prepared for the New Zealand Theatre Federation.

Published Sources
Arts and Community, vol.5 no.4, May 1969 (editorial)
Bond, Russell. 'Dedicated Worker for the Development of Drama', *Dominion*, 26 Jan. 1974 (obituary)
Downes, P. and Harcourt, P. *A Dramatic Appearance: Radio Broadcasting in New Zealand: A Documentary*, Wellington, 1976, pp.115–6

Evening Post, 22 Jan. 1974 (obituary)

Firth, Muriel. 'First Lady of the Theatre', *NZ Woman* (Stitch), April 1965

McNaughton, H. D. 'Nola Millar, dynamic force', *The Press*, 24 Jan. 1974 (obituary)

Mann, Nonnita. 'The New Theatre Arts Council Interim Training School', *Act*, July, Aug. Sept. 1970

Millar, Nola. 'Producing Shakespeare for a College Audience', *Education*, vol.10 no.10, Nov.1961, pp.306–11

'Nola Leigh Millar', *NZ Libraries*, vol.37 no.2, April 1974 (obituary)

Wiseman, Dorothy. 'A Beret is her Trademark', *Weekly News*, 26 July 1971

ALICE MINCHIN

1889–1966

Alice Ethel Minchin was the first librarian at the Auckland University College. She was born on 5 November 1889, at Rangiahua in the Hokianga. Her father, Charles Humphrey Minchin, an Irish gentleman, had immigrated to New Zealand to become a farmer. Her mother Edith (born Fennell), the daughter of missionaries in India, had been educated in India and in Europe. When Charles Minchin died, the family moved to Cambridge; Alice attended Prince Albert College in Auckland and Cambridge District High School, before travelling to Bath, England, in 1906, where she lived with her aunt and uncle and was a pupil at Bath Girls' High School, returning to New Zealand in 1908. After two years at Wellesley Street normal school in Auckland, she taught in country schools until 1915, when she was appointed cataloguer at the Auckland Public Library. There she received her basic library training. At the beginning of 1918 she took up the post of librarian at Auckland University College, where she was to stay until her early retirement in 1945.

During 1932–33 she had the happy experience of spending a year overseas as a Carnegie Fellow, and graduated Bachelor of Arts in Library Science from the University of Michigan's department of library science, one of the first two New Zealanders to hold such a qualification.

Back in Auckland her tenure of the college post was marked by constant struggles to get adequate funds, not only for books, but also for staff salaries, which remained for many years the lowest in the country, just as the library itself was the smallest among the university colleges. Her tenacity was remarkable in view of the entrenched attitudes of the college council, male chauvinists to a man; their dismissive treatment of her well-argued appeals was the more galling because her library was fully catalogued and organised on recognised principles, well ahead of the other college libraries.

When she retired, she gave her reason as ill health. It is to be supposed that this was caused largely by years of frustration rather than by some physiological condition. She spent the following year in Wellington as the senior lecturer in cataloguing and classification at the newly opened New Zealand Library School, pending the return of the principal, who was attending a course overseas. At the end of that year she returned to Auckland, where she lived, busy with gardening and her many other interests, until 1966, when she suffered a stroke and died, without recovering consciousness, on 26 July.

She was a handsome woman, with many friends and admirers, though she never married and said she had never wanted to. Although never a member of the Communist Party, she was closely involved with the New Zealand Society for Closer Relations with the USSR in the early 1940s.

In her professional life she never accepted the inferior role which male tradition would have assigned to her, and in her private life she was independent and unconventional in her attitudes and her actions.   *Olive A. Johnson*

Unpublished Sources
Information has been provided by family members, friends, and former colleagues of Alice Minchin.
Annual Reports, Library, University of Auckland
NZ Collection, MS Files, Library, University of Auckland
Records, School of Library Science, University of Michigan

Published Sources
McEldowney, J. *The NZ Library Association, 1910–1960*, Wellington, 1962
'The Opening of the Library School, 18 February 1946', *NZ Libraries*, vol.9 no.2, March 1946 pp.15–20
Scholefield, G. H. (ed.). *Who's Who in New Zealand*, Wellington 1951, 1961, 1964

PERRINE MONCRIEFF

1893–1979

Perrine Moncrieff, a vigorous advocate for conservation in New Zealand, came from an upper-class British family which included artists (Sir John Millais was her grandfather) and naturalists. With her husband, Captain Malcolm Moncrieff, and their two sons, she emigrated to New Zealand in 1921, settling in Nelson. Here they sought outdoor pleasures (sailing, bird-watching, and tramping) as an alternative to society life in Britain.

The family soon leased a property in Tasman Bay where they built a comfortable bach for the summer months. In the 1930s they were able to buy the land and immediately made it a scenic reserve. The threat to the bush from frequent fires, damage by introduced animals such as opossums, and the continuation of milling to provide more farmland was of great concern to Perrine. Once the idea of a national park had been suggested to her, she worked tirelessly for that cause:

Gradually the idea of a National Park gained favour and about that time the Member of Parliament for Nelson presented our case to the Government. Now, what would happen? At this anxious time somebody came up with a brilliant suggestion . . . The forthcoming year, 1942, would be the Tercentenary of the visit of Abel Tasman to New Zealand. What about calling it the Abel Tasman National Park and suggesting that the government of New Zealand request the Queen of the Netherlands [a wartime ally] to become its patron. Thereafter all went smoothly . . .

The creation of the Abel Tasman National Park was Perrine's greatest achievement. She was a member of the park board until forced to resign at the age of eighty-one by a national ruling which excluded members aged over seventy years.

Perrine became an active conservationist as soon as she arrived in New Zealand. By 1925, she had published *New Zealand Birds and How to Identify Them*. It was a popular handbook for decades, reaching its fifth edition in the 1960s. In 1923, she was a founding member of the Native Bird Protection Society, forerunner of the Royal Forest and Bird Protection Society, and became one of its regional vice-presidents in 1927. Impatient with the society's inability to deal adequately with the preservation of forest as well as of native birds, in 1928 she set up the Nelson Bush and Bird Society. This group campaigned successfully for the preservation of many areas around Nelson, including Lake Rotoroa, and the springs and bush at Maruia. In 1953 Perrine received the Loder Cup, an annual award for the protection and cultivation of New Zealand flora.

But she felt much was lost because of the lack of funds, and often the lack also of public interest. Throughout her life she made generous donations to conservation causes, even acquiring personally a large area of coastal bush at Okiwi, which she donated to the Crown for a reserve known as Moncrieff Bush. (The Moncrieffs also donated part of Haulashore Island to the city of Nelson in memory of their eldest son Alexander, who died of polio in 1925.)

Perrine knew the areas she tried to save. She tramped throughout Nelson and the West Coast and visited bird habitats such as Okarito, Stephens Island, and Hen Island. She often went tramping with her friend Gladys Bisley, a founding member of the Nelson Bush and Bird Society, and in their seventies they walked the Milford Track. The Dun Mountain behind Nelson, known for its interesting geology, was a favourite haunt, and they opposed any suggestion by mining companies to reopen mines on the mountain.

In 1933, Perrine began the campaign to have Farewell Spit, a wetland of international importance, made a sanctuary; the tidal flats were granted this status in 1938, with the spit being made a nature reserve. Perrine continued to lobby over the years on issues concerning the spit, including a ban on grazing by cattle and stricter policing of poaching and trespassing.

Perrine led the way for women in many organisations: she became president of the Philosophical Society of Nelson, chaired the school committee of her boys' school, and for her services to the Nelson Institute and Museum was made an honorary life member. She became the first woman president of the Royal Australasian Ornithological Union in 1932, having contributed several articles on New Zealand birds to its journal, *Emu*. Her last contribution was a comprehensive account of the birds of Nelson Province, published in 1938. She was a founding member of the New Zealand Ornithological Society in 1940, but resigned after two years because she disagreed with society policies such as breeding native birds in captivity, making known where rare birds were to be found, and the banding of birds.

Perrine had an international outlook as a naturalist, and always extended her campaigns overseas by writing articles or calling on influential people and organisations, such as the International Council for Bird Preservation. In a 1944 article she wrote:

By what means can New Zealand be educated from without, and the public conscience awakened from the sleep of ignorance and apathy to a sense of the

Perrine Moncrieff on Stephens Island, 1933, holding a tuatara and wearing the practical tramping trousers she designed herself. *Runa Claasen*

responsibility this country owes to the rest of the world for the unique flora and fauna with which she has been entrusted?

Perrine saw wardens as an essential means for enforcing legislated protection, and became one of the earliest honorary rangers herself, for two areas near Nelson. She also served as an honorary ranger for the Department of Internal Affairs from 1947 to 1962, the only woman to do so in Nelson Province, and was said to carry out her duties rigorously.

Her interests were many, and if there was no group to further them, she founded one: the Herb Society, the Nelson Spinners' and Weavers' Guild, and the Humic Compost Society, which became the Soil Association of New Zealand. She became a justice of the peace in 1943. She ran the Girl Guides in Nelson, did radio talks, wrote nature columns and articles for Nelson and Christchurch newspapers, supported Arbor Day, and gave illustrated lectures on birds.

The focus of her life was, however, the battle for the protection of New Zealand's flora and fauna. Her efforts were rewarded by official honours from a number of sources. Perrine died in December 1979, mourned by the many friends to whom she had shown warmth, generosity, and inspiration in her untiring fight for issues she believed in.   *Janet McCallum*

Quotations
para.2 P. Moncrieff, *People Came Later*, p.129
para.8 P. Moncrieff, 'The Destruction of an Avian Paradise', p.16

Unpublished Sources
Assistance was provided by Peg Fleming and John Cunningham.
Correspondence between Perrine Moncrieff and Captain Sanderson, Royal Forest and Bird Protection Society Records, MS Papers 444, ATL
Department of Internal Affairs files 46/15/9, 46/29/12, National Archives, Wellington

Perrine Moncrieff, correspondence in private possession
Radio New Zealand Sound Archive, Timaru
Published Sources
Emu, vol.33, 1933–4; vol.37, 1938; vol.80, part 3, July 1980
The Loder Cup Committee. *The History of the Loder Cup: A Review of the First Twenty Five Years*, Wellington, 1960
Moncrieff, Perrine. *People Came Later*, Nelson, 1965
Moncrieff, Perrine, 'The Destruction of an Avian Paradise', *Journal of the Society for the Preservation of the Fauna of the Empire*, June 1944

ELEANOR MONTGOMERY

c. 1900

Lucien: Elise, my gentle Elise is Valentine Roland? The wit of Paris? The voice of the people?

Elise (proudly): Yes, Valentine Roland, whose spirit will still live on earth when these hands you now clasp are but dust!

Lucien: Elise, my angel, forgive me! Why dids't thou not confide in me?

Elise (sinking on the couch): Confide in the man who said 'Man worships the star, but it is the tender violet alone he would wear on his breast'?

Lucien (kneeling at her feet): Words spoken in ignorance of the gift Heaven had sent me! How could I, a simple mortal, believe that the most glorious of intellects, the loveliest of women, should shed her benediction on his humble home?

In this scene, the climax to Eleanor Elizabeth Montgomery's one-act play, *Madame Beranger*, Lucien Beranger has discovered a passionate letter composed by his wife, Elise. In fury, he accuses her of infidelity and so discovers that the letter is fiction and his quiet and dutiful wife is in fact the writer Valentine Roland, popular novelist and inspiration of Republican France. It is tempting to detect in this play, one of the few to be written and published in New Zealand before 1900 and the only one by a woman, some identification between author and subject, and some wishful thinking in the denouement.

Little is known of the author's life. She was the daughter of Frances Reid (born in Scotland, died in Palmerston North in 1898). Her father was Captain Henry Montgomery (born in London in 1819), and the family lived at Brunswick near Wanganui where they farmed and took an active interest in Liberal Party politics. Eleanor's birth date is unknown and her first official appearance is in the 1899 Electoral Rolls, as housekeeper to her brother William, a Palmerston North JP. She remains listed amongst ratepayers until 1907, when it appears that William left for Canada, and at this point Eleanor simply vanishes (though her name appears on the flyleaf of a presentation copy of her book *The Songs of the Singing Shepherd*, dated February 1912).

In her father's obituary (*Wanganui Herald*, 2 October 1891) she is described as 'the well-known authoress of poems, dramas and short stories of considerable merit'. None of her short stories have been traced. Of her plays, one (*Madame*

Beranger) is held in the Parliamentary Library, and another, in manuscript, at the National Library. The latter, a three-act play entitled 'At Bay', records the machinations of Monteith, gambler and seducer, to ruin the happiness of Margaret Beresford and her true love, Gerald:

Monteith (aside): Ten thousand furies! Margaret!
Margaret (aside): John Monteith! Alive! Here! Ah!
Gerald (aside): They know each other! What's this man to her?

Several volumes of Montgomery's poetry are also held at the National Library: *Songs of the Singing Shepherd* (1885), *Hinemoa* (1887), *The Land of the Moa* (1890), *The Tohunga and Incidents of Maori Life* (1896). *A Tribute to Tennyson, The Pilgrim of Eternity* (1892) is in the Auckland Public Library. Her verse, blending Wordsworth, Longfellow, melodrama, and Maoriland, is studded with such titles as 'The Dying Girl to the Skylark' and such lines as:

> *Hau! I hear Tu's voice fierce calling*
> *Hau! Why sleep the chiefs of Taupo?*

or

> *O Ellen! Blissful shade arise*
> *To bless thy lonely Malcolm's eyes!*

The most interesting piece is 'The Retrospect', a dramatic verse romance, set on a farm in the Wanganui Valley.   *Fiona Farrell Poole*

Unpublished Sources
Biographical information from Wanganui Museum and Palmerston North Electoral Rolls
Published Sources
Montgomery, E. E. M. *Madame Beranger*, Wanganui, 1887

LUCY MOORE

1906–1987

A list of Lucy Beatrice Moore's achievements conveys little of the intrepid woman she was. Lucy died in 1987, still with the same passion for botany she had had in the 1920s and 1930s.

Becoming a botanist, however, was no easy achievement for Lucy Moore. She grew up in Warkworth, the daughter of Harry Moore, the local librarian, who was a keen amateur naturalist. Her mother, Janet, remained based in the home, baking, sewing, and keeping in touch with a wide extended family. From the time when, at thirteen, Lucy left home to go to the nearest secondary school, Epsom Girls' Grammar in Auckland, Janet Moore wrote regularly about homely everyday matters. Such stability must have been supportive for the young student trying to take her life in new directions.

From her secondary school days Lucy's future looked promising. A Junior and a Senior National Scholarship gained at school were followed by a University

National Scholarship when she was a student at Auckland University College. She graduated MSc with first-class honours in 1929, and this should have been the opening to a range of opportunities.

However, she was at first unsuccessful in her attempts to work as a botanist. She was not awarded an International Federation of University Women fellowship in 1930, receiving a letter which stated that her 'academic qualifications were not really quite on the level of the five who were placed on the short list'. All awards for 1930 went to students in Europe.

Applications for positions at Canterbury and Victoria university colleges were similarly unsuccessful. This was in spite of the fact that, between 1928 and 1938, her botanic research output was extremely prolific and praised by eminent botanists such as Dr Leonard Cockayne. As she reflected wryly in a letter to Dr H. H. Allan, following rejection by Victoria:

They put a nice little note in with the papers they returned, showing that they did think I would have done the job if a better man [sic] had not been offering . . . On the island [a field trip to Mayor Island], just for that week I let myself pretend perhaps I might be a botanist.

So the nine years from 1929 to 1938 were spent mainly as a demonstrator in zoology at Auckland University College. Immediately after her graduation she turned initially to school teaching. At the Auckland Diocesan School for Girls she was offered a position teaching mainly home science subjects, along with a request to help with games coaching. She taught there for one term. She was also accepted for teachers' training college but attended for only one day as she found that the atmosphere 'exceeded her wildest imaginations'. It was clearly with relief that she was able to return to the world of scientific research through being awarded the Duffus Lubecki Scholarship annually between 1929 and 1931. She was able to combine this work with her demonstrating commitments.

Lucy Moore, the university-based academic, was balanced by Lucy Moore, the botanical explorer. Her early days around the Mahurangi Peninsula had developed in her a love for the study of plants in their native habitat.

The first series of trips – as field-work for the Duffus Lubecki Scholarship – were to Mt Moehau at the tip of the Coromandel Peninsula, and most were with her close friend and fellow botanist, Lucy Cranwell. Getting to Mt Moehau was no small enterprise. Lucy described it as:

NSS Co. Steamer to Coromandel, service car with Dick Goudie to Colville and a few miles further by the clay road that would be impassable if wet. From the hill within sight of Port Charles it was a matter of walking, carrying everything we had, as far as Stony Bay. The leading ridge from there gave the most direct access to the Moehau trig (892 m).

Tramping equipment in the 1920s and 1930s was rather different from that provided at the outdoor shops of today. Lucy wore schoolboy's navy serge shorts. Sleeping-bags were unlined canvas sacks, and tents were usually erected from a flysheet and branches. She also had to carry her precious botanical specimens, which would have been ruined in an unframed canvas haversack. She therefore carried them in 'a good pile of newspaper strapped between 3-ply boards'.

Lucy Moore, 'The mother of New Zealand botany', cradling a hebe on Maungapohatu trig, January 1932. *Lucy Moore Papers*

Until Lucy Moore's departure for Wellington in 1938 to a position in the botany division of the Department of Scientific and Industrial Research, the two Lucys, as they were known in botanical circles, made a number of forays into remote parts of the country in order to contribute to information about native flora. Moehau was followed in 1930 by Maungapohatu (1359m), deep in the heart of the Urewera country.

The Second World War made further calls on Lucy Moore. She developed a project involving the extraction of agar from seaweed, in order to grow cultures for bacteria. Japan had previously been the world supplier of agar. This was no laboratory exercise. In order to encourage assistance from the children of the native schools of the East Coast, Lucy travelled around the coast from Te Kaha to Gisborne by foot, cream cart, and the occasional service car, visiting schools along the way.

After the war Lucy changed her research field to the tussock-lands of Molesworth, in Marlborough, moving to the botany division of the DSIR at Lincoln in 1960. She retired in 1971 and spent the last sixteen years of her life back at her family home, 'Huamara', at Warkworth.

Throughout her career, Lucy maintained a keen interest in New Zealand native plant species. She worked with Dr. H. H. Allan on Volume I of the *Flora of New Zealand*, then produced Volume II of the series with Dr Elizabeth Edgar.

453

Her retirement project was *The Oxford Book of New Zealand Plants*. Her published papers range over 'marine and terrestrial ecology, the taxonomy of flowering plants, seaweeds and barnacles; plant geography, flower biology, carpology, and the history of New Zealand botany'.

She died in 1987, happy among her relatives, friends, and especially her beloved plants.

Lucy the woman has been described by relatives as a very private person. However, her diaries show that she was a devoted friend and family member. She hated 'socialising', as a diary entry after attending a Mahurangi Regatta Club dance in 1930 showed: 'Again I resolve never to dance again. I find it repulsive with no joy at all and so beastly hot and dusty,' and another comment in 1941 during the journey around East Cape:

To my great private consternation, found myself projected into a tennis and garden party at one of the station homesteads away up the Whakaangiangi Valley.

Her former colleagues acknowledged her feminism:

Lucy in a sense was a pioneer for Women's Liberation, not by any overt direct action but by her own work contributions and attitudes during her long career in the Public Service.

After long years of scant recognition, Lucy's achievements were recognised during the latter part of her life. Had she ever bothered to record her titles in full she would have been: Lucy Beatrice Moore, MBE, MSc (1st Class Hons), DSc (Cantuar), FLS (Fellow of the Linnaean Society), FRSNZ (Fellow of the Royal Society of New Zealand). *Rae Julian*

Quotations
para.4 Letter, 22 May 1930, L. Moore Papers
para.5 Letter, 3 Dec. 1936, L. Moore Papers
para.6 Diary entry, 17 Feb. 1929, L. Moore Papers
para.8 1985 Lucy Cranwell Lecture, given by Dr Lucy Moore, published in *Auckland Botanical Society Newsletter*, vol.41 no.2, July 1986, pp.22–3
para.9 'Was a double Tararua crossing 54 years ago special?', unpublished paper, dated 21 April 1987, Lucy Moore Papers
para.13 E. Godley, 'Lucy Beatrice Moore', *Proceedings of the Royal Society of New Zealand*, vol.116, June 1988, p.55
para.15 Diary entry, 15 Jan. 1930, L. Moore Papers; letter to Norman Potts, 16 March 1941, L. Moore Papers
para.16 DSIR, *Botany Division Newsletter*, no. 114, 1987

Unpublished Sources
Information has been provided by members of the family, which include the author.
L. Moore Papers: Lucy Moore's papers are to be held at AIM.

RINA MOORE

1923–1975

Rina Moore was the first Maori woman to qualify as a doctor, and a psychiatrist who expressed controversial views on a number of social issues.

Rina Winifred Ropiha was born in Auckland in 1923, the only daughter of Rhoda Walker (Whanau a Apanui) and Tipi Tainui Ropiha (Ngati Kahungunu). Both her parents were the offspring of mixed marriages. Her father, a qualified surveyor, was the first Maori to be Secretary of the Department of Maori Affairs. His work was the basis of the Hunn Report (a review of the conditions of Maori people, especially the impact of urbanisation). Her mother was a nurse who had worked among the Maori people in remote rural areas. She was the hub of the household, organised, efficient, and a perfectionist.

Rina had a middle-class suburban childhood in Remuera, where she and her younger brother Peter were brought up as Pakeha. Their parents believed it was important for Maori to get the best European education, to enable them to cope with the modern world. They had an English nanny until Rina was eight. After school she learned ballet, elocution, ballroom dancing, and piano.

Her parents made tremendous sacrifices to set aside funds to give the children these opportunities, and approval was forthcoming only for achievement. Discipline was strict, and parental control over the children was tight. Rina was under great pressure from her parents to study hard and succeed in her chosen profession. She was expected to be an example to and leader for the Maori people, and to give the benefits of her skills and knowledge back to the community. Sometimes she visited marae with her adored father, but she used to resent being held up to the Maori as an example of possible achievement.

In 1943 Rina went to the University of Otago to study medicine. In her second year of studies she married Ian Moore, a law student from Nelson and had her first child in the following year. The couple's finances were stretched, but both families provided help and support. Her mother came to Dunedin to look after the baby for six months while Rina continued her studies. To complete the practical part of her degree, Rina commuted to Wellington during the week while her husband and baby stayed with her in-laws in Nelson. That was a tough year, at a time when post-war propaganda was centred on 'women at home' and 'the family'.

After graduation in 1948, Rina started work as an assistant medical officer at Ngawhatu, a psychiatric hospital in Nelson. It was the best job available, but a fortuitous choice, given her natural empathy with people which was the key to her success as a psychiatrist.

At Ngawhatu she worked mainly with the women patients. She also tried to break down public fears and prejudices about 'madness'. She explained mental illness as an extreme of the mood swings experienced by 'normal' people, and breakdowns as similar to physical illness – and not necessarily a lasting psychiatric condition.

It was her belief that psychiatric patients needed to be accepted within the community (a concept which has since been implemented with half-way houses), and she spent time setting up links between the hospital and the community.

Intelligent, articulate, and vivacious, Rina was an excellent communicator, and in the 1950s became a much sought-after public speaker. She was outspoken on a number of controversial issues. For example, at a time when New Zealand had one of the highest illegitimacy rates in the world, she strongly advocated sex education in schools. It was to be another thirty years before such a view gained wide acceptance.

Rina Moore. *Geoffrey Wood*

In the late 1950s Rina was invited to participate in a series of hui with young Maori leaders, discussing issues such as urban migration, high crime rates, mental health, and education. As she got older she realised that she had, like many migrants to the cities, missed out on much of her Maori heritage. However, despite many attempts she never mastered the Maori language.

In 1963 she had worked at Ngawhatu for fifteen years, and had been Medical Officer there for some time. Any further promotion was inhibited by her lack of a post-graduate degree, which would have required several years of overseas study. This was not a feasible option as she now had four children (one daughter and three sons) and a husband who was bound to his legal practice in Nelson.

Frustrated that she could not progress further, she resigned and set off alone for an overseas trip to Europe and Asia. Her itinerary included Khatmandu and Moscow – unusual destinations at that time.

On her return she set up a Family Advisory Clinic – a private psychiatric and counselling clinic – in her own home. Her children remember how intrusive this was. They would come home from school to find their playroom (now the waiting-room) full of patients and Rina in consultation in the living-room.

In 1966 Rina discovered she had cancer of the breast and lymph nodes. She refused to have her breast removed, but agreed to tumour removal and radio-therapy. Medical opinion was then against her, but today such conservative treatment has gained credibility. The fact that she lived nearly ten more years vindicated her decision. She was scared of dying in pain and from time to time suffered from depression.

At perhaps the high point of her career, she wrote four papers for the fourth International Congress on Social Psychiatry held in Israel in 1972. All were accepted. They covered issues such as urban migration, education, health, and mental health: problems facing Maori people and lower socio-economic groups, and relevant to minority races worldwide.

After this success she returned home to be a housewife with a part-time job (again at the clinic), at a period when her children were all leaving home. Her feelings of frustration grew, and she experienced bouts of heavy drinking. However, she slowly rebuilt her private practice and also took up golf, photography, and writing to put her life back together.

In 1975 she suffered a mild stroke and it was soon apparent that the cancer had struck again, this time in the brain. She died later that year, at the age of fifty-two.
                                                                          Karin Beatson

Unpublished Source
Information was provided by family members and friends. The author is Rina Moore's daughter.

HARRIET MORISON

1862–1925

Harriet Russell Morison was born in Ireland in 1862 and came to New Zealand in 1867. Her father was a master tailor and her first employment was as a tailoress. She was an active Christian, and became a lay preacher for the Bible Christian denomination, and later a chairwoman of the Unitarian Church Committee. Feminism, unionism and religion were to be interwoven threads throughout her life.

On 11 July 1889 Morison was present at the inaugural meeting of the country's first women's union, the Tailoresses' Union of New Zealand, held in the Dunedin Choral Hall. The Revd Rutherford Waddell (who had preached his famous sermon 'The Sin of Cheapness' on the evils of sweated labour in the clothing trade in September 1888) was elected president of the new union, John Millar (who was also secretary of the Federated Seamen's Union) became secretary, and Harriet Morison became vice-president.

In 1890 Morison tried unsuccessfully to organise a union for domestic servants, in an attempt to give them the dignity of skilled labour. She also became secretary of the Tailoresses' Union, a post she held until 1896. During this time she organised the tailoresses into one of the larger and more active unions in New Zealand. Branches were established in Christchurch, Wellington, and Auckland in 1890, and within twelve months the national membership of the union was around 2,500. In 1891 the several branches were federated under the name 'New Zealand Federated Tailoresses' Union', and the union's national headquarters was registered in Dunedin in 1898. When the Auckland branch flagged in 1891, and again in 1892, Harriet Morison went to Auckland to revive it. She was especially interested in getting employers there to operate the 'Dunedin' or 'Southern' log, which was a record of appropriate hours of work and payment negotiated by the union. Her efforts were successful:

As a result of Miss Morison's sojourn in Auckland, the minimum wage had been increased to 7/6 per week, a healthy public opinion had been created, and there was every chance of the Southern log being adopted.

The Tailoresses' Union was one of the first three unions to affiliate itself to the Otago Trades and Labour Council when this was formed in 1890. It was also the third largest contributor of financial support to the Maritime Strike from August to November 1890, donating £107.10s to the Strike Defence Fund.

Morison also tried to found a convalescent home for her members. This scheme was unsuccessful, but a benefit fund to assist sick members was established, and by 1894 a reading-room and a luncheon room were part of the union's suite of rooms in Dunedin. The reading-room was a precursor of the Omand and Freeman Library, which was founded by public subscription.

Unionism was not Morison's only channel for improving the lot of women workers. She was an organiser of ambulance classes for women, and an active worker for women's suffrage. In her public speeches for the suffrage cause she often linked her religion and her feminism: at one meeting she said that 'Jesus Christ was the first founder and head of the women's franchise movement'. At another she maintained that

the laws of the past had been framed almost solely in the interest of property, trade, monopolies, while laws affecting humanity had been very little considered. Men had made the laws as they now exist; women would make laws for the protection of humanity.

Harriet Morison was a founder member of the Women's Christian Temperance Union (WCTU). It was in Dunedin that the WCTU first established contact with women workers, and Morison was instrumental in collecting their signatures on suffrage petitions. Historian Patricia Grimshaw records that there was a 'distinct correlation between the number of signatures obtained in an area and the strength of the local women's trade union'.

Helen Nichol, the local franchise superintendent of the WCTU, was a personal friend of Harriet Morison. Morison and Nichol believed that women's suffrage was worth fighting for in its own right, not just as a means of furthering the temperance cause. They took the initiative in founding New Zealand's first Women's Franchise League, a suffrage organisation which was independent of the temperance movement. The Dunedin Women's Franchise League continued to exist after the vote was won in 1893, and seems to have operated as a charitable organisation for women, running a soup kitchen and sewing quilts and counterpanes for the poor.

Morison also led the successful women's campaign against Henry Smith Fish's bid for the Dunedin mayoralty in 1892. Fish was the chief parliamentary spokesman for the liquor trade and an active anti-suffragist.

In 1896 Morison's pioneering work for women's unionism in New Zealand came to a sad end when she was dismissed from her position of secretary of the Tailoresses' Union. In addition to the usual duties of a union secretary, Morison had been expected to raise funds for the union. In 1896 a carnival which she had organised for this purpose made a loss, and she was accused of mismanaging and even misappropriating funds. It is unlikely, however, that she was guilty of any impropriety. 'The incident was rather an example of either inefficiency or overwork blown up out of proportion by petty infighting and buck passing.'

Following her dismissal Morison lost her high public profile, although she did not retire completely from community activism. She was an official visitor to Seacliff Hospital for fourteen years, and maintained her involvement with the church. In 1906, however, she returned to public view in a role she had long campaigned for – factory inspector. Once again she was in the forefront of social change.

In 1908 she moved to Auckland to become officer in charge of the Women's Employment Bureau in the Department of Labour, a position she held until her retirement in 1921. She died at New Lynn in 1925. *Christine Dann*

Quotations
para.3 J. Salmond, 'The History of the New Zealand Labour Movement', vol.2, p.489
para.6 P. Grimshaw, *Women's Suffrage in New Zealand*, pp.55, 111
para.7 P. Grimshaw, p.49
para.10 P. Harper, 'The Dunedin Tailoresses' Union', p.38

Unpublished Sources
J. D. Salmond, 'The History of the New Zealand Labour Movement from the Settlement to the Conciliation and Arbitration Act (1840–1895)', PhD thesis, Otago, 1928
P. A. E. Harper, 'The Dunedin Tailoresses' Union: 1889–1914', BA Hons research essay, Otago, 1988

Published Sources
Daybreak, vol.1 no.20, 20 April 1895
Grimshaw, Patricia. *Women's Suffrage in New Zealand*, Auckland, 1972
NZ Herstory 1978, Dunedin, 1977
Roth, H. and Hammond, J. *Toil and Trouble: The Struggle for a Better Life in New Zealand*, Auckland, 1981

ELLA MORRIS

1887–1962

Ella Morris was a tall, well-built woman, whose physique matched her kind and generous spirit.

Ella Florence Wood was born in Palmerston North on 23 February 1887, the second of seven children. Her father, Joseph Thomas Wood, was architect for the Palmerston North Borough Council. Her mother, Mary Jane Presnell Wood (born Shennen), was fluent in five languages and led the All Saints Church choir. Ella was twelve when her mother died suddenly. Her elder sister, Edith, looked after the family, enabling Ella to finish primary school and begin work as a tailoress.

During her fifteen-year career in the clothing industry, she rose to the position of head costumier at C. Smith's department store in Palmerston North. Her duties included the designing of women's fashion clothing and the supervision of the sewing of the garments. She had to travel out to the homes of customers to take measurements, discuss styles, and complete final fittings. So that she might more easily negotiate the Manawatu countryside, her employers provided a car. Ella used the car to advantage. In order to accumulate new design ideas, she would drive to the Woodville races, where she would spend the day sketching the race-day fashions.

In 1915, Ella's sister Edith died suddenly, three weeks after giving birth to her first-born son, Percy. Ella was determined to raise the baby. She left work and was supported financially by her father and brother-in-law. Within the year, however, Percy contracted polio and his father, Tom Harrison, died suddenly of a stroke. Shortly afterwards Ella learned of a rural housekeeping position in the Wairarapa and applied, on the condition that she could take the crippled Percy with her. She was interviewed by the sister of her prospective employer who decided she was perfect for the job.

Her new employer, Robert James Sutherland Morris, was a widower with three adult daughters. Despite the fact that all three daughters still lived at home, 'Toro Ranch' homestead, at Haunui, was thought too demanding for them to cope with. Ella was the same age as the eldest daughter when she moved into the Morris home in 1916. A year later, she became Robert Morris's wife, some twenty-four years his junior. Their daughter (1918) and the much-wanted son (1920) were born in quick succession. Percy died in 1919.

The isolation of Ella's new home did not prevent her paying regular visits to her extended family in Palmerston North. She would drive the thirty miles to Eketahuna and then on to Woodville before putting the Landrover car and her family on the train in order to travel through the Manawatu Gorge. Her relations remember her arriving majestically in the large vehicle, swooping into the house, gathering all her 'darlings' to her substantial bosom then distributing chocolates and sweets to one and all.

In the early 1920s, Ella and Robert decided to retire from the farm, which Robert owned jointly with his three brothers, and move to Feilding, where they had built a large home in the style of a 'majestic manor'. But as the Depression took hold the farm became no longer economically viable; they were forced to walk off the land and sell the Feilding house in order to meet debtors' demands.

There followed drastic changes for the family. Robert took labouring jobs on Hawke's Bay farms and later worked as a blacksmith for the Public Works Department on the East Coast railway line. The family, now with a third child, moved to public works cottages at Kiwi Creek, and later at Kotemaori. Then in 1934 Robert died, at the age of seventy-one.

Ella, a widow with three children, had now to find ways to support her family in a pre-pension era. She put all her skills to the test by taking in sewing and boarders. It was cheaper to live in the remote Hawke's Bay countryside, and Ella elected to remain at Kotemaori for the next three years. However, by the time her youngest son was of secondary school age, she moved to Wellington. She supported him through Wellington College by running a series of boarding-houses in the vicinity of Athletic Park.

Ella's generous nature ensured that the young post office workers who became regular boarders were well cared for. Her cooking was renowned for both its quality and quantity. Yet life was still a struggle and particularly so once

Ella Florence Morris, 1915.
Kay Morris Matthews

she retired. During the latter part of her life, she lived in rented rooms around Wellington and during this time derived much pleasure from visiting her children and their families. Despite the long hours of travelling, she would arrive resplendent in tailored dresses with ruffled inset, high-heeled lace-up shoes, and felt hat complete with feather. On these occasions she baked to her heart's content and enjoyed the evening card-playing sessions, although by this time her eyesight was rapidly deteriorating.

Ella Morris died in Wellington in 1962. She was seventy-five years old.

Kay Morris Matthews

Unpublished Sources
Information was provided by family members: Richard Wood, Maryella Wakelin, Emma Kenward, John Morris. The author is Ella Morris's granddaughter.
Roie Pearson, 'Family Papers', an account by Ella Morris's daughter, is in the author's possession.

MARY ANN MÜLLER

1820–1901

At twenty-two, London-born Mary Ann Wilson married James Whitney Griffiths, with whom she had two sons. Separated from her husband, she emigrated with her sons to New Zealand on the *Pekin*, arriving in Nelson in January 1850. There she looked after her own and the four children of Dr Stephen Lunn Müller, who had been ship's surgeon on the *Pekin* and whose wife had died on the voyage out. They married in December 1851, after Griffiths' death. Her husband became Resident Magistrate, and Provincial Secretary in Nelson.

Mary Müller wrote under the pen-name of 'Femina' for the *Nelson*

Examiner, whose owner-editor Charles Elliot preserved her anonymity. Her husband, who was 'rigid in his views as to the impropriety of women manifesting an interest in politics' and was opposed to women's suffrage, knew nothing of her writing and the identity of 'Femina' was kept secret until after his death, when an announcement and photograph appeared in December 1898 in *The White Ribbon* (the periodical of the Women's Christian Temperance Union). In July 1900 *The White Ribbon* wrote: 'To Mrs Mary Muller belongs the honour of being the pioneer worker for the enfranchisement of women in New Zealand.' She died in July 1901 in Blenheim, aged eighty-one.

Mary Müller's ideas on property rights for women were influential in initiating the Married Women's Property Protection Acts of 1860 and 1870, which extended protection to deserted or dispossessed wives who could prove their case to a magistrate. In 1869 she issued a pamphlet, *An Appeal to the Men of New Zealand*, which was much discussed and often reprinted in New Zealand, and which evoked an encouraging letter from John Stuart Mill. In it she addresses 'the common sense of New Zealand men – of New Zealand law-givers', saying:

We ask you, our rulers; to disembarrass yourselves of those tenets of Government built up during ages upon a system of credulous trust in those principles which guided our ancestors . . . Women are now educated, thinking beings, very different from the females of darker ages . . . Let the laws be fitted to the people and times. Do you still persecute for religious opinions? Do you still burn for witchcraft? Why when the broad road of progress is cleared for so many human beings, is the Juggernaut car of prejudice still to be driven on, crushing the crowds of helpless women beneath its wheels? . . .

Why has a woman no power to vote, no right to vote, when she happens to possess all the requisites which legally qualify a man for that right? She may be a householder, have large possessions, and pay her share of taxes towards the public revenue; but sex disqualifies her. Were it a question of general knowledge and intelligence as compared to men, women might submit unmurmuringly; this is not the case. The point is, Is she as capable as our bullock-drivers, labourers, and mechanics? It may surely be confidently asserted that when a woman is possessed of sufficient skill and management to retain unassisted the guidance of her family, and remain a householder she develops more than a moderate degree of capability . . . The true position is that educated thinking members of the state are degraded below the level of the ploughman, who perhaps can neither read nor write . . .

Our women are brave and strong, with an amount of self-reliance and freedom from conventionalities eminently calculated to form a great nation. Give them scope. At present their grasp and power of mind is 'cribbed, cabined and confined' to one narrow groove. It is weakened and famished by disuse, and only a close observer can detect the latent force, the unspent energy lying dormant in many seemingly ordinary characters.

Mark the sudden questions of a bright eager girl, or the quiet remark of

TRICESIMO TERTIO ET TRICESIMO QUARTO

VICTORIÆ REGINÆ.

No. XXXVII.

****

ANALYSIS.

Title.
Preamble.
1. Short Title.
2. Provisions of "Married Women's Property Protection Act 1860" extended.

3. Custody of children under ten years of age.
4. Maintenance of children may be ordered.
5. Time to be defined in order.
6. Destitute Persons Relief Act to apply.

An Act to extend the Provisions of "The Married Women's Property Protection Act 1860." Title.

[*12th September* 1870.]

WHEREAS it is expedient to extend the powers given to Resident Magistrates and Justices of the Peace in Petty Sessions by section two of "The Married Women's Property Protection Act 1860" hereinafter called "the said Act" to other cases besides that which is mentioned in the said section Preamble.
BE IT THEREFORE ENACTED by the General Assembly of New Zealand in Parliament assembled and by the authority of the same as follows—

1. The Short Title of this Act shall be "The Married Women's Property Protection Act 1870." Short Title.

2. In addition to the case provided for by the second section of the said Act the same section and all other the provisions of the said Act shall extend and be held to apply to the following cases that is to say— Provisions of "Married Women's Property Protection Act 1860" extended.

    (1.) When a wife is subjected by her husband to cruelty without adultery
    (2.) Where the husband of any woman shall be guilty of living in open adultery
    (3.) Where the husband of any woman shall be guilty of habitual drunkenness
    (4.) Where the husband shall habitually fail to provide a a maintenance for his wife and children without such failure being caused by sickness or other unavoidable cause

Mary Ann Müller's 1869 pamphlet, *An Appeal to the Men of New Zealand*, was influential in securing the 1870 Married Women's Property Protection Act. *New Zealand Statutes some sensible matron upon a political matter in the newspaper before her, and see the cold stare of surprise, or hear the rebuke about women seeking to step beyond their province, with which the paterfamilias stops the innovation, and can you marvel that the girl turns to gossip about the new fashions, or the mother takes refuge in discussion upon servants, sewing machines and other minor domestic details? Women of the middle class suffer most from this open, systematic 'putting down': . . . We do but begin now: still, having begun, let us make good strides in the noble race for knowledge – knowledge of all kinds tending to the welfare of our community, and some knowledge of and share on the Government of our country is imperative. And where, in what land upon the face of the earth, was there ever a finer field for educating people in the art of government?*

The appeal ends:

. . . how frail a hope seems these few pages, penned in jealous secrecy from every human eye, for such is the ban we live under that a woman naturally learns to shrink from drawing down upon her devoted head the avalanche of man's condemnation and travels on with 'bated breath' hiding her noblest, highest aspirations! Yet there is a hope . . . It is the cry of aliens for naturalization, the wail of the fettered for freedom . . . The change is coming, but why is New Zealand only to follow? Why not take the initiative?

She does not appear to have been active politically in the latter part of her life, but followed and supported campaigns for women until her death. At the age of seventy-eight, in 1898, Mary Müller wrote to Kate Sheppard:

I like to feel in touch with those carrying on this struggle. Old and failing, it is cheering to watch the efforts of those younger and abler women striving bravely to succeed in obtaining rights, so long unjustly withheld. It was a triumph to obtain the Suffrage: The Married Woman [sic] Property Act was to me even greater for I had suffered greatly.

Aorewa McLeod

Quotations
para.2 'Outlines of the Woman Suffrage Movement in New Zealand', *The White Ribbon*, July 1900, pp.9–10 (signed 'W.S.S.')
para.3 M. Müller, *An Appeal to the Men of New Zealand*
para.10 M. Müller. Letter to Kate Sheppard, quoted in B. Harper, *Petticoat Pioneers*, pp.163–4
Published Sources
Grimshaw, Patricia. *Women's Suffrage in New Zealand*, Auckland, 1972
Harper, Barbara. *Petticoat Pioneers: South Island Women of the Colonial Era*, Book Three, Wellington, 1980
Müller, Mary Ann ('Femina'). *An Appeal to the Men of New Zealand*, Nelson, 1869

KATERINA NEHUA

1903 – 1948

'Splash!' That remarkable Maori Mrs Nehua capped her Sydney endurance swimming record by remaining afloat in Brisbane for seventy-two hours, twenty-one minutes. The swim was done in a closed bath and under much pleasanter conditions than her open-air swim in cold, bleak water in Sydney. The American ladies who have specialised in this sort of thing for some years and were directly responsible for the revival of the craze recently, have been badly licked, their Maori rival having beaten the best of them by hours.

This item appeared in an Australian newspaper in April 1931, after endurance swimmer Katerina Nehua broke her previous world record of seventy-two hours and nine minutes.

Endurance swimming – a phenomenon of the Depression of the 1930s – originated in the United States, from where it spread to Australia and New Zealand. The rules were simple: contestants were to remain afloat at all times, without touching the sides or bottom of the pool, but they were not required actually to swim any distance. Whoever endured immersion in the water for the longest period won what was usually quite a large cash prize. Crowds flocked to watch the events, which in Australia attracted entries from several well-known international distance swimmers.

In January 1931 New Zealand's Katerina Nehua entered a contest held at Manly Baths in Sydney. She had previously competed in a similar event in the Bay of Islands, remaining afloat for a period of twenty-five hours. Now she was resident in Sydney with her husband Joseph Darley and four small children, the youngest a baby only nine weeks old and recently weaned from the breast. The prize money offered for the Manly event was £500 to the winner and £100 to the runner-up. Katerina and her family were living in a substandard dwelling on the outskirts of the city, and Joseph had been out of work for nine months. She needed money desperately, money to feed and clothe her family and to keep a decent roof over their heads.

Katerina and Joseph spent what little money they had left on the tram fares from their Collaroy home to the baths, where the officials gave them chocolate and beef tea before the contest began. Because they could not afford to pay for the special grease with which contestants usually coated themselves prior to entering the water, Katerina applied a mixture of glycerine, olive oil, and black axle grease to her body. As she entered the water, she was heard to comment that she was 'determined to stay in the water until they carry me out'.

It was 9.45 am on a Friday morning when Katerina began her marathon swim. Forty-seven hours and fifty-two minutes later, she began to show signs of distress and was then forced to leave the water. By that stage, the only remaining competitor was English Channel swimmer Mercedes Gleitz, who lasted another twenty-two minutes before also retiring from the pool. But the heroine of the event and favourite of the large crowd was Katerina. Impressed by her courage and determination, Mercedes Gleitz added £100 from her own winnings to the £100 Katerina received as runner-up. Both women were then taken home by ambulance.

Over the next eighteen months, Katerina entered a dozen or so similar contests and enjoyed considerable success, becoming a well-known personality in the process. But such incredible feats of endurance didn't become any easier with time. In March 1931, Katerina first broke the world record when she spent seventy-two uncomfortable hours in the cold water of Rushcutters Bay, Sydney, in an open-sea contest. Describing her feelings during the last few hours of the effort, she said she was 'afraid to go near the boat for nourishment, as the temptation to hold on to the side might have been too much for her'.

Katerina Nehua, 1931.
Alexander Turnbull Library

In April 1931 at the Municipal Baths in Brisbane, Katerina broke her own world record with a time of seventy-two hours and twenty-one minutes. Later that year tentative arrangements were made for an endurance swimming attempt in Auckland, to be sponsored by the manufacturers of 'Speedo' swimsuits. Katerina would have her return fare and all expenses paid as part of the deal, and in return would use and endorse only 'Speedo' swimwear. Unfortunately for Katerina, who had been feeling homesick, the trip never eventuated.

For Katerina, endurance swimming was a practical means of supporting her family during the tough years of the Depression – years spent apart from the extended family and community she missed so much. And she welcomed the publicity as an opportunity to bring her people into the limelight. 'I am proud to be able to uphold my Maori race in this class of sport.'

Although known in her personal life as Katherine Darley, professionally she used her mother's maiden name, Nehua. Born in 1903 to Mereana and

Hareparau Waetford of Whakapara in the Bay of Islands, Katerina married Joseph Darley, an English-born farmer, in 1923. She was a member of the Nga Puhi tribe, and a direct descendant of Eru Patuone, the older brother of Tamati Waka Nene, and his wife Te Hoia. While living in Sydney in 1940, she and her daughters participated in a gathering to commemorate the one hundredth anniversary of the signing of the Treaty of Waitangi. Present were other descendants of treaty signatories, including a great-granddaughter of James Busby.

Katerina was only forty-four years old when she suffered a heart attack in June 1948 and died at her home in Woollahra, New South Wales. She was already a widow by then, and left five daughters, the youngest only sixteen years of age.

After she set her first world record in 1931, Katerina had been invited by a Sydney radio station to broadcast a message to Australian and New Zealand audiences. She spoke about her attitude to her achievements:

Some folk think that endurance swimming is quite a simple thing to do, when really it is not, for a person requires courage and plenty of it, to stay in the water overnight. Therefore my advice to young people who might like to try endurance swimming is don't.

I hope to come to Auckland shortly and attempt a record swim there, and add more laurels to my Maori race.

Hello Mother. I hope you are quite well, and also my brothers. I hope to be there with you all very shortly, so cheer up Ma, we will have a gay party very soon.

Arohanui and best wishes
Goodnight
Katerina.

Tui MacDonald

Quotations
para.1 *Daily Telegraph*, 24 March 1931 (in MS Papers 2754, folder 1/5, ATL)
para.11 K. Nehua, Notes for a radio address on Station 2UW Sydney on 1 April 1931, MS Papers 2754, folder 1/3, ATL

Unpublished Source
Katerina Nehua, MS Papers 2754, ATL

Published Sources
Curtis, Vicki. 'Katerina Nehua: Endurance Swimmer', *Turnbull Library Record*, vol.19 no.1, May 1986

GRACE NEILL

1846–1926

Elizabeth Grace Campbell was born into a wealthy Scottish landowning family in 1846. She died in Wellington in 1926 after a life which included the conventional female experiences of matrimony and motherhood, but which encompassed as well a diversity of paid employment and a prominent role in New Zealand's nascent welfare bureaucracy.

As for many other genteel British women, the newly respectable profession of nursing offered Grace release from family expectations. It provided her with saleable skills and with experience of authority and command. After finishing her training, she became matron of the Pendlebury Hospital for sick children. Marriage in her thirties to Dr Channing Neill resulted in the birth of a son in 1882, but this did not restrict her to domesticity and family life. She extended her nursing skills with a period of midwifery training among the poor of Battersea, England in 1886.

After joining her doctor husband in Queensland later that year, Grace Neill was widowed in 1888. Reluctant to accept her mother's offer of a comfortable home in England, she turned to journalism to support herself and her small son (who by this time was old enough for boarding-school). After serving in a number of short-term official positions in Queensland, Neill was introduced to William Pember Reeves, Minister of Labour in New Zealand's Liberal cabinet. Her appointment in March 1894 as New Zealand's first female inspector of factories began a thirteen-year career in the New Zealand public service as its senior woman official.

For a while Neill was the only woman official in Wellington's government buildings. Her curiosity value was shown by a request that she enter the building before or after the men employed there so as to avoid causing them embarrassment. Even the redoubtable Neill felt obliged to accede to this curious (and, we might now think, offensive) request, though by the end of her career she was able to remark on the number of 'bright faces and pretty frocks' flitting up and down the stairs of the old building.

Although Neill remained only one year in the Department of Labour, the success of her appointment justified the extension of the female inspectorate and the establishment of a women's labour bureau. However, Neill's personal qualities and experience were needed in another, more challenging role, and in April 1895 she was transferred to the Department of Hospitals and Charitable Institutions. This was the forerunner of our modern Health Department, one of the first agencies of state welfare in New Zealand. Since Neill was the third member of a minute department, her work-load was vast, but the opportunity for personal influence all the greater.

In her new position, Neill's special responsibilities brought her into contact with hospital and asylum nurses and with female recipients of public charity. She frequently deputised for the Inspector-General of Hospitals on official inquiries, and sometimes wrote the departmental report to parliament. She often had to travel around New Zealand on inspections, at a time when travel to more remote locations was not at all usual or easy for a lone woman. She appears to have commanded widespread respect, even among the notoriously touchy hospital and charitable aid boards with whom she had to deal, and in 1898 the visiting Fabian investigator, Beatrice Webb, commended her abilities. Something of Neill's formidable character shows through in her later boast that she loved

. . . to bully the male if he be placed in the position of superior officer. It was real plums to twist & twiddle Ministers & Premiers & make them think they were having their own way all the time. Catch me allowing any public official

Grace Neill. *Alexander Turnbull Library*

to treat me as 'putty', however soft my outer coat might be. They knew I could take it off on occasions.

Neill was a strong supporter of women's rights and was later to take great pride in her position as an enfranchised New Zealander. However, her background, self-sufficiency, and successful struggle as a solo parent did little to generate sisterly feeling toward the less competent. She particularly feared the 'cancerous growth of pauperism, and many another social evil', and criticised 'brazen faced beggars of the female sex' who, she alleged, took advantage of poorly administered charities. Denouncing the 'pernicious custom of aid becoming a pension', she conceded that:

An able-bodied woman deserted or left a widow with an infant in arms may possibly require temporary assistance, but there are instances where that assistance has gone on steadily for from four to seven years.

Since women featured more heavily than men in the charity lists, they were ready targets for Neill's hostility, though she did concede that there were genuinely destitute, 'independent spirited' women who hesitated to seek aid. Neill shared with many of her contemporaries a belief in the 'deserving' and 'undeserving' poor, but those involved in the day-to-day administration of charities proved less confident about the distinction.

For Neill, a more satisfying side of her work involved the reform of nursing, and the New Zealand profession quite rightly regards her as one of its founding mothers. Herself trained to Florence Nightingale's ideals of dedication and service, she warned of the dangers threatening nursing from an influx of girls without the dedication of their predecessors. 'It cannot be too strongly impressed upon a probationer', she insisted, 'that the main function of a nurse is to serve – to serve others.' In the long term, such attitudes would severely constrain the profession, but Neill also had practical goals to improve the status of nurses. She was convinced that there was a need for a comprehensive system of hospital training followed by a final examination conducted by an independent board of examiners.

Neill achieved her objective with the 1901 Nurses Registration Act. The entire responsibility for this, the world's first national registration act for nurses, went to Grace Neill, who drafted regulations for the conduct of examinations, defined the curriculum, appointed examiners, and designed the medal of the New Zealand registered nurse. Within two years 320 names were on the register, among the first being Neill herself.

This measure was followed in 1904 by legislation to register midwives, another of Neill's initiatives. The final years of her inspectorate were taken up with the establishment of state maternity hospitals in which midwives would be trained to a high level. Her aim, she later said, was a 'State hospital for mothers, managed by women and doctored by women', where the wives of working men would get rest, good food, and nursing care at a moderate price. Neill faced persistent opposition from doctors, who saw the St Helen's hospitals (as they were called) as threats to their own incomes and, ultimately, to their control of family health. The necessary speed and economy with which the hospitals were established meant that some of the buildings chosen were old and unsuitable for their purpose, and Neill was also criticised for this. The stress told. Facing a choice between resignation or breakdown in health, Neill retired in December 1906, handing over her responsibilities to Hester Maclean.

Neill's appointment to New Zealand's public service came at a time when women's distinctive concerns were beginning to impinge upon politicians and administrators. It acknowledged the need for capable women to deal with problems affecting women and children. But as Neill's position became institutionalised, her sphere of influence narrowed. The transformation of the omnicompetent woman inspector into director of nursing services was anticipated by Neill's growing preoccupation with nursing matters.

Tall, red-headed, a woman of considerable physical presence, and (unusual for women of her time) a cigarette smoker, Neill herself provides us with an assessment of her life:

Why on earth when I was young I did not content myself like a proper minded Early Victorian with Shakespeare & the musical glasses, or marry the dear old man with £40,000 a year & a blue satin drawing room, or make a cult of some harmless ist or ism! Then when I was sixty I could have developed into a more or less amiable old lady with a lace cap, a taste for knitting, local gossip & bridge with a decent cloak of religiosity. But the fates willed otherwise & made me a nondescript combatant against drink, poverty, factory owners & the medical profession in NZ . . . I have had a jolly good life, heaps of variety in experiences [,] sound constitution & good health above the average & have no

*business to growl when at the age of sixty-three I am forced to 'taper off' . . .
take it easy and look on at the game instead of playing.*

This was written in 1909. Neill still had seventeen years to live and to her 'heaps of variety' she added the wartime control of a children's ward at Wellington Hospital during her seventies. She died in 1926, blind and crippled with arthritis. Unorthodox to the last, her request was for cremation without hearse, flowers, ostentation or religious rites.　　　　　　　*Margaret Tennant*

Quotations
para.4 *NZ Free Lance*, 8 Dec. 1906
para.6 Grace Neill to Agnes Bennett, 20 March [1912?], Agnes Bennett Papers
para.7 Annual Report, Department of Hospitals and Charitable Institutions, *AJHR*, 1897, H-22, p.32
para.8 J. O. C. Neill, *Grace Neill*, p.41
para.10 *Evening Post*, 10 Aug. 1912
para.12 Grace Neill to Agnes Bennett, 16 Feb. 1909, Agnes Bennett Papers

Unpublished Sources
Agnes Bennett Papers, MS Papers 1346, folder 211, ATL
Agnes Bennett, 'Pioneers who have passed away', ICN Review, among material held by Registered Nurses Association, Wellington
Grace Neill's will, in possession of family

Published Sources
Annual Reports, Department of Hospitals and Charitable Institutions, *AJHR*, 1895–1906, H-22
Campbell, Helen. 'Mrs Grace Neill. Her Life and Work and her Contribution to New Zealand Nursing', *NZ Nursing Journal*, 15 June 1946, pp.146–9
Neill, Grace. Interview, *Evening Post*, 31 March 1894
Neill, J. O. C. *Grace Neill. The Story of a Noble Woman*, Christchurch, 1961
Tennant, Margaret. 'Mrs Grace Neill in the Department of Hospitals, Asylums and Charitable Institutions', *NZJH*, April 1978, pp.13–14

SARAH NEWDICK

1822–1870

On 29 January 1840 Captain Hobson, lieutenant governor of New Zealand, arrived at Kororareka in the Bay of Islands. Kororareka, then the capital of New Zealand, was later renamed Russell.

Sarah Mackey, aged about eighteen, and her brother Hugh, aged sixteen, arrived at Kororareka this same year on the ship *Shamrock*, a coastal trader that plied the seas between Sydney and New Zealand. It seems that Sarah and Hugh were the only members of their family to come to this country. Both were born in County Donegal, Ireland.

Sarah married Richard Newdick at St Paul's Church in Auckland on 20 March 1843. The Revd John Frederick Churton officiated.

Life in those early years of settlement was never easy. Stark, unremitting drudgery was the lot of the working classes. For women the burden was particularly heavy. They lived and worked in the most primitive of conditions, and they bore children year in, year out, with no end in sight as to when their childbearing days would be over.

Between 1844 and 1852 Sarah bore five children.

Auckland Lunatic Asylum, c.1890s. Sarah Newdick was first admitted to the Whau Asylum (later the Auckland Lunatic Asylum at Avondale) in 1854, and spent much of the remaining sixteen years of her life there. *Auckland Institute and Museum*

On 21 October 1854, she was admitted to the Auckland Asylum. Her condition was described in the register as 'melancholia'. Her desperation was so great that she had attempted to drown herself. Her menses had ceased for five months.

'Daily improved', was the notation for 5 December 1854. Menses appeared on 12 November and on 5 December she was removed by her husband to convalesce.

From the entry of 21 December 1854 we find that she was living with her brother from her release until 17 December, when she again showed symptoms of her old complaint. She was readmitted to the asylum.

The entry for 1 February 1855 reads, 'Menses reappeared middle January and she appears much better.' In April 1855, Sarah was released.

Sarah's sixth child was born in 1857, and on 9 December 1858 she was re-admitted to the asylum. Her seventh child was born in 1862.

Sarah Newdick died in the asylum in 1870, sixteen years after she was first admitted. The last entry in the asylum register is on 19 June 1870. It states that she died at a few minutes to 4 o'clock in the later stages of emaciation.

Her death notice appeared in the *New Zealand Weekly News*, on 25 July 1870: 'On June 19 at the Lunatic Asylum, Sarah Newdick, beloved wife of the late Richard Newdick, aged 48 years.' *Sherryle Buckby Lane*

Unpublished Sources
Auckland Centennial Roll, 1840–1940, APL
Marriage Register, St Paul's Church, AIM
Register, Auckland Asylum, National Archives Records Centre, Auckland

MARJORY NICHOLLS

1890–1930

Marjory Lydia Nicholls, the first woman to win the Plunket Medal for oratory at Victoria University College, was born in Wellington on 29 July 1890. Her mother's maiden name was Susan Sampson; her father, Harry Nicholls, was secretary to the Wellington Harbour Board and a notable amateur actor.

Marjory was educated at the Terrace School and Wellington Girls' College, where she was a prefect and editor of the school magazine. Olga Harding, the school's historian, called her an outstanding pupil, distinguished for her 'penetration of mind . . . shrewdness of judgement . . . and generosity of spirit'.

At Victoria University College, Marjory's talents and personality made her prominent in student activities, particularly in the Debating Club. She edited and contributed to the magazine *The Spike*, started a play-reading group, and produced two plays. In 1913 she was the first woman ever to enter for the prestigious Plunket oratory contest. According to the historian J. C. Beaglehole, men students were rather taken aback when Marjory Nicholls, 'the gifted and radiant one', carried off the medal with a speech on Joan of Arc. They had wanted to encourage women, but had never expected this.

Marjory left Victoria shortly afterwards, without taking a degree, because of ill health and eye strain. There was clearly no lack of ability to complete a degree.

The remaining seventeen years of her life were spent in travelling, writing, teaching, dramatic work, and following an interest in art. These pursuits were often connected and mutually enriching.

Marjory made a number of extensive journeys over several continents. While travelling on a ship she met the man she married in 1920, a Scotsman named John Hannah, who was a partner in a hardware firm in Ceylon. But the marriage was very brief as her husband died twelve weeks later of enteric fever.

While on her travels, Marjory followed her interest in theatre and studied in England under Edith Craig, daughter of the great actress, Ellen Terry. She also studied at the Pasadena Theatre in California.

On her return to New Zealand she taught English and sometimes drama at a number of schools: Wellington Girls' College, Chilton House, and Samuel Marsden Collegiate School in Wellington, and Chilton St James School in Lower Hutt. Her lively personality, sense of humour, and wide reading were remembered with joy by some of her pupils sixty years later. At Wellington Girls' College there is now an annual Marjory Nicholls prize for oratory.

Her work in the theatre was central to her life. She was a foundation member of the National Repertory Theatre Society, acted in a wide variety of roles, and also produced plays. She put her knowledge of stage production and acting at the service of the schools in which she taught and aroused a lasting interest in drama in some of them. In addition, she taught elocution and lectured for the WEA.

Marjory Nicholls published three volumes of poetry, which received good reviews. These were *A Venture Into Verse* (1917), *Gathering Leaves* (1922), and

Thirdly (1930), which appeared a few days before her death. She also studied painting under D. K. Richmond and was a gifted and popular lecturer. Marjory Nicholls was killed in a street accident when she was on her way home from a concert on 1 October 1930. In her will she left £200 to be spent on pictures by New Zealand artists, which were to be given to the women's common room in Victoria College. Her trustees used some of the money to commission a leading portrait painter, Mary Elizabeth Tripe, to paint a portrait of her. This portrait hung for years in the common room, but in 1988 it was moved to Women's Studies House at the university.

Marjory Nicholls was clearly a woman of many talents. Perhaps too many, her friend Eileen Duggan suggested in an obituary article: 'too many fairies came to her cradle'. However, an assessment of her achievements is difficult, since there were very limited career opportunities for a woman of her interests in New Zealand at the time. Although she was a gifted teacher, her lengthy travels precluded a proper career in teaching. Men who won the Plunket oratory contests often went on to a career in politics or the law, but no woman entered the New Zealand parliament until after Marjory's death, and there were few women lawyers. In any case, her real interests and her chief gifts lay in the theatre. But professional theatre did not exist here in her lifetime.

In 1928 Robin Hyde wrote an article about Marjory Nicholls in which she described Marjory's Sydney Street flat with its blue Delft plates and souvenirs of her visits to the East. 'Etching and Indian Brass and a Taffeta Gown' was the headline, and Hyde's description of Marjory herself ended with 'and charming lady in general'. It was Marjory Nicholls' personality which made the most powerful and lasting impression on people: her warm sympathy, her witty conversation, her ringing laugh, her kind heart.   *Beryl Hughes*

Quotations
para.2 O. Harding, *One Hundred Years: A History of Wellington Girls' College*, Wellington, 1982, p.62
para.3 J. C. Beaglehole, *Victoria University College: an essay towards a history*, Wellington, 1949, p.122
para.12 *The Spike*, no.59, 1931
para.13 *NZ Truth*, 6 Dec. 1928

Unpublished Sources
'A Family Called Nicholls', booklet produced by family members, sometime in the 1980s (in private possession)
Letter from Margaret Nicholls (niece) to author, 20 Feb. 1989

Published Sources
Art in New Zealand, vol.3 no.2, March 1931 (obituary)
Evening Post, 2 Oct. 1930 (obituary)
Hughes, B. and Vial, J. 'A Portrait of Marjory Nicholls', *Women's Studies Journal*, vol.5 no.1, Sept. 1989, pp.74–9
NZ Free Lance, 6 Dec. 1930 (obituary)
G. H. Scholefield (ed.). *A Dictionary of New Zealand Biography*, Wellington, 1940

KIRSTINE NIELSEN

1873 - 1937

Mette Kirstine Bruun was born in 1873 in the town of Vejle, on Vejle Fjord in Denmark. Her father was a post office official, and blue-eyed, dark blonde Kirstine was one of eleven children. She grew into a tall and capable woman, consistently warm-hearted and pleasant.

As soon as she was old enough she went out to work, and in 1894 she married Hans Nielsen, a foundry worker, who was born in 1868. He was a tall, slender, brown-haired man, not very robust, but vital and sociable. They had three sons and one daughter.

After some years Hans began to suffer from indifferent health. Kirstine's sister, Jensine, had emigrated to New Zealand with her husband Morris Cohr. They settled at Ngamoko where Morris operated a sawmilling plant on the eastern slopes of the Ruahines, a short distance from the headwaters of the Manawatu River and a few miles from the Scandinavian settlement of Norsewood. In 1906 Hans left Denmark to work for Morris Cohr in Ngamoko, in the hope that he would regain his health in a better climate. Two years later Kirstine and the children joined him; there was a wonderful reunion in Wellington followed by the journey home by train to Ormondville, and then by Fred Smith's coach to Ngamoko. Hans had bought a dairy-farm of seventy-four acres on the opposite side of the Manawatu River to the Cohrs.

Domestic and farm life in pioneer New Zealand was hard and primitive for Kirstine, coming as she did from the gentle landscape of Denmark and her cosy, sociable town life. When she arrived the air was hazy with the smoke from bush-fires, charred trees lay about, there was very little pasture and the mountains – an unusual sight for a Dane – were very close. Like other isolated women in New Zealand, she missed her neighbours at home, and it was during this first experience of living in a remote region and with little English, that she started to think about other women in the same situation. How did they fare without close neighbours? How could their lonely lives be made fuller and richer? She turned to her traditional sources of creativity: needle-work and handcrafts, 'making beauty from nothing'. She shared these skills with every woman or group with whom she came in contact.

Hans' farming prospered, and in 1912, Kirstine, longing to see her homeland again, went back to Denmark for a visit. But things had changed – the back garden of her old home was now part of the railway-yards, old friends had gone and nothing seemed the same anymore. She had been too long away, the gap could not be bridged, and she was glad to return to New Zealand.

A few years later Hans, in poor health again, had to stop farming. He bought three and a half acres in Arthurs Road in Norsewood, where their house was on a rise facing a beautiful view over downland. And there, on the sunny verandah or under the shade of her big camelia tree, Kirstine's many Pakeha and Maori friends would find her, absorbed in her handcrafts, with the rich smell of the coffee she roasted from beans to welcome them.

Kirstine's granddaughter remembers her Danish fondness for smoked eel and her delight when Maori friends brought her some as a present, and her delicious Danish cooking.

Kirstine became friendly with Miss Jerome Spencer, the founder of New Zealand's Country Women's Institutes, and in July 1922 she attended a public meeting in the Norsewood Library to consider the formation of a women's institute in Norsewood, the second institute to be formed in New Zealand. She was elected to the committee and one year later took over the work of the president, Mrs Hinds. At last Kirstine could realise her dream of bringing isolated country-women together, and she threw herself into teaching and assisting all who were interested in handcrafts. She also started an institute for Maori women at Rakau-tatahi, seven miles west of Takapau. The women there so appreciated her efforts that they seldom passed her door without leaving a small gift.

Kirstine was in her element in Norsewood, organising many activities in the community, such as persuading the government to purchase the Lutheran Hall. But there was one project which never left her mind. In Denmark 'health seals' were sold to the public to be placed on letters, and the money from these sales was used for health care in the community. She returned from her visit to her homeland full of enthusiasm for a similar scheme in New Zealand.

Danish 'health seals' gave Kirstine Nielsen the idea for New Zealand health stamps such as the one depicting health camp founder Dr Elizabeth Gunn.

In 1926 she gained support for the system from the Norsewood Institute, and it was agreed that she should approach the government. So Kirstine travelled to Wellington and discussed the matter with Lady Fergusson, the wife of the governor general. The proposal was then outlined in a letter written by Kirstine's son (whose English was good), and it was eventually taken up by the Post and Telegraph Department. It was decided that the issue of a stamp proper, having a postage as well as a charity value, would be preferable to the issue of a seal. Such stamps were in use in a number of countries and they had been approved for international use at the Postal Convention of Stockholm in 1924.

In 1929 the first New Zealand health stamps were issued and profits from their sale allocated to the children's health camp movement. Begun in 1919, health camps took in children who were malnourished, debilitated through sickness, or at risk from tuberculosis, and gave them a six to eight-week period of outdoor life, good food and rest. The sale of health stamps provided both funds and publicity to the camps which, over the next two decades, became permanent structures located all over New Zealand.

Kirstine was president of the Norsewood Institute until 1932 and was very proud indeed when a fine chair with her name on it was presented to her in recognition of her work for the institute. She left Norsewood with Hans in 1937 and died in Hastings in 1938, aged sixty-five.   *Yvonne du Fresne*

Unpublished Source
Information was provided by Mrs E. Anderson, Kirstine Nielsen's granddaughter.

Published Source
Macgregor, Miriam. *Petticoat Pioneers: North Island Women of the Colonial Era*, Wellington, 1973

NANCY NORTHCROFT

1913-1980

As town planner for Christchurch City, and later for the new Canterbury Region, Nancy Northcroft was one of a small number who established town planning as a recognised profession in New Zealand in the 1940s and 1950s.

Family, friends, and professional colleagues remember her as very methodical, a clear thinker, completely professional in everything she undertook to do, and a person of great integrity. As a planner she was strong-minded, but not dogmatic. In her obituary a colleague described her as someone who 'led from the front'. She is also remembered for her ability to get on with people, her fairness, and her sense of humour.

Nancy Northcroft was born in Hamilton in 1913. She and her older sister Joan attended the small private Sonning School run by Mrs Whitehorn. When their lawyer father joined an Auckland firm in 1921, the family moved to Auckland where the girls attended the Auckland Diocesan Girls' School. Nancy became head prefect. An abiding enthusiasm for cricket dated from membership of the school's cricket team. She was later to become a life member of the Riccarton Cricket Club and for many years was official scorer for the club's senior team.

Nancy's father was an important influence in her early life. Overseas for the First World War for three years when Nancy was very young, he spent as much time as he could with his two young daughters on his return. He encouraged them in a range of activities and interests such as yachting and tramping, as well as academically. However, when Nancy wished to study law and become a lawyer herself, her father prevented it, apparently regarding the law as an unsuitable occupation for women. Architecture was more acceptable, and Nancy, despite a lack of aptitude for the mathematical side of her studies, obtained a bachelor's degree in architecture from the University of New Zealand in 1940. She worked before and after completing her degree in the Auckland architecture office of Keith Draffen. There were then very few women architects in New Zealand.

In 1942 Nancy Northcroft won a British Council scholarship and set off with two other women on a cargo boat to Britain. The journey was adventurous, with boats in the same convoy apparently being torpedoed, but the passengers arrived safely in London. The scholarship period was spent studying housing in and around London and in Scotland, despite the interruptions of war. The immense amount of war damage, and the need to rebuild and recreate communities, led Nancy to expand her architectural interests into town planning.

In 1943 she joined the small core staff of the Association for Planning and Regional Reconstruction in London. This was a research and teaching organisation, and the job enabled Nancy to study for a Diploma in Town Planning, which she completed in 1946, and to develop research and teaching skills which became invaluable later in her career.

Returning to establish a career in New Zealand in 1948 was difficult. Town planning was not a recognised discipline in its own right (most town planning work being carried out by surveyors), and there was also some prejudice against women, particularly at the senior level which Nancy's qualifications justified. Nancy was unable to convince the Hamilton City Council either that it needed a planner, or that her skills were suitable. She was on the point of returning to Britain when the Christchurch City Council advertised for a planner. Thoroughly disheartened, she nonetheless applied and, to her surprise, got the job. She remained chief planner for the Christchurch City Council from 1948 to 1954.

The framework for city development she helped to lay down is apparent in Christchurch today. It is largely due to sound planning over the past forty years that the city has become the pleasant place and tourist attraction it now is. In the dual role of first chief executive and chief planner for the nascent Canterbury Regional Planning Authority from 1954 to 1962, Nancy Northcroft also left her mark. The regional authority was one of the first in the country, and was something of a planning success story. Nancy's outstanding contributions included the adoption of the Rural Area Protection Policy in 1959, and the Master Transportation Plan in 1962. Nancy Northcroft's last fourteen professional years were as a partner in the multi-disciplinary firm of Davie Lovell Smith in Christchurch. In this position she undertook planning work all over New Zealand for a range of clients and became widely known. She suffered from poor health in these later years, but kept it very much to herself.

In Christchurch, she became involved in a range of other activities and interests. She was particularly involved in the Geographical Society, the Anglican Church, and a number of women's organisations including the Te Wai Pounamu Maori Girls' College, the Soroptimist Club of Christchurch, and the New Zealand Federation of University Women. She was a justice of the peace and the first woman to become president of the New Zealand Planning Institute. She was the first recipient of the Institute Gold Medal on her retirement in 1978, and in that year she was also awarded the OBE for services to the community.

Nancy Northcroft did not regard herself as a feminist and was critical of the emergence of feminist philosophy amongst young women planners in the late

1970s. However, both her career as a planner and her involvement and commitment to many women's organisations contrast with this expressed view. Although she never married, she was heard to remark, towards the end of her professional career and with characteristic humour, that she could really have done with a husband at home to manage her household and other day-to-day responsibilities.

Sylvia Allan

Unpublished Sources

Information was provided by Michael Davie and Kim McCracken of Davie Lovell Smith, Christchurch; Derek Edmondson, Gabites and Porter, Wellington; Joan Upton, Ngaruawahia (Nancy Northcroft's sister).

Published Sources

Douglass, M. 'Retirement of Nancy Northcroft', *Town Planning Quarterly*, no.47, June 1977
Edmondson, D. 'Nancy Northcroft, OBE, Obituary', *Town Planning Quarterly*, no.60, Sept. 1980

KATE NUNNELEY

1875–1956

Kathleen Mary Nunneley, one of New Zealand's earliest and most successful tennis champions, was born at Market Harborough in Leicestershire in 1875. Little is known of her early life except that she began her tennis career while only a teenager, winning several titles before she had turned fifteen. In 1891 she won the Brighton Handicap singles title and then in 1893 she recorded victories in

Kate Nunneley, c.1889. *Alexander Turnbull Library*

provincial tournaments in Liverpool, Leicester, Northampton, Nottingham, and Wellingborough. Although she never competed for the All England title, she had the honour of defeating Wimbledon champion Blanche Bingley before she left England for New Zealand in 1895.

Kate Nunneley had an immediate impact on the game of tennis in New Zealand. After settling in Wellington, she joined the Thorndon Lawn Tennis Club and took part in her first New Zealand Lawn Tennis Association tournament in December 1895. Equipped with an extremely powerful forehand drive, a strong service, and an accurate backhand, she had little trouble winning both the singles and doubles titles.

She was then chosen to represent New Zealand at the New South Wales Championships in 1896, where she won both the ladies' championship and handicap singles titles.

Kate Nunneley's success in her first overseas competition and in subsequent New Zealand championship tournaments confirmed that she was one of Australasia's leading women players. In all, she won the New Zealand ladies' singles title on thirteen consecutive occasions between 1895 and 1907.

She also won ten ladies' doubles titles, nine combined doubles titles, and was a key member of the first New Zealand women's tennis team, which made a triumphant tour of New South Wales in 1909.

By the time she made her first trip to England at the end of the First World War, she had given up playing tennis at the highest level. Some years later she decided to have the gold medals which she had won at New Zealand tournaments mounted on a casket. The so-called 'Nunneley Casket' was presented to the New Zealand Lawn Tennis Association in 1928, and since then has become the trophy for the annual inter-provincial women's team tennis competition.

In 1935 Kate Nunneley retired from her position as a senior staff member of the Wellington public libraries, where she had worked for thirty years. In later years she maintained her involvement with tennis by helping young players and making donations to the game. A keen spectator at the Wellington Lawn Tennis Association's courts, she returned to England to see the Wimbledon tennis tournament in both 1949 and 1953. Her contribution to women's tennis was officially recognised when she was made a life member of the Wellington and the New Zealand Lawn Tennis Associations. She was also a life member of her own tennis club in Thorndon.

She died of a heart and lung disorder at the age of eighty-one in the Wellington Public Hospital on 28 September 1956.   *Margaret Hammer*

Unpublished Sources

Dept. of Internal Affairs. 'An Encyclopaedia of New Zealand: Sports and Pastimes Collection', 1966, MS Papers 2000, folder 17, pp.1269, 1273–5, ATL

NZ Biographies Scrapbooks, vol.4, 1958, p.97; vol.5, 1975, p.178, ATL

Published Sources

Elenio, Paul. *Centre Court: A Century of New Zealand Tennis 1886–1986*, Wellington, 1986

NZ Illustrated Magazine, vol.1, Dec. 1899, pp.201–2, 204–6

The Thorndon Club Inc. 1879–1979: A History, Wellington, 1979

ROTIRA TE REWA OTENE

?1868-1978

Rotira Te Rewa Otene was born in Waimana in about 1868. She was from Tuhoe. As a young woman Rotira and some other Tuhoe people came to live among Te Atianga-a-Mahaki in Gisborne. Rotira had two husbands. She had no children of her own but raised eight whangai.

Rotira wore a moko. It is said that she was one of the last kuia in Gisborne to have her moko incised by the traditional method.

Rotira died in 1978 aged 110 and is buried at Puha Tiko Tiko, north of Gisborne.

Her story is told by Ruby Te Hei and Sarah McGhee.
She was a very nice looking lady, but she was big. Very strong build, about five foot. Her hair was white. Sometimes she wore it tied up in a headscarf. She had amazing skin. It only seemed to crinkle in the last couple of years. She looked the same, even towards the end. And she loved jewellery. She always had her greenstone earrings. She had a walking stick, it was old manuka. It had a clear sort of thing like an eye in it. I think she just used it really for us, because she wasn't leaning on it until her last years. Then she had a proper stick, but before then it was a rakau. Oh yes. I had a lot of those.

She walked every day, too. Two miles at least. She was fit, eh? She could chop wood or do anything. She liked music too. She used to play the button accordion and the mouth-organ. And she could dance.

She didn't drink. Not very much, only when there is something on at home, like a card game. Then she'd have a drink. It was gin. She liked gin. She smoked roll-your-owns. Pocket Edition and Zig Zag papers. She used to swear, but only when she was really annoyed, that's all.

She spoke Maori to us. We'd get a smack because she'd be talking Maori to us and I'd answer back in English. She'd get angry. She couldn't read or write. She used to have X crossed for her sign. But she could play cards. Canasta, bridge, five hundred. You have to be able to count to do those things.

Nanny lived with Johnny Smith. One time when the old man went to Te Karaka on that white horse of his, she says, 'Bring back some bread, butter and things.' He goes to the pub and comes back drunk without any things. So when he gets home and he wants Nanny to serve him his kai, she cuts a block of wood and puts it right in front of him on his plate. He says, 'He aha, he aha?' What's this, what's this? and she says, 'Sit down. He tika ra, that's your kai for tonight. You didn't bring the butter and some bread.' And away they go, arguing.

Most of the time we'd have to get up early. She'd have breakfast ready for us. Porridge and sometimes tea and bread, or fried bread, maybe meat, it all depends. You haven't tasted fried bread until you have tasted our old kuia's. Hers melted in your mouth. As a treat sometimes she made kororirori. She

481

Rotira Te Rewa Otene. *Ruby Te Hei*

*made the very dry mixture of flour, made it quite stringy, or if you like lumpy
you make it lumpy. Rub it together and boil it in the water like macaroni or
dumplings or dough boys. Then you serve it up with sugar and cream or golden
syrup and cream.*

*She often used to cook for the shearing gangs. She would not just cook up
meat and spuds, she would always have greens of some sort. Watercress and
puha. She used to like making toroi – preserved puha. She used to collect it,
then clean it, and cook and cook it until it's soft. She'd drain that water out
because it's sour. Then she'd put fresh water in and break the puha up.
Mukumuku [crush]. Then she added salt, then mussels and sometimes
muttonbird. A muttonbird would go that green colour, but it doesn't harm it.
Then she put it into crocks, with a cloth over the top because you don't seal it.*

*She'd tahu meat like wild pork in from the bush. She'd preserve them in
fat. An over-abundance of meat, she'd chop it up into portions. Then she'd
have the stewing pan or a big pot of boiling hot fat, and deep fry the pieces of
meat until they're absolutely pakapaka – crisp. Then once it's cooled down, the
fat is scooped off all the other debris. The meat is laid down in pots and the
clean fat is melted and poured over it. When you use it later, you just scrape off
the fat and heat the meat up or placed on top of puha or watercress. That meat
lasts for a whole year. She did the same with the pauas. Lay them down nice
and black, but you had to take that pewa [roe] off. Then bang them. We lay
them down in pork fat. No salt. Much the same way, stored for a long time.*

*When we harvest the potatoes it was an all-day job. She put them in the
pakoro which is a separate shed with a roof on. Some people used to have*

482

pakoro in the bank, but we had an old shed. First of all it would be lined with manuka. We'd collect all the frondy parts, the brush parts. The pakoro was covered with raupo too, out of the swamps. Nanny would supervise the laying of the potatoes. We used to cart them to her, and she'd place them in the pakaro carefully because we probably bruised them. We had a garden down by Uncle Wi's. Two acres. Potatoes, kumara, corn, and onions. She drove the horse in behind the plough. She would take turns and D'Arcy would share and give her a break. I'd be on the horse going down the lines, steering. I'd go to sleep and go crooked. D'Arcy used to pick up big clumps of dirt. Chuck them at me on the back of the head. All I could feel was this donk!

She loved eeling. She was the best. She fished by the moon by the Maori calendar. Hardly ever used the hinaki [eel weir]. For Nanny it was mostly bombing. If the word went round that she was going to mahi tuna [looking for eels], everyone down tools and off we went. I don't know that we got many, but we had fun with her.

She always used to bury her money, eh? Bury it in those old baking powder tins in the back. About four or five hundred pounds, she'd have in that tin. Because Lovey and I did the garden and in this particular place in the bank, she had those creepy flowers there. She said, 'Don't touch that side – you can do anywhere else.' So I was weeding and thought, 'Nanny's always telling us don't dig here.' I started digging and bang, there's something buried there. So I dug it up. It was a baking powder tin. I opened it and saw all the money. When Nanny calmed down I told her I had found it and that's when I got a good hiding.

She used to love the buggy rides. Johnny Smith had one. She'd say, come on, and off to town. When we saw our friends we hid our faces. Too shamed. Don't want to be seen in that old thing. Once a month she goes to town and come back with a little something for us. We get those round tins, full of boiled lollies.

She goes to church. She used to take us every first of the month. Murae, they call it. Ringatu. We used to go for a feed. She used to say, 'A he makihakiha.' We think she don't know what we're thinking, like we're only going there for kai, but she knew we were, makihakiha, hopeless case.

Nanny was clear about tapu things. You couldn't go and eat on her pillow, things like that. Never see a comb on a table. She was very strict with our clothes. We wash our underwear, and hang it up. She goes with her stick, pow, do it again. To me it's clean, eh? No. Two or three times we wash it again. No washing clothes at night. Or sweeping. Especially if you've got manukiri [visitors] or people visiting us. You don't dare sweep with a broom because that's rude.

She cut our hair, the clippings go down the toilet, down the long drop. You can't burn or bury it. Too tapu. You don't leave it around, so down the toilet it went. Very Ringatu.

She had eight whangai. The youngest one was John, a Pakeha-looking boy. He was a mischief boy. One day he took a gun and shot a milking cow. He would have been almost eight years old. He come back and acted out how the cow staggered around. So Nanny had to go and look for it. She found it when she came back and we wondered what's Nanny going to do to him. She put John in a hole. Cover him right up to his neck and she left him there all afternoon. He never done anything naughty for a long time after that.

What I remember about her most was the way she cared for us. The love she gave us and the patience she had. I think I'm a better person today because of it.

Ruby Te Hei, Sarah McGhee & Cushla Parekowhai

PALLISER BAY WOMAN

c.1200

She was born in about the twelfth century AD, locality unknown, tribal affiliation uncertain, died later in the twelfth or early thirteenth century AD, aged thirty-five to forty years, and was buried at the mouth of the Makotukutuku River, Palliser Bay. The physical and social environment in which this woman spent her life has been reconstructed by archaeologists who in 1970 excavated the site of the coastal village where she was interred.

Although she is nameless, examination of her skeletal remains has provided details that give her individuality. In life she stood 162.6 cm tall (about 5′ 4″), was fairly robust and right-handed. She had given birth to between two and four children. By the time of her death she was suffering from quite severe wear on her teeth. The pulp cavity of some of her molars was exposed and this had led to abscessing. Evidence of arthritis in the spine may be linked to the deterioration of health that accompanied these infections. Her diet (or the sand that blew into her food) was clearly very abrasive.

During the twelfth and thirteenth centuries, the small community in which she lived occupied a group of sleeping huts and cooking sheds on the north bank of the ponded mouth of the Makotukutuku River, one of several coastal hamlets in Eastern Palliser Bay. Although seasonal trips were made to catch birds such as tuis and parakeets and to gather berries from the forested valleys of the Aorangi Mountains that formed its backdrop, the coastal village was permanently occupied because of proximity to its gardens and seafood resources. The gardens were located on the old raised beach ridges and swales just behind the village. Their shallow stony soils which had formed under coastal scrub had been cleared by fire, with unwanted stones piled along the plot boundaries. Of the tropical crops introduced by her ancestors, this woman grew mainly the kumara and gourd, best suited to the harsher climate and light soils of the area. In autumn the kumara harvest was carefully stored within enclosed pits close to the cooking sheds.

When not occupied by gardening, she gathered seafood from the intertidal platform, especially paua, topshells, limpets, and crayfish. Some of the fish eaten at the village were caught inshore using circular hooks of bone and shell, but when sea conditions were suitable the men caught fish such as barracouta and kahawai by trolling lures behind canoes. Rats and eels were trapped close to the village and domestic dogs were killed to supplement the meat of sea mammals such as dolphins and seals. During the summer months, food gathering included items for preservation. The long hours of daylight were fully occupied with the splitting of eels and other oily fish for drying, and the weaving of kete for storage. This woman's activities were more closely affected by seasonal changes than those of her tropical Polynesian ancestors. However, her heavy work-load in summer and autumn would have slackened in winter and she was fortunate to have fresh water and firewood close at hand throughout the year.

Her death, in her fourth decade, would not have been unexpected since few adults survived long, given their physically demanding life-style. She was buried in the vicinity of several family members and a pet dog, along the seaward edge of the village. The grave was a small scoop in the gravel in which her body was placed, tightly trussed, on its left side. Several large stones formed a pillow beneath her head. There were no apparent burial offerings.

Helen Leach & Philip Houghton

Published Source
Leach, B. F. and Leach, H. M. (eds). *Prehistoric Man in Palliser Bay*, National Museum of New Zealand Bulletin 21, Wellington, 1979

Shell midden, Palliser Bay. *Atholl Anderson*

MAY PALMER

1886–1977

Alice May Palmer was born in 1886 and lived to ninety. She had a brilliant school record, a successful career in the public service (in terms of what was open to women), and was the first woman to make her mark on the Public Service Association.

May was born in Gordon, near Gore on 6 August 1886, the eldest child of Alice Palmer (born Shepard) aged twenty-two, and Walter Henry Palmer, clerk of court, aged twenty-four. Two sons, Darcy and Arthur Henry, completed the family. May entered Southland Girls' High School in 1900 with an Education Board scholarship, boarding with a Mrs John Mackinnon of Crinan Street, Invercargill. In 1903 she was dux. In 1904 she was dux again, this time of Southland Boys' High School. It was then board policy that all senior girls went to the boys' high school to have 'their courses of study mapped out by Mr T. D. Pearce, Rector'. Her record sheet shows her as passing the Junior Civil Service Examination and being a 'Junior Scholar, Credit List'.

On 22 June 1905 May became a clerical cadet in the Department of Education in Wellington, by then having also passed the Senior Civil Service Examination. George Hogben was one of the few department heads, if not the only one, who appointed women to permanent clerical positions.

Between 1906 and 1911 May, while continuing to work full time, completed

Office work became an increasingly popular choice for women after leaving school, though few followed May Palmer's example by becoming office holders in their union. May Palmer was the 'Ladies Representative' in the PSA from 1914 to 1935. *Gordon Burt Collection, Alexander Turnbull Library*

486

a Bachelor of Arts degree at Victoria University College. She was capped in 1912, one of seven women and twelve men to graduate BA.

A foundation member of the Public Service Association (PSA), May was elected to the national executive in 1914 as a ladies' representative 'for all women outside Wellington'. The association created two special positions for women in response to the actions of the new public service commissioner, the first to head a politically independent service, who had stopped girls from sitting the public service entry exams and fixed a lower female maximum for women already in the service. There are *Public Service Journal* reports of May using her public speaking skills, honed in the University Women's Debating Society, in the service of justice for women. At the first PSA annual dinner on 22 July 1914, held at the Oriental Bay Kiosk, she replied to the toast, 'the ladies' ('an unusual situation of a member of the fair sex responding,' reports the *Journal*). She said that 'women are content to be judged on the merit of the work they perform and should not be kept on the bottom rungs of the ladder simply on account of their sex'.

May continued to serve as ladies' representative on the PSA executive, with one break of five years, until 1934. In August of that year she was elected in a contested election as one of the two executive vice-presidents of the association. She was the first woman to reach high office; in fact the second woman vice-president was not elected until 1978 and the first woman president until 1988. She did not stand for any position after the 1935 council meeting.

Although entry, status, and promotion conditions for women improved little, and from time to time deteriorated, during May's service, she made astonishing personal progress – for a woman. In 1916, after nearly eleven years' service, she moved from Class VII to Class VI into a newly created position of statistical clerk, the only woman in the department to have reached this level. (She entered as a cadet in Class VIII-VII.) Eight years later she moved into the professional division to become sub-editor of the *New Zealand School Journal*, a step achieved by contributing articles (written in her own time) 'displaying singular ability'.

In 1937, after nearly thirty-two years' service, she became acting editor of the *School Journal* and the *New Zealand Education Gazette*. She remained 'acting' until her retirement in October 1940, with thirty-five years' service. (Men stayed on until the age of sixty and in some cases sixty-five.) Dr C. E. Beeby, director of education from April 1940, wrote recently of the

unusual qualities of the woman that enabled her to progress from the clerical branch of the Department to a professional post, a rare achievement in those days and by no means common even now.

He also noted: 'Incidentally, I never did discover why she remained "acting" for so long, and by the time I came to power, she was close to retirement.'

Despite the modesty of her salary, May saved enough to go on a world trip with a woman friend before retirement and to buy a house after she retired. She lived for nearly thirty-seven years after her retirement on what must have been a rapidly shrinking superannuation. For the first twenty-three years she lived in her own house at Eastbourne; then, at the age of seventy-eight, moved into a flat in the basement of the Karori house of her niece and her husband. She continued to play bridge, read, entertain friends, and visit her club. Her last years were spent in Silverstream Hospital. Her niece says she was as alert and clear-headed as ever when she died there on 25 June 1977 in her ninety-first year.

Margaret Long

Quotations
para.2 Olive Deaker, *History of Southland Girls' High School*, 1978
para.5 *Public Service Journal*, 15 Aug. 1914, p.iii
para.7 *Education Gazette*, 1 Dec. 1940, p.210
para.8 Letter to author from C. E. Beeby, 25 July 1989

Unpublished Sources
Interview with Joan and Malcolm Wheatley, Raumati
Letters to the author from C. E. Beeby; Barbara Clark (archivist, Southland Girls' High School); Bert Roth; University Grants Committee

Published Sources
Education Gazette, Dec. 1940
Evening Post, 28 June 1977 (death notice)
McLauchlan, Gordon (ed.) *Encyclopedia of New Zealand*, Part 33, Auckland, 1986, p.910
NZ Gazette, 1911–40 (Public Service Classification List)
NZ Herstory 1984, Auckland, 1983
Public Service Journals, 15 Aug. 1914, p.iii; 20 July 1915, p.iii; 20 Aug. 1915, pp.34, 42; 20 Oct. 1915, p.31; 20 Nov. 1915, p.44; Oct. 1934, p.512
Roth, Bert. *Remedy for Present Evils*, Wellington, 1987
The Spike, The Victoria College Review, no.21, June 1912, p.21: no.22, Oct. 1912, pp.42, 65

GUIDE BELLA
BELLA TE HOARI PAPAKURA

?1870–1950

Bella Te Hoari Papakura was born Ihapera Te Hoari Thom at Whakarewarewa, Rotorua, in 1870 or 1871. Her mother was Rakera of Ngati Wahiao, Tuhourangi, and her father was William Thom, a Pakeha. Bella received a comprehensive formal education, including three years' secondary schooling at Hukarere Maori Girls' College in Napier.

In 1910 Bella was a member of a concert party, led by her sister Maggie Papakura, which went to Australia and England to perform as part of the celebrations for the coronation of King George V. Before that time Bella had become a guide at Whakarewarewa. She is remembered as being a senior guide who taught and influenced many young Ngati Wahiao women.

Guide Bella lived in Whakarewarewa village itself. She had a small whare opposite the Catholic church called Te Awai-a-Manukau. Bella had no children of her own, although she had three husbands. However, she adopted and raised one child. In later life Bella suffered a stroke and spent eleven years in Rotorua Hospital. Bella died in February 1950, and is buried at the Whakarewarewa village cemetery.

Her story is told by Guide Bubbles Mihinui:

Bella and Maggie Papakura were half-sisters. When Bella was born her mother became very sick and the family thought she would die. In those days if a husband was widowed, you'd match them off to the deceased person's surviving sibling. So what they did was marry Bella's father off to another cousin. To take it the Maori way, from his first wife he had Bella. But his second wife was a sister to the first wife and she had Maggie Papakura. So Bella and Maggie were not only first cousins, but half-sisters too. (Bella's mother Rakera in fact rallied and later remarried.)

Now that I'm older I realise how much Bella really gave me. Her sister Maggie Papakura was able to go to Oxford University and see the globe, but Bella was able to hold her own in both the Maori and Pakeha worlds too.

Guide Bella Papakura. *Emily Schuster, Maori Arts and Crafts Institute*

Bella was in the background all the time, working and teaching in her own quiet way. I feel of all the guides, Bella had the most influence. She was our mentor as well as our kuia.

In those days there were six of us training to be guides. Our uniform was a red skirt and a tapa silk blouse. It wasn't white, but more of an ecru colour. Our silk blouses laundered up beautifully and were very cool. We also wore red scarves. Red is a very warm and welcoming colour. We had badges too. And at one time we used to wear a band around the sleeve with an ID number. You had to display it prominently so that if people wanted to lay a complaint they took down your number.

I remember we were still serving our apprenticeship and it would be a scorching hot day at the height of the season. Bella would say to us, 'Well, when it's nearly sunset, and cooler in the evening, come up to my place.' She had a little meeting-house up on the hill and you could look down onto the reserve, out over Pohutu and up to the model pa. There she would tell us some of the old stories about the area.

For instance, there were several burial caves up in the reserve. She showed us where some of them are but she said, and I've never forgotten this, 'Don't ever talk about these caves in ordinary conversation. Not all your visitors need to know everything. You can assess when people might have a specialist interest, like historians or conservationists, then you can choose exactly what ought to be said.' This is why I put Bella on a pedestal, because for the younger ones she was forthcoming with her knowledge. Bella always believed in taha Maori me te taha Pakeha. She didn't separate them. Her teaching was all done the old Maori way by observation and participation.

Bella and her generation of guides had a caring attitude. She hated the word 'tourist' because it has cheapening connotations. She said, 'Think of it in Maori terms, any stranger to our place is manuhiri – a visitor. Treat them all like that and people will respond.' Maori, whether we know it or not, communicate well with body language. That's what Bella used to get her point across. Every single one of her visitors were able to relate to her without any words at all.

In those earlier years, most of our visitors came from the British Isles and Europe, and because it took such a long time to get here, people didn't rush. They stayed not just for a week, but for three months or more. The average visitor at that time did things in a more leisurely way and we were able to spend time with them. These days visitors are only given forty-five minutes to go through the attractions and the guides don't get a chance to develop any meaningful relationship. In Bella's day it was different. The friendship was more lasting.

There was a natural amphitheatre up at the pa, steep banks for seating and the performance space divided off into sections with little manuka fences. This is where Bella did the poi. She was wonderful poi dancer. We'd have a tangata whaikorero [speech maker]. He'd speak to our visitors and Bella would translate. Oh how it all came out. Beautiful English. Listening to her I heard a quality and poetry of language that's rarely spoken now.

There used to be a special song sung by the Whaka guides that was called 'Pakete whero mau mai i a koe' [The red kerchief that you wear]. Bella composed a poi to this song for the 1934 Waitangi Day celebrations. For a long time only the guides at Whaka could perform it, because 'Pakete whero' has got an off-beat. This is because Bella likened her poi to the hoof beats of galloping horses – she loved the races. So Bella's poi became the recognised signature of the Whaka guides. She also worked closely with Alfred Hill in the composition of 'Waiata Poi'.

I suppose the fact that we actually lived in the thermal area makes Whaka

490

unique. It was not just an attraction, it's a part of our life.

Guiding wasn't a job, it was a vocation. We weren't there to tell visitors the geysers were so many degrees centigrade. None of us knew that anyway. We were there to talk about them from our perspective. What the geyser meant to us, and how our ordinary and not so ordinary lives depended on it.

Bella taught me that, and it's wisdom difficult to match.

Bubbles Mihinui & Cushla Parekowhai

Published Source
Makereti. *The Old Time Maori*, Auckland, 1986

GUIDE MAGGIE MAKERETI PAPAKURA

1872-1930

Makereti was born in Whakarewarewa, Rotorua, on 20 October 1872. She was the eldest of three; her paternal half-sister Ihipera (Bella) became a famous composer and guide; her paternal half-brother Tiki excelled at rugby. Makereti's parents were Pia Ngarotu Te Rihi, of chiefly Ngati Wahiao and wider Te Arawa descent, and William Arthur Thom, a scholarly Englishman. She was raised by her mother's paternal aunt and uncle, Marara Marotaua and Maihi Te Kakau Paraoa, in the bush at Parekarangi. They instructed her closely in traditional Maori lore and custom; these teachings continually influenced her life.

At ten years of age, she was sent to a private school for young ladies in Tauranga. From here, she moved to Hukarere Maori Girls' College in Napier, where she flourished as a writer and scholar. Later in her life, her bookshelves, lined with Keats, Rousseau, Shelley, Austen, Gibbon, Byron, Robespierre, and countless others, were frequently remarked upon by visiting Europeans.

She was married for a short time to James Dennan, and her son, William Aonui Dennan, was born in 1891. By 1894, as a young mother, Makereti was working as a tourist guide in the Whakarewarewa thermal reserve. During this time, she demonstrated her creative wit and initiative by renaming herself. She was guiding some overseas visitors who insisted on knowing her *Maori* name. They were by the bubbling dainty Papakura geyser, so she replied, 'My name is Papakura' – and the name remained.

The pinnacle of her guiding career came in 1901, with the visit of the Duke and Duchess of Cornwall and York. Her mentor, the dowager guide Sophia, escorted the Duke, and Makereti charmed the Duchess and the press with her dulcet voice and vivacious beauty. Over the next decade, Makereti featured prominently in the media of the day; magazines, calendars, booklets, postcards, newspapers, and notable 'society columns' on both sides of the Tasman published her pictures and followed her life. She published her own guide book, *Maggie's Guide to the Hot Lakes* (n.d., c.1903), which was a huge success.

Makereti was a fearless campaigner for a number of Maori causes. Single-handedly, she attempted to disrupt and expose a grave-robbing operation in the

Maggie Papakura (Makereti), centre, and members of her concert group, including Dick Papakura, far left, Bella Papakura, seated left, and Lena Papakura, seated right. *Emily Schuster, Maori Arts and Crafts Institute*

Rotorua district, and she was a forceful advocate of the Maori right to snare, hunt and fish in traditional areas. She also supported liquor control in the Maori community, and was an active health lobbyist.

A polished entertainer and skilled entrepreneur, she established the Rotorua Maori Choir with the Revd (later Bishop) Fred Bennett in the early 1900s. This became the basis of the touring concert party she took to Clontarf, Sydney, in 1910. Later that same year, the group journeyed to London, and the coronation of King George V and the Festival of Empire celebrations; again, the press was overwhelmed by Makereti's charisma and quick repartee. She accompanied the party home in 1912, then returned almost immediately to England, where she married Richard Staples-Browne, a wealthy Oxfordshire farmer and landowner, whom she first met in 1907.

During the First World War, Makereti opened her grand farmhouse, Oddington Grange, to convalescent Anzacs. For their fallen comrades, she raised funds for a memorial which stands in the little Norman church at Oddington – an Italian *pietà* supported by an elaborate stand of traditional Maori carving.

In 1924, after a quiet divorce, Makereti shifted into Oxford, to attend the university as a 'home student' in the new discipline, anthropology. The richness of all her taonga Maori – carved panels, canoe prows, feather garments and basketry, jade ornaments and weaponry – furnished her unique salon, the New Zealand Room, where colonial scholars met every Thursday night.

Enrolled as a Bachelor of Science candidate, Makereti returned to Whaka-rewarewa in 1926, spending four months with her family, checking her manuscript which the kaumatua endorsed after considerable debate. She kept impeccable records of these discussions. Her thesis examination was scheduled for 5 May 1930; she died suddenly on 16 April, three weeks before the event. Her work was published posthumously, in 1938, as *The Old Time Maori*.

E te whaea, te tohunga, takoto mai ra koe i te poho anuanu o tawahi; tangi tonu atu matou mou; moe mai, moe mai.* *Ngahuia Te Awekotuku*

Beloved mother revered wise one, lie there in that cold place so far away; we miss you; rest on.

Unpublished Sources
Information was provided by family and friends.
Makereti archive, Pitt Rivers Museum, Oxford
T. E. Donne Scrapbook, ATL

MERE KINGI PARAONE

?1835-1942

Mere Kingi Paraone was born in Tarere, Manutuke, in about 1835. Her mother was Hine Whati-o-Rangi of Ngaitawhiri and her father was William Brown, a Pakeha. Mere Kingi had three husbands and six children. Her first husband, Komene, was an elder brother to Te Kooti. Mere Kingi lived all her life in the Poverty Bay area. She is remembered as being a kuia whose everyday beliefs about the world gave deep expression to the spiritual dimensions of Maori experience and thought.

Mere Kingi died in July 1942, aged over a hundred years, and is buried at Tuarakena, Manutuke, Gisborne.

Her story is told by Heni Sunderland:
She was my great-grandparent, Granny Mata, she raised me till I was seven. She was a big woman, very tall and very old. She was born at Tarere and she lived most of her life in Tarere. I don't recall her ever speaking about her childhood. When I come to think of it, I never heard her talk about her father, William Brown. I'm sad about that now. I would have liked to have known more about William Brown. She's a Ngaitawhiri. That's her tribe on this side of the river. But when I knew Granny Mata she was living at Manutuke.

I don't know who did Granny Mata's moko. Never heard. She liked pretty things. She had tartan skirts and tartan shawls. I suppose it was fashionable in those times. My Aunty gave my sister all of Granny's tartan shawls, about three of them. She was to wrap all her babies in. Granny Mata was a midwife. She gave me my name, Heni Materoa.

I remember distinctly Granny talking about three women. Mere Whaitiri, or Mere Waewae as we know her, Granny Tiakiwhare, and my grandmother, Granny Motoi, these three women. She was their midwife. They had very hard times when they had their babies. And to each of those women, after their second child, she said to them, 'You will have no more children.' And no more children did they have. I've lived to regret that I never asked what she did as a midwife – because if you ask they tell you. When the baby was born, they held it by the feet and threw them out to clear the nose. That's how they got rid of all the mucus. She talked about the kinds of massage that they gave the babies. The other thing I heard was that as a midwife they were very strict with themselves. They never gazed at the placenta.

She used to smoke a pipe, Granny Mata. Didn't smoke cigarettes, smoked a pipe. I never knew her to drink. And she didn't play cards. Never saw a drink in our house as we grew up. It wasn't until after my father died. My brother was the first one to bring a bottle of beer to our house.

She was happy about machines; she lived with the times. My dad used to pick her up in the car and fetch her to town. No sweat. The other thing about Granny Mata was that Lady Carroll used to come to her house when I was little. I remember this lady came to the house in a grand car. I don't know about those old Maori – Pakehas would come, they'd talk to them in Maori, and Pakehas seemed to understand.

All the old people had lovely gardens. Vegetable gardens, where flowers seemed to grow among them. Fuchsias was one of the her favourites, with all those beautiful pinks and purple inside. Because she made the pillowcases. Granny Mata used to draw a free-hand picture of a fuchsia and embroider them. Put me to shame. Oh yes. And she always waiata. That was their way of life. Sit on the verandah and waiata like that.

Being Anglican, Granny Mata knew the prayer book off by heart. Neither could she read or write, but nevertheless she memorised it because that was the way. Granny was more like a Ringatu. After our koroua died, Granny Mata would never sit at the table without saying grace.

The other thing about Granny Mata – and these are the rather special things about her – she never ate a meal after sunset, never. You had to pull the blinds down if anybody was still sitting there. She'd say, 'E hoa, kei roto koe i te whare nei, kei raro te kehua nei.' You're sitting in here eating and the ghost is just under there. Every mouthful you have, she made sure that we pulled the blinds down. Superstitious. But she herself never ate after dark, never.

Sunday, Granny Mata didn't do any extra things. She'd peel more potatoes on the Saturday. Sunday was the Sunday. This is the way. Morning prayers, prayers before meals, saying thank you to God. When I think now I could be picking kiwifruit on Sunday, that would be probably frowned on by her. But they were flexible in their time. They gave way to us kids. They gave way to a lot of things. But she was very strict about the church to herself, and very orderly in her life. The things that stand out vividly for me about Granny Mata was their way of life.

We had an easy life, a rich life. When I say a rich life, I compare my childhood with a lot of children today. Never never did we go home from school and there was nobody home. There were no double standards when we grew up. What they believed in, what they taught us, was how they did. You just become part of that too. For instance, if people came to the house and she had something nice to eat, or something extra, that something was put out for the visitors. That generation were like that – whatever they had, wouldn't stay in a cupboard.

The ritual thing was real. For instance, I can remember my brother Joe and I were planting our first watermelon seeds. These were always given to God. Then they'd say to us, 'Korero ki a ratou – talk to the seeds to bear fruit, plenty fruit, round as a big full moon.' Because they know the Maori calendar and Rakaunui was the time for first planting. Now when they say that corns have ears, that potatoes have eyes – you never ever forget it. It's a lesson that's all there for you, to do just what they teach.

When we plant kumara was another ritual. I know all the days that we plant. On the Mawharu for big kumara. Rakaunui for long keeping. But Mawharu was the day for the big-size kumara. Why I remember Mawharu, is because we always had to plant some rows, two rows, maybe four, that day. We didn't keep church Harvest Festival the same way as the Anglican Pakehas' church. You see, food was never ever taken in the church. We always used to have a church bazaar special for the vicar's stipend. That's why we planted those special rows, for the church. That was our way of keeping Harvest Festival.

Then eeling, we learned about that when we were kids, because they took you out with them. You learned why this night was a good night for eeling. Then we had to have worms, so you'd go along with them to dig for worms and sit down and thread them. When you come home with the eels, you sort them out. You know, the very small ones, the next hei rara to grill, hei pawhara [to dry] for long keeping. You learned because you did it all with them. This is why I say what a rich life we had. Because you became self-reliant, very early in life. You knew exactly what to do. At eleven or twelve you'd be old enough to go out on your own and they didn't have to worry.

We didn't go to the marae when we were small. We all milked cows, so we never came up to the pa. I spent more time at the pa when I was in my teens. They didn't use the word kawa o te marae. The kawa of the marae was the kawa o te whare. I don't remember being sat down and told this – you just picked it up by observation and by listening as you went. You soon knew the things that you were to do and were not to do at the marae. For instance, you learnt very fast that you don't go across when people are speaking because the kuias give you such a yell and then you don't do that. When the ope [visitors] are coming and the whaikorero [speech-making] is on, never, ever go across the marae atea [open space]. They tell you, that is one part of the marae that is absolutely tapu. I never heard the word paepae as a child neither. But I always knew the front part of the house was the paepae. As a girl growing up, when I did go to the marae, our kaumatuas never sat in a place of prominence. They

Mere Kingi Paraone of Ngaitawhiri
photographed with one of her mokopuna
when approaching her hundredth birthday in
1937, *Auckland Weekly News*, 9 June 1937.
Auckland Public Library

didn't. They just sat around but they knew who they were. They knew all the
speakers. It's rather different now.

The other thing I remember about Granny Mata was that she never used
hot water. Why I say this, I suppose, is for their generation there were some
people who were quite special. For instance, if that fantail flies direct to
Granny Mata, she'd say straight out, 'Ko wai?' She seemed to know where to
go. Who of her relatives were so ill. And if they'd been taken off, she'd let us
know. You follow what I'm saying? So probably that is why I say she never ever
used hot water. Not for her bodily functions. But Granny Mata was very, very
fussy with washing. She used olive oil for her face, a little bit on her hair. I
don't ever remember her being a sick woman. Never lost any of her faculties,
right up to the end.

I would say that she would have been a centenarian when she died. She
just slipped away. She's the first person that I said the Committal prayer over. I
say to Granny in Maori, you came into the world with nothing and you go out
with nothing. I've never ever forgotten that. It is one of the privileges that I
had. It is one of those rare privileges because from that day on I haven't got the
mataku kehua [fear of ghosts] thing.

Heni Sunderland & Cushla Parekowhai

Published Sources
Binney, Judith and Chaplin, Gillian. *Nga Morehu: the Survivors*, Auckland, 1986
MacKay, J. A. *Historic Poverty Bay and the East Coast; North Island, New Zealand*, Gisborne, 1949

JEAN PARK | *1888–1977*

HETTY WEITZEL | *1900–1971*

After the First World War and the 1917 Russian Revolution, fears of foreign invasion and of militant socialism were rife in New Zealand. Teachers particularly were under pressure to demonstrate their loyalty and to inculcate ideas of 'good citizenship' in the minds of the youth of the nation. In 1921 two young women in the teaching profession, Hetty Weitzel and Jean Park, found themselves at the centre of a growing controversy.

Hedwig Weitzel was born on 17 September 1900 in Palmerston North, the first New Zealand-born child of newly arrived German settlers Gustav and Friederich Weitzel and his wife Maria (born Benninghoven). A brass-founder by trade, Gustav Weitzel soon turned his hand to farming, moving the family to the Horowhenua area when Hetty was about two years old.

By 1912 the family had moved to Wellington, where Gustav Weitzel seems to have returned to his old trade. Although he had become a naturalised New Zealander in 1902, the family experienced anti-German hostility during the war. After Gustav Weitzel died in 1917 the family appears to have suffered some serious financial setback which resulted in Maria Weitzel and several of her children joining the Socialist Party. This was a small Wellington-based group, dedicated to industrial syndicalism and revolutionary struggle. Early in 1921 Maria Weitzel and two of her children emigrated to the United States.

Against this turbulent home background, Hetty Weitzel pursued a successful academic career, attending Wellington Girls' College from 1914 and graduating BA in economics and philosophy from Victoria University College in 1920. In 1921 she was enrolled as a trainee teacher at Wellington Teachers' College. She was described in reports at this time as intelligent, retiring, and unassertive, although letters she wrote from Sydney in 1922 reveal a fun-loving, flirtatious side to her personality.

On 19 August 1921 in the Wellington magistrates' court Hetty Weitzel was convicted of selling seditious literature, having sold a copy of the Australian newspaper *The Communist* to a police constable in the Wellington Communist Hall on 19 June. On 2 April she had joined the Socialist Party, at a meeting in which it voted to transform itself into the New Zealand Communist Party. Shortly after her conviction the authorities dismissed her from Wellington Teachers' College, causing her financial hardship and ending any expectations of a teaching career in New Zealand.

The matter might have ended there, but the minister of education, C. J. Parr, used the Weitzel case as a pretext for extending the hunt for subversive and disloyal elements in the teaching profession. In the next two months he instigated inquiries at both Wellington Teachers' College and Victoria University College into the influence and activities of communists; women students at the teachers' college were singled out for special investigation. Parr also introduced an oath of allegiance, compulsory for all teachers in the Dominion, in his Education Amendment Act, 1921–22.

The inquiries at the teachers' college and the university had found no evidence of communist infiltration. Unsatisfied, Parr sought other ways of rooting out the communist elements from among the nation's teachers; his attention fell on Jean Park.

Jean Gladys Park was a second-generation New Zealander, born on 15 February 1888 at Masterton to Gavin McIntyre Park and his wife Mary (born Atkinson). Her father worked for the post office and the family moved around, from Masterton to Napier to Taupo. The family's fortunes after the mid-1890s are unclear.

Jean Park's entry to the teaching profession was more arduous than Hetty Weitzel's. After a year as pupil-teacher at Hokitika District High School in 1909–10, she was a student at Wellington Teachers' College from 1911 to 1912 and in 1913 began as an assistant at Hutt District High School. Over the next thirty-one years she taught at eight different schools in the Wellington area, finishing as headmistress of Houghton Bay (later Houghton Valley) School from 1931 to 1944. Jean Park never obtained a tertiary qualification, although she may have studied extramurally at Victoria University College.

The October 1921 issue of *National Education*, the monthly magazine of the New Zealand Educational Institute (NZEI), carried a letter from J. G. Park, then at Carterton District High School, protesting against the dismissal of Hetty Weitzel. While dissociating herself from Hetty Weitzel's political views, Jean Park saw the dismissal as an example of sinister political interference with teachers. She drew comparisons with the political control over teachers in Germany and questioned the status of the order in council by which Hetty Weitzel had been convicted. It was not a law made by the people for the people.

Reaction was swift. The Carterton District High School Committee demanded that the Wellington Education Board hold an inquiry into Jean Park's conduct. There were other allegations: that she had told her pupils that Nurse Edith Cavell had been a spy, and that they should read the *Maoriland Worker*, a weekly journal dealing with industrial unionism, socialism, and politics. An inquiry held in private in December cleared Jean Park of all charges. In January 1922 Parr called for a new, public inquiry into Park's conduct and claimed the right to cancel or suspend her teaching certificate. In February Jean Park, with the backing of the NZEI, sought an injunction restraining the minister. In June the injunction was granted in the Supreme Court.

The Park case heralded the end of the campaign against allegedly disloyal teachers. There was widespread revulsion against a patriotism that verged on fanaticism, and condemnation of 'village heresy hunts'; teachers have not since been subjected to such overt political interference.

Up until 1922 Hetty Weitzel and Jean Park had met only briefly and then just to pass the time of day. Thereafter, it seems, their paths did not cross again.

In early 1922 Hetty Weitzel moved to Sydney to continue her teaching training, and joined the Communist Party of Australia. She taught at the Communist Sunday School organised by Hector Ross, whom she married in Sydney on 15 December 1923. In 1924–5 the couple visited New Zealand to assist in reorganising the fragmented New Zealand Communist Party.

Hetty Ross was a prominent member of the Communist Party of Australia throughout the 1920s. She was on its central committee, and was party organiser and convener of the women's department of the party. She was also active in journalism, writing for and editing the *Workers' Weekly* and the *Woman Worker*, and as a member of the Sydney Militant Women's Group produced the *Women's Road to Freedom*, a policy statement on women's relationship to the class struggle.

In 1930 Hetty Ross left Sydney to teach in the country, and in 1931 she divorced Hector Ross. Although she remained a communist, she never figured as prominently in party affairs again. A teacher all her life, she spent thirty years on the executive of the Australian Teachers' Federation. During the Depression and after, she played a leading role among teachers in the campaigns against salary reductions and the Married Women's Dismissal Act. She was the chairperson of the Equal Pay Committee set up in 1936.

In 1961 Hetty Ross said of her forty-year membership of the Communist Party:

By belonging to such a movement, I am glad to say, I can feel that my life has had some significance. I am sorry for those people who drift along as lost individuals. I prefer to be one of the thousands who have been able to play a small part in creating a mighty force.

Hetty Ross died in Sydney on 26 October 1971 from pneumonia; she had been suffering from Parkinson's disease.

In March 1922, while awaiting the outcome of her case against the minister of education, Jean Park was transferred from Carterton to Petone District High School. In 1926 she moved to Island Bay School, where she worked until her appointment to Houghton Bay School in 1931. Between 1925 and 1939 Jean Park was a prominent member of the NZEI, both at branch and national level, and for much of the same period was also on the national executive of the New Zealand Women Teachers' Association. She championed the cause of women teachers: she opposed the differentiation in salaries for men and women teachers, and the absence of opportunities for women both to enter the school inspectorate and to obtain administrative positions in the Department of Education.

Jean Park was adept at grasping the complex technical details of subjects such as salaries, gradings, superannuation, and leave regulations. She served on numerous national committees set up to examine these matters, as well as joining delegations to the minister of education, and writing reports and articles published in *National Education*. During the Depression she was on the national executive of the NZEI, and worked hard to alleviate the hardships suffered by teachers, in particular married women who were in danger of losing their jobs.

At her first NZEI annual general meeting in 1925, Jean Park had moved that at least six of the eleven-member executive of the NZEI should be women. The motion was lost. Fourteen years later she put a similar motion; again it was lost. She had also put her name forward for vice-president of the NZEI but, when the motion on the composition of the executive was defeated, she withdrew her candidacy in protest. She never attended another annual general meeting of the NZEI.

Little has yet been established about Jean Park's activities following her retirement in 1944. In 1962 it was reported that 'she still maintains her interest in questions of social justice and lends her support to any cause where she considers it to be at stake'. She died from a stroke on 20 January 1977 at Piki-te-Ora private hospital in Wellington.   *Brigid Pike*

Quotations
para.17 *People's Voice*, 8 March 1961, p.7
para.20 J. G. Park, 'The Park Case Re-examined', p.3

Unpublished Sources
Correspondence, H. Weitzel to F. Tuohy, June–Oct. 1923. Conrad Bollinger Papers, MS Papers 2151, folder 442, ATL
Minutes of Socialist Party, Wellington. Gerald Griffin Papers, Acc 86–43, 2/20, ATL

Published Sources
Johnston, Audrey. *Bread & Roses: A Personal History of Three Militant Women and their Friends 1902–1988*, Sutherland, NSW, 1990
'Miss Park is Dead', *National Education*, vol.59 no.625, April 1977, pp.50–1; vol.59 no.627, Aug. 1977, p.157
Openshaw, R. 'Executive and Judiciary in Conflict: Park v. Minister of Education', *NZ Law Journal*, 4 Sept. 1979, pp.352–5
Openshaw, R. 'Lilliput under Siege: New Zealand Society during the "Red Scare", 1919–1922', *History of Education Quarterly*, Winter 1980, pp.403–24
Openshaw, R. 'The Highest Expression of Devotion: New Zealand Primary Schools and Patriotic Zeal during the Early 1920s', *History of Education*, vol.9 no.4, 1980, pp.333–4
Park, J. G. 'The Park Case Re-examined: From the Chief Protagonist – Some Corrections', *Public Service Journal*, vol.49 no.3, March 1962, p.2

HELEN PASKE

1948–1989

On 14 March 1989 the New Zealand parliament suspended a sitting of the House so that members could attend a funeral. It was not, as might be expected, the funeral of a senior statesman, but of a journalist, a woman of just forty years. Her name was Helen Paske.

At the end of the service the governor general, the prime minister, the leader of the Opposition, most of the Cabinet, and the mayor of Wellington all joined the rest of the congregation in singing (some hummed) the women's movement anthem, 'I am Woman'. Even in death, Helen Paske was a pioneer on behalf of her sex.

Helen Mary Paske was born in England in 1948. Her first challenge came early: from birth her eyesight was very poor. The problem was only partially rectified at the age of three by what Helen later described as 'agee jar strength spectacles'. By then she had already developed a phenomenal memory to compensate for her lack of eyesight. As a journalist, she was able to recall the finer detail of even the most esoteric subject.

When she was fifteen, Helen was fitted with her first pair of contact lenses. It was, says her mother Joan, 'a turning point in her life; the beginning of a social personality'. An article the year before her death summed Helen up as 'vivacious, articulate, intelligent, and also decidedly assertive'. Obituaries spoke of her

500

'exuberance' and 'zest for life'. Yet as a child, Helen Paske was decidedly introverted; a bookworm and a loner. This was partly due to her 'different' appearance: the hateful spectacles and her determinedly straight hair, then so unfashionable. There was also the fact that she had been uprooted from her beloved Yorkshire at a 'difficult' time, the age of six. At school in Wellington she did not make friends easily. 'I remember,' says Joan, 'the house being full of people and Helen sitting reading.'

The Paskes were a family of achievers. Helen's mother, Joan, was the first woman president of the New Zealand Educational Institute. Her father, Les, came to New Zealand as an industrial chemist and was later to become a Wellington city councillor.

Like most parents of very bright children, they placed high expectations on their daughter. Joan recalls:

Something she never let me forget was once when she was in the fourth form and she came home one day and said she had got 99 per cent in a Latin exam. And I, being very puffed up with pride but still a Yorkshire woman, said, 'Oh well done dear, but what happened to the other mark?' It was still rankling to the day she died.

Always, says Helen's husband, Sir Kerry Burke, there was a strong anxiety about failure. But early on she showed the ambition that was to make her a pioneer among women journalists. Half-way through her fifth form year she decided she would be dux of Wellington East Girls' College, 'or die in the attempt'. According to Joan:

She became dux to spite the school. She really was unhappy there. She was an oddball, a very bright girl who didn't do the conventional things and was picked on because of it.

At university Helen gained a BA, later complemented by a Diploma in Business Administration. She became a journalist almost by accident, starting as a proof-reader at Wellington's *Dominion* newspaper simply to pay for her student flat. By the age of twenty-five she was chief sub-editor of the *Sunday Times* and by 1977 deputy editor. But it was through her weekly *Sunday Times* columns that her talent as a writer emerged. Sharp, irreverent, and witty, they displayed early on the remarkable range of subject matter that so distinguished her work. And she began to report women's issues in a way that was entirely new:

It wasn't the patronising nonsense that was traditional for the women's pages. Nor was it immoderate rhetoric . . . It was hard-nosed analysis of the problem and the arguments. It was also the work of someone who recognised and felt the pain of others, and had the magical gift of being able to convey it elegantly in readable and often witty form.

Through her work for Mediawomen, an organisation she helped found, and other activities, Helen maintained a total commitment to the advancement of women – her last editorial, a week before her death, was about pay equity. The pioneering work she did by being one of the first women to accept the challenge of appearing on television programmes such as *Newstand* and *Fourth Estate* can never be underestimated: 'By putting forth her views clearly and forcefully – and entertainingly – she did a great deal to raise the self-esteem of women in New Zealand.'

Marriage to a politician – Sir Kerry was a cabinet minister and later Speaker of the House – placed high demands on Helen's time. But she managed to combine electorate duties, motherhood of young Tom (born in 1985), and her own executive career. At the *Listener* she had worked her way in four years to assistant editorship.

Helen Paske *loved* writing – about anything. She would sit at her kitchen table with her big old green typewriter and the wit would simply flow. She rarely had to do a second draft. For many people, the most cherished Helen Paske articles were the tender and very funny stories she wrote about life with her much-loved Tom.

A piece of her very best writing has yet to be published. It is the letter she dictated for three-year-old Tom the night before she died, to be given to him when he is eighteen, in 2003.

Always a courageous and inspiring fighter of her cancer, Helen stopped in this, her last intellectual act, only to breathe into her oxygen mask. There was no going back for editing or correction. Professional in this as in all things, she met her last deadline without faltering.   *Pamela Stirling*

Quotations
para.8 Margaret Shields, funeral address, copy in author's possession
para.9 Pamela Stirling, funeral address

Unpublished Sources
Interviews with Helen Paske's parents, Joan and Les Paske, and with her husband, Sir Kerry Burke. The author was a colleague and friend of Helen Paske.

Published Sources
Booth, Pat. 'Kerry Burke: Minister of Crisis', *North and South*, June, 1987
Dominion Sunday Times, 19 April 1989 (obituary)
NZ Listener, 1 April 1989 (obituary)

IRENE PAULGER

1899–1966

Irene Doris Paulger was born in Christchurch, the illegitimate daughter of Annie Paulger, on 13 September 1899. She was brought up by her grandparents on a dairy farm near Inglewood in Taranaki, and subsequently trained as a teacher in Dunedin. For two years she taught at the Nuhaka Native School in Hawke's Bay, then in April 1925 she went to Maungapohatu, in the heart of the Urewera. There she opened the government school, and devoted the rest of her life to the community and its Tuhoe people.

Paulger's dedication was derived from her close association with the Presbyterian Maori mission, although she herself was not a missionary. She developed the state school, building on the work of the earlier mission school, which

Irene Paulger went to teach at
Maungapohatu in 1925. *New Zealand Herald*

had begun in 1918 but had closed in 1924. Her arrival coincided with the end
of a typhoid epidemic, which had claimed the lives of two children. She opened
the school in May 1925 with a roll of thirty-eight, while the Health Department
still had a tent hospital in the school grounds. She herself became nurse, postmistress, registrar of births and deaths, and 'mother' to several children. Because
of the poverty in the community, many families had to leave to find work and
the school roll began to fall in the early 1930s. As a consequence, Paulger
boarded several of the children in the schoolhouse to enable them to continue.
The Department of Education paid her a small allowance of five shillings a week
for each child.

She adopted four children. The youngest was Te Riini, who was born in the
schoolhouse. Paulger assisted at her birth, as she did with many others. Paulger
had also adopted Te Riini's older sisters, Hiki and Meri, and their brother Mare
– children of Te Puhi Tatu (Materoa Kahukura). The Maungapohatu people, in
their turn, adopted her, naming her Huhana after the old chieftainess Huhana
Tutakangahau, who had originally given the land to found the school.

In the early days, Paulger lived (with another teacher) in a two-roomed cottage that possessed no facilities. They bathed once a week (on Fridays) in the
river, as did the rest of the community, the only difference being that the
teachers made a Heath Robinson shower of kerosine tins behind a shed. Later,
they got a bath, which had to be filled from the river. They cooked on a camp
oven outside the back door; after seven and a half years, they were sent a stove
and a chip heater by the Department of Education. Maungapohatu was considered 'the most isolated' school in the country.

The settlement was also unique: it was the community led by the visionary
prophet, Rua Kenana Hepetipa, who was believed by the people of Maungapohatu to be the Maori Messiah. Paulger had to learn to co-operate with him. She

taught many of his own children, and he supported the school and its strict disciplines. But during the early 1930s, as she and the families struggled to keep the children at school, she also faced difficulties with him. In a report to the Department of Education in 1934, concerning some children under his care who were regularly absent because he depended on their labour, she asked that her name be kept out of the affair. She said simply, 'Rua is Rua and we have to live in the place'.

'Huhana' Paulger loved Maungapohatu. She shared in all the activities of its life, helping to birth the children and conducting the Presbyterian part of the burial services for the dead. She even made the coffins. She became the head teacher at the school from May 1931, and she remained there until ill health forced her to leave in 1947.

Paulger then went to Birkenhead in Auckland, where she taught at the primary school. She lived with her unmarried mother. The two women always called themselves sisters, to hide the truth of Irene's birth. When Irene died, on 6 June 1966, she predeceased her mother, who then registered Irene's grandparents as her parents. Such was the stigma of illegitimacy for a woman who had triumphed over it.

Judith Binney

Quotation
para.5 I. Paulger to Director of Education, 24 Feb. 1934, E44/4 II, Maungapohatu Native School Files
Unpublished Sources
'Maungapohatu Maori School History', compiled by 'F.K.B.', typescript, APL
Maungapohatu Native School Files, National Archives, Auckland
Published Source
NZ Herald, 24 June 1966

ISABEL PEACOCKE

1881-1973

Isabel Peacocke was 'a real Kiwi' journalist and author, hailed by Pat Lawlor as a writer of 'prodigious output' and 'one of the most active and cheerful women in New Zealand'. Although she wrote verse, light romances, newspaper articles, stories for magazines, plays and radio broadcasts for station 1YA, her specialty was children's books; between 1915 and 1939 she produced one almost annually. These were published (and frequently sold out) in England, but sufficient numbers reached our shores for the writer to be rated sixth – after Edith Howes and Charles Dickens – in a survey of children's favourite authors by the Canterbury Public Library in December 1926.

Her best-remembered titles include *My Friend Phil* (1915); *Dicky, Knight-Errant* (1916); *Patricia-Pat* (1917); *Robin of the Round House* (1918); *The Misdoings of Micky and Mac* (1919); *Quicksilver* (1922); *The Adopted Family* (1923); *Little Bit O' Sunshine* (1924); *His Kid Brother* (1926); *Brenda and the Babes* (1927); *The Runaway Princess* (1929); *The Cruise of the Crazy Jane* (1932, 1984); *Cathleen with a 'C'* (1934); and *Marjolaine* (1935). These were family rather than school stories, the dominant form of junior fiction at the time.

Peacocke preferred to explore human nature and relationships, particularly between adult and child. 'The main thing in a book is humanity,' she declared, 'human nature as it is found every day, which is not perfect by any manner of means.' Readers identify with her characters, who make the most of life and have plenty of faults. In this Peacocke broke from the traditional moralising and didactic style of writing for children; she allowed her characters to be themselves.

Peacocke's books were also unusual for their urban rather than rural or bush settings. A proud Aucklander, Peacocke revelled in this city and its harbour and island environs. In *The Runaway Princess*, she acclaims Auckland as 'the largest, most prosperous and beautiful of all the cities in New Zealand'; in *Dicky, Knight-Errant*, it is 'the seething heart of things'. Themes include irresponsible parents, the maternal role, snobbery, the differences and difficulties between the 'haves' and 'have-nots', and education. In her treatment of these subjects Peacocke appears a libertarian, caring most for children's rights and development, and less for the elite and the social distinctions they demanded. James B. Ringer has noted the few Maori characters in Peacocke's books. When they do appear, they are patronised.

Peacocke's real characters, and her ability to tell and sustain a tale (although frequently 'soppy'), sprang from an understanding of children gained over many years. At sixteen she began her own school, teaching small girls. Later (1906–16) she taught at the Dilworth Ulster Institute in Auckland, a home and school for boys whose parents were in 'straitened circumstances'. Here, Peacocke took her 'charges' on nature expeditions to Mt Hobson, Mt St John, and St Heliers; she also established 'one of the greatest delights of those first, homesick lads' – the tradition of telling stories before 'lights-out'. She dedicated a Sydney story, *My Friend Phil* (1915), her first important work and one which enchanted Robin Hyde in childhood, to the boys – 'my comrades all'.

Her father, Gerald Loftus Peacocke, had left New Zealand to study law in London, gave it up for writing, then married an Englishwoman, Emily Mitchell, in 1872. With three children he returned to Auckland where he became editor of the *New Zealand Farmer*. Isabel Maud was one of three more children; she was born on 31 January 1881 at Devonport on the North Shore, and enjoyed childhood friendships with Elsie K. Morton and Ewen W. Alison (also to become writers). From the age of five she attended the infant department of Devonport school. She took up writing stories in pencil in the back of an old account book. 'At the age of nine or thereabouts' she wrote her first novel in ink on six or eight pages of a brand-new exercise book. It 'dealt with "high life", of course', she confessed, 'and was stiff with titles, being, I don't doubt, an unwitting burlesque of that type of story common to the *Family Herald*, which I blush to say, I read surreptitiously at that time.' Peacocke recalls her early childhood years in *When I Was Seven* (1927).

The Peacocke family moved from the North Shore to Remuera in 1901. Before this, in her teenage years, Isabel Peacocke wrote much verse; some appeared in the Sydney *Bulletin*. Her first article was published in the *New Zealand Herald*. She also contributed to the *New Zealand Illustrated Magazine* in 1900 and the *Atom Quarterly: a magazine written and illustrated by the girls of New Zealand* from 1901 to 1903. In 1908 Peacocke's poem 'Welcome to the American Fleet' was set to music by Rupert Morten and sung in the Auckland Town Hall. Her first book, a collection of poems including earlier work from the *Bulletin*, was *Songs of the Happy Isles* (1910). By 1922 the writer was not only reminiscing about old Auckland and the old North Shore in Auckland's daily papers, the *New Zealand Herald* and *Auckland Star* (which she wrote for until she was elderly), but was also writing for magazines in Australia, Great Britain (*Windsor Magazine*), and America; in the last two countries, her adult novels *Cinderella's Suitors* (1918) and *The House at Journey's End* (1925) were serialised. She also adapted classic stories such as Charles Kingsley's *Water Babies* for the *Whitcombe's Story Book* series for children.

In 1920 Isabel Peacocke married George Edward Cluett, an inventor (of Cluett clips, which superseded nails in some Auckland buildings). Peacocke's husband was interested in her writing, and seemed to provide much of the impetus for her books. In 1924–5 they travelled to South Africa, Europe, and England, where Peacocke's publisher, Ward, Lock & Co, gave her a 'swell party' in London at the Waldorf Hotel. On her husband's death in 1937, Peacocke appeared to lose the incentive for longer works; from then on she wrote more for newspapers and magazines.

Writers' groups became important to Peacocke around 1925. She was a foundation member of the Penwomen's Club, organised in Auckland in 1925 by Mrs E. Macky, who modelled it on the League of American Penwomen. First meetings were held on the top floor of a city building; members sat on apple-boxes. The motto of this group was 'Sincerity in Art and Friendship'; the aim, to stimulate creative work in the arts and to foster comradeship among women

This scene from Isabel Maud Peacocke's novel
Brenda and the Babes (1927) was captioned
'. . . and almost invariably a rent somewhere
to be repaired.' *Dorothy Neal White
Collection, National Library*

with equal interests. Peacocke was president of this group in 1930–31. She founded the Writers' Club, Auckland rival to the New Zealand League of Penwomen, and was also a member of PEN, a foundation vice-president (1932–73) of the New Zealand Women Writers' and Artists' Society, and from 1925 a member of the Authors', Artists', and Playwrights' Association, London.

Peacocke was also vice-president of the Auckland Women's Forum, and during the Second World War served with the Women's War Service Auxiliary, and the Emergency Precaution Scheme. The latter, a largely female group, was responsible for organising air raid practices and preparing the public for emergencies. She was also interested in the work of the YMCA and the Childhaven Association. For relaxation she enjoyed gardening and long tramps over the countryside with her dog, from which she was inseparable. She left the family home in Remuera in 1960 to live at the Mt Roskill Masonic Village, where she died in 1973.   *Celia Dunlop*

Quotations
para.1 *NZ Woman's Weekly*, 13 April 1970, p.47; P. Lawlor, *Confessions of a Journalist*, pp.189–90
para.2 *NZ Woman's Weekly*, 13 April 1970, p.47
para.4 J. Berry, *Dilworth School*, p.6
para.5 I. Peacocke, 'My First "Novel"', p.5

Published Sources
Bagnall, A. G. (ed.). *NZ National Bibliography to the Year 1960*, vol.4: 1890–1960 P–Z, Wellington, 1975
Berry, John. *Dilworth School: The First 70 Years, 1906–1976*, Auckland, 1976
Elder, Ann. 'Reprint Plan Surprises City Authoress', *Auckland Star*, 11 Aug. 1972, p.7
'Forty Busy Years of Authorship', *NZ Herald*, 2 April 1957, p.20
Gilderdale, Betty. *A Sea Change: 145 Years of New Zealand Junior Fiction,*, Auckland, 1982
'Her Children's Books Covered 40 Years', *NZ Herald*, 15 Oct. 1973, p.3 (obituary)
'Is Yours Here? Children's Favourite Authors', *Sun* (Christchurch), 16 April 1927, p.20
Lawlor, Pat. *Confessions of a Journalist: With Observations on Some Australian & New Zealand Writers*, Auckland, 1935
Lee, Joy. 'Penwomen's Progress', *NZ Woman's Weekly*, 1 June 1959, p.71
Newcomb, Elizabeth. 'Penwomen's Club Widens Its Scope', *NZ Woman's Weekly*, 24 June 1963, p.6
Peacocke, Isabel Maud. 'My First "Novel"', *NZ Life*, vol.2 no.1, Oct./Nov. 1922, pp.5–6
Petersen, G. C. (ed.) *Who's Who in New Zealand* (7th edn), Wellington, 1961
Renshaw, Judith. '40 Years of Authorship – and a Pen in her Hand Still', *NZ Woman's Weekly*, 18 Jan. 1960, p.24
Ringer, James B. *Young Emigrants: New Zealand Juvenile Fiction 1833–1919*, Hamilton, 1980
Scholefield, G. H. (ed.). *Who's Who in New Zealand* (4th edn), Wellington, 1941; (5th edn), Wellington, 1951
Spilman, Sherrilyn. 'Deterred by Half-Adults Aged Ten', *NZ Woman's Weekly*, 13 April 1970, pp.45, 47

MAUD PEMBER REEVES

1865–1953

Maud Pember Reeves was an active socialist, campaigning for women's citizenship rights and family welfare.

Born at Mudgee, New South Wales, on 24 December 1865, Magdalen (Maud) Stuart Robison was the third child of Mary and William Smoult Robison.

The family came to New Zealand in 1867 when William Robison became manager of the Bank of New South Wales in Christchurch. After attending Christchurch East School, Maud was a foundation pupil at Christchurch Girls' High School. At nineteen, she married William Pember Reeves, a political journalist on the *Lyttelton Times*. When he became editor, Maud was, for a time, lady editor of the weekly *Canterbury Times*.

Maud had three children, Amber (1887), Beryl (1889), and Fabian (1896). After Beryl's birth, Maud became a student at Canterbury University College, studying English under Professor John Macmillan Brown, and his assistant, O. T. J. Alpers, who found her an outstanding student. She actively supported her husband in his political career. In 1887, he was elected to parliament and in 1890 became a cabinet minister in the Liberal government. Maud formed the Women's Section of the Christchurch Liberal Association and became its president.

When the family moved to Wellington in 1890, Maud joined Ellen Ballance, the premier's wife, in enlisting support for women's suffrage. She wrote to support Sir John Hall when he presented his Female Suffrage Bill in 1890: 'We are going to have our franchise after all. Isn't it glorious? . . . My husband is to be relied on. I have seen to that.' Tall and striking, with a clear voice and a lively wit, she was in demand as a platform speaker. In 1892, she joined the Canterbury Women's Institute, formed to promote women's rights. After women were enfranchised in September 1893, Maud was active in educating and encouraging them to use the vote.

Another move for the family came in 1896 when W. P. Reeves became New Zealand's Agent-General in London. Maud was attracted to London life, and New Zealand visitors found her a vivacious hostess. She and her husband aligned themselves with the non-revolutionary, intellectual socialism which was advocated by the Fabian Society. Maud joined the Fabian Society in 1904, served on the executive from 1907 to 1919, and retained membership for life. When H. G. Wells antagonised G. B. Shaw by trying to reform the society in 1906, Maud was one of his supporters. While Wells accused the Fabians of 'arrested development' and set out to expose their faults in scathing pamphlets, Maud played a conciliatory role, helping to prevent a rift. At the same time, she pressed successfully for her own reform measure, requiring members to support equal citizenship for women and men.

In 1907, Maud helped to form the Fabian Women's Group (FWG). Advocating equal opportunity under socialism and economic independence for women, Fabian women organised seminars and published tracts. With some training in social investigation from Beatrice Webb, they prepared themselves for public responsibility. Maud was active as a speaker, writer, and committee member. Her sympathies lay with women who, particularly as mothers of small children, were economically disadvantaged. In a paper introducing a series on 'The Disabilities of Mothers as Workers', Maud said:

If we consider the economic position of women at the present time, we see that it is in a chaotic state; and it is safe to say that any body of men would find it intolerable. The great majority of women are working as hard, or harder, than

Maud Pember Reeves. *Family Collection*

their strength will allow, and are earning no wage but that of a vague right to
be kept by a husband who may or may not be able to fulfil his obligation.

A period of anxiety when her elder daughter, Amber, a brilliant student at
Cambridge, had an affair with Wells and bore his child, was followed by still
more intense activity with the Fabian Society. In 1909, under the wing of the
FWG, she started a survey of the health of mothers and children of low-income
families in the borough of Lambeth. With medical help from Dr Ethel Bentham,
Maud and her sister, Effie Lascelles, visited over thirty families twice a week for
nearly four years. An interim report, *Family Life on a Pound a Week*, was published as a tract by the FWG in 1910 and in 1913 Maud's book, *Round About
a Pound a Week*, became a best-seller. It provided data for Maud's advocacy of
state assistance for mothers and foreshadowed much welfare legislation.

Maud was responsible for involving the Fabian Society in women's suffrage
activities. When defending the cause, she drew freely on her experience of New
Zealand's successful campaign.

In wartime, when national health became a major concern, Maud's expertise was utilised. In 1916, she was the only woman on a committee of inquiry
into the high cost of food and, from 1917 to 1919, she was employed by the
Ministry of Food to develop propaganda for voluntary rationing and to be
Director of Women's Services.

When her son, Fabian, was killed in 1917, Maud took solace for a time in
spiritualism. After English women gained partial voting rights in 1918, Maud
was again speaking on 'The Education of Women as Voters'. She served on the
Council of the National Union of Societies for Equal Citizenship.

Her husband's declining health and other family demands, her delight in
bridge, and travel dominated Maud's later years. In 1925, she accompanied

509

W. P. Reeves on a return visit to New Zealand. Widowed in 1932, Maud lived for a time with her sister in Cambridge. She died in London on 15 September 1953.

Ruth Fry

Quotation

para.4 Undated letter, M. Pember Reeves to Sir John Hall (possibly August 1890), Sir John Hall Papers, MS Papers 1784, folder 199, ATL

para.6 M. Pember Reeves, *Summary of Eight Papers and Discussions upon the Disabilities of Mothers as Workers*, London, 1910, p.4

Unpublished Sources

Blanco White papers (including letters and family tree), in family possession

Fabian Society Records, Nuffield College, Oxford; Fabian Society, London

W. P. Reeves, Papers 1852–c.1929, MS Papers 129, ATL

Published Sources

Alpers, O. T. J. *Cheerful Yesterdays*, London, 1928

Canterbury Times, 1889–90

MacKenzie, N. and J. *The First Fabians*, London, 1977

Pugh, Patricia. *Educate, Agitate, Organize: 100 Years of Fabian Socialism*, London, 1984

Reeves, Maud Pember. *Round About a Pound a Week*, London, 1979 (first published 1913)

Sinclair, K. *William Pember Reeves, A New Zealand Fabian*, Oxford, 1965

Votes for Women, Fawcett Library, City of London Polytechnic

LILLIAN PETERSEN

1900–1973

Lillian Petersen was born Riria Konore (Lillian Connley) in Pahi on the Pouto Peninsula in 1900. She was a descendant of Hakiputatomuri and Kuiteao of Ngati-Uri-O-Hau. Lillian was married three times and had one child. Fishing and hunting were her two passions, and she spent much of her life on the Kaipara Harbour. In 1964 she held the New Zealand 'all comers' record for a mako shark caught on an 80-pound line. That same year Lillian also held the Kawau Island Deep Sea Fishing Club women's record for marlin. Her record-breaking 435-pound fish was caught on the east coast between Kawau and Great Barrier Island off Lillian's favourite boat, the *Lillian A*.

In later life Lillian was a patient of Professor Herbert Green at National Women's Hospital. She died of cervical cancer on 2 March 1973, and is buried at the Garfield Road cemetery, Helensville.

Her story is told by her son and grandson, George and Cameron Smith.
Her full name was Riria Konore or Lillian Connley. Her mother was a Kena from round the back of Pahi. Lillian came to Helensville when she was about sixteen years old. In those days she worked as a stewardess on the steamers that ran from here to Dargaville. I think this was where she learned about the Kaipara. She knew that harbour really well. She had an intuitive weather knowledge. In the evening before we were due to go fishing, she'd often say, 'I don't like the look of the sky.' She would study the sunset or the clouds saying,

'It's no use fishing tomorrow.' She had a great knowledge of tides and sea conditions too.

She knew that when the tide was coming in we'd fish this spot and when the tide was going out we'd fish that spot. She had her favourite fishing places around Takatu Point, Kawau Island out to Little Barrier. If she wasn't absolutely happy with the location, the anchor would come up and she'd shift the boat forward fifteen metres. She would always let the anchor down herself. By doing that I'm sure she could tell what sort of line to set. Whether you had a running sinker with two or three hooks, or whatever the case may be. She had a peculiar knack. There would be several people fishing in the same place and no one would be catching anything, but there she'd be hauling them in right, left and centre. If there were fish around, she'd catch them.

Quite often when we went fishing, she'd get in the dinghy off the back of the boat. One day she's out there fishing away and suddenly she's hauling the dinghy in, then she grabbed the shotgun and some cartridges, and out she goes again. Next minute you could see this fin circling, circling the dinghy. It was a grey nurse shark, about six feet long, but she didn't bat an eyelid, she just upped both barrels and took it out.

She could handle the boat in any conditions. I remember coming back from Great Barrier Island on one trip where we got caught in a storm and she took the boat from the Barrier to Kawau Island with a tail sea. This is the worst sea imaginable where the waves are rolling in from behind you. If the swell rolls in from the front or the side you can see the big waves coming, but with a following sea you can't see anything. The sea can actually pick the boat up and lift the rudder out of the water. We must have been out there in that heavy sea about four and a half hours. Lillian was magnificent and steered us all the way home.

When we were on the boat Lillian was always totally responsible, particularly when she was with us kids. If we were going swimming off the boat, she'd be out in the dinghy playing around, making sure the kids didn't go too far. When we were fishing she always set the kids' lines first. Made sure we had some gear over. But if you got your line caught up in hers, she would give your line an extra yank. I used to think that I had the biggest fish in the world on it. She'd always do that, and laugh.

Sometimes we used to go to a regatta up at Pahi, on the northern side of the Kaipara Harbour. There they had women's power-boat races, which Lillian always used to win. Three laps around the circuit and the trophy would be hers. On the way back we'd stop at Old Man's Nose where there is a huge bed of rock oysters. She'd take a hammer and screwdriver and sit on the reef and chip away at the oysters, eat one and put one in the container.

When we were living on the boat, she made us take her remedies too. If you cut yourself you had kerosene swabbed on your cuts, or if you ever got constipated, she used to serve you up tinned fruit salad and this special *something. It sure freed you up! Quite often when we were out fishing she would get a fresh snapper and boil it on the spot, always in sea water. A big fat steaming snapper with butter on it, beautiful. We used to go down the Kaipara Harbour and pick sacks and sacks of scallops too. Several boats would go out and we would get all these scallops, stay the night at Shelly Beach and have a big cook up. These days there's hardly a scallop in the harbour. So it wasn't long before the limits were put on.*

Lillian Petersen of Ngati-Uri-o-Hau.
Cameron Smith

We'd go out with Lillian and she would always take more than the regulation allowed. We would stop at the mouth of the Hokio River, off-load the excess under the stopbank, and steam quietly into the wharf. Sure enough, she knew the fisheries inspector guy would be there waiting for her. He'd stay and have a beer and then he'd get on his boat and head off. When the coast was clear, we'd all go down the stopbank and bring these bags of scallops back. On a Monday morning, I regularly got one of those 10-pound billies full of shelled scallops or a couple of smoked fish or a big snapper to deliver around the district. Everyone got their share. There'd always be something for the local families.

Actually it didn't matter who went past, swaggerman, hitch-hiker or anyone that wanted a feed, she was the first to help them. Give them a meal and get them on their way with a little extra food and a dollar or two. She was a very generous person.

When it came to the farm, she was a better farmhand than most of the men. She had an amazing way with animals. Lillian could work her hunting dogs with a whistle and a kind word. She would never yell and scream at them. They were so quiet and well trained. When she shot a duck, the dogs would slip away and retrieve it. They were taught never to damage the bird, but to hold it very gently in their mouths. She used to spend hours out at the back of the house throwing an old slipper for the dogs to retrieve.

I can remember at night when she'd go out to feed the stock. There would be this troop of birds and animals all following her. Turkeys, ducks, geese, and half a dozen pet lambs would trail along squawking and bleating and cackling. During the shooting season she'd look into the sky and call down the wild ducks. All of a sudden there would be hundreds of these wild ducks flying in to see her. They just zoomed in like bombers. She used to buy a sack of maize, about three bushels a month, just to feed the ducks. She had a couple of irrigation ponds on the farm where the wild ducks took sanctuary. She would not allow shooting on those ponds.

As kids we learnt a lot from her. You were always her equal and you knew she really cared. Although she was always busy she was still interested in what you were doing. There was always something to be done, but she spent hours with the kids. Took us fishing or for walks in the bush. She was tremendously independent. She would never rely on other people and I don't think she ever asked for favours. Yet she would always give willingly to others.

Lillian didn't drink herself, and never smoked neither. She wasn't an ardent church-goer, although she did believe in God. None of us ever knew what that really meant, but she took all her fishing secrets with her to the grave. She was never happier than when she was on the sea.

George Smith, Cameron Smith & Cushla Parekowhai

Published Sources
Forrest, Logan. *Pouto; 105 Years 1879–1984*, Pouto School Reunion Committee, 1984
Rodney and Waitemata Times, 2 March 1973 (obituary)

ELEANOR PETRE

1825–1885

Mary Ann Eleanor Petre was the wife of one of the prominent younger members of the New Zealand Company, the Hon. Henry William Petre. She lived in New Zealand from 1843 to 1855 and for the first two years kept a diary, now in the Alexander Turnbull Library, which is a valuable source of information about the Wellington and Hutt settlements for that period.

She was born Eleanor Walmesley at Middleton Hall, Essex, and educated at New Hall Convent. At sixteen she was brought home to be married to her neighbour and childhood friend, Henry Petre, a member of one of the oldest Roman Catholic families in England, whose father, Lord Petre, was a patron of the New Zealand Company. Henry had just returned from accompanying the first company colonists to Wellington and intended to go back quickly with his bride. It appears that the marriage, if not quite arranged by the families, had been long expected and desired by them; at all events it proved a very happy union. After a few weeks' honeymoon the couple embarked by the *Thomas Sparkes* and landed in New Zealand in late January 1843.

The couple lived briefly in Wellington before moving to 'Herongate' farm in Petone, where Henry began farming and stock-breeding. As the leading Roman Catholics of the district, they were also at once drawn into organising that denomination. Their domestic chaplain, Father O'Reilly, seems to have been the first priest in the district since Bishop Pompallier's visit in 1840.

Their family grew rapidly, eventually numbering sixteen children, and 'Herongate' was both often flooded and too small. About 1848 they moved to a larger house which they called 'Woburn Farm'; the surrounding area of Lower Hutt is still known by that name. There they remained until 1855, when Henry decided to return permanently to England to resume his life as a sporting gentleman. (He was an outstanding horseman and breeder of horses.)

Apart from the record left in her own diary, Eleanor is seen in the letters of Charlotte Godley, who knew her in 1851, and in the rather sentimental and inaccurate memoirs of her own eldest daughter, Lucy, who wrote a family history in 1907. The diary and letters show Eleanor as a woman of sunny, almost childlike, charm and great physical energy. Charlotte Godley wrote:

Mrs Petre, herself, is very young-looking and with wild spirits, and enjoys a ball, or a ride, or a scamper of any kind, and is sometimes very pretty . . . He is very pleasant . . . and seems moreover duly impressed with a high idea of her excellencies; which indeed are manifold, for there is nothing she cannot do, all learnt out here, from receiving company, down to cooking the dinner they are to eat; and all pleasantly and well, and so as to be very much liked.

She also walked, rode, or drove her pony-trap all over the district, even during the periods of tension between Maori and settlers in the mid-1840s. She often mentions visiting or talking with Maori on her rambles and displays no prejudice towards them. Indeed, her diary records significant details about some of the inter-racial incidents. Being uncritical and artless, she simply scribbled down what she had seen and heard; she does not seem to reflect the views of the New Zealand Company, despite her husband's association with it.

The following extract was written on 13 December 1843, at a time of dangerous tension between Maori and settlers in Wellington. On this occasion, Eleanor, Miss Fitzgerald, and Miss Swainson had rambled up the road to Porirua and climbed a hill. Miss Fitzgerald, rather timid and perhaps a nuisance to the other two, was left to rest while they explored further. Upon their return:

We found Miss Fitzgerald tête a tête with a one-eyed Maori and soon after fell in with a party of three carrying their potatoes to Petoni they joined us and seeing our dresses nearly covered with burrs sat down round us and picked them off then we started down the hill and when we were nearly down we saw Miss Fitzgerald standing at the top looking down with terror. A great old Maori

seeing this went back and gave her his hand saying 'qua pie de Parkeha'
[? Ka pai te Pakeha – The Pakeha is good] and most gently did this untutored
savage in his blanket looped up on one shoulder lead civilisation down the hill.

Eleanor's diary also provides a lively picture of the Petres' social life and their friendship with several other prominent families, particularly the Wakefields, Cliffords, Daniells, and Fitzgeralds.

The most dramatic episode of Eleanor's New Zealand life was the night of the great earthquake in January 1855. The entire family, servants, and local Maori took refuge on the lawn at Woburn, where amid the din and terror Eleanor gave birth to her fifth child while comforting all around her.

The family returned to live at Cowes on the Isle of Wight but the memory of New Zealand remained warm, and two sons later returned to the colony, one of them (Frank Petre) to become a notable colonial architect and engineer. Their daughter Lucy records that the children often played at being back in New Zealand again. *Susan Butterworth*

Quotation
para.5 C. Godley, *Letters from Early New Zealand*, p.71
para.7 E. Petre, *Diary*, 13 Dec. 1843

Unpublished Sources
Mrs Philip Wellesley Colley (born Lucy Petre), *The Life of the Honourable Henry W. Petre and Eleanor Walmesley his wife*, 1907, MS COL, ATL
Petre, Mary Ann Eleanor. *Diary 1842–1844*, MS Papers, ATL

Published Source
Godley, Charlotte. *Letters from Early New Zealand* (ed. J. R. Godley), Christchurch, 1951

NGOI PEWHAIRANGI

1922–1985

Ngoi Pewhairangi was born Kumeroa Ngawai in Tokomaru Bay, Tairawhiti, in 1922. Her mother was Wikitoria Te Karu and her father was George Ngawai of Ngati Porou. Ngoi was educated at Tokomaru Bay School and later at Hukarere Maori Girls' College in Napier.

Ngoi was married to Ben Pewhairangi of Tokomaru Bay and had one child. Ngoi joined her husband in a shearing gang and then became involved with the well-known Tairawhiti cultural group Te Hokowhitu-a-Tu. After the death of her aunt, Tuini Ngawai, the founding leader of Te Hokowhitu-a-Tu, Ngoi took over leadership of the group. It was at this time that she began writing original songs.

In the early 1970s Ngoi was a grass-roots supporter of the fledgling Nga Puna Waihanga (Maori Writers and Artists Association). She was also active at various New Zealand Polynesian festivals, at which she often judged kapa haka (haka group) participants in the cultural competitions. In the late 1970s Ngoi was appointed to the Maori and South Pacific Arts Council (MASPAC) as the representative for Tairawhiti. She took a lead role in MASPAC affairs, vigorously promoting all aspects of Maori art, culture, and craft. In 1978 Ngoi received a

QSM in recognition of her services to Maori people. She became the script-writer and adviser for the innovative Maori language television programme *Te Reo*. For this series Ngoi adapted many teaching principles from her pioneer work in the Atarangi method of Maori language learning. During this period Ngoi was also deeply involved in the development of Te Kohanga Reo as a nationwide Maori language learning programme for pre-school children.

In more recent years Ngoi composed a number of waiata which have performed exceptionally well on the New Zealand charts. She wrote the popular song 'E Ipo' especially for the Maori singer Prince Tui Teka. But the song which attracted most attention was the now classic best-selling New Zealand single, 'Poi E'. Written in collaboration with Dalvanius Prime, 'Poi E' was released in 1983 by the Patea Maori Club and was a resounding triple platinum success, sitting at the top of the New Zealand charts for some time.

Ngoi Pewhairangi is remembered as a woman of many achievements. Her song-writing was merely one feature of a remarkable and creative artist committed to sharing her expert knowledge of tikanga Maori. She died in January 1985, and is buried at Ngaiopapa, Tokomaru Bay.

Her story is told by Henare Te Ua:
We've always just known her as Ngoingoi Pewhairangi. I think most people know her better just as Ngoi. It was only in later years, when her reputation spread beyond Tairawhiti, that she became known as Ngoingoi. But everybody knew her as Ngoi, or as Aunty Ngoi.

My memories of Ngoi are of this rather shortish woman – not a tall lady. Fairly well built. Her trademark was the dark glasses that she always wore. Ngoi had that lovely way of tossing back her head. I think it was a trait that belonged to that generation. When they're talking to you, their head would rise up, and Ngoi's dark glasses would lift like her eyebrows. You never really saw her eyes, so you couldn't tell what she was thinking about. She had a distinct resemblance to her whanaunga [kin] and her great mentor, Tuini Ngawai. Ngoi and others of her generation had a certain style that was distinctly part of the Ngati Porou whanui.

Like a lot of our people, she had tones of voice, depending on what the occasion was. I know she used to startle different audiences. Here was this respected and dignified person, coming on stage, head held back. People would whisper, here she is, and Ngoi would get to the mike and say, 'Talofa lava!' Everybody would just burst with laughter, because they expected some great big tauparapara [oratorical chant]. She used to rock people. But this is part of what I would call Ngati Porou humour. Ngatis are famous, at the most reverential occasions, for just changing gear, so that you'd come out from the depth of serious things and relax into the light-hearted. Ngoi had that ability.

The New Zealand Polynesian Festival came as a result of a huge hui held by Maoridom in 1970. The occasion was a powhiri to welcome the Queen and the Duke of Edinburgh at Rugby Park in Gisborne. All the tribes of Maoridom were there – Taitokerau, down the island, right to Murihiku, and so on. They were all there. It was a spectacular occasion and each tribal area had an opportunity to perform – to show the strength of their own iwi in haka, waiata, and so on. At the end of that visit, a lot of people asked why do we wait until Pakeha royalty arrives before we do this sort of thing? Why perform to the best of our ability only for Kuini Pai? Why don't we have cultural competitions on a regular basis? So out of that discussion grew the New Zealand Polynesian Festival. Now Polynesian was brought in because it would embrace our whanaunga o nga moutere o Te Moananui-a-Kiwi – the Pacific and the Pacific Islands people. Nineteen-seventy-two saw the first one of these festivals being held in Rotorua. It was going to be held annually, but very soon it was realised the cost was going to be enormous. So after 1973, it was decided to hold it on a biennial basis. In many of those early festivals, Ngoi was one of the judges.

Within the festival there were certain areas in which each group has to take part. Haka, waiata tawhito, action song, poi, whakaheke, whakawatea, costuming, and so on. Of course, Ngoi's expertise used to be in the waiatas. They were so various. All different. At the end of the festival when all the groups had performed and the different finalists short-listed, invariably there would be a time when the judges had to do their final collating of points, certificates had to be written out and so on. It was here that there were some marvellous impromptu performances. In 1979 when the festival was held in Lower Hutt, there was one of these pregnant pauses, everybody waiting, who's won the festival? Napi Waaka is the MC. He's a great performer too, and he calls out for Ngoi to come up and sing. So he starts singing a Pakeha song, 'You always hurt the one you love'. But at the end of every line he'd pause and in impeccable Maori, Ngoi'd come in and translate the lot, just adding extra emphasis on certain words, to bring out the meaning. Well, the place just packed up.

It's that sort of humour for which I remember Ngoi. Because she could go from the depths of nga mea hohonu [profound things], and then – flick – change the tone and be in that light-hearted playful mood. I think that's how she endeared herself to many different people. It didn't matter whether they were kaumatua or te rangatahi [youth], whether they were Kohanga Reo kids or crack haka exponents. She had that wonderful warmth and a real love for people. She had that beautiful facility to move among everybody.

That's only a little wee sketch of Ngoi as I knew her. Perhaps one of my regrets is that there wasn't an opportunity of knowing her as Dalvanius did. Dalvanius went looking for this legendary figure, writer, composer, and song-maker – Ngoi Pewhairangi. He tentatively asked her, 'Can I come and see you, maybe stay a night?' Dalvanius ended up living with her for a fortnight. He had all the tunes in his head and she had the words. Just one of the songs that came out of that short collaboration was 'Poi E'. It was her use of the language which I think made Ngoingoi a significant contemporary Maori composer. In her field this is a space occupied by very few people.

Ngoi Pewhairangi. *Gisborne Herald*

When we go back to composers like Tuini Ngawai, Apirana Ngata, and all the others from the [East] Coast, they all came out of a particular era. A time when Maori language could skilfully describe the wisdom of the past and the promise of the future. And of course this ability continued and flowed on, so what we're waiting for now is to see whether or not there are successors. Are there uri or inheritors of people like Ngoingoi, Tuini, and Apirana, in whose songs the concerns of the people remain?

For me, the song which encapsulates the essential Ngoi is 'Ka noho au'.

> *Ka noho au i konei*
> *Ka whakaaro noa*
> *He pehea ra te huri a te ao katoa*
> *Nga rongo kino e tukituki nei*
> *Nga whakawai e hau nei nga tamariki*

Where she sits and ponders, wondering what on earth is happening to us as a people these days. Where are we going to? Who are we turning to? What will become of our youth?

It's a song full of questions, but when you look inside the lyrics, the answers are there. 'Ka noho au' is a marvellous song, because the words become a beautiful epic poem. They stand up in their own right, as strong and powerful poetry. Add to it the actual melody and it's an inspirational work. Remembering, of course, that Ngati Porou were the masters of action songs. So marry Ngoi's words with Ngati Porou actions and the melodic line, and you've got far more than the action song. So the short answer to which of Ngoi's songs speaks to me best, it is 'Ka noho au', because that one was written, although we didn't know it then, when she was reaching the twilight of her years.

Ngoi's involvement with the Kohanga Reo movement is something I can't really talk about. I don't know very much of that side of her. The other involvement with which I became familiar was when she was a member of what's commonly called MASPAC, the Council for Maori and South Pacific Art.

On her instigation some years ago, the Aotearoa Weavers had their inaugural hui at Ngoi's marae, Pakirikiri. Weavers from throughout the country were all brought together – not only the guns like Rangimarie Hetet, Diggeress Te Kanawa and so on, but anybody who had a love of raranga kete and whariki [the weaving of kits and mats]. That hui was a roaring success and now it's become a continuing thing. So within MASPAC she had a great influence.

So these are my own little reminiscences. Other people could talk about the Ngoi Pewhairangi who was with the mokopuna, sweeping out the dining hall, and add another dimension to the person we all knew and loved as Ngoi. She was made up and gifted with all those different feathers as it were.

Henare Te Ua & Cushla Parekowhai

Published Sources
Broadsheet, April 1984; March 1985
Dominion, 30 Jan. 1985 (obituary)
Gisborne Herald, 28 Dec. 1984; 29 Jan. 1985 (obituary); 2 Feb. 1985; 31 Jan. 1987
Hawke's Bay Herald Tribune, 30 Jan. 1985 (obituary)
Patea Maori Club, *Poi E* (sound recording), Maui Records, 1983
Prince Tui Teka, *E Ipo* (sound recording), RCA, 1982
Tu Tangata, June/July 1985; Feb./March 1986; Oct/Nov. 1986
Wedde, Ian and McQueen, Harvey. *The Penguin Book of New Zealand Verse*, Auckland, 1985

PINEPINE TE RIKA

?-1954

Pinepine Te Rika was the first wife of the Tuhoe prophet, Rua Kenana Hepetipa. She was the daughter of the Ruatahuna elder Te Rika (Te Wharenui) and his wife Tuhiwai Taheke. Her tribe was Tuhoe, her hapu was Ngati Kuri, and her marae, Te Uwhiarai. By 1898 she had borne Rua three children. Te Whatu, their eldest son, was then about thirteen; Toko, their second, was about ten; and Whakaataata (Meri Tukua), their eldest daughter, was about eight. Altogether, Pinepine bore her husband seventeen children.

Pinepine became Rua's tapu wife because she had shared with him the vision on the sacred mountain of the Tuhoe, Maungapohatu. Te Puhi Tatu, who married Te Whatu, narrated Pinepine's account of how she climbed the mountain; this narrative dates from about 1905. An angel appeared before Rua and Pinepine, when they were at their home near Maungapohatu, to urge them to take the path onto the mountain. Te Puhi explained: 'It was that thing, that diamond, that was the reason' ('Ko te mea ke ra hoki, ko te taimana'). The hidden diamond on the mountain is the mauri whenua of Tuhoe, the talismanic source of the power and the knowledge of the people. 'That was the reason Tai [Rua] and Mami [Pinepine] climbed up there' ('Koia ke ra hoki te piki a Tai raua ko Mami ki reira'). The diamond was revealed on the mountain by Whaitiri, the Tuhoe ancestress and guardian of the mountain. In Te Puhi's account, at the revelation of the stone, Pinepine and Rua saw Christ and his 'sister' ('Te Karaiti raua ko tana tuahine'), Whaitiri. This narrative is seminal to the history of Rua, because it identifies him as the chosen leader and Tuhoe Messiah. Equally, this vision set Pinepine apart from all other women.

She became tapu. She was unable to cook food for herself, because cooked food violates tapu, the state of being under the influence of divine forces. A female companion, Te Kuini (Marumaru), therefore always accompanied her and fed her. She used feeding sticks or a rautao (platter of leaves), which would then be destroyed. From 1907 and the foundation of Maungapohatu as the City of God on earth, Pinepine lived in a separate house from her husband. Her first house was built inside the wahi tapu (the tapu inner area) of Maungapohatu. She was carried outside for her meals. She always washed her hands before leaving this sanctuary to remove its tapu. Her own house was particularly tapu; it is said that on entering it everyone had to remove their clothes and leave them outside, lest they become contaminated. They sprinkled themselves and their clothes with water from vessels placed by the doorway, on entering and on leaving. As Rua's tapu wife, she was also the guardian of the Kawenata, the Covenant, the large illustrated English-language Bible which Rua had been given by the Tuhourangi hapu of Te Arawa, when they recognised him as the leader who had been prophesied. She was known to the people as 'our Holy Mother'.

If Pinepine had become a tapu woman, she was also identified as King Solomon's wife, Pharaoh's daughter, who had lived apart in her own house in Jerusalem. When Maungapohatu was reconstructed (like Jerusalem) and the inner sanctuary area cleared of all buildings but Rua's house, she retained her separate home. A new house was built for her, near to the House of the Covenant; only she could enter the House of the Covenant. When the community's new meeting-house was constructed (in 1914), she was not able to enter it, being in a permanent state of tapu. Sometimes at night, the assembled company saw her peeping sadly through the rear windows at them.

The police assault on Maungapohatu on 2 April 1916 caused the death of her son Toko. She was convinced that he had been murdered by one of the police. She was a crucial witness. In the assault Toko was wounded by the police rifles and he fled to the back of her house where she hurriedly bandaged his wrist. She then ran into her house. When she came out, fleeing with the heavy Kawenata, she saw her son crawl under the wash-tubs at the back of her house. He died with more wounds in his body; the last shot, which she claimed to have heard as she fled, was fired in cold blood. Her evidence given at the time was buried under the orchestrated perjuries of the senior police, but it points to an unpalatable truth.

Pinepine's world was structured by the Scriptures and by the Maori cosmology. Most of her life was bound by the constraints of tapu upon her. Even after Rua lifted the tapu from her, about the time they moved to Matahi to live

Pinepine Te Rika. *E. Murphy Album, Alexander Turnbull Library*

in 1933, she remained apart from the others. As an old lady, she had to learn to cook again for herself. It is told of her with fond amusement that she always burnt the food. But wherever she lived, Pinepine was associated with bright beds of flowers, which she planted to lead up to her welcoming doorway. When she died at Matahi, on 9 August 1954, it was thought that she was ninety-six years old. Pinepine's life had spanned a world of vast changes for her people but, for her, guidance had always come from God.   *Judith Binney*

Quotations

para.2 This version of Pinepine's account (originally told in Maori in 1978) may be found in Judith Binney, 'Maori Oral Narratives, Pakeha Written Texts: Two Forms of Telling History', *NZJH*, vol.21 no.1, April 1987, p.22

para.3 Haremate Roberts of Tataiahape, talking with Judith Binney, 17 May 1978

Unpublished Source

Best, Elsdon. 'Genealogies of the Tuhoe as of 1898', pp.26–7, MS, ATL

Published Source

Binney, J., Chaplin, G., and Wallace, C. *Mihaia, the Prophet Rua Kenana and his Community at Maungapohatu*, Wellington, 2nd (corrected) edn, 1987

MARY PLAYER

1856–1923

Mary Crampton came to New Zealand from Kilkenny, Ireland, as an assisted immigrant aboard the *Woodlark*, arriving in Wellington in 1874. Years later, she told her daughters that she had been 'pressed' by the New Zealand government agent in the southern Irish port of Waterford. Aged only eighteen, Mary had lightheartedly put her name on the list of prospective immigrants. Despite the anguished efforts of her parents, the contract remained binding. Her sister wrote thirty-three years later:

I shall never forget the day you sailed away for New Zealand. It is fresh in my memory as if it was today. Dear mother fainted away, had to be carried home and she took to her bed and never got better after . . .

The *Woodlark*'s voyage was notorious. It incurred official censure for the behaviour of some women of 'bad character' on board. There was a galley fire, an outbreak of scarlet fever, and food was short.

After several years of working in Wellington, Mary married Edward Player in 1877. Her father-in-law (also Edward Player) was much concerned with social issues of the day and associated with Samuel Parnell's efforts to improve working conditions. Mary had married into a family with literary and political interests which fostered her own growing social awareness.

Irish-born Mary Player, left, seen here with her sister Joannah, came to New Zealand in 1874. *Gladys Rainbow*

The marriage was happy, but with only modest means and a growing family of six children, Mary worked outside the home as well. A natural skill as a midwife and nurse took her increasingly into the community. Over the years she did much to search out and relieve cases of distress among working people. Mary was constantly made aware of the effect that poor working conditions had upon women's health and this became her abiding concern.

She was a member of the Wellington Ladies' Christian Association (WLCA) and a Blue Ribboner (part of the American-based Blue Ribbon Army, committed to total abstinence). The WLCA was the first independent women's group in Wellington, set up in 1878 with the aim of creating a fund for a home for destitute women. The association's work eventually led to the establishment of the Alexandra Home for Friendless Women and the Levin Memorial Home for Girls.

In 1894, she set up, with others, the Women's Social and Political League. At the first meeting (12 April 1894) she was elected president and subsequently re-elected. At a meeting in July 1894, she read a paper on 'Domestic Servants and the Necessity of Establishing a Government Labour Bureau for Women'. A resolution was passed, and early in 1895, Mary and one other member called on the minister of labour who welcomed the idea. The bureau for women was established soon after.

In September 1895 Mary resigned as president and as a member of the league. Louisa Seddon, wife of the Liberal premier, Richard Seddon, was elected in her place. Richard Seddon spoke in a celebratory speech to the league of an association 'founded by women holding strongly Liberal views . . . [and] believing in temperance . . . [who] also believe great political principles to be of first importance.' It seems unlikely that Mary Player, who was committed rather to the improvement of conditions for women, agreed with these views, which presumably now dominated the league. There is little indication that she continued to be involved in her own community.

Her home life and circumstances now became more demanding. In 1895, with five children to care for, she gave birth to twins, one of whom survived only to die after three months of ceaseless crying. Then in 1897 Mary, aged forty, had her last child. Four years later her husband became ill with cancer. On his death in 1905 Mary was left homeless, with no income. She took on full-time case nursing, often living in.

In her last years Mary moved in turn to her married daughters' homes, delivering her own sixteen grandchildren. Throughout her life she had given unstintingly to those around her, and worked to improve the lives of women.

Gladys Rainbow

Quotations
para.1 Alice Player to Mary Player, 30 Oct. 1906, letter in author's possession
para.7 *NZ Mail*, 18 Oct. 1895
Unpublished Sources
Information was provided by family members; the author is a granddaughter of Mary Player.
Annual General Report of the Women's Social and Political League of Wellington, 1894–5, in author's possession
Published Sources
AJHR, 1874, D-2, pp.45–6
Evening Post, 11 Jan. 1924 (obituary)

Grimshaw, Patricia. *Women's Suffrage in New Zealand*, Auckland, 1972

Lake, J. *Alexandra, 1879–1979, Commemorating 100 Years of Community Service*, Wellington, 1979

Millen, Julia. *Colonial Tears and Sweat*, Wellington, 1984, pp.76–80

NZ Mail, 18 Oct. 1895; 23 April 1896

Wellington Ladies Christian Association Reports 1885–1927, ATL

ANNA PLISCHKE

1895–1983

Anna Plischke came to New Zealand from Vienna in 1939, with her architect husband Ernst Plischke, and one of her two sons by an earlier marriage. Unlike many of the refugees from Europe at that time, the Plischkes came to employment: New Zealand was short of architects and Ernst Plischke was brought here initially to work on the 1940 Centennial Exhibition, and subsequently worked for the Housing Department. He was a brilliant, innovative and perfectionist architect, whose modern designs influenced New Zealand architecture substantially, although he was never fully accepted; equally, he never adapted completely to colonial 'she'll be right' habits.

Anna Plischke before she left Europe.
Tup Lang

Anna, however, loved her new country. Her family in Austria were well-to-do Jewish merchants (Hugo Schwitzer and Hedwig Nossal). After completing an arts degree at Vienna University, Anna married businessman Robert Lang, and her life was that of high society in Vienna – wealthy, intellectual, social. She married Ernst Plischke (after a divorce) in 1935. Always strong-minded and independent, she found New Zealand invigorating after the rigidity of the world she had left, and threw herself into making a new life for her husband and son.

Anna had already had some experience in landscape gardening in Vienna, and in Wellington she created a beautiful garden around the turn-of-the-century house the Plischkes bought in Brooklyn. As Ernst Plischke began to take on private commissions for houses around Wellington, she undertook the landscaping of their gardens. Landscaping to her meant not only planning – carefully creating the right visual effect of these 'international' houses in their New Zealand setting – but also doing the work, lugging the rocks, shifting the soil, and digging in the plants. In her work she was both sensitive and practical, as her own words indicate:

With every plant I always try to find a place where it looks its best; of course the growing conditions that a plant wants also have to be taken into consideration . . . but for me the most important considerations are always these: how does this particular plant look in this particular place; how will it look with the other plants; and how will it appear from where one is most likely to look at it? What is the good of a fine gladiolus if it turns its blooms towards the sun and away from you. (Nobody can blame it for that; and as this side happens to be just where you and the path are not, the only thing you see is the back of the gladiolus, which is annoying.) But if you had planted a dahlia or a lily instead of the gladiolus, you could have avoided this slight, as they are not so fond of the sun.

Anna Plischke was a woman of deep religious faith, who became a Catholic on her marriage to Ernst. She had also great personal strength, making courageous choices – to divorce her first husband in order to marry Ernst Plischke, to leave Austria, to adapt fully to New Zealand. A friend wrote:

I came to regard her as a very wise woman indeed. She had a very serious cancer operation, followed by a long convalescence . . . she once said 'the most important of the virtues is courage'. She had plenty of courage herself, she needed it after the cancer. But I thought it a slightly odd choice at the time. Since then, I have come to feel the strength of the case for courage.

She had need of courage too, when the time came for Ernst Plischke to leave New Zealand, on his appointment as Professor of Architecture at the Academy in Vienna in 1962. Anna had no wish to leave her family, her garden, or her chosen country, for a small flat in Vienna. But she had always supported her husband fully, and she did so now. She died in Vienna in 1983.

Bridget Williams

Quotations
para.3 Anna Plischke, 'A Garden for Pleasure', *Design Review*, no.6, 1951
para.4 Nan Parsons, 'Anna', typescript in author's possession
Sources
Information was provided by Henry and Tup Lang (Anna Plischke's son and daughter-in-law), and Roy and Nan Parsons.

MARY POLSON

1897-1971

Mary Victoria Cracroft Wilson was born in 1897 at Culverden, North Canterbury. The Cracroft Wilsons had long been prominent in both farming and politics in Canterbury. Her maternal grandfather, Sir John Hall, was also a former New Zealand prime minister who had been active in obtaining the vote for women in 1893, and her mother was known for her involvement in public activities, particularly those concerning women. For eight years Mary was educated at the Brondesbury School in London, where she became a head girl. During the First World War she worked for the VAD (Voluntary Aid Division) in the nursing service. After the war she returned to New Zealand with her mother, and in 1920 she married her first husband, Arthur Grigg, a soldier and farmer. They had three children. Mary Grigg was widowed in 1941. Less than two years later she married William Polson, a National Party MP for Stratford, Taranaki.

Although coming from a political family, Mary Polson did not have any political ambitions. She states that it was only when her first husband entered parliament in 1938 that she became interested in politics. When Arthur Grigg died, his widow was elected unopposed to fill the vacant mid-Canterbury seat in January 1942. (As she noted herself, she was fortunate in that not only was she able to afford to send her children to boarding-schools, but also they were of an age to look after themselves.)

On entering parliament Mary Grigg became the National Party's first woman representative, though the fourth woman to take a seat. She was also the first woman in the party, since its formation in 1936, to have her name put forward for selection as a nominee. Out of the first eleven women parliamentarians, seven entered parliament through a by-election and/or the death of a close male relative. Mary Grigg was no exception to this trend.

Farming issues were of the most concern to Mary Grigg. The greater part of her maiden speech was devoted to this subject. She said that her other parliamentary interests were housing, health, and education. She often looked at these questions from a woman's viewpoint; for example, she was concerned with the effect of the labour shortage on wives and children. The women MPs from both sides of the House worked together on a number of issues. In 1942 they urged that the number of women police be increased and that they be issued with a uniform, and that women be allowed to sit on juries. It was also in 1942 that Mary Grigg and Mary Dreaver (Labour MP for Waitemata) joined forces to promote the Women's Land Service uniform that Mary Grigg had designed.

Before her election to parliament, Mary Grigg was active in community life in the Canterbury area. She was president of the Ashburton Plunket Society, a member of the Red Cross executive, and president of the Mt Somers Ladies' Guild. In 1941 she topped the election poll for the Ashburton Hospital Board and became its first woman member. When Arthur Grigg rejoined the army, his wife took over his parliamentary duties in the electorate. She was also the first woman member of the National Party's Dominion executive and was chairwoman of the women's section of the Canterbury National Party division.

Mary Polson (later Polson-Grigg), left, with Mary Dreaver recruiting for the Women's Land Service, 1942. The Land Service uniform they are wearing was designed by Mary Polson. At the time Mary Polson was the National MP for Mid-Canterbury, Mary Dreaver the Labour MP for Waitemata. *New Zealand Listener*

After Mary Grigg's second marriage in 1943 to William Polson (who was later knighted), she did not seek re-election in the September general election. Her parliamentary career lasted only twenty months, but she continued to be active in the National Party. In 1945 the Polsons supported Hilda Ross in her first election campaign and in 1949 she and Mary Polson co-wrote the National Party's election manifesto. She was awarded an MBE in 1946.

Vanya Bootham

Unpublished Sources
NZ Biographies, vol.4, 1971, p.3, ATL
Vanya Bootham. 'Women Political Candidates in the New Zealand General Elections 1919–1951', BA Hons research essay, Victoria, 1989

Published Sources
Gustafson, Barry. *The First 50 Years: A History of the New Zealand National Party*, Auckland, 1986
NZ Listener, 17 July 1942, p.12; 30 Oct. 1942, p.9
The Press, Christchurch, 17 Dec. 1941, p.6

MIRIA WOODBINE POMARE

1876–1971

Lady Miria Woodbine Pomare was a most remarkable and gracious woman, who will be remembered for her life of service to both the Pakeha and Maori communities. She was 'the last of a generation that blazed the trail to the new world'.

Miria Pomare was born on 24 December 1876 and died at the age of ninety-four on 7 September 1971. She was the eldest of three daughters (Miria, Meri and Heni) and two brothers (James and Eru), born to James Woodbine Johnson and Mere Hape in Manutuke, Poverty Bay.

Her father, James Woodbine Johnson of 'Wairakaia', Manutuke, had emigrated to Poverty Bay with his brother Randall in 1867 and established one of the finest farms and fruit orchards in that district. James Woodbine Johnson's upbringing, at Whepstead Hall, Lavenham, Suffolk, England, was that of a privileged English rural family. His reasons for travelling to the new world were not social and economic necessity but rather challenge and excitement. This may be somewhat surprising, given that only two years previously, James had graduated from Trinity College, Cambridge, but then his original intentions may have been to stay for only a limited period. He stayed, however, to farm and to play an important role in the development of Poverty Bay as its first representative on the Auckland Provincial Council (1873–5) and first chairman of Cook County (1877–9).

Miria Pomare's mother, Mere Hape, was Maori of Rongo Whakaata and Te Aitanga-aa-Mahaki descent from Manutuke. Mere was a warm and hospitable mother and home-maker. With her strong local tribal links, she ensured that Miria was not only a fluent Maori speaker but was also well versed in tikanga Maori (Maori customs) and thoroughly comfortable in te ao Maori (the Maori world). Miria accompanied her to various Maori functions and celebrations, and these experiences no doubt stood her in good stead in later years and established her tangata whenua roots. Miria also had a close affinity with her grandmother (Mere's mother), Maora Pani, who lived to 114 and who remembered well the arrival of Captain Cook at Young Nick's Head in 1769.

Besides her Maori upbringing, Miria's father arranged for her the type of education that he felt was right and proper for an English child of her time, namely a live-in governess, Miss Palethorpe, who taught her French, music (piano), literature and needlework. Education at home was followed by secondary school at Gisborne High School where she boarded. Miria's favourite pastimes at this stage of her life were riding and hunting – very much the pursuits of the English landed gentry.

Miria Johnson married Dr Maui Pomare (of Te Atiawa and Ngati Toa descent) in January 1903. Miria and Maui made their home at 'Hiwiroa', Western Hutt, the home which will be remembered for its warmth and generous hospitality over many decades. Their house nestled in an eight-acre estate that lay on Te Rangihaeata's old track to the Hutt Valley.

Dr Maui Pomare had graduated in medicine at Battle Creek, Michigan, in 1899, and returned to New Zealand in 1900 to become the first Maori Medical Officer of Health in the time of the Seddon government. Wellington was his base but as a medical officer of health he travelled widely. By dint of his overseas training, he had acquired a fair understanding of western culture and, more importantly, how this knowledge might be used to assist the health of the Maori community at a time when the Maori population had slumped to an all-time low of around 40,000 due to European afflictions.

Both Miria and Maui Pomare accomplished much in the twenty-seven years

Lady Miria Woodbine Pomare, 1949. *S. P. Andrew Collection, Alexander Turnbull Library*

of married life they had together until his death in 1930. They had three children, Ana, Naera and Te Rakaherea. Whilst Maui's life became very busy and public due to his duties as a politician, Miria's life was no less busy as a mother, a staunch supporter of her husband, and as a tireless worker in numerous community activities, whether they be Maori or Pakeha. Because of her upbringing and early education, Lady Miria was equally comfortable whether at state functions or on the marae. She won the respect of all through her dignity and charm, no more so than when her husband Maui was knighted in 1922 for his services to the country.

It was during the war years 1914–18 that Miria's leadership qualities and organisational skills in community affairs first came to the fore as honorary president of the Soldiers' Fund, which had over seventy committees throughout New Zealand and the Cook Islands. This work involved sending comforts to soldiers overseas, knitting, and organising receptions for returned soldiers. She received the OBE for this work in 1918, the first New Zealand woman to be given this honour.

This work was just one example of a life's commitment to community work. She was an office-bearer in groups as various as the Red Cross, Lower Hutt Anglican Boys' Home, Women's Reform League, YWCA and the English Speaking Union. She was chairperson of the Anglican Maori Mission and one of the founders of the Ngati Poneke Welfare Mission and Club. Indeed, much of Lady Miria's energies and interests in her later years were channelled into the life and welfare of the Ngati Poneke Club, for which she had a great love and affinity.

Lady Miria died on 7 September 1971 at Lower Hutt where she had spent the greater part of her life and her ashes were laid beside those of her husband, Sir Maui, and sons Te Rakaherea and Naera at Manukorihi Pa, Waitara. She was truly a remarkable woman and a 'woman of two worlds'.

Eru Woodbine Pomare

Quotation

para.1 Rt Revd Manu Bennett, address at the funeral of Lady Miria Woodbine Pomare, 1971, in private possession

Unpublished Sources

Information was provided by family members, including M. O. W. Pomare and M. H. Pomare. The author is Lady Miria Woodbine Pomare's grandson.

Hui Whakamahara ki a Maui Pomare. Souvenir of Pomare Memorial Meeting, Waitara, 27 June 1936, p.2, in private possession

Published Sources

Dominion, 1 Oct. 1971

Harper, Pauline. 'Lady Pomare – A Life of Service', *NZ Woman's Weekly* (undated clipping in the author's possession)

1841–1933

Born Jane Kelly in the Bay of Islands in 1841, Heni Pore was both witness to and a participant in some of the major events in New Zealand's history. Heni was the daughter of an Arawa woman of the Ngati Uenuku-Kopaku hapu, and of an Irish sea captain. After one of his forays south in the 1820s, Hongi Hika had taken back with him to the Bay of Islands a young woman called Maraea, the daughter of Te Ngahoe and Rangitauninihi of Mokoia Island. Later, Maraea was married by the Revd Richard Taylor to William Thomas Kelly, and a daughter was born to the couple.

Heni was only a young child when her father was drowned at Mangonui. She was later sent to the Church of England mission station at Paihia, and was living there in 1845 at the time of Hone Heke's raid on Kororareka. In later years she was able to remember vividly the sight of Kororareka ablaze with flames and the sound of the guns of HMS *Hazard* firing on the township. The following day, Heni and her mother were amongst those evacuated by ship to Auckland where they settled for the next few years.

During that time Maraea married Thomas Russell, a shipbuilder, and Heni became known as Jane Russell. She was educated for a while at a convent, attended several other schools for short periods, and spent some time as a pupil at Wesley College. An intelligent and well-educated young woman, Heni was offered employment as an assistant teacher of Maori girls at Three Kings College in Auckland.

In 1855 she was married to Te Kirikaramu, also of Arawa, and bore five children in quick succession. After war broke out in the Waikato in 1863, Heni left her husband and, along with her children, mother, and sister, joined her brother Te Waha-Huka in fighting for the King movement. They joined forces with the Koheriki hapu of Ngati Paoa and spent several months living in the Hunua Ranges. Heni took an active part in the skirmishes with British troops, using firearms with efficiency, often while carrying her baby in a blanket on her back.

Finally their group managed to break through the cordon of British troops to link up with the main body of the Kingite force. Heni's many talents included skill in embroidery, and during this time she produced a beautiful flag for the Kingite movement. Of red silk with a white cross and star and the name 'Aotearoa' embroidered on it, the flag was captured during 1863 by the Forest Rangers and is now held by the Auckland Museum.

In 1864 Heni fought during the battle of Gate Pa at Tauranga, reputedly the only woman to do so. She had also assisted in the construction of the pa. It was during this battle that Heni performed an act of mercy which was later to add to her reputation as a fearless, compassionate, and honourable fighting woman. This is her description of the incident:

I was in the firing-trench when I heard the wounded officer lying in our lines calling for water. There were other wounded soldiers distressed for want of water. When I heard these cries I could not resist them. The sight of the foe with their life-blood flowing from them seemed to elate some of our warriors, but I felt a great pity for them, and I remembered also a rule that had been made amongst us that if any person asked for any service to be performed, the request must not be refused; it would be an aitua to ignore it – that is, neglect to comply would bring misfortune. So I rose up from the trench, slung my gun, and was about to run back to the cooking-place where we kept our water when my brother asked me where I was going. I told him that I heard the dying men crying for water and I could not disobey the call. He said not a word, but stood with his gun-butt planted on the ground and his hands gripping the muzzle and watched me earnestly while I ran to fetch the water. I had to go about 10 yards to the rear of the trench, and as our fence was almost demolished I was in view of the troops. I found that a small tin in which I had some water had been capsized, but that there was still the iron nail-can full. It was so heavy that I had to spill about half of it before I could conveniently carry it to the soldiers. I carried it in my arms to where the Colonel was lying. I did not know then that he was a Colonel, but I could tell by his uniform that he was a senior officer. He was the nearest of the soldiers to me. I went down by his side, took his head on my knees, and said 'Here's water' in English. I poured some of the water in one hand which I held close to his lips so that he could drink. He said 'God Bless You', and drank again from my hand. I went to the three other soldiers

Hine Pore (Jane Foley), heroine of Gate Pa, 1864, pictured here with the flag she made for the King movement. *National Museum/ Te Whare Taonga o Aotearoa*

*and gave them water one by one in the same way. Then, placing the nail-can so
that it would not spill, I ran back to the trench.*

Gate Pa was not the end of Heni's fighting career. She later joined a party
under Major William Mair which was hunting the killers of the interpreter James
Fulloon. She also took part in a series of skirmishes at Matata, Te Teko, and
various places on the East Coast.

After the wars, Heni settled down to a very different life – running the
'Travellers Rest' Hotel at Maketu with her second husband, Dennis Foley.
Another four children were born of that marriage. After a few years the Foleys
moved to Katikati, where in 1890 Heni was widowed after Dennis drowned.

Heni then moved to Rotorua, where she was licensed as an interpreter and
became renowned as an expert on matters involving Maori land title. She was
also a staunch supporter and office-holder in the Rotorua branch of the Women's
Christian Temperance Union.

In 1933, Heni died in Rotorua at ninety-two years of age. A stained-glass
window in Lichfield Cathedral, England, is dedicated to the brave conduct of
Heni Pore. *Tui MacDonald*

Quotation
para.6 J. Cowan, *The New Zealand Wars and the Pioneering Period*, vol.1, p.149

Published Sources
Auckland Star, 26 June 1933
Cowan, James. *The New Zealand Wars and the Pioneering Period*, Wellington, 1922
NZ Herstory 1982, Dunedin, 1981

RUHIA PORUTU

c.1840

Ruhia Porutu was born in Taranaki sometime before 1840. She was a Ngati Awa
woman who was married to Ihaia Porutu, son of Rira Porutu, a rangatira from
Pipitea and a Whanganui-a-Tara signatory to the Treaty of Waitangi. Ruhia had
only one child who died in infancy.

She was the owner of a finely made kaitaka (cloak), which is regarded as
an excellent example of a kakahu paepae-roa.* In kakahu paepae-roa the
garment is turned after weaving in order that the whatu rua run in a vertical
direction from top edge to bottom. Ruhia's kaitaka is heavily trimmed in taniko.
A principal feature of this border is the triangle-shaped niho taniwha design. The
cloak is of exceptional weave and it is likely that many women made it together.
At this time the kaitaka has been entrusted to the National Museum. A portrait
of Ruhia Porutu herself painted by Gottfried Lindauer remains in the private
possession of one of her descendants.

Her story is told by Mairatea Tahiwi, on viewing Ruhia's cloak at the National
Museum.

*The Maori terms in this paragraph all refer to different types of weaving used in cloaks.

The cloak is just as I remember it. As little children, my father wrapped both my brother and I in it. We were about five or six years old and I can remember my father sitting us together on the couch for a photo. It felt heavy but the fabric was soft as silk.

In the beginning the cloak belonged to my ancestress, Ruhia Porutu. The story of the cloak has been told many, many times. But as I remember it, back in the 1840s many Maori folk were beginning to realise that their land was being taken by the Pakeha. For Ruhia and her people over in Petone, there was another threat which could have just as easily devoured their land. It was dis-covered that the Hutt River flooded dangerously. The people were a bit anxious about the risk.

So they had built a cottage for a Dr Evans who was on the ship Adelaide *coming to Wellington. This Dr Evans was a doctor of engineering, I believe. Maybe the people had built the place for him because they thought this Pakeha engineer might have the ability to redirect the river. Anyhow, as was the custom, his newly built house was very tapu.*

About this time, so the story goes, two immigrant boys, Thomas Whilmore McKenzie and friend, attempted to enter the house built for Dr Evans. But of course the building was still tapu. The foolishness of the Pakeha children was observed by Rira Porutu, a rangatira from Pipitea. Old Rira questioned whether the coming of the white man was advantageous to the Maori at all. Rira watched the disrespectful high jinks with troubled gaze. When the two boys were about to cross over the threshold, old Rira with anger mounting in his heart grabbed Orokiwi [Horokiwi], his greenstone mere, and made to strike them. But just as things were getting serious, his daughter-in-law Ruhia took off her cloak and threw it over the two boys. She then put her head to the ground, we are told, appealing to the old man to spare their lives.

Ruhia herself had already accepted Christian beliefs, and the sight of her pleading for the Pakehas melted the old man's heart. So Rira let them live and the McKenzie boy grew up among the Maori almost as one of Ruhia's own.

I don't know much about Ruhia herself, except that way back she was a Ngati Awa from Taranaki and she lived at Pipitea. I can't say anything about how she came to Wellington; perhaps a marriage was arranged to bring the two people together. However, she married Rira Porutu's son, Ihaia. They had one child, but it died. I'm not sure who Ruhia's parents were, but she had some land out in the Hutt, called Te Momi. It's where the original Hutt High School was, near the railway.

Henare Porutu was Ihaia's brother. From Henare Porutu, the cloak passed to my father Arthur Pitt-Porutu. It was a great treasure to him. We always kept it in a special drawer at our home in Naenae and my father brought it out on rare occasions. Sometimes, when we had a visitor, the cloak came out and my father started to talk about it. We always realised this person would be someone Father liked and trusted. I don't remember my father ever putting the cloak on anyone, except once on this special friend of mine. We grew up in the Hutt together. She was like a sister to me, because I had none of my own. One day when the cloak had been brought out, Father put it about her shoulders. When she had gone, Father said to me that from that time on she would always be a true and faithful friend. And she was.

Ruhia Porutu's cloak. *National Museum/ Te Whare Taonga o Aotearoa*

The cloak was cared for at home until my father died. He left it to my brother, Arthur Pitt, who put it in the care of the museum. I was left the portrait of Ruhia painted by Gottfried Lindauer. It's fairly likely that Ruhia never sat for the portrait but was probably painted from a photograph.

In the painting the artist has draped the cloak so that the border is at the top. It's worn half-folded so the taniko hangs upside down. The cameo Ruhia wears in the picture shows her husband Ihaia's portrait. It's lovely to have the image of them both. I don't know much about how the cloak was made, except that it's very old and dates well back to the 1830s.

These days the cloak has been in the museum for a long time. When the marae at Pipitea was opened, there was some discussion about the story of Ruhia Porutu and her cloak. It was decided that, because I was one of the last left in line with Ruhia, the people would like me to accompany the priest and wear the cloak at the opening of the house.

Taki Marsden was the Maori vicar at the time and we took the cloak out of the museum the night before. He came up with me and said he would like to do it in the Maori way. He gave a prayer and explained to me that it was a little chant of thankfulness for the ways we knew. The cloak then came back with us to my home and lay beside my bed that night. Anyway, after the ceremony was over, I wanted to get it back to the museum as soon as possible. It was very busy on that day, but Martin Winiata and two or three young girls helped me put it away. The children rolled it up so it was safe and Martin said the appropriate prayers.

The cloak was taken back to the museum and that was the last time it was ever worn in public.

Mairatea Tahiwi (born Pitt-Porutu) & Cushla Parekowhai

Published Sources
Early Settlers' and Historical Assn of Wellington, *Newsletter*, May 1970
Priestley, Dinah. *Old Thorndon*, Wellington, 1988

ANIMERATA POULGRAIN

?1890–1958

Animerata Poulgrain was born at Kaitara, Gisborne. Her mother was Riria Kehukehu of Nga Ariki, of Te Aitanga-a-Mahaki tribe. Her father was William Poulgrain, a Pakeha. She never went to school and was educated at home. Animerata had five husbands and eighteen children. All her life she lived among her extended family in the small rural community of Puha, twelve kilometres north-west of Te Karaka, Gisborne. She died in 1958 and is buried at Kaitara.

Her story is told by her youngest daughter, Paare Stevens.
Her full name was Animérata Poulgrain, but she was also well known as Puti. It's not a nickname. The old people had what's known as an ingoa karangatanga. It's a term they have to describe a name used by the family.

She was stocky, about five foot two, with very pale skin and sharp, bright, brown eyes. She wore the old-fashioned long skirts to the ankle most times, but then, when the fashion changed for the shorter dress, she wore that. Even when she was sixty she kept up. I wouldn't call her mod, but she was flexible. She smoked Pocket Edition and rolled her own too.

Mum really liked her gambling. Cards and horses. Up all night for three or four day card-games. She'd never miss the races either. If there was a meeting in Gisborne, she'd get there come hell or high water. It didn't matter if she had to beg, borrow or steal. Needless to say the day before the races, she was visiting all her family, touching them up for a few bob. She followed the circuit from the Gisborne races down to Napier, Hastings and back. Race days were crazy days. Early in the morning you have your cup of tea, and everybody's got

*to tell their dreams. No matter how silly or insignificant, you'd have to come
out with it. Tell her your dream and she'd work them out. You had to. She was
tinny about it, she didn't study any form, it might be the unusual things like a
Chinese man walking past in a checked shirt. She'd interpret the sign.*

*With the big winnings a certain amount was put aside for the next day's
races. The rest went into the bottom of the tin trunk. She'd have separate little
bundles and each bundle was for a specific purpose. A purpose only she knew.
The tin trunk was kept in her room under the bed. It was something like a glory
box where she had her best linen and very important papers, like marriage
certificates, whakapapa, and her winnings from the races.*

*The other thing she loved was reading. We'd have a kerosene lamp and
she'd put the book behind the lamp and it must have magnified it or something,
but that's how she read with her nose to the lampshade. She read detective
stories and Agatha Christie. Historical romance and the cowboys. When she
was reading Dad would say, 'Come on Mum, tell us the story,' and she'd sit
down and tell him all about it. But it would be in the language because Dad
could only understand that. So we'd get Zane Grey in Maori. Neat.*

*I remember, too, we loved listening to the 'Green Hornet' on the radio.
We stayed up late to be with her, listening. The radio was in the kitchen, but
we didn't have one of our own until later. Mary, my eldest sister, was the first.
So we used to walk around to their place. Mum always wanted to know what's
happened to the Phantom Drummer. It used to be a spooky one. You can
imagine me late at night riding piggy-back, hanging around their necks in the
old-fashioned shawl.*

*When we were children and her eyesight was still good, she made all our
petticoats, pinnies, and bloomers. She'd boil old Snowball cloths, flour bags, in
caustic soda to remove all the printing, then she'd crochet a lace trim around
the bottom. But the clothes you wore around at home and not at school still had
the words on them. So if you'd bend over there'd be 'Snowball' on the bum.*

*She had a good garden too. Carnations, roses, everything. If there was a
flower, Mum would have it. I remember about the middle of September after
the frost, we had to get up early, even before the sun came up, and plant the
watermelons. It really started the night before. We'd soak the seeds in sugar
and water in a jar. In the morning you're still rubbing sleep out of your eyes,
and you're pushing these silly seeds into the ground. Usually as the watermelons
were getting bigger and bigger, you could hear her talking to the plants. She
knew just which patch belonged to who and where. Then there was paddocks
full of kumara, potatoes.*

*But the job that I hated most was maize picking. Because there was rows
and rows and rows of it. May was plucking maize time. We had a stick on a
leather thong that you strapped around your wrist and you'd have this nail
sticking out. You just grabbed the corn, slick it through the husk, pull it down,
and break off the cob. Easy. But you had to do that hundreds of thousands of*

Animerata Poulgrain. *Paare Stevens*

*times. Then you threw the cobs into heaps so they could be bagged and taken
on horseback to the crib.*

*Mum wouldn't supervise the maize picking but she did the cooking for the
workers. There was heaps of kai. That used to be a treat. You worked hard and
you eat hard. A big basket full of food would come out to the paddock. She
would bring pikelets, scones, tarts, sandwiches, whatever. The best time,
though, was when there was cold kumara, dried pipis, and smoked eels. She
was a good cook. Great cook. I remember her doing kotero potato cakes. When
we would dig up a root of Maori potatoes, there'd be one or two squishy ones.
She'd save these somehow and then they'd be hung in a bit of mutton cloth or
muslin and dried; then it was ground into potato flour, and she made these
pancakes. We called them sugar buns and they were very sweet.*

*The other one she did was kanga waru. It's like a long skinny pudding
thing cooked in a maize husk. She'd grate the maize until it was fine, like you
can buy cornmeal now. Kanga waru is not fermented. It's just the mature corn
grated down. Then she would add sugar, butter, and egg, I think. Mix it and
roll it up in corn husks. Tie it tightly, and steam them. Oh yes, they were
lovely. She made kanga pungarehu too. She'd use old mature corn. Might have
been in the pakoro for what, three or four years? Anyhow the corn would be
put in the pot with water and some wood ash. You had to keep stirring all the
time, otherwise it would set like cement at the bottom. This takes all the husk
off the corn, and if you've got a proper Maori corn, all the kernel skins come off
and they float up to the top. Then you take it off the heat and reboil it. This
time with sugar and water. The kernels will then swell to about double their
size. If it's the Maori corn, kanga pungarehu was really pretty. The kernels*

were different colours. Might be white, black, red. All different.

Then there was the eeling. First thunder in February it starts, when the matamoe [eels] are going back to the sea. We used to make an eel weir the width of the river. Wooden stakes would be intertwined with manuka bush to make a good sort of V-shaped fence. Then we'd put the net in at the bottom where it'd been narrowed. And away they'd go. It depended on how fast the eels would be coming downstream. But up at the top of the weir there would be little holes dug out into the bank. Matamoe in one pit and the mongrel eels, as we call them, in the other. Matamoe was the king. That's the one we were going for. Never mind the others really. Sometimes we even threw them back, it got that fussy.

But as kids our job was to sort out the little wee fishes, the cockabullies. That's what us little ones would do. All the cooks, Mum and the rest, kept the big fires going. Those setting the net were always wet. They've got to have dry clothes for them to get into. Mum and them would have all these clothes hanging out, drying. On top of the fire we'd have grills. Mum used to cut up meat on long sticks, very much like you use a skewer. Only these ones were big long sticks. She put them over the embers and under the embers there would be a hole dug out with the potatoes all in. Oh it was a great time, not only our family, but everybody. They'd all come down to the river and sleep in the camp, in tents. Everybody helping everybody else.

She didn't have a role on the marae locally, but she knew what you should do and shouldn't do on the marae. Like table manners. You never took food off the table, when you went visiting. When the hakari [feast] is set out on the table you would eat what was in front of you and never reach over somebody else. You only eat to satisfy yourself and never, ever take a snack for later on. That was very rude. Not only rude, but selfish because there were other people coming along. Those sorts of things we were taught and yes, the proper way to eat different things like kereru. Start from the head and work your way down. You must eat the head, you weren't to pick, and eat the best part first.

She wasn't a public person, but she had strong views and opinions. She'd talk privately to the family and they took note of what she said. Before any huihui, she'd get the family together to find out what everybody thought. You all had to be there, and say what you wanted, and how you wanted, and they talked till it was satisfied. Then, when you got to the marae, everybody knew exactly what was going to be done. But Mum organised the whole thing.

She spoke her mind. She was pretty forceful, a sort of woman you can't say no to easily. Because she was very strong-willed. Obstinate even, hard-headed, a taringa maro. She could have had the whole pa up in arms against her, but if she said no, it meant no. There were times when she could be very comforting, like most old people, then there were times when she could speak firmly. No nonsense whatsoever. But I think Mum always had a sense of humour. With all the kids she had, she needed it. Paare Stevens & Cushla Parekowhai

HINE POUPOU

c.1600s

Hine Poupou, daughter of a chief of Ngati Kuia of Rangitoto, D'Urville Island, was living on Kapiti Island with her husband Manini-pounamu, and his younger brother, Te Hiki-paroa. Waking early one morning she found herself completely alone, her husband and brother-in-law having abandoned her. Manini-pounamu had tired of his faithful wife and, with the intention of marrying another woman, had returned to Rangitoto. Hine Poupou's parents were told that their daughter had met her death on Kapiti.

Meanwhile, Hine Poupou, the deserted wife, was making preparations to swim the sea of Raukawa, Cook Strait. She feared her safety might be endangered by the island's other inhabitants if she were to remain, and, although she had no canoe, she resolved to follow Manini-pounamu across the water.

With care, she plucked from a flax-bush the rito-harakeke, the young shoot of the plant. Had it snapped, the omens for her trip would have been unfavourable. But the rito-harakeke came out whole and strong, indicating a successful journey lay ahead of her.

So, with confidence in her gods, and determination, Hine Poupou continued her preparations. Standing at the southernmost tip of Kapiti, looking out to sea towards Rangitoto, she recited a maro – an incantation for success in her undertaking, for aid during the journey, and for strength and endurance to sustain herself.

After gathering up some bundles of harakeke which she tied around her waist to help her float, she cast herself into the sea and struck out strongly towards her home. As she swam she continued to murmur her karakia, and eventually, assistance did arrive in the form of Kakai-a-waro, the tribal taniwha, or dolphin of her Ngati Kuia people. Kakai-a-waro found her, far out in the sea of Raukawa, and guided and supported her over the long days and nights of her journey.

Hine Poupou stopped first at Toka-Kotuku, the Brother's Rocks. Then, rested and warmed by the sun, she repeated her incantations. Swimming on, she broke her journey next at Papanui-a-Puta, a rock outside the entrance to Pelorus Sound. Then she was back into the water for the last leg of her marathon trip.

At last Hine Poupou reached the shores of Rangitoto and the safety of her father's house. Father and daughter wept together. Although he was overjoyed to find his beloved child still alive, her father's anger was quickly aroused by the story of his son-in-law's treachery.

During her swim, Hine Poupou had observed an extensive hapuka fishing ground, previously unknown to her people. She asked her father to organise an expedition to the area, knowing that both Manini-pounamu and Te Hiki-paroa would join the trip. Concealed in the bottom of her father's canoe, Hine Poupou was among the group that set out for the fishing ground. As the fishing proceeded, she began chanting a powerful karakia to the taniwha of Raukawa. The resulting storm which lashed the hapuka grounds carried off many of the canoes into rough seas. Manini-pounamu, his brother, and all of his men were drowned; Hine Poupou and her father returned safely to Rangitoto, where, eventually, she remarried, and lived to a great age.

More than two hundred years have elapsed since this great and courageous feat. Since then, the image of Hine Poupou far out at sea, long black hair floating in the water, has been observed by several residents of the sounds. On Kapiti, two rocks on the cliff face at the southern tip are named 'Nga Kuri a Hine' – representing the animals left behind, howling on the beach for their heroic mistress.

Several versions exist of Hine Poupou's story. All agree on one fundamental fact: she did swim from Kapiti to Rangitoto after being abandoned by her husband. This version is faithful to a written account by the late Kipa Hemi Whiro, kaumatua of Ngati Kuia, of Okoha, Pelorus Sound.   *Tui MacDonald*

Sources

The author, who is Ngati Kuia herself, drew on Ngati Kuia oral tradition. A written account by the late Kipa Hemi Whiro, kaumatua of Ngati Kuia, of Okoha, Pelorus Sound, is contained in *The Marlborough and Nelson Districts*, Wellington, 1909.

ANNIE QUIN

1875–1955

Hawera in the 1930s and 1940s, when I grew up there, took pride in its achievement in music and drama. Central to both these activities was the Quin family and at the heart of that family was Annie Quin: Hawera's 'mother of music', the local paper called her. She was a big woman. I remember her commanding presence as a conductor, always bringing the best from her choirs, from our school choir, from *The Pirates of Penzance*, even encouraging the Presbyterian choir – simply by being in the congregation – to render extracts from *The Messiah* with greater verve. (Did she get special dispensation for this? The barriers between Catholic and Protestant were formidable, but Mrs Quin surmounted them.) She was always available for any musical venturing. In a small community traumatised by the Depression and then by the excitement and casualties of war, Mrs Quin was a steady point of reference.

Annie Winifred Flynn was born at New Plymouth on 12 July 1875. She was the eldest of Mary Jane (born Hall) and John Flynn's family of ten children. Her mother, daughter of a Fencible, was born at Auckland. Her father came from Ireland, following the gold-rushes from Ballarat to Gabriel's Gully before settling in New Plymouth. He fought and was wounded in the Taranaki wars. In 1879 the Flynn family moved to Hawera where John drove the stage-coach to New Plymouth via the coast road.

Annie's musical career started early. From her family Mary Jane formed the Flynn Family Orchestra. Each member could play at least two instruments; Annie, particularly gifted, played the piano, organ, and double-bass, and also taught music. In 1893 Joseph Higham formed a women's orchestra in Hawera and Annie became the double-bass player. She continued as bass player in many subsequent Hawera orchestras and as a piano accompanist for the silent movies and later for the 'Competitions'. She was also organist at the Roman Catholic church. As an accompanist she was able to play at sight, by ear, and to transpose with ease; as a conductor, which was the role she most enjoyed, she always established immediate rapport with her choir.

Annie Flynn married William Alphonsus Quin, a local accountant, in 1901. He was a reserved, studious man, keenly interested in local history. But he had no ear for music and, even worse for his family, little business acumen. He turned, unsuccessfully, from accountancy to dairy farming at Te Whareroa on the outskirts of Hawera, where he and Annie raised seven children. William Quin died on 22 September 1943; Annie on 29 December 1955, aged eighty.

The public facts acclaim Annie Quin, but the memoirs of her daughter, Veronica de Lacey, reveal not the person I remember – then in her sixties, serene, dignified, assured – but an overworked woman who struggled to maintain her family and in the process used music as a tool of trade rather than a means of self-fulfilment. 'The trivial round, the common task' did not furnish all she could have asked. Raising children in straitened circumstances, working exhausting hours on an unpromising farm, and, after the evening milking, journeying by gig to and from Hawera to play for the movies, left her with little profitable time to herself. Mozart was her favourite, but she had no time to practise and eventually arthritis in her fingers – a legacy from hand milking – meant that she was unable to play as she would have wished. Although she was a bread-winner, she had no money of her own. There came a Sunday in winter when, after attending early Mass at St Joseph's, the prospect of the cold ride home with shivering children was too much. 'We are leaving the farm,' she said, 'I've had enough.'

The Hawera Ladies Orchestra, 1894. Annie Quin, then Miss Flynn, is centre back, *New Zealand Graphic*, 4 August 1894. *Auckland Public Library*

It was a bold statement; it was customary to leave that sort of decision to the husband, and emotions, no matter how strongly felt, were not generally voiced. However, she prevailed. The family moved in 1920 back to Hawera, into a large dilapidated house which Annie put to rights.

Faith, ambition for her children, and the use she could make of music for others sustained her. Her marriage vows were irrevocable; husband and wife were both fiercely loyal, but, apart from mutual regard, shared religious beliefs, and affection for their children, they had little in common. Annie Quin could have become bitter, she might have allowed her talent to be consumed by toil. Instead she blossomed into the Mrs Quin I remember – 'Hawera's mother of music' – and mother too of that remarkable Quin family which performed so ably in the British Drama League festivals. She could do little to ease her own life but she enhanced that of others – always encouraging, always available.

In that regard she was not, of course, unique. Other New Zealand communities have relied on their Mrs Quins. She therefore has her place in New Zealand history, alongside those more widely known.   *Frances Porter*

Unpublished Sources
The author has drawn on her own knowledge of Hawera and on information provided by family members.

GUIDE RANGI
RANGITIARIA DENNAN

1896–1970

Rangitiaria Dennan, known always as Guide Rangi, was born Rangitiaria Ratema at Ngapuna in 1896. Her mother was Rimupai from Tuhourangi of Arawa and her father was Te Mango Ratema from Ngati Hinekura of Ngati Pikiao. Rangitiaria was educated at Hukarere Maori Girls' College in Napier. When she left Hukarere, Rangitiaria spent a brief time teaching at Torere and Ruatoki Maori schools. Ill health forced her to give up teaching and she became a trainee nurse at Napier Hospital. Failing health again caused Rangitiaria to abandon her chosen career and she returned home to Whakarewarewa.

In 1921 Rangitiaria began guiding visitors around the thermal attractions on a part-time basis. A year later she became a full-time guide. In a career spanning over forty years, Rangitiaria escorted many people around the Whakarewarewa thermal areas. In 1957 she received an MBE for services as a guide.

Rangitiaria was married to Te Aonui William Dennan, son of Makereti (Maggie) Papakura, and had no children. She died in 1970 and is buried at the Whakarewarewa village cemetery.

Her story is told by Emily Schuster:
Aunty was born in a little whare near Ngapuna. There were three or four other children but they all died in infancy. So her grandfather, Tene Waitere, was

quite concerned. And when his daughter became pregnant again, a tapu was placed on her. Aunty was a tapu child right up until the age of about eight or nine. When she was born, the tapu wasn't lifted from her because the tohunga that her parents consulted had died. That's why she had this period of isolation before she was cleansed.

Aunty said the biggest thing in her childhood was being brought up with the old people. It instilled in her nga mahi tapu [an awareness of sacred things] that was hard for such a young thing, but it was something that she had to come to terms with. She had to make all these personal adjustments. She couldn't say to people who didn't understand, 'You can't do this to me.' If you were born a tapu child, you can't eat ordinary kai. If the kai had been passed over the head of another person, she would just get up and leave. She'd say, 'I'm not well.' The thing with tapu is that it's instinctive. You know exactly how far the tapu applies to you. As Aunty said, the ones that you listen to are the pakeke [elders], you take what they're saying and apply this knowledge in your own way. But you never make that knowledge public, because it's what gives you your inner strength. So she led this lonely life.

As a child she was taken by the old people and brought up in the bush. When she was growing up, the birds in the bush, the wetas, and all the ngangaras [insects] were her mates. All the natural resources, the kiekie and the flax, were her playthings. Aunty knew about pawhara and how to eat it. In the month of September kiekie has a beautiful flower, it's delicate mauve with lovely blue stamens. Very mushy stamens. Aunty would tie kiekie leaves together to encase the flower. Then she would leave it like that for a couple of hours while off doing other things. When she came back to the flower, it'd got very soft. Aunty would eat all the custardy inside.

Then of course there was the karaka berries. The flesh of the karaka is orange and mushy like persimmon and has a beautiful sweet perfume. Aunty would get the karaka berries and boil them in the ngawha [boiling pools] all day. Then she'd soak them in cold water for two days. You've got to chill the karaka nuts right down, then you can eat them to your heart's content. That's what the Pakehas say was poisonous, toxic. Of course it's poisonous if you eat them untreated but the Maoris have eaten karaka berries for years.

When Aunty was fourteen years old, she went away and had the schooling. She became a prefect at Hukarere Maori Girls' College in Napier. Then she left school and applied to go nursing. She was always in the children's ward. When the other nurses couldn't get through to the Maori children Aunty could settle the kids down, no problem. But Aunty was never a robust person, she was always a sickly child herself. That weakness affected her teenage years. Working on the wards, she felt her health was giving in. The matron of the hospital said that she couldn't cope physically with the demands of nursing. Aunty said that was one of the saddest days of her life.

Then she came home to Rotorua and had nothing much to do. An old

Guide Rangi (Rangitiaria Dennan). *New Zealand Woman's Weekly*

guide, Guide Susan, said to her, 'Well, come out to Whaka and see what it's like. You're good at talking to people.' That was how she chose the profession. It was an outdoor life. Gave her a lot of fresh air, physical fitness, and kept her mentally alert. From then on she was a guide. As Aunty guided people around the attractions, she shared with them the knowledge she had and talked about Maori life so that outsiders could understand.

Aunty could taniko and she could whatu [weave] a cloak, but she would never get down on the floor. She just couldn't handle flax for either whariki [mats] or kits, but she was a meticulous gardener. Any hour of the day or night, she'd be in the garden. Roses were her favourite. A pink and a yellow creamy one were the two she loved. She liked all flowers and plants that kept bright *colour during the summer months, because that is the height of the tourist season. When she was talking with visitors and tourists, she would often bring them back to this house. Sometimes she would be given little mementoes by people who appreciated being here. Cricket balls, a Pakistani shuttlecock, the Australian League team's football, the Queen's signature. Aunty always said to the people who came to see her, 'Inside this whare is my home. It's a Maori world but my people have learned to walk with one foot in another world. Outside in the garden with the flowers and the trees there's the Pakeha world and that's you.'*

Once she met the Prince of Wales. She had taken him for a walk around Whaka, but on that day she was out in her karikari clothes doing her gardening. She was on the roadside sweeping and mowing her lawns. There used to be a drain along the front where she always lit a fire to burn the rubbish and the cabbage tree leaves. The reason Aunty had a cabbage tree growing was that the tukohu [cooking basket] is a little woven basket for cooking in the ngawha, made from cabbage tree leaf. The tukohu is not made from flax because the flax in the boiling water leaches out the bitterness. Anyway, Aunty looked up from her smoky fire and saw the Prince strolling along the street and invited him in.

I remember when we grew potatoes by the acre. At harvest time the men would go ahead and loosen the earth around the plants, but Aunty was always the one who struck a nest of field mice. The baby mice would be almost naked – bald. When Aunty found the nest you'd never see such a change in a person. She'd talk to the baby mice and bring the kids over and show them. Then when we finished sorting the potatoes, she'd put them back. Aunty had no children and anything small and just born was precious to her.

When we used to go out and catch pigeons, our job as kids was to pluck the birds and put the feathers in the right containers – one for each of the different colours. Then Aunty and the old man would cook the pigeons over an open fire. In the summer months when there was a big storm we used to go down to the beach and collect the long bull-kelp that was washed up on the shore. When it was still pliable we used to split it in half – open it up and dry it out. Then we'd make all these poha bags. When the kereru [pigeons] had been cooked on a spit over kongakonga [glowing embers], they'd be put in these kelp bags and the birds became preserved in their own fat. You could put up to a dozen birds in a bag.

I remember during the Second World War we also used to get pipi by the bag. Aunty would leave the shellfish in the kits and dunk them in the ngawha just to open the shells. Then we'd take out the meat and thread them on a string. These strings would be hung in the sun until they were completely dried. After this the pipis were packed and sealed in tins and sent off to the battalion [Maori Battalion]. They tasted just like salted chewing-gum.

During the war Aunty became a member of the St John's Ambulance. She never drove a car or an ambulance in her life but she was given the manual of how to do repair work on the motor. In the end, Aunty was made a serving sister of St John's.

Aunty spoke Maori all the time. When she went to school she had to learn to speak Pakeha, but Aunty always said tenei te ao o te Pakeha [this is a Pakeha world]. She reckoned we had to learn to live in the Pakeha world. But you don't have to be absorbed or get lost in it. Aunty always claimed that Rotorua and district had benefited by tourism. She saw Rotorua grow from a village to the city it is today, but we still live in the Whakarewarewa village. Aunty's descendants are working and walking in two worlds. We haven't lost our identity. Aunty said no Maori is a lost person, because you're tangata whenua and you've always got somewhere to go. This is your whenua and no one can take that away from you.

Because Aunty lived on her own and was busy guiding or working the garden, our family cooked the meals. Sometimes if she knew there was a pot left over and a boil up, next morning she'd come over for breakfast. Aunty enjoyed life, there's no doubt about that. She could always see the humour in it.

But in about 1965 Aunty got sick and went into hospital. She was suffering with cataracts and she also had throat problems. When she finished nursing and started guiding she always had chronic laryngitis. As she got older her eyes started to play up and she went into hospital. At that time she was at the height of her career. People would never leave her alone. But she was told that she had to slow down. We had to make her have a total rest. Now and again she'd get spasms and want to go guiding. Her mental deterioration happened slowly. I nursed her for five years.

Then one day Aunty said, 'By kare I'm tired' and went to lie on the sofa, and that afternoon she died. It was a lovely way to go. Quiet and peaceful.

Emily Schuster & Cushla Parekowhai

Published Sources
Barnett, S. and Sullivan, J. *In Their Own Words; from the Sound Archives of Radio New Zealand*, Wellington, 1968
Dennan, Rangitiaria. *Guide Rangi of Rotorua*, Christchurch, 1968
Dominion, 19 Aug. 1952; 15 Aug. 1970
NZ Herstory 1977, Dunedin, 1976
NZ Woman's Weekly, 30 May 1966
NZ Weekly News, 24 Aug. 1970; *NZ Weekly News*, 31 Aug. 1970
Zambucka, K. *Faces from the Past; the Dignity of Maori Age*, Wellington, 1971

IRIAKA RATANA

1905-1981

Iriaka Ratana was the first Maori woman to serve as a member of parliament. In 1949, a by-election was held to fill the vacancy in the Western Maori electorate caused by death of the sitting member, Matiu Ratana, Iriaka's husband. The first candidate chosen by the Labour Council to contest the by-election was a non-Ratana Labour Party member. However, Iriaka threatened to stand in opposition to him as an Independent candidate, as the Maori seats had in recent years been the preserve of the Ratana movement. Rather than risk the possibility of a split vote, the nomination was altered in Iriaka's favour. She was successfully elected, consolidating her victory the following year in the general election by polling the largest number of votes gained by any candidate.

Iriaka Ratana, c.1949. *New Zealand Free Lance Collection, Alexander Turnbull Library*

A descendant of the Tuwharetoa and Whanganui peoples, Iriaka was born in 1905 and grew up in the Ratana movement. As a young woman she travelled extensively around the country with the prophet Tahupotiki Wiremu Ratana and his followers. She married Matiu, one of T. W. Ratana's sons, and the couple brought up six children. Together they ran a dairy farm at Whangaehu, Wanganui, under the Maori Land Development Scheme. After Matiu was elected to parliament for Western Maori, Iriaka continued to run the farm herself.

When Iriaka delivered her maiden speech in parliament in 1950, she declared her priorities to be the problems of Maori people as a whole, and not just those of her own electorate. Commenting on the post-war migration to the towns and cities, she listed housing and health as two of the most pressing priorities. Her speech was well received in parliament and she was praised for her eloquence.

In 1955 Iriaka addressed the annual conference of the Maori Women's

Welfare League. She spoke of the feeling of apprehension and strangeness she experienced in those first early weeks when she was acutely conscious of her unusual position:

You know what it is to be a member of parliament in your first weeks in there?
I didn't know who was who, I didn't know my whereabouts. I had never met
or discussed anything with the Minister of Maori Affairs.

I felt like packing up and going home, but I thought to myself, 'No, I was
going to stand on my feet and see if I could do something to help my people.'

When I first became a member of parliament, I think I was hardly three
weeks in the House when I made my maiden speech, and I won't forget that
because it was a great ordeal.

At first there was opposition to the break in tradition represented by a woman taking political office. But Iriaka's personal qualities and the work she carried out ensured that she continued to be elected with a large majority until her retirement from politics in 1969. At the age of sixty-four, she stepped down and was succeeded by Koro Wetere, another member of the Ratana Church.

One of Iriaka's achievements was the Amendment to the Maori Purposes Act, 1954 (section 5, Ratana Settlement) which made possible the redevelopment of Ratana Pa and its surrounding land. Another of her initiatives was the Amendment to the Maori Purposes Act, 1967 (section 9, Amalgamation of titles to Wanganui Vested Lands), which gave protection to large areas of Maori land. She encouraged the settlement and development of rural blocks of land and pushed for wider availability of loan finance to fund that development.

During her twenty years in the House, the Labour Party occupied the Opposition benches. In that time, Iriaka involved herself in the settlement of disputes surrounding confiscated lands in Taranaki and Waikato. She also worked to strengthen relationships between the iwi of both areas. She was actively involved in health and education and supported the welfare work of the Maori Women's Welfare League and the Maori Council. She maintained a lifelong commitment to the Ratana movement. In 1971 her services to her people were recognised with the award of an OBE.

In December 1981 Iriaka died in Wanganui Base Hospital after a long illness. She was buried at Aramoho Cemetery, Wanganui.   *Tui MacDonald*

Quotation
para.4 Maori Women's Welfare League Records, 1952–1970, MS Papers 1396, folder 2, ATL

Unpublished Source
Maori Women's Welfare League, MS Papers 1396, ATL

Published Sources
Horn, Pauline, Leniston, Margaret, and Lewis, Pauline. 'The Maiden Speeches of New Zealand Women Members of Parliament', *Political Science*, vol.35 no.2, Dec. 1983
NZ Herstory 1984, Auckland, 1983

CATHERINE REDMAYNE

1825–1869

Miss Redmayne returned today from Jacob's River, but I regret to say not fully recovered from an unfortunate accident which she met with when proceeding there, having been thrown off her horse and broken one of the small bones of her wrist. The two concerts which she gave in Invercargill met with but moderate patronage, which may be chiefly attributed to the inhabitants being much scattered about, and the bad state of the roads, which of course makes our ladies loath to venture out at night.

To be a lone woman musician, entertainer, and music teacher in Otago in the 1850s and 1860s required considerable courage. Endeavouring to bring musical entertainment to Southland in 1859, Catherine Redmayne travelled by the ship *Geelong* from Dunedin to Invercargill, and between venues she travelled by horseback in treacherous conditions. For two concerts which she gave at the new Court House she borrowed a piano from one of the settlers and encouraged local amateur singers to perform solo or in choruses. After performing at a ball designed as the finale to her Invercargill visit, she was invited to entertain in Riverton. Travelling there by horseback on the rough roads, Catherine fell and injured her arm. Her pioneering spirit did not allow this to prevent her from giving a concert in Riverton a few days later.

Two years prior to her first Southland tour, on 26 November 1857, Catherine Redmayne arrived in Otago aboard the *Bosworth*, accompanied by her parents and two sisters. One month later she placed an advertisement with the Otago *Colonist* offering to give 'Lessons in Singing and the Pianoforte, according to the principles taught in England', becoming the first private music teacher in Dunedin to advertise publicly for pupils.

Within six months of settling in Dunedin, Catherine advertised her first concern with the title 'Grand Sacred and Miscellaneous Concert'. This took place at the School Room on 13 April and attracted an audience of more than two hundred. It was not the first public concert in Dunedin; acrobatic theatrical shows had visited the city and there had been a charity concert in 1852, but concerts offering a variety of items ranging from popular songs of the time to classical excerpts were a rarity and were welcomed by the small community of settlers. The first Redmayne concert included in the programme such choruses as Haydn's 'The Heavens are Telling', as well as vocal duets, and solo songs accompanied by the pianoforte (Catherine Redmayne) or the concertina (Mr Richardson). These were well received, but the item which brought the house down with rapturous applause was a concertina duet which ingeniously imitated the sound of the bagpipes. Naturally, in a community of predominantly working-class Scottish immigrants, such items from 'home' were at a premium. Indeed, a reviewer's otherwise enthusiastic notice was barbed with the observation that the concert lacked 'good old Scotch songs' and hoped that they would be included in future concerts.

550

Catherine's next advertised concert, 'A Grand Competition Concert' in which 'A Prize of Five Guineas' was offered to the best solo singer, did not come to fruition, possibly for lack of competent or willing competitors. Her second 'Sacred and Miscellaneous Concert', on 28 May 1858, contained music by Handel and Mozart, as well as quartets, duets, and solos of a light nature. She sang most of the solos and shared the pianoforte accompaniment with a Mr Calcutt.

Public pressure, along with poor attendance at the second 'Sacred and Miscellaneous Concert', contributed to a change in her programmes. Catherine's 'Indian Mutiny Fund Concert' on 19 July was rich with Scotch songs, well-known ballads, and favourite waltzes; it included the well-loved 'Imitation Bag-pipes' item which was repeatedly encored. Calling for support for the British during the Indian uprising, the concert raised nearly £28. The music was enthusiastically received, so much so that members of the audience were criticised for 'the vulgar practice [of] thumping their feet upon the floor, which is by no means a harmonious accompaniment'.

Catherine Redmayne also expressed her patriotic fervour through poetry. Of her four poems published in the Otago *Colonist*, 'The Indian Fund' is the most supportive of British colonialism:

> *Hail, hail ye valiant men,*
> *Of a thousand battles gained and won!*
> *Whose watchword is Onward, onward! still,*
> *Through every good, and through every ill:*
> *Whose arms can stay a giant's stride,*
> *Brave sons of England's boast and pride:*
> *Whose ships can wing the stormy sea,*
> *And ride triumphant in victory!*

In a later poem Catherine extolled the virtues of toil as the means for building a strong future for Otago, a sentiment which may also be applied appropriately to Catherine Redmayne's musical career:

> *We all alike are pioneers,*
> *Upon this virgin shore,*
> *Where each must track his ploughshare well,*
> *Or else no garnered store.*

From October 1858, as well as organising and participating in 'Concerts', Catherine Redmayne gave 'Soirees', 'Literary and Music Entertainments', and 'Lectures', travelling north to Lyttelton and Christchurch, south to Invercargill, and around the Dunedin district. By 1863 she preferred lectures to concerts, and in that year gave a series of nine public lectures around Otago in which she sang, accompanying herself on the pianoforte.

Catherine Redmayne returned to England in 1864 and is reported as having given a lecture on the Isle of Man on the subject of Otago and its gold-fields. She must have returned to New Zealand subsequently, for she died in childbirth in 1869 on the West Coast. There is no record of her having married.

Suzanne Court

551

Quotations

para.1 *Otago Witness*, 24 Sept. 1859
para.3 *Colonist*, 25 Dec. 1857
para.4 *Colonist*, 2 April 1858; *Otago Witness*, 17 April 1858
para.6 *Otago Witness*, 24 July 1858
para.7 *Colonist*, 2 April 1858
para.8 *Colonist*, 30 April 1858

Unpublished Sources

Lister, Clare. 'The Life of Catherine Redmayne from 1857 to 1864', BMus (Hons) research essay, Otago, 1989
Pearson, Ethel. 'The History of Music in Dunedin to 1925', MA thesis, University of Otago, 1941

Published Sources

Campbell, Margaret (Ethel Pearson). *Music in Dunedin*, Otago, 1945
The Cyclopedia of New Zealand, Christchurch, 1905

ROSEMARY REES

1876-1963

Rosemary Frances Rees was born in 1876. Her father, W. L. Rees, was a barrister and an MP. Rees worked as an actress in New Zealand and in 1910, aged thirty-four, she went to England to act, including appearances in two plays she wrote. During the war she was in charge of the 'Lena Ashwell Dramatic Party', a touring theatrical company which spent fourteen months of the war based at Rouen entertaining the troops. The strain of the work told on Rees, and she had two physical breakdowns during this time.

When peace was declared she returned to New Zealand on a troop-ship, entertaining the passengers en route. She organised her own theatrical company to tour the provinces of New Zealand; Ngaio Marsh was also a member of the troupe, and described it as 'one of the earliest attempts to found a permanent theatre in this country'. New Zealand audiences were unreceptive to what Rees's company had to offer; she put it down to a belief on their part that 'this company can't be any good or it wouldn't come here'. The company had to fold up because Rees was unable to pay salaries. She then went to Australia looking for work in the theatre.

While she was waiting for an opening, she wrote short stories and then decided to write a novel: 'I said to myself: "You may not be able to produce anything of much literary merit; but why not endeavour to produce a book just as well as your own limitations allow . . ."' Five weeks later she had written the manuscript of *April's Sowing*, which was published in 1924 by Herbert Jenkins. Rees returned to New Zealand to live and during her long writing career, which ended with *The Proud Diana* (1962) in the year before her death, she wrote thirty-one novels. All of these were published by English firms, and many went into American editions. By 1936 her English publishers estimated that 100,000 copies of her novels had been sold in Britain alone.

Like Louisa Baker before her and Essie Summers after her, Rosemary Rees was a highly successful and popular romantic novelist. She discovered a story pattern which her readers obviously enjoyed and which she continued to use throughout her writing life. Early in the novel, a woman and man meet; there is an attraction between them, but that is tempered by a feeling of dislike. What could develop into love is thwarted, often by misunderstanding on the part of one about the other, sometimes by the intrusion of another man or woman who appears to divert the attention of one of them. In Rees's novels there is often the distance of class: a poor woman in a lowly position – a governess, shop assistant, or lady's help – is sought out by an older and richer man. She thinks his attentions are insincere because of the differences between them. Against such odds the two must finally be brought together because they are destined for each other. As the heroine of *Life's What You Make It* (1927) observes of the man she will marry: 'Aeons ago in the dawn of the world she had lost this man who was her mate.' The complications of each novel differ; the outcome is always the same.

Rosemary Rees had a keen eye for changes in her audience's views on certain issues. In particular, over the four decades she was writing, her portrayal of Maori characters changes in accordance with the way that Pakeha thinking was changing. In the 1920s the Maori in her novels were dirty and primitive; by the 1940s she presented them as kind and well-mannered, if subservient. Likewise, Rees recognised that people's views on morality changed. In the 1920s divorce and premarital sexual activity were unacceptable in her novels; by the late 1940s some characters live together without marriage and without condemnation, though the hero and heroine still do not.

Rees was the most astute judge of her place in literary history; in 1936 she wrote to J. C. Andersen, who was preparing a New Zealand Authors' Week, asking if she was to be included: 'I am the best selling New Zealand author.' He included her. Robin Hyde reported meeting her at this event: 'likeable, clever Rosemary Rees . . . made no bones about writing to sell: "The highbrows take themselves much too seriously. Come along and have a cup of tea."'

Heather Roberts

Quotations
para.2 N. Marsh, *Black Beech and Honey Dew*, Auckland, 1966, p.141
para.3 R. Rees, 'How I Wrote My First Novel', Rees Papers, ATL, p.4
para.4 R. Rees, *Life's What You Make It*, London, 1927, p.255
para.6 Letter to J. C. Andersen, 22 March 1936, NZ Author's Week Correspondence, 1936, J. C. Andersen MS Papers 148, ATL; Robin Hyde, 'NZ Authoresses', in *Mirror: the home journal of New Zealand*, vol.18 no.8, Feb. 1938, p.20

Unpublished Sources
Rosemary Rees, 'Biographical Notes', Rees Papers, qMS, ATL
Rosemary Rees, 'How I Wrote My First Novel', Rees Papers, qMS, ATL

ELSIE REEVE

1885–1927

Elsie Reeve was born in the Hawke's Bay district in 1885, one of the three daughters of Alfred and Cornelia Reeve. Brought up probably in Auckland, where her father was a dentist, Elsie moved at the end of her schooling to London to study design at the School of Art attached to the Regent Street

Polytechnic Institute. After studying textile design for several years she was awarded the school's highest honour (a silver medal) and a scholarship which entitled her to another year of study. She now learned metalwork, concentrating on the technique of enamelling.

Elsie returned to New Zealand shortly before the First World War. Settling in Wellington, she made and possibly exhibited enamelled jewellery that attracted such patronage as that of Lady Ward, a popular figure in Wellington's social life. Elsie returned to England in about 1914, and remained there for the duration of the war, doing clerical work with the office of the Admiralty in London.

By 1922 Elsie had returned to New Zealand, settling in Auckland where she advertised her work in the *Ladies Mirror*, providing a Remuera address. Later that year she acquired space in the city centre from which she operated a successful business for almost five years.

Elsie was a confident and energetic woman who spent much of her time promoting the development of craft in Auckland. In July 1923 she was appointed convener of a special meeting of the Auckland Lyceum Club's Arts and Crafts Circle. At this meeting Elsie organised a lecture by a Wellington craftsman, arranged demonstrations of 'many beautiful and skilful crafts' by her female contemporaries, and 'demonstrated her own exquisite art jewellery'.

Elsie's 'art jewellery' had by 1922 become much more diverse than her prewar work. She now used gold as well as silver, and incorporated precious and

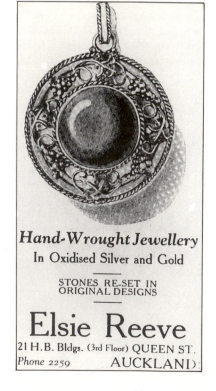

Hand-Wrought Jewellery
In Oxidised Silver and Gold

STONES RE-SET IN
ORIGINAL DESIGNS

Elsie Reeve
21 H.B. Bldgs. (3rd Floor) QUEEN ST.
Phone 2259 AUCKLAND

One of Elsie Reeve's advertisments. The pendant featured is typical of her work in which berries, vine leaves and tendrils were common motifs. *Ladies Mirror*, 1 August 1924 semi-precious stones as well as pearls in her designs. Elsie exhibited her jewellery as a working member of the Auckland Society of Arts from 1922 until her sudden death in Wellington in 1927. Her prices realistically reflected the time spent on each piece as well as the materials; she had a good business sense to back up her skills.

By 1922 Elsie had developed a personal style that is characterised by her use of berry, grape, vine tendril and vine leaf motifs with which she framed her stones and pearls. Her style and use of non-precious materials provides a link with the English arts and crafts movement with which she would have been familiar while in Britain and working within her crafts circle in New Zealand. Although quite individual, her work is similar to that of an Australian contemporary, Rhoda Wager, who worked in Sydney.

As jewellery began increasingly to be mass produced, the work of Elsie Reeve had originality and presence. She is thus a significant figure in the early years of the studio jewellery movement. *Angela Lassig*

Quotations

para.4 *Ladies Mirror*, vol.2 no.3, 1 Sept. 1923, p.19

Unpublished Sources

Auckland Society of Arts, Annual Exhibition Catalogues, 1922–27, and Minutes of Monthly Meetings, Auckland Society of Arts, Inc. Records, MS 19, AIM. The minutes for 21 April 1927 include an obituary.

Published Sources

Ladies Mirror, vol.1 no.1, 1 July 1922, p.33; vol.1 no.2, 1 Aug. 1922, p.44; vol.1 no.3, 1 Sept. 1922, p.37; vol.1 no.4, 2 Oct. 1922, p.43; vol.2 no.3, 1 Sept. 1923, p.19 (incomplete holdings, AIM)

TUMANAKO TE PUNA REWETI

1903 – 1980

Tumanako Te Puna Reweti (Aunty Hope) was born at Orakei Pa, Auckland, in 1903 and educated at St Mary's Convent in Ponsonby. At school Tumanako studied music, and later received a certificate from Trinity College of Music, London. Tumanako had no children of her own, but raised three whangai. She never married.

During the Second World War Tumanako served as a driver and motor bike dispatch rider in the Maori Unit of the Women's National Service Corps and the Women's War Service Auxiliary.

Tumanako was active in the Maori Women's Health League, which was founded after the war to promote Maori health, parenting skills, and childcare. Tumanako was also a foundation member of the Waitemata District Council of the Maori Women's Welfare League and later served on the Waitemata Regional Executive.

Tumanako was well known for her voluntary welfare and community work in the Freemans Bay area of Auckland. She received a British Empire Medal and a Silver Jubilee Medal for her services to Maori people. In 1977 she was also awarded life membership of the Labour Party. In her later years Tumanako was one of the kaumatua who gave awhina (help) and support to the protest group during the 501-day occupation of Takaparawha (Bastion Point).

Tumanako died on Anzac Day 1980, and is buried at Rewiti, Helensville.

Her story is told by Danny and Josie Tumahai.

Danny Tumahai: *I was brought up by Tumanako [Hope] at a very early age. She was Reweti. Her father was Te Puna Reweti and her mother was Ani Paora. Tumanako was Te Puna Reweti's only child and she belonged here at Orakei. I was a week old when she came and picked me up. We were at Panmure and she came out on this motor bike and picked me up. I don't know how – I look at someone riding a motor bike and wonder how many times she must have dropped me on the road! In my young days I was brought up with Hope at the old papakainga [village] down on the flat by the urupa [cemetery]. This place was known as Orakei Pa. From there we shifted up on to Bastion Point.*

Hope put me through my schooling years, and even though I was very young, I was starting to see what she was on about. We were coming away from the pa system and we had to accept the city life because that was starting to spread, starting to come right into our pa down below. Hopey could see that and she yearned to move from the marae into the city. Hope was always interested in people. It didn't matter who they were. She had a lot of interest in and aroha for these people. Especially if they were in the streets with nowhere to go.

At the Second World War she moved to the city and took on jobs working for the P & T [post office]. She drove trucks delivering mail and joined the women's army. She worked herself up to three stripes, as a motor bike dispatch rider. In the army she had this love for trucks and vans and motor bikes and things that women wouldn't usually do. I can remember going with her one day, when we moved an aeroplane. I was only young, just a little boy. We moved an aeroplane wing from Whenuapai to the Manukau Harbour. She was driving an articulated truck – it was really frightening backing up to the wharf, as if we were going to back right over the edge into the water.

Josie Tumahai: *My earliest memory of Hopey was when I was about six or seven and I lived up in Rewiti in Helensville, by our other Kaipara whanau. Hopey used to come on Princess Te Puea's big army truck. She used to drive Princess Te Puea out to the sandhills at Muriwai to collect bones from the old urupa. Then they'd take the bones back to be buried in the Taupiri Mountain. Anyhow, we used to have beautiful gardens that grew vegetables. When our vegetables got big, who would turn up and walk around the whole section, saying, 'I'll have that one, kid, and I'll have that one, kid'? Aunty Hope. I used to really dislike her. I used to say to my Mum, 'I don't like that lady. Here she comes again to take our kai.' Hopey was the one that kept up the ties. When she used to come and pinch our kumara, she was really keeping the ties open with us there at Rewiti and the rest of our whanau here at Orakei. It's all right jumping up and down saying this is our land, but you've got to know who the people are that you're doing this jumping for.*

Danny Tumahai: *When Hope moved from the pa, she wanted to go and work with the people in the Freemans Bay area. That's where she was really at home. In Freemans Bay she moved to about three houses and every house that she moved to was a little bigger than the last one. These homes were always filled by people from off the streets. People who had nowhere else to go. She put them up sometimes. I have to say it was to my annoyance, because I knew that it was starting to take its toll. But there was no stopping her. This was her life – that's the way she wanted to handle it.*

Josie Tumahai: *Hopey took on all the street kids – well, what we call street kids, but they weren't street kids to her. She just helped them and treated them like human beings. I think how she got them right again was because her houses were at street level. Her premises weren't flash by any means, but she cared for these kids and she did all this without the assistance of government or anything like that.*

Danny Tumahai: *When she moved to the city, she hardly ever came back to Orakei. There were some people who felt that perhaps Aunty Hopey has lost her mana, but as years went on even they saw what she was really about, her awhina was not only for her own people, but it was for everybody. I suppose I could explain it better like this: If there were a protest march coming down Queen Street for the right to occupy some land, then she would walk with these people, and right at the very head of it. And in the afternoon if there was another march coming down the other way and they were the opposition, then she would be in that march too. She just liked marching.*

So Hopey didn't have political interests of her own, but if she was confronted with a situation like that she could handle it. She was always with the person who was being pushed down, she felt she had to go and help them. She always wanted to comfort them. Even during the Bastion Point occupation. I don't know how many times I went to get her to go back home – not that I was against what was happening at Bastion Point, but Hope was getting on in age, and I wanted her not to be up there in the cold. So I used to go and get her and she says, 'All right, all right, I'll go home.' I see her get a cab and go and then I would turn on the TV that night and see that she had come back again. She was back with the protesters to awhina them. She had so much aroha for the people. Especially those who needed that kind of help.

Josie Tumahai: *I used to say to her, 'What are you doing up at the Point?' And she says, 'I know they're doing wrong, but when they fall, who are they going to have? I want to be there for them, I want to be there to pick them up.' And I never challenged her any more. I let her do what she wanted to do. There is logic to it.*

557

On the day of the Bastion Point eviction, Danny went and took her off. He's the right one to have brought her off, but the loud-mouths would have loved for her to stay because there were jibes flying, telling him to leave her there. I think that she knew all the kaumatua were here and irrespective of

This portrait of Tumanako Reweti hangs at the marae at Takaparawha.
Danny and Josie Tumahai

that, she stayed on the losing side. She always knew that the rest of the kaumatua would proceed with the take [cause] in the way they did. Kaumatua don't protest. Hopey did all the protesting for them. She wasn't outspoken, but she always supported people with take. When meetings were on she would always encourage you to go, but you would wonder why because she bloody well talked all the way through and you couldn't hear a damn thing. She made friends with everybody.

I used to love going to poukais [King movement meetings] with Hopey. We used to go down to the Waikato with clothes in the back of the car and drop them off at the gardens in South Auckland. She knew everyone working on the gardens. She'd toot her horn and they'd all come off the spud patches and she'd dole out clothes to the workers. When we got to all the different marae on the way, she'd stuff her little kit with all these dried eels and these would be our little munchies on the way back.

Aunty Hope could've had heaps of things if she'd wanted them. She owned land everywhere and she'd hock it off like nobody's business. Then she'd get the money and go to the car saleyards and buy a useless old bomb. She was truly incredible. But it was never for her personally, it was always for everybody else. When she went out she dressed beautifully. Fur coat, you name it. She always looked immaculate. But it wasn't like that. Hope wore clothes from second-hand shops. She'd buy a beautiful lace-front blouse, and it wouldn't fit her, so she'd split it up the back and have it pinned. And then she'd have something over the top. When she died we found everything was pinned. Hope was the original punk rocker!

Hopey didn't have a great sense of church. I think it was because she showed her church in what she did and in the way she treated people. Whereas other people may go to church and think very much church, but what do they show in the way they live their life?

But Hope was different. She used to sell poppies every Anzac Day down at the bus terminal – that was her area. She used to go from there up to the war memorial where they have the Anzac Day parade. She did that for years and years. Anyway, one Anzac morning Hopey was late getting to the cenotaph. It turned out she had died. On the day that she always paid special attention to – Anzac Day.

Danny Tumahai: *I think it was at her tangi that we really saw appreciation for the work that Hope did amongst the ordinary people living in the city of Auckland. When Hopey died the mayor came and asked if he might sleep the night beside the casket. So he arrived in his big Rolls Royce and then went home and came back in his pyjamas.*

Josie Tumahai: *The whole hui was her. You had Lange, Muldoon, and all them from parliament. You had the 'down and outs', the little old people with their dogs, the Head Hunters, the Black Powers, the whole works. Every nationality possible, all came down to Hopey's tangi. I thought this was tremendous, the lowly mixing it with the highly, all on common ground.*

Danny Tumahai: *That's the way I remember her, standing for unity amongst people. I think she would have wanted us to try and recognise each other with more tolerance and compassion. Hopey's greatest wish in all the world was for aroha and peace.* Danny Tumahai, Josie Tumahai, & Cushla Parekowhai

Published Sources
Auckland Star, 25 April 1890 (obituary)
Bastion Point; Day 507 (motion picture), dir. Merata Mita, Awatea Films, Auckland, 1980
Dominion, 28 April 1980 (obituary)
Evening Post, 28 April 1980 (obituary)
Inner City News, 14 Dec. 1979
NZ Herald, 28 April 1980 (obituary)
NZ Listener, 24 June 1978
Thursday, 26 Sept. 1974

LILLIE RICHARDSON *1868–1937*

ETHEL RICHARDSON *1869–1946*

FANNY RICHARDSON *1872–1954*

Lillie, Ethel, and Fanny were the daughters of George Frederick Richardson, runholder of 'Oaklands' in Southland, surveyor, and minister in the Atkinson government (1887–1891), and Lillie Richardson (born Augusta Marie Isobella White), the granddaughter of a British Admiral. Brought up presumably on 'Oaklands', the three girls moved with their mother and two brothers to Wellington in their late adolescence to join their father. It was here in 1890 that they pleaded with their father for permission to go on the government steamer *Hinemoa* to the sub-antarctic islands – 'because Pa knew Captain Fairchild so well'. Permission was granted; the sisters were aged between eighteen and twenty-two. They were high-spirited, adventurous, and unusually independent for young women of that period.

Ethel wrote an account of their journey in a 'six weeks log'. The early pages point out that it is *'not meant for all hands and the cook to read but only me and mine'*. The log is illustrated and documents shipping positions and conditions on the voyage, as well as describing the wildlife and scenes they encountered. This was a trio of Victorian tomboys in high buttoned boots, long skirts, and tight bodices, who thought nothing of capturing a strange horse at Bluff and, after fashioning a makeshift bridle of flax, each going for a bareback gallop.

They were familiar with the sea and ships, having earlier been on a circumnavigation of the North Island, and seemed to have no difficulty springing in and out of longboats in rough seas, or hitching their skirts into their long bloomers to ramble over the tussock and rocks of the barren islands. They played hide-and-seek with sea-lions, and squelched through bog to fetch grass for the cow on board.

The voyage took them to the Auckland, Campbell, Antipodes, and Bounty Islands – 'The various depots for the benefit of castaways all examined.' On Enderby Island, in the Auckland group, the *Hinemoa* released sheep and goats to provide food for possible 'castaways'. It was on this island that the *Derry Castle* was wrecked in March 1887. The girls examined the straw huts made by the survivors, who had lived there for several months.

The Richardson sisters were probably the first women to set foot on many of these islands. They were keen nature lovers, and knowledgeable about the fauna and flora they saw. Ethel wrote of Jackson Bay, on the West Coast:

O! the ferns, the ferns, they were so lovely – nobody can tell what they are like you must see to know and have eyes that can see too – millions of kidney ferns up the stem of almost every tree and plastered all over the ground in beds and beds and such bunches of umbrella ferns O! that's all I can say – we hopped around with delight, pure joy at such a lovely place.

Running down the track at Jackson Bay, 15 October 1890. An excerpt from Ethel Richardson's sketchbook journal of the sisters' expedition to the sub-antarctic islands.
Cynthia Cass

Of a storm in Milford Sound she wrote:

It was blowing like fury (I counted sixty waterfalls on one mountainside) and any waterfalls that shot clear of the face were blown up into sprouts of mist that looked like dozens of cannons fired out of the rocks in all directions – truly the dowdiest wretch in the world must have been rejoiced at such a sight.

The long hours at sea were spent flirting mildly with some of their shipmates, and entertaining themselves in various ways. Ethel carved a draughts set of native wood, lowering half the counters, impaled on a pen nib, into an ink bottle to colour them black. All three sisters took their violins on board, and practised them. An illustration showing a lonely goat bleating on an overhanging rock ledge with seagulls wheeling above and the sea far below bears the caption: 'This is meant to represent the sound of a piece of Lillie's music.'

Lillie was later to marry the ship's carpenter, Andrew Knox, and move to a sheep station at Pahiatua. They raised two children. Her consuming passion was horses, and it was said that she valued them above people.

Ethel was a draughtswoman with the Department of Lands and Survey, and spent the latter part of her life in a small cottage at Waiho Gorge at Mt Cook in order to be near a married man whom she secretly admired. She lived from her oil and water-colour paintings, which she sold to tourists through the Hermitage Hotel.

Fanny also remained single and lived in Wellington, where she devoted her time to painting in water-colours. She was a regular exhibitor at the Academy of Fine Arts and illustrated for the *Forest and Bird* magazine. She was an aunt much loved by many for her sense of humour.   *Cynthia Cass*

Quotations
All quotations are from Ethel Richardson's log, except for:
para.4 Annual Reports of the Marine Department, *AJHR*, 1890, 1891, H-18
Unpublished Source
Ethel Richardson's log is in the possession of the author, who is Lillie Richardson's granddaughter.

DOROTHY KATE RICHMOND

1861–1935

D. K. Richmond's interest in art was apparent early. At five, she was spending 'a great deal of time setting up "picture bricks" – cubes with six sides and piece of picture on each. She knows every little scrap of each of the pictures and pounces on them like a little hawk.'

Her father was James Crowe Richmond, civil engineer, politician, and painter. Art was his passion, and from the beginning he encouraged his daughter's talent. Her mother, Mary (born Smith), died when Dolla (as she was known) was four. The large Richmond-Atkinson clan gave her a strong female network which nurtured her throughout her life. Central amongst them was James's sister, Jane Maria Atkinson, who wished for her own daughters Dolla's 'gift for art'.

The Richmonds and Atkinsons were independent-minded intellectuals. Education was a priority – for daughters as well as for sons. Her father wrote: 'I also want her to have some art or profession by which if necessary she may earn a living and at all times feel as much independence as mortals have a right to feel.' Art and art teaching were both classed as suitable occupations for middle-class women; they were also seen by the Richmonds as a means of support.

Spending her early years in the midst of the clan at Nelson, New Plymouth, and Wellington, Dolla and her two older siblings, Ann Elizabeth (Alla) and Maurice, went with their father to England in 1873. Initially the twelve-year-old Dolla and Alla went to Miss Cranch's in Blackheath, where the discipline was strict and the drawing master ineffectual. They moved to Frau Professor Schulz-Bodmer's in Zürich (where their father was pleased to learn that they would also receive training in 'household work'), and on to Dresden to the warmth and custody of Jane Maria's friend Margaret Taylor.

Here, in 1875, Dolla discovered her artistic abilities for herself. As well as classes during the day with her female cousins, she had drawing classes with a Mr Simonsson. 'I don't like him very much but I like his lessons awfully. I have begun to draw heads from statues now, it is so beautiful.' Her sister also described Dolla's admiration of the German artist Ludwig Richter: 'his most charming works are his illustrations of fairy tales and his delicious pictures of German peasants and curly headed boys and girls.'

Back in London in 1877, Dolla was to get 'a fair start in painting' before returning to New Zealand. After a time at Bedford College for women, she secured a place at the Slade School of Art, University College. Submitting a portfolio of her work, she was encouraged by the Slade Professor, French painter Alphonse Legros, and soon promoted to the 'Life School', a class restricted to students with advanced drawing skills. In June 1879, Dolla received a silver medal and £3.3s for the best painting from the antique. She was subsequently awarded a prestigious Slade scholarship. Whether to stay in Europe and continue with her art education or return to New Zealand posed a continuing problem. As her father wrote to a friend: 'I half dread lest a rival should have been introduced into my home whose dwelling is and must be Europe, while mine . . . must be New Zealand.'

Financial considerations seem to have been the determining factor and the family returned to New Zealand by January 1881. The two sisters seemed to their uncle, C. W. Richmond, to have 'walked out of one of Walter Crane's books'. Since the death of her mother, when Dolla was only four, her elder sister, Alla, had become a surrogate mother. The close bond between the sisters remained, and on their return to what seemed the alien cultural environment of Nelson, the two sisters clung to each other 'like limpets and drowning straws'. Dolla set herself up to teach drawing, as she had been taught, importing £50 worth of casts and photographs for the purpose. Her own subjects were usually flowers and portraits; landscapes, decidedly a male preserve (and her father's forte) she approached more tentatively. In March 1881 Dolla was appointed to teach drawing at the newly established Nelson College for Girls.

To advance her career, she was overseas from 1885 to 1886 – fitting a pattern of travel becoming popular with New Zealand artists. During the 1890s, back in New Zealand, Dolla established herself professionally as an artist, and assisted in the care of her ailing father. James died in 1898. Dolla was elected to the council of the New Zealand Academy of Fine Arts in Wellington in 1898.

She returned to England in 1899, and attended Elizabeth and Stanhope Forbes' Newlyn School of Art. For the next few years she spent much time painting in Europe with Frances Hodgkins. Both artists were daughters of New Zealand painters, and may have met early on; in Europe they became good friends and painting companions. To Frances, Dolla was 'the dearest woman with the most beautiful face and expression', and the older painter gave the younger unwavering support, having faith in her talent. It was Dolla's ability to support and guide young artists that later endeared her to her pupils when she taught art in Wellington:

I remember her as one of the loveliest people I ever met, . . . not only to look at but as a character. I looked forward all week to the painting lesson with her. It didn't matter what one painted – she made one see the beauty in everything, and she encouraged us to feel we could tackle anything . . . Her paintings were very like her . . . serene and gentle and beautiful. She never struck me as being old, though she was rather bent – I can see her still, loping along Fitzherbert Terrace in her long black skirt and cloak, and carrying a bag of painting things.

Unlike Frances Hodgkins, Dolla always came back to New Zealand – torn perhaps between the stimulus of painting in Europe and support provided by the family networks in New Zealand. After 1903 she was to remain permanently in New Zealand. She never married, but remained close to the ever-extending Richmond-Atkinson clan – a source of wisdom and inspiration for the younger generations.

In 1904 Dolla and Frances Hodgkins held a joint exhibition in Wellington. Dolla was to participate fully in the Wellington art scene until her death. A long-standing member of the Academy council, she also encouraged the teaching of art at Wellington Technical College, judged exhibitions, championed the idea of a National Art Gallery, and was a regular Academy exhibitor. Private tuition was an assured source of income, and she taught a special class at Miss Baber's (later Samuel Marsden Collegiate).

After her return from Europe, she could command good prices. A strong personal approach marked her work, although she adapted her style to local changes in taste. Maori, for example, began to feature in her genre subjects. From 1906 she shifted from painting in oils to water-colours, and landscape became her primary subject.

D. K. Richmond died in 1935, a talented, independent woman, and a successful artist.   *Ann Calhoun*

Quotations

para.1 G. Scholefield, *Richmond-Atkinson Papers*, J. C. Richmond to M. Richmond, 10 Dec. 1866, p.222

para.2 G. Scholefield, J. M. Atkinson to Emily E. Richmond, 28 June 1876, p.422

para.3 G. Scholefield, J. C. Richmond to Miss Ann E. Shaen, 22 Aug. 1873, p.351

para.4 G. Scholefield, J. C. Richmond (circular letter), 31 March 1874, p.369

para.5 G. Scholefield, D. K. Richmond to R. H. and J. W. Richmond, 19 Dec. 1875, p.409; Ann E. Richmond to R. H. Richmond, 4 April 1876, p.416

para.6 G. Scholefield, J. C. Richmond to A. S. Atkinson, 12 Dec. 1876, p.430; J. C. Richmond to Ann Shaen, 20 March 1876, in F. Porter, *Born to New Zealand*, p.309

para.7 G. Scholefield, C. W. Richmond to Emily E. Richmond, 14 Jan 1881, p.480; A. E. Richmond to Annie Atkinson, 24 March 1882, in F. Porter, p.335

para.9 Quoted in E. H. McCormick, *Portrait of Frances Hodgkins*, 3rd edn, Auckland, 1990, p.41; Tosti Murray, *Marsden: The History of a New Zealand School for Girls*, Wellington, 1967, p.225

Unpublished Sources

Richmond-Atkinson family papers, Acc 77–253, ATL (The above quotations will mostly be found in the ATL collection but are sourced to G. Scholefield's edition and to *Born to New Zealand*, for easier access.)

Published Sources

McCormick, E. H. *The Expatriate: A Study of Frances Hodgkins*, Auckland, 1954

Nunn, Pamela G. *Victorian Women Artists*, London, 1987

Porter, Frances. *Born to New Zealand: A Biography of Jane Maria Atkinson*, Wellington , 1989

Scholefield, G. H. (ed.) *The Richmond-Atkinson Papers*, vol.2, Wellington, 1960

MARY RICHMOND

1853–1949

Mary Elizabeth Richmond was born in New Plymouth on 30 August 1853, two weeks after her parents arrived from England. The families of her father, C. W. Richmond, and her mother, Emily Atkinson, intermarried frequently and provided Mary with a large number of cousins, among them the artist Dorothy Kate Richmond. As the eldest of a family of nine, she was accustomed to taking responsibility for others from an early age. Her grandmother wrote to her: 'What a life of usefulness you may look forward to, the eldest of such a family.' This was an accurate prediction; usefulness within the family and on a wider stage was the keynote of Mary's life.

Some of Mary's women relatives in the lively Richmond-Atkinson clan were involved in good works, educational and community affairs, and politics. Her aunt, Jane Maria Atkinson, had a strong concern for the education of girls and with Mary's mother tried to promote a girls' college in Nelson. Emma Jane Richmond (1844–1921), second wife of Mary's uncle Henry, was active in charitable work, particularly for women prisoners. She became a member of the Taranaki Education Board in 1886, the first woman in the country to hold a position of this kind. Mary's cousin, Arthur Richmond Atkinson, was married to Lily Kirk (1866–1921), who joined in its early days the Women's Christian Temperance Union, a feminist organisation (she was elected Dominion president in 1901), and was one of the leaders of the women's suffrage campaign in Wellington province. These women, as well as Mary's father, who was a lawyer, a member of the House of Representatives, and a judge, provided her with examples of serving the community and also with useful contacts.

Mary Richmond was educated at the Misses Greenwood's school in Nelson and then in Geneva and Florence. She followed her sister Margaret in joining the staff of Wellington Girls' High School (later Wellington Girls' College) in 1884 and remained until 1890. After a brief engagement which ended when her fiancé died, she attended Newnham College, Cambridge, one of the foremost colleges for women in England. She left Newnham after one term because of illness in the family.

Her next important venture was to attend the Froebel Institute in London in 1896 to train as a kindergarten teacher. On returning to Wellington, she opened a kindergarten in a Sunday school room on the corner of Bowen Street and the Terrace and ran it from 1898 to 1912.

The children in her kindergarten came from prosperous families. For some years there had been free kindergartens for poor children in Dunedin. Mary decided to establish free kindergartens in Wellington; in 1905, she began to raise money for them and showed her organising ability by dividing the city into twenty centres, each with members and associate members committed to raising funds. As a result, the Wellington Free Kindergarten Union was formed, which for some years was called the Richmond Free Kindergarten Union in her honour.

For many years Mary's life was largely concerned with education. She became president of the Froebel Society in Wellington in 1905 and from 1906 to 1916 served on the board of governors of Wellington Girls' College, the first woman to do so. In 1907, she represented New Zealand at an Imperial Education Conference in London.

Her prominence in educational work in Wellington led newspapers to seek her opinions and to report her speeches at length. Her public pronouncements showed reservations about the value of higher education for women and ambivalence about the position of women. She wanted to see women in the Department of Education, on school committees, and on education boards, but blamed women alone for their virtual absence from these bodies. New Zealand women, she said in 1911, knew nothing, did nothing, and cared nothing about education.

Mary Richmond, seated centre, with her kindergarten in the Congregational Church Hall on the corner of Bowen Street and The Terrace in Wellington, 1904. *Miss Erica Hoby Collection, Alexander Turnbull Library*

(Teachers and 'the wonderful mothers of the past' were excluded from this condemnation.)

She believed that the intellectual girl was well provided for, but that the 'ordinary girl' lacked sound domestic training and that higher education unfitted girls for domestic life. She proposed that all girls except those of exceptional academic ability should take a compulsory 'Ordinary Girls' course. Every girls' high school must have a creche and a kindergarten attached and all 'OGs' would do a year's work in each. The following year, she said that natural motherhood was being bred out of girls. 'The old fashioned prejudice of man against the learned woman has more in it than appears at first sight.'

It is hard to list all Mary's many interests. She belonged to the Women's Social Progress Movement, was a member of the Hospital and Charitable Aid Board and its first woman office-holder, a member of the Society for the Protection of Women and Children, and the first president of the Pioneer Club. With others of her family, she was involved with the evangelical Forward Movement. She contributed to its journal, *The Citizen,* and for nearly eight years edited the League of Mothers' magazine.

An able speaker, Mary Richmond was also a fluent writer. Plays, articles, songs for kindergarten use, and, above all, rather mediocre verse poured from her pen over many decades.

Her interests were not confined to New Zealand. During several long stays in England she was active in various movements, including the British League of Unitarian and other Liberal Christian Women, on whose behalf she spoke all over the country. While in the United States, she visited schools and the famous colleges for women, Wellesley and Radcliffe.

Throughout her life Mary was closely involved in her family network, to an extent that she sometimes found oppressive. On a trip overseas as a young woman, she wrote to a sister:

I badly want to be free . . . this minding of the family is bad for the spirits and the body . . . the only thing I have gained by my trip is experience in nursing inflammation of the lungs.

But as she aged, she greatly enjoyed the visits of her young relatives. She took pride in her distinguished family and with her sister Emily prepared a two-volume typescript of family letters. Emily, her admiring shadow, who shared a home with her for many years, seems to have suffered more from immersion in the family than Mary, whose talents had won general recognition.

To the end of her life, Mary retained an interest in outside affairs. At eighty-seven, she planned study circles for the Women's Social Progress League; at ninety-one she joined the newly formed Religious Drama Society. Her many years of service were recognised a few months before her death by the award of a CBE, given her by the Governor-General at her bedside in Bowen Street Hospital.

Beryl Hughes

Quotations
para.1 F. Porter, *Born to New Zealand*, p.255
para.7 *Evening Post*, 8 April 1911
para.8 *Evening Star*, 2 Nov. 1912
para.12 F. Porter, p.307

Unpublished Sources
Richmond-Atkinson family papers (especially Acc 77–173, boxes 2 and 22, and Acc 84–56, 1/10, 2/1, 4/15, 6/8), ATL
Wellington Free Kindergarten Association Papers, MS Group 52, ATL
Published Sources
Dominion, 4 July 1949 (obituary)
Evening Post, 8 April 1911
Evening Star, 2 Nov. 1912
Harding, Olga. *One Hundred Years: A History of Wellington Girls' College*, Wellington, 1982
Porter, Frances. *Born to New Zealand: A Biography of Jane Maria Atkinson*, Wellington, 1989
Scholefield, G. H. (ed.). *Who's Who in New Zealand* (4th edn), Wellington, 1941

MERE RIKIRIKI

?1866–1926

Atareta Kawana Ropiha Mere Rikiriki was a prophet and healer of great standing in the Rangitikei-Whanganui district, notably during the first twenty years of this century. She was a descendant of Maata, an 1840s medium and healer from Oroua on the Manawatu River, who in an early Christian-reactive tradition cast out ngarara (lizards). She was a chief of Ngati Apa, based near Parewanui, near Scotts Ferry at the Rangitikei River mouth west of Bulls; through her Ngatitauwira hapu she had strong Rangitane connections. She was born about 1866; her mother was Mere Rikiriki Kawana Ropiha.

It was in the Rangitikei River that Mere Rikiriki is said to have baptised herself seven times in a special ritual invoking the Holy Ghost. From the traditions of Te Atihau nui a Paparangi and Ngati Apa we learn that it was this small woman, with a light moko and plaited hair, who not only foretold the coming of the prophet Ratana but also laid the foundations for his teachings. She was thus part of a prophetic tradition embracing Tawhiao, Te Kooti, Tohu, Te Whiti, Te Maiharoa and Ratana. Te Kooti, for example, had foretold not only the rise of Rua Kenana, but also the coming of a leader in the west who would restore the Maori to a new footing for self-respect and mana. Te Whiti and Tohu, both of whom had close links with Ngati Apa, gave her the name Mere Rikiriki at Nukumara, in South Taranaki.

For some time Mere Rikiriki's prophecy pointed to one of her followers, Panau Tamatai (whom she called Mihia), as a future leader, but he disobeyed God's word, fell from grace and became a cripple. Others around Mere Rikiriki acting as apostles were Mawe Anaru, Mareikura, Ruka and Moe. It eventually became clear that the chosen one was her kinsman T. W. Ratana, a farmhand working on family land near the Turakina River.

He sought Mere Rikiriki's counsel as he struggled with his destiny. She passed on her faith-healing gifts and gave names to two of his sons, Arepa and Omeka (Alpha and Omega), whom she refused to touch or baptise because of their great spiritual power. It was while Ratana was camping with them on the beach near the mouth of the Whangaehu River that he was given one of his most salient signs, the beaching of two large whales. Mere Rikiriki's teachings led

Ratana to adopt his Christian-based beliefs and his strong emphasis on the Treaty of Waitangi.

By 1918 Ratana's fame as a prophet, healer and leader had spread far beyond his tribal area and his farm, located between the Whangaehu and Turakina Rivers. Although Ratana the place became a healing and spiritual centre for the Ratana movement, which continues to this day, by 1928 Ratana himself had moved, as foretold, from his spiritual to his earthly mission, in politics.

Another significant, but much less known, spiritual legacy of Mere Rikiriki is the Maramatanga movement. While Ratana's religious emphasis was on repudiation of the past and destruction of old tapu, Maramatanga blends traditional Maori belief and Catholicism. The movement's founder was a relation and contemporary of Ratana, Hori Enoka, who became Mareikura. The close bonds between this family and the Kingitanga remain to this day.

By 1912 Mere Rikiriki, herself an Anglican, had formed the Holy Ghost Mission church based at Wheriko (Jericho) church, at wind-swept but then populous Parewanui. Some of the movement's traditions and observances draw directly on her life: 27 July 1910, for example, is still commemorated at the meeting-house Matarangirei, Parewanui, as the ra or day she made manifest the word of God. Her mana may be appreciated by King Tawhiao's presentation to her of a still-prized flag 'E Te Iwi Kia Ora', which carries a white crucifix and brown boat on a blue background. She died on 13 March 1926 at Parewanui. The strength of the movement is found today among Maori communities at Levin, Wanganui, Ohakune, Hastings and Auckland, where many of the descendants of the original group reside. Mere Rikiriki was married to Inia Te Rangi, and though she bore no children, the mokopuna of her brothers Tamati and Tiemi maintain the line today.

She is remembered by her mokopuna as:

– *A marvellous person – she could see right through you and she could see a long way off.*

– *She was all the time within herself in a room . . . It was an old bedroom with an armchair and photographs of her old people, mostly of her brothers and her grandfather.*

– *She was probably meditating there. There was a feeling, I don't know, a spiritual quality. We children used to play 'tangi' and look at the tupuna on the walls and cry.*

– *We used to hear her singing the waiata.*

– *She had her humorous side too.*

There are a few physical remnants of the great village at Parewanui. However, the legacy of Mere Rikiriki has two significant strands, one essentially non-denominational, non-racial and also political, the other Catholic and traditional Maori. Together, they still wield considerable influence spiritually and culturally today.   *David Young*

Unpublished Sources
The author talked to Morgan Kawana, Elizabeth Reti, Ruth Harris, and other members of Mere Rikiriki's whanau. All quotations are from these interviews.

Sinclair, Karen. 'Maramatanga: Ideology and Social Process among the Maori of New Zealand', PhD thesis, Brown University, 1976

Published Sources

Elsmore, Bronwyn. *Mana from Heaven: A Century of Maori Prophets in New Zealand*, Tauranga, 1989

Henderson, J. *Ratana, the Man, the Church, the Political Movement*, Wellington, 1972

Jones, Pei Te Hurinui. 'Maori Kings', in *The Maori People in the Nineteen-Sixties: A Symposium*, ed. Erik Schwimmer, Auckland, 1968, pp.132–73

TE KIATO RIWAI

1915–1967

Although it was just daybreak, Te Kiato (Kia) Riwai had already placed her first tray of small cakes in the oven at her tiny city flat in Cashel Street, Christchurch. She busied herself creaming the butter and sugar for the next batch of baking. By eight o'clock her freshly baked cakes and biscuits would be packed in a basket ready for the long journey by tram to her cake and confectionery shop in Redcliffs.

Kia considered the day before her. On this particular day her cousin's wife would come to the shop with Kia's two young nieces. It was one of those occasional visits that Kia thoroughly enjoyed. The women would work together through the morning and then take the children to the nearby beach. In the late afternoon, on her way back to town, Kia would stop off at her old school, Te Wai Pounamu College. There, she would visit the girls and staff as well as attend to some business of the Old Girls' Association.

After tea, Kia planned to attend an Otautahi Cultural Club evening. She was extremely pleased that the club was doing well. She remembered back to the pre-war years when she played her part in getting the club up and running.

Kia looked forward to the late evening. After the picture theatre traffic had died down, her cousin would take her out for her daily driving lesson in his Morris Cowley van. She liked the van, which was about First World War vintage. Unlike modern cars, the van was sedate and manageable. She smiled as she thought about her driving lesson. After being stopped on several occasions, she and her cousin had finally convinced traffic and police officers that the car's very slow speed was simply that of a nervous woman learning to drive, not of burglars casing the city shops! How much easier life as a single woman would be with her own transport.

Kia was born on the Chatham Islands in 1915, one of eight children born to Mere Riwai. In the mid-1920s her family came to New Zealand to live in Brougham Street, Christchurch, near relatives from the Chathams who had already settled there.

Kia's early education at Te Wai Pounamu College was not completed because of the Depression, but she maintained strong links with the college throughout her adult life. In 1941 she established the Te Wai Pounamu Old Girls' Association of which she was the second president, a position she held for twenty-five years. Kia also gave many years' service as a member of the school's board of governors.

As a young woman, Kia played team sports, including outdoor basketball and hockey for the Otautahi Maori Club. She was chosen for the New Zealand hockey team, but could not play because of measles. Kia also loved to play cricket, and looked very handsome in the knee-length box-pleated shorts, white shirt, and peaked cap of her club, Mai Mai.

Kia was active also in the administration of the Otautahi Maori club, which was a social centre for Maori people living in Christchurch. In many ways the club's activities were a response to the dislocation of whanau from traditional hapu and iwi structures. Kia and her cousin Mary Hargreaves made an awesome team in the running of the club and the organisation of events. Kia preferred to work behind the scenes, and her gentle but firm manner complemented Mary's tougher, more direct style.

At the outbreak of the Second World War, Kia was prominent in the formation of the Otautahi Concert Party, which raised funds for the war effort and farewelled soldiers going overseas. She also established a club for soldiers on leave.

When the New Zealand government eventually accepted women volunteers for war service overseas, Kia was selected as a member of the VAD (Voluntary Aid Division). The women received nursing training in New Zealand before being posted overseas. While on leave before her posting, Kia confided to a friend that, as part of their instruction about their duties, the trainee nurses were left in no doubt that it was preferable for New Zealand soldiers to receive favours from New Zealand nurses than from foreign prostitutes.

Once overseas, Kia served in the hospital at Caserta in Italy, and later worked in a hospital in Kent, England, caring for ex-prisoners of war. Before returning to New Zealand on the hospital ship *Maunganui*, Kia was posted to a hospital in Folkestone for soldiers on leave. She was awarded the British Empire Medal for her war service and invited back to England for the Victory Parade.

After the war Kia ran her own cake and confectionery shop for six years. The business provided security and suited her well. It allowed her to work in the shop until early afternoon, and have the remainder of the day free for her activities in the local Maori community. She was thus able to strengthen her community links and networks again after her absence overseas.

In 1952, Kia was appointed Welfare Officer in the Department of Maori Affairs, Christchurch. By this time she had a driver's licence, although her driving was erratic, and in her work she clocked up many miles in her car. During this period of her life, Kia was awarded the MBE for her outstanding service to Maori people.

Soon Kia was working to set up branches of the Maori Women's Welfare League in the South Island, the first being in Tuahiwi, Christchurch, Rapaki, and Taumutu. When the executive members of the league visited the South Island, Kia drove them everywhere. On their arrival at Otakau, the executive told, with some horror, tales of their frightful trip over Arthur's Pass with this 'lunatic' driver. Kia, however, was blithely unaware of the panic about her when she sallied forth on the road.

Ten years after joining the Department of Maori Affairs, Kia took up the position of Senior Welfare Officer for the South Island. During the fruit-picking season, she would spend several months in the Nelson/Motueka area, providing advice and services to the seasonal Maori workers, especially the young women, who flocked into the area.

Kia set up culture groups and encouraged local competitions. Her assessment was that the dislocation felt by the young seasonal workers was similar to that experienced in Christchurch thirty years earlier. She felt that the way to achieve stability during the season was by helping these loosely bound groups to forge new friendships and feelings of self-esteem. The culture competitions flourished, inspiring Kia to promote the idea of competitions for culture groups from throughout the South Island. The first of these was held in 1965. On top of her heavy official workload, Kia still maintained her Maori committee work in and around Christchurch.

Kia took a special interest in the trade training schemes established by the Department of Maori Affairs. Trade trainees stayed at Rehua Hostel, and Kia was a key supporter of the plan to build a marae on the site. After her death, a community hall was added to the marae complex at Rehua, and named Te Kiato Riwai in recognition of her work for the trade trainees.

In the last months of her life, Kia had a mastectomy. She never fully recovered from the operation, and died on 31 August 1967, aged fifty-two. Her tangihanga was at Rehua marae, and a service held in Christchurch Cathedral was attended by friends and relatives from throughout New Zealand.

Kia Riwai was a woman of considerable charm and warmth of character, who brought a comforting, steady influence into her community welfare work. Some were irritated by her slow, measured response to Maori issues. In later years, some mistook her slowness for lack of ability, and failed to appreciate the extent of her contribution to the Maori communities throughout Te Wai Pounamu (South Island). Kia is now widely respected for her work and for her energy and commitment in initiating positive responses to the breakdown of traditional social systems.

Miriama Evans

Unpublished Source
Information was provided by a number of friends, relatives and colleagues of Kia Riwai.
Published Source
Te Ao Hou, no.61 (1967–8), p.3

HILDA ROSS

1893 – 1959

Hilda Ross was born Grace Nixon in 1893 in Whangarei, the daughter of Adam Nixon, a fireman. Her early childhood was spent in Sydney, but in her youth she returned to Auckland where she studied music. In 1904 she married Harry Campbell Ross and adopted the names Hilda Cuthberta. A year later they moved to Hamilton where their two sons were born. Harry Ross established his own furnishing company and for a while Hilda Ross taught music to help supplement their income.

Hilda Ross cited the 1931 Napier earthquake as the time she first became involved in the community affairs of Hamilton. She had in fact been active much earlier, particularly in the interests of children. During the 1918 influenza epidemic she cared for the sick. In 1927 she was instrumental in founding the Waikato Health Camp movement for children; in her Christmas holidays she regularly helped out in the camps. The Depression years also saw her working to help the needy. Her interest in music led her to found the Hamilton Choral Society and she played for the Operatic Society and the Orchestral Society.

After the death of her husband in 1940, Hilda Ross entered local politics. In 1941 she won a seat on the Hamilton Hospital Board. Three years later she was elected Hamilton's first woman borough councillor. In 1945 she became the deputy mayor of Hamilton, but resigned from the council the same year when she entered parliament.

Hilda Ross first won the Hamilton seat for National on 26 May 1945 in a by-election – only the second woman to represent the National Party. In 1946 she stated that a woman getting into parliament 'is like getting a camel through the eye of a needle'. It was particularly difficult for a National Party woman to become an MP, because of the party's reluctance to put women candidates forward in safe blue-ribbon seats.

When the National Party came into office in 1949, Hilda Ross was appointed the Minister for the Welfare of Women and Children. This was a new position, and one without departmental responsibilities. At first, Hilda Ross had little to do, but was not willing to be a token woman in the cabinet. She worked hard for the benefit of women and children. Many people came to her with their problems, believing that because she was a woman they would get a more sympathetic hearing.

Hilda Ross was always ready to help those in need (making gifts from her own purse if necessary), but she was quick to resist anyone she thought was trying to impose on her. A firm, kindly but decisive woman, she gave credit where credit was due, regardless of party. In her maiden speech she spoke of the possibilities for bipartisan co-operation amongst the women MPs. She also stated that it was the welfare of the community that was of interest to her, not party political warfare.

Her greatest honour came in 1956, when she was made a Dame Commander of the British Empire. She acknowledged it as recognition of work done by a woman, for women. Dame Hilda Ross represented Hamilton for four years, until her death in 1959. She gave New Zealand women an important legacy by helping to break down the prejudice against women in parliament.   *Vanya Bootham*

Quotation
para.4 Quoted in B. Gustafson, *The First 50 Years*, p.284

Unpublished Sources
Ann M. Burgin. 'Women in Public Life and Politics in New Zealand', MA thesis, Victoria, 1967
NZ Biographies: 1953, vol.3, p.108; 1959, vol.3, pp.110–20; 1976, vol.2, pp.105–6, ATL
Vanya Bootham. 'Women Political Candidates in New Zealand General Elections 1919–1951', BA
  (Hons) research essay, Victoria, 1989

Published Sources
Evening Post, 3 Jan. 1956, p.8; 7 March 1959, p.7
Gustafson, Barry. *The First 50 Years: A History of the New Zealand National Party*, Auckland, 1986
McLintock, A. H. (ed.) *An Encyclopaedia of New Zealand*, vol.3, Wellington, 1966

NZ Herald, 29 May 1945

NZ Parliamentary Debates, vol.268, 27 June–3 Aug. 1945

Scholefield, G. H. (ed.). *Who's Who in New Zealand*, Wellington, 1951

Tourist and Publicity Dept. *Biographies of Members of the House of Representatives*, Wellington, 1960

Weekly News, 25 May 1955

ETTIE ROUT

1877–1936

Ettie Rout campaigned for 'safe sex' seven decades before the term was coined and long before the concept was an acceptable one – especially for a woman to propose.

In the First World War, having discovered that venereal disease was a major problem for the New Zealand Army, she set out to find means by which soldiers could protect themselves from infection. Her means were ultimately adopted officially by the New Zealand Expeditionary Force, but she received no credit; in fact her name was banned from the columns of New Zealand newspapers for the duration of the war. To many (including most New Zealand women), she was 'the most wicked woman in Britain'; to the soldiers, however, she was 'a real guardian angel of the Anzacs'.

Ettie Rout was born in Tasmania on 24 February 1877 – along with her twin sister, Nellie (another sister followed two years later). Her father had a hardware shop and the family were Congregationalists. They came to New Zealand when Ettie was seven and settled initially in Wellington, where Ettie won a scholarship to high school but had to forfeit it because of her father's bankruptcy. The family later moved to Christchurch and, at Gilby's College, Ettie studied shorthand and typing. She mastered these with such skill that she soon joined the staff of the college, and then set up her own business in Chancery Lane as a freelance shorthand typist. She was one of the first women appointed by the government to take down evidence in the Supreme Court and on commissions of inquiry, and won a reputation as the fastest in the field, often working through the night to be able to present a transcript the next morning.

She was a 'physical culture' enthusiast, attending classes at the Christchurch School of Physical Culture, run by Fred Hornibrook, the bombastic Irishman whom she later married. A keen tramper and swimmer, as well as a successful businesswoman, she tended to berate other women for being so conformist that they let themselves be kept in submission. She urged them to get rid of the artificial constraints – like corsets and lack of fitness – that stopped them from taking the place God intended them to have as 'the equals of men, physically and mentally'.

To her, non-conformity was second nature. She wore short skirts, men's coats and hats, sandals, and trousers for tramping and cycling; she also bobbed her hair years before it was fashionable to do so.

A free thinker and socialist, she became involved in the labour movement in 1907 when she was engaged by the farm workers and their employers jointly to take down evidence in the Arbitration Court and provide a verbatim report

Ettie Rout, wearing the badge of the New Zealand Volunteer Sisterhood, the group of women she organised to work among the troops overseas in 1915. *Jane Tolerton*

of their dispute case. She was by no means an unbiased reporter, not only giving her services free to the union, but also advising the farm workers' advocate throughout the case. In 1910 she was founding editor of the Labour paper *Maoriland Worker* (which later became the *Worker,* then the *Standard*).

In 1915 she set up the New Zealand Volunteer Sisterhood, a group for women who wanted to go overseas and work among the troops. The government opposed the movement; policy decreed that only trained nurses should be allowed to go overseas. Undeterred, Ettie raised the money to send the first group to Egypt in October 1915; she herself left in December.

She arrived in Cairo in March 1916 and discovered that venereal disease was a major problem among the New Zealand soldiers. Most of the New Zealand troops, however, left for France a month later. Ettie ran canteens for the mounted troops who remained. Concerned that the men's physical and psychological health should be better looked after, she not only provided rest and recreation facilities, but trekked across the desert to deliver food (especially huge barrels of fruit salad) to men on patrol.

Her health broke down under pressure of hard work; the malaria she contracted was to plague her intermittently for the rest of her life. At the end of 1916 she visited England, and found not only that the venereal disease problem was very bad, but also that the army authorities were still doing very little about it.

In June 1917 she really took up her campaign, moving to England to learn everything she could about venereal disease prophylaxis methods. She visited the foremost experts – 'You need not apologise for talking plainly,' she wrote with characteristic directness to one doctor, 'I have been inoculated against all moral shock' – and put together a prophylactic kit (containing calomel ointment, Condy's Crystals, and condoms).

These doctors, who treated venereal disease as a medical problem rather than a moral one, formed one side of the debate about how to fight its spread. The other camp believed that venereal disease was punishment for immorality and that the fear of catching it was necessary to the maintenance of social virtue.

To Ettie,

the question at root seems simple to decide. Is sexual relationship a necessity for the troops or is it not? The troops have certainly decided, Yes. Then our duty is to make that relationship accessible and harmless. Why get into moral tangles?

Ettie had set out to be a catalyst, confining her own actions to research and lobbying. But, in spite of the fact that the New Zealanders had the highest venereal disease rate among the colonial troops, the army authorities took no action, hamstrung, they said, by the failure of the New Zealand government to confront the issue.

Frustrated, Ettie decided to write a series of articles to publicise the issue back home and push the government into action. Only one article was ever published, in the *New Zealand Times* on 24 October 1917. But that was enough. The outcry came mainly from a wide range of women's groups, outraged at Ettie's suggestion that soldiers be provided with prophylactic kits and licensed brothels.

A deputation of women asked the prime minister to get Ettie away from the New Zealand soldiers. The government was unable to comply, but it could defuse the situation by cutting off from the New Zealand public any information about Ettie's activities overseas. In early 1918 the cabinet banned Ettie from the pages of New Zealand newspapers under the War Regulations. Editors faced a fine of £100 if they mentioned her in their columns.

About a month after her article was published in New Zealand, General Richardson, the officer in charge of administration of the New Zealand Expeditionary Force in Britain, finally decided to issue kits. While selling kits had brought wrath down on Ettie's head, there was no outcry when the army started handing them out – not only free, but as a condition of getting a leave pass – because there was no publicity about it. Nor was it ever made known in New Zealand that the army had adopted the kit Ettie had put together.

With one plank of her prophylactics programme achieved, Ettie left for France in April 1918 to look for a brothel to organise as a 'safe sex' spot for New Zealand soldiers.

Many New Zealand First World War veterans remember her rounding up her countrymen on the platform of the Gare du Nord as they arrived from the front. She checked whether they had their kits – and advised them not to have sex with 'boulevard girls'; Madame Yvonne's *maison* in Rue St Lazare made 'safe and suitable provision for the sexual needs of the troops', the little card she handed out said, adding that she inspected it regularly with a (French) doctor.

Ettie ran a total social service for the troops in Paris: offering accommodation, looking after gear and money (she made a practice of getting men to hand over their money and drip-feeding it back to them so that they would not spend it all immediately), advising on cheap places to eat, and visiting those who fell ill. In her reception room at New Hotel, where she had taken over several floors, she sat behind a table (with a German groundsheet for a tablecloth) and greeted a line-up of Australians and New Zealanders who came with a myriad of problems and requests. As each came forward, she clasped him and kissed him on the cheek. With her system in full swing, she claimed that New Zealanders had the lowest venereal disease rate for any troops coming to Paris.

After the Armistice Ettie continued her operation in Paris, joined by Fred Hornibrook, who had spent the previous year as prophylaxis lecturer to the troops (the idea and the speech notes provided by Ettie). In mid-1919 she went to Salisbury Plain, in England, where New Zealand troops were massed before sailing home, and gave lectures and individual counselling sessions – often on how to tell wives or girlfriends about having contracted venereal disease.

In 1919 Ettie and Fred went to Villers-Brettóneux, a little town on the Somme which had been almost totally destroyed in the war. Working under the auspices of the American Red Cross, they set up a canteen in the dilapidated schoolhouse and provided a daily hot meal for about 200 children.

In May 1920, the couple settled in London and married. Ettie continued her campaign. Her 1922 book *Safe Marriage*, advising women on venereal disease prophylaxis and birth control methods, was banned in New Zealand. She also wrote books on diet, exercise, and Maori culture. Fred became a very well-known physiotherapist, his prominent clients including Winston Churchill, H. G. Wells, and Arnold Bennett.

In 1936 Ettie returned briefly to New Zealand before moving on to Rarotonga, where she died of an overdose of quinine.

The obituary published in a number of New Zealand newspapers called her 'one of the best known of New Zealand women' – a curious statement since the press had not been allowed to mention what she was 'best known' for at the height of her notoriety and she had been out of the country for about twenty years.

Ettie's 'safe sex' campaign – run at a time when syphilis was a killer disease, and the less dangerous but much more widespread (and incurable) gonorrhoea was responsible for much infertility in women – has obvious parallels in the current debate on how to contain the spread of AIDS. 'Safe sex' or no sex, condoms or celibacy – the divide in the debate remains the same. And Ettie's advice, stated with characteristic exasperation, is as timely now as it was seven decades ago:

we shall never conquer this greatest of national perils simply by spreading pious fluff over the landscape. Cannot we simply take our courage in our hands now, and face the facts of life as they really are?

Jane Tolerton

Quotations
para.2 F. A. Hornibrook, *Without Reserve*, pp.113–4; E. Rout, *Two Years in Paris*, p.28
para.4 E. Rout, letter published in *Lyttelton Times*, 16 July 1904
para.10 E. Rout to Dr Archdall Reid, 22 July 1917, AD 24/46, National Archives, Wellington
para.12 E. Rout to Col. Samuel, 26 Aug. 1917, AD 24/46, National Archives, Wellington
para.24 *Evening Post*, 19 Sept. 1936 (obituary)
para.25 E. Rout, 'Venereal Disease Among Our Troops', unpublished article written 29 Aug. 1917, AD 24/46, National Archives

Published Sources
Charity, F. H. 'Ettie Rout, M. A. and Easy Notoriety: A Sketch and Some Thoughts', *Quick March*, 25 May 1918, p.11

Hornibrook, F. A. *Without Reserve*, London, 1935

Rout, E. A. *Maori Symbolism*, London, 1926

Rout, E. A. *The Morality of Birth Control*, London, 1925

Rout, E. A. *Native Diet: with practical recipes*, London, 1926

Rout, E. A. *Restoration Exercises for Women*, London, later renamed *Stand Up and Slim Down*, and
finally published in 1959 as *Health Culture for Women*

Rout, Ettie. *Safe Marriage*, London, 1922, later published as *Practical Birth Control*, 1926

Rout, E. A. *Sex and Exercise*, London, 1925

Rout, E. A. *Two Years in Paris*, London, 1923

Rout, E. A. *Whole-Meal: with practical recipes*, London, 1927

PUHI ROYAL

1899–1972

Puhi Royal was born Elizabeth Te Puhi o Rakaiora Taiaroa at Puketeraki,
Otago, in 1899. She had ancestral links with the people of Ngai Tahu, Ngati
Mamoe, and Ngati Kuri.

Puhi left school at fourteen having received primary education only.
Towards the end of the Second World War she worked as a clerk at the War
Office in Wellington. In the early 1950s Puhi was closely involved with the
organisation and activity of the Maori Women's Welfare League. She was a significant force in setting up the small but dynamic Puriri branch of the league in
Rotorua. From 1953 to 1962 Puhi represented Waiariki district at the league's
national conference. In 1955 she was elected one of two league vice-presidents.
Through her voluntary work with the league, Puhi vigorously promoted the
interests of her people.

Puhi was married to prominent Maori public servant Rangi Royal, first
controller of Maori Welfare, and had five children. She died in 1972 and is
buried in the Rotorua public cemetery.

Her story is told by her daughter, Taini Jamieson:
Her Maori name was Te Puhi o Rakaiora. I don't think she had another name
after that, it was long enough.

There were thirteen in Mum's family and they all lived down south. Mum
was brought up by my great-aunt who was Irihapeti Tini Parata. They lived
out at Puketeraki on one side of the harbour and the rest of the family lived on
the other, down at Taiaroa Heads. Mum came to Rotorua with the South
Island crowd that travelled up to a hui for the Prince of Wales. That would
have been about 1922. I don't think she ever went back. She met my father,
and they married. She didn't mind staying because she had family here already.
Mum had five children, but one boy died. We lived at Grey Street, Rotorua.
There wasn't much money and even as kids Mum made sure that we shared the
household work.

I remember coming home from school on wet days, and we used to paddle
in all the streams and walk in all the water. Mum would always have a big pot

of soup on the range, and we'd have to soak our feet in hot water and mustard. I don't know why, but we'd put our feet in the basin and soak until our toes turned pink. The other thing I remember was having to take castor oil when we got bound. Mum had all the old family recipes. Every spring we used to be dosed with sulphur and treacle mixed up. We used to take a spoonful of that to clear the blood. Everybody took it, every now and then. As a kid I always had a cold. At night if you coughed and coughed, Mum'd come in with a spoonful of sugar with a drop of eucalyptus in it. This was supposed to clear the throat. Oh, we hated that. Then there was the trusty Lane's emulsion to build you up and cod liver oil with malt. We couldn't afford to get sick.

In Grey Street we always used to have people popping in. We were the only house with a telephone and everybody used to come and use it. Dad was always bringing people home, especially from the office. We had a great big wooden table which would seat about ten people and Mum would provide for everybody. She used to do the washing all by hand. Scrub away in a big wooden tub and boil up the copper. Women at home had it hard in those days. We had two big verandahs on our home. Mum and Dad had one covered in and they slept out there with our big white dog, called Puhuruhuru. When it was very hot, we kids used to fight about who got to sleep on the uncovered verandah at the back.

When Dad came back from the war, we moved to Wellington. We lived in Wilton Road, just up from the reserve where the state houses are. Mum got a job in the army headquarters office. When Mum decided she was going off to work, Dad was not pleased, but he accepted it. She was the type of person that once she made her mind up, that was that.

When we were in Wellington, Mum used to get hungry for kaimoana. She had a special little place for getting paua and mussels. It was out on the coast past the naval station at Shelly Bay. They used to drive right round to where you could sit on the beach and look across the harbour to the city. In those days we used to be able to pick the paua up off the sand. Mum got very irate when somebody came down and discovered her little patch.

In Wellington Mum must have been very lonely, because my father was hardly ever home. He did a lot of travelling, and when Mum was not working she would go with him. But most times she stayed behind. It was at this time that Mum became involved with setting up the Maori Women's Welfare League. We used to have Rotorua people in the Wilton Road house all the time. The people used to group at Mum's place and have a good old gossip. Catch up on the Maori news.

Her interest in the league wasn't a political thing, it was really motivated by the recognition of need and the wish to do something for the welfare of Maori women. She was concerned at the way people were leaving their tribal areas and going to the city, because it seemed they were looking for more excitement. She would say that if Maori people didn't have education and

Puhi Royal. *Taini Jamieson*

couldn't get a decent job, then they wouldn't be able to get all the material things they wanted. She thought you could do without such comforts, but if Europeans had flash houses, wringer washing-machines, and fridges, Mum reckoned Maori people should have them too. She was a great believer in education as a way forward for the people. Mum only went to standard two herself, because that was all her family could afford at the time, but that never stopped her.

At the league meetings in Wilton Road they used to have little competitions. Mum would make pikelets, or paraoa [bread]. Something like that for the competition night. All the women enjoyed competing against each other and then getting stuck into the kai after. But they really worked hard, fund-raising and planning their next project. Looking back, I think she would have been pleased at the progress being made by Maori women. How they've projected themselves and achieved. Often you don't hear much about Maori women and their success.

I think Mum would be sad too, about the number of Maori women who have gone off the track and got lost a bit, especially with their smoking and the high incidence of lung cancer. Mum would have had a lot more to say about health issues concerning Maori women. As I remember it, I was learning all the time from her. The thing that she taught was to be honest about whatever you're doing. As Mum always said, the truth is what will get you in the end.

Taini Jamieson & Cushla Parekowhai

Unpublished Source
Maori Women's Welfare League, MS Papers 1396, ATL

RUA-PUU-TAHANGA

c.1600

Rua-puu-tahanga probably lived in the seventeenth century and all we can ever know of her comes from oral tradition. Her story portrays a beautiful aristocrat of indomitable will.

Taranaki was her home, Ngaati Ruanui her tribe. As a young woman she was beautiful, with fair skin and hair, and dedicated to ceremonial virginity as the puhi of her tribe. Tuurongo, son of Taawhao, came all the way from Kaawhia to court her and it was arranged that they would marry at his home after he had made suitable preparations for their wedding. When she arrived, however, Tuurongo was made to appear improvident and incompetent, nothing but a 'leaky calabash' unable to accommodate or feed her retinue. So she switched her affections and married Tuurongo's half-brother, Whatihua, and settled down at his home on the shores of Aotea Harbour.

After a time Whatihua took another wife, Apakura, and fed her with succulent eels caught with the aid of a magic talisman that belonged to Rua-puu-tahanga. This enraged Rua. Taking her child Uenuku, she set off down the coast for home, hotly pursued by Whatihua as soon as he found she had gone. Encumbered by her child and seeing that she was being overtaken, she scooped a hole in the sand and left the baby in it. By the time Whatihua had recovered his child, the mother was swimming across the Kaawhia Harbour to Te Maika.

Leaving the child with others, Whatihua continued his pursuit southwards. Rua-puu-tahanga pressed on past Lake Taharoa and along the beach known as Harihari, across the Marokopa River mouth and the Kiri-te-here Stream to the sheer cliffs below Moeaatoa Mountain where she paused. A little stream spurting forth from the foot of the cliff is still known as Rua-puu-tahanga's pee.

Then she came to the lair of the taniwha named Raakei-of-a-hundred-eyes, a fearful place where the rising tide dashes into the monster's cave. In her desperation she did not hesitate but threw herself in and was thrown by the waves to stand safely on the other side. When Whatihua arrived the tide was higher. On the far side stood Rua-puu-tahanga who shouted, 'E hoki i konaa! Ka mate koe i te whaainga ki taku hika tau kee' (Go back lest you die in pursuit of my charms now lost to you).

Free of Whatihua, she pressed on to Mookau where she married a man who bore the name of that place. Their child, named Kura-moonehu, was later to marry Rooraa, son of Maniapoto, the eponymous ancestor of Ngaati Maniapoto.

We do not know why she left again and went home to Paatea, where she made a third marriage to Porou, a man of her own people, and had two sons, named Wheke and Nguu. When she was old and about to die she said to Wheke and Nguu, 'When I die do not bury me but lay me out on a raised burial platform on the marae. If visitors arrive and my head falls, you will know that the strangers are your brothers.' And it came to pass as she had said.

Today the tribes of Waikato and of Taranaki alike trace their descent from Rua-puu-tahanga.

Bruce Biggs

Unpublished Source

Pei Te Hurinui Jones. 'Etehi korero o Tainui' (some Tainui history), 1940–1944, Ms notebook in private possession, Te Kuiti, pp.4, 187

Published Sources

Jones, Pei Te Hurinui. *Mahinarangi (the moon-glow of the heavens): a Tainui Saga*, Hawera, 1946

Kelly, Leslie G. *Tainui, the Story of Hoturoa and his Descendants*, Wellington, 1949

Pomare, Sir Maui. *Legends of the Maori*, vol.2, Wellington, n.d.

Smith, S. Percy. *History and Traditions of the Maoris of the West Coast North Island of New Zealand prior to 1840*. Memoirs of the Polynesian Society, vol.1, New Plymouth, 1910

White, John. *The Ancient History of the Maori, His Mythology and Traditions*, vol.4, Wellington, 1888

NELLE SCANLAN

1882-1968

Nelle Margaret Scanlan was born in Picton in 1882, one of the three children of Michael Scanlan, a police sergeant, and Ellen Scanlan (born Kiely). The family moved to Blenheim, where Nelle attended the convent school. She began her working life as a secretary in Palmerston North, and set up her own typing business there. She also contributed articles to the *Manawatu Times*, and, when war broke out and all the paper's journalists enlisted, she was asked to join the staff. In 1921 she was the only woman and the only New Zealand journalist at the Arms Limitation Conference in Washington. She wrote: 'Because New Zealand had given the vote to women first, Americans were surprised that I wasn't an ardent feminist. I wasn't.'

From 1923 until 1948 she lived in England, writing fiction and earning a living as a freelance journalist, contributing articles particularly about famous people and royalty. During that time she would return to New Zealand every five or six years, as did her contemporary, Ngaio Marsh. Nelle Scanlan had written two novels set in England when her publisher, Jarrolds, suggested that she write a book about New Zealand. Scanlan replied, 'Oh, no, they're never popular out there,' but the publisher insisted she think abut the idea further. From that was born her Pencarrow quartet: *Pencarrow* (1932), followed by *Tides of Youth* (1933), *Winds of Heaven* (1934), and the final volume, *Kelly Pencarrow* (1939). Scanlan wrote fourteen other novels, some set in New Zealand and others in England and America, but with none of them did she achieve the fame that the Pencarrow series brought her. The novels were republished a number of times during the 1940s and 1950s.

Scanlan returned to live in New Zealand in 1948 and continued producing fiction until her last novel in 1952, *The Young Summer*, set in London. She bought a cottage at Paraparaumu Beach and lived in retirement there, producing her autobiography, *Road to Pencarrow*, in 1963. She died in Calvary Hospital, Wellington after a severe heart attack, in 1968, aged eighty-six.

Nelle Scanlan was one of a number of New Zealand writers producing historical fiction during the 1930s. In her quartet, Scanlan traces the fortunes of one family, the Pencarrows (named after the headland at the entrance to Wellington Harbour), from the arrival of Bessie and Matthew Pencarrow in the 1840s through four generations to the late 1930s. The family story is set against a background of social and political events in New Zealand and Europe, Bessie and Matthew buy a farm in the Hutt Valley and have five children. This gives a good base for the family to be involved in the most important events of the succeeding years: the farm is prosperous and another is bought in the Wairarapa. The children move into influential positions, particularly Miles, who becomes a lawyer and partner in a big firm and marries the boss's daughter. He and Norah have eight children, who extend the Pencarrow influence further, this time in the city rather than in the rural areas.

Nelle Scanlan. *Alexander Turnbull Library*

The occupations of each new generation of Pencarrows is a recurring problem, particularly for the adults who have fixed notions of what the family should be involved in. The law and farming are obvious choices but, given the number of children involved, there are aberrations: a nun, a journalist, and a pilot. The family law firm and the two family farms take up many of the male Pencarrows, even though some are less suited to such occupations than others. For every square peg, however, there is a Pencarrow such as Kelly, son of Miles and Norah, who is addicted to farming, or Michael, Kelly's son, who keeps the law firm afloat.

The Pencarrow women have even fewer choices than their brothers. This does not matter for Bessie, who works as hard as her husband in breaking in a new farm and bringing up five children. It becomes something of a problem in the next generation, when Bessie's daughter, Kitty, inherits her mother's energy and organising skills but has nowhere obvious to direct them. The family is now too well off for its daughters to need to go out to work. In the end she marries the 'amiable and pliant' Robert Herrick and organises their life, including a spell running a boarding-house in Blenheim when Robert is too ill to work any longer as a stock and station agent.

The same difficulty faces Genevieve, one of Miles and Norah's daughters, who wants to marry her cousin but is not allowed. Her energies are finally used in the family law firm, when a lull occurs in the number of male Pencarrows wanting to be lawyers. Genevieve's choice of occupation, an unusual one in the 1930s, is explained by Scanlan thus: 'Her revolt, if it could be called such, was against the peculiar hypocrisy that seemed ingrained in the relationship between parents and children', rather than from any feminist views. Other Pencarrow women with the same spirit as Kitty and Genevieve sometimes find themselves in difficult marriages because they have not learned to submit.

Though each member of the large Pencarrow clan receives some attention in the course of the four novels, Scanlan can focus in detail on only a few, and thus the novels are more the stories of first Bessie and Matthew; then Miles, Norah, and Kitty in the second generation; followed by Kelly, Maisie, and Genevieve in the third generation; and Bittie (Kelly and Maisie's daughter) and her husband, Martin, in the fourth.

Nelle Scanlan had no equal in her popular appeal during the 1930s. As her contemporary, Alan Mulgan, remarked:

opinions differ about the literary merits of her Pencarrow [books] but sales speak their own voice . . . Miss Scanlan has done more than any other writer to induce New Zealanders, to read New Zealand fiction.

At a time when many New Zealanders, and Nelle Scanlan was on her own admission one of these, doubted the ability of artists to interpret their own experiences, she showed them it could be done and done well. *Heather Roberts*

Quotations
para.1 N. Scanlan, *Road to Pencarrow*, p.74
para.2 N. Scanlan, *Road to Pencarrow*, p.181
para.7 N. Scanlan, *Tides of Youth*, London, 1934, p.45
para.9 A. Mulgan, 'The New Zealand Novel', p.11

Published Sources
Evening Post, 7 Oct. 1968 (obituary)
Marlborough Express, 7 Oct. 1968 (obituary)
Mulgan, Alan. 'The New Zealand Novel' in J. C. Andersen (ed.) *Annals of New Zealand Literature*, Wellington, 1936
Scanlan, Nelle. *Road to Pencarrow*, London, 1963
Weekly News, 21 Oct. 1968 (obituary)

ANNIE SCHNACKENBERG

1835–1905

'Strong, talented and pious': with these words, missionary Cort Schnackenberg described Annie Jane Allen. Cort was to decide they were ideal qualities for a wife; but they were also traits which Annie would bring to her later career as one of the most significant feminists of the nineteenth century.

Born in 1835, Annie Jane was the daughter of Elizabeth and Edward Allen, who emigrated from Leamington, Warwickshire, arriving in Auckland on the *Black Eagle* in 1861. The Allens were one of the pioneering farming families of

Mt Albert; they were also devout, and the first Methodist religious services in the
the district were held in the kitchen of 'Allendale', the Allens' farmhouse. Back
in England, Annie had played the organ and taken Sunday school at the Wesleyan chapel. Within days of her arrival in New Zealand she was recruited to
assist in the Wesleyan mission at Kawhia, and embarked on the long journey by
bullock dray, Maori canoe, and on foot.

At this remote spot, Cort Schnackenberg laboured to bring salvation to the
Maori, making long trips into the Waikato interior in search of converts. Amy,
his wife, attended to the domestic side, the care of several half-caste children,
and the school.

Miss Allen is a great help [wrote Cort to former mission wife Eliza White]. The
flies made unmerciful attacks upon the stranger, but she has come off victorious
and is now quite well and busily engaged. She has charge of the school, for
which she possesses great abilities.

Amy Schnackenberg had breast cancer, and Annie's duties increased as Amy
succumbed to the disease. She died in late 1863, and within months Cort proposed to Annie, his 'beloved Jane'. His church brethren cautioned him to proceed
discreetly, but Cort was by temperament a passionate man, and at the age of
fifty-two he was impatient. 'I know of no law to forbid our marriage at the
present time', he wrote to her father. '. . . and I want my beloved Jane in my
work.'

The couple married in May 1864, and within a year Annie was back at
'Allendale' waiting to 'become a Mother within a month or two'. Rina was born
in 1865 and another four children were born over the next seven years. Annie,
said Cort, was not just busily engaged in child-rearing and

the duties of a housewife, but in preaching, writing, account keeping, singing
sacred music . . . [she] has ability above the common order – is of very essential
help to my missionary and ministerial labours, as also in letter-writing –
especially spelling and official communications with the government.

The Waikato wars of the 1860s had a devastating effect on the Schnacken-
bergs' work. Congregations dwindled, pupils stopped coming to the mission
schools, and the Maori were 'cowed and sullen'. The mission was removed to the
relative safety of Raglan. According to the Methodist historian, William Morley,
'the faithful pastor was almost heartbroken, and his reports pathetic.'

Descendants record that the Schnackenberg house was the first Pakeha
dwelling entered by King Tawhiao after the Waikato wars. When Tawhiao and
his followers visited Raglan, Cort

decided that the wisest course was to pay a friendly visit to the King and take
his wife and children with him . . . King Tawhiao was so pleased with his
reception that he paid a return visit to the Schnackenberg home . . .

Annie gave Tawhiao's policemen breakfast and the rest of the party tea. Wrote
Cort:

Tawhiao and the chiefs sat at the table with us, and made themselves as agreeable as possible. They were somewhat surprised, I think, and delighted because they could converse with Mrs Schnackenberg in Maori as well as with me . . . All appeared pleased, and on leaving Tawhiao expressed a desire to come again in the evening and listen to some singing and music on the harmonium, but they did not return.

Cort had exhausted himself in his mission work and his heart began to fail. In 1880, he asked Annie to take him to Auckland to die, although the local Maori begged her not to. He died on board ship while crossing the Manukau Bar: 'Mrs Schnackenberg supposed he was resting in quiet sleep; but thinking he slept longer than usual, looked, and found the happy spirit had fled.'

Annie returned to her family home in Mt Albert with her children, then aged between seven and fifteen. She was able to draw a missionary pension, but at forty-five she was still a young woman and accustomed to the challenge of an active mission. She was also very strongly evangelical, and this provides the explanation for the direction her life was to take. Within months of her husband's death Annie is recorded as a Sunday school teacher at the Mt Albert Methodist Church. She began to be active in church affairs, and by 1882 she was a church leader at the Pitt Street Methodist Church. This would have brought her into contact with women such as Mary Ellen Wilson, Jessie Wiseman, and Elizabeth Caradus, who would provide the driving force behind all the new initiatives for social reform for women in Auckland over the next decades.

Temperance was the cause which first attracted Annie Schnackenberg and it would remain an important focus all her life. In 1885 she was a founding member of the Auckland branch of the Women's Christian Temperance Union (WCTU), formed after the visit of WCTU travelling envoy Mary Leavitt; between 1889 and 1897 she was branch president.

The union acted as a surrogate church for women who were denied leadership roles in the traditional churches. In the WCTU, able women such as Annie Schnackenberg could lead prayers, read addresses, and urge their members to deeper worship. 'The evangelical department is the very backbone of our organisation,' said Annie Schnackenberg, exhorting members to intensify their religious observance. 'Let me emphasise the importance of our daily practice of noontide prayer . . . this is the golden chain which binds us as workers to God and to each other.'

In the WCTU she was Scientific Temperance Instruction Superintendent, and worked assiduously but unsuccessfully to get temperance included in the curriculum in schools. 'It was most essential that every child should understand the poisonous nature of alcohol and its baneful effects on the human system.'

In 1891 Annie was appointed national president of the WCTU and held the post until 1901. She was thus at the helm when the historic suffrage legislation was passed, and chaired a huge celebratory public meeting in Auckland.

Nineteenth-century feminism had a moral purpose: the purification of humanity. Feminists believed women had superior natures and could by their efforts elevate men to the same exalted plane. Winning the vote was seen as a precondition for the cleansing of society. Women must use the vote, said Annie, 'to raise the moral standard of the colony'.

Remember, said *The Prohibitionist*, that the 'vote is A SACRED POSSES-SION for the protection and welfare of your sex, your homes and the moral benefit of the community at large'. Annie Schnackenberg, along with other suffragists, argued trenchantly against party politics as undercutting the moral responsibility of voters. 'Every voter,' she said, 'should ask himself or herself how would Jesus Christ use His vote if He lived today, and act as He would have us act.' Immediately after the first election involving female electors in 1893, Annie Schnackenberg wrote to Kate Sheppard expressing her satisfaction that

so many men have been returned who are of sound moral principles . . . in my opinion the women voted for character without regard to the politics of the candidates and so in many instances the best men have succeeded.

None of the suffragists pursued the aims of the Social Purity campaign more single-mindedly than Annie Schnackenberg. Other feminists such as Amey Daldy and Kate Sheppard had a broad platform and actively supported issues which were not critical to the spiritual transformation of society, for example equality in employment and access to divorce. But in the WCTU and later the National Council of Women (NCW), of which she was a founding vice-president, Annie Schnackenberg primarily promoted the issues which were central to the Social Purity ethos: the raising of the age of consent for women, the repeal of the Contagious Diseases Act, and prohibition. After the inaugural NCW convention, Annie was able to report to the WCTU that she had put forward resolutions on Social Purity questions and they were all carried. 'The WCTU is many-sided, waging a ceaseless and peaceful war against vice in all its known forms.'

Feminist historian Phillida Bunkle describes how the WCTU believed the 'male' idea of sex for pleasure degraded women; therefore they strove to eliminate 'any influence that stimulated the sexual imagination and all forms of sexual expression except for the purposes of reproduction within marriage.' To this extent, she argues, they attacked sex itself.

Annie Schnackenberg took the extreme position of campaigning for the age of consent to be raised to twenty-one years, and said it should be called the 'age of protection . . . because it ought never to be possible for a girl or woman to consent to her own ruin'. On the subject of the infamous Contagious Diseases Act, she was eloquent:

[A]ny law or Act of Parliament which interferes with the rights and liberties of women only to make it safer for men to sin, is a disgrace to a community calling itself Christian.

In one year she took three WCTU petitions against the act to parliament.

The Contagious Diseases Act allowed for the compulsory detention of prostitutes (but not of men) so that they could be inspected and treated for venereal disease. The discriminatory nature of the act rankled with feminists, but their main objection was that any state regulation of 'vice' implied condoning it. In their view, venereal disease was a punishment for transgressing God's moral order.

Alcohol was seen by the WCTU as a body pollutant which undermined self-control. It was blamed for immorality, defective children, dirty homes, profligacy, and poverty. While some feminists were in favour of state regulation and temperance, others such as Annie Schnackenberg wanted it to be totally outlawed. '[S]till King alcohol reigns,' she said, 'devastating the land.' She was interested in the subject of scientific food reform, not so much for its own sake, but because it was believed that wholesome food would 'destroy alcohol liquor craving'.

Annie Schnackenberg's experience with the Maori and proficiency in their language were valuable assets to the WCTU. In 1898 she reported to the Auckland branch that she had visited Orakei and succeeded in getting six Maori women to sign a pledge that they would not 'drink anything that causes us to get drunk, neither will we be tattooed or smoke tobacco'. Although the law prohibited the supply of what she called 'bad water' to Maori women, they found ways of gaining access to it.

The WCTU was the only major women's organisation which involved Maori women in its structure, although it was not until 1898, and then only after protests from Maori members, that they attended the annual national convention. By the end of the century there were nine Maori branches with 113 members. In one year they succeeded in getting 600 Maori to pledge themselves not to drink alcohol.

In 1898 Annie was appointed the WCTU's national superintendent of Maori work. She travelled widely in the Rotorua and Bay of Plenty regions promoting the union, and worked closely with Heni Pore (Jane Foley), who had fought with the Kingites in the wars. Visiting women at Whakarewarewa, Annie reported that 'some of the men came to hear the visitor speak in their own tongue; it is an advantage when one is going about among the people.' Her daughter reported that when Annie spoke there was great excitement: 'One of the leading Maoris rushed up to the platform and seizing Mrs Schnackenberg's hand proceeded to rub noses with her.' To her Maori friends she was Mihi Nakipeka and she translated her Christmas greetings and letters into Maori.

Annie Schnackenberg was indefatigable. At the turn of the century she was simultaneously national president of the WCTU, on the committee of the WCTU publication, *The White Ribbon*, superintendent of Maori work, WCTU delegate on the NCW, an executive member of the Auckland Women's Political League, and acting president of the Auckland YWCA.

In 1904 Annie failed to attend the national conference of the WCTU for the first time in many years, the reason being 'her declining health'. She died on 2 May 1905 and was buried beside her husband in the Symonds Street cemetery.

Sandra Coney

Quotations

para.1 C. Schnackenberg to E. White, ?1862, Schnackenberg Papers
para.3 C. Schnackenberg to E. White, ?1862, Schnackenberg Papers
para.4 C. Schnackenberg to E. Allen, 21 April 1864, Schnackenberg Papers
para.5 C. Schnackenberg to Mr Volkner, 12 April 1865, Schnackenberg Papers; C. Schnackenberg, 17 June 1872, Schnackenberg Papers
para.6 W. Morley, *History of Methodism*, p.175; W. Morley, p.175
para.7 G. Sexton, 'Mrs A. J. Schnackenberg', p.31; NZ *Wesleyan*, 1 Aug. 1878, p.173
para.8 NZ *Wesleyan*, 1 Oct. 1880, pp.221–2
para.11 *The White Ribbon*, vol.3 no.33, March 1898, p.4

para.12 *The White Ribbon*, vol.2 no.21, March 1897, p.3

para.14 The President's Address, Minutes of the WCTU 9th Annual General Meeting, 1894, WCTU Papers, Acc 79-57, ATL

para.15 *The Prohibitionist*, no.89, 21 Oct. 1893; *The White Ribbon*, vol.3 no.33, March 1898, p.4; A. Schnackenberg to K. Sheppard, 13 Dec. 1893, Sheppard Collection, Canterbury Museum

para.16 Minutes of the WCTU 9th Annual General Meeting, 1894, WCTU Papers, Acc 79-57, ATL

para.17 P. Bunkle, 'Origins of the Women's Movement', p.62

para.19 *The White Ribbon*, vol.2 no.20, Feb. 1897, p.4; quoted in B. Holt, *Women in Council*, p.18

para.20 *The White Ribbon*, vol.1 no.1, July 1895, p.5; Auckland WCTU minutes, 14 Nov. 1893, ATL

para.21 Minutes of Auckland Branch of the WCTU, 25 May 1898, WCTU Papers, Acc 79-57, ATL; *The White Ribbon*, vol.2 no.18, Dec. 1896, p.9

para.23 *The White Ribbon* (n.d.); G. Sexton, p.31

Unpublished Sources

Auckland YWCA Archives, MS 1131, AIM

H. K. Lovell-Smith Papers 1869-1968, MS Papers 1376, ATL

Kenderdine Scrapbooks, AIM

Memoirs of Mrs K. E. Astley (Rina Schnackenberg), in possession of Mrs Mary Ford

National Council of Women of New Zealand Records, MS Papers 1371, ATL

Schnackenberg Papers, St John's College Library

K. W. Sheppard Papers, Canterbury Museum

Women's Archives, NCW, AIM

WCTU Papers, Acc 79-57, ATL

Published Sources

Bunkle, Phillida. 'The Origins of the Women's Movement in New Zealand: The Women's Christian Temperance Union 1885-1895', in P. Bunkle and B. Hughes (eds), *Women in New Zealand Society*, Auckland, 1980

Coney, Sandra. *Every Girl: A Social History of Women and the YWCA in Auckland*, Auckland, 1986

Fry, Ruth. *Out of the Silence: Methodist Women of Aotearoa 1822-1985*, Christchurch, 1987

Holt, Betty. *Women in Council: A History of the National Council of Women of New Zealand 1896-1979*, Wellington, 1980

Jensen, J. H. and Barber, L. H. 'The Schnackenberg Family Papers', *Auckland-Waikato Historical Journal*, no.51, Sept. 1987, pp.24-7

Morley, William, *The History of Methodism in New Zealand*, Wellington, 1900

NZ Wesleyan, 1 Aug. 1878, p.173; 1 Oct. 1880, pp.221-2

Sexton, Gladys. 'Mrs A J Schnackenberg 1835-1905' *Women's Viewpoint*, vol.1 no.1, June 1960, pp.41-4

FANNY SCOTT

1896-1967

The story of my early life, told in *Hot October*, is visibly the story of my mother's shaping influence. For many people, inside and outside her family, Fanny Scott was a potent fertilising force, expanding their sense of the possibilities in their own lives and challenging them to think more openly, to abandon traditional assumptions. When her children were students, we often brought friends to stay, visits memorable for the adventurousness and excitement of the discussions and speculations Fanny sparked around her. Our friends often marvelled at the range and depth of her conversations. Most parents in the 1940s and 1950s, like New Zealand society itself, were conservative, moralistic, even puritanical; Fanny by contrast was full of questions.

Fanny Scott. *Lauris Edmond*

Her morality was of another kind; it engaged with the growth and expansion of the minds of the young, with finding 'the truth' behind convention and orthodoxy, not with seeking protection from it. Her influence on a wide group was a natural extension of the habits and philosophy of her work as a parent, and an earlier, shorter career as a teacher. Visitors to our house were struck by the extraordinarily open, frank, and vital relationships she had with each of her children. I was temperamentally the most like her and shared her interest in language and in writing (plays first, in her case, poems in mine), and this made her communication with me particularly intense. Later in our lives, when she was alone and I was struggling to write but too busy with my own children to give much time to it, we exchanged opinions, sympathy, encouragement, samples of work. She was the only person I talked to of this private and precious occupation – as she had always been the person to whom I could most freely and satisfyingly explain myself.

Born in 1896 in Norsewood, Hawke's Bay, Fanny Price grew up on a farm in Raukawa, the eighth in a family of twelve born to parents who had come to New Zealand as children of assisted immigrants in the 1870s. It was a family that lived by the pioneer principles of hard work, independence of mind, strong family loyalty, personal responsibility – this, a cardinal virtue, meant 'facing up to things', speaking out, telling the truth. All became articles of faith in Fanny's instruction of her own children – and instruct she did, in the most convinced and compelling way. She had learned authority from her father, partly by a kind of inverse example; he was an intelligent, lively-minded, bossy man but for many years a compulsive drinker and gambler. Fanny was his most articulate and forthright opponent; they had a permanent furious quarrel. Yet in many ways she was like him and when at fifteen she became a pupil-teacher in Wairoa, in charge of a class of Maori boys bigger and in some cases probably older than her, she took firm hold and kept it.

From her mother she learned the domestic skills of pioneering women, managing a large family with little money, and nothing ready-made; she made all her own and her children's clothes, often cutting up and refashioning used garments, not to mention making the family bread, soap, jam, and bottled fruit, covering furniture, and making curtains and mats. She also took from her childhood, and probably from her mother, Clara Price, a sense of family cohesion, an urge to defend her own children with, if necessary, great ferocity. As a parent and a personality she had in an exceptional degree the traditional woman's ability to stimulate and encourage people around her. We must make the best of ourselves; I must learn the piano and practise an hour a day from seven years onwards. I also learned elocution, as speech training was called; Lindsay learned the piano and ballet dancing, Clive the violin; for a while, because I liked singing, I learned that too. For years we had to learn by heart and recite for her a poem a day. We were shy, so she made us go and play with other children till we found out how to make friends. There was compulsion in all this, but there was pleasure too; she created a climate of intense moral rigour around her, along with powerful emotional bonds. She influenced us by showing how deeply she cared that we confront our difficulties and grow from them. However expansive her appreciation, you had to earn it, and to think for yourself – though disagreeing with her did not actually change the relentless momentum of the programme of self-development she pursued with and for us.

Being a parent, teaching, stimulating, appraising – it was all one really, for Fanny, her life's work. At training college in Wellington, where she was a student from 1916 to 1918, she found a group of friends for whom she was again the forthright voice, the one who spoke out; indeed she once saved the five of them from expulsion by being the only one to tell the entire truth about a weekend escapade at the beach.

The man she married – my father – was himself the child of parents who had come to Hawke's Bay as assisted immigrants in the 1870s, but to take up businesses, a tradition Lewis Scott carried on in the post office store in Maharahara where he and Fanny first lived, and where three of us were born. He was already modestly successful (he owned a horse and gig, and a motor bike and side-car). When they moved to Greenmeadows and he took up his father's trade of painting and paper-hanging, he established a substantial business which his men were still running at the time of his death. He was a fanatically hard worker and for much of our childhood Fanny was virtually the only parent. He was proud of his intelligent, amusing, authoritative wife, as he was of her tall elegant style, and he was content to serve her and his family by devotion to work.

But he also brought an adventurousness of mind to the marriage and the household. His mother had been known as a 'seer'; Lewis began to read occult literature and went on to the utopian genre, to political reform and in particular Social Credit. Fanny eagerly embraced these ideas; for her, diet reform and medical unorthodoxy became the most important, especially in 1946 when she was found to have TB, a dreaded disease. By then she and Lewis had moved into semi-retirement on a small citrus orchard in Tauranga. She went into hospital: the only known treatment was prolonged rest, a year or more in isolation wards. Not for Fanny; after a few days she decided she would cure herself using the natural health methods she and Lewis already practised. Even when new and effective drugs were discovered in 1952, she refused hospital treatment.

She was in her early fifties. During the next ten years she needed all the courage and strength of character she had so tried to instil in her children. In 1953 Lewis died of bowel cancer and two years later John, her late child, a brilliant student but a fragile personality, also contracted TB. More seriously, he became schizophrenic and committed suicide in 1955. Alone and devastated, Fanny at last went into hospital and was cured, though she continued to have severe breathing difficulties. Her life became somewhat nomadic. She lived in various houses Lewis had left in Napier; she tried a spell in a boarding-house in Wanganui and there met and became engaged to a retired photographer with whom she lived informally for several years, not caring too much about the break with convention. He died in 1960.

Her last years were spent in an open ward in Wairoa Hospital; Lindsay's family lived nearby and she made frequent trips to visit the other two families. She died in Lower Hutt in 1967 while staying with Clive. She was seventy, physically worn out but as intellectually enterprising as ever.

These years were a time of great suffering and constant mistakes. With the young families she was often interfering, demanding; she discriminated between one grandchild and another; she was unfair to the parent who was not from her own family. In fact she is a classic example of a woman condemned by her historical situation, the beliefs of her time, to use her powers to promote the growth of others, not to develop talents latent in herself. Deprived of her sphere of influence, she lost her occupation, as well as discovering her dependence. However, she was a woman of courage and spirit. She disciplined her fiery temperament, she learned at last to stand aside from her children, she 'faced up' to her own most fundamental fear, that of being alone. George Powell, husband of her closest sister, visited her often in Wairoa and described her as still slim and graceful, a beautiful woman, and in her maturity more charming, more interesting and invigorating, than she had ever been.   *Lauris Edmond*

Published Sources
Edmond, Lauris. *Bonfires in the Rain*, Wellington, 1991
Edmond, Lauris. *Hot October*, Wellington, 1989

MARY SCOTT

1888–1979

Mary Scott was born Mary Clarke in 1888 in Napier, the third of three children. Her father died when Mary was a baby, and her mother worked as a music teacher. Mary's primary relationship was with her sister, with whom she 'ran rather wild'. In 1902 Mary, her mother, and her sister moved to Auckland to be with her brother. Mary attended Auckland Grammar, and then Auckland

University College, where she was taught psychology, economics, and history by Joseph Grossmann, the husband of Edith Searle Grossmann. Mary Clarke graduated with a first-class MA degree and went to Gisborne, and then to Christchurch to teach. In Christchurch she began what was to be a lifelong friendship with Alan and Marguerita Mulgan. In 1913 she was the first woman to climb the Remarkables, which she did with her brother.

She went back to Gisborne to nurse her sick mother, and there met Walter Scott, whom she married in 1914. The Scotts bought a bush farm at Pirongia, twenty-five miles from Te Awamutu; Mary's sister, who had married Walter Scott's brother, bought a neighbouring farm. Mary and Walter Scott had four children and continued farming in the area until 1958, when their son took over the farm. In the mid-1930s Mary Scott worked in the Te Awamutu library, to be near her children who were at school in the town. At the same time she began contributing columns and stories to newspapers, including the *Manchester Guardian*. These were collected in Scott's four 'Barbara books', which appeared between 1936 and 1954 and were the beginning of her prolific literary production. When Mary Scott died in 1979, aged ninety-one, she had written thirty-five books, most of which were produced at the rate of one a year between 1953 and 1978.

Mary Scott. *Alexander Turnbull Library*

Mary Scott became a best-selling author with her first novel, *Breakfast at Six*, which was published by Hurst and Blackett in 1953. By that time her children had grown up and left home, and Scott, by her own account, now had time to devote herself to longer pieces of fiction. *Breakfast at Six* went immediately into a second edition and was reprinted in 1954 and 1956. It was also produced in Dutch and German translations, as were many of Scott's succeeding novels. In 1957 Mary Scott changed publishers to Paul's Book Arcade, marking a move which became more common in the 1950s amongst New Zealand writers to have their work published in their own country. For Scott it made financial sense too, as her public was largely a New Zealand one and her New Zealand royalties were higher if her work was published here.

Mary Scott's novels are stories of rural New Zealand, of communities similar to those in which she lived, and about people who were familiar to her. In the foreword to her autobiography she writes: 'I have always drawn upon actual people and actual happenings.' *Breakfast at Six* (and most of the novels which follow it) tells of the lives of Susan and Paul, who buy a backblocks farm, raise a family, and make a living there. They are surrounded by other families who share with them the joys and difficulties of farming inhospitable terrain, bringing up children far from schools and doctors, and the incidents which unite small communities. Apart from Susan and Paul, other characters appear through the novels, in particular Susan's friend, Larry. Larry and her husband, Sam, farm a neighbouring property, but it is not farming that unites the two women, but rather a love of impropriety and a delight in each other's company. They share the life of being farmers' wives, of being tied to a domestic routine when each wishes sometimes for other things. Together they take on challenges which alone they might not have attempted: running a farm holiday scheme to raise money during a rural downturn in *Board But No Breakfast* (1978), or sorting out a younger sister's love life in *Dinner Doesn't Matter* (1957).

Scott wrote about other families in her novels, but it was with Paul and Susan and the neighbourhood in which they lived that she achieved her popularity. Her excursion into thriller writing with Joyce West, herself an established writer of historical fiction, was greeted less kindly by readers. The two women wrote five novels, beginning with *Fatal Lady* in 1960 and ending in 1965 with *Who Put It There?* The novels are set in New Zealand, and follow a fairly common thriller pattern with easily distinguishable villains and heroes. Scott explained the move as being 'for fun'. Both writers are, however, better remembered for their prowess in other fictional forms than they are for writing thrillers.

Scott, as perhaps one would expect from someone with a first-class degree in English literature and French, was her own most stringent critic. While others noted her 'gaiety and life . . . [and] flashes of perception', Scott dismissed her novels by saying that 'they have had far more success than they deserve'. Her English lecturer at Auckland University College had talked to her about her 'fatal fluency': the less she knew the more fluently she wrote. Scott saw her novels as being written out of that facility, yet she was writing about things that she knew deeply. It is this familiarity with her subject matter that is the hallmark of her work; she wrote about something which, perhaps surprisingly, other New Zealand writers had not tackled: the ordinary life of rural New Zealand. It was also a topic which has international appeal; as one commentator remarked rather grudgingly in 1981, this was perhaps because 'her bucolic novels reinforce the popular . . . notion of New Zealand as a land of blue skies, green grass and generally untroubled people'. While Scott's characters do not suffer large tragedies or significant rewards in their lives, they do experience the setbacks and joys which are common to most people, whether they live in country or town. It is this aspect of her novels, together with their rural setting, which has made her one of New Zealand's most widely read authors.   *Heather Roberts*

Quotations
para.1 M. Scott, *Days That Have Been*, p.28
para.4 M. Scott, p.11
para.6 J. Stevens, *The New Zealand Novel*, p.45; M. Scott, p.199; M. Scott, p.199; K. du Fresne, 'German Connections'

Published Sources
du Fresne, Karl. 'German Connections', *NZ Listener*, 20 June 1981
Scott, Mary. *Days That Have Been*, Auckland, 1966 (autobiography)
Stevens, John. *The New Zealand Novel 1860–1965*, Wellington, 1966

SARAH SELWYN

1809–1907

Sarah Harriet Richardson, daughter of Sir John Richardson, a judge of the Court of Common Pleas, and his wife Harriet (born Hudson), was born on 2 September 1809 at 'Wanlip Hall', Leicestershire, and spent her childhood in London. She had no formal education, but her reminiscences suggest a reserved, observant personality, musical and artistic, with considerable sensitivity to her surroundings and to the social and political events of the time. Chronic asthma forced her father to resign his judgeship in 1824 and the family spent considerable time in Malta. In July 1839 Sarah married George Augustus Selwyn, curate at the parish of Windsor and tutor at Eton, whose future seemed to lie in 'preferment and prosperity in England'. She enjoyed life at Windsor and Eton, where in 1840 their son William was born. Her reservations regarding Selwyn's acceptance of 'Episcopal Office in New Zealand' in July 1841 are implicit in her comment that 'George . . . was quite ready to take his education and his wife and all besides into any sphere to which he might be called by lawful authority'.

Sarah's life in New Zealand began on 24 June 1842 at the Church Missionary Society station in Paihia, where the family was welcomed into the busy, hospitable home of the Revd Henry Williams. Within a fortnight she had moved to her first home at Waimate and the bishop had departed for six months on a tour of inspection through the North Island to Wellington and Nelson, leaving his chaplain, the Revd W. C. Cotton, in charge of the youthful party of catechists who had accompanied him from England. As Sarah reflected:

When George is really gone and I am left with all this charge on my shoulders I shall feel more thoroughly alone than ever I did in my life before: but people are used to being alone in N.Z. and it seems so clearly the most helpful thing for me to do, to keep things strait and going forward at home, that I doubt not it will be well one way or another.

Besides providing 'homey' surroundings for 'George's young staff', Sarah, known to the local Maori as 'Mata Pihopa' (Mother Bishop), busied herself learning their language and attending to the sick 'in a very humble way'.

Although she has little to say on the matter, the stress of keeping things going forward at home and the anxiety of the bishop's long absence took toll on Sarah's health. She had accepted that 'a public life was to be mine from the day I landed', but her home was also St John's College, established by Selwyn in 1843 for the 'religious and useful education' of young men of both races, but particularly for candidates for Holy Orders. Here she felt that she was living in a box 'ceiled walled and floored with Kauri wood'. The bishop set up a retreat for her in the stone store at Kerikeri, where unbroken quiet replaced 'the inevitable noise of wooden buildings'. In October 1843 the Selwyn family left for Auckland to spend the summer with Mary Ann Martin, invalid wife of the Chief Justice, while the bishop made another long journey which took him as far south as Stewart Island.

Mary Ann Martin was ten years younger than Sarah, who had enjoyed her lively company on the long voyage to New Zealand on the *Tomatin*. On her part Mary Ann found the bishop's wife 'staid and so very good', probably reflecting Sarah's contentment in remaining quietly in the background in the presence of her husband's forceful personality. Mary Ann's letters are strong and practical, and she speaks of Sarah's need, now that she was pregnant, for a quiet, comfortable, and congenial home where, removed from all domestic responsibilities, she could be cared for:

And this is a comfort in a strange new land, for it is the lack of sympathy that is the most trying part of a woman's lot. People fancy at home that our sufferings are to be of a more material order – salt pork and dampers and the like . . . No – the ordeal at first, is the loss of so many of the blessed home charities, that were more to us than meats and drinks, and though so far from wishing to hinder the noble spirits we are linked to, we would urge them on, and strengthen their hands, yet the poor frail nervous body, sinks under hours and weeks and months of loneliness.

Sarah's health improved after the birth of a second son, John, in May 1844.

In December St John's College was translated to Auckland and the Selwyns lived for a time at Parnell, within half a mile of the Martins. During 1845 Sarah 'enjoyed quiet and her husband's society both of which are rare enjoyments to her' at Otaki; the Selwyns briefly took Archdeacon Hadfield's place while he lay ill in Wellington. In June 1846 the bishop moved his family to St John's College at Bishop's Auckland (the name he gave to land he purchased at Tamaki). Here Sarah's responsibilities included the supervision and training of the married Maori couples and their children, and the primary school for children of the local working people. With Mary Ann Martin's assistance, she compiled reading books for use in the school and proof-read translations of parts of the Bible and a Maori grammar by the Revd Robert Maunsell, produced at the college press – 'a rare help in the language for me'.

Over the years Sarah accompanied the bishop on a number of journeys by land and sea in New Zealand and to the Melanesian Islands, but she spent many long months watching and waiting for his return. Mary Ann Martin, who could measure her husband's absences in weeks, shared her loneliness as their friendship grew:

Dear Mrs Martin and I have much talking, much laughing and some reading together . . . She has an excellent understanding, and so cultivated a mind, such strong feeling and such a merry heart, that she can suit a grave, a wise, or a lively mood . . .

The strength of this friendship must have supported Sarah through the sorrow of the death of a daughter, Margaret Frances, in February 1851. The child was born on 5 September 1850, just twelve days before the bishop left for Sydney; he did not return to Auckland until April 1851.

The friends had been joined by Sarah's cousin, Caroline Abraham, in August 1850. The measure of the support and relief that Dr Abraham and his wife gave to the toil-worn Selwyns is reflected in Sarah's comment two years later:

You can hardly fancy a more cosy and happy party than the two pair of Husbands and wives, when we do get an opportunity of a little esoteric talk together. We are so entirely happy and comfortable in all relations one to another, as spouse to spouse, as friend to friend, as cousin to cousin, as clergyman to Bishop . . . The warm cooperation and ready sympathy always at hand are so great a support to my dear Husband who has for the most part been little understood and less supported . . .

Caroline soon came 'down from her aesthetic heights to our level of divine drudgery', teaching the community's children with 'a mind ever alive to the best way of making a stew – or boiling bones to jelly to feed hungry lads'.

The women were also to become involved in the issues which engrossed their husbands' plans and actions 'for laying the foundations of the Government and the Church in New Zealand' with the welfare and rights of the Maori people very much at heart. They 'used dutifully to listen', for example, to the discussions on the proposed system for church government and constitution, founded on voluntary compact, which Selwyn and Martin formulated over several years. There is ample evidence that it was informed listening and Sarah, though professing not to understand the subject, wrote that Governor Grey 'counts me a deputy Bishop in George's absence'.

But the issue which was to arouse Sarah's active response was the Waitara purchase of March 1860 when Governor Gore Browne, responding to settlers' pressure for land, enforced the purchase of Maori land in Taranaki based on individual tenure. The clergy were acutely conscious that their role was to stand aloof from politics, but Bishop Selwyn sent 'a solemn protest' to the governor. Formal public statements by other public figures and missionary organisations, published in pamphlet form, were responded to by politicians and landowners seeking to justify the action of the New Zealand government. Sarah, Mary Ann Martin, and Caroline Abraham made their contribution to this pamphlet war with *Extracts of Letters from New Zealand on the War Question*, which throws 'much inner light' on the reaction of Bishop Selwyn and his supporters to the situation. The letters were written directly to family members and friends in England or between Sarah Selwyn in Auckland and Caroline Abraham in Wellington. The writers knew that the information they were sending would be made available to influential people in England.

The bishop, 'disliking all private communications to people in power', shrank from the proposal that he should write home officially to the Duke of Newcastle and to Gladstone. But Sarah's published letter of 30 August 1860 to her cousin Mary Anne Palmer champions Selwyn's cause and stresses that the bishop's main objection to the governor's actions lay in the purchase of Maori land based on individual instead of tribal right, a change in policy that departed from the land guarantee of the Treaty of Waitangi, but added that she 'did not pretend to justify the Maories in all that has followed'. Selwyn was gravely concerned about the result, that the government had

rushed into a bloody quarrel without trying all other methods of settling the dispute first; assuming that the natives are rebels before they have done one single thing to prove themselves to be so, and denying them the ordinary privileges of British subjects, which the Treaty of Waitangi declares them to be . . . Oh! we are sinking so low in the eyes of the Maories. Where is our good faith? Where our assurances that the Queen would never do them wrong? . . . it goes to our hearts to see a noble race of people stigmatized as rebel, and driven to desperation, by the misrule of those who are at the same time lowering their own people in their eyes.

Sarah was back in England when the pamphlet was published for private circulation in London in 1861. Torn between her wish to be with her husband at a time when the bishop and clergy were experiencing 'great odium by the part they have taken in the matter' and her desire to be with the two schoolboy sons she had not seen since 1855, she had sailed for England in the troop-ship *Boanerges* on 5 February and arrived at Portsmouth in May. From the beginning of her life in the new colony, Sarah Selwyn saw her role as 'to follow suit, not to choose and then see the best side of things' but clearly she, and her two close friends, were quite prepared to express openly their own opinions on broader matters.

A tribute from Archdeacon J. F. Lloyd, who was closely associated with the Selwyns from the time of his arrival in Auckland in 1849, sums up the measure of Sarah's contribution to her husband's endeavour as Bishop of New Zealand:

I do not think I have ever met anyone equal to Mrs Selwyn. She is an admirable woman, though you do not find out her worth until after a long and intimate acquaintance with her.

In 1868 Selwyn was appointed Bishop of Lichfield where he died on 11 April 1878. Sarah spent her long widowhood in an old house in the cathedral close, 'making no display, seeking no publicity, yet showing her keen and intelligent interest in events both past and present'. She died there on 24 March 1907. Her tranquil portrait hangs in the Lady Chapel dedicated to her memory in Lichfield Cathedral. Worshippers today still speak to interested visitors of her 'gentle Christian influence'.   *June Starke*

Quotations
para.1 W. H. Tucker, *Memoir*, vol.1, p.54; S. Selwyn, 'Reminiscences', p.26
para.2 S. Selwyn to M. A. Palmer, 24 June–1 July 1842, G. Selwyn Papers, Micro MS 613/9
para.3 Letter, 6 Sept. 1842, G. Selwyn Papers, Micro MS 613/9
para.4 M. A. Martin to Rev. E. Coleridge, 23 Feb. 1844, Letters from Bishop Selwyn and Others, vol.4
para.5 M. A. Martin to Rev. E Coleridge, 10 Oct. 1845, Letters from Bishop Selwyn and Others, vol.4; S. Selwyn, Reminiscences, p.5
para.6 S. Selwyn to F. Selwyn, 21 Nov. 1845, G. Selwyn Papers, Micro MS 613/9

para.7 S. Selwyn to Mrs Coleridge, 3 June 1852, S. Selwyn to Rev. E. Coleridge, 21 May 1852, Letters from Bishop Selwyn and Others, vol.4

para.8 S. Selwyn to Mrs Coleridge, 27 May 1850, Letters from Bishop Selwyn and Others, vol.3

para.10 S. Selwyn to M. A. Palmer, 30 Aug. 1860, *Extracts of Letters from New Zealand on the War Question*, pp.25–6

para.11 S. Selwyn, Reminiscences, p.150; p.96

para.12 J. F. Lloyd to E. Lloyd, 4 Feb. 1861, J. F. Lloyd MS Papers 1786, folder 2, ATL

para.13 J. H. Evans, *Churchman Militant*, p.203

Unpublished Sources

G. A. Selwyn Papers, 1831–1909, Micro MS 613, ATL

Letters from Bishop Selwyn and Others 1842–1867, qMS, ATL

S. Selwyn, Reminiscences 1809–1867, qMS, ATL

Published Sources

Evans, J. H. *Churchman Militant*, London, 1964

Extracts of Letters from New Zealand on the War Question (printed for private circulation), London, 1861

Starke, J. J. 'I must write a pamphlet, or I shall burst', *Turnbull Library Record*, vol.19 no.1, May 1986

Tucker, H. W. *Memoir of the Life and Episcopate of George Augustus Selwyn*, *D.D.*, London, 1901

ELIZABETH SEWELL

1940–1988

Elizabeth Louise Simes (also known as 'Bid') was born and raised in Christchurch, the eldest of three daughters. She went to school in Christchurch at Elmwood Primary, and in Timaru as a boarder at Timaru Girls' High School. On leaving school she spent a brief period (1958–9) nursing at Christchurch Public Hospital where she completed her Junior Hospital Nursing Finals. In 1959 she married Jim Sewell and soon had three children: Brett, Penny, and Hamish.

By 1965 she had formed a small jewellery business with the assistance of her mother, Thelma Louise Simes. The business was successful and enabled Elizabeth to support herself and her family following her separation in 1965 and eventual divorce. At the end of the 1960s it also enabled her (until the expense became too great) to learn to fly a single-engine aircraft, and in the 1970s to devote much of her time and energies to the women's movement. The business was run from the garage and involved the manufacturing of copper jewellery, some with silver and gold plating, and lampshades. Elizabeth designed the jewellery and employed two staff. She sold initially to friends and local markets and eventually to outlets throughout New Zealand.

In 1971, as well as running the business and raising three children, Elizabeth took up part-time university study. Between 1971 and 1978 she completed six papers towards a BA, specialising in American Studies.

During the 1970s Elizabeth became increasingly active in the women's liberation movement, and was at the forefront of many of its activities. Her participation and commitment grew both from her personal experience, and her increasing political awareness. In 1972, with Diane Roberts, Elizabeth wrote the Values Party's manifesto statement on women.

In response to the passing of the Contraception, Sterilisation and Abortion

Act in 1974, Elizabeth set up the Pregnancy Counselling Service which provided services to women facing unwanted pregnancy. In 1977, when the 'Birch' amendment to the act was passed making legal abortions virtually inaccessible to women in New Zealand, Elizabeth founded the Sisters Overseas Service (SOS). The service provided counselling and support, and made the necessary arrangements for women to travel from Christchurch to Sydney for safe, legal abortions. Elizabeth supervised its two staff and twenty volunteers, organised the publicity, and personally provided counselling to many women. At its peak, SOS in Christchurch received twenty calls a day from women seeking assistance.

In 1977 Elizabeth was one of five women who co-ordinated the United Women's Convention in Christchurch which was attended by over 2,500 women. The conference was the focus of much controversy when it voted to exclude the media; it was also the target of a campaign from conservative religious groups to subvert feminist discussion at the conference.

In the second half of the 1970s Elizabeth worked hard and without payment on many women's issues. She ran seminars on women's health and politics, and was involved in the establishment of both a battered women's support group and the first women's refuge in New Zealand. She was a member of Mayoress of Christchurch Judith Hay's Committee on Women, the Women's Electoral Lobby, and the group that produced *A Guide to Getting On* for women wanting to influence the political system. Through her involvement in the guide and following her move to Wellington, Elizabeth also became involved in the running of the Women's Appointment File, which promotes the appointment of women

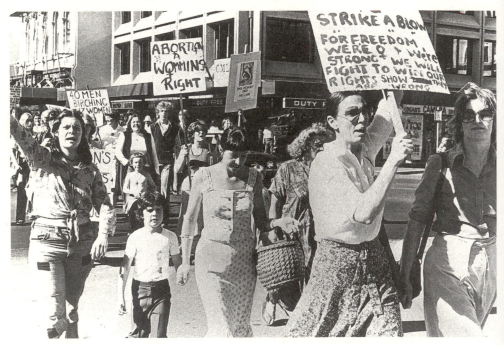

Elizabeth Sewell, second from right, marching for abortion rights in Christchurch, 1970s. *Press*

to government boards and committees by maintaining a list of women and their credentials. The file, now administered by the Ministry of Women's Affairs, was initially maintained by volunteer women representing a range of women's organisations.

In 1979, as her children approached adulthood, Elizabeth sold her jewellery business and moved to Wellington. There she took up a position as research assistant and private secretary to Marilyn Waring, the high-profile feminist member of parliament in the National government. Marilyn was not eligible for research assistance, and paid Elizabeth's salary herself. Elizabeth worked for Marilyn for twelve months, and during that time developed nationwide contacts, in-depth knowledge of government policies, and personally helped many women who approached Marilyn for assistance. She left in 1980 to take up an appointment as national executive director of the Young Women's Christian Association (YWCA). During this period, Elizabeth was also a member of the Hecate Collective, a Wellington-based women's health group.

Elizabeth worked for the YWCA until 1984, providing high-profile leadership both nationally and internationally. She coaxed the often conservative organisation into taking a more active role in the women's movement, and recruited many feminist and professional women into volunteer and paid positions. Following her lead, the YWCA placed new emphasis on the issues of women and unemployment, and combated sexual abuse against women. In 1983 it organised a national conference on sexual violence against women which brought together women from a wide range of organisations working in the field of sexual abuse. Elizabeth was also instrumental in establishing a national network of trained self-defence tutors in a coalition between Sue Lytollis and the YWCA. Eventually, however, Elizabeth's spirited commitment to feminism proved too much for the YWCA and the two parted company.

Elizabeth began her brief career as a senior public servant in February 1985, when she was appointed director of the Consumer Affairs Unit in the Department of Trade and Industry. Her task was to undertake public consultation on behalf of Minister of Consumer Affairs Margaret Shields on the need for a Ministry of Consumer Affairs. The ministry was formed in 1986 and Elizabeth was appointed as its first head, a position she held until her death in 1988. She worked hard to form the new small ministry into a credible government department with strong community links.

Every summer for the last fifteen years of her life, Elizabeth spent a month resting and re-energising with her family and close friends at a secluded beach in Golden Bay. She was an avid reader, enjoyed socialising and debating with friends, had a delightfully astringent sense of humour, and was a competitive backgammon player.

In September 1987 Elizabeth was diagnosed as having terminal cancer. She chose to maintain her existing life-style and continued to work as her strength allowed. Her feminist-based commitment to maximising control over her life extended also to her death. She actively pursued self-healing techniques, along with conventional medicine. Elizabeth died at her home in Wellington on 30 May 1988, in the care of her children, her companion Vincent Burke, and her close friends.   *Annette Dixon*

Unpublished Sources
Elizabeth Sewell, Papers, Acc 89–326, ATL
Interviews with Penny Fenwick, Jennifer Cato, Diane Shannon, Jenny Heal, Diana Crossan, and Nedra Johnson
Louise Simes, Acc 88–214, ATL
Published Source
Waring, Marilyn. 'Letters to my Sisters: In Memory', *NZ Listener*, 16 July 1988

HELEN SHAW

1913 – 1984

Since 1932 my bible fuel and light had been contained in A Room of One's Own, *a 'book to be put in the hands of girls'. If it was not in my destiny to be endowed with, or to earn, the five hundred pounds a year Virginia Woolf advocated for a woman writer, I had at least a room of my own, and there I began writing stories.*

Helen Shaw's 'room of my own' was in a boarding-house in Papanui Road, Christchurch – a house distinguished by the oddity of some of its inhabitants, described by Shaw as 'Dostoyevsky-like'. Throughout Shaw's stories, old houses and their elderly occupants act as the environment or shaping force of the story. In 'Praise the Lord Wilson', Wilson's little girl Polly goes exploring in Miss Barclay's large dark house and comes across 'a dusty vision of Miss Barclay's sister playing the eggbeater while thin threads of saliva spun out of her mouth'. The dust-jacket of Shaw's first collection of stories, *The Orange Tree and Other Stories*, shows the detail of an old New Zealand house, wooden lace on the verandah; in the 'octagonal shaped turret room' ('The Blind') or the 'small bellshaped room encircled with windows' ('The Three Strange Miss Vinings') of this house, the significant events of her stories occur.

Born in 1913, Helen Shaw was brought up in Timaru. Her father was a solicitor who got into financial difficulties and resolved them by going to the war; he was never heard of again. Shaw grew up with her maternal grandparents, the Gows; their house, containing Helen Shaw and her mother Jessica, her Aunt Lilian, and her grandparents, is probably the forerunner of all the rambling dusty mansions inhabited by elderly children and their even more elderly parents in her fiction.

When she left school, Shaw went to training college in Christchurch, but after qualifying she decided to abandon teaching and took up hairdressing to earn an income while she wrote. At the beginning of 1937 Shaw submitted a children's story, 'The Truth of the Chinese Vase', to the *Press Junior*, a children's supplement edited for *The Press* by Jean Stevenson. It became the first of many of Shaw's stories to be published by the *Press Junior* from 1937 to 1940. Shaw and Stevenson, later Jean Bertram, became close and lifelong friends, and shared a flat in Carlton Gore Road with a gate to the river.

Towards the end of this time Frank Hofmann, the celebrated photographer, visited *The Press* to sell some photographs, met Stevenson and through her Shaw.

In 1941 Shaw travelled to Auckland to marry him. She lived in Auckland for the rest of her life, but all her fiction is suggestive of the large, settled, layered families, with their roots in colonial New Zealand, amongst whom she grew up in the towns of the South Island.

Her first collection, *The Orange Tree and Other Stories*, was published in 1957. Shaw is often associated with Mansfield and in her essay 'Short Stories' (1978) describes herself as having worked largely in isolation but with 'an influence that comes simply from being published in the company of others. Your work will be measured by theirs.'

Shaw's patrician families and their decaying houses have an historical relationship to Mansfield's writing but also register the passing of time as deterioration and threat. In the concluding essay to her later collection *The Gipsies* (1978), Shaw wrote: 'The present is continually vanishing. The past is continually being created or being remembered, but often in a fragmented not cohesive state.' In *The Gipsies*, which includes some stories from the earlier collection as well as stories published in periodicals, the fragmentation of the past is accompanied by the destructive threat of the present; Paola Rosa's spirit, in the title story, contained in his house and garden and venerated by the present-day transients who live there, is to be displaced by a motorway.

Shaw's story writing, accomplished and distinctive, seems only ever to have been occasional. She described the difference between her two collections as that between innocence and experience, and said: 'To publish a collection of stories is in a sense to close a door on what has been achieved.' In fact she seems to have moved away from writing fiction and towards poetry in the latter decades of her life, publishing a considerable number of volumes of poetry, and guest-editing issues of *Ocarina*, and *Poet*.

Her poetry has been described by James Bertram as 'shimmering, abstract, rather mystical verse'. Much of it was published by or associated with the Tagore Institute of Creative Writing International, or by small presses in New Zealand, such as the Griffin Press who published *Leda's Daughter* (1985). Two more substantial volumes, *Ambition of Clouds* (1981) and *Time Told from a Tower* (1985), collected poems published in periodicals. Shaw's poetry is highly abstract and imagistic, and perhaps expresses the quality she aimed for in her stories ('a surface of layers, layers of surfaces') in its least mediated form.

> *Poems are cries*
> *are your cries*

Shaw also undertook editing the letters and work of D'Arcy Cresswell in the 1960s and 1970s, and edited *Dear Lady Ginger*, an exchange of letters between Lady Ottoline Morrell and D'Arcy Cresswell, in 1981. Helen Shaw died in Auckland in 1984.

Lydia Wevers

Quotations
para.1 H. Shaw, *The Gipsies*, p.109
para.2 H. Shaw, *The Gipsies*, p.110; H. Shaw, *The Orange Tree and Other Stories*, Auckland, 1957, pp.53, 13, 68
para.6 H. Shaw, *The Gipsies*, p.109
para.7 H. Shaw, *The Gipsies*, p.111
para.8 H. Shaw, *The Gipsies*, p.112

para.9 James Bertram, *NZ Listener*, 3 March 1979, p.60; H. Shaw, *The Gipsies*, p.111; H. Shaw, 'The Young Woman Calls on the Passerby', *Ambitions of Clouds*, Christchurch, 1981, p.7

Unpublished Source
Information was provided by Jean Bertram.

Published Source
Shaw, Helen. 'Short Stories: An Essay', in *The Gipsies and Other Stories*, Wellington, 1978

KATE SHEPPARD

1848-1934

Although we are still political outcasts, the Promised Land is in sight! Year by year we have been winning our way . . . our forces have been growing in numbers, not by any transient wave of enthusiasm, but by sheer, logical reasoning, and the hard work performed by our members.

These were Kate Sheppard's words to the annual convention of the Women's Christian Temperance Union (WCTU) in March 1893 as she presented her annual report as franchise superintendent. While still frustrated in her goal to win the right to vote for New Zealand women, Kate Sheppard was resolute. For six years her hard work, persistent reasoning, and sheer effort had built a nation-wide campaign. To her belongs much of the credit for the victory which was won in September 1893.

Born in Liverpool in 1848 but raised and educated in Scotland, Catherine Wilson (generally known as Kate) came to New Zealand in 1869 with her mother and other members of her family. Two years later she married Walter Allen Sheppard, a thirty-five-year-old storekeeper and Christchurch city councillor. They had one son, Douglas, in 1880. Kate was well positioned, having a sympathetic and comfortable domestic base from which to engage in public life. A member of the Trinity Congregational Church, Kate was an independent thinker with a keen sense of social responsibility and justice. Her convictions led her to seek broad solutions rather than short-term remedies for immediate problems. She had a strongly held desire that women could and should participate in the political and social world, and little time for notions which relegated women to purely decorative or domestic functions. 'It is time that the *doll* era has passed away, and the *womanly* period had dawned', she wrote in 1891.

Kate Sheppard was, above all, an extremely able organiser. She joined the Christchurch branch of the WCTU soon after it was established in 1885. Two years later, at the age of thirty-nine, she took national office as superintendent of the franchise department. It was in this capacity that she led the hard-fought struggle for the vote. From the time Kate Sheppard took office she worked steadily and with effect, directing the efforts of a large and diverse organisation towards specific goals. She concentrated first on persuading the WCTU membership that in all aspects of their work they were reliant on and 'affected by enactments in Parliament'. Without exercising a direct influence on those who held power, Kate Sheppard argued, women's concerns would be continually overridden. As a preliminary to achieving any kind of social reform, women needed the vote; she urged that 'every earnest worker should strive for political power',

In her first year as franchise superintendent Kate Sheppard organised a petition – the first of a succession which were presented over the following six years – impressing on parliament and on the public generally how keen was women's desire for the vote. She also forged an alliance with Sir John Hall, who was to become the suffrage campaign's chief advocate within parliament. In conjunction with these initiatives, Kate Sheppard also published her first suffrage pamphlet outlining the case for women's suffrage. The first of her *Ten Reasons why the Women of New Zealand should Vote* simply stated:

Because a democratic government like that of New Zealand already admits the great principle that every adult person, not convicted of a crime, nor suspected of lunacy, has an inherent right to a voice in the construction of laws which all must obey.

From these first efforts Kate Sheppard consolidated and nurtured a campaign, searching always for new ways in which to extend and broaden support. Faced with defeats in 1888, 1891, and 1892, she did not succumb but determinedly worked at building sympathetic public opinion, urging members of the WCTU to take up yet another petition, address another public meeting, and write another letter to the editor. Working hard herself, she motivated others to work untiringly in the cause.

As well as being an able organiser, Kate Sheppard was also a consummate publicist. In addition to writing pamphlets and petitions she inaugurated and was the first editor of the WCTU's page in the fortnightly *Prohibitionist*. As 'Penelope', Kate Sheppard presented a lively mixture of accounts of local events with reports of progress on suffrage and temperance campaigns overseas. Readers could not help but be aware that they were part of an international movement. Kate Sheppard was also to become the first editor of the WCTU's own publication, *The White Ribbon*, in 1895. Sheppard's style was lively, succinct, and reasonable. She made no apology for her views and directly addressed her opponents' arguments, being quick to point out contradictions and inanities. Reporting the failure of the 1891 Women's Suffrage Bill she wrote:

The Hansard report of the debate on the second reading of the bill in the House of Representatives shows that our opponents have mended their manners somewhat? We find no longer remarks as to the mental inferiority of women to men. Indeed the chief objection seems to have been a fear that women would lose the charm and delicacy which distinguishes them. Curiously enough, the very men who deny the suffrage to women for fear the delicate bloom of their modesty should be impaired, are simply rampant when it is proposed to do away with the employment of girls as barmaids. We think that the modesty of women will be safer in their own charge than in the hands of either Mr. Fish or Mr. Swan, and for these men to constitute themselves guardians of the delicacy of women is little short of an insult.

Three years, two more petitions, many public meetings, and much lobbying were to pass before the Electoral Bill finally gained the support of the majority of members in both houses of parliament and received the governor's assent on 19 September 1893. Premier Richard Seddon, an arch-opponent of the women's franchise, telegraphed Kate Sheppard with the news, assuring her that the women of New Zealand now had no reason for doubting the government's sincerity in the matter. In' her final column for 1893, Kate Sheppard labelled the year a 'Red-letter one' in which 'the political freedom of one-half of . . . [the] population has been brought about'.

In 1894–5 Kate Sheppard travelled to England, visiting members of her family and attending an international WCTU convention in London in June 1895. She received invitations to speak to conferences, public meetings, and organisations both on this occasion and again in 1908 when she returned to England and visited America. As the leader of the campaign in the first nation-state where women had been enfranchised, her experience and accomplishment as a speaker put her in great demand. While overseas Kate Sheppard also became personally acquainted with feminist leaders such as Millicent Garrett Fawcett and Carrie Chapman Catt, the president of the International Woman's Suffrage Alliance. It was in England in 1894 that the idea of forming an ongoing national women's organisation was suggested to Kate Sheppard by Eva McLaren of the International Council of Women.

Kate Sheppard and Anna Stout accepted provisional responsibility for such an organisation, and the first full meeting of the National Council of Women (NCW) took place in Christchurch in April 1896. Kate Sheppard was elected president and continued to be a leading member of the NCW until it went into recess in 1905. After suffrage, the issue which she advocated most vigorously was women's economic independence. In 1899 her paper at the NCW meeting in Auckland was a plea for married women's economic independence.

Asked to reflect on the impact of women's suffrage at its twenty-first anniversary in 1914, Kate Sheppard wrote with the same vigour that she had shown two decades earlier:

Woman must be free to work for humanity in whatever capacity for which God has fitted her. And so we ask to-day, as we have asked for years past, for the removal of all the civil and political disabilities of women . . . for economic equality or partnership between husband and wife; for the co-guardianship of children by wife and husband; for equal pay for equal work and equality of opportunity for men and women to fill all Government posts, capacity for the work and not sex to be the test . . . And for the furthering of these and other reforms, we want to see women sitting side by side with men in the legislative assemblies, helping to make laws which will be beneficial to the community as a whole.

In 1917 when the NCW was revived it was Kate Sheppard who once again became president.

Kate Sheppard the person, in contrast to Kate Sheppard the public figure, has left little trace in the historical record. Her only son and grandchild predeceased her. There are few personal papers. In an obituary Jessie Mackay

Kate Sheppard. *Alexander Turnbull Library*

spoke of Kate Sheppard's 'golden mean in temperament', her sweetness, and of how her 'firm arguments were advanced with a good humoured patience that disarmed prejudice and warded off hostility'.

Walter Allen Sheppard died in 1915; ten years later, aged seventy-seven, Kate married William Sidney Lovell-Smith, a long-time supporter of women's suffrage and author of *Outlines of the Women's Franchise Movement in New Zealand* (published in 1905 under the name of W. S. Smith). They lived in Riccarton. Kate Lovell Smith died at her home in July 1934.

Charlotte Macdonald

Quotations
para.1 *The Prohibitionist*, 8 April 1893
para.2 *The Prohibitionist*, 20 June 1891
para.3 K. Sheppard, *Franchise Report for 1893*, H. K. Lovell-Smith Papers, ATL
para.4 *Ten Reasons why the Women of New Zealand should Vote*, Item 503 'Franchise Scraps', K. W. Sheppard Papers, Canterbury Museum
para.6 *The Prohibitionist*, 26 Sept. 1891
para.7 *The Prohibitionist*, 30 Dec. 1893
para.10 *Evening Star* (Dunedin), 19 Sept. 1914
para.11 *The White Ribbon*, 18 Aug. 1934

Unpublished Sources
Sir John Hall, MS Papers 1784, ATL
H. K. Lovell-Smith, MS Papers 1376, ATL
K. W. Sheppard Papers, Canterbury Museum

Published Sources
Grimshaw, Patricia. *Women's Suffrage in New Zealand*, Auckland, 1972
Mackay, Jessie. 'Kate Wilson Sheppard', *The White Ribbon*, 18 Aug. 1934, p.9 (obituary)
The Prohibitionist, 1891–4
Sheppard, Kate. 'Economic Independence of Married Women', introduced by Tessa Malcolm, *Women's Studies Journal*. vol.5 no.1, Sept. 1989, pp.3–24

MAUD SHERWOOD

1880-1956

Maud Kimbell was born in Dunedin, the daughter of Elizabeth and Alfred Kimbell, a fruiterer. The family moved to Wellington when she was a child and it was there that she first attended art classes. Taught by Mabel Hill and James Nairn at Wellington Technical College, she displayed a precocious talent, easily passing the South Kensington examinations for art education, established in England. Following Nairn's death in 1904, Maud was appointed to the staff at the college. Six years later, in April 1910, she held her first solo exhibition at McGregor Wright's gallery. At this point she decided to take up a scholarship for study abroad.

Although she initially set her sights on London, arriving there in January 1912, Maud soon crossed the channel to Paris. She studied briefly at Colarossi's, where Frances Hodgkins was a tutor, before entering the studio of Tudor Hart. During the summer she accompanied his sketching group (which included fellow expatriates Cora Wilding and Owen Merton) on a tour of England. A year later she travelled independently to Concarneau in Brittany, then to Holland and Bruges. Characteristic of *plein air* painters, her subject matter was picturesque, recording small villages with local fishermen and their families. She preferred to use water-colour, applying it to paper in a broad and fluid impressionist manner not unlike Hodgkins' own.

Towards the end of 1913 the artist left Europe for Australia, establishing herself in Sydney where her mother and sister were living. In August 1917 she married businessman Alfred Sherwood, but the marriage ended some three years later. Meanwhile, Maud Sherwood won local recognition for her animated compositions, based chiefly on still life studies and the model, which she exhibited with Sydney's Society of Artists and the Society of Women Painters. In 1924 she was the sole woman representative on the committee of the Water Colour Institute, a group to which leading art establishment figures (such as Sydney Long and Arthur Streeton) belonged. The same year, Sherwood's work was included in a show of Australian art at the British Empire Exhibition in Wembley.

Loath to cut her ties completely with New Zealand, the artist regularly dispatched work to the Academy of Fine Arts in Wellington and in 1925 held a comprehensive exhibition there. This comprised images from her first experience of Europe, those based on Australia, such as *The Beach, Dee Why, Sydney* (1923), and a number she produced during the months spent in Wellington preparing for the show. On returning to Sydney she once again looked towards Europe for stimulation and professional advancement. Initially accompanied by another artist from New South Wales, Gladys Owen, in February 1926 she embarked on a trip that would last for seven years.

Sherwood spent time in Naples, Florence, and Venice, amongst other places. However, it was to an American friend's villa in Capri that she repeatedly returned until 1931, when she lived and worked in an apartment overlooking the Borghese Gardens in Rome. During this sojourn Sherwood was represented at the Salon des Indépendants, Paris (1928), the Prima Mostra Internazionale d'Arte

Coloniale. Rome (1931), and the Royal Academy, London (1932). Equipped with credentials which would enhance her reputation in Australia, she returned to Sydney, which she regarded as her home for the remaining twenty-three years of her life.

Her first solo show in that city was held in August 1933 at the prestigious Macquarrie Galleries. The vibrant water-colours and dense charcoal drawings of European subjects earned her considerable praise from reviewers. They also prompted William Moore in his *Story of Australian Art* (1934) to declare that:

with all its broadness and boldness, there was a sureness in draughtsmanship which left no doubt as to her power to give weight and distinction to her varied compositions.

The travels in search of appropriate motifs did not cease as Sherwood grew older. With the aid of a caravan she explored and recorded the rugged back-country areas of New South Wales. She also took up relief printing and produced linocuts such as *Petunias* and *Venetian Fishing Boats*, which parallel the bold graphic designs of Thea Proctor and Margaret Preston. Water-colour, however, remained her preferred medium, used in the last years for a series of flower studies which retained the authority of her earlier work.

Maud Sherwood was regarded in the 1930s as a leading Australian artist, but it is her country of origin which has subsequently acknowledged this woman's achievement.   *Anne Kirker*

Quotation
para.6 W. Moore, *The Story of Australian Art*, vol.1, Sydney, 1934, p.109

Unpublished Sources
Maud Sherwood Papers, 1912–1960, MS Papers 1976, ATL

Published Sources
Maud Sherwood 1880–1956 (exhibition catalogue), Robert McDougall Art Gallery, Christchurch, 1985

HARRIET SIMPSON

1822–1907

Harriet Simpson, her husband Joseph, and daughter Bessie arrived in Canterbury on the *Charlotte Jane* in December 1850, employed in the service of Charles and Georgiana Bowen. They soon left the Bowens' service because they could get better wages than the £40 a year the Bowens offered. Joseph obtained work in Lyttelton and later went on to the gold-rushes in Australia where he died.

In November 1856 Harriet applied for the post of nurse at the Lyttelton Hospital. She wrote in her application:

Should I be fortunate in gaining the appointment I would make it my best endeavour to do all in my power for the comfort of the sick that would fall to my care and to carry out all your wishes.

Dr Donald, who was in charge of the hospital, recommended her appointment and she commenced her duties that year.

Lyttelton Hospital was situated in the old Customs House building. The number of patients would swell when ships arrived in port with sickness on board, but usually there were about six patients to be looked after. Dr Donald was pleased with Harriet's work, and wrote to the Canterbury Provincial Council in 1858 praising her. No extra nursing had been required since her appointment and on several occasions Harriet stayed up all night nursing patients.

Harriet also took charge of the five Berry children who had left England in 1859 with their parents on the *Clontarf*. There were thirty-six deaths on the voyage out to Lyttelton, including two of the Berry children, their mother, and a stillborn baby. Their father, James, was sent to the Lyttelton Hospital on arrival and died from consumption in June 1860. The children were left to the care of the provincial council and remained at the hospital. Harriet offered to look after them if allowed extra rations.

As the population of Canterbury increased, the hospital suffered badly from overcrowding. Harriet wrote to the provincial secretary on 6 September 1861:

. . . it is impossible to find room for the Hall and Loft have patients sleeping in them for my Self I am compelled to make use of a shake down in the Kitchen which has another patient also in it . . . I alone have 17 cases to cook feed nurse . . .

In January 1862 Harriet handed in her notice – she was to marry Captain David Ritchie that March. A condition of the marriage was that the Berry children could be taken into her new home, as well as Mr Thompson, a cripple whom she looked after.

In 1864 Harriet was appointed matron of the Christchurch Female Home. The home was inaugurated by Maria Rye, who came to New Zealand from

The Christchurch Home for Women of Respectable Character, where Harriet Simpson (Ritchie) was matron in the 1860s. *Canterbury Museum*

England to further the objectives of the Female Middle Class Emigration Society. The society's original aim was to recruit young women to go to the colonies as governesses, to arrange and in part finance their passages, and to find them appointments on arrival. There was much concern about the fate of these women after their arrival; it was feared some of them would turn to prostitution as they often had no family or friends.

The Female Home (initially called the Christchurch Home for Servants of Respectable Character) was set up to provide a safe and respectable home for women of good character during temporary lack of employment or convalescence after discharge from hospital. It had a servants' registry attached. Harriet with her nursing experience was ideally suited for the job.

Harriet and David Ritchie moved to the home which opened in a house on Worcester Street on 25 January 1864. Harriet's salary was £100. During the first year 190 employers registered, and 320 servants were employed through the registry. Harriet was commended for the conscientious discharge of her duties and excellent management. During the next year 218 women stayed in the home and 288 servants were employed. Applications had numbered 545 for servants, the demand far outweighing the supply. Harriet was praised as indefatigable in her endeavours for the prosperity of the home. The home moved to Peterborough Street and was extended to accommodate invalids from the country; a repository for fancy and plain needlework was started on a commission basis. At the beginning of 1867 Harriet left. The home was closed eighteen months later.

David Ritchie was lost at sea, and in the late 1870s Harriet set up as a dressmaker in Armagh Street and took in boarders. She was known for her philanthropy. She died on 30 September 1907.   *Jo-Anne Smith*

Quotations
para.2 Letter 671/56, Canterbury Provincial Council Records
para.5 Letter 1627/61, Canterbury Provincial Council Records

Unpublished Sources
Canterbury Provincial Council Records: Inward Correspondence to Provincial Secretary, Letters 671/56, 363/58, 625/60, 1627/61, Canterbury Museum
Ellen Bruce, 'Recollections', MS typescript, Canterbury Museum
G. R. Macdonald Biographies, Canterbury Museum
W. R. Norris, Christchurch Hospital MS, Canterbury Museum

Published Sources
The Press, 20 Aug. 1863; 3 Dec. 1863; 24 Feb. 1865; 11 March 1865; 27 Oct. 1865; 28 March 1866; 25 June 1869

MIRIAM SOLJAK

1879–1970

'If you've got your housework done, dear,' Miriam Soljak used to say to her daughter, 'it's a sign you're neglecting the movement.' There was a great deal of housework in Miriam Soljak's life – she and her husband Peter had seven children and erratic income – but she never let it interfere with her lifelong commitment to the Labour movement.

She was born Miriam Cummings in Thames in 1879, to parents of strong but divided principles who brought their two sons up Protestant, their five daughters Catholic. From primary school, Miriam became a pupil-teacher, attended a training school in New Plymouth, and began teaching in Northland. In her first school, at Pakaru, some classes were taught in Maori; she boarded with a part-Maori family and gained a fluency in the Maori language and a deep concern for Maori culture and welfare that would last her life through.

In Rotorua in 1908 Miriam married Peter Soljak. Recently arrived from Yugoslavia, Peter Soljak had little education or command of English but he was able to turn his hand to anything. In Northland he traded in kauri gum, built stone fences, dug ditches; later, at Tauranga, he worked land at Gate Pa and carried flax by tow-boat to the rope works and shells to the lime works. It all entailed constant moving about: the family lived in eight different houses in the Tauranga district alone. For some time after her marriage Miriam was able to resume her teaching career. At Kawakawa, so highly valued was her knowledge of Maori, she was provided with a school house and day care for her three young children. It was the birth of her fourth child that ended her career as a teacher.

When the First World War broke out, the pride Miriam took in both the Maori and Pakeha elements of her New Zealand heritage was sorely tried and the injustice of New Zealand's nationality law as it affected women was harshly borne in on her. She learned that by her marriage she had exchanged her own nationality for that of her husband. Moreover, although Peter Soljak had come to New Zealand partly to avoid conscription into the army of the hated Austrian Empire, he and his wife were now classed as Austro-Hungarians, enemy aliens obliged to register with the police and submit to various restrictions on their travel and possessions. When Miriam's youngest child was due, she was refused admission to the maternity hospital.

The registration of aliens was maintained after the war, and in February 1919 an angry Miriam, on threat of prosecution, was forced to register. She insisted that the constable who witnessed the document write on it that she did so 'under protest'. The indignation she felt would sustain her efforts over the next twenty years to secure for New Zealand women their own independent nationality, irrespective of marriage. Her efforts undoubtedly helped put the issue on the Labour Party's agenda. In 1927 Peter Fraser sent her, 'with compliments', a signed copy of his bill reforming women's nationality. In fact the New Zealand government could not alter its nationality law, which was part of a general law operating throughout the whole British Commonwealth.

When the family moved to Auckland in 1920, Miriam's political awareness developed sharply. She found an ideological home in the Auckland Women's Branch of the New Zealand Labour Party, of which she was an active, sometimes turbulent member in the late 1920s. The branch shared her commitment to pacifism, specifically the abolition of compulsory military training, and to improving the position of women: motherhood endowment, maternal mortality, child welfare, and sex hygiene were all debated with fervour. In 1926 Miriam helped organise a successful demonstration outside the Auckland Town Hall to protest the withholding of unemployment relief from women workers. She was authorised to speak to churches and heads of secondary schools on compulsory military training. She drew the branch's attention to the problems facing urban Maori and in turn explained Labour policy, in Maori, to Maori groups. As delegate to the Labour Party Conference in 1929 she put forward a remit in favour of birth control which earned the branch the tag 'those dreadful women'.

The end of the decade, however, marked an abrupt end to her work with the Auckland Women's Branch. She was censured for controversial public statements in its name and the life membership she had been voted was expunged from the minutes. Her abrasive style and refusal to compromise also caused a breach with old Labour allies such as Bob Semple and Michael Savage. For a time in the mid-thirties she turned to the Communist Party.

She also clashed head-on with the Roman Catholic Church. Angered by a priest whose advice to her on family limitation was 'submit or abstain', she wrote a series of letters as 'Zealandia' to the *New Zealand Herald* advocating birth control. She became and remained for the rest of her life a member of the Rationalist Association; when the Family Planning Association was formed, she was a foundation member.

'If you've got your housework done . . . it's a sign you're neglecting the movement' — Miriam Soljak. *Connie Purdue*

In 1936–7 Miriam's concern for women's nationality was sharply revived when she spent almost a year with one of her sons in England. Although Peter Soljak had naturalised in 1929, she had to travel abroad on a passport stamped 'wife of alien, now naturalised' and to report to the British police. Her divorce from Peter Soljak, finalised in 1937, made no difference to this status; her nationality of birth would only be restored to her by a new nationality law in 1948.

On her return to New Zealand, up to and during the Second World War, Miriam Soljak continued to promote women's rights and the peace movement. When the war was over, she settled with a wounded son at Point Chevalier.

Once again she became an active member of the Labour Party, which at last rewarded her loyalty by the gold badge for long service. Miriam Soljak died at the age of ninety-one in 1970.   *Dorothy Page*

Unpublished Sources
Information was provided by two of Miriam Soljak's children, C. Purdue and L. Soljak.
M. Dobbie, Manuscript on early years of the Family Planning Association, in private possession
Minutes of the Auckland Women's Branch of the NZ Labour Party, qMS, ATL

Published Sources
Boese, K. M. *Kawakawa School Centenary; including Pakaru, Whangae, 1873–1973*, Kawakawa, 1973
Page, D. 'Women and Nationality: Feminist Organisations in the Inter-war Period', in B. Brookes, C. Macdonald, M. Tennant (eds), *Women in History*, Wellington, 1986
Purdue, C. (ed.). *Women in the Labour Cause: the History of the Auckland Women's Branch, NZLP, 1925–1975*, Auckland, 1975

GWEN SOMERSET

1894–1988

Gwendolen Lucy Alley was born on 16 November 1894 in Springfield, North Canterbury, the second child of Frederick Alley and Clara (born Buckingham). There were seven children in the family, several of whom achieved distinction and one, Rewi Alley, became world famous. When Gwen was three, the family moved to Amberley, where her father was headmaster of the district high school. He was strict with his children, but some of Gwen's attitudes and ideas came from him. She wrote: 'To him, education was not merely a fact-finding routine but the fulfilment of each child's inborn capacity . . .' Her mother (a member of the first National Council of Women in 1892) allowed the children more freedom, and in the holidays they built dams and tree-houses and bathed naked in the creek.

After the family moved to Christchurch, Gwen began at the age of fourteen to attend Christchurch Girls' High School, an experience which in some ways she found claustrophobic and a poor preparation for life. At the age of sixteen, she became a pupil-teacher in a Christchurch primary school, where she disliked the rigid discipline and corporal punishment. In 1915–16, she attended teachers' college and then, while continuing with primary school teaching, attended classes at Canterbury University College.

Attending a WEA summer school in Oxford, North Canterbury, in early 1921, she said, changed the course of her life. Not only was she invigorated by contact with James Shelley, Professor of Education at Canterbury College, but she was led to apply for a teaching position in Oxford. Here she began to develop her ideas on education.

Finding that many children had been working on the farm each morning since 4 am and needed relaxation at school, Gwen started the day with singing and dancing. Her teaching methods were too free for some of the parents, but the inspectors and headmaster pointed out that Gwen was providing music, physical education, and handwork, which were prescribed in the syllabus.

In 1923, she achieved her wish to teach beginners when she was appointed infant mistress. Acting, gardening, and pottery became standard activities and, since there was little supplementary reading for young children, Gwen wrote her own booklets. Later, she wrote of this time:

There was always a sharing of the living and moving outside world, always an empathy, a two way communication. We were not enclosed like bottled fruit while trying to pursue unreal, irrelevant, even unnecessary 'subjects' and routines.

She removed the teacher's table and chair as symbols of authority and sat on children's chairs herself. The children loved the freedom they were given to carry out their own ideas. One of them began each day with the prayer, 'Please God, don't make it Saturday.'

In 1931, Gwen married Crawford Somerset, who shared her views on education. His book, *Littledene*, gives an excellent picture of the life and institutions of Oxford and the surrounding district. Their two sons, Anthony and David, were born in the next few years. A former pupil of Gwen looked after the house and children while Gwen continued to teach.

A Carnegie Fellowship was awarded jointly to the Somersets in 1936. They attended the First World Conference in Early Childhood Education in England, and visited educational institutions, including nursery schools, and art galleries and theatres in Europe and the United States.

After one more year in Oxford, the Somersets became co-directors of the Feilding Community Centre for Further Education. Gwen had been closely involved with the activities for adults while in Oxford and, with adult education now the core of their work, she and her husband turned their hands and minds to whatever appeared valuable to the community.

They ran classes on a variety of topics, including child development and art appreciation. They supported local clubs in their activities and on late shopping nights they showed films, borrowed from the National Film Library, to the children of shoppers. Gwen was keenly interested in drama, and she and Crawford established the Feilding Community Players, a drama group which built a little theatre out of a tin shed and presented both one-act and full-length plays, including *The Merchant of Venice*, *A Midsummer Night's Dream*, and the Gilbert and Sullivan opera, *H.M.S. Pinafore*.

Another of Gwen's interests was the creation of a play group for children under five, which she ran with the help of secondary schoolgirls. This was the first time she had worked in pre-school education.

Gwen's life changed direction when Crawford accepted a post in the department of education at Victoria University College, Wellington, in 1947. Many organisations were eager to enlist her help but she decided to work in the pre-school field. She already had contacts with the Nursery Play Centre movement, which had started in Wellington in 1941. In 1948, she was elected first president of the New Zealand Federation of Nursery Play Centres, inspiring the four associations with her progressive ideas and encouraging an interest in adult education in the movement. At the request of the Play Centre Association, she wrote *I Play and I Grow*, published in 1949 and revised many times. She wrote many booklets for play centre parents and edited the *Play Centre Journal*. Her direct, easy style was well suited to spreading new ideas on child development and family relationships among parents.

Gwen also became active in the WEA, serving on an advisory committee for adult education for thirty years, and in the Free Kindergarten movement; she lectured on child development at the Wellington Free Kindergarten Training College for years and became Dominion adviser to kindergarten associations throughout the country. Her work was recognised by the award of an MBE in 1964.

Early in 1970, two years after her husband's death, Gwen went to Nairobi to care for her son Anthony's three children, whose mother had died, and stayed there for two years.

Gwen exemplified her belief that education should be a lifelong activity. She continued her interest in pre-school education throughout her eighties and early nineties, writing new material for pre-school groups and revising some of her early work. Her autobiography, *Sunshine and Shadow*, was published in 1988. To the end of her long life, she maintained an interest in her family and friends and in young children. At ninety, she still planned eagerly for her garden. She died on 31 October 1988.

Victoria University of Wellington awarded Gwen the honorary degree of Doctor of Laws in 1975, the first honorary degree it awarded to a woman. The house in Kelburn Parade which the family occupied for twenty years was bought by the university, moved to another site on campus, and named Somerset House after two outstanding people.   *Beryl Hughes*

Quotations
para.1 G. Somerset, *Sunshine and Shadow*, p.25
para.5 G. Somerset, *Sunshine and Shadow*, p.163

Published Sources
Somerset, G. *I Play and I Grow*, Wellington, 1949
Somerset, G. *Sunshine and Shadow*, Auckland, 1988
Somerset, G. *Vital Play*, Auckland, 1976
Somerset, G. *Work and Play in a Preschool Playgroup* (7th revised edn), Auckland, 1975

MARY STANLEY

1919–1980

Mary Stanley was a poet whose talent manifested itself briefly in her collection *Starveling Year* (1953). This minuscule thirty-one-page booklet is all but invisible on the library shelf between the solid collected works of her male contemporaries.

Born in 1919, Mary grew up in Thames, the eldest of four. She became an ardent girl guide, sang in the church choir, played the piano well, and was 'always writing'. A strong character, close to her mother, she fought continuously with her father who would not brook opposition. Dux of Thames High School, she went to university in 1935 and later trained as a teacher. She married a young accountant shortly before he was killed in the war.

Mary was lovely, her expression serene, her hair honey-coloured. She had a beautiful speaking voice which she never raised in class. After the war she married teacher and poet Kendrick Smithyman. For a time they lived with their son Christopher in a fibrolite bach on Pine Island (now Herald Island) in Auckland Harbour. Mary had already developed the arthritis which was to cripple her increasingly; coping was a struggle, but she was happy writing. The poem 'Householder' says:

> And yet I like this house under the pines.
> We have mended the roof, painted the walls, set all
> in order. Only the garden will not be tamed.

Settled finally on Auckland's North Shore with three sons, Mary made their small house a pleasant place with books, pottery, flowers, and her family piano. Mary and Kendrick shared a passion for gardening, gourmet cooking, and literary discussion – her sister once found them talking to each other in rhyming couplets.

Mary resumed teaching in the 1960s. Colleagues appreciated her personality and ability to involve children in her love of the arts. Her rich experience of life is reflected in poems which celebrate passion and conjugal affection, but also convey the pain and separateness of romantic love:

> . . . At the end we come home
> to the same bed, fallen like stones or stars
> in a country
> no one travels.

Mary's poetic use of the particularities of a woman's life was unusual in the 1940s. Her work includes 'For My Mother', a deceptively simple portrait of a complex relationship, and salutes to her sons. 'The Wife Speaks', classically balanced, crystallises a moment in which the speaker feels herself at one with the cycles of nature and all men and women leading domestic lives. As A. W. Stockwell wrote in 1953: 'Poetry of her quality, written from a woman's point of view, is sufficiently rare to make it doubly welcome in this country.'

Why did she stop writing? Lack of organisation? Or feeling overwhelmed by close contact with male writers who, she believed, trivialised her work? There are no simple answers. Housework is demanding, but Mary grew up in a household where tidiness was an obsession. Her father used to polish his gardening fork until it shone; his daughter insisted on ironing the family pyjamas.

Forced by poor health to stop teaching in the 1970s, Mary fought her arthritis bravely with doctors and fringe cures – lecithin, diets, gold, copper, mussels, acupuncture – but lived in pain. For the most part Kendrick contrived to nurse her at home as she wished. She died of a heart attack in 1980.

Jill McLaren

Quotations
Poems quoted are from *Starveling Year*.
para.6 A. W. Stockwell, Review, *Landfall* 26, 1953, p.140
Unpublished Sources
Interviews with Ruth Evans, Kendrick Smithyman, Bernard and Barbara Stanley

Published Sources

Ensing, Riemke. Introduction, *Private Gardens: An Anthology of New Zealand Women Poets*, Dunedin, 1977

Joseph, Michael. 'Mary Stanley, 1919–1980', *Islands* 28, 1980

Stanley, Mary. *Starveling Year*, Christchurch, 1953

THE WIFE SPEAKS

Being a woman, I am
not more than man nor less
but answer imperatives
of shape and growth. The bone
attests the girl with dolls,
grown up to know the moon
unwind her tides to chafe
the heart. A house designs
my day an artifact
of care to set the hands
of clocks, and hours are round
with asking eyes. Night puts
an ear on silence where
a child may cry. I close
my books and know events
are people, and all roads
everywhere walk home
women and men, to take
history under their roofs
I see Icarus fall
out of the sky, beside
my door, not beautiful,
envy of angels, but feathered
for a bloody death.

ELEANOR STEPHENSON

1808–1883

In April 1840 Eleanor Baker was settled on her own land beside the Orira River in the Hokianga, possibly the first woman alone to buy land in the new colony.

How had she come there? An unlikely pioneer, this Quaker widow in her early thirties, her children left behind in England. Married at eighteen to John Baker, she had borne seven children in nine years, buried four small boys and then her husband.

Perhaps her Quaker upbringing had shaped Eleanor's yen for independence – Quakers accorded equal status and education to daughters. Born into a staunchly Quaker family at Bristol on 4 April 1808, Eleanor Hancock had attended a Quaker boarding-school for three years.

For whatever reason, Eleanor exchanged the familiarity of home and family for a lonely, raw, and rigorous life as a Hokianga settler. She had some funds, for she purchased one hundred acres of land. In a later appeal to the governor, seeking to revive her claim to land at Orira, she explained her purchase 'as the only means of obtaining a peaceful residence and food'. Peaceful indeed, for her land was in a very isolated place. Before the end of her first year Eleanor lost everything when her house burned down. The Wesleyan missionaries over at Mangungu took her in but she soon started anew on her own land.

At Mangungu she met George Stephenson, carpenter, sawyer, and Wesleyan lay missionary. They married in 1842 and Eleanor moved to her second New Zealand home at Kaipara. Here George, a mild and unassertive man, had been cutting kauri and running a trading station for some years.

Eleanor and George moved to Auckland after only a few years. George worked as carpenter and builder, but in 1849 Eleanor claimed that their four little children were principally dependent on her. She gave no hint of the source of her income.

Unless Eleanor received money from England, she somehow accumulated it in Auckland. In 1854 she paid £500 to buy a farm on the Northland coast. The purchase deed specified that Eleanor held the land in her own right, free of the control of her husband.

'Waiaua', Eleanor's farm, occupied a fine sweep of coast, an elevated table-land with its own sheltered bay. Much of the land was bush-covered. A visitor in 1857 wrote that the Stephensons kept pigs, a few sheep and cattle, grew Indian corn, and had a small store for the natives.

After ten years Eleanor moved on to another remote and picturesque place – Moturoa Island in the Bay of Islands. This time one of her Baker sons (all three children left in England had by now emigrated to Auckland) bought it on her behalf. Eleanor and some of the family farmed Moturoa, while her husband apparently stayed at 'Waiaua' with the others.

Eleanor moved yet again, leaving a son at Moturoa. Nearly seventy now, she was not content with a grandmotherly role. Back in Auckland she bought several properties and let money out on mortgage.

To her end, Eleanor claimed independence. Her will described her as a widow, though her husband outlived her by years. Nearly all her legacies were to women, with the stipulation that they were to be 'free from the debts, control and engagements of any husband'.

Although Eleanor succeeded in establishing unusual independence for a married woman of her time, she apparently confined herself to family interests. Her death in 1883 was marked by the briefest of notices: 'At Rocky Nook, on 7 June, Mrs Eleanor Stephenson, aged seventy six years.'   *Meryl Lowrie*

Quotations
para.4 E. Stephenson to the Colonial Secretary, Auckland, 4 July 1849, OLC 1/1031, National Archives, Wellington

Unpublished Sources
Eliza White, Journal 1835, Micro MS 612, Reel 3, ATL
Land records and Eleanor Stephenson's will, Lands and Deeds Dept., Auckland
Old Land Claims 1031, 610–11, National Archives, Wellington
Quaker records, Friends' House, Euston Road, London
William Woon, Journal 1840–42, qMS, ATL
Published Sources
NZ Herald, 8 June 1883
Stewart, J. T. 'A Trip in Northern NZ, July–August 1857', *Bay of Plenty Historical Review*, vol.32 no.1

JEAN STEVENSON

1884–1948

When Jean Stevenson died in 1948, her obituary described her as 'one of the Dominion's great women leaders'. Jean Stevenson had piloted the Young Women's Christian Association (YWCA) through thirty years of phenomenal growth. Her genius lay in her ability to initiate new projects, and to inspire other people to carry them through.

In many ways she was an unlikely leader. She was never physically robust and suffered from recurrent ill health. Neither was she flamboyant or aggressive in personality. The origin of her strength was her deep Christian faith. On her retirement as general secretary of the New Zealand YWCA in 1937, Jean quoted Robert Browning's poem:

> *Religion's all or nothing – it's no smile*
> *O'contentment, sign of aspiration, sir,*
> *No quality of the finelier-tempered clay*
> *Like its whiteness or its lightness; rather stuff*
> *O' the very stuff, life of life, and self of self.*

Jean Stevenson took this concept of total commitment into her own life and never deviated from it. She believed 'in the perfectability of human life', and she saw the YWCA with its foundation in fellowship and individual development as a vehicle for realising this goal.

Jean was the oldest of thirteen children in the Stevenson family of Roslyn, Dunedin, and attended Girton College, a private girls' school. She then worked for eleven years in the office of the family firm, Irvine Stevenson, makers of jams and pickles, and to supplement her practical training took a university course in chemistry and an American correspondence course in advertising. Profiles of Jean during her career describe her as one of the earliest businesswomen in Dunedin. This background proved of great value in her YWCA work and motivated an abiding concern for the welfare of working women.

Jean was recruited to the YWCA in 1911. She trained in Adelaide and at the YWCA's New York training school, before taking up the newly created position of industrial secretary for Australia and New Zealand in 1919. As a result of the war, increasing numbers of young women were moving into areas of work which had hitherto been the exclusive domain of men. 'Practically nothing', said Jean, 'is yet known of the general effect of the stress of industrial life on the health of women workers.'

In 1924, she was appointed to the post of general secretary to the Auckland YWCA. In three short years, Jean was able to put the Auckland YWCA on the map, generating huge public support for the projects she initiated. Her concern for working women led to the establishment of a holiday house on the Manukau Harbour and a successful campaign to raise money for a huge three-storey hostel.

Jean inaugurated major swimming and athletic associations for women, centred on industries such as clothing and shoe manufacture and retailing. Two hundred girl athletes from nine city businesses took part in the first sports meeting held by the Inter-House Girls Sports Association; by 1929, 600 athletes performed before crowds of over 12,000.

An ardent champion of young working women at a time of rapid social change, Jean was often called to their defence. When Auckland girls were accused of aping men by bobbing their hair, she struck back:

I can see no reason for supposing that because a woman cuts her hair she does it with the idea of imitating men, any more than if she wears a collar and tie. I take it she cuts her hair because it is cool and convenient . . . I should be sorry to think that a woman's 'most precious quality – her womanliness' depended either upon the length of her hair or the length of her skirt.

In answer to criticisms of working women she reminded the public that they were essential to the economy: 'Everything we wear today is made by the young girls of our community.' She added cuttingly:

We think it necessary to find food and shelter and care and rest for our horse, but do not always find out whether the wages of our girls are sufficient to provide them with these things.

Later, during the Depression, she disagreed with those who argued that unemployed women should accept starvation wages.

Some people seem to think that a girl should go into a house and work for seven people for 2s 6d a week . . . This was not enough to keep the wheels of industry turning . . . Every girl is a consumer. There should be other ways of meeting the situation.

Jean Stevenson made these statements as general secretary of the New Zealand YWCA, a position she took up in 1932, at the height of the Depression. It was a mark of Jean's organisational and financial acumen that the YWCA not only survived these difficult years, but expanded. Business and professional women's clubs were started by her in 1932 as a means of organising a new constituency of white-collar women – office workers. Jean had dreams that the clubs would encourage women to 'more effectively participate in the civic and national life of their country'. Although this aim was never fully realised, in a few years the clubs developed into a nationwide federation of Business and Professional Women's Associations, independent of the YWCA.

Ill health forced Jean Stevenson to retire in 1937, but a recuperative holiday in the East led to postings in Burma and India for the next nine years. She returned to New Zealand in 1947 and died in Wellington on 19 April 1948.

Sandra Coney

Quotations
para.1 *Otago Daily Times*, 22 April 1948
para.2 J. Stevenson, 'A Good-bye Message', *NZ Girl*, 10 Dec. 1937, p.3
para.4 S. Coney, *Every Girl*, p.106
para.7 S. Coney, p.113; p.111; p.204
para.8 S. Coney, p.206

Unpublished Sources
Auckland YWCA Archives, MS 1131, AIM
Women's Archives, NCW, AIM

Published Sources
Coney, Sandra. *Every Girl: A Social History of Women and the YWCA in Auckland*, Auckland, 1986
Every Girl, 10 Dec. 1926; 10 Jan. 1927
Law, Ethel, *Down the Years*, Wellington, 1964
The NZ Girl, 10 Dec. 1937

ADELA STEWART

1846-1910

Adela Blanche Stewart, with her husband, Hugh, and their only child Mervyn, aged seven, arrived in Auckland from Belfast in 1878 as part of a planned migration from Northern Ireland under the leadership of Hugh's brother, George Vesey Stewart. She was thirty-two years of age, daughter of a British army officer, James Anderson, and had received part of her education in Paris. With her husband, then an officer in the Royal Artillery, she had been stationed in the Mediterranean, the West Indies, and Bermuda.

The Stewarts built a house eight miles from Katikati, calling it 'Athenree' after the family property in Ireland. This name was later given to the township which developed around the house. The farm was initially 300 acres, but was extended to 500 acres.

From time to time Adela had domestic help, but there were considerable periods when she had to cope with household work, gardening, and poultry rearing with only the assistance that Hugh and Mervyn could spare her. In some ways she was well equipped for her new life. Her early travels probably made her adaptable; certainly she was willing to try her hand at almost anything. Like nearly all women at the time she could sew, but she had no experience of cooking before she emigrated.

From the time of sailing to New Zealand on the *Lady Jocelyn*, Adela kept a diary on which her book *My Simple Life in New Zealand* was based. This work allows the reader to observe the development of her practical skills and the ways in which she solved the problem of her need for the social life she enjoyed in a thinly settled area.

Some of her early attempts at cooking were unsuccessful. Acting on wrong

A coach outside Athenree Post Office c.1910. The township near Katikati grew up around Adela Stewart's homestead. *Alexander Turnbull Library*

instructions, she boiled peaches with sugar all day long to make jam: 'the result was a dark unattractive looking and tasting compound.' After practice, she made between 500 and 1500 pounds of jams, jellies, bottled fruit, and marmalade a year. She became in time an accomplished cook. Using in an emergency a camp oven (a 15-inch round iron pot on legs), she once fed unexpected guests a meal of sheep's head broth, cutlets with tomato sauce, boiled mutton with caper sauce, vegetables, jelly, stewed peaches, cream, and coffee. Cooking for farm workers as well as family, for many visitors and for huge parties, she regularly made butter and bread, brewed beer, and made wine.

Gardening and poultry keeping became particular pleasures and she was skilled in many kinds of handcraft. She made a drawing-room carpet while supervising her son's lessons, and provided fancy work on a large scale for church bazaars. An energetic woman who enjoyed activity, she ran a confirmation class and a French club and was always ready to teach others her skills or to learn new ones.

For Adela one of the main drawbacks of 'Athenree' was its relative isolation. She seized all opportunities for arranging dances, picnics, and other festivities and invited friends for long visits. An uninvited guest was Te Kooti, who arrived with 'a strong armed bodyguard' and demanded beer. 'So sorry we have none,' Adela replied, and served him tea in the drawing-room.

Adela gives a lively picture of the effects on 'Athenree' of the volcanic eruption at Tarawera. Always practical, she gathered what she calls 'the strange slate-pencil scrapings-like stuff' and packed it into tin matchboxes to send to friends around the world.

The land the Stewarts had bought was poor. After a long struggle they established a sheep farm and made the garden and orchard into a show place.

But as Adela grew older, the difficulty of finding satisfactory domestic help, and of entertaining in the way she needed to satisfy her sociable nature, became too burdensome. They sold 'Athenree' and returned to England with their son in 1906.

Adela's book, *My Simple Life in New Zealand*, was published in 1908 by Robert Banks and Son, London. It gives a brisk, cheerful, and highly readable account of her experiences and provides a valuable picture of domestic life and the process of settling. Although Adela did not have the worries of poverty and a large family that many pioneer women had to endure, she led a busy life and proved a competent, resourceful woman. She was clearly a leader in social activities in the district and the centre of her close-knit household.

Hugh Stewart died in 1909. Adela returned to visit his relatives in Katikati and died there in February 1910.   *Beryl Hughes*

Quotations

para.5 A. Stewart, *My Simple Life*, p.25
para.7 A. Stewart, p.85–6
para.8 A. Stewart, p.98

Published Sources

Burke, J. B. *Burke's Peerage, Baronetage and Knightage*, London, 1967
Stewart, Adela. *My Simple Life in New Zealand*, London, 1908. All quotations are from the facsimile edition of this book (Auckland, 1971).

CATHERINE STEWART

1881–1957

Catherine Campbell Sword was born in 1881 and educated in Glasgow. Her working-class background remained an important influence throughout her life. As she said in 1940:

Perhaps I am too sympathetic to the working class, but I cannot forget that I am one of them. We hear a lot about sacrifice, but the workers do not require to learn anything about that. All down the years of industrial history they have been bludgeoned, coerced and starved into submission.

Catherine began her public work at a very young age. From 1897 to 1900 she was engaged in the weaving industry and in social service work. She was a foundation member of a women's co-operative guild in Glasgow; although the guild later failed, it continued its educational work as a women's study circle. As a young woman, Catherine read widely in economics, psychology, sociology, and comparative religions. Her reading, added to her early experiences, confirmed her as a strong socialist. She also had an active interest in women's rights, and became a member of the Women's Suffrage Political Union, although she severed her connection with the union when she discovered they wanted a property vote only. She was three times taken into custody for her suffragette activities, but each time was told by police officials to go home and behave herself – perhaps a reaction to her rather frail appearance.

At eighteen, Catherine married Charles Stewart, and by the time she was twenty-four she had three sons. Although her husband informed her that politics was something that she, as a woman, could not understand, Catherine did not allow marriage and motherhood to stifle her political curiosity. By rising at 5 am to do the housework and persuading her relations to mind the children, she managed to attend lectures at Glasgow University and also meetings of the Glasgow City Council, where she earned the title of 'the lone woman in the gallery'.

In 1921, the Stewarts emigrated to New Zealand. The following year she began her political career in Wellington by joining the Socialist Party. In 1928 she became secretary of the After-Care Association for subnormal children, representing this association on the National Council of Women. During this period she became active in the New Zealand Labour Party, and was co-founder of the Elizabeth McCombs Club, a Wellington-based Labour Party club for women which became, for a short period, the centre of women's educational and political activity within the party. She was also the first president of the Melrose-Houghton Bay branch of the Labour Party.

At fifty-seven, Catherine Stewart entered parliament. In the 1938 general election Wellington West was a new electorate which she won, as Labour Party candidate, with a majority of 956. She held the seat until she was defeated in the 1943 election.

Catherine made few speeches in the House. Unlike her colleague, Mary Dreaver, who was an uncritical supporter of her party in government, Catherine Stewart's beliefs sat, at times, uneasily with Labour's social democratic doctrine. She believed that democracy could only be achieved by the destruction of capitalism and the development of socialist states throughout the world. She was a true socialist, as her speeches show:

I saw in the city of Glasgow the suffering resulting from this iniquitous system of private enterprise . . . The days of huge profits and small wages can no longer be tolerated.

As a member of the war-time government, she continued to state her belief that only capitalists gained from war:

Let us never forget that through all the suffering and sorrow of warfare there is always a small minority of people who reap fortunes through the blood of their fellow men and women. I lay that charge here this evening on the heads and shoulders of the group of financiers and big businessmen who have always engineered war.

As well as fighting capitalism, she worked constantly to improve the position of women in society. She often used humour to get her message across:

Budgeting for a home is a much more difficult task than men realise. Even the Minister of Finance will admit that his task is a simple one in comparison. After all, he is using other people's money.

She felt strongly the need for wives to be financially independent: 'There is nothing so degrading . . . as to be financially dependent on another person. Even if [her] husband is the best, and kindest man in the world . . . A woman needs an income of her own.'

Catherine was sometimes overtly critical of the Labour government. She was never scared to air her differences openly. For example, she argued in parliament that the 1940 budget was harsh on the elderly and low-income families, suggesting that these groups were being 'robbed' in order to pay for the war.

Her implacable stand against wealth and exploitation continued throughout her years in parliament, making her position on the Labour benches at times difficult. John A. Lee, who was soon to be expelled from the Labour Party, said of her: 'I wonder if she hasn't more courage than most of the men.'

Catherine Stewart died in 1957 – a warm, principled woman who worked throughout her life for the fulfilment of socialist ideals, and for improvement in the lives of the oppressed.   *Liz Gordon*

Quotations

para.1 *NZ Parliamentary Debates*, 1940, vol.257, p.482
para.3 *NZ Listener*, 28 July 1939, p.11
para.6 *NZ Parliamentary Debates*, 1939, vol.255, p.309
para.7 *NZ Parliamentary Debates*, vol.254, p.349
para.9 *NZ Parliamentary Debates*, 1941, vol.259, p.392; *NZ Listener*, 27 June 1941, p.43
para.10 J. A. Lee, *Diaries*, p.216

Published Sources

Lee, John A. *The John A. Lee Diaries 1936–1940*, Christchurch, 1981
NZ Herald, 10 Aug. 1973
Scholefield, G. H. (ed.). *Who's Who in New Zealand*, Wellington, 1951
The Press, 17 Oct. 1938

FRANCES STEWART

1839–1916

Frances Ann Stewart was an active member of her Wanganui community, serving on various church and voluntary associations, and writing prolifically, though usually anonymously, on social affairs in the Wanganui press. As the first woman member of a hospital board, she also began an important tradition in New Zealand whereby hospital boards, more than any other local authorities, have provided a political outlet for women's concerns and abilities.

Born in Sydney in 1839, Frances came to New Zealand with her parents, Martha and Stephen Carkeek. Her father at the time of her birth was the commander of the revenue cutter *Ranger*. In 1865 she married John Tiffin Stewart, a prominent surveyor. After spending their early married years in Foxton, the couple moved with their family to Wanganui in 1889. As her children grew up, Frances, like many other women activists, had more time to devote to public interests. In the 1890s she was appointed official visitor to the Jubilee Old People's Home in Wanganui and, in 1896, she offered herself as candidate for the Wanganui Borough Council. Stewart's real aim was to gain a seat on the local hospital and charitable aid boards, since before 1909 all such boards were appointed by the territorial local bodies, rather than being decided through ratepayer election. Despite Stewart's lack of success in the local body elections, Wanganui borough councillors decided in 1897 to appoint her one of their two representatives on the boards. From this position, Stewart waged a campaign for the better training of nurses and improved management and greater levels of comfort at the Old People's Home. None of her agitation made her popular with her male colleagues, and she ultimately spent only two years on the boards, commenting in 1900 on how stressful the experience had been.

This portrait of Frances Stewart was taken in 1907 when she was sixty-seven.
Barbara Marshall

Stewart was a strong-minded and articulate woman, who sought a greater voice for women on local bodies, in parliament, and within the church. She was in favour of women's suffrage and supported temperance. However, it is questionable whether she can be characterised as 'feminist', even within the maternally based feminism of her time. She stood aloof from the main feminist organisation in Wanganui, the Women's Political League, suggesting that such bodies were doing more harm than good to the women's cause. She was suspicious of the involvement of single women in women's issues, suggesting that

any sound reformation of the relations between men and women must proceed from women who have fulfilled well their relations as they now exist . . . only those who have worked well in harness will be able to work well out of harness.

She saw little need for the education of girls beyond the age of twelve, and, herself the parent of ten, placed the blame for children's failings fairly and squarely on the shoulders of mothers, even where fathers were guilty of drunkenness and neglect. She would have judged herself on her achievements as a mother, and in her numerous letters to the press most frequently identified as such: 'A New Zealand Mother', 'Indignant Mother', 'Mother of the Old School' (as well as 'Deep Thinker', 'Grievance', and 'A Country Settler's Wife'). Stewart epitomises the contradictions and ambivalences which characterised many women activists of her time.   *Margaret Tennant*

Quotation
para.3 Unidentified press cutting [1893?] in F. Stewart, 'Scrapbook of Cuttings'

Unpublished Sources
Bronwyn Labrum. '"For the Better Discharge of Our Duties": The Women's Movement in Wanganui 1893–1903', BA Hons research essay, Massey, 1986
Frances Stewart. 'Scrapbook of Cuttings', in possession of Mrs B. Marshall
Published Source
Tennant, Margaret. *Paupers and Providers, Charitable Aid in New Zealand*, Wellington, 1989, Ch.4

MARGARET STODDART

1865–1934

Margaret Stoddart was the first of many women artists in Canterbury to practise water-colour painting with professional purpose. Belonging to the pioneer generation of New Zealand born painters, she enrolled in 1882 at the Canterbury College School of Art in its opening year and when only twenty was elected to the Council of the Canterbury Society of Arts. The society bought her flower paintings and the Canterbury Museum acquired studies of New Zealand flora. As a young woman she was seen as one of the colony's promising painters.

In common with many women artists of her time Margaret came from an enterprising, prosperous, and cultured family. Her aunt was a painter in Edinburgh. Edward Chudleigh described her mother as a clever woman and noted tersely in his diary that the Stoddart sisters had 'clear good brains'. Her father, Mark Stoddart, was an admiral's son from Edinburgh who, after emigrating to Australia, had come to New Zealand in 1851 and set up a sheep run at Rakaia Terrace. Charlotte Godley described him as a 'gentle-manlike man, fond of drawing, poetry, reading and so on'. In 1862 he married Anna Schjott, a governess and daughter of a Norwegian clergyman, and they settled at Diamond Harbour where Margaret was born on 3 October 1865. When the couple returned to Scotland for a visit in 1876 with their two sons and four daughters, Margaret attended Edinburgh Ladies College.

Her real education, however, was at home in New Zealand. Her father was a naturalist and Margaret shared his keen-eyed interest in flora and the landscape. It was in the mountains which she knew so closely and loved so much that Margaret became a painter. She learned the lie of the land and discovered hidden plots high up where alpine flowers grew. As a young woman, she kept albums (now held at the Canterbury Museum) in which she recorded trips she made around Banks Peninsula and into the high country. In 1892 she joined a climbing party which scaled Mt Torlesse and in 1896 recorded a journey along the West Coast road beyond Bealey and Craigieburn. It was on such expeditions that she sketched the landscape and collected specimens for the studies of native plants and flowers which she gave to the museum in 1907. In 1886 and 1891 she visited friends in the Chatham Islands, and in 1894 went to Australia where she was received as one of the colony's leading flower painters.

In 1897 Margaret returned to Europe and by 1898 could be contacted through Dora Meeson at her address in London. Dora was the first 'lady member' of the Canterbury Society of Arts to leave New Zealand to pursue her career in Europe. Margaret visited Norway (the home of her mother's family) and followed the sketching routes through Europe, taking in France, Switzerland, Italy, and Capri. Her teachers included Norman Garstin, who took outdoor sketching classes and counted Frances Hodgkins and Dorothy Kate Richmond amongst his pupils. She stayed at St Ives, a thriving artists' colony in Cornwall, and working there she developed the impressionistic direction of her own painting. In Christchurch, as a member of the Palette Club and student of Alfred Walsh, she had already been an enthusiastic outdoor sketcher. It may also have been at St Ives that she took lessons from an Australian, Louis Grier, and an American, Charles Lasar.

Times were hard for colonial women artists who sought to establish a reputation in England. Frances Hodgkins recorded with admiration how Margaret was managing to live on a pound a week when she and Dorothy Kate Richmond called on her in 1902 at St Ives. However, that year at an exhibition held by New Zealand artists in London she sold four water-colours and was singled out for special praise by the *Sunday Times*. She exhibited with the Royal Birmingham Society of Artists in 1898 and 1899, and was accepted by the Royal Society of British Artists in 1899 and 1900. She exhibited with the Royal Institute of Painters in Watercolour as well as at venues in Paris and Rome. In 1906 her work was shown at Baillie's Gallery as well as with the well-established Society of Women Artists and at the traditional prestigious Royal Academy. Viewed from New Zealand at this time, these events constituted success; after nine years in the closed shop of the London art world, she had achieved perhaps a little more and certainly no less than her fellow expatriates.

In 1906, aged forty-one, Margaret rejoined her mother and sister Agnes at the 'Big House' at Diamond Harbour; they ran the household and she continued to pursue her painting. After her mother's death and the sale of the property in 1913, she moved to the Cashmere Hills above Christchurch. Settling back into New Zealand life and exhibiting regularly with the art societies, she joined the

Margaret Stoddart, left, boiling a billy on the West Coast Road, April 1896. *Canterbury Museum*

Society for Imperial Culture and became one of the first members of the Christchurch Women's Club.

Apart from exhibiting in Paris at the Salon des Artistes Francais, she channelled her energies into artistic life in Canterbury. Whilst regularly showing her flower paintings Margaret continued to travel and paint in the South Island's high country. In her later years she went on sketching trips with Cora Wilding and the young Olivia Spencer Bower. Seeking characteristic regional features in her painting, she captured the starkness and bold austerity of the Canterbury mountains, plains, and dry river beds.

It was as a flower painter and as a landscapist who developed impressionistic and regional painting that Margaret Stoddart made her contribution to cultural life in New Zealand. Although belonging to a generation of expatriate painters, she returned to New Zealand and her painting flourished in her native landscape. She became a well-loved Canterbury artist and enjoyed the admiration of contemporaries and the respect of younger painters including Evelyn Page and Rita Angus. Toss Woollaston recalled how she instilled in younger artists the need for varied brushwork, always a distinctive feature of her own painting. To Olivia Spencer Bower she was an example of an older woman artist who never stopped responding to a new challenge. She died in Hanmer on 10 December 1934.   *Julie King*

Quotations
para.2 E. R. Chudleigh, Diary 1886–87, 5 Aug. 1887 (see also 20 June 1887), Canterbury Museum; Charlotte Godley, *Letters from Early New Zealand 1850–1853*, ed. J. R. Godley, Christchurch, 1951, p.318

Unpublished Sources
M. O. Stoddart, Albums, Canterbury Museum
R. Burgess, 'Margaret O. Stoddart (1865–1934)', Canterbury Public Library

Published Sources
Harper, Barbara. *Petticoat Pioneers: South Island Women of the Colonial Era*, Book Three, Wellington, 1980, pp.221–5
King, J. 'Margaret Stoddart: Landscapes of a Canterbury Flower Painter', *Art NZ*, no.31, 1984, pp.46–9
Thompson, S. L. & Shelley, J. 'Miss M. O. Stoddart', *Art in NZ*, vol.8 no.2, Dec. 1935, pp.99–101

ALICE STOTT

1867–1933

Who was Alice Zelda Stott? Like most of our foremothers, she was not among the few women selected by a reluctant patriarchy to become 'famous'. She is in that sense typical of that large group of working-class women whose lives become invisible, forgotten except by family and remaining friends. In another sense her life was atypical, lived at the intersection of cultures in conflict, of swift adaptations for survival, of the worlds of the nineteenth and twentieth centuries.

Much of her life remains unknown. Her birth, on 1 August 1867, was registered to George Stott and Rachel Waterhouse, her place of birth given as Waimea East. George had married Rachel bigamously at Richmond in 1858, having abandoned a wife and three children, one of whom was also called Alice, back in Manchester. The Waterhouses had arrived in Nelson on the *Martha Ridgeway* in 1841 when Rachel was eleven, and George came in 1858. Seven children were registered to George and Rachel, an unusual attention to form during a time when registration was not always complied with. Some of these children were surprisingly dark, in particular Alice and her brother Thomas, born in 1865. The family explained this by claiming Spanish descent – a claim which was quite false.

When the children were small, George and Rachel packed the family on horses and left for the West Coast, apparently because of a 'scandal' which made life in the Nelson area difficult. The nature of this scandal is unknown. The dark-skinned children may have been adopted from Maori in the area, or George may have added a Maori wife to the family. After years of prospecting for gold on the Coast, George died in 1895, of 'softening of the brain and exhaustion', followed by Rachel in 1904 at the Lyell. One daughter is said to have drowned while panning for gold in the Buller, but the others survived into adulthood.

Alice is next heard of in 1894, when she married John Laurie, born in Timaru in 1864 and descended from Cornish quarry-workers. Her occupation is given as 'domestic servant' in Nelson, while John is identified as a miner. John, a keen sportsman, earned money as a bare-fist boxer, runner and walker throughout the South Island, moving from place to place according to chance. Alice and John lived for a time at the Lyell, where they ran a beer tent and where their eldest son was born. By 1899, John was bookmaking, and is said to have prudently left the country when the police bore down on him at Nelson. He set off for Kalgoorlie and the gold-strikes of Australia, followed by Alice, pregnant and with three small children. Their youngest child, Allan, was born in a tent at Kalgoorlie, where Alice managed childcare in a wild environment of prospectors, heat, and few amenities. The three older children attended school in the area, being transported there by goat-cart, as a family photograph shows.

John Laurie died suddenly in 1903, either from drinking poisonous water or from a ruptured appendix. Alice, widowed with four small children, managed to get to Sydney – family stories indicate that the miners took up a collection for the fare. In Sydney she put the children into the Salvation Army orphanage – a receipt dated 1903 shows that she paid £1/10- for three months' board. She then went to sea, working as a cook-stewardess on various ships to support the children and to earn the passage money for her eventual return home. Family stories indicate that she worked on ships sailing the South China Seas and also possibly between Australia and California. She met George William Dighton from Queensland and they returned to New Zealand, taking the children out of the orphanage. They married in 1904 and the children took 'Bill''s name.

The family settled in Napier and in about 1914 took in another child – Annie Stott, Alice's niece. Annie was one of Thomas Stott's four children; when his wife Amelia left him, Annie and her brother Jack had been fostered by a relation who worked for the Barton Bros. Circus. From the age of eight Annie was in training as a trapeze artist but suffered from asthma. According to family stories, her father Thomas wrote to Alice when the circus was in Napier, asking her to get Annie out of the circus. Alice kept Annie until 1917, when she returned to her father on the West Coast. In 1915 Alice adopted a baby, Mick. She was then forty-eight years old and continued periodic work at sea, as well as taking in boarders and doing occasional crop-picking. Bill worked as a road contractor, though work was not always regular. In about 1915 the family moved to Wellington, where they lived at a variety of addresses. Alice's daughters, Girlie and Ivy, followed her to sea and married sailors. Her son Jack fought in the First World War and then became a schoolteacher, Allan became a surveyor, while Mick fought in the Spanish Civil War and then settled in Australia. Alice continued to take in a number of boarders and sometimes went to Nelson for the hop-picking. The date of her last job at sea is unclear, but she continued in paid work until shortly before her death in 1933. She is buried with her brother Thomas at Karori Cemetery.

Alison J. Laurie

Sources
Information has been obtained from family stories and records. The author is Alice Stott's granddaughter.

ANNA STOUT

1858–1931

Anna Paterson Logan was born on 29 September 1858 at 'Ferntree Cottage' on Royal Terrace in Dunedin. Her mother, Jessie Alexander Logan (born Pollock), and father, John Logan, clerk to the superintendent of Otago, had emigrated from Greenock, Scotland, in 1854. As a girl, Anna was strongly influenced by her Presbyterian upbringing and her parents' interest in prohibition and other social reforms. She was remembered as being 'strong and courageous, not afraid of criticism, or even sneers' and had 'fine, almost delicately carved features'.

On 27 December 1876, eighteen-year-old Anna married a thirty-two-year-old barrister and member of parliament, Robert Stout, at her parents' home in London Street. At first, the young couple lived at the London Street property where most of their six children were born. During the first year of her marriage, Anna's loneliness during Robert's absences in Wellington and her longing for her husband are revealed in a letter that she wrote to him:

Please do write me longer letters, and let them be more juicy, not so cut and dry as if you were afraid to write your thoughts and feelings to me. You always begin about letters; next, weather; third, politics; and lastly, a lecture on looking after myself. You can't tell how I long to hear what you are thinking and feeling. When I get your letters I always know there is nothing that makes me feel as if you were with me. You can't tell how I am longing for you, or you would write me more, and with more feeling. Surely you are not getting tired of me already. The year is not up yet, remember. Anna.

During the early years of her marriage, Anna was kept busy bearing and bringing up her children, but domestic staff enabled her to embark on a long career in voluntary work. In 1885 she became a foundation member of the Women's Christian Temperance Union; in 1886 a foundation member of the

New Zealand Alliance. Anna had a strong commitment also to the advancement and protection of women. She believed that men and women should have equal political and legal rights, equal pay for equal work (but only where women succeeded in doing the work equally well), and equal opportunity for educational advancement. In 1892 she became one of two presidents elected to lead the first Women's Franchise League in Dunedin. To a colleague she once commented: 'If ever I am false to the woman's cause I hope you'll send me over the edge of the wharf.'

In 1886, while he was premier of the colony, Robert was made Knight Commander of the Order of Saint Michael and Saint George (KCMG), and Anna became Lady Stout. In February 1895, the Stout family arrived in Wellington to settle permanently. Robert became Chief Justice in June 1899, and in July the foundation stone was laid for their grand residence at 238 Wellington Terrace.

In 1894, Eva McLaren, foreign corresponding secretary to the International Council of Women, wrote to Kate Sheppard, suggesting that she and Lady Stout assist in forming a National Council of Women to co-ordinate the activities of women's organisations in New Zealand, with Kate taking the lead and Anna as vice-president. In April 1896 the first convention of the NCW was held, under the auspices of the Canterbury Women's Institute. Anna Stout was elected one of the first vice-presidents.

In Wellington in 1895, Anna formed the Southern Cross Society for the purpose of educating 'women from all classes and of all shades of opinion'. She was especially interested in the education of Maori women. Her egalitarian sentiments were radical for one who mixed in élite social circles in the capital city. Anna was also a foundation member in Wellington of the Society for the Protection of Women and Children, devoted to protecting women and children from maltreatment, supplying legal assistance in obtaining redress, and improving the legal rights of women. She believed that 'in all social matters it is necessary for the protection of the weaker to put more rigid restrictions on the stronger' and that men should 'stand upon an equality with women in the divorce law'.

We have too long excused the stronger sex, and blamed and punished the weaker, when we all know that, if the stronger were subject to equal punishment, it would act as a lever to keep them on the right path.

Anna Stout was 'quite prepared to face all the ridicule that jealousy and ignorance might cast' and noted that 'all reforms and reformers had in their time undergone ridicule'. She was fearless and outspoken in her views, and as a result frequently became involved in controversy. Anna expressed disappointment that the first convention of the NCW in 1896 had been 'confined to political questions' and that, with one exception, the societies invited and represented were political organisations:

The Council was intended to represent, and should represent, all societies of women, and its object in the meantime was to have all women engaged in industrial, professional, social and political work organised, and afterwards represented by delegates in the Council.

Their president, Kate Sheppard, retaliated by stating that it was 'true that all the subjects dealt with were political, but it is difficult in a democratic country to draw the line between political and social', and that five of the eleven societies which attended were in fact social organisations and industrial bodies *had* been invited to co-operate. The following year, Anna refused to attend because for a second time the venue was Christchurch and she again publicly attacked the NCW over the same issues. Her charges were refuted by the 1897 convention in open council and rebutted by Kate Sheppard in the press.

Anna Stout's concerns extended not only to all classes of people but to other races. Over the question of Chinese immigrants, she crossed swords publicly with her husband. Although Robert Stout was president of the Anti-Chinese League, Anna opposed the Undesirable Immigrants Bill of 1896 because, in her view, the Chinese were

desirable immigrants on account of their honesty, sobriety, industry, thrift and kindness . . . If the Chinese in the colony lived in insanitary surroundings, it was the fault of the defective inspection.

On 5 March 1909 Anna and Robert Stout sailed with their daughter from Wellington to the United Kingdom. There, Anna was described as

a lady who combines with a most charming and attractive personality, a keen intelligence, a thorough and exact knowledge of literature and art; and whose outlook on life has been broadened and sweetened by actual contact with people in all grades of society.

Robert returned to New Zealand later that year but Anna remained in

Anna Paterson and Robert Stout on their wedding day, 27 December 1876. *Alexander Turnbull Library*

England until 1912: four of their children were studying there but Anna also became actively involved with the highly publicised and bruising English suffrage campaign. She joined the International Council of Women, the London Lyceum, and the Women's Social and Political Union, spoke at meetings, and published articles in the press and elsewhere in defence of the women's cause. In doing so, she struck up friendships with the Pankhursts and other feminist leaders. Anna fought for the female franchise in England by appealing to the conservative values of the ruling classes and by presenting New Zealand as a successful model:

Instead of becoming addicted to masculine habits, as the result of the suffrage, the New Zealand women have developed a much higher standard of womanhood and the duties and obligations of motherhood . . .

This was manifested by the growth of societies for the protection and promotion of the health of women and children, the increase in the New Zealand birth rate, and the decline in infant mortality. Women were still 'very womanly and domesticated women', men were 'very manly men', and

the united and loyal comradeship of men and women have secured for New Zealand reforms in legislation which are making the Dominion a paradise for men as well as women and children.

Upon her return to New Zealand, however, for the domestic audience Anna ceased to present the results of female suffrage in glowing terms. Instead, on the twenty-first anniversary of women's suffrage in New Zealand, she put herself out of step with most former campaigners by expressing deep disappointment and disillusionment with 'the selfishness and apathy of the unthinking and irresponsible women' and 'the doormat and doll type of women':

When in England, and amongst the leading women thinkers of the day, who have made almost a religion of the vote, one cannot help but think that New Zealand women were emancipated before they had realised the great power and responsibility which the vote had placed in their hands for the uplifting of their sex and the protection of their children.

At this time of her life, Anna Stout belonged to a formidable array of organisations: the Plunket Society, the League of Nations Union, the English Speaking Union, the Pioneer Wellington Club, the Lyceum Club, the Wellington Women's Club, the Society of Fine Arts, the Women's National Reserve, and numerous educational and charitable committees. In 1922 she published a pamphlet opposing compulsory notification of syphilis, possibly fearing the reimposition of the double moral standard associated with the recently repealed Contagious Diseases Act. In 1920, she gave the University of Otago £500 to establish the Anna Paterson Stout Scholarship for women in economics, history, and home science, and in 1926 she donated £50 to Victoria University College as a bursary for women undergraduates to commemorate her golden wedding anniversary.

In later years, Anna became very deaf and used a silver ear-trumpet 'which was very convenient at times when she did not want to hear what was being said'. Anna Stout died on 10 May 1931 at Queen Mary Hospital at Hanmer Springs of a cerebral haemorrhage. She was survived by her four sons and two daughters, Robert having died the preceding year. An old fellow-worker paid Anna tribute:

Of all the daughters born in Dunedin there stands out one who loved her nation and who possessed clear vision and generous impulse.

Roberta Nicholls

Quotations

para.1 *The White Ribbon*, 18 June 1931, p.2c; W. H. Dunn and I. L. M. Richardson, *Sir Robert Stout*, p.55

para.2 Dunn and Richardson, p.55

para.3 *The White Ribbon*, 18 June 1931, p.2c

para.6 Lady Anna Paterson Stout, *Southern Cross Society: Its Objects* [Address by Lady Stout delivered at the inaugural meeting of the Southern Cross Society, Wellington, August 22, 1895], Wellington, 1895, p.1, p.2

para.7 *The White Ribbon*, June 1896, p.4

para.8 *Lyttelton Times*, 18 April 1896

para.9 Dunn and Richardson, p.197

para.10 Anna Stout, 'What the Franchise has done for the Women and Children of New Zealand', *The English Woman*, vol.6 no.16, May 1910, pp.7–8, 124–9; Lady Stout, *Woman Suffrage in New Zealand*, London, 1911, p.21; Dunn and Richardson, p.198

para.11 *Evening Star* (Dunedin), 19 Sept. 1914, p.11

para.13 M. L. Greig, 'Wives of the Prime Ministers of New Zealand', manuscript, 1962, ATL; *The White Ribbon*, 18 June 1931, p.2

Published Sources

Dunn, W. H. and Richardson, I. L. M. *Sir Robert Stout: A Biography*, Wellington, 1961

The White Ribbon, 18 June 1931 (obituary)

BATHIE STUART

1893–1987

Bathie was aptly named by her Scottish grandmother when she was born in Hastings in 1893; in Gaelic 'beatha' means life. Even when she was well into her nineties, Bathie gave the impression she was twenty years younger. Active, independent, and always well presented, Bathie lived unconventionally. She confessed to being 'somehow unusual' for her time, never 'backward' like many of her fellow New Zealanders.

The daughter of Ellen and Alec Stuart, a farmer, Bathie was educated privately by a governess and tutors. She studied music, piano, voice, and drama at St Mary Philomena's Academy in Dunedin before turning professional at the age of fourteen by joining 'Tom Pollard's Juveniles', a musical troupe of children. After travelling through Australasia performing in operettas, she returned to Dunedin to appear in opera.

Bathie married Crofton Umbers, a government accountant, in Dunedin in 1912; their one son, Graham, was born in 1913. In 1917 the family moved to Wellington, and the following year both Crofton and Bathie contracted influenza; Crofton died, Bathie recovered. She never remarried. Later Graham became a boarder at King's College, Auckland.

Hercus Plimmer, a Wellington music critic, urged Bathie to go back on the stage and introduced her to Henry Hayward, owner of a chain of movie theatres throughout New Zealand. In the 1920s, theatrical acts and musical items were part of the entertainment offered at the cinema. Bathie began her new career on the Hayward circuit at Everybody's Theatre in Wellington, opening as 'Bathie Stuart and Her Musical Maids'. Later, Bathie went to Rotorua to choose four women who could perform with her as well as teach her Maori songs and poi dances. 'Bathie Stuart and her Maori Maids' became extremely popular: 'the gates of fame are swinging wide for you', telegraphed Hayward after she had filled the Majestic Theatre in Wellington for four weeks. In 1925 Bathie was chosen by Beaumont Smith, an Australian producer, to play the female lead in *The Adventures of Algy*, a silent feature film set in Sydney and New Zealand.

Although uninterested in pursuing a film career, Bathie travelled to Hollywood with Miss New Zealand, Dale Austen, and her chaperone in 1927. She worked there as a public relations agent for Hayward, gathered material on the stars for the *Sporting and Dramatic Review*, and recorded a prologue consisting of a haka and chants, as well as further chants and songs for the soundtrack to Universal Studios' film *The Devil's Pit*, which had been shot in New Zealand. She also gave a talk on New Zealand to the Los Angeles Pen Women's Club; a booking agent present was so impressed by her presentation (which included a

Bathie Stuart filming *New Zealand* with Robert Steele, 1948. *Stills Collection, New Zealand Film Archive*

Maori welcome) that she promised to arrange lecture appointments for her in the United States. But first, Bathie returned to New Zealand and informed the Tourist and Publicity and Railways Departments that they needed to appoint a representative in California, an area, she told them, which was progressing in leaps and bounds and which had a climate that tourists would find attractive. When they asked her to suggest someone suitable, she replied, 'Me'.

Armed with a New Zealand Railways pass which entitled her to free second-class travel on American trains, Bathie returned to California, set up tourist offices in San Francisco and Los Angeles, and by 1930 had started on her lecture circuit.

She also worked for the New Zealand government on its stand at the New York World Fair in 1939. Bathie's lecture on New Zealand initially consisted of Maori chants, poi dances, and slides for illustrations. However, in 1948, during one of her frequent trips back to New Zealand to visit her son Graham, Bathie stayed on to help Robert Steele, an independent Auckland film-maker, shoot a film about New Zealand which she could use in her lecture instead of slides. Although Steele was the cameraman, the idea was Bathie's: 'Nobody else had those kinds of ideas in those days.' When the Maori women were performing the poi dance on film, Bathie sang the poi song in the lecture theatre, and, when the men did the haka, she spoke the words to it. The move to film was a success. At the age of fifty-five, Bathie had just started her film-making career. Increasing age never deterred her from setting out on new projects.

Robert Steele also assisted Bathie on her next film, *Polynesia*, which looked at life in Hawaii, Western Samoa, Tonga, Tahiti, and the Cook Islands. However, by 1959 Bathie had decided that she could probably use a 16mm camera just as effectively as any cameraman, and so after some tuition shot *Melanesia* by herself. Other travel/adventure films made by Bathie were *Asia's Shining Cities*, *The New Malaysia*, and *The New China*, the latter being filmed when she was seventy-two.

Bathie had already visited China in 1931, so her 1965 documentary high-lighted the developments made since then. As a New Zealand citizen she was able to get a visa and join a Canadian tour group. Uncomfortable with organised group travel, Bathie shot some film en route but then returned to Hong Kong, and got permission to re-enter China alone. She retraced her steps through Soochow, Hangchow, Canton, Shanghai, and Peking, carrying all her own equipment, and consequently shot an extra 4,000 feet of film. *The New China* was shown in American schools and colleges as well as on her lecture circuit. Because it was impossible to get any first hand information about China in the United Sates, she found that Americans had difficulty in reconciling their propaganda image of the Chinese with her images. Where are the slums? asked her audiences. Her response was: 'There aren't any in China now; there are poor people and poor areas, but no slums, not like the slums in New York in 81st Street.'

Bathie continued to give over 150 lectures a year throughout the United States and Canada until her retirement in 1975 at the age of eighty-two. She also made radio broadcasts and appeared on television travel and adventure programmes such as *Bold Journey*, *Safari*, *Golden Voyage*, and *World Adven-*

ture. Few women were accepted as travelogue presenters during this period, but Bathie's clear articulation, her Standard English pronunciation, and her knowledge of Maori songs and dances gave her a distinct edge over her American competitors.

In her retirement Bathie lived alone in a trailer (caravan) park called Treasure Island overlooking Laguna Beach, California. The interior of the trailer felt like the cabin of a boat to her, and the community at Treasure Island consisted of other interesting, often film-oriented, individuals of all ages and nationalities. In 1986 Bathie was awarded the Queen's Service Medal, belated recognition of her achievements in promoting New Zealand.

Bathie died in 1987, on the same day as Fred Astaire. It is easy to imagine Bathie's spirit dancing with Fred's on into her next life: she was always one to do things in style.

Julie Benjamin

Unpublished Sources

Bathie Stuart file, NZ Film Archive Library, Wellington. The former director, Jonathan Dennis, also provided information.

Interview by the author with Bathie Stuart, Feb. 1984, Laguna Beach (copy at NZ Film Archive Library). All quotations are from this interview.

Private papers in the author's possession

LAURA SUISTED

?–1903

Laura Jane Suisted contributed stories and articles to the *Otago Witness* in Dunedin for nearly twenty-five years from about 1880. She contributed widely to magazines and newspapers in this country and overseas and won prizes for original fiction in *Sharlands Trade Magazine*. Her stories of life in New Zealand deal with the isolation of women left alone and the difficulty of forming relationships in pioneer communities. They also express both awe and delight at New Zealand's natural environment.

Laura Eyre came from Yorkshire, and first appears in the New Zealand record in 1864, when she married James Suisted, an Otago station manager. In 1869 Laura and James moved to Westport, where James and his brother ran a butchery business. 'St Leonards', the home they established there, was Laura's base for the rest of her life.

In 1884, Laura took her place as the first woman in the parliamentary press gallery, sending lively notes, published under the pseudonym of 'Scribbler', to the *Otago Witness*. She reported on parliament for nine sessions, her notes appearing in many newspapers in New Zealand and Australia. They include Laura's views on political matters, but also her comments on the human side of political life and the joys and trials of being a parliamentary reporter. In October 1884, she attacked those who denied women an intellectual role in life:

But what think you . . . That because a woman works with head as well as hands, she must of necessity lose her womanly sweetness and grace? That to cultivate and turn to profitable account the natural gifts with which she may be

Parliament sitting about the time Laura Suisted was a member of the parliamentary press gallery and before women were allowed to stand as candidates, c.1890s. *Alexander Turnbull Library*

endowed . . . implies loss of domestic habits, or neglect of household duties?
That in as much as she studies early and late . . . she must therefore become
hard and masculine in style and tone? . . . You know them not these toilers and
brainworkers among womankind. Believe me, those who rank highest in
intellectual power will be found also to possess every true womanly attribute in
a more worked degree than their detractors would care to acknowledge.

In 1893, she made a trip alone to England, Sweden, and Norway. While there she wrote for New Zealand papers about politics and society and, after her return, she wrote and published a book recounting her experiences, *From New Zealand to Norway*. Many friends expressed concern at her travelling such a long distance alone, and she was asked on her return whether she thought 'it really an easy matter nowadays for a lady to travel about the world alone? To which I reply concisely: "*That* depends upon the lady."'

Laura was one of the first women to join the New Zealand Institute of Journalists and was a member of both the Society of Authors and the Institute of Journalists in London. She was elected a corresponding member of the Victorian branch of the Royal Geographical Society of Australasia and wrote an article on Antarctic exploration. She died at her home in Westport in September 1903.

Laura was obviously dedicated to her career as a writer, although there was no financial necessity for her to work (James Suisted was a successful businessman, a longstanding chairman of the Westport Harbour Board, and served a term as mayor of Westport). Nor did she tailor her career around her role as a wife. She travelled extensively to cover parliament and even went to the other side of the world alone. She maintained interests in all facets of life, from the natural world, to politics, to the reality of women's lives. She herself admits to being unorthodox:

let me plead guilty to what the strictly orthodox would doubtless term 'sadly unconventional tastes and habits' – but the outcome of such has usually proved only the innocent acquirement of much useful knowledge.

Maud Cahill

Quotations
para.3 'Jottings from the Seat of Government', *Otago Witness*, 18 Oct. 1884, p.26
para.4 L. Suisted, *From New Zealand to Norway*, p.66
para.6 Suisted, p.31

Unpublished Sources
L. Suisted to H. A. Atkinson, 3 Feb. 1888, Atkinson Papers, MS Papers 91, ATL
L. Suisted to John Ballance, 24 Aug. 1892, Ballance Papers, MS Papers 25, ATL

Published Sources
The Cyclopedia of New Zealand, vol.5, Christchurch, 1906, pp.164–5
NZ Free Lance, 19 Sept. 1903, p.3a (obituary)
NZ Mail, 15 Sept. 1893, p.11b; 17 Nov. 1893, p.22c
Otago Daily Times, 29 Nov. 1864, p.4d; 8 Sept. 1903, p.6f (obituary)
Otago Witness, 9 Sept. 1903, p.23 (obituary)
Scholefield, G. H., *A Dictionary of New Zealand Biography*, vol.2, Wellington, 1940, pp.348–9
Suisted, Laura. *From New Zealand to Norway*, Dunedin, 1894

MARY SUTHERLAND

1893–1955

Forestry is not a common career for women in New Zealand. Yet the science of forestry in this country owes much to the first woman to be employed as a forester.

Mary Sutherland came from Britain, where she had obtained her science degree in forestry at the University College of North Wales, served in the Women's Land Army during the First World War, worked as a forester on two Scottish estates, and worked as assistant experimental officer with the British Forestry Commission. Emigration to New Zealand in about 1924 gave Mary firsthand experience of the strongly conservative attitudes and male prejudice in the New Zealand Forest Service. In those days 'all forestry [was] subject to camp conditions, and there [was] no place for a woman in a forestry camp'. Mary persevered, despite being merely tolerated at first, and received a permanent appointment in 1925, employed at Wellington and Rotorua offices on investigative work in silviculture.

During field-work Mary often wore 'her British Forestry Commission kit of off-white leather jacket, leather belt with rings and snaps, riding breeches and high boots'. It was rather an unusual outfit for a woman in those days, but no doubt serviceable, and it came to be accepted by her colleagues as an integral part of her personality.

Mary Sutherland.
New Zealand Forestry Institute

Field-work conditions during the 1920s and 1930s were less comfortable than they are today. During a three-week introductory course for rangers at Whakarewarewa in 1924, Mary was distanced from her colleagues not only by chauvinistic pride but also by the 'practicalities' of accommodation. Although it was mid-winter, all the twenty rangers and senior rangers, except her, camped in tents in a horse-paddock, while Mary's lodgings were at the Geyser Hotel along with the chief inspector, visiting officers, and part-time specialists. It was no doubt more comfortable than tent life but the message was clear that she was not quickly going to be accepted on grounds of merit. And there was always going to be a financial disincentive for the Forest Service to send Mary into the field under these conditions.

Mary's good grounding in biology, her common sense and quiet unassuming character, her intelligence and friendliness, and a strong Scottish doggedness saw her through the difficulties. She could also match her male counterparts in all aspects of their work, including field-work. On the introductory course her knowledge of botany came to the aid of senior foresters in their lectures and by the end of the three weeks she had won the respect and friendship of her peers.

The Depression years of 1933–6 led the Forest Service to make severe cutbacks, including in Mary's specialty area of research. She was laid off, and spent these years working at the Dominion Museum in Wellington. Nineteen-thirty-seven saw her back with the Forest Service again, this time as a botanist. She began her pioneering work in agricultural forestry in 1946 when she was seconded to the new position of Farm Forestry Officer with the Department of Agriculture. The *New Zealand Journal of Agriculture* published many of her articles relating to the use of and improvement in trees grown for shelter-belts, weed control, and timber on farms. Her foresight and talent have benefited farmers across the country. She also had to make field inspections of the department's many land holdings, deal with a large volume of correspondence, and write several bulletins dealing mainly with farm forestry plantations.

The New Zealand Institute of Foresters (NZIF), established in 1927, lists Mary among its inaugural members. She firmly supported the institute's aims and activities, serving as a councillor in 1935 and as vice-president in 1940–41. Her design of a sprig of fruiting rimu was voted into the NZIF official seal. Shy as she was, she needed some encouragement before she showed the design to members at one of the early institute meetings. She was also appointed a Fellow of the Society of Foresters in Great Britain in 1928.

Mary's career was cut short when ill health suffered during field-work in Central Otago during 1954 led to her death on 11 March 1955. Mary's contribution to forestry is remembered each year in the Mary Sutherland Award granted to a student member of the New Zealand Institute of Foresters.

Mary Sutherland broke new ground for all women in forestry – she was not only the first woman forester in New Zealand, but the first in the British Empire and possibly in the world. *Pip Lynch*

Quotations
para.2 F. E. Hutchinson, 'Mary Sutherland: An Appreciation'
para.3 F. E. Hutchinson, 'Mary Sutherland'

Unpublished Sources
Information was provided by: Janice Griffin, Dept. of Conservation; Brian Mackrell, NZ Deerstalkers Association; Paul Mahoney, Historic Places Trust; John Novis, NZ Institute of Foresters; Julia Risk, Ministry of Forestry; M. M. Roche, Massey University; G. C. Weston, DSIR.

Published Sources
Hutchinson, F. E. 'Mary Sutherland: An Appreciation', *Newsletter*, NZ Institute of Foresters, vol.8 no.3, July 1976
NZ Journal of Agriculture, vols 74–88, 1947–54

MARY SWAINSON

1826–1854

The only daughter of William Swainson and his wife Mary (born Parkes), Mary Frederica Swainson left vivid and entertaining accounts of her life in a shipboard diary and in letters to grandparents and friends in England and to her wandering father and brothers.

In Britain, William Swainson was a naturalist of some distinction (a member of the Linnean Society and Fellow of the Royal Society), although his paid occupation had largely been in the Mediterranean Army. After his wife died, he turned his thoughts to emigration. Joining the committee of the New Zealand Company, he purchased 1100 acres in the Hutt Valley, and in 1841 arrived in New Zealand. There he established himself as a farmer, with his four eldest children and his second wife, Ann (born Grasby). (The youngest son, Edwin, was considered too young to emigrate, and remained in England with foster parents. He published *Ferns of New Zealand* in 1846.)

To the young Mary, emigrating at fifteen, everything was an adventure – she was an enthusiastic settler. She wrote home about domestic things, and the prices of essentials. The letters contain requests for shoes, clothing, and sewing materials for the family, also for seeds – pansies, irises, violets – for her garden. Her stepmother would have been in charge of housekeeping, possibly with the help of servants, but it seems that Mary had an active role in what was apparently a volatile family.

She also writes of people and social occasions, including balls and horse-racing on Petone beach, and indulges in a little gossip:

Have you met young E. Jerningham Wakefield? – we hear he has become a London dandy, a sudden transition from being almost synonymous with a native! His is certainly the best book on NZ, but too personal, and his own conduct what it ought to have been, not what it was. However the natives in reality are very fond of him, there is no humbug *in that,* his *account of the country & mode of the life of the settlers & natives is very good, and I think as truthful as it could be.*

All the young Swainsons had been encouraged to draw and to take an interest in natural history. Mary in particular was regarded by William Swainson as likely to carry on his work. On sketching expeditions with her father, she was taught discipline and technique to supplement her own sharp observation. The native fuschia, she writes, was

Mary Swainson's sketch of her house in the Hutt Valley, 1841–4. *Alexander Turnbull Library*

. . . now in full flower and . . . very beautiful – the calyx is green, tinged with purple when it first opens, and before it falls off the tree it becomes red – not however the bright red of the one we have in England. This grows to the size of a tree, and we frequently burn it for firewood. It is one of the most beautiful shrubs we have and I long to be able to paint well enough, that I may send some home.

Her letters showed a warm interest in Maori, their customs and language. She was, however, to experience at first hand the land conflicts of the period, when the chief Te Kaeaea of Ngati Tama felled timber and built a pa in the Hutt, to assert Ngati Tama's claim to the land. In 1846 two neighbouring settlers were killed in the ensuing skirmishes.

Eventually Ngati Tama left the land, and the Swainsons remained in possession of 'Hawkshead'. Mary replanted her garden, and resumed her interest in collecting fossils and shells. She continued painting and sketching, and writing the letters that fostered friendship across the world. She was also much in demand in fashionable Wellington, refusing several suitors before she married Captain John Marshall in 1849.

They lived at 'The Glen' at Kaiwharawhara, between Wellington and the Hutt Valley, and had two sons. Mary wrote to Mary de Lys in England, on 24 February 1854:

. . . New Zealand is very beautiful, and to me the sea has great charms, and I love to watch the waves come rolling in. I wish you could go with us on a coast trip we are about to take, quite in a primitive style however. In a cart with our baggage, so we cannot take very long journeys. The road until you get to the sea side is very beautiful. My nurse girl and the two children with my husband as coachman comprise the party.

A few months later she was dead, of scarlet fever. Years later, Mary de Lys remembered her parting from Mary as one of the saddest days of her life.

Sheila Natusch

Quotations
para.4 M. Marshall to her uncle, 22 Nov. 1846, Letters mainly to her father and husband . . . , ATL
para.5 M. Swainson to her grandmother, 18 Oct. 1842, Mary Swainson to her grandparents . . . , ATL
para.8 M. Marshall to Mary de Lys, Feb. 1854, Letters to Mary de Lys . . . , p.26, ATL;

Unpublished Sources
M. F. Marshall, Journal of a voyage to New Zealand in the Barque *Jane*, MS, ATL
M. F. Marshall, Letters mainly to her father and husband 1842–1853, MS, ATL
M. F. Marshall, Letters to Mary de Lys and Isabel Percy, 1843–1854, MS, ATL
Mary Swainson to her grandparents in England, 1840–1854, qMS ATL

Published Sources
Natusch, S. and Swainson, G. *William Swainson F.R.S., F.L.S. &c of Fern Grove*, Palmerston North, 1987

MARY ANNE SWAINSON

?1833-1897

Mary Anne Arrowsmith was born in Brough, Westmorland, England, the younger of two daughters of Henry Abel Arrowsmith, a schoolmaster, and his wife Isabella (born Parkin). Little is known of her early life. Her father emigrated to America but the family soon lost touch with him. Her sister, Sophia, married a Dr Wigan of Tasmania; her mother lived first with them and later with Mary in Wellington.

Mary probably arrived in Wellington in 1855 or 1856. She married George Frederick Swainson at St James Church, Hutt, on 27 December 1859. Swainson, a surveyor, was the second son of the eminent naturalist and artist William Swainson and his first wife, Mary (born Parkes). He worked in the survey department of the provincial government until 1863 and as commissioner of native reserves in Wellington from 1864 to 1867.

In nine years the Swainsons had five children – two daughters and three sons. The second daughter died of convulsions at twenty-three months, five weeks before the birth of the first son on 22 April 1865.

In 1869 Mary opened a school for girls on the corner of Woodward Street and Wellington Terrace. Her four children were all under ten, the youngest under a year. Precisely why she embarked on this venture is unclear, but financial reasons were probably compelling. George had left the government service and was working as a surveyor on his own account. He also seems to have had a drinking problem. In 1870 he was living and working in Rangitikei and on the night of 5 October died suddenly from 'serous apoplexy' [*sic*] in a Marton hotel. As he died intestate, leaving an estate valued at under £600, the family must now have been totally dependent on the income from Mary's school.

Fortunately, there was no shortage of pupils and before long she moved to a larger house further up the Terrace. By 1877 she was looking for even larger premises. That year also brought the 1877 Education Act, which established a free, secular, and compulsory system of primary education. Mary foresaw that she might lose pupils to local state schools. Realising, however, that there was a need for a school with religious affiliations and one that provided boarding facilities, she build a new home and school in Fitzherbert Terrace, Thorndon. It opened as a boarding- and day-school early in 1878 and from the beginning was closely associated with the Anglican pro-cathedral of St Paul's.

It was a secondary as well as a primary school, predominantly for girls, although a number of boys attended until ready for secondary school. The fees were £21 a term for boarders and four guineas for day pupils. The curriculum was similar to that of early nineteenth-century denominational schools in England: religious instruction, 'the classics', reading, writing, arithmetic, spelling, history, and geography. Music, singing, drawing, French, and dancing were all 'extras'. Over the years Mrs Swainson gathered around her such dedicated teachers as May Taylor, Fanny Irvine-Smith, Mary Galwey (Mrs Henry Smith), Mlle Baradeux (Mme Bendall), Phoebe Myers, Esther Mary Baber, and Robert Parker.

646

Mrs Swainson with some of her girls, 1896.
Te Kura

In the first twenty years, the boarding roll fluctuated from twelve to twenty, with the boarders coming in the main from Hawke's Bay, Wanganui, Rangitikei, Manawatu, and Wairarapa. They slept in several small dormitories on the first floor and were expected to take cold baths in the early morning. Although waited on at table, they helped out whenever there was a shortage of domestic staff. They went to concerts and plays and, along with the day pupils, were encouraged to help those less fortunate than themselves.

At all times Mrs Swainson demonstrated genuine affection and concern for each pupil and insisted on a duty toward 'Godliness and good learning'. She invariably dressed in a full black frock and wore a heavy gold and greenstone brooch at the neck. Towards the end of her life she took only the occasional scripture or sewing class but remained headmistress of the school until her death on 3 August 1897. She died of heart failure hastened by the strain following an operation for cancer of the breast a fortnight earlier. The litany desk in St Paul's was given in remembrance of her, and her 'loving pupils' subscribed to a stained glass window in 'thankful memory'.

Her daughter Mary Jessy Swainson was headmistress of the school from 1897 until 1906, and in 1920 it was acquired by the diocese of Wellington and became known as the Samuel Marsden Collegiate School. It moved to Karori in 1926 but a preparatory school was maintained in Fitzherbert Terrace until 1936. The boarding establishment began to be phased out in 1990 and, although boys can enrol in the pre-school department, it has remained essentially a school for girls.

Prior to 1878, Mrs Swainson's school was not remarkably different from others of its kind. She had the courage and foresight, however, to provide an alternative to schools in the newly created state system, and the energy and skill to ensure it survived the educational changes of the time. In doing so, she founded one of New Zealand's oldest girls' schools.   *Diana Beaglehole*

Unpublished Sources
Swainson papers, Acc 87–162, Box 1, ATL

Published Sources
Murray, Tosti. *Marsden: The History of a New Zealand School for Girls*, Wellington, 1967
Natusch, Sheila and Swainson, Geoffrey. *William Swainson of Fern Grove FRS, FLS&C: the anatomy of a nineteenth-century naturalist*, Wellington, 1987

GISA TAGLICHT

?1898–?1981

Dance teacher Gisa Taglicht (born Frankl) came to New Zealand from Vienna in 1939. To understand her background one must go back to Central Europe after the First World War, where freedom from the hardships and anxieties of war brought the demand for new freedoms – freedom in dress, freedom of expression in the arts, and freedom in movement, including modern dance.

Barefoot dancing began as a sensational break with old traditions. Isadora Duncan introduced new dance forms; Dr Rudolf Bode's theories in rhythmical gymnastics and modern dance revolutionised the approach to movement; Rudolf Laban's philosophies of physical, emotional, intellectual, and spiritual functions were adopted by young teachers of movement and dramatic art. There were recitals, congresses, discussions, and lectures: Gisa Taglicht was in the midst of it all. She had studied Eurythmics with one of the best teachers, Eleanor Thordis, and later worked as her assistant as well as running a dance school of her own.

Gisa Frankl was a member of a prosperous, well-respected Jewish business family in Vienna. Her interest in dance began in 1919 when she joined a gymnastic club run by her future husband Adolf Taglicht, also from a notable Jewish family. The marriage was not, however, happy, and in time the couple lived apart. Gisa Taglicht formed another relationship, which endured over many years. The Nazi regime, however, forced Gisa to flee Europe. By 1940 she was settled in Wellington, employed by the YWCA to teach movement and rhythmical gymnastics.

The beautiful, flowing, rhythmical movements she introduced had an effect on movement teaching throughout the country. Hitherto, movement teaching had been mainly angular movements – 'drill' or physical jerks. 'Madame Taglicht' believed that everybody had it in themselves to move with grace, if only they were shown how, and that this grace should be part of everyday life. The newly appointed superintendent of physical education at the Department of Education, Philip Smithells, recognised the value of her work, and incorporated it into the training of physical education teachers.

From her earliest days in Wellington, Gisa Taglicht taught a wide range of students in private classes, in public classes for YWCA, and for diverse groups such as kindergarten teacher trainees, and postgraduate nurses.

From 1955 she taught at residential schools for the New Zealand Drama

Council, and later with the drama school of the New Zealand Players and the New Zealand Opera Company. Actors and singers learned relaxation, along with fluidity of gesture and movement on stage. She was herself dramatic, dressing theatrically, moving beautifully, and expressing herself eloquently through her gestures.

Gisa Taglicht's ideas on relaxation were revolutionary in their time. She argued that the human body had to be given a chance of complete rest and inactivity, especially with the speed of present day living. Techniques for this, she said, had to be taught. When the Parents' Centres were set up in the early 1950s, they engaged her to teach relaxation techniques in childbirth.

She was an influence too on the first modern dance group in New Zealand, New Dance, formed in 1945. The founders of this group, Olive and Philip Smithells, Rona Bailey, and Edith Sipos, had all been students of Gisa's. They were also inspired, however, by the American modern dance, which sought to express ideas through movement. Gisa was not sympathetic to these concepts.

In her forties when she arrived in New Zealand, Gisa Taglicht was constantly torn between her love of Europe and love of New Zealand. After the war she visited Europe many times, studying and lecturing in England and the United States. But her hunger for her homeland was not assuaged by mere visits. She returned to Austria permanently in 1964, settling in Salzburg to be with her old friend and teaching movement until her health gave out. She had given New Zealand twenty years of her teaching and stylish personal example; her influence on physical education, dance, theatre, and opera endures today.   *Tup Lang*

Gisa Taglicht with a group of her dancers on the Makara hills. The sequence featured in a National Film Unit production *Rhythm and Movement* (1948). *National Dance Archive*

Sources

The article on which this essay is based appeared first in *Dance News*, no.22, Sept. 1982. Most of the personal information comes from Gisa Taglicht's pianist, Joan Stevens, and her brother Hans Frankl. Gisa Taglicht's papers are in the National Dance Archive, C/-Tup Lang, 81 Hatton Street, Karori, Wellington.

TAKIORA LUCY LORD

1842-1893

During the Taranaki wars of the 1860s some of the campaigns were fought out over rugged and difficult bush terrain. For soldiers such as Major von Tempsky, Lieutenant-Colonel McDonnell, and Colonel Whitmore, the use of Maori guides and scouts who were familiar with the territory was essential in the execution of their manoeuvres. One of the most renowned of the guides who assisted government troops during that period was a young woman known as Takiora, or Lucy Lord.

Although by descent she was of Taranaki's Ngatiruanui tribe, Takiora was born in the Bay of Islands, the daughter of Kotiro Hinerangi and William Lord. Kotiro had been living in Kororareka under the jurisdiction of Hone Heke, and while there was a pupil of Samuel Marsden's Mission School. As a young girl she was married to a Scotsman, Alexander Gray, and two daughters were born of that marriage. The eldest, Te Paea, in later years became celebrated as Guide Sophia of Whakarewarewa. After the death of Gray, Kotiro lived with and subsequently married William Lord, a whaler and storekeeper. In 1842, their daughter Lucy Elizabeth was born.

Two years later, Kotiro was one of the main participants in events which led directly to the opening of Hone Heke's campaign against British rule. Annoyed at receiving a message from Heke ordering her to leave William Lord, Kotiro, in angry defiance, is reputed to have compared the famed Nga Puhi chief with the head of a dead hog. The disturbance caused by this dire insult led in turn to Heke's challenge to British authority and the subsequent attack on the Kororareka flagstaff in 1844.

By the 1860s Takiora had established herself in Taranaki on the land of her mother's people, and had married a man of the Whanganui tribe, Te Mahuki. Her husband was a guide for the government troops and was described as von Tempsky's most popular scout. After Te Mahuki's death, Takiora herself continued working successfully as a scout. She was a close and trusted friend of von Tempsky, and both she and Te Mahuki are portrayed in several of his paintings of the Taranaki campaigns.

During the year of 1866, as the military action against Titokowaru intensified, Takiora's value increased in the eyes of both von Tempsky and McDonnell, the commander of the government forces. Wiremu Katene Tuwhakaruru, a Ngaruahine guide highly valued for his bushcraft and military skills, had left the government's service, and spent the next few years as one of Titokowaru's most trusted lieutenants. Takiora guided McDonnell and von Tempsky on many long

Two images, both claimed to be Takiora or Lucy Lord, also known as Wikitoria of Nukumaru. *Taranaki Museum*

and arduous marches through the most difficult bush terrain. Some of the marches were of several days' duration, the weather was cold and wet, and the troops themselves raw and inexperienced. Von Tempsky frequently tried to ensure Takiora's physical safety by leaving her in camp if the information she provided was considered to be sufficient. McDonnell praised her ability to navigate successfully through the dense Taranaki bush and depended heavily on her route planning talents.

As the surviving members of Titokowaru's community were being hunted down, shot, and imprisoned during the year of 1869, Takiora continued her intelligence-gathering activities. There is some hint from her own writings during this period that doubts about her role were beginning to creep in. In her 'Notes taken during the troublous times', she recounts an episode in which she reported the return of some of Titokowaru's followers to their own land. She guided troops out to the area, with the object of taking prisoners, but, contrary to her wishes, two elderly men were shot to death on the spot. An old woman who was captured at the same time wept, lamenting her loss and blaming Takiora. 'I did not remonstrate as I knew wrong had been done.'

As a salaried government employee, Takiora received up to £10 per month, and later Native Minister Donald McLean gifted to her two blocks of confiscated land, some of which she may have had good claim to in any case.

In 1878 she married Joseph Dalton, a surveyor, and the couple began farming on her land at Normanby, north of Hawera. They then entered into a lengthy correspondence with government departments and the West Coast Royal Commission into Confiscated Lands, attempting to get legal title to another block of land they were living on. As Louisa T. Dalton, she petitioned the Commission repeatedly, emphasising her consistent loyalty, her need to be granted land for herself and her relatives, and the promises made that her loyalty to the government would be recognised.

Sir William Fox, who headed the commission, was not particularly sympathetic, however, pronouncing that he knew 'of no special circumstances in her case which necessitates her being specially treated, or differently from that of other members of the hapu'.

Whether or not Takiora was fairly rewarded for her professional services is not clear. What does emerge, however, is a picture of a strong woman who operated in an almost totally male setting, and who was a staunch ally and a respected adviser to a succession of the military's top commanders. She survived several years of intensive and wearying campaigns, which saw many hundreds of casualties on both sides and the end of some eminent military careers. Her resilience must have stood her in good stead in her later battles to obtain title to the land she felt was hers.

On 7 September 1893, the following obituary appeared in the *Taranaki Herald*:

There passed away at the local hospital on Sunday last, a half caste woman who has had an eventful career. We refer to the death of Mrs Lucy Takiora Dalton. She had been residing on her own land in the Normanby district for many years. She was an intelligent woman, and in the accounts of the times we find her as Lucy Grey, acting as guide during the war in 1868. She was afterwards for some time in the employ of the Government. Her remains were interred in the Henui cemetery.

Tui MacDonald

Quotations
para.6 L. Lord, 'Notes', ATL
para.9 Letter, 3 April 1882, MA 68/4a, National Archives, Wellington

Unpublished Sources
Lucy Lord, Manuscript by Takihora, Maori Woman Guide, 1868, MS 230, Taranaki Museum
Lucy Lord, Notes taken during the troublous times, 1868, W. F. Gordon Papers, MS 1918, ATL
Royal Commission appointed under 'The Confiscated Lands Inquiry and Maori Prisoners Trials Act 1879' (West Coast North Island), MA 68/4a, National Archives, Wellington

Published Sources
Belich, James. *I Shall Not Die: Titokowaru's War, New Zealand 1868–1869*, Wellington, 1989
Taranaki Herald, 7 Sept. 1893 (obituary)

TARORE

?1824-1836

Twelve-year-old Tarore enjoyed reading in Maori from her copy of St Luke's Gospel to 'Mother' Brown at the Church Missionary Society school near Matamata Pa. Alfred and Charlotte Brown had set up their mission station early in 1835 and since then many changes had taken place in Tarore's life.

Her father, Ngakuku, a nephew of Ngatihaua chief Te Waharoa, had become Alfred Brown's leading assistant and accompanied him on peacemaking expeditions. The copy of St Luke which Tarore treasured had Ngakuku's name written on one of the pages. She kept it in a small bag which hung around her neck.

Tribal warfare between Ngatihaua and Arawa of Rotorua caused the missionaries to close the Matamata station. On 18 October 1836 Tarore, her father, her younger brother, and a party of twenty school children left Matamata, intending to travel to Tauranga over the steep track which crossed the Kaimai Range near the Wairere Falls.

As night fell they stopped at a hut near the foot of the falls, but unfortunately their camp-fires were seen by some Rotorua warriors who waited until dawn to attack the sleeping party. A barking dog woke them in time for them to escape and hide in the fern and bush. Ngakuku snatched up his son and carried him on his back, but Tarore was caught and murdered by the warriors.

Sadly Ngakuku carried the body of his only daughter back to the Matamata mission station, where Alfred Brown gave her a Christian burial just outside the pa. The law of utu required her relatives to seek revenge for her death but Ngakuku, influenced by the Christian message of peace and forgiveness, said:

*There lies my child. She has been murdered as a payment for your bad
conduct, but do not rise to seek payment for her. God will do that. Let there be
a finishing of the war with Rotorua. Now let peace be made.*

The warriors took Tarore's copy of St Luke back to Rotorua. From there it was sent to Otaki and used to teach Tamihana Te Rauparaha (known as Katu), the son of Te Rauparaha, and his cousin Matene Te Whiwhi to read. These two men travelled to the Bay of Islands to ask for a missionary to be sent to Otaki and afterwards took the Christian message of peace to the southern part of the South Island. When Bishop Selwyn visited the southern tribes in 1844 he found them already holding Christian services.

In 1839 Tarore's father Ngakuku was baptised with the name of William Marsh and became a trusted Maori teacher.

Uita, the Rotorua warrior who had murdered Tarore, is said to have learned to read from her copy of St Luke. He became a changed man, was baptised, and joined a Christian settlement at Kuranui, near Matamata. Ngakuku accompanied Alfred Brown on a visit there in 1849 and met Uita. Brown wrote in his journal:

In the evening they were engaged together worshipping God at their prayer meeting, and are apparently on the most friendly terms. Surely the source of this must be looked for in something deeper than natural feeling. Who but the Christian loves his enemy?

In 1976 Tarore's grave was located at the site of Matamata Pa by Kathleen Holmes-Libbis, secretary of the Hamilton Bible Society. The following year a headstone and plaque were unveiled at a special service which commemorated the story of Tarore's death, the sequel of her father's forgiveness of her murderer, and the spread of Christianity through the influence of her copy of St Luke.

A hundred and fifty years after the event, a re-enactment of Tarore's story took place at the Raungaiti Marae at Waharoa, near Matamata, and a pilgrimage was made to her grave. *Joan Stanley*

Quotations
para.5 A. N. Brown, 'Journal', 20 Oct. 1836, vol.1, pp.89–90
para.8 A. N. Brown, 17 Jan. 1849, vol.2, p.31
Unpublished Source
A. N. Brown. 'Journals 1835–1850', qMS, ATL

Published Sources
Carlton, Hugh. *Life of Henry Williams*, edited and revised by James Elliot, Wellington, 1948
Matheson, A. H. *The Wairere Track: An Ancient Highway of Maori and Missionary*, Tauranga, 1975
Stanley, J. 'William Marsh (Ngakuku): A Christian Convert and Teacher', *Journal of NZ Federation of Historical Societies*, vol.2 no.5, Sept. 1987
Woods, Sybil. *Samuel Williams of Te Aute*, Christchurch, 1981

EVELYN TARULEVICZ

1895–1984

In 1875 a fourteen-year-old Swiss boy, Alfred Scherer, sailed with his family on the *Lammershagen* and arrived in Wellington three months later. In the same year a little eight-year-old girl, Frederika Gernhoefer, the youngest of a large family who sailed from Hamburg on the *Humboldt*, reached Wellington. They were a Protestant family whose ancestors had fled from religious persecution in Austria and settled in East Prussia; Gottlieb Gernhoefer and his family then left a militaristic Germany to find safety and peace in New Zealand. These two families both bought land in Taranaki near Mt Egmont, and set to work felling the heavy bush for timber, building their houses, and gradually developing farms. Alfred and Frederika met and were married in 1885. The couple worked hard on the farm as their family grew.

My mother Evelyn was born in Midhurst, Taranaki, in 1895, their seventh child. By 1901 the family had saved enough for a larger farm and they sailed from New Plymouth to the Manukau Harbour with their farm animals. They bought 1,000 acres of land near Waharoa. This block was covered by scrub, gorse, and mud, into which their animals rapidly vanished. The children would ride through the tracks on their ponies rounding up the cattle. Years of work transformed the land into several lush dairy farms. All the children were expected to work – a large family was an advantage on the farm. Evelyn enjoyed caring for the animals, but when her pet calf was butchered she vowed never to eat meat again and was a vegetarian for the rest of her life. With ten in the family, there were enough Scherer children to supply most of the pupils for the small country school. The children all rode horses to the school, which had just one teacher and only one other pupil. Evelyn was proud of her proficiency certificate from primary school; she then went to Hamilton to attend Hamilton High School for two years.

When she left school to earn her living at the age of fifteen, she was employed as an assistant to a photographer, Mr Jenkinson in Ward Street, Hamilton, and from him learned the art and business of photography. When Mr Jenkinson died, she bought the business and continued to work as a photographer for the next sixty years. She was now financially independent, and in 1921 bought her first car. This enabled her to go tramping in the bush with her friends. They also started skiing on Mt Ruapehu and she became a member of the first Ruapehu Ski Club. With friends she sailed down the Wanganui River from Taumarunui to Pipiriki, taking a camera to record the trip. They had to use whole-plate negatives, and the exercise was cumbersome, but beautiful photographs were taken.

Evelyn Scherer (later Tarulevicz), right, sitting on the boat, with friends on holiday, Wanganui River, 1929. *Tania Gunn*

In 1931 Evelyn and her younger sister set off to see the world, leaving a manager in charge of the business. In England they bought a little car and drove from Lands End to John o' Groats, and then toured Europe. Her sister started to work and Evelyn decided to visit Russia alone.

In Moscow she met an exciting stranger, Jan Tarulevicz, an American journalist who had fled from Russia as a boy following the revolution. Where she travelled, he travelled. They were married in London after a whirlwind courtship and then returned to New Zealand. A daughter was born in 1932 and a son the following year. Unfortunately, Jan could not get New Zealand citizenship, and eventually had to leave the country. Evelyn continued her photography business, developing a special skill in child portraits. She and the children lived in the big family home by the Waikato River while her parents were alive. She was a strong fearless swimmer and taught her children to swim in the river. With a child on either side putting a hand on her shoulder as necessary, they triumphantly swam across the river.

In 1937 Evelyn and her children sailed to New York to meet her husband, but he was delayed in Shanghai and not able to join her there. She came home, visiting China and New Guinea on the way. The next year the whole family spent several months together in Indonesia and plans were made to settle in the United States. Evelyn returned to Hamilton to make arrangements. But the year was 1939. No visas were obtainable and soon the war broke out. During the war her husband was lost.

Evelyn set to work to raise her two children while she continued her profession as a photographer. Private schools, music lessons, seaside holidays, skiing trips: this was a rich and varied upbringing. Christmas and birthday presents were books, which were always exchanged and discussed at length. With her help, both children went to university and on to professional careers.

Evelyn was now a truly independent woman. She gave both time and money generously to her church, friends, and family. She was passionate about beauty, whether natural or created. An early conservationist, she was a member of the Royal Forest and Bird Protection Society for many years. Travel was her other love. She visited Western Australia and Darwin to see the wild flowers. She made five trips around the world which included the Trans Siberian Railway, Treetops in Africa, Machu Picchu in Peru, and Easter Island. She enjoyed a winter in the snows of Montreal and a summer in the Australian outback, but she always came back to Hamilton and the photography business which gave her financial security. She worked until she was seventy-six, and only retired when forced to by the rebuilding of the area in which her studio was located.

After she retired she made a trip to Canada to help care for her grandchildren; on the way back she travelled in Africa, India, and Thailand. Evelyn spent the last five years of her life gardening and looking after her 'old' friends. She died suddenly at the age of eighty-nine.   *Tania Gunn*

Unpublished Sources
Information came from the family records of Evelyn Tarulevicz and family members. The author is
  Evelyn Tarulevicz's daughter.

MARY TAYLOR

1817–1893

'Mary [Taylor] . . .', wrote her friend Charlotte Brontë in 1841, 'has more energy and power in her nature than any ten men . . . It is vain to limit a character like hers within ordinary boundaries – she will overstep them. I am morally certain Mary will establish her own landmarks . . .' Charlotte knew her Mary well. Determined to avoid the 'long, slow death' imposed on middle-class women by Victorian conventions of dependence, submissiveness, and domesticity, she would stay 'outside the cage – though it is somewhat cold'. She would 'shut [her] eyes for a cold plunge', and 'when I come up again', she added vigorously, 'I [will] tell you all what it's like.'

Mary was born on 26 February 1817 to Yorkshire banker and cloth manufacturer Joshua Taylor and his wife, Anne (born Tickell). The 'peculiar, racy, vigorous' Taylors, 'of good blood and strong brain, turbulent . . . intractable . . . but sound, spirited and true-bred . . .', were 'of the furious Radical party', Republicans and Nonconformists, with strong independent views, which they were convinced 'were the opinions of all the *sensible* people . . . .'. The children were 'licensed to express themselves vociferously before their elders'. Mary thus grew up with 'an energetic and active mind, proving the possession of courage, independence [and] talent'; she was frank, forthright, and uncompromisingly honest.

Mary first met Charlotte Brontë and Ellen Nussey at Roe Head School in 1831. Ellen remembered her as 'not talkative . . . but industrious and always ready with lessons'. Already she showed her unusual quality, in quiet rebellion against what she saw as useless studies; she preferred 'to accept the penalty of disobedience'.

The failure of her father's bank and subsequent reduction in the family's standard of living may have reinforced the 'fiercely persistent desire for financial independence' which governed the rest of Mary's life. She proclaimed her philosophy thus to Charlotte: 'A woman who works is by that alone better than one who does not', adding that a woman who 'does not wish to [earn] is guilty of a great fault – almost a crime – a dereliction of duty which leads rapidly and almost certainly to all manner of degradation.' She had to admit, though, that employment opportunities for women in England were limited – 'teaching, sewing, or washing'. And as she 'can not and will not be a governess, a teacher, a milliner, a bonnet-maker or a housemaid', she would leave. After the death of their father in 1840, Mary and her brother Waring decided on the 'outrageously odd' plan of emigrating to New Zealand.

Perhaps because of family pressures, Mary did not immediately take up this scheme. Instead, she accompanied her sister Martha to school in Brussels where she studied German, French, and music. After Martha's death in 1842, Mary moved on to Germany, 'activity being in my opinion the most desirable state of existence – both for my spirits, health and advantage'. There she began tutoring boys in English. These 'resolute and intrepid proceedings' stunned even Charlotte; 'opinion and custom run so strongly against what she does', she wrote, adding hopefully, 'Often genius like Mary's triumphs over every obstacle without the aid of prudence . . .' She was right; Mary was busy and successful, teaching forty-two lessons a week and making 'more than I need to live on . . .'.

Yet she was not satisfied. She had 'established [her] right to be doing odd things' but she was 'alone and melancholy'. She would go to New Zealand after all, to join Waring, and 'bid adieu to [her] confounded patrie . . . for ever and a day . . .'. And so she sailed on the *Louisa Campbell*, arriving in Wellington on 26 July 1845.

Mary adjusted to the primitive surroundings which greeted her with remarkable rapidity. Initially she continued in the traditional occupation of teaching, astonishing the locals by living in the house of a widower as tutor to his daughter without having any intention of marrying him. Her letters, however, are full of enthusiastic descriptions of her more 'unwomanly' activities: buying land, building a house for rent, and dealing in cattle. She also began to write both fiction and non-fiction, finding 'the faculty does not in the least depend on the leisure I have; much more on the *active* work I have to do'. With the arrival of her cousin Ellen Taylor in August 1849, the fulfilment of more exciting ambitions became possible. Out of the 'dozens of schemes' considered, the two women typically selected the 'most healthy but the most difficult of accomplishment', the establishment of a women's clothing and drapery shop.

With capital provided by the Taylor menfolk, Mary and Ellen launched into business, 'heart and soul'. Mary wrote full and lively accounts of the enterprise to Charlotte. For fifteen years she had wished to earn her own living; now she was doing so and the prospect filled her with joy. She gloated over their new house in the heart of the commercial centre and 'by far the best . . . on our acre', and over the 'moving, cleaning, shopkeeping' which made them tired every night – so much better than being 'ennuyee'! Mary did all the buying, getting 'as fierce as a dragon', and the housework, shopwork, and accounting were shared.

The buildings which housed Mary Taylor's shop on the corner of Dixon and Cuba Streets, Wellington, c.1866. *Alexander Turnbull Library*

Together they revelled in learning new skills. 'We like it and that's the truth!' Mary was indeed 'in her element' in New Zealand, where the sight of gentle-women in trade aroused more amusement than ire. Mary gaily asserted that she 'pass[ed] here for a monkey who has seen the world', and Ellen wrote: 'Our keeping shop astonishes everybody here.' But there was no question of social ostracism: Mary noted wryly that Ellen found 'herself better received than ever she was in her life before', and one old settler remembered Mary herself as 'a good conversationalist' and 'an English lady whom it was a pleasure to meet'.

Sadly, Mary's happiness was to be short-lived, for in December 1851 Ellen died of consumption. Mary's letter to Charlotte 'wrung my heart so – in its simple, strong, truthful emotion'. Yet she did not give up, despite her 'dreary solitude'. She bought the shop outright from Ellen's brother and courageously continued alone. 'Fortunately', she wrote, 'the more I work the better I like it.' By 1853, her shop was listed in the *Wellington and Southern Provincial Almanac* as one of the 'Principal Stores' and it was apparently 'very well patronised'. In 1854, Mary 'got an addition to my store by which you may see I'm getting on in the world', and she also employed an assistant. Although the tone of her letters in the 1850s is greyer than before, she was able to write in 1857 a measured judgement of her achievements

and the effect of my position on me. First of all it agrees with me. I am in better health than at any time since I left school . . . it is just the difference between everything being a burden and everything more or less a pleasure . . . in former days . . . There was always plenty to do but never anything that I really felt was worth the labour of doing.

Nevertheless, Mary was never able to adapt herself to the cultural barrenness of the new colony. 'Do you know that living among people with whom you have not the slightest interest in common is just like living alone, or worse', she wrote to Charlotte. Without Ellen, Mary found some solace in books but 'I never see a human being to whom it would ever occur to me to mention anything I read to them'. Most of her neighbours were 'narrowminded and ignorant', though she admitted: 'This is my fault in part for I can't take interest in their concerns.' Perhaps she never intended to stay in New Zealand permanently; in any case, having sold her shop to her assistant and invested some of her profits in land, she departed from Wellington in May 1859. By 1860, she was back in her own house in Yorkshire where she passed the rest of her life.

The writing she had begun in New Zealand resulted in *The First Duty of Women*, a book on the feminine condition, designed 'to inculcate the duty of earning money' on every woman 'to protect herself from the danger of being forced to marry'. Her novel, *Miss Miles*, which appeared in 1890, preached the same doctrine. Although they did not 'revolutionize society and faire epoque' as Mary had once hoped, still the books were her 'children' and gave her enormous delight. Mary took no part in satisfying public curiosity about the Brontës, having long since destroyed most of Charlotte's letters. She died in 1893, having 'followed her inspiration, courageously and apparently without regrets', literally to the ends of the earth. She had indeed tried all things, and had not, on the whole, found them empty.   *Pat Sargison*

Quotations
para.1 J. Stevens (ed.) *Mary Taylor*, p.18; C. Brontë, *Shirley*, p.384; J. Stevens, p.58
para.2 C. Brontë, p.170; J. Stevens, p.159; W. Gérin, *Charlotte Brontë: The Evolution of Genius*, Oxford, 1967, p.70; J. Stevens, p.51
para.3 C. K. Shorter, 'Mary Taylor', p.234
para.4 A. Hammerton, 'Mary Taylor in New Zealand', pp.74–5; J. Stevens, p.94; J. Stevens, p.80; J. Stevens, p.19
para.5 J. Stevens, p.40; J. Stevens, p.51; J. Stevens, p.45
para.6 J. Stevens, p.50; J. Stevens, p.54; J. Stevens, p.36
para.7 J. Stevens, p.86
para.8 J. Stevens, p.88; J. Stevens, pp.87–100; J. Stevens, p.58; J. Stevens, p.82; J. Stevens, p.99; J. Stevens, p.91; *Dominion*, 4 Dec. 1937
para.9 J. Stevens, p.106; J. Stevens, p.110; 'Old Hand's Reminiscences', *NZ Free Lance*, 14 July 1926, p.8c; J. Stevens, p.121; J. Stevens, p.130–1
para.10 J. Stevens, p.95; J. Stevens, p.131
para.11 M. Taylor, Preface to *The First Duty of Women*, pp.iii, 209; J. Stevens, p.74; J. Stevens, pp.86, 109; M. Peters, *Unquiet Soul: A Biography of Charlotte Brontë*, London, 1977, p.348; C. Brontë, p.385

Published Sources
Brontë, Charlotte. *Shirley* (ed. A. & J. Brook), Harmondsworth, 1974
Fraser, Rebecca. *Charlotte Brontë*, London, 1988
Gérin, W. *Charlotte Brontë: The Evolution of Genius*, Oxford, 1967
Hammerton, A. J. 'Mary Taylor in New Zealand: A Case Study', in his *Emigrant Gentlewomen: Genteel Poverty and Female Emigration, 1830–1914*, London, 1979, pp.71–91
Shorter, C. K. 'Mary Taylor', in his *Charlotte Brontë and her Circle*, London, 1896, pp.234–322
Stevens, Joan (ed.). *Mary Taylor, Friend of Charlotte Brontë: Letters from New Zealand and Elsewhere*, Auckland, 1972
Taylor, Mary. *The First Duty of Women: A Series of Articles reprinted from the Victoria Magazine, 1865 to 1870*, London, 1870
Taylor, Mary. *Miss Miles, or A Tale of Yorkshire 60 Years Ago*, London, 1890

TE AKAKURA RU

1893–1930

Te Akakura was the rangatira (chiefly) wife of the Tuhoe prophet Rua Kenana Hepetipa. She was also known as the 'Queen of Sheba', that is she unto whom King Solomon gave all her desires.

Te Akakura was born in 1893. She was the daughter of Ru Hoani, a Tuhoe elder from Ruatahuna, and the high-ranking Tuhoe chieftainess Te Raumiria Te Haunui, from Ruatoki. She traced her lineage from her mother. Her hapu was Ngati Rongo, and her marae, Tauarau. She was called Patu as a small child, and the name remained with her, for she grew into a strong-willed and beautiful woman.

Te Akakura attended Ruatoki Native School for only two years, 1902–3. She had, however, been brought up in association with the Anglican mission, and she first married a young man, Hena Rakuraku, from a leading Anglican family at Ruatoki. Two months after their marriage he died, and Rua then came to Ruatoki to claim her. As their elder daughter put it, 'She was only a widow a very short time and my father went over to get her. He fought for her. He had already prophesied – he spoke about her.' Hena's death had been attributed to

Te Akakura Ru of Ngati Rongo, the chiefly
wife of prophet Rua Kenana, with her son.
Alexander Turnbull Library

Rua's powers of makutu (cursing), and a taiaha (spear) fight took place between
Rua and Hena's father, Rakuraku. Te Akakura's great-uncle, Numia Te
Ruakariata (Numia Kereru), who was the senior Tuhoe chief of Ruatoki, also
strongly disapproved of her marriage to Rua. But Te Akakura went with him.
She remained with him all her life.

The earliest photographs of Te Akakura as Rua's wife date from April 1908.
She was his third wife. She was considered his legal wife, because a Ringatu
ceremony took place, although no formal registration of the marriage exists.
They had three children: Henare, probably born on 17 March 1911; Te Akakura,
probably born on 1 July 1914; and their youngest, Noti (Patu), probably born
in 1919.

Te Akakura lived with Rua (and his other wives) during the years in which
Maungapohatu was constructed as the City of God on earth. The people re-
enacted, under Rua's direction, the entire history of the Israelites of the Old and
New Testaments, sealing anew their covenant with God. As the builder of New
Jerusalem, Rua was King Solomon to Te Akakura's Sheba. When he made his
second ritual home at Maai, about half a mile away from the old community,
she moved there with him. Among the wives she is remembered as the dominant
presence. She was Patu Maori; one of Rua's other wives, Wairimu, who was
part-European, became known as Patu Pakeha because the two women often
quarrelled. But generally Te Akakura was considered a good companion and
friend.

She was renowned for the influence she had with her husband. On one occasion, as his adopted son Hillman later narrated, she intervened to persuade Rua

to help Te Ripo Horomona, who had brought up their younger daughter, and who now lay ill at Matahi in the Bay of Plenty.

Patu [Te Akakura] said to Rua, 'Rua, think about that woman.' We'd got word that she was just dying. Te Ripo. And the old man said, 'What good is that woman to us?' And Patu says, 'Don't you remember our daughter? . . . old Te Ripo look after that baby, and she's a woman now.' And the old man says, 'Oh well, I'll see.' And he send me down from Maungapohatu. He says, 'You go down and have a word with this woman.' The whole day I came from Maungapohatu. I got into Matahi . . . She sit up in her bed, just thinking about Rua. Trying to help him eh? Put out her hand to me – where I came from. From Rua. Rua might have given me something for her. So I shook hands with her. She went out of her bed that very day. She was well. And there she was lying in bed to die! Ai. That's how Patu did things, eh? That's all I had to do – just shake hands, nothing else. I don't know what's on me, or what. That very day she got out of bed.

Several songs composed around 1916, when Rua was in jail in Auckland, also stress Te Akakura's authority and influence over him. This one was composed by the women of Maungapohatu about Rua:

> *Matakai mai e Aka i Ruatoki*
> *Aroaro ra i ai te rere mai a te manu*
> *He mea ra tuki mai na Te Akakura!*

> *From Ruatoki, Aka, you hold me in your gaze*
> *Like the bird flying straight to me*
> *Released for that purpose by Te Akakura!*

Te Akakura was also famous for her disobedience to her husband. At the beginning of 1928, against his instructions, she insisted on going through on a truck from Ruatahuna with a party of Maungapohatu elders to attend a tangi (funeral) at Te Whaiti. Rua had forewarned disaster. The truck came off the road shortly after leaving the tangi and two of the elders were killed. Te Akakura herself suffered serious back injuries, and had to be brought home to Maungapohatu on a litter. She was thought to have recovered, but she may not have done. She died three years later, on 17 December 1930, of spinal cancer.

Rua married Te Akakura because of her chiefly lineage among Tuhoe. She always kept her independence. She retained her land, against his advice. She returned to Ruatoki, often for long periods. She sent her elder daughter to be educated there by the Anglican mission, and ensured that she later attended Turakina Maori Girls' College. Te Akakura was also a powerful voice in persuading Rua to accept a Presbyterian mission school at Maungapohatu in 1918. But if she called the people of Maungapohatu 'backward' when compared with Ruatoki, she also remained with them. She is, in turn, remembered by them for her independent will, her love of life, and her commitment to their community and its prophetic leader.
                                                                          Judith Binney

Quotations
para.3 Te Akakura Rua, cited in J. Binney and G. Chaplin, *Nga Morehu*, p.176
para.6 Abridged from Binney and Chaplin, pp.177–8
para.7 Binney and Chaplin, p.177

Unpublished Sources
Elsdon Best, 'Genealogies of the Tuhoe as of 1898', MS ATL, p.33
Ruatoki Native School Files, National Archives, Auckland

Published Source
Binney, Judith, and Chaplin, Gillian. *Nga Morehu*, Auckland, 1986

TE MAIAIREA TE RIRI WAIRUA PURU

c. 1660

'Ko Te Amaru tera' (That's The Amaru). That is the reply which would be given when strangers marvelled at the woman walking in the mist of Murihiku – the woman who seemed to be walking in a world of her own where there was no mist. For her the sun shone, so great was her tapu.

She was called the Amaru because in her time she was the oldest descendant of the ariki lines, the highest-ranking families of Kati Mamoe (also known as Ngati Moa), an ancient tribe of Te Wai Pounamu, the South Island. That was the title appropriate to her rank, by which she was known to her people. Her actual name was Te Maiairea Te Riri Wairua Puru. She lived twelve generations ago in Murihiku (Otago-Southland). Te Maiairea married Nekeneke Puauau of the Waitaha, an even more ancient South Island tribe. He was the last descendant of the ariki lines of Waitaha. Two children were born to them. When they were staying at Hauroko Lake (in what is now Fiordland National Park), Nekeneke is said to have deliberately struck his head on a rock and died so that his blood would forever flow in the lake. His gift to the gods was to ask them to protect his children and his children's children.

The tribes of Waitaha, in the southern end of the South Island, and Kati Mamoe, in the north, had both felt the pressure from the invasion of the South Island by the tribal groups Ngai Tara and Ngai Tahu who had crossed to the South Island between three and five generations before. Some of these immigrants were related to Kati Mamoe. As Kati Mamoe gave ground to the new arrivals they moved south into the Waitaha lands. Nekeneke Puauau could see his people withdrawing into the more remote areas where they would become even fewer. This was perhaps the reason for his sacrificial action, to return the mana of his people to the sacred waters of the lake.

Nekeneke Puauau and Te Maiairea's descendant six generations later was Kohuwai of Kati Mamoe, who married Honekai of Ngai Tahu, whose daughter Kura was the mother of Tuhawaiki, also known to Europeans as 'Bloody Jack', paramount chief of Ngai Tahu. In this way the mana of Waitaha, Kati Mamoe, and Ngai Tahu continued and became one.

Te Maiairea and her people had come from Turakautahi, a village near Christchurch. In the south they lived in various villages during the seasonal cycle. Kumara and other crops introduced from the Pacific Islands do not grow in Murihiku so while there was a winter village in which the tribal groups lived for a month or two, there was no agriculture. A good substitute was to cook and dry the underground stems of kauru (cabbage tree), which were dug just before the flowering in October, cooked and dried, then kept for winter use.

It may have been on an expedition to gather birds that Te Maiairea was again at Hauroko. While she was there she died. Her people, because she was too tapu to be taken back to the winter village at Oraka (Colac Bay), or because they knew the story of Nekeneke Puauau, took the hut she was living in and made a bier from its framework for her to sit on in a cave on what is now known as Mary Island. They covered the bier with para fern (king fern) leaves to show it was tapu. Te Maiairea they tied up in a crouched position, wrapped around with her Kati Mamoe cloak made with a half-hitch weave and decorated with strips of kaka skin with feathers diamond-hitched to the warp. In 1967 her resting place in the cave was rediscovered. With the agreement of the Murihiku Tribal executive, the burial was recorded, and then, with the help of the Fiordland Park Board, was protected with a metal grille. A radio-carbon date for the house wood gave a determination of about AD 1660. The genealogical date is twelve generations from the present.   *David Simmons*

Unpublished Source
Nekeneke Renata, direct descendant of Nekeneke Puauau and Te Maiairea, provided the name, and
    stories about Te Maiairea.

Published Sources
Shortland, E. *The Southern Districts of New Zealand*, London, 1851
Simmons, D. R. 'The Lake Hauroko Burial and the Evolution of Maori Clothing', *Records of Otago
    Museum: Anthropology*, no.5, 1968

TE PUEA HERANGI

1883–1952

Te Puea Herangi, a key figure of the Kingitanga, was one of the most dynamic and inspiring leaders of this century. She was born at Whatiwhatihoe in the Waikato in 1883. Her mother was Tiahuia, a daughter of King Tawhiao, and her father Te Tahuna Herangi. He was the son of Hariata Rangitaupua, a chieftainess of Ngati Maniapoto, and William Nicholas Searancke, an English surveyor.

In her twenties, Te Puea settled on land at Mangatawhiri and began dairy farming, soon becoming established as a leader of the small community there. About this time she began working with her kuia and kaumatua, collecting and recording waiata, whakapapa, and korero tawhito (songs, genealogies, and history).

In 1911, Mahuta, who had succeeded Tawhiao as king, gave Te Puea her first opportunity to demonstrate her gifts for organisation and leadership. He decided to support Maui Pomare's bid for election to parliament in the Western Maori electorate. Rather than do so openly, Mahuta conveyed to Te Puea his wish that she undertake the election campaign. The sitting member, Henare

Kaihau, was himself an influential figure in the Kingitanga. Although there had been some dissatisfaction with his performance, opposing his re-election was no easy commission for Te Puea and it was to make her enemies. Pomare was successfully elected, however, and Te Puea's influence and strength became more widely recognised. Mahuta died two years later and was succeeded by his son, Te Rata. By that time, Te Puea's leadership role in the Kingitanga was more firmly established, even if that recognition did not yet extend to all of Waikato.

The smallpox epidemic of 1913 had a tragic effect on Te Puea's settlement and on others along the Waikato River. With very little money or support, she organised camps to nurse those affected by what was often a fatal disease. Very few hospitals at the time would accept Maori patients. The reluctance was mutual, with most Waikato Maori fearful and suspicious of the medical profession. Later, during the 1918 influenza epidemic, Te Puea devoted herself again to nursing the sick. This epidemic had an even more devastating effect on Maori settlements. Many children were orphaned and old people left without anyone to care for them. Te Puea gathered them all up and brought them to live in the Mangatawhiri community.

Her leadership of the Waikato-Maniapoto anti-conscription movement in 1917 brought her into conflict with the government and into the public eye. Te Puea's stand was inspired by the words of Tawhiao. She would quote one of his sayings from after the wars of the 1860s, when he spoke out strongly against war:

The killing of men must stop, the destruction of land must stop. I shall bury my patu [club] in the earth and it shall not rise again . . . Waikato lie down. Do not allow blood to flow from this time on.

Taking her stand against conscription, Te Puea opened up Mangatawhiri as a refuge for the men who refused to enlist. When the police party came to arrest those called up for overseas service, she led her people in a non-violent protest. One of the young men forcibly removed by police was her future husband, Tumokai Katipa.

From the early 1920s on, Te Puea's aims were to re-establish the mana and strength of the Kingitanga, to achieve economic strength, and to build a marae at Ngaruawahia. Waikato were almost landless – a result of the confiscations of the 1860s. Attempts to procure compensation from the government were not to result in a settlement until 1946. So funds for her projects were slowly raised in a number of ways. Her people took up contracts for scrub-cutting, road-making, and gum-digging. A touring concert party travelled the North Island giving performances. Not only was the tour a financial success, but it also contributed to a revival of interest in haka, waiata, and poi.

The land at Ngaruawahia was eventually purchased; Te Puea and her people struggled for several years against the odds to build Turangawaewae. In March of 1929 the main meeting-house Mahinarangi was opened at an historic hui of 6,000 people. Te Puea's genius for organisation and hospitality was obvious, and her reputation grew deservedly.

When in the late 1920s she decided to support Sir Apirana Ngata's land development schemes, she encountered opposition. Te Puea believed the schemes offered a way for Waikato to farm large blocks of land successfully in the manner they had done last century before the land was taken. But apart from her own family and community, there was widespread opposition to such close co-operation with the government. In some parts of Waikato Te Puea was nick-named 'Mrs Kawanatanga' (Mrs Government).

Nevertheless, she and her followers spent the next few years toiling at the job of bringing various blocks into production. As always, Te Puea led by example, clearing gorse, collecting kauri gum, planning and organising the direction of the work. These were the years of the 1930s Depression; Te Puea helped her people to have goals to work towards, shelter, and a livelihood. And they were able to live and work in the way they preferred – communally.

Through her association with Ngata, Te Puea came to realise the value of having friends in power. After Labour became the government in 1935, she enjoyed good relationships with Prime Minister M. J. Savage and his successor Peter Fraser. She understood the benefits of cultivating and lobbying politicians, and did so effectively for the benefit of the Kingitanga. From the 1930s until her death in 1952, Te Puea was one of the government's most prolific correspondents.

During the 1940s she turned her energies towards the settlement of Te Raupatu o Waikato – the confiscated lands grievance. In 1928, the Commission into Confiscated Native Lands (Sim Commission) had published its findings. It found that confiscation had been excessive in the case of Waikato and recom-mended compensation. This was to be paid in the form of an annual amount to be administered by a trust board, for the benefit of the descendants of those whose land was taken. After the release of the commission's report, attempts to finalise a settlement had been unsuccessful, and eventually resolution of the matter was held over until the end of the Second World War.

In April 1946, Prime Minister Fraser and the Minister of Native Affairs, H. G. R. Mason, attended a hui at Turangawaewae. The settlement was dis-cussed and debated over several days and an offer made: £6,000 a year for fifty years and £5,000 a year thereafter in perpetuity. Te Puea played a leading role in the negotiations, and the offer was eventually accepted, although agreement was not unanimous. A section of Waikato held strongly to the belief that, as land was taken, only land was acceptable compensation. In Te Puea's eyes, settlement of the Raupatu grievance meant that finally funds were available to continue economic development, to pay for the upkeep of Turangawaewae, and to enable her people to pursue educational goals. And it also meant official recognition of the validity of their grievance, and of the principle that unjust treatment by government should be rectified, however much time had elapsed.

Although her health was frequently bad during the last years of her life, Te Puea maintained her active involvement with the life of Turangawaewae. She continued to direct the activities of the Kingitanga and involved herself in projects such as the purchase of a sawmill and the lost cause of keeping the Wai-kato 'dry'. She took pleasure in the company of her mokopuna and friends from the old days. One of the most longstanding and loyal of Te Puea's friends was Ngeungeu Beamish Zister. In February 1990, she shared her personal memories of Te Puea with Merimeri Penfold:

My friend was Te Atarua, her youngest sister. We went to Mercer School. We all lived down the river banks. Te Painga was what we used to call it then.

Mercer was Te Painga. There was a very big Maori settlement.

Te Puea and my elder sister – they were sent to a ladies' school in Auckland and they boarded with a Maori family called the Mackies. They were not very happy because of weekends and times when they were made to do gardening and so on. Anyway, Mahuta got to hear of it, so they were brought home, back to Mercer.

Te Puea was a lovely girl, a bit of a tomboy. Everybody was in love with her. All the married men and all them out here were after her. Oh yes, she was very good looking, a very loving sort of girl.

She had a Maori look and she had a Pakeha look about her – kaore tino Maori te ahua [her appearance wasn't totally Maori] – because her father was a Searancke.

She used to travel around, up and down the river. You know, Waikato's a big place. Right from Tuakau to Taupo. And everybody knew she was a relation. She was the daughter of Tawhiao's daughter. Everybody was chasing after her, oh yes, she was spoilt all right.

Friday Herewini, my uncle, was Te Puea's first husband. She must have been quite young then. They were both handsome people, a very handsome couple. She never had any children, never. Anyway, in the end there were family troubles.

She had husbands after that – she had several men of course. She had one Pakeha husband [Roy Seccombe] and all the rest were Maori. This is way back, I'm talking about.

When we were at Mercer, Friday and the Herewinis had a band. They were great bandspeople. Te Puea used to dance a lot, but she was a little bit cumbersome. She was a big girl. She'd get up to dance with a partner, then she'd pull somebody else up to take over.

And she was sick. She got very sick. She went down to Taupo and they nursed her back. She married a wonderful husband from Taupo – that was the best husband. I thought he was really lovely – Iwikau [Te Tahi Iwikau]. He was a Tuwharetoa. They were all in our lot anyway, we were all related.

They lived at Mercer. It was a great place then in those days. He was a good man, handsome, but freckle-faced. He helped her out on the farm. I was at school then and Atarua was at Grammar. They'd come to town, Iwikau and Te Puea, and call for me at school in a taxi. They'd take me out to lunch, there'd always be three or four of them because they wouldn't go around by themselves. I'd be in seventh heaven.

Iwikau left after it came to fisticuffs. He came to see me in Auckland and said, 'I'm going back.' I was terribly upset. That was the last time I ever saw him. Te Puea went after him, but they married him off to somebody else. Anyway that was the end.

Later, Ngeungeu Zister moved to Wellington to work, but kept in touch with Te Puea. She also contracted tuberculosis.

I got very sick. I got leave for twelve months and I was in the sanatorium. I made up my mind I wasn't going to die. Hera, that's Te Puea's elder sister, she was living in Otaki then, and her family used to come and look after me in the sanatorium. Bring me up Maori kai and cook it. Hera was a wonderful person, a beautiful woman. Te Puea came down two or three times to the sanatorium. She was thinking then of starting Ngaruawahia.

Te Puea and Hera came to the hospital to get me out. I went back to the office after I got better, but the doctor said I should be outside.

Then Te Puea came for me. 'I want you to come home, come back and help me.' And I said, 'What for?' 'Oh,' she said, 'we're going to take up this land in Ngaruawahia – I want you to come and help me.' So I said, 'All right'.

Princess Te Puea Herangi. *Alexander Turnbull Library*

Ngeungeu Zister returned to Waikato and worked alongside Te Puea as she struggled to build Turangawaewae.

She had an iron will. She said, 'I want you to come and teach our people. I'm going to do it, everybody's trying to put me off. I want you to help me make this the talk of the world.' She made up her mind and she did it. So I came back. We lived in bag huts and all sorts.

When she was building Turangawaewae her husband was Dave Katipa [Tumokai Katipa]. He was years younger than she was. He was a good helper, a wonderful worker, he did a lot. They looked after all these children together.

Te Puea had a very hard time at Ngaruawahia. The Pakehas didn't want a marae there. They didn't want to give them work or anything. I worked as her social secretary.

There were plenty of people about. When it came to teaching them to cook and all that, she was wonderful. She taught them everything. She took all these orphans, a lot of them there had lost their parents with one thing and another. We had a lot of people come and live on the marae. They built houses – went and got tree ferns, ponga, we had a lot of ponga houses and they were good houses too.

She always talked to me a lot. If she got a letter from somebody, wanting something, she'd say, 'Have a look at this.' And I'd say, 'No, you don't do that – do this.' I used to advise her.

When Labour tried to get her to stand for parliament, I talked to her. I said, 'You're a rangatira. After you join them how do you think they'll treat you? You'll be no rangatira then.'

She was very loveable – most people loved her. She had a wonderful personality. Even the Pakehas took to her. She was a very humble person. I was with her from when I was a kid until she died.

Te Puea Herangi died in 1952 aged sixty-eight. She lay in Mahinarangi for seven days and was buried on Taupiri Mountain as heavy rain fell. With her death, Waikato lost their beloved leader, an ariki of vision, deep spirituality, and much humility. An inspirational woman, she possessed great strength, initiative, and tenacity of purpose. Such was her energy and drive that she often said of herself, 'I have no recreations, when I am not working, I sleep.'

Tui MacDonald with Ngeungeu Zister

Quotation
para.5 Quoted in M. King, *Te Puea*, p.77

Unpublished Sources
Interview with Ngeungeu Zister, by Merimeri Penfold, Feb. 1990
Report of 1927 Commission re Waikato Confiscations, MA1 5/13/9, National Archives, Wellington

Published Source
King, Michael. *Te Puea*, Auckland, 1977

WHETU TE WHATA

1876–1945

Whetu Karehau Taimona, known as Hemo, was born in Kokohuia, in the Hokianga. She was one of a very large family and spent her childhood in Kokohuia. On 6 October 1892, at the age of sixteen, Hemo married Tango Raumati Te Whata. Because of the ways of those times, Hemo and her husband moved to the settlement of Waipoua, south of the Hokianga Harbour, to work in the kauri gum-fields.

Their two daughters, Reiha and Maro, who was nicknamed Tuha, were born there. Hemo and her husband longed for a son, and when she fell pregnant once more they were both hopeful it would be a boy. Hemo's labour with this baby was long and difficult. After two weeks, Hemo asked her husband to seek assistance from the tohunga Te Rekauere at Otaua. This was a journey on horseback of many hours.

Tango Te Whata rode his horse along the coast to Waimamaku, north of Waipoua. There he spoke of his wife's plight with Iehu Moetara, a chief of great mana. Iehu told him to move on to Otaua. Tango told him he thought his horse was too tired, but Iehu told him all would be well. Tango moved on inland and at Omanaia he met another local chief called Huru Titore and told him about his wife. Titore told him to keep going to Otaua, to Rekauere. Tango mentioned his horse was too tired, but Titore assured Tango all would be well. Tango moved on to Otaua where he met Te Rekauere and explained his wife's request for special assistance. Te Rekauere told Tango he must return home and gave him a bottle to gather water. Tango was told not to speak to anyone or let anyone touch him on his return journey. Te Rekauere gave Tango a special branch as a horse whip as Tango was concerned about his very tired horse.

On his journey home Tango passed through Omanaia and saw Titore, who asked how things had gone at Otaua. Tango did not reply but kept going. Tango arrived back at Waimamaku where Moetara was waiting for him. When Moetara asked how things were, Tango did not reply. Moetara moved toward him but Tango backed away. Moetara caught his horse and they both travelled out to the coast from Waimamaku. While travelling along the sea-shore they both witnessed a meteor, or falling star, falling into the sea. Moetara told Tango he would find the water for his bottle where the star fell into the water. Tango asked how he would get there, and the reply was that he should just go.

Tango got off his horse and walked down to the water. The water kept receding in front of him, further and further back, building higher. Tango was by now quite fearful that the wall of water would break over him. He reached the spot where he thought the star had fallen, stopped, lifted the bottle from Rekauere, and let three drops of water fall into it. He stepped back three steps, turned his back on the wall of water, and walked ashore. All the time he could hear the water and feel it lapping at his heels as he walked back to dry land. Tango returned to his wife, gave her the water in the bottle to drink, and she was safely delivered of their eldest son.

Hemo related this story to her daughter, Meti, to illustrate how powerful

670

Mana Maori was in her life. Hemo's helper at the birth of all her children was her husband, Tango. They both came back to live in Kokohuia eventually.

Hemo was a very skilled midwife and helped deliver many, many babies in the Kokohuia, Waiwhata, and Waimamaku area. Her daughter tells of the birth of her own daughter Maraea. Although many other women had asked Hemo to be their midwife, Meti had asked one of her cousins to assist when she went into labour. The labour proved to be longer and more difficult than expected, and after two days it was decided to take Meti to the Rawene Hospital, about eighteen miles away, to have the baby. The car carrying the expectant mother ran out of petrol at Omapere, quite close to Hemo Te Whata's home. A figure was seen walking towards the car – it was Hemo, making her way to Waimamaku some five miles away to see her daughter Meti. She came up to the car and the moment she touched it, Meti gave birth to Maraea. Needless to say, mother and new daughter were able to go straight home to Waimamaku.

Hemo Te Whata is remembered with great affection by many people, especially her niece Ani Iraia. She remembers Hemo as a loving, kind person who always had huge mahinga (gardens) with home-grown sugar-cane, popcorn, strawberries, melons, corn, and all manner of vegetables. Hemo's grandson, Daniel Ambler of Waimamaku, has fond memories of staying with his grandmother when he was a child and enjoying life in her small, cosy home. He remembers eating delicious crabs, caught from the shores of the Hokianga Harbour. He also remembers the woven mats in her home and her lovely flower gardens.

Hemo Te Whata's contribution to family and community life in the Kokohuia area has living proof in the lives of her many children, grandchildren, and great-grandchildren, many of whom still live in the Hokianga area.

Kiri Matthews

Unpublished Sources
Information was provided by Meti Ambler (Hemo's daughter), Daniel Ambler (grandson), and Ani Iraia (niece).

GREVILLE TEXIDOR

1902–1964

Anyone who can make Janet Frame 'impressed and quietly depressed' by the 'assurance and sophistication' of her stories deserves recognition in our literary history. But both the work and the recollection of Greville Texidor seemed to fade from public consciousness in the twenty years between her death and the eventual republication of most of her stories in 1987.

Both in her own fiction and in accounts of her life, Texidor is an exotic figure in the landscape of New Zealand writing. Painted by Augustus John, associated with a contortionist, active in the Spanish civil war, Texidor brought with her to New Zealand, and to New Zealand fiction, horizons of glamour, adventure, and romance. Although Texidor lived in New Zealand for only eight years, most of her writing was done here, and a substantial part of it is set in this country. One of her stories, 'An Annual Affair', about a community picnic where all the men get drunk and the women become ever more tight-lipped as they look after the kids, was included in Oxford University Press's first volume of *New Zealand Short Stories*, edited by Dan Davin; her short novel, *These Dark Glasses*, was published by the Caxton Press. Thus, however engagingly foreign Texidor appears, it is as a New Zealand writer that she makes her claim on history.

Texidor's mother, Editha Prideaux, was a painter who arrived in New Zealand as a child and left to go to the Slade School of Art in London in her late twenties. She married a barrister, William Arthur Foster, had two daughters, Greville and Kate, and, after the suicide of her husband at the end of the First World War, moved into artistic company in Hampstead. Greville said she was drawn by Augustus John as a child, her sister was an art student, and the family was acquainted with a number of Hampstead painters including Mark Gertler and Stanley Spencer.

Texidor spent some time dancing in a variety chorus in Europe and New York, toured with a German contortionist, and was married a couple of times, latterly to a Spanish industrialist (Manuel Texidor) in Buenos Aires. The Texidors moved to Spain in 1933, and were living in Tossa de Mar when they separated. It was in Tossa de Mar, prominent as a place of refuge for intellectuals and artists in opposition to European facism, that Texidor met her third husband, Werner Droescher. As Anarchists, the couple were involved in the Civil War doing propaganda and relief work.

This itinerant, politically engaged European experience is the material for some of Texidor's writing, although all her work focuses on the outsider, the transient, the foreigner, in a way which connects stories apparently distinct. Texidor's novella *These Dark Glasses* (1949) is the diary of Comrade Ruth Brown, who spends one summer at Calanques in a community of intellectuals, artists, and refugees. The contradictions, pretensions, and shifting emotional climate of Calanques are presented from the subjective viewpoint of Ruth Brown, on the fringe, observing 'the mercilessly lighted cabaret of the beach thinly disguised with books and dark glasses'. *These Dark Glasses* is Texidor's longest fictional work. Like her other stories about Spain, and about English girls working and travelling in Europe (for example, 'Jesus Jiménez', 'Santa Cristina', and 'Maaree'), it takes place in an environment of significant political and historical events. Ruth Brown's diary highlights the condition of people engaged with movements larger than individual lives; at the same time, its focus is the 'view', the 'dark glasses' of the individual. This representation of the community through the individual is characteristic of Texidor's work.

In order to escape both Germany and internment in England, Texidor and Droescher left Europe for New Zealand, arriving in Auckland in May 1940. Droescher worked on a farm in North Auckland, and Texidor made shirts in a factory. Fortunately, they met in New Zealand the local equivalent of the European society they were used to: Kendrick Smithyman, Frank Sargeson, Maurice Duggan, and other New Zealand writers befriended the Droeschers, and it was Sargeson who pushed and encouraged Texidor to write. While living in New Zealand Texidor wrote thirteen stories and a novella as well as some uncollected

Greville Texidor, 'an exotic figure in the landscape of New Zealand writing'. *NZ Post Collection, Alexander Turnbull Library*

fragments; during this time seven of the stories were published, in New Zealand, and also in Australia and England.

In 1947 Texidor moved to Australia; she later wrote from there to Sargeson, saying that since he had 'given up being responsible for it I have never written another thing'. But as the recent collection of her work shows, Texidor's fictional country is the polyglot, shifting geography of her own life, given an opportunity for expression perhaps by the very condition of expatriation in which she found herself in Auckland in 1940. Texidor killed herself in Australia in 1964.

In her novella 'Goodbye Forever', Lilli, a young Viennese landed in New Zealand during the war, asks:

To live, what for? And the rain and nothing nice to see anywhere. Unheated cinemas and draughty dance halls. And hardly enough money to pay the rent. To live just to eat and sleep. And no love.

All Texidor's fiction is preoccupied with that question – 'To live, what for?' It is a question that belongs perhaps particularly to the condition of itinerancy and expatriation in which she lived and wrote.   *Lydia Wevers*

Quotations
para.1 Janet Frame, *An Angel at My Table: An Autobiography*, vol.2, Auckland, 1985, p.173
para.5 G. Texidor, *These Dark Glasses*, p.29
para.7 K. Smithyman, 'Introduction', in G. Texidor, *In Fifteen Minutes*, p.20
para.9 G. Texidor, *In Fifteen Minutes*, p.196

Published Sources

Sargeson, F. 'Greville Texidor: 1902–1964', *Landfall*, 74, June 1965, pp.135–8

Texidor, Greville. *In Fifteen Minutes You Can Say A Lot* (edited with introduction by Kendrick Smithyman), Wellington, 1987

Texidor, Greville. *These Dark Glasses*, Christchurch, 1949

BLANCHE THOMPSON

1874–1963

Blanche Edith Lough was born at Amberley, the youngest twin daughter of Henry Lough and Harriet Waters. Harriet had been a governess and Henry worked as an accountant for the Salt Water Creek Harbour Board in North Canterbury, until the Waimakariri flood of 1868 ruined the port, disintegrating their sod cottage in the process. The young couple, then with two children, moved to Amberley and started farming.

Blanche, her twin sister Bertha, and their six older brothers and sisters received their early formal education in a sod school at Glasnevin, five miles north of Amberley. Their grandfather, who had been a schoolmaster in England, established the school in 1866 for his own family and children from neighbouring farms.

When she was twelve years old, Blanche was sent to a primary school in Amberley. It was a long walk, bitterly cold and wet in winter and dusty in

Blanche Lough (later Thompson), left, with her twin sister Bertha, first women cycle riders in Christchurch, *c.*1892.
Ngawi Thompson

summer, unless she was lucky enough to hitch a ride on a passing railway jigger. There Blanche learned to play the piano, encouraged by her musical parents. When she was fifteen, the whole family moved to Christchurch, where Blanche continued her piano lessons and eventually taught pupils of her own.

Her elder brothers became interested in the new craze of bicycling, and the twin sisters were soon keen to try. In August 1892 a group of young women in Christchurch formed the Atalanta Cycling Club for women, with Blanche as the captain. Kate Sheppard, then in her forties, and Bertha were amongst those on the committee. They encountered much hostility from the public as they pedalled about the city and environs. Blanche recalled that at times her older brothers used to accompany club members on cycle outings to ward off stone-throwing objectors. Her brothers also used to go out in front waving flags, warning people (gig drivers in particular) that the women were coming.

At nineteen, Blanche met Horace Thompson, who had recently returned to New Zealand from six years in England and Europe where he had been apprenticed to piano-makers. She married him in 1893. He was a proficient cellist, and they formed a small musical group of piano and string instruments and played at social functions around the city. For a time they were resident musicians at the somewhat controversial community established by Professor A. E. Bickerton at Wainoni.

Blanche's motivation to help others was rooted in her own experiences of tragedy; her first-born children, twin boys, died the day after they were born. Her three daughters, Rona, Piri, and Ngawi, were each born eight years apart, with many miscarriages in between.

During the 1918 influenza epidemic Blanche worked all day in a food relief kitchen, in spite of the risk to her own health. Rona was instructed to have the copper boiling ready for Blanche to strip off and boil her clothes at the end of the day. Her contributions to the community were an integral part of her character and her life; she worked voluntarily for the Red Cross, and was one of a small group of women who started the Richmond Free Kindergarten in Christchurch. Although she was motivated by compassionate concern for others, her matter-of-fact personality and wry sense of humour sometimes infuriated her children; she routinely explained cause of death as 'shortage of breath'.

In later years, Blanche made several long sea voyages to England, accompanying first Piri (who was embarking on a career as a concert pianist), then Ngawi for specialist surgery (she had contracted polio). Later Blanche returned to England to help Piri during her second pregnancy which ended in a still birth, and again when Piri's second child was ill and subsequently died. On one occasion Blanche was away from Horace and Rona for almost two years.

Coming from a family that was eager to try new things, Blanche was eager to learn to drive. Her husband was amongst the first in the country to own and drive a motor car, and Blanche was quick to follow suit. She is credited with being the first woman in the South Island to drive a motor car. In 1906 she won a silver teapot as first prize in a ladies' driving contest held at the Addington Showgrounds Motor Gymkhana.

Blanche was willing to accept and embrace change, both technological and social. For example, she would get cross with people who criticised young mothers for having washing-machines, instead of making do with a copper; she was genuinely pleased for others' good fortune.

In later years Blanche became an avid air traveller and tried to train as a pilot; with age against her, she had to content herself with being a passenger. Nevertheless, she remained an enthusiastic traveller all her life, from railway jigger to aircraft. When she died in Wellington, in 1963, her body was flown to its final resting place in Christchurch.

Clare Simpson & Ngawi Thompson

Source
Information came from family sources, and in particular from Ngawi Thompson's memories of her mother.

ROSA THOMPSON

1917–1971

In the 1980s, every prison in New Zealand had to have the services of a social worker, and to provide equal employment opportunities to all staff, according to Department of Justice policy. Yet in 1960, when Rosa Thompson was appointed as a prison social worker, she created an historical precedent as the first such female worker in a male prison in New Zealand.

She was born Rosa Haiat in Manchester, England, the youngest of five children, whose father was a cotton importer. The family spent time in the Middle East, settling permanently in England when the Depression caused a slump in the cotton trade.

Rose left school at sixteen with no qualifications, drifting into various jobs until 1939 when she joined the Women's Army Corps. A year later she transferred to the NAAFI (Navy, Army and Air Force Institutes), and with Effie, another Manchester girl, she toured the Italian Alps setting up canteens for the troops.

After the war Effie married a New Zealander, Owen Nicholas, and Rosa visited her in Auckland. Here Rosa got a job as a health education officer and organised a welfare service for unmarried mothers. Through her work she met A. W. S. (Bill) Thompson, another recent immigrant who was then head of the Health Department's Auckland office. In 1951 his marriage ended and he and Rosa were married. Their only child Gillian was born in 1952.

In 1954 Rosa began noticing problems with her sight, co-ordination, and comprehension. A harrowing series of misdiagnoses eventually led to the realisation that she had a brain tumour. Fortunately this was benign, and after an operation in Scotland she made a complete recovery.

Back in New Zealand, where Bill was now Director of Clinical Services at the Health Department in Wellington, Rosa looked for employment when Gillian started school. Her work with soldiers had given her an understanding of the stresses suffered by men isolated from normal social contact. In 1957 she began doing voluntary social work at Mount Crawford (Wellington Prison), asking no pay until she had proved her worth. She was aided by the interest and support of the superintendent, Lew Gorman, the chaplain, Les Clements, and the psychologist, Tony Taylor, although they were doubtful of the wisdom of allowing a female social worker into a potentially dangerous male environment.

The Secretary for Justice at this time was S. T. Barnett, who made a number of radical changes to penal policy. He placed a strong emphasis on the rehabilitation of prisoners, and was responsible for the introduction of chaplains and psychologists into the prison service. Although his policy did not explicitly include the use of social workers, the climate was right for this type of experiment.

Rosa Thompson, 1960. *New Zealand Family Doctor*

In appearance Rosa was an unlikely candidate for work in a male prison, being four foot eleven inches tall and slightly built. However, her sharp mind, good humour, courage, and matter-of-fact approach to the job proved highly successful in dealing with the needs of prisoners and their families, even though she had no formal training as a social worker. She also had strong convictions about her relationship to the prisoners. She always referred to them as 'clients', and invariably addressed them as 'Mr ...', emphasising that they had as much right to help and counselling as any other member of society.

By 1960 her efforts had convinced the Department of Justice to make her position official, although the salary was low. In 1965 the social worker's position was added to the professional staff at Mount Crawford prison, and her hours gradually increased from sixteen to thirty. In addition she made her home telephone number available to prisoners' families, and dealt with many urgent crises out of working hours.

Sadly her career and her life ended in 1971. She had been ill for some time and believed she had cancer. Her traumatic experience with the brain tumour had given her an exaggerated mistrust of doctors and a great fear of serious illness, and she died from an overdose of sleeping tablets at the age of fifty-three.

Gill Winter

Unpublished Sources

The author (who is Rosa Thompson's daughter) is grateful to the following for information: Irene Ralph, secretary at Wellington Prison, 1959–67; Blanche Sherbourne (Rosa Thompson's sister); Professor A. and Mrs M. Taylor, Wellington. The Department of Justice also provided access to Rosa Thompson's personal file.

Published Sources

Department of Justice. *Crime and the Community: A Survey of Penal Policy in New Zealand*, Wellington, 1964

NZ Family Doctor, July 1960; June 1965; Feb. 1966; May 1967 (articles by Rosa Thompson relating to her prison work)

Report of the Penal Policy Review Committee, Wellington, 1981

HELEN THOMSON

1905–1989

If an epitaph had to be compressed to one word, Helen Thomson's would be, simply, 'Teacher'. In her work, standards, and ideals, she represented many women of her generation, women who dedicated their lives to teaching. She taught for forty-two years, mainly at New Plymouth Girls' High School, then continued actively working for the school until her death.

Helen Thomson was born at her family's farm in Kaimata in 1905, and was initially taught at home by a governess. She was a pupil at New Plymouth Girls' High School from 1917 to 1922, after one term at its prep school. She said about her school-days:

I was very small and very shy and an inadequate follower of my sister Meg who worked much harder and took a much greater part in school games than I did. Meg became captain of the hockey team, senior athletic champion, swimming champion and head girl . . . My only sports prize was for winning the sack race for under thirteen, when all in front fell down.

As a pupil I automatically accepted rules which even in those days were silly and inappropriate. Black woollen stockings were far too hot in summer, a boater hat was difficult to manage when riding a horse or bicycle, and pleated serge tunics below the knee were awkward for games enthusiasts.

She described her teachers, all unmarried, as 'excellent', 'splendid', and 'inspiring', and said her Taranaki Scholarship to university was the result of skilled teaching rather than her own hard work. At the University of Otago she studied principally mathematics, graduating in 1927 with both a BA and a BSc.

After teaching for a brief time at Nelson College for Girls, Helen Thomson was appointed to the Stratford Technical High School. In 1936, she began teaching at New Plymouth Girls' High School, and there she stayed, becoming first assistant in 1950 and often acting as principal until she retired in 1970.

Other teachers have given long service: Helen Thomson was different in that she worked in and influenced almost every aspect of school life, in spite of a heavy timetable of maths teaching. From coaching basketball, later to become netball, and encouraging girls in life-saving, to administration and acting as principal, she seemed to embody the school. And throughout her teaching career, and for the rest of her life, she worked through the school's old girls' association to improve amenities for successive waves of schoolgirls.

She is remembered by former pupils with much affection and respect, but also with fear:

Miss Thomson was a strict disciplinarian with the knack of being able to strike fear and terror into the heart of any would-be wrong-doer. She was one teacher who could appear on stage in school assemblies, look around and say 'Gels' and have the whole school's instant attention. No one, but no one, wanted to tangle with Miss Thomson. It was not until I had to go into hospital and received a very kind letter from her explaining the work I was missing and expressing her best wishes for my speedy recovery, that I, even as a self-centred fourth former, recognised a kindness and interest hitherto unsuspected.

Other past pupils spoke of her 'rod of iron' but also described her as a role model –

a phrase we hadn't heard of then, but it fitted her. She gave the strong sound educational grounding which allowed us to go farther in the educational system and become part of that generation which began to manage career and family.

One of the things which made her remarkable was her capacity to continue learning and growing, and to talk candidly about her changing attitudes. When she returned to New Plymouth Girls' High School as a teacher, she found that little had changed: 'Girls were to show the staff unquestioning obedience, just as I had in my schooldays.' Under two long-serving principals, Miss D. N. Allan and Miss A. R. Allum, Helen Thomson did not question the old system of an academic élite, with music for the gifted, but little respect or standing within the school for those who were not in the top academic forms.

I had been taught to teach the subject, not the girl. I was so sad when I came to realise this and realise how many of the less academic or as yet unmotivated girls had slipped through the net, as it were, because I hadn't understood.

But with the advent of a free-thinking and strong-minded principal, Miss Jean Wilson, in 1968, Helen Thomson began to change her own thinking:

She was like a shot of explosive. Suddenly our school was opened up to revolutionary educational ideas. Each subject became equally important and girls were encouraged to experiment and choose. The old streaming was abolished. Each girl was encouraged to develop as an individual, to enjoy self-esteem, to become self-reliant and to play a responsible part in the school community.

This was the most positive and progressive educational thought I had met in my limited experience. I agreed entirely with Miss Wilson's aims, once I understood them.

Mrs Maisie Heward began teaching at the same school in 1952 to support her three small children. In the mid-1950s she entered into an arrangement to share Helen Thomson's house.

There I saw clearly how selfless and devoted Helen was. She was intensely loyal to her own school, to the point where she almost seemed to deny she had needs of her own. In the new educational era ushered in by Jean Wilson, we all saw Helen blossom. When it was time for the school history, everyone drew on her encyclopaedic memory, which had been fostered by her ongoing active involvement in the old girls' association, and her genuine concern for generations of former pupils.

Helen Thomson always maintained that she had been doubly fortunate. She had worked for a school she loved, and she had gained 'a ready made family' in the Heward children, who had given her so much interest and pleasure.

After her death in 1989 her school held a ceremony to celebrate her life. It was the end of an era.   *Christine Cole Catley*

Quotations
para.2 C. Cole Catley, *Springboard for Women*, p.27
para.6 C. Cole Catley, p.152
para.7 C. Cole Catley, p.201
para.8 C. Cole Catley, p.201
para.9 Letter to the author from Maisie Heward.

Unpublished Sources
The author, a former pupil at New Plymouth Girls' High School, interviewed many former pupils of
    Helen Thomson for the history she wrote of the school.

Published Sources
Cole Catley, Christine. *Springboard for Women*, Picton, 1985

BEATRICE TINSLEY

1941–1981

The scientific work of Beatrice Tinsley brought her international acclaim, and was described as 'opening doors to the future study of the evolutions of stars, galaxies, and even the Universe itself'. Yet this outstanding astrophysicist and cosmologist is still little known in her own country.

This is partly because she left New Zealand for the United States at the age of twenty-two, soon after she had graduated from the University of Canterbury, and because of her premature death, at the age of forty, from melanoma cancer. Largely, however, her lack of recognition is due to the very nature of her professional work. Her research into the evolution of galaxies was far removed from the orbits of most New Zealanders.

Beatrice Muriel Hill was born on 27 January 1941 in Chester, England, the second of Jean and Edward Hill's daughters. The family emigrated to New Zealand in 1946, living in Christchurch, Southbridge, and then New Plymouth from 1950. Edward Hill, an Anglican clergyman, was also mayor of New

Plymouth from 1953 to 1956. Jean Hill was a writer, who had a religious novel published. The family's interests were unusually intellectual, and their home was filled with books and music. Beatrice's violin teacher urged her to become a professional musician, but although she later played for two years in the National Youth Orchestra she regarded music as her recreation.

From 1953 to 1957 Beatrice attended New Plymouth Girls' High School, where she is remembered as a person of exceptional character as well as intellect: warm, genuinely concerned for the well-being of others, conscientious, and phenomenally hard-working. A physics teacher, Joyce Jarrold, remembers the fourteen-year-old Beatrice asking to borrow some seventh-form physics textbooks.

I knew she was bright, but I was sceptical. When you teach, you're mostly trying to din something in. Very occasionally you realise that you are dealing with a mind that is infinitely superior to your own. Beatrice came into that category.

While still only sixteen, she became dux of her school and won a Junior University Scholarship.

As a young woman who had been brought up in provincial middle-class New Zealand in the stable 1950s, Beatrice shared the hopes and expectations of her peers: she would become a débutante, fall in love and marry, with a white wedding and the traditional reception, and have children. But alongside these conventional aspirations was her determination to continue her studies and to make some contribution to the world's understanding of astronomy.

At the University of Canterbury Beatrice studied physics, chemistry, and mathematics, writing to her parents that: 'The fascinating thing about theoretical physics is that you can never learn about it fast enough because there's always more being discovered to learn.'

In 1961 Beatrice Hill married a fellow student and physicist, Brian Tinsley, also from New Plymouth. The following year she gained first-class honours for her MSc thesis. The couple now sought postgraduate positions where they could both work at the same centre. Inevitably this would take them away from New Zealand.

Brian Tinsley accepted a position in 1963 at the South West Centre for Advanced Studies in Dallas, now part of the University of Texas. But there was no suitable work for Beatrice, who found that in macho Dallas she was not taken seriously. She made the difficult decision to commute to the astronomy department of the University of Texas in Austin, 200 miles away, returning for long weekends.

Beatrice completed her PhD thesis by the end of 1966, in less than a third of the usual time. Entitled 'Evolution of Galaxies and its Significance for Cosmology', it was regarded by her professors as 'extraordinary and profound', and as embodying 'two of the most monumental discoveries of this century: that the Universe is populated with billions of galaxies, and that they are receding from one another.' It became the foundation for modern studies of galactic evolution, and established Dr Tinsley as a world leader in modern cosmology.

Fellow astronomer Dr Sandra M. Faber, of the Lick Observatory in

California, has noted that Beatrice Tinsley's thesis was greatly in advance of her time.

She had had to learn a great many disciplines – stellar evolution, stellar atmospheres, the interstellar medium, galaxies, computer programming – and pull them all together to formulate her conclusions. This was at a time when these disciplines were still rather separate from one another, without much shared knowledge between fields.

Beatrice Tinsley graduating PhD, 1966.
Edward Hill

While Beatrice was still working on her PhD thesis, she had discovered she was unable to have children. The Tinsleys decided to adopt a baby whose birth was due in August 1966, and whose parentage they knew. Beatrice managed to type her thesis, and sit her oral examination, in between caring for the new baby, Alan. Two years later the couple adopted a daughter, Teresa.

Beatrice knew that having the children would keep her from full commitment to astronomy for some years; however, with her prodigious energy and the availability of temporary childcare, she expected to be involved in part-time teaching, conferences, summer schools, and writing papers. More than twenty of her scientific papers were researched, written, and published during these years when her children were young. Always concerned with social issues, she also became secretary of the first Dallas branch of an organisation called Zero Population Growth.

What she had not foreseen, however, was that even her great joy in the children could not fully compensate her for being denied professional opportunity, even professional recognition, in Dallas. 'The University of Texas in Dallas has kept me at the nearest possible level to nothing,' she wrote to her father. 'To be rejected and undervalued intellectually is a gut problem to me . . .' There was so much she knew she could contribute – *must* contribute – to astronomy. In deep distress she made the decision to initiate an amicable divorce, in 1974, leave the children with their father, and devote herself full time to her scientific work.

The excellence of her teaching and her publications had brought Beatrice invitations from Cambridge University and from many American universities. She eventually accepted an assistant professorship at Yale in 1975, becoming professor of astronomy in 1978, just when her melanoma was diagnosed. She continued to work productively almost up until her death on 23 March 1981. A world-wide network of colleagues and students mourned her as a mentor and friend, as well as a truly remarkable cosmologist.

After her death, the American Astronomical Society created the Beatrice M. Tinsley Medal in her honour, awarded for outstanding research in astronomy and astrophysics. In her short working career of fourteen years, Beatrice had written some one hundred scientific papers as a single or joint author. Most are concerned with the evolution of galaxies and the effect this has on attempts to determine the origin and size of the universe.

The University of Texas at Austin has established the Beatrice M. Tinsley Visiting Professorship in Astronomy, 'to recognise her extraordinary accomplishments'.

Christine Cole Catley

Quotations
para.1 *Beatrice M. Tinsley Centennial*, p.12
para.4 C. Cole Catley, *Springboard for Women*, p.156
para.6 E. Hill, *My Daughter Beatrice*, p.37
para.9 *Beatrice M. Tinsley Centennial*, p.5; p.11
para.10 E. Hill, p.xii
para.13 E. Hill, p.76
para.16 *Beatrice M. Tinsley Centennial*, p.12

Unpublished Sources
Interviews with family, friends, and colleagues

Published Sources
Cole Catley, Christine. *Springboard for Women*, Picton, 1985
Hill, Edward. *My Daughter Beatrice*, New York, 1986
The Beatrice M. Tinsley Centennial Visiting Professorship in Astronomy, booklet published by the University of Texas in Austin, USA, 1985

ANNIE TOCKER

1889–1980

Annie Constance Tocker was a key figure in the early development of New Zealand's social welfare services. Recognising the need for training, she took whatever opportunities were available to equip herself for the task, and later drew on her wide experience to train the staff who worked with her. At a time when women were unwelcome at an administrative level in the public service, male colleagues recognised her, not always sympathetically, as a militant feminist. Her competence and dedication, however, won their respect.

Annie Tocker's home town was Greytown, where she was born on 6 May 1889, went to school, and worked for four years as a librarian and assistant to the town clerk. In 1914, following a call to social work, she entered the

Methodist Deaconess House in Christchurch. After two years' training, she worked as a deaconess in East Christchurch where she encountered many family problems, caused to a large extent by the absence of fathers and husbands at the war.

Feeling herself inadequately equipped, she trained as a nurse at Christchurch Hospital from 1918 to 1921. She went on to qualify in midwifery and to work in the venereal disease clinic at the Jubilee Home. While in Christchurch, she gained a plumber's licence and qualified as a health inspector, becoming an Associate of the Royal Sanitary Institute (London). In 1923 she moved to Wellington, working first at St Helen's Hospital and then as a sister at Wellington Hospital. During 1925 she was acting lady superintendent of Deaconess House in Christchurch, but now felt that her training and experience could be used in a wider field of social work.

Her opportunity came with the passing of the Child Welfare Act in 1925 and the subsequent establishment of the Child Welfare Branch (later a division) of the Department of Education. In February 1926, Annie Tocker was appointed as a child welfare officer. Her work was mainly in Wellington, but she had short spells in Invercargill and Napier, and, in 1927, was sent to establish an office in Hawera. From 1940 till her retirement in 1949, she was the senior woman officer in the Wellington District Office. During this time, Annie exercised her authority to the full, often ignoring the fact that, even in her work with girls and unmarried mothers and in pioneering the new adoption procedure, she was subject to a male controlling officer. According to one male administrator, she caused two superintendents and the director of education, Dr Beeby, 'considerable concern from time to time through her liking for appearing to be much more of an authoritative figure than she was entitled to be'. Her sharp sense of humour enabled her to ride through many a crisis. She was, in fact, an extremely able and hard-working public servant, and a humane and caring social worker. In working with clients, she acknowledged the futility of an authoritative attitude:

We had to learn that it was often better to leave children in their own home and guide the parents towards more adequate care than use the law to sever basic family relationships.

She saw to it that her staff were well prepared, not only in their understanding of the law as it affected children but also in such matters as relationships with the public and liaison with other agencies.

The wide range of committees on which Annie Tocker served included the Public Health Committee of the New Zealand Registered Nurses' Association from its inception in 1928 until 1949, the Mayor's British Children's Overseas Committee (1940–5), the Metropolitan Relief Committee (1940–9), the Registered Nurses' Executive Council (1943–5), the Mayor's Committee on Social Conditions and By-laws (1943), and the Wellington branch of the National Council of Women. Her concern for the social disruption caused in Wellington by the large influx of American servicemen on leave led her to work closely, from 1940 till the end of the war, with the Police Anti-Vice Squad. 'Girls flocked to Wellington from all parts of the country. We had the job of picking them up and getting them back home again before they got into trouble.'

After her retirement, Annie was a member, from 1951 to 1955, of the Women's Borstal Association. Living in Karori, she kept up her interest and love of gardening, and became a resident at Wesleyhaven in 1974. She died on 13 October 1980.

Ruth Fry

Quotations
para.4 L. G. Anderson to R. W. Widdup, 14 Oct. 1980, Methodist Archives; A. Tocker, 'Recollections from 1926', p.23
para.5 A. Tocker, 'Recollections from 1926', p.23

Unpublished Sources
Tocker, A. Written Reminiscences, typescript in Methodist Church Archives, Latimer Square, Christchurch

Published Sources
Chambers, W. *Not Self – But Others: The Story of the New Zealand Deaconess Order*, Auckland, 1987
Tocker, Annie C. 'Recollections from 1926', *NZ Social Worker*, vol.5 no.4, Oct. 1969, pp.21–23

RANGI TOPEORA

?1790–?1870

A well-known chieftainess of the Ngati Toa tribe, Rangi Topeora, also known as Topeora, figured prominently in the affairs of her people on the Kapiti Coast. She was born at Kawhia, probably in the late eighteenth century. Her mother, Waitohi, was a sister of Te Rauparaha, and her father was Te Rakaherea. Her brother Te Rangihaeata was a senior warrior under Te Rauparaha.

Topeora belonged to the Ngati Te Maunu and Ngati Kimihia sub-tribes of Ngati Toa and to the Ngati Huia sub-tribe of Ngati Raukawa. A woman of high rank, she could trace direct descent from Hoturoa, captain of the Tainui canoe. Topeora marched with Te Rauparaha during the migration in the 1820s from Kawhia to the shores of Cook Strait and crossed to Kapiti Island.

She has been described as an imperious lady who was venerated by her people as an Ariki-tapairu, a queen-like woman. Proud, domineering, and beautiful, she had a number of exciting relationships. One of her earliest passions was for a chief of Te Atiawa tribe of Taranaki named Rawiri Te Motutere. He was noted as one of the handsomest men of his day, and many women fell in love with him. Tradition says he had to cover his face with a mask because of the constant attention he received from women. Others say he wore a mask to preserve his complexion. Topeora fell in love with him long before she saw him, but her efforts were to no avail. In her sorrow she composed and publicly sang a waiata-aroha (love-song) for him.

According to James Cowan her first husband was Te Rangikapiki, a Ngati Raukawa man of high rank. Their son, Matene Te Whiwhi O Te Rangi, became an influential chief of the Ngati Toa and Ngati Raukawa tribes.

In 1818 Topeora fell in love again with a Taranaki warrior chief named Te Ratutonu. In the siege of Tapuinikau in Taranaki, his tribe was defending the pa and her people were the besiegers. Topeora demanded him as her husband and a truce was called. Te Ratutonu was permitted to enter the enemy camp under a guarantee of safety. At the same time another woman called Nekepapa also desired him. A dispute arose. Quick of mind, Topeora ran to meet him and cast her topuni (dog-skin mat) over his shoulders and claimed him as her husband.

Later she took as husband Hauturu, whose actions triggered Topeora's pitiless temper. When Hauturu's attentions strayed to another woman, Topeora became enraged with jealousy and condemned the unfortunate woman to death. Some Pakeha whalers attempted to intervene, pleading with Topeora and offering trade goods in exchange for the woman's life. But Topeora's heart had hardened. At her command Topeora's people carried out her wish.

At the battle of Waiorua, on Kapiti Island, in 1824, she showed her influential position in the tribe. Wearing only a rapaki (garment worn from the waist to the knees) and exposing her bare breasts, she climbed upon the gateway of the pa and stood with her legs astride. Holding a taiaha (long wooden weapon) in her hands, she stood defiantly before the approaching enemy, forcing them to pass between her legs. This act illustrated an old Maori custom of degradation. Topeora composed a great song of triumph from this incident.

She became renowned throughout the land for her compositions of poetical songs. These included kaioraora (cursing songs), where she expressed the utmost hatred of her enemies and condemned them to horrible deaths. Others were love-songs of great beauty and sophistication. She was also a famous singer.

Topeora was involved in the 1836 peacemaking between Ngati Raukawa, Ngati Toa, and Ngati Tama. A dispute had arisen between these tribes over the sale of Maenene pa on Kapiti Island by Te Rauparaha to Thomas Evans, and several chiefs had died. Topeora, who strongly opposed the sale, agreed that her son Matene be involved in peace negotiations.

As a leading figure of her tribe, Topeora was one of the few women who signed the Treaty of Waitangi. It is thought she was at least in her early fifties when she signed on 14 May 1840 at Kapiti.

In her day Topeora was one of the few women who spoke formally on the marae. On 29 August 1846 she spoke, in the absence of her brother Te Rangihaeata, of the aggressions of Pakeha and of the reluctant resistance of Maori at the time.

In her early days Topeora supported Governor Grey's plan to build a road through the Horoki Valley to Paekakariki Beach. She asked her people to assist, but Te Rangihaeata would not agree. Despite her people's opposition she placed pegs along the line of the proposed road. No one dared to interfere with her road pegs. Subsequently the road was built, and in acknowledgement Grey presented Topeora with a horse and trap brought over from Sydney. Topeora handed this gift to her cousin, Kahe Te Rau O Te Rangi.

In her later years, Topeora became known as 'Queen of the South' by the early European settlers, and 'Te Kuini' by the people of Otaki. When Bishop Selwyn baptised her in the 1840s at Otaki, she selected the name Queen Victoria, and Albert for her husband.

To her last days at Otaki she took pride in wearing traditional Maori attire A painting by Gottfried Lindauer shows Topeora in a beautiful taniko-bordered cloak, wearing precious Maori treasures.

As an old woman she was a frequent visitor to the villages on the Wellington harbour. She sometimes came by sea in her great canoe, or by an old war track from Paekakariki over the Johnsonville hills.

Topeora died at Otaki probably in the 1860s or 1870s.   *Raina Meha*

Quotations
para.13 G. Lindauer and J. Cowan, *Pictures of Old New Zealand*, p.187

Published Sources
Burns, P. *Te Rauparaha: A New Perspective*, Wellington, 1980
Lindauer, G. and Cowan, J. *Pictures of Old New Zealand*, Auckland, 1930

ELIZABETH TORLESSE

1835 – 1922

Elizabeth was the sixth child of sixteen born to Margaret and Thomas Revell. Margaret Revell was five months pregnant when, with her nine surviving children, aged from twenty-four to two, she left Ireland for England in 1852. Thomas Revell, who was twenty-four years older than his wife, stayed behind in Ireland to finalise their affairs, which were in some disarray.

Margaret and the children sailed for New Zealand on the *Minerva* in October 1852. Henry Torlesse, an Anglican parson's son, joined the ship at Plymouth. On arriving at Lyttelton on 2 February 1853, the Revells stayed at the Immigration Barracks there, while the three eldest sons went to the land they had purchased at Kaiapoi, called 'Korotueka'.

Elizabeth went as a lady help to a family at Governors Bay, while her elder sister looked after the family, still at the barracks. Thomas Revell arrived in July 1853, but it was not until 24 December 1853 that the family walked over the Bridle Path to Heathcote, then travelled by bullock dray to Kaiapoi, a trip that took all day. Settling at 'Korotueka', the Revells lived first in a small whare, the children all sleeping in one room. Elizabeth worked with her brothers and sisters to make a garden, plant fruit trees, and clear land to grow wheat, which they then scythed and threshed by hand, and ground in a hand-mill to make flour.

On 16 June 1857 Elizabeth married Henry Torlesse, and went to live at 'Fernside', near Rangiora. A year later Henry decided to prepare for ordination into the Church of England and they moved to a smaller house nearby, called 'Stoke Lodge', with seventeen acres.

Henry was ordained a deacon on 25 September 1859, and placed as deacon and schoolteacher at Okains Bay on Banks Peninsula. The Torlesses were received with hostility by some of the men at Okains Bay, who said they did not want a church, and organised disturbances during the services. Henry won them over, impressing them with his sporting skills, and began a night-school for men. In addition to school and church duties at Okains Bay, he ran schools and services at Duvauchelle and Little Akaloa and was away a good deal of the time. Elizabeth took Sunday school and school on Monday mornings. In addition to their increasing family (Elizabeth gave birth to four daughters while they were at Okains Bay), they took in boarders to give them some extra income.

Henry was ordained as a priest in December 1862. His family reluctantly returned to Christchurch, just three weeks after Elizabeth had given birth to her fifth child. Elizabeth rode side-saddle on her horse, while Henry carried the baby on his mule. They rode from Akaroa Harbour, over the hills to Lyttelton Harbour, crossed by boat to Lyttelton, and drove in a carriage to Rangiora.

On 1 January 1864 Henry was appointed chaplain of the hospital, gaol, and lunatic asylum in Christchurch, with a stipend of £300 a year. Late in 1864 the Anglican Church had taken steps towards setting up a refuge for 'fallen women', and Henry took charge (under the Synod) of this project, with Elizabeth's full support. She set up a women's committee to collect funds, street by street, in Christchurch, Lyttelton, and surrounding areas. She wrote in a letter to her mother-in-law on 13 May 1864:

We do not for a moment hope to stem the tide of sin but we want to have a home where those poor girls who have once fallen & are now anxious to leave the miserable life & try & regain by quiet industry & good conduct the position that they have lost.

Land was leased next door to where Elizabeth and Henry were living in Antigua Street (now Rolleston Avenue), a house built, and in December 1864 the Female Refuge was opened. Elizabeth supervised much of the day-to-day running of the refuge while Henry acted as chaplain. Eleven women entered the refuge during the first year. Laundry was taken in to provide an income for the running costs of the refuge, and also for the women so that they were not destitute when they left.

In June 1867, Henry resigned from his chaplaincy and the refuge due to poor health and was appointed vicar at St Cuthberts in Governors Bay. He attributed many of the refuge's successes (women who had not returned to prostitution) to Elizabeth's efforts. Henry's health deteriorated even further, and Elizabeth spent a lot of time nursing him. When she went to Christchurch for the birth of her last child in 1869, Henry was expected to die.

They decided to move back to 'Stoke Lodge'. Living on a pension of £55 a year, they could not afford servants. Elizabeth cared for Henry, did the housework, made butter, and looked after the livestock and the garden. The eldest children helped look after the younger children and Henry gave lessons when he was able.

On 17 December 1870 Henry died. Elizabeth was left with eight children to provide for, the eldest aged only twelve. During her thirteen years of marriage she had given birth to ten children, two of whom died as infants. She had shifted house six times, and coped with Henry's absences and ill health, lack of money, and her responsibilities as a clergyman's wife. A strong faith in God and the work they were doing sustained her throughout.

After Henry's death, Elizabeth supported herself and her family on a small pension and by taking in boarders. She died on 22 September 1922, aged eighty-seven.
Jo-Anne Smith

Quotations
para.7 Letter, 13 May 1864, contained in Sister Frances Torlesse, Letter of 16 Oct. 1920
Unpublished Sources
Information was provided by family members.

Elizabeth Torlesse, Memoirs, Ms typescripts, Canterbury Museum
G. R. Macdonald Biographies, Canterbury Museum
Henry Torlesse, Typescript of diary, 1870, in private possession
Sister Frances Torlesse, Letter of 16 Oct. 1920 (includes extracts of letters written by Elizabeth and
Henry Torlesse in 1864), typescript, Canterbury Museum
W. Norris, Christchurch Hospital, Ms, Canterbury Museum
Published Sources
Lyttelton Times, 10 Feb. 1866; 7 June 1867
The Press, 4 June 1864; 11 Feb. 1867

JESSIE TORRANCE

1879–1941

Sister Jessie Torrance was well known in the parish of Knox Church, Dunedin, where she was nursing sister for twenty-five years. She was most conspicuous in winter, as she lugged bags of coal and blankets to the homes she visited, using the free tram travel which was Knox Church's only contribution to her transport.

Jessie was born in 1871, at Russell Street, Dunedin, the third child of Scottish immigrants. Her mother, Eliza Wright, left the family farm in Lossiemouth at the age of eighteen to travel to New Zealand. Just over a year later, in 1865, she married John Ainslie Torrance who was eleven years older than her. He was a printer by trade, but had been chaplain on the immigrant ship *Ben Lomond*. Although he was never ordained, he was an elder and lay preacher in the Presbyterian Church, and was employed by the Patients' and Prisoners' Aid Society as chaplain and social worker to Dunedin's hospital, gaol and asylum. Jessie thus grew up in a religious household, committed to a very practical Christianity. As she grew older, she played an increasing part in the support her family offered to ex-patients and prisoners. Her niece remembers the house as a 'very happy one, full of laughter and big shining eyes'.

In 1903 Jessie entered nursing training at Dunedin Public Hospital. By 1906 she was a charge nurse, and about this time led a deputation of nurses to the board to state that scrubbing drainage sumps should not be undertaken by nurses who dealt with ill and vulnerable patients. As a result she was demoted; her staff were so enraged that they insisted on doing her duties. At the next board meeting, a decision was made to employ outside contractors to clean the drains.

Private nursing followed. Then with the development of the Plunket Society in Dunedin after 1907, Jessie Torrance became one of its earliest nurses. By this time, she was sharing a house with her younger sister, Martha (Mattie), a music teacher, an arrangement that was to last until her death.

Jessie's second clash with authority was less effective than her first. She fell out with Plunket's founder, Dr Frederic Truby King, who maintained that all babies were alike in thriving on humanised milk (diluted cow's milk with added lactose). Jessie Torrance insisted, from her experience, that no one regime suited all babies, whose individual needs should be recognised. She resigned from the Plunket Society in protest when her views were not heeded.

The St John Ambulance Brigade then asked her to join them, and she remained there for thirteen years, including during the First World War. In 1921, she was appointed nursing sister at Knox (Presbyterian) Church, a position which included lecturing to the students of the Missionary Training Unit. A deaconess herself, she also tutored other nurses who wished to become deaconesses. But the focus of her energy was nursing and social work in the area surrounding Knox Church. Her commitment was such that it was only ill health that forced her retirement at the age of seventy-five, after twenty-five years of devoted work. She died three years later, in 1949.

Jessie Torrance's life was one of hard work and good works, lived with grace and good humour. But she is especially remembered and honoured in her family for her challenges to authority which symbolised both her independence and her concern for the well-being of others. *Claire-Louise McCurdy*

Unpublished Source
Information was provided by May Huia Cameron (Jessie Torrance's niece and the author's grandmother).

Published Sources
Angus, John. *A History of the Otago Hospital Board and its Predecessors*, Dunedin, 1984
Chisolm, Revd Jas (ed.) *Memorials of John A. Torrance*, Dunedin, 1908
Olssen, Erik. *A History of Otago*, Dunedin, 1984
Otago Daily Times, 14 Dec. 1949 (obituary)

MONA TRACY

1892–1959

Mona Tracy was a journalist and writer of children's books. She is remembered as a 'personality', a woman of beauty and character who was somewhat 'gypsy-like'. In her was 'the blood of the Highlands, that mixture of the mystic and realist', wrote George Burns, editor of the *Christchurch Star*. She was proud but not arrogant, quick to defend a right, and sociable, frequently hosting functions at her Christchurch homes. Intense, ebullient, and voluble (also a heavy smoker), she was interested in everything and everyone, a friend of all. In the Depression she worked long hours in a relief depot for the unemployed. During the Second World War she reduced her age by seven years to be eligible for the Women's Auxiliary Air Force, where she rose to the rank of corporal. She was also a member of the Arthur's Pass National Park Board from 1938 to 1948, one of only two women members up until 1979.

Her 'all devouring industry' and vitality produced a great range of work: articles, short stories, serials, and poetry for the more enterprising Australasian newspapers and magazines; radio broadcasts; children's historical novels; and non-fiction. Much of her writing was done at a rented sod cottage in Allandale, at the head of Lyttelton Harbour, where she lived with her husband W. F. Tracy, a barrister and solicitor. She was president of the local Women's Division of the Farmers' Union, and also found time to be a great cook, tend the cottage's old-world garden, carpet her lounge (by hooking sheep's wool through canvas), and do exquisite embroidery.

Mona Innes MacKay was descended from Gaelic Covenanters who came to New Zealand from Nova Scotia in the days when Kororareka was known as Blackguard Beach and Auckland was 'but a collection of wooden shanties'. Like the settlers described by Fiona Kidman in *Gone North* (1984), they took up land at Waipu, becoming a peaceful community which toiled during the week, read their Bibles behind drawn blinds on Sundays, and privately distilled a little 'scotch'. Tracy's father, John William MacKay, was an itinerant mine assayer who followed the 'gold fever'. Her mother, Katherine J. MacKay (born Bilston), a journalist for Australian and New Zealand newspapers and magazines, wrote as 'Katrine', cookery editor of the *Weekly Press*, and in 1929 published *Practical Home Cookery Chats and Recipes*.

Mona was born at Kensington, South Australia, and grew up in Paeroa among Maori families, an influence which was to show up in her children's books. Memories of her childhood in this small country town are of the bush 'which came down to our very doors', and of the Martha, Talisman, and Waihi mines of the Ohinemuri gold-fields, which worked around the clock and drew a 'kaleidoscope procession' of people along the Paeroa-Waihi road. She moved to Auckland to finish her schooling, and at thirteen gained a job on the *Auckland Weekly News*, later training as a general reporter on the *New Zealand Herald*, one of the first women to do so. She visited Australia briefly, then moved with her mother to Christchurch and became a 'lady reporter' to the Christchurch *Press* in May 1917. She worked at the law courts and on women's news; through the former she met her future husband. In 1920 Mona left *The Press* and full-time work for their marriage, and for research and writing.

In 1925, in addition to caring for her two small children, Terence and Romany, Tracy published *Piriki's Princess and Other Stories of New Zealand*, the first of several children's books published in New Zealand by Whitcombe & Tombs Limited; it contained work first published in the *Christchurch Sun*. Later followed the racy romantic adventure stories which earned her the title of 'The New Zealand Henty': *Rifle and Tomahawk; a stirring tale of the Te Kooti rebellion* (1927); *Lawless Days; a tale of adventure in old New Zealand and the South Seas* (1928); and *Martin Thorn – adventurer* (1930). These books, unusually for children's writing at the time, featured strong Maori characters and the issues of mixed marriage, loyalties, and race. Also, 'a spirited adventurous girl' appears in each. *The Story of the Pacific* (1925), written by Tracy for secondary schools, was part of *Whitcombe's Historical Story Book* series, a subseries of the wider *Whitcombe's Story Books* series for which Tracy also adapted material.

While Mona Tracy wrote for magazines such as *New Nation, New Zealand Railways Magazine, Art in New Zealand*, and *New Zealand Artists' Annual*, some of her most colourful writing appeared in *Aussie*. Here, in September 1923, she took over 'The Voice of the Enzed Woman' column, writing merrily under pen-names, the best of which was 'Sally Forth'. Her lively articles commented on the fate of women, women's interests, and fashions – like her beaded dress which came to grief in the clutch of a man whose ballroom prowess was matched only by his performance on the football field (1927). In the same year she concluded that 'the financially independent wife is the happiest wife'. Historical snippets were often about whaling and Maori personalities, such as an old chief who in the census dramatically increased the population of his settlement by including as members of his family every pig, dog, fowl, and cat in the pa (1926).

Mona Tracy strove for perfection, particularly in her poetry.

Hers was a constant struggle to find the word or phrase that precisely expressed her thought, to convey the exact shade of meaning, to create the atmosphere she felt.

Robin Hyde described Tracy's 'Dusk on Akaroa Town' as a 'lilting little song . . . that everyone remembers and puts into New Zealand's few poor wing-clipped anthologies'.

One of Mona Tracy's favourite pastimes during the 1920s and 1930s was holidaying at Arthur's Pass and on the West Coast. She tramped all over this area researching old records, enjoying a beer in the pub with the old gold-diggers, and recording their colourful memories. From this material she wrote newspaper serials, and broadcasts for radio station 3YA. After her death it was published as *West Coast Yesterdays* (1960). *Historic Kawau* (1927) is another non-fiction work.

Mona Tracy's writing and interests show she was a woman of adventure, compassion, and foresight, especially in her views on women. She died in Christchurch in 1959, after an illness.   *Celia Dunlop*

Quotations

para.1 Letter from Mrs E. E. Scott to author, 15 Jan. 1990; G. Burns, Introduction to *West Coast Yesterdays*, p.7

para.2 P. Lawlor, *Confessions of a Journalist: with Observations on some Australian and New Zealand Writers*, Auckland, 1935, p.250

para.3 Sally Forth, 'A Story of My People', *Aussie*, 15 Aug. 1925, NZ Section, p.III

para.4 S. Forth,'Where Are They Now?', *Aussie*, 15 Feb. 1926, NZ Section, p.XII; S. Forth, 'The Goldfields of the Past', *Aussie*, 15 March 1927, NZ Section, p.V

para.5 P. Lawlor, p.251; E. Locke, 'Children's Historical Fiction', p.8

para.6 S. Forth, 'Making Wives Independent', *Aussie*, 15 Nov. 1927, NZ Section, p.XIII

para.7 G. Burns, p.7; R. Hyde, *Journalese*, Auckland, 1934, p.65

Unpublished Sources

Letters from relatives, and people who knew Mona Tracy (in author's possession)

Published Sources

Auckland Star, 10 March 1959 (editorial)

Bagnall, A. G. (ed.) *New Zealand National Bibliography to the Year 1960*, vol.IV, Wellington, 1975

Burns, George. Introduction to *West Coast Yesterdays*, Wellington, 1960

Locke, Elsie. 'Children's Historical Fiction in New Zealand', *Historical News*, March 1976, pp.7–10, 16

The Press, 24 Feb. 1959, p.2 (obituary)

The Press 1861–1961: The Story of a Newspaper, Christchurch, 1963

Tracy, Mona (Sally Forth). 'The Voice of the Enzed Woman' column, and articles, in *Aussie: The Cheerful Monthly* (Sydney), 1925–1927

BELINDA TRAINOR

1958–1986

Belinda Christine Trainor was born in Invercargill. Her parents were lighthouse-keepers and her very early years were spent at Portland Island, Puysegur Point, Tiritiri Matangi, and Coromandel. By the time she started school the family was living in East Tamaki, but most of her schooling was in Northcote, where they moved next and stayed throughout her childhood.

At Northcote College Belinda was a successful student and also became involved in many school activities: drama, public speaking, editing the school newspaper and magazine, and the counselling of younger students. Her passion for challenging injustice became clear during these years.

In 1976, she was awarded an American Field Scholarship and was placed with a white family in a predominantly black area in Louisville, Kentucky. The family was not well-off and relied on the mother's income as a civil rights worker. Belinda became involved in this work and by her return home had decided to study political science at university.

During the years 1978–80 she completed a BA degree in political science at Canterbury University. She spent some time as an arts faculty representative, wrote for the student paper *Canta*, and was a member of the Working Women's Council and the University Women's Group. Income came from working as a bar-person.

Her standard of undergraduate work was recognised with the awarding of a University Senior Scholarship to help with MA studies. She had not found the university especially sympathetic to her political views, which encompassed Marxism and feminism. She greatly valued the unstinting support of two faculty members, but it did not entirely offset the stress of hostile reactions to her views. With the high level of work and motivation necessary for maintaining both high achievement and personal integrity, life had become so serious that her ability to make friends and her wicked sense of humour and fun had been overwhelmed. She decided to take a year off and go to Australia on a working holiday.

While in Australia Belinda developed health problems, and it is thought that this was when she contracted the virus which caused cardiomyopathy. On her return to Canterbury to begin her MA studies she was admitted to hospital where the condition was diagnosed. In spite of the illness, her MA was completed with first-class honours in 1984.

Women's health and the attitudes of a male-dominated medical profession had always been an area of interest: her MA thesis was titled 'Patriarchal Reproduction: An Analysis of Male Social Power'. In 1985 Belinda was selected for a Commonwealth Scholarship, to be taken up at Essex University in England, to complete a PhD. Her cardiomyopathy was known to the scholarship commitee from the beginning, but nine days before she was due to leave the scholarship was withdrawn because of her heart condition. This was a terrible blow to her confidence in her ability to manage the illness.

However, now living in Auckland and identifying as a lesbian, she moved on from this disappointment. By 1986 she was writing and teaching outside the academic context about health from a feminist perspective – particularly contraception, reproductive technology, and retrograde changes to the public health system. Her writing was published in *Broadsheet* magazine and she taught a course in women's reproductive health at the Auckland WEA. She was excited at discovering ways to combine her ability to communicate with people with her academic knowledge and skills. She was also becoming interested in lesbian political debates.

But as 1986 progressed her health deteriorated. A passionate critic of high-tech and privatised medicalised health treatments, Belinda needed a heart transplant; the irony of this was not lost on her. Money was raised by family and friends to send her to St Vincent's Hospital in Sydney for a transplant operation. She was desperately ill by the time she went, there was no immediate donor, and she died in Sydney on 7 October 1986.   *Pat Rosier*

Unpublished Sources
Information was provided by family and friends.
Belinda Trainor, 'Patriarchal Reproduction: An Analysis of Male Social Power', MA thesis, Canterbury, 1984

Published Sources
Broadsheet, no.144, Nov. 1986, p.7 (obituary)
Trainor, Belinda. 'Give to the Rich Deal to the Poor', *Broadsheet*, May 1986, pp.23–5
Trainor, Belinda. 'Having or Not Having Babies – What Power do Women Have?', *Women's Studies Journal*, vol.3 no.2, March 1988, pp.44–72
Women's Studies Journal, vol.3 no.2, March 1988, p.43 (obituary)

JILL TREMAIN

1946–1974

At the bottom we crossed left (no choice) over crevasses to the shelf, and paused for a rest and a drink. The scenery was still wonderful, white cloud billowed from the west, reaching with the long arm of the wind, to curl about Sefton and the Footstool. Down-valley, pink-grey hogsbacks marched towards us in ever increasing numbers. The shelf of crevasses became a picture of shapes in the evening sun as we crossed avalanche debris to the glowing orange of Empress Hut.

This excerpt, written after a traverse of Mt Cook, illustrates the talents of Gillian Gwen Tremain. An exceptional mountaineer, she was also a painter, a poet, and a fashion artist. A close friend and mountaineering companion says of Jill that her life was

a cup to be filled, not a measure to be drained.

Her great love for the mountains was expressed as much by her poetry, painting and sketches as by her many trips to remote areas and her important climbs. She was an almost perfect companion, always prepared to give rather than take, a good listener, quiet but strong and courageous. To be with her in the mountains and to share her philosophy was to know life better.

Jill's formal education began at a small Miramar primary school, continued at Wellington East Girls' College, and finished with a commercial art course at Wellington Polytechnic. 'A bit of a loner' as a child, not particularly robust until her seventh year, she was an average student. Yet she was an inspiration to many: 'she was very strong – physically and mentally; very beautiful – physically . . . everyone it seemed fell in love with her . . .'

Her family first led Jill into the outdoors, on a ski trip when she was fifteen or sixteen. She then made contact with the Wellington Tramping Club and later the Hutt Valley Tramping Club, which included a strong mountaineering contingent:

She had this almost double life. Drawing fashion stuff for Kirks in Wellington during the week and tramping every weekend . . . Over the years tramping was superseded by climbing – every Christmas she'd take off six–eight weeks and do long climbs in the Alps with the clubs. I don't know what drove her to do so much though I think the companionship of similar people may have been part of it.

Like many other mountain people, Jill had to get 'into the hills' regularly – the other side of busy city life and nine-to-five work. Although no one else in the Tremain family was very active in the outdoors, Jill had their support. Her father had always admired and encouraged his daughters and took Jill along to tramping club meetings in the early days, although he did not tramp himself.

In 1966, three years after she had started tramping, Jill set her sights on the highest peaks of the Southern Alps where she did most of her serious mountaineering. A first ascent of the East Face of Footstool was followed by ascents of Zurbriggen's Ridge (Mt Cook), East Ridge of Mt Cook, Grand Traverse of Mt Cook, Mt Tasman, Mt Douglas, and a Dampier-Vancouver traverse. In 1969 she travelled to Europe, climbing near Zermatt and Grindelwald, and ascending Mont Blanc among other peaks. In Britain Jill's skills as an outdoor instructor were recognised by colleagues when she worked at the Plas Y Brenin Outdoor Centre in Wales and at Scotland's Benmore Centre. Back in New Zealand Jill Tremain became a household name, synonymous with adventure, courage, and determination, through her 1971 winter traverse of the Southern Alps with Graeme Dingle. The progress of this intrepid pair was reported in news broadcasts and interviews, as described in more detail in *Two Against the Alps*, written by Graeme and illustrated by Jill.

Nineteen-seventy-three saw Jill and four other New Zealand women mountaineers, Vicki Thompson, Margaret Clark, Bev Price, and Faye Kerr, preparing for the eleven-member Indo-New Zealand Himalayan Expedition the following year. The expedition's main aim was to climb Mt Hardoel (7035 m). The morning of 30 May 1974 dawned perfectly, but while moving up the mountain from Camp One, Jill, Vicki, two Indian women mountaineers, and their sherpas were hit by a tremendous avalanche. No trace of the women was found.

For Jill, the mountains had always been more than just places to climb. Her artist's eye took in form, texture, and hue, often sketched in quiet moments. Words, too, found an outlet through her pen, in her many letters to friends and family, with whom she shared her travels and thoughts. Her diary records her impressions of her last mountain:

Went for a short walk this afternoon – very pleasant, but cold, almost up to next glacier. Stood for a long time and looked at Hardoel and surroundings. Felt more familiar among the mountain scenery. With glasses on and off studied various ways as far as I could see them. The sunlight revealed more of the mountain's shape and grandeur as the shadows lengthened with the afternoon . . . I walk on the crest of the moraine wall as some animal has done before me. I stop again and look and listen – the mountain is magnificent – if I stay here much longer I can see I am going to want to climb it.

Jill made a significant contribution to the clubs and organisations she was involved with, and felt a responsibility to those coming after her. Many young New Zealanders have watched the hypothermia awareness film which she helped to make. Jill's buoyant spirit was inspired by the poems and quotes she collected and kept nearby. She followed her dreams and in so doing expanded the realms of possibility for others.   *Pip Lynch*

Quotations
para.1 J. Tremain, 'A Traverse of Cook', p.457
para.2 G. Dingle, 'Obituary', p.122
para.3 P. Stewart to author, Aug. 1989; G. Dingle to author, 7 June 1989
para.4 P. Stewart to author, Aug. 1989
para.8 J. Tremain, Diary, 3 May 1974

Unpublished Sources
Jill Tremain, Diary, privately held
Letters to the author from Graeme Dingle and Pauline Stewart (Jill Tremain's sister)

Published Sources
Bates, Margaret. 'Obituary', *NZ Alpine Club Bulletin*, no.61, 4 Sept. 1974
Dingle, Graeme. 'Obituary', *NZ Alpine Journal*, vol. 27, 1974, pp.122–23
Dingle, Graeme. *Two Against the Alps*, Christchurch, 1972
Evening Post, 17 or 18 June (possibly July), 1974
Tremain, Jill. 'A Traverse of Cook. Without the Peaks', *NZ Alpine Journal*, vol.23 no.2, 1970, pp.456–7

WAIPAARE TUHAKARAINA

1912–1978

Waipaare Graham, affectionately known as Barley by her family and friends, was born on 18 October 1912 at Piarere in the Hinuera Valley near Matamata, and was educated at Piarere primary school.

In 1938 Barley Graham married George Tuhakaraina (Tu) at Te Puna, north of Tauranga. At first her husband drove a truck which collected cream cans from local farms. Then came a move to Tauranga where George found work as a bus driver. Barley was kept busy looking after their two children, Bernadette and Damian. Later the family returned to Te Puna to farm a property belonging to George's father.

Early in 1950 the couple decided to move to Barley's ancestral land at

A 1936 concert party at Piarere in the Hinuera Valley, Waikato. Barley Tu (Waipaare Graham), far left, with Rau Wilson, Camelia Dehar, Peggy Martin, Lulu Penetito, Marie Penetito and Wahi Penetito. *Camelia Penetito*

Piarere. They lived in a tent and Barley helped her husband milk a few cows while they built a house for the family. Barley became deeply involved in community affairs. With her husband she regularly attended services held at the Church of the Holy Angels in Matamata, and she became an active member of the Catholic Women's League.

When the Waharoa branch of the Maori Women's Welfare League was started in 1965, Barley was a foundation member and acted as counsellor and adviser. She was always ready to support young Maori women in a practical way. In 1967 five girls, including Barley's niece Kanakana King, were presented as debutantes at a ball organised by the league at Tauranga. Quietly Barley organised dressmakers, flowers, jewellery, partners and their outfits, rehearsals and transport. A few years later she encouraged young women to enter the local 'Mrs Matamata' contests run by the Plunket Society and again helped them with their outfits and made sure that their husbands supported them.

In 1968 a combined committee of the Waharoa Maori Women's Welfare League and the National Council of Women sponsored the Waharoa Homework Centre at which Maori pupils could receive assistance with their homework after school hours. Barley became honorary treasurer on the Homework Centre Committee, a position which she held for ten years. She was responsible for helping to raise funds for the project with street stalls, and paddy's markets. Several treadle sewing machines were obtained for the centre and Barley helped the girls with their sewing homework.

Promoting Maori culture and crafts was very important for Barley, who was a fluent Maori speaker and an expert in weaving bodices, headbands and taniko designs. She used her artistic talents and quiet organising ability to arrange displays such as the Maori Women's Welfare League's prize-winning entries in the Maori courts section at the Waikato Winter Show.

Barley's special love was floral art and she was responsible for many displays at the Anglican Flower Show and other floral art festivals and exhibitions in the Matamata district. Her own home was full of lovely arrangements using native foliage and plant materials.

Barley was always busy at home with farm and household tasks, making floral arrangements, weaving Maori designs and working in her garden where she grew a profusion of flowers. As her health deteriorated she was no longer able to milk the cows, so the task was taken over by her granddaughter Lucy Bennett. Shortly before her death on 6 October 1978, while a patient in Waikato Hospital, she made twelve beautiful sprays for the National President and the Executive of the Maori Women's Welfare League who were visiting the Raungaiti Marae.

As a tribute to her memory her husband presented a carving known as the Waipaare Tu Trophy as the major prize in the Maori Culture competitions held annually at the Matamata Agricultural and Pastoral Show.

Joan Stanley

Unpublished Sources
Information was supplied by: Lucy Bennett (granddaughter of Barley Tu), Sarah Cotter, Joan Leggatt, and Molly Pond, all of Matamata.
Pond, Molly, *A Matamata Folk Story — They Named It Mataroa* (privately held manuscript)
Published Sources
Matamata County Mail, 3 Aug. 1967, 5 Sept. 1971. Also several undated cuttings in the possession of Molly Pond, Matamata
Matamata District Chronicle, 3 May 1976 ('Sunny Break Greets Queen'), 9 July 1978 (obituary), 5 Dec. 1988 (obituary, George Tuhakaraina)

BESSIE TURNBULL

1885–1988

Bessie Turnbull, the youngest of eleven children, was born and lived all her life in Mosgiel. Her parents ran a small bakery. As an adult she worked in the Mosgiel Woollen Mill. Bessie's vivid recollections of working-class life were recorded when she was 101:

Well they said I was like my father, what the Scottish call spare bones; he didn't have any over growing fat about him. He was the head of the house and had to be waited on.

My mother hadn't an easy time at all because every two years for a while she had a baby . . . and a shop, and books and orders to make up, and cook for the men that were working in the bakehouse. She didn't have much time to herself. In fact it was a selfish life on the part of my father – I told him that too. *I tell you there's no married woman would put up with that with her man today.*

Mother wanted a piano for the eldest girls. And he just held up his hands. He said, 'those are what is going to help me in my bakehouse, I'm not buying no piano for them.'

We were taught properly at the East Taieri school. I suppose I was a cheeky imp like all the other kids, I wasn't a model kid by any means. I thought it was only right when I did wrong I should be punished for it and that kept me from getting out to play at night with my mates, when I had to write out all these words on my slate.

I never got to high school, yet I had good passes and all. Bad times had come and my father took ill and my mother took in white cotton sewing to make ends meet because there were no pensions in those days.

When I left school I wanted to be trained as a teacher but my mother didn't have the means to educate me and dress me as the teachers were supposed to be dressed, you know, better than anybody else. So I had to knock that nonsense out of my head and I got an opening in the factory. I stayed there for fifty-seven years.

Quarter to eight you had to start work, you used to finish at half past five. An hour off for dinner. And morning tea – we stole the time. We weren't supposed to take the time, but we used to go out one by one. I think it was

Bessie Turnbull, second from left, with her sisters Kate, Susan, Liza and Jean. *B. Turnbull Collection*

someone in the engine-room used to boil the water up for the girls to make a pot of tea. We used to go outside and sit around the lav. But there was always a scout on to tell you if there was any of the bosses coming around.

I only made about 12/- the first fortnight, you weren't paid for learning. I just put my mind to it, and the next pay I got it was 24/- for the fortnight. I was as proud as Punch. I can still see me getting home with this 24/-, it was tightly rolled in my hand, and handing it to mother.

We made socks, hundreds and hundreds and thousands of dozens of pairs of socks in our shed. The work had to be done right or you got it back to do over and over again and you got nothing for it. Oh, they were hard. Generally on a Saturday morning we used to scrub our board and surroundings in the factory and never got a penny for it. When the unions started, the factories had to pull up and look after their workers. Mind you, I haven't got time for some unions because I don't think they are very straight.

I made some great friends at the mill. I stood up for myself and for the other girls and many a one used to thank me. Well, it was only fair if they were putting out good work they should get the praise for their efforts. We loved when it came to Saturday . . . we could have a long lie-in on the Sunday morning, to get our brains cleared again.

The people were more friendly one with the other in those days. They might have an evening once now and again singing and if anybody had an accordion or concertina to play we might have a dance in the kitchen.

I never got married, though I had boyfriends. I thought it was my duty to stand by my mother and give her a good ending in life. I think that was what kept me from ever marrying.

Fifty-seven years I worked in the factory. I liked my work and I did my best I could because my mother always told me not to be a looker-on – 'do your work properly and honestly and you can look any man or woman in the face' – that's the advice she gave me.

I'm not saying I had an easy life. I've had to work for my living. I was in the working class and I'm not sorry to say I enjoyed it and I've had a lot of pleasure with my workmates and I'm not thinking of looking for a higher place in heaven than anybody else.

Recorded by Helen Frizzell

Source

This essay contains extracts from interviews recorded with Bessie Turnbull in 1986 for Presbyterian Support Services – Otago's Oral History Programme, where the tapes are currently stored. They are available to bona fide researchers.

Extracts from the tapes were combined with photos to produce the Bessie Turnbull Exhibition, which is on permanent display at the Otago Early Settlers Museum, Dunedin. A tape containing interview extracts accompanies the exhibition.

MARGARET URQUHART

1857–1945

Margaret Kane was born in 1857 to Jane (born Kerr) and Daniel Kane at Dalry, south of Kilbirnie in Ayrshire, Scotland. The eldest of 'fourteen living to adulthood', she was needed from an early age to assist at home. Living at Kilbirnie she would regularly go for five-mile walks to the shops at Dalry or Beith.

When Margaret was sixteen she came to New Zealand with the rest of her family on the *Invercargill*, arriving at Port Chalmers on 16 October 1874. Before marrying, Margaret became a nanny or governess to a Jewish family, the Isaacs of Royal Terrace, Dunedin. She was also required to help dress Mrs Isaacs and comb her hair when the latter was entertaining or going out.

In 1881 Margaret married John Urquhart, who had been born in Inverness, Scotland, in 1850. He was a foreman bridge builder with the New Zealand Railways and was paid one guinea a week. They had five children: Janet (1882), Angus (1884), Annie (1886), Grace (1888), and John (known as Jack) (1889). John was killed on a railway jigger while returning from work in 1889; an unscheduled train was on the line and he had not been notified. His death occurred before Jack was born.

It is not known how Margaret managed for money at first, but she and her children spent their weekends with her parents on the farm they leased in Green Island, where they had cows and a milk run. So the family got free meals at weekends. Margaret had a sewing-machine and hemmed sheets and pillowcases for other people. She also had a quarter-acre section with hens, apple trees, berry fruits, and a large vegetable garden. She made her own wine, a glass of which was offered at family weddings and Hogmanay.

Margaret's brother and her husband's cousin built a small shop on the corner of her property at 57 Cutten Street, South Dunedin. She sold groceries from this shop for a period. When her two eldest children went to the normal school in Moray Place, she rented a house in Maclaggan Street for a few years to save on tram fares. At this time she took in boarders as well. When Margaret returned to her own home and as her children left home, she took in boarders again. Many were cadets and employees of the New Zealand Railways.

At the suggestion of the manager of the DIC department store where Margaret had long had an account, she began a service whereby women could purchase goods at DIC and charge them to her account (provided she had given them an 'order'). They then paid her off in weekly instalments. Some women came to her house to make their payments, particularly if they did not want their husbands to know, and she went to the homes of others to collect the payments. Margaret did not charge the women interest, but received a 10 per cent discount on purchases, as did all account customers, and a further 2.5 per cent if the account was paid before the last day of the month.

It is thought that Margaret offered this form of credit from the 1900s till the 1930s, a period when women could not easily obtain credit and could 'bind' their husbands only for 'necessaries'. Lay-by did not become available until the 1930s.

In later years her daughter Grace, who was not in paid employment, went to the homes to collect money. Among these was the home of a wealthy family who lived in Belmont Lane and owned a large run 'up country'. Grace had to go in the afternoon when the husband was away and was only paid if the wife had been given her dress money.

When the old age pension was introduced, Margaret did not collect hers as she said it was charity. She died in 1945 near Middlemarch, where her daughter Grace farmed with her husband.   *Margaret Aitken*

Source
Information was supplied by family members.

| ELLEN VALPY | *1827–1904* |

| CATHERINE VALPY | *1820–1919* |

| ARABELLA VALPY | *1833–1910* |

| JULIET VALPY | *1835–1911* |

Ellen, Catherine, Arabella, and Juliet Valpy arrived in Dunedin on the *Ajax* in January 1849 with their father, Judge William Henry Valpy, their mother, Caroline (born Jeffreys), and their brother, William Henry. A fifth daughter, Caroline, remained in England with her husband Henry Hensley. William Valpy had retired from the Indian Civil Service and emigrated to New Zealand for health reasons; he became an influential gentleman-colonist, and was said to be one of the richest men in Otago.

The four daughters are remembered for a number of charitable, social, and cultural works in the local community. Brought up in the Church of England, they leaned to the evangelical, involving themselves with the China Mission, the local Benevolent Institution, the Tract Depot, the Salvation Army, and the Band of Hope Coffee Rooms.

All the daughters, like their mother, were to some degree artistic. Ellen Penelope Valpy was a painter, and her water-colours survive in the Hocken Library and the Otago Early Settlers Museum. Her paintings are delicate and slight, offering glimpses of an empty land.

Ellen married her cousin Henry Jeffreys in Dunedin in 1852, and in the following year they moved to Australia with their baby daughter, Caroline. The marriage appears to have broken down, and Ellen returned to her parents' home, 'Forbury', in Dunedin in 1860, accompanied only by a son, Henry. Caroline had died in 1854, and other children born to the marriage appear not to have survived infancy. However, a second son, Edmond, was born six months after her return.

Whatever plans Ellen had for taking up painting and teaching as a means of support came to nothing. She lived in Oamaru while her sons were growing up. But with the hospitalisation of her elder son for recurring bouts of mental instability she moved back to Dunedin. A few years later her younger son died of typhus. These events caused her to turn for financial support to her sister Catherine, whom she joined in a variety of charitable work.

Catherine Henrietta Elliott Valpy was the musician of the family. Her main instrument was the piano but for sixty or seventy years she played whatever instrument was available at almost every church service in the Taieri district, as well as playing for family and friends. In 1852 she married James Fulton and moved to his farm 'Ravensbourne' on the Taieri Plain. Eight children were born to her, and her life was devoted to family, farming, and the community – especially that centred on the local Presbyterian church.

In 1879 James was elected to the House of Representatives, and in 1889 was appointed to the Legislative Council; Catherine later attended the sessions daily with the wives of other parliamentarians to follow the passage of the Woman Suffrage Bill through the House. When James died in 1891, her active promotion of women's suffrage ceased. But at elections after the bill was passed in 1893, she ferried her women neighbours to the polling booths to ensure that they could exercise their rights.

Her other activities reflect the interests of a devoutly religious woman. She was the Dominion president of the Women's Christian Temperance Union from 1889 to 1892. She helped found the Dunedin branch in May 1885 and was its first president. For a number of years, she organised and chaired the Tract Depot which 'freely distributed . . . the very best Gospel reading matter'; she also helped run the Band of Hope Coffee Rooms with her sisters Ellen and Arabella.

Arabella Jeffreys Valpy is remembered for the invitation she issued to General William Booth which brought him to introduce the Salvation Army to New Zealand. She wrote to him in London in April 1882:

Dear Sir, Can you see your way to send to the rescue of perishing souls in this respectable and highly favoured city? Herewith please find draft £200. The Lord reward you and yours.

A wellwisher.

For this she was lambasted by the *Otago Daily Times* on 11 May 1883: 'Some illiberal Dunedinite, with more zeal than discretion is endeavouring to bring down upon us, the Salvation Army . . .' For the rest of her life Arabella maintained a keen interest in the work of the Salvation Army and contributed to Army funds.

Unlike her sisters, Arabella did not marry. For some years she lived with her mother, who had been widowed in 1852. She was generous with her considerable fortune, and devoted herself to charitable work. Catherine described her as a 'warm friend to the sailors', who at her own expense 'hired a building in Dunedin for a Sailors' Coffee Room, which she worked well for several years'.

Juliet Anna Owen Valpy was still in her early teens when the family arrived in New Zealand. Her first husband, William Mackworth, Governor Grey's aide-de-camp, met and fell in love with her when she was only fifteen. At her father's request he did not propose for two years. The pair eventually married in September 1852 in a joint wedding with Catherine and James Fulton. Mackworth died a few years later, whereupon Juliet returned to her family in Dunedin with a daughter, Wilhelmina.

She then married Bayly Pike, a run-holder with property also in Caversham. Four children were born to them, but Pike was something of a rogue who swindled his brothers-in-law and spent his wife's inheritance. Juliet was assisted by Arabella, particularly in later years when Wilhelmina suffered nervous fits severe enough for her to be hospitalised. Juliet did not share to the same extent in the altruistic concerns of her sisters. *Rosemary Entwisle*

Quotations
para.8 Obituary monograph, 'Miss Arabella Valpy', Otago Early Settlers Museum
para.9 Letter, A. Valpy to General William Booth, 5 April 1882 (copy in Otago Early Settlers Museum)
para.10 C. Valpy, 'Autobiography', p.45
Unpublished Sources
C. H. E. Fulton, Diaries of Catherine Henrietta Elliott Fulton, 1845–46, in private possession
C. H. E. Fulton, Diaries of Catherine Henrietta Elliott Fulton, 1857–1917 (photocopies), 162/87, Hocken
C. H. E. Valpy, 'Autobiography of Mrs James Fulton (Catherine Henrietta Elliott Valpy) written in 1915', M. 1/846, Hocken
Francis Crossley Fulton, 'First of the Fultons in New Zealand: A Peep into the Past', in private possession
J. L. Patterson, 'Woman Suffrage in Dunedin 1890–93', BA Hons research essay, Otago, 1974
Published Sources
Bradwell, C. R. *Fight the Good Fight: The Story of the Salvation Army in New Zealand 1883–1983*, Wellington, 1982
Eldred-Grigg, S. *A Southern Gentry: New Zealanders Who Inherited the Earth*, Wellington, 1980
Hocken, T. M. *Contributions to the Early History of New Zealand (Settlement of Otago)*, London, 1898

VAN CHU-LIN

1897–1946

Van Chu-Lin was only eighteen when she arrived in Wellington in 1915. At that time, according to Census figures, there were only about seventy Chinese women in the whole country. Restrictive immigration legislation against the Chinese meant that Chinese women, already discriminated against in their own culture, were even further disadvantaged.

Her husband Chun Yee Hop, a Chinese general store proprietor, had come to New Zealand in the late 1890s and was a community leader among the Tsengshing [Zengcheng] county folk. He was also long-time president of the powerful Chee-Kung Tong (Chinese Masonic Association), a close-knit fraternity widespread among expatriate Chinese communities. In New Zealand, the Chee-Kung Tong was the most influential socio-political organisation among the Chinese, transcending the smaller groups which were usually based on county of origin.

There was very little glamour or mystique in Chu-Lin's life, however. It was a joyless chronicle of daily struggle for subsistence and of eternal bondage to childbearing and family drudgery.

Chu-Lin was born in the Sun Tong [Xintang] village of Tsengshing county of South China, a short distance north-east of the city of Canton. Her father was an oil vendor, who carried a pole with a bucket of cooking oil on one end and a bucket of fuel oil on the other, and hawked all day in the streets. Chu-Lin was his only child and also exceptionally pretty. When Chun Yee Hop asked to marry Chu-Lin, her father was initially reluctant. Chun was twenty-eight years her senior, and he already had a principal wife. Chun was insistent, for he wanted an heir and had returned to China with the explicit aim of finding a new young wife. He promised to take Chu-Lin with him to New Zealand, and guaranteed generous remittances every year.

They were married in Sydney on 19 January 1915. Chun used the name of Ah Young, a naturalised New Zealander, so that he could bring Chu-Lin into the country without her having to sit the English test or pay the poll-tax. They arrived in Wellington in August, on board the *Ulimaroa*. Chu-Lin soon became pregnant, but her first-born died and then she had a miscarriage. Meanwhile the irregularity of her entry was somehow found out, and she was only allowed to stay after a lengthy legal battle in 1917.

Chu-Lin helped her husband to run his Chinese foodstuffs store, first on Lambton Quay and then in Willis Street. His political activities also took up a great deal of his time, although Chu-Lin, as a woman, was excluded from all but the public ceremonial aspects. Her full-time job was to procreate and to rear the children, a task which she could barely manage.

In 1929, fourteen years after she first set foot in New Zealand, Chu-Lin and her husband set sail on the *Ulimaroa* with their ten children (seven girls and three boys) and made the homeward trip to China. The explicit reason was to give the children a Chinese education, but there may also have been the implicit aim of relieving Chu-Lin of the burden of child-rearing.

Chun had a principal wife at home in China, and she could well be asked to look after his children as well as oversee their Chinese education. The cost of living in China was also considerably lower. Within a year, Chu-Lin returned to New Zealand with the three boys, leaving the girls in China with the principal wife. The two eldest daughters, who could be useful in the shop helping with English correspondence and translation, were summoned back in the early 1930s. The others remained in China until forced to leave when the Japanese invaded the southern Chinese countryside. It was not until 1940 that the last of the girls returned to New Zealand. One remarked how shocked she was to see how her parents had aged.

Chun was not over-excited to see his daughters. After leaving the seven girls in China, he and Chu-Lin continued to have more children once they returned to New Zealand. Chu-Lin apparently dreaded the prospect of more babies, and after her eleventh child was given some contraceptive jellies, which were obviously a dismal failure.

Her health suffered, and after the thirteenth child, doctors insisted that she go to the hospital for all subsequent deliveries. (All the previous births were home deliveries, and she often started to work a few hours after giving birth.) Confinement in hospital was the only 'holiday' that Chu-Lin ever knew, and she reportedly 'loved every minute of it'.

Chu-Lin was by nature a gentle person, but the burden of so many children made her ill-tempered. She was always busy, either cooking, making noodles, going to the market to buy food, washing clothes, tending the babies, putting the children to sleep, or disciplining them. Her daughters never remember her sitting down, except to sew or darn, and she often fell asleep over her handiwork through sheer exhaustion. She also demanded that her children work hard. The older ones had to look after the younger ones, and after working past midnight in one of the family shops, they would be woken up by their mother early next morning with 'Get up, do work!' Most of the children were pulled out of school as soon as it was legal. They were needed to work in the shops.

By the 1930s, the family shop was in Riddiford Street, Newtown. The parents lived upstairs with the younger children; as there were only four rooms, they could not accommodate the entire family. The older children lived in another shop in Kilbirnie. They did all the writing and keeping of accounts, for Chu-Lin could not read or write either Chinese or English, and Chun Yee Hop could only write some Chinese.

The big event for the family was Sunday dinner, for which Chun would always cook a proper Chinese meal. The children all enjoyed the good food and the atmosphere of temporary contentment. Communication between parents and children was minimal, however, and it was usually in the form of basic commands. Chu-Lin was too busy to talk to her daughters, and never verbalised how she felt about her life. She had very few friends, and attended hardly any social functions, although the Chinese women in Wellington knew one another well. They simply had no time to socialise. Anne Wong, the minister's wife, who was bilingual, was the one person that Chu-Lin would turn to in times of need.

As her husband became older Chu-Lin had to go to the market to buy supplies for the family shop as well as shoulder more of the business responsibilities. Chu-Lin worked hard to keep the family going, but she also had one great ambition: to save up a couple of hundred pounds to be sent back to China so that her parents could buy an adopted heir to take her place. Unfortunately she never fulfilled this dream. She seldom spoke to her daughters, but she confided that she was worried that her parents would be uncared for, since she was their only child and had gone so far away.

Even with the help of her older daughters, Chu-Lin was weighed down by her business and family responsibilities. And all the time she was having more children. She died aged forty-nine, survived by eighteen children and her seventy-seven-year-old husband.

Many-ing Ip

Unpublished Sources

Interviews with Doris Chung, Chu-Lin's daughter, and Kirsten Wong, Chu-Lin's granddaughter.

NZ Census & Statistics Office, *Register of Aliens, 1917*, Wellington, 1917

Record Book of Chinese Arrivals at Wellington, 1917–1930, Labour Department Records L31/3, National Archives, Wellington

Record Book of Chinese Arrivals at Wellington, 1930–61, L31/4, National Archives, Wellington

ELSIE WALKER

1911–1928

A young girl is taken, in the dead of night, from her home in a quiet little country village, and her dead body is found 150 miles away in a lonely spot outside Auckland, and the only explanation offered by the police is that she, with no previous knowledge of car-driving, drove the car all night, over a range of mountains, past yawning ravines, round hairpin bends, under the shadow of impending cliffs and through a maze of roads in the Waikato, and having arrived at her journey's end crawled under a clump of bushes and died of exhaustion, or, as one sapient representative of the police suggested, died of fright when bitten by a rat.

The provocation for this scalding attack on the minister of justice, by solicitor H. D. Cooney, was the mystery and judicial muddle surrounding the death of a young rural domestic. Elsie Walker's life had been ordinary and obscure, but her death led to a raging controversy, and a massive campaign by women's groups.

In October 1928, two boys chasing rabbits in wasteland near Auckland found the body of seventeen-year-old Elsie Walker under a bush. One night, several days earlier, she had walked out of the kitchen door of the Bayly farm-house near Te Puke to empty the rubbish bin and she had not come back. The Bayly family car went missing and was later found abandoned on a back road at Papatoetoe.

How she got to Auckland, who drove the car, how she died, and, if it was by foul play, who was responsible, were all questions which exercised the police, the courts, and the public imagination.

The police argued for the scenario lampooned by Mr Cooney. There was a bruise on the top of Elsie's head, but the pathologists held that the injury was insufficient to cause death. To add to the enigma, there was semen on her under-clothes, although she was still a virgin.

If the death was not accidental, the prime suspect was William Bayly, son of the family for whom she worked and to whom she was related. He was living in Auckland at the time and early evidence did not place him anywhere near the family farm.

A coroner's inquest was held, the coroner deciding that Elsie had either dis-turbed a thief or been sexually assaulted, and that she died from an accidental or deliberate blow on the head. He also slammed the police for their conduct of the case and called for an inquiry.

A three-month Royal Commission followed, which decided that the police had acted promptly and thoroughly. The coroner had gone further in his recon-struction of the death than the evidence allowed. If the cause of death was not known, then no one could point the finger at Bayly.

But the Elsie Walker case would not go away. Two women, who had origin-ally testified that they had not seen Bayly at the farm for days before the tragedy, now came forward saying that they had seen him on the train to Te Puke on the night in question. They had consulted their priest and he said they should not camouflage the truth. There was a suggestion that one of the women had discussed a sum of £10,000 with Mrs Bayly.

The public, already keenly interested in the case, now went into full cry. They demanded the inquest be reopened, but the minister of justice replied that the law did not allow this.

In Auckland, women's groups saw the case as a women's issue. The Society for the Protection of Women and Children and the National Council of Women (NCW) organised a public meeting in the Town Hall which was attended by 800 people.

At the emotional meeting, Ellen Melville, president of the NCW, said that the women of Auckland were seriously disturbed about the case:

The fact that girls of very young age go about the world today in a manner quite unaccustomed when the Coroners Act was passed in 1908 makes it all the more desirable that they should be protected.

Fellow NCW member Blanche Carnachan also deplored the fact that no woman was present 'when the dead body of Elsie Walker was undressed', arguing that this supported the council's campaign for women police.

The NCW started a petition which, when delivered to parliament, contained over 15,000 signatures and weighed thirteen and a half pounds. The *Sun*, describing its presentation in the House, called it a 'triton among minnows' and the largest received for many years. It was not deemed weighty enough, however, to lead to the reopening of the Elsie Walker case, although a year later the minister did amend the law. Just how Elsie Walker died would forever remain a mystery.

Sir Vincent Meredith, who acted for the police at the original inquest, theorised in his autobiography that Elsie died after she resisted an attempt at seduction which occurred in the dark garage at the back of the Bayly house. Her assailant then panicked and removed her body in the car. Meredith points out that William Bayly could produce no alibi for his whereabouts at the time in question, and relates how a housemaid at his boarding-house told him Bayly's bed was not slept in one night, although she could not be definite about which night.

Bayly went down in criminal history for quite a different matter. On 30 July 1934 he was hanged for murdering Samuel and Christobel Lakey, the couple who lived next to his farm at Ruawaro. Mrs Lakey's body was found by neighbours in the duck-pond and Samuel had disappeared. By some masterly forensic work, the police eventually discovered that Bayly had shot Mr Lakey, burned his body in an oil drum at the back of his cowshed, and scattered the remains (and a few overall buttons) on his kitchen garden.   *Sandra Coney*

Quotations
para.1 Unidentified, undated newspaper clipping, NCW scrapbooks, AIM
para.12 Unidentified, undated newspaper clipping, NCW scrapbooks, AIM
para.13 Unidentified newspaper clipping, 24 Oct. 1929, NCW scrapbooks, AIM
para.14 *The Sun*, undated, NCW scrapbooks, AIM

Unpublished Source
Minutes and scrapbooks of the Auckland Branch of the NCW, AIM

Published Sources
Leary, L. P, *Not Entirely Legal*, Christchurch, 1977
Meredith, Sir Vincent. *A Long Brief: Experiences of a Crown Solicitor*, Auckland, 1966
Wilson, H. J. *The Bayly Case*, Wellington, 1934

MRS WALKER OF CRONADUN

c. 1930s

On cold days Mrs Walker sat with her feet in the oven. Her circulation was poorly, she would say when she thought an explanation was needed, which was not often. She burned only wood in her stove. It was clean, the warmth was easily tempered, and she wanted only wood-ash for her garden. Vegetables flourished where the fine white ash was added to the soil. Mrs Walker disliked coal. It burnt too fiercely, it was hard to control, it was dirty and smelt of carbon. It made her oven too hot to be used as a foot-warmer. Sure there was coal aplenty up in the hills behind her house. The coal lorries went directly past her door several times each day carrying loads of shining nuggets or dusty slack from the mine to the railway station. Mrs Walker could have had a load of coal dropped off at any time of any day and paid for it with a song. But she wouldn't touch it. The word 'pollution' was not used much in the early 1930s, but she knew what it was and she would have none of it. In another age, Mrs Walker would have been a 'greeny'.

Her house was one of a scattered few at Cronadun in the Inangahua Valley, hedged in by mountains on both sides. It was a small house of the most basic kind, with each room leading into the next one. Yet the upkeep of that house and garden filled her days and, as far as anyone could judge, she was a contented woman. The bare wooden floors were covered with brightly coloured mats made by her own hands. Every woman in her neighbourhood made mats from used sacks, but Mrs Walker raised her craft almost to an art form. She embroidered hers with wool recycled from old jerseys and cardigans, dyed and redyed with the help of leaves and plants from her garden. The coarse weave made it possible to count the threads and she worked out her own designs. For special places – beside her bed, in front of the fireplace in the best room, under the pedals of her precious harmonium – she had mats made completely of wool. Those miniature carpets were her pride and joy. They carried her brightest colours, her most intricate designs, her strongest sacks firmly reinforced and backed.

The local farmers' wives felt slightly reproached when they visited her house, but, they told themselves, she didn't have to contend with men's boots coated with mud from the cowyard and she had more time than they did. No cows to milk, no separating to be done, no calves to feed, no children with insatiable appetites to be fed at least two hearty meals a day and always emptying her cake tins. Privately Mrs Walker thought that most of them overfed their children: porridge every morning followed by bacon and eggs or chops or stew before they went off to school; lunch tins full of thick sandwiches cut the night before (meat again, she suspected); and, at the end of the day, ploughman's meals of meat and vegetables at which any eight-year-old worth his salt could polish off at least three large potatoes. Mrs Walker had ideas about children's diet. It was a pity that she had no children of her own: this barred her completely from sharing her theories with the fertile women around her.

Whatever Mrs Walker felt about her own apparent infertility, she kept strictly to herself. Her husband worked in the local dairy factory, hard-working, good-natured, something of an extrovert. Was it his 'fault' or hers? No doubt, in a valley where large families of healthy children were a source of fulfilment, if not complacency, especially to women, there must have been some speculation. But it would be strictly pillow talk. It would be hard to conceive of a group of people more circumspect than those valley people. Their emotional lives were a secret from one another and, in not prying, they believed they were showing one another an essential respect. The invisible walls around each one were as impenetrable as the mountains that dominated their skyline.

One such protective bulwark was the formality with which they addressed one another. The women virtually never used first names. No matter how drawn to one another they might be, no matter what the level of friendship, they remained Mrs McMahon, Mrs Smith, Mrs Walker. They shook hands. The casual kiss or hug was no part of their relationship. They were not given to intimacy. When they confided their distress or suffering to another, it was invested with a kind of sacred quality because it was done so rarely. Only at a time of death was it legitimate to open the emotional doors to admit other people and reveal the depths of one's grief. Even then it was the woman who showed emotional control who was to be most commended. She was 'so strong, so resigned'. It was inevitable, then, that if Mrs Walker agonised for children, if her infertile marriage was a source of humiliation for her, she gave no outward sign.

For all that, the children of the neighbourhood beat a path to her door. For one thing, she had built up a reputation as a healer. Local mothers gradually came to accept that it was no reflection on themselves if they sent their children to Mrs Walker. Doctors, after all, lived in town and charged money. Mrs Walker knew all about home-made ointments for burns, natural anaesthetics for tooth-ache, herbal drinks for persistent coughs (though sometimes she did resort to a spoonful of Baxter's Lung Preserver). She knew how to make a pack with sugar and soap to draw the pus from a boil, how to cut an ingrown toe-nail, what was the right mix of sulphur and treacle to take if one wanted to be rid of stubborn pimples. And over and above her knowledge, she had a soft, soothing voice, healing hands, and unshakeable confidence in her own prescriptions.

But there was another side of Mrs Walker that these country children loved, a side that adults scarcely knew about. She could act the clown. She made finger puppets and toys that had mocking eyes and wide cunning grins. And she always seemed to have a new gadget of one kind or another. By far the most exciting of these was her electric comb. She herself had fine, wispy hair, but she'd read an advertisement about this new technology which guaranteed a head of thick curls. It never made the slightest discernible difference to her own thin hair but it brought endless joy to her young visitors. First of all the batteries had to be carefully inserted, then the tiny switch turned on – and the humming sound would begin. Then, as you began to comb, your head would suddenly become a mass of shimmering blue lights, crackling, sparking, and hissing wildly. Even when you took the comb away, your hair would keep on firing and spitting. Sometimes it just stood straight up on your head in the most alarming way. And Mrs Walker would clap her hands and crow with laughter.

Mrs Walker virtually never left her house. She was too busy altogether for visiting. But there was one exception. On the last Tuesday of every month she put on her hat and coat and attended the meeting of the Country Women's Institute. It was the one occasion when the local women met for an hour or two. But even that meeting had a formal structure. For one thing, there was always a competition: the best oven cloth or peg bag or apron made from a sugar bag, the best embroidered tea-towel from a flour bag, the finest drawn-thread hankie from a salt bag. Or it might be the best recycled article of clothing from an old coat, the most original use for a leaking gumboot, the cleverest way to use wool picked from barbed-wire fences – always the most original this, the most ingenious that, the most unlikely something else. Mrs Walker shone. She showed the other women that there could be real pride in the humbling, if not humiliating, drudgery that was theirs, the task of constantly recycling and making do. In this as in everything else, she inspired tired women, worn out from too much work and too little money, with a hope that life had wider dimensions and they themselves had the resources to explore them.   *Pauline O'Regan*

Source
This portrait was drawn from the author's memory of a woman's life in a rural community in the 1930s.

ISABEL WALMSLEY

1900–1985

Isabel Gubbins was born in Dunedin on 20 September 1900, the first of the four children of Isabella and George Gubbins, who was a metal tradesman at the Hillside Railway workshops. At fifteen, while a student at King Edward Technical College, Isabel began keeping a personal diary, and continued to do so until her last illness in 1985. After a few years' secretarial work, she turned twenty-one and began nursing training at Wairau Public Hospital. She later recalled the joy of being 'free and independent – a new and heady experience for a young girl brought up in a rather sheltered atmosphere'.

Her training interrupted by several years' treatment for tuberculosis, she passed her finals with her younger sister Doris in 1928, and, after nursing at Cashmere (in the same sanatorium where she had previously been treated) and at Pleasant Valley and Orangapai in Otago, took a nurse-receptionist's position with a Dunedin doctor. She also began having occasional pieces published in periodicals such as *The Dairy Exporter*.

Later in 1934, half in fun, Isabel answered an advertisement for a 'blonde young lady aged thirty–thirty-five . . . view matrimony'. On 14 January 1935, she married MacGregor Walmsley. Her freedom and independence had ended.

Gregor was tall, handsome, deaf, and eccentric. His interests were eclectic, and he set up as a consultant in diet reform, aptitude testing, and vocational guidance. He was capable of considerable mental, and occasionally physical, cruelty. Her diaries enabled Isabel to survive nineteen years of marriage, documenting and analysing the turbulent relationship which she could never quite bring herself to end, nurturing her fragile self-image in the face of his cold hostility. Optimism repeatedly breaks through:

Mrs MacGregor Walmsley: rather skinny, but full of pep; rather discontented but still cherishing a few illusions; feeling rather badly-treated but . . . There's always hope! *Me chin's up!*

During the first year of her marriage, Isabel received a total of £4/9/6 (almost her only pocket-money) for published sketches, poems, and photos. When one of Gregor's aptitude tests revealed that she had superior 'artistic ability', he replaced her box Brownie with a better camera. At the kitchen sink, late at night, with makeshift equipment, she would spend many hours successfully combining elements from a number of shots into one satisfying composition.

In 1938 her sympathetic mother-in-law paid for Isabel's first trip abroad – to California, with a Walmsley cousin. She loved travel, and on her return published and broadcast a number of lively stories and articles.

The couple had moved to Timaru on their marriage, and later settled in Christchurch. In 1940 Isabel joined the largely male Christchurch Photographic

'Delicacy', one of Isabel Walmsley's photographic prints. This was later used by Liberty's of London. *Jenny Chisholm*

Society and soon made it plain that she was there as a serious photographer. In 1956, now a widow, she became the first New Zealand woman to be an Associate of the Royal Photographic Society. Eleven of the twelve prints she submitted were accepted; only nine were required for her to qualify.

I carried [the notification of the award] around in my pocket all day, afraid to open it. Late in the afternoon I fortified myself with a glass of sherry and slit the envelope.

That evening she looked again at the letter.

It was addressed to Mrs I E Walmsley ARPS. To think I had spent agonising hours afraid to open it, and there was the whole story on the envelope!

From being a regular winner of club and national photographic awards, Isabel progressed to judging photographic competitions for club and A & P shows. She lectured widely, and continued to explore the photographic medium through new techniques. For twenty years she was on the committee of the Christchurch Photographic Society; she wrote regularly in photographic journals, and edited her own club's quarterly. Always her main concern was to inspire and encourage younger photographers.

Journeys in Europe, the United States, and Mexico satisfied Isabel's passion for travel and gave her further opportunities for carefully observed descriptive writing. Gregor, she wrote, had refused to allow her to have children, considering her unfit to be a mother (he would have been a disaster as a father), but in her eighties she was still publishing delightful children's stories in a city newspaper.

Isabel once wrote that perhaps the only things that she and Gregor had in common were their love of cats and their interest in mystical religions. Her little Siamese cat Lulu kept her company after the death of her dearly loved widowed younger sister, but soon after Lulu died, Isabel followed, aged eighty-five. Surrounded as she was by friends in the Christchurch Photographic Society, the Sumner Writers' Group, and the 'Super-Sixties' Club, she reveals movingly in her last diaries both the loneliness and weariness of old age and her unflagging enthusiasm for the activities that had given her satisfaction and a sense of achievement throughout her life.   *Jenny Chisholm*

Quotations
para.7 I. Walmsley, 'A Moment of Triumph', published short story, date and publication unknown
All other quotations are from Isabel's diaries.
Unpublished Sources
Isabel Walmsley's diaries and papers, in the author's possession
Published Source
Mihajlovic, Marie. 'At Home With NZ's Sole Woman ARPS', *NZ Woman's Weekly*, 9 Feb. 1970

MARY WATSON

1896–1968

Mary Isaline Watson kick-started her mobile home-help service into existence in 1938.

After hearing that the farm wives in the district were having difficulty in getting domestic help, she dreamed up the idea of a travelling home help as the most logical answer. As she was the eldest of ten children of a Scottish pioneering family, and later the wife of a farm labourer, she was no stranger to hard work.

She bought an Alldays Alton two-stroke motor cycle which earned her the nickname Two-Stroke Watson from the local people. For this she designed a side-car on which she mounted a National washing-machine. Advertising herself as 'Happy Day Washer', she would be seen five days a week, in leather coat and goggles, driving between farms in the Grassmere/Seddon district of Marlborough. She did all her own motor cycle maintenance.

Upon arrival at the farmhouse she would park as close as possible to the laundry, run out a lead from the washer to a power point in the house, and, with a hose for water, was ready to do the washing. A vacuum cleaner and iron were also carried in the side-car.

She was fast and efficient. Once finished, she would move on to her next customer. Over the years she had four motor cycles, her last being a yellow

Mary 'Two-Stroke' Watson kick-started her mobile home help service into action in 1938.
Anne Morrison

55-cubic-inch Indian Scout. Because of its striking colour her nieces and nephews called her Aunty Canary.

On becoming the agent for the National washing-machine, her work-load increased. When the ordered washers arrived at a depot in Blenheim, she would have to pick up and deliver them to her customers in the Seddon district. During the Second World War she took on the weekly rural mail service. One day was devoted entirely to delivering 'His Majesty's Mail'. Mary Watson took this responsibility very seriously, and did not see that carrying the mail in the washing-machine, along with some small grocery orders for the housewives, presented a somewhat comical picture. Another 'duty' she took seriously was that of dispatch-rider as part of the local Emergency Precaution Service during the same war.

By 1950 she had given up her home-help service. From her earnings she had bought a house for herself and her husband, Herbert. Her housekeeping had always been, and still was, impeccable, with her linen starched and her floors gleaming. Though she never had children of her own, she devoted many hours to children, by working as a Red Cross leader in Seddon for many years and teaching local children sewing and embroidery. Her work in this craft was of such a high standard that she won 142 first prizes around the country. Her pieces included two portraits in silks, one of Charles Kingsford-Smith and the other of Jean Batten, of which it was said that it was difficult to tell the reverse side. The embroidery she did for St Andrew's Church in Seddon is still in use today.

Mary Watson gave unstintingly of her time to causes, particularly to her church of which she was a dedicated member, right up till the illness that hospitalised her shortly before her death on 19 April 1968, aged seventy-one.

Anne Morrison

Unpublished Source
Information was provided by friends and relatives of Mary Watson.

Published Source
Johnson, S. 'Washday was "black Monday"', *NZ Woman's Weekly*, 29 June 1981

MIRIKA POWHIRIHAU WEHIPEIHANA

1902–1978

Mirika Wehipeihana was born at Kuku, Ohau, in 1902. Her people were Ngati Tukorohe and Ngati Raukawa of Horowhenua.

In 1924 Mirika graduated as a general nurse from the Waikato School of Nursing. The following year she completed postgraduate study in midwifery at St Helen's Hospital, Wellington. In 1926 Mirika's first appointment was as district nurse for the East Coast area. Based at Tikitiki, Mirika worked in association with Apirana Ngata. Together they developed a successful community health education programme, where Mirika began marae-based group instruction for Maori women on aspects of infant welfare and preventive family health care.

As a Maori nurse, Mirika found she was able to maintain her professional responsibilities while working co-operatively with Maori people. Discussing the perceived difficulty of nursing predominantly Maori patients, Mirika herself once said:

Strictly speaking a nurse may enter any place, but sometimes when the Ringatu . . . were holding a meeting I was not allowed to enter their meeting house that day or the next. I used to work in with them in their religious observances and sometimes I had to work in with their tohunga too.

In 1930 Mirika left the East Coast for a brief period and undertook specialist training in the treatment and prevention of tuberculosis. She returned to Tikitiki in 1934 and became the tuberculosis control nurse for the Waiapu County. She supervised the pilot segregation hut scheme for the treatment of tuberculosis, which allowed Maori patients to receive treatment in a controlled environment without entirely removing them from their own communities. By 1940 this method of treating tuberculosis had been adopted nationwide by the Health Department. In 1947 Mirika received an MBE in recognition of her work on the segregation hut scheme.

After her work on the East Coast, Mirika moved to Opunake where she practised as a public health nurse until 1961. During this time, Mirika's hours often extended well beyond her regular shifts. Despite this, she managed to maintain her passion for sport and 'felt quite justified enjoying a round of golf during working hours'. Mirika's ability on the golf course once caused her to be reported in the local press. This minor achievement was subsequently noted by her employers at the Health Department Head Office and Mirika received an official censure. Undeterred, she changed her name to Miss Brown for future tournaments and 'her handicap continued to improve'.

In late 1961 Mirika moved to Wanganui where she worked part time until her retirement in 1967. She was a diabetic and treated herself with insulin injections to the thigh. She died on 6 July 1978 and is buried at Tukorohe.

Mirika's story is told by her brother and sister, Hare Hemi Wehipeihana and Arihia (Butty) Goldsmith.

Her real name was Mirika Powhirihau, but we always called her Daddie. We all have nicknames, every one of us. That's just the way we are down here. Daddie wasn't actually known as Ngati Raukawa at all. She became Ngati Porou. A 'Ngati' for short. Even her own people called her that. When she came back to Raukawa to visit, our old people would always laugh and say, 'Ah, go home, Ngati, go back to the Coast.'

Daddie didn't speak Maori when she left home, but when she got up the Coast, she really learned the Ngati Porou way of talking. Daddie became entirely fluent in the language. In those days, she was a favourite of Sir Apirana Ngata. Ngata encouraged her and in return she did so much for his people. Over the years that she was up the Coast, she fought to lower the incidence of TB. But they had to do what she said. She'd say to Ngata, 'It's no good, the people are going to die.' He said, 'So what are you going to do?' She said, 'Let me have the right to go to your people's houses and instruct them and the situ-

Nurse Mirika Wehipeihana (Aunty Daddie) of
Ngati Tukarohe and Ngati Raukawa, c.1926.
Hare Hemi Wehipeihana

ation will improve.' From that time on they never considered her an outsider.

*Up and down the Coast she was the nurse and the doctor for all the
people. She brought all their babies into the world. Not the way they do it now,
but the real Maori way. When Daddie was doing midwifery she made the
woman squat down on her knees. The patient would be supported by someone
else, usually another woman, who would push their knees gently, but firmly,
against the labouring woman's tummy. Daddie would be massaging the
patient's back, talking to her all the time. Then after the woman had given
birth, Daddie would be ready to collect all the whenua [placenta]. We are
careful with that and bury it somewhere safe. Now I'm not sure what they do
with it. I still think it is the best way.*

*When she lived up the Coast, the place she stayed was mostly Ringatu.
Daddie had one little house where you cook and eat and that and another house
where you dress and sleep. She said that was the Ringatu style. You sleep in one
place and you eat in one place, you didn't do it all together like we do now. She
had this little room, joining the house, for her surgery. This is where she held
the clinic and did her work.*

*She kept everything spick and span. All her instruments were clean and
sterilised. After she'd treated her patients she'd sit down and talk to them. She'd
explain to them what their symptoms were. Then she'd tell them what they had
to do and they'd have to do it. As she said, if they didn't follow her instructions
– well, God help them.*

*Sometimes she'd keep patients for a few days, until everything was all
right, then she'd say you can go home now. But she'd continue visiting them
until they'd made a recovery. Daddie would always tell you what was wrong
and then she'd show you what to do. Now she said, 'You follow the treatment
otherwise you can bloody well die!' She wasn't hard-hearted, it was just her*

way. She'd give her last ounce of energy trying to help you but you had to listen to her. She was really tough. Plus she was a damn good nurse. She was a professional and knew what she was doing.

If you put something to her and she didn't think you were right, she'd tell you off. She wasn't argumentative, but when she put her foot down, you couldn't even give her the time correctly. If she thought that the local people were at risk in a particular area, she made sure they did something about it. She used the authority of the Health Department all the time to give her recommendations extra clout. If she went into a hospital and saw the treatment was wrong for the people, then she would tell the authorities. She did that in New Plymouth Hospital. She went there and there were some elderly pakeke [elders] who wanted to go home, but they couldn't because they were too ill. Daddie made sure that the Maori people provided kai that suited them, boosted their morale, and then they got well. Then the Pakeha Health Department could see how sometimes the culture overruled their system of health.

I remember Daddie going on about those little bedside lockers, where they used to have specimen bottles. She'd say, 'Inside these, patients are expected to keep kai, and their dirty clothes, and their haircomb – all in the one place.' But of course this is how we were brought up. We don't wash our clothes where we wash our dishes, but the Pakehas couldn't care less. To them personal hygiene means as long as it's sterilised it's okay. The attitude has actually changed in the last few years, but I remember Daddie getting really wild about it.

On the Coast the people got to know her, because she more or less was one of them. She lived with them and she visited them. She cared for them and she growled at them, but she loved them too. The Coast people didn't have any bad feeling for her because they knew what she was like. Daddie was rough and tough, but good. Every time they called her, she went. Whether it was early in the morning, or late at night. She went. If ever she was called out at night and had to cross the river, one of the local boys would go with her. While she was up on the Coast she did a lot of her travel by horse. When the people eventually got a road it was nothing more than a metal track. Daddie got a little Morris. It was a good car, that little Morris. Daddie used to travel around quite a lot. Out to Hicks Bay, Te Araroa, and right up to the Cape. Even though Daddie liked the car, there were places where she still had to use the horses.

In the latter part of her life, Daddie married a Pakeha, Arthur Brassey, but she never ever wore her wedding ring and she never changed her name neither. No, she said, she was not going to change her name, she still wanted to be known as Nurse Wehipeihana.

Daddie never had any children. Work was more important to her. She was a career woman. All her working life she was determined to help with improving the health and welfare of Maori people. She was as good as a doctor. If it came to the crunch and there was no one around, she could do anything.

Hare Hemi Wehipeihana, Butty Goldsmith & Cushla Parekowhai

Quotations
para.3 Unpublished obituary, in possession of Hare Hemi Wehipeihana
para.5 Unpublished obituary
Unpublished Sources
Certificates, correspondence, personal papers, in possession of the Wehipeihana family, Levin
Typescript, NZ Pan Pacific Women's Association, Maori Women's Biographies, qMS 1952, ATL

ELIZABETH ANN WHAREPAPA

?1849–1921

A letter to my children and grandchildren, and their children and grandchildren:

I write this before some of you are born. However, it seems appropriate for us to talk, as I near the end of my time, to allow you to see my life and the direction it took. I am only able to share snippets of my life as writing tires me.

It is 1863, but I shall return to a time when even I was not born. The year was 1831. Captain John Reid, my dear papa, went out to New Zealand and met with a fine chief, Te Pomare. A friendship developed between them and now papa is keen to meet with Te Pomare's son, Hare Pomare, who is visiting London with a group of his brethren. Papa has invited Hare Pomare and his Ngapuhi kindred to visit with us at our Marylebone residence. I am looking forward to the visit because I have heard much of the beauty of New Zealand natives and, as yet, I have not set eyes on any.

I have met him. He is such a ruggedly handsome man and the tattoos on his face are quite beautiful. I am sure that our children will have these markings too. Goodness! I am being forward but he has quite captured my imaginings. We are unable to communicate without an interpreter except by signs and some sort of Maori-English. I am also unable to say his name properly, Kamariera Te Hautakiri Wharepapa, so I call him 'Mari'. In return he calls me 'Rihipeti'. Papa still sees me as a child (I am nearly sixteen) despite the fact that I have been in service at the estate which papa manages, these past two years. Mari visits almost daily and he calls me his 'sweet-faced English girl'. I do believe that he is fascinated by my smallness and my blue eyes.

Today is 31 March 1864. Mari and I were married at St Anne's parish church, Limehouse (on the north side of the Thames, a few miles below Tower Bridge), and I am delightfully happy despite my apprehension about leaving England and the knowledge that the arrival of our first child is in a couple of months. My dear Mari is so handsome and I am quite the envy of my friends.

Early this morning, 31 May 1864, off Cape Good Hope, our daughter, whom Mari and I have named Maraea Good Hope Wharepapa, was born. We have been at sea on the clipper ship *Flying Foam* since 4 April and our daughter's arrival is the happiest event to date. I have been ill with seasickness, which has been a common complaint, and being heavy with child has not helped matters.

Fourteen days out from Gravesend stories of a ghost appearing in the women's quarters were going about. A thorough investigation revealed that the 'ghost' was a certain third mate, Mr Brock. Three weeks out we also had some of the crew plotting mutiny. This came to a head on 17 April during Crossing-the-Line festivities when drink got a little out of hand and the sailors got into a fight. Captain Perkins ordered the offenders to be placed in irons but his order was refused by the rest of the crew. The captain then called upon the passengers to assist him and his officers in restoring discipline. Although I and the other women and children were cleared from the decks when the fracas first broke out I know that my dear Mari and several of the other passengers armed themselves with revolvers and other weapons and formed themselves into a strong defence party. Some of the crew have been placed in irons and there is much discontent. The events of that particular incident were relayed to me by some of the English-speaking passengers as Mari and I are still unable to communicate clearly in a common language. His English is very much better than my Maori though.

Elizabeth Ann Wharepapa.
Powhiri Rika-Heke

Evening, 13 July 1864, and I am weary with the constant anticipation that the last four days have brought. We rounded North Cape on 9 July in fine, warm weather which quickly deteriorated to a fierce head wind which has tried the patience of both crew and passengers alike. Nothing can be more tantalising than to be coasting along the land and everyone looking forward to the time when they could be treading it and not being able to get to the right port. Auckland is now in sight some sixteen miles ahead and the wind coming right at us. The chances are that we might anchor in the harbour and we may not. Maraea is such a sweet baby and Mari such a caring husband and father that the waiting is more bearable than it might otherwise be. Mari assures me that we will spend a little time in Auckland before making our final journey, the destination being some 150 miles further north. Although I long to be in my own place I am anxious too because there are no English people in the valley which is to be my home.

April 1872. I have been living in the Mangakahia Valley these past nine years and in all that time I have had no direct contact with Europeans. My patience has been pressed since coming to New Zealand but I have sought God's help and He has lent me His hand in times of trial. I have spent these years teaching Mari and the children rudimentary English and he has taught me Maori. I get along comfortably with the Maoris but I know that if there were a school and a clergyman at hand I would feel lighter. I have tried to help the Maoris to be civilised and more industrious, which is a much easier task now that I can talk to them in their own language.

I often receive letters from my dear friend, Charlotte Weale, who lives in Bridport. She has helped me to see the light in times of despair and darkness. I have learned to be patient and to bear up by asking God's help. Charlotte always urges me to turn to Him when my isolation becomes too much for me. She has just sent me some pretty pictures to amuse the children and some stories which I shall read to them. I do wish that I had adult company to talk with in proper English but I suppose that I should be grateful for the children. I now have five daughters who are so fine and bring me such joy.

My dear friend Mrs Colenso, who lives in Paihia, also writes and keeps me informed of the goings on in New Zealand. She sent me some seeds last year and I now have a delightful garden with vegetables which are 'English'. I have a nice crop of parsnips and carrots and other vegetables for winter's use. I have planted some parsley, mint, sage, and rosemary. Maoris have such different tastes. I also have some pigs which are unlike the wild beasts roaming the bush. It was lovely to have bacon which tasted like the bacon I remember from home. I have learnt to be a good farmer's wife and I know that if I had a few English people near me to talk to and a church and a clergyman at hand I would get along more brightly.

2 July 1872. What a wonderful day this has been. Dr Gennes Fraser has arrived in the valley to set up our first school. He has been riding for two days and speaks so little Maori that if I had not been at the meeting with the locals where he was to read a letter from the native minister he would have been quite lost. At last Mari's plea to Queen Victoria that 'all our children and all our youth may be taught' will come true. I am to be Dr Fraser's interpreter and teacher of Maori. Mari has been elected as chairman of the school committee and the school will open with a roll of thirty-five children and some adults. Although I am delighted by this recent turn of events I am also experiencing some disquiet because my relationship with Mari has become quite strained. I fear that he is dissatisfied because we have not had a son and, though he loves the girls very much, a chief needs a son to carry on the line. It is like this in England too.

9 December 1877. I suppose you all think me very evil but I can assure you that I think of you often. As Mrs Colenso is coming to Auckland at Christmas I should like one of you to come with her, that is if your papa will consent. I suppose he will not but you can only ask. Write and let me know. I shall feel pleased to see any of you. My new home, which your dear papa has so generously provided, is in Parnell and I would be so happy to see you children here with me. Although he has given me the freedom to leave Mangakahia I know he will never allow any of you to live with me. That makes me very sad. However, you can visit with me when your papa says so and, of course, when you are older.

30 August 1920. Dear Mari has been dead a year now and I am about to marry my own Charles Samuel Lakey whom I have lived with these past forty

years or more. My Mary Faith and her husband Thomas are to be our witnesses at the ceremony. Charles and I have a family of our own who have grown up knowing their 'Uncle Mari' and their Wharepapa sisters because of the many visits that Mari and his relatives have made to our home during these past years. I have also been fortunate to have my grandchildren come to stay when they have been attending the St Stephen's Boarding School at Parnell. Mari and Charles got along quite splendidly in the end.

My first family are all grown and married with children of their own. Maraea Good Hope married William Rudolph and is living in the Mangakahia. Edith Harriet married Pererika Heke from Whangaroa and also lives in the Mangakahia. Hora Eliza Ann married William Archibald Alison and lives in the Mangakahia too. Mary Faith married Thomas Ryan and lives on the Barrier. And, finally, Susan married Wati Ruwhiu from Otaua and moved to Te Araroa in 1912. Though they are grown women and mothers they will always be my darling daughters.

It is time for me to end this musing and to prepare for my wedding. I know that what I have done has not always met with the approval of either the Church, my family and friends in England, or my children, but Mari's support has helped me to live with my decisions in a way that may have been intolerable otherwise.

I trust that you will know me from my writings and that you will not judge me too harshly.

Your ever affectionate mama, and great-grandmama, Lizzie Wharepapa.

Powhiri Rika-Heke

Unpublished Sources
Written by Elizabeth Wharepapa's great-great-granddaughter, from family information, letters left by
    Elizabeth Wharepapa, and letters to Elizabeth Wharepapa from Charlotte Weale.
Published Sources
Mackrell, Brian. *Hariru Wikitoria! An Illustrated History of the Maori Tour of England*, Auckland,
    1985

ELIZA WHITE

1809–1883

It was the fate of missionary wives to enter a life of hard labour, loneliness, and privation but to leave little trace of it for posterity. Their husbands kept diaries, maintained record books, and conducted voluminous correspondences. A good deal of this has been preserved, so that a clear picture of missionary activities and the personalities of the male protagonists exists. The women remain elusive. Restricted by religious and social prescriptions about their proper sphere, they rarely played a public role. Accepting their place as 'helpmeet' to their husband, missionary wives were also unlikely to have the sense of significance which leads to a decision to record one's life in a diary. The passage of time has intensified the silence. Descendants were less likely to preserve what their female ancestors had written, and there were no biographers promoting interest in female subjects.

Eliza White is an exception. She did leave a record, and its very rarity makes it precious. From the moment she boarded the *Sisters* at Deal in England, on 16 September 1829, bound for the Wesleyan mission station on the Hokianga, she kept a journal as a way of communicating with her parents in England. Eliza's youth and sense of adventure may have made her alert to the fact that she was taking part in events which would shape history. A shipboard entry in Eliza's journal hints that she recognised the extraordinary and even heroic nature of the task she was facing:

I have entered on a new scene – left the parental roof, and the friends and guides of my youth, to become a wife – forsaken my native land and embarked for a distant barbarous clime as the partner of a Christian missionary.

There are omissions in what Eliza chose to record. The scandals surrounding her husband William and his eventual dismissal from the mission at Mangungu are barely mentioned, but her record of daily life is important, and her thoughts and fears, however circumspectly expressed, create a vivid and sometimes harrowing picture of the life of a mission wife.

Eliza was born on 11 July 1809, the daughter of Thomas and Elizabeth Leigh of Earith in Huntingdonshire. Her father was a coal and timber merchant. The Leighs were Baptists, but attended Wesleyan services, and Eliza was converted to Wesleyanism at the age of sixteen. In 1827 she attended a missionary meeting and, according to her obituary, 'her sympathies were greatly stirred'. Back home, she expressed her feelings in a poem:

O may my life, my all, be spent
In telling heathens Thou was sent
To save their souls from sin and hell,
That they might in Thy presence dwell.

Increase the spark that now I feel,
Into a flame of holy zeal;
And may I hear the negro say –
'Dear missee, teach me how to pray'.

William White had gone back to England in 1825 looking for a wife. The work of the Whangaroa mission where he had first worked had been hampered because only one of the mission men was married. Single men in the field were prey to 'temptations of the most powerful kind, and delicate nature', said a fellow missionary. Luke Wade confessed in tears that he had slept with a Maori woman. White denied having done so, even though a woman had complained to another missionary, John Hobbs, that White had not given her the gown he had promised in return for her sexual favours.

It took William White four years' searching to find his bride. The Leighs provided hospitality for visiting Wesleyan preachers, so perhaps this was how Eliza met William, for he was preaching at nearby Higham Ferrers in 1827. Eliza was undoubtedly the answer to William White's prayers, for at least one prospective wife had already declined to accompany him to New Zealand, but he also provided Eliza with a means of realising her dream. Perhaps her ambition made her blind to the potential difficulties in the union. She had not yet turned twenty, and was seventeen years younger than the difficult, volatile White. White's biographer describes her as a

young, impressionable girl from a relatively prosperous village family . . . It does not seem possible that she can have had the slightest real understanding of the kind of man he was.

On board ship William quickly displayed his temperament by falling out with the ship's doctor and refusing to dine at the same table. Eliza noted that William 'found it difficult to command his temper', but nevertheless reacted with the loyalty she was to maintain for all their married life. Observers of the strife which surrounded the Mangungu mission, and in particular White, noted Eliza's capacity to support her husband without ever losing the friendship of even his bitterest enemies.

Eliza stayed in her cabin most of the voyage, plagued by seasickness, heat, and cockroaches. She was the only female on board, and by the time the *Sisters* reached the Bay of Islands in early 1830, she was seven months pregnant. The arrival of the vessel was an occasion for great excitement among the Maori of the bay. One hundred clambered on board. Eliza wrote:

They were very curious to get a sight of Whitey's [the Maori called White 'Te Waiti'] wife, and when I went on deck to get into the boat, [I] was completely surrounded by them. Some got in the rigging and examined my countenance and dress with great earnestness.

On the journey to Mangungu, two Maori carried Eliza on a covered sedan chair – 'they were as careful over me as they probably could be' – while two others went ahead 'to break the branches of trees down to make way for my carriage'. At Mangungu she discovered that she and White were to live in 'a nice little rush house', the former home of the mission servant. With experience, she was to describe it as 'cold and very inconvenient'.

On the ship, Eliza had longed for the company of other women. 'A female companion', she wrote, 'will be a treasure to me after so long a separation from my own sex.' At Mangungu, John Hobbs's wife Jane was also pregnant and the two women became very close, establishing bonds they would sustain, despite the differences which emerged between their husbands. 'I loved you and respected you . . .' wrote Eliza simply when Jane was at the mission in Tonga. Eliza was very fond of Jane's children and one daughter recorded that:

'Mata Waiti' (to me) was my first friend . . . She was a sweet and pretty young woman. It was a happy time when my mother watched me from the gate to that where Mrs White stood to welcome me . . .

Eliza's love of children was not to be speedily satisfied with the birth of her own. Soon after her arrival, she gave birth to a stillborn girl. She was 'much affected at this circumstance, as I had often anticipated its birth . . .'. Her childbirth history continued to be tragic and she frequently expressed her grief in her journal. A son was born alive but died unexpectedly at eight months. Then, in 1833,

I was confined with a little girl – whose feeble voice once uttered a plaintive cry, and was silent in death! This stroke seemed for a moment more than my nature could bear.

The child had been strangled by the umbilical cord. John Hobbs wrote that: 'the overwhelming sensations of the Mother, whose labour had from the nature of the circumstances been of the severest kind, were beyond description . . .'

A few weeks later, when the same complication occurred during Jane Hobbs's labour, the missionaries knew what to do, and Jane was safely delivered of a boy. Eliza wrote:

Every bone in my bleeding heart was opened afresh, and I was obliged to give vent to my griefs. None but a Mother bereaved of All her children in a foreign land can conceive how deeply – how acutely I feel when holding this precious babe in my arms!

Happily, in 1834, John Ebeneezer White was born. Eliza wrote to Jane Hobbs (by then in Tonga) that he was 'very healthy, very lively and very good . . .'. But she could not forget her dead children. She rationalised her loss as a test or punishment by God. She needed

to pray to be saved from idolizing [her baby] I have had many warnings but my treacherous heart yet cleaves to the dust this child seems to occupy so much of my time and attention . . .

Another son, Thomas Leigh, was born in 1836. After this birth Eliza wrote to Jane Hobbs that she was 'not likely to have any more', and no further children were born to the Whites.

The mission wives attended each other's births, acted as midwives for settlers' wives, and dispensed medicine to both races. Eliza painted a graphic picture of the delivery of one baby. She had just gone to bed, she wrote, when the mission women were told that Mrs Mitchell was in labour:

. . . we went immediately – the lads pulled well – Mrs W [Woon] and I remarked to each other how much concerned some of our English friends would feel if they knew of our situation – two females in a boat, late at night, on a large River – in a thick fog – with New Zealanders for our companions – but we felt perfectly safe, and one lad sat at the stern as pilot. We found our dear friend ill, and after a severe time she was safely delivered at 7 o'clock of a fine Girl. I dressed the little stranger – we sat on a while with our friend, and returned home.

The tone of this entry is typical of Eliza. She was undaunted by the dangers of her life, and the warlike Maori. She wrote:

I can sit down with a party [of Natives] with as much comfort as though they

725

were a party of my English Friends, and I believe the Anger of the fiercest chief might be allayed by a basin of sweet tea.

One of Eliza's main tasks at the mission was the conversion, education, and training of Maori girls and young women. For this task it was necessary to learn the Maori language and on the voyage out she had had her first lessons from her husband. Six months later she was still bemoaning her lack of progress: 'I daily feel my almost entire ignorance of this language to be a great hindrance to my usefulness.' Eventually she became completely proficient in the language, helped write a school-book for printing on the mission press, and translated *Pilgrim's Progress*. On one occasion she noted: 'I have only seen one white person about five minutes today excepting my baby. I should soon lose some of my native language if it were not for my books.'

Eliza White. *Hemus and Hanna photo/YWCA Collection, Auckland Institute and Museum*

Reading was one of Eliza's few personal pleasures. For entertainment she walked on the beach when the tide was low – 'over stumps and roots of trees', went on picnics, rode her horse Pompey White, and read voraciously. It was a way of keeping up to date what was happening in England, but it was also a relaxation. This did not come easily to Eliza. Her strong religious commitment – she described herself as 'Methodist to the backbone' – meant she measured herself constantly against an ideal of the perfect Christian pilgrim. When she fell short, she chastised herself:

I feel unhappy this evening on account of reading some unprofitable pages from Addisons Monks – I fear if fictitious works were often in my way I should be overcome with temptation . . . I have many struggles with this besetting sin.

Most of Eliza's days were spent in what she described as 'domestic drudgery'. Although eventually ten Maori 'domesticks' lived with the Whites and did most of the washing, cleaning, and fetching of firewood, Eliza attended to the cooking, sewing, and ironing. The diet included a great deal of pork, kumara traded from the Maori, and dried peaches. She wrote in 1833:

We have several geese on the settlement and 4 Turkeys, with a great many fowls which lay an abundance of eggs, so that we just now are living almost luxuriously for New Zealand. We have also one Cow in milk and I can make about 1/4lb of butter a week between myself and Mrs Whitely we generally use goats milk for Tea, which is almost as rich as cream.

She recorded making 'bread for my family, now 14 in number', and bemoaned the work caused by a constant stream of visitors since there were 'no inns in the land'. About this, wrote Eliza, 'I sometimes feel very vexed and William says I look so – do not therefore be surprised if you should hear what an unamiable woman Mrs W is!'

Despite several entries such as this which suggest that housework was not Eliza's favourite occupation, she completely accepted the restraints placed on her role because of her sex. Suffering acutely from the heat, she said she envied the Maori women whom she could see cooling off in the harbour. 'A bathe would be a great luxury this hot season', she wrote, but she did not dare do so. When William's brother Francis arrived from England, and preached in English, Eliza was frustrated because 'only about one twentieth of his hearers could understand him', but it was not possible for Eliza herself to preach.

I heartily wished I could lend brother my knowledge of their language and almost felt a wish that it were common and proper for Women to preach but my own judgement is so decided on this point, except in very peculiar circumstances I think it very indecorous . . .

From her first days at Mangungu, Eliza conducted a school for Maori girls with Jane Hobbs. She occasionally despaired at the difficulty of the task. The young women were eager to learn and Eliza described how 'they came to me today and said Mother, read "*Buka, Buka*" . . .' But there were deep cultural differences in matters such as sexual habits, dress, hygiene, ownership of property, and behaviour. Eliza related that one of her charges 'stole some pork out of a pot which was boiling for Sunday dinner and went into the bush to eat it'. When Eliza remonstrated with Kapohia, her favourite pupil,

she was very obstinate: I told her my little girls in Europe did not speak to me as she did . . . When we reprove them for doing wrong, they either laugh at us, or cover their heads, sit down and cry.

At the end of three years, Eliza felt little had been achieved: 'I know not one Native female who has derived any real benefit from my instruction.' But later in the same year she reported a distinct improvement. There had been a marked increase in the number of Maori coming to church and being baptised and married. She was moved when the Maori women prayed 'extempore', and she started an infant school with three pupils. By 1836 Eliza was able to record that seventy women were attending prayers with her on Sunday.

Eliza's husband was indefatigable in his efforts to spread the Gospel and was very successful at it. 'The natives', wrote Eliza, 'are ready to tear Mr White in pieces for missionaries.' By 1836 he had established missions at Waingaroa, Kawhia, and Raglan. This work took him away from Mangungu for long periods. Eliza found the separations very trying. If her husband's expected arrival time passed, she was filled with 'dark forebodings and distressing fears – frequently have I felt desolate as a widow'.

White's success can be explained by his popularity with the Maori. A former carpenter, he was a physically robust man with a strong personality. He supported the concept of Maori rule in the Hokianga, and wanted the chiefs to pass a law prohibiting the landing of spirits in the area, which Europeans would have to obey. In September 1835 he called the first temperance meeting in New Zealand, attended by large numbers of Maori, which Eliza recorded in her journal. After this, the Whites gave up drinking wine at the dinner table.

White's opposition to the sale of Maori land obstructed the plans of the European settlers and earned him the intractable opposition of the Additional British Resident, Thomas McDonnell. McDonnell had a sawmill at nearby Horeke, and White further earned his displeasure by organising a sizeable timber-milling operation at the mission, staffed by local Maori. The proceeds went into developing the mission and buying back Maori land sold to Europeans by their relatives. Eliza noted that McDonnell

seems most inveterate against Mr White because he has such influence with [the] Native, who he had advised not to sell their possessions, but keep them for their children . . . if it were not for this advice the white people would try to make them sell their land for nought, and soon treat them as they have been used to do to the aborigines of New South Wales *and* Van Dieman's Land.

In 1835 the rumours and controversy surrounding White came to a head. Personality conflicts between the missionaries, aggravated by White's requirement that they work at the sawmilling enterprise despite church prohibitions on missionaries engaging in commercial operations, had led to a stream of accusations and counter-attacks being sent home to missionary headquarters in London. Meanwhile McDonnell resorted to more direct tactics. He waved a cutlass at William White and said, Eliza records, that 'were it not for *Mrs White* and *John!* he would bring his large guns and blow the mission station up!!' Finally McDonnell set up a committee of Europeans to hear charges against White of immoral relations with Maori women (including the wives of Maori preachers and the Whites' own servants). The committee included employees of McDonnell and enemies of White. Concerned at the bias, White withdrew, but his missionary colleagues agreed with the verdict of guilty and this was conveyed to London along with their own accusations that White had misapplied mission funds.

In early 1836, the Turner family arrived to replace White as head of the mission. Eliza recorded unemotionally that she and William *removed most of our goods and chattels to the* Raupo *House on the hill, to leave our present large and commodious dwelling for Mrs T's large family – they all arrived to a late tea.*

But other entries showed that she was deeply distressed by the events. When some of McDonnell's letters passed through her hands she scrawled biblical injunctions on the envelopes, such as 'thou shalt not bear false witness against they neighbour', and to Mrs Hobbs she talked of 'this painful subject which has disturbed my mind for years'.

It seems probable that she did not believe the accusations of adultery and rape against her husband, as she later directly accused another missionary of infidelity to his wife. If she had believed her husband was guilty of the same sin, it seems unlikely she would have taken such a bold step.

Following William's dismissal the Whites sailed to Sydney, then London, where William pleaded his case with the missionary authorities, but to no avail. The church determined that the dismissal should stand. The Whites returned to New Zealand and settled on land next to the Mangungu mission where William, to the considerable chagrin of the missionaries, continued to preach, sometimes clad in his clerical robes and collar. He attempted to establish a European model settlement in the Hokianga, and with his brother Francis traded in timber. But at this he did not prosper, and when he lost an entire cargo of timber in a shipwreck on the Hokianga bar, his fortunes entered a decline from which they never recovered.

We know little about Eliza at this time except that she had a school attended by the children of Francis and Jane White and sometimes of the Hobbs. Her niece, Hannah (White) Martin, writes that Eliza was 'very well educated and refined, and we had the very best teaching possible'.

With the outbreak of the war in the north, Eliza and her children were evacuated to Auckland, where Eliza was able to find another outlet for her missionary impulses. She maintained an interest in the Maori missions, attending Maori services at the Native Institution in Grafton Road and providing practical support for the missions. Eliza probably played a part in recruiting Annie Allen to assist Cort Schnackenberg at Kawhia.

Her husband's disgrace did not disqualify Eliza from carrying out church work. Indeed, her ability to remain true to her purpose after such a severe test as her husband's dismissal (following which he has 'added to his crimes a fearful list', according to missionary Thomas Williams) embued her with a special saintliness. She was highly regarded in church circles. Her determination to carry on also demonstrates considerable strength of character. A weaker person might have preferred to retire into obscurity, and the option of burying herself in domesticity presented a means of honourable retreat. Eliza did not take it. She had an ambition, conceived at the age of sixteen, and she pursued it unwaveringly until the end of her life.

Eliza developed her own mission in the city, visiting the sick at the hospital and lunatic asylum, the poor in their homes, and the elderly at the refuge. She held mothers' meetings and 'was often found walking long distances on errands of mercy after she had passed her three-score years and ten'. The prison was also on her visiting circuit, and the matron said that some women 'completely broke down, and cried bitterly, as she read the "Old, old Story", and pleaded for them in prayer'.

Eliza held interdenominational prayer meetings in her house in Vincent Street and in 1878, at the age of sixty-nine, founded the Ladies Christian Association of which she was president. The association continued the work Eliza had begun and also conducted a night school for 'the larrikin class' which required 'much patient waiting on God'. Seven years later, it became the Young Women's Christian Association, the second to be formed in New Zealand.

William had died in 1875, aged eighty-one. He was extreme to the end; his obituary noted that his health had deteriorated after a forty-mile horse ride followed by a day's gardening. Eliza then lived alone in Vincent Street with an elderly servant and, suffering from deafness, employed an ear-trumpet to hear the services at the nearby Pitt Street Methodist Church. She died on 27 February 1883 of spinal disease and was buried alongside William in the Symonds Street cemetery.

Sandra Coney

Quotations

All unreferenced quotations come from Eliza White's journal.

para.3 *NZ Wesleyan*, 2 April 1883, p.79
para.4 W. Walker, quoted in J. Owens, *The Wesleyan Mission*, p.48
para.5 M. Gittos, *Mana at Mangungu*, p.37
para.8 E. White to J. Hobbs, undated, St John's College Library
para.9 E. White to J. Hobbs, 17 Oct. 1834, ATL; E. Kirk, 'Wesleyan Missionary Society Station', ATL
para.10 John Hobbs, Journal, 21 Jan. 1833, quoted in J. Owens, p.452
para.12 E. White to J. Hobbs, undated, St John's College Library
para.24 E. White to J. Hobbs, undated, St John's College Library
para.27 H. Martin, 'Grandma Martin's Story', ATL
para.29 Quoted in G. Ramsden, *Marsden and the Missions*, p.114
para.30 *NZ Wesleyan*, 2 April 1883, p.79
para.31 S. Coney, *Every Girl*, p.4

Unpublished Sources

Eliza White, Journals 1829–1836, St John's College Library
Eliza White to Jane Hobbs, n.d., St John's College Library
Eliza White to Jane Hobbs, 17 Oct. 1834, in Wesleyan Missionary Society, miscellaneous correspondence, MS Papers 66, folder 17, ATL
Emma Kirk (Hobbs), 'Wesleyan Missionary Society Station at Mangungu', qMS, ATL
Hannah Martin (White), 'Grandma Martin's Story', 1955, qMS, ATL
J. M. R. Owens, 'The Wesleyan Mission to New Zealand 1819–1849', PhD thesis, Victoria, 1969
Murray Gittos, 'First There Were Three', unpublished typescript, n.d., MS 1153, AIM
William White, Journals 1823–1835, St John's College Library

Published Sources

Coney, Sandra, *Every Girl: A Social History of Women and the YWCA in Auckland*, Auckland, 1986
Gittos, Murray. *Mana at Mangungu*, Auckland, 1982
Lee, Jack. *Hokianga*, Auckland, 1987
Morley, William. *The History of Methodism in New Zealand*, Wellington, 1900
NZ Herald, 26 March 1883 (obituary)
NZ Herald, 26 Nov. 1875 (obituary, William White)
NZ Wesleyan, 2 April 1883 (obituary)
Owens, J. M. R. *The Wesleyan Mission to New Zealand*, Auckland, 1974
Ramsden, George Eric. *Marsden and the Missions: Prelude to Waitangi*, Dunedin and Wellington, 1936
Williment, T. M. I. *John Hobbs 1800–1883*, Wellington, 1985

MARGARET WHITE

1868–1910

Margaret Matilda White was probably the first woman photographer to set up a professional studio in New Zealand, establishing premises in Newton, Auckland, in the last years of the 1890s. At that time, women were barred from joining the Auckland Photographers Society, and thus were effectively denied access to the benefits of a professional guild. The ban remained until 1917 – seven years after Margaret White's death – when Una Garlick's undeniable talent finally forced a change.

Margaret White was born in Belfast, Northern Ireland, on 9 January 1868, the third child and only daughter of Mary Jane (born Davison) and John White. Following the death of her husband in 1869, Mary Jane White remarried and, in 1886, emigrated to New Zealand with her three children, her husband (Alexander Orr Polley), and his two sons. The family arrived in Auckland on 17 March on board the *Ionic* and settled in Upper Pitt Street.

Although the 1893 Electoral Roll classifies Margaret White's occupation as 'home duties', at some stage during this period she trained and worked as a nurse, first at an Auckland private hospital and then at the Auckland Mental Hospital in Avondale. She was, at the same time, developing her interest in photography.

Margaret Matilda White, 'female assistants', Avondale Mental Hospital, c.1890s, one of a series of photographs. *Auckland Institute and Museum*

There is some evidence that she trained with John Hanna in his Queen Street studios, perhaps working with him as a part-time apprentice from as early as 1890.

During the five years before she established her studio, Margaret White travelled extensively on horseback, accompanied by a female companion and carrying glass-plate camera equipment. During these tours, probably undertaken between periods of working as a nurse, she took photographs in localities ranging from Whangarei, through Albany and Auckland, to Kihikihi (where, in 1894, she photographed the tangi of Rewi Maniapoto) and Gisborne. Although these included some landscape compositions, the majority were commissioned group portraits.

Many aspects of Margaret White's photographic style mirrored the rather formal conventions of the time. Within these, however, she developed an innovative and modern sense of composition and introduced numerous personal motifs and pictorial devices. Her most extraordinary series of images – those of fellow nurses and attendants at the Auckland Mental Hospital in the late 1890s, and those of Maori people – initially arose out of formal commissions. But they demonstrate just how sensitive and innovative her photography could be. For the Auckland Mental Hospital commission, White satisfied the client's requirements with a series of interesting but conventional group portraits and studies of buildings. That completed, she moved on to produce a group of images of the nurses and attendants scattered in odd arrangements within the hospital grounds. These complex, unsettling images are an acute expression of contemporary social reality.

Margaret White's most important series of photographs of Maori was of the Maori troops who took part in the 1897 Diamond Jubilee celebrations. Unlike many contemporary photographers and artists, White appears to have approached Maori people with openness and sensitivity to the cultural and social realities of her subjects.

Although business was good, the Margaret Matilda White Studio was short-lived. Her marriage to Albert Reed in 1900 saw her close the studio and move to Mackaytown, near Waihi, with her husband. There she continued with her photographic work, producing commissioned group portraits for local schools and the Volunteer Fire Brigade, and a series of studies of the Waikino and Karangahake mining plants.

Gradually, however, domestic routines and the birth of her two sons meant that she had less time for photography. By the time of her early death in 1910 – the result of tetanus poisoning – her work seems to have been limited to domestic 'snaps'. She was not, at the time of her death, widely known or referred to as a photographer. Indeed, in professional terms, she remained largely invisible throughout her life. Her most interesting work has only recently become known, and Margaret White is now increasingly regarded as an important figure in the development of photographic practice in this country.   *Tim Walker*

Unpublished Source
Tim Walker, 'Margaret Matilda White (1868–1910) Photographer', unpublished catalogue, 1982
Published Sources
City Group. 'Margaret Matilda White', *Photofile*, Spring 1988

Walker, Tim. 'A curious dislocation: Margaret Matilda White's photographic manner', *Art New Zealand*, no.53, Summer 1989–90

Walker, Tim. 'Margaret Matilda White (1868–1910): An Introduction' in 'Six Women Photographers', *Photoforum New Zealand*, no.56, 1987

MAATA WICKLIFFE

1906–1985

Maata Wickliffe was born Maata Hurihanganui at Whakarewarewa, Rotorua, in 1906. Her parents were Hurihanganui Ngarimu and Karaihe Hori Ngarae. Maata's people were Ngati Wahiao, Tuhourangi, Ngaiterangi, Ngai Tahu, and Ngatiwhaoa.

As a young woman Maata played the lead role of Hinemoa in the classic early New Zealand feature film *The Romance of Hinemoa*. Directed by Danish film-maker Gustave Pauli, *The Romance of Hinemoa* was made in 1925 on location in Rotorua, and featured an all-Maori cast. Maata's handsome cousin Matt Hona played opposite her as Hinemoa's chiefly lover, Tutanekai. All but one reel of the film appears to have been lost. The surviving reel was discovered in 1981 by a London barrister. Returned to this country, it has been restored by the New Zealand Film Archive.

For many years Maata was a guide at the Wairakei thermal area. During this time she worked closely alongside her partner and husband, Matauranga Wickliffe. Maata had no children of her own but raised three whangai.

Maata then returned to Rotorua and lived in Whakarewarewa village where she gave long and valued service to Wahiao marae. Maata Wickliffe died in 1985, and is buried at the Sala St Cemetery, Rotorua.

Her story is told by Louie Waaka and Charlie Hurihanganui.
There was five of them in her family, three girls and two boys. Maata was the eldest. As a young woman she had beautiful jet-black eyes, long, long hair, and a lovely smooth complexion. Her father was Te Hurihanganui. Naturally we thought that Hurihanganui was our family name, but Maata said no, actually it wasn't. Originally we were Ngarimu. I said, 'Well how did we come to be Hurihanganui?' And she said because in our koroua's days, if anything extraordinary or tragic happened, that father would change his name to remember the event. Once when one of our kuia fell in a ngawha [boiling pool], was badly scalded and died, her family then all changed their names.

But for us the cataclysmic occasion was the eruption of Tarawera. That's what Hurihanganui means, and it was Maata who told me. When she made the Hinemoa and Tutanekai film, that was well before our time. So we don't know what that was like.

We have to begin when she finished guiding over at Wairakei and came back to Rotorua and settled here. That's when she started working for the marae. We were building our dining-room at the time, and paying it off by running lunches for visitors to the village.

Te Rau Aroha was the name of the dining-room. It was run like a restaurant. Order from your table and the kai would be brought out to you.
Maata's staff weren't uniformed. They just wore ordinary day frocks, but
everybody was very tidy to serve the tourists. There weren't any starched tablecloths, because that meant added expense. Maata arranged for the laundry to
be done by ourselves. Everything was economical, so the dining-room could
raise money to do whatever we wanted to do in the village itself. The menu at
the dining-room was written up on a blackboard. Maata's lunches were just
ordinary luncheons. Fresh salads and meat. Hot veges. Maata used to put them
in the hangi behind the dining-room. She'd make steak and kidney pies, and
when it was a cold day, dish up stew and mashed potato. Always plenty of
bread, cup of tea, and sweets. There'd be big cream sponges, apple shortcake,
and steamed puddings were easy because she had the ngawha out the back.

Maata always kept her expenses down by making things out of almost
nothing. Say she had a cake left over from the day before, she'd always keep
that and make trifle up with it. She didn't run up big bills with the catering.
She always made do with what she had.

She didn't try any Maori kai on the tourists. It was only for ourselves
really. When we had tangis, Maata just used to close the dining-room to visitors
and cater for the family.

Maata was absolutely straight up and down. Very, very honest. She
handled all the money. Pita Awatere was the one that taught her. She took a
three-week pressure-cooker course in bookkeeping and accounting, run by the
Maori Affairs. Come auditing time she'd get the books ready and send them in.
The auditor had no problem. Everything was accounted for.

Maata also helped form the Puarenga branch of the Maori Women's
Welfare League. She was the instigator of getting the Maori women settled in
Sala Street. That was a welfare league housing project for the Maori mothers.
In recognition of her work for the people and the marae, they tried to get her to
accept an OBE but she refused. No, she said, and she was adamant too, but the
authorities tried and tried.

She declined because she felt that she wasn't doing it for herself. She was
doing it for everyone. She was really a very shy person who turned her back on
public honours.

For a long time after her husband died, Maata never came out of her
house. It was her time of mourning and she spent that period in the house
spinning flax and doing cloaks. She was a lovely weaver and made beautiful
kakahu [cloaks]. When the need came and we wanted whariki [mats], she made
it her business to learn to raranga [weave]. Some of the whariki in the meeting-
house are hers. At the same time, she was totally aware that we had a kuia
from Te Puke helping with the weaving. When these old women weave, they
don't fool around with food. So Maata delegated to us the responsibility of
making lunch. She'd say, 'I know you won't be here all day, because you've got

Maata Wickliffe (Hurihanganui) as Hinemoa
and Matt Hona as Tutanekai in the 1925
feature film *The Romance of Hinemoa*.
Stills Collection, New Zealand Film Archive

your babies, but can you make sure that there's something for the kuias' lunch?'
She had that ability to delegate tasks to people but in a very nice way. She
always managed to give you the impression that she was only asking you
because she knew you could do it. Half the time you didn't have a clue, but
because of the way she asked, you gave it a go.

It wasn't until almost at the end of her life, that I suddenly realised what a
wealth of knowledge she had, but unfortunately it was too late. When she was
on her deathbed, things came out all of a sudden. You'd be sitting there
chatting and she'd quietly mention something interesting. You just had to sit
there and listen as best you could. She had a terrific mind and mine was so dull
I couldn't remember. She'd go from one point to another and jump to
something else and I'd get confused. So it's gone. It's a shame because all the
time now we're searching, searching for our family history.

Louie Waaka, Charlie Hurihanganui & Cushla Parekowhai

Unpublished Sources
'New Zealand Premier to attend showing of Maori film', press release, Gaumont Co. Ltd, 1926, NZ
    Film Archive, Wellington
Published Sources
Otago Daily Times, 25 Sept. 1981
Romance of Hinemoa (motion picture), dir. Gustave Pauli, Gaumont Co. Ltd, London, 1926
Tu Tangata, Nov./Dec., 1981; Feb./Mar. 1982

MARGARET WILLIAMS alias OPIUM MAG

c. 1850s – 1920s

'This is the holder of the record', an Auckland police officer claimed, exhibiting a list of seventy-four-year-old Margaret Williams' 213 criminal convictions, dating from 1876 to 1924. Margaret Williams arrived in Dunedin from England in 1876, aged about twenty-six years. With no family, friends or prospects of regular employment, she soon began working as a prostitute, settling in the 'Devil's Half Acre' or Chinese quarter of town. While living and working there, she became addicted to alcohol and opium smoking, earning herself the nickname 'Opium Mag'.

Her life-style and addictions brought her into frequent contact with the police and the courts. Described by the local press as a 'degraded looking woman', or as an 'unfortunate who was trembling from the effects of opium', Mag often pleaded to be let off her charges. However, the police and the courts maintained that gaol was the best place for her and that she should be locked up for her own safety, as 'some day she would be found lying dead in the streets'. Consequently, Mag spent more than four of her first seven years in the colony in the Dunedin prison. Most of her sentences were short, ranging from a week to three months' imprisonment. Such short sentences reflected the minor nature of her offences: abusive language, vagrancy, drunkenness, and soliciting for the purposes of prostitution.

Mag's lack of family and friends, and her life-style, led her to travel up and down the country, never spending more than a few years in any one centre. From Dunedin, Mag made her way to Auckland and back again, receiving several sentences in each major town in which she stopped. During her two and a half years in Wellington, she was convicted and imprisoned on ten separate occasions, spending twenty-four months in gaol. The sentences were for the usual minor offences of drunkenness, vagrancy, and having insufficient legal means of support. Only on one or two occasions did her offences become more disruptive; she broke a window in Auckland's Queen Street, smashed a bucket while locked in a police cell, threw a rock at a man who had annoyed her. Yet, by 1909, her long list of convictions led the Auckland Supreme Court to declare her an habitual criminal and an incorrigible rogue.

Mag finally settled in Auckland in 1916 where she remained until her death sometime after 1926. She was obviously destitute during the last decade of her life, and on at least one occasion was convicted of soliciting alms from passers-by. Her lack of money also forced her to continue to work as a prostitute and, although in her sixties, she received convictions for prostitution-related offences until 1920. Mag's alcohol problems never diminished and, despite prohibition orders and a year spent at an Inebriates' Home, she continued to be convicted for drunkenness. Her last court appearance was in 1926, when, aged seventy-six, she was charged with being an idle and disorderly person, only two days after being released from prison. She was convicted and sentenced to three months' imprisonment, her 214th conviction and at least her 140th term in gaol.

Bronwyn Dalley

Quotations
para.1 *NZ Herald*, 23 October 1924, p.7
para.2 *Otago Daily Times*: 6 Jan. 1880, p.2; 4 Jan. 1878, p.3; 20 June 1879, p.3
Unpublished Sources
Heather Lucas, '"Square Girls": Prostitutes and Prostitution in Dunedin in the 1880s', BA Hons research essay, Otago, 1985
Ingrid Clausen, 'Crime and Criminals in Dunedin 1880–93', BA Hons research eassay, Otago, 1983
J. M. A. Tuck, 'The Devil's Half Acre: 1900–1910', BA Hons research essay, Otago, 1983
Published Sources
Macdonald, Charlotte. 'The "Social Evil": Prostitution and the Passage of the Contagious Diseases Act (1869)', in B. Brookes, C. Macdonald and M. Tennant (eds), *Women in History: Essays on European Women in New Zealand*, Wellington, 1986, pp. 13–33
NZ Herald, 1881–99, 1905–12, 1916–27
NZ Police Gazette, 1877–1930
Otago Daily Times, 1877–83, 1886–8, 1990–04, 1912–14

RHODA WILLIAMS

1880-1972

Dorothy Rhoda Williams visited New Zealand for only a short time in 1911, but recorded in a diary and sketches her expedition over the Milford Track. Accompanied by her friends Jim and Barbara Dennistoun, Rhoda spent eight days walking from Lake Te Anau to the Milford Sound, then back along the same route. This account of early 'tourism' in New Zealand is the more interesting for being a woman's view.

The first entry in the diary conveys her energy and enthusiasm:

Motored with 5 females 52 miles in a 28 h.p. Darracq [early French car] to Manapouri Lake. Got there as sun was setting behind Cathedral Peaks moon rising. Very *lovely. Went on 12 miles in twilight to Lake Te Anau. Beautiful moon and* vile *roads.*

The following day they packed their 'swags' and crossed the Clinton River in a boat. On the first day they covered twelve miles and spent the night at the Pompolona Huts – 'one large kitchen with huge wood fire and the ladies hut with 10 bunks opening off it'. For supper that night they ate 'lentil soup – cold mutton, carrots and potatoes, tinned apricots and tea'.

It took the party three days' tramping to reach Milford Sound, often walking for up to eight or nine hours and covering approximately nineteen miles a day. Rhoda often went for a further walk by herself at the end of the day to draw and write. Her diary is illustrated with sketches and water-colours of such scenery as Mitre Peak, and Quintin Huts.

Throughout her diary Rhoda comments on the number of women walking the track: 'went to bed at 8 and there were 9 other ladies!'. One illustration shows her friend Barbara sitting at Mitre Peak in a surprisingly formal outfit of a calf-length skirt, jacket, and large hat. The women must have needed extra energy to drag their long, and often wet, clinging skirts along the track.

Their tramp lasted eight days. One of the most strenuous parts of the trek occurred on the final day.

We climbed over several foaming currents and got very wet and enjoyed ourselves immensely and got to the pass at 10 – very good – 2 and a half hours. We went down the other side and got to the Pompolona Huts at 12 – very wet indeed. We had lunch and got into dry things again and tramped down 10 miles to Glade House. Such a lovely walk through the best bush we have seen.

'Barbara and Mitre Peak'. Rhoda Williams' sketch of her friend Barbara Dennistoun on an expedition to Milford Sound, 1911. *Canterbury Museum*

Rhoda had come to New Zealand to visit her sister Margaret Wallis, who was married to the then Bishop of Wellington. She returned to England shortly after her trip. She married Robert Leatham Barclay, a director of Barclay's Bank, in 1924, and had one daughter. She died in 1972 at the age of ninety-two.

Her diary bears the inscription:

Tis glorious to have them for my own
These naked crags, these rugged snow-clad heights.

> *These shattered pinnacles, and misty peaks*
> *Mine to recall at will, mine for all time.*

Philippa Fogarty & Caroline Etherington

Source

Diary of D. Rhoda Williams, Journey over Milford Track, 1911, Acc. 256/83, Canterbury Museum. All quotations are from this diary.

ANNE WILSON

1802–1838

Anne Catherine Hawker was born in Ireland on 24 November 1802 to Francis (later Major) Hawker of the Twelfth Dragoons and his wife, Frances (born Cripps). By 1814 the family was living at Fort Henry on Jersey where Anne met John Alexander Wilson whom she married in 1828. 'Under [the] gentle influence' of his wife, Wilson was converted to Christianity and brought to consider missionary employment. He was accepted by the Church Missionary Society, and, to the horror of Anne's family, posted to 'that outlandish place', New Zealand. On 21 September 1832, the couple, with their two young sons, boarded the *Camden*, a convict vessel bound for Australia. 'The more I hear of [the heathen]', wrote Anne, 'the more my heart seems drawn to them.' She would indeed need all her powerful evangelistic faith and courage in the years ahead.

During the four-and-a-half-month voyage, the Wilsons experienced severe storms, illnesses, and the opprobrium of almost everyone else on board, their efforts to bring religion to their shipmates being largely unappreciated. They finally arrived at Paihia on 12 April 1833 aboard the *Byron*. 'We have thus begun housekeeping in the savage land', wrote Anne. '. . . I feel great responsibility lays on me . . .'

The Wilsons served as missionaries in the Bay of Islands (1833 and 1837), Puriri (1834–5), and Tauranga (1836 and 1838). Anne's life revolved round her children (two more sons being born in 1834 and 1838), teaching in Maori schools, and 'household affairs', where she was responsible for training Maori girls and 'constantly [had] to keep them to their work'. Her husband was frequently absent and Anne was left to cope alone with the trials of missionary life: isolation amid often 'far from congenial fellow labourers', mostly people from a very different social class; frequent family illnesses which filled her with 'inexplicable horror'; and the disappointments occasioned by the many 'failures' in Christian behaviour of the 'poor deluded people' they had come to save. Anne never mastered the Maori language and found it difficult 'to express anything spiritual', thus making her feel at times 'a fruitless branch' in her labours.

Anne was devoted to her husband, and this made the 'anguish of parting extremely painful'. 'It seemed my heart would break and violent floods of tears followed', she confided in her journal after one such separation. Eighteen-thirty-six was the worst year, when tribal wars kept John in Tauranga while Anne and the children returned to the comparative safety of Puriri. 'I do not think I have ever felt so anxious about your safety before', she wrote to John. 'I cannot bear the thought of your being so constantly exposed in perilous situations.' She tried 'to be submissive . . . as it is his duty to go' and wrestled with her conscience through her journal, accusing herself of being a 'faithless creature', full of 'pride and selfseeking'. 'Oh when shall I truly . . . say sincerely "Thy will be done"', she cried. Yet it was 'a comfort to know that [John was] one of the chosen of the Lord . . . engaged in His particular service' and, despite all her 'afflictions', her faith in the rightness of the cause never failed. .

Throughout this period Anne suffered increasing ill health, deriving, as she felt, from continual anxiety. She had frequent headaches and pain in her side, caused 'by a complaint of the heart', and in 1837 discovered a 'small hard lump under [her] left arm'. By then she was 'convinced . . . I shall never recover'. She was right. Her death agonies are described in harrowing detail by Charlotte Brown, but 'though her bodily sufferings were peculiarly severe . . . she was not suffered . . . to fall from her God and Saviour'. Anne died on 23 November 1838 as she had lived, the 'most striking feature of her character . . . Simplicity of faith'. She had been 'an endeared and highly valued friend and assistant, an affectionate and tender mother and a wife whose worth [her husband] could surely appreciate', a 'companion after [the Lord's] heart and his own'.

Pat Sargison, with assistance from Max Armstrong

Quotations

para.1 'Obituary of Mrs Wilson', p.173; M. G. Armstrong (ed.), 'My hand will write what my heart dictates', title page; Armstrong, p.8
para.2 Armstrong, p.33
para.3 Armstrong, p.109; Armstrong, p.45; Armstrong, p.51; Armstrong, p.27; Armstrong, p.88
para.4 Armstrong, p.58; Armstrong, p.96; Armstrong, p.75; Armstrong, p.91; Armstrong, p.57; Armstrong, p.75; Armstrong, p,53; Armstrong, p.43; Armstrong, p.81; Armstrong, p.51
para.5 Armstrong, p.110; Armstrong, p.102; Armstrong, pp.97,110; 'Obituary of Mrs Wilson', pp.171–3; Armstrong, p.114; Armstrong, p.31

Unpublished Sources

M. G. Armstrong (ed.), 'My hand will write what my heart dictates': The Letters and Journal of Anne Catherine Wilson (1802–1838), Missionary Wife in New Zealand. MS Papers 3943, ATL

Published Sources

Armstrong, M. G. 'Mrs J. A. Wilson', *Auckland-Waikato Historical Journal*, no.38, April 1981, p.16
Boyd, R. H. 'The Rev. John Alexander Wilson (1809–1887), *Auckland-Waikato Historical Journal*, no.38, April 1981, pp.14–16
'Obituary of Mrs Wilson, wife of Mr J. A. Wilson, catechist of the Church Missionary Society in New Zealand', *Church Missionary Record*, vol.10 no.8, Aug. 1839, pp.170-73
Stanley, Joan. '"Giving honour unto the wife . . .": The Story of The C.M.S. Missionary Wives in the Thames Valley, Waikato and Bay of Plenty Districts', *Journal of NZ Federation of Historical Societies*, vol.1 no.11, July 1981, pp.7–11
Wilson, J. A. *Missionary Life and Work in New Zealand, 1833 to 1876, being the private journal of the late Rev. John Alexander Wilson*, Auckland, 1889

ELIZA WOHLERS

1812–1891

Born in 1812 to Hannah and William Hanham of Bridport, England, dressmaker Eliza had at the age of twenty-seven 'married and gone to New Zealand' with her carpenter husband Richard Palmer. Little is known of their first years in the colony, except that Eliza was left widowed and childless, and that she had acquired some fluency in the Maori language.

Eliza Wohlers. *Sheila Natusch*

By 1849 she was living in Wellington. Her description by a Wesleyan missionary's wife commended her to the bachelor missionary J. F. H. (Johann) Wohlers of Ruapuke in Foveaux Strait, who had been making enquiries for a suitable young woman to be his wife. A meeting was arranged in Wellington in July 1849, and the couple were married two months later. Wohlers, from a Lutheran community, had trained with the North German Mission Society in Hamburg, and following his ordination in 1842 had come to New Zealand to carry out non-denominational mission work for the society. His marriage to Eliza was a no-nonsense, but highly successful partnership. It produced a daughter, Gretchen, and brought new life to the dispirited southern settlement she moved to.

The island of Ruapuke in the 1830s had been the refuge for many Maori fleeing raids by the Ngati Toa chief Te Rauparaha, who had come down from the North and laid waste to many South Island pa, notably around Akaroa and Kaiapohia. Foveaux Strait was also an area early frequented by European sealers and whalers, who introduced respiratory diseases and alcohol to the local population. To the German pastor, arriving in 1844, Ruapuke seemed a dying place. Whaling in the area had declined, leaving small 'European' settlements – of Pakeha men and their Maori women – on both sides of the strait, living off the land (potato crops and livestock) and the sea.

The Wohlers' mission was Christianity, but they also brought knowledge of

741

new ways in a new world. To Pastor Wohlers' efforts to combat ill health and poverty were added Eliza's skills: with the help of her medicine chest she nursed many a sick baby or child back to health; at sewing sessions at the mission house local women learned to make 'simple and decent European clothes'; she also instructed them in 'health, cleanliness and decency'. The boys learned to farm and the girls to make butter. Their parents turned up in the reading class too.

But life on the island wasn't always easy for the Wohlers. At Easter 1850 the mission house was burned to the ground, and Eliza found herself, also badly burned, bedding down with the pigs in a nearby shed. There were hints of a revival of muru (the custom of plundering the victims of misfortune) after the fire, but there was nothing left to plunder. Wohlers had only a small and sporadic salary from the home mission, which had a policy that missions should be self-supporting. He eked out this income with his duties as deputy-registrar of births, deaths and marriages for the Foveaux Strait district and as teacher at the Ruapuke Native School. Eliza also taught at the school, instilling the basics of reading and spelling, as well as the singing of English hymns.

As time went by, the couple's material conditions improved. Thanks to the practical and energetic Eliza, the rebuilt mission house was spotless, ordered, and comfortable. She also built up the garden and orchard with cuttings and seeds sent to her by friends. They had also made an impact on the morale of the local community. People from Ruapuke and other Foveaux Strait communities, both Pakeha and Maori, attended church services and came to the mission for visits. It was later said of Eliza that she had 'ruled somewhat like a queen over the little community . . . creating a social and economical revolution on the island'. Whatever else the new regime of health, hygiene, and hope had brought to Ruapuke people, Eliza was able to write in her one surviving letter: 'We think they love us'.

Sheila Natusch

Quotations
para.2 S. Natusch, *Brother Wohlers*, p.119
para.4 S. Natusch, p.127
para.6 J. Wohlers, *Memories*, p.219; E. Wohlers to the North German Mission Society, J. F. H. Wohlers Papers, MS Papers 428, ATL

Published Sources
Natusch, Sheila. *Brother Wohlers*, Christchurch, 1969
Natusch, Sheila. *On the Edge of the Brush: Pioneer Women of Southland*, Invercargill, 1976
Wohlers, J. F. H. *Erinnerungen aus meinem Leben*, Bremen, 1883
Wohlers, J. F. H. *Memories of the Life of J. F. H. Wohlers*, Dunedin, 1895 (trans. John Houghton)

SUSAN WOOD

1836–1880

Susan Nugent Wood was well known in southern New Zealand in the 1860s and 1870s as a writer of verse, essays, and short stories. She gave public lectures and readings of her work to raise funds for community projects.

Much of her writing draws on her eventful, often tragic, life, and reveals a great deal about the physical and emotional conditions, aspirations, and values of a middle-class pioneer woman striving to uphold domestic moral order in a raw gold-fields society.

Susan Lapham was born on 21 August 1836 in Lisdillon, Tasmania, to Anglo-Irish parents, Susan (born Butler) and Samuel Lapham, and died at Riverton, Southland, on 30 November 1880. She grew up in a remote area of Tasmania (probably the penal settlement of Maria Island), where her father was a farmer and probation officer. He was dismissed in 1850 for leniency towards an Irish political prisoner who had earlier been accused of making advances towards the fourteen-year-old Susan. After two difficult years the family moved to Victoria. In 1854 she married John Nugent Wood, son of a clerical English family, and pastoralist at Mt Gambier, South Australia. From 1855 he was an official on the Victorian and Otago gold-fields, rising from clerk to warden, and later to resident magistrate. Because his appointments were so extensive, it is difficult to pinpoint everywhere Susan Wood lived in Otago. She was probably at Tuapeka in 1861, and certainly at Queenstown, Nokomai, possibly Naseby, and from 1869 at Switzers.

She had no formal schooling and attributed her education to poring over old books and to a bush childhood. She identified strongly as an Australian, and in her early years in New Zealand she was desperately homesick for 'the wattle's flowery branches . . . In my own land far away'. Her new country she described as 'these cold and gloomy regions [where] Life is sad and dark to me'. Later, however, she developed an affection for Otago's beauty.

By today's standards much of her writing seems to be sentimental or morbid. She had a strong interest in the supernatural and one of her public lecture topics was 'Ghosts'.

Some of her writing appears to be an outlet for her grief over real events such as the deaths in infancy of her first three children and fears for the two survivors; her own ill health and the prospect of an early death from tuberculosis; the couple's dwindling financial expectations; an unspecified scandal which appears to have occurred just before their coming to New Zealand; the extreme physical and social conditions of gold-fields life; the unrealistic expectations placed on her husband by his superiors.

Her writing also expresses her middle-class Christian morality, which gave meaning to suffering: submission, self-discipline, and endurance would bring a reward in the world to come. She promoted the concept of the 'good woman': subservient to her male partner, yet with a power over him to uplift domestic life for the betterment of society. She was a feminist in the nineteenth century sense of claiming equal value for women's role and the right to develop their talents, but she rejected the 'crowing hen' as foolish and outside God's order. Susan Wood derived comfort and self-confidence from a belief that she was fulfilling the requirements of the 'good woman', and saw herself as an example to other women at a time when society was in upheaval:

the Women of Australia have a 'work' of their own to do . . . In their hands lies the power of raising the moral and intellectual condition of the land they live in; of making the social life a clear bright stream, reflecting the images of peace and purity, instead of the defiled turbid torrent which I fear it is fast becoming.

Susan Lapham (later Nugent Wood), c.1850.
Stephanie Cox

However, not all her work is gloom or preaching. She writes light-heartedly of domestic life, focusing on her warm relationship with her husband, her love for her children (even if there are continual reminders of her dead daughters), her friendships and wider family relationships, the beauties of nature and of everyday life and pleasures, including reading and writing.

Susan Wood's work was published in local periodicals, the *Otago Witness*, the *Saturday Advertiser*, and in three small books: *Woman's Work in Australia* (Melbourne, 1862), *Bushflowers from Australia* (London, 1867), and *Waiting for the Mail* (Melbourne, 1875).   *Rosemarie Smith*

Quotations
para.4 'The Australian's Lament', *Bushflowers from Australia by a Daughter of the Soil*, London, 1867, p.65
para.7 'A Daughter of the Soil' (S. Nugent Wood), *Woman's Work in Australia*, Melbourne, 1862, pp.3–4

Published Sources
Scholefield, G. H. (ed.) *A Dictionary of New Zealand Biography*, vol.2, Wellington, 1940, p.540
Western Star, 1 Dec. 1880 (obituary)

RUMATIKI WRIGHT

1908–1982

One of the first Maori welfare officers, founding member of the Maori Women's Welfare League, and pioneer in Maori pre-school education, Ruth Wright had a passionate desire to understand and support the needs of her people.

Born Rumatiki Gray in 1908, Ruth (as she was generally known) was affiliated to Rangitane, Ngati Awa, Ngaiterangi, and Aupouri. She grew up within Ngati Kurawhatea. Her Pakeha grandfather, Robert Gray, married Ngatoko; their son, Robert, married Ngaraiti Tuatini, and Ruth was their daughter. She was brought up on the Wanganui River by her maternal grandfather, Tuatini Te Waiho, until she was fourteen.

After attending Pipiriki Native School, Ruth worked in the flour mill up the river, and also as a domestic servant. She married Angus Wright in 1926 at the age of eighteen. They farmed a large area of land between Raetihi and Pipiriki in difficult times, and had four children, William, Douglas, Maria and Angus. Ruth worked in the laundry at the local hospital to pay for her children to go to boarding-school; Angus, the baby, lay at her side in a laundry basket.

Ruth was acutely aware of the widespread effects of the Depression, particularly on the Maori people in terms of land loss and under-development. Her experience at this time led to the belief that solutions had to be provided in Maori terms, working from the grass-roots. Like Te Puea, she had the mental and physical resources to tackle all obstacles, and she also expected great achievements of others – possibly too great for those who lacked her stamina or her vision.

Like many rural women of her time, Ruth had a formidable range of domestic and farming skills which helped to stretch the family's resources and were a useful basis for her future work. She sewed and did handcrafts, fenced and milked, and was a superb horsewoman. Her paid work outside the home honed her organisational skills and made her familiar with conditions in the workplace.

During the Second World War, Ruth was one of a number of women whose abilities were recognised and used in the Maori war effort. After the war, Ruth was appointed as a welfare officer in the Department of Maori Affairs, under the Maori Social and Economic Advancement Act (1945). She was working in Taranaki when Nurse Cameron was forming health leagues in Rotorua. The leagues were a means of imparting health information and skills to women at a time when tuberculosis and other life-threatening diseases were widespread. The need for special attention to Maori health was emphasised, and Maori women were invited to join the leagues. Ruth supported the concept and started forming health leagues in Taranaki for Maori women and their communities.

Ruth then became convinced of the need for a national organisation that could become a vehicle for the larger aspirations of Maori women and also attend to the great variety of local needs. She and other supporters persuaded the Department and the Minister of Maori Affairs that health and other areas of concern to Maori women were best dealt with in ways which were culturally appropriate and which they initiated. With the assistance of departmental staff, Maori Women's Welfare League branches were formed throughout the country, a constitution was drawn up, and the structures for a national organisation put in place.

In September 1951 the first conference of the Maori Women's Welfare League was held in Hamilton and chaired by Ruth, although she declined to be considered for office; Whina Cooper was elected as the league's first president. The department provided administrative assistance and the services of Ralph Love, and later Mira Petricevich (Szaszy), as Dominion secretary. This link with the department was later to have disadvantages as the league grappled with increasingly sensitive issues of land, language, and race relations in the late 1950s; however, it enabled the league to establish and implement policy in the early days.

In her work as a Maori welfare officer, Ruth continued to provide support to league branches and to the welfare officers detailed to assist the league in their areas. Her faith in the capacity of women to tackle sensitive social and national issues was fully justified. For example, the league was quick to appreciate the threat to health and the ocean food-chain posed by nuclear testing in the Pacific; their concern was not, however, shared by many in authority.

The league became independent from the department in 1960. Ruth again became an important anchor during the period of consolidation which followed, despite any qualms she may have had about the league's future security. She worked long hours in a support and planning role at its Hawkestone Street office in Wellington, balancing this commitment with other work in Hamilton.

In 1958, Ruth visited the Soviet Union as a member of a goodwill party of New Zealand women. This gesture of détente was quite bold in view of the Cold War ideology prevalent in New Zealand at that time, and was to have later repercussions for her career. She bore the criticism stoically. Meanwhile, she was determined to use the insights she had gained on her trip to improve early childhood education for Maori children, so that they could flourish intellectually and culturally.

Her opportunity came with the growth of the pre-school work of the Maori Education Foundation. Under its auspices Ruth formed and nurtured a large number of independent pre-school groups in remote areas of the Waikato and Maniapoto, and encouraged each group to express the style and values of its own community. The success of these autonomous models made them the focus of educational research in the 1970s, and led to visits by Maori pre-school organisers and league members to Aboriginal communities in Australia to discuss an indigenous approach to pre-school education.

Despite her practical skills and the huge areas she covered, Ruth never learned to drive: she had no affinity with cars. In the early days she rode or walked everywhere. Later, she became an adept user of public transport, with an extensive network of helpful drivers and contacts. She was noted and admired for the compactness of her luggage at hui or on journeys. She was never without her writing materials and diary, and assiduously recorded requests, events, the day's work, and future plans. She wrote while travelling or waiting – anywhere there was space or time – and took teasing about her addiction to scribbling in good part.

Ruth's small, chunky, neatly suited figure – hair in a bun, hands gloved – hid an enormous energy and charisma. She seemed to expand at meetings and with women. She liked sharing knowledge and ideas, and invested those of others with significance. She left women feeling confident and purposeful, enlarged with the gift of their own extended insights.

Ruth wore her Maoriness with confidence and pride, while also acknowledging her dual heritage. She strove for knowledge and excellence in both cultures and was at home in both. She enjoyed being 'correct' in the protocol and etiquette of Pakeha society, and disliked sloppy preparation or dress for important gatherings. While she was at ease anywhere, she especially enjoyed the excitement of large formal events.

She had a deep throaty chuckle and a habit of reinforcing a point by touching one's arm or leaning forward to share a confidence. She was a wonderful mentor and travelling companion – informative, supportive and

Rumatiki Wright. *Taini Jamieson*

resourceful; impressive as a speaker, and an astute observer and commentator. While she radiated warmth, she was also a very private person who did not readily talk about her personal life and feelings. She had a few cherished familiars, among whom was her relative and friend, Iriaka Ratana MP, who was often seen with her, head to head, deep in conversation.

While she gave loyalty where it was due within organisations and hierarchies, Ruth had a slightly sceptical attitude to those exercising authority. A keen sense of the ridiculous often helped to blunt the frustration she felt both as a worker and as a woman. At the same time, she was deeply respectful of 'sanctified' authority and treasured her awards: the MBE and OBE she received for her services to the Maori people.

As she had advised others to do, Ruth worked to consolidate family land and to ensure its future management. Wherever she worked she paid regular visits to her home at Raetihi, returning to it as a well-spring and a refuge – and keeping an eye on things.

Ruth had planned another of her working holidays in Australia, but she collapsed and died at a tangi at Pohara, Tokoroa, on 14 December 1982. She was seventy-four.

Her obituary spoke of Ruth as the 'Mother of the League'. From her work over the years she gained an appreciation of the challenge facing Maoridom, and of the strength and resilience of Maori women. She called on that strength and directed it towards the well-being of Maori women and children, and the future of their race.

Ruth Wright was an exciting, innovative, supportive colleague and friend, who remains part of my life.

> *Who shines the stars to light the way,*
> *Who weaves the cloak to warm the land,*
> *Who sets the mind to slake its thirst,*
> *Who links the hands that rock the world.*

Joan Stone

Unpublished Sources
Information was provided by Marama Laurenson (Ruth Wright's granddaughter), Bill and Taini Wright (her son and daughter-in-law), Anne Delamere, Sir Ralph Love, Geraldine McDonald, John Booth, Marion Antonievich.
Maori Women's Welfare League Records, 1952–1970, MS Papers 1396, ATL

Published Sources
Auckland Star, 17 Dec. 1982 (obituary)
Stone, Joan and David. 'A Race Relations Controversy', in J. E. Ritchie (ed.), *Race Relations: Six New Zealand Studies*, Wellington, 1964

ADELE YOUNGHUSBAND

1878–1969

Pioneer surrealist painter Adele Younghusband was born Adela Mary Roche on 3 April 1878. Her father, Hungerford Roche from Dublin, was a farmer at Ngaroto near Te Awamutu; her mother's family, the Malcolms, emigrated from London and bought an isolated piece of land on Great Barrier Island. Fanny Osborne, who painted the island's endemic flora, was Adele's aunt. However, Adele's own early interest in art was not to develop and flourish until she was in her forties.

Adele married Frank Younghusband on 1 August 1905 in Christchurch. The marriage was not a success and the couple later separated. With three children to support, Adele turned to portrait photography, learning from F. Gaze of Hamilton. She joined the Auckland Society of Arts in 1913.

In December 1919, at the age of forty-one, she established herself in Whangarei. Advertising 'as a photographer of undoubted merit', she took over a studio where her patrons were 'assured of really first class work, perfect in technique, taste and pleasure'. That studio became the venue of the newly formed Whangarei Arts and Literary Society, of which Adele was the secretary. She and George Woolley set up the Art Studios where she undertook the dark-room work and retouching and George taught classes in painting and drawing.

Unhappy in the partnership, Adele moved to Dargaville in 1927, then on to Devonport and Hamilton. Here in 1934 she was a founding member of the Waikato Society of Arts and, the following year, its representative on the National Society of Arts.

An exhibition of her paintings was arranged for her in Sydney in 1937, and she went on to study with George Bell in Melbourne, returning to New Zealand early in the war years. A successful 'one-person' show at the Auckland Society of Arts in October 1941 was followed by twenty years of active painting. Always individualistic, always experimenting, her work in the twenties and thirties was nevertheless formal and orthodox. By modification and simplification, her work moved away from the natural and progressed into the surrealistic and abstract.

At the age of eighty-five, Adele was present at an exhibition of her work in Hamilton. Her death on 4 April 1969 ended an association of over fifty years with northern arts societies.

Not great art, not always successful, her best work is, however, a satisfying pattern of colour, light, and design on a variety of subjects and themes, using a variety of media. Her linocuts are vivid and forceful.

A. C. Hipwell said of Adele that:

Surrealism becomes the only true vehicle of personal expression, and judgement from this angle places Adele Younghusband not only a New Zealand born pioneer in this field but as a very successful surrealist painter.

Mim Ringer

Quotations
para.8 A. C. Hipwell, 'Adele Younghusband', p.8

Unpublished Source
Auckland Society of Arts, records and catalogues, APL

Published Sources
BP Magazine (Sydney), 1 Sept. 1937
Hipwell, A. C. 'Adele Younghusband: A New Zealand Surrealist', *Art in NZ*, no.54, Dec. 1941
Northern Advocate, 3 December 1919
Waikato Times, 15 Aug. 1934; 2 April 1963

MISS Y AND MISS Z

1890

Miss Y was a worker at Clarke's steam laundry in the North-East Valley, Dunedin, in 1890. She worked in the ironing room, ironing shirts. It was heavy, hot work. The irons weighed nine or ten pounds each; Miss Y and the other ironers stood all day. The room was over-heated from the stoves which were kept burning all day to heat the irons. In summer the temperature was particularly unbearable. Working days started at 8 am and finished at 6 pm, six days a week, the only holidays being Sundays, Christmas Day, and sometimes New Year's Day. The only break in the day was a half-hour for dinner at midday.

Miss Y was paid by the piece: how much she earned depended on how many shirts she ironed in a day. On average she took home £1 a week. Miss Y was one of twenty-five women employed in the laundry along with an engineer and a lad who drove the express (the engine that made the steam). The youngest workers – two girls aged twelve and the next aged sixteen – earned less though they worked the same hours.

Miss Z also worked at Clarke's steam laundry. Like Miss Y and the other young women there, she got sick from time to time with the strain of standing all day in a hot and poorly ventilated room (there were windows down one side only which allowed no ventilation at all when the wind blew from the south).

Despite the unpleasantness of the job, Miss Z preferred laundry work to domestic service because it enabled her to spend the evenings with her parents. She was the eldest in the family.

Miss Y and Miss Z appeared as witnesses before the 1890 Sweating Commission set up to investigate wages and conditions of work, especially for women workers, in the wake of the Revd Rutherford Waddell's revelations of the appalling conditions in which women were employed in sewing workshops in Dunedin. Miss Y and Miss Z were asked specific questions about their work and conditions at their workplace, and their replies were recorded verbatim. Like most of the workers who appeared before the commission, these two young women were protected by anonymity from potential reprisals from their employers. Their real identities remain unknown.

Asked if they had any complaint to make about their employment, Miss Y and Miss Z only asked that the dinner break be extended to an hour. 'We need the rest in the middle of the day', Miss Y explained.   *Charlotte Macdonald*

Source
AJHR, 1890, H-5, p.26. The quotation is from this source.

Wages and conditions in workshops such as this 1911 clothing factory and the Dunedin laundry where Miss Y and Miss Z worked were the focus of the 1890 Sweating Commission. *Steffano Webb Collection, Alexander Turnbull Library*

INDEX TO NAMES

Page references in bold type indicate photographs.

INDEX TO SUBJECTS

The following groupings help the reader to make connections between essays.

They are at times only guidelines. Childlessness, for example, lists only those essays in which childlessness is discussed, not all the women in the book who are childless.

The groupings refer to main items in the essays – the subject's occupation, for example, or a central issue discussed in the essay. Minor references may occur in other essays which are not listed in the subject groupings.

ARTS
Performing arts:
  Actors: Dronke, Rees, Stuart, Wickcliffe
  Composers: Howie, Katene, Papakura, B., Pewhairangi, Topeora
  Dance teacher: Taglicht
  Drama teachers: Dronke, Escott
  Entertainers: Papakura, B. & M., Redmayne
  Films: Stuart, Wickcliffe
  Music teachers: Buckman, Dreaver, Howie, Redmayne, Ross, Thompson, B.
  Musicians: Drewet, Quin, Ross, Thompson, B., Tinsley, Valpy
  Oratory/Public speaking: Colclough, Connon, Cunnington, Daldy, Devanny, Geddes, Millar, Nicholls, Palmer
  Singers: Basham, Grennell, Hato, Laughton, Stuart
  Opera singers: Alda, Buckman, Howie
  Theatre: Escott, Irvine-Smith, Marsh, N., Millar, Nicholls

Visual arts and crafts:
  Art societies: Angus, Arndt, Clark, Field, Gardner, Hill, Joel, Jones, Macalister, Reeve, Stoddart, Younghusband
  Art teachers: Crabb, Hill, McIntosh, Richmond, D. K., Sherwood
  Artists: Abraham, Angus, Arndt, Bullock, Clark, Crabb, Field, Haszard, Hill, Hocken, Hodgkins, Joel, King, M., Marsh, N., Richardson, Richmond, D. K., Sherwood, Stoddart, Swainson, M., Valpy, Younghusband
  Designer: Alcorn
  Floral art: Tuhakaraina
  Handcrafts: Jones, McIntosh, McMurray, Nielsen, Tracy, Tuhakaraina, Mrs Walker, Watson
  Jewellery: Reeve, Sewell
  Photography: Buckland, Frank, Kent, Kidson, Tarulevicz, Walmsley, White, M., Younghusband
  Printmaking: Arndt, Haszard
  Sculpture: Butler, Kidson, Macalister
  Weaving: Brown, Hoterene, Lough, Marsh, A., Porutu, Tuhakaraina, Wickcliffe
  Woodcarving: McMurray

COMMERCE
See also Labour, Service Occupations, and Trades
Businesswomen: Alcorn, Barron, Frank, Hellaby, Rout, Sewell, Stevenson, Taylor, Watson
Financier: Urquhart
Shopkeepers: Ah-Chan, Alcorn, Barron, Caradus, Chunyu, Doo, Riwai, Taylor, Urquhart, Van Chu-Lin

COMMUNITY SERVICE

Community involvement: Bartlett, Clark, Humphries, Moncrieff, Northcroft, Polson, Pomare, Reweti, Tuhakaraina
Entertaining: Barker, Busby, Geddes, Hobhouse, Stewart, A.
Overseas relief work: Greig
Philanthropists: Bannerman, Clark, Daldy, Geddes, Hellaby, Pomare, Simpson, Stout, Valpy, White, E.

CRIME AND THE LAW

Criminal convictions: Aves, Bock, Dean, Kaaro, McKenzie, F., Williams, M.
Homicide: Aves, Dean, Walker, E.
Justices of the Peace: Dreaver, Drewet, Henderson, Northcroft
Law office worker: Greig
Lawyers: Benjamin, Henderson, Melville

DEPRESSION, 1929–1935

Ah-Chan, Alcorn, Aves, Basham, Begg, Boyd, Douglas, Geddes, Glen, Humphries, Jacob, Melville, Morris, Nehua, Quin, Stevenson, Sutherland, Te Puea Herangi, Mrs Walker, Wright

EDUCATION

Adult education: Cunnington, Hetherington, Somerset
Education boards: Richmond, M.
Education of girls: Atkinson, Barnicoat, Baxter, Benjamin, Bennett, A., Colclough, Connon, Cruickshank, Edger, Ellis, Freeman, Griffin, Hetherington, Hobhouse, Lohse, Pomare, Richmond, D. K., Richmond, M., Stewart, F., Swainson, M. A., Thomson, Turnbull
Educationalists: Ashton-Warner, Daldy, Laughton, Somerset, Stout
Inspector: Hetherington
Physical education: Heap, Rout
Preschool education: Daldy, Glen, Kelsey, Pewhairangi, Richmond, M., Somerset, Wright
Teacher education: Heap, Hetherington, Irvine-Smith
Teachers: Allan, Ashton-Warner, Aubert, Bain, Buckland, Burton, Colclough, Colenso, Connon, Cook, Cruickshank, Daldy, Edger, Escott, Freeman, Greig, Griffin, Grossmann, Heap, Henderson, Hetherington, Hobhouse, Howes, Irvine-Smith, Johnstone, Jones, King, M., Laughton, Lohse, McIntosh, Mackay, McKenzie, M., Mactier, Mander, Moore, L., Nicholls, Park/Weitzel, Paulger, Peacocke, Rangitiaria Dennan, Scott, F., Scott, M., Soljak, Somerset, Stanley, Swainson, M.A., Taylor, Thomson, White, E.
University graduates: Allan, Barkas, Barnicoat, Baughan, Baxter, Benjamin, Bennett, A., Bush, Chunyu, Connon, Cook, Cruickshank, Duggan, Edger, Freeman, Gordon, Greig, Griffin, Grossmann, Gunn, Henderson, Hetherington, Irvine-Smith, Kidson, King, I., McDonald, McKenzie, M., Melville, Millar, Minchin, Moore, L., Moore, R., Northcroft, Palmer, Papakura, M., Park/Weitzel, Paske, Plischke, Scott, M., Sewell, Somerset, Sutherland, Thomson, Tinsley, Trainor
University lecturers: Duggan, Tinsley

FAMILY AND PERSONAL LIFE

Adoption: Morris, Paulger, Simpson, Stott, Te Puea Herangi, Tinsley
Adultery: Colenso, Grey, Kendall, Morris, White, E.
Arranged marriages: Ah-Chan, Brown, Gillies, Maitai, Petre
Childlessness: Angus, Mrs Walker, Walmsley
Divorce: Alda, Angus, Barclay, Burr, Daldy, Greig, Humphries, Mahupuku, Papakura,
   M., Park/Weitzel, Plischke, Sewell, Sherwood, Soljak, Tinsley, Younghusband
Foster parents and whangai: Bennett, F., Brown, Elkington, Gillies, Jacob, Katene,
   Maitai, Otene, Papakura, B., Reweti, Te Puea Herangi, Wickliffe
Friendship: Bethell, Mahupuku, Mansfield
Illegitimacy: Gibb, Hyde, Lee, Mansfield, Paulger, Pember Reeves, Redmayne, Stott
Improvident husbands: Barron, Burr, Caradus, Cherrington, Colclough, Dean, Ellis,
   Grossmann, Johnstone, Lee, Quin, Stephenson, Stott, Swainson, M. A., Valpy
Lesbians: Gregory, Trainor
Marriage: Alda, Allan, Ashton-Warner, Atkinson, Barker, Burr, Cherrington,
   Colclough, Colenso, Daldy, Dronke, Edger, Field, Fraser, Grey, Grossmann, Haszard,
   Kendall, King, I., Lee, Maher, Newdick, Paske, Plischke, Quin, Scott, F., Soljak,
   Stanley, Suisted, Taglicht, Tarulevicz, Thompson, B., Tinsley, Topeora, Tracy,
   Turnbull, Walmsley, Wehipeihana, Wharepapa, White, E., White, M., Wilson, Wood
Mixed marriages: Barclay, Donnelly, A., Dorling, Geddes, Karetai, Laughton,
   Mahupuku, Moore, R., Pomare, Pore, Poulgrain, Takiora, Wharepapa
Motherhood: Allan, Atkinson, Bartlett, Baxter, Bennett, F., Busby, Doo, Dorling,
   Douglas, Edger, Field, France, Gordon, Graham, Grey, Grossmann, Hellaby,
   Henderson, Hill, Hobhouse, Lee, McDonald, Moore, R., Paraone, Paske, Scott, F.,
   Stewart, F., Tinsley, Van Chu-Lin, Wharepapa, Wood
Sexuality: Anon, Devanny, Grossmann, Schnackenberg
Widows: Barker, Barron, Blanch, Bullock, Christeller, Deans, Donnelly, E., Drewet,
   Gibb, Gilmer, Hill, Maher, Morris, Neill, Player, Ross, Schnackenberg, Simpson, Stott,
   Stuart, Swainson, M. A., Torlesse, Urquhart

FARMING AND THE NATURAL ENVIRONMENT

Communes: Drewet
Conservationists: Baker, Boyd, Gilmer, Johnstone, Moncrieff, Tarulevicz, Mrs Walker
Farming: Bartlett, Beaufoy, Bennett, F., Blanch, Boyd/Abraham, Burr, Climo,
   Donnelly, A., Donnelly, E., Gibb, Johnstone, Karetai, Kennard, McMurray,
   Marsh, A., Matenga, Nielsen, Petersen, Polson, Quin, Ratana, Scott, M., Stephenson,
   Te Puea Herangi, Tarulevicz, Tuhakaraina, Wright
Forestry: Sutherland
Gardening: Baker, Bethell, Dorling, Fisher, Gilmer, Hill, King, I., King, M., Laughton,
   Plischke, Poulgrain, Rangitiaria Dennan
Goldmining: Climo, Donnelly, E., Stott, Wood
Gum digging: Hoterene, Te Whata
Horticulture: Chunyu
Landscape architecture: Plischke
National parks: Moncrieff, Tracy
Poultry farming: Dorling
Runholders: Barker, Deans, Petre, Stewart, A.
Stockbreeder: Arnold
Tobacco farming: Hall
Town planning: Northcroft
Viticulturalist: Ah-Chan

FEMINISM AND SOCIAL REFORM

Activist: Cook

Feminism: Begg, Benjamin, Bullock, Cunnington, Devanny, Griffin, Henderson, Howard, Mackay, Macpherson, Melville, Moore, L., Morison, Paske, Schnackenberg, Sewell, Tocker, Trainor

Pacifism/Peace movement: Angus, Bain, Baker, Burton, Cook, Douglas, Gibson, Macpherson, Soljak

Prison reform: Baughan, Bullock, Cunnington, Edger, Thompson, R.

Socialism: Cunnington, Devanny, Douglas, Gibson, Henderson, Howard, Macpherson, Park/Weitzel, Pember Reeves, Rout, Stewart, A., Trainor

Suffrage: Baker, Bullock, Caradus, Daldy, Edger, Gibson, Henderson, Mackay, Macpherson, Morison, Müller, Pember Reeves, Schnackenberg, Sheppard, Stewart, A., Stewart, F., Stout, Valpy

Temperance and prohibition: Benjamin, Bullock, Caradus, Ellis, Henderson, Mackay, Mactier, Player, Schnackenberg, Stewart, F., Stout, Valpy, White, E.

Unemployed: Cook

Women's rights: Bain, Bartlett, Caradus, Colclough, Daldy, Grossmann, Müller, Neill, Northcroft, Pember Reeves, Sewell, Stewart, C., Stout, Taylor, Wood

HEALTH AND WELFARE

Abortion: Aves, Gordon, Sewell

Alcohol and drug abuse: Ashton-Warner, Ellis, Johnstone, Lee, Moore, R., Williams, M.

Ambulance driver: Barclay

Birth control: Bush, Dean, Ellis, Macpherson, Soljak, Trainor, Van Chu-Lin

Cancer: Buckland, Campbell, Chunyu, Devanny, Donnelly, A., France, Katene, McDonald, Marsh, N., Melville, Moore, R., Paske, Petersen, Riwai, Sewell, Tinsley

Charitable aid: Lee, Mee, Neill, Player

Childbirth: Abraham, Barker, Barron, Boyd, Busby, Campbell, Climo, Collard, Donnelly, E., Gordon, Hobhouse, Hoterene, Hyde, Kennard, Lee, McMurray, Mansfield, Newdick, Player, Redmayne, Te Whata, Thompson, B., Trainor, Van Chu-Lin, White, E.

Dietician: McKenzie, M.

Doctors: Barkas, Bennett, A., Bush, Cruickshank, Gordon, Gunn, Moore, R.

Epidemics: Bagley, Cherrington, Cruickshank, Gillies, Hoterene, Lambie, Maude, Ross, Stuart, Te Puea Herangi, Thompson, B.

Health camps: Gunn, Nielsen, Ross

Health stamps: Nielsen

Homeopathy: Aubert, Bennett, F., Colenso, Maitai, Scott, F., Sewell, Stanley, Trainor, Mrs Walker

Hospital boards: Campbell, Cunnington, Dreaver, Gilmer, Henderson, Richmond, M., Ross, Stewart, F.

Nursing: Graham, Holford, Mee, Player, Rangitiaria Dennan, Sewell, Simpson, Tocker, Torrance, Walmsley, White, M.

District nursing: Aubert, Bagley, Cameron, Maude, Wehipeihana

Midwives: Bagley, Bicknell, Blanch, Cherrington, Gillies, Graham, Holford, Hoterene, Karetai, Paraone, Paulger, Player, Te Whata

Nursing administrators: Bicknell, Lambie, Maclean, Neill

Nursing education: Lambie, Maclean, Neill

Polio: Cherrington, Morris, Thompson, B.

Prison visitors: Baughan, Bullock, Cunnington

Psychiatric illness: Angus, Anon, Ashton-Warner, Bennett, F., Cherrington, Climo,

Gregory, Grey, Hyde, Newdick, Valpy
Psychiatry: Barkas, Christeller, Moore, R.
St John Ambulance: Barclay, Torrance
Sex education: Bush, Moore, R., Rout
Social work: Aubert, Begg, Bethell, Cunnington, Maude, Riwai, Thompson, R., Tocker, Torrance, Wright
Suicide: Gregory, Hyde, Johnstone, Scott, F., Texidor, Thompson, R.
Tuberculosis: Briggs, Lee, Mansfield, Maude, Scott, F., Te Puea Herangi, Walmsley, Wehipeihana

IMMIGRANTS

Chinese in New Zealand: Ah-Chan, Chunyu, Doo, Stout, Van Chu-Lin
Colonisers: Abraham, Aubert, Bannerman, Barker, Beaufoy, Boyd/Abraham, Burr, Busby, Deans, Donnelly, E., Fraser, Gibb, Graham, Hadfield, Hobhouse, Johnstone, Kennard, King, M., McMurray, Martin, Newdick, Nielsen, Petre, Player, Redmayne, Schnackenberg, Simpson, Stephenson, Stewart, A., Stott, Suisted, Swainson, M., Swainson, M. A., Taylor, Torlesse, Wharepapa, Wohlers
Germans in New Zealand: Christeller, Dronke, Lohse, Park/Weitzel, Plischke, Taglicht, Tarulevicz
New Zealand Company: King, M., Petre, Swainson, M.
Pacific Islanders in New Zealand: Cherrington
Refugees: Christeller, Dronke, Plischke, Taglicht, Texidor
Yugoslavs in New Zealand: Soljak

LABOUR

See also Commerce, Service Occupations, and Trades

Factory inspectors: Morison, Neill
Factory work: Turnbull
'Sweating': Y, Miss and Z, Miss
Trade unions: Daldy, Garmson, Howard, Humphries, Morison, Palmer, Rout, Turnbull
Women and employment: Colclough, Cook, Daldy, Gibson, Grossmann, Henderson, Macpherson, Morison, Paske, Player, Riwai, Soljak, Stevenson, Taylor

LITERATURE AND SCHOLARSHIP

Children's authors: Clark, Glen, Howes, Lough, Peacocke, Tracy, Walmsley
Collectors: Frank, Hocken
Editors: Henderson, Maclean, Macpherson, Palmer, Paske, Pember Reeves, Richmond, M., Rout, Sheppard, Somerset
Historians: Irvine-Smith, Papakura, M.
Letter writers: Abraham, Douglas, Fraser, Hobhouse, King, I., Martin, Selwyn, Swainson, M., Taylor
Librarians: Bartlett, Bryant, Chunyu, France, Greig, Hall, McDonald, Millar, Minchin, Nunneley
Novelists: Ashton-Warner, Devanny, Ellis, Escott, France, Grossmann, Hyde, Lancaster, Mactier, Mander, Marsh, N., Rees, Scanlan, Scott, M., Taylor
Playwrights: Montgomery
Poets: Bain, Baughan, Bethell, Briggs, Duggan, France, Hyde, Lough, Mackay, Mactier, Montgomery, Nicholls, Redmayne, Shaw, Stanley, Tracy, Wood
Short story writers: Hyde, Lancaster, Mansfield, Shaw, Suisted, Texidor, Wood

Writers: Barker, Bullock, Carter, Deans, Fisher, Gibson, Gordon, Kent, Maclean, Macpherson, Martin, Moncrieff, Müller, Peacocke, Richmond, M., Rout, Somerset, Stewart, A., Stout, Taylor, Walmsley

MAORI

Crafts: Brown, Hoterene, Marsh, A., Pewhairangi
Education: Laughton, Moore, R., Pomare, Riwai
Fishing/Eeling: Brown, Hoterene, Little Papanui Woman, Otene, Palliser Bay Woman, Paraone, Petersen, Poulgrain
Food planting, gathering and preparation: Brown, Hoterene, Little Papanui Woman, Maitai, Otene, Palliser Bay Woman, Paraone, Poulgrain, Rangitiaria Dennan, Te Maiairea Te Riri Wairua Puru
Health services: Bagley, Bush, Cameron, Lambie, Martin, Royal, Wehipeihana
Kotahitanga Movement: Mangakahia
Land: Abraham, Hadfield, Martin, Pore, Selwyn, Te Puea Herangi, White, E.
  Bastion Point: Hyde, Reweti
  Maori Land Court: Donnelly, A., Karetai
Maoritanga: Elkington, Ellis, Gillies, Heketa, Irvine-Smith, Jacob, Moore, R., Papakura, B. & M., Pewhairangi, Riwai, Te Puea Herangi, Te Whata
Maramatanga: Rikiriki
Medicine: Aubert, Brown, Maitai, Rikiriki, Royal
Meeting houses: Jacob, Laughton, Marsh, A., Rikiriki, Te Puea Herangi, Wickliffe
Missions: Aubert, Colenso, Hadfield, Kendall, Laughton, Martin, Schnackenberg, Tarore, White, E., Wilson
Moko: Brown, Heketa, Katene, Maitai, Otene, Paraone
Music: Grennell, Hato, Howie, Katene, Papakura, B. & M., Pewhairangi, Topeora
Pakeha-Maori: Ata-hoe, Makariri
Pre-contact social conditions: Little Papanui Woman, Palliser Bay Woman, Rua-Puu-Tahanga, Te Maiairea Te Riri Wairua Puru
Prophets: Kaaro, Pinepine Te Rika, Rikiriki
Ratana religion: Hoterene, Ratana, Rikiriki
Ringatu religion: Otene, Paraone, Wehipeihana
Tapu: Ellis, Pinepine Te Rika, Rangitiaria Dennan, Te Maiairea Te Riri Wairua Puru
Treaty of Waitangi: Busby, Kahe Te Rau O Te Rangi, Nehua, Topeora
Tribal affiliations:
  Nga Puhi: Nehua, Wharepapa
  Ngai Tahu: Gillies, Royal, Te Maiairea Te Riri Wairua Puru
  Ngaitawhiri: Brown, Paraone
  Ngati Apa: Rikiriki
  Ngati Hao: Kaaro
  Ngatihaua: Tarore
  Ngati Hine: Hineamaru
  Ngati Kahungunu: Donnelly, A.
  Ngati Koata: Elkington
  Ngati Kuia: Poupou
  Ngati Kuri: Hoterene
  Ngati Mamoe: Te Maiairea Te Riri Wairua Puru
  Ngati Maru: Brown
  Ngati Porou: Pewhairangi, Wehipeihana
  Ngati Raukawa: Jacob, Topeora, Wehipeihana
  Ngati Ruanui: Rua-Puu-Tahanga, Takiora

MEDIA

PLACES

Kaikoura: Boyd
Katikati: Stewart, A.
Manawatu: Bennett, F., Burr, Morris
Marlborough: Watson
Milford Track: Williams, R.
Mosgiel: Turnbull
Nelson region: Arnold, Atkinson, Barnicoat, Bartlett, Climo, Frank, Hall, Hobhouse, Kidson, Matenga, Moncrieff, Moore, R., Müller, Stott
Norfolk Island: Colenso
Northland: Cherrington, Dorling, Drewet, Hadfield, Hineamaru, Hoterene, Kaaro, Kendall, Mander, Petersen, Pore, Stephenson, Te Whata, Wharepapa, White, E.
Otago: Bannerman, Buckland, Karetai, Kennard, Little Papanui Woman, Makariri, Wood
Otaki: Briggs, Hadfield, Jacob
Pacific Islands: Cherrington, Lambie
Palliser Bay: Palliser Bay Woman
Poverty Bay: Paraone
Rotorua: Barclay, Cameron, Hato, Papakura, B. & M., Rangitiaria Dennan, Royal, Wickliffe
Southland: Blanch, Dean, Te Maiairea Te Riri Wairua Puru, Wohlers
Stewart Island: Baker
Sub-Antarctic Islands: Richardson
Taranaki: Atkinson, Basham, Briggs, Gordon, Holford, King, M., Quin, Rua-Puu-Tahanga, Takiora, Thomson
Thames: Ah-Chan
Urewera Country: Laughton, Mansfield, Paulger, Pinepine Te Rika, Te Akakura Ru
Waikato: Johnstone, Marsh, A., Scott, M., Te Puea Herangi, Tuhakaraina
Waimate: Cruickshank
Wanganui: Aubert, Bullock, Chunyu, Cruickshank, Gunn, McMurray, Rikiriki, Stewart, F.
Waitangi: Busby
Wellington: Abraham, Alcorn, Angus, Aubert, Basham, Bennett, A., Butler, Campbell, Carter, Crabb, Douglas, Heketa, Hetherington, Humphries, Irvine-Smith, Kahe Te Rau O Te Rangi, Katene, Maher, Millar, Nicholls, Nunneley, Palmer, Park/Weitzel, Paske, Petre, Player, Plischke, Pomare, Porutu, Royal, Sewell, Stout, Swainson, M., Swainson, M. A., Taglicht, Taylor, Tocker, Topeora
West Coast, South Island: Graham, McMurray, Maher, Stott, Suisted, Mrs Walker

POLITICS

Cabinet ministers: Howard, Ross
Communist Party: Cook, Devanny, Minchin, Park/Weitzel, Soljak
Governors' wives: Barker, Grey
Labour Party: Bartlett, Devanny, Dreaver, Gibson, Henderson, Howard, Macpherson, Ratana, Reweti, Soljak, Stewart, C.
Local government: Campbell, Dreaver, Gilmer, Henderson, Melville, Ross
Maori Parliament: Mangakahia
Members of Parliament: Dreaver, Henderson, Howard, Polson, Ratana, Ross, Stewart, C.
National Party: Polson, Ross
Parliamentary candidate: Melville
Political secretaries: Gilmer, Sewell

Resident's wife: Busby
Treaty of Waitangi: Busby, Kahe Te Rau O Te Rangi, Nehua, Topeora
Wives of Members of Parliament: Field, Paske, Pember Reeves, Pomare, Stout, Valpy

PUBLIC INSTITUTIONS

Arts institutions:
   Canterbury School of Fine Arts: Angus, Marsh, N., Stoddart
   New Zealand Academy of Fine Arts: Angus, Arndt, Butler, Crabb, Field, Hodgkins, Richardson, Richmond, D. K., Sherwood
   Wellington Technical School: Alcorn, Arndt, Burton, Butler, Hill, McIntosh, Sherwood
Cawthron Institute: Kidson
Charitable institutions:
   Christchurch Female Home: Simpson
   Christchurch Female Refuge: Torlesse
   Otago Benevolent Institution: Mee, Valpy
Hospitals:
   Christchurch Hospital: Maude
   Lyttelton Hospital: Simpson
   St Helens hospitals: Bennett, A., Holford, Neill
Psychiatric hospitals:
   Ashburn Hall: Anon, Mee
   Auckland Asylum: Newdick, White, M.
   Seacliff Hospital: Anon, King, I., Morison
Schools:
   Auckland Girls' High School: Heap
   Christchurch Girls' High School: Connon, Edger, Grossmann, Henderson, Somerset
   Girton College: Freeman, Stevenson
   Nelson College for Girls: Atkinson, Barnicoat, Bartlett, Edger, Kidson
   New Plymouth Girls' High School: Thomson, Tinsley
   Otago Girls' High School: Benjamin, Buckland, Freeman
   Samuel Marsden Collegiate: Swainson, M. A.
   Te Wai Pounamu College: Katene, Riwai
   Turakina Maori Girls' College: Laughton, Te Akakura Ru
   Wanganui Girls' College: Cruickshank

PUBLIC SERVICE

Dept of Education: Fisher, Greig, Palmer, Tocker
Dept of Health: Bagley, Bicknell, Gordon, Lambie, McKenzie, M., Maclean, Neill, Wehipeihana
   School Medical Service: Gunn
Dept of Justice: Thompson, R.
Dept of Labour: Morison, Neill
Dept of Lands and Survey: Richardson
Dept of Maori Affairs: Riwai, Wright
Dept of Scientific and Industrial Research: Kidson, Moore, L.
Ministry of Consumer Affairs: Sewell
National Library Service: Greig, McDonald
New Zealand Forest Service: Sutherland
New Zealand Native Office: Takiora
War Office: Royal

RELIGION

Bishops' wives: Abraham, Hadfield, Hobhouse, Selwyn
Christian Science: Cunnington
Church of England: Abraham, Bartlett, Bethell, Colenso, Cunnington, Hadfield, Jacob, Maude, Selwyn, Torlesse, Wilson, Wharepapa
Church of Jesus Christ of Latter Day Saints: Elkington
Congregational Church: Daldy, Edger, Kelsey
Deaconesses: Bethell, Tocker, Torrance
Evangelist: Mactier
Forward Movement: Edger, Richmond, M.
Free Church: Bannerman
Jewish: Benjamin, Christeller, Joel, Taglicht
Maramatanga: Rikiriki
Methodist/Wesleyan: Burton, Caradus, Kennard, Schnackenberg, Tocker, White, E., Wohlers
Missionaries: Aubert, Bannerman, Begg, Colenso, Hadfield, Kendall, Laughton, Schnackenberg, White, E., Wilson, Wohlers
National Spiritualist Church: Dreaver
·Nun: Aubert
Presbyterians: Burton, Deans, Gibb, Henderson, Kaye, Laughton, Paulger, Stout, Torrance, Valpy, Watson
Prophets: Kaaro, Pinepine Te Rika, Rikiriki
Ratana: Hoterene, Ratana, Rikiriki
Ringatu: Otene, Paraone, Wehipeihana
Roman Catholics: Barron, Douglas, Duggan, France, Frank, Gregory, Hato, Petre, Plischke, Quin, Tuhakaraina
Salvation Army: Collard, Valpy
Unitarian Church: Atkinson, King, M., Morison
Vicar's wife: Torlesse

SCIENCE

Astrology: Dreaver
Astrophysics: Tinsley
Botany: Baker, Baxter, Moore, L., Sutherland
Chemistry: Kidson
Ornithology: Moncrieff

SERVICE OCCUPATIONS

See also Commerce, Labour, and Trades

Boarding-houses: Graham, Morris, Simpson, Stott, Torlesse, Urquhart
Cookery: Carter, Stewart, A., Wickliffe
Domestic service: Beaufoy, Fraser, Garmson, Gibson, Hobhouse, Maher, Player, Simpson, Stewart, A., Urquhart, Walker, E.
Home help service: Glen, Watson
Hotel and accommodation house keepers: Barron, Burr, Donnelly, E., Gibb, Humphries, Jacob, Kennard, Maher, Morris, Pore
Postmistresses: Dorling, Drewet, Gibb, Graham, Kennard, Paulger
Prostitution: Lee, McKenzie, F., Torlesse, Williams, M.
Shorthand typists: Cherrington, Gregory, Rout, Scanlan

Social work: Aubert, Begg, Bethell, Cunnington, Maude, Riwai, Thompson, R., Tocker, Torrance, Wright
Tourist agent: Stuart
Tourist guides: Papakura, B., Papakura, M., Rangitiaria Dennan, Wickliffe

SPORTS

Basketball: Grennell
Cricket: Allan, Dawson, Northcroft, Riwai
Cycling: Alcorn, Barnicoat, Thompson, B.
Deep sea fishing: Petersen
Golf: Grennell, Wehipeihana
Hockey: Dawson, Riwai
Horse racing: Briggs, Poulgrain
Mountaineering: Barnicoat, Baughan, Du Faur, Scott, M., Tremain
Show jumping: Briggs
Skiing: Geddes, Tarulevicz
Swimming: Kahe Te Rau O Te Rangi, Maitai, Nehua, Poupou
Tennis: Nunneley
Tramping: Moncrieff, Tremain, Williams, R.

TRADES

See also Commerce, Labour, and Service Occupations
Baker: Riwai
Dressmakers: Alcorn, Burr, Lee, McKenzie, F., Simpson
Hairdressing: Shaw
Printing trades: Gibson
Tailoresses: Morison, Morris

TRANSPORT

Aviatrix: Batten
Motor car driving: Barclay, Hall, Marsh, N., Morris, Reweti, Riwai, Thompson, B.
Motor cycle driving: Watson
Railways: Collard, Urquhart
Ship's cook: Stott
Shipwrecks: Matenga
Voyages: Player, Richardson, Wharepapa

WARS

Boer War: Bain
Inter-tribal wars: Tarore, Topeora
New Zealand wars (nineteenth century): Abraham, Atkinson, Burr, Johnstone, King, M., Martin, Pore, Schnackenberg, Selwyn, Swainson, M., Takiora
Sino-Japanese war: Ah-Chan, Hyde, Van Chu-Lin
Spanish Civil War: Texidor
Vietnam War: Cook
World War I: Arndt, Arnold, Bagley, Bain, Baker, Barnicoat, Baxter, Bennett, A., Bicknell, Cameron, Carter, Griffin, Gunn, Kelsey, Maclean, Papakura, B., Pember Reeves, Polson, Pomare, Rout, Soljak, Te Puea Herangi, Torrance
World War II: Baker, Barclay, Basham, Begg, Benjamin, Bennett, A., Bryant, Bush,

Campbell, Dreaver, Geddes, Gilmer, Griffin, Jacob, Moore, L., Northcroft, Peacocke, Polson, Rangitiaria Dennan, Reweti, Riwai, Soljak, Stewart, C., Thompson, R., Tocker, Tracy, Wright

WOMEN'S ORGANISATIONS

Canterbury Women's Institute: Cunnington, Garmson, Grossmann, Pember Reeves
Christchurch Women's Club: Stoddart
Civic League: Melville
Country Women's Institute: Bartlett, Jacob, Nielsen, Mrs Walker
Fabian Society: Cunnington, Pember Reeves
Family Planning Association: Bush, Soljak
Federation of University Women: Bennett, A., Griffin, Northcroft
Maori Women's Welfare League: Cameron, Jacob, Marsh, A., Ratana, Reweti, Riwai, Royal, Tuhakaraina, Wickliffe, Wright
Medical Women's Association: Bush
National Council of Women: Bain, Begg, Bullock, Bush, Caradus, Cunnington, Daldy, Dreaver, Geddes, Gibson, Griffin, Henderson, Jacob, Lambie, Mackay, Melville, Schnackenberg, Sheppard, Stout, Tocker, Walker, E.
New Zealand Army Nursing Service: Bagley, Bicknell, Maclean
New Zealand Nurses' Association (formerly Trained Nurses Association, then Registered Nurses' Association): Bagley, Bicknell, Holford, Lambie, Maclean, Maude, Tocker
New Zealand Women Writers' and Artists' Society: Peacocke
Pan-Pacific and South East Asian Women's Association: Griffin, Henderson
Parents' Centre: Campbell
Penwomen's Club: Peacocke
Plunket Society: Campbell, Geddes, Gordon, King, I., Stout, Torrance
Public Service Association Women's Committee: Greig
Society for the Protection of Women and Children: Benjamin, Edger, Geddes, Richmond, M., Stout, Walker, E.
Southern Cross Society: Stout
Wellington Ladies' Christian Association: Player
Women Teachers' Association: Henderson, Park
Women's Borstal Association: Tocker
Women's Christian Temperance Union: Caradus, Daldy, Edger, Henderson, Mackay, Morison, Pore, Schnackenberg, Sheppard, Stout, Valpy
Women's Division of Federated Farmers: Cherrington, Hall, Tracy
Women's Electoral Lobby: Sewell
Women's Franchise League: Bullock, Caradus, Daldy, Morison, Stout
Women's Health League: Cameron, Reweti
Women's Political League: Bullock, Daldy, Gibson, Player, Stewart, F.
Women's Refuge movement: Sewell
Women's Social Progress League: Richmond, M.
Workers' Education Association: Cunnington, Somerset
Young Women's Christian Association: Begg, Burton, Bush, Caradus, Cook, Geddes, Griffin, Jones, Kaye, Mactier, Sewell, Stevenson, Taglicht, White, E.

INDEX TO AUTHORS